SMITH & WOOD'S EMPLOYMENT LAW

Eleventh Edition

IAN SMITH MA, LLB (CANTAB)

of Gray's Inn, Barrister
Emeritus Professor of Employment Law at the University of East Anglia
An editor of Harvey on Industrial Relations and Employment Law

AARON BAKER BA JD (ST LOUIS), BCL (OXON)

Reader in Law at Durham University

OXFORD
UNIVERSITY PRESS

OXFORD
UNIVERSITY PRESS

Great Clarendon Street, Oxford, OX2 6DP,
United Kingdom

Oxford University Press is a department of the University of Oxford.
It furthers the University's objective of excellence in research, scholarship,
and education by publishing worldwide. Oxford is a registered trade mark of
Oxford University Press in the UK and in certain other countries

Eighth edition 2003
Ninth edition 2007
Tenth edition 2010

Impression: 2

British Library Cataloguing in Publication Data

Data available

ISBN 978-0-19-966419-1

Printed in Great Britain by
Ashford Colour Press Ltd, Gosport, Hampshire

PREFACE AND RECENT DEVELOPMENTS

When the prior edition of this book came out in 2010 we wrote that employment law evolves so quickly that a textbook on the subject requires updating every three years. Nothing could better illustrate this rapid evolution than our decision, based on the experience of these last three years, to move to a two-year window for future editions.

Although the Equality Act 2010—whose pending-but-not-certain passage posed the chief threat to the finality of the previous edition—entered into law in much the form we wrote about, various small changes, non-implementations, and judicial interpretations soon rendered our discussion less than definitive. The Coalition government did not take long to make its presence felt, and the courts and tribunals did their accustomed part to make this 2013 edition feel almost overdue. As a result we will be working on the next edition by the time the first few employment law students flip past this preface on the way to their first assigned reading.

Of course, we suffer under no illusions that this acceleration will prevent the book from arriving in law school lecture theatres already missing key developments. As we wrote this eleventh edition the Enterprise and Regulatory Reform Bill was working its way through Parliament (it is in the Report stage in the House of Lords right now) and has already seen substantial amendments since we handed this edition over to the publishers. None of those changes contradict what this edition says about the Bill, but we were cautiously non-committal, so readers need to consult the Act in its final form. This edition also discusses several consultations that have not run their course at the time of writing ('The Equality Strategy: Building a Fairer Britain', 'Modern Workplaces—Flexible Parental Leave', and 'Charging Fees in Employment Tribunals and the Employment Appeal Tribunal', to name three). These will almost certainly produce changes to employment law, some as early as this year. One consultation came out too late for us to discuss but will surely produce significant changes before the next edition: 'Fitness for work: the Government response to "Health at work—an independent review of sickness absence."' This announces plans to provide, by 2014, a 'health and work assessment and advisory service' to give independent health assessments for workers off work for four weeks or more, and to provide occupational health advice to workers and their employers; definitely one to watch.

Then, inevitably, there are the judicial decisions. Shortly after this book went to press, the Supreme Court handed down its decision in *Societe Generale v Geys*, [2012] UKSC 63, which settled the question of whether an employment contract can be terminated by an employer's repudiatory breach without the employee accepting the repudiation. We discuss the issue in Chapter 6 (section 4 (ii)), suggesting that the better view is the one indicated in *Gunton v Richmond LBC* [1980] ICR 755, rejecting 'automatic termination' and requiring acceptance. This is the direction the Supreme Court took in *Geys*, foreclosing yet another opportunity for employment lawyers to count angels on the head of a pin. Although less immediately binding, in that we await domestic articulation of its implications, the decision of the European Court of Human Rights (ECtHR) in *Eweida v UK* [2013] ECHR 48420/10, will perhaps have a more significant practical impact. The ruling joined several important cases on religion or belief discrimination, all discussed in Chapter 5 (section 6), finding that all had reached the correct result except the *Eweida* case itself. The UK Court of Appeal (*Eweida v British Airways* [2010] EWCA Civ 80) had held that indirect discrimination was not established where the claimant could not identify a belief-holding group—beyond the individual claimant—that was disadvantaged by the challenged policy; our discussion of the case in this book questions the justice and sustainability of this requirement. Fortunately, the ECtHR rejected the requirement, finding that Article 9 imposed no such hurdle for the claimant. This cannot have the automatic effect of changing UK law, but it means that continuing to apply this logic could amount to a treaty violation. Perhaps more dramatically, *Eweida* appears to have binned the accepted (but difficult to defend) doctrine, for cases of workplace burdens on religious practice, to the effect that no violation of Article 9 occurs where the claimant could avoid the burden by resigning and going to work elsewhere.

Countless further cases clamour for admission, such as *Davis v Sandwell* [2013] EWCA Civ 135 (written warnings underlying a dismissal can only be reconsidered if allegedly issued in bad faith or 'manifestly inappropriate') or *Bancroft v Interserve* [2012] UKEAT 0329_12_1312 (dismissal at the behest of a third party is unfair in the absence of investigation into whether request was justified). Alas, as the host of editors descends the gates must close leaving an unlucky few outside the palisade. We will afford them ample refuge in 2015 when we next attempt to catch up with the galloping vanguard of employment law.

ITS

AB

March 2013

CONTENTS

TABLE OF STATUTES

TABLE OF STATUTORY INSTRUMENTS

TABLE OF EUROPEAN LEGISLATION

TABLE OF CASES

1

INTRODUCTION

1 GENERAL

Employment law has been the subject of as rapid a transformation as can have happened to any legal subject in recent times, and is certainly one of the most difficult areas of law in which to keep up to date. In some ways it is a curious mixture of ancient and modern, for much old law lies behind or at the basis of new statutory law and in some cases the old law continues to exist alongside the new (eg the continued existence of the separate actions for wrongful dismissal and unfair dismissal, the former being a common law action and the latter entirely a creation of statute). To take one small example, as late as 1969 it could still be seriously debated before the Court of Appeal[1] whether a general hiring of an employee (ie one not subject to any express time limitation) was a hiring only for a year, under the old 'presumption of a yearly hiring' which used to apply in the nineteenth century and before, principally in order to guarantee year-round employment for agricultural labourers, but which is now totally irrelevant to modern employment law. Ghosts can still clank their chains, particularly in the law relating to contracts of employment where a strictly contractual approach may not always lead to a realistic result. However, the subject is unrecognizable from what it was only 40 years ago with the enormous increase in statute law and the ever increasing volume of case law on the modern statutes. Thus, the intending student must be able to exercise the lawyer's skill in dealing both with extensive case law and with major statutes, sometimes of astounding complexity. Moreover, he or she must be able to deal with this mass of law with a certain amount of intelligence and discernment, for example being able to tell when a line of old cases, authoritative in themselves, may be so out of line with the modern approach to employment or industrial relations that they are unlikely to be applied in practice, or to tell when a case on a modern statutory provision is merely *illustrative* (however interesting) rather than setting a definite precedent on a point of interpretation, for if this distinction is not borne in mind the student will soon find himself or herself buried alive under the case law, particularly in an area such as unfair dismissal where so much is vested in the discretion of the tribunal and, furthermore, where any actual point of law which does arise should normally be approached primarily by reference to the wording of the statute; the student will soon realize when reading this book that while a desire to escape from over-legalism

---

[1] *Richardson v Koefod* [1969] 3 All ER 1264, [1969] 1 WLR 1812, CA.

in decision making on employment matters has been one of the dominant themes of modern employment law, it is regularly frustrated by the avalanche of modern legislation, often of great complexity. Case law of course remains important, but equally clearly some cases are more equal than others. While the approach of this book is avowedly legal, treating the subject as it now has to be treated as an important area of substantive law which leads in practice to a very considerable amount of litigation, at the same time it must be realized that in certain ways this is law with a difference; this must be reflected in the approach of the student, and it is hoped that it is reflected in this book, which in turn reflects the love–hate relationship to the law adopted by so many employment relations practitioners.

As well as a whole new body of law, employment law is also subject to a separate jurisdiction exercised by employment tribunals (with appeal to the Employment Appeal Tribunal (EAT), and only then into the ordinary court structure, with appeal to the Court of Appeal and then to the Supreme Court). Even though tribunals gained some common law jurisdiction (on termination of employment) in 1994, not all matters may go to a tribunal, for many common law actions must still go to the ordinary courts (eg an action for breach of the contract of employment during employment, or an action by an employer for an injunction to restrain illegal industrial action). However, the large majority of cases which are brought do in fact go before the tribunals, and for over a decade now the numbers of such cases have increased alarmingly.

This has led to a mushrooming in specialized sources and materials in employment law, many ephemeral, but some of major practical use to the industrial lawyer. The two main series of law reports are the Industrial Cases Reports (ICR)[2] and the Industrial Relations Law Reports (IRLR);[3] preference will be given to citation of these reports throughout this book. The Industrial Tribunal Reports (ITR) commenced publication in 1966 and have now ceased, to avoid further duplication. The leading academic journal is the *Industrial Law Journal*,[4] and the principal updating aids, so vital in this rapidly developing subject, are:

(1) The IDS Brief—published twice per month; IDS also publish occasional supplements with the brief, covering recent developments in one particular topic, and the more substantial IDS Handbooks which aim to update the reader on the major areas of the subject.

(2) The *Industrial Relations Law Bulletin* (IRLB)—also published twice a month, covering recent case law and 'guidance notes' on particular topics.

---

[2] These are the official reports, published by the Incorporated Council of Law Reporting for England and Wales; until 1974 they were called the 'Industrial Court Reports'.

[3] Published by LexisNexis UK. See also now their stablemate, the *Equality Law Reports*.

[4] Published for the Industrial Law Society by Oxford University Press.

(3) Various websites—some are of course private, subscription sites, but of particular use as open public services are the websites of the Department for Business, Innovation and Skills, the Office of Public Sector Information (particularly for new statutory instruments) and the Information Commissioner (for developments in relation to data protection issues).[5]

The leading practitioner work is *Harvey on Industrial Relations and Employment Law*,[6] a five-volume looseleaf work (updated seven times per year, with a monthly bulletin) which is used extensively by practitioners, advisers and tribunals, and is frequently cited in court judgments (especially in the EAT).

Codes of practice are of ever increasing importance in employment law, allowing the statute to lay down merely the general principle on a topic and then amplifying that principle in a way that is likely to be of more use to the people concerned; so far, they have been used in the fields of unfair dismissal, employment protection, union rights, picketing, the closed shop, health and safety at work and disability discrimination, and they should be consulted whenever appropriate. Also, much useful information can be obtained from the annual reports of ACAS. In the collective sphere the Donovan Report[7] should still be consulted in any historic context, for it formed the analytical background to many of the reforms (successful or unsuccessful) in this area. Finally, many of the bodies connected with industrial relations in the widest sense publish from time to time reports or studies with important impacts upon the legal framework.[8]

2 A BRIEF HISTORY OF LEGAL INTERVENTION AND THE LEGISLATION

(i) ORIGINS

The subject of employment law may be split, for convenience if not for accuracy, into three principal areas—industrial safety law, individual employment law and the law relating to employment relations. Each has a different legal and social background, and until recently the level (and type) of legal involvement was markedly different in each. Industrial safety law has a history of statutory intervention dating back to the beginning of the nineteenth century, with a formidable volume of case law on the statutes and on the actions which could be brought by an injured employee. Individual

---

[5] These are at, respectively, <http://www.bis.gov.uk/>; <http://www.opsi.gov.uk>; and <http://www.informationcommissioner.gov.uk>. In more specialized contexts, the websites of the Equality and Human Rights Commission, ACAS and the Health and Safety Executive may be of use.

[6] Published by LexisNexis Butterworths.

[7] Report of the Royal Commission on Trade Unions and Employers' Associations (Cmnd 3623, 1968).

[8] The annual reports of ACAS, the CAC, the Certification Officer, the European Court of Human Rights and the Health and Safety Commission are particularly useful sources of information.

employment law, however, was based almost entirely upon the common law concept of the contract of employment; it attracted little statutory intervention and even much of the common law, though extensive in theory, was a dead letter in practice, principally due to the inadequacies of the remedies for breach of the employment contract by the employer. Employment relations law was characterized by the voluntary principle and the abstention of the law (once legislation had been used in the latter part of the nineteenth century and the first part of the twentieth to legalize the operations and purposes of trade unions and to protect them and their members from tortious liability for industrial action);[9] it is true that wage negotiation in certain industries used to be encouraged by Wages Councils which were the creation of statute, but even here the law merely provided a minimum framework and did not attempt to impose legal rights and duties on the substance of the negotiation itself.

Major developments have occurred in the last four decades which have changed this previous picture, in some areas out of all recognition. In the industrial safety sphere, the first of two revolutionary changes came with the Health and Safety at Work etc Act 1974 which creates administrative machinery, provides for more effective enforcement procedures and widens the general duties owed by employers (and others). Secondly, the substance of our safety laws has now been subject to major reform from a different source, namely the EU, with increased emphasis on attempting to harmonize laws on major safety matters throughout the Community.[10] Due to constraints on the size of a book such as this, industrial safety law is no longer covered here in detail.

Individual employment law has been the subject of major revision by the provision of new statutory rights for those in employment (and, in the area of sex, race, disability, sexual orientation, religion/belief and age discrimination, for those seeking employment); moreover, these rights (which usually have little or no dependence upon the theoretical contractual basis of employment) are now the subject of *realistic* enforcement procedures through the tribunal system and so are doubly preferable to most common law rights. These rights are many and various, from what is now a relatively minor matter such as minimum periods of notice according to length of service, to the more important employment protection rights; clearly the most important is the right not to be unfairly dismissed, and these cases have always constituted a major part of the tribunals' caseload.

Employment relations law suffered a great upheaval under a Conservative government with the Industrial Relations Act 1971, which unsuccessfully attempted to impose an overall legislative framework on industrial relations, giving rights and imposing duties by law as is done in some other jurisdictions. The Act was repealed

---

[9] This culminated in the Trade Disputes Act 1906 which gave a trade union complete legal immunity and its officers and members an immunity applying to all acts 'in contemplation or furtherance of a trade dispute'. This underpinning of the voluntary system and the withdrawal of the law from industrial disputes lasted until the Employment Act 1982.

[10] See Smith, Goddard, Killalea and Randall *Health and Safety: the Modern Legal Framework* (2nd edn, 2002).

in toto in 1974 (except for the unfair dismissal provisions, which were re-enacted), but ironically we then saw under the same Labour government the enactment of significant new legal rights for trade unions which were capable of having an effect on some of the most fundamental aspects of collective labour relations, such as recognition, bargaining information, standardization of terms and conditions throughout an industry, prior consultation on impending redundancies and direct union involvement in safety procedures. Certainly, where employment relations remain on a collective level (and there has been a significant decline in collective bargaining over the past three decades), such relations are still on a voluntary basis and voluntary procedures remain paramount; however, this field is no longer devoid of legal intervention, and the modern legislation has also played an important part in setting up machinery for the settlement of certain industrial disputes (in particular, the Advisory, Conciliation and Arbitration Service and the Central Arbitration Committee) and subsequently in placing stringent limitations on what the previous Conservative government saw as unacceptable forms of industrial action or unacceptable purposes behind such industrial action, while at the same time they sought ever greater deregulation of the labour market itself.

(ii) THE EARLY LEGISLATION

The whole subject is thus heavily overlaid with modern statutes.[11] In the employment law area, this process started with the Contracts of Employment Act 1963 (consolidated in 1972) which introduced new rules on notice periods, required an employer to give his employee a written statement of terms of employment, and laid down for the first time the statutory rules on 'continuity of employment' which were to take on much greater significance when more extensive employee rights were later enacted which depended on the concept of continuity (either for qualification for rights or computation of benefits, or both). The first of these rights was the right to a redundancy payment under the Redundancy Payments Act 1965. As well as attempting to introduce a new, but politically unacceptable, framework for industrial relations, the Industrial Relations Act 1971 was notable for introducing the new law on unfair dismissal, and this was re-enacted by the Trade Union and Labour Relations Act 1974 which repealed the 1971 Act and (1) restored the essentially voluntary nature of industrial relations (abolishing, in the process, the National Industrial Relations Court which had adjudicated cases arising under the 1971 Act) and (2) consolidated the law relating to trade union immunities and internal affairs; the 1974 Act was itself amended by the Trade Union and Labour Relations (Amendment) Act 1976 which made the immunities more watertight, abolished the statutory action against a union for unfair expulsion or exclusion, and tightened up the law on the closed shop.

---

[11] The statutes currently in force are set out, with annotations, in *Harvey*, Division Q.

The Employment Protection Act 1975 made significant steps forward in many directions. On the collective side, it gave statutory backing to ACAS, set up the CAC and introduced the important new trade union rights mentioned above; it also set up the Employment Appeal Tribunal (to take the place of the NIRC) and modernized the provisions relating to wages councils. On the individual employment side, it introduced new employment protection rights (eg guarantee payments, time off work for union purposes, a right not to be discriminated against on trade union grounds and the rights relating to maternity pay and leave) and it made significant alterations to the law on unfair dismissal (particularly as regards the available remedies). By this time, the statute law was something of a jungle and indeed was on one occasion castigated in the House of Lords as a bad example of legislation by reference, in that it was frequently the case that a point of law could only be discovered by referring to separate but complementary provisions in two or more Acts. The *individual* aspects were therefore consolidated into the Employment Protection (Consolidation) Act 1978 which covered particulars of terms of employment, employment protection rights, termination of employment, unfair dismissal, redundancy payments, and industrial (now employment) tribunals and the EAT, and was for years the principal statute.

(iii) THE CONSERVATIVE GOVERNMENTS 1979-97

The Employment Act 1980 marked a major change of direction after the election in 1979 of a Conservative government under Mrs Thatcher with a radically new political agenda based on free market economics. Although it adopted, at the very beginning of that government, a 'softly, softly' approach, avoiding a rerun of the Industrial Relations Act 1971, it started the remarkable transformation of employment law that marked the 1980s. On the collective side, it affected statutory trade union rights by repealing the provisions of the Employment Protection Act 1975 relating to the statutory recognition procedure and the extension of terms and conditions of employment by the CAC ('Schedule 11 claims'). It also affected the internal government of trade unions by allowing financial support for union elections and by reinstating a statutory right of complaint to a tribunal for people unreasonably expelled or excluded from a union where there was a closed shop in operation. The law relating to picketing was altered, and new curbs introduced on secondary industrial action. On the individual side, the Act altered certain aspects of unfair dismissal law (principally those relating to the burden of proof, the closed shop and compensation) and made changes in the rules governing maternity rights and guarantee pay.

The Employment Act 1982, an altogether 'drier' statute by a more established government, contained some new provisions (eg altering the law of unfair dismissal in cases where the persons dismissed were on strike) and a host of minor amendments. However, it was principally designed to tighten up the 1980 Act in two areas—the closed shop and the law on industrial disputes. With regard to the former, it imposed more stringent procedural requirements of balloting, radically increased the compensation payable to an employee unfairly dismissed because of a closed shop, and made it more likely that in such a case compensation will in fact be paid by the union rather than the employer. Also, new provisions were introduced to discourage the inclusion of union-labour-only requirements in contracts and tenders. In the area of industrial disputes, the Act basically left alone the restrictions introduced by the 1980 Act (though with a tightening-up of the definition of 'trade dispute' on which the statutory immunities are based); however, the radical change in the 1982 Act was the removal of the union's complete immunity from suit in tort (which the unions had had, with the exception of the years of the Industrial Relations Act 1971, since the Trade Disputes Act 1906), so that now the union itself may be sued (subject to statutory maxima on the damages recoverable) if it contravenes the strengthened laws on industrial disputes.

The Trade Union Act 1984 (following the 1983 election when 'giving unions back to their members' was a prominent Conservative theme) was the third major statute passed by the previous government, but in large part marked a significant departure. While Part II can be seen as following on from the Employment Acts 1980 and 1982 by allowing an employer to sue a union (for damages or an injunction) if the union takes strike or other industrial action without the now obligatory strike ballot, Parts I and III were different in that the causes of action contained within them are vested in the union *members*. Part I obliged a union to hold secret ballots for high union offices and Part III introduced compulsory periodic reballoting on whether a union should continue to operate a political fund. This Act was therefore aimed at the *internal* affairs of a trade union particularly as the events surrounding the miners' strike and certain other major industrial disputes tended to show a greater degree of readiness on the part of union members (or of whole sections of a union) to resort to legal action in order to secure compliance with the union's rules. This process was taken a stage further by the Employment Act 1988 (following the 1987 election and the experiences of the miners' strike of 1984–85, a major event in the evolution of employment law at the time), which tightened up some of the provisions of the 1984 Act (in relation to balloting) and introduced certain new statutory rights for union members (eg rights to ballots before industrial action, to inspect union accounts, to restrain unlawful expenditure by the union and not to be unjustifiably disciplined); to assist in the enforcement of rights against a union, the Act also established the office of Commissioner for the Rights of Trade Union Members. In one respect, the Act harked back to the early legislation of that government, for it took the changes to the law on the closed shop to their logical conclusion by removing *all* legal protection from it as an institution, so that it is now no longer possible for a union to establish or maintain a legally effective, post-entry closed shop.

While the Employment Act 1989 was largely a tinkering measure, the Employment Act 1990 in several ways set the seal on a decade of change,[12] taking several themes

---

[12] Highly recommended reading to set this series of statutes into their political context is Auerbach *Legislating for Conflict* (1990), commented on in Foch et al 'Politics, Pragmatism and Ideology: The Wellsprings of Conservative Union Legislation' (1993) 22 ILJ 14; and Davies and Freedland *Labour Legislation and Public*

first developed in 1980 to their logical conclusions. In particular, it rendered illegal the *pre*-entry closed shop, made illegal *all* secondary action and attacked *un*official industrial action. Thus, by 1990 laws were in place which many Conservatives would have liked to have seen in 1980, had they been able to wave a magic wand. Crucially, of course, by that time there had also been a significant decrease in union membership, a radical decrease in union influence and a very noticeable move away, in many areas, from collectively negotiated terms and conditions of employment, towards more individual contracting, flexibility in employment and more use of what used to be called atypical employments. Indeed, by the early 1990s the encouragement of such moves had been adopted as government policy,[13] along with continuing deregulation.

After the fourth Conservative election victory in 1992, another Bill was expected, though possibly of a tinkering nature again, meant politically to show that the government had not run out of steam in the hitherto politically profitable area of industrial relations. However, the Trade Union Reform and Employment Rights Act 1993 turned out to be far more than that. It again addressed union elections and ballots, and the financial affairs of unions; it recast members' rights on disciplining and expulsion; further restrictions were introduced on industrial action (including strike notice and a Citizen's Charter right for individuals to challenge industrial action in the public sector). In the individual field, it altered the laws on maternity, employment particulars, redundancy consultation and transfers of undertakings in response to changes in EC law, and introduced two new heads of unfair dismissal. As a logical, but much criticized, further measure to deregulate the labour market, it finally abolished wages councils.

Outside the above mainstream legislation, the 1980s also saw very significant changes in social security laws relevant to employment law (especially payment through the employer, through statutory sick pay and statutory maternity pay), and the Wages Act 1986 introduced new laws on deductions from wages that saw quite remarkable development in the early 1990s. In the field of discrimination law there were, again, consistent developments, but this time largely through the intervention of EC law rather than changes in domestic legislation. If all of this does not provide the reader with enough excitement in life, there are always the Transfer of Undertakings Regulations ...

Given this quite remarkable series of statutes (and, often, their supporting regulations and orders) we have at least been fortunate in having five major consolidations in the period 1992–96, bringing some order to the chaos. The Trade Union and Labour Relations (Consolidation) Act 1992 consolidated the morass of laws (ancient and modern) on collective labour law, replacing in particular the Trade Union and Labour Relations Act 1974 and most of the Conservative Employment Acts 1980–93. Social

---

Policy (1993). The political progress of the three governments of Mrs Thatcher is set out in excellent and highly readable form in Young *One of Us* (1990).

[13] Employment for the 1990s (Cm 540, 1988); People, Jobs and Opportunity (Cm 1810, 1992).

security law was consolidated into the Social Security Contributions and Benefits Act 1992 and the Social Security Administration Act 1992; it took a particularly strong river to clean out those Augean stables. The law relating to individual employment matters was finally consolidated in the Employment Rights Act 1996 which replaced the Employment Protection (Consolidation) Act 1978 (as, by then, heavily amended) and the Wages Act 1986, with the law relating to tribunals and the EAT being consolidated at the same time in the Employment Tribunals Act 1996. Outside that framework lay the Equal Pay Act 1970, the Sex Discrimination Act 1975, the Race Relations Act 1976, the Disability Discrimination Act 1995 and the Pensions Act 1995.

(iv) NEW LABOUR: CHANGE AND CONTINUITY

The 1997 General Election saw the end of a period of 18 years of Conservative administrations and a landslide victory for New Labour. Dramatic though this political reversal of fortunes was, it was far removed from the previous return of a Labour government in 1974, when the Trade Union and Labour Relations Act 1974 (sweeping away the previous Conservative government's employment laws) was the first statute passed by that incoming government. Instead, New Labour seemed to put a relatively low priority on employment law changes (reflecting the equally low priority of the subject at the election), and it had been made clear for some time by the 'modernizers' within the party that there were to be no wholesale repeals of the reforms of the Thatcher administration.[14] Indeed, the first statute passed was the Employment Rights (Dispute Resolution) Act 1998 (reforming tribunal procedures and establishing the ACAS arbitration alternative to tribunals for unfair dismissal cases) which was inherited at Green Paper stage from the previous government. The National Minimum Wage Act 1998 enacted one of New Labour's relatively few election commitments on employment law, and the Working Time Regulations 1998 were an obligation under EC law (the previous government's challenge to the legality of the backing Directive having failed in the European Court of Justice); the Public Interest Disclosure (or 'Whistleblowers') Act 1998 was also in many ways relatively uncontroversial and commanded widespread support. It was only with the publication of the White Paper 'Fairness at Work'[15] that a clear idea could be obtained of the likely direction of the new government in this area. Again, however, in spite of some reforms important in themselves, this was hardly a major sea change, and even then the government were accused of some backsliding by the unions on the eventual form of

---

[14] 'The abolition of the closed shop was one of the many employment law reforms of the 1980s that were justified and will remain … Other measures which will remain include those on picketing, secondary action, ballots and notice before strikes, unofficial action, elections for certain trade union offices and rights to join the trade union of one's choice and not to be unjustifiably disciplined': Fairness at Work (Cm 3968, May 1998), p 22. For the background political changes, especially in relations with the trade unions, see McIlroy 'The Enduring Alliance? Trade Unions and the Making of New Labour 1994–1997' (1998) 36 BJIR 537.

[15] See n 14. See generally Taylor 'Annual Review Article 1997' (1998) 36 BJIR 293.

the resulting statute, the Employment Relations Act 1999, especially in relation to the union recognition procedure and the mere lifting of the limit on the unfair dismissal compensatory award (from £12,000 to £50,000), rather than its abolition as had been mooted in the White Paper. The introduction to the White Paper said that this Act was not to be seen as merely a first step in reforms, because it 'seeks to draw a line under the issue of industrial relations law' and this was largely the case in the first Labour government, at least in relation to purely domestic legislation. However, the second New Labour government (after their emphatic re-election in 2001) did see a renewed increase in the pace of domestic legislation with the enactment of the Employment Act 2002, a bad example of 'Henry VIII' drafting, ie requiring supplementation by a huge raft of statutory instruments over a prolonged period. The two main themes of this Act were the extension of family-friendly policies (a major plank of New Labour policy, covering longer maternity leave, paternity and adoption leave and the right to request flexible working) and a fairly desperate attempt to halt the inexorable rise in tribunal applications by further reforms of tribunal procedure and (more radi-cally) new 'standard procedures' for grievances and discipline/dismissal which must be exhausted by both parties before going to a tribunal (backed by a regime of auto-matic unfairness, striking out of tribunal claims and significant increases or decreases in compensation).

At the same time as these domestic developments, EC law was becoming more active. Prior to Mr Blair's second election victory in 2001 there had been transposed one Directive in the Part-time Workers (Prevention of Less Favourable Treatment) Regulations 2000, and not long afterwards the transposition of a second 'atypical worker' Directive in the Fixed-term Employees (Prevention of Less Favourable Treatment) Regulations, though a third and complementary Directive on agency workers did not then find favour with member states and was rejected. Going beyond this area of mainstream employment law, EC law was also by this time powering discrimination law, leading to an upgrading of existing sex, race and disability discrimination law (in particular introducing a statutory reversal of the burden of proof and a wider definition of indirect discrimination) and the introduction of new laws to combat employment-related discrimination in the areas of sexual orientation, religion or belief, and age. The Information and Consultation Directive 2002 led to enactment of the Information and Consultation of Employees Regulations 2004 giving a legal right to require mechanisms for informing and consulting the workforce (where no such mechanism already exists) in firms of 150 or more employees by 2005, in firms of 100 or more by 2007, and finally in firms of fifty or more by 2008. The other major EC law development was the updating of the Acquired Rights Directive, leading to the renewed Transfer of Undertakings (Protection of Employment) Regulations 2006 which introduced some useful reforms but were also a disappointment in other ways, this being an area where the government could only make changes which were allowed by the Directive itself.

The domestic law agenda of this second New Labour government was unadventurous after the Employment Act 2002 (the Employment Relations Act 2004 being largely a miscellany of technical amendments to industrial relations law), but at the 2005 election there was once again considerable emphasis by New Labour on further developments in family-friendly policies and the work–life balance. A year after Mr Blair's third election victory, this fed through into the Work and Families Act 2006 which gave extended maternity rights (including the raising of the statutory maternity pay period to nine months, as a stage towards an eventual one year) and paternity rights, and (significantly, given changes to the UK's demographic pattern) extended the right to request flexible working to those with caring responsibilities for the elderly and infirm.

The Employment Act 2008, as well as making several technical amendments (particularly to the national minimum wage legislation) addressed one major problem in employment law by that time. The 'standard procedures' for grievances and dismissal (introduced by the 2004 Act to attempt to drive down the tribunal application figures) had proved to be an inflexible, bureaucratic and (at times) counterproductive failure, to such an extent that they were even producing exasperated criticism by the judges having to try to make sense of them, in language sometimes bordering on the unjudicial. They stand as a warning of two dangers in employment law—trying to impose a one-size-fits-all solution to the myriad forms of employment and assuming that legal provisions alone can resolve an employment law problem. To avoid at least a level of facial egg, the government commissioned an independent review of them (the Gibbons Report) which grasped the nettle and recommended total repeal, a relief to all involved. This was done in the 2008 Act,[16] though (in a good example of 'legislate in haste, repeal at leisure') it has taken years to purge the system of the last cases to be governed by them. Fortunately, however, it is no longer necessary for this edition to consider them and their voluminous case law. Finally, two other legislative developments occurred towards the end of this government. First, the EU finally agreed a directive on temporary working and this was transposed into domestic law in the Agency Workers Regulations 2010. Secondly, a further major consolidation exercise resulted in all six heads of discrimination being put into one place, the Equality Act 2010; in addition to the mammoth task of consolidation, the then government introduced a limited number of substantive changes to the law in this Act, though at the time of writing several of these have either not been brought into force or are actively being considered for repeal by the successor Coalition government.

(v) THE COALITION GOVERNMENT

The 2010 election proved inconclusive in the sense that Labour lost it but the Conservatives did not win it. The result was a Conservative/Liberal Democrat Coalition, a factor that has had an effect in employment law because of the compromises that have had to be made to possible reforms in this area. It is certainly true that

---

[16] See Sanders 'Part I of the Employment Act 2008: "Better" Dispute Resolution? (2009) 38 ILJ 30.

the Conservative side of the Coalition have not been able to make certain changes that their backbenchers would have liked to see; on the other hand the Liberal Democrats have had to agree to other changes that in a wider sense could be seen as not exactly 'liberal' as the price of progress of some of their ideas, in particular extending even further the laws on flexible and family-friendly working.[17] Part of the Coalition agreement was a review of employment law. Possibly as a result of the novelty in this country of Coalition politics, this has not had the sort of ideological consistency of the reforms of Mrs Thatcher's governments *but* when the eventual proposed changes are taken as a whole they do amount to a relatively large scale of reform, if only of an incremental nature. At the time of writing (December 2012) the power to make many (but not all) of these changes is being established by the Enterprise and Regulatory Reform Bill but this will still leave nearly all the substantive changes to Regulations. These are likely to come into force over a considerable period in 2013 and 2014, with changes to flexible working being scheduled for 2015. They will have to be taken into consideration by the reader during the currency of this edition.

3 MACHINERY (1): PRACTICAL DISPUTE RESOLUTION

As seen above, the voluntary and non-legal nature of British industrial relations has been its dominant characteristic, and there is not an overall statutory framework for compulsory conciliation and arbitration leading to enforceable awards and agreements as may be found in certain other countries. Moreover, we do not formally distinguish between what are conceptually two different types of industrial dispute—those about the negotiation of new and improved terms of employment (disputes of interest) and those about the interpretation, application and enforcement of existing terms (disputes of right).[18] Arguably there should be separate procedures for dealing with these, particularly as the second type is inherently more amenable to legal adjudication, but in this country any such differentiation will be the exception rather than the rule, and so both kinds of dispute tend (in areas where collective bargaining is still the norm) to be subject to voluntarily negotiated procedures of varying quality (or ad hoc arrangements), leading as has been seen to non-enforceable collective agreements. However, although the law has been non-interventionist (except for the period covered by the

---

[17] The Prime Minister's office commissioned a report into employment law by a businessman, Adam Beecroft, which suggested extremely wide-ranging reforms, including an a element of American-style dismissal at will, or at least on the payment of a set amount of money. This report was eventually dropped, as was confirmed with some pleasure by the Liberal Democrat Secretary of State for BIS, Vince Cable, *but* one cynical interpretation is that the whole point of the Beecroft review was to spook the Liberal Democrats into agreeing to other, less radical reforms which otherwise they may have opposed.

[18] Report of the Royal Commission on Trade Unions and Employers' Associations (Cmnd 3623, 1968) para 60.

Industrial Relations Act 1971) it has not abstained totally, and has attempted in various ways at various times to provide certain residual machinery to facilitate industrial relations and minimize industrial conflict. Wages councils were historically used (prior to their abolition in 1993) to aid collective bargaining in under-unionized trades, and since the Conciliation Act 1896 there has existed machinery (in various forms, but before 1975 principally under the Department of Employment and its predecessors) for industrial conciliation. Since the Industrial Courts Act 1919[19] there has also existed machinery for industrial arbitration, previously under the Industrial Court (a tripartite arbitral body, not to be confused with the NIRC, set up by the Industrial Relations Act 1971) which was renamed the Industrial Arbitration Board between 1971 and 1974, under the 1971 Act; once again, however, the arbitration has always[20] been basically voluntary, ie by the consent of the parties. Since 1975, these conciliation and arbitration services have been largely provided by the Advisory, Conciliation and Arbitration Service (ACAS), and are considered below.

In the resolution of employment disputes by the intervention of an outside agency there is an important conceptual distinction. On the one hand there is conciliation which is where the conciliator attempts to bring the parties together in the hope that a common discussion will reveal a means of settlement acceptable to both parties; one variation of this is 'mediation' where the mediator takes a more active role in putting forward detailed solutions, though still with a view to settlement by agreement.[21] These functions are now within the jurisdiction of ACAS, which was originally established by the Employment Protection Act 1975 and is the successor to the conciliatory functions of the Department of Employment (and the Commission on Industrial Relations which functioned under the 1971 Act). On the other hand there is arbitration, which is where the arbitrator fulfils a quasi-judicial role in that the parties have agreed to submit their dispute to that person for his or her *decision* on what should be the result; he or she therefore has to look into the relevant facts and law, and it is clearly understood that the parties will abide by the decision. This function is now within the jurisdiction of both ACAS and the Central Arbitration Committee (CAC), which also was established by the Employment Protection Act 1975 and is the successor to the Industrial Court and the Industrial Arbitration Board; as we shall see, it may conduct voluntary arbitrations,

---

[19] Now the Trade Union and Labour Relations (Consolidation) Act 1992, ss 215–16, in relation to courts of inquiry.

[20] Except for the period 1940–59 when, initially as a result of wartime measures aimed at avoiding industrial disruptions, some arbitration was compulsory. In 1951 Order 1376 replaced Order 1305 of 1940; some 1,270 cases were heard before its revocation in 1959: see Cooper's *Outlines of Industrial Law* (6th edn, 1972) 446–51; Kahn-Freund *Labour and the Law* (1983) 151–3.

[21] Mediation may be used particularly (1) where issues cannot be presented in a sufficiently clear-cut manner for arbitration (eg major changes of work, linked to a pay settlement) or (2) where one or both of the parties is or are unwilling to submit the matter formally to arbitration (on the principle that a party who agrees to arbitration must ultimately be able to afford to lose). Either way, mediation must be properly understood by the parties—it does not result in an 'award' by the mediator, though there may be considerable moral pressure to comply with the mediator's suggestions.

but also has certain powers of unilateral arbitration under statute and has now been given important new jurisdictions in relation to the statutory recognition procedure, European Works Councils and the informing and consulting of employees.

(i) THE ADVISORY CONCILIATION AND ARBITRATION SERVICE

The composition of ACAS is governed primarily by Part VI of the Trade Union and Labour Relations (Consolidation) Act 1992. It is directed by a Council consisting of a chairman and between nine and 15 members (three or four representing employers, three or four representing unions and the rest 'independents'). ACAS itself is set up as a body independent of the government, in particular independent of the Department for Business, and appoints its own staff. It maintains a central office in London and regional offices in Scotland, and in five regions in England and Wales, and must produce an annual report for the Secretary of State for Business to lay before Parliament.

Amongst its staff, it maintains 'conciliation officers'[22] who have particular responsibility for conciliating in statutory actions brought by individual employees.

The functions of ACAS are set out in Part IV of the 1992 Act; in addition to the detailed functions considered below, there is a statement of its general duty in section 209, as follows:

It is the general duty of ACAS to promote the improvement of industrial relations.

This apparently simple formulation has in fact gone through three phases, with considerable symbolic significance (if little practical effect). From 1975 to 1993 the section continued 'and in particular to encourage the extension of collective bargaining and the development and, where necessary, reform of collective bargaining machinery'. That may well have been the ethos of the 1970s, but after a decade in the 1980s of overt government hostility to any such aims it was hardly surprising that the previous government took the opportunity in the Trade Union Reform and Employment Rights Act 1993 to repeal that wording. They substituted 'in particular by exercising its functions in relation to the settlement of trade disputes under sections 210 and 212 [ie by conciliation and arbitration]'. ACAS had certainly proved useful to the previous Conservative government in certain disputes (a measure of that use being that they were never seriously threatened with abolition, unlike most tripartite bodies of the 1970s), and this formulation reflected that. However, it arguably placed too much emphasis on reactive, problem-solving work ('fire fighting' in IR jargon), and too little on long-term advice work ('fire prevention') which ACAS wanted to enhance. With the change of government in 1997, an increased emphasis on fire prevention could be seen to be consistent with the present government's 'partnership' ideas in the White Paper 'Fairness at Work'. As a result, the Employment Relations Act 1999 removed the

---

[22] Trade Union and Labour Relations (Consolidation) Act 1992, s 211; they are known as Conciliation Officers Tribunals (COTs) to distinguish them from those specializing in collective conciliation.

1993 wording and left ACAS with the widest possible general duty as set out above. Of course, the cynic could argue that the extent to which ACAS can increase their proactive work will depend not on a change to their statutory remit but on the resources they are to be given; over the past decade there has also been some controversy, with those resources first being depleted significantly but then largely restored when the previous government realized they needed ACAS to dig them out of the hole caused by the failure of their system of 'standard procedures' for grievance and dismissal.

The specific statutory functions[23] of ACAS are as follows.

(a) Collective conciliation

Where a trade dispute[24] exists or seems imminent ACAS may, at the request of one or more of the parties or on its own initiative, offer its assistance for the purposes of conciliation or mediation. In doing so, it may also refer the parties to a third person for conciliation, and it must where possible encourage the parties to use any existing negotiation or disputes procedures.[25] The traditional form of conciliation is carried out by an individual ACAS officer working directly with the parties, but in recent years there has been an increase in the use of a hybrid form, referred to as 'advisory mediation', aimed at encouraging a cooperative and problem-solving approach by the parties themselves, possibly on a longer term basis; this tends to be done by the setting up of a joint workshop or joint working party, chaired by the ACAS officer, and may be particularly appropriate for resolving disputes over matters such as handling organizational change.[26] In addition to these forms of voluntary conciliation, ACAS also has statutory conciliation functions at certain stages in union claims for disclosure of bargaining information or under the statutory recognition procedure, both of which are considered in Chapter 9.

One area of potential difficulty for ACAS in the context of collective conciliation may arise if it transpires in a particular dispute that the employer is seeking to bring a legal action against the union, initially for an injunction to restrain the industrial action or threat of it and then possibly in a suit for damages. In such a case, any ACAS

---

[23] These services always were in the past free to the parties, but s 251A of the 1992 Act (inserted by the Trade Union Reform and Employment Rights Act 1993) gave a power to charge fees *and* a power for the Secretary of State to require the charging of fees for some or all services. This change was not wanted by ACAS itself.

[24] The wide definition as originally contained in the Trade Union and Labour Relations Act 1974, s 29 (and now in the Trade Union and Labour Relations (Consolidation) Act 1992, s 218) continues to apply for this purpose; the narrowed definition for the purpose of immunity from tort action in industrial disputes enacted by the Employment Act 1982 and now in the 1992 Act, s 244 does not apply here. Perhaps an example of governmental propensity to have cake and consume same.

[25] Trade Union and Labour Relations (Consolidation) Act 1992, s 210. In 2011/12, 972 collective conciliation cases were received and 754 completed. Of these cases, 46% concerned pay or other terms of employment, 12% recognition, 10% redundancy, 10% other union issues, 10% dismissal/discipline and 10% changes in working practices: *ACAS Annual Report 2011/12*. Independent research carried out in 1985 and published in 1988 showed a high level of satisfaction with the service provided, by both unions and employers: *ACAS Annual Report 1987* p 26.

[26] See Kessler and Purcell 'Joint Problem Solving' (ACAS Occasional Paper No 55).

intervention would have to be more circumspect. However, there is another side to it, since such ACAS intervention might in practice be more likely to resolve an impasse than legal proceedings, and at one stage the suggestion was made tentatively that the law should be amended to include provision for a judge to stay proceedings in any action arising from an industrial dispute in order for ACAS to attempt conciliation[27] which, if successful, might well make considerable savings in cost, time, acrimony and accusations against the courts of partiality in industrial disputes; however, this interesting suggestion has never been taken up. It can be further noted that where the parties engage lawyers the lines of communication may be lengthened and the process of conciliation made more difficult.

(b) Individual conciliation

ACAS, through its conciliation officers, has a statutory duty to attempt to conciliate in cases brought before tribunals by individuals claiming unfair dismissal or denial of employment protection rights; this also applies to cases of all the heads of modern discrimination law and to the various rights enacted by the legislation for the protection of trade union members, including the statutory redundancy handling procedures.[28] The ACAS regional offices receive copies of originating applications to the tribunals and a conciliation officer must attempt to settle a case without reference to a tribunal if requested to do so by the parties or if, in the absence of a request, he thinks there may be a reasonable prospect of success.[29] In all cases, the conciliation officer must consider encouraging the use of established grievance procedures within the firm. In unfair dismissal cases, the officer must in theory seek to promote a settlement primarily by way of reinstatement or re-engagement, and only attempt a monetary settlement if that is impracticable, or not wanted by the ex-employee.[30] The conciliation process is confidential, in that anything said to the officer during it is not admissible evidence

---

[27] *ACAS Annual Report 1983* para 1.16.

[28] Employment Tribunals Act 1996, s 18. See ACAS *Individual Employment Rights—ACAS Conciliation between Individuals and Employers.*

[29] For many years the total number of such (ET1) cases received by ACAS was stable at about 35,000 pa. However, they started to climb alarmingly in the 1990s, reaching 79,332 cases received in 1994. This was at a time of some decrease in numbers of staff and placed a severe strain on other ACAS functions. The figures took another lurch upwards in 1995 to 91,568, topped 100,000 in 1996 and stood at 165,093 in 2001–02. This was the background to attempts by successive governments to lessen reliance on the tribunal system, first in the Employment Rights (Dispute Resolution) Act 1998 and then in the Employment Act 2002. At first this seemed to be working, with a decrease to 81,833 in 2004–05, but there was a further lurch upwards in 2005–06 to 109,712. In 2011/12 that figure stood at 72,075, but when pre-claim cases (below) are added the total figure was 94,090. Of the cases received in 2011/12, 56% were primarily for unfair dismissal, 27% for working time issues, 14% for redundancy and 28% for discrimination; one odd figure is that 70% of cases included an element of unpaid wages or other benefits (taking the figures well over 100%) but this is because such claims are frequently added to other primary claims. Of the cases completed in the year, 43% were settled, 24% were withdrawn and only 21% proceeded to a tribunal hearing: *ACAS Annual Report 2011/12.*

[30] Employment Tribunals Act 1996, s 18(4). This is wholly ineffective in practice, as can be seen from the consistently low rate of re-employment (whether by order or by agreement): see Ch 7, heading 6; Williams and Lewis *The Aftermath of Tribunal Reinstatement and Re-engagement* (DE Research Paper No 23) pp 31 and 39.

in subsequent tribunal proceedings without the consent of the person who said it.[31] It must be emphasized that if the conciliation is successful in leading to an agreed settlement as a consequence of action taken by a conciliation officer under his statutory duties, that will bar any future tribunal proceedings in the matter,[32] so that the claimant should be certain that he or she is happy with the terms of the proposed settlement before irrevocably agreeing with it. For this reason alone, it is vital that ACAS should behave, and be seen to behave, entirely impartially as between the claimant and the employer when conducting negotiations.

In this respect, a serious problem arose for ACAS through the rise throughout the 1980s of the number of cases submitted to them *without* any formal application having been made to a tribunal. In these cases (referred to as 'non-ET 1' cases in the jargon) the employer would often be wanting ACAS to record an agreement already reached, in order to achieve legal finality, but doubts could arise as to whether the employee had really understood the terms of the agreement. A conflict arose between law and practice. Legally, it was clear from the cases that there was no statutory obligation on an ACAS officer to ensure that it was a *fair* settlement and so an employee could not later challenge the binding nature of the settlement on the grounds that ACAS had not explained his rights to him properly or given him independent advice.[33] On the other hand, it was the established ACAS view that their officers should not simply act as rubber stamps for possibly inequitable settlements and should at least enquire whether the employee understood his position and his rights.[34] Eventually, however, the considerable rise in non-ET 1 cases placed such a strain on resources that ACAS had to reconsider its policy. This was done in 1990 and the current position is that: (1) officers will only act in non-ET 1 cases where the employee claims infringement of specified employment rights; (2) they will decline to conciliate where any qualifying period is clearly not satisfied; (3) they will not become involved where employment ended voluntarily or where a redundancy occurred under fairly applied customary arrangements or agreed procedures; and (4) (most importantly) they will not have any

---

[31] Further, anything communicated to the ACAS officer in this process is covered by the defence of absolute privilege in the law of defamation: *Freer v Glover* [2006] IRLR 521, QBD.

[32] ERA 1996, s 203(2); there are equivalent provisions in the discrimination legislation and the other provisions where ACAS conciliation appears. Because of the form on which they are recorded, these are known as 'COT3 settlements'.

[33] In *Moore v Duport Furniture Products Ltd* [1982] ICR 84, [1982] IRLR 31, HL, it was held (1) that the action of the conciliation officer in recording an agreement to accept compensation of £300 on the standard form COT3 was sufficient to bar further proceedings, and (2) that where an officer is presented with such an agreement already worked out by the parties, his duty is only to verify the fact of agreement and record it—he is not under a further duty to enquire into the 'fairness' of the agreement or to give the applicant any further advice. Likewise, an ACAS official is under no legal duty to explain the law to the applicant and is not bound to adopt any particular formula or approach: *Slack v Greenham (Plant Hire) Ltd* [1983] ICR 617, [1983] IRLR 271. This approach was strongly reaffirmed in *Clarke v Redcar & Cleveland BC* [2006] IRLR 324 where equal pay claimants were trying to evade a COT3 settlement after receiving further legal advice that they had settled for too little, arguing unsuccessfully that the ACAS officer should have told them that it was too little.

[34] *ACAS Annual Report 1984* p 63.

role to play in *any* case (whether or not a non-ET 1 case) where a firm agreement has already been reached independently, *unless* the terms of the agreement are capable of being changed as a result of conciliation.[35] One result of this, to provide a mechanism for dealing with non-ET 1 cases, was the introduction of the concept of the 'compromise agreement' which allows the parties themselves to reach a binding agreement which rules out a tribunal application, providing the statutory criteria are satisfied, the most important being that the individual has received advice from an independent adviser as to the effect of the proposed agreement.[36] There are now therefore two forms of legally binding settlements, the longstanding ACAS COT3 settlement and the compromise agreement. At the time of writing, the Coalition government intend to raise the profile of compromise agreements (in order to increase even further the level of settlement on which the whole system depends), including by renaming them 'settlement agreements'.

One very important development in individual conciliation arose from the repeal of the 'standard procedures' for grievance and dismissal, which were abolished in April 2009. Welcome though that was, it was only the start for ACAS because the Gibbons Report which had recommended abolition envisaged as part of a replacement system (along with a revised ACAS code of practice and a greater emphasis on 'mediation') more active intervention by ACAS *before* disputes get to the issuing of tribunal proceedings. To this end, ACAS have established a system of 'pre-claim conciliation' (PCC), ie intervention *before* an ET1 tribunal claim form has been issued, which in most cases is bound to harden attitudes. In a sense, it is a very *old* idea (in traditional ACAS parlance, fire prevention rather than firefighting), but there are two potential problems—(1) the rise in the number of tribunal applications may jeopardize it, because ACAS have a statutory *duty* to conciliate in those cases which may soak up resources meant for PCC;[37] (2) all parties concerned (employer, trade union, advice workers, ACAS) still have to operate this system against the background of very tight timetables because one thing that the government would *not* consider as part of the abolition of the standard procedures was any relaxation of the inflexible three-month time limit for most employment claims. The Coalition government intend, at the time of writing, to address both of these issues in the Enterprise and Regulatory Reform Bill. If these fundamental proposals proceed, the whole system will change, in that PCC will become ACAS's primary *duty*, relegating the traditional ET1 cases to a mere power (with the availability of conciliation dependent on resources). The emphasis will therefore be on early attempts at resolution. On the question of timing, this is to be dealt with by providing that when

---

[35] *ACAS Annual Report 1991* p 45. As a result of this change, the non-ET 1 caseload declined from 17,724 in 1989 to only 2,431 in 1992.

[36] Employment Rights Act 1996, s 203(3)–(4) provides the template for the rules on compromise agreements in all the relevant legislation.

[37] In spite of this, the early experience of PCC has been encouraging and in 2011/12 ACAS received 23,777 requests for PCC; the resolution figure was 55%: *ACAS Annual Report 2011/12.*

a case goes to PCC the clock of the time limit in question will stop (the proposal being for up to one month). The intention is to bring in these radical changes in 2014.

(c) Arranging arbitration

Under section 212 of the Trade Union and Labour Relations (Consolidation) Act 1992, ACAS may arrange arbitration for an actual or anticipated trade dispute if one or more of the parties request it *and* all parties consent to it.[38] This is clearly voluntary arbitration, and the resulting decision will not be legally enforceable per se,[39] though in practice the arbitrator's decision is invariably complied with. ACAS does not automatically have to arrange arbitration; as well as being satisfied that all parties consent, it must also consider whether conciliation might be successful instead, and should not arrange arbitration unless satisfied that existing negotiation and disputes procedures have been exhausted (unless there are special reasons why arbitration should be used *instead* of such procedures). The conciliation stage is important—if successful it removes the need for an arbitration; if unsuccessful the ACAS conciliation officer then has the task of determining with the parties the precise terms of reference for the arbitrator, for it is important in an arbitration that the terms are not themselves a subject for dispute; in fact, the terms of reference are usually kept as simple as possible and, further, nothing of what has happened or been said at the conciliation stage is made known to the arbitrator, who approaches the issue afresh. The usual practice is for ACAS to appoint one person to conduct the arbitration (from the panel of approximately 80 appropriate people whom they use), though occasionally a board of arbitration may be convened; officials and employees of ACAS are *not* used, though ACAS do of course provide the necessary secretarial and administrative services.[40] It is also possible for a voluntary arbitration to be referred to the CAC, though this option has effectively now fallen into disuse. Legal representation at an arbitration is unusual (and indeed usually discouraged if suggested) and although the proceedings may be conducted in a relatively structured manner (aimed at giving both sides a full opportunity to expand upon their written submissions and to query the other side's case), matters of procedure are largely for the arbitrator to determine and will not normally include legalistic forms, such as prolonged cross-examination.

Certain particular aspects in arbitration might be noted here briefly. First, references may come from *standing* arbitration agreements, usually taking the form of a clause in the disputes procedure section of a collective bargain stating that in the absence

---

[38] Mumford 'Arbitration and ACAS in Britain: A Historical Perspective' (1996) 34 BJIR 287.

[39] Pt I of the Arbitration Act 1996 does not apply to this form of arbitration: s 212(5). One rare example of binding arbitration on terms and conditions of employment was contained in the Pilotage Act 1987, s 5 and the Terms of Employment of Pilots (Arbitration) Regulations 1988, SI 1988/1089, but it was meant to be a temporary expedient; see Smith 'The Pilots' Compensation Scheme: A Study in Arbitration, Interpretation and Causation' (1994) 32 BJIR 379.

[40] In 2011/12 there were only 21 references to arbitration: *ACAS Annual Report 2011/12*. On the use of third-party intervention, see Millward et al *Workplace Industrial Relations in Transition* (1992) 194–6 and 208–11.

of agreement on a disputed point through internal procedures, the matter shall be referred to ACAS for conciliation and/or arbitration. This may be a general reference, or the clause itself may cover the procedure that is to be adopted. Second, it is possible for parties to a dispute to approach ACAS to ask them simply to *nominate* an arbitrator to conduct an arbitration which has already been agreed upon, without going through the normal conciliation procedures; such arbitrations do not figure in the annual ACAS statistics.[41] Third, at times there has been considerable interest in and publicity about the form of arbitration variously known as 'pendulum', 'flip-flop', 'straight choice' or 'final offer', where the arbitrator is constrained to choose between acceptance in full of one side's case or that of the other.[42] The aim of this is said to be to narrow the field of dispute and ensure that each side puts forward a realistic (rather than a bargaining) case, capable of being accepted in full. While this may be a natural form of adjudication in disputes of right, ACAS is by no means convinced that it is a panacea in disputes of interest such as pay determinations where flexibility in the arbitration may be just as important. Although ACAS will arrange such an arbitration if the parties desire it, it does *not* adopt it as its policy, preferring to encourage responsible bargaining in other ways and pointing out consistently that the fact that an arbitrator is normally given full discretion in coming to his award does *not* mean in practice that all he or she does is to split the disputed area down the middle, with half a baby to each.

(d) Arbitration in unfair dismissal and flexible working cases

Although voluntary arbitration has always been available to the parties to a dismissal dispute, it has in the past worked on an informal basis (with a disappointed complainant employee still able to go to a tribunal for a further hearing), and in recent years has declined in numbers along with arbitration generally. Faced with the steep rise in tribunal applications, the previous government explored the possibility of a revamped ACAS-run arbitration scheme to act as an *alternative* to tribunal proceedings.[43] This idea was taken up by the previous government, and made possible by the Employment Rights (Dispute Resolution) Act 1998, section 7 (inserting the Trade Union and Labour Relations (Consolidation) Act 1992, section 212A) which gives ACAS the power to produce a scheme for promulgation by the Secretary of State by order. Although this power has existed since August 1998, the finalized scheme did not

---

[41] This, however, can lead to a problem: the resulting arbitration is *not* an ACAS arbitration within the Act and so the exclusion of the Arbitration Act 1996 by s 212(5) (n 39) does not apply. Thus the 1996 Act could be applicable (if the agreement to arbitrate is in writing) and so the resulting decision could be legally binding (and any recourse to the courts excluded) under that Act, possibly without the parties realizing it at the time.

[42] See the *CAC Annual Report 1984* ch 3 for a discussion of this development. The aim is to avoid the damage arbitration is said to do to conciliation. Parties in negotiation anticipating arbitration tend to 'stand off' leaving a wide band of discretion for the arbitrator. Final offer arbitration encourages them to adopt a more realistic position, even perhaps to reach agreement. While this is a natural process in disputes of right, where the arbitrator has usually two positions to choose from, it is less certain in its application to disputes of interest. There is considerable North American experience in public sector arbitration.

[43] Resolving Employment Rights Disputes: Options for Reform (Cm 2707, 1994).

come into force until 2001.[44] It is based on a high level of agreement between the parties and has to be entered through a COT3 agreement or compromise agreement making it clear that the parties (particularly the claimant) understand that they are giving up completely their right to go to a tribunal. ACAS then organize an individual arbitrator to hear the case; the hearing is deliberately informal (with legal representation discouraged), the arbitrator has the powers of award of a tribunal *but* there is no appeal from the arbitrator's decision. In a sense, this system was an attempt to turn the clock back to a time where disputes were always supposed to be settled internally (going to a tribunal being a sign of failure), but it was always debatable whether this was possible now. The scheme faced considerable hostility from employment lawyers (the lack of an appeal being a particular bugbear) and, from a very slow start, things only went downhill[45] and so the present position is that in practice this is no real alternative to a tribunal for an unfair dismissal claim. In spite of this, the scheme was extended in 2003 when the new right came into force to request flexible working and not be unreasonably refused.[46] In theory this ought to be particularly appropriate for an arbitral approach but to date there has been little or no experience of it.

(e) Advice

The statutory power to give advice, contained in the Trade Union and Labour Relations (Consolidation) Act 1992, section 213, was altered by the Trade Union Reform and Employment Rights Act 1993. It used to contain eleven particular categories of relevant areas, including matters affecting collective bargaining, worker organization and recognition of unions. It now reads more simply:

> ACAS may, on request or otherwise, give employers, employers' associations, workers and trade unions such advice as it thinks appropriate on matters concerned with or affecting or likely to affect industrial relations.

As with the change at that time (considered above) to the general duty of ACAS, this alteration was likely to have little practical effect, but could be seen (in its removal of express references to collective means of resolving employment problems) to be symbolic. Again, references to such matters have not been reinstated by the present government.

The power to advise remains wide and will doubtless continue to be heavily used.[47] It covers general advice, specific replies to queries (for example on the meaning of modern employment laws), in-depth surveys and projects, giving conferences or

---

[44] It is now contained in the ACAS Arbitration Scheme (Great Britain) Order 2004, SI 2004/753, *Harvey* R [1977].

[45] From its inception in 2001 until 2009 only 61 cases were lodged: *ACAS Annual Report 2008–09*.

[46] See the ACAS (Flexible Working) Arbitration Scheme (Great Britain) Order 2004/2333, *Harvey* R [2149].

[47] This advice function has always been of great importance in practice: Armstrong 'Evaluating the Work of ACAS' [1985] Employment Gazette 143 and 'Asking ACAS' (ACAS Occasional Paper No 56; Dix, Hawes and Pinkstone).

seminars and the publishing of advisory booklets.[48] Diagnostic work within a company on a longer term basis may in fact be the result of one particular problem which arose and was settled through ACAS conciliation—the approach may have been made for the ACAS officer to attempt to find a settlement for the immediate problem on the understanding that the whole area in dispute would be looked at, either by the officer himself or, increasingly, by the setting up of a joint working party or workshop under the aegis of ACAS. This latter approach (more recently known as 'advisory mediation', see above) has expanded and largely replaced the older ideas of externally conducted 'IR audits' for two reasons—(1) it fits the current employment relations realities better, reflecting their more diverse nature with less chance of one desirable model being appropriate, but (2) at the same time it enables ACAS still to make a distinctive contribution towards ideas of *joint* resolution of problems and employee involvement, even in areas where formal bargaining with unions is no longer the norm.[49]

The ACAS Helpline came to renewed prominence with the repeal of the standard procedures for grievance and dismissal in 2009. As part of the government's replacement system (aimed at returning to a more voluntaristic and less prescriptive way of resolving individual disputes), the Helpline was expanded by about 50% in order to undertake a subtly different function – previously its function had been largely to give factual information (eg as to a dismissed employee's legal rights) but the idea now is that it should operate more proactively to steer enquiries into the available choices for resolving the possible dispute behind the enquiry (eg pre-claim conciliation, see above) *instead* of issuing tribunal proceedings.[50]

(f) Powers of inquiry

ACAS may on its own initiative hold an inquiry into aspects of industrial relations generally or in any particular industry or firm.[51] It may add its advice to its eventual findings, and is empowered to publish both if it thinks publication desirable (after hearing any representations on the question by those involved). In cases of greater public interest, however, the Secretary of State may decide to appoint a Court of Inquiry under the Trade Union and Labour Relations (Consolidation) Act 1992, section 215 (originally the Industrial Courts Act 1919). This is a more formal procedure than that adopted by ACAS and results in the laying before Parliament and publication of a formal report.[52] In appointing such a court, the Secretary of State lays down rules regulating its procedure, which may include powers to compel witnesses to provide information or give evidence on oath.

---

[48] For the current list of publications, set <http://www.acas.org.uk> under 'our publications'. The website also gives details of the e-learning packages for use in advice and training.

[49] Kessler and Purcell 'Joint Problem Solving—Does it Work? An Evaluation of ACAS In-depth Advisory Mediation' (ACAS Occasional Paper No 55).

[50] In 2011/12 the Helpline received 924,787 enquiries.

[51] Trade Union and Labour Relations (Consolidation) Act 1992, s 214.

[52] Use of this device is rare; a notable example was the Report of the Court of Inquiry under Scarman LJ into the dispute between Grunwick Processing Laboratories Ltd and APEX (Cmnd 6922, 1977).

(g) Codes of practice

Pursuant to its powers of inquiry and advice, ACAS is empowered by the Trade Union and Labour Relations (Consolidation) Act 1992, section 199 to issue codes of practice. The procedure is that a draft code will be drawn up with a view to comment by interested parties. The final draft is then submitted to the Secretary of State, who, if he approves, may lay it before Parliament. If no objection is taken to it, the Secretary of State may then bring it into force by order. Codes of practice are of increasing import-ance in modern employment law, to attempt to fill out the bare bones of the legislation and give practical advice on how to put that legislation (often of considerable legal complexity) into effect. A code of practice is not law in itself, so a person will not be liable for its breach; like the Highway Code in motoring cases, however, breach of its terms may be used as evidence against an employer in any proceedings before a tribunal or the CAC.[53] The first three codes of practice issued by ACAS covered disci-plinary practices and procedures in employment, disclosure of bargaining information and time off work for trade union duties and activities. Arguably, the COP No 1 on discipline and dismissal has been one of the most important documents in modern employment law, laying down many of the most fundamental principles for unfair dismissal law, and being the basis (or even model) for most of the internal procedures adopted by employers.

The original three codes of practice were reissued in 1998, but only in order to bring them up to date with current legislation, and not to make any substantive changes. The Code of Practice No 1 on discipline and dismissal was then reissued in 2000, in an expanded form also covering grievance procedures and the statutory right to be accompanied at a disciplinary or grievance hearing, and again in 2004 to take into account the new standard disciplinary and grievance procedures. It then, of course, had to be reissued yet again in 2009 when those procedures were repealed(!). At that stage, it constituted an important part of the government's policy for a replacement for the failed procedures. The idea is that the code will resume the primacy it always had in *practical* dispute resolution. To that end, the new code is actually shorter than its pre-decessor (to be more user-friendly to non-lawyers), though backed by the much longer 'Discipline and grievances at work: the ACAS guide' which, though not having the for-mal status of a code of practice, is likely to be of great practical significance in fleshing out the principles set out in the new code. All of this may appear to be essentially an exercise in returning to the past *but* there is one innovation. Wanting to 'beef up' the code (as a replacement for the failed procedures) the government have provided in the Employment Act 2008, section 3 (adding a new section 207A to the Trade Union and Labour Relations (Consolidation) Act 1992) that if a tribunal finds that a party before

---

[53] Trade Union and Labour Relations (Consolidation) Act 1992, s 207(2). Under s 203 the Secretary of State for Employment may himself issue codes of practice (after consultation with ACAS) and any such COP may replace part or all of one already issued by ACAS. This power has been used to issue the COPs in the politically contentious areas of picketing, the closed shop and union ballots and elections.

it has unreasonably failed to comply with a code of practice, it may increase or decrease any award or compensation by up to 25%. The novelty of this is that the ACAS Code No 1 (for all its immense practical effect) has *never* previously had any element of legal enforceability, being meant to operate purely in the context of 'best practice'. How (and on what principles) this new discretion will be operated by the tribunals remains to be seen at the date of writing. It is to be hoped that it will not increase the 'legalism' of tribunal hearings even more.

(ii) THE CENTRAL ARBITRATION COMMITTEE

The CAC, successor to the Industrial Court and the Industrial Arbitration Board, was established by the Employment Protection Act 1975 and its procedure is now governed by Part VI of the Trade Union and Labour Relations (Consolidation) Act 1992. It is a permanent arbitration body, independent of both ACAS and the sponsoring department and sitting centrally in London and elsewhere as the need arises. It consists of a chairman and deputy chairmen and a panel of persons appointed from both sides of industry. It will normally sit with a chairman or deputy chairman and two 'wingmen', though if it cannot reach a unanimous decision, the power of decision lies with the chairman or deputy chairman, acting as an umpire. It may sit in public or in private, and its decisions made in the exercise of its statutory functions (but not its consensual arbitrations) must be published; these decisions are given in the form of arbitral awards, with the emphasis upon a statement of 'general consideration' and then the terms of the award, rather than in the form of a closely reasoned legal judgment. If a question arises as to the interpretation of one of its awards, any party to it may refer the matter back to the CAC for decision. The functions of the CAC were progressively lessened by the previous Conservative government (which had a general distaste for third party intervention in industrial disputes) and were restricted to the following:

(1) To arbitrate on matters voluntarily submitted to it by the parties through ACAS;[54] the CAC may thus be an alternative to the (more usual) single arbitrator and such a reference may be ad hoc or may be because reference to the CAC is formally built into the relevant procedure agreement between employer and union;

(2) To enforce the disclosure of certain bargaining information.

The workload of the CAC was therefore drastically reduced from its high point as a major player in employment relations under the Labour governments of the 1970s.

The CAC has, however, seen a revival in its use under the present government, being involved in three major developments. The first, and most high profile, is the new statutory recognition procedure under the Employment Relations Act 1999 (see Chapter 9); jurisdiction to adjudicate on disputes arising from this procedure is given

---

[54] Trade Union and Labour Relations (Consolidation) Act 1992, s 212(1)(b).

to the CAC.[55] The second development was the transposition of the European Works Councils Directive 94/45/EC. More significantly, however, the CAC was given important functions under the Information and Consultation of Employees Regulations 2004, in relation to questions both of interpretation and enforcement.[56] These important new functions are likely to be sensitive and contentious, as can be seen from three further factors. The first is that when the CAC is operating the recognition procedure, it now has separate procedural requirements as to appointment, composition and decision taking,[57] aimed at increasing openness and minimizing challenges to its decisions. The second is that its decisions in relation to disputes over European works councils or the information and consultation of employees are subject to appeal on a point of law to the EAT.[58] The third is that, in expanding its membership to cope with the likely increase in its case law, the government were keen to stress (again) openness and adhesion to the 'Nolan principles' on open competition for public appointments. Moreover, the possible legal complexity of these new jurisdictions was reflected in the choice as Chairman (to replace the long-serving previous Chairman, Professor Sir John Wood, the original co-author of this work, on his retirement) of not just another eminent employment lawyer, but a High Court judge, Burton J.

(iii) THE CERTIFICATION OFFICER

In addition to ACAS and the CAC the other principal institution which the reader is likely to encounter in the areas of industrial relations and trade union law is the Certification Officer (CO). The office was established by the Employment Protection Act 1975 and is now governed by Part VI of the Trade Union and Labour Relations (Consolidation) Act 1992, though with major changes made by the Employment Relations Act 1999. It takes its name from the major function at that time of certifying trade unions as 'independent', such certification being the key to enjoyment of the new statutory rights given to unions and their members by that Act; the procedure of certification is considered in Chapter 9. However, it becomes immediately obvious that in fact this official is, if not misnamed, at least inadequately named, since his functions now extend far beyond certification (which is now of course quantitatively far less important). In fact, he resembles more the old institution of the Registrar of Trade Unions, with a wide supervisory jurisdiction which may be generally split

---

[55] In exercising these functions, the CAC 'must have regard to the object of encouraging and promoting fair and efficient practices and arrangements in the workplace': Trade Union and Labour Relations (Consolidation) Act 1992, Sch A1, para 171.

[56] In 2011/12 the CAC received 52 applications; 43 concerned trade non-recognition, 4 disclosure of information, 1 European consultation and 4 information and consultation of employees: *CAC Annual Report 2011/12*.

[57] Trade Union and Labour Relations (Consolidation) Act 1992, s 263A. In particular, there *must* be a side member for each side of industry; where there is a split of opinion, but a majority have the same opinion, that is to be the decision (and so the chairman only has the power of umpire to decide the case if there is no majority opinion).

[58] Transnational Information and Consultation of Employees Regulations 1999, SI 1999/3323, reg 38(8); Information and Consultation of Employees Regulations 2004, SI 2004/3426, reg 35(6).

into two functions—administrative and judicial. The administrative functions include the listing of trade unions, dealing with the mechanics of union amalgamations, and receiving the audited annual returns and actuarial reports on members' superannuation schemes that are required of trade unions under the Trade Union and Labour Relations (Consolidation) Act 1992. In addition, however, the CO has judicial functions, in that he has the power to adjudicate on complaints brought by individuals of infringements of the laws relating to (1) political expenditure by a union, the running of a political fund and the necessary balloting thereon; (2) the balloting required for a union amalgamation; and (3) the balloting required for the appointment of union officers. Although the CO is funded and provided with staff through ACAS, he operates independently of it (and of the Department for Business, Innovation and Skills). He is expressly empowered to regulate his own procedure on any application or complaint to him, and he produces an annual report on his activities, which is an important source of up-to-date information and statistics on trade unions and their operations. At the time of writing, the Coalition government have proposed merging the office of the CO with the CAC.

4 MACHINERY (2): JUDICIAL DISPUTE RESOLUTION

The large majority of all employment and employment relations litigation is handled by employment tribunals, which from inauspicious beginnings under the Industrial Training Act 1964 have expanded to assume wide new jurisdictions under the modern employment legislation and now have common law jurisdiction over breach of contract claims, at least on termination of employment.[59] They started life as 'industrial tribunals' but were renamed 'employment tribunals' in 1998,[60] for no apparently compelling reason. As 'industrial juries' they were originally designed to provide a means of speedy resolution of employment cases which will often turn very heavily upon their particular facts, and the Donovan Report in 1968[61] referred to their potential advantages as being ease of access, informality, speed and inexpensiveness. Rules of procedure (including pre-trial procedures, such as the simplified pleadings)

---

[59] Employment Tribunals (Extension of Jurisdiction) Order 1994 SI 1994/1623 (in Scotland SI 1994/1624); see *Harvey* Division R [778], [788]. One serious limitation in high value claims is that the maximum awardable is £25,000, a figure that has not been raised since 1994. Moreover, a claimant in such a claim cannot claim the *first* £25,000 in a tribunal (in which, for example he or she is claiming unfair dismissal) and then claim the rest in a court because the tribunal decision establishes an estoppel: *Fraser v HLMAD Ltd* [2006] ICR 1395, [2006] IRLR 687, CA.

[60] Employment Rights (Dispute Resolution) Act 1998, s 1. The Industrial Tribunals Act 1996 was renamed the Employment Tribunals Act 1996. All references to these bodies pre-1998 (in cases and legislation) will of course be to 'industrial tribunals'.

[61] Royal Commission on Trade Unions and Employers Associations (Cmnd 3623, 1968).

are drafted with this aim in mind, and the tribunals have wide powers to decide most cases in a common-sense way, having regard to 'good industrial practice'. The paradox here, however, is that while the tribunals' procedure may be simplified, the law which they have to apply is often of great complexity and there has in the past been major controversy over how 'legalistic' the proceedings and decisions of tribunals should be. Simple, common-sense access to quick justice may be a worthy aim, but there is still a lot of hard law which must be complied with in most of the statutory actions.

The original idea of quick and informal justice in a tribunal was consistent with another theme in this area, namely the undesirability of appeals to complicate the matter. Tribunals have always been given primacy on questions of fact, and so one important feature of this whole system is that an appeal from a tribunal decision lies to the EAT only on a question of *law*.[62] As seen below, this rule is applied rigorously and indeed may well affect the ultimate disposal of an appeal because, even if it is successful, a common order will be for the matter to be remitted to the tribunal for final decision on the facts, ie the EAT will not normally *decide* the case for itself.

(i) EMPLOYMENT TRIBUNALS

Tribunals sit in most local centres of population, under the auspices in England and Wales of 21 local offices, all under the control of the Head Office in London, and in Scotland four local offices under the control of the Head Office in Glasgow. Under the original model, a tribunal consists of three people, a legally qualified chairman (now known as an employment judge) and two lay members, one from a panel kept by the Secretary of State representing employers' interests and one from a panel kept representing employees' interests. The theory is that, although expressly appointed from each side of industry, the lay members are to act as independent members of the bench, not in a partisan manner, and so they are full members of the tribunal which decides its cases if necessary by a majority (even in the unusual case of the judge being in the minority). One of the principal functions of the side members is to use their employment experience to help the tribunal to come to a sensible and practicable decision; however, this approach must not be taken too far, and the Court of Appeal has warned that knowledge of the employment background and industrial common sense (though of great importance in many cases) may *not* be used to take a decision directly against the plain meaning of a statutory provision, even if the side members consider the end result of applying that plain meaning to be unfair or ridiculous.[63]

This original model has, however, been under attack for some years. This started when the Trade Union Reform and Employment Rights Act 1993 amended these provisions as to the composition of a tribunal by establishing a class of case to be heard by a chairman *alone*; this was partly to deal with withdrawn or non-contested cases, but

---

[62] Employment Tribunals Act 1996, s 21.
[63] *British Coal Corpn v Cheesbrough* [1988] ICR 769, [1988] IRLR 351, CA.

it also covered Wages Act cases, applications for interim relief and the common law proceedings that may now be heard by a tribunal, *unless* they raise matters of fact or law such that they should be heard by a full tribunal. This process was taken further by the Employment Rights (Dispute Resolution) Act 1998 which extended the categories of chairman-alone hearings (covering, for example, guarantee payments and redundancy payments and cases involving union subscriptions) against the background of a significant increase in tribunal applications.[64] However, arguably the most significant change came in 2012 when the Coalition government added to the list of judge-alone jurisdictions cases of unfair dismissal, for many lawyers the prime area for the use of side members with their industrial expertise. There is still a power to sit with side members[65] but the legislation now makes judge-alone very much the normal default setting in these cases.

The tribunal is administered by a clerk who is a permanent official. The claimant may conduct his case before the tribunal in person or be represented by any other person (sometimes a lawyer, sometimes a trade union official, and the respondent employer may often be represented by a member of the firm's personnel or legal staff);[66] there is no legal aid for representation, though a dismissed employee may be eligible to obtain free preliminary advice from a solicitor, and may also be able to turn to his or her trade union or to the CAB.

Costs are not usually awarded; this has generally been thought to be a fundamental and desirable element of the tribunal system. However, there is always some pressure politically to curb what are seen as unworthy or time-wasting applications (at the very least adding a significant 'nuisance value' to applications, leading—so the argument goes—to too many undeserving cases being bought off by employers, regardless of their merits). In recent years, this has coincided with the desire of successive governments to curb the major increase in the number of tribunal applications. There has always been a residual power to award costs. Originally this only covered frivolous or

---

[64] Applications rose sharply from 34,697 in 1990–91 to 71,821 in 1992–93; they peaked at 130,408 in 2000–01. In 2004–05 they fell to 86,181 which seemed to give some credence to the government's dispute resolution reforms in the Employment Act 2002, *but* any hopes of a permanent decrease were then dashed when they increased again to 115,039 in 2005–06. In 2007–08 they reached 189,303 (artificially swelled by large, multiple equal pay cases in the public sector). In 2011/12 the figure was 186,300, without that artificial swelling.

[65] As the President of the Scottish EAT Lady Smith pointed out forcefully in *McCafferty v Royal Mail Group* UKEATS/0002/12.

[66] Dickens et al *Dismissed: a Study of Unfair Dismissal and the Industrial Tribunal System* (1985) found that 23% of applicants had legal representation, 22% had trade union representation and 9% had some other form of representation; 41% of employers had legal representation, 52% had internal company representation and 5% were represented by an employers' association. The Genn Report (*The Effectiveness of Representation at Tribunals*; Report to the Lord Chancellor, 1989) found broadly the same, with 28% of applicants having legal representation, 16% trade union representation and 18% some other form of representation; 42% of employers had legal representation, 49% internal company representation and 8% employers' association representation. The report has a wealth of information on the effects of representation; see Mullen (1990) 53 MLR 230 and Genn 'Tribunals and Informal Justice' (1993) 56 MLR 393. See also Banerji, Smart and Stevens 'Unfair Dismissal Cases in 1985–86—Impact on Parties' [1990] Employment Gazette 547; Tremlett and Banerji *1992 Survey of Industrial Tribunal Applications* (1994).

vexatious conduct by a party; in 1980 this was widened to cover cases brought 'otherwise unreasonably' and in 2001 the current rule was introduced under which costs may be awarded where the party or their representative acted 'vexatiously, abusively, disruptively or otherwise unreasonably, or the bringing or conducting of the proceedings by the paying party has been misconceived'.[67] The significance of the 'misconceived' heading was that for the first time a costs application could be made based on the weak *merits* of the case, not just the way it was handled. Even this change was not thought enough by the then government when drafting the Employment Act 2002. At original Bill stage, this contained the remarkably radical proposal to introduce an ordinary costs rule (loser pays) into the tribunals, as a major assault on increasing applications. This, however, proved to be too controversial and was withdrawn. However, the Act did lead to two other significant changes in the Rules of Procedure. The first was to allow an employer to claim costs based not on its legal expenditure, but on its own in-house costs in dealing with the case. The second was to allow the making of what elsewhere are called wasted costs orders against paid representatives whose conduct has needlessly wasted tribunal time. Costs have thus become a live issue again, with these wider powers. On the other hand, employment judges remain generally wary of introducing wider costs rules into their jurisdiction and, in spite of these changes, actual orders for costs remain relatively rare.[68]

Apart from specific rules, such as that on costs, the tribunals have wide powers to determine their own procedure by virtue of the Rules of Procedure.[69] In recent years, there has been much emphasis on case management in tribunals with the judge expected to play an active part at this preliminary stage. Successive governments have wanted to increase the use of strike-out powers in the case of weak claims, if only to reduce the running costs of the tribunal system but this aspect above all others has led to what could be seen as a conflict between executive and judiciary because to a significant extent tribunal judges have been loath to comply and the higher courts have always stressed the unusual and draconian nature of a strike-out, particularly in the light of the right to a fair hearing in Article 6 of the European Convention on Human Rights.[70]

At the time of writing, we are expecting new Rules of Procedure to come into force in 2013 as a result of a comprehensive review undertaken by a previous President of the EAT, Underhill J; these are aimed at reducing technicality and making the rules easier to understand, especially for litigants in person. In addition to this, two other major

---

[67] Rule 40(3).

[68] Even by 2011/12 the proportion of cases where costs were awarded was still only 0.5%; the mean award was £1,730.

[69] Details of the ET procedure rules lie outside this work; for comprehensive coverage, see *Harvey* Division PI.

[70] The leading EAT authority is *Balls v Downham Market High School* [2011] IRLR 217 and in *Tayside Public Transport Co v Reilly* [2012] IRLR 755 the Inner House of the Court of Session reaffirmed that normally there should be no strike-out if any facts remain in contention.

changes in the pipeline (also scheduled for 2013) are (i) a new scheme enacted for the levying of fees to bring a tribunal claim (to be recouped from the respondent if successful but forfeited if unsuccessful) and (ii) the levying of what will in effect be a fine (payable to the state, again to help finance the tribunal system) on a losing employer if there are 'aggravating factors' to the case.[71]

One final point concerns the aggregate effect of all of these changes. If one adds together the demise of side members in so many cases, the consequent emphasis on the position of the judge alone (no longer simply the tribunal 'chairman'), the attempts to extend the costs regime, the charging of fees and the inexorable lengthening of hearings with arguably a significant decrease over the years of the original inquisitorial nature of tribunals,[72] the question might well be asked—are these really still tribunals as originally understood, or simply courts by another name?

(ii) THE EMPLOYMENT APPEAL TRIBUNAL

Appeal from a tribunal decision lies to the EAT, a body set up under the Employment Protection Act 1975.[73] The EAT, a superior court of record, consists of a High Court or circuit judge and either two or, more unusually, four lay members, once again giving equal representation to both sides of industry, though once again the members should not act in a partisan manner and the decision of the EAT is by simple majority, if necessary.[74] Where a tribunal has consisted of an employment judge sitting alone, an appeal may be heard by the judge alone. The constitution of the EAT is laid down in the Employment Tribunals Act 1996, which expressly gives it the powers of the High Court *and* those of the employment tribunals.[75] Its procedure is contained in the EAT Rules laid down in Regulations.[76] As in the case of tribunal proceedings, the parties may be represented by anyone and costs are not normally awarded, unless the EAT considers that the appeal was 'unnecessary, improper, vexatious or misconceived' or there was 'unreasonable delay or other unreasonable conduct in bringing or conducting the proceedings'.[77]

---

[71] This would be 50% of the amount awarded to the successful claimant, subject to a maximum of £5,000. Although 'aggravating factors' are not defined, this fine would probably be particularly appropriate if the employer has ridden roughshod over internal procedures.

[72] In *Arnold Clark Autos Ltd v Middleton* UKEATS/0011/12 Lady Smith in the Scottish EAT struck down a decision by a tribunal to call witnesses itself when dissatisfied with the parties' evidence and in doing so went as far as to suggest that an inquisitorial approach is now never appropriate—'Employment tribunals are not investigative bodies. It is not for them to decide what issues are to be looked into'.

[73] Now the Employment Tribunals Act 1996, Pt II.

[74] This has caused some debate, particularly after the case of *Nethermere (St Neots) Ltd v Gardiner* [1983] ICR 319, [1983] IRLR 103 (extending rights to homeworkers), the argument being that if appeal to the EAT is so stringently confined to a point of law, then should there be two non-lawyers with the power to outvote a High Court judge?

[75] Sections 28, 33.

[76] SI 1993/2854, *Harvey* R [714]. These rules are supplemented by the EAT *Practice Direction* reissued in May 2008 and set out at *Harvey* PI [1761].

[77] Rule 34A; r 34C allows a wasted costs order against a paid representative personally.

The most important point about the appeal to the EAT is that it is an appeal on a point of law *only*;[78] this is a deliberate policy to minimize appeals. The practical significance of this is that the parties must ensure that they argue the facts properly and fully before the tribunal, for if they do not and they lose on the facts (for example, by not calling all the relevant evidence or by not presenting it sufficiently persuasively) they may not take the matter to the EAT for a second chance. To appeal to the EAT, the party must be able to show that the tribunal was wrong in law. It has been authoritatively stated in *British Telecommunications plc v Sheridan*[79] by the Court of Appeal that this means one of two things—either (1) an ex facie error of law or (2) that the tribunal's decision was perverse. There had been said to be a third category, ie where the tribunal misunderstood or misapplied the facts,[80] but that was specifically disapproved in *Sheridan*, since it would have permitted the EAT to allow an appeal simply by taking a different view of the facts.[81] The judicial approach to perversity has undergone considerable changes over time, against the background of the obvious point that this is the only way that an appellant can legitimately convert fact into law. In the early years of the tribunals' expanded jurisdiction after the inception of unfair dismissal law in 1971, the appellate courts tended to take a wider, more interventionist approach that if (particularly) the industrial members of the bench agreed that they would not have decided the case that way, the decision was perverse. At a time when the new law was bedding in and basic ground rules were being established, this approach could be seen as natural, but by the mid-1980s a large element of revisionism (based on the idea that the system was becoming too legalistic) led to a review of this crucial element of perversity appeals. It was now that the current narrow approach to perversity came in (with the corresponding warnings to the EAT not to reverse a tribunal decision merely because they think it wrong on the facts). In *RSPB v Croucher*[82] Waite P went as far as to call cases of perversity 'exceptional' and said:

> We have to remind ourselves of our duty and our functions as an appellate tribunal. We have to remember that it is our duty loyally to follow findings of fact by an industrial tribunal which has enjoyed the advantages, which can never be ours, of having seen witnesses, sensed the atmosphere prevailing in a particular work-place, gauged the qualities of the different personalities, weighed the impact of their effect each upon the other; and that cases must be

---

[78] The EAT will not hear appeals where the dispute has in fact been resolved, even if one or both of the parties wish to have a particular point resolved as a matter of principle: *IMI Yorkshire Imperial Ltd v Olender* [1982] ICR 69. Likewise, if there is no real dispute between the parties, who want a ruling for some extraneous purpose: *Baker v Superite Tools Ltd* [1986] ICR 189.

[79] [1990] IRLR 27, CA.

[80] *Watling v William Bird & Son Contractors Ltd* (1976) 11 ITR 70, per Philips J.

[81] If there can be said to be *no* evidence to support a particular finding of fact, that is an error of law under head (1). Note, however, that delay by a tribunal, even if extreme, is not a separate head of appeal even when allied to human rights arguments: *Bangs v Connex South Eastern Ltd* [2005] IRLR 389, CA.

[82] [1984] ICR 604, [1984] IRLR 425; the passage cited is at 609 and 428, respectively. Note, however, that on its facts this case was later restrictively construed in *John Lewis plc v Coyne* [2001] IRLR 139.

very rare indeed where we take upon ourselves to reach the conclusion that a tribunal has arrived at a result not tenable by any reasonable tribunal properly directed in law.

This narrow approach to perversity was approved by the Court of Appeal in *Neale v Hereford and Worcester County Council*[83] where May LJ said that an appellate court should only reverse a tribunal's decision if it could be said 'My goodness, that must be wrong.'[84] Indeed, even this well-known explanation was thought possibly too liberal in *Piggott Bros & Co Ltd v Jackson*[85] by Lord Donaldson MR who thought that it might tempt an interventionist EAT into the forbidden land of fact. However, his preferred solution (that perversity could normally only be shown by an error of law or a *total* lack of evidence) was arguably capable of removing perversity as a separate heading. Subsequently, Wood P in the EAT in *East Berkshire Health Authority v Matadeen*[86] complained that *Piggott* was causing difficulties in appeals, and sought to lean back towards the *Neale* approach, stating that the EAT could interfere if the members[87] were satisfied that the tribunal decision was not a permissible option, or was one which offended reason, or was one which no reasonable tribunal could have reached, or was so clearly wrong that it could not stand. This formulation would leave perversity as a freestanding ground, which seems now to have been accepted at Court of Appeal level, though with the clear warnings that any perversity challenge must be fully particularized, and should only be upheld by the appellate body if an 'overwhelming case' has been made out.[88]

In addition to such policy considerations, perversity appeals also face another problem; it is now well established that a tribunal must not simply substitute its own view of what would have been reasonable in the circumstances for that of the employer, but must consider (in an unfair dismissal case) whether dismissal was an option which *a* reasonable employer might have chosen, even if others might not (the 'range of reasonable responses' test, see p 505 below). Thus, if a tribunal's decision on reasonableness is to be challenged as perverse the appellant has, in effect, a double hurdle—he must show that *no* reasonable tribunal could possibly have come to the conclusion that *a* reasonable employer could have decided to dismiss (where the appellant is the employee) or that *no* reasonable employer could have decided to dismiss (where the appellant is the employer).

---

[83] [1986] ICR 471, [1986] IRLR 168, CA; moreover it was held in *Campion v Hamworthy Engineering Ltd* [1987] ICR 966, CA that if a case goes to the Court of Appeal on perversity, that court's function is to apply the *Neale* test to the tribunal's decision, *not* to consider whether the EAT's decision on the point was correct.

[84] This is known in some quarters as the 'Biggles test' (see (1987) 16 ILJ 213) due to a flippant remark in the *Harvey* bulletin that although this statement is entirely consistent with the modern approach, its phraseology may appear over-reliant on the writings of Captain W E Johns ('Gosh' said Biggles as a shell ripped off his right leg).

[85] [1992] ICR 85, [1991] IRLR 309, CA.   [86] [1992] ICR 723, [1992] IRLR 336.

[87] One strong argument by Wood P is that the lay members are there to contribute their industrial expertise, and are capable of applying such tests of perversity 'when viewed against appropriate industrial experience and practice', ie at least a nodding recognition of the earliest approach.

[88] *Yeboah v Crofton* [2002] IRLR 634, CA; this case is now frequently cited in this context.

Appeal on a point of law is thus tightly circumscribed and the point has been made repeatedly that the EAT must exercise considerable self-restraint in cases where it disagrees profoundly with the decision of the tribunal on the facts but where there is no definable error of law; in such a case it must not interfere.[89] Likewise, there have been repeated warnings by the Court of Appeal to appellants and, more particularly, their legal advisers that points of fact are not to be dressed up in the garb of points of law in order to bring an appeal.[90] Moreover, this is backed by an important procedural device. Starting originally with perversity appeals but now applying to all appeals, a notice of appeal is subject to a 'sift' by a judge or the Registrar which is partly to decide (as a matter of case management) which of several procedural routes should be adopted, but which can also be used to ensure that there is a proper point of law at issue; if not, the appeal may be struck out at that stage (subject to a right to have this decision reconsidered at a short oral hearing).[91]

Three further points about the EAT are worth noting. The first is that it will be most reluctant to admit fresh evidence unless, exceptionally, the existence of the fresh evidence could not have been reasonably known of or foreseen (akin to the 'reasonable diligence' test applied generally by the Court of Appeal);[92] this rule is not to be circumvented by remitting the case to the tribunal for a rehearing including the otherwise inadmissible evidence.[93] This reinforces the point made above that it is essential that all relevant evidence is placed before the tribunal at the hearing. The second point is that, although the EAT is empowered on appeal to substitute its own decision for that of the tribunal if it allows the appeal,[94] if the decision on appeal entails the finding of further facts or the reconsideration of certain existing facts the proper course will normally be to remit the case to the tribunal for further consideration in the

---

[89] *Retarded Children's Aid Society Ltd v Day* [1978] ICR 437, [1978] IRLR 128, CA; *Martin v Glynwed Distribution Ltd* [1983] ICR 511, [1983] IRLR 198, CA; *O'Kelly v Trusthouse Forte plc* [1983] ICR 728, [1983] IRLR 369, CA; *Spook Erection v Thackray* [1984] IRLR 116, Ct of Sess. The decision of the EAT in *Woods v WM Car Services (Peterborough) Ltd* [1981] ICR 666, [1981] IRLR 347 (upheld on appeal: [1982] ICR 693, [1982] IRLR 413, CA) is a good example of the necessary self-denial; see also the judgment of Mummery P in *Stewart v Cleveland Guest (Engineering) Ltd* [1996] ICR 535, [1994] IRLR 440. This will be particularly so in matters of procedure which fall primarily within the discretion of the tribunal chairman: *Dietmann v London Borough of Brent* [1987] IRLR 146, CA.

[90] See, eg, *Hollister v NFU* [1979] ICR 542, [1979] IRLR 238, CA; *Thomas and Betts Manufacturing Ltd v Harding* [1980] IRLR 255, CA.

[91] EAT Practice Direction, paras 9.5, 9.6. The institution of this process is explained in detail by Burton P in 'The Employment Appeal Tribunal: October 2002–July 2005' (2005) 34 ILJ 273. *Star Wars* fans may think of this as the Revenge of the Sift.

[92] *Borden (UK) Ltd v Potter* [1986] ICR 647 (overruling the previous 'reasonable explanation' test in *Bagga v Heavy Electricals (India) Ltd* [1972] ICR 118); for an example of the application of this test (and the further requirement that the new evidence would have an important influence on the outcome of the case) see *Wileman v Minilec Engineering Ltd* [1988] ICR 318, [1988] IRLR 144. Similarly, the EAT will not normally allow a party to argue a point of law not taken at the tribunal, unless it is a point that the tribunal should have considered on its own motion: *Langston v Cranfield University* [1998] IRLR 172.

[93] *Kingston v British Railways Board* [1984] ICR 781, [1984] IRLR 146, CA.

[94] Employment Tribunals Act 1996, s 33.

light of the EAT's decision.[95] The third point is that as a matter of precedent the EAT is not bound by a previous decision of its own.[96] Thus, there have been many instances, in cases raising bona fide matters of law, of a later EAT decision altering the direction of an area of law away from previous authorities. There is thus a difficult balance to maintain between certainty and legal development, and the student of employment law must realize that in practice the doctrine of precedent is not as strong here and so, for example, it cannot always be assumed beyond doubt that an ageing EAT decision will always be applied without question.

Finally it should be noted that at the time of writing the Enterprise and Regulatory Reform Bill proposes to alter the constitution of the EAT by providing that normally it is to sit judge-alone. This is consistent with the approach of the present government to tribunals, considered above, and marks another stage in the process of the demise of lay participation in adjudication on employment disputes.

---

[95] *O'Kelly v Trusthouse Forte plc* [1983] ICR 728, [1983] IRLR 369, CA. A hybrid is that it is now accepted that the EAT may adjourn its hearing and remit the case to the tribunal to amplify its reasons, if that will help the EAT to come to a final decision: *Burns v Consignia plc (No 2)* [2004] IRLR 425, approved by the Court of Appeal in *Barke v SEETEC Business Technology Centre Ltd* [2005] IRLR 633, CA.

[96] *Secretary of State for Trade and Industry v Cook* [1997] ICR 288, [1997] IRLR 150.

2

CONTRACTS OF EMPLOYMENT (1): STATUS, FORMATION, CONTINUITY AND CHANGE

OVERVIEW

Coverage of the substantive law of employment must always start with an analysis of the most fundamental jurisdictional point of all—who is an 'employee'? This has taxed the courts and tribunals for decades and, if anything, has actually become more difficult in recent years because of the increasingly diverse nature of the UK's workforce. What used to be thought of as 'atypical' forms of employment have in many contexts actually become quite typical and one of the themes of this first part of this chapter is the way that the law has had to keep up with changing models of 'employment'. Even the old 'employee/self-employed' division is now complicated by increasing use in modern statutes of the term 'worker'. Part-time, fixed-term and agency workers have featured prominently recently and consideration is given to these specifically. Two more technical areas are then considered. The first concerns the 'section 1 statement' of basic terms and conditions which has been an obligation on employers since 1963 but which is still not always given. The second concerns the difficult question of the extent to which an employer can seek to impose limitations on an employee even after employment ends; this entails the law on restraint of trade clauses and their more recent variant, the garden leave clause. The chapter concludes with an examination of the rules on continuity of employment and changing contracts. Although continuity differs in being a statutory concept, it is often of practical importance alongside the common law question of status—for example, in order to bring an unfair dismissal action it is usually necessary for the claimant (1) to have been an employee *and* (2) to have had at least two years' 'continuous service' with the employer.

1 THE RELATIONSHIP OF EMPLOYER AND EMPLOYEE; OTHER FORMS OF ENGAGEMENT

The fact that someone is an employee of someone else is a major jurisdictional factor in several areas of law, for example in tort law on the question of vicarious liability, and in the fields of taxation and social security on the questions of assessment, payment and contributions. In employment law, both ancient and modern, it is often of fundamental importance; most of the common law on employment only applies to employees, and it has hitherto usually been the same with the important statutory rights which usually require the claimant to be an employee and to have served a certain qualifying period as such.[1] As the only definition of 'employee' in the Employment Rights Act 1996 and the Trade Union and Labour Relations (Consolidation) Act 1992[2] is 'an individual who has entered into or works under (or, where the employment has ceased, worked under) a contract of employment', the question of what constitutes a contract of employment is left to the courts and tribunals. The major divide here is between employment and self-employment, between a contract of employment and a contract for services (although other relationships such as agency or partnership could perhaps be used to avoid the relationship of employer and employee and the concept of the 'office holders' has occasionally caused problems for such individuals trying to enforce statutory rights).[3] A person with a contract for services is usually referred to as an 'independent contractor' and there may be several reasons why an individual may wish to be classed as such; the prime one is usually taxation, for there may well be tax advantages in being self-employed, of a legal nature (ie tax avoidance through being assessed under Schedule D with its payment at least partly in arrears and more generous allowances) or an illegal nature (ie tax evasion through part- or non-disclosure of income, not being under the PAYE system for Schedule E taxation of employees).[4] From the employer's point of view it may be desirable to hire independent contractors, for this relieves him of the administrative tasks involved in deducting PAYE deductions and national insurance contributions from wages, and may relieve him of certain other administrative burdens (eg statutory sick pay and statutory maternity pay); further, it

---

[1] For the arguments in favour of freeing statutory employment rights from their present basis on the contract of employment, see Hepple 'Restructuring Employment Rights' (1986) 15 ILJ 69; for a criticism that courts tend still to lean too strongly on contractual principles when interpreting employment statutes, see Anderman 'The Interpretation of Protective Employment Statutes and Contracts of Employment' (2000) 29 ILJ 223.

[2] Sections 230(1) and 295 respectively.

[3] In *Lincolnshire County Council v Hopper* [2002] ICR 1301 a registrar of birth, deaths and marriages was unable to claim unfair dismissal. See generally the discussion of different kinds of office holding by Morison P in *Johnson v Ryan* [2000] IRLR 236 where, on the facts, it was held that a rent officer could so claim.

[4] Technically this terminology ('Schedules D and E') did not survive the replacement of the Income and Corporation Taxes Act 1988 by the Income Tax (Earnings and Pensions) Act 2003 and the Income Tax (Trading and Other Income) Act 2005, but it is retained here because it is deeply ingrained through long usage, and likely to remain the current jargon for the next 20 years! For tax treatment in general, see *Harvey* Div BII.

may have certain VAT advantages and help to avoid the need to negotiate with unions (indeed in an area of large-scale self-employment such as the building industry it may be a longstanding cause of weak unionism generally).[5]

Advantages to the individual, however, tend to be of a short-term nature, and categorization as 'independent' may have certain serious longer term disadvantages, for most of the industrial safety legislation, some of the most important social security rights (particularly those relating to unemployment and disability) and much of the modern employment protection legislation only applies to employed persons—to put it shortly, the independent contractor may be in a better monetary position while working, but at a grave disadvantage if he falls off a ladder or is sacked. Moreover, categorization as independent may indirectly affect the rights of third parties too, for example a passer-by injured by the acts of that person, for the action then lies only against that independent contractor and *not* against the employer who may in the realities of the case be the only person worth suing.[6]

(i) DEFINITION OF THE RELATIONSHIP

In spite of the obvious importance of the distinction between an employee and an independent contractor, the tests to be applied are vague and may, in a borderline case, be difficult to apply.[7] Historically, the solution lay in applying the 'control' test, ie could the employer control not just what the person was to do, but also the manner of his doing it—if so, that person was his employee.[8] In the context in which it mainly arose in the nineteenth century, of domestic, agricultural and manual workers, this test had much to commend it, but with the increased sophistication of industrial processes and the greater numbers of professional and skilled people being in salaried employment, it soon became obvious that the test was insufficient[9] (for example in the case of a doctor, architect, skilled engineer, pilot, etc) and so, despite certain attempts to modernize it,[10] it is now accepted that in itself control is no longer the sole test, though it does remain a factor and perhaps, in some cases, a decisive one.[11] In the search for a substitute test,

---

[5] Bird 'The Self Employed: Small Entrepreneurs or Disguised Wage Labourers?' in Pollert (ed) *Farewell to Flexibility* (1991).

[6] There are certain exemptions to this general rule, where an employer can be liable for the acts of his independent contractor, but they are narrow and, in some cases, uncertain: see Grubb (ed) *The Law of Tort* (2002) pp 115–17.

[7] The tests to be applied are a matter of law, but the *application* of those tests is a question of fact; where it arises in a statutory action, this means that the decision on categorization lies almost entirely with the employment tribunal with little chance of a successful appeal from their decision: *O'Kelly v Trusthouse Forte plc* [1983] ICR 728, [1983] IRLR 369, CA; *Lee v Chung* [1990] ICR 409, [1990] IRLR 236, PC.

[8] See, eg, *Performing Right Society Ltd v Mitchell and Booker (Palais de Danse) Ltd* [1924] 1 KB 762; *Mersey Docks and Harbour Board v Coggins and Griffiths (Liverpool) Ltd* [1947] AC 1, [1946] 2 All ER 345, HL.

[9] *Cassidy v Ministry of Health* [1951] 2 KB 343, [1951] 1 All ER 574, CA (a surgeon).

[10] See, eg, *Zuijs v Wirth Bros Ltd* (1955) 93 CLR 561 (concerning the control which could be exercised over a circus acrobat).

[11] Particularly where the control demonstrates the reality of the relationship (eg in a case where there is more than one possible employer): *Clifford v Union of Democratic Mineworkers* [1991] IRLR 518, CA. In *Quashie v*

ideas have been put forward of an 'integration' test, ie whether the person was fully integrated into the employer's concern, or remained apart from and independent of it.[12] Once again, this is not now viewed as a sufficient test in itself, but rather as a potential factor (which may be useful in allowing a court to take a wider and more realistic view). The modern approach has been to abandon the search for a single test, and instead to take a multiple or 'pragmatic' approach, weighing up all the factors for and against a contract of employment and determining on which side the scales eventually settle.[13] As Cook J put it, in his much-cited judgment in *Market Investigations Ltd v Minister of Social Security*[14] the question ultimately is whether the person in question is performing the services as 'a person in business on his own account'; factors which are usually of importance are as follows—the power to select and dismiss, the direct payment of some form of remuneration, deduction of PAYE and national insurance contributions,[15] the organization of the workplace, the supply of tools and materials (though there can still be a labour-only subcontract) and the economic realities (in particular who bears the risk of loss and has the chance of profit); however, even this is not an exhaustive checklist, and a court or tribunal must still look at the overall picture in the particular case.[16]

A further development in the modern case law (particularly concerning atypical employments) has been the idea of 'mutuality of obligations' as a possible factor, ie whether the course of dealings between the parties demonstrates sufficient such mutuality for there to be an overall employment relationship. It is true that such an approach can be disadvantageous to certain particularly irregular workers, making it more difficult to establish that they are employees,[17] but on the other hand it has the positive aspect

---

Stringfellows Restaurants Ltd [2012] IRLR 536 a lapdancer was held to be an employee on the basis of a high level of control by the club, outweighing the otherwise casual nature of her work. Control may also be particularly important in vicarious liability in tort, in a case where employer A 'borrows' an employee from employer B and injury is caused by the employee while working for the latter: *Hawley v Luminar Leisure Ltd* [2006] EWCA Civ 18; if control is actually shared, there may even be joint vicarious liability now: *Viasystems Ltd v Thermal Transfers Ltd* [2005] IRLR 983, CA, see Brodie (2006) 35 ILJ 87.

[12] *Stevenson Jordan & Harrison Ltd v McDonald and Evans* [1952] 1 TLR 101, CA, per Denning LJ.

[13] *Ready Mixed Concrete (South East) Ltd v Minister of Pensions and National Insurance* [1968] 2 QB 497, [1968] 1 All ER 433; *Construction Industry Training Board v Labour Force Ltd* [1970] 3 All ER 220; *Global Plant Ltd v Secretary of State for Health and Social Security* [1972] 1 QB 139, [1971] 3 All ER 385; *Hitchcock v Post Office* [1980] ICR 100; *Andrews v King* [1991] ICR 846, [1991] STC 481 (a fascinating tax case on the legal position of the archaic system of agricultural gang labour).

[14] [1969] 2 QB 173, [1968] 3 All ER 732, approved and applied by the Privy Council in *Lee v Chung* [1990] ICR 409, [1990] IRLR 236.

[15] Though perhaps a potent factor, this is not decisive (being primarily a matter between the person and the tax and insurance authorities) and so the non-deduction of these sums does *not* inevitably point to an independent contract if the other factors are against it: *Davis v New England College of Arundel* [1977] ICR 6; *Airfix Footwear Ltd v Cope* [1978] ICR 1210, [1978] IRLR 396; *Thames Television Ltd v Wallis* [1979] IRLR 136; conversely, deduction of these amounts does not per se mean that the relationship is one of employment: *O'Kelly v Trusthouse Forte plc*, see n 7.

[16] *Hall (Inspector of Taxes) v Lorimer* [1994] ICR 218, [1994] IRLR 171, CA.

[17] *O'Kelly v Trusthouse Forte plc* [1983] ICR 728, [1983] IRLR 369, CA; *Wickens v Champion Employment* [1984] ICR 365.

that it is capable of extending employed status to groups of atypical workers (especially of an external or part-time nature) if the relationship with the employer is sufficiently longstanding and stable; thus in *Nethermere (St Neots) Ltd v Gardiner*[18] outworkers making garments at home on a piecework basis were held to be employees of the garment manufacturer, largely because of the regular, longstanding arrangement which showed the necessary mutuality of obligations (to do and to be provided with the work) in practice, even though the outworkers were not covered by a formal contractual obligation to undertake a particular quantity of work; this is an important development, capable of extending employee status (and thereby employment rights) to workers employed otherwise than on a nine-to-five basis on the employer's premises. On the other hand, 'mutuality' was used as an argument *against* employee status for 'casual, as required' power station guides in the rather regressive decision of the House of Lords in *Carmichael v National Power plc*,[19] where it was seen as an irreducible minimum for the existence of a contract of employment; indeed, the current approach is to view it as a requirement for any kind of contract to arise between the parties, leading on to a consideration of other factors to see if the contract was one of employment.[20] On a more general level, however, this whole idea of an 'irreducible minimum' is rather worrying because it could cut across the usual approach of weighing *all* the factors (all factors are equal, but some are more equal than others) and could be seen as the higher courts searching for a philosopher's stone in this area. It was seen again in *Express & Echo Publications Ltd v Tanton*[21] where the Court of Appeal viewed personal service as an irreducible minimum. While it is true that *Tanton* was 'explained' and restrictively interpreted by the EAT in later cases,[22] the Court of Appeal showed a similar approach again in *Montgomery v Johnson Underwood Ltd*[23] in relation to a necessary amount of control by the employer. We have therefore seen qualifications on the pure 'balancing of factors' approach in the higher courts, but some reluctance to go down such a route in the (specialist) EAT.

Given the vagueness of the tests, there is considerable scope for an 'instinctive' approach in this area, ie that the judge knows a contract of employment when he sees one. In *Cassidy v Ministry of Health*,[24] Somervell LJ said:

One perhaps cannot get too much beyond this, 'Was the contract a contract of [employment] within the meaning which an ordinary person would give under the words?'

---

[18] [1984] ICR 612, [1984] IRLR 240, CA.
[19] [1999] ICR 1226, [2000] IRLR 43, HL, applied in *Stevedoring Haulage Services Ltd v Fuller* [2001] IRLR 627, CA, where the employer had set this argument up in advance by saying in the hiring contract that there were to be *no* mutual obligations between the parties.
[20] *Stephenson v Delphi Diesel Systems Ltd* [2003] ICR 471; *Cotswold Developments Construction Ltd v Williams* [2006] IRLR 181.
[21] [1999] ICR 693, [1999] IRLR 367, CA.
[22] *MacFarlane v Glasgow City Council* [2001] IRLR 7; *Byrne Bros Ltd v Baird* [2002] ICR 667, [2002] IRLR 96.
[23] [2001] IRLR 269, CA.
[24] [1951] 2 KB 343, [1951] 1 All ER 574, CA at 352 and 579 respectively; see also McKenna J's third condition for a contract of employment in the *Ready Mixed Concrete* case, see n 13. *Withers v Flackwell Heath Football Supporters' Club* [1981] IRLR 307.

This may be unsatisfactory from an analytical point of view, but it probably reflects the practical position and indeed may not be as unsatisfactory as it first seems when considered in the context of the modern statutory rights where it falls to be applied by employment tribunals which may be expected to apply industrial experience in their resolutions.[25] The real problem with a vague test or tests is, however, that it can make advising in advance very difficult; not only is this a problem for the lawyer, but also it concerns an area of fundamental importance for both employer and employee who need to be certain as to the legal basis of their relationship. The parties' primary contact on this matter is likely to be, not with lawyers or tribunals, but with government departments and agencies, in particular HM Revenue and Customs[26] and the DSS; given the practical importance of such contacts, there has unfortunately been evidence in the past of different departments and agencies giving different advice and using different criteria on a person's employment status.[27] In the context of taxation, the Revenue has published a leaflet 'Tax: Employed or Self-Employed'[28] which attempts to clarify the distinction between employment and self-employment, using the criteria set out above. While stressing that no one factor is a conclusive test, it suggests that you are an employee if you can answer 'yes' to the following questions:[29]

- Do you have to do the work that you have agreed to undertake yourself?
- Can someone tell you what to do, and when and how to do it?
- Are you paid so much an hour, a week or a month?
- Can you get overtime pay?
- Are you expected to work set hours, or a given number of hours a week or month?
- Are you expected to work at the premises of the person you are working for, or at a place or places they decide?

It is then suggested that you are self-employed if you can answer 'yes' to the following questions:

- Are you ultimately responsible for how the business is run?
- Do you risk your own capital?

[25] *Challinor v Taylor* [1972] ICR 129; *Thames Television Ltd v Wallis* [1979] IRLR 136. One limitation on this is now that, since April 2012, unfair dismissal cases are to be heard primarily without side members, who were always that repository of such industrial experience.

[26] In many cases, the parties will in practice consider that they have successfully created the relationship of self-employment if the Revenue have accepted it and not required the employer to operate the PAYE system. As stated above, however, this is not legally conclusive and the Revenue can later decide to reconsider, the second principle of tax law being that the Revenue cannot be estopped (the first principle being that they always win eventually).

[27] See Leighton 'Observing Employment Contracts' (1984) 13 ILJ 86.

[28] IR56. See also IR53 'Thinking of Taking Someone on?'

[29] The leaflet does not, however, explain what is the position if you answer 'yes' to half of these questions and to half of the next set of questions!

- Are you responsible for bearing losses as well as taking profits?
- Do you provide the major items of equipment you need to do your job?
- Are you free to hire other people, on terms of your own choice, to do the work that you have agreed to undertake?
- Do you have to correct unsatisfactory work in your own time and at your own expense?

While these are not authoritative statements of law, and ultimately the decision on a person's status may have to be taken by a court or tribunal, it is to be welcomed that at least an attempt is being made to standardize the rules of the game (in the most import-ant context in which in practice the issue initially arises, ie tax and NI contributions), though one might be cynical and say that in marginal cases a game is precisely what it remains.[30]

In addition to the general points made above, two particular problems may be noted here, one a specific and recent cause of controversy and the other a general problem that has vexed the courts and tribunals for many years. The first (specific) issue arises if the contract in question contains a 'delegation' or 'substitution' clause, stating in some way that the work need not actually be performed by that individual. The problem is that there is an immediate clash with the idea that *personal* service is at least one of the hallmarks of a contract of employment. As seen above, the initial response was a strong one in *Express & Echo Publications Ltd v Tanton*[31] that any power to delegate was fatal to employment status. This was then construed restrictively by the EAT and when the matter was reconsidered by them generally in *Staffordshire Sentinel Newspapers Ltd v Potter*[32] an important distinction was drawn: if the clause only applies where the individual *cannot* do the work (and so, for exam-ple, must arrange a suitably qualified replacement to take the shift) there can still be a contract of employment, but a *general* power to delegate (or indeed not do the work at all)[33] at the individual's own discretion is inconsistent with a contract of employ-ment. Welcome though this clarification was, it left one particular loose end—what if an employer cynically inserted such a clause into what would otherwise be a normal contract of employment, thus deliberately *avoiding* employment liabilities? In *Staffordshire Sentinel* it was said that a tribunal could avoid such a clause if it was a

---

[30] With the Revenue permanently having the service, through their ability to raise an assessment on the basis that they have decided upon (usually employment and Schedule E), leaving it up to the employer and/or 'employee' to appeal and challenge the correctness of that basis. In the light of this, the National Federation of the Self-Employed have argued for a registration system for self-employment, with registration under it being conclusive of a person's status, and at one point the Institute of Directors put forward the most radical proposal, that people should simply be able to *elect* to be self-employed. Neither of these suggestions has been taken up officially.

[31] See n 21.   [32] [2004] IRLR 752.

[33] This is sometimes known informally as the 'duvet test', ie can the individual decide to stay down his or her (or indeed somebody else's) duvet that morning.

sham, but what is meant by a 'sham'? When tested, the EAT felt obliged to hold that it will only be a 'sham' if it could be proved that the employer deliberately inserted it to evade legal liabilities;[34] the mere fact that the clause had never actually been activated in practice (ie the individual had always turned up and done the work himself) was not sufficient. This difficult point caused contradictory decisions at EAT and Court of Appeal level for some time but eventually came before the Supreme Court in what is now the leading case, *Autoclenz Ltd v Belcher*,[35] in which the facts raised the point neatly. The contractual arrangements for car valeters were entirely consistent with employment status *except* that the employer inserted both a delegation and a substitution clause (neither of which had in practice ever been used). The Supreme Court in effect struck these clauses down and held that the valeters were not only 'workers' (their principal contention) but also 'employees'. In doing so, they approved the decision of the Court of Appeal below that the answer to this conundrum lies not in trying to apply the inherently difficult concept of a 'sham' (which fits commercial law more than employment law) but in considering more widely whether the clause in question reflected the true agreement between the parties at the time of contracting. Where the offending clause had simply been inserted by the employer because of its superior bargaining position and it was clear from the outset that it would play no part in practice in the actual employment, it could be overlooked when deciding on employment status. Giving the leading judgment, Lord Clark accepted that this involved a level of purposive interpretation which would not normally be adopted in commercial contracts. He approved a passage from Aikens LJ in the Court of Appeal to the effect that in the employment context, employers will often have the power to dictate contract terms which the employee has to accept in order to take the job and that in this area 'it may be more common for a court or tribunal to have to investigate allegations that the written contract does not represent the actual terms agreed and the court or tribunal must be realistic and worldly-wise when it does so'. Expanding on this, Lord Clark said that the true nature of the agreement will often have to be gleaned from all the circumstances of the case, of which the written agreement is only a part. Thus, although delegation or substitution clauses are not per se illegal and may be proper in certain contracts, this decision of the Supreme Court shows that the scope for their *abuse* has been severely limited.

The second (longstanding) problem concerns the emphasis (or lack of it) which can be placed upon the statements and intentions of the parties themselves. They may stipulate (orally or in writing) that their contract shall be viewed one way (usually as

---

[34] *Real Time Civil Engineering Ltd v Callaghan* (2006) UKEAT/516/05. The classic definition of a 'sham' in a commercial setting is where *both* parties intend to deceive the outside world: *Snook v London and West Riding Investments Ltd* [1967] 2 QB 786, CA per Diplock LJ. This also caused severe problems in the initial case law.

[35] [2011] ICR 1157, [2011] IRLR 820, SC, approving *Protectacoat Firthglow Ltd v Szilagyi* [2009] IRLR 365, CA and disapproving *Consistent Group v Kalwak* [2008] IRLR 505, CA. See Bogg, 'Sham Self-employment in the Supreme Court' (2012) 41 ILJ 328.

an independent contract)—how is the court or tribunal to treat that?[36] In the past the usual approach has been to ignore the statements of the parties and apply an objective test,[37] and this can be seen in the decision of the Court of Appeal in *Ferguson v John Dawson & Partners (Contractors) Ltd*[38] where a man taken on at a building site with no written contract but on an oral understanding that he was on the 'lump', ie a labour-only subcontractor, who was later injured, was held to have been in fact an employee (and so able to rely on certain industrial safety provisions in order to bring his action). The majority, Megaw and Brown LJJ, took a clearly objective approach and said that a declaration by the parties, even if incorporated into the contract, should be *disregarded entirely* if the remainder of the contractual terms pointed to the opposite conclusion (though for the purpose of their decision, they were prepared to adopt the less stringent approach that such a declaration or statement can be a relevant, but certainly not conclusive, factor). Lawton LJ dissented strongly, stating:[39]

> I can see no reason why in law a man cannot sell his labour without becoming another man's servant even though he is willing to accept control as to how, when and where he shall work. If he makes his intention not to be a servant sufficiently clear, the implications which would normally arise from implied terms do not override the prime object of the bargain. In my judgment, this is just such a case.

In a subsequent Court of Appeal case, *Massey v Crown Life Insurance Co*,[40] however, a different approach was taken. In that case a branch manager who was an ordinary employee asked to change the basis of his contract to self-employment (for tax purposes); the employer consented to this and negotiated a new agreement. When the agreement was subsequently terminated, the manager tried to claim unfair dismissal on the basis that he was in fact an employee all along, but the Court of Appeal held unanimously that he could not do so, since the new agreement had effectively altered the basis of his engagement so that he was no longer an employee. It must be said at the outset that the desire to avoid a position whereby a person could claim various tax advantages, and then argue exactly to the contrary to obtain unfair dismissal benefits at a later stage, obviously played a part in this decision[41] but, in spite of that, the approach to the problem was different from that of the previous Court of Appeal. Lord Denning MR said:[42]

> It seems to me on the authorities that, when it is a situation which is in doubt or which is ambiguous, so that it can be brought under one relationship or the other, it is open to the

---

[36] There may be the added complication that the employee is now trying to *change* the basis of the contract, eg where he initially agreed to be self-employed, but has now been injured or dismissed and so needs to show that he was in fact an employee in order to claim the appropriate remedy.

[37] For examples, see *Davis v New England College of Arundel* [1977] ICR 6; *Tyne and Clyde Warehouses Ltd v Hamerton* [1978] ICR 661; *Thames Television Ltd v Wallis* [1979] IRLR 136.

[38] [1976] 3 All ER 817, [1976] IRLR 346, CA.

[39] [1976] 3 All ER 817 at 828, [1976] IRLR 346 and 351.

[40] [1978] ICR 590, [1978] IRLR 31, CA, applied in *BSM (1257) Ltd v Secretary of State for Social Services* [1978] ICR 894 and *Calder v H Kitson Vickers & Sons (Engineers) Ltd* [1988] ICR 232, CA.

[41] See also the dissenting judgment of Lawton LJ in *Ferguson v John Dawson & Partners (Contractors) Ltd*, n 38.

[42] *Massey v Crown Life Insurance Co* [1978] ICR 590 at 595, [1978] IRLR 31 at 33.

parties by agreement to stipulate what the legal situation between them shall be.... So the way in which the parties draw up their agreement and express it can be a very important factor in defining what the true relation was between them. If they declare that one party is self-employed, that may be decisive.

His Lordship distinguished the *Ferguson* case quite simply 'on its facts' and Lawton LJ did likewise (pointing primarily to the lack of a written agreement or, indeed of any particularly reliable evidence as to the relationship in that case), adding:[43]

> *Ferguson* clearly established that the parties cannot change a status merely by putting a new label on it. But if in all the circumstances of the case, including the terms of the agreement, it is manifest that there was an intention to change status, then, in my judgment, there is no reason why the parties should not be allowed to make the change.

However, this wider approach in *Massey* was called into question in the further Court of Appeal case of *Young & Woods Ltd v West*[44] where a sheet metal worker who had been engaged on a self-employed basis (and had been treated as such by the Inland Revenue) was held to have in fact been an employee so that after his dismissal he could claim unfair dismissal. The court did not indicate that *Massey*'s case was wrong, and did not take as purely an objective approach as the majority in *Ferguson*'s case would have liked to do. They did, however, seek to narrow the effect of *Massey*'s case; in particular they did not accept that if the parties deliberately set out to create a relationship of self-employment, that intention should normally be put into effect by a court or tribunal. A further contribution to this question was made by Lord Hoffmann in *Carmichael v National Power plc*,[45] where 'casual, as required' power station guides were held not to be employees; pointing out that in reality many employment relationships will not be contained purely in written form, but will also need to be discerned from correspondence and conduct, he envisaged a significant role for the parties' intentions, at least as a factor:

> The evidence of a party as to what terms he understood to have been agreed is some evidence tending to show that those terms, in an objective sense, were agreed. Of course, the tribunal may reject such evidence and conclude the party misunderstood the effect of what was being said and done. But when both parties are agreed about what they understood their mutual obligations (or lack of them) to be, it is a strong thing to exclude their evidence from consideration.[46]

Thus, the position now seems to be that, as a matter of practice, the declared intention of the parties may be more important if (1) there has been a deliberate *change* in the basis of employment, (2) the work in question was of an unusual nature so that an

---

[43] [1978] ICR 590 at 597, [1978] IRLR 31 at 34.   [44] [1980] IRLR 201, CA.
[45] [1999] ICR 1226, [2000] IRLR 43, HL.
[46] [1999] ICR 1226 at 1235, [2000] IRLR 43 at 47. Lord Hoffmann disapproved the view of the majority of the Court of Appeal that the relationship had to be considered purely objectively, disregarding the parties' understandings.

ambiguity as to its true nature might be found more easily[47] or (3) the arrangement has been entered into in a relatively informal manner and has to be construed in the light of several factors and circumstances, as in *Carmichael*. On the question of the policy behind the earlier decisions, the court in *Young & Woods Ltd v West* thought that the danger of allowing employers to avoid the employment protection legislation simply by labelling people as self-employed was an important consideration. They recognized the fears expressed (particularly in *Massey's* case) of injustice being caused by allowing a person to claim to be self-employed for tax purposes during employment, but then to claim on dismissal to have been an employee all along in order to claim unfair dismissal, but suggested that this could be overcome by a court or tribunal finding that the person was employed (thereby permitting the unfair dismissal action) but then informing the Revenue of that fact, thereby inviting a reassessment of his tax liability for the past years of his employment under Schedule E;[48] knowledge that this is a possibility could be a considerable disincentive to the person who is thinking of trying to alter his or her status at this late stage.

(ii) THREE PARTICULAR APPLICATIONS

In addition to these general principles relating to the existence of a contract of employment, three particular applications points are worthy of mention. The first is that, although some of the cases cited on this problem are tort cases concerning vicarious liability, some care may be needed, for the test for vicarious liability is not necessarily identical to that for the existence of an employment relationship in employment law. It is true that it *looks* the same—was there a contract of employment?—but the factors behind it may be different, for in tort (for example, in a 'borrowed servant' case,[49] where employer A lends B a crane plus driver and, while acting under B's orders the driver injures C—should A or B be liable to C?) the court is essentially looking at the liability question at one moment in time, whereas in an employment case (eg on redundancy rights or unfair dismissal) the tribunal may have to assess the legal consequences of a potentially long-term relationship; it may be, therefore, that 'static' ideas of control may be more important in a tort case than in an employment case where more factors

---

[47] Both (1) and (2) were considered by Stephenson LJ in *Young & Woods Ltd v West* to have been important aspects of *Massey's* case; on the latter factor, Mr Massey's position as a manager with a separate agency agreement was more unusual employment than Mr West's job of sheet metal worker (working alongside other people doing exactly the same work, but as employees). The Court of Appeal found that Mr West's circumstances did not raise the sort of ambiguity necessary if the label of self-employment was to be decisive.

[48] Thus it could be that the ex-employee would end up owing more to the Revenue than he gained in compensation for unfair dismissal. In *Young's* case, Ackner LJ said that Mr West had probably won a 'hollow, indeed an expensive, victory'. The problem from the employer's point of view is that if this happens he will end up liable to pay the employer's NI contributions that should have been paid over the course of the employment; moreover, if the employee is unable to pay the back tax, the Revenue could seek to recover it from the employer on the basis that he should have been operating the PAYE system all along.

[49] *Mersey Docks and Harbour Board v Coggins and Griffiths (Liverpool) Ltd* [1947] AC 1, [1946] 2 All ER 345, HL.

may need to be taken into account to achieve a realistic result. Thus, in the borrowed servant example, it may be that, on the facts, B is liable to C,[50] whereas it is clear that for unfair dismissal or employment protection purposes, A remains his employer. Thus, tort precedents may have to be used with care in other contexts.[51]

The second point is that various practical problems may arise over the use of independent contracting, particularly in a system of labour-only subcontracting as on the 'lump' in the building industry.[52] The Court of Appeal showed some hostility to this in *Ferguson's* case, particularly as there was clear suspicion in that case of unlawful tax evasion; as it stood, that case could perhaps have been developed by subsequent courts as a way of curbing the overuse of subcontracting by placing stringent limits upon its legal recognition, but even the majority did not feel that they could go as far as to strike down such an agreement as an illegal contract and, in the light of the subsequent case law discussed above, a major judicial assault on the lump and other such practices is unlikely.[53] Legislative reforms have been suggested in order to rule out all but bona fide contractors but, except in the area of income tax where provisions have been introduced to extend the PAYE system and counter unlawful tax evasion, little has been done specifically. Indeed, the legal issues that have tended to arise recently in relation to the building industry have come from a general change in some legislation to the use of the term 'worker' (rather than 'employee') which can cover many contractors, even though their tax status is that of a self-employed independent (see head (vi) below).

The third point concerns the position of company directors. An ordinary director will not normally be under a contract of employment, even when in receipt of directors' fees. However, there is nothing to prevent a director from being 'employed' (even by his own one-man company)[54] if the relationship is in fact over and above that of ordinary director, as in the case of an executive or managing director. However, the mere fact that a director performs some duties for the company may not be enough[55]

---

[50] *Donovan v Laing, Wharton and Down Construction Syndicate Ltd* [1893] 1 QB 629, CA; *Sime v Sutcliffe Catering Scotland Ltd* [1990] IRLR 228, Ct of Sess. For variations on this, see *McDermid v Nash Dredging and Reclamation Co Ltd* [1987] ICR 917, [1987] IRLR 334, HL and *Interlink Express Parcels Ltd v Night Trunkers Ltd* [2001] EWCA Civ 360, [2001] RTR 338, [2001] 20 LS Gaz R 43, CA. Control was vital in *Hawley v Luminar Leisure Ltd* [2006] EWCA Civ 18 in holding a nightclub liable for the violence of a bouncer who had been supplied by a security company to whom that function had been contracted out. If there is actually joint control by A and B, there can now be joint vicarious liability: *Viasystems Ltd v Thermal Transfers Ltd* [2005] IRLR 983, CA.

[51] For a clear indication of this, see Denning LJ's judgment in *Denham v Midland Employers' Mutual Assurance Ltd* [1955] 2 QB 437, [1955] 2 All ER 561, CA and more recently, the decision of the Court of Appeal in *Morris v Breaveglen Ltd* [1993] ICR 766, [1993] IRLR 350, CA.

[52] Clark 'Industrial Law and the Labour-only Sub-contract' (1967) 30 MLR 6; Drake 'Wage Slave or Entrepreneur?' (1968) 31 MLR 408; Mordesley 'Some Problems of the "Lump" ' (1975) 38 MLR 504.

[53] In *Costain Building and Civil Engineering Ltd v Smith* [2000] ICR 215 an agency-supplied building engineer was held not to have been lawfully appointed by her union as a safety representative because he was not an 'employee' as required by the relevant regulations.

[54] *Lee v Lee's Air Farming Ltd* [1961] AC 12, [1960] 3 All ER 420, PC.

[55] *Stanbury v Overmass and Chapple Ltd* (1976) 11 ITR 7, IT. However, there may be a presumption of employed status if the director is required to work full time for the company in return for a salary: *Folami v Nigerline (UK) Ltd* [1978] ICR 277.

and if he wishes to establish a contract of employment (for example to be able to claim unfair dismissal when his services are dispensed with) he must show further factors. Thus in *Parsons v Albert J Parsons & Sons Ltd*[56] the Court of Appeal held that a director was not 'employed', in spite of working full time for the company, since the company records did not contain a written contract of employment for him or memorandum setting out the terms of an oral contract,[57] his sole remuneration was that categorized in the accounts as 'directors' fees' and he had been treated as self-employed for tax and national insurance purposes. One problem has been the possible argument that a director should not be classed as an 'employee' because to do so would be inconsistent with the employment right that that person is trying to claim; the area in which this has arisen to date is the state guarantee for moneys outstanding to employees on a company's insolvency,[58] where it was initially held by the EAT that it would be improper to allow the de facto owner of a one-man company to claim from the state on his company's insolvency.[59] However, the Court of Appeal later reaffirmed strongly that there was no such rule of law, and that in each case it remains a question of fact—the person's status as a controlling director may well be a *factor* against employment status, but must be balanced against other factors such as the bona fides of the contract, the degree of control exercised by the company, the position of any other directors and the conduct of the parties.[60]

(iii) ATYPICAL WORKERS—DOMESTIC LAW

It has long been clear that atypical workers such as 'outworkers' (ie people who perform work for another at home rather than in a factory) may have their employment protection, etc, rights jeopardized by a finding that they are independent contractors.[61] Part-time workers in factories may have had problems in the past with the old '16 hours per week' rule for computing continuity of employment until its repeal in 1995,[62] but at least there was usually no question that they were in fact 'employed', whereas in the case of an outworker even that might be in doubt, for if on the facts it appears that the work is brought to them, and accepted, purely on an ad hoc basis, the tribunal

---

[56] [1979] ICR 271, [1979] IRLR 117, CA; *Morley v C T Morley Ltd* [1985] ICR 499; *Eaton v Robert Eaton Ltd* [1988] ICR 302, [1988] IRLR 83.

[57] As was required by the Companies Act 1985, s 318.

[58] See Ch 3, heading 6, p 217.   [59] *Buchan v Secretary of State for Employment* [1997] IRLR 80.

[60] *Secretary of State for Trade and Industry v Bottrill* [1999] ICR 592, [1999] IRLR 326, CA (director held to be an employee for insolvency guarantee purposes; reasoning in *Buchan* disapproved), as explained and amplified in *Secretary of State for Business, Enterprise and Regulatory Reform v Neufield* [2009] IRLR 475, CA (directors again held to be employees for insolvency purposes in spite of 90% and 100% shareholdings in their companies) where the Court of Appeal approved guidance given by Elias P in *Clark v Clark Construction Initiatives Ltd* [2008] IRLR 364.

[61] Collins 'Independent Contractors and the Challenge of Vertical Disintegration to Employment Protection Laws' (1990) 10 OJLS 353.

[62] See further discussion under 5(i), p 102.

might take the view that the outworker was not in fact 'employed'.[63] Where, however, the outworker works on a regular basis the EAT held in *Airfix Footwear Ltd v Cope*[64] that there is no reason why there should not be a finding of a contract of employment, even though the work is done elsewhere than on the employer's premises, if there is sufficient mutuality of obligations; as seen above, this approach was approved by the Court of Appeal in *Nethermere (St Neots) Ltd v Gardiner*.[65] While an arrangement such as homeworking is still generally considered 'atypical', it is increasingly recognized that nine-to-five employment throughout the year in a manufacturing factory is becoming *less* typical, and so increasingly the law has had to consider the position of those working under more diverse and less full-time conditions. In particular, much of the recent job creation in the economy has been in forms hitherto thought to be atypical, but fast becoming the norm in many sectors of the labour market.[66] At the same time, with the decline of traditional manufacturing industries and the expansion of the service and IT sectors, the nature of the employing concern has been changing, with larger numbers of people now being employed by what hitherto would have been considered 'small firms'.[67]

Part-time and temporary work is now more prevalent[68] and in some areas teleworking (the modern form of more traditional homeworking) is being increasingly considered.[69] Generally, the workforce has become more flexible[70] and indeed

---

[63] *Mailway (Southern) Ltd v Willsher* [1978] ICR 511, [1978] IRLR 322; there is also a possible argument, adverted to in the *Airfix* case (n 64 below) that there could be a *separate* contract of employment for each job where it is only on a sporadic basis, but no overall contract.

[64] [1978] ICR 1210, [1978] IRLR 396. See generally Ewing 'Homeworking, a Framework for Reform' (1982) 11 ILJ 94; and Hakim 'Homeworking in Britain' [1987] Employment Gazette 92.

[65] [1984] ICR 612, [1984] IRLR 240, CA.

[66] See, eg, Fredman 'Labour Law in Flux: The Changing Composition of the Workforce' (1997) 26 ILJ 337.

[67] This was strikingly demonstrated by research undertaken in the late 1990s when considering whether to decrease the then exemption for small firms from the Disability Discrimination Act 1995. This showed that 1m employers in the private sector (95% of the total number of employers in the UK) employing 4.5m workers were firms employing fewer than 20 people: *Disability Discrimination Act 1995: Employment Provisions and Small Employers* (DFEE, 1998).

[68] As long ago as 1998 a major survey found that there were 6.6m part-time workers, comprising 1.3m men and 5.3m women, or 8% of the male workforce and 44% of the female workforce; of those aged between 25 and 49, 47% of men said they worked part time because they could not find full-time work and 34% did not want full-time work, whereas 8% of women said they worked part time because they could not find full-time work and 90% did not want full-time work: (1998) Labour Market Trends 600. According to the same survey, in 1998 there were 1.8m in temporary jobs (8% of the workforce), comprising 880,000 men and 967,000 women: (1998) Labour Market Trends at 598. The literature on this is voluminous. See, eg, Millward et al *Workplace Industrial Relations in Transition* (1992) pp 337ff; Dickens 'Working Time and Employment Equality' (1992) 21 ILJ 146; views can vary, however, as to how to define 'part-time work' and therefore how prevalent it is: see Hakim 'Employment Rights: A Comparison of Part-time and Full-time Employees' (1989) 18 ILJ 69 and the reply by Disney and Szyszczak (1989) 18 ILJ 223.

[69] For the extent of this, see Hotopp 'Teleworking in the UK' (2002) Labour Market Trends 311.

[70] *ACAS Annual Report 1987* pp 14, 18; Hakim 'Trends in the Flexible Workforce' [1987] Employment Gazette 549; Labour Flexibility in Britain, the 1987 ACAS Survey (ACAS Occasional Paper No 41, 1988); Wareing 'Working Arrangements and Patterns of Working Hours in Britain' [1992] Employment Gazette 88; McGregor and Sproull 'Employers and the Flexible Workforce' [1992] Employment Gazette 225; Dickens *Whose Flexibility?*

encouraging such flexibility has long been government policy,[71] since it is seen as a way of encouraging more use of individual contracting, flexible pay and payment by results, the antithesis of the collective approach to wage determination. However, this development may cause strains in applying laws evolved basically against the background of full-time, 'normal' employment. While it is important to remember that, for better or for worse, the juristic basis here remains the traditional contract of employment, it is also important to ensure that there is not too much scope for employers to use devices such as temporary or part-time work in order to evade statutory obligations.[72] It has been argued for some time now that in Britain we are in danger of evolving a two-tier labour force—those in traditional full-time employment with a fair degree of job security and statutory protection, and (increasingly) those in part-time, temporary or otherwise atypical employment with little security, and hitherto generally excluded from statutory protection.[73] In fact, the principal moves towards protection of part-time employees have come through EC law. Initially, this was under EC sex equality laws which apply because of the disparate effect on women of rules prejudicing part-timers; the most notable success lay in the enforced removal (first by court action and then by amending regulations) of the requirement of working 16 hours per week in order to gain continuity of employment (for the purposes of qualifying for the major statutory rights).[74] This approach is now largely being superseded by EC law directives aimed at giving protection *directly* to specific forms of atypical employees, relieving them of the necessity of going through the hoops of a discrimination action; this development is considered separately below.

One legal device that has shown some signs of evolving as a possible remedy in cases where part-time or sporadic work (for example, on a series of short-term contracts) appears to be being misused is that of the 'umbrella or global contract', ie a finding that although the employee was only actually working for certain periods (possibly on an

---

(1992); Beatson 'Progress towards a Flexible Labour Market' (1995) Employment Gazette 55; Nolan and Walsh 'The Structure of the Economy and Labour Market' in Edwards (ed) *Industrial Relations, Theory and Practice in Britain* (1995); Collins 'Regulating the Employment Relation for Competitiveness' (2001) 30 ILJ 17; Leighton and Wynn, 'Classifying Employment Relationships—More Sliding Doors or a Better Regulatory Framework?' (2011) ILJ 5.

[71] See Employment for the 1990s (Cm 540, 1988) and People, Jobs and Opportunity (Cm 1810, 1992) for the previous Conservative government's policy; Fairness at Work (Cm 3968, 1998) for the previous Labour government's policy.

[72] *Lewis v Surrey County Council* [1987] ICR 982 at 998, [1987] IRLR 509 and 516, HL, per Lord Ackner. One employer's ace wheeze, to avoid employment responsibilities (such as SSP), of putting an employee onto 'daily contracts' (sic) for a total period of nine months was kicked into touch by the Court of Appeal who applied the Employment Rights Act 1996, s 86(4) which states that any contract for less than a month which in fact lasts for more than three months is deemed to be for an indefinite period (thus requiring notice to end it): *Brown v Chief Adjudication Officer* [1997] ICR 266, [1997] IRLR 110, CA.

[73] Dickens 'Falling through the Net: Employment Change and Worker Protection' (1988) 19 IRJ 139. One view is that this movement has been a pragmatic reaction to market conditions and business uncertainties rather than deliberate and widespread managerial policy: Sisson and Marguison 'Management: Systems, Structures and Strategy' in Edwards (ed) *Industrial Relations, Theory and Practice in Britain* (1995) 113.

[74] See further discussion in this chapter under heading 5(i), p 102. See also the enforced extension to part-timers of rights under occupational pension schemes, see Ch 5, heading 3(vi).

irregular basis), there was sufficient mutuality between the parties to justify a finding that in law there was one overall contract governing the whole period in question. This argument in fact failed in one of the leading cases, *Hellyer Bros Ltd v McLeod*,[75] where trawlermen who had sailed exclusively for one company for many years were held unable to claim redundancy payments when dispensed with, since the facts only established a series (albeit a long series) of separate contracts for each voyage. It is thus not automatically a panacea, but two recent cases concerning an unlikely pairing of a lapdancer and a care worker have shown that it remains alive and well and potentially available to a court or tribunal faced with a too-obvious attempt by an employer to use contractual sleight of hand to avoid employment responsibilities.[76]

Casual work has always caused problems legally, especially as there is a persistent folk myth among many employers that *because* a person is termed 'casual', *therefore* they cannot have any employment rights. It is important to realize, however, that 'casual' is not a legal term of art, that the word appears nowhere in the Employment Rights Act 1996, that the only legal distinction is between those who do and those who do not qualify for employment rights, and that a casual worker may or may not so qualify, depending on the facts. On the other hand, it has to be accepted that casual workers can have more problems than most in meeting qualification conditions, obviously in relation to continuity of employment, and more fundamentally in relation to employee status. Although the general trend in the past in the case law has been towards extension of legal rights to casuals, this development has suffered some setbacks. In *Clark v Oxfordshire Health Authority*[77] a 'bank' nurse (being offered and accepting work or as when it was available at any of the authority's hospitals) who was paid at standard rates and charged to PAYE and NI contributions, but who was not guaranteed any regular work, was held by the Court of Appeal *not* to be an employee (after three years working in the authority's hospitals, with only four breaks totalling 14 weeks) and so unable to claim unfair dismissal.[78] In *Carmichael v National*

---

[75] [1987] ICR 526, [1987] IRLR 232, CA. The possibility of such a finding was, however, considered to be an important possibility (for countering the abuse of short-term contracts by an employer) by Lord Ackner in *Lewis v Surrey County Council*, n 72, above. Continuity of employment was preserved by the Court of Appeal in *Flack v Kodak Ltd* [1986] ICR 775, [1986] IRLR 255 and *Cornwall CC v Prater* [2006] IRLR 362, CA in cases of irregular, sporadic contracts by the alternative device of resorting to the ERA 1996, s 212(3)(b) ('temporary cessation of work'), see further discussion in this chapter under heading 5(ii), p 105.

[76] *Quashie v Stringfellows Restaurants Ltd* [2012] IRLR 536; *Pulse Healthcare v Carewatch Care Services Ltd* UKEAT/0123/12. In the latter case the care home sought to evade employment status for care workers working consistently to provide a high level of care by putting them onto 'nil-hours contracts', with any engagement technically only by the day; this was struck down with little hesitation by the EAT.

[77] [1998] IRLR 125, CA.

[78] There was, however, a major qualification in the judgment. In the tribunal this issue had arguably been confused by considering not just whether there was an employment contract, but whether there was an umbrella contract covering the whole period (above). What had not been considered was whether there was a series of *individual* contracts (for each stint at one of the hospitals), possibly *linked* by the rules on continuity of employment (see now *Cornwall CC v Prater*, see n 75); the result of the decision was a remission to the tribunal to consider this possibility.

Power plc[79] a question was raised as to the employment status of two power station guides employed on a 'casual, as required' basis to show parties around when the need arose, given uniforms and charged to PAYE and NI contributions. The Court of Appeal split, with the majority finding that they were employees, in a thoughtful decision in favour of extending employment status, perfecting the potentially informal relationship by finding implied terms that (1) the employer would offer each guide a reasonable amount of the work available and (2) each guide would accept a reasonable amount of the work offered. However, on further appeal the House of Lords disapproved this completely and held that the guides were not employees, largely due to lack of a level of mutuality of obligations which Lord Irvine LC said was an irreducible minimum for any contract of employment. This was taken one step further in *Stevedoring and Haulage Services Ltd v Fuller*,[80] where the employer in effect achieved this result in advance by putting a clause into the hiring contract that no mutual duties (to offer work or to turn up for it) were to arise under it. This is a serious blow to any prospect of further extension of employment status by judicial action, and it is clear that there are difficulties in attaining a fair balance in this area. In the light of this any further moves towards extending employment status and ensuring that employment protection laws continue to apply widely to an ever more diverse workforce are for the moment having to come from legislation, which is considered below.

One other form of engagement currently which has recently caused problems at common law of a surprisingly fundamental nature is agency working. This has traditionally been seen by employers as *the* way to keep staff out of employment status and to achieve a high level of flexibility. Although the relationship legally between the agency and the worker has been far from straightforward,[81] it was thought to be clear that the worker could *not* be the employee of the client. This made particular sense (and continues to do so) when the nature of the work is such that the identity of the worker is unimportant, there is a high level of rotation of staff to the particular client and the demands are fluctuating (ie classic 'temping'). The situation, however, began to become more difficult through the evolution of a very different form of agency

---

[79] [1999] ICR 1226, [2000] IRLR 43, HL. The principal speech is by Lord Irvine LC; the other speech by Lord Hoffmann is of interest on the fact/law distinction as applied to the existence of a contract of employment, holding that the Court of Appeal had been wrong to interfere with the tribunal's decision for the employer *at all*.

[80] [2001] EWCA Civ 651, [2001] IRLR 627. Dockers who had been made redundant as full-time employees and rehired on a casualized basis, could not claim statutory rights, even though in fact working consistently for the same employer, because of the clause in the contract. How much of a sham would such a clause have to be in practice before a tribunal would feel able to ignore it?

[81] The leading case is *McMeechan v Secretary of State for Employment* [1997] ICR 549, [1997] IRLR 353, CA, where it was held that the relationship is a question of fact (ie no rules of law either way) and that there could be two distinct employments with the agency—a general one (to be on the books) and an individual one covering a particular assignment. In *Bunce v Postworth Ltd* [2005] IRLR 557, CA, however, an agency-provided worker working wholly under clients' control was held not to be an employee of the agency at all, through lack of control *and* mutuality of obligations.

working, where the work is specialized, the worker's own skills are a key point, labour is in short supply, and when the client discovers a good worker it will want to *keep* him or her. In such a case, the agency in practice is little more than a recruiter; from that stage on, the client takes over 'running' the worker as the agency soon recedes into the background (remaining technically the conduit for payment). That individual worker then works nine-to-five, 52 weeks a year, for that one client for a significant period of time, by the end of which he or she is virtually indistinguishable from the client's permanent employees doing similar work.[82] It is well known that in similar circumstances a self-employed 'consultant' who ends up working permanently for the one 'client' can transmute over time into an employee. Could that happen with an agency worker?

In *Montgomery v Johnson Underwood Ltd*[83] an agency worker was held not to be the employee (for unfair dismissal purposes) of the agency because once supplied to the client, she worked for that one client for two years, subject to little or no control, supervision or direction by the agency. A case such as this suggested that, if the worker is not to be cast into the outer darkness with no rights against anyone, a sympathetic tribunal might be tempted to look for another candidate for 'employer' and there is only one—the client. This was generally thought to be legally impossible (without the deliberate, separate hiring of a good temp onto the permanent staff) until the bomb-shell case of *Motorola Ltd v Davidson*,[84] where the EAT held that it was a possibility. The worker in question was a skilled telephone repairer who was recruited by an agency to the client's own specifications. He then worked wholly for the client for two years, entirely under its control and with no further contact with the agency. When he gave cause for concern, he was disciplined under the client's own disciplinary procedures (though termination was effected through the agency). On his complaint of unfair dismissal, the tribunal held that on these facts there was a contract of employment with the *client*, against whom the action lay. The client's appeal against this finding was dismissed by the EAT. This decision certainly caused a renewal of interest in this area though it was only a first instance decision. It was, however, followed by three Court of Appeal decisions which strongly suggested that there could have been an evolving con-tract of employment with the client over time. In *Franks v Reuters Ltd*[85] this was obiter, as it was in *Dacas v Brook Street Bureau*[86] where the court split on the matter. In *Cable & Wireless plc v Muscat*,[87] however, the court upheld a tribunal decision that an agency worker *had* become the direct employee of the client after two years' service. Thus, by 2007 it appeared to be a distinct possibility that consistent use over time (though *quaere* how long?) of an agency-provided worker could lead to a formal employment relationship with the client.

---

[82] Particularly as good HR practice tends to be to treat 'outsiders' as much like your own as possible; legally, this is exactly what the client should not do.

[83] [2001] EWCA Civ 318, [2001] IRLR 269, [2001] ICR 819; see also *Bunce v Postworth*, see n 81.

[84] [2001] IRLR 4.   [85] [2003] EWCA Civ 417, [2003] IRLR 423, CA.

[86] [2004] ICR 1437, [2004] IRLR 358, CA.   [87] [2006] ICR 975, [2006] IRLR 354, CA.

What happened then was a volte-face that was rapid even by employment law standards. Quite simply, the EAT in a series of cases refused to apply this line of authority and consistently held that *no* such contract had evolved. This reached its height in the judgment of Elias P in *James v Greenwich BC*,[88] where an agency worker was supplied to the council, worked for it consistently for three years, tried to claim unfair dismissal when replaced, but was held by the tribunal and EAT not to have been the council's employee at all. When this decision was appealed,[89] the Court of Appeal unanimously *upheld* the EAT's decision. They said that *Dacas* had not been a good case in which to consider this fundamental point and (more significantly) that *Cable & Wireless* had been a case on unusual facts (true!) which had laid down no general principle. They agreed with Elias P that the test for transmutation into an employee by the finding of an implied contract with the client is not merely that the agency worker ends up *looking* like a direct employee, but the much tougher test that it must be *necessary* to find such an implied contract in order to make sense of the situation *at all*. In a normal case (where, for example, payment remains through the agency, with whom the client still deals) there will be *no* such necessity, no matter how long the engagement lasts. Thus, in practical terms, *James* has stopped this movement towards direct client-employment of agency-provided individuals. This obviously came as a major relief to large-scale users of agency workers and as an equally major disappointment to those wanting greater employment rights for agency workers. In his judgment in *James*, Mummery LJ expressed some sympathy with the latter view but said that litigants must not have unrealistic expectations as to what the courts, as opposed to Parliament, can do to change the law here.

Since this decision Parliament has enacted the Agency Worker Regulations 2010 which are considered below *but* it is important to note that, although these Regulations provide important new rights for agency workers, they do *not* govern the employment status (or otherwise) of such workers for other purposes such as general statutory rights, which thus remains subject to the above case law.

(iv) ATYPICAL WORKERS—EU INTERVENTION ON PART-TIME, FIXED-TERM AND AGENCY WORK

The principal developments extending legal protection to certain types of employment are now coming from the EU. One original idea was for a single, overarching Directive covering all atypical workers, but this was always found politically unacceptable, and so the successful approach has been to propose individual Directives on specific categories of work, primarily through the medium of 'Framework Directives' which are agreed between the social partners (ETUC, UNICE and CEEP) and then merely promulgated by the relevant EU bodies.[90]

---

[88] [2007] IRLR 168; see also Judge Clark's judgment in *Cairns v Visteon* [2007] IRLR 175.

[89] [2008] IRLR 302, CA.

[90] This has two main effects in employment law. The first is that the drafting may be vague and aspirational (being more like a supranational collective agreement than a statute) which causes problems for transposition

(a) Part-time workers

The Part-time Workers Directive[91] is transposed into domestic law in the Part-time Workers (Prevention of Less Favourable Treatment) Regulations 2000[92] in relation to its primary requirement of a regime of non-discrimination. Thus, a part-time worker has a right not to be treated less favourably than a comparable full-time worker, as regards the terms of his contract or by being subjected to any other detriment by any act, or deliberate failure to act, of his employer, unless the treatment in question is objectively justified.[93] In assessing whether treatment has been less favourable the pro rata principle may be applied[94] (for example, half pay for half time, not one-third pay) which could make less than pro rata 'part-timer rates' unlawful and may cause technical problems with terms of employment other than pay (for example, in trying to pro rata holidays or bank holiday entitlements, or a firm's car). There may be some scope here for the objective justification defence, but at a more general level it may be difficult to argue for any widespread use for that defence, given the aim of the Directive to enhance the position of part-time work generally—why should part-timers be treated any less favourably than on a pro rata by time basis? A part-timer is defined quite simply as any worker who 'having regard to the custom and practice of his employer in relation to workers employed by the worker's employer under the same type of contract is not identifiable as a full-time worker'.[95] This covers anyone working fewer hours than full time and so is not confined to those working, for example, half time. There must normally be a comparison with a comparable full-time worker, except where a worker changes from full time to part time or has a period of absence for full-time work and returns part time, in which case the comparison may be with their own previous

---

into UK law with its literalist tradition. The second is that this vagueness means that it is unlikely that many parts of such Directives will be precise enough to support direct effect (see *Gibson v East Riding of Yorkshire Council* [2000] ICR 890, [2000] IRLR 598, CA where even the relatively precise provisions of the holiday entitlement in the Working Time Directive were held to be insufficient).

[91] Directive 97/81/EC, applied to the UK by Directive 98/23/EC. For a strong critique of its minimalist approach, see Jeffrey 'Not Really Going to Work?' (1998) 27 ILJ 193.

[92] SI 2000/1551, *Harvey* R [1288]. One immediate point to note is that these Regulations apply to 'workers', not just 'employees'; for the significance of the wider 'worker' definition, see this chapter under heading 1(vi), p 67 . For an assessment of the first ten years of the Regulations, see Bell, 'Achieving the Objective of the Part Time Workers Directive? Revisiting the Part-time Workers Regulations' (2011) 40 ILJ 254.

[93] Regulation 5(1), (2). There must be an actual comparator; there is no provision in the Regulations for a hypothetical comparator and EC law does not require it: *Carl v University of Sheffield* [2009] IRLR 616. The Directive says that a part-timer must not be less favourably treated *solely* because of being part time; the English EAT have held that there is no such restriction in the regulations (*Sharma v Manchester CC* [2008] IRLR 336), but this conflicts with an obiter statement to the contrary by the Scottish Court of Session (*McMenemy v Capita Business Services* [2007] IRLR 401).

[94] Regulation 5(3). It is specifically provided that a part-timer does not qualify for overtime rates until he has completed normal full-time hours, ie he cannot claim such rates at the expiry of his own part-time hours: reg 5(4). For an example of how complex an argument can be as to what is pro rata, see *Elsner-Lakeberg v Land Nordrhein-Westphalen* C-285/02 [2005] IRLR 209, ECJ.

[95] Regulation 2(2). Regulation 2(3) sets out categories of persons not to be considered as being under the same type of contract.

full-time terms.[96] The normal requirement of comparability lay behind the leading case on the Regulations, *Matthews v Kent and Medway Towns Fire Authority*[97] which, though an individual action, was a test case for 12,000 part-time ('retained') firefighters and their union's longstanding campaign for equal treatment, especially access to the full-time firefighters' pension scheme. When the Regulations were passed, their expectation was that this campaign would now be successful, but they then had the mortification of losing at tribunal, EAT and Court of Appeal levels. Even when the case went to the House of Lords, the judges split 3–2, in the firefighters' favour.[98] The point at issue was whether there was a true comparison, because part-time firefighters largely only fight fires, whereas full-timers have much broader duties (for example in relation to licensing, safety promotion and education). The panels up to Court of Appeal level and two of their lordships held that this ruled out a comparison; three of their lordships held that, on balance, there still was a valid comparison. The case shows that a comparison cannot be too easily assumed from a shared title ('firefighter'). Beyond that, one view is that the case establishes little and really only concerned a dispute over fact. However, it may be significant for one passage in Lady Hale's speech where she says that in a case such as this one should start with the similarities of the *core* duties, not with the dissimilarities. To start with the latter may lead to a finding of no comparison largely because of factors inherent in being part time in the first place.

A worker may present a complaint to an employment tribunal that his or her employer has infringed the Regulations; in such a case the burden of proof is on the employer and if the tribunal finds the complaint established it may make a declaration to that effect, award compensation and/or recommend action to be taken by the employer within a specified time to obviate or reduce the adverse effect on the complainant.[99]

As seen above, less favourable treatment of part-timers because of their status has already been under attack from existing law for many years, on the basis that it constitutes indirect sex discrimination which would be difficult to justify objectively. This has been known to good employers for a long time, and so it is arguable that these Regulations are largely pushing at an already opened door. They should get rid of any lingering attachment of the less-than-good employer to ideas of 'part-timer rates' for

---

[96] Regulations 2(4), 3, 4. In *Wippel v Peek & Cloppenburg* C-313/02 [2005] IRLR 211 the ECJ held that being a 'work on demand' casual worker meant that by definition there was no full-time equivalent and so no cause of action under the Directive. A worker who considers that the employer may have treated him or her less favourably on the ground of being part-time has a right to a written statement by the employer of the reasons for the treatment in question: reg 6.

[97] [2006] ICR 365, [2006] IRLR 367, HL.

[98] The final judge count was 11–3 in favour of the fire authority, but sadly for them the 3 were in the House of Lords.

[99] Regulation 8(1), (6), (7). The complaint must be presented within three months, with the usual discrimination law 'just and equitable' ground for extension of the period: reg 8(2)–(5). Compensation is such as is just and equitable having regard to the infringement and the worker's loss; it is not capped, but may not include injury to feelings and is subject to mitigation and compensatory fault (as in the case of unfair dismissal): reg 8(9)–(13). If an employer fails without reasonable justification to comply with a recommendation, compensation may be increased: reg 8(14).

these 'peripheral' staff and their major advantage legally is that a worker still faced by such antediluvian treatment now has a *direct* cause of action before a tribunal, rather than having to go through the hoops of a sex discrimination action. The Directive does, however, have a secondary aim, much more difficult to transpose into UK law. As is clear from the recitals to the Directive and its second half, it aims generally to increase the value placed on part-time work within organizations and to encourage the facilita-tion of movement between full-time and part-time working, which may include 'timely information' on such job opportunities and 'access by part-time workers to vocational training to enhance career opportunities and occupational mobility'. Moreover, it is made clear that part-time working is to be viewed as a realistic and valued option not just for hewers of wood and drawers of water (or even stackers of shelves), but 'at all levels of the enterprise, including skilled and managerial positions'. This sentiment sits easily alongside successive governments' family-friendly and work/life balance policies, but is difficult to put into the usual format of black letter law. The original idea was to produce a code of practice but this was dropped and the eventual solution was DTI (now BIS) Best Practice Guidance.[100] This covers matters such as widening access to part-time work, making more jobs available on that basis, jobsharing, taking requests to change to and from part time seriously, providing information to staff, training and other measures to facilitate part-time working. Some of this advice is potentially far-reaching and in places could be seen as placing an informal onus on an employer to *justify* any refusal of part-time working. Moreover, it pre-empted legislative moves towards the right to request a contract variation in the Employment Act 2002[101] and remains available to those not covered by that new right, ie those without a child under 17 or not caring for the infirm. Of course, the lawyer might be tempted to dismiss this all as non-legalistic wishful thinking, but it is possible that in the future employment lawyers will have to take this form of 'soft law' more seriously, especially as it comes from a directive. It is true that the guidance has no direct form of enforcement, but increasingly in areas such as this employment lawyers are having to think laterally and try to envisage how soft law might be *used* in other contexts. Two are mentioned here: (1) a refusal of part-time working might be attacked as indirect sex discrimination which would require the employer to justify the refusal, at which point the guidance could be powerful evidence (particularly if it suggested that part-time working should be possible in those circumstances); (2) the guidance might be relevant as evidence of reasonable or unreasonable employer action in a case where the refusal was made in such circumstances as to result in the employee leaving and claiming constructive dis-missal. Thus, to write the guidance off as 'only' soft law might be a very short-sighted view.

---

[100] 'Part-time work: the law and best practice', available at <http://www.bis.gov.uk/er/pt-detail>. The first half contains guidance on the Regulations; the second half contains best practice guidance on the second part of the Directive. *Quaere* whether there could be an issue under EC law as to whether this format is sufficient to transpose the Directive properly.

[101] Employment Act 2002, s 47; see Ch 4, heading 3(xi), p 287.

(b) Fixed-term employees

The Fixed-term Worker Directive[102] has two principal objectives: to establish a regime of non-discrimination and to require member states to have laws to prevent the perceived abuse of keeping individuals on successive fixed-term contracts for unreasonable periods. The first objective is thus very similar to that in the Part-time Worker Directive but the second is legally much more precise. Both of these objectives are transposed into domestic law in the Fixed-term Employees (Prevention of Less Favourable Treatment) Regulations 2002.[103] With regard to the first, a fixed-term employee has a right not to be treated less favourably than the employer treats a comparable permanent employee as regards the terms of his or her contract or by being subjected to any other detriment by any act, or deliberate failure to act, of his employer, unless the treatment in question is objectively justified.[104] As with the part-time provisions, the pro rata principle may be applied in determining whether there has been less favourable treatment.[105] The Regulations define a fixed-term contract by adopting the Directive's definition which extends that hitherto used by domestic law—in the latter a contract was only for a fixed term if it was time limited (ie until an expressed or ascertainable date) but the Regulations cover contracts terminating (1) on the expiry of a specific term, (2) on the completion of a particular task or (3) on the occurrence or non-occurrence of any other specific event (other than reaching retirement age);[106] heads (2) and (3) extend the definition to what have usually been referred to as 'purpose' or 'task' contracts (eg employment 'until this building is demolished'). There

---

[102] Directive 99/70/EC; *Del Cervo Alonso* C-307/05 [2007] IRLR 911, ECJ; *Impact v Minister for Agriculture and Food* C-268/06 [2008] IRLR 552, ECJ; *Rosado Santana v Consejeria de Justicia de la Junta de Andalucia* C-177/10 [2012] 1 CMLR 534, CJEU; *Kucuk v Land Nordrhein Westfalen* C-586/10 [2012] ICR 682, [2012] IRLR 697, CJEU.

[103] SI 2002/2034, *Harvey* R [1551]. These are explained in the DTI 'Fixed-term Work: a guide to the regulations', available at <http://www.berr.gov.uk/er/fixed/fixed-pl512>. In *Duncombe v Secretary of State for Children, Schools and Families* [2011] ICR 495, [2011] IRLR 840, SC Lady Hale commented that, although the Regulations are important for their stated aims of countering discrimination and abuse, they are not meant to outlaw the proper use of short-term contracts. Note that unlike the Part-time Worker Regulations (above) these Regulations are deliberately restricted to applying only to 'employees', not to 'workers'.

[104] Regulation 3(1), (3). Provided this comparison is shown these provisions apply and it is no defence that the employer treats other forms of non-permanent staff equally badly: *Cure v Coutts & Co plc* [2004] All ER (D) 393 (Oct). It is not a 'detriment' to be put onto a fixed-term basis in the first place: *Webley v Department of Work and Pensions* [2005] ICR 577, [2005] IRLR 288, CA. Regulation 3(2) particularizes the right not to be less favourably treated in relation to any period of service qualification for a condition of service, the opportunity to receive training and the opportunity to secure any permanent position in the establishment. With regard to the last, the employee has a right to be informed by the employer of available vacancies in the establishment, by advertisement or other reasonable form of notification: reg 3(6), (7).

[105] Regulation 3(5).

[106] Regulation 1(2). The Regulations in fact went much further and applied this wider definition to fixed-term contracts generally in the Employment Rights Act 1996, see Ch 7, heading 2(i), p 479. As under that Act, a fixed-term contract retains its status as such even if it also contains a notice provision: *Allen v National Australia Group Europe Ltd* [2004] IRLR 847.

must be a comparison with a comparable permanent employee.[107] An employee may present a complaint to an employment tribunal that his or her employer has breached this part of the Regulations.[108]

A key issue under these Regulations will be justification for continuing disparity of treatment (especially in relation to terms and conditions other than pay), for at least two reasons: (1) there is less likelihood of a straight pro rata solution than there is with part-timers and (2) there are known problems of mismatch between those on *short* fixed-term contracts and major, long-term benefits primarily intended for long-term permanent employees (for example, generous sickness benefits and pension entitlements). Thus, justification is likely to be a much more live issue here than under the part-time provisions. It may be affected by three particular points under the Regulations:

(1) There is a specific provision (inserted at a late stage) that, in determining whether a fixed-termer has been less favourably treated than a permanent employee without justification, one can look at whether the terms of the fixed-termer's employment *taken as a whole* are at least as favourable as those of the comparator. This allows the employer to rely on a 'package' approach, rather than a term-by-term approach.[109] This may be particularly useful where the employer pays the fixed-termer *more* (eg a higher hourly rate) to reflect the fact that he or she does not qualify for longer term benefits.

(2) Employees on short-term contracts may lawfully be excluded from particular benefits by attaching qualifying periods to those benefits, *provided* that the period in question does not discriminate between fixed-term and permanent employees.[110]

(3) Ultimately an employer could rely on straightforward objective justification for the disparity in treatment. The BIS Guide to the Regulations suggests a general three-stage test for justification (which must be considered on a case-by-case basis), namely whether the employer can show that the less favourable treatment is to achieve a legitimate objective, is necessary to achieve that objective and is an appropriate way to achieve it. Specific guidance is given on when it may be justifiable to exclude those on short-term contracts from pension schemes (where the benefit to the employee may be marginal and the administrative

---

[107] Regulation 2. An employee who considers that the employer may have treated him or her less favourably on the ground of being fixed-term has a right to a written statement by the employer of the reasons for the treatment in question: reg 5.

[108] Regulation 8. Such a complaint as to procedure and remedies is subject to the same rules as those applying to a complaint under the Part-time Worker Regulations 2000, see earlier.

[109] Regulation 4. This package approach is unusual—there is no mention of it in the Part-time Worker Regulations and it is *not* permitted in equal pay law, where the applicant can demand equality on a term-by-term approach (see Ch 5, heading 3(iii), p 357). There is guidance in the BIS Guide (n 103) on applying the package approach; one problem may be how to quantify the monetary worth of the benefit forgone.

[110] Regulation 3(2)(a); Directive 99/63/EC, cl 4(4) (which adds 'except where different length-of-service qualifications are justified on objective grounds').

problems for the employer great) and from contractual redundancy/assurance schemes (which may be argued to be constructed to compensate permanent employees for the *unexpected* loss of their jobs, this being inappropriate at the end of a deliberately defined period of a fixed-term contract).

One final point to note on this first objective of removing discrimination is that one piece of institutionalized discrimination had to be removed. Prior to October 2002 when the Regulations came into force it was possible for the employer of an employee on a fixed-term contract of two years or more to get the employee to sign away his or her rights to a statutory redundancy payment at the end of it. This has now been repealed,[111] so a fixed-term contract can no longer be used for this purpose (common though it was in the past).

Moving on to the second objective of the Directive, the placing of limits on the unfair use of successive fixed-term contracts, the government adopted a hybrid of two of the three approaches permitted by the Directive. A worker kept on successive fixed-term contracts for four years or more is deemed in law to be a permanent employee, unless the employer can objectively justify keeping that person on a fixed-term basis.[112] Justification is not defined, the BIS Guide contenting itself with repeating the general threefold test (above) here too. It would clearly need a strong business case which, after four years, may well be wearing thin. One possible candidate would be where the post is paid for by 'hot money funding', ie where it is supported by some outside source providing the money on, for example, a one- or two-year basis only, with no guarantee that it will continue into the future. At the time of writing, unfortunately the only reported case considering justification arose on very unusual facts and in it the Supreme Court upheld as justified a nine-year maximum *duration* for teaching contracts at EU international schools (that limit being provided for by EU rules) without giving any general guidance as to how justification is to apply to more typical cases.[113] One exception provided by the Regulations is that these provisions generally can be disapplied by a collective or workforce agreement and replaced by other controls on abuse, in the form of one or more of the following: (1) a different maximum period for successive contracts; (2) a maximum number of successive contracts; or (3) the laying down of what are to be objective grounds for renewal of fixed-term contracts.[114]

---

[111] Schedule 2, Pt I, repealing the Employment Rights Act 1996, s 197(3)–(5). Also abolished were exclusions of those on fixed-term contracts of three months or less from statutory sick pay, guarantee payments, medical suspension and minimum notice.

[112] Regulation 8. There have to have been *successive* contracts and so an initial contract of five years would not be converted on the fourth anniversary. Where there have been successive contracts, the conversion occurs on that anniversary. Major uncertainty here is caused by the fact that 'successive' contracts are defined simply by adopting the normal statutory rules on continuity of employment (see this chapter, heading 5, p 101), under which quite substantial gaps between contracts can be 'forgiven', especially where the contract themselves are for relatively long periods.

[113] *Duncombe v Secretary of State for Children, Schools and Families* [2011] ICR 495, [2011] IRLR 840, SC.

[114] Regulation 8(5). A 'workforce agreement' is an agreement between an employer and his employees or their representatives, satisfying the conditions (as to form, duration and the election of representatives) in Sch 1 to the Regulations.

An employee who considers that he or she has become a permanent employee under these provisions is entitled to a written statement from the employer acknowledging this or giving reasons why the employer contends that the contract remains fixed-term. If a dispute arises, the employee may present an application to an employment tribunal for a declaration of permanent status.

What is likely to be the effect of the Regulations? It is possible that they will have a greater effect than the Part-time Worker Regulations because, while part-time working had for some time been exposed to scrutiny under the law of indirect sex discrimination, this had not happened in relation to fixed-term working and so the possibilities for disparate treatment have remained greater, particularly as in managerial folklore such working has tended to be viewed as a prime way of keeping workers at arm's length legally, and of providing a reservoir of flexible staff with few or no legal rights. Ironically, shortly before the Regulations were drafted there arose the first reported case of a successful attack on disparate treatment of fixed-termers based on sex discrimination. In *Whiffen v Milham Ford Girls' School*[115] a school faced with making compulsory redundancies adopted the hitherto common policy of not renewing fixed-term contracts first, and then (and only then) applying fair selection criteria to the permanent staff in order to make the last few redundancies. This was held to be unjustified indirect sex discrimination. As with the Part-time Worker Regulations, a major advantage now is that an employee in that position no longer has to go through the complexities of a sex discrimination action, but can instead complain directly under the Fixed-term Employees Regulations that this was unjustified discrimination against fixed-termers.[116]

The Regulations do *not* ban the use of fixed-term contracts, and bona fide use may continue; this point was affirmed by the Court of Appeal in *Webley v Department of Work and Pensions*,[117] partly by reference to some of the recitals to the backing Directive which accept that time-limited contracts can be to the benefit of both parties. What the Regulations may do, however, is to alter the economic balance of advantage in using them—if they can no longer be used to lower labour costs, increase flexibility, make redundancies easier and cheaper and keep those advantages for year after year by keeping individuals on them, what are their remaining advantages? It may be that in many circumstances employers are to be advised to minimize their use (possibly sharpening up probation and redundancy procedures instead), reserving them for where the real need arises and objective justification could if necessary be shown. Doubtless it will be a long time before this sea change percolates down to line manager level, where assumptions about the continued desirability of fixed-term engagements may persist that are now either totally inaccurate or, at least, greatly exaggerated. It may

---

[115] [2001] ICR 1023, [2001] IRLR 468.

[116] As happened in *Dorset CC v Omenaca-Labarta* [2008] UKEAT/92/08.

[117] [2005] ICR 577, [2005] IRLR 288, CA; the court upheld a practice by the DWP of putting temporary staff (not recruited through the formal Civil Service procedures) onto 51-week contracts only, thereby avoiding unfair dismissal claims.

now be that, if a manager indicates that he or she wishes a new or replacement post to be on a fixed-term basis, an advising lawyer or HR professional will need to start the advice by asking one key question—'Why?'

(c) Agency workers

For several years there was considerable controversy over EU proposals for an agency worker Directive, extending to such workers a regime of equality with the permanent staff of the client for the time being, akin to that applying to part-timers and fixed-termers. UK employers' association were strongly opposed, on grounds of cost and administrative inconvenience, pointing out that the UK is by far the heaviest user of agency labour in the EU. One particular flashpoint (if there was to be a directive at all) was how long a worker should have to be with the one client before the proposed Directive should apply; UK employers wanted a period of months (to exclude all short-term hirings) whereas the EU authorities have tended to want a short qualifying period (weeks only), if any. The matter seemed to go to sleep but in 2008 suddenly came back onto the EU political radar when it was linked to negotiations on amendments to the Working Time Directive. Putting it rather brutally (but reflecting the nature of the political horse-trading involved) the position evolved that the 'price' for the UK keeping its major derogations in the Working Time Directive was to agree to a Temporary Agency Work Directive.[118] It principally requires a regime of equal treatment in EU-based legal rights and terms and conditions ('at least those that would apply if they had been recruited directly by that undertaking to occupy the same job'); there are then further requirements on access to employment, collective facilities, training, representation and information. One key point is that Article 5(4) permits member states to impose a qualifying period before the equality regime applies; the UK government, the CBI and TUC agreed that in the UK this was to be 12 weeks, thus excluding genuinely short-term agency workers.

The Directive was transposed into domestic law in the Agency Workers Regulations 2010 [119] which came into force in October 2011. They apply wherever an 'agency worker' is supplied by a 'temporary work agency' to work for a 'hirer'. The most important limitation to note at this definitional stage is that a 'temporary work agency' (usually known colloquially as an employment agency) does not include an agency which introduces workers to employers for *direct or permanent* employment.[120] The principal

---

[118] Directive 2008/104/EC.

[119] SI 2010/93. There is substantial BIS guidance on the application of the Regulations: Agency Workers Regulations Guidance (URN/11/905).

[120] These definitions are contained in regs 2, 3 and 4. An agency worker is defined as an individual (a) who is supplied by a temporary work agency to work temporarily for and under the supervision and direction of a hirer and (b) has a contract with a temporary work agency which is—'(i) a contract of employment with the agency or (ii) any other contract to perform work and services personally for the agency'. Note that the last part of this definition frees the application of the Regulations from a formal contract of employment. Hirings through intermediaries are covered but there is an exemption for client/customer relationships of a professional or business nature.

substantive provision is in reg 5(1) which states that a qualifying agency worker is enti-tled to the same basic working and employment conditions as he or she would have been entitled to for doing the same job, had they been recruited by the hirer *other* than through an agency. This provides an initial contrast with the Regulations on part-time and fixed-term working, namely that here there is no need for a comparator employee (though it is provided that if there is such a comparator and the agency worker works under the same terms and conditions as that person, that is a defence for the hirer or agency). The reference to equality of basic terms looks initially wide, but it is a major limitation of the Regulations that they only apply to certain *specified* terms. These are set out in reg 6(1) as (a) pay, (b) duration of working time, (c) night work, (d) rest periods, (e) rest breaks and (f) holidays. Heads (b) to (f) obviously mirror the normal working time rights[121] and so it is not surprising that the key right is (a) and that this is further defined. The general rule is that 'pay' means 'any sums payable to a worker of the hirer in connection with the worker's employment, including any fee, bonus, commission, holiday pay or other emolument referable to the employment, whether payable under the contract or otherwise'.[122] Once again, the apparently open nature of this defin-ition is immediately qualified by a list of exceptions, including occupational sick pay and pensions, redundancy payments, certain statutory payments, any bonus, incentive payment or reward not directly attributable to the work (such as loyalty or long-service payments) and any payment under a financial participation scheme. What these have in common is that they are longer term benefits meant for long-term employees and quite simply *inappropriate* for short-term, temporary workers. Two particular points should be noted. The first is that bonuses are a particular problem, appearing under both what is included and what is excluded. It is thus the case that it is the nature of the particular bonus that must be considered. According to the BIS Guidance:

> The key question is whether the bonus or incentive payment or reward is directly attribut-able to the amount or quality of work done. If it is for another reason … such as to encourage the worker's loyalty or to reward long-service then it is outside the scope of the entitlement to the same terms and conditions relating to pay.

Obviously, this could lead to differences of opinion in any given case. The second point is that, controversially at the time, there was written into the Regulations a general exception to the right to pay equality in any case where the worker has a permanent contract of employment with the agency which states that the right to equal pay is not to apply *and* (effectively instead) during any workless period the agency not only takes reasonable steps to obtain other work but also agrees to pay the worker a 'minimum amount of remuneration' for at least four weeks.[123] That amount is then defined as at least 50% of the pay paid to the worker in the best paid reference period within the 12 weeks preceding the end of the previous assignment (with an absolute minimum of the national minimum wage). Some concern has been expressed as to how widely

---

[121] See Ch 4, heading 2(iii), p 234   [122] Regulation 6(2). The exceptions are in reg 6(3).
[123] Regulation 10.

this could be used by employers to avoid the statutory protection; the basic obligation to pay during workless periods is hardly likely to be attractive to an agency *but* a
major client with considerable bargaining power could make it a condition of using a
particular agency that it operates this system.

The other issue which arose as to possible evasion of the new rules was as a result
of the negotiated position that the above rules were to apply only once the worker has
been with the hirer for 12 weeks. This is incorporated into the Regulations in reg 7(2)
which defines a 'qualifying agency worker' as one working 'in the same role with the
same hirer for 12 continuous calendar weeks, during one or more assignments'. This
raised three forms of possible evasion—(1) altering the role undertaken by the worker
during the 12 weeks, (2) using separate contracts of up to 11 weeks with breaks in
between in the case of any particular worker[124] and (3) structuring the assignments
themselves in such a way as to negate the rules. These three possibilities are covered
separately by anti-avoidance provisions which are of very considerable complexity and
take up a large proportion of the Regulations. With regard to (1), reg 7(3) enacts a presumption that the worker has been in the same role unless the worker has started a new
role with substantially different work or duties and the employer has informed him or
her of the new type of work in writing. With regard to (2), arguably the major threat,
reg 7(5)–(11) unsurprisingly had to enact more complicated sub-rules. The approach
here is to deem there to be continuity of employment through seven stipulated forms
of absence. These cover any break of up to six weeks (to stop evasion by a series of
short breaks with little disruption to the employer), sickness/injury absence (up to
28 weeks), pregnancy/maternity leave (up to 26 weeks), the taking of other leave to
which the worker is statutorily or contractually entitled (eg parental leave), jury service, customary breaks (particularly customary holidays and shutdowns) and periods
of strike, lockout or other industrial action at the hirer's establishment.[125] With regard
to (3), reg 9 addresses the possible use of the structure of assignments (possibly by the
use of intermediaries such as companies related to the principal hirer) to disrupt the
acquisition of rights by an individual agency worker. It addresses the problem that,
in spite of the above sub-rules, a hirer may still be able to organize assignments so as
to avoid qualification by the individual (lawfully but only just). However, if a *pattern*
of doing so over a period of time emerges, reg 9 may bite because, most unusually, it
then concentrates on whether the hirer's *intention* was to evade the rules. If the worker
has completed two or more assignments with the hirer (or with a connected organization) or has worked in more than two roles during an assignment, then an inquiry is
to be made as to whether the 'most likely explanation' for this is that the hirer or the
agency intended to prevent the worker from being (or continuing to be) entitled to

---

[124] When (prior to 1995) there was a statutory requirement that an employee had to work 16 hours per
week in order to qualify for the major statutory rights such as unfair dismissal, the use of 15-hour contracts
for part-timers was common.

[125] This is a précis of complex provisions, which need to be consulted directly in any given case. The BIS
Guidance at p 18 sets out how these provisions are to affect what it terms the 'ticking of the clock'.

the equality requirement of the Regulations. In so deciding, there can be taken into account the length and number of assignments, the number of new roles given to the worker, the number of times he or she has returned to work in the same role for the hirer and the period of any breaks. If the correct inference from this is that the necessary intent to evade the Regulations is shown, the end result is that the worker is to be treated as having completed a qualifying period which would have been completed but for the structuring of the assignment(s). It can also mean that a worker does not have to complete a further qualifying period if returning to the hirer in these circumstances. A good example of the possible working of these complex provisions is given in the BIS Guidance; having stated that the Regulations do not prevent the use of 11-week contracts or gaps of more than six weeks as such, it then states:

> For example, an agency worker completes 2 or more assignments with the same hirer, where they have already worked for 11 weeks with a 6 week break and then a further 11 weeks with another 6 week break. If the agency worker is then taken on for a third assignment, this could be considered an attempt to avoid the completion of the qualifying period but it would need to be clear that the attempt was deliberate. This would be a matter for the tribunal in the event of a claim.

As with the Regulations on part-time and fixed-term working, there is a second part to the protection to be given under the Directive, but here it is less extensive. It simply consists of (1) a right for agency workers to have access to collective facilities and amenities provided for employees such as canteen or similar facilities, childcare and transport services[126] and (2) a right for an agency worker to be informed during an assignment of any relevant vacant post with the hirer, in order to give him or her the same opportunity as a comparable worker to find permanent employment.[127]

An agency worker who considers that any of these rights has been infringed has a right of action to a tribunal and, in preparation for this has a right to request a written statement from the agency as to why they have been treated in the way they were.[128] The tribunal can, if a complaint is upheld, make a declaration to that effect, award compensation and/or recommend future action to be taken by the respondent. Where the breach is of the principal right in reg 5 to equality of basic terms and conditions, both agency and hirer can be liable to the extent that each is 'responsible for that breach'; however, an agency is given a defence if it shows that it took reasonable steps to obtain information from the hirer about these terms and conditions and to ensure that the worker was treated by the hirer in the proper manner.

---

[126] Regulation 12. This is a 'day-one' right, not requiring 12 weeks' service, and is (unusually here) amenable to a justification defence for the employer.

[127] Regulation 13. Once again, this is a day-one right.

[128] Regulations 18 and 16 respectively. There is the usual three-month time limit for a tribunal claim, extendable on the discrimination law 'just and equitable' basis, the usual ban on contracting out of the Regulations and protection from detriment or unfair dismissal for asserting these rights.

(v) ASSOCIATED EMPLOYERS

When considering the relationship of employer and employee, 'the employer' will normally be readily identifiable. If an employee decides voluntarily to change employer (eg to further their career), it is accepted that he or she will in doing so lose the rights he or she has accrued already and have to start again with the new employer. However, in the realities of modern business in the private sector, the employer is likely to be a body corporate and here it may be more difficult to identify 'the employer' in that the particular company for which the employee works may itself be merely one part of a larger organization. Such an organization may be split down into smaller units for reasons (usually financial) which have little to do with employment law. It is, therefore, important that there should be provisions ensuring that employees do not lose their rights as a result of the composition of the employing concern and that an excessively technical view should not be taken of who or what constitutes the employer. Such provisions also serve as an anti-avoidance device, ensuring that employers cannot gain by dividing undertakings artificially into small units.

The provisions in question are those relating to 'associated employers', whereby two or more units (such as companies within one group) can be treated as one employer. The most important application of the concept of associated employers is in the context of continuity of employment (a vital factor in modern employment rights, both as to qualification to claim the right in question, such as unfair dismissal or a redundancy payment, and quantification of the employee's entitlement under that right). Thus, if an employee transfers (or is transferred) from the employment of one employer to the employment of an associated employer, their continuity of employment is *preserved*, and time spent with the first employer can count as time with the second employer.[129] The concept goes further, however, and can be found elsewhere in the employment legislation. Thus for example offers of 'suitable alternative employment' (important in redundancy law and in relation to maternity leave) may be made by the employer or an associated employer.[130]

From these examples, it is easy to see the importance of the concept of associated employers. The definition is contained in the Employment Rights Act 1996, section 231:

> any two employers are to be treated as associated if one is a company of which the other (directly or indirectly) has control, or if both are companies of which a third person (directly or indirectly) has control.

'Control' is thus crucial, and there must be voting control in some form, not just de facto influence, however strong.[131] An extension to this narrow approach was suggested by

---

[129] See this chapter, heading 6, p 113. To be an 'associated employer', it is not essential that the company in question was already employing labour when the employee in question transferred to it: *Lucas v Henry Johnson (Packers and Shippers) Ltd* [1986] ICR 384.

[130] See Ch 4, heading 3 and Ch 8, heading 1, pp 267 and 589.

[131] *Secretary of State for Employment v Newbold* [1981] IRLR 305; *Umar v Pliastar Ltd* [1981] ICR 727. This even applies when the person in question owns 50% of the shares in one of the companies, for that is *not a*

the EAT in *Zarb and Samuels v British and Brazilian Produce Co (Sales) Ltd*[132] where it was held that control by a third person could include control by third *persons*, so that if two or more persons between them own more than 50% of the voting shares of the two companies *and* in practice act together, that may satisfy the definition. However, this approach has caused considerable difficulties, since the Court of Appeal in *South West Launderettes Ltd v Laidler*[133] questioned the correctness of *Zarb* and declined to apply it where on the facts it may have been possible to do so. The position is not absolutely clear because it was not necessary for the court to decide the matter and in the subsequent case of *Harford v Swiftrim Ltd*[134] the EAT applied *Zarb* (on the basis that it has been consistently followed) and expressly refused to apply the criticisms of it in *Laidler*. A different division of the EAT under Wood P then declined to follow *Harford* in *Strudwick v Iszatt Bros Ltd*,[135] stating obiter that if necessary they would have followed the criticisms in *Laidler* and held against any concept of plural control (largely because of the major problems of discovery, evidence and proof that are capable of arising under such a concept). On the other hand, *Zarb* was applied again by a later EAT in *Tice v Cartwright*,[136] which perhaps showed that the present position (until we have a definitive ruling of the Court of Appeal) is that *Zarb* remains there to be used where common sense and justice demand that two organizations be deemed to be one, especially where (or in this case) the facts concern a very restricted shareholding in a family concern, where the necessary de facto control and common action can be shown.

One significant problem which arose under this definition was that it only refers to *companies* as being associated employers. What was to be the position where the two employers in question were *not* companies (eg in the public sector, bodies such as health trusts, local authorities or universities) or if *one* of the employers was not a company (eg where one farmer runs two farms, one constituted as a company and the other as a partnership)? There were conflicting EAT decisions on this point. One view was that the definition was not exhaustive (only governing the position where the two employers in fact are companies) so that other bodies can be 'associated' if that is the practical position.[137] The other view was that the definition *was* exhaustive, so that only companies can be associated.[138] This conflict was resolved in *Merton London*

---

voting majority and so the companies are not associated: *Hair Colour Consultants Ltd v Mena* [1984] ICR 671, [1984] IRLR 386; *South West Launderettes Ltd v Laidler* [1986] ICR 455, [1986] IRLR 305, CA; cf, however, *Payne v Secretary of State for Employment* [1989] IRLR 352, CA, where one person held 50% as a nominee of the other person.

[132] [1978] IRLR 78. For this principle to apply, it must be the same group of persons exercising control in the case of each company claimed to be associated: *Poparm Ltd v Weekes* [1984] IRLR 388, approved by the Court of Appeal in *South West Launderettes Ltd v Laidler*, n 131.

[133] [1986] ICR 455, [1986] IRLR 305, CA.   [134] [1987] ICR 439, [1987] IRLR 360.

[135] [1988] ICR 796, [1988] IRLR 457; *Russell v Elmdon Freight Terminal Ltd* [1989] ICR 629, EAT.

[136] [1999] ICR 769.

[137] *Hillingdon Area Health Authority v Kauders* [1979] ICR 472, [1979] IRLR 197.

[138] *Southwood Hostel Management Committee v Taylor* [1979] ICR 813, [1979] IRLR 397.

Borough Council v Gardiner[139] where the Court of Appeal held that the definition is exhaustive, so that an employee who was unfairly dismissed by a local authority could only claim to have his compensation calculated by reference to the two years he had worked with that authority, not by reference to the 10 years he had previously served with three other local authorities. Thus, except under the first part of the definition ('vertical' associated employers) where one of the employers can be any sort of person provided that he, she or it has control of the company which is the other employer, the bodies claimed to be associated must be companies, which is a significant limitation on the definition in the absence of any special statutory exception; the most important such exception now is that employees in local government service are covered by Regulations which deem their employment to be continuous, for redundancy rights purposes, when they move from one local government body to another.[140]

(vi) 'WORKER' AND THE WIDER DEFINITION OF EMPLOYMENT

It can be argued that the traditional legal dichotomy between 'employee' and 'independent contractor' is now too simplistic to fit our diverse workforce, and leaves too many people potentially in a hole in the middle. One way to avoid (or at least mitigate) this, would be to move the goalposts and extend the definition of 'employee'.

This is not a new idea, and it has in the past been done in one of two ways, namely to use the term 'worker' instead (with a correspondingly wider definition) or to retain the term 'employee' but add to the normal definition (ie as a person under a contract of employment). Trade union legislation has always used the term 'worker', defining it as 'an individual who works ... (a) under a contract of employment or (b) under any other contract whereby he undertakes to do or perform personally any work or services for another party to the contract who is not a professional client of his'.[141] The extension in (b) is highly significant. Discrimination legislation has always used the term 'employment' but applied it to employment under a contract of employment or apprenticeship or a contract personally to do any work;[142] in other words, it confusingly uses the term 'employee' where it in effect means 'worker'. The Transfer of Undertakings (Protection of Employment) Regulations 2006 use the term 'employee' but define it as working 'for another person whether under a contract of service or apprenticeship or otherwise but

---

[139] [1981] ICR 186, [1980] IRLR 472, CA.

[140] Redundancy Payments (Continuity of Employment in Local Government, etc) (Modification) Order 1999, SI 1999/2277; *Harvey* R [1186]. See also the Redundancy Payments (National Health Service) (Modification) Order 1993, SI 1993/3167; *Harvey* R [755] which performs a similar function in the now-fragmented structure of the NHS, and the ERA 1996, s 218(7) which preserves continuity through the movement by teachers between schools maintained by a local education authority and that authority.

[141] Trade Union and Labour Relations (Consolidation) Act 1992, s 296; the 'Wages Act' provisions or deductions from wages use a similar term and definition, see now the ERA 1996, s 230(3) and the recovery of commission by a self-employed investment consultant in *Robertson v Blackstone Franks Investment Management Ltd* [1998] IRLR 376, CA.

[142] Equality Act 2010 s 83(2). This definition does not contain the express exclusion of a professional client.

does not include anyone who provides services under a contract for services'.[143] While these definitions contain subtle differences (with the TUPE definition being arguably narrowest, with its exclusion of *anyone* under a contract for services), they do show a deliberate extension of statutory coverage. Perhaps surprisingly, the case law on them has been relatively scarce, though the leading authority of *Mirror Group Newspapers Ltd v Gunning*[144] emphasizes the element of 'personal service', and states that that must be the dominant purpose of the contract in question. A good example of the interplay between the traditional 'employee' category and the wider definition arose on unusual facts in *Percy v Board of National Mission of the Church of Scotland*[145] where a female Church of Scotland minister who was obliged to stand down because of an affair with a married church elder conceded that she could not claim unfair dismissal because she was not an 'employee'[146] but succeeded in bringing a claim for sex discrimination, using the wider definition. In *Cotswold Developments Construction Ltd v Williams*[147] this area was reviewed by the EAT under Langstaff J who suggested that a useful approach would be to consider first whether there was the required minimum level of mutuality of obligations between the parties for there to be a contract at all, secondly (if there was) whether the level of mutuality and control was enough to produce a contract of employment, thirdly (if not) whether there was a sufficient obligation of personal service on the part of the individual to qualify him or her as a 'worker' and fourthly (if so) whether the usual proviso (that the work must not have been done in the course of the individual's business or profession) applied on the facts. This was followed by further consideration and guidance from Elias P in *James v Redcats (Brads) Ltd*[148] where a parcel courier (using her own van, working only for the respondent firm, arranging her own timetable and holidays, paid per parcel delivered and accepted by HMRC as self-employed) was held to be a 'worker' for the purposes of a claim of breach of the national minimum wage.

---

[143] SI 2006/246, reg 2(1).

[144] [1986] ICR 145, [1986] IRLR 27, CA, applied by the EAT in *Sheehan v Post Office Counters* [1999] ICR 734 in holding that a sub-postmaster was not covered by the disability legislation. The provision of legal services was held by the House of Lords to be capable of coming within the similar definition in the Northern Ireland fair employment legislation in *Kelly and Laughran v Northern Ireland Housing Executive* [1998] ICR 828, [1998] IRLR 593.

[145] [2006] ICR 134, [2006] IRLR 195, HL.

[146] There has always been an issue whether a church minister is employed directly by a divine authority or by an earthly body more amenable to the jurisdiction of a tribunal. For many years the accepted view was that a minister or priest is *not* an employee but the Court of Appeal reviewed this and held not only that there was no such rule but that on the facts a Methodist minister was indeed an employee: *President of the Methodist Conference v Preston* [2012] IRLR 229, CA. It is thus possible that the concession on non-employment status in *Percy* would now be wrong. The position of Church of England clergy was finally regularized by the Ecclesiastical Offices (Terms of Service) Regulations 2009, SI 2009/2108, which give parallel employment rights, *as if* employees. This of course does not apply to ministers of other denominations or religions.

[147] [2006] IRLR 181. See generally Davidov 'Who Is a Worker?' (2005) 34 ILJ 57.

[148] [2007] IRLR 296.

This whole matter took on more significance when the wider 'worker' definition was adopted by the previous Labour government in the Public Interest Disclosure Act 1998,[149] the National Minimum Wage Act 1998[150] and the regulations on working time and part-time workers.[151] The aim generally has been to move away from the traditional coverage of employees only, especially as many of the individuals most in need of protection will come into the middle ground of 'atypicals' that has caused so many problems of definition in the past. Arguably, the 'worker' definition is a more inclusive one, prima facie covering atypical working unless there is good reason why it does not. The way that this is put in the DTI (now BIS) guides on the national minimum wage and working time may be significant—they both state that it is only the '*genuinely* self employed' who will not be covered by these laws. Clearly, there will be as many problems defining this as there are currently in defining a person under a contract of employment; however, it does give a flavour of the intent of the legislation which can be seen graphically from the two leading cases (both of which concerned the entitlement to statutory holiday pay of individuals who, prior to the Working Time Regulations, would have had no such claim). In *Byrne Brothers (Farmwork) Ltd v Baird*[152] self-employed building workers (under a subcontracting contract which stated that no holiday pay was due) were effectively laid off by a Christmas/New Year closure by the one firm that they worked for. Even though they were clearly not employees (being Schedule D labour-only subcontractors in the longstanding tradition of the building industry) they successfully sued the firm for paid annual holiday for the period in question under the Working Time Regulations 1998; they were under *a* contract, performing work personally for that firm, and in practical terms were subordinate workers (dependent for work on that firm) and so not genuinely in business on their own account. This result was then seen again when the matter reached the Court of Appeal in *Wright v Redrow Homes (Yorkshire) Ltd*[153] and direct labour subcontracting bricklayers were held entitled to holiday pay because (looking at the realities of the engagement rather than the technical meaning of the ill-fitting contract that they had been given) the intention of the parties was that the individual bricklayers themselves were to perform the work in question. While it is true that there was criticism of some of the reasoning in *Byrne Brothers* for over-emphasizing the policy reasons for a wide interpretation, and an affirmation that what the 'worker' definition requires is an obligation to work personally (not

---

[149] This is because the Act puts new sections into the ERA 1996 and adopts the latter's definition of 'worker'.

[150] Section 54. In *James v Redcats (Brands) Ltd* (n 148) it was thought important for the effectiveness of the national minimum wage legislation that a broad approach be taken to the definition of 'worker', to include *just* the types of individuals most in need of its protection.

[151] SI 1998/1833, reg 2(1); SI 2000/1551, reg 1(2). The wider definition is, however, not used in the Fixed-Term Employees (Prevention of Less Favourable Treatment) Regulations 2002.

[152] [2002] ICR 667, [2002] IRLR 96.

[153] [2004] ICR 1126, [2004] IRLR 720, CA. Subsequently to this decision, the employers (with advice) sought to amend their terms of hiring deliberately to exclude 'worker' status, but when a further challenge arose it was held that they had failed to do so: *Redrow Homes (Yorkshire) Ltd v Buckborough* [2009] IRLR 34.

just a vague understanding), the end result is very much in line with the earlier decision. Taken together, they may serve as a cautionary tale, particularly at the dodgier
end of the self-employment spectrum.

Finally, one possible further development here has come to nothing. In the
Employment Relations Act 1999, section 23, the government took a power to extend
any or all employment rights to individuals other than employees. A DTI working
party was set up and at one point there were some hopes that it might look into the
whole questions of employment status,[154] even extending the 'worker' definition more
widely. However, when a report was finally issued[155] it contained little other than vague
exhortations to employers to treat employees nicely, and legally was completely anodyne. There is, for the time being, to be no return to the drawing board in this complex
area.

(vii) EMPLOYEE SHAREHOLDERS

Finally on status, one other development should be noted, though it is still only at a formative state at the time of writing. In 2012 the Chancellor of the Exchequer announced
that the Coalition government is to enact a new form of hiring, the 'employee owner'.
The idea here is that the employer would be able to offer to take on an individual as
basically an employee *but* with lesser employment rights. In particular, the individual
would opt out of the protection of unfair dismissal law (except for the categories of
automatic unfairness or where the dismissal constituted unlawful discrimination), the
right to a statutory redundancy payment and the rights to request flexible working
and employer-sponsored training; also, where relevant, the individual would have to
give longer notice when returning from maternity or adoption leave. Why would the
individual agree to do so? The answer is that the quid pro quo for these opt-outs would
be the right to receive shares in the employer's business to a value between £2,000 and
£50,000 which on resale (ie on termination of employment) would be free from capital
gains tax. The idea is clearly to give the individual a stake in the business while at the
same time limiting the employment obligations on the employer that normally come
with taking on an employee. This rabbit was pulled out of the hat with little warning
and at the time of writing the government are consulting on how it is to work (one particular issue being how the shares are to be valued on termination, a known problem
with existing private sector employee share schemes). The basic law here is contained
in the Growth and Infrastructure Bill and the details are likely to emerge during the
currency of this edition; the key question will be whether this will prove to be a significant addition to the variations of employment status or merely an exercise in what
could unkindly be termed gesture politics.

---

[154] As had been suggested in the White Paper 'Fairness at Work' (Cm 3968) para 3.18.
[155] 'Success at Work: Protecting Vulnerable Workers' (DTI, 2006).

2 FORMATION

(i) THE CONTRACTUAL BASIS OF EMPLOYMENT

We have already seen that the relationship of employer and employee arises out of a contract. This, however, was not always so, for before the latter half of the nineteenth century the relationship was viewed more as one arising out of the 'status' of being a servant. Blackstone refers to master and servant as being one of the three great relationships in private life, along with husband and wife and parent and child,[156] and the extensive legislation governing supply and conditions of employment, dating back to the Statute of Labourers 1351, was not finally abolished until 1875.[157] The movement towards contract proceeded throughout the nineteenth and twentieth centuries, becoming firmly established. In *Laws v London Chronicle*[158] Lord Evershed MR said:

> A contract of service is but an example of contracts in general, so that the general law of contract will be applicable.

No sooner was this established beyond real doubt than the trend was arguably reversed. Since 1963, and particularly since the concept of unfair dismissal was introduced in 1971, the employment relationship has been increasingly overlaid with statutory criteria, rights and duties, to such an extent that it is certainly open to doubt whether we should still accept that contract law alone provides the underlying structure of employment law, or whether we should talk instead of a modern 'status' relationship of some sort or, at the least, of a *sui generis* Law of Employment which of necessity looks to contractual theories for guidance in given areas.[159] Against that, it must be stressed that employment remains for the most part a voluntary relationship, and the content of most of the terms of employment remains to be negotiated by the parties, either individually or through the medium of collective industrial relations. The contract theory remains paramount and, if anything, of renewed importance, given the moves over the last three decades in many areas away from a collective model of wage and conditions

---

[156] 1 Bl Com 422.   [157] See Wedderburn *The Worker and the Law* (3rd edn, 1986) 141.

[158] [1959] 2 All ER 285 at 287, [1959] 1 WLR 698 at 287, CA. This case demonstrates the purely contractual approach to summary dismissal, which can also be seen in the more colourful case of *Pepper v Webb* [1969] 2 All ER 216, [1969] 1 WLR 514, CA.

[159] For general discussion, see Rideout 'The Contract of Employment' [1966] CLP 111; Khan-Freund 'A Note on Status and Contract in British Labour Law' (1967) 30 MLR 635; Napier 'Judicial Attitudes towards the Employment Relationship' (1977) 6 ILJ 1; Kerr 'Contract Doesn't Live Here Any More?' (1984) 47 MLR 30; Honeyball 'Employment Law and the Primacy of Contract' (1989) 18 ILJ 97; Anderman 'The Interpretation of Protective Employment Statutes and Contracts of Employment' (2000) 29 ILJ 223; Barmes 'The Continuing Conceptual Crisis in the Common Law of the Contract of Employment' (2004) 67 MLR 435; Freedland 'From the Contract of Employment to the Personal Work Nexus' (2006) 35 ILJ 1; Honeyball and Pearce 'Contract, Employment and the Contract of Employment' (2006) 35 ILJ 30. In particular, Professor Hepple argues that the statutory rights should be freed from their existing contractual basis, in order to avoid 'a multitude of common law snares': 'Restructuring Employment Rights' (1986) 15 ILJ 69.

determination, towards an emphasis on individual contracting; we therefore now have to consider the character of the contract, its formation and its content.

The employment relationship is by its very nature bilateral, at its simplest work for wages,[160] so much of the case law on this aspect of contract is of little practical importance. It is extensively dealt with in the contract textbooks which should be consulted as required. Form used to be of supreme importance in apprenticeship contracts whose impact has greatly declined and still is in the particular case of merchant seamen, but it will be noted later that one of the major features of the modern legislation is a revived interest in form generally. Legality in the field of employment law concerns principally the doctrine of restraint of trade, a relatively rare oasis where the courts over many decades have adopted an important stance based on public policy. It merits detailed treatment below, along with the way in which the general doctrine of illegality has been imported into unfair dismissal law, occasionally doing it considerable violence. The question of 'intent to create legal relations' plays a major part in the sphere of collective agreements, where it is discussed, being largely responsible for the longstanding rule that collective agreements are not legally binding.

One further significance of the contractual base is that certain tenets of contractual interpretation or modification (common law or statutory) may be argued by one party or the other to good effect. Thus, for example, in *Levett v Biotrace International plc*[161] a managing director benefiting from valuable share options was wrongfully dismissed and then told by the company that those options had lapsed under a clause in his employment contract providing for such lapse on termination of employment. However, the Court of Appeal interpreted the clause as only applying to *lawful* termination (thus preserving their benefit for him), relying on the general contractual rule of construction that a party should not be able to take advantage of his own breach of contract. Similarly, the general contract law rules on penalty clauses could apply to a provision in a contract of employment stating that a set amount must be paid by the employee to the employer in the case of some particular act or default by that employee, for example a failure to give notice when leaving; under ordinary contract principles, such a clause would be void unless the employer could show that it was a genuine pre-estimate of loss to the employer, which in the employment context could be difficult.[162]

Further, two uncertainties arise in the area of statutory coverage of ordinary contract law. The first is whether the Unfair Contract Terms Act 1977 could be relied on in an

---

[160] Even here, however, complications can arise in cases of partial performance by an employee, eg when taking part in industrial action short of a strike (such as a go-slow or refusal to perform certain duties)—is he still entitled to payment, and if so how much? See Ch 10, heading 2, p 695.

[161] [1999] ICR 818, [1999] IRLR 375, CA.

[162] *Giraud (UK) Ltd v Smith* [2000] IRLR 763. See also *Murray v Leisureplay plc* [2005] IRLR 946, CA where a relatively indulgent approach was taken to what was argued to be a penalty clause, in a case where a stricter approach might have jeopardized the widespread practice of putting 'golden parachute' clauses into the contracts of executives to facilitate termination and minimize litigation.

employment case. At first this was thought unlikely, but in *Brigden v American Express Bank Ltd*[163] Morland J held that the Act can apply, though he went on to find that a clause stating that an employee could be dismissed within the first two years without implementation of the disciplinary procedure was *not* an exclusion clause within section 3 of the Act (with its requirement of reasonableness). However, a finding that the Act applied required the rather artificial reasoning that the employee dealt with the employer 'as a consumer' and when the matter arose for the first time before the Court of Appeal in *Commerzbank AG v Keen*[164] (a case where the Act was being used to attack a clause in a bonus scheme which stated that no bonus would be payable if the employee was not in the employer's employment at the date the bonus was calculated) they held that in relation to a normal term in a contract of employment it cannot be said that the employee deals as a consumer or on the employer's standard terms of business (the alternative bases for the Act to apply). The decision in *Brigden* was said to be unsatisfactory, and so it now appears that the Act is very unlikely to play any significant role in mainstream employment law. The second uncertainty is whether the Contracts (Rights of Third Parties) Act 1999 could apply. Employment contracts were of course not primarily the contemplation of its framers, but it does provide that third party rights can be established against employers or ex-employers (but not employees). As such rights can generally be excluded or modified by agreement, the lawyer drafting an employment contract may wish to cover this point in any case where a third party right might arise, especially where one of the benefits in the contract might apply to a spouse or dependant of the employee, for example use of a company car or coverage by medical insurance, life insurance or pensions.[165]

(ii) RECRUITMENT ISSUES

The recruitment of staff has traditionally been an area of little legal involvement, being largely left as a matter for employer discretion, with few rights at common law for job applicants.[166] Given that the common law basis for employment is contractual, the refused applicant has by definition no contract on which to sue and so even the implied term of trust and respect (so important in safeguarding the legal rights of persons once employed) could not be relied on at this inchoate stage.[167] This common

---

[163] [2000] IRLR 94, relying on Watson 'Employees and the Unfair Contract Terms Act' (1985) 14 ILJ 323.

[164] [2007] IRLR 132, CA.

[165] Smith and Randall *Contracts Actions in Modern Employment Law* (2nd edn) p 30; Milgate 'Third Party Rights' [2000] Employment Law Journal 5.

[166] See the well-known quote from Lord Davey in the foundation case on common law liabilities, *Allen v Flood* [1898] AC 1, HL (set out at Ch 5, heading 1, p 301), asserting the employer's right to refuse employment for any reason or none.

[167] One of the stranger cases on direct enforcement of contracts of employment was *Giles & Co Ltd v Morris* [1972] 1 All ER 960, [1972] 1 WLR 307 where specific performance of the execution of an offered job was ordered, largely so that the individual would then, as an employee (technically, if not actually), have common law rights on his 'dismissal'. On the other hand, in *Wishart v National Association of Citizens Advice Bureaux*

law abstentionism is now subject to four particular qualifications, three by statute and the fourth arising from separate developments in relation to employment references. Important though these are in their contexts, we still do not have any overarching 'law of recruitment'.

The first and most important intervention of the law is, of course, through the discrimination statutes. Recruitment is a vital area in which to counter discrimination and it has always been clear that it is covered by the laws on sex, race, disability, sexual orientation, religion or belief and age discrimination, which are considered below in detail in Chapter 5.

The second, and very different, form of statutory intervention has come under the Data Protection Act 1998. This Act, materially increasing the coverage of previous legislation, ostensibly does not affect the process of recruitment but can apply to documentation produced and/or stored as part of that process. However, the guardian of the Act, now renamed the Information Commissioner, has tended to take a wide view of this remit and has issued guidance which arguably strays significantly into the process itself. This guidance is in the form of the 'Employment Practices Data Protection Code Part I: Recruitment and Selection'.[168] It covers advertising, handling applications, verification of details, shortlisting, interviews, pre-employment vetting and retention of treatment records. It should be consulted in detail on any of these matters, and is likely to have considerable practical significance for HR practitioners. Among its key recommendations (showing its overall approach) are to (1) make a staff member responsible for compliance, (2) make serious data protection breaches by employees handling their information a disciplinary offence, (3) only request data about an applicant that is relevant to recruitment, (4) ensure that job applicants sign a consent form if documents are needed from a third party, (5) inform applicants if automated shortlisting is the sole basis of decision, (6) retain interview notes,[169] (7) establish a retention period for recruitment records[170] and (8) dispose of salary information from previous employers. This part of the Code has a slightly ambiguous position in employment law. Unlike Part 3 on employee monitoring (which could well be relevant

---

Ltd [1990] ICR 794, [1990] IRLR 393, CA the Court of Appeal refused to enforce a job offer which was withdrawn in the light of references; there was no subsisting employment relationship to which any argument of trust and confidence could attach; 'instead there is a stillborn relationship to which one party strongly objects' (per Mustill LJ).

[168] This is available on <http://www.ico.gov.uk>. The other three parts of the Code are on employee records, monitoring of employees and information about workers' health.

[169] This would be advised by a lawyer anyway, in case of a later complaint of discrimination by a disappointed applicant (the time limit normally being three months). As these notes may now be obtainable under the Data Protection Act those conducting interviews must be advised to be careful what appears in them, including 'pen portraits' of the applicant in the margin.

[170] Together with point (3) this shows an application of the general data protection tenet that a data controller should only gather and retain information that is necessary for the purpose; a variant of that here is that not all information relevant at the recruitment stage will be relevant later—any that is not should not automatically be transferred into the successful applicant's personnel file (see also point (8)).

in an unfair dismissal action, eg by an employee dismissed for internet abuse),[171] Part I is unlikely to link indirectly into mainstream employment law, at least in the case of unsuccessful applicants because they have no subsisting contract on which to sue (and successful applicants are less likely to have a grievance, though it is not impossible). Its effect will therefore be primarily within its own context of enforcement under the Data Protection Act itself; here, the Code states that (while it is not law per se and does not *have* to be followed) an employer who does follow it knows that there has been compliance with the Act.

The third form of statutory intervention, dating back much further though with some topicality, is under the Rehabilitation of Offenders Act 1974 whereby a person whose conviction or convictions is or are 'spent' is to be treated as not having been convicted. The key point here is of course that a spent conviction does *not* have to be disclosed on a job application form, even in response to a direct question.[172] This is of importance because if the Act does not apply any false answer at the recruitment stage is likely to be considered fraudulent, leading if necessary to a later lawful dismissal (even if the individual thought at the time that he or she had good reason to be sparing with the actualité).[173] Also of major importance here, however, is the Rehabilitation of Offenders Act 1974 (Exceptions) Order 1975[174] which sets out certain professions, offices, employments and occupations which are *not* subject to the Act, so that in these cases a conviction can never become spent and must always be disclosed when asked. This has always covered areas such as the legal profession, medical profession and law enforcement agencies. More recently, however, there have been significant extensions of the exempted categories in the light of contemporary concerns about cases of sexual or physical abuse; the Order now also covers wide categories of those employed to care for children and vulnerable adults. This necessary change in the law for this purpose was accompanied by administrative changes to establish systems whereby the suitability of applicants for jobs involving contact with children and vulnerable adults could be checked against criminal and other records. This was done first of all by the establishment of the Criminal Records Bureau and the Independent Safeguarding Authority, but the Coalition government took the view that this system was inadequate and replaced it in late 2012 with the Disclosure and Barring Service which operates a stronger system of obligations on an employer to check applicants before appointing them to work in what are defined as 'regulated activities'.[175]

---

[171] See Ch 3, heading 3(vii) and Ch 7, heading 5(ii), pp 159 and 515.

[172] Rehabilitation of Offenders Act 1974, s 4. The rehabilitation periods necessary for a conviction to become spent are set out in s 5.

[173] This general rule is strongly set out in *City of Birmingham District Council v Beyer* [1978] 1 All ER 910, [1977] IRLR 211. It was applied to concealment of a non-spent conviction in *Torr v British Railways Board* [1977] ICR 785, [1977] IRLR 184. On the other hand, dismissal because of discovery of a spent conviction is likely to be unfair: *Property Guards Ltd v Taylor* [1982] IRLR 175.

[174] SI 1975/1023.   [175] Protection of Freedoms Act 2012 Pt 5 chapters 1–3.

The fourth intervention of the law has been in relation to employment references. Hitherto this involvement of the law has been primarily in relation to possible tortious liability for negligent misstatement. Ever since the foundation case of *Hedley Byrne & Co Ltd v Heller & Partners Ltd*[176] it has been arguable that the referee owed a duty of care to the potential employer requesting the reference, but for many years there was no development of this in relation to the employee subject to the reference, probably because the tradition in the UK was that the applicant for the job did *not* see the reference at any stage. The resurgence of interest here of late has been for two reasons—first, it was held in *Spring v Guardian Assurance plc*[177] that the referee owes a duty of care to the *applicant* for the job who, if turned down because of a negligently bad reference may be more likely to contemplate legal action (especially in the financial services sector which has spawned most of the case law) particularly as, secondly, under the Data Protection Act 1998 an employment reference may now be seen by an individual. We have thus seen serious changes here (both in the law and the likelihood of it being used), though wholly in relation to the rights of the *subject* of the reference, not its recipient. These matters are considered in Chapter 3, in relation to the employer's duty to exercise care, along with the difficult question whether the law now imposes any positive duty on an employer or ex-employer to *give* a reference (the common law position in the past having been that there is no such duty at all).[178] Apart from tortious liability, there has been little law on references in the purely employment contract context, except for one important point of definition. When an employer makes an appointment 'subject to satisfactory references' this simply operates in the law of contract as a condition precedent. However, the question could arise as to what is meant by 'satisfactory'. In *Wishart v National Association of Citizens Advice Bureaux Ltd*[179] the Court of Appeal held that this only meant satisfactory *to the employer*, ie a subjective test; it is not open to a refused applicant (already pushing a rock uphill in trying to enforce employment) to argue that the reference *ought* to have been satisfactory to a reasonable employer. Finally, there has recently been one other form of legal involvement in references, but again in the slightly separate context of data protection law. The Employment Practices Data Protection Code Part 2: Employment Records contains advice (in Section 2, part 9) on the handling of reference-giving. It suggests that an organization should have a policy on who can give references and in what circumstances.[180] Moreover, an employer should not provide confidential information about an individual unless

---

[176] [1964] AC 465, [1963] 2 All ER 575, HL; the case in fact concerned a reference, but as to commercial-creditworthiness, not individual employability.

[177] [1994] ICR 596, [1994] IRLR 460, HL.   [178] See Ch 3, heading 3(iii), p 149.

[179] [1990] ICR 794, [1990] IRLR 393, CA.

[180] *Spring's* case (n 177) is a prime example of how corporate references should not be given—inaccurate, unchecked statements were made (highly prejudicial to the subject) in an ad hoc exercise by a manager just collecting others' opinions. While there is no law against a bad reference, this could be a recipe for a *negligently* bad reference. Some organizations (especially in the public sector) have policies as to the only information they will give, and the only form in which they will give it, regardless of what the requesting organization may ask.

sure that that is their wish, and when employment ends should establish whether the departing employee wishes references to be provided in the future. Breach of this guidance could mean a breach of the Data Protection Act, but it is possible that the Code could also be used as evidence for collateral purposes more specifically within employment law. Apart from tortious liability for negligent misstatement (above), one interesting cross-over can be seen in *TSB Bank Ltd v Harris*[181] where an employee who left employment when they discovered that highly unfair references were being sent to potential future employers successfully claimed constructive dismissal (for the purposes of an unfair dismissal action); in such circumstances it is possible that any breach of the Code could now be evidence in such an action.

Finally, one variant of this tortious liability is still in its infancy but may see further developments. In *Cheltenham BC v Laird*[182] it was held that a job *applicant* is under a duty of reasonable care when answering questions (especially those in a health question-naire) posed by the putative employer. The council had sued its ex-managing director for failing to divulge a history of mental/stress problems which she had not disclosed in a pre-appointment health questionnaire; she had taken sick leave for similar reasons not long after being appointed, ending in early retirement at the council's expense. While the claim failed on the facts because the questionnaire was not sufficiently pre-cise to *require* this disclosure (and the background here is the well-established rule that a (non-director) employee need not volunteer information and so it is for the employer to discover it),[183] the case does establish the duty on the applicant and the judge con-sidered that breach of that duty could lead not just to dismissal (if appointed) but also to an action for damages.

3 FORM

(i) FORM GENERALLY

According to a doctrine peculiar to English law a contract must be under seal or based upon consideration. A promise gratuitously to perform services will not be action-able unless it is by deed. Subject to this, however, a contract of employment may be entered into orally at common law, and statute has not intervened to alter this general position. However, some particular contracts of employment or contracts relating to employment may have to be in writing. Thus, under Part II of the Employment Rights Act 1996, an employer and employee may agree for the former to make deductions from the latter's wages, provided that the agreement is either contained in a written

---

[181] [2000] IRLR 157.

[182] [2009] IRLR 621, QBD. The employer had sought damages for almost £1m for waste of council resources and the cost of the early retirement.

[183] See Ch 3, heading 4(iv), p 170, and in particular *Nottinghan University v Fishel* [2000] ICR 1462, [2000] IRLR 471.

contract (or in a contract whose effect has been notified to the employee in writing) or otherwise evidenced in writing signed by the employee prior to the making of the deductions.[184] Certain other provisions of the 1996 Act also require writing; thus under section 71 and the Maternity and Parental Leave etc Regulations 1999 a woman claiming to exercise her right to take maternity leave must inform her employer of her intention in writing if so requested by the employer. Similarly, an employee may consent in writing to work beyond the maximum 48 hours per week under the Working Time Regulations 1998.

(ii) NOTICE OF TERMS OF EMPLOYMENT

Although English law is basically informal about the form of a contract of employment, Part I of the Employment Rights Act 1996 (first passed as early as 1963 as the Contracts of Employment Act) provides that an employee to whom the Act applies must be given written particulars of the salient terms of his employment. These provisions were amended and extended by the Trade Union Reform and Employment Rights Act 1993, in order to comply with an EC Directive on information concerning employment conditions,[185] which the previous government were ready to agree to, for two reasons: (1) the existing law was already largely in compliance; and (2) the extensions necessary (which stressed the need to give these written statements on an individual basis) were in line with their policy of encouraging more individual contracting, at the expense of collective negotiation of terms.

(a) The status of the written statement

The incontrovertible starting point is that the written ('section 1') statement is *not* per se the contract of employment; it is, however, evidence of the terms of the contract. This may seem a technical distinction (especially in a case where a longstanding statement appears to be the *only* tangible evidence), but it has the important consequence in law that it leaves the door open for an employee to argue in later proceedings that the statement was inaccurate as to the real terms on a given matter. The question then becomes how compelling the statement is to be as evidence. It is certainly not conclusive,[186] but it is possible to point to earlier cases where courts showed themselves ready to incorporate terms from the written statement into the individual contract of employment, particularly where the statement appeared to have been accepted without protest for a reasonable period of time.[187] Later cases have, however, shown a tendency to treat

---

[184] Section 13, see Ch 3, heading 5(v), p 211. There are exceptions in s 14 and obviously certain statutory deductions (such as income tax under PAYE) do not need written consent.

[185] Directive 91/533/EEC; see Clark and Hall 'The Cinderella Directive' (1992) 21 ILJ 106 and Kenner 'Statement or Contract?—Some Reflections on the EC Employee Information (Contract or Employment Relationship) Directive' (1999) 28 ILJ 205.

[186] *Turriff Construction Ltd v Bryant* (1967) 2 ITR 292; *Parkes Classic Confectionery v Ashcroft* (1973) 8 ITR 43; see Dumville and Leighton 'From Statement to Contract' (1977) 6 ILJ 133.

[187] *Camden Exhibition and Display Ltd v Lynott* [1966] 1 QB 555, [1965] 3 All ER 28, CA.

the statement with more circumspection in circumstances where a major dispute has arisen as to the accuracy of a particular term, especially where 'acceptance without protest' is relied upon by the employer as showing the correctness of the statement. In *System Floors (UK) Ltd v Daniel*[188] Browne-Wilkinson J put the position thus:

> It seems to us, therefore, that in general the status of the statutory statement is this. It provides very strong prima facie evidence of what were the terms of the contract between the parties, but does not constitute a written contract between the parties. Nor are the statements of the terms finally conclusive: at most, they place a heavy burden on the employer to show that the actual terms of contract are different from those which he has set out in the statutory statement.

This case concerned the less typical situation of the *employer* arguing that the statement did not properly reflect the contract; the burden is less heavy in the more typical case where it is the employee contesting the correctness of the statement, for as against him the statement will be (in Browne-Wilkinson J's words) 'no more than persuasive, though not conclusive, evidence'. It is therefore open for him to adduce hopefully more persuasive evidence that the real term was other than that contained in the employer's statement (for example evidence of what was said at the job interview, in letters of appointment, or even what was accepted in practice from the beginning of the employment). This can be seen from the subsequent decision of the Court of Appeal in *Robertson and Jackson v British Gas Corpn*[189] in which the above dicta by Browne-Wilkinson J were approved and the employee successfully challenged the accuracy of the section 1 statement on the basis that it did not reflect what was agreed at the commencement of employment on the bonus that was to be paid. At one stage, Ackner LJ seems to go further and say that the statement was not *even* evidence of the terms, but that must be taken in the light of the facts of the case, particularly the fact that the statement was not given until seven years after the commencement of the employment. In the more usual case, where the statement has been given at the time of or shortly after the commencement of employment and not dissented from, it certainly will be evidence, possibly compelling, for in practice these statements assume considerable importance in many employments.

One case that has caused some difficulty in this area is *Gascol Conversions Ltd v Mercer*[190] where the employer had sent written terms of employment to the employee who had signed them and a receipt which was attached; the Court of Appeal held that this constituted a written contract, governing inter alia the question of hours which was in dispute. The result of such a decision is that the written term in question is

---

[188] [1982] ICR 54, [1981] IRLR 475. This approach can also be seen in *Jones v Associated Tunnelling Co Ltd* [1981] IRLR 477 in the context of alterations to contractual terms, considered below.

[189] [1983] ICR 351, [1983] IRLR 302, CA; note Leighton (1983) 12 ILJ 115. The case is also of particular interest on the incorporation of terms from collective agreements; see Ch 3, heading 2(ii), p 132.

[190] [1974] ICR 420, [1974] IRLR 155, CA; cf *Hawker Siddeley Power Engineering Ltd v Rump* [1979] IRLR 425. See Hepple (1974) 3 ILJ 164.

binding and not to be supplanted by evidence of extraneous matters or implied terms. However, this decision does not compromise the principles set out above, since it appears that the employee actually signed the written instrument as the new terms of his contract of employment, not just the attached receipt. It is common for section 1 statements to be signed for, but merely signing for receipt will *not* constitute a binding written contract, unlike in *Mercer's* case where the crucial extra step of signing *as the contract* was present. This view of *Mercer's* case (and the distinction between signing a contract and signing a receipt) has been accepted in the later cases.[191] It is thus possible for what would normally be a section 1 statement to be transformed into a formal written contract by the parties signing it as such, but if they are to do so it is doubly important that they should ensure that the terms are correct.

(b) Requirements of the written statement

The obligation on an employer to give the section 1 statement arises whenever a person is taken on as an 'employee', thus excluding (as usual in statutory employment laws) the self-employed. Certain categories of employee are excluded; thus, this part of the Act does not apply to certain types of mariners,[192] employees working wholly outside Great Britain,[193] or those employed for less than one month.[194]

Wherever this part of the Act applies, the employer is given the period of two months from the beginning of the employment in question in which to deliver to his employee the necessary written statement,[195] though in practice many employers will have the statement ready at the beginning, often as part of a 'starter pack' for new employees (along with other documents, such as a health and safety statement, disciplinary rules and company handbook). Where there is, subsequent to the giving of notice of particulars, a change in them the employer has one month in which to issue a statement of the change.[196]

The initial notice must identify the parties and specify the date of commencement of employment and whether any employment with a previous employer is to count as part of the employee's continuous employment.[197] Section 1(4) then provides that certain particulars of the terms of employment must be stated (and if there are no agreed particulars

---

[191] *System Floors (UK) Ltd v Daniel*, n 188; *Robertson and Jackson v British Gas Corpn*, n 189.

[192] Section 199.

[193] This appears to be the case on general principles, in spite of the repeal of the Employment Rights Act 1996, s 196 (by the Employment Relations Act 1999).

[194] Section 198.   [195] Section 1(2), as substituted by the 1993 Act.

[196] Section 4; see heading 6 later in this chapter on changing the terms of employment.

[197] This should now be viewed with caution by an employee, for a simple assurance of continuity of employment by a new employer (where such continuity is not preserved by a provision in the relevant statute) is not enough to safeguard continuity for the purpose of a later claim for a statutory right (especially a redundancy payment); *Secretary of State for Employment v Globe Elastic Thread Co Ltd* [1979] ICR 706, [1979] IRLR 327, HL, overruling *Evenden v Guildford City AFC Ltd* [1975] 3 All ER 269, [1975] ICR 367, CA; see Ch 8, heading 1(iv), p 586.

under any of the heads that fact must be stated too).[198] These particulars are—the scale or rate of remuneration; the intervals at which remuneration is to be paid; terms and conditions relating to hours of work (and possibly 'normal working hours'); any terms and conditions relating to holidays (including public holidays and holiday pay) with sufficient information to enable the entitlement to be calculated precisely, incapacity for work due to sickness or injury, and pensions and pension schemes; the length of notice which the employee is obliged to give and entitled to receive to determine the contract; the title of the job which the employee is employed to do;[199] how long the employment is to last if it is not permanent; the place of work; any collective agreements affecting terms and conditions; and, where the employee is to work outside the UK for more than a month, the period abroad, currency for remuneration, any additional remuneration or benefits, and any terms and conditions relating to his return to the UK. In addition section 3 provides that the employer must include a note specifying any disciplinary rules and procedures, how and to whom the employee may apply if dissatisfied with a disciplinary decision relating to him or if seeking redress of any grievance relating to his employment, and any further steps in the employer's grievance procedure, though these requirements do not apply to any rules, procedures, etc, relating to health and safety at work. Also under section 3 the note must state whether a contracting-out certificate is in force for the employment, for the purposes of the Pension Schemes Act 1993.

Two changes were made by the Trade Union Reform and Employment Rights Act 1993 and the Employment Act 2002 relating not to what has to be specified, but how it is to be notified to the employee. Prior to 1993, the employer was given a wide power to refer in the section 1 statement to other documentation, provided it was reasonably available to the employee. Thus, even on major terms such as pay, the statement could refer, for example, to a collective agreement. Increasingly, this technique was used where the firm produced a company handbook, to which frequent reference could be made.[200] However, that power of reference was restricted in 1993 and now only applies to (1) any particulars relating to sickness, sick pay or pensions, when reference may be made to some other document reasonably available, and (2) the length of notice, when reference may be made to the general law[201] or any relevant collective agreement.[202]

---

[198] Thus, the obligation is to notify terms that exist, not to have a particular term in the first place: *Morley v Heritage plc* [1993] IRLR 400, CA (no term on accrued holiday pay).

[199] This is not necessarily a full 'job description', but the employer should approach it with care, because the more specific the title is the less the employer will be able lawfully to demand flexibility on the part of the employee, a factor which could be of importance in a redundancy or unfair dismissal case; conversely, the wider the title, the more difficult it may be to establish that a dismissal is for redundancy. This one example of the job title (in addition to other clear examples such as job location clauses) shows how important it is for both employers and employees to treat contracts and/or written statements not as tedious bureaucracy, but rather as documents which may be decisive in actions before tribunals for modern statutory rights.

[200] Company handbooks became increasingly popular with employers and ACAS have published advice on producing them (Advisory Booklet No 9). However, there can be difficulties with the contractual status of different parts of such a handbook (see Ch 3, heading 2(ii), p 138).

[201] The legal minima are set out in the Employment Rights Act 1996, s 86, see Ch 6, heading 2, p 425.

[202] Section 2(2), (3).

Other than that (and the note on disciplinary and grievance procedures), the rule is that the particulars required must be specifically included in a 'single document'.[203] Similarly, any changes must be notified specifically in a written statement, subject to the same exceptions. As stated above, this change was consistent with the previous government's stated policy to encourage the extension of individual contracting and flexibility in the setting of terms and conditions but it could lead to an unrealistic requirement being imposed (at least technically) when employment is entered as process rather than a single transaction;[204] moreover (whether by design or oversight) this change also removed the previous provision stating that a full contract can fulfil the function of the written statement. Some tidying up on this was done by the Employment Act 2002, which added a new section 7A, stating that where the employer gives the employee a document in the form of a contract of employment or a letter of appointment, that document contains all the information required by section 1 and it is given within the normal two-month period, that discharges the requirement of giving the written statement. This goes some way towards rationalizing the position, but does not go back to the pre-1993 right to refer to any other documents. It may still be necessary, for example, to consider whether a letter of appointment referring to a company handbook could be construed as 'one document'.

(c) Enforcement

Contractual rights may of course be enforced by an ordinary common law action and so, for example, a claim that the employer should be paying more in wages under the contract may be tested by bringing an action for those wages in the county court (or in a tribunal, under the guise of the underpayment being a 'deduction for wages'), which may involve a determination by the court or tribunal of the correct contractual term on wages, which in turn may involve a determination of the accuracy of the written statement on the question of wages. In addition to this, however, the Act provides for the *direct* enforcement of the requirement to give the written statement.

Under section 11 the method of direct enforcement of these provisions is by reference of the issue to a tribunal. Where either no statement has been given under section 1 or 4 or a statement does not comply with those sections the employee may refer the matter, and where a statement has been given but a dispute has arisen as to the particulars which ought to have been included or referred to in it so as to comply with the statutory provisions, either the employer or the employee may refer the matter. By section 12 the tribunal is given wide powers to determine what particulars

---

[203] Section 2(4). There is a peculiarity in the new drafting. The old s 5 used to state specifically that the need to give a statement did not apply if the employer instead gave a full written contract covering the relevant matters; no such provision now appears, so it must be assumed to be implied that such a written contract constitutes a 'written statement to the employee' under s 1(1).

[204] Particularly as Lord Hoffmann emphasized in *Carmichael v National Power plc* [1999] ICR 1226, [2000] IRLR 43, HL, that at common law it may be necessary to look at several sources to determine and continue a contract of employment.

ought to have been included, or whether any particulars which were included are to be confirmed, amended or substituted. These powers of the tribunal should be a considerable incentive for the employer to comply with the requirements of section 1 in the first place; if he does not do so, and a dispute later arises with his workforce over a particular term of employment (for example overtime arrangements) it would be possible for them to take him to a tribunal under section 11 and invite the tribunal to write into their statements the version of the term on overtime that *they* say they originally agreed—if they were successful that would in practice end the dispute in their favour.[205]

However, two problems have arisen as to the construction of these powers. The first arises from the fact that they are declared to be only for the purpose of deciding what 'ought to have been included or referred to in the statement *so as to comply with the requirements of [these provisions]*'. This means that in a section 11 claim the tribunal may only declare what ought to have been included in the sense of what was agreed on these various enumerated matters between the parties; it cannot therefore go further and *interpret* any terms expressed in the written statement, for that would be to usurp the functions of the ordinary civil courts to whom traditionally the employee had to turn for interpretation and enforcement of his contractual rights.[206] This distinction was accepted in early case law[207] and has recently been reaffirmed by the Court of Appeal in *Southern Cross Healthcare Co Ltd v Perkins*[208] which illustrated the point neatly on its facts. The employees' section 1 statements covered the question of holiday entitlement by granting 20 working days, plus up to five more days for long service by an individual. The claimants were on the maximum of 25 days when in 2009 the statutory entitlement to holidays under the working time legislation went up to 28 days. Did the term in their statements mean that they were entitled to five days for long service on top of the new 28-day entitlement, or did their entitlement merely have to go up to 28 days in total (which would have swallowed up their long service extra)? The parties locked horns on the issue and the claimants brought tribunal proceedings to have the term construed and its true meaning decided. The tribunal and EAT found for the claimants' construction, but when the case came before the Court of Appeal, the issue of whether the tribunal had jurisdiction at all came to the fore. Applying the principle

---

[205] Note, however, that it is essential that there should be a dispute between the parties; it is an abuse of procedure to bring a s 11 claim where there is no dispute, merely the parties wanting a ruling on a particular matter for some extrinsic purpose: *Baker v Superite Tools Ltd* [1986] ICR 189 (parties wanting a ruling as to whether the workers involved were employed or self-employed, for use in dealings with the Revenue).

[206] Unless the matter has arisen on termination of the employment, in which case a tribunal may have jurisdiction to determine a contract claim under the Employment Tribunals Extension of Jurisdiction Order 1994 SI 1994/1623 or the case may be brought before a tribunal during employment under Pt II of the Employment Rights Act 1996, concerning deductions from pay. This would now cover the case of *Cuthbertson* (see n 207).

[207] See *Cuthbertson v AML Distributors* [1975] IRLR 228, IT; *CITB v Leighton* [1978] IRLR 60. Arguably, in some cases a tribunal or court succumbed to the temptation to stray into enforcement; see *Owens v Multilux Ltd* [1974] IRLR 113.

[208] [2011] ICR 285, [2011] IRLR 247, CA.

set out above, the court allowed the employers' appeal and held that what the claimants were wanting the tribunal to do was to construe and enforce the term in question, but it had no power to do so. That exercise, going beyond merely ensuring compliance with section 1, remained the province of the ordinary courts. Not surprisingly in the light of this, the court declined even to give any indication as to what its view would have been on the construction issue.

The second problem was potentially more far-reaching, for while it was clear on the wording of section 12 that a tribunal could determine a case where there was a partial or total *failure* by the employer to include the necessary terms in the statement, it was argued that it did not have jurisdiction where the employer had indeed given terms but the employee claimed that they were *inaccurate* (ie that they did not reflect what had actually been agreed).[209] This very narrow view was supported by the ambiguous third sentence in the above dictum by Kilner Brown J in *Leighton*'s case, and could be seen in the judgment of the EAT in *Brown v Stuart, Scott & Co Ltd*,[210] though in each case the pronouncements were obiter. It is true that the wording of section 12 was not explicit on the point (though the use of words such as 'amend' and 'substitute' surely points in the direction of including claims that particulars are inaccurate); however, it certainly seemed that the narrow view was contrary to Parliament's intention and an unnecessary restriction on the tribunals' jurisdiction. As originally drafted, the Employment Bill 1982 contained a provision which would have stated expressly that tribunals could hear complaints about particulars which had been included or referred to in statements, but this provision was removed as unnecessary when the position was rectified by the decision of the Court of Appeal in the important case of *Mears v Safecar Security Ltd*.[211] It is made clear in this case that a tribunal *does* have jurisdiction to hear complaints of inaccurate particulars. However, on its facts the case concerned the *failure* to give particulars[212] and in this context too the case is important for its clarification and extension of existing principles. Here, Stephenson LJ said that the complaint could be either (1) a complaint that the statement does not contain a term which had actually been agreed, or (2) a complaint that a term had not been included where in fact there had been no express agreement. In the latter case, a tribunal must consider all the facts to determine what term should be implied,[213] and normally there will be sufficient evidence for them to be able to do so (in particular, evidence of general working practices which are obvious at the latest by the end of the two-month period that the employer has in which to give the

---

[209] See Mogridge 'Giving Written Particulars of Employment—a Valueless Exercise' [1981] NLJ 1250.

[210] [1981] ICR 166.

[211] [1982] 2 All ER 865, [1982] IRLR 183, CA. The case includes a detailed explanation by Stephenson LJ of the original drafting of ss 11 and 12.

[212] The particulars in question related to the payment (or non-payment) of sick pay; this aspect of the case is considered at Ch 3, heading 5(ii), p 194.

[213] The case is also important on this general question of the implication of terms into contracts of employment (see Ch 3, heading 2, p 125), for the approach of the Court of Appeal was not constrained by old contract law notions of the intent of the parties or business efficacy.

written statement). However, a further problem arose because the court went further and said obiter that the obligation upon the tribunal to declare the relevant particulars (on a complaint of failure to give them) applied even in the untypical case where there is no clear evidence at all, in which case the tribunal might ultimately be left to 'invent' them, on the basis of what would be reasonable and sensible terms in all the circumstances. However, the Court of Appeal subsequently disapproved strongly of that extreme position in *Eagland v British Telecommunications plc*,[214] where it was reaffirmed that the tribunal's function is only to declare what has already been agreed in some way, not to impose upon the parties terms which have not been agreed. They adopted the distinction drawn by Wood P in the EAT in the case between 'mandatory' and 'non-mandatory' particulars.[215] In the case of the latter, if there is no evidence at all of any agreement, the tribunal should simply state that there is no term on the matter.[216] Mandatory terms cause more difficulty. They said that it is most unlikely that this problem will arise (an employment relationship with *nothing* ever said about pay?), but if it did a tribunal would have to look at what the law would normally include as the ordinary requirements of an employment relationship (the obvious example being the implication of a term of reasonable notice if there was no evidence of any agreement). However, Leggatt LJ in a short, concurring judgment stated what must eventually be the bottom line if no power of invention is allowed:

> If an essential term, such as a written statement must contain, has not been agreed, there will be no agreement.

The question of the enforcement of the section 1 statement arose in the previous Labour government's deliberations on new methods of dispute resolution in order to lessen recourse to tribunals. They took the view that too many essentially contractual disputes are taken to tribunals, a view borne out by the statistics at the time[217] and that one reason for this was that it is still the case that in too many such disputes the employee had not been given either a contract or a written statement of terms (the giving of which might have settled the issue in dispute at the beginning). This view was backed by research showing that, in a survey of 2,700 completed tribunal cases, 82% of employers but only 60% of employees said that terms had been given in writing, and that only 51% of employers and 28% of employees said that there were written procedures at the workplace for dealing with the issue or issues that had led to the tribunal

---

[214] [1993] ICR 644, [1992] IRLR 323, CA.

[215] [1990] ICR 248, [1990] IRLR 328. According to Parker LJ, giving the leading judgment in the Court of Appeal, mandatory terms (as the section stood pre-1993) are those relating to the parties, date of commencement, continuity of employment, rate of pay, intervals for payment, notice and job title; non-mandatory terms are those relating to hours of work, holidays, sickness/sick pay and pensions. Of the particulars added in 1993, those relating to termination of non-permanent employment, place of work and applicable collective agreements appear to be mandatory; the extra particulars relating to employment abroad appear to be split.

[216] *Morley v Heritage plc* [1993] IRLR 400, CA.

[217] In 2008/9, ACAS dealt with 30,634 claims for unlawful deductions from wages and 31,637 claims for breach of contract on termination, amounting together to 26.4% of all claims: *ACAS Annual Report 2008/9*.

application.[218] One obvious problem was that under existing law a section 1 statement could only be enforced by the individual employee (in section 11 proceedings); these remained rare. The Employment Act 2002 addressed this issue of insufficient enforcement in a novel way. Under section 38, where a tribunal hearing a case finds in favour of the employee and discovers that the employer was in a breach of the duty to give written particulars it must award extra compensation of between two and four weeks' pay (unless there are exceptional circumstances making that unjust or inequitable). The important point here is that there is *no* causative element, ie it need not be shown that the employee won the substantive claim *because* there was no section 1 statement; thus, this provision simply gives a new responsibility to tribunals to police the giving of these statements.

4 LEGALITY AND RESTRAINT OF TRADE

(i) THE DOCTRINE OF ILLEGALITY GENERALLY

All contracts having objects contrary to statute or common law, or which entail the passing of an illegal consideration, are void. So, for example, an agreement by which an employee purports to permit his employer to make deductions from his remuneration will be void unless there is compliance with the provisions of Part II of the Employment Rights Act 1996.[219] So too will a purported agreement to waive a breach of duty imposed by statute on an employer.[220] Sundry other forms of illegality may theoretically apply to contracts of employment as well as to contracts generally even if in practice they are less likely to do so. One which could arise directly in the context of employment is the rule that a contract of employment must not contain 'servile incidents', which may best be described as harsh terms showing a lack of mutuality, as where a cinema company obtained sole use of an actor's stage name[221] or where the defendant borrowed money from a moneylender on terms which made it impossible for him to change employment, deal with his possessions, change address, etc, without prior permission.[222]

One particular application of notions of illegality has caused problems in the field of employment law. These problems arise when one of the parties (usually the employer)

---

[218] Findings of the 1998 Survey of Employment Tribunal Applications (Employment Relations Research Services No 13, 2002; available on the BIS website).

[219] *Kearney v Whitehaven Colliery Co* [1893] 1 QB 700, CA (case on the now-repealed Truck Acts); see Ch 3, heading 5(v), p 209.

[220] *Baddeley v Earl of Granville* (1887) 19 QBD 423; for a strong case, see *Wheeler v New Merton Board Mills Ltd* [1933] 2 KB 669, CA.

[221] *Hepworth Manufacturing Co v Ryott* [1920] 1 Ch 1, CA; however, some cinema contracts have validly imposed highly personal restraints on employees' diets, health, personal life, etc, probably on the ground that they were in the interests of both parties; *Gaumont-British Picture Corpn v Alexander* [1936] 2 All ER 1686. A tie to pay back the cost of training is not illegal (*Strathclyde Regional Council v Neil* [1984] IRLR 11).

[222] *Horwood v Millar's Timber and Trading Co Ltd* [1917] 1 KB 305, CA.

to a tribunal action concerning modern statutory rights such as redundancy payments or unfair dismissal argues that the contract of employment in question was in some sense illegal, usually because it contained some element of unlawful tax evasion (for example under-declaration of income payable under it, or the payment of non-declared extra amounts of income). If this is proved, it can lead to a decision that the contract itself is void and, as such a contract is necessary before an applicant can show that he was an 'employee' for the purpose of claiming his statutory rights, that the applicant's claim must be struck out.[223] The doctrine of illegality in the law of contract is a complicated subject at the best of times,[224] but in the sphere of employment law can have particularly drastic effects by depriving tribunals of jurisdiction, even where the element of illegality might be incidental and (in the case of tax evasion) where the amount of money concerned is small. Moreover, it can lead to the problem, which arises generally under the doctrine of illegality in contract law, of one party to the contract (here usually the employer) benefiting from his own illegality, eg in a case where the evasion scheme was in fact initiated by the employer who later used it to try to defeat an employee's claim for unfair dismissal. The starting point here is that the general argument that the doctrine of illegality should not apply to contracts of employment (either at all, or at least to the extent of prejudicing statutory actions) on the grounds of employment law policy has clearly been disapproved by the EAT.[225] Thus, the doctrine is applicable and in a series of cases the tribunals have had to work out its effects. It may of course apply to forms of illegality other than tax evasion, as for example in *Coral Leisure Group Ltd v Barnett*[226] where it was claimed that an ex-employee could not maintain an action for unfair dismissal because part of his job had entailed hiring prostitutes for the employer's clients, thus falling foul of the law on immoral contracts, and in *Hounga v Allen*[227] where deliberate breach of a work permit requirement from the beginning of the hiring of an au pair made the whole employment illegal. In this sort of case it is easier to apply the basic common law distinction that contracts illegal in inception are void, but contracts which are legal in inception but later performed

---

[223] *Napier v National Business Agency Ltd* [1951] 2 All ER 264, CA; *Jennings v Westwood Engineering Ltd* [1975] IRLR 245; *Tomlinson v Dick Evans 'U' Drive Ltd* [1978] ICR 639, [1978] IRLR 77. Note, however, that it has been held (thankfully) that merely getting the tax status *wrong* (eg where employer and employee both treated it as self-employment but it is later held by a court or tribunal to have been employment) does *not* render the whole contract void for illegality: *Enfield Technical Services v Payne* [2008] IRLR 500, CA.

[224] Especially as the purely contract law cases tend to be on abstruse facts.

[225] *Newland v Simons and Willer (Hairdressers) Ltd* [1981] ICR 521, [1981] IRLR 359. It is of course possible for a statute to state expressly that contravention of its terms shall *not* make any resulting contract void for illegality (see, for example, the Company Securities (Insider Dealing) Act 1985, s 8(3) and, in particular, the Social Security Contributions and Benefits Act 1992, s 97 which covers industrial accidents in the course of illegal employments); it is unfortunate that the Employment Rights Act does not have such an exclusory provision. A later challenge that to apply the doctrine of illegality to employment cases was in breach of the Human Rights Act 1998 failed: *Soteriou v Ultrachem Ltd* [2004] IRLR 870.

[226] [1981] ICR 503, [1981] IRLR 204.

[227] [2012] IRLR 685, [2012] EqLR 679, CA. Unlawful working by an asylum seeker also led to a finding of illegality in *Vakante v Addey & Stanhope School* [2005] ICR 231, [2004] IRLR 1065, CA. These cases concerned discrimination claims rather than claims for unfair dismissal; see later in this chapter.

in an illegal manner may not be.[228] However, that distinction may be more difficult to apply to the more usual cases of tax evasion. The tendency has fortunately been to treat them as illegal only in performance, with the result that 'innocence' is a defence, and so in practice the determining factor has been whether the employee *knew* of the evasion being practised by the employer—if not, he can still claim his statutory rights;[229] moreover, it is clear that knowledge here means actual, subjective knowledge, so that it is an error of law for a tribunal to consider whether the employee ought to have realized what was happening.[230] The most difficult case here is *Corby v Morrison* where the primary ground for ruling out a claim for unfair dismissal by an ex-employee who had received £5 per week without deduction of income tax was that the contract of employment was illegal *in inception*, which renders the knowledge or otherwise of the employee irrelevant; the EAT did give as a secondary ground of judgment that, even if it was only illegal in performance, she knew what was going on and so was ruled out anyway. This second ground of judgment was emphasized in the explanation of the case subsequently in *Newland v Simons and Willer (Hairdressers) Ltd,*[231] but the first ground was not disapproved. However, in *Hewcastle Catering Ltd v Ahmed*[232] the Court of Appeal clearly leaned towards treating tax evasion cases as illegality in performance, to which the doctrine should be applied sparingly. Beldam LJ stated that the modern law is that it applies only if in all the circumstances it would be an affront to the public conscience to allow the claim to proceed; further, the defence will not be allowed if the defendant employer's conduct in participating in the illegal contract is so much more reprehensible than the employee's conduct that it would be wrong to allow the employer to rely on it. This is an important case because of the facts—the employees were waiters at the employers' club who were involved in operating the employers' VAT fraud, *but* they did *not* derive any personal benefit from it. After the

---

[228] In *Coral Leisure*, the EAT held that the tribunal had jurisdiction to hear the claim. The ex-employee had not been taken on to hire prostitutes, and it was not part of his contract to do so (merely one of the ways in practice of discharging his functions); the contract was therefore not illegal in inception. Dicta in the case suggest that, because it was only illegal in performance, *therefore* it was not void, but it is submitted that the better view is that that means that it *may* not be void, and that the ground for the decision is that, given that the illegality was only in performance, that particular form of illegality (hiring prostitutes) was not sufficiently grave to justify invalidating the whole contract.

[229] *Tomlinson v Dick Evans 'U' Drive Ltd,* n 223; *Davidson v Pillay* [1979] IRLR 275. In *Wheeler v Quality Deep Ltd (in liq)* [2004] EWCA Civ 1085, (2004) The Times, 30 August, CA a determining factor against applying the doctrine was the employee's inability to speak English and lack of knowledge of the UK tax and NI system. *McConnell v Bolik* [1979] IRLR 422 has an interesting twist in the story in that the case concerned non-declaration of income by the employee, so that the crucial question was the state of the *employer's* knowledge. The knowledge in question is as to the facts; lack of knowledge of the illegality of the transaction (ie a mistake of law) will not help the party: *Salvesen v Simons* [1994] ICR 409, [1994] IRLR 52.

[230] *Corby v Morrison* [1980] ICR 564, [1980] IRLR 218; *Newland v Simons and Willer (Hairdressers) Ltd* [1981] IRLR 359.

[231] See n 230; the same judge presided over the EAT in both cases. *Newland's* case was clearly viewed as one of illegality in performance, and was remitted to the tribunal to make more precise findings of fact on the employee's knowledge of the evasion.

[232] [1992] ICR 626, [1991] IRLR 473, CA.

employers were caught (and the employees gave evidence against them), the employees were dismissed and the employers raised illegality as a defence. Had the court simply applied the existing test (did they *know* of it?) the defence would have succeeded, but on the two wider principles above the court was able to disallow it since (1) public policy did not demand its application and (2) the employers were clearly the more guilty. While this decision does not go as far as to say that an employee with knowledge (though possibly only an unwilling minion) *cannot* be debarred from an action if he made no personal gain, it did allow a decision to be taken much along those lines on the facts. Moreover, it may permit further developments towards what, it is submitted, would be the best solution (given that the doctrine has to apply at all), namely that any incidental tax evasion should only ever make the contract illegal in performance and that for the illegality then to make the contract void the employee must have known of *and benefited from* the evasion to such an *extent* (in comparison with the gain to the employer) that the court or tribunal has no option but to declare the whole contract void.

Finally, three points might be noted. The first is that on general principles it is not every form of illegality that can render a contract void—the illegality must be sufficiently grave or of such a nature as to show (in the case of illegality through contravention of a statute) that the intention of the legislation is to affect contracts if necessary, not just to penalize the conduct in question in other ways.[233] It is this principle that prevents, for example, a lorry driver's contract of employment being totally void as soon as he exceeds a speed limit. However, it cannot help a claimant before a tribunal in a case involving tax evasion, for it has so far been the approach of the courts (subject to any possible new emphasis on the respective moral blameworthiness of employee and employer, see above) that *any* element of tax evasion (even if concerning only small amounts, or only extra remuneration[234] on top of basic wages on which full tax may have been paid) is grave enough to activate the rules on illegality; likewise the tribunals have not accepted the argument that protection of tax revenue can be adequately left to the tax authorities and legislation and does not need to be reinforced by the striking down of contracts, though it has been accepted that employers may be deterred from making illegal payments and then trying to rely on them to defeat statutory claims by the power of a tribunal at the end of the day to transmit the evidence that they have received to the Revenue.[235] The second point is that a slightly different approach to

---

[233] The authority usually cited for this is the judgment of Devlin J in *St John Shipping Corpn v Joseph Rank Ltd* [1957] 1 QB 267, [1956] 3 All ER 683. One potentially controversial question now may be whether a contract to work hours in excess of the maxima in the Working Time Regulations could be argued to be illegal; this is probably *not* the intent of the Regulations (except to the extent of the excess?), and the results of so holding could be harsh and unpredictable for the employee.

[234] If, however, the tax evasion applies only to extraneous payments (eg gifts) which are *not* part of contractual remuneration, the validity of the contract is not affected: *Annandale Engineering v Samson* [1994] IRLR 59.

[235] A course advocated in *Corby v Morrison* and put into effect in *Newland v Simons and Willer (Hairdressers) Ltd* (n 230). A similar device has been suggested to deter a person from claiming to be self-employed for tax purposes while working, but then turning round and claiming to have been in reality an employee all along

illegality was taken in the case of *Hyland v J H Barker (North West) Ltd.*[236] In this case the employee had taken illegal payments for a period of only four weeks (out of a total period of employment of 16 years); it was accepted that this did not render the whole contract void *but* that did not help the employee much since it transpired that those four weeks fell during his final year before dismissal and thus (as the contract was void for those four weeks) he could not show the year's continuous employment ending with the date of dismissal that was then required in order to bring proceedings for unfair dismissal. The case shows a possibly unfortunate combination of the restrictive rules on illegality and continuity of employment and also, more generally, the harsh effects of the doctrine of illegality in this field; it also leaves open the question as to how major and/or longstanding the illegality has to be to render the *whole* contract void (not just part of it, the timing of which could be entirely fortuitous). The third point is that, as a matter of statutory construction and policy, it has been held that the purely contractual doctrine of illegality as such cannot be used to defeat a discrimination claim because (unlike unfair dismissal) such a claim does not depend on the existence of a contract of employment; however, in such a claim it is still possible for a tribunal to consider whether the claim is so connected to illegal conduct by the claimant that it could not give a remedy without appearing to condone that activity and, if that is the case and the illegality is sufficiently serious, to rule out the claim on wider grounds of public policy.[237]

In addition to these general applications of the doctrine of illegality, much case law has been produced by one particular area of it, the area of restraint of trade. Indeed now that this has been held to apply to harsh and one-sided contractual conditions during employment as well as after it,[238] it has probably made much of the ancient law on servile incidents redundant. The classic restraint of trade clause in a contract of employment is where the employee agrees not to work in the same trade or not to solicit his employer's customers in a certain area for a certain period, after the termination of his employment with that employer. It is to the doctrine of restraint of trade, and the validity or otherwise of such an agreement, that we now turn.

(ii) THE DOCTRINE OF RESTRAINT OF TRADE

The doctrine of restraint of trade is a legal device to attempt to hold the balance between two competing factors—an employee's freedom to take employment as and when he

---

when later dismissed and wanting to bring an action for unfair dismissal—he may end up with a tribunal finding in his favour outweighed by the hefty tax demand: *Young & Woods Ltd v West* [1980] IRLR 201, CA (see this chapter heading 1(i), p 44).

[236] [1985] ICR 861, [1985] IRLR 403.

[237] *Leighton v Michael* [1995] ICR 1091, [1996] IRLR 67, [2001] ICR 99; *Hall v Woolston Hall Leisure Ltd* [2000] IRLR 578, CA; *Vakante v Addey & Stanhope School (No 2)* [2005] ICR 231, CA; *Hounga v Allen* [2012] IRLR 685, [2012] EqLR 679, CA.

[238] *Schroeder Music Publishing Co v Macaulay* [1974] 3 All ER 616, [1974] 1 WLR 1308, HL; *Clifford Davis Management Ltd v WEA Records Ltd* [1975] 1 All ER 237, [1975] 1 WLR 61, CA.

wishes, and an employer's interest in preserving certain aspects of his business from disclosure or exploitation by an employee or, more usually, an ex-employee.[239] Both factors are important, and indeed the law will protect the employer if necessary by the implication of a term of fidelity in the contract of employment thereby restraining the employee inter alia from divulging confidential information.[240] However, the employer may wish to go further and extract an express promise from the employee (1) not to disclose certain information and, more important, (2) not to place himself in a position in which he may do so, for example by not working for a competitor for a certain period of time within a certain area after leaving the employment. It has been reaffirmed by the Court of Appeal that if the employer wants this protection of actually being able to restrain future employment by a competitor for a certain period (known in the jargon as 'barring out relief') it must be done through an express restraint clause; reliance merely on the implied duty of fidelity will not be enough.[241]

It is thus established that an employer can stipulate for protection against having his confidential information passed on to a rival in trade. But experience has shown that it is not satisfactory simply to have a covenant against disclosing confidential information. The reason is because it is so difficult to draw the line between information which is confidential and information which is not; and it is very difficult to prove a breach when the information is of such a character that a servant can carry it away in his head. The difficulties are such that the only practicable solution is to take a covenant from the servant by which he is not to go to work for a rival in trade. Such a covenant may well be held to be reasonable.[242]

The question then arises whether any given restraint clause is valid and enforceable against the ex-employee, or void. The modern law on restraint of trade is to be found in *Nordenfelt v Maxim Nordenfelt Guns and Ammunition Co*[243] and *Esso Petroleum Co Ltd v Harper's Garage (Stourport) Ltd*,[244] a case on 'solus' agreements in the garage trade, in which the House of Lords reconsidered the whole doctrine. In the *Nordenfelt* case it was established that a restraint clause is to be considered void unless the party alleging its validity can prove that it is (1) reasonable as between the parties and (2) in the public interest. The two principal forms of agreement which have been subject to the doctrine are agreements by the vendor of a business not to compete with the purchaser of it, as in the *Nordenfelt* case, and by an employee not to act in a certain way after finishing the employment, and it has been clearly stated that it will be more difficult to establish the validity of a restraint clause in the latter case, with which we are primarily concerned

---

[239] The leading work on this area is Brearley and Bloch *Employment Covenants and Confidential Information: Law, Practice and Technique* (3rd edn, 2009) which gives an excellent exposition of the law and practice.

[240] This topic is discussed at Ch 3, heading 4(iv), p 173.

[241] *Caterpillar Logistics Services (UK) Ltd v de Crean* [2012] ICR 981, [2012] IRLR 410, CA.

[242] *Littlewoods Organisation Ltd v Harris* [1978] 1 All ER 1026 at 1033, CA, per Lord Denning MR.

[243] [1894] AC 535, HL, as explained by a subsequent House of Lords in *Mason v Provident Clothing and Supply Co Ltd* [1913] AC 724, HL.

[244] [1968] AC 269, [1967] 1 All ER 699, HL.

here, for it concerns not a commercial transaction at arm's length, but rather a transaction, potentially between parties of different bargaining strengths, which could have a major effect on an individual's livelihood (future and present) to the disadvantage of himself and the public interest.[245] For present purposes, the decision in the *Esso Petroleum* case clarified the law in two major ways. The first was to confirm that not all agreements which restrain a person's freedom of action are subject to the doctrine, for some are so accepted as normal incidents of particular businesses or transactions that they are not subject to challenge.[246] The test for deciding what is subject to the doctrine and what is not subject is not entirely clear, but what is important for present purposes is that the House of Lords said clearly that restraint clauses by employees in favour of employers are definitely subject to the doctrine. The second major effect of the case was to revive the ailing second limb of the rule in *Nordenfelt*'s case, ie public interest. This had been so neglected as to have been virtually ignored,[247] but this can no longer be so and indeed Lord Reid and Lord Hodson intimated[248] that certain past cases which were decided on the first limb, reasonableness as between the parties, might well have been better decided on the second limb. In the employment context this could be of some importance, as there might be certain forms of agreement as we shall see below, such as labour stabilization agreements between employer and employer, which might be eminently reasonable as between the parties, but would now be subject to challenge on the wider ground of the public interest.

Thus, an employee might validly bind himself in a contract of employment as to his future activities, usually when he enters the contract, but also possibly during its currency[249] or at its termination, provided in the latter case that the agreement is genuinely referable to the contract of employment, and not just an afterthought 'in gross'.[250] Moreover, it is now established that a clause restraining certain activities by the employee *during* employment may be subject to challenge as well as one restricting activities upon termination of the employment; in *Schroeder Music Publishing Co v Macaulay*[251] an agreement whereby the plaintiff, a young and unknown songwriter, gave his exclusive services to the defendants for five years without any obligation on the latter to publish his works or provide him with any livelihood, and whereby the

---

[245] See particularly *Herbert Morris Ltd v Saxelby* [1916] 1 AC 688, HL, per Lord Parker at 710 and Lord Shaw at 714.

[246] Tied houses in the brewery trade are valid, whereas 'solus' agreements in the garage trade, not being so widely accepted, have been the subject of several legal cases.

[247] 'Their Lordships are not aware of any case in which a restraint, though reasonable in the interests of the parties, has been held unenforceable because it involved some injury to the public', *A-G of Commonwealth of Australia v Adelaide Steamship Co Ltd* [1913] AC 781, PC, at 795 per Lord Parker. One exceptional case was *Wyatt v Kreglinger and Fernau* [1933] 1 KB 793, CA, followed by *Bull v Pitney-Bowes* [1966] 3 All ER 384, [1967] 1 WLR 273.

[248] [1968] AC 269 at 300 and 319, [1967] 1 All ER 699 at 709 and 721.

[249] *RS Components Ltd v Irwin* [1974] 1 All ER 41, [1973] ICR 535.

[250] *Stenhouse Australia Ltd v Phillips* [1974] AC 391, [1974] 1 All ER 117, PC.

[251] [1974] 3 All ER 616, [1974] 1 WLR 1308, HL, followed in *Clifford Davis Management Ltd v WEA Records Ltd* [1975] 1 All ER 237, [1975] 1 WLR 61, CA.

defendants could terminate or extend the contract at their election but the plaintiff could not, was held to be void as in restraint of trade. That was, however, an unusual case, and any more normal restraints during employment, for example not to work for competitors or not to disclose information, might well be held to be so common as to require no justification, under the *Esso Petroleum* case, and indeed certain standard ones would possibly be implied by operation of law even if not expressed.[252]

Given that restraint clauses in contracts of employment are amenable to challenge, the next relevant questions are: what interests warrant protection? how extensive can the restraint be if it is to be valid? and what remedies are available to the parties?

(iii) PROTECTABLE INTERESTS

The clearest starting point is that an employer cannot simply restrain an ex-employee from competing with him in an ordinary manner; it must go far beyond that, and in the employment context this has traditionally meant that the restraint must be necessary to protect either (1) trade secrets or (2) customer connections.

There appears to be no case in which a covenant against competition by a servant or apprentice has as such ever been upheld by the court. Wherever such covenants have been upheld it has been on the grounds, not that the servant or apprentice would, by reason of his employment or training, obtain the skill or knowledge necessary to equip him as a possible competitor in the trade, *but* that he might obtain such personal knowledge of, and influence over, the customers of his employers, or such an acquaintance with his employer's trade secrets as would enable him, if competition were allowed, to take advantage of his employer's trade connection or utilize information confidentially obtained.[253]

From this basic principle, certain important points arise. The first is that although 'trade secret' is difficult to define, it is an important concept and must be distinguished from the employee's own skill and general knowledge of the trade (albeit gained in the employer's service),[254] knowledge of general business methods and organizations,[255] and information which lacks confidentiality (for example through having been published),[256] none of which merit lawful protection. The subject matter must be something more in the nature of a secret process or formula or the detailed design of a machine (albeit from parts the individual specifications of which are generally known)[257] and in modern circumstances may also cover highly confidential information

---

[252] See Ch 3 under the duty of fidelity.

[253] *Herbert Morris Ltd v Saxelby* [1916] 1 AC 688 at 709, HL, per Lord Parker. For a modern reaffirmation of this principle, see *Faccenda Chicken Ltd v Fowler* [1986] ICR 297, [1986] IRLR 69, CA.

[254] *Herbert Morris Ltd v Saxelby*, n 253; *Mason v Provident Clothing and Supply Co Ltd* [1913] AC 724, HL; *Faccenda Chicken Ltd v Fowler*, n 253.

[255] *Commercial Plastics Ltd v Vincent* [1965] 1 QB 623, [1964] 3 All ER 546, CA.

[256] *Mustad v Dosen* [1963] 3 All ER 416, [1964] 1 WLR 109n, HL (though in fact decided in 1928).

[257] *Haynes v Doman* [1899] 2 Ch 13, CA; *Forster & Sons Ltd v Suggett* (1918) 35 TLR 87; and see the detailed knowledge of current research carried on by the plaintiffs in *Commercial Plastics Ltd v Vincent* [1965] 1 QB 623, [1964] 3 All ER 546, CA.

of a non-technical or non-scientific nature (disclosure of which to a competitor could cause significant harm)[258] or detailed knowledge of the workings of a specialized business.[259] Particularly difficult questions may now arise in the computer and information technology industries, in deciding what remains confidential at the cutting edge and what is merely the (expert) employee's own knowledge, or indeed general knowledge in such a rapidly developing field.[260] The second point is that the phrase 'customer connections' is even more intangible; naturally, an employee in constant touch with customers may in certain circumstances attract a personal following, be they a solicitor's clerk,[261] estate agent,[262] bookmaker's assistant,[263] or milkman,[264] sales representatives and canvassers might well be subject to valid restraints. Every case will depend heavily upon the facts, and in essence what must be shown is that there is a *real* possibility of *misuse* of the employee's knowledge of customers; if this is missing, for example because the employee's contact with the customers was insufficiently direct or influential, the restraint will be void.[265] However, once this elusive element is established, it may well be reasonable to restrain the ex-employee from soliciting not only his particular customers at the date of termination of employment, but also any other persons who were the employer's customers at any other time during the period of employment or some specified part thereof,[266] though it will not generally be reasonable to restrain solicitation of persons who might become the employer's customers at some time after termination,[267] as for example by a clause restraining a commercial traveller from soliciting anyone in the relevant trade in the area in which he used to travel for the employer, not limiting it to those who were the employer's customers, or from whom he had attempted to solicit custom for the employer.[268]

The third point is that if the restraint clause cannot fairly be said to protect a trade secret or customer connection, the longstanding view has been that it should be void on the basis that it concerns no protectable interest known to the law, unless the court is to establish a new one. In *Kores Manufacturing Co v Kolok Manufacturing Co*,[269] two neighbouring employers producing similar goods agreed that neither would employ anyone who had been employed by the other within the previous five years.

[258] *Lansing Linde Ltd v Kerr* [1991] ICR 428, [1991] IRLR 80, CA.

[259] *Littlewoods Organisation Ltd v Harris* [1978] 1 All ER 1026, [1977] 1 WLR 1472, CA.

[260] *FSS Travel and Leisure Systems Ltd v Johnson* [1998] IRLR 382, CA.

[261] *Fitch v Dewes* [1921] 2 AC 158, HL.

[262] *Scorer v Seymour-Johns* [1966] 3 All ER 347, [1966] 1 WLR 1419, CA.

[263] *SW Strange Ltd v Mann* [1965] 1 All ER 1069, [1965] 1 WLR 629.

[264] *Home Counties Dairies Ltd v Skilton* [1970] 1 All ER 1227, [1970] 1 WLR 526, CA; *Dairy Crest Ltd v Pigott* [1989] ICR 92, CA.

[265] *Bowler v Lovegrove* [1921] 1 Ch 642; *SW Strange Ltd v Mann* [1965] 1 All ER 1069, [1965] 1 WLR 629.

[266] *G W Plowman & Son Ltd v Ash* [1964] 2 All ER 10, [1964] 1 WLR 568, CA, applied in *Home Counties-Dairies Ltd v Skilton* [1970] 1 All ER 1227, [1970] 1 WLR 526, CA; *John Michael Design plc v Cooke* [1987] 2 All ER 332, [1987] ICR 445, CA.

[267] *Konski v Peet* [1915] 1 Ch 530.

[268] *Gledhow Autoparts Ltd v Delaney* [1965] 3 All ER 288, [1965] 1 WLR 1366, CA.

[269] [1959] Ch 108, [1958] 2 All ER 65, CA.

As this mainly concerned labourers there was no question of trade secrets or customer connections, and the sole purpose of the agreement was to encourage a stable labour supply. The Court of Appeal held it to be void on the ground that it was, on its facts, unreasonable as between the parties,[270] but it is submitted that conceptually the prime reason for invalidity should have been that it concerned no known protectable interest, and there are dicta in the judgment in support of this. This has, however, caused recent controversy and a change in the law, at least partially, because of moves by employers to prevent solicitation by leaving employees of *other employees*, especially in highly competitive areas such as the City and/or in the case of highly marketable executives. At first, the traditional view was taken that such anti-solicitation clauses were not permitted. In *Hanover Insurance Bros Ltd v Schapiro*[271] certain standard clauses preventing solicitation of customers were enforced against the company's departing chairman and managing director, but a clause stating that they would not, within one year of leaving, solicit any *employees* to join them in their new venture was held to be unenforceable, the court giving its opinion that staff preservation was not a protectable interest. However, that was swiftly followed by an unreported Court of Appeal case, *Ingham v ABC Contract Services Ltd*[272] in which it was held that an employer does have a 'legitimate interest in maintaining a stable trained workforce in what is acknowledged to be a highly competitive business'. In the light of this, an injunction was granted in *Alliance Paper Group Ltd v Prestwich*[273] by a Chancery judge to enforce a covenant not to entice away certain employees, on the basis that the remarks on protectable interests in *Hanover* were obiter (the actual decision having been that the clause was too wide in any event), and that it was *Ingham* that was to be followed on this point. Likewise, when it went before the Court of Appeal again in *Dawnay, Day & Co Ltd v De Braconier d'Alphen*,[274] where three Eurobond dealers broke away from their employer to join a similar competing venture, the court upheld the decision of Walker J to enforce (inter alia) covenants prohibiting for one year solicitation of certain other employees, again expressly on the basis of the employer's interest in maintaining a stable, trained workforce, within the bounds of reasonableness. Thus, this form of staff retention may now be seen as joining trade secrets and customer connections as a third protectable interest *but* with limits. It does not necessarily mean that *Kores v Kolok* is wrong, and simple attempts to stabilize non-key and non-specialist staff (ie just for administrative convenience) may still not be valid. The cases so far have concerned the solicitation of *senior* staff, in highly competitive industries subject to high turnover and 'head-hunting'

---

[270] This case is expressly mentioned by Lord Reid and Lord Hodson in *Esso Petroleum Ltd v Harper's Garage (Stourport) Ltd* [1968] AC 269, [1967] 1 All ER 699, HL as one which should have been decided on the other limb of the *Nordenfelt* test, public interest. It is interesting to note that the agreement was between employers; the existence of such contracts is difficult to discover.

[271] [1994] IRLR 82, CA.   [272] (1994) unreported.   [273] [1996] IRLR 25.

[274] [1998] ICR 1068, [1997] IRLR 442, CA. This case was also notable for deciding that a joint venture had sufficient interest to protect. For extensive discussion of these cases, see *TSC Europe (UK) Ltd v Massey* [1999] IRLR 22.

of people with instantly marketable skills and knowledge.[275] It is possible that this legal development is confined to such cases, though with two caveats—there could also be arguments for a valid protectable interest in relation to a more junior employee if (1) that person, though junior, is a key employee in terms of skills, for example in computer technology[276] or (2) that person is a member of a whole *team* being enticed away by the departing employee (sometimes known as a 'swarming' case).

(iv) THE EXTENT OF THE RESTRAINT

Once there is a legally protectable interest, the question which then arises concerns the extent to which the employer can bind the employee's future conduct in order to protect that interest. Cases on this are as infinitely variable as are the facts upon which they are based, but certain important factors can be discerned. The terms of the restraint must be no more than is reasonably necessary to give the employer adequate protection,[277] and in approaching this the court might first look at the type of business concerned to see how much protection it warrants;[278] in this context it might be significant if the business is either specialized in its product or service or localized in its area of operation. The position of the employee is also a matter for consideration. The closer his contacts with customers or prospective customers the easier it will be to justify a restraint.[279] Similarly the higher the employee is in the hierarchy of employees the easier it will be. Thus in *M and S Drapers v Reynolds*[280] where the restraint was imposed on a collector salesman, the court rejected the analogy with a managing director based on *Gilford Motor Co v Horne*[281] and held that in the light of its particular circumstances the restraint was unreasonable. It is nothing more than a question of fact for again, in *G W Plowman & Son Ltd v Ash*,[282] a restraint on a sales representative was accepted as valid.

---

[275] In *Alliance Paper Group* the restraint related to company employees 'in a senior capacity' and in *Dawnay, Day* to directors or senior employees; in each case the court held that such phrasing was sufficiently precise to be enforceable, on the elephant principle, ie that you cannot define it but you know one when you see it. By contrast, in *Hanover* a non-solicitation clause applying to 'any employees' was too wide.

[276] Readers of Joseph Heller's *Catch 22* will know that the whole Mediterranean theatre of war was in fact run by ex-PFC Wintergreen, not the general staff.

[277] *Herbert Morris Ltd v Saxelby* [1916] 1 AC 688, HL; the longstanding test was reaffirmed by Millett J in *Allied Dunbar (Frank Weisinger) Ltd v Weisinger* [1988] IRLR 60, where he disapproved an attempt to replace it with a more flexible concept of 'proportionality' between the extent of the restraint and the benefit of the employer. For a good factual example, see *Scully UK Ltd v Lee* [1998] IRLR 259, CA.

[278] The business in question must be that in which the employer is actually engaged, and not one in which it might be interested at some future date: *Bromley v Smith* [1909] 2 KB 235; however, it may be valid for the employer to protect the business carried out by its subsidiaries, provided the restraint does not go wider than that and apply to activities not covered by the group: *Stenhouse Australia Ltd v Phillips* [1974] AC 391 at 404, [1974] 1 All ER 117 at 125, PC.

[279] It was felt in *SW Strange Ltd v Mann* [1965] 1 All ER 1069, [1965] 1 WLR 629, that a bookmaker's clerk built up no real contact with clients as business was largely conducted on the telephone.

[280] [1956] 3 All ER 814, [1957] 1 WLR 9, CA.   [281] [1933] Ch 935, CA.

[282] [1964] 2 All ER 10, [1964] 1 WLR 568, CA.

Given that the business merits some protection from an employee such as the one in question, the major factual problem is how wide the terms of the restraint may be in terms of geographical area and duration of time. There are no rules of law here; a 25-year worldwide restraint was valid in the context of the international armaments trade in the *Nordenfelt* case;[283] but a one-year restraint was held to be void in the context of the plastics industry in *Commercial Plastics Ltd v Vincent*[284] partly on the ground that it was unlimited in area. The only general rule is that the two factors of geographical area and duration of time tend to be complementary, in that the wider the geographical area, the shorter the period of time that might be considered reasonable, and vice versa as in *Fitch v Dewes*[285] where a restraint that a solicitor's clerk in Tamworth would *never* practice as such within seven miles of Tamworth Town Hall upon ceasing the employment was held to be valid in the light of the restricted area. Further than this, all that can be said is that the drafting of a restraint clause may require a delicate balance in order to protect the lawful interests of the employer whilst at the same time achieving no more protection than is reasonably necessary for that purpose in all the circumstances. After warning of the dangers of 'home-made' restraint clauses, Pearson LJ said in *Commercial Plastics v Vincent*:[286]

> It would seem that a good deal of legal 'know-how' is required for the successful drafting of a restraint clause.

(v) ENFORCEMENT

In looking to see if a restraint agreement is valid and enforceable, the court is entitled to look at the realities and effect of any stipulation so that, for example, an employer may not disguise a restraint clause by providing that the employee is at liberty to solicit any customers but must pay a premium or commission for any of the employer's customers solicited.[287] Moreover, this point is reinforced by the fact that restraint of trade as a doctrine is not confined to bilateral contracts involving the party concerned,[288] and for present purposes the significance of this is that two or more employers cannot evade

---

[283] See also the permanent, worldwide restraint on a servant of the royal household, preventing disclosure of any personal information on the royal family in *A-G v Barker* [1990] 3 All ER 257, CA.

[284] [1965] 1 QB 623, [1964] 3 All ER 546, CA; other grounds of invalidity were that the clause covered work in the whole field of PVC not just that part which was secret, and it applied to any employment not just research. On the importance of geographical area, see also *Greer v Sketchley Ltd* [1979] IRLR 445, CA; and *Marley Tile Co Ltd v Johnson* [1982] IRLR 75, CA. A longer period is more likely to be reasonable in the case of a non-solicitation of customers' clause than a non-competition clause: *Dentmaster (UK) Ltd v Kent* [1997] IRLR 636, CA (citing *Office Angels Ltd v Rainer-Thomas and O'Connor* [1991] IRLR 214, CA). The judgment of Slade LJ in *Office Angels* is now often cited as a good summary of the basic law.

[285] [1921] 2 AC 158, HL.

[286] [1965] 1 QB 623 at 647, [1964] 3 All ER 546 at 555; though cf the possible qualification in head (v) below.

[287] *Stenhouse Australia Ltd v Phillips* [1974] AC 391, [1974] 1 All ER 117, PC.

[288] See, eg, *Nagle v Feilden* [1966] 2 QB 633, [1966] 1 All ER 689, CA and *Edwards v Society of Graphical and Allied Trades* [1971] Ch 354, [1970] 3 All ER 689, CA.

the doctrine by agreeing between themselves to do that which if done between each one of them and his employees would be void. The facts of *Kores v Kolok*[289] are set out earlier under head (iii); the indirect restraint there, which would clearly have been invalid if put directly into the contracts of employment of the individual employees affected, was held to be void, thus increasing the legal protection given to the employee. However, the question then arose whether the employee could himself challenge such an agreement, for the agreement in *Kores v Kolok* had in fact lasted for 23 years and was only finally challenged because one of the parties became dissatisfied with it. In *Eastham v Newcastle United Football Club Ltd*,[290] a case concerning the 'retain and transfer' system whereby the restrictive agreement between the club and the Football Association and League could have a major effect on the livelihood of the individual players, Wilberforce J held that the individual does in fact have the right to challenge such an agreement even though he is not a party to it, and this was accepted as correct by Lord Upjohn in *Pharmaceutical Society of Great Britain v Dickson*.[291]

If the restraint clause is void, it cannot be enforced by the employer, but there are two ways in which a court might be able to save a clause even if it is prima facie void. The first is that, although such a clause must normally be construed strictly, it may be the case that the potential invalidity arises from an ambiguity in the wording which, read one way, could mean that the restraint is too wide; if, however, it is possible to read the clause realistically in the sense in which the parties obviously meant it, and in that sense it is valid, the court may feel able so to validate it. In *Home Counties Dairies Ltd v Skilton*[292] the agreement was not to 'serve or sell milk or dairy products' and it was pointed out that taken literally this could stop the ex-employee from working in a grocer's shop as well as in the capacity of milkman, and was therefore potentially void for being too wide, but the Court of Appeal held that the true meaning, in the light of the intention of the parties at the time of entering the agreement, was only to restrain future employment as a milkman, and as such the clause was valid. Likewise in *Marion White Ltd v Francis*[293] it was held that a clause restraining employment in the hairdressing business 'in any way' which could conceivably have prevented the ex-hairdresser from working as, for example, a receptionist or bookkeeper, in fact was intended by the parties to refer only to actual hairdressing and as such was narrow enough to be valid. This power of construction was applied quite liberally by the majority of the Court of Appeal in *Littlewoods Organisation Ltd v Harris*[294] (in which Lord Denning MR suggested that the restraint clause in *Commercial Plastics Ltd v Vincent*[295] which the court had regretfully held to be too wide might have been validated in this way), but was

---

[289] [1959] Ch 108, [1958] 2 All ER 65, CA; see also *Mineral Water Bottle Exchange and Trade Protection Society v Booth* (1887) 36 Ch D 465, CA.

[290] [1964] Ch 413, [1963] 3 All ER 139, HC of A.

[291] [1970] AC 403 at 433, [1968] 2 All ER 686 at 701, HL.

[292] [1970] 1 All ER 1227, [1970] 1 WLR 526, CA.

[293] [1972] 3 All ER 857, [1972] 1 WLR 1423, CA.   [294] [1978] 1 All ER 1026, CA.

[295] [1965] 1 QB 623, [1964] 3 All ER 546, CA.

treated much more circumspectly by a subsequent Court of Appeal in *J A Mont (UK) Ltd v Mills*[296] on the grounds that otherwise an employer would have little incentive to phrase covenants in appropriately restricted terms in the first place; clearly the matter is one of balance.

The second possible way to validate a potentially void clause is if the offending part may be severed, leaving the valid remainder capable of enforcement. The concept of severance is a difficult one best dealt with in detail elsewhere.[297] Suffice it to say that where a contract in restraint of trade contains some stipulations which are void and some which by themselves would be valid, it may be possible to sever the void ones and enforce the valid ones. However, the court will not rewrite the contract, and may only be prepared to sever where each stipulation is distinct in itself. In *Mason v Provident Clothing and Supply Co Ltd*[298] Lord Moulton said:

> It would in my opinion be pessimi exempli if when an employer had exacted a covenant deliberately framed in unreasonably wide terms, the courts were to come to his assistance and by applying their ingenuity and knowledge of the law, carve out of this void covenant the maximum of what he might validly have required.

From this it has been argued that the courts should be less willing to sever in an employer–employee restraint case, but any such general principle was disapproved by the Court of Appeal in *T Lucas & Co Ltd v Mitchell*[299] where severance of words within a clause was allowed and the valid part of the restraint enforced.

If the restraint clause is held to be valid (either generally or via one of the above validation methods) it may be enforced against the employee, subject to the caveat that if the employer is in fact in breach of the contract of employment, for example by wrongfully dismissing the employee, he loses the benefit of any restraint clauses contained in it.[300] Provided this is not so, the employer may sue the employee for damages (and

---

[296] [1993] IRLR 172, CA.

[297] Contrast *Attwood v Lamont* [1920] 3 KB 571, CA with *Goldsoll v Goldman* [1915] 1 Ch 292, CA.

[298] [1913] AC 724 at 745, HL.

[299] [1974] Ch 129, [1972] 3 All ER 689, CA; see also *Sadler v Imperial Life Assurance Co of Canada Ltd* [1988] IRLR 388 and *Scully UK Ltd v Lee* [1998] IRLR 259, CA. Severance was allowed with little difficulty in *Stenhouse Australia Ltd v Phillips* [1974] AC 391, [1974] 1 All ER 117, PC, where the relevant stipulations were not only separate in content but also expressed in separate clauses in the agreement, and in *Hinton & Higgs (UK) Ltd v Murphy* [1989] IRLR 519, Ct of Sess, where the contract itself contained a clause inviting severance if any particular restriction was held to be too wide, though the validity of the latter point was later doubted in *Living Design (Home Improvements) Ltd v Davidson* [1994] IRLR 69, Ct of Sess. In *Marshall v NM Financial Management Ltd* [1997] ICR 1065, [1997] IRLR 449, CA severance was allowed at the request of the *employee* in order for him to rely on a linked clause in his favour.

[300] *General Billposting Co v Atkinson* [1909] AC 118, HL; *Spafax Ltd v Harrison* [1980] IRLR 442, CA; *Rex Stewart Jeffries Parker Ginsberg Ltd v Parker* [1988] IRLR 483, CA; *Briggs v Oates* [1990] ICR 473, [1990] IRLR 472; *Cantor Fitzgerald International v Bird* [2002] IRLR 867 (where it was reaffirmed that repudiatory breach of the term of trust and respect short of dismissal could justify the employee in leaving and claiming to be free of the restraint clause). In *Rock Refrigeration Ltd v Jones* [1997] 1 All ER 1, [1997] ICR 938, the Court of Appeal held that this still applies even if the employer has stated that the clause is to apply on termination 'however caused'; possibly significantly there are dicta in the case that they only so held because they were *bound* by

indeed either party may seek a declaration on the validity of the clause in question);[301] in practice, however, the real importance of the action to the employer is that he may seek an injunction to restrain the employee from acting in breach of the clause, and in an urgent case may be granted an interlocutory injunction (provided he can show that he will suffer immediate loss, so that the 'balance of advantage' lies in his favour, within the principles in *American Cyanamid Co v Ethicon Ltd*).[302] Normally, the court will not grant an injunction to enforce a contract of employment on the basis that it is a personal contract not amenable to such enforcement;[303] one longstanding exception to this, however, is the rule in *Lumley v Wagner*[304] that the courts will enforce a valid negative restraint clause, provided that to do so will not have the effect of specifically enforcing the actual contract. This will normally mean that an injunction *will* lie for breach of a restraint clause,[305] but in an untypical case an injunction could be refused as in *Page One Records Ltd v Britton*[306] where the dismissed manager of a pop group, The Troggs, sought to enforce a clause in their agreement that they would not engage

---

General Billposting, not because they agreed with the principle. For an argument that *General Billposting* is too sweeping and that decisions here should be more responsive to the justice of the case, see Freedland (2003) 32 ILJ 48. One open question for a long time was whether it would apply to a dismissal which was not a breach of contract by the employer (ie with proper notice, therefore not wrongful) but which was later held to have been *unfair* by an employment tribunal. From a strictly contractual view, unfairness under the statute would have no effect on the restrictive covenants which would remain enforceable by the employer against the unfairly dismissed employee but as a matter of policy it might be thought unjust that an employer guilty of unfair dismissal could still benefit from the restraint clause and interfere with the dismissed employee's future employment. When the matter finally came before a court these arguments were fully rehearsed and Hickinbottom J held that a dismissal lawful at common law but unfair under statute does *not* destroy a restraint clause: *Lonmar Global Risks Ltd v West* [2011] IRLR 138.

[301] Even if the period of restraint is already over, provided the applicant can prove that he still has a worthwhile interest in pursuing it (eg where an employer has other employees who are subject to the same clause): *Marion White Ltd v Francis* [1972] 3 All ER 857, [1972] 1 WLR 1423, CA.

[302] [1975] AC 396, [1975] 1 All ER 504, HL; there was disagreement in the Court of Appeal as to whether these principles apply to a restraint of trade case in *Fellowes & Son v Fisher* [1976] QB 122, [1975] 2 All ER 829, CA, the majority applying the 'balance of convenience' principle and Lord Denning MR declaring that the case came within an exception to the new rules, whereby the court could apply the old principles and look at the relative strength of each party's case; in *Lawrence David Ltd v Ashton* [1991] 1 All ER 385, [1989] ICR 123 the Court of Appeal affirmed that *American Cyanamid* normally does apply to restraint cases, but in *Lansing Linde Ltd v Kerr* [1991] ICR 428, [1991] IRLR 80, CA, an exception was established where full trial is not likely to occur quickly enough. The requirement of showing real harm (not just breach of a reasonable restraint) where the application is interlocutory was stressed by Lord Johnston in *Jack Allen (Sales & Service) Ltd v Smith* [1999] IRLR 19, OH.

[303] *Whitwood Chemical Co v Hardman* [1891] 2 Ch 416; CA; cf *Hill v CA Parsons & Co Ltd* [1972] Ch 305, [1971] 3 All ER 1345, CA. Section 236 of the Trade Union and Labour Relations (Consolidation) Act 1992 provides that no injunction may be granted compelling an employee to work. See Ch 6 on remedies for wrongful dismissal.

[304] (1852) 1 De GM & G 604, 42 ER 687; see also *Warner Bros Pictures Inc v Nelson* [1937] 1 KB 209.

[305] Normally, damages will not be considered a sufficient remedy instead; likewise, an injunction should not normally be refused on the ground that the defendant is willing to undertake not to use the trade secrets, etc until final judgment: *Johnson & Bloy (Holdings) Ltd v Wolstenholme Rink plc* [1987] IRLR 499, CA (a case on the duty of confidentiality generally, but the principles should apply to a restraint of trade clause case).

[306] [1967] 3 All ER 822, [1968] 1 WLR 157; *Warren v Mendy* [1989] ICR 525, [1989] IRLR 210, CA.

any other person or firm as manager during a five-year period and would not act as such themselves; Stamp J held that, as they had to have a manager in order to operate, to enforce the clause would be to force them to employ him, and so no injunction could be granted.

It can be seen from this discussion that restraint clauses are not simple, either in their framing or in their enforcement, especially as they tend to operate on an 'all or nothing' basis. It is probably this that has led to the search for other, more reliable, ways to safeguard the employer's confidences when an employee leaves the employment. One way that has attracted interest is the 'garden leave' clause, which operates on the basis of a very long notice requirement, during which the employee is paid in full (even though not actually working), but with an express obligation on the employee not to work for anyone else during the notice period. Such clauses may be more certain (though more expensive) than restraint clauses and are considered in Chapter 6.

5 CONTINUITY OF EMPLOYMENT

(i) THE CONCEPT OF CONTINUITY AND THE TREATMENT OF PART-TIME EMPLOYEES

The concept of 'continuous employment' is an important one in that many accruing rights, privately negotiated or statutory, depend upon it either for qualification for a particular right, or for computation of benefits to be received under it. Thus, various periods are laid down by statute for the purposes of qualification for written particulars of employment and minimum rights during notice, qualification for redundancy pay, computation of redundancy pay, qualification for protection from unfair dismissal, quantification of a basic award for dismissal, and qualification for various other employment protection rights. These matters are considered in detail elsewhere, but are mentioned to show the direct effect of the provisions that govern the question of statutory continuity (now contained in sections 210–219 of the Employment Rights Act 1996).

Four preliminary points should be noted. The first is that continuity of employment means generally with one employer,[307] and this has been construed widely to include continuity where the employee has changed department, job, seniority or even the terms of his contract of employment during the period, provided that he has remained with the same employer.[308] The second is that the Act governs which weeks count in

---

[307] *Lee v Barry High Ltd* [1970] 3 All ER 1040, [1970] 1 WLR 1549, CA; *Harold Fielding Ltd v Mansi* [1974] 1 All ER 1035, [1974] ICR 347. It also means in relation to one contract of employment: *Lewis v Surrey County Council* [1988] AC 323, [1987] ICR 982, HL.

[308] *Wood v York City Council* [1978] ICR 840, [1978] IRLR 228, CA; *Jennings v Salford Community Service Agency* [1981] ICR 399, [1981] IRLR 76; continuity is a purely statutory concept, exhaustively covered by the statutory provisions which are not to be qualified by courts or tribunals: *Carrington v Harwich Dock Co Ltd* [1998] ICR 1112, [1998] IRLR 567 (applying Lord Denning MR's judgment in *Wood v York City Council*,

computing a period of employment, and generally if a week does not count it will break continuity, so that the employee then loses his accrued period and must start again from scratch;[309] however, there is the qualification that certain weeks (particularly those spent on strike or, for the purpose of redundancy, abroad)[310] do not count, but at the same time are deemed not to break continuity, and thereby the position is effect-ively rendered neutral (the employee is not unduly penalized by losing all accrued continuity, but at the same time does not benefit because he cannot actually use the relevant period for any purpose of computation). The third is that there is a statutory presumption of continuity, unless the contrary is shown; thus, in cases of doubt (for example where there is a possibility that some relevant weeks may not count and so break continuity) the burden of proof is on the employer to show that the employee did *not* have the necessary continuity of employment.[311]

The fourth, and much the most significant, point is that this area underwent major change in 1995 due to a conflict with EC law. In domestic law the concept of con-tinuity had always been used to achieve the secondary, less obvious aim of exclud-ing part-timers from employment protection rights such as redundancy and unfair dismissal. This was done by providing that a week did not count unless during it the employee actually worked (or normally worked) for 16 hours or more (or between eight and 16 hours after five years' service). Thus, no matter how long the part-time employee worked, they never accumulated the necessary continuous period of employ-ment for the major rights (for example two years, as it then was, in order to claim unfair dismissal) if they did not work the necessary hours. This was longstanding, deliberate policy by successive governments. However, the tide of EU law was running strongly in the opposite direction (towards extending rights to atypical employees). Although the Maastricht opt-out which was in operation at the time could be used to prevent any direct EU pressure for more such rights by employment law Directives, the then government could not rule out the possibility of a challenge under already-applicable EC law, in particular that relating to equality of pay and treatment. This happened in *R v Secretary of State for Employment, ex p Equal Opportunities Commission*,[312] in which the House of Lords held that (1) the Equal Opportunities Commission (the

---

above, and doubting the decision in *Roach v CSB (Moulds) Ltd* [1991] ICR 349, [1991] IRLR 200); *Sweeney v J & S Henderson Ltd* [1999] IRLR 306, EAT (going further and disapproving *Roach*).

[309] Section 210(4).   [310] Sections 216 and 215 respectively.

[311] Section 210(5). The effect of the presumption was considered in *Nicoll v Nocorrode Ltd* [1981] ICR 348, [1981] IRLR 163 where the EAT held that where it is unclear whether an employee had worked the necessary number of qualifying weeks, the employee need only show that *some* weeks during the qualifying period count and the burden of proof then passes to the employer to prove that there were weeks that do not count and so break continuity. However, there is an exception—in *Secretary of State for Employment v Cohen* [1987] ICR 570, [1987] IRLR 169, the EAT held that the presumption does *not* apply to a 'transfer of busi-ness' case under s 218 (see later discussion), though Scott J emphasized that although the burden of proving continuity through such a transfer lies on the employee, a tribunal should not apply an unrealistically high *standard* of proof.

[312] [1995] 1 AC 1, [1994] ICR 317, HL; see Villiers and White (1995) 58 MLR 560.

predecessor to the Commission for Equality and Human Rights) had locus standi to challenge the legality of the hours limits, (2) those limits were contrary to Article 119 and the Equal Pay Directive 75/117 (in relation to redundancy payments) and the Equal Treatment Directive 76/207 (in relation to unfair dismissal) and (3) in neither case was the discriminatory effect on women justified on the government's assertions that such limitations were necessary socially and economically in order to promote the extension of part-time employment, in the absence of substantive *evidence* that this form of deregulation had had that effect. This bombshell decision had certain loose ends but the government soon realized that they could not sensibly hold any tenable line simply by amending the hours limits, and so by the Employment Protection (Part Time Employees) Regulations 1995[313] removed these limits altogether. Thus, the major statutory rights can now be claimed by part-timers and this in turn has had serious long-term effects on the law relating to continuity of employment.

(ii) WEEKS WHICH COUNT

(a) 'Any week during the whole or part of which the employee's relations with the employer are governed by a contract of employment'

(Employment Rights Act 1996, section 212(1)). As stated immediately above, this used to be a far more complex provision, linking continuity to the performance or normal performance of 16 hours work or more per week (or eight hours for more than five years). The emphasis now, however, is on looking only at the continuing existence of the contractual relationship, and whether it covers the week(s) in question. Thus, in *Clifford v Devon County Council*[314] a dismissed employee was able to claim unfair dismissal even though for part of the two years prior to the claim she had only worked seven and a half hours per week and, most startlingly of all, in *Colley v Corkindale*[315] an employee working one five-and-a-half-hour bar shift every *alternate* Friday was also allowed to bring an unfair dismissal action. Under the previous law the latter claim would have been doubly inadmissible, due to (1) the number of hours and (2) the existence of the alternate weeks when no work was done or expected, which would have broken continuity anyway.[316] The test now is thus a far more general, less technical and (above all) contractual one than before. It is suggested therefore that the proper approach is to construe the amended provision afresh, and to forget the substantial body of case law on the previous provisions. That is not to say that the same result may not be reached in any given case. Thus, for example, there is still a requirement that the contract in question must be continuous, and so continuity might still be broken in a case of regular

---

[313] SI 1995/31.   [314] [1994] IRLR 628.   [315] [1995] ICR 965.

[316] Thus, in *Lloyds Bank Ltd v Secretary of State for Employment* [1979] 2 All ER 573, [1979] ICR 258, an employee working one week on and one week off was *not* covered by the normal continuity rules, and only succeeded in the claim under the special 'saving' rule in s 212(3)(b) by a strained interpretation which is now probably untenable (see below). This is a good example of the sort of technicality which hopefully should now arise less frequently.

but separate contracts, as in *Hellyer Bros Ltd v McLeod*[317] where trawlermen were held not entitled to redundancy payments on the collapse of their part of the fishing industry, for although they had sailed for one particular owner for many years the court held that the proper construction was that they had been engaged on a series of separate crew agreements, each covering one voyage. Arguably this case would still be decided the same way now and so, although the continuity rules are now simpler, they still cannot be taken for granted. This was further emphasized in *Booth v United States of America*[318] where maintenance workers were put on to a series of fixed-term contracts totalling more than two years, but with very deliberate two-week gaps between each; their eventual claims for redundancy payments and unfair dismissal were disallowed for lack of continuity—the gaps broke normal continuity, which (for technical reasons, see below) could not be covered by one of the 'deemed continuity' provisions, and the bottom line was expressed by Morison P as follows:

> If, by so arranging their affairs, an employer is lawfully able to employ people in such a manner that the employees cannot complain of unfair dismissal or seek a redundancy payment, that is a matter for him. The courts simply try and apply the law as it stands. It is for the legislators to close any loopholes that may be perceived to exist.[319]

(b) A week during which there is no subsisting contract of employment, but which is covered by special statutory provisions

In order to avoid unfortunate gaps or 'hiccoughs' in continuity, certain exceptions have always been specifically created by the legislation, and these are now contained in the Employment Rights Act 1996, section 212(3). The three specific cases covered by this subsection are as follows.

(1) Where the employee is incapable of work through sickness or illness (subsection (3)(a)). Incapable has been held to refer to the job in question and a temporary lighter job need not break continuity.[320] Absence from work does not normally, in default of express provision in the contract, terminate the contract.[321] If the contract has not been determined then the weeks of absence count under subsection (1) anyway. This head is an extension stretching into the period after the contract has been determined.[322] It is limited to

---

[317] [1987] 1 WLR 728, [1987] ICR 526, CA.

[318] [1999] IRLR 16. This is a particularly harsh decision because, although the employees were formally 'terminated' and had to complete new application forms for the next contract (after a break which the employers insisted had to be for a minimum of two weeks—strangely), in fact when they returned they were given the same employee number and used the same tools and equipment, and even the same lockers. What a coincidence.

[319] [1999] IRLR 16 at 18. There was nothing in the White Paper 'Fairness at Work' covering this matter. As it has been allowed to continue, the moral of the story seems to be that the more cynical the manipulation of these rules, the more likely the employer is to win.

[320] *Collins v Nats (Southend) Ltd* (1967) 2 ITR 423; *Donnelly v Kelvin International Services* [1992] IRLR 496.

[321] For the law as to the payment of sick pay, see Ch 3, heading 5(ii), p 193.

[322] There must be a causal link between the absence from work and the incapacity through sickness or injury: *Pearson v Kent County Council* [1993] IRLR 165, CA.

26 weeks after a week counting under subsection (1) and must be followed by a week so counting. Theoretically an employee could have a solitary week of employment followed by 26 weeks of illness and a further week of employment which would both maintain the continuity and permit a further 26 weeks of absence through illness to count.

(2) Where the employee is absent from work on account of a 'temporary cessation of work' (subsection (3)(b)); this has been in practice the most important special case, but it is a phrase not without difficulty. No time limit is laid down. The phrase was considered by the House of Lords in *Fitzgerald v Hall, Russell & Co Ltd*[323] where it was held that it refers to cessation of the *employee's* work for some reason, so there is no requirement that the employer's business in which the employee is engaged should have ceased. It was also held that each case under this head must be looked at in the round and, if necessary, with hindsight, to establish whether it was 'temporary' (the statute giving no guidance on this). Thus, if both parties obviously envisaged that it would be only temporary that would be cogent evidence, but the lack of it would not mean that the arrangement would necessarily be construed to be permanent:

> The effect of that case is that the tribunal is enjoined to look at the matter as the historian of a completed chapter of events, and not as a journalist describing events as they occur from day to day. The importance of that is this, that things are seen, as they unfold, quite differently from the way in which they are seen when one looks back and considers the whole of the chapter in context. What at the time seems to be permanent may turn out to be temporary, and what at the time seems to be temporary may turn out to be permanent.[324]

The essence of most successful cases is that the employee has been 'stood off' in the sense that he was to be recalled later. The fact that a job is taken in the period of cessation does not destroy the position,[325] but it is plainly not meant to cover the situation where an employee moves to a new employer, fails to settle, and quickly moves back to his old job. It may cover situations such as extra holiday periods taken as periods of absence with the employer's agreement at the employee's expense, and, more particularly, periods when the workplace is closed or no work is available[326] (which may

---

[323] [1970] AC 984, [1969] 3 All ER 1140, HL, approving *Hunter v Smith's Dock Ltd* [1968] 2 All ER 81, 3 ITR 198. 'Work' here means paid work; if that is missing, the paragraph may apply and it is not the tribunal's function to enquire into *why* the paid work is missing: *University of Aston in Birmingham v Malik* [1984] ICR 492. However, at the end of the day it must be the case that there is a 'cessation of work' available for the employee to do: if the work remains but for some reason he is not eligible to do it, the paragraph does not apply: *Bryne v Birmingham City District Council* [1987] ICR 519, [1987] IRLR 191, CA. It is that cessation that must then be 'temporary', not the employee's absence: *Flack v Kodak Ltd* [1986] ICR 775, [1986] IRLR 255, CA. This can have the unfortunate effect that if the work remains available but the employer *refuses* at certain times to offer it to a particular employee (in order deliberately to break continuity, eg by insisting on gaps between fixed-term contracts), then subs (3)(b) cannot apply and the employee may be unable to claim statutory rights: *Booth v United States of America* [1999] IRLR 16 considered earlier.

[324] *Bentley Engineering Co Ltd v Crown* [1976] ICR 225 at 228, [1976] IRLR 146 at 148; in this case, periods of two years and 21 months were held still to be temporary. The correctness of this decision has been doubted over the years by commentators, but it was reaffirmed by the EAT in *Holt v E B Security Ltd* UKEAT/0558/11.

[325] *Thompson v Bristol Channel Ship Repairers and Engineers Ltd* (1969) 4 ITR 262; affd (1971) 5 ITR 85, CA; *Bentley Engineering Co Ltd v Crown* [1976] ICR 225, [1976] IRLR 146.

[326] *Hunter v Smith's Dock Ltd* [1968] 2 All ER 81, 3 ITR 198.

arise through many causes such as a natural calamity like a fire,[327] or the disruption of supplies of materials). In *Ford v Warwickshire County Council*[328] it was held to cover the case of a schoolteacher who had been employed on eight consecutive fixed-term contracts for the academic year (September to July); thus, the periods of the summer vacations were held not to break continuity so that she could claim unfair dismissal and a redundancy payment when she did not receive a ninth contract. In interpreting the subsection, the House of Lords took a basically similar approach to that in their earlier decision in *Fitzgerald v Hall Russell Ltd* (above), holding that 'temporary' means 'transient' and adding that the application of subsection (3)(b) was not defeated either by the fact that the absences were easily foreseeable in advance or by the fact that the case concerned a series of fixed-term contracts (rather than a series of contracts terminable by notice). The 'transience' requirement makes it clear that the principle in the case cannot be applied so widely as to give previously unheard of rights to genuinely casual/seasonal workers (who, for example, only work for three or four months of each year—there, the gaps would be anything but transient); however, the case may give food for thought to any employer seeking to avoid the application of employment laws by putting an employee on a series of short-term contracts, if it transpires that in fact the gaps are relatively short by comparison with the periods of work (provided that it remains the case that it is the *work* that is temporarily unavailable, not just the fact that it is not being done by that employee).[329] The application of hindsight and an overall view of events, permissible under this subsection, could easily work to the employer's disadvantage in such a case, though it must be remarked that the categorization of transience as a matter of fact for the tribunal would make it difficult to give definite advice in advance in a marginal case on whether the sub-paragraph will apply,[330] the lawyer being faced with the unanswerable question 'How long is short?'

In seeking to answer that question, two quite different approaches are possible. As stated above, *Fitzgerald v Hall Russell Ltd* sets out a 'broad-brush' approach, looking at all the circumstances throughout the period of employment in order to see if any particular gap can be categorized as temporary. However, in *Ford v Warwickshire County Council*, Lord Diplock suggested a narrower 'mathematical' test of looking at whatever period is relevant to the claim in question[331] and, in the case of any gap during that time, comparing its length mathematically with the periods of work on either side

---

[327] *Newsham v Dunlop Textiles Ltd (No 2)* (1969) 4 ITR 268.

[328] [1983] ICR 273, [1983] IRLR 126, HL, overruling *Rashid v ILEA* [1977] ICR 157.

[329] See *Booth v United States of America*, n 318.

[330] See, eg, the facts in *Berwick Salmon Fisheries Co Ltd v Rutherford* [1991] IRLR 203 where salmon netters had been employed for 30 weeks on, 22 weeks off, until their final two seasons when they only worked for 23 weeks on, 29 weeks off. This point now has a particular resonance under the Fixed-term Employees (Prevention of Less Favourable Treatment) Regulations 2002, SI 2002/2034, under which these continuity rules are applied in order to calculate whether an employee has been kept on 'successive' fixed-term contracts for four years, thus becoming a permanent employee unless the employer can objectively justify continued use of fixed-term contracts (see this chapter under heading 1(iv), p 59).

[331] For example, if the question arose as to entitlement to a redundancy payment, that period would be the last two years before the date of dismissal.

of it to see if it was temporary. This latter approach could produce anomalies[332] and the matter was reconsidered by the Court of Appeal in *Flack v Kodak Ltd*[333] a case on very different facts from those in *Ford*. This case concerned a series of highly irregular work patterns over periods varying from three to 11 years (the employees having been laid off and taken back on again intermittently, depending on season and demand). The tribunal applied the mathematical approach (even to the extent of expressing the gaps as percentages of their surrounding periods in work) and found that in the case of each employee continuity was broken in the vital qualifying period for redundancy payments. However, the EAT and the Court of Appeal held that this was the wrong test to apply, that the 'broad brush' approach should be taken and that the matter should be remitted to another tribunal for reconsideration. The question is where this leaves the law. Although Lord Diplock's statement in *Ford* as to the mathematical test was said to be obiter, it is clear from later cases that that test has not been disapproved. In *Sillars v Charrington Fuels Ltd* the EAT[334] suggested that the mathematical test should apply to cases like *Ford* of regular gaps, and the broad-brush approach to cases like *Flack* of irregular gaps. Unfortunately, the matter was not fully resolved when the case went to the Court of Appeal[335] for it was there held that (the case being one of seasonal employment with long, regular gaps) the mathematical test was one which it was *open* to the tribunal to have used. Although the distinction drawn by the EAT appears to have been thought too simplistic by the Court of Appeal, if one is looking for a rough rule of thumb it may not be a bad one, pending further authoritative guidance on the matter. The continued vitality of the 'temporary cessation' exception in cases of irregular employment can be seen from *Cornwall CC v Prater*[336] where it was held that a children's home tutor who had undertaken assignments for the council on an ad hoc basis over the years (with no expectation of any particular level of work, but who expected to have to complete an assignment once she had undertaken it) but with no overall contract could claim statutory rights because (1) there was enough mutuality of obligations to produce a separate contract of employment for each assignment and (2) these separate contracts could then be put together under paragraph (3)(b).

A lockout is covered, and so are non-strikers laid off because a strike has disrupted production so that work is not available.[337] However, section 216(1) expressly provides that absence through strikes does not count (although, of course, by section 216(2)

---

[332] If in the relevant period, for example, the employee had a gap of eight weeks with periods in work of only two weeks on each side, that would not be 'temporary' on a straight mathematical comparison. If, however, that was because of short time in times of difficulties prior to his redundancy, and came as a series of late hiccoughs after years of unbroken service, the end result (no redundancy pay because not continuously employed for two years counting back from the date of dismissal) would be ludicrous.

[333] [1986] ICR 775, [1986] IRLR 255, CA.

[334] [1988] ICR 505, [1988] IRLR 180.

[335] [1989] ICR 475, [1989] IRLR 152, CA. The mathematical approach was also applied to the facts of *Berwick Salmon Fisheries Co Ltd v Rutherford* [1991] IRLR 203, see n 330.

[336] [2006] ICR 731, [2006] IRLR 362, CA; see Davies (2006) 35 ILJ 196.

[337] *Macartney v Sir Robert MacAlpine & Sons Ltd* (1967) 2 ITR 399.

continuity is not broken by a strike), and so cannot be made to count by calling it a 'temporary cessation of work'. This, however, was qualified in *Clarke Chapman-John v Walters*[338] where a period on strike was followed, in the employee's case, by a short period laid off pending a phased return to work; it was held by the NIRC that during that short period he was not on strike, so the predecessor of section 216(1) did not apply, and it could be construed as a 'temporary cessation of work', albeit the direct result of the actual strike.

(3) Where the employee is absent from work in circumstances such that, by arrangement or custom, he is regarded as continuing in the employment of his employer for any purpose (subsection (3)(c)). Under this head any unique local practices are covered, and some potentially unfortunate breaks in continuity avoided. It appears that the agreement or custom must exist when the absence begins, not as an ex post facto afterthought;[339] once this is satisfied the cause of the absence appears to be immaterial—it could be something ad hoc, such as leave of absence for personal reasons[340] or a long-term agreement that the employer might keep the employee on a 'reserve-list' to be called upon when necessary.[341] One area of current interest where reliance has been sought on subsection (3)(c) is contractual career break schemes. These are not covered by statute; where they have been introduced voluntarily (for example as part of a family-friendly package of terms and conditions) they have caused novel problems legally .[342] One question has been whether the employee taking the break could claim that his (or, more likely her) continuity of employment was preserved under this subsection, on the basis that the scheme constituted an 'arrangement' to regard the employment as continuing. This finally came before the courts in *Curr v Marks & Spencer plc*,[343] where the employee had taken a four-year break (for family purposes) under the employer's scheme. She had commenced her employment with them in 1973 and took the leave from 1990 to 1994. When she was made redundant in 1999 the employers calculated her entitlement to a redundancy payment only back to 1994; she claimed back to 1973

---

[338] [1972] 1 All ER 614, [1972] ICR 83.

[339] *Murray v Kelvin Electronics Ltd* (1967) 2 ITR 622; *Todd v Sun Ventilating Co Ltd* [1975] IRLR 4; cf *Cann v Co-operative Retail Services Ltd* (1967) 2 ITR 649. 'Arrangement' requires some form of advanced discussion or agreement to the effect that the parties regard the employment as continuing; mere acquiescence or expectation that the employer would periodically lay the employees off is not enough: *Booth v United States of America* [1999] IRLR 16. An exception was created to the rule (that an 'arrangement' must already exist at the time of the absence) in *Ingram v Foxon* [1984] ICR 685, [1985] IRLR 5 where it was held that the subsection covered an agreement to reinstate on the understanding that continuity would be deemed to be unbroken; this was disapproved in *Morris v Walsh Western UK Ltd* [1997] IRLR 562 but then a different EAT again in *London Probation Board v Kirkpatrick* [2005] ICR 965, [2005] IRLR 443 reconsidered the matter and preferred *Ingram* to *Morris*.

[340] *Moore v James Clarkson & Co Ltd* (1970) 5 ITR 298; *Taylor v Triumph Motors* [1975] IRLR 369, IT.

[341] *Puttick v John Wright & Sons (Blackwall) Ltd* [1972] ICR 457; *Normanton v Southalls (Birmingham) Ltd* [1975] IRLR 74, IT.

[342] An interesting parallel can be seen with PHI schemes (Ch 3, heading 3(vii), p 161), which at one point were being enthusiastically introduced as an aid to headhunting, without working out their complex legal implications.

[343] [2003] ICR 443, [2003] IRLR 74.

(capped to the maximum 20 years) on the basis that she had continuity through the break. The scheme itself provided that an employee taking the break had to resign and forfeit continuing staff benefits (for example staff discount, loans and share options), but that the employers undertook to take the employee back into an equivalent position and that in each year of the break the employee would do two weeks' paid work (to keep up skills). A tribunal found against this employee, a sympathetic EAT allowed her appeal, but the Court of Appeal (while expressing some sympathy for her position and some criticism of the employers for not making the continuity point clear) restored the tribunal's decision. Reaffirming the point that an 'arrangement' must be mutual,[344] they held that here there was no meeting of minds to the effect that the employment was to be considered as continuing, primarily in the light of the requirement on the employee to resign, and the freezing of all employee benefits. Given that this probably represented a fairly typical career break scheme, this case shows that severe problems of continuity are to be expected with such schemes, *unless* an employer (wishing to use one as a positive recruiting tool) very deliberately drafted it so as to preserve continuity by contract.[345] This apart, semble a scheme would only come purely within the wording of the subsection if employment was accepted as continuing 'for any purpose' (for example for pension purposes, as instanced by the Court of Appeal) which was not the case here.

(iii) INDUSTRIAL DISPUTES

The Act defines strikes and lockouts in similar language.[346] A lockout involves the closing of a place of employment, the suspension of work or the refusal by an employer to continue to employ any number of his employees. A strike involves cessation of work by a body of employees acting in combination, a concerted refusal to continue work. In the case of both strikes and lockouts these actions must be in consequence of a dispute and in each case the aim of the action must be to coerce the employees or employers, as the case may be, to accept or not to accept terms or conditions of or affecting employment. Both definitions also expressly include similar action taken to aid other employers or employees in dispute.

If an employee is on strike during a week or any part thereof, that week does not count as a period of employment by virtue of section 216(1); however, a compromise is achieved by section 216(2) which provides that the employee's *continuity* of employment is not broken by a strike. In the case of a lockout section 216(3) provides that continuity is not broken by the fact that an employee is absent from work because of

---

[344] See n 339, particularly *Booth v United States of America* [1999] IRLR 16.

[345] Even here there is a problem—continuity for statutory purposes cannot be established by contract where the statutory definition is not satisfied (see this chapter under heading 3(ii), p 80), so the employer would need to draft a scheme operating purely in contract even when giving (wholly or partly) the statutory entitlement.

[346] Employment Rights Act 1996, s 235. Note that these definitions are only for stated purposes; they do not apply to the unfair dismissal provisions relating to industrial action, see Ch 10, heading 2(ii), p 698.

a lockout, but the paragraph says nothing about whether such a period can *count*, so that that question must rely on whether the contract of employment subsists during the lockout.[347] If it does not, presumably the period will not count, though of course continuity will not be broken.

During the currency of a strike, the employer may in fact dismiss the employees, but this in itself will not affect continuity of employment for the following reasons: (1) section 216 makes no distinction between strikes where there are dismissals and those where there are not; (2) the definition of 'employee' for the purposes of section 216, in section 230, includes an ex-employee; and (3) it was held in *Bloomfield v Springfield Hosiery Finishing Co Ltd*[348] that section 216 applies to persons who were employed at the *outset* of the strike, and that for present purposes the strike is to be considered as continuing as long as there is the possibility that normal employment will be resumed at the end of the dispute; this may mean in practice until the employer replaces the striking employees with others, closes down the department in question, or until the employees concerned find permanent employment elsewhere. Thus, if the striking employees are in fact re-engaged, their continuity will be safeguarded even if they were dismissed during the strike. Similar principles should apply to a lockout.

As noticed above, a further extension of this is that if a striker is temporarily laid off at the end of a strike until the business picks up and there is work for him to do, that employee is not on strike during that period, but he may be considered to be absent on account of a temporary cessation of work under section 212,[349] and so not only is his continuity safeguarded, but he may also count the period of lay-off.

(iv) CHANGE OF EMPLOYMENT

Normally when an employee terminates his job with an employer and goes to work for another employer, his continuity ends and he must start to build up continuous service with the new employer from scratch.[350] However, there may be ways in which the continuity can be carried over, so that he is regarded as being employed by the new employer as from the date when he commenced employment with the old employer. The Employment Rights Act 1996, section 218 lays down six classes of case in which employment may be deemed to be continuous even though there is a change in employment. The six cases are as follows:

(1) Where the trade of business or undertaking is itself transferred. Subsection (2) provides that continuity is unbroken; this is of general application, but particularly important in cases of redundancy. However, to be relied upon at all, the criteria for its application must be satisfied; one is that the employee in question must have been

---

[347] *E and J Davis Transport Ltd v Chattaway* [1972] ICR 267, 7 ITR 361.
[348] [1972] 1 All ER 609, [1972] ICR 91.
[349] *Clarke Chapman-John v Walters* [1972] 1 All ER 614, [1972] ICR 83.
[350] *Lee v Barry High Ltd* [1970] 3 All ER 1040, [1970] 1 WLR 1549, CA.

in the relevant employment 'at the time of the transfer' (which raises the problem of a gap in employment over the period of the transfer),[351] but the primary one is—was it a transfer of business, or merely the disposal of certain assets? If the latter, the provision does not apply, even if the employee goes with the asset, so that, for example, the sale of an operating factory may not come within subsection (2) if it is seen merely as the disposal of a surplus asset, particularly if the original employer carries on his business in other establishments.[352] In *Lloyds v Brassey*[353] Lord Denning MR said:

> The meaning of [this provision] was considered by the Divisional Court in *Kenmir Ltd v Frizzell*, where Widgery J said 'In deciding whether a transaction amounted to the transfer of business, regard must be had to its substance rather than its form … the vital consideration is whether the effect of the transaction was to put the transferee in possession of a going concern, the activities of which he could carry on without interruption.' I think that it is the right test. If the new owner takes over the business as a going concern—so that the business remains the same business but in different hands—and the employee keeps the same job with the new owner … his period of employment is deemed to continue without a break in the same job.

This basic distinction between a transfer of business and a transfer of assets was approved and applied by the House of Lords in *Melon v Hector Powe Ltd*[354] to a case of the sale by the original employer of one of their two factories to another employer in the same trade; in the circumstances it was held that the tribunal had correctly decided that this was merely a transfer of assets, not a transfer of business. However, certain forms of business may be *sui generis*, and in *Lloyd v Brassey* the Court of Appeal held that in the case of farming the essence of the business is the land itself, so that sale of the land constitutes transfer of the business, not just the disposal of an asset; this idea was applied by analogy to the transfer of the tenancy of a hotel in *Young*

---

[351] This was for a long time complicated by the decision of the Court of Appeal in *Teesside Times Ltd v Drury* [1980] ICR 338, [1980] IRLR 72 which permitted a gap to count, but for three different reasons; in *Clark & Tokeley Ltd v Oakes* [1998] 4 All ER 353, [1998] IRLR 577, the Court of Appeal subsequently held that it is Stephenson LJ's judgment in *Teesside Times* that is to be applied, ie that there is no hard-and-fast rule, that a 'transfer' may well take place over an extended period of time, and that continuity will be preserved, provided that the employee was still in employment at the start of that process (a question of fact for the tribunal).

[352] *Kenmir Ltd v Frizzell* (1968) 3 ITR 159; *Woodhouse v Peter Brotherhood Ltd* [1972] 2 QB 520, [1972] 3 All ER 91, CA; *Crompton v Truly Fair (International) Ltd* [1975] ICR 359, [1975] IRLR 250. There must be a legal transfer of sorts, it is not enough merely that de facto control has been given to someone else: *S I (Systems and Instrumentation) Ltd v Grist* [1983] ICR 788, [1983] IRLR 391. Continuity is preserved even if there is a gap between the two employments, provided that gap is related to the machinery of the transfer: *Macer v Abafast Ltd* [1990] ICR 234, [1990] IRLR 137. Note that the presumption of continuity in s 210(5) does *not* apply to a 'transfer of business' case under s 218: *Secretary of State for Employment v Cohen* [1987] ICR 570, [1987] IRLR 169.

[353] [1969] 2 QB 98 at 103, [1969] 1 All ER 382 at 384.

[354] [1981] ICR 43, [1980] IRLR 477, HL. Notice that in this case it was the *employees* who were arguing that there was no transfer of business, in order to be able to claim their redundancy rights from the original employer; this claim was upheld by the House of Lords. See to like effect *Ward v Haines Watts* [1983] ICR 231, [1983] IRLR 285 (concerning sale of the goodwill of a professional practice).

v Daniel Thwaites & Co,[355] but attempts to apply it more widely to other businesses have failed.[356] The question whether there has been an actual transfer is to be considered from the point of view of the dealings between the employers; if their dealings do not disclose such a transfer subsection (2) does not apply even if the employees carry on doing the same work and from *their* point of view it appears to be a transfer. In *Woodhouse v Peter Brotherhood Ltd*[357] a factory was sold and the new owner carried on using the same plant and equipment and indeed completed the order for one of the old employer's contracts, but it was held by the Court of Appeal that from the employer's point of view this was no transfer, and it was irrelevant that from the employee's point of view their 'working environment' had continued unchanged. One major factor pointing towards a transfer might be the sale of goodwill[358] which was one of the missing factors in the *Woodhouse* case. The term 'business' is defined in section 235 as including a trade or profession and any activity carried on by a body of persons, whether corporate or unincorporate.[359] It has been held to cover the transfer of *part* of a business (for example where an employer carries on business in place A and place B and sells off his whole business in place A, as in *G D Ault (Isle of Wight) Ltd v Gregory*),[360] but only if that part is genuinely severable (in its nature or location)[361]—if not, the transaction might well be viewed as again merely the disposal of an asset. Finally, it should be noted that continuity through a business transfer may also be materially affected by the Transfer of Undertakings (Protection of Employment) Regulations (first passed in 1981 and reissued in 2006). These are capable of having a far more radical effect, being based on a regime of *compulsory* transfer if they apply (not just the preservation of continuity *if* the employee transfers), and are dealt with separately in Chapter 8.

(2) Where an Act of Parliament causes one corporate body to replace another as employer: subsection (3).

(3) Where the employer, not being corporate, dies and the personal representatives carry on the business: subsection (4).

(4) Where the 'employer' is a partnership, personal representatives or trustees, and the composition of the body involved changes: subsection (5). This provision safeguards continuity when, for example, a partner retires and another is appointed. A more difficult case, however, arises where the partnership is dissolved but *one* of the

---

[355] [1977] ICR 877.

[356] *Port Talbot Engineering Co Ltd v Passmore* [1975] ICR 234, [1975] IRLR 156 (maintenance contracts); *Bumstead v John L Cars Ltd* (1967) 2 ITR 137 (petrol station).

[357] [1972] 2 QB 520, [1972] 3 All ER 91, CA.

[358] *HA Rencoule (Joiners and Shopfitters) Ltd v Hunt* (1967) 2 ITR 475; *Kenmir Ltd v Frizzell* [1968] 1 All ER 414, [1968] ITR 159.

[359] Explained by Diplock LJ in *Dallow Industrial Properties Ltd v Else* [1967] 2 QB 449 at 458, [1967] 2 All ER 30 at 33.

[360] (1967) 2 ITR 301.

[361] *McCleod v John Rostron & Sons* (1972) 7 ITR 144; *Newlin Oil Co Ltd v Trafford* [1974] IRLR 205, 9 ITR 324; *Gibson v Motortune Ltd* [1990] ICR 740.

partners carries on the business. On a narrow construction of subsection (5) it was held in *Harold Fielding Ltd v Mansi*[362] that this was not covered and so continuity was not preserved. The opposite conclusion was reached in the later cases of *Allen & Son v Coventry*[363] and *Jeetle v Elster*[364] but primarily on the alternative ground that, irrespective of subsection (5), such a change could constitute a 'transfer of business' under subsection (2); in each case the EAT criticized the reasoning on subsection (5) in *Mansi* but without actually overruling it. Eventually, however, the issue arose again in *Stephens v Bower*[365] where the Court of Appeal upheld *Jeetle* and disapproved *Mansi* as a matter of presumed parliamentary intent.

(5) Where the employee is taken into the employment of an associated employer:[366] subsection (6).

(6) Where an employee of the governors of a school maintained by a local education authority or that authority itself is taken into the employment of the governors of another such school or the authority: subsection (7).

6 CHANGING THE TERMS OF EMPLOYMENT

We have already seen that section 4 of the Employments Right Act 1996 states that changes in the terms and conditions relevant to the section 1 statement must be notified to the employee within one month. However, it is important to realize that section 4 only adds a procedural requirement—it does *not* give the employer any substantive right to alter the terms of employment simply by issuing an amending notice. Any such variation must first be lawful and effective under the ordinary law of employment contracts. A first possibility is that there may be certain, untypical, cases where the employment contract itself is drafted to give the employer a right of unilateral variation.[367] In *Wandsworth LBC v D'Silva*[368] the Court of Appeal recognized that in purely contractual terms such a clause could be valid and effective but expressed the view obiter that particularly clear language would be necessary to reserve such an unusual power for one party to the contract and that courts should seek to avoid any unreasonable exercise of such a power. However, in *Bateman v ASDA Stores Ltd*[369] the

---

[362] [1974] 1 All ER 1035, [1974] ICR 347; *Wynne v Hair Control* [1978] ICR 870.

[363] [1980] ICR 9, [1979] IRLR 399.   [364] [1985] ICR 389, [1985] IRLR 227.

[365] [2004] 148 Sol Jo LB 475, CA.

[366] For the definition of associated employers, see this chapter, heading 1(v), p 65.

[367] The terms and conditions of employment of senior civil servants may be varied unilaterally by the government under the Civil Service Orders in Council. In an ordinary contract of employment, it would be an interesting question as to whether a term allowing unrestricted unilateral variation ('You are employed to do what I say, on any terms I may decide upon') could be held to be void for uncertainty.

[368] [1998] IRLR 193, CA; see also *Securities and Facilities Division v Hayes* [2001] IRLR 81, CA and Smith and Randall, *Contract Actions in Employment Law* (2nd edn, 2011) 43.

[369] UKEAT/0221/09. See further Reynolds and Hendy, 'Reserving the Right to Change Terms and Conditions; How Far Can an Employer Go?' (2012) 41 ILJ 79.

well-known supermarket had a major legal win on this point. They were proposing changes to the terms and conditions of a large section of their staff: 9,330 employees agreed but 8,700 did not. The management went ahead and purported to impose the changes on the refuseniks under a clause in their company handbook which said that the company 'reserved the right to review, revise, amend or replace the contents of this handbook and introduce new policies from time to time reflecting the changing needs of the business and to comply with new legislation'. In spite of the broad wording, the reference to changing 'policies' (not specifically contractual terms) and arguments that this power was only meant to apply to technical changes, the EAT held (applying *Wandsworth*) that it unambiguously gave the power of unilateral variation of major terms claimed by the employer.[370] From the employee perspective, it is to be hoped that this decision lies at the end of the spectrum of legally acceptable means of change. Less drastically, a second possibility is that it may be that a particular 'variation' in fact falls within the managerial discretion to order changes,[371] either because it is within an area of flexibility envisaged by the contract or because it falls within the scope of an implied term that the employee will adapt to necessary changes in what remains essentially the same job.[372] However, both of these possibilities show the basic problem here, that contracts are essentially static whereas work and work methods may change (sometimes rapidly), and the possibility may equally arise that the employer may wish to effect changes which are *not* envisaged by the contract. In such a case there has to be a legally effective variation; if this does not happen, an employee may insist upon adhering to the original contract and may bring a common law action to underline that adherence (for example by bringing an action in the county court for his wages, which are due by virtue of his being willing and able to continue performing his duties under the original, unamended contract)[373] or (in the case of a pay cut) proceedings before a tribunal on the basis that the change constitutes an unlawful 'deduction' from wages. In such a case, an employer who is insistent upon forcing through changes may have to grasp the nettle, dismiss those who still refuse to accept changes and take his

---

[370] In *Wandsworth* it was pointed out that, even if such a clause was contractually valid, an oppressive application of it might breach the implied term of trust and confidence (see Ch 3, heading 3(iv), p 151). On the facts in *ASDA* the EAT held that there had been no such conduct, especially as the employer had undertaken an extensive consultation exercise with the staff and guaranteed that no existing employees would suffer a decrease in pay.

[371] As in the case of the introduction of a no-smoking policy in *Dryden v Greater Glasgow Health Board* [1992] IRLR 469, which was held not to be a breach of contract, so that the employee who left was not constructively dismissed.

[372] This was the case with the computerization of Inland Revenue procedures; this was held to be merely an updated version of the plaintiff tax officers' existing jobs (with which they were expected to cope), *not* a substantive variation of their terms of employment: *Cresswell v Board of Inland Revenue* [1984] ICR 508, [1984] IRLR 190; see Ch 3, heading 4(ii), p 165.

[373] As in *Burdett-Coutts v Hertfordshire County Council* [1984] IRLR 91 where dinner ladies who had refused to accept a unilateral decrease in their hours of work successfully sued their employer for arrears of wages due under their original contract.

chances before an employment tribunal by seeking to show that the dismissals were fair because of the business's need to alter working patterns.[374]

From the employer's point of view, these uncertainties can be avoided if it can be shown that the employee in question in fact agreed to the proposed variation in the contract. How is that to be shown? Obviously the clearest case is where the employee has expressly agreed to the variation, either individually or collectively (through negotiations with his union). However, there remains a middle ground (especially where union representation is not involved), which is where the employer 'proposes' a variation simply by announcing it (possibly by reissuing an amended section 1 statement), thus putting the onus on the employee to *object*. If the employee does not object, that gives rise to the argument that he has impliedly assented to the variation. If such an argument were easily accepted, the contractual rights of an employee would mean little and so it was held in *Jones v Associated Tunnelling Co Ltd*[375] that the question of the correct interpretation to be placed on a lack of objection following a unilateral change in terms by the employer must be approached realistically; if the term in question is of immediate practical importance (for example a reduction in wages or alteration of working hours) and the employee fails to object, that may show implied assent on his part, but in the case of other terms of little immediate importance (for example as to sick pay or possible future changes in the workplace) it may be expecting too much of an employee to make immediate objection (even if he understands the full significance of the changes) and so a tribunal in such a case should be slow to infer assent merely from lack of objection. A particularly useful summary of the legal position here is contained in the following passage from the judgment of Elias P in *Solectron Scotland Ltd v Roper*[376]:

> The fundamental question is this: is the employee's conduct, by continuing to work, only referable to his having accepted the new terms imposed by the employer? That may sometimes be the case. For example, if an employer varies the contractual terms by, for example, changing the wage or perhaps altering job duties and the employees go along with that without protest, then in those circumstances it may be possible to infer that they have by their conduct after a period of time accepted the change in terms and conditions. If they reject the change they must either refuse to implement it or make it plain that by acceding to it, they are doing so without prejudice to their contractual rights. But sometimes the alleged variation does not require any response from the employee at all. In such a case

---

[374] This is one of the most difficult areas of unfair dismissal, for it is well established that dismissal because of refusal to accept a necessary business reorganization can constitute dismissal for 'some other substantial reason' within the Employment Rights Act 1996, s 98 (see Ch 8, heading 1(ii), p 566 and, again concerning dinner ladies and cost-cutting councils, *Gilham v Kent County Council (No 2)* [1985] ICR 233, [1985] IRLR 18, CA) but to take the final step and hold that that dismissal was *fair* is to give priority to the employer's business considerations over what the employee would normally expect to be his contractual rights (particularly the right not to have his contract altered except by agreement).

[375] [1981] IRLR 477, applied in *Harlow v Artemis International Corpn Ltd* [2008] IRLR 629, QBD where an employee managed to show that, over many years, he had *never* agreed to any changes to the (contractual) redundancy rights contained in his original contract.

[376] [2004] IRLR 4.

if the employee does nothing, his conduct is entirely consistent with the original contract continuing; it is not only referable to his having accepted the new terms. Accordingly, he cannot be taken to have accepted the variation by conduct.

This 'only referable to acceptance' test was applied in *F W Farnsworth Ltd v Lacy*[377] but with a twist in the facts. The employer was seeking to enforce a restraint of trade clause against a departing employee but that clause was not in his original (2003) contract. It had been put into a 'revised' contract given to him in 2009 but which he claimed he had never signed or returned to the employer. He argued that he had at no point accepted the new contract and so, as his silence was not only referable to implied agreement, he was not bound by the restraint clause. However, the twist in the facts was that the 2009 contract had also contained for the first time a valuable right to private medical insurance which the employee had taken up. On that basis it was held that he must be taken to have implicitly accepted the whole contract and so the clause could be enforced against him.

Finally, there is one other tactic that has featured largely in employer received wisdom in the past, but which has always been legally more complex than employers have assumed. This is to dismiss all the employees in question (by giving lawful notice) and then re-engage them on the new terms. Purely as a matter of contract law, this can work to substitute the new terms, but there are two reasons under statute law why it can be legally dangerous: (1) it is possible that the employees could claim unfair dismissal from the old contract and seek compensation to reflect the net loss of value to them of the new contract;[378] (2) this tactic has been held to constitute a 'redundancy' under the wider EC law definition used in the law on collective redundancies and so if (as will usually be the case, given that the employer is looking to force the change through) there has not been the obligatory period of consultation with trade union or workforce representatives (where 20 or more employees are involved), the employer may lay himself open to protective awards which could total a significant amount if large numbers of employees have been subject to this tactic;[379] moreover, in any case where the Information and Consultation of Employees Regulations 2004 apply an employer using this tactic (or the previous one of simply announcing changes, leaving it to employees to object) as an alternative to discussions with the employees involved may fall foul of the requirement of informing and consulting worker representatives on 'decisions likely to lead to substantial changes in work organization or in contractual relations'.[380]

---

[377] [2012] EWHC 2820 (Ch).

[378] This is because of the rule in *Hogg v Dover College* [1990] ICR 39 that an employee can be 'dismissed' from a particular contract and so can claim unfair dismissal even if still in that employer's employment but under a different contract; see *Alcan Extrusions v Yates* [1996] IRLR 327. Note, however, that the dismissal must still be proved to have been unfair; if the employer had pressing business reasons for the changes and handled it reasonably, that could still be a fair dismissal for 'some other substantial reason', see Ch 8, heading 1(ii), p 566.

[379] *GMB v Man Truck and Bus UK Ltd* [2000] ICR 1101, [2000] IRLR 636. For the law on collective redundancies (including the wider EC law definition and liability for protective awards), see Ch 8, heading 1(iii), p 572.

[380] SI 2004/3426, reg 20(1)(c); see Ch 9, heading 5(ii), p 684. This particular obligation is a strong one because the information and consultation must be 'with a view to reaching agreement' (reg 20(4)(d)). Failure by the employer can lead to a fine up to £75,000.

In addition to these statutory implications, the courts have recently had to struggle with a further problem here—what is the position of employees who are *unsuccessful* in the reselection procedure? Given the commonplace nature of the tactic of dismissing all and getting them to 'reapply' for their jobs (which may have a subtext not just of forcing through changes to terms and conditions, but also of trying to effect a major reorganization while at the same time disguising redundancies and not being bound by the usual rules of fair selection for redundancy) it is curious that we have not seen more case law on it.[381] When the point finally arose directly before the EAT in *Ralph Martindale & Co Ltd v Harvis*,[382] it looked as though the law was to be developed in such a way as to give the unsuccessful employee at least some legal redress. The EAT accepted the basic conceptual problem here that the normal redundancy selection rules cannot apply (because *all* are selected—QED) *but* indicated that the tribunal in such a case should impose a 'duty of care' on the employer to ensure that the 'rehiring' exercise is carried out fairly, for example by the use of open procedures with objective reselection criteria. However, when the matter came before the EAT again three years later, this novel approach was not built upon, but in fact disapproved. In *Morgan v Welsh Rugby*[383] it was held that *Ralph Martindale* established *no* general principle and that a dismissal under this fire-and-rehire tactic was fair even though the employer had departed from the reselection procedure it had adopted. More importantly, a year later the EAT under Underhill P reconsidered the law in greater detail in *Samsung Electronics UK Ltd v Monte-d'Cruz*[384] and held (again finding fair dismissal on the facts) as follows:

(a) There is no absolute requirement of objectivity in selection; there will often be a heavy element of judgment and 'good faith assessments of an employee's qualities are not normally liable to be second guessed by an employment tribunal'.

(b) The employer is to be given considerable discretion in choosing who to retain, especially if the jobs have been changed and there are also external candidates (who, in the absence of discrimination, have no rights).

(c) This is an area where a tribunal can easily fall into the 'vice of substitution' (ie improperly substituting its own view of what should have been decided) especially using language such as 'It would have been better to' or 'The claimant was clearly the best candidate'. It is not the job of the tribunal to second-guess the employer and the question is not whether it would have been reasonable for the employer to have acted differently, but whether it was *unreasonable* to act as he did—a much tougher test.

---

[381] The EAT had harsh words for the tactic in *Church v West Lancashire NHS Trust* [1998] ICR 423, [1998] IRLR 4, but then the case was disapproved on its principal issue (of 'bumping' redundancies) in *Murray v Foyle Meats Ltd* [1999] ICR 827, [1999] IRLR 562, HL.

[382] [2008] UK EAT/166/07.   [383] [2011] IRLR 376.   [384] UKEAT/0039/11.

(d) There is good *practice* in relation to holding interviews, treating candidates equally and adhering to set procedures and selection criteria *but* that does not translate into legal requirements.

This gives an employer very considerable leeway in operating this system and is bound to make the eventual decision difficult to challenge, unless (as the EAT put it) 'the failures in process identified had led to some serious substantial unfairness to the claimant'. Indeed, in *Morgan* it was put even higher in terms of capriciousness, favouritism or nepotism. This raises a high bar for the ex-employee in an unfair dismissal action. Obviously, sound advice to the employer is to have demonstrably defensible procedures for the reselection exercise, which should make a challenge effectively impossible, but the bottom line is that even if this is not done the position of the unsuccessful employee is weak.

3

CONTRACTS OF EMPLOYMENT (2): CONTENT AND WAGES

OVERVIEW

At the heart of the contractual element of employment lies the question of the terms of the contract. As in all contracts, it is usually desirable that these are express and clear, but in employment law this is often not the case. Thus, the chapter explores where express terms come from, especially if they are not in fact all neatly set out in writing, and then goes on to consider how terms become implied. Here, several significant differences between ordinary commercial contracts and employment contracts will be seen, both in the scale of the use of implied terms in employment law to 'perfect' the bargain and in the sheer strength of some of these frequently implied terms which (contrary to contract law orthodoxy) can in practice be just as important as express terms. Having looked at where these terms come from, the chapter goes on to consider the principal duties that they impose on employers and employees. Some of these are old and/or obvious, such as the employer's duty to pay wages and the employee's duty of obedience to lawful orders. On the other hand some are more recent and more at the cutting edge of modern employment law. The implied term of trust and respect by the employer is the prime example. The chapter concludes by considering specifically the legal provisions (common law and statutory) on what will often be the most important element of the employment relationship, namely the obligation to pay wages.

1 EXPRESS TERMS

While the employer and employee are generally free to determine the content of the terms of employment, there are now legislative provisions in Part I of the Employment Rights Act 1996 requiring the employer to give written notice of certain basic terms. These provisions were considered in Chapter 2, where it was seen that while this notice does not itself constitute the contract it will be strong evidence as to its terms and indeed if it is signed as such by the employee it may be construed as the written contract, according to *Gascol Conversions Ltd v Mercer*.[1] For present purposes, the importance of these provisions is that they require that major terms be put down in writing and probably encourage the employer to give the employee an individual written contract of employment; as with all contracts, written terms are generally to be preferred for the certainty that they bring,[2] and the legislation attempts to minimize the incidence of 'factory gate employment' where an employee was taken on without having the relevant terms settled, leaving potentially important matters to later decision by the courts. Certainty, however, can work both ways, and if the parties set something down in writing they should ensure that it is accurate, for once it is expressed there is less room for further extrinsic evidence as to their intentions. As an example of this, in *Nelson v BBC*[3] the contract stated that the employee could be required to work when and where the corporation demanded, but when the corporation closed down the Caribbean service in which he worked, they claimed that it was to be implied that he was only employed for the purposes of that one service and therefore that he was redundant; the tribunal and the EAT accepted this, but the Court of Appeal rejected it, since the express term was in unrestricted language, and as a basic principle of contract law it was impossible to imply a restriction of the kind that the tribunal had found. On the other hand, even in contract law there are exceptions to the rule against extrinsic evidence, particularly where a written contract does not completely cover all the matters upon which the parties had previously agreed. Thus, in *Tayside Regional Council v McIntosh*[4] a job advertisement for a vehicle mechanic stated that a clean driving licence was essential and this was restated at interview. When later the employee lost his licence and was dismissed, he pointed to the fact the written terms which he had been given upon appointment made no mention of a driving licence, but the Scottish EAT refused to accept that that meant there was no express term as to a licence. The basic distinction between these two case examples (out of many) is that in the latter extrinsic evidence was being properly used to amplify a written agreement which was incomplete, whereas in the former it was being used improperly to alter the meaning of an existing written term.

In line with normal contract law, it should also be remembered that, to be an express term, it does not have to be in writing, and so an alternative argument may be that something that was said (or promised) went beyond extrinsic evidence and was

---

[1] [1974] ICR 420, [1974] IRLR 155, CA; see Ch 2, heading 3(ii), p 79.

[2] For a particularly salutary example, see *Stubbes v Trower, Still & Keeling* [1987] IRLR 321, CA where solicitors, in offering articles, omitted to state expressly that the applicant had to pass the requisite examinations before beginning, and the Court of Appeal refused to find that there was an implied term to that effect on the facts; in the words of one commentator, you cannot always rely on common sense and implied terms to rectify a contractual oversight.

[3] [1977] ICR 649, [1977] IRLR 148, CA; see the discussion of this case in *Cowen v Haden Ltd* [1983] ICR 1, [1982] IRLR 314, CA which shows the importance of the proper construction to be placed upon the express term in question.

[4] [1982] IRLR 272. This is consistent with the view expressed by Lord Hoffmann in *Carmichael v National Power plc* [1999] ICR 1226, [2000] IRLR 43, HL that it may be necessary to look to several sources to discern the whole contract of employment.

actually an *oral* express term. Naturally, there may be major problems of proof in such a case (with the defendant swearing blind that no such thing was ever said) and as a matter of fact there may be a difference between things said on a relatively formal occasion (such as a recruitment or promotion interview) and things said more informally.[5] One other minefield can arise where, as a drafting matter, a written contract seeks to establish an express term by reference to some other document. The safest way to do this is to incorporate it specifically by reference and attach it to the contract (or state where it can be found). In *Jowitt v Pioneer Technology (UK) Ltd*[6] the contract promised the employee coverage by a long-term disability scheme which the employer had had underwritten by an insurance company. However, instead of specifically incorporating that policy into the contract, the employer tried to précis the policy in his own words in the contract itself. In doing so, he got a key element wrong and ended up promising much more than the policy itself underwrote. When the employee made a claim on this benefit, the employers tried to limit their liability to what the policy actually covered (ie what they had *meant* by their précis), but the Court of Appeal agreed with the employee that all that mattered to him was what *his* contract actually said. The employer was thus left to shoulder the wider (uninsured) liability that he had managed to create by his poor drafting.

Three current uncertainties relating to express terms of contracts of employment are worth mentioning at this stage. The first is whether there is any requirement that an express contractual right for an employer (however clearly expressed) must be *exercised* reasonably. The traditional view is that there can be no such requirement; a contract is a contract, and if the employee agrees a term he must abide by it, even if its application by the employer seems harsh (eg where an employer activates an unrestricted mobility clause to require an employee to move hundreds of miles with little or no warning).[7] However, modern case law has suggested a significant modification of that position and this is considered later in this chapter under heading 2(i); if this trend continues, it will be of major importance and marks another departure of contracts of employment from orthodox contract law.

The second uncertainty is whether an employer can, in effect, try to pre-empt any attempts by the employee to add to the written terms by casting the employment contract in terms of an 'entire contract'.[8] In the leading case on this developing area of contract law generally, Lightman J put it thus:

> The purpose of an entire agreement clause is to preclude a party to a written agreement from threshing through the undergrowth and finding, in the course of negotiations, some

---

[5] In *Judge v Crown Leisure Ltd* [2005] IRLR 823 the Court of Appeal held against an employee who alleged that he was contractually entitled to a pay rise promised to him at the end of the firm's Christmas party (hic!).

[6] [2003] IRLR 356, CA.

[7] *Rank Xerox Ltd v Churchill* [1988] IRLR 280.

[8] One form of this would be a clause stating to the effect that 'This agreement constitutes the entire agreement between us with regard to its subject matter, and supersedes any previous agreement (whether verbal or written) made between us at any time'.

(chance) remark or statement (often long-forgotten or difficult to recall or explain) upon which to found a claim, such as the present, to the existence of a collateral warranty. The entire agreement clause obviates the occasion for any such search … For such a clause constitutes a binding agreement between the parties that the full contractual terms are to be found in the document containing the clause and not elsewhere, and that, accordingly, any promises or assurances made in the course of the negotiations (which, in the absence of such a clause, might have effect as a collateral warranty) shall have no contractual force, save in so far as they are reflected and given effect in the document.[9]

Should this development in commercial contracts law apply equally to employment contracts? There is an argument that it should not; commercial contracts are *expected* to be certain and preferably reduced to clear written terms (hence the general dislike of implied terms in ordinary contract law, see below) whereas an employment relationship is likely to be far more amorphous, easily entered and possibly rapidly evolving. An entire contract clause could lead in practice to an even greater danger of the contract terms and employment realities diverging radically than is already inherent in our present contract-based law on employment. However, the little authority that currently exists shows a spectrum of approaches. At the pro-employer end, in *White v Bristol Rugby Club Ltd*,[10] a professional rugby player signed up by a club under a contract which provided for an advance on earnings tried to avoid going through with the engagement by arguing that if he returned the advance he was free to go elsewhere. His primary argument was that there was an oral express term to that effect, arising from discussions that he had had before signing the contract with the club's chief executive. The contract, however, contained an entire agreement clause, stating that the contract contained the whole agreement and that the parties had not relied on any oral or written representations made by other persons.[11] The judge held that this clause was applicable and, as a matter purely of construction, covered the circumstances here, so that no oral term could arise. This forced the employee back on to arguments relating to the terms of the contract *as they stood*, and whether under these he had a right not to go through with the engagement; it was held that he did not. In the middle of the spectrum in *Fontana (GB) Ltd v Fabio*[12] a general manager's contract made no reference to any right to pension contributions (in fact it contained a clause stating that there were to be none) but the manager said that there had been on oral agreement to such a right. When later dismissed, he claimed arrears of pension contributions alongside an unfair dismissal claim. The contract contained a clause stating that it *substituted* previous

---

[9] *Inntrepreneur Pub Co v East Crown Ltd* [2000] 3 EGLR 31 at 33.

[10] [2002] IRLR 204, QBD.

[11] There is some discussion in the judgment (at paras 30–5) as to whether the latter half of the clause (no reliance) could be subject to the Misrepresentation Act 1967, s 3 which subjects a clause of a contract excluding or restricting liability for misrepresentation to the reasonableness test that applies under the Unfair Contract Terms Act 1977. The relationship between s 3 and an entire agreement clause remains subject to conflicting authority, as the judge here did not have to decide the issue because the first half of the clause was effective anyway.

[12] (July 2002, unreported), EAT; see Employment Lawyer No 94 (September 2002).

agreements and arrangements, whether written, oral or implied. Did this preclude his claim? The EAT held that it did not; they accepted that an entire contract clause can apply to an employment contract but, applying *White v Bristol Rugby Club Ltd*, held that as a matter of construction this particular clause was not strong enough to preclude this claim because it did not expressly claim that the contract contained all the terms. At the pro-employee end of the spectrum, in *RNLI v Bushaway*[13] the EAT had little difficulty in avoiding an entire agreement clause (in a far more run-of-the mill context than that of a well-known rugby player) by finding ambiguities in the clause's application, allowing a finding that it had not been what the parties had really intended. The result therefore seems to be that a court or tribunal will be likely to apply an *unambiguous* entire contract clause which clearly covers the facts in question. Presumably, such a clause is to be construed strictly; indeed as a matter of policy it should be construed particularly strictly in an employment case. Where one applies, it would have a strongly dampening effect on any later arguments based on custom and practice, and instead of using collateral warranty arguments the party trying to 'add' to the written contract would be forced back on to other arguments, such as that the representations claimed to have been made are relevant to construing written clauses in the contract (difficult in *Fontana* because the written clause said there was *no* entitlement to pension contributions) or that there had been a legally valid *variation* of the original agreement (difficult in a case where it is a *pre*-contractual representation that is being relied upon). Clearly, both parties will have to be careful what they sign if the agreement contains one of these clauses.[14] To the extent that they are used in specifically negotiated contracts for the engagement of higher and/or key employees, this may be fair enough, but if it were ever to be the case that they were being put into many, far more standard, contracts as a matter of course (where they could cause many more difficulties and potential injustices) the employment-related courts and tribunals might have to look at them afresh in this context, with a more critical eye.[15]

The third uncertainty concerns the extent to which an employer may use express terms to reserve to himself a right of unilateral variation. Flexibility in employment has been a nostrum of modern managerialism for some time now, and there will certainly be cases where an employer can lawfully claim to have carefully built in flexibility and an ability to change a particular term or, alternatively, that the matter has been so drafted as to remain non-contractual (so that change remains in the

[13] [2005] IRLR 674; the case concerned the transmutation of an agency worker into a permanent employee; the entire agreement clause was not permitted to stand in the way of the EAT's decision, which was in effect to look behind the wording of the original contract, at what had happened in practice.

[14] Normally, it will be the employee who stands to lose, but it could be the employer—on the facts of *Tayside Regional Council v McIntosh*, n 4, if there had been an entire agreement clause the employer would have had difficulty relying on the requirement of a clean driving licence which had only been mentioned in the job advertisement.

[15] If the effect of such a clause was ever to threaten an employee's *statutory* rights, it might be attacked as an attempt to contract out of the protection of the statute, which might be void; see particularly the Employment Rights Act 1996, s 203(1).

employer's discretion).[16] The question is whether a point could be reached where such phrasing became so unconscionable and vague as to be unenforceable; the contractual doctrine of uncertainty would be inappropriate in an employment context because it would render the whole contract void (to the employee's disadvantage), and so far this point has not had to be fully explored by the courts. The nearest that they have come is in *Wandsworth London Borough Council v D'Silva*[17] where, after upholding the employer's contention that a sickness absence policy in a code of practice remained non-contractual and so within the employer's power to change, Lord Woolf MR said obiter that, although a party to the contract could reserve a right of unilateral variation, it would take clear language to do it and a court should, in construing the contract, try to avoid a construction allowing a power of unilateral variation of significant employee rights which could produce an unreasonable result. This can be seen in *Land Securities Trillium Ltd v Thornley*[18] where the employer claimed that a significant change to the employees' duties (from exercising her profession as an architect to managing an office) was permissible under a clause requiring her to perform to the best of her abilities 'all the duties of this post and any other post you may subsequently hold' but the EAT construed this narrowly as only referring to any other post that she had *agreed* to undertake. While this is a significant decision, whether a court could go further in the case of an absolutely clearly drafted power of unilateral variation that was equally clearly inequitable in its result remains to be seen.

2 THE IMPLICATION OF TERMS

(i) THE PROCESS OF IMPLICATION

Even when the statutory provisions for written particulars are complied with, there will be areas left in a contract of employment where no terms are expressed, so that if a dispute arises in one of these areas the court or tribunal may have to have recourse to implied terms. The implication of terms is a concept of application to the whole law of contract, but in the context of employment it has evolved along more specialized lines. Starting from orthodox contract theory, the basis of implication is subjective, in that the court or tribunal should look at the likely intention of the parties at the time of contracting, and should not imply terms simply because they appear (objectively)

[16] *Airlie v City of Edinburgh District Council* [1996] IRLR 516, EAT (terms of a bonus scheme expressly subject to variation by employer after consultation with the workforce; no requirement of agreement before revision, provided consultation carried out).

[17] [1998] IRLR 193, CA. See Ch 2, heading 6, p 113 and in particular the decision for the employer in *Bateman v ASDA Stores Ltd* UKEAT/0221/09.

[18] [2005] IRLR 765. The EAT also held that a reference to 'any other duties that may reasonably be required of you' was to be construed in the circumstances of the individual employee (here, a professional who feared losing her skills), not the employer's commercial reasons for the change.

reasonable when the case is viewed in hindsight.[19] The two classic tests for an implied term are (1) that it is necessary to give 'business efficacy' to the transaction as must have been intended by both parties[20] or (2) that it is so obvious that it goes without saying, so that if an officious bystander had suggested that it be expressed the parties would have testily suppressed him with a common 'Oh, of course!'[21] Moreover, it has been clearly stated that the presumption is against the adding to contracts of terms which the parties have not expressed, particularly if the term in question is of a novel nature.[22] This traditional view of implied terms has, however, been considerably modified in the case of contracts of employment where, historically and in particular before the Contracts of Employment Act 1963, so many terms (often the basic ones) were not expressed and where the process of implication has been much used to fill in the details once it was clear that an employment relationship existed.[23] It has been modified in three main ways:

(a) Inferred terms

Although cases will of course arise where courts find implied terms on the above traditional grounds,[24] there are also cases where they appear to have been more willing to imply terms because they appear reasonable in all the circumstances, rather than because of the supposed subjective intention of the parties, which, in the reality of a vague hiring, may have been non-existent. There is still a large role for the genuine factual implied term but in this context the court or tribunal may feel more ready to imply, or, more accurately perhaps, infer, a term because it seems reasonable in all the circumstances. This more objective approach can clearly be seen in the reasoning of the Court of Appeal in *Mears v Safecar Security Ltd*.[25] The case primarily concerned a complaint of failure to give the obligatory written statement of terms of employment, and the question of whether wages are to be paid during sickness,[26] but (although certain rather extreme dicta that ultimately a tribunal may have to 'invent' a term were

---

[19] *Reigate v Union Manufacturing Co (Ramsbottom) Ltd* [1918] 1 KB 592 at 605, CA, per Scrutton LJ.
[20] *The Moorcock* (1889) 14 PD 64 at 68, CA per Bowen LJ.
[21] *Shirlaw v Southern Foundries Ltd* [1939] 2 KB 206 at 227, CA, per McKinnon LJ; see *Spring v National Amalgamated Stevedores and Dockers Society* [1956] 2 All ER 221, [1956] 1 WLR 585.
[22] *Luxor (Eastbourne) Ltd v Cooper* [1941] AC 108 at 137, HL per Lord Wright.
[23] Certainty of terms is classically a prerequisite for a binding contract, but this too has been qualified almost to the point of extinction in contracts of employment: see *Powell v Braun* [1954] 1 All ER 484, [1954] 1 WLR 401, CA; and *National Coal Board v Galley* [1958] 1 All ER 91, [1958] 1 WLR 16, CA. The problem is that the result of applying it could be to make the whole contract of employment void (regardless of how long the employee had actually been working for the employer), which is simply not an option in employment law. On the other hand, the doctrine of certainty might apply to one particular aspect or term of the contract, where the rest of the agreement is not in issue: see *Fontana (GB) Ltd v Fabio*, n 12 above.
[24] See, eg, *Ali v Christian Salvesen Food Services Ltd* [1997] ICR 25, [1997] IRLR 17, CA, where the question was whether it was possible to imply a term into an 'annualised hours' contract as to what was to happen to an employee leaving part of the way through the year, the parties having failed to cover the point expressly. The EAT thought it was, but the Court of Appeal held to the contrary and the loss lay where it fell.
[25] [1982] 2 All ER 865, [1982] IRLR 183, CA.
[26] See Ch 2, heading 3(ii), p 84 and this chapter heading 5(ii), p 194.

later disapproved)[27] it also contains important guidance on the implication of terms into contracts of employment, showing that in the case of such contracts the normal concepts of implied intention of the parties and business efficacy may have little part to play. Instead, a tribunal may have to take a broader approach and be ready to insert a reasonable term based on all the evidence of the relationship between the parties *and* what had happened in practice *since* the employment began (particularly where it is important that *some* term be included, eg whether or not such pay is payable, or where the employee could be made to work).[28] It is true that this case arose under the Employment Rights Act 1996, section 11, and much of what is said about implying terms is inextricably linked to the court's approach to the tribunal's powers to declare or amend terms of employment under that section, but it is submitted that their approach to the implication of terms should be applicable to a common law action as well as a statutory one—it would be ridiculous if different principles were to apply depending on which forum the employee happened to choose; after all, on the facts of the case, the employee could just as easily have gone to the county court and *claimed* sick pay. The same approach can be seen in the later decision of the Court of Appeal in *Courtaulds Northern Spinning Ltd v Sibson*[29] where, in the context of the necessary implication into a contract of employment of a location/mobility clause (where the contract was silent on the matter, but the question was vital for deciding a point on constructive dismissal) Slade LJ said:

> [I]n cases such as the present where it is essential to imply some term into the contract of employment as to place of work, the court does not have to be satisfied that the parties, if asked, would in fact have agreed the term before entering into the contract. The court merely has to be satisfied that the implied term is one which the parties would probably have agreed *if they were being reasonable.* (Emphasis added)

(b) Imposed terms

The contract of employment has long been surrounded not only by terms implied or inferred from the facts of any given employment, but also by a quite distinct form of 'implied term', namely the term which will be imposed by the law onto most or all contracts of employment simply because the relationship of employment exists (except in so far as the parties are free to exclude it expressly and do so), which once again has little to do with any supposed intention of the parties. In *Lister v Romford Ice and Cold Storage Co Ltd*[30] Viscount Simonds said that the question whether there was an implied term that the employer would ensure that the employee was insured had little to do with the facts of a particular contract or any question of business efficacy, but depended instead on more general considerations relating to the very nature of

---

[27] *Eagland v British Telecommunications plc* [1993] ICR 644, [1992] IRLR 323, CA.
[28] See the facts of *Jones v Associated Tunnelling Co Ltd* [1981] IRLR 477.
[29] [1988] ICR 451, [1988] IRLR 305, CA; the dictum cited is at 460 and 309, respectively.
[30] [1957] AC 555, [1957] 1 All ER 125, HL.

contracts of employment. This approach is clearly seen in the following two dicta. In *Sterling Engineering Co Ltd v Patchett*[31] Lord Reid said:

> There are cases in which it has been said that the employer's right to inventions made by an employee in the course of his employment arises from an implied term in the contract of employment. Strictly speaking, I think that an implied term is something which, in the circumstances of a particular case, the law may read into the contract if the parties are silent, and it would be reasonable to do so; it is something over and above the ordinary incidents of the particular type of contract. If it were necessary in this case to find an implied term in that sense I should be in some difficulty. But the phrase 'implied term' can be used to denote a term inherent in the nature of the contract which the Law will imply in every case unless the parties agree to vary or exclude it.

In *Scally v Southern Health and Social Services Board*[32] Lord Bridge referred to the clear distinction between

> the search for an implied term necessary to give business efficacy to a particular contract and the search, based on wider considerations, for a term which the law will imply as a necessary incident of a definable category of contractual relationship.

In *Malik v BCCI SA (in liquidation)*[33] Lord Steyn referred to such terms as 'default rules' which are standardized terms that are incidents of all contracts of employment.

It is this form of 'implied term' that will be discussed below under the headings of 'Employer's implied duties' and 'Employee's implied duties', and it could well be argued that the phrase 'implied term' should be discarded, and these duties viewed simply as incidents of the law of employment.

(c) Overriding terms

One of the most interesting recent developments in this area is the possible development of the concept of 'overriding terms' in a contract of employment, ie that certain terms may be so important that they will be applied by the courts irrespective of the parties' intentions.[34] This would have the radical effect that they could even be used to qualify or attack clear express terms of the contract, something that in orthodox contract law

---

[31] [1955] AC 534 at 547, [1955] 1 All ER 369 at 376, HL.

[32] [1991] ICR 771, [1991] IRLR 522, HL; the decision in this case is considered under heading 3(vii), at p 157.

[33] [1997] ICR 606, [1997] IRLR 462, HL; the decision in this case is considered under heading 3(iv), at p 154.

[34] This would mark them off from the above discussion of imposed terms, since the latter (as in the above dictum from Lord Reid) are conceived of applying 'unless the parties agree to vary or exclude them'; see also per Lord Steyn in *Malik v BCCI*, n 33. For an interesting argument that the courts should go even further and hold that the employment relationship gives rise to *fiduciary* duties (which could not be excluded), see Clarke 'Mutual Trust and Confidence, Fiduciary Relationships and the Duty of Disclosure' (1999) 28 ILJ 348. The current judicial approach, however, is entirely to the contrary, finding no fiduciary duties in an ordinary employment relationship: *Nottingham University v Fishel* [2000] ICR 1462, [2000] IRLR 471: see Sims (2001) 30 ILJ 101. *Fishel* was approved by the Court of Appeal in *Ranson v Customer Systems plc* [2012] IRLR 769, CA.

no 'implied' term should be able to do. The prime candidate for beatification as an overriding term is the implied term of trust and respect[35] which, if applied widely, could be seen as having the effect that even where an employer has the contractual right to insist on something, he must do so *reasonably*. If not, the employee would be able to leave and claim constructive dismissal, through the employer's breach of that implied term. Perhaps the clearest example is an unrestricted mobility clause. Can the employer simply insist on the literal wording and require the employee to move his place of work from Norwich to Carlisle over a weekend and with no prior warning, or can the employee claim that that insistence (though technically within the employer's contractual power) is in breach of the term of trust and respect on the facts? Orthodox contract law is, of course, on the employer's side,[36] but there have been developments. Where there is no express mobility clause and a court is having to imply one, there may be less problem in attaching implied conditions such as reasonable notice.[37] However, what may eventually prove to have been the crucial step was taken by the EAT in *United Bank Ltd v Akhtar*,[38] where there was an express clause allowing the employer to move the employee to any branch in the UK. In spite of that, the EAT held that the employee could claim constructive dismissal when the employer ordered him to move from Leeds to Birmingham on only six days' notice and refused to grant his request for more time because of his personal circumstances. As well as finding an implied term of reasonable notice, the EAT held even more fundamentally that the employers' conduct in exercising their contractual rights was a fundamental breach of the implied term of trust and respect:

> We take it as inherent that there may well be conduct which is either calculated or likely to destroy or seriously damage the relationship of trust and respect between employer and employee which a literal interpretation of the written words of the contract might appear to justify, and it is in this sense that we consider that in the field of employment law it is proper to imply an *overriding obligation* [of trust and respect] which is independent of, and in addition to, the literal interpretation of the actions which are permitted to the employer under the terms of the contract.[39] (Emphasis added.)

At first sight, the subsequent EAT decision in *White v Reflecting Roadstuds Ltd*[40] may appear to resile from *Akhtar*, for it was held that an employee who resigned after a

---

[35] See heading 3(iv), at p 151.

[36] This straightforward approach was applied as late as *Rank Xerox Ltd v Churchill* [1988] IRLR 280.

[37] *Prestwick Circuits Ltd v McAndrew* [1990] IRLR 191, Ct of Sess; however, the Court of Appeal had earlier declined to add any 'reasonable exercise' conditions to an implied mobility clause in *Courtaulds Northern Spinning Ltd v Sibson* [1988] IRLR 305, CA.

[38] [1989] IRLR 507. See also *French v Barclays Bank plc* [1998] IRLR 646, CA where the termination of an interest-free bridging loan to a relocated employee when it became too onerous was held to be in breach of the term of trust and respect, even though the granting of such a loan was clearly expressed to be discretionary.

[39] At 512, per Knox J. There was an unreported tribunal decision in Cambridge in 1990 where an employee was dismissed for refusing to work 12 hours per day, seven days per week, for nine weeks; the employer had the power to require this under the strict terms of the contract, but the tribunal held that to do so was unreasonable, and the dismissal was unfair, on similar reasoning: see Earnshaw [1992] NLJ 1011.

[40] [1991] ICR 733, [1991] IRLR 331.

transfer on to a lower paid job which was permitted by the contract could not claim constructive dismissal. However, it is suggested that that was because the employee argued simply that a contractual right such as this must always be exercised reasonably; this was too much to accept and Wood P said that *Akhtar* does not establish any such sweeping principle. However, at the end of his judgment, he recognized that there was a problem with unconscionable action by an employer and offered the following solutions:

> As Knox J emphasised in *Akhtar* a purely 'capricious' decision would not be within the express mobility clause. Likewise, in the present case if there were no reasonable or sufficient grounds for the view that Mr White required to be moved … then there would be a breach of the clause. Secondly, it must be emphasised that as a result of the *Woods* decision[41] there is the *overriding implied term* as to the relationship of trust and respect between employer and employee and this is where communication is so important.[42] (Emphasis added.)

The implication must therefore be that in a case such as this the employee may have a good argument if it is couched properly (in terms of the term of trust and respect, *not* simply as a general allegation of unreasonableness), and that *White* does not negate *Akhtar*.[43]

In addition to mobility and flexibility clauses, similar ideas of the use of the overriding term of trust and respect to qualify or restrain reliance by an employer on his strict contractual rights have been seen in relation to the imposition of disciplinary measures,[44] the exercise of a power to suspend an employee[45] and (most strikingly of all) in the administration of employee pension funds.[46]

The other principal candidate so far for an overriding term is the employer's obligation to take care for the employee's health and safety. The leading case, *Johnstone v Bloomsbury Health Authority*,[47] shows very different approaches to the matter, which

---

[41] Ie *Woods v WM Car Services (Peterborough) Ltd* [1981] ICR 666, [1981] IRLR 347, the leading decision of Browne-Wilkinson P in the EAT on trust and respect; see heading 3(iv), at p 153.

[42] [1991] ICR 733 at 742, [1991] IRLR 331 at 335.

[43] In the unreported decision in *St Budeaux Royal British Legion Club v Cropper* (EAT 39/94) *Akhtar* was applied to hold that a flexibility clause applied in a 'high-handed and irresponsible manner' by the employer (when cutting hours) was a breach of the term of trust and respect.

[44] The idea being that the exercise by an employer of his discretion under a disciplinary procedure must be subject to requirements of reasonableness and proportionality: *BBC v Beckett* [1983] IRLR 43; *Cawley v South Wales Electricity Board* [1985] IRLR 89; *Stanley Cole (Wainfleet) Ltd v Sheridan* [2003] ICR 297, [2003] IRLR 52.

[45] *McClory v Post Office* [1992] ICR 758, [1993] IRLR 159. Previously, an express lay-off clause had been held to be subject to an implied limitation to a reasonable period in *Dakri & Co Ltd v Tiffen* [1981] ICR 256, [1981] IRLR 57, but a subsequent EAT had refused to follow this in *Kenneth MacRae Ltd v Dawson* [1984] IRLR 5.

[46] *Imperial Group Pension Trust Ltd v Imperial Tobacco Ltd* [1991] ICR 524, [1991] IRLR 66 where Browne-Wilkinson V-C (applying his own previous decision in *Woods v WM Car Services (Peterborough) Ltd* [1981] ICR 666, [1981] IRLR 347) held that the black and white of pension fund deeds and rules should be impliedly subject to the limitation that they must be exercised in good faith and so as not to undermine the employees' trust and respect: see Nobles (1991) 20 ILJ 137.

[47] [1991] ICR 269, [1991] IRLR 118, CA; see Dolding and Fawlk (1992) 55 MLR 562. At the time of writing, this is once again topical, but in the context of maximum hours under the working time legislation.

in turn shows well the conceptual difficulties yet to be addressed. This was the highly publicized case of the legal challenge to excessive hours by junior hospital doctors. The doctor plaintiff's contract stated a standard working week of 40 hours, but a further 48 hours on call, which was regularly required, sometimes up to 100 hours per week. He argued that this had a detrimental effect on his health[48] and was a breach of the employer's duty to take reasonable care for his health and safety. The proceedings in fact concerned an interlocutory application by the employers to have the claim struck out, as disclosing no cause of action. By a majority, the Court of Appeal allowed it to proceed. Leggett LJ, dissenting, applied orthodox contract law, stating that reliance on a clear express power could not make the employer in breach of an implied term (ie the traditional primacy of express terms; the doctor had signed the contract and must abide by its clear terms). The problem and fascination of the case is that the two majority judges differed in their reasoning. Browne-Wilkinson V-C took a middle path; he said that the extra 48 hours in question were an 'optional right' for the employers, not an absolute right and, while there must be no blatant conflict between an express term and an implied term, it was not improper to read in a term that, in exercising their *discretion* to call for further hours, the employers had to have regard to the employee's health and safety. However, possibly the more significant judgment for the future is that of Stuart-Smith LJ who held more simply that, although the contract gave the power to require work of up to 88 hours on average, that power had to be exercised subject to other contractual terms, in particular that relating to health and safety. The difference between the two majority judgments would be shown if a contract required a mandatory 88 hours, for Browne-Wilkinson V-C accepted that in that case that express term would have to be allowed to stand, whereas Stuart-Smith LJ would still have been prepared to make it subject to the requirement of health and safety.[49]

(ii) PARTICULAR SOURCES OF TERMS

(a) Collective bargains

Although its use as the primary form of setting terms and conditions of employment has declined markedly in recent years,[50] collective bargaining in the past was of central importance, and still is in areas retaining such coverage and yet the precise legal

---

[48] Let alone the prospects for a patient (treated in the hundredth hour) of a long and prosperous life.

[49] The judge makes the significant point that even where the contract stipulates high hours, that still only gives the employer a *power* to call for them: 'There is no obligation to require the men to [work] for 88 hours in the week, and if by so doing he exposes him to foreseeable risk of injury he will be liable': [1991] ICR 269 at 277, [1991] IRLR 118 at 121, CA.

[50] As early as 1992 it was found that 'the decline in the extent of union recognition naturally fed through into a fall in the proportion of employees covered by collective bargaining. This had shrunk to 54 per cent in 1990 from 71 per cent six years earlier. As most employees outside the scope of the survey [ie those employed by small firms] are almost certainly not covered, it is clear that only a minority of employees in the economy as a whole had their pay jointly determined by management and trade unions': Millward et al 'Workplace industrial relations in transition' (the ED/ESRC/PSI/ACAS Survey) (1992) p 102. Twelve years later, the 2004 Workplace

effect of a collective bargain on the contracts of employment of employees potentially affected by it has always been a topic of some difficulty. The bargain is often classified as performing two functions—regulating the relationship between the bargainers, ie employers' association or employer and trade union, and settling provisions (for example wage rates and hours) intended for the individual contracts of the employees who are covered. The collective bargain itself is generally not enforceable by the union or employer,[51] and, as the individual is a third party not privy to the agreement, it will not generally be directly enforceable by an employee, particularly as the union is not viewed as acting as the employee's agent during negotiations;[52] in *Burton Group Ltd v Smith*[53] the EAT considered that any agency relationship must be capable of inference from the particular facts of the case and does not arise merely from the relationship of union and member. Thus, the employee will only be legally entitled to any parts of a collective bargain which in some way became terms of his individual contract of employment.[54]

A term may be incorporated into a contract of employment from a collective bargain either expressly or impliedly. Express implication may come through the parties agreeing in writing that all or part of a particular collective bargain shall be binding upon them, as in *National Coal Board v Galley*.[55] In the past, this fitted in with the statutory requirements for written particulars in Part I of the Employment Rights Act 1996 (see above, under 'Form') which allowed the employer to refer the employee to some other document which the employee has reasonable opportunities of reading, and this 'other document' could well be the relevant parts of the current collective bargain. There may now be less scope for this approach, because of the amendments to Part I in 1993 and 2002 restricting the employer's right to refer to other documents (except in relation to sickness, pensions and disciplinary notice and guidance procedures); on the other hand, there was added to the list of matters to be notified in writing 'any collective agreements which directly affect the terms and conditions of the employment', which could be significant in any argument for the incorporation of terms other than those which now have to be given individually.

In *Marley v Forward Trust Group Ltd*[56] the EAT caused a considerable stir by holding that where a collective bargain was expressed to be binding in honour only,

---

Employment Survey found that (in workplaces with more than 10 employees) only 34% of employees were union members (64% in the public sector; 22% in the private sector). At that time there were 7.56m members; by 2011 this had declined further to 7.26m.

[51] *Ford Motor Co Ltd v Amalgamated Union of Engineering and Foundry Workers* [1969] 2 QB 303, [1969] 2 All ER 481 (see Selwyn (1969) 32 MLR 377); Trade Union and Labour Relations (Consolidation) Act 1992, s 179; see Chapter 1; *National Coal Board v National Union of Mineworkers* [1986] ICR 736, [1986] IRLR 439.

[52] *Holland v London Society of Compositors* (1924) 40 TLR 440; cf *Edwards v Skyways Ltd* [1964] 1 All ER 494, [1964] 1 WLR 349.

[53] [1977] IRLR 351.   [54] *Hulland v William Sanders & Sons* [1945] KB 78, [1944] 2 All ER 568, CA.

[55] [1958] 1 All ER 91, [1958] 1 WLR 16, CA.

[56] [1986] ICR 115, [1986] IRLR 43, EAT; revsd [1986] ICR 891, [1986] IRLR 369, CA, applying *Robertson and Jackson v British Gas Corpn* [1983] ICR 351, [1983] IRLR 302, CA.

a contractual term purporting to incorporate a provision from the bargain was itself therefore of no legal effect; fortunately, this startling decision was quickly reversed by the Court of Appeal and orthodoxy re-established. However, some care may be needed with this form of incorporation (where it is still viable), for reference to a particular aspect of a collective bargain (for example sickness) does not necessarily incorporate other aspects of it (for example the right to lay off employees) which may need specific incorporation,[57] and indeed the parties must be clear which particular collective agreement they are wishing to incorporate, which may not be as simple as it sounds where either there has been a series of agreements over a period of time or where there is, at any one time, more than one agreement possibly applicable; the latter possibility could well arise where there is both national and local bargaining within an industry, or where there has been a tendency over time to move the emphasis from national to local bargaining.[58] Moreover, in *Burroughs Machines Ltd v Timmoney*[59] the Court of Session, reversing the EAT, treated a contractual reference to a particular clause in a collective bargain as an independent term of the contract which merely relied on the clause for its exposition and definition, so that the employees continue to be bound by part of the clause that allowed the employer to lay them off in certain relevant circumstances, even though the employer had in fact left the employers' federation which was a party to the collective bargain. In this case the principle of the independent effect of a collective bargain term once incorporated worked to the employee's disadvantage. However, it is equally likely (if not more so) to work to the employer's disadvantage as can be seen from *Robertson and Jackson v British Gas Corpn*[60] where the Court of Appeal held that employees could still claim a bonus which had been incorporated into their contracts even though the collective agreement whence it had originally come had been unilaterally abrogated by the employer. The lesson is clear for an employer wishing to resile from the terms of a collective agreement—it may not be enough just to abrogate the agreement if in fact some of its provisions have been incorporated into individual contracts of employment; he may have to go further and show that those contracts have themselves also been *varied* (which will principally mean by consent, see Chapter 2, heading 6) to exclude or amend the terms in question.

In the absence of express reference, a tribunal or court may be asked to incorporate a term of a collective bargain by implication, and this may raise difficulties, for if one thing is certain it is that implication is by no means automatic. On a structural level, it cannot be argued that an agreement is incorporated simply because the employer

---

[57] *Jewell v Neptune Concrete Ltd* [1975] IRLR 147, IT; *Cadoux v Central Regional Council* [1986] IRLR 131, Ct of Sess; *Alexander v Standard Telephones and Cables Ltd (No 2)* [1991] IRLR 286.

[58] This problem can be seen on the facts of *Gascol Conversions Ltd v Mercer* [1974] ICR 420, [1974] IRLR 155, CA (see Ch 2 heading 3(ii), p 79). Site level bargaining was taken into account by the EAT in holding a site bonus to be contractually binding in *Donelan v Kerrby Constructions Ltd* [1983] ICR 237, [1983] IRLR 191.

[59] [1977] IRLR 404.

[60] [1983] ICR 351, [1983] IRLR 302, CA. See, to like effect, *Gibbons v Associated British Ports* [1985] IRLR 376.

belongs to an employers' association that bargained for that agreement.[61] Further, it must be remembered that vague reliance upon implied terms from collective bargains (whether national or local) cannot oust or qualify clear express terms of a contract of employment covering the matters in question.[62] In the old case of *Young v Canadian Northern Rly Co*[63] an employee sued the company for wrongful dismissal on the basis that his dismissal for redundancy was not in accordance with the agreed seniority provisions in a collective bargain; he was not a member of the union, but claimed that the company's practice was to observe the terms of the agreement and apply them to all employees, whether or not members of the union. The Privy Council held for the company, refusing to incorporate the necessary collective terms into his contract of employment. They said that he had not shown that the company's implementation of the collective bargain was due to contractual liability, that it was equally explicable on grounds of company policy, and that any remedy for breach, as in this case, was industrial and not legal. It may be argued that this is too strict an approach, making it too difficult to incorporate a collective bargain even in cases where there are no other clear, obvious terms in the contract of employment itself. All that can be said is that each case will depend on its own facts, and that one of the factors that may sway a court or tribunal is whether the clause of the bargain in question is really relevant to the individual circumstances of the employee claiming the benefit of it; if it concerns larger questions relating primarily to employment relations, such as recognition of one or more unions,[64] machinery for resolving collective disputes,[65] longer term policy planning on matters such as retraining or redundancy[66] or the allocation of staff numbers to particular duties,[67] the court or tribunal might decide that the clause is not to be incorporated into the contracts of the individuals concerned. On the other hand, if the correct inference is that it was envisaged that those conducting the bargaining would be binding those concerned in some relevant matters, the resulting clause might well

---

[61] *Hamilton v Futura Floors Ltd* [1990] IRLR 478, OH. There is a similar rule in the law relating to recognition, see Ch 9, heading 3(i), p 664.

[62] *Gascol Conversions Ltd v Mercer*, n 58.

[63] [1931] AC 83, PC; *Land v West Yorkshire Metropolitan County Council* [1979] ICR 452, [1979] IRLR 174; revsd on other grounds [1981] ICR 334, [1981] IRLR 87, CA.

[64] *Gallagher v Post Office* [1970] 3 All ER 712. Though cf *City and Hackney Health Authority v National Union of Public Employees* [1985] IRLR 252, CA where it was thought arguable (on an interlocutory application) that a clause from a Whitley Council agreement concerning shop stewards *was* incorporated into a steward's individual contract of employment.

[65] *National Coal Board v National Union of Mineworkers* [1986] ICR 736, [1986] IRLR 439; the judgment of Scott J is a useful affirmation of the principle.

[66] *British Leyland UK Ltd v McQuilken* [1978] IRLR 245. In *Alexander v Standard Telephones and Cables Ltd (No 2)* [1991] IRLR 286 the court refused to incorporate a term in a collective bargain covering seniority in the redundancy procedure, though in *Anderson v Pringle of Scotland Ltd* [1998] IRLR 64 the Court of Session thought that it was at least arguable (in interlocutory proceedings) that a redundancy handling clause in a collective government had been incorporated (*Alexander* not cited). Quaere whether a term quantifying individuals' severance payments might be appropriate for incorporation.

[67] *Malone v British Airways* [2011] ICR 125, [2011] IRLR 32, CA.

be incorporated into the individual contracts and so binding, as with the 'no-strike' clause in *Rookes v Barnard*.[68] How difficult this distinction may be in practice can be seen from *Kaur v MG Rover Group Ltd*[69] where one part of a major restructuring and flexibility deal with the unions (itself cast largely in aspirational terms) contained the remarkably precise statement by the management that there would (in return for the flexibility) be *no* compulsory redundancies. When, nine years later and in a very different economic situation, such redundancies were threatened, an employee brought a test case claiming that they would be in breach of her contract of employment. The judge at first instance caused quite a stir by holding that this statement had indeed been incorporated into her contact; on appeal, however, the Court of Appeal revised this decision and took the more traditional view that that part of the agreement was primarily concerned with large-scale issues of redundancy handling and, in spite of the unusual working, was not appropriate for incorporation into individual contracts.

One of the strongest arguments in favour of incorporation would be custom and practice, evidenced by previous changes in the individual's contract in line with changes in the collective bargain; likewise, the collective bargain may itself be used as evidence of custom and practice within an industry where for some reason it becomes necessary to decide on such matters.[70] In *Henry v London General Transport Services Ltd*[71] (a relatively rare modern case on this point) a management buyout involved negotiations with a recognized trade union leading to a 'framework agreement' worsening certain terms and conditions as a cost of retaining jobs. In the past, the company had negotiated annually with the union and changes in terms (beneficial or not) had always ensued from this, though the contracts were silent on the matter. When, two years later, 94 of the employees brought claims for unlawful deductions for wages on the basis that the new terms had never been incorporated into their contracts the Court of Appeal held that there was a custom or practice of change coming through dealings with that union; that custom was 'reasonable, certain and notorious' (see below) and so incorporation was proved and the claims failed.[72] This form of incorporation may thus defeat objection by dissidents who are union members; it has always been a known problem in the case of the non-unionist within a union shop. Ostensibly a similar principle should apply (especially if the non-member had taken the benefit in the past of union-negotiated increases in pay), but what little scrap of authority that exists on the point suggests a different approach.

---

[68] [1964] AC 1129, [1964] 1 All ER 367, HL. No-strike clauses may now only be incorporated into individual contracts in restricted circumstances: Trade Union and Labour Relations (Consolidation) Act 1992, s 180.

[69] [2005] IRLR 40, CA.

[70] *Howman & Son v Blyth* [1983] ICR 416, [1983] IRLR 139.

[71] [2002] ICR 910, [2002] IRLR 472.

[72] One complication was that in the past any new terms negotiated by the union had been put to a ballot of members; in the difficult circumstances of the buyout this had not been done. Was it an essential part of the custom and practice? This point was remitted to the tribunal. However, as an alternative the tribunal had held that the two-year delay meant that the employees had acquiesced to the new terms anyway and so lost their right to object; the Court of Appeal indicated that this was probably correct.

In *Singh v British Steel Corpn*[73] the employee resigned from the union which subsequently negotiated a new shift system which the employee did not want to work; he refused to work it and was dismissed. One of the questions in the case was whether the new union agreement could be considered to have been incorporated into his contract which would have thereby been modified and would have obliged him to work the new shift system. The tribunal held that it was not incorporated so he remained subject to his original contractual terms. The fact that he was no longer a member of the union obviously weighed heavily with the tribunal, and it will be recalled that in *Young v Canadian Northern Rly Co*, above, the employee was also a non-member and the fact that the employer in practice treated all employees alike was to little avail. To deny a non-unionist the rights (or, as in *Singh's* case, the obligations) under a collective bargain by not incorporating terms may perhaps seem just, but on the other hand, to say that *because* he was a non-member, therefore the term will not be incorporated would appear to be based principally on an agency theory (that the union always acts as agent of its members), which as seen above has been rejected in other contexts.

One final point to note is that the fact that incorporation of collective agreement terms is accomplished contractually may affect not just the incorporation itself, but also the *interpretation* of such terms. Although they may in practice have their origins in a loosely drafted collective agreement, probably the result of compromise and horse-trading, once they are incorporated into a contract they take effect as contractual terms and are to be interpreted as such. In *Hooper v British Railways Board*[74] a sick pay term was incorporated into an employee's contract from an agreement of the Railway Staff Joint Council; the problem was that it was (according to the employers) badly drafted, did not reflect what the employers considered to be the actual basis of agreement and (when applied literally) produced arguably a bizarre result. The employers argued that the fact that the term came from a collective agreement should be taken into account when interpreting and applying it, and that the court should also look at the real intent of the employers at the time, and at how it had subsequently been applied in practice. The Court of Appeal, however, disagreed and held that it must be construed in the normal contractual way, ie objectively as it stood, and *not* by reference to any subsequent behaviour of the parties. The case, with its relatively strict contractual approach, shows that even though collective agreements are not themselves legally binding, the drafting of any clauses within them that may be incorporated into individual contracts (either expressly or by implication) should be approached with care.

(b) Custom

Trade usage or custom may have a role to play in filling a gap in the expressed terms of a contract of employment,[75] or perhaps in the interpretation of a particular term (for

---

[73] [1974] IRLR 131, IT.   [74] [1988] IRLR 517, CA.

[75] Where this is the case, the Court of Appeal in *Mears v Safecar Security Ltd* [1982] ICR 626, [1982] IRLR 183, CA took a broad approach to the evidence that can be taken into account to imply the necessary term,

example an incorporated clause in a collective bargain, as already discussed),[76] as in the old cases of *Sager v H Ridehalgh & Son Ltd*[77] (custom that the employer might deduct sums from weavers' wages for bad work held to be part of the individual weaver's contract) and *Marshall v English Electric Co Ltd*[78] (established practice of using suspension as a disciplinary measure held to be incorporated). To be thus accepted, a custom must be certain, general (eg in a trade or a particular area) and reasonable, but the legal basis for its incorporation into a contract of employment is not certain—is it automatically incorporated once it is certain, general and reasonable? Or does it have to be known to and, perhaps freely accepted by the employee? In *Marshall v English Electric Co Ltd* there was a division of opinion, Lord Goddard accepting automatic incorporation, but du Parcq LJ (dissenting) considering that mere operation is not enough, there being some further element of acceptance necessary. *Meek v Port of London Authority*[79] is some authority in favour of a requirement of knowledge, but is a rather unusual case since it involved a change of employer and a custom (the payment by the employer of the employee's income tax if payable) which did not affect the employee when he commenced employment and had in fact been discontinued by the time the employee might be affected by it. It appears therefore that, although evidence of knowledge and acceptance might be most useful in establishing a binding custom, in some cases a custom might be applied without proof of them, and in particular in three instances:

(1) Where the custom is so notorious that the court or tribunal may take judicial notice of it.[80]

(2) Where it is so well established that the employee must be said to have accepted employment subject to it. In *Sagar v H Ridehalgh & Son Ltd* the practice of deductions from pay for bad work was widespread in Lancashire factories, and Lawrence LJ said:[81]

> I think that it is clear that the plaintiff accepted employment in the defendant's mill on the same terms as the other weavers employed at that mill ... Although I entirely agree with the [first instance judge] in finding it difficult to believe that the plaintiff did not know of the existence of the practice at the mill, I think that it is immaterial whether he knew or not, as I am satisfied that he accepted his employment on the same terms as to deductions for bad work as the other weavers at the mill.

in particular allowing evidence of actual working practices adopted or continued after the employment had commenced (following *Liverpool City Council v Irwin* [1977] AC 239, [1976] 2 All ER 39, HL and *Wilson v Maynard Shipbuilding Consultants AB* [1978] ICR 376, [1977] IRLR 491, CA); this involves stretching ordinary contract law, where terms are not normally to be construed by later conduct, but this may be essential in employment law: *Stevedoring and Haulage Services Ltd v Fuller* [2001] IRLR 627 at 628, CA, per Tuckey LJ.

[76] *Parry v Holst & Co Ltd* (1968) 3 ITR 317; *Dunlop Tyres Ltd v Blows* [2001] IRLR 629, CA, where it was said that later conduct could be used as a guide to interpreting an ambiguous collective agreement.

[77] [1931] 1 Ch 310, CA.   [78] [1945] 1 All ER 653, CA.

[79] [1918] 1 Ch 415. The decision in *Henry v London Transport Services Ltd* [2002] EWCA 488, [2002] ICR 910, [2002] IRLR 472 reaffirmed the 'certain, general and reasonable' formulation but did not address this point of knowledge because it concerned whether the custom existed at all.

[80] *George v Davies* [1911] 2 KB 445.   [81] [1931] 1 Ch 310 at 336, CA.

Much here may depend upon the certainty and generality of the custom, so that the mere fact that it has happened before in one firm may be insufficient.[82] Also there is the 'reasonableness' limb of the test which might be important.[83]

(3) Where a practice grew up while the employee was in that employment and he impliedly accepted it (eg by accepting benefits under it). This might be a less certain area, for it should not cover unilateral practices, and might be subject to du Parcq LJ's caveat in *Marshall v English Electric Co Ltd* that mere continuance at work may not be enough for acceptance, for it might be caused by other factors such as fear of dismissal.

One particular application of custom and practice merits special mention. This concerns the question whether payments ostensibly made by the employer on an ex gratia (ie non-contractual) basis, if made frequently or consistently, can be argued to become contractual through custom and practice, so that in future they can be *demanded* by the employees. In *Quinn v Calder Industrial Materials Ltd*[84] the employers had paid enhanced redundancy terms on four occasions between 1987 and 1994, pursuant to a management policy document but in each case as a result of an individual decision by senior managers. When redundancies were made in 1994 no such enhanced terms were offered and the employees claimed them as a contractual right by virtue of custom and practice. The EAT rejected this argument, on the basis of insufficient evidence that the employers intended the policy to have contractual effect. A similar result was reached in *Warman International v Wilson*,[85] and in *Hagen v ICI Chemicals and Polymers Ltd*[86] the court refused to incorporate a security of employment policy statement into individual contracts. However, these are ultimately decisions on the facts, and incorporation is legally possible. In *Albion Automotive Ltd v Walker*[87] the employers' predecessor (Volvo) had carried out six redundancy exercises between 1990 and 1994. Enhanced terms had been agreed with the union for the first, but in fact they were then given on each occasion. In 1995 the current employers took over the business and in 1999 made the applicant employees redundant, offering only the statutory redundancy payments. The applicants claimed the enhanced terms in a breach of contract action and won. Upholding the tribunal decision in their favour, the Court of Appeal pointed particularly to the facts that the policy was known to the employees; it had originally been adopted by agreement and reduced to writing; it had been applied frequently, and

[82] *Spencer Jones v Timmens Freeman* [1974] IRLR 325, IT; *Samways v Swan Hunter Shipbuilders Ltd* [1975] IRLR 190, IT.

[83] *Hardwick v Leeds Area Health Authority* [1975] IRLR 319, IT.

[84] [1996] IRLR 126. The EAT relied on the statement of Browne-Wilkinson P in *Duke v Reliance Systems* [1982] IRLR 347 that a unilaterally adopted management policy cannot become contractual on the grounds of custom and practice unless it is at least shown that the policy had been drawn to the attention of the employees or had been followed without exception for a substantial period.

[85] [2002] All ER (D) 94 (Mar).   [86] [2002] IRLR 31 at 42.

[87] [2002] IRLB 702 at para 9. There is the interesting twist that Albion were liable for their *predecessor's* custom and practice; this may be a salutary lesson for lawyers advising on a TUPE transfer.

automatically on each occasion; the employees had a reasonable expectation of benefiting from it; and the manner in which it was communicated implied contractual intent. Future cases on this important point will depend heavily on their facts, and mining the difficult middle ground between *Quinn* and *Albion*.

In the light of this uncertain legal position it is perhaps fortunate that the scope for custom in establishing terms of contracts of employment is much diminished in modern conditions, particularly in the light of the growing number of areas which are covered by statutory provisions or compulsory written terms, bearing in mind that the orthodox approach is that a 'custom' could not be used to overturn or alter a clear express term.[88]

(c) Works rules, company handbooks and policy statements

An employer may lay down works or company rules, and it is possible that these may become, in whole or in part, terms of the contract of employment particularly if the employee expressly agrees to abide by them or have some particular aspect of his employment governed by them, or if they are sufficiently brought to his notice when entering the employment. Also, some matters covered in a rule book may now be matters of which written notice must be given by statute, and so they may be strong evidence of the terms of employment by virtue of that (see above, under 'Form'). However, it is clear from *Secretary of State for Employment v Associated Society of Locomotive Engineers and Firemen (No 2)*[89] that not all such rules will have contractual effect. Lord Denning MR said:

> Each man signs a form saying that he will abide by the rules, but these rules are in no way terms of the contract of employment. They are only instructions to a man as to how he is to do his work.

The distinction between contractual and non-contractual rules is significant because if a rule is contractual, (1) it cannot be altered unilaterally by the employer, for that would require consensual variation in some form, and (2) the employee could, in the absence of such variation, insist upon continuing to work that rule and refuse to operate some other rule; if the rule is non-contractual, (1) it can be changed unilaterally by the employer for, being non-contractual, it remains in the sphere of managerial prerogative,[90] and (2) if an employee refuses to operate the amended rule, he is refusing to obey a proper order and so at common law could be dismissed and under the statutes would quite possibly be fairly dismissed. Thus, the more the rules are considered to be contractual, the more restraints are placed upon the manager's prerogative, and where a rule is not expressly made contractual in some way a court

---

[88] Although the dividing line between unacceptable alteration and acceptable interpretation may be a thin one, see *McColl v Norman Insurance Co Ltd* (1969) 4 ITR 285.

[89] [1972] 2 QB 455, [1972] 2 All ER 949, CA.

[90] See, eg, *Wandsworth London Borough Council v D'Silva* [1998] IRLR 193, CA where it was held that the council's sickness absence procedures were non-contractual and so could be lawfully altered by the council.

or tribunal may have to make a difficult decision whether it is to be considered contractual by implication. A particularly good example (in an area which had plagued personnel managers for several years prior to the smoking ban) is *Dryden v Greater Glasgow Health Board*[91] where the employers introduced a no-smoking policy into the hospital and the employee, a heavy smoker, left and claimed constructive dismissal. Her claim failed because the EAT held that the no-smoking policy was in the realm of working rules and employer discretion, and so there was no breach of contract on which to base constructive dismissal:

> There can, in our view, be no doubt that an employer is entitled to make rules for the conduct of employees in their place of work, as he is entitled to give lawful orders, within the scope of the contract.[92]

This longstanding law on 'works rules', itself rather an old-fashioned phrase, thus retains substantive significance and may be seen in two more current developments in managerial practice. The first is the modern tendency in medium and large firms to produce company handbooks; while these are in many ways a Good Thing (being readily available, relatively informal and much more of a guide to new employees) and are encouraged by ACAS, they could cause problems in that they may well mix together some matters that are formal contractual terms and others that are mere guidance or rules made within the managerial discretion, without any clear differentiation. *Keeley v Fosroc International Ltd*[93] is a good example of this problem. The handbook clause in question was under the heading 'Employee benefits and rights' and said that employees with two years' service were 'entitled' to an enhanced redundancy payment *but* its amount was to be left to collective and individual consultation. In spite of this lack of certainty, the Court of Appeal held that this clause *was* contractually enforceable, especially as redundancies were common in the firm and this clause was viewed as part and parcel of an employee's remuneration package.

The second development has been the increased use by employers of 'policies' of various kinds.[94] Again, these may or may not have contractual effect, though the cases

---

[91] [1992] IRLR 469.

[92] [1992] IRLR 469 at 471, per Lord Coulsfield. The employee's second argument (if, as found, there was no contractual entitlement to smoke) was that the introduction of the policy was in breach of the implied term of trust and respect, but this failed on the facts since the employer had adopted a reasonable procedure for introducing it. One might be tempted, however, to the mischievous thought that formal approval for such a blatant exercise in managerial prerogative might have been more controversial had the case not concerned the politically correct matter of the current Jihad against smokers.

[93] [2006] IRLR 961, CA. The 'handbook' may now in fact be electronic (eg as part of an employer's intranet); where, however, there is a changeover from hard copy to electronic, that does *not* give an employer carte blanche to make changes to any parts which had contractual status, ie the change is only to the *format* of the handbook, not to its substance: *Harlow v Artemis International Corpn Ltd* [2008] IRLR 629, (QBD).

[94] See the Code of Practice on sickness absence in *Wandsworth London Borough Council v D'Silva*, n 17 above. One variation of this problem is where a policy is initially non-contractual but is applied so frequently and/or consistently that it is later argued to have become incorporated into contracts by custom and practice: see p 137 above.

so far have not accorded them great legal significance. In *Secretary of State for Scotland v Taylor*[95] prison officers tried to oppose a unilateral decrease in their retirement age by arguing that it was a breach of contract because it contravened their employer's equal opportunities policy which included a reference to age discrimination; the Scottish EAT held that the policy was part of the contract (largely because the employer was hoist by its own petard by having introduced it in a way consistent with contractual intent), but as a matter of construction further held that the parties could not have intended it to outlaw an otherwise lawful retirement provision in the contract. Perhaps more significantly, when in *Grant v South-West Trains Ltd*[96] an attempt was made to establish sexual orientation discrimination as a breach of contract (again because it appeared in the firm's equal opportunities policy) Curtis J held that the policy was not part of the contract at all; it was merely a statement of aims and aspirations. Given the prevalence of various forms of policies, circulars, codes of practice or (God forbid) mission statements, this distinction is likely to be troublesome for some time to come.

In dismissal law, however, the practical effect of these matters may be diminished by the fact that the modern law on unfair dismissal is not concerned with technical questions of breach of contract but rather with the overall merits of the dismissal, and in this context it is clear that, whilst breach of the rules (whether contractual or not) may well be important in any given case, it will only be *evidence*, not a determinative factor, and the existence of works rules will in no way preclude a tribunal from looking into the overall fairness of the employer's actions. Thus, for example, in *Laws Stores Ltd v Oliphant*[97] the disciplinary section of the works rules said that cases of gross misconduct (including the disregard of till procedures which was in question) would normally result in immediate dismissal, but the EAT held that such a provision (or even one more mandatory) could not limit a tribunal's jurisdiction and held the dismissal, on the facts of the particular case, to be unfair. This case is perhaps an example of the decline in the purely contractual approach to employment.

---

[95] [1997] IRLR 608, EAT, upheld by the House of Lords (where the incorporation point was not argued): [2000] IRLR 502.

[96] [1998] IRLR 206, ECJ. One distinction with *Taylor* was that in the latter the employer's circular introducing the new equal opportunities policy had stated that it was being introduced into the employees' contracts of employment. There was no such evidence of contractual intent in *Grant*. Note that this *Grant* litigation was separate from and parallel to the main litigation which involved an ultimately unsuccessful argument before the ECJ that EC law on sex discrimination should also cover sexual orientation; see Ch 5, heading 4.

[97] [1978] IRLR 251. An equally good example is the imposition of a disciplinary penalty by the employer—he may technically have had the contractual power to impose the penalty in question, but it is still open to the employee to argue that on the facts of the case it was excessive (thus, for example, justifying the employee in walking out and claiming constructive dismissal): *BBC v Beckett* [1983] IRLR 43; *Cawley v South Wales Electricity Board* [1985] IRLR 89.

3 IMPLIED DUTIES OF THE EMPLOYER

(i) TO PAY WAGES

This obligation is so fundamental that the law relating to it is considered separately in Section 5.

(ii) TO PROVIDE WORK

The general common law position has been that there is no obligation to provide work for the employee to do; there is only the obligation to pay the wages which may be due under the particular contract of employment concerned. The classic, if now rather nostalgic, statement of this rule was given by Asquith J in *Collier v Sunday Referee Publishing Co Ltd*:[98]

> Provided I pay my cook her wages regularly, she cannot complain if I choose to take any or all of my meals out.

This means that in such a case the employer will not be in breach of contract by failing to provide work and so may, for example, normally give salary in lieu of notice.[99] However, the law recognized that in certain contracts the opportunity to work is of the essence, and so certain exceptions to the general rule evolved. In particular, it was held that there may be an obligation to provide work for an actor or singer where the publicity involved may be as important as the remuneration,[100] for an employee paid on a piecework[101] or commission[102] basis where actual work is necessary for him to earn his living, and possibly for an employee engaged to fill a specific office (particularly of a professional nature).[103] Outside such exceptional cases, however, the general rule applied, as can be seen in *Turner v Sawdon & Co*[104] where a sales-man on a fixed-term contract at a fixed salary was given no work to do but still paid

---

[98] [1940] 2 KB 647 at 650, [1940] 4 All ER 234 at 236.

[99] *Konski v Peet* [1915] 1 Ch 530. It is possible that in some cases, where the contract does not envisage dismissal with wages in lieu (either expressly or impliedly), such a dismissal will be a breach of contract *but* as damages have been paid in anticipation (by paying the wages due in the notice period) this will be a technical breach only and of little legal significance (except possibly where a restraint of trade clause is in issue): *Rex Stewart Jeffries Parker Ginsberg v Parker* [1988] IRLR 483, CA. See Ch 6, heading 2, p 427.

[100] *Fechter v Montgomery* (1863) 33 Beav 22; *Bunning v Lyric Theatre* (1894) 71 LT 396; *Marbé v George Edwardes (Daly's Theatre) Ltd* [1928] 1 KB 269, CA; the obligation may be to provide not just work, but work of a particular kind or standard, eg a leading part in a play as in *Herbert Clayton and Jack Waller Ltd v Oliver* [1930] AC 209, HL.

[101] *R v Welsh* (1853) 2 E & B 357; *Devonald v Rosser & Sons* [1906] 2 KB 728, CA.

[102] *Turner v Goldsmith* [1891] 1 QB 544, CA; *Bauman v Hulton Press Ltd* [1952] 2 All ER 1121.

[103] *Collier v Sunday Referee Publishing Co Ltd* [1940] 2 KB 647, [1940] 4 All ER 234.

[104] [1901] 2 KB 653, CA. Quaere whether the position would be different if it was more urgent that the employee should keep in practice, as for example in the case of a surgeon.

his salary and it was held, distinguishing *Turner v Goldsmith*,[105] that this was merely a contract to retain the employee so that the employer was not in breach of contract, in spite of the employee's assertions that denial of work would make him deteriorate as a salesman. However, some doubt was cast on this principle in *Langston v Amalgamated Union of Engineering Workers*[106] where an employee involved in an industrial dispute was suspended on full pay by his employer. To succeed in his claim against the union involved under now repealed legislation[107] he had to show that the dispute had induced a breach of contract, and this would only have been so if he had a contractual right to be provided with work since the employers were continuing to pay his salary. The Court of Appeal thought that the duty to provide work might exist, and in a strong judgment Lord Denning MR said that the previous authorities such as *Collier v Sunday Referee Publishing Co Ltd* were out of date, that the courts now recognize a 'right to work' and that this was one application of it. However, it must be remembered that this decision was only at an interlocutory stage, so that the Court of Appeal had to decide only if there was an arguable case on this point—they then did not have to *decide* the point, and the judgments of the other two members of the court, Cairns and Stephenson LJJ, are much less emphatic on the point than that of the Master of the Rolls. The case was remitted to the NIRC which held in the employee's favour[108] but on much more restricted grounds than those explored by Lord Denning, for Sir John Donaldson P held that this case came within one of the existing exceptions to the old rule, since under the contract the employee was to be paid premium payments for night shifts and overtime, so that he came within the pieceworker exception in that denial of actual work meant denial of opportunity to earn the premium payments. Thus, in its result, the case is in fact compatible with the old common law rule and its established exceptions.

This question of whether and when there is a right to work (or more accurately, whether a contract requires the provision of work in addition to the payment of wages) had been dormant for many years, but was revived in an unusual context in *William Hill Organisation Ltd v Tucker*.[109] The case concerned an attempt by an employer to construct an implied 'garden leave clause'[110] from the terms of the employee's contract,

---

[105] [1891] 1 QB 544, CA.

[106] [1974] 1 All ER 980, [1974] ICR 180, CA; see also *Breach v Epsylon Industries Ltd* [1976] ICR 316, [1976] IRLR 180; *Bosworth v Angus Jowett & Co Ltd* [1977] IRLR 374.

[107] Industrial Relations Act 1971, s 96.

[108] [1974] ICR 510, [1974] IRLR 182. It is made clear in the President's judgment that the employee had to work such shifts and hours as the employer stipulated, which made it easier to construe overtime as a contractual requirement; it is submitted, however, that purely voluntary overtime is not an essential part of a contract, and so failure to provide it should *not* be a breach of contract, and so not subject to the reasoning in *Langston's* case.

[109] [1999] ICR 291, [1998] IRLR 313, CA.

[110] A 'garden leave clause' is an alternative to a restraint of trade clause, whereby an employer puts an employee onto long notice with a provision that during that notice he can be sent home by the employer (to avoid damage to the employer's business) *but* cannot take any other work while still technically employed by that employer; see Ch 6, heading 2, p 430.

quite simply because they had omitted to put an express clause in. The contract contained a long (six months') notice provision; when the employee left with only one month's notice, the employers applied for an injunction restraining him from taking work elsewhere during the six-month period, on the basis that they were prepared to pay his wages *and* had a common law right to require him during that period to do no work for them or anyone else. The Court of Appeal held that that depended on whether his contract only required payment of wages (as the employers argued) *or* required the employers to provide him with work as well (in which case the employers would be in breach of contract and the employee could leave to take up other work); they thus revived the old controversy, and for good measure seemed to take an expansive view as to who can claim to have a sufficient interest in actually performing their work in order to claim that the contract is to be interpreted as requiring work to be provided, not just payment. Far from restricting it to theatrical or piecework/commission workers, they held that this employee, a senior 'spread betting' dealer with a betting organization, *did* have a right to be provided with work; there was thus no inherent right for the employer to put him on garden leave,[111] and so the employer's application for an injunction was refused. Factors leading to that conclusion were that the appointment was a specific and unique one, that the skills involved were those requiring constant practice and experience and that the contract contained certain provisions (as to obligations on the employee in carrying out his duties, training and an express power of suspension) which the court thought consistent with an obligation to provide work, provided that it was available. While the first point (a specific appointment) could point to a narrow future application of this case and some of the points on construction of the contract terms are, with respect, highly arguable, it is likely that most contention in any future cases will be over the second point—who will be considered to be in a job whose skills need constant honing and exercise, so as to come within a widened class of employees with some form of 'right to work'?[112]

Two further points might be mentioned. The first is that this uncertain area of law will only be relevant where there is no express term covering the provision of work, and where such provision is important to either of the parties, they are advised to incorporate a clause in the contract putting the matter beyond doubt. The second is that this topic may be allied to the question of the continuation of wages during stoppages of work and for present purposes it might be noted that at common law suspension without pay will only be lawful if there is an express or implied term in the

---

[111] As Morritt LJ stated at the end of his judgment, the answer of course is for the employer to use an *express* garden leave clause wherever there might arguably be a right to work (more often now, in the light of this case?). In *SG&R Valuation Services Co v Boudrais* [2008] IRLR 770, QBD there was no express clause *but* it was held that the employee's misconduct (soliciting customers before leaving employment) negated his right to be provided with work and the employer was allowed to keep him on a de facto garden leave for the (long) period of his notice.

[112] A similar case in a different context is *Land Securities Trillium Ltd v Thornley* [2005] IRLR 765 where one factor in construing a flexibility clause narrowly was that the employer was trying to use it to move the employee away completely from her professional work, in which she had an interest.

particular contract to that effect; that failure to provide work may constitute a lay-off, thus activating certain statutory provisions (principally concerned with redundancy—Employment Rights Act 1996, sections 147–154); and that in the absence of continuing contractual payments the employee may be eligible for a statutory guarantee payment under the 1996 Act, sections 28–35.

(iii) TO EXERCISE CARE—GENERALLY AND IN RELATION TO WORK-RELATED STRESS CASES AND EMPLOYMENT REFERENCES

On a general level, this matter will normally relate to care for the employee's health and safety for the employer's common law duty of care is one of the bases of the law relating to the compensation of an injured employee. However, four particular applications of it are important also in mainstream employment law. The first is that one of the commonly accepted aspects of this overall duty is that the employer must provide competent and safe fellow employees,[113] for example to protect the employee from practical jokers; one effect of this is that there may be a positive common law obligation upon the employer to be rid of a potentially dangerous employee and this should be a good defence to an allegation of unfair dismissal by that employee, provided the necessary procedures are used in effecting the dismissal. The second is that the general duty of care may be construed as including an obligation upon the employer to pay attention to complaints from an employee that a particular appliance, method, etc is unsafe and to act reasonably in dealing with matters of safety; if the employer does not do so, not only may the employee be justified in walking out and claiming, for the purposes of unfair dismissal, to have been constructively dismissed[114] but also that dismissal may well be automatically unfair.[115] The third is that the employer may be under an obligation to indemnify the employee against expenses necessarily incurred in the course of his employment, which may include the cost of defending legal proceedings, though not where the fault was purely that of the employee and only collateral to the performance of his duties;[116] there is, however, no implied obligation to insure the employee's activities to any greater extent than is required by law.[117] The fourth is that the specialized duty of care will in general not extend to a duty to take care of the

---

[113] *Wilsons & Clyde Coal Co Ltd v English* [1938] AC 57, HL; *Hudson v Ridge Manufacturing Co Ltd* [1957] 2 QB 348, [1957] 2 All ER 229.

[114] *British Aircraft Corpn v Austin* [1978] IRLR 332; cf *Lindsay v Dunlop Ltd* [1980] IRLR 93.

[115] Employment Rights Act 1996, s 100, see Ch 7, heading 5(iv), p 523.

[116] *Burrows v Rhodes* [1899] 1 QB 816; *Re Famatina Development Corpn* [1914] 2 Ch 271, CA; *Gregory v Ford* [1951] 1 All ER 121.

[117] *Lister v Romford Ice and Cold Storage Co Ltd* [1957] AC 555, [1957] 1 All ER 125, HL. In a case where insurance cover is likely to be important, the employee is advised to make the position clear with the employer, especially since the decision in *Merrett v Babb* [2001] EWCA Civ 214, [2001] QB 1174, that when the employer went out of business the individual employee could be liable in damages for bad advice given during employment.

employee's belongings;[118] any possible liability for loss of the employee's goods would
have to arise on ordinary principles of tort if there was evidence of particular proximity
between the particular employer and employee, not just on the employment relationship per se, or possibly under the Workplace (Health, Safety and Welfare) Regulations
1992, regulation 23 which provides for 'suitable and sufficient accommodation' for
clothing not worn during working hours.[119]

In addition to these longstanding applications of the general implied duty on the
employer to exercise care, two areas of considerable modern concern have taken this
duty much further on than its origins in physical injury to the employee in a workplace
accident. These are the expanding law relating to workplace stress-induced injuries
(still largely a health and safety issue, but going well beyond traditional accident-based
liability) and the possible liability for a negligently written reference (which expands
the duty into the employee's, or ex-employee's future financial interests).

The expanding case law on psychiatric injury from mental stress at work has been a
major feature of personal injury litigation in recent years. It has developed separately
from the longstanding law on 'nervous shock' in the law of tort,[120] and at a journalistic
level has been much discussed in the press as an example of our alleged 'compensation
culture'. Clearly this is an area where it was always going to be difficult to strike the
right balance. The dam appeared to burst with (ironically) a first instance decision in
a single case, *Walker v Northumberland County Council*.[121] A social worker succeeded
in a claim for damages for common law negligence against his employers, based on
the second, debilitating nervous breakdown that he suffered due to the ever-increasing
workload placed on him and the failure of the employer to provide help which had
been promised after the first breakdown. This widely reported decision (unfortunately
not appealed) caused considerable consternation in personnel circles, especially with
its ruling that the employer could not raise as a defence that the increased workload
was caused by externally imposed financial cutbacks. It raised the interesting prospect
of the old common law contractual and tortious duty of care at work taking on a new
role as possibly the only counterweight to what has seemed over time an irresistible
movement in so many kinds of work to demand more and more of fewer and fewer
employees and call it economic efficiency.

It also showed the continuing vitality of the common law in areas not yet covered
by protective legislation. Interest in, and concern about, this novel form of liability

---

[118] *Deyong v Shenburn* [1946] KB 227, [1946] 1 All ER 226, CA; *Edwards v West Herts Group Hospital Management Committee* [1957] 1 All ER 541, [1957] 1 WLR 415, CA.

[119] *McCarthy v Daily Mirror Newspapers Ltd* [1949] 1 All ER 801, CA (on the equivalent provision under
the old Factories Acts).

[120] Nervous shock cases tend to arise from trauma (eg being involved in an accident caused by the
defendant) whereas stress cases tend to arise from a process over time, eg incessant excessive work demands.
Of course, there could still be liability to an employee for trauma-induced mental injury at work, but here there
is no special protection for an employee, who must still comply with the normal rules for nervous shock: *White
v Chief Constable of South Yorkshire Police* [1999] 2 AC 455, [1999] 1 All ER 1, HL.

[121] [1995] IRLR 35, [1995] 1 All ER 737.

grew exponentially, straddling employment law and personal injury litigation, and was eventually subject to detailed review in what is now the leading case, *Sutherland v Hatton*.[122] This was in fact four conjoined appeals which gave the Court of Appeal the opportunity to consider the law here generally. The judgment of the court given by Hale LJ (as she then was) contains a survey of the background to this kind of litigation, anchoring it firmly into the principles of negligence and the duty of care on the employer, as extended into the area of mental rather than physical injury. Of crucial importance, at paragraph 43, the judge reduces all of this to 16 'practical propositions' which have become the *locus classicus* on this whole subject. While these should be read in full by anyone dealing with it, the key points are as follows: (1) the ordinary principles of employer's liability apply to this novel area, which therefore focus on foreseeability of the injury to the employer; (2) mental disorder will be inherently more difficult to foresee than physical injury and an employer will normally be entitled to assume that the employee can withstand the normal pressures of the work; (3) there are no inherently dangerous jobs in relation to stress and so much will depend on whether the demands on that employee have been excessive, perhaps evidenced by a history of sickness (including by other employees) and complaints; (4) the employer is normally entitled to take what the employee says at face value (eg if he or she is denying difficulty in coping); (5) the employer will only be in breach of duty if he has failed to take steps which he could reasonably have been expected to take, which may involve consideration of the size and resources of the firm and the need to treat other employees fairly as well; (6) an employer who offers a confidential counselling service is unlikely to be found to be in breach of duty;[123] (7) if the only way to avoid the danger was to dismiss or demote the employee, an employer will not be in breach of duty by allowing a willing employee to continue working;[124] (8) causation must be proved, which means showing that the injury was caused by the breach of duty, not simply by the stress itself; (9) on causal grounds, where the stress was caused only partly by the work (eg where the employee also had difficulties outside work) the employer must only pay for his share and if necessary the court must apportion the blame when awarding damages.

---

[122] [2002] ICR 613, [2002] IRLR 263, CA.

[123] This proposition was thought particularly important in personnel management; it was elaborated further in *Hartman v SE Essex Mental Health NHS Trust* [2005] IRLR 293, CA where it was held that if the employee disclosed problems to a counsellor in confidence, telling the counsellor not to disclose them to managers the employer is *not* fixed with knowledge of them for the purpose of establishing foreseeability of harm. However, a counselling service will not always be a panacea, and the Court of Appeal subsequently took a more cautious approach, especially where the real cause of problems was the workload itself, not the employee's personal difficulties with it: *Daw v Intel Corpn Ltd* [2007] IRLR 535, CA; *Dickins v O2 plc* [2009] IRLR 58, CA.

[124] This point has caused problems in health and safety law generally—the traditional approach was that the relationship is not teacher/pupil, that an employee is an adult and so able to make his own decision to carry on working in the knowledge of the danger (*Withers v Perry Chain Co Ltd* [1961] 3 All ER 676, CA). However, in *Coxall v Goodyear GB Ltd* [2002] IRLR 742 there was liability (for a physical injury) for allowing a willing employee to continue working, and the court envisaged a possible duty on the employer ultimately to dismiss if no other way round the danger could be found.

There was a further appeal to the House of Lords (sub nom *Barber v Somerset CC*)[125] but this turned out to be largely a question of the *application* of these principles to the facts of one of the four cases in the original appeal. Thus, it is still to the principles set out by Hale LJ that the lawyer must look as the essential starting point, as accepted by the Court of Appeal in *Hartman v SE Essex Mental Health NHS Trust*.[126] What these principles seek to do is to hold liable the bad employer but at the same time to give viable defences to the good employer who either could not have foreseen what was about to happen or who generally tried to cope with it. Contrary to journalistic arguments about our 'compensation culture', *Sutherland v Hatton* can make these cases far from easy for the claimant, especially where he or she did not show clear signs of difficulties (perhaps deliberately concealing them), then suddenly imploded (perhaps after only one or two altercations with a manager), went off 'with stress' and never returned; in such a case the end result may well be no liability on the employer.[127] Given the amount of concern expressed about the levels of stress litigation after *Walker v Northumberland CC*, the judgment in *Sutherland v Hatton* seemed to provide a balanced and highly desirable settlement of the law.

There are, however, two possible threats to that settlement. The first is the possible effect of disability discrimination law. If the stress-induced injury is sufficiently serious to constitute a 'disability'[128] then different rules come into play in addition; once a claimant alleges breach of this Act, the question becomes not whether the employer could have foreseen the injury but what steps were taken post-injury by way of 'reasonable adjustments' (in particular to ease the way back into employment for the employee absent with the stress-induced condition). While this may be a considerable complication in a case, it is a longstanding one, relatively well understood by employment lawyers who often have to operate on the cusp between employment law and discrimination law. However, the second threat came like a bolt from the blue and is capable of constituting a most unfortunate '*Sutherland v Hatton* by-pass', destabilizing the law in this area. In *Majrowski v Guy's and St Thomas's NHS Trust*;[129] the claimant sued for damages for stress-induced injury in relation to alleged bullying and harassment by a line manager. As this was not over a long period and he seemed to have done little by way of complaint, he would probably have failed for lack of foreseeability under *Sutherland v Hatton*; moreover, he had brought his action four years later, and so an ordinary personal injury action would have been statute barred anyway. In the light of this, his lawyers sued instead under the Protection from Harassment Act 1997.

---

[125] [2004] ICR 457, [2004] IRLR 475, HL.

[126] See n 123. This is again an interesting case factually because it concerned six conjoined appeals with facts going across a whole spectrum of difficult types of stress case, including one of mental injury caused by trauma at work. While most of the litigation here will be in tort, *Sutherland v Hatton* is potentially of general application, as the EAT held in *Marshall Specialist Vehicles Ltd v Osborne* [2003] IRLR 672 when applying it in a constructive dismissal case to determine whether the stress in question justified the employee leaving the employment.

[127] As in *Pratley v Surrey CC* [2003] IRLR 794, CA and *Bonsor v UK Coal Mining Ltd* [2004] IRLR 164, CA.

[128] See Ch 5, heading 7(i), p 389.   [129] [2006] IRLR 695, HL.

This Act was clearly meant to give protection to individuals from *stalking* activities; it makes 'harassment' a criminal offence (without defining it) backed by restraining orders, but almost as a side effect attaches a right of civil action for the victim, subject to a *six*-year limitation period and with the possibility of damages merely for 'anxiety' caused by the harassment. Ostensibly, this Act had nothing to do with employment law but on the other hand the Act is so vague and broadly drafted that nothing excludes it from that area either. When the claimant here brought his action under the Act rather than at common law, the trial judge rejected the claim, saying that it was inappropriate in the employment context. The Court of Appeal reversed this by 2–1, with a strong dissent denying the applicability of the Act at all, but a further appeal to the House of Lords held unanimously that the Act applies to facts such as these. Although only one judge so held with approval, the others feeling compelled to come to that result as a matter of statutory interpretation (and expressing sympathy as a matter of policy with the dissenting judge in the Court of Appeal), the result is clearly that this avenue is now open to a claimant where the cause of the occupational stress is alleged to be harassing action by another at work. The results of this are as follows: (1) although the Act is cast in terms of liability on the actual perpetrator, in a civil action the claimant can sue the employer for being *vicariously liable* for the perpetrator's actions, and vicarious liability is *strict* (requiring no foreseeability by the employer, or indeed any fault at all);[130] (2) 'harassment' is not defined and remains purely a question of fact (with a potentially difficult borderline between active management of an underperforming employee and unlawful harassment);[131] (3) the time limitation is not three years but six (a long time for memories to fade and relevant staff to turn over); (4) damages can be awarded merely for anxiety, thus breaking the link with the mental *injury* which was so important in *Sutherland v Hatton*; (5) if the cause of the harassment was sex, race, disability, sexual orientation, religion or belief or age the normal expectation would be action under the relevant discrimination law where the employer would have the defence that all reasonable steps were taken to prevent that or things like it happening, but under the 1997 Act (which apparently can be used as an alternative to a discrimination action as well as to a common law negligence action) there is *no* such defence available to the employer. While several of their lordships in *Majrowski*

---

[130] Majrowski did not sue the individual manager at all, and there was no requirement to do so. Moreover, vicarious liability will be particularly applicable in one of these cases since the law was changed in *Lister v Hesley Hall Ltd* [2001] ICR 665, [2001] IRLR 472, HL to replace the old 'expressly or impliedly authorised' test for when a employee is acting in the course of employment with a much wider 'reasonable work connection' test. If the bullying manager was doing it in working hours, the employer will now almost certainly be vicariously liable, with little chance of showing that the manager was acting 'on a frolic of his own', ie purely personally.

[131] Lady Hale said that it was important for the courts to draw 'sensible lines between the ordinary banter and badinage of life and genuinely offensive and unacceptable behaviour'. The only limitations in the Act are that it must be such that a reasonable person would think the course of conduct amounted to harassment of another (s 1(2)) and that there must indeed be a *course* of conduct (s 1(1)), so that a one-off event is not covered (see *Banks v Ablex Ltd* [2005] IRLR 357, CA).

tried to play down the floodgates arguments against allowing the 1997 Act to apply in the employment context,[132] the exact limits of liability are likely to remain disputed. In *Sunderland CC v Conn*[132a] the Court of Appeal showed a more wary approach, holding that two instances of bad temper by a supervisor (only one of which was aimed at the claimant) fell far short of the threshold required to constitute 'harassment' under the Act. In doing so, they said that where that threshold lies may well vary with the nature of the employment, and that it must be serious enough to be potentially *criminal* under the *primary* provisions of the Act. This quasi-criminal standard was then downplayed by a subsequent Court of Appeal in *Veakins v Kier Islington Ltd*[133] where a more general emphasis on 'oppressive and unacceptable conduct' was preferred but then in the first instance decision in *Dowson v Chief Constable of Northumbria Police*[134] the quasi-criminal test was again applied. In spite of these arguments, however, (and judicial comments that liability under the 1997 Act is not to be found readily) the genie is now out of the proverbial bottle and available for use.

The second area of considerable current interest concerns the application of a duty of care to the giving of references by an employer or ex-employer. There could, of course, be liability for a negligently written reference to the new employer,[135] but the question arose whether the employee as the *subject* of the reference could sue in negligence, for breach of a duty of care. The House of Lords in *Spring v Guardian Assurance plc*[136] (reversing a more cautious decision by the Court of Appeal) held that there could be such a duty on the employer giving a reference; it lies both in tort (according to Lord Goff on a *Hedley Byrne*-style assumption of responsibility, and according to Lords Lowry, Slynn and Woolf on the basis that this extension of liability is fair, just and reasonable, and concerning a sufficiently proximate relationship) and also in contract, based upon a breach of this implied term. This decision does not prevent the giving of a bad reference, only a negligently bad reference, and their Lordships were not persuaded by the argument that to impose liability would deter people from writing references. Subsequent case law has explored this new form of liability to the subject of the reference. One key question is how comprehensive a reference needs to be in order to discharge the duty of care. This point was addressed in the most important explanatory case to date, *Bartholomew v London Borough of Hackney*[137] where the Court of

---

[132] The Act has been used by employers to protect their staff against threats from outsiders, eg animal rights extremists; in *First Global Locums v Cosias* [2005] IRLR 873 it was successfully used to restrain an ex-employee who had reacted to being disciplined and dismissed by making death threats against fellow employees.

[132a] [2008] IRLR 324, CA.

[133] [2010] IRLR 132, CA.   [134] [2010] EWHC 2612 (QB).

[135] Under the ordinary principles of *Hedley Byrne & Co Ltd v Heller & Partners Ltd* [1964] AC 465, [1963] 2 All ER 575, HL.

[136] [1994] ICR 596, [1994] IRLR 460, HL. The decision was by 4–1, with Lord Keith dissenting. The majority held that a duty of care did exist on the facts, but this does not mean that an action will always succeed in such circumstances—the question of causation must also be established (did the employee fail to get new employment because of the negligent reference?); where the plaintiff was one of many applicants, that may be difficult to prove.

[137] [1999] IRLR 246, CA, applied in *Kidd v Axa Equity and Law Life Assurance Society plc* [2000] IRLR 301 and *Jackson v Liverpool City Council* [2011] IRLR 1009, CA. In *Legal and General Assurance Ltd v Kirk*

Appeal adopted from defamation law the rule that the reference must be true, accurate and fair, but need not necessarily be full and comprehensive. The latter part of this means that the subject has no right to insist on particular information being in it; content remains a decision for the referee provided that the end result is not misleading (either positively or through the effect of an omission). This has been particularly important when addressing a well-known problem here—what is the referee to say when the employee left while still subject to unfinished disciplinary investigations? In *Bartholomew* a reference was requested by a potential employer on an individual who had left the referee's employment in a negotiated termination while under investigation for financial irregularities. The reference stated this as a fact and the individual was refused the post. When he sued under *Spring* the Court of Appeal held for the defendant referee; the reference was factually accurate, it did not give a misleading impression and the individual had no right to demand that it should have contained further explanatory or exculpatory material. However, in *Cox v Sun Alliance Life Ltd*[138] an ex-employer giving a reference overstepped an important line here by going beyond a factual statement that allegations had been made (at a very late stage) against the individual and gave the impression that there was substance to them (so that he may well have been dismissed if he had not resigned), even though these allegations had *not* been investigated, or even put to the individual for his reactions. The Court of Appeal upheld his claim in negligence; the basis for this was that if value judgments are to be made as to guilt and included in the reference they must (to satisfy the duty of care) be made on the basis of reasonable investigation. Mummery LJ made an interesting analogy here with the law of unfair dismissal where a dismissal for suspected misconduct will only be fair after a reasonable investigation has led to a positive belief in guilt;[139] if a dismissal requires this, so does a later reference. Short of such an investigation, the referee ex-employer should stick to factual statements and to value judgements only on any parts of the investigation that had been completed.

The law's application to employment references has thus developed out of all recognition in the last decade, though entirely in relation to the reference's subject, not its recipient. This is likely to continue because of another development in a different field. Traditionally references on employees were wholly confidential and so,

---

[2002] IRLR 125 it was held that, the action lying in tort, an actual reference must have been given in order for a cause of action to arise: the employee cannot sue on the basis that the ex-employer is *proposing* to give a reference in terms to which he or she objects. However, in a different context, it was held in *TSB Bank Ltd v Harris* [2000] IRLR 157 that an employee (still in employment) discovering that misleading references were being given about her could leave and claim constructive dismissal on the basis of breach of the implied term of trust and respect.

[138] [2001] EWCA Civ 649, [2001] IRLR 448. Part of the ex-employee's complaint was that a form of reference had been agreed as part of a termination settlement but the employer had ignored this. There could be a problem with an agreed reference as part of a settlement (a common practice)—if it was misleadingly incomplete, to hide misdeeds by the departing employee, there could be *Hedley Byrne* liability to the *recipient* (the new employer); presumably the fact of agreement between referee and subject would be no defence to such liability, provided that damage and causation could be proved.

[139] *British Home Stores Ltd v Burchell* [1980] ICR 303n, [1978] IRLR 379; see p 519 below.

even if the subject suspected that poor opinions were being expressed by the referee (for example if turned down for several jobs, having named the same referee), it was quite likely that he or she would never actually know that or be able to prove it. Now, however, there has been a major change almost by a side-wind. By virtue of the Data Protection Act 1998 an employment reference, though unavailable to the subject in the hands of the referee, *can* be demanded by the subject in the hands of the recipient (the only exception being if it refers to third parties who have their own confidentiality interest, though this is unlikely in an employment reference).[140] Whatever the logic of this strange position may be, it is capable of revolutionizing the practice of reference writing, though whether overall for the better may be arguable. The discoverability of references may well lead to yet more litigation in this area by their subjects.

Finally, one continuing problem is whether there is any implied obligation on an (ex-) employer to *give* a reference; it has normally been thought that there is no such obligation, but in the speech of Lord Woolf in *Spring* there is a passage suggesting that in certain circumstances (where references are known to be an essential element of recruitment) it may be necessary to imply just such an obligation.[141] As with the whole of the case, this could be seen against the factual background of the plaintiff seeking new employment under the financial services sector rules (with their mandatory references), but equally both these remarks and the case itself are expressed in general terms potentially applicable either to employment generally or at least to types of employment where references play an important part in recruitment. On the other hand, Lord Slynn pointed out that it is open to the reference-giver to state specifically the parameters within which the reference is given (and any limitations on his knowledge of the employee) or, ultimately, to rely on the *Hedley Byrne* aspect of the case to make his agreement to the employee to give the reference subject to an express disclaimer of liability. Further judicial guidance on these important points in the general context (ie not just in the financial services sector) is needed.

(iv) TO TREAT THE EMPLOYEE WITH RESPECT

In modern employment law there has been a restatement of implied duties of mutual respect between employer and employee. In certain employments, particularly of a domestic nature, this may require positive courtesy[142] while in others it may mean treating each other with such a degree of consideration and tolerance as would allow the contract to be executed. This is, of course, a vague concept which will vary with the circumstances, and if there is a more concrete area of dispute in any given case

---

[140] Data Protection Act 1998 s 7 and Sch 7 para 1. For the Information Commissioner's advice as to handling requests for references, see Ch 2, heading 2(ii), p 76.

[141] [1994] ICR 596 at 647, [1994] IRLR 460 at 481. In addition, the ECJ have held that if an employer *refuses* to give a reference to retaliation for a sex discrimination complaint made by the employee, that itself can constitute unlawful sex discrimination: *Coote v Granada Hospitality Ltd* C-185/97 [1999] ICR 100, [1998] IRLR 656, ECJ, applied in *Coote (No 2)* [1999] ICR 942, [1999] IRLR 452, EAT.

[142] *Wilson v Racher* [1974] ICR 428, [1974] IRLR 114, CA.

questions of want of 'respect' will be of secondary importance.[143] However, an obligation upon the employer to treat the employee with respect and not to act in a manner
likely to destroy or seriously damage the relationship of trust and confidence without
good cause may be seen as a corollary of the employee's general duty of faithful service,
as confirmed in *British Telecommunications plc v Ticehurst*.[144] Given that the line is
still strongly held that employment is *not* a fiduciary relationship and so generalized
mutual duties of good faith are not to be incorporated that way,[145] the development
of this implied term has meant that more particular duties can be imposed when
necessary in order to govern the employment relationship, in particular to restrain
inequitable exercises of contractual power by the employer; at times, such duties come
very close to fiduciary or 'good faith' ones but by using a more acceptable contractual
analysis.[146] Moreover, it is argued above[147] that there are developments suggesting not
only that this is a well-established and much-used implied term, but that it is assuming
an overriding nature, capable of qualifying the ability of an employer to rely on a literal
application of his rights under a contract of employment.

The development of such a term is perhaps not so surprising, for the advent of the
law on unfair dismissal has restricted the employer's prerogative to dismiss so that good
personnel management has become an essential, not an optional extra.[148] The overall
requirement of fair dismissal procedures, for example, has meant that more notice has
to be taken of the employee's viewpoint, and the employer is expected not just to assess
conduct and issue warnings, but also to take more positive action to assist or train
the employee to meet any required standards of competence or conduct. Moreover, in
one important area of unfair dismissal law, the concept of an implied duty of respect
has taken on definite significance; this is in the area of 'constructive dismissal'. This is

---

[143] As in *Donovan v Invicta Airways Ltd* [1970] 1 Lloyd's Rep 486, CA.

[144] [1992] ICR 383, [1992] IRLR 219, CA; see p 185.

[145] *Nottingham University v Fishel* [2000] ICR 1462, [2000] IRLR 471.

[146] For the evolution of the term generally, see Lindsay J: 'The Implied Term of Trust and Confidence' (2001)
30 ILJ 1 and see Cabrelli 'The Implied Duty of Mutual Trust and Confidence: An Emerging Overarching Principle'
(2005) 34 ILJ 284 for an argument that this remains a separate implied term, not an adjunct of the term of reasonable care. Terminology may be significant; the term tends to be expressed in the negative (*not* to act in such a way as
to *destroy* trust and confidence/respect) because a positive formulation (that the employer *must* act in a particular
way) could suggest a wider, reasonableness test at which courts have baulked (see p 128). If necessary, however,
the term *can* place positive obligations on the employer: *Transco plc v O'Brien* [2002] ICR 721, [2002] IRLR 444,
CA. One balance for the employer is the qualification that the employer must not behave in the way in question
'without reasonable and proper cause': *Hilton v Shiner Ltd* [2001] IRLR 727.

[147] See p 127.

[148] In *Cantor Fitzgerald International v Bird* [2002] IRLR 867 breach of the term came from the manner of
the employer's dealings with the employees when changing their contracts; in *Stanley Cole (Wainfleet) Ltd v
Sheridan* [2003] ICR 297, [2003] IRLR 52 it came from the imposition of an unjustified disciplinary penalty.
Horkulak v Cantor Fitzgerald International [2003] IRLR 756 (upheld in relation to remedies in [2004] IRLR
942, CA) was notable for its firm disapproval of the idea that if the employer paid a high enough salary it
could treat the employee any way it wanted; ie trust and respect always applies, even in the City; similarly, in
McBride v Falkirk Football and Athletic Club [2012] IRLR 22 a football club could not excuse bad treatment of
its manager simply on the basis that an 'autocratic style of management' is the norm in the sport.

discussed in detail in Chapter 7, but the essence of it is that the employee can claim to be dismissed, even though he walks out, if he can show that the employer's conduct was such that he was 'entitled' to do so.[149] In *Western Excavating (ECC) Ltd v Sharp*,[150] a case which served to emphasize the underlying contractual nature of the employment relationship, the Court of Appeal held that this meant *contractually* entitled, ie where the employer's conduct went as far as to repudiate the whole contract; on the face of it, this narrowed the concept of constructive dismissal, for mere unreasonableness by the employer would not be enough per se, but the effect of this case has been considerably reduced by praying in aid the implied term of respect, for if there is such a term and the employer behaves unreasonably (ie with unacceptable disregard for the employee), the employer can be held to have broken the implied term, to have repudiated the contract, and therefore to have constructively dismissed the employee even within the narrower view taken in *Western Excavating (EEC) Ltd v Sharp*.[151] Reliance on the implied term in this context is common and can arise on a wide variety of facts, to such an extent that it can constitute something of a 'wild card' in employment law, often requiring the employer to think in terms not just of whether contemplated or proposed conduct (for example changes to working practices or terms and conditions) is strictly lawful under the wording of the individual contracts, but whether objection could legitimately be made by affected employees to the *manner* in which the management propose to pursue their goals. This potentially restraining effect may be a significant factor in good personnel/HR practice. Moreover, the trend in recent years has been for the implied term to be used more widely than just in its original home of constructive dismissal. Action which breaches it also constitutes repudiatory conduct generally which may give rise to other arguments or causes of action. Thus, for example, the implied term has been the basis for extending compensation for wrongful dismissal,[152] for freeing a employee from a restraint of trade clause after leaving because of the employer's conduct,[153] and even for recovering personal injury damages in cases of occupational stress caused by such conduct.[154]

---

[149] Employment Rights Act 1996, s 95; a similar definition applies to redundancy claims—s 136. For an application of similar ideas of a duty of trust and confidence in a common law claim, see *Bliss v South East Thames Regional Health Authority* [1987] ICR 700, [1985] IRLR 308, CA.

[150] [1978] 1 All ER 713, [1978] ICR 221, CA.

[151] There is an excellent explanation of this role for the implied term of respect in the judgment of Browne-Wilkinson J in the EAT in *Woods v WM Car Services (Peterborough) Ltd* [1981] ICR 666, [1981] IRLR 347 (approved by the Court of Appeal [1982] ICR 693, [1982] IRLR 413). If employer conduct is bad enough to breach this term, that will invariably be repudiatory conduct for these purposes: *Morrow v Safeway Stores plc* [2002] IRLR 9. See also the modern case law set out at pp 127-30, and in particular the extension of this term to the area of employees' pension rights in *Imperial Group Pension Trust Ltd v Imperial Tobacco Ltd* [1991] ICR 524, [1991] IRLR 66.

[152] *Clark v BET plc* [1997] IRLR 348; see p 454.

[153] *Cantor Fitzgerald International v Bird* [2002] IRLR 867.

[154] *Gogay v Hertfordshire County Council* [2000] IRLR 703, CA; *Eastwood v Magnox plc* [2004] ICR 1064, [2004] IRLR 733, HL.

The implied term of trust and respect finally received the approval of the House of Lords in *Malik v BCCI SA*[155] where it formed the basis for an unusual claim at common law for 'stigma damages', the employees' argument being that they had had their future job prospects materially damaged (as ex-managers in the collapsed BCCI bank) by reason of the fraudulent conduct of the bank's operations while they had been employed by it, which had breached the term of trust and respect. Lord Steyn referred to the term as a 'sound development' which had met with widespread approval, and which had to be applied to a wide range of situations in order to strike a balance between the employer's interest in managing the business and the employee's interest in not being unfairly and improperly exploited.[156] Shortly afterwards, however, in a fashion not uncommon in cases of major developments in the common law, serious uncertainty was introduced into this area as a sideeffect of the subsequent House of Lords decision in *Johnson v Unisys Ltd*.[157] The principal aim in this decision was to strangle at birth a new head of recovery of wide, general damages for 'stigma' loss *on dismissal*. This had been enthusiastically taken up by claimants' lawyers after *Malik* and was viewed by their Lordships as a highly undesirable development which was to be stopped. They did so by restricting stigma damages to breaches of contract *during* employment (ie confining *Malik* to its own facts). This was achieved in two ways: (1) by holding that a common law wrongful dismissal action is not to be used to outflank the statutory action for unfair dismissal, which is what Parliament intended should be the principal remedy for unfairness in termination (including stigma), with its deliberate imposition of short time limits and a cap on the amount that can be recovered; and (2) by holding that the term of trust and respect is aimed at ensuring that the contract can *continue* in a reasonable and proper manner and so is not applicable at the dismissal stage where, by definition, questions of continuance no longer arise. It was this second ground that caused problems. If confined to the moment and mechanics of dismissal (as used in the case itself to rule out stigma damages from the manner of dismissal) it was unobjectionable. However, if ever applied more widely to the whole process leading up to dismissal, it could be disastrous for the proper treatment of employees under discipline and indeed for constructive dismissal (where the employee would normally want to rely on immediately pre-termination employer misconduct as justifying leaving). This loose end of what was meant by the implied term not applying 'on termination' caused

---

[155] [1997] ICR 606, [1997] IRLR 462, HL; see Brodie 'The Heart of the Matter: Mutual Trust and Confidence' (1996) 25 ILJ 121 (cited with approval in the case) and 'Beyond Exchange: The New Contract of Employment' (1998) 27 ILJ 79; and 'Mutual Trust and the Values of the Employment Contract' (2001) 30 ILJ 84; and 'Mutual Trust and Confidence: Catalysts, Constraints and Commonality' (2008) 37 ILJ 329.

[156] The Northern Ireland Court of Appeal in *Brown v Merchant Ferries Ltd* [1998] IRLR 682 and the English Court of Appeal in *Transco plc v O'Brien* [2002] EWCA Civ 379, [2002] ICR 721, [2002] IRLR 444 adopted Lord Steyn's formulation of the implied term which stressed that the test was an objective one, ie whether the employee could properly conclude that the employer was repudiating the contract, not whether the employer had intended so to act. It was also established in *Malik* (n 155) that the repudiatory conduct does not in law have to be aimed directly at the employee.

[157] [2001] UKHL 13, [2001] ICR 480, [2001] IRLR 279.

problems for some time and led to a division of opinion in the Court of Appeal.[158] Fortunately, however, the issue was fairly quickly considered by the House of Lords in *Eastwood v Magnox plc*[159] which concerned appalling behaviour by the employer during employment (leading to serious mental injury) *but* culminating in dismissal. The case thus posed the question neatly: if a narrow interpretation was adopted (only applying the so-called '*Johnson v Unisys* exclusion zone' at the moment of dismissal) the damage had already been done and the employee could sue; if a wide interpretation was adopted (with the exclusion applying to any facts leading up to an eventual dismissal) the employee's action would be invalid. The House of Lords unambiguously chose the narrow interpretation and held for the employee. Lord Nicholls put it as follows:

> Identifying the boundary of the '*Johnson* exclusion area', as it has been called, is comparatively straightforward. The statutory code provides remedies for infringement of the statutory right not to be *dismissed* unfairly. An employee's remedy for unfair dismissal, whether actual or constructive, is the remedy provided by statute. If before his dismissal, whether actual or constructive, an employee has acquired a cause of action at law, for breach of contract or otherwise, that cause of action remains unimpaired by his subsequent unfair dismissal and the statutory rights flowing therefrom. By definition, in law such a cause of action exists independently of the dismissal.[160]

(v) TO DEAL PROMPTLY AND PROPERLY WITH GRIEVANCES

In *W A Goold (Pearmak) Ltd v McConnell*[161] two salesmen whose commission-based pay had been hit by a change in sales methods, tried to raise this as a grievance; in the absence of a proper procedure[162] they tried to do so on several occasions in an ad

---

[158] In *Eastwood v Magnox plc* [2002] IRLR 447 the Court of Appeal used a wide interpretation to rule out an employee's action, but on very similar facts a different Court of Appeal in *McCabe v Cornwall CC* [2003] IRLR 87 adopted the narrow view and allowed the employee's action to proceed.

[159] [2004] ICR 1064, [2004] IRLR 733, HL. This common law claim was heard at the same time as the appeal in *Dunnachie v Kingston upon Hull CC* [2004] ICR 1052, [2004] IRLR 727, HL where it was held that non-financial loss for injury to feelings cannot be awarded in an unfair dismissal action (see Ch 7, heading 6(ii), p 539). The end result is that such damages (and 'stigma' damages more widely) cannot be claimed either at common law or by statute if they arise on termination.

[160] At para 27. Lord Nicholls saw the statutory cap on compensation for unfair dismissal as one of the problems here (leading to a claimant's lawyers wanting to use a common law action as well if actual damages exceed that cap). Giving the other principal judgment, Lord Steyn was even more critical, tracing many of the problems back to *Johnson v Unisys* itself (in which he dissented) and saying that this whole area needs reforming by Parliament. In *Edwards v Chesterfield Royal Hospital NHS Trust* [2012] ICR 201, [2012] IRLR 129 SC the Supreme Court applied *Eastwood* and held that the disciplinary procedures leading to the dismissal come within the '*Johnson* exclusion zone' and so cannot found a common law action separately from the dismissal; this had the important effect of disallowing 'loss of career' damages of £4.7m.

[161] [1995] IRLR 516.

[162] As employees, they should have had a written note of the appropriate grievance procedure in their written ('section 1') statement of terms and conditions; see Ch 2, heading 3, p 80. This point was used by the EAT to demonstrate Parliament's intention that there should be proper such procedures, properly administered.

hoc manner with their manager and then with the new managing director, but with no results. When eventually they sought an interview with the company chairman and were refused they walked out. Upholding the tribunal decision that this was a constructive dismissal and unfair, the EAT held that it is an implied term in a contract of employment that employers will reasonably and promptly afford a reasonable opportunity to their employees to obtain redress of any grievances they may have. Moreover, this is a fundamental term, breach of which will be sufficiently serious to justify the employee in terminating the employment.

This declaration of a new (possibly overriding?) implied term was of particular significance for three reasons. First, it was a very good example of the use of implied terms set out above, as a way of the courts governing certain basic contents of the employment relationship and imposing certain standards of behaviour in employee relations. Secondly, although this point is not mentioned in the judgment of Morison J, the case could be seen as following on from at least two previous decisions in which failures to take up specific forms of complaints arising in the high-profile areas of health and safety[163] and sexual harassment[164] had been held to constitute fundamental breaches of contract for the purpose of establishing constructive dismissal when the complainant left. *Goold* in effect consolidates such disparate cases into one general principle and in doing so places new emphasis on the efficient administration of grievance procedures. Thirdly, it fits in well with two subsequent developments elsewhere, namely the extension of the ACAS Code of Practice No 1 in 2000 to cover grievance procedures as well as disciplinary procedures. This was followed by the unsuccessful experiment (in the Employment Act 2002) of making exhaustion of the statutory grievance procedure compulsory. Although that experiment was abolished in April 2009, part of its replacement was a further reissuing of the ACAS Code of Practice No 1 which again clearly covers grievance procedures (this time primarily as a matter once again of best practice rather than overly prescriptive law, though with provision for an uplift or decrease of compensation for breach of statutory rights such as unfair dismissal of up to 25% if the employer or employee unreasonably fails to comply with the Code[165]). For these reasons, grievance procedures have been given an ever higher profile in recent years and proper exhaustion of them by both parties will now usually be very advisable.

(vi) TO PROVIDE A REASONABLY SUITABLE WORKING ENVIRONMENT

In *Waltons & Morse v Dorrington*[166] a non-smoking secretary in a solicitors' firm was moved into a room close to heavy smokers which she found a problem. Her complaints

---

[163] *British Aircraft Corpn v Austin* [1978] IRLR 332.

[164] *Bracebridge Engineering Ltd v Darby* [1990] IRLR 3.

[165] Trade Union and Labour Relations (Consolidation) Act 1992, s 207A, inserted by the Employment Act 2008 s 3.

[166] [1997] IRLR 488.

had only partial effects and eventually she was told to put up with the solution or leave. She left and claimed constructive dismissal, which was upheld by the EAT who held that it is now an implied term of all contracts of employment that the employer will provide and monitor for employees, so far as is reasonably practicable, a working *environment* which is reasonably suitable for the performance by them of their contractual duties. This term goes beyond the longstanding term of health and safety (above) (on the facts, for example it would probably have been too soon to show distinct health risks to her), and in formulating it (much more along 'welfare' lines) the EAT adopted much of the phraseology of the Health and Safety at Work etc Act 1974, section 2(2)(e) which provides that the employer must take reasonable care for 'the provision and maintenance of a working environment for his employees that is, so far as reasonably practicable, safe, without risks to health and adequate as regards facilities and arrangements for their welfare at work'. Moreover, although not mentioned in the judgment, this implied term is also consistent with (1) modern health and safety Regulations, especially the Management of Health and Safety at Work Regulations 1999 with their emphasis on proactive measures such as risk assessments in workplaces, and (2) the clear coverage of the 'working environment' (not just traditional health and safety) in Article 118a of the Treaty of Rome (now Article 137), under which the Working Time Directive was validly passed, even though it does not concern health or safety directly.[167] This new implied term is potentially very wide and is likely to need much interpretation in the future case law on it.

(vii) FURTHER DEVELOPMENTS: ADVICE, CONFIDENTIALITY AND PHI SCHEMES

As seen above, it is, of course, always open to the courts to extend the scope of these imposed duties on employers. In that context, three developments merit mention. The first is that in *Scally v Southern Health and Social Services Board*[168] the House of Lords upheld the finding of an implied term that the employer would *inform* the employee of valuable (but obscure) rights under his pension scheme; when the employer failed to do so and the employee lost those rights due to a time limitation, the employee could therefore sue the employer for breach of contract. Clearly, the facts of this case were unusual, but Lord Bridge drew a principle that there could be such an implied term where (1) the terms of the contract had not been negotiated individually, but resulted from negotiation with a representative body or were otherwise incorporated by reference, (2) the employee could only avail himself of a valuable right under the contract by taking certain action, and (3) the employee could not, in all the circumstances, reasonably be expected to be aware of the term unless it was brought to his attention. Obligations to

---

[167] See Ch 4, heading 2(iii), p 234.
[168] [1991] ICR 771, [1991] IRLR 522, HL. If this case applies, the obligation on the employer is only to use reasonable care to advise, not to guarantee receipt of the information: *Ibekwe v London General Transport Services Ltd* [2003] IRLR 697, CA.

inform or warn are common in modern health and safety law,[169] and it was interesting to see this development in mainstream employment law (albeit in the specialized context of pensions), because the traditional approach was much more in the nature of caveat employee.[170] However, subsequent case law has not shown a desire to extend *Scally*, which may eventually turn out to have been the highwater mark here, or indeed to be restricted to its own facts. In *University of Nottingham v Eyett*[171] it was held that there was no duty on an employer to advise an employee about to retire that his pension would be higher if he delayed slightly (when all that that employee had enquired about was his entitlement on his preferred date of retirement) and in *Hagen v ICI Chemicals and Polymers Ltd*[172] there was again held to be no obligation to give positive advice on pension entitlements through a TUPE transfer; for good measure, the Court of Appeal held in *Outram v Academy Plastics*[173] (alleged breach of duty by employer as pension trustee in not advising the employee to rejoin the scheme when he renewed employment after a break) that if there is no duty under the contract of employment (given this restrictive treatment of *Scally*) the employee will not be allowed to argue for a wider duty in tort. Thus, unless a case arises which is much closer to the facts of *Scally* (which is now seen as heavily dependent on the inability of the employees to discover the true facts without information from the employer) it is unlikely that any duty to advise will be held to have arisen. One interesting point here is that in *Hagen* the claimant employees in fact succeeded on the separate ground that certain information that they had actually been given was misleading and so, they having relied on that to their provable detriment,[174] the employer was liable in tort for negligent misstatement. Thus, if an employer *chooses* to give information which the employee will reasonably and foreseeably rely on care must be taken as to its accuracy. This distinction is well shown by the contrasting decisions in *Crossley v Faithful & Gould Holdings Ltd*[175] and

---

[169] A good example is the decision of Waite J in *Pape v Cumbria County Council* [1992] 3 All ER 211 that there was a common law duty on the employer to warn cleaning staff of the danger of dermatitis from certain cleaning chemicals (*General Cleaning Contractors Ltd v Christmas* [1953] AC 180, [1952] 2 All ER 1110, HL applied).

[170] In *Lister v Romford Ice and Cold Storage Co Ltd* [1957] AC 555, [1957] 1 All ER 125, HL there was no obligation on the employer to organize all matters of insurance (see heading 4(iii), p 167) and in *Reid v Rush & Tompkins Group plc* [1990] ICR 61, [1989] IRLR 265, CA it was held that the employer was under no duty to warn the employee of the risk of economic loss (through not insuring himself adequately when working abroad). The question of insurance cover for the employee should preferably be covered expressly in the contract whenever it is likely to be an issue, especially since the decision in *Merrett v Babb* [2001] EWCA Civ 214, [2001] QB 1174 that when a firm of surveyors went bankrupt one of their employees could be personally liable to a client to whom he had given bad advice; unfortunately he was not insured as he was no longer covered by the firm's previous policy.

[171] [1999] ICR 721, [1999] IRLR 87. See also *Marlow v East Thames Housing Group Ltd* [2002] IRLR 798.

[172] [2002] IRLR 31.   [173] [2001] ICR 367, [2000] IRLR 499, CA.

[174] This element in *Hagen* was unusual—the employees could show causation on the basis that, if their true position had been known to them, they would have objected to the TUPE transfer *and* then the employers would *not* have gone through with it. Normally, employees will have no such de facto power of veto, the transfer would happen anyway and so what they may or may not have been told in advance would have no causative effect on their later loss, which would have happened anyway.

[175] [2004] ICR 1615, [2004] IRLR 377, CA.

Lennon v MPC.[176] In the former, a senior employee arranged his early retirement in a way that was less advantageous than it might have been; he did not know this but his employer did, and when he finally found out the true position he sued the ex-employer for not telling him. In line with the above case law, his claim was dismissed on the basis that there is no positive obligation in general on an employer to advise an employee as to his or her best interests. However, *Lennon* fell on the other side of the line because there a police officer changing forces had asked an HR officer which was the best way to do so (to preserve certain accrued benefits) and the officer had *undertaken* to find out for him. When the wrong option was advised and he lost the benefits he successfully sued his old force for damages for their loss, on the basis that there was sufficient 'assumption of responsibility' to activate liability under the modern approach to negligent misstatement. The distinction between these two very instructive cases is clear legally, but in practice there could be major issues of fact as to who said or promised what to whom.

The second development is the possible extension of ideas of confidentiality in employment. There is a well-developed implied duty of confidence *on* an employee, but there may evolve an equal and opposite duty *towards* an employee. In *Dalgleish v Lothian and Borders Police Board*[177] an interdict was granted, preventing the employers from divulging employees' names and addresses to the council who were chasing community charge defaulters, partly on the ground that this information was confidential, not in the public domain, and was held by the employers only for the purpose of the employer–employee relationship. Another sign of such ideas was the decision of the European Court of Human Rights in *Halford v United Kingdom*[178] that interception of telephone calls at work constituted a violation of the Convention rights to respect for private life and family life, home and correspondence. Clearly, such arguments are now likely to be buttressed by the Human Rights Act 1998, so that such matters may now be justiciable before the national courts and tribunals. In practice, however, changes in the direction of greater recognition of ideas of employee privacy or confidentiality in personnel/HR practice are likely to come from a further, independent source not reliant on contractual or human rights ideas, namely data protection law as revamped by the Data Protection Act 1998. Although in itself lying primarily outside employment law, much effort was put into the production by the Information Commissioner of an Employment Code of Practice giving best practice advice on the impact of the legislation in the employment context. A significant amount of this advice is clearly of relevance to the establishment of a level of confidentiality for employees while at work that has hitherto only been argued for in theory. It is perhaps not fanciful to say that the overall approach is based on a simple yet important principle that the employer employs the employee; it does not own him or her.

---

[176] [2004] ICR 1114, [2004] IRLR 385, CA.   [177] [1991] IRLR 422, Ct of Sess.
[178] [1997] IRLR 471, European Court of Human Rights (ECtHR).

The Code is split into four parts. We have already seen Part I: Recruitment and Selection in the previous chapter.[179] Even at this initial stage there are provisions clearly premised on an element of employee confidentiality, in particular the advice to (1) only ask for information that is directly relevant to recruitment, (2) destroy information afterwards unless it is definitely necessary to keep as part of a personnel file and (3) only ask for sensitive personal data (especially on health record) once a prima facie decision has been made to appoint that person. Part II: Employment Records continues this approach into the question of what information to keep (and how to keep it) on employees once appointed. Key points here are to (1) only keep such records as are necessary (and inform employees what is kept), (2) ensure security of records, limiting access only to those managers who need to have it, (3) use absence records, not detailed schemes records, where possible, (4) have systems to cope with access requests by employees and third parties, (5) provide references to third parties only where the employee wishes this, (6) ensure that disciplinary records are accurate and only used when necessary and for proper purposes (for example in later investigations) and (7) have a disposal policy for old or spent information. Medical records are dealt with separately in the fourth part of the Code, being in the more specialized category of 'sensitive personal information'. However, it is the third part 'Monitoring at work' which is likely to be most controversial in the context of confidentiality. It covers not just obviously intrusive forms of monitoring such as the use of telephone tapping or CCTV cameras, but the much wider and more sensitive areas of monitoring for email and/or internet abuse. Here, the simple approach that the machinery belongs to the employer, who can therefore do as he wants, is not sufficient because we are seeing the evolution of at least formative ideas that an employee at work has certain rights or expectations of privacy, especially where personal use is not wholly banned. Key suggestions in the Code are to (1) have clear business reasons for any monitoring, (2) have a policy on the use and abuse of electronic communications and publicize it to staff, (3) keep access to information obtained restricted, (4) use an 'impact assessment' (similar to a health and safety risk assessment) to determine what monitoring is justified by the benefits, (5) ensure that workers and others know the extent of monitoring, (6) where possible monitor traffic, not content,[180] (7) try to use software solutions to present abuse at source (especially downloading of offensive material) and (8) in dealing with any allegations of internet abuse, remember that inappropriate websites can be accessed by mistake. Technically, of course, a code such as this is only relevant to data protection issues, and breach of it for no good reason would only be of direct concern in an enforcement action under the Data Protection Act 1998. However, the cross-over into employment indirectly could be considerable for three reasons: (1) in fact the Codes are likely to have a major impact on personnel/HR practice, just as much as if they had

---

[179] See Ch 2, heading 2(ii), p 74.
[180] Although sensible generally, this might not be possible in a case of alleged harassment by electronic means where the content would be vital.

been produced under employment law; (2) the Code on Monitoring could well have a major impact in any case concerning discipline or dismissal for email or internet abuse (for example where the employee has breached a well-known and consistently applied employer policy, drafted in line with the Code);[181] (3) an interesting point would arise if ever an employee sought to use breach of his or her rights or expectations under the Code(s) (especially that on monitoring) to privacy at work as a reason for walking out and claiming constructive dismissal—would the courts evolve an implied term either to protect privacy generally or (less controversially) to abide by the Codes? If so, the cross-over would become formal, not just informal.

The third development concerns a modern trend in the employment of more senior employees of offering permanent health insurance ('PHI') as part of the remuneration package; paid for by the employer, this can offer major benefits to an employee who becomes permanently incapable of work through illness, but its relationship with ordinary sickness procedures and notice provisions has proved troublesome (as has the potentially difficult relationship between employer, employee and the insurance company providing the scheme)[182] especially where the PHI has been in the nature of an 'add-on' without thought as to its possible legal effects. In *Aspden v Webbs Poultry and Meat Group (Holdings) Ltd*[183] the plaintiff was a senior manager who was subject to the firm's PHI scheme for senior staff—if incapable of work for more than 26 weeks, he would be entitled to three-quarter salary until death, retirement or ceasing to be an employee. However, on engagement he had been given a standard contract which did *not* take the separate PHI scheme into account and in the case of long-term illness provided for six months' sick pay and then for dismissal. When he became ill (after altercations with the firm over reorganizations) the employers, who suspected he might have been exaggerating his illness, exercised their contractual power of dismissal before he could qualify for the PHI benefits. The employee brought an action for wrongful dismissal; normally this would have been doomed to failure because of the terms of the contract, but Sedley J upheld the employee's claim that on the facts of the case there was an implied term that, save for summary dismissal for cause,[184] the employer would not terminate the contract while he was incapacitated, so as to

---

[181] Particularly in the light of the hard line already taken by the EAT to such misconduct in *Thomas v Hillingdon London Borough Council* (2002) The Times, 4 October.

[182] In *Marlow v East Thames Housing Group Ltd* [2002] IRLR 798 the insurance company stopped paying the PHI benefits when it thought the employee was no longer incapable of work; the employee could not challenge this directly (the PHI scheme contract was between the employer and the insurance company) but established that the employer was contractually bound to take all reasonable steps to pursue her claim, on the basis of the implied term of trust and respect.

[183] [1996] IRLR 521.

[184] This was expressed in *Aspden* to be the important protection that the employer needs in such a case; for an example of its application, see *Briscoe v Lubrizol Ltd* [2002] EWCA Civ 508, [2002] IRLR 607. However, it now needs to be expanded to cover summary dismissal for cause *and* dismissal for bona fide redundancy, neither of which mean that the employer is trying to frustrate the PHI scheme, and so neither of which would be contrary to the implied term: *Hill v General Accident Fire and Life Assurance Corpn plc* [1998] IRLR 641, OH.

deprive him of the PHI benefits. The judge acknowledged that this was on the edge of permissibility for the use of implied terms, but was necessary because otherwise an unrestricted power to terminate would completely negate the working of the PHI scheme which clearly applied to the plaintiff but had been completely overlooked when his contract had been given to him. Although an adventurous decision, it has been followed by the Outer House of the Court of Session[185] and approved obiter in the Court of Appeal;[186] it marks yet a further move away from strict contract doctrine in the employment field.

One point of considerable importance for future developments here is whether the *Aspden* principle will be applied outside the PHI context. It operates by, in effect, placing a restriction on the employer's normal power to dismiss by giving notice where to do so would negate valuable PHI rights; might it evolve into a wider principle, applying to deliberate attempts by the employer to use the doctrine of notice to deprive the employee unfairly of *any* valuable rights or expectations? This would be a major inroad into the traditional law on dismissal by notice,[187] but there are signs of such an extension (certainly where there is a close analogy to PHI rights) in *Jenvey v Australian Broadcasting Corpn*[188] where an employee, alleging that his employment had been deliberately terminated in a way and at a time so as to ensure that he could not claim valuable redundancy rights, successfully bought a common law breach of contract action for the value of those rights. Elias J held that there had been a breach of a specific implied term that, where an employer has resolved to dismiss an employee by reason of redundancy, the employer will not (other than for good cause) dismiss that employee for some other reason. Thus, any advance of the law here is suitably cautious and incremental, not based on any wide generalized principle; on the other hand, the case does extend the PHI cases by analogy into an area not previously covered. As in any area of controversy, however, developments are not all in one direction, and the subsequent decision of the Privy Council in *Reda v Flag Ltd*[189] was far less adventurous. It concerned complex contractual provisions for the termination and payment of two senior executives of a Bermudan company; there were three stipulated forms of termination, each with a different compensation package spelled out. When the company dismissed them expressly under one of these (with a substantial payment) but with the effect that they could not benefit from a new share option scheme being introduced, they argued on analogy with *Aspden* that this was unlawful and that they were entitled to the benefit of the scheme. The Privy Council turned down their claims. At first sight this appears to go against the flow of the previous cases but it is suggested that the case is best viewed

---

[185]   *Adin v Sedco Forex International Resources Ltd* [1997] IRLR 280, Ct of Sess.

[186]   *Brompton v AOC Int Ltd* [1997] IRLR 639, CA. In *Villella v MFI Furniture Centres Ltd* [1999] IRLR 468 a similar argument succeeded again, this time where dismissal was used to try to avoid continuing with PHI payments already being made, as in *Briscoe v Lubrizol Ltd* (n 180 above) where the Court of Appeal accepted the *Aspden* principle as established law.

[187]   See Ch 6, heading 2, p 424 and Smith and Randall *Contract Actions in Modern Employment: Developments and Issues* (2000) 93–5.

[188]   [2003] ICR 79, [2002] IRLR 520.   [189]   [2002] UKPC 38, [2002] IRLR 747.

as reliant on its facts—the termination agreement was highly specific and was not to be assailed by reliance on implied terms (whereas such an assault may be more feasible in more normal cases where the employer is just (ab)using the ordinary doctrine of notice, with no large pay-offs); *Aspden* was distinguished, not disapproved (and none of the other above case law was mentioned); and in any event on the facts the court clearly thought little of the merits of the employees' cases, and said that the employers had had sound commercial reasons ('reasonable cause'?) for acting as they had done. In fact, in the only subsequent case to consider *Reda* (and then only briefly) the Court of Appeal took a narrow approach to it, as being largely explicable on its facts,[190] and so it is suggested that it should not be seen as stopping further development in this area in suitable cases, though it does show that radical arguments such as these are not to be relied on too readily or too widely. Suitability here may well be heavily reliant on the substantive merits of the case. In *Jenvey* the employer had in fact dismissed the employee in a way that was automatically unfair (partly as revenge for tribunal proceedings brought by him over a dispute), but then pleaded that as the reason why he could not claim to have been redundant and so qualified for the enhanced redundancy rights. Faced with this deeply unattractive argument that the employer could rely on its own automatically unfair dismissal to negate the employee's rights (or at least expectations) Elias J ended his judgment with the following instructive passage:

> It follows that I find for the claimant. I confess that I am pleased to be able to do so. The defendant's position lacked merit. It would in my view have been a gross injustice if ABC were to be better off as a result of dismissing the employee for an unlawful reason than it would have been had it dismissed him lawfully by reason of the redundancy that had arisen. The need to preserve the integrity of the legal process recognised in the old adage 'hard cases make bad law' may sometimes compel a court to accept a particular injustice because it cannot properly be remedied in line with legal principle. Fortunately, I am satisfied that I can here do justice without any improper distortion of the legal rules.

4 IMPLIED DUTIES OF THE EMPLOYEE

(i) OBEDIENCE

In the days before employment was explained in terms of a contract, the servant's duty of obedience was taken to be a natural element of employment and indeed if one delves far enough back it was accompanied by the master's right to discipline and perhaps chastise the erring servant. It is now explained as an aspect of the contract of employment that the employer may give and the employee should obey a lawful order, and indeed it has been argued that this should be taken a step further and viewed not as a duty of obedience, but rather as an example of cooperation. The term 'lawful'

---

[190] *Horkulak v Cantor Fitzgerald International* [2005] ICR 402, [2005] IRLR 942, CA.

order is often used but in this context it means primarily an order which is reasonably within the ambit of the employment in question so that, once again, in any given dispute much or all will depend on the terms of the individual contract of employment, whether express or implied; the task of deciding what is the scope of the employment may be facilitated by the requirements in section 1 of the Employment Rights Act 1996 of written particulars of terms of employment, particularly of the title of the job which the employee is employed to do (section 1(4)(f)). Thus, the employer cannot give orders outside the proper scope of the employment, for example orders of a 'personal' nature such as regulating the length of the employee's hair or his out-of-work activities (unless he can show some special considerations bringing such matters within the scope of employment, such as danger in having long hair when working machines or some form of special interest, employment-related, in outside activities). Also, this principle means that the employer cannot order the employee to change his contract, so that if it is clear that he is not contractually bound to be mobile or work overtime, it will not be 'lawful' to order him to work elsewhere[191] or put in hours above the basic.[192]

Questions of obedience are naturally bound up with the law on dismissal, and at common law principally with the employer's right to dismiss summarily. In general, refusal to obey a proper order would usually justify summary dismissal and although such matters tend to change over time with different social attitudes this is still the basic position with regard to the common law action for wrongful dismissal. However, the statutory action for unfair dismissal is now far more important and the question of fairness depends upon all the factors in the case, not just whether the employee was technically in breach of contract.[193] In the light of this, although the employer may still dismiss summarily in cases of grave misconduct, a single act of disobedience may not necessarily render the dismissal fair, for although it would qualify as a reason concerning 'conduct' within section 98(2) of the Employment Rights Act 1996, the tribunal must go further and consider, under section 98(4), whether the employer acted reasonably in treating it as a sufficient reason for dismissal in all the circumstances of the particular case.

The duty of obedience at common law is subject to two particular qualifications. The first is that the employer may not order the employee to do something illegal;[194] if he does so the employee is entitled to refuse to obey the order, and any purported summary dismissal will be wrongful, and of more importance, very likely to be held to be unfair, as in *Morrish v Henlys (Folkestone) Ltd*[195] where the employee was dismissed

---

[191] *O'Brien v Associated Fire Alarms Ltd* [1969] 1 All ER 93, [1968] 1 WLR 1916, CA; *Courtaulds Northern Spinning Ltd v Sibson* [1988] ICR 451, [1988] IRLR 305, CA; cf *Stevenson v Teesside Bridge and Engineering Ltd* [1971] 1 All ER 296 and *United Kingdom Atomic Energy Authority v Claydon* [1974] ICR 128, [1979] IRLR 6.

[192] *Pengilly v North Devon Farmers Ltd* [1973] IRLR 41.

[193] *Farrant v Woodroffe School* [1998] ICR 184, [1998] IRLR 176.

[194] *Gregory v Ford* [1951] 1 All ER 121. Semble there must be a clear order if the employer is to be in breach of this principle: *Buckoke v Greater London Council* [1970] 2 All ER 193, per Plowman J; affd by the Court of Appeal: [1971] 1 Ch 655, [1971] 2 All ER 254, CA.

[195] [1973] 2 All ER 137, [1973] ICR 482.

because he refused to falsify accounts. The second qualification is that the employer may not order the employee into danger; in *Ottoman Bank v Chakarian*[196] an employee was held to have been justified in disobeying an order to stay in Constantinople where he had previously been sentenced to death and was in danger of being apprehended a second time. However, it appears that for this exception to apply there must be immediate and personal danger so that in *Bouzourou v Ottoman Bank*,[197] expectation merely of general hostility from the Turkish authorities was not enough to justify refusal of an order to work in Mersina; likewise with an unspecific fear of IRA activity if sent to work in Eire in *Walmsley v UDEC Refrigeration Ltd.*[198]

(ii) ADAPTATION TO NEW METHODS AND TECHNIQUES

As was pointed out in the previous chapter when considering changes in the terms of employment, problems may arise from the fact that jobs change but contracts tend to be static. What is to happen if the employer introduces new working methods or techniques which the employee is unwilling to accept? In such a case, the employee may argue that the changes are sufficiently fundamental to fall outside the scope of his existing contract; if this is so, the employer must be able to show a consensual variation of the relevant terms before he can insist on the employee accepting the changes.[199] There is extensive case law on this point in the law on redundancy,[200] where the courts have consistently given considerable latitude to employers to alter work practices without being held to have altered the job itself. A second possibility is that the employer may have envisaged the possibility of future changes and in the light of that either framed the contractual terms (particularly the job title/description) flexibly, or given himself express contractual authority to make the changes in question. However, the question remains what is to happen where neither of these solutions applies, ie where the changes are not fundamental enough to alter the job itself, but changes in methods or techniques are not expressly covered by the contract? Can the employee refuse to adapt?

It appears that in most cases he will not be able to refuse, for he will not be deemed to have a right to continue as he always had indefinitely. There is little case law directly on this point, but it is possible that if necessary the courts would develop an implied term of adaptation. Signs of this can be seen in the judgment of Walton J in *Cresswell v Board of Inland Revenue.*[201] In that case, Inland Revenue officers and clerks refused to operate a new computerized system of PAYE administration when their employers could not guarantee that there would be no compulsory redundancies. They sought

---

[196] [1930] AC 277, PC.　　[197] [1930] AC 271, PC.　　[198] [1972] IRLR 80, IT.

[199] On variation, see Ch 2, heading 6, p 113. If no such variation is forthcoming, the employer may have to dismiss the objector employee and defend an unfair dismissal action on the ground that the dismissal was fair because of the business need to change; see Ch 8, heading 1(ii), p 566.

[200] See Ch 8, heading 1(i), p 551.

[201] [1984] ICR 508, [1984] IRLR 190. Napier 'Computerisation and Employment Rights' (1992) 21 ILJ 1.

a declaration that their employers were in breach of contract in requiring them to operate the computers. It was held, however, that the change to computers was not sufficient to fall outside their contractual duties of tax gathering and that on the facts they were expected to adapt to the new methods:

> There can really be no doubt as to the fact that an employee is expected to adapt himself to new methods and techniques introduced in the course of his employment.[202]

However, if such an implied term is to be developed, it should be noted that Walton J added a requirement of reasonableness, continuing the same passage as follows:

> Of course, in a proper case the employer must provide any necessary training or retraining.... [I]t will, in all cases, be a question of pure fact as to whether the retraining involves the acquisition of such esoteric skills that it would not be reasonable to expect the employee to acquire them.

Cresswell was a common law action, but this reasonableness approach could be particularly important in an unfair dismissal action. In *Smith v London Metropolitan University*[203] a university lecturer in theatre studies was involved in a personality clash with a colleague in that department, as a result of which she was required by the university to move into the English department and teach English literature. She maintained that that was outside her experience and competence and refused to do so, as a result of which she was disciplined and dismissed. When she claimed unfair dismissal the university argued that she had been in breach of the implied term of reasonable adaptation. The tribunal agreed but the EAT allowed her appeal; they held that that implied term applies to adaptation to new methods of performance of existing contractual duties, whereas on the facts here working in the English department would constitute a new *job*, which is not covered by this term.

(iii) THE DUTY OF CARE

An employee owes to his employer an implied duty of care in carrying out his job. The basic authority for this is usually said to be *Harmer v Cornelius*[204] even though that case actually concerned a representation that the employee possessed the necessary *skill* for the job, for in subsequent cases skill and care have been treated as roughly equivalent. This duty of care applies generally[205] and could cover, for example, care in

---

[202] pp 518 and 195, respectively.

[203] [2012] IRLR 884.

[204] (1858) 5 CBNS 236. It was held in *Cheltenham BC v Laird* [2009] IRLR 621, QBD that a job *applicant* owes a duty of care when answering questions posed by the employer (eg as to previous health record); the employer's claim for breach of this duty failed on the facts (see Ch 2, heading 2(ii), p 77).

[205] Theoretically breach of this duty could found an action for damages by the employer against the employee: this is most unlikely to happen, though for an example of it, on rather special facts, see *Janata Bank v Ahmed* [1981] ICR 791, [1981] IRLR 457, CA. In *Cheltenham BC v Laird* [2009] the employer had unsuccessfully claimed almost £1m from the employee.

using the employer's equipment. However, its principal legal significance arises where an employee in the course of his employment injures a third party or his goods. In these circumstances the employer may be sued for damages by the third party as being vicariously liable for the tort of the employee. Once sued, however, the employer has a legal action against the employee for an *indemnity*, and this has caused some difficulty.

The employer's cause of action arises in two ways:

(1) He may sue the employee for breach of contract, for in incurring him in liability to pay damages, the employee is in breach of his implied duty of care. The leading case on this is *Lister v Romford Ice and Cold Storage Co Ltd*[206] where it was clearly held that this implied duty exists, and the employer's insurers were awarded an indemnity against the employee who had negligently run down a third party (his own father as it happened) who had sued the employer for damages. In the House of Lords, the employee attempted to mitigate this harsh application of the duty of care by saying that in modern employment law there is a further implied term that the employer will ensure that the employee is insured against liability such as this, but this was rejected by a majority of three to two.

(2) He may sue the employee in tort, for where the employer has been held vicariously liable he and the negligent employee are in law joint tortfeasors, so that he may sue the employee for contribution or a full indemnity under the Civil Liability (Contribution) Act 1978; under this statute, the court may award such contribution as it thinks 'just and equitable having regard to the extent of [the employee's] responsibility for the damage'.

The decision in *Lister's* case caused some consternation and was at the time heavily criticized on the grounds that the principal rationalization for vicarious liability is the practical one that it is the employer or his insurer who can afford to pay the damages and that a finding by a court that the employee was negligent may be just a means of fixing liability onto the employer or his insurers; on both of these grounds, a right of indemnity would be inconsistent.[207] Two ways round the decision in *Lister's* case have been suggested. The first was in *Harvey v R G O'Dell Ltd*[208] where McNair J held that the right of indemnity did not apply to an employee driving a vehicle in the course of his employment when such action was not work he was employed to do but was merely a special occasion on which the employee had assisted his employer by undertaking an unusual task; this, however, is to take a very refined view of what an employee is engaged to do. The second arises from the fact that at common law (before the new cause of action was added by statute in 1935) the rule was that there could be *no* contribution between joint tortfeasors;[209] there was, however, one longstanding exception to this

---

[206] [1957] AC 555, [1957] 1 All ER 125, HL.
[207] Glanville Williams 'Vicarious Liability and the Master's Indemnity' (1957) 20 MLR 220 and 437.
[208] [1958] 2 QB 78, [1958] 1 All ER 657.
[209] The rule in *Merryweather v Nixan* (1799) 8 Term Rep 186.

where the party seeking contribution was wholly innocent[210] and only liable by some operation of law such as vicarious liability—*Lister*'s case was an example of this exception, hence the common law indemnity. Thus, if some fault can be attributed to the employer who is seeking contribution, the case does not fall within the exception, but comes instead within the rule and so contribution cannot be claimed; such fault could arise, for example, if the employer had given the employee some task beyond his competence or had failed to give him proper instruction, as in *Jones v Manchester Corpn*[211] where an inexperienced doctor had caused physical injury to a patient who had sued the employing hospital board for damages, but when the board sought an indemnity from the doctor the Court of Appeal, by a majority, refused to allow it since the hospital had also been at fault in failing to provide adequate supervision for the doctor. The practical problem is that, even if one can circumvent the contractual action in this way, the court still has the discretion to apportion under the 1978 Act, and so an indemnity may still in the end be awarded against the employee, unless the court could be persuaded that it would not be 'just and equitable' to do so; 100% indemnities under the Act were awarded against employees in *Ryan v Fildes*,[212] *Semtex Ltd v Gladstone*,[213] *Harvey v R G O'Dell Ltd* (above) and in *Lister*'s case itself.

In the light of these problems, the effects of *Lister*'s case were investigated by a committee of the then Ministry of Labour[214] which concluded that while legislation could alter the position, there was no urgency since in general employers would not seek indemnities because of the effect on employment relations, and insurers (who were most likely to be interested, since when they pay the damages awarded against the employers they are 'subrogated' into their insured's shoes and can exercise their insured's rights in their own favour—it was an insurance company which brought the action in *Lister*'s case, not the employers) have a 'gentleman's agreement' not to exercise these subrogated rights to indemnity against employees (in personal injury cases, where there is no wilful misconduct or collusion). This remains the position and there has been no amending legislation. However, the rights against employees still exist in law (even if not generally exercised by employers or their insurers in practice) as can be seen from *Morris v Ford Motor Co Ltd*[215] where a third party who was neither the employer nor an insurance company, claimed to have acquired the important right of subrogation through a peculiar indemnity clause in a cleaning contract. The third party then sought to sue the negligent employee who had (indirectly) caused him to pay damages, but the Court of Appeal by a majority refused to allow it. There was no *express* subrogation clause in the cleaning contract, so Lord Denning MR disallowed an implied one on the grounds (1) that subrogation was an equitable concept and it would not be equitable to allow it in this case and (2) that no clause would be implied in the light of employment realities, and James LJ also disallowed it on ground (2). However,

---

[210] *Adamson v Jarvis* (1827) 4 Bing 66; *Pearson v Skelton* (1836) 1 M & W 504.
[211] [1952] 2 QB 852, [1952] 2 All ER 125, CA.   [212] [1938] 3 All ER 517.
[213] [1954] 2 All ER 206, [1954] 1 WLR 945.   [214] See Gardiner (1959) 22 MLR 652.
[215] [1973] QB 792, [1973] 2 All ER 1084, CA.

this case does *not* remove the legal right to indemnity in the employment sphere, for two reasons—first, it contains no assault on *Lister*'s case, only upon the concept of subrogation which does not directly affect the actual right to indemnity; second, the majority could only decide the case this way because there was no express subrogation provision—if there had been it could not have been negated by an implied term to the contrary, so James LJ at least would presumably have had to decide the other way and that would have produced a majority in favour of the indemnity. The possibility of an indemnity being claimed from a negligent employee therefore continues to exist even if it is rarely enforced in practice.[216] This raises two further points of interest—first, no concerted action has been taken by trade unions to secure insurance cover for employees (the term claimed in *Lister*'s case), and second, it appears to be noone's business or interest to clear up an area where the formal legal position is in no way in accordance with general assumptions or practice.

(iv) GOOD FAITH

An act which is inconsistent with the terms of the contract, express or implied, and which is injurious to the employer and his interest will amount to a breach of the duty of faithful service. Thus, a manager whose acts were injurious to the interests of the theatre he was employed to manage was held to have been rightly dismissed at common law,[217] and conversely a court saved from attachment an employee who refused to produce material documents in his possession which he held merely in his role of employee, for the court would not infer that he could produce the documents without violating the duty he owed to his employer.[218] In particular, an employee must not place himself in a position in which his own interests conflict with his duty to his employer.[219] The clash of interest and duty can be seen most clearly in the leading case, *Boston Deep Sea Fishing and Ice Co v Ansell*.[220] The defendant had been employed as managing director of the plaintiff company and he had contracted with a firm of shipbuilders for the supply of certain vessels and had taken from them a commission in respect of the transaction, of which his employers knew nothing. He also possessed shares in an ice-making and

---

[216] For a rare recent example, see *Padden v Arbuthrot Pensions and Investments Ltd* [2004] EWCA Civ 382 where the Court of Appeal held that an employee who had committed fraud against a client was liable to indemnify the employer against any claim brought by the client. One limitation here, however, is that if what the employee has done is to incur the employer in a criminal or administrative *fine* it may be contrary to public policy to permit the employer to shift some or all of that fine onto another party (here, the employee): *Safeway Stores Ltd v Twigger* [2010] EWCA Civ 1472.

[217] *Lacy v Osbaldiston* (1837) 8 C & P 80.

[218] *Eccles & Co v Louisville and Nashville Railroad Co* [1912] 1 KB 135, CA.

[219] *Pearce v Foster* (1886) 17 QBD 536, CA provides a good example; see generally Stephens 'An Agent's Duty to Account' (1975) 28 CLP 39.

[220] (1888) 39 Ch D 339, CA. Note that one of the main propositions established in this case, that at common law the employer may rely on misconduct unknown to him at the date of dismissal and only discovered subsequently in order to justify dismissal, does *not* apply to proceedings for unfair dismissal: *W Devis & Sons Ltd v Atkins* [1977] 3 All ER 40, [1977] ICR 662, HL.

fish-carrying company which paid bonuses to those of its shareholders who, being own-ers of fishing vessels, used the company's ice or its services as a carrier. He was held to the strictest accountability but, apart from that, there was clearly a breach of his duty faithfully to serve, since the temptation to use the company's ice or its services as a car-rier conflicted or might conflict with his duty to consider his employer's interests in preference to his own. It was held that he was properly dismissed, and he had to account to his employer for his profits. It is true that this case concerned a managing director and directors may be under a special fiduciary duty anyway,[221] but the general principle may apply to any employee who misuses his employer's property in a way which shows breach of fidelity (for example by borrowing from the till when not allowed to do so: *Sinclair v Neighbour*),[222] or improperly exploits his position of employment in order to make a secret profit or gain. In *Reading v A-G*,[223] Sergeant Reading who was stationed in Egypt agreed on a number of occasions to accompany lorries to certain destinations, his uniform guaranteeing that such lorries would avoid inspection by the police. These lorries contained illicit spirits and as a result of his services Reading secured almost £20,000. When the military authorities arrested him, they impounded the money and when he was released from prison he brought a petition of right claiming return of the money by the Crown. The House of Lords not surprisingly held against him, for he had misused his position in the service of the Crown and had to account for his profit.

Although secret profits and interests may have to be disclosed, and in certain circumstances an employee may have to inform his employer about matters in his knowledge which affect confidential interests of the employer,[224] the duty of fidelity must not be taken too far. Except for the case of directors who are under a fiduciary duty,[225] a contract of employment is not a contract uberrimae fidei requiring total and voluntary disclosure. Thus, an employee is not under a general duty to declare facts which may prove inimical to the employer, including his own misconduct or unsavoury aspects of his own background. This rule, dating back to the well-known authority of *Bell v Lever Bros Ltd*,[226] was strongly reaffirmed in *Nottingham University v Fishel*[227] where the employers were seeking to recover damages from their employee,

---

[221] *Cook v Deeks* [1916] 1 AC 554, PC; *Cranleigh Precision Engineering Ltd v Bryant* [1964] 3 All ER 289, [1965] 1 WLR 1293; *Industrial Development Consultants v Cooley* [1972] 2 All ER 162, [1972] 1 WLR 443; *Thomas Marshall (Exports) Ltd v Guinle* [1978] ICR 905, [1978] IRLR 174. Under longstanding rules of com-pany law, a director with an interest in a contract with the company is under a duty to disclose that interest to the board of directors.

[222] [1967] 2 QB 279, [1966] 3 All ER 988, CA.   [223] [1951] AC 507, [1951] 1 All ER 617, HL.

[224] *Cranleigh Precision Engineering Ltd v Bryant* [1964] 3 All ER 289, [1965] 1 WLR 1293.

[225] *Regal (Hastings) Ltd v Gulliver* (1942) [1967] 2 AC 134n, [1942] 1 All ER 378, HL; *Horcal Ltd v Gatland* [1984] IRLR 288, CA; *Item Software (UK) Ltd v Fassihi* [2005] ICR 450, [2004] IRLR 928, CA.

[226] [1932] AC 161, HL. Most of these cases involve attempts by an employer to recover golden handshakes given to employees who, after leaving, are discovered to have been defrauding the employer. Note that a 'spent' conviction does not have to be disclosed anyway, under the Rehabilitation of Offenders Act 1974, s 4 (for the application of this Act to unfair dismissal cases, see Ch 7, heading 5(ii), p 517).

[227] [2000] ICR 1462, [2000] IRLR 471. See also (for another good factual example) *Helmet Integrated Sys-tems Ltd v Tunnard* [2007] IRLR 126, CA.

a leading scientist, who had been undertaking private work abroad without telling them, also using other university employees. Their victory was distinctly Pyrrhic because the primary breach of contract (working abroad in university time) had in fact benefited university research so that there was no damage; there was a secondary breach by using the other employees which gave rise to damages but not to any great amount. On the crucial allegation (for present purposes) that he was in breach by not telling them the truth, the court held that it was important *not* to erect any contractual duties on employees to fiduciary levels and that special duties of disclosure should only exist if expressly provided for in the contract, which was not the case here. Thus, the university's claim under this head failed, very much along the lines of *Bell v Lever Bros Ltd*. However, this rule has always been subject to the qualification that the employee must not positively *mislead* the employer as to such matters,[228] and in the important case of *Sybron Corpn v Rochem Ltd*[229] it was further (1) suggested that there may be a duty to disclose the employee's own misconduct which has been fraudulently concealed, and (2) held that there may be on the facts of the case a positive duty to disclose the misconduct of *other* employees (particularly in the case of an employee high in the company's hierarchy, with responsibility for those other employees) even if that involves of necessity disclosing his own misconduct.[230] In *Tesco Stores v Pook*[231] a senior manager (*not* a director) defrauded the company to the tune of £0.5m, for which he was sentenced to imprisonment. When the company sought to recover another £0.3m in relation to a bribe that he had taken, he counterclaimed for share options that he said he had been denied by the company. The judge dismissed this counterclaim, partly by finding an implied term that the options would not be exercisable if the employee committed dismissible fraud, but also by holding that, at his level of seniority, he had been in breach of contract himself by not disclosing the bribe. While it is true that a bribe may give rise to a fiduciary duty to account for it, and once a fiduciary duty arises it is easier to find a duty to disclose, the judge also relied on *Sybron Corpn*, even though there was no question of misconduct by other employees. What seemed to be relevant here was the employee's *seniority* and the overall point of interest is whether a case such as this is showing a movement towards extending duties very similar to fiduciary ones down *below* board level, at least to

---

[228] Hence the importance, on recruitment, of the employer asking the right questions (eg at an interview) so that the employee cannot simply refrain from volunteering information and obtain the employment sub silentio. Deliberate fraud in gaining employment will usually be a fair ground for dismissal: *City of Birmingham District Council v Beyer* [1978] 1 All ER 910, [1977] IRLR 211. Moreover, in the light of *Fishel* (n 227) an employer may be advised to include in the appointed employee's contract a clause specifically requiring disclosure (eg of any other employment or activities to be undertaken) if it is likely to be a significant issue.

[229] [1983] 2 All ER 707, [1983] IRLR 253, CA.

[230] Applying *Swain v West (Butchers) Ltd* [1936] 3 All ER 261, CA. A case possibly going further is *RBG Resources plc v Rastogi* [2002] EWHC 2782, Ch D (see Lewis (2004) 33 ILJ 278) where it was thought arguable that a senior manager may have a duty not just to disclose misconduct by others but to *investigate* it initially, with a view to disclosing it.

[231] [2004] IRLR 618, Ch D.

senior managers. If so, arguably the result is that, although *Bell v Lever Bros* has not been subject to frontal assault, there have been moves in recent years to undermine it, particularly where the facts of the case (in *Pook* the bribe) can be used to convince the court that it is 'special' enough to be treated as an exception. On the other hand, the courts may have to be careful that they do not go too far and erect positive duties on ordinary employees that are too onerous. While it is true that in recent years the law has taken major steps to protect those who *choose* to whistleblow,[232] it would be a different matter for the law to develop so as to impose on ordinary employees an actual *obligation* to whistleblow.

From this general discussion of fidelity, we must now turn to four specific ways in which an employee might be in breach of his duty—by competition, misuse of confidential information, making his own inventions and failing to serve the employer in good faith.

(a) Competition

The courts will be most reluctant to impose restraints on a person's spare time and generally an employee's skills are his own (even if learned in the employer's time) so that normally there is no legal objection to an employee taking other employment in his spare time. The courts will, however, interfere in the untypical case where the use of the employee's skill and knowledge can be clearly shown to be harming the employer. This was the situation in the leading case of *Hivac Ltd v Park Royal Scientific Instruments Ltd*.[233] Certain employees of the plaintiff company worked in their spare time on a similar kind of highly specialized work for the defendant company, the two firms being in direct competition. There was no evidence that any of the employees (who were not parties to the action) had divulged any confidential information. It was found that the employees had agreed to do and had done work which they knew must harm their employers, that this was a breach of their duty of fidelity and that the defendant company would be restrained from employing them. The court made something of the fact that because of the abnormality of the times and the operation of an essential work order, the employees could not easily be dismissed, but it is doubtful how far this is relevant, as the principle remains that where the employee harms his employer the law may interfere:

> It would be most unfortunate if anything we said should place an undue restraint on the right of the workman, particularly a manual workman, to make use of his leisure for his profit. On the other hand, it would be deplorable if it were laid down that a workman could, consistently with his duty to his employer, knowingly, deliberately and secretly set himself to do in his spare time something which would inflict great harm on his master's business.[234]

---

[232] See p 179.   [233] [1946] Ch 169, [1946] 1 All ER 350, CA.

[234] [1946] Ch 169 at 178, [1946] 1 All ER 350 at 356, per Lord Greene MR. This dictum was applied by the EAT to an unfair dismissal claim in *Nova Plastics Ltd v Frogatt* [1982] IRLR 146, reinforcing the requirement of definite harm to the employer before an ordinary employee can be said to be in breach of this duty; see also *Helmet Integrated Systems Ltd v Tunnard* [2007] IRLR 126, CA.

There may, therefore, be cases where the courts will restrain competition, but even then it will only be during the course of employment, and will not apply to competition by an ex-employee.[235] If the employer wishes to fetter competition after the employee leaves him it will have to be by an express restraint clause[236] and, as we have seen in the previous chapter, even then the clause will only be valid if there is some definite element of trade secrets, customer connections or staff preservation to protect, for the courts will not allow a clause which is aimed simply at stifling competition.[237]

If an employee engages in improper competition that may be a valid reason for dismissal, though as always in the realm of unfair dismissal the fact that it is a breach of contract is not conclusive (as it might have been at common law for wrongful dismissal) and the dismissal must still be fair in all the circumstances, including the procedure adopted.[238] If the employer finds that the employee is soliciting customers with a view to setting up in business when he leaves, that too may be a valid ground for pre-emptive dismissal, but once again the evidence of this will have to be clear, and may require reasonable investigation by the employer before this step is taken;[239] if the further elements of trade secrets or other confidential information being at risk are not present, however, merely planning to leave employment to work for a competitor or to set up in competition will probably not be a fair ground for dismissal.[240]

(b) Misuse or disclosure of confidential information

During the course of employment the employee is under an implied duty not to misuse confidential information belonging to his employer[241] and this is a duty which may continue to operate after the termination of his employment; however, it was pointed out by the Court of Appeal in what has for some time now been viewed as the leading modern case on the subject, *Faccenda Chicken Ltd v Fowler*,[242] that there is a

---

[235] *JA Mont (UK) Ltd v Mills* [1993] IRLR 172, CA. The combination of the duty on an *existing* employee not to compete and a long notice provision produces a 'garden leave clause': see Ch 6, heading 2, p 429.

[236] This was reaffirmed by the Court of Appeal in *Caterpillar Logistics Services (UK) Ltd v de Crean* [2012] IRLR 410, CA where an attempt to extend this form of 'barring out' relief to cases of breach only of this implied term (ie with no express restraint clause to rely on) was rejected.

[237] *Herbert Morris Ltd v Saxelby* [1916] 1 AC 688, HL; *Faccenda Chicken Ltd v Fowler* [1986] ICR 297, [1986] IRLR 69, CA.

[238] *Gibson v National Union of Dyers, Bleachers and Textile Workers* (1972) 7 ITR 324; *Golden Cross Hire Co Ltd v Lovell* [1979] IRLR 267.

[239] *Hawkins v Prickett* [1976] IRLR 52, IT.

[240] *Harris and Russell Ltd v Slingsby* [1973] 3 All ER 31, [1973] ICR 454; *Laughton and Hawley v Bapp Industrial Supplies Ltd* [1986] ICR 634, [1986] IRLR 245; cf, however, *Marshall v Industrial Systems and Control Ltd* [1992] IRLR 294 where a managing director, proposing to leave, had suborned two other employees and approached customers (*Laughton* distinguished), and *Adamson v B & L Cleaning Services Ltd* [1995] IRLR 193 where the foreman of a contract cleaning firm tendered for a contract in competition with his employer prior to leaving to set up his own firm, and was fairly dismissed.

[241] *Bents Brewery Co Ltd v Hogan* [1945] 2 All ER 570; see generally Bryan 'The Employee and Trade Secrets Law' (1977) 30 CLP 191.

[242] [1986] ICR 297, [1986] IRLR 69, CA, noted Hepple [1986] 15 ILJ 183; applied in *Roger Bullivant Ltd v Ellis* [1987] ICR 464, [1987] IRLR 491, CA and *Johnson & Bloy (Holdings) Ltd v Wolstenholme Rink plc* [1987] IRLR 499, CA.

difference in the content and extent of the duty—in the case of an existing employee the obligation of confidentiality is wider (covering matters such as the employee's own particular skills and knowledge acquired generally during the employment) than in the case of an ex-employee whose obligations to his ex-employer are restricted to the kind of trade secrets or confidential customer connections that could be the subject of a valid restraint of trade clause.[243] To cover this latter case (of an ex-employee), in any employment where questions of confidentiality are at all likely to be material the employer is well advised to extract from the employee such an express restraint clause (or a garden leave clause) which is not only more certain, but which may in practice be more effective for, provided that it is valid, it will stop the ex-employee actually entering employment where he may be tempted to divulge confidential information, whereas the implied duty of fidelity could only be used to seek to prevent him from divulging such information once he is in the employment in question. An express clause is thus preferable, but if the employer omits to negotiate one or if there is an express clause which stops short of imposing any actual restraints on the employee, the courts will usually find an implied term as in *Robb v Green*[244] where a manager secretly copied out lists of his employer's customers, left the employment and set up in competition using the lists: the Court of Appeal upheld the injunction which had been granted restraining the ex-employee and Lord Esher MR said:

> I think that in a contract of service the Court must imply such a stipulation as I have mentioned (ie, that the servant will act with good faith towards his master), because it is a thing which must necessarily have been in view of both parties when they entered into the contract. It is impossible to suppose that a master would have put a servant into a confidential position of this kind, unless he thought that the servant would be bound to use good faith towards him; or that the servant would not know, when he entered into this position, that the master would rely on his observance of good faith in the confidential relation between them.

Thus, in *Sanders v Parry*[245] an assistant solicitor who set up independently, taking away from his employer one of the practice's main clients whose affairs he had looked after, was held to have broken his implied duty of good faith.

In general, the same rules will apply to this implied duty as apply to express restraint of trade clauses, and these are considered in the previous chapter; in particular, the duty will apply essentially to trade secrets and customer connections (those being recognized by the law as protectable interests, with increasingly the addition of staff preservation), there must be a genuine element of secrecy attached to the information in question, the

---

[243] Thus, in *Wallace Bogan & Co v Cove* [1997] IRLR 453, CA solicitors leaving their employer to set up their own firm played it 'by the book', doing nothing to infringe the higher duties before leaving; but *then* writing to clients of the old employer announcing the existence of the new firm. *Held*—no general restriction on this form of competition after employment, in the absence of a restraint of trade clause.

[244] [1895] 2 QB 315, CA; the passage cited is at 317.

[245] [1967] 2 All ER 803, [1967] 1 WLR 753. Contrast on the facts *Wallace Bogan & Co v Cove* [1997] IRLR 453, CA, n 243.

duty will not apply to ordinary skills or knowledge gained during employment, and it will not be allowed in order simply to stifle bona fide competition.[246] However, even though essentially the same principles apply, the express clause remains preferable, for it will normally restrain the ex-employee from entering certain forms of employment during a particular period, and so breach of it will readily be shown, whereas the implied duty allows other employment, only restraining the ex-employee from improper disclosure and this may be far more difficult to *prove*, particularly where there is no tangible evidence such as the deliberate copying out of plans or lists (as in *Robb v Green*).[247] This problem arises because of the difficult borderline between the ordinary use of information and expertise, albeit gained in the previous employment, which is permissible,[248] and the improper misuse of confidential information which may be restrainable; this may be further complicated if the ex-employee is using some information from each category, and the principle has been stated by Lord Denning in *Seager v Copydex Ltd*[249] thus:

> When the information is mixed, being partly public and partly private then the recipient must take special care to use only the material which is in the public domain. He should go to the public source to get it; or, at any rate, not be in a better position than if he had gone to the public source. He should not get a start over others by using the information which he received in confidence.

The difficulties of applying such a principle to any particular set of facts, for example where a technical director has left his employer and gone to work for a competitor on similar work, are great, and in the light of this it may be the case in practice that although there is no legal requirement that the ex-employee should have carried the information away in some tangible (particularly written) form before the duty can be used to restrain him (and so in some cases evidence of deliberate solicitation of customers prior to leaving has been sufficient),[250] the presence of evidence of such

---

[246] The assumption has also been hitherto that, like a restraint clause, the implied duty will lapse if the employee is wrongfully dismissed, under the rule in *General Billposting Co Ltd v Atkinson* [1909] AC 118, HL (see Ch 2, heading 4(v), p 99). However, *Campbell v Frisbee* [2002] EWCA Civ 1374, [2003] ICR 141 raised at least the possibility of a coterminous equitable obligation of confidence on an ex-employee (in particular not to divulge *personal* information about the ex-employer) which might survive an employer repudiation. The case itself was not determinative because all that the Court of Appeal were doing was to disapprove an order for summary judgment in favour of the claimant (the model Naomi Campbell); the matter was not dealt with on its merits: see Clarke (2003) 32 ILJ 43.

[247] If, however, it *is* the case that the employee leaves with written material containing confidential information, he may expect short shrift from a court, even if he argues that at least some of the information could have been carried away in his head: *Johnson & Bloy (Holdings) Ltd v Wolstenholme Rink plc* [1987] IRLR 499, CA, applying *Roger Bullivant Ltd v Ellis* [1987] ICR 464, [1987] IRLR 491, CA where Nourse LJ stated that it was still of great importance that the principle in *Robb v Green* should be steadfastly maintained.

[248] *Spafax Ltd v Harrison* [1980] IRLR 442, CA; *Faccenda Chicken Ltd v Fowler*, n 242.

[249] [1967] 2 All ER 415 at 417, [1967] RPC 349 at 368, CA. This dictum refers particularly to the position of a third party, which is considered below, but the principle is applicable to the ex-employee himself.

[250] *Wessex Dairies Ltd v Smith* [1935] 2 KB 80, CA; *Thomas Marshall (Exports) Ltd v Guinle* [1978] ICR 905, [1978] IRLR 174; cf *Hawkins v Prickett* [1976] IRLR 52, IT.

conduct could be extremely persuasive and indeed in the lack of it the employer could have grave problems of proof. Considering this problem in *Printers and Finishers Ltd v Holloway*[251] Cross J said, in the context of the ex-employee's knowledge of the general workings of the employer's business:

> Recalling matters of this sort is, to my mind, quite unlike memorising a formula or list of customers or what was said (obviously in confidence) at a particular meeting. The employee might well not realise that the feature or expedient in question was in fact peculiar to his late employer's process and factory; but even if he did such knowledge is not readily separable from his general knowledge of the flock printing process and his acquired skill in manipulating a flock printing plant, and I do not think that there was anything improper in his putting his memory or particular features of his late employer's plant at the disposal of his new employer. The law will defeat its own object if it seeks to enforce in this field standards which would be rejected by the ordinary man.

The employer failed on this particular part of the case, essentially because his case was too vague (as in *Baker v Gibbons*),[252] and this is likely to be the case wherever the employer lacks compelling evidence such as deliberate subterfuge and compilation of information.[253]

If an employee or ex-employee is misusing confidential information, what remedies are available to the employer? If the employee is still in employment, it might well be a good reason for dismissal which is likely to be held to be fair.[254] If he has already left employment, the employer may seek an injunction to restrain him from passing on information or damages for breach of the implied duty as in *Sanders v Parry*.[255] A complication might arise if the ex-employee passes on confidential information to a third party, for example a competitor with whom he has taken employment or a company which he has set up in order to take advantage of his illicit knowledge. This, however, has not proved a problem, for the original employer may sue that third party, seeking an injunction restraining him from taking advantage of the information either on the narrower ground of inducement to breach of contract[256] (particularly if the employee in question is still in employment with the original employer) or on the

---

[251] [1964] 3 All ER 731 at 736, [1965] 1 WLR 1 at 6.

[252] [1972] 2 All ER 759, [1972] 1 WLR 693.

[253] This is as a matter of evidence; there is, however, no legal principle that an employee is free to use *anything* carried away only in his head: *Johnson & Bloy (Holdings) Ltd v Wolstenholme Rink plc* [1987] IRLR 499, CA, disapproving dicta in favour of such a principle by Scott J in *Balston Ltd v Headline Filters Ltd* [1987] FSR 330.

[254] *Smith v Du Pont (UK) Ltd* [1976] IRLR 107, IT.

[255] [1967] 2 All ER 803, [1967] 1 WLR 753. See Goulding 'Springboard Injunctions in Employment Law' (1995) 24 ILJ 152. In *Johnson & Bloy (Holdings) Ltd v Wolstenholme Rink plc* [1987] IRLR 499, CA it was held that a plaintiff employer in such a case should normally be entitled to an injunction—it is not enough for the defendant to offer an undertaking not to use the information to compete with the plaintiff (with the prospect only of damages if there is in fact unlawful competition).

[256] *Bents Brewery Ltd v Hogan* [1945] 2 All ER 570; *Hivac v Park Royal Scientific Instruments Ltd* [1946] Ch 169, [1946] 1 All ER 350, CA. The injunction may even order the new employer not to proceed with contracts already entered into: *PSM International plc v Whitehouse* [1992] IRLR 279, CA.

wider ground of breach of confidence. The exact basis and extent of this latter equitable concept are still arguable and some fundamental questions await a definite answer[257] (for example whether there is a breach if the recipient of the information is ignorant of its source or confidential nature and, if so, what the remedy should be). Whatever be the details and developments, however, it is capable of being a useful weapon against a third party in cases such as these, as a further ground for an injunction or damages,[258] or, perhaps of more value, as a ground for ordering an account of profits[259] and delivery up or destruction of the material in question.[260] Thus, to take a useful example from an Australian jurisdiction, in *Ansell Rubber Co v Allied Rubber Industries*[261] the plaintiff company made rubber gloves from machines whose parts and principles were known, but the actual construction of which was secret. One of their employees, A, left their employment and set up the defendant company using identical machines, and a fellow employee, G, remained in employment while helping A to do so. In the subsequent action, the court held (1) that the construction of a machine is capable of being a matter of confidence, albeit made from known components; (2) that A was in breach of his contractual duty of fidelity through misuse of confidential information, G was likewise in breach for that reason and through improper competition while still employed, and the defendant company had received and misused confidential information and so was in breach of confidence; (3) that the plaintiff company should be awarded damages against A and G, an account of profits against the defendant company and injunctions restraining any further use of the information and the machines.

One exception to the duty not to misuse or divulge confidential information arises where disclosure by the employee or ex-employee is in the public interest. This might arise where the employer is committing a criminal offence, but it might also go wider than this. The exception evolved at common law, but is now also covered by statute.

(i) *Common law* In *Initial Services Ltd v Putterill*[262] the ex-employee gave to a newspaper details of an unlawful price-protection ring involving the employers (contrary to the Restrictive Trade Practices Act 1956) and of price rises attributed to

---

[257] On breach of confidence generally see *Saltman Engineering Co Ltd v Campbell Engineering Co Ltd* [1963] 3 All ER 413n, (1965) 65 RPC 203, CA; *Seager v Copydex Ltd* [1967] 2 All ER 415, [1967] RPC 349, CA; *Sun Printers Ltd v Westminster Press Ltd* [1982] IRLR 292, CA: Report on Breach of Confidence (Law Com No 110).

[258] *Seager v Copydex Ltd (No 2)* [1969] 2 All ER 718, [1969] 1 WLR 809, CA. Causation must be proved: *Universal Thermosensors Ltd v Hibben* [1992] 3 All ER 257, [1992] 1 WLR 840.

[259] *Peter Pan Manufacturing Corpn v Corsets Silhouette Ltd* [1963] 3 All ER 402, [1963] RPC 45. In a rather more sensational context, the possibility of an action for an account of profits through misuse of confidential information was mentioned as a further remedy for the government against Mr Peter Wright, author of *Spycatcher*, in the light of its failure to have it suppressed in other jurisdictions; no such proceedings were brought in the event.

[260] *Industrial Furnaces Ltd v Reaves* [1970] RPC 605.

[261] [1967] VR 37; the judgment of Gowans J contains an extensive review of the relevant British and US authorities on confidential information. For a more recent example, see *PSM International plc v Whitehouse* [1992] IRLR 279, CA.

[262] [1968] 1 QB 396, [1967] 3 All ER 145, CA.

Selective Employment Tax in order to disguise higher profits. The Court of Appeal held that this was capable of constituting proper disclosure in the public interest, and Lord Denning MR clearly envisaged that this exception went beyond crime and fraud and applied wherever disclosure was justified in the public interest. This principle was applied in *Fraser v Evans*[263] and *Hubbard v Vosper*[264] but was subject to restriction in *Beloff v Pressdram Ltd*[265] by Ungoed-Thomas J who thought that it only applied to the disclosure of 'misdeeds of a serious nature' by the employer. However, this restrictive view was later disapproved by the Court of Appeal in *Lion Laboratories Ltd v Evans*[266] where it was held that public interest disclosure could apply to a wide range of matters, of which 'iniquity' on the part of the employer was only one example. Moreover, disclosure in the public interest may be particularly justified where that disclosure is to a regulatory body with power of investigation and control of the employer's business.[267] This whole area became topical with increasing concern being expressed over attempts by certain employers to prevent any form of disclosure by employees by the incorporation of 'gagging clauses' into their contracts, for example banning them from talking to the press about anything concerning their employment, and making it a disciplinary offence to do so.[268] Particular concern arose over the use of such clauses by the newly independent trusts and other bodies in the NHS.[269] While at one level the incorporation of an express clause could be likened to the (lawful) use of a restraint of trade clause (rather than relying on the general implied term of confidentiality), the suspicion was quick to arise that these clauses were really intended to go further and prevent *any* disclosure or, as it has come to be known, whistleblowing.

(ii) *Statute* Although the above common law will continue to apply by way of a defence to a civil action, concerns such as those above allied with certain moves (eg the Nolan Committee) towards more openness about standards in public life led to calls for more direct protection for the *individual* employee making disclosures in

---

[263] [1969] 1 QB 349, [1969] 1 All ER 8, CA.

[264] [1972] 2 QB 84, [1972] 1 All ER 1023, CA.

[265] [1973] 1 All ER 241 at 260. The earlier authorities would have restricted it to criminal acts or danger to the state: *Weld-Blundell v Stephens* [1920] AC 956, HL. Note that an employee may in certain circumstances be under a statutory duty to disclose certain material, eg under the Health and Safety at Work etc Act 1974, ss 27 and 28.

[266] [1985] QB 526, [1984] 2 All ER 417, CA. This is an interesting case on the application of the public interest defence, containing inter alia a statement by Stephenson LJ that not all that is interesting to the public may be disclosed in the public interest, and a reminder that the press may have a private interest of their own in making disclosures, which may be a factor to be taken into account.

[267] *Re a Company's Application* [1989] ICR 449, [1989] IRLR 477.

[268] Lewis 'Whistleblowers and Job Security' (1995) 58 MLR 208.

[269] Vickers 'Whistleblowers and the NHS' (1995) NLJ 57. One such clause even prevented employees from contacting their MP without going through (protracted?) internal procedures. One irony is that, at the same time as concern was mounting about this practice, doctors were themselves being placed under a contractual *obligation* to blow the whistle on allegedly negligent colleagues (though not of course on the activities of the increasing legions of hospital administrators, a breed who have rapidly overtaken undertakers, farmers, estate agents and solicitors to rival bankers in the public hate stakes).

the public interest. This came about through a Private Member's Bill, backed by the government as a commitment in the White Paper 'Fairness at Work', which became the Public Interest Disclosure Act 1998.[270] This operates by way of additions to the Employment Rights Act 1996 to establish special protection from dismissal[271] or action short of dismissal[272] imposed because the worker[273] has made a 'protected disclosure'. This is the disclosure of information which, in the reasonable belief of the worker making the disclosure, tends to show a criminal offence, a failure to comply with a legal obligation, a miscarriage of justice, a health and safety danger, environmental damage, or deliberate concealment of any of these.[274] As with the wider view of the common law, this goes well beyond criminal offences and to that extent the protection is wide. Indeed, in its first fifteen years this increasing width led to arguments that it was being applied more widely than Parliament had intended (particularly at the suit of employees dismissed before serving the qualifying employment for unfair dismissal) and too far away from its roots in protecting the *public* interest, especially as *Parkins v Sodexho Ltd*[275] (the first major EAT decision) applied 'failure to comply with a legal obligation' to complaints about the employee's own contractual terms and conditions, potentially extending the scope for complaint substantially. Recently, however, two developments have shown a deliberate narrowing of the ambit of whistleblowing. First, case law has established that to be a protected disclosure at

---

[270] Lewis 'The Public Interest Disclosure Act 1998' (1998) 27 ILJ 325, 'Whistleblowing at Work: on What Principles Should Legislation Be Based?' (2001) 30 ILJ 169 and 'Providing Rights for Whistleblowers: Would an Anti-discrimination Model Be More Effective?' (2005) 34 ILJ 239.

[271] Employment Rights Act 1996, s 103A; such a dismissal is automatically unfair, as is any later selection for redundancy for this reason; there is no qualifying period or upper age limit; the cap on the compensatory award for unfair dismissal has been removed completely in these cases and interim relief is available. According to Public Concern at Work (the charity that was the architect of the Act) in the first three years of this new law, there was a success rate of 46% before tribunals; the highest award was £805,000, the lowest £1,000 and (perhaps most significantly) the average was £107,117, a remarkably high figure.

[272] Section 47B.

[273] The 1998 Act adopts the wider definition of 'worker' in the Employment Rights Act 1996, s 230(3), ie a person under a contract of employment *or* under any other contract to do or perform personally any work or services for another (other than a client or customer of any profession or business undertaking carried out by the person); see Ch 2, heading 1(vi), p 67. In an appropriate case the protection can apply to victimization after termination of employment: *Woodward v Abbey National plc* [2006] EWCA Civ 822. For good measure, s 43K specifically includes agency workers, homeworkers, work trainees and certain specified NHS staff who might not otherwise have qualified. Although the terminology of unfair dismissal is of course being used, the Act can go wider than the employment relationship because there is no requirement that the divulged information must show evil-doing by the worker's employer (though of course in many cases that will be so).

[274] Section 43B(1). These matters may occur in the UK or abroad: s 43B(2). The reference to the reasonable belief of the worker means that there can still be a protected disclosure if some or all of the allegations are later not substantiated: *Darnton v University of Surrey* [2003] ICR 615, [2003] IRLR 133; *Babula v Waltham Forest College* [2007] IRLR 346, CA. However, a worker may not use improper means (eg computer hacking) to try to find evidence leading to that reasonable belief: *Bolton School v Evans* [2006] EWCA Civ 1653. The further requirement that the disclosure must have been made 'in good faith' may import an element of motive, so that a disclosure for another purpose (eg revenge) will not be covered, even if true: *Street v Derbyshire Unemployed Workers' Centre* [2005] ICR 97, [2004] IRLR 687, CA.

[275] [2002] IRLR 109.

all the actions of the employee must disclose *information* showing the wrongdoing in question; the corollary of this is that the protection is not extended to mere *allegations or adverse opinions* about the employer by the employee.[276] Secondly, the Coalition government took the opportunity of the Enterprise and Regulatory Reform Act 2013 to take the unusual step of reversing *Parkins v Sodexho* by statute; this was done by reading into the above definition of a protected disclosure that it must be 'in the reasonable belief of the worker making the disclosure *and in the public interest*', thus arguably bringing it back to the original aim of the 1998 Act.

The drafting makes it clear that the Act is also meant to strike a balance and not simply to allow the whistleblower to go straight to the press on all occasions, especially where the press in question are waving chequebooks.[277] To that extent, it has advantages to an employer too in emphasizing that disclosure is primarily and initially meant to be internal.[278] This is achieved by establishing the forms of disclosure that have the protected status, with four categories of disclosure to named persons, backed up by two categories of wider disclosure which are subject to much more stringent conditions. The four 'normal' categories are disclosure:

(a) in good faith, to the employer or where the worker reasonably believes that the relevant failure relates solely or mainly to the conduct of another person or to any other matter for which another person has legal responsibility, to that person;[279]

(b) to a legal adviser, in the course of obtaining legal advice;[280]

(c) in good faith, to a Minister of the Crown (where the worker's employer is appointed by a Minister);[281]

(d) to a person prescribed by order by the Secretary of State, where the worker reasonably believes that the relevant failure falls within the order and that the information disclosed (and any allegation contained in it) are substantially true.[282]

Obviously, cases may well arise where one of these is not appropriate (particularly where the person to whom disclosure is primarily meant to be made is actually the

---

[276] *Cavendish Munro Ltd v Geduld* [2010] IRLR 38; *Goode v Marks & Spencer plc* UKEAT/0442/09. In the former case the example was given that if a nurse made a complaint that needles were being left unsafely on wards, that could constitute whistleblowing; if, however, the nurse merely aired the opinion that health and safety was not taken seriously at the hospital, that would not be.

[277] '[The Act] will encourage resolution of concerns through proper workplace procedures, but it will protect those who, in the last resort, have to go public': Fairness at Work (Cm 3968, 1998) para 3.3.

[278] Although there is no obligation in the Act for an employer to have a formal whistleblowing policy, this may well be advisable so that complaints/disclosures can be dealt with effectively in-house, thus avoiding the possibility of a protected disclosure to the press.

[279] Section 43C.   [280] Section 44D.   [281] Section 43E.

[282] Section 43F. See the Public Interest Disclosure (Prescribed Persons) Order 1999, SI 1999/1549, *Harvey* R [1183].

culprit—in this context of course, the employer) and so the Act then establishes two longstops, where the worker is in effect allowed to 'go public':

(1) 'disclosure in other cases'[283]—this applies where (a) the worker makes the disclosure in good faith, (b) he reasonably believes that the information disclosed (and any allegations contained in it) are substantially true, (c) he does not make the disclosure for personal gain, (d) any one of a series of conditions is met[284] and (e) in all the circumstances of the case, it is reasonable for him to make the disclosure;[285]

(2) 'disclosure of exceptionally serious failure'[286]—this applies where (a) the worker makes the disclosure in good faith, (b) he reasonably believes that the information disclosed (and any allegations contained in it) are substantially true, (c) he does not make the disclosure for purposes of personal gain, (d) the relevant failure is of an exceptionally serious nature (undefined) and (e) in all the circumstances of the case, it is reasonable for him to make the disclosure.[287]

The question of gagging clauses is then dealt with directly and briefly by a provision which states that any provision in any agreement between a worker and his employer[288] (*including* a settlement of legal proceedings) is void in so far as it purports to preclude the worker from making a protected disclosure.[289]

Finally, one possible further statutory development should be noted which would operate in the opposite direction, ie to *increase* the liability of an individual (possibly an employee) in relation to the use of information. The Law Commission have suggested that it should become a *criminal* offence (triable on indictment) knowingly to use or disclose a trade secret belonging to another without that other's consent.[290] Clearly this

---

[283] Section 43G.

[284] The conditions are that (1) the worker reasonably believes that he will be subjected to a detriment by his employer if he makes the disclosure to him or to a prescribed person; or (2) that, where there is no prescribed person, the worker reasonably believes that it is likely that evidence relating to the relevant failure will be concealed or destroyed if he makes disclosure to his employer; or (3) that the worker has previously made a disclosure of substantially the same information to his employer or a prescribed person: s 43F(2).

[285] In deciding on reasonableness, regard is to be had to (1) the identity of the person (or tabloid?) to whom disclosure is made; (2) the seriousness of the relevant failure; (3) whether the failure is continuing or likely to occur in the future; (4) whether the disclosure is made in breach of a duty of confidentiality owed by the employer to any other person; (5) in a case of previous disclosure (under s 43G(2)(c)) any action which the employer or prescribed person has taken or might reasonably be expected to have taken as a result; and (6) in a case of previous disclosure to the employer, whether the worker complied with any disclosure procedure whose use by him was authorized by the employer: s 43G(3). The final head shows the possible importance of a whistleblowing policy in ensuring that disclosure follows the correct internal channels, rather than spilling out too easily into the public arena.

[286] Section 43H.

[287] In deciding on reasonableness, regard is to be had in particular to the identity of the person to whom the disclosure is made: s 43H(2).

[288] Whether or not a 'worker's contract' (under the extended definition in the Employment Rights Act 1996, s 230(3)).

[289] Section 43J. A disclosure not protected under the Act would not come under this provision and so a gagging clause covering it would be valid *unless* a court were persuaded to strike it down at common law.

[290] Misuse of Trade Secrets (Law Com No 150, 1997). One other possibility raised in the paper is an offence of dishonest acquisition of trade secrets. See generally Colling 'Should the Use and Disclosure of Trade Secrets Be Criminalised?' (1998) 27 ILJ 147.

would need a carefully drafted public interest defence; the consultation paper came before the Public Interest Disclosure Act 1998 and so contained its own proposed draft of such a defence (including 'any use or disclosure of information which under the law of confidence would be justified on grounds of public interest'), but any developments in this area would now need to be consistent with the 1998 Act; of equal interest would be how it was proposed to define 'trade secret', still a notorious area of difficulty in the civil context after a century of case law. It may be that we hear little more about this proposal.

(c) The employee's inventions

In the absence of an express term in the contract of employment, the common law position was that the employer was entitled to the benefit of inventions made by his employee if they were referable to the employment. Thus, in *British Syphon Co Ltd v Homewood*[291] the defendant discovered a new type of soda syphon and applied to patent it; he was employed by the plaintiffs as a chief technician to advise them generally on their business, but he had not been asked to make any new designs and there was no express agreement between them on the matter of inventions. Roxburgh J held that the plaintiffs were entitled to the benefit of the invention which had arisen out of the employment. This was a strong implied term at common law, usually explained on the basis of fidelity, and it would apply if the parties were silent or if an express term was void through being too wide; moreover, it would continue to apply even if the employee went ahead and patented the invention, for then it was held that he held the patent on trust for the employer.[292] It was even held that the employee might be under a continuing duty to do anything necessary to assist the employer to realize the patent.[293] Not every invention belonged to the employer, however, and much might depend on the nature of the invention and the position of the employee, but the employee was only really safe if the nature of the invention was clearly outside the employer's business interest;[294] however, if it was safely outside those interests, the fact that it was made during working hours or with the employer's materials would not deprive the employee of it[295] and indeed even an express term giving the benefit of *any* invention to the employer might be void as in restraint of trade.[296] Section 56(2) of the Patents Act 1949 appeared to mitigate this possibly harsh implied term by allowing the comptroller to apportion the benefits of an invention between employer and employee unless satisfied that one party was absolutely entitled, but this was construed restrictively by the House of Lords in *Sterling Engineering Co Ltd v Patchett*[297] so that it did

---

[291] [1956] 2 All ER 897, [1956] 1 WLR 1190. See also *British Reinforced Concrete Engineering Co v Lind* (1917) 86 LJ Ch 486.

[292] *Triplex Safety Glass Co Ltd v Scorah* [1938] Ch 211, [1937] 4 All ER 693.

[293] *British Celanese Ltd v Moncrieff* [1948] Ch 564, [1948] 2 All ER 44, CA.

[294] *Re Selz Ltd* (1953) 71 RPC 158.   [295] *Mellor v Beardmore* (1927) 44 RPC 175.

[296] *Electrolux Ltd v Hudson* [1977] FSR 312.

[297] [1955] AC 534, [1955] 1 All ER 369, HL.

not apply to the majority of employment cases where, by the operation of the implied term, the employer was already absolutely entitled to the invention. The whole area of patent law was overhauled, however, by the Patents Act 1977, and so the common law will now only apply (1) to inventions made before the commencement of the relevant parts of the Act;[298] (2) where the Act does not apply, in particular where the employee was not 'mainly employed in the United Kingdom', but, under the conflict of laws rules, the matter remains generally governed by English law.[299]

For present purposes, the modern legislation made two innovations—it sets out in section 39 when an invention will belong to the employer, and provides in sections 40 and 41 a scheme for compensating an employee inventor which is quite independent of contractual obligations. Now, therefore, most disputes as to employee inventions will be solved by a process of statutory interpretation, not by recourse to the common law rules. Section 39(1) provides that an invention belongs to the employee except in two specified instances when, for the purposes of the Act and all other purposes, it belongs to the employer; these are:

(1) if it was made *in the course of the normal duties of the employee* or in the course of duties falling *outside his normal duties, but specifically assigned to him*, and the circumstances in either case were such that an invention might reasonably be expected to result from the carrying out of his duties; or

(2) if the invention was made in the course of the duties of the employee and at the time of making the invention, because of the nature of his duties, he had a *special obligation to further the interests of the employer's undertaking.*[300]

Unlike the common law position, this owes nothing to concepts of fidelity, and contentious points now are likely to be whether the invention was reasonably to be expected, and in what circumstances an employee is under the special obligation mentioned in paragraph (b) (a director under a fiduciary duty would presumably be covered, but the question is how far coverage will extend outside that special case).[301] By section 42, any agreement purporting to diminish the employee's rights in an invention under section 39 is unenforceable to the extent that it does so diminish those rights.

---

[298] Patents Act 1977, s 43(1); the 'appointed day' was 1 June 1978—Patents Act 1977 (Commencement No 2) Order 1978, SI 1978/586.

[299] Section 43(2).

[300] Emphasis added. For a rare example of litigation under these provisions, see *LIFFE Administration & Management v Pinkava* [2007] ICR 1489, CA where it was held that the invention (in fact, unusually, a business method) had been made in the course of the employee's 'normal employment' and belonged to the employer. The court affirmed that these statutory provisions are to be construed as they stand, not by reference to the earlier case law.

[301] For detailed discussion of these provisions, see the Commentary section in the *Encyclopedia of United Kingdom and European Patent Law* and Phillips 'Employee Inventors and the New Patents Act' (1978) 7 ILJ 30; *Reiss Engineering Co Ltd v Harris* [1985] IRLR 232.

Sections 40 and 41 provide in addition a statutory scheme for compensation for an inventor employee. Under this scheme, the employee may make a claim to the Patents Court or the Patents Office within a year of the expiry of the patent for compensation in one of two circumstances:

(a) where the invention belonged to the employer under section 39 and proved to be of 'outstanding benefit'[302] to that employer; or

(b) where the invention belonged to the employee under section 39 and he assigned or exclusively leased it to the employer but received benefits from that contract which were 'inadequate in relation to the benefit derived by the employer from the patent'.

The court or comptroller is then empowered to award such compensation to the employee as will secure for him a 'fair share' of the actual or anticipated benefits derived from the patent. 'Fair share' is not defined, but section 41 lays down criteria to be considered. In the case of (a) above, these are:

(i) the nature of the employee's duties, his remuneration and any other advantages from his employment or the invention;

(ii) the employee's effort and skill in making the invention;

(iii) the effort and skill of any third party involved;

(iv) the significance of any contributions of the employer towards the invention (for example advice, facilities).

In the case of (b) above, they are:

(i) any conditions in any licences granted under the Act in respect of the invention or the patent;

(ii) any extent to which the invention was a joint project with a third party;

(iii) any contributions by the employer (as in (iv) above).

An order for compensation may be for a lump sum or for periodic payments or both.[303] Any agreement purporting to exclude the employee's right to statutory compensation is ineffective, but these provisions do not apply where the matter is already governed by a collective agreement.[304]

The position with regard to copyright in material produced by an employee is governed by the Copyright, Designs and Patents Act 1988, section 11, which provides

---

[302] 'Outstanding' is not capable of definition and remains a question of fact in each case: *Memco-Med Ltd's Patent* [1992] RPC 403. It is a superlative term, not merely a comparative one, and so the burden of proof is a high one: *British Steel plc's Patent* [1992] RPC 117.

[303] The first reported cases of applications by employees under s 40 are set out and discussed in Wotherspoon 'Employee Inventions Revisited' (1993) 22 ILJ 119.

[304] Patents Act 1977, s 40(3).

that, although the first owner of copyright is the author, 'where a literary, dramatic, musical or artistic work or a film is made by an employee in the course of his employment, his employer is the first owner of any copyright in the work subject to any agreement to the contrary'. This straightforward provision does not attempt any more ambitious schemes of recompensing employed authors, such as that seen above in the patents legislation, being content instead to leave the matter as essentially one for agreement between the parties. It substantially re-enacts the pre-existing law which was contained in the repealed Copyright Act 1956, section 4, whose effect can be seen from the case of *Stevenson, Jordan and Harrison Ltd v MacDonald and Evans*[305] where an accountant employed by the plaintiff company wrote a book on business management; part was based on public lectures given during his employment, part was composed while engaged on a particular assignment for the employer, and the rest was written after leaving the employment. The Court of Appeal held that the lectures were not given pursuant to his contract of employment, but that the second part (composed whilst on the assignment) was produced in the course of his employment, and so the copyright in that part lay with the employer who could restrain publication of it.

(d) Failure to serve the employer faithfully

It has been seen above that the employee must obey proper orders of the employer and that there is a general duty of fidelity upon the employee. This does not give the employer an unrestricted prerogative and in general he will be bound by the terms of the contract of employment which he cannot change unilaterally. Thus, he cannot make the employee work overtime if it is purely voluntary or change the terms of employment (for example by making a day worker work nights where there is no such provision in the contract); to this extent the employee may stand upon the terms of the contract, and, if necessary, withdraw his goodwill, even if this has a disadvantageous effect on the employer's business. However, there may be cases where a lack of cooperation by the employee may be construed not as a lawful insistence upon observation of the contract, but instead as in fact collective industrial action aimed at prejudicing the employer's business. Although the employee may argue that this form of action (known, for example, as 'going slow', 'working to rule' or 'working to contract') is merely the insistence on the contractual minimum, it is clear that in some cases it can, in fact, be a *breach* of contract, in particular the implied duty to serve faithfully. The line between the two arguments can be a thin one, but it exists.

Strict adherence to contractual terms (on a collective level, as part of industrial action) was held capable of being a breach of contract by the Court of Appeal in *Secretary of State for Employment v ASLEF (No 2)*,[306] though the reasoning of the three judges varied. However, the leading case is now *British Telecommunications plc*

---

[305] (1952) 1 TLR 101, CA; see also *Beloff v Pressdram Ltd* [1973] 1 All ER 241.
[306] [1972] 2 QB 455, [1972] 2 All ER 949, CA. The case concerned long-repealed provisions of the Industrial Relations Act 1971.

v Ticehurst[307] where a college manager took part in industrial action, first by way of a go-slow and work to contract, and then escalating to a rolling campaign of strikes. The question arose[308] whether this action was lawful under the contract and the Court of Appeal held that it was a breach of the implied term 'to serve the employer faithfully within the requirements of the contract'. Adopting that formulation from the judgment of Buckley LJ in the *ASLEF* case, Ralph Gibson LJ said:

> It is, in my judgment, necessary to imply such a term in the case of a manager who is given charge of the work of other employees and who therefore must necessarily be trusted to exercise her judgment and discretion in giving instructions to others and in supervising their work. Such a discretion, if the contract is to work properly, must be exercised faithfully in the interests of the employers.

And later:

> The term is breached, in my judgment, when the employee does an act, or omits to do an act, which it would be within her contract and the discretion allowed to her not to do, or to do, as the case may be, and the employee so acts or omits to do the act, not in the honest exercise of choice or discretion for the faithful performance of her work but in order to disrupt the employer's business or to cause the most inconvenience that can be caused.[309]

Although the case concerns a manager, it is suggested that the key to this is not managerial status but, much more generally, employee *discretion* in how to perform the work. It may be that, if a job was exhaustively defined in the contract, there could still be a work to contract that would not be in breach,[310] *but* in modern conditions most jobs are not like that; in such circumstances, the decision in *Ticehurst* shows that such action is very likely to be a breach of the implied duty of faithful service in the contract.

Finally, it may be noted that in at least one area the employee may be under a positive obligation to cooperate with his employer, for under the Health and Safety at Work etc Act 1974, section 7(a), there is a statutory duty upon every employee 'as regards any duty or requirement imposed on his employer or any other person by or under any of the relevant statutory provisions, to cooperate with him so far as is necessary to enable that duty or requirement to be performed or complied with'.

---

[307] [1992] ICR 383, [1992] IRLR 219, CA.

[308] Whether or not such action is a breach of contract is not particularly relevant in the context of unfair dismissal, since the special provisions on dismissal during industrial action (Ch 10, heading 2(iii), p 698) apply to strikes 'or other industrial action', with the latter *not* depending on proof of breach of contract. However, this case concerned the equally vital question as to whether the employer can *refuse to pay* employees taking industrial action, where the question of breach is central; that aspect of the case is considered at heading 5(i), p 168.

[309] [1992] ICR 383 at 398, [1992] IRLR 219 at 225, CA. In *Burgess v Stevedoring Services Ltd* [2002] UKPC 39, [2002] IRLR 810 the Privy Council also adopted the narrower views of Buckley LJ in *ASLEF*, rather than the wider views adopted by Lord Denning. While this case is interesting (given the scarcity of recent authority on this abstruse point), it was under Bermudian legislation which has no UK counterpart and *Ticehurst*, n 307 (the leading UK case) was not discussed.

[310] It could, of course, still constitute 'industrial action' for statutory purposes, see n 308.

5 THE LAW RELATING TO WAGES

(i) THE RIGHT TO WAGES AT COMMON LAW

The obligation upon the employer to pay the wages which are due is a basic term of the contract of employment; details of the scale, rate or method of calculation of the remuneration should be given to the employee in writing,[311] and he has a statutory right to receive an itemized pay statement upon payment of wages or salary.[312] However, it must be stressed that the details of the obligation upon the employer depend entirely upon the terms of the contract of employment, and there cannot be said to be any overall legal obligation to pay wages as such, since wages are not necessarily the consideration to be supplied by the employer for the work done or service rendered by the employee. Thus, at common law there can be a valid contract of employment, even though no set wages are payable, where the employee is to be rewarded by a commission,[313] by fees, by the receipt of tips from customers[314] or by being given the *chance* to earn a salary.[315] Likewise, there will be no set wage or salary where the employee is paid on a piecework or hourly basis (with or without an agreed guaranteed minimum wage), though in such a case there may be an implied term that the employer shall provide a reasonable amount of work for the employee to do.[316] Moreover, in an extreme case it might be that the correct construction of the contract is that, in the circumstances, nothing is payable to the employee as in *Re Richmond Gate Property Co Ltd*[317] where the managing director of a company in liquidation had never had the question of his remuneration determined by the directors as required by the company's articles, and so Plowman J held that, in the circumstances, he was not entitled to receive anything for services rendered prior to the liquidation. Also, in certain older cases[318] it was held that an agreement which gives the employer the right to fix remuneration, gives him the right to give *no* remuneration. However, this is unlikely to be the case now, for where there is some reference to remuneration, or some discernible understanding that there would be remuneration, or where the contract is just vague on the subject, the employee may be able to recover a reasonable sum on a quantum meruit basis, as

---

[311] Employment Rights Act 1996, s 1(4); on the significance of different forms of remuneration, see Freedland 'The Obligation to Work and to Pay for Work' (1977) 30 CLP 175.

[312] Employment Rights Act 1996, s 8.

[313] *Phillips v Curling* (1847) 10 LTOS 245; *Clayton Newbury Ltd v Findlay* [1953] 2 All ER 826n, [1953] 1 WLR 1194n; *Bronester Ltd v Priddle* [1961] 3 All ER 471, [1961] 1 WLR 1294, CA.

[314] *Pauley v Kenaldo Ltd* [1953] 1 All ER 226, [1953] 1 WLR 187.

[315] *Gaumont-British Picture Corpn v Alexander* [1936] 2 All ER 1686.

[316] See heading 3(ii), p 141.

[317] [1964] 3 All ER 936, [1965] 1 WLR 335.

[318] *Taylor v Brewer* (1813) 1 M & S 290; *Roberts v Smith* (1859) 4 H & N 315. See, however, the explanation of these cases by Vaughan Williams LJ in *Loftus v Roberts* (1902) 18 TLR 532, CA.

in *Way v Latilla*[319] where the plaintiff, who had obtained gold mining concessions for the defendant (yielding a £1m profit) on the vague understanding that the defendant would 'look after his interests', was held by the House of Lords to be entitled to £5,000 commission on a quantum meruit basis when the defendant refused to pay him anything. Likewise, in *Powell v Braun*[320] a secretary who had been offered an unspecified annual bonus (having regard to the firm's performance) in place of the usual increase in wages was held by the Court of Appeal to be entitled to a reasonable amount on a quantum meruit basis for the two years during which her employer had failed to pay any bonus at all, thus establishing that a quantum meruit action may be used to recover additional remuneration as well as ordinary wages or salary. Some of these stranger forms of remuneration (or, indeed, possible non-remuneration) may of course now have to be read subject to the national minimum wage legislation (see Chapter 4), but that only specifies a minimum *amount* that must eventually be payable and does *not* mean that these forms in themselves are illegal.

One theoretical problem concerning the common law right to wages has arisen where the employee does not complete the relevant obligation in the contract of employment. In strict theory it may be that *no* remuneration is payable (even on a quantum meruit action), as in the old case of *Cutter v Powell*[321] where a sailor who contracted for 30 guineas to act as second mate for a certain voyage died in the course of that voyage and his widow failed to recover any of the amount agreed upon, since the court held that partial performance of an entire obligation did not give rise to a right to any of the remuneration. This principle is most unlikely to apply to a case today, for most contracts are divisible, not entire, certainly to the extent of definite periods for payment of remuneration.[322] Even if this were not so, an employee could attempt to circumvent *Cutter v Powell* in several ways—first, by claiming that the employer had received substantial performance of the contract and so was not relieved from payment;[323] second, if complete performance was prevented by the employer, by bringing a quantum meruit action;[324] third, where the contract was frustrated,[325] by claiming a just amount under the Law Reform (Frustrated Contracts) Act 1943, section 1(3); fourth, by claiming that his wages or salary are to be deemed to accrue from day to day (even though not so payable under the contract) under the Apportionment Act 1870, section 2 which thus apportions 'all rents, annuities, dividends and other periodic payments in the nature of

---

[319] [1937] 3 All ER 759, HL. See also *Craven-Ellis v Canons Ltd* [1936] 2 KB 403, [1936] 2 All ER 1066, CA.

[320] [1954] 1 All ER 484, [1954] 1 WLR 401, CA.

[321] (1795) 6 Term Rep 320, followed in *Sinclair v Bowles* (1829) 9 B & C 92 and *Vigers v Cook* [1919] 2 KB 475, CA.

[322] Details of the periods for payment must be given to the employee in writing: Employment Rights Act 1996, s 1(4).

[323] *Hoenig v Isaacs* [1952] 2 All ER 176, CA; *H Dakin & Co Ltd v Lee* [1916] 1 KB 566, CA; *Bolton v Mahadeva* [1972] 2 All ER 1322, [1972] 1 WLR 1009, CA.

[324] *Planché v Colburn* (1831) 5 C & P 58.

[325] See heading 5(iii), p 199.

income'—section 5 states that 'annuities' include 'salaries and pensions', and it appears that 'salaries' should be taken to include wages.[326]

In addition to this theoretical problem, three points might be mentioned particularly about the employee's right at common law to be paid his wages. The first is that an action for wages due, brought in the ordinary courts or a tribunal, might be used not just as an individual's remedy but also as a way of testing the legal position in what is in essence a collective dispute between employer and workforce (possibly by the device of bringing an action by one named individual, which is viewed in reality as a test case affecting an entire class of employees). In *Burdett-Coutts v Hertfordshire County Council*[327] the county council purported to vary the terms of employment of school dinner assistants without their consent (indeed, in the face of their positive dissent); they continued to work under protest, accepting the lower wages under the new terms, but brought an action in the High Court claiming, inter alia, the payment of the arrears of wages that were due under the pre-existing terms of employment; the judge held that on the facts they had *not* impliedly accepted the employer's variation by continuing to work, and gave judgment for the arrears. The validity of such an action was accepted by the Court of Appeal in *Miller v Hamworthy Engineering Ltd*[328] (enforced short-time working, not covered by the terms of the contract and not agreed to by the employee or his union) and, more importantly, in the short but emphatic decision of the House of Lords in *Rigby v Ferodo Ltd*[329] (unilateral reduction in wages by the employer, not agreed to by the employee or his union). The point about such an action (or the threat of it) is that it may oblige the employer (who wishes still to force through the new terms) to dismiss the employees formally, and then have to defend an action for unfair dismissal.[330]

However, this will only work if the employee is held to have been contractually in the right. This is because the second point is that in *Cresswell v Board of Inland Revenue*[331] Walton J held that where an employee refuses to perform duties that he is contractually obliged to perform, the simple principle 'no work, no pay' applies, so that an action for wages will then fail. Of course, such a principle begs the monumental question— what duties *is* the employee contractually obliged to perform? In fact, the case hinged on this question, and whether a requirement that the staff start to operate a newly

---

[326] *Moriarty v Regent's Garage Co Ltd* [1921] 1 KB 423 (reversed on other grounds: [1921] 2 KB 766, CA). See Matthews 'Salaries in the Apportionment Act 1870' (1982) 2 LS 302. 'Day to day' was held to mean working days, not calendar days, in the year, at least when claiming holiday pay under the Working Time Regulations: *Leisure Leagues UK Ltd v Maconnachie* [2002] IRLR 600 (disapproving *Thames Water Utilities v Reynolds* [1996] IRLR 186 on the basis that it was decided before those Regulations were introduced).

[327] [1984] IRLR 91. See also *Gibbons v Associated British Ports* [1985] IRLR 376.

[328] [1986] ICR 846, [1986] IRLR 461, CA.

[329] [1988] ICR 29, [1987] IRLR 516, HL.

[330] As in *Gilham v Kent County Council (No 2)* [1985] ICR 233, [1985] IRLR 18, CA; see Ch 8, heading 1(ii), p 566 on the application of unfair dismissal laws to this class of case.

[331] [1984] ICR 508, [1984] IRLR 190.

computerized system had or had not altered the nature of the job.[332] The principle has acquired particular significance in a series of cases concerning deductions from wages due to industrial action—if the employee fails wholly or partly to carry out his duties, what can the employer do? An employee in breach of contract may be sued by the employer, but this is unlikely in practice; instead, the employer will wish to avoid paying some or all of the wages in the first place. If the employee fails to perform any of his duties (either through being on strike, or through only being willing to perform certain of his duties, which the employer refuses to allow, sending him home instead), then as in *Cresswell* the employer need not pay any wages. However, the position becomes more complex when the employee is permitted by the employer to perform *part* of his duties.

Here, there are two possibilities. If the part not performed is discrete and quantifiable, it seems clear that the employer may refuse to pay the amount of wages representing that part. Thus, in *Royle v Trafford Borough Council*[333] where a teacher participating in industrial action refused to accept a further five pupils into his class but continued to teach his existing 31 pupils, the education authority were allowed to deduct 5/36ths of his salary. Similar results were reached in *Sim v Rotherham Metropolitan Borough Council*[334] (amounts deducted from teachers' salaries representing their refusal to cover for absent colleagues as part of industrial action) and *Miles v Wakefield Metropolitan District Council*[335] (registrar normally working 37 hours per week refusing to perform marriage ceremonies in the three hours on a Saturday morning as part of industrial action; employer held correct to deduct 3/37ths of his salary). However, there has been a significant divergence of view on the reasoning behind these deductions.[336] In *Sim* Scott J held that in such a case the employee could sue for his wages in full, but subject to the employer's right of equitable set-off of the amount representing the duties not performed (for which the employer could have sued the employee in separate proceedings). However, in *Miles* the House of Lords took the more fundamental approach that with regard to the three hours in question the employee had *no* right to the pay in the first place since he had failed to provide the consideration for his part of the contract, namely being ready and willing to work. In the case of a quantifiable failure to perform duties, these two approaches produce the same result, but the position becomes more difficult in the case of a more generalized and nebulous failure (for example as part of a general go-slow or withdrawal of goodwill). This could be particularly important if (1) the industrial action is 'guerilla' in nature,[337] being aimed at inconveniencing the

---

[332] This aspect of the case is considered at heading 4(ii) and Ch 8, heading 1(ii), p 165 above and p 566. One significance of applying such a general principle is that the employer has a freestanding right not to pay wages—it does not constitute a 'suspension' and so the employer does not have to comply with any contractual procedures that may exist before he can impose a suspension (so that *Gorse v Durham County Council* [1971] 2 All ER 666, [1971] 1 WLR 775 was distinguished in *Cresswell*).

[333] [1984] IRLR 184.   [334] [1986] ICR 897, [1986] IRLR 391.

[335] [1987] ICR 368, [1987] IRLR 193, HL.

[336] See the notes on *Sim* and *Miles* by McMullen (1988) 51 MLR 234 and Morris (1987) 16 ILJ 185.

[337] This may now be more difficult to arrange lawfully because of the requirement of strike notice, introduced by the Trade Union Reform and Employment Rights Act 1993; see Ch 10, heading 4(vii), p 748.

employer while at the same time allowing the employees still to earn most of their wages, (2) it involves employees who have some discretion in how they perform their work and (3) they work in open premises from which the employer cannot simply lock them out. Under the above cases, the employer could counter the action by deducting a 'reasonable sum' (as in *Sim*) representing duties not carried out. However, two later Court of Appeal decisions (*Wiluszynski v London Borough of Tower Hamlets*[338] and *British Telecommunications plc v Ticehurst*)[339] have established that if the employer makes it *clear* that he will not accept the defective performance by the employees, he may lawfully refuse to pay anything *at all* (even if the employees have attended work and performed most of their duties). In *Wiluszynski* this was explained as following on from the reasoning in *Miles* (above), and the important decision in *Ticehurst* takes this further in two ways: (1) it links it in with an implied term that employees with a discretion how to perform their work will exercise that discretion so as to advance the employer's business, not so as to frustrate it;[340] (2) it shows the efficacy of one particular employer tactic when faced with guerilla action, namely to give an ultimatum that the employees must work normally as from a certain date, otherwise the employer will refuse to pay at all as from that date. One final point on this area should be noted; if the employer permits imperfect performance by his employees in such a way as to suggest acquiescence in it, he may be held to have waived the employees' breach and so lost his right to deduct (whether partially or totally).[341]

The third point raises legal complications out of proportion to its commonplace nature. What is to happen if the employee is mistakenly overpaid? Can the employer recover the overpayment?[342] What if the employee has already spent the money? Can the employee simply keep quiet about it? Such problems could arise where payment is in cash, but may be more likely to arise now, with payment by direct debit more common. The starting point is that, in the ordinary law of restitution, payments made under a mistake of law are not generally recoverable, but those made under a mistake of fact are. Thus, the first point is to categorize the mistake. Simple inadvertent overpayment (whether by quill pen or computer) is likely to constitute a mistake of fact, thus giving the employer a prima facie right to recover. This was the case in *Avon County*

---

[338] [1989] ICR 493, [1989] IRLR 259, CA; see also *MacPherson v London Borough of Lambeth* [1988] IRLR 470.

[339] [1992] ICR 383, [1992] IRLR 219, CA.

[340] This aspect of the case is considered at heading 4(iv), p 185; as pointed out there, most jobs today are likely to have some discretion in them, rather than being wholly governed by the contract; and so this case doubts the legality in most cases of any form of 'work-to-contract', 'work-to-rule' or 'withdrawal of goodwill'.

[341] *Bond v CAV Ltd* [1983] IRLR 360 (employer's action in not insisting on the employee working on disputed machinery and allowing him to continue working on other machinery held to constitute waiver of the employee's breach).

[342] On a technical level, a deduction to recover an overpayment is not an illegal deduction under the Employment Rights Act 1996, Pt II (heading 5(v), p 214) since it is covered by an exception in the Employment Rights Act 1996, s 14(1); however, that subsection does *not* give a positive right to recover and so the overall legality of recovery by the employer remains a common law matter, subject to the following rules.

Council v Howlett[343] where an employee off sick was inadvertently overpaid. The principal defence to the employer's action for repayment was estoppel by representation, in relation to the whole of the overpayment in spite of the admission by the employee that he had only spent *part* of the overpaid amount.[344] This defence succeeded. However, in the subsequent House of Lords decision in *Lipkin Gorman v Karpnale Ltd*[345] (not itself an overpayment of wages case), Lord Goff said that in future cases such as *Howlett* should be dealt with, not on grounds of estoppel, but on grounds of a general defence of 'change of position' in the law of restitution. He said that such a defence should now be evolved in case law and so is likely to be uncertain for some time. However, one relatively certain point is that such a defence would allow only that part of the overpayment actually spent innocently to become irrecoverable, rather than the defence of estoppel which would operate, potentially unfairly, on an all-or-nothing basis.

All of this operates on the assumption that the employee has spent the money innocently. The one thing that he must not do is simply keep quiet about it if he does realize that he has been overpaid, because that can render him guilty of theft, by virtue of the Theft Act 1968, section 5(4) which provides that:

> Where a person gets property by another's mistake, and is under an obligation to make restoration (in whole or in part) of the property or its proceeds or of the value thereof, then to the extent of that obligation the property or proceeds shall be regarded (as against him) as belonging to the person entitled to restoration, and an intention not to make restoration shall be regarded accordingly as an intention to deprive that person of the property or proceeds.

The Court of Appeal held in *A-G's Reference (No 1 of 1983)*[346] that this section (which does not actually create an offence, but rather supplies what might otherwise be the missing elements for a charge of theft under section 1) can apply to payment by direct debit of sorts as well as to payment in cash, and so provided the prosecution can prove dishonesty[347] the employee may be found guilty of theft through deliberately keeping

---

[343]　[1983] 1 All ER 1073, [1983] IRLR 171, CA.

[344]　A peculiarity of the case, commented on adversely by Cumming-Bruce LJ, was that the evidence showed that the defendant had in fact spent *all* the overpayment before realizing that he was not entitled to it. However, at the trial, counsel for the defence was instructed to proceed on the basis of only *part* expenditure, since the defendant's backers were using this as a test case, seeking to establish (for the purpose of others who had been overpaid) that even partial expenditure could defeat the employer's right to repayment.

[345]　[1991] 2 AC 548, [1992] 4 All ER 512, HL. Lord Goff was of course no stranger to the law of restitution. In *National Westminster Bank plc v Somer International Bank (UK) Ltd* [2001] EWCA Civ 970, [2002] QB 1286, [2002] 1 All ER 198 (a commercial case) it was held that even where estoppel is still used a court can (in its equitable jurisdiction) rule that only the part actually spent has become irrecoverable; if this is correct, *Avon CC* and *Lipkin Gorman* would now produce the same result.

[346]　[1985] QB 182, [1984] 3 All ER 369, CA. The Theft Act 1968, s 5(4) made a definite change here, for under the pre-1968 law an employee keeping an overpayment was not guilty of theft: *Moynes v Coopper* [1956] 1 QB 439, [1956] 1 All ER 450.

[347]　Dishonesty is covered by *R v Ghosh* [1982] QB 1053, [1982] 2 All ER 689, CA, and is a question whether (1) the conduct in question is dishonest by the standards of ordinary people and (2) the defendant realized that it would be thought wrong by those standards. While this may often be obvious in one of these

the overpayment, though the Court of Appeal expressed some disquiet at the involvement of the criminal law in such cases which have the flavour predominantly of civil debt. However, there should only be criminal liability where the defendant deliberately kept it, or spent it *after* realizing that he had been overpaid. If he had already spent it before so realizing, then in civil law the employer would have lost his right to restitution according to the above cases and so section 5(4) ('is under an obligation to make restoration') would not apply.

(ii) WAGES DURING SICKNESS AND STATUTORY SICK PAY

In most cases, questions of pay during sickness will be governed expressly by the contract of employment, some form of 'topping up' of state sickness benefits being now very common and usually clearly set out (for example as to how many weeks per year are payable, whether there is any waiting period before it is payable, whether there is a qualifying period for new employees, and at what rate it is payable, bearing in mind receipts from the state).[348] However, there have been cases where the question of whether sick pay is payable has arisen where there has been no express agreement on the matter. The question then arises whether a term is to be implied covering sick pay and, as a matter of law, this has caused problems. Theoretically, the basis of the law here is the general common law tenet that the employee's consideration for wages is 'service' (ie being ready and willing to serve), not the actual performance of work,[349] and this could lead to the inference that, in the absence of anything to the contrary, wages should continue to be paid during sickness even though the employee is unable actually to perform his work. This view that there is a presumption that sick pay is payable was accepted by Pilcher J in *Orman v Saville Sportswear Ltd*[350] and was consistent with the judgment of the Court of Appeal in *Marrison v Bell*,[351] as explained in later cases.[352] Such a presumption could be rebutted by factors such as payment on

---

cases, there could be latitude for a defence of no dishonesty if, for example, the employee kept the overpayment because he was already owed money by the employer who was refusing to pay him it. A jury might be sympathetic.

[348] See the statistics in the White Paper 'Income during Initial Sickness' (Cmnd 7864, 1980) which introduced the idea of statutory sick pay.

[349] *Warburton v Co-operative Wholesale Society Ltd* [1917] 1 KB 663, CA; *Henthorn v CEGB* [1980] IRLR 361, CA; *Miles v Wakefield Metropolitan District Council* [1987] ICR 368, [1987] IRLR 193, HL; Elias 'The Structure of the Employment Contract' [1982] CLP 95; cf, however, the different views expressed by Napier 'Aspects of the Wage Work Bargain' [1984] CLJ 337.

[350] [1960] 3 All ER 105, [1960] 1 WLR 1055.

[351] [1939] 2 KB 187, [1939] 1 All ER 745, CA.

[352] *Petrie v MacFisheries Ltd* [1940] 1 KB 258, [1939] 4 All ER 281, CA; *O'Grady v M Saper Ltd* [1940] 2 KB 469, [1940] 3 All ER 527, CA. The problem was that Scott LJ expressed his views on sick pay so strongly in *Marrison v Bell* that it was reported (in the law reports and the newspapers) as laying down a definite right to wages during sickness as a matter of law, leading to claims for it by people who could show little or no contractual backing for entitlement to it; this was rectified in the above two cases.

a piecework basis,[353] a clear custom that nothing was offered or expected[354] or some form of notice by the employer that he would accept no, or restricted, liability to make any payments.[355] However, it was still arguable that it was putting matters too highly to say that there was a presumption, and fortunately the matter was clarified by the Court of Appeal in *Mears v Safecar Security Ltd*,[356] an important case not only on sick pay but also on the jurisdiction of tribunals on complaints of failure to give any or proper particulars of the terms of employment[357] and on the whole question of the implication of terms into contracts of employment.[358] In this case it was clearly held that there is in law no presumption that sick pay is payable; if there is no express provision, a tribunal or court must look at all the facts of the case to determine the correct inference. Applying that approach, the Court of Appeal upheld the EAT's decision that nothing was payable on the facts of the case given that it was the employer's well-known practice not to pay, the applicant had been ill during the course of employment and had never asked for payment, and he had only brought his claim seven months after leaving employment, not really expecting to get anything. Stephenson LJ, giving the judgment of the court, did say that there might be a residual presumption that sick pay was payable in a case where there were no factors either way to guide the court on the correct term to be implied, but that this was inherently extremely unlikely to happen, since usually there will be some evidence at least of past custom and practice.

A clear contractual term covering sick pay entitlement is a good example of the benefits to be gained from a well-drafted contract of employment,[359] or proper compliance with the obligation to give written notice of terms of employment. As stated above, such terms are common and, indeed, were for many years an important area for the improvement of terms and conditions by negotiation (for example by increasing payment rates and the entitlement per year, and decreasing or eliminating any qualifying periods), particularly in times of wage restraint (though with some evidence in the 1990s of retrenchment by employers and the worsening of sick pay terms in times of recession). Thus, except in the odd case unfortunately leaving sick pay as a matter to be implied (or not), it could have been said that there was little *law* on sick pay, merely a question of construction of individual contracts. However, that has not been entirely the case since 1983 when there came into force the present scheme of statutory sick

---

[353] *Browning v Crumlin Valley Collieries Ltd* [1926] 1 KB 522; *Hancock v BSA Tools Ltd* [1939] 4 All ER 538.

[354] *O'Grady v M Saper Ltd*, n 352.

[355] *Petrie v MacFisheries Ltd*, n 352 above.

[356] [1982] 2 All ER 865, [1982] IRLR 183, CA, applied by the EAT in *Howman & Son v Blyth* [1983] IRLR 139, where the implication of a term raised questions as to amount and duration of payment.

[357] Employment Rights Act1996, Pt I; see Ch 2, heading 3(ii), p 84. The case was brought before a tribunal under s 11 to determine the correct contractual term; it was not a common law claim for actual payment.

[358] See heading 2(i), p 125.

[359] One complication in some modern cases has been the provision by the employer of permanent health insurance (PHI) on top of the normal sickness provisions in the contract, without really thinking through how the two are to fit together; see heading 3(vii), p 161.

pay (SSP) under the Social Security and Housing Benefits Act 1982 (now Part XI of the Social Security Contributions and Benefits Act 1992).[360]

This scheme came into being pursuant to a White Paper[361] which showed that contractual sick pay terms are common and quantitatively more important than state social security benefits in the maintenance of income during short-term sickness,[362] that such contractual schemes operated usually by taking into account amounts received from the state[363] and that most illness was in fact short term.[364] From these findings, the government formed the view that the existing system was administratively inefficient:

> given that the great majority of claimants have available a second source of income from their employer, there is duplication of administrative machinery between employers and DSS in that evidence of incapacity has to be provided for both schemes and two sets of arrangements for the calculation and payment of income have to be maintained.[365]

The new scheme was therefore designed to prevent duplication in the large majority of claims—where an employee is sick, the employer must now by law pay an amount equivalent to what that employee would have received from the state. As originally enacted, SSP was payable for a maximum of *eight* weeks (either in one period of illness or cumulatively over several illnesses) in one tax year. However, the scheme was viewed as such a success by the government that the Social Security Act 1985 contained a major extension, so that the maximum entitlement is now 28 weeks (put on to a rolling basis, ie not tied now to the tax year); the overall effect of this is that now the employer is liable for the payment of all short-term sickness benefit due to one of his employees (with the principal function for the DSS now being the payment of long-term benefits such as incapacity benefit once the extended SSP entitlement has been exhausted in the case of a major illness or disability). Under the original scheme, the employer recouped the full amount of the money paid out as SSP, by deducting it from his NI contributions. However, this position was gradually altered by the Statutory Sick Pay Acts 1991 and 1994, so that the current position is now that in most cases there is *no* recoupment, so that the employer actually *pays* the SSP; the only exception is that if in any income

---

[360] As amplified by the Statutory Sick Pay (General) Regulations 1982, SI 1982/894, *Harvey* R [198].

[361] 'Income during Initial Sickness' (Cmnd 7864, 1980).

[362] Contractual sick pay terms were relatively uncommon in 1948 at the inception of the National Insurance System, but by 1974 (the year used in the White Paper for statistical purposes) 80% of full-time male workers and 78% of full-time female workers were covered by them; in the large majority of cases, employees qualified to claim sick pay either immediately upon becoming employed or at the most within six months.

[363] In 1974, in the case of male workers, for example, full pay without deduction was payable in only 11.5% of cases; full pay *less state benefits* was payable in 55% of cases; some other scheme operated in the remaining 33.5% of cases (eg topping state benefits up to 85% of full pay).

[364] 'only a very small proportion of people who qualify for (state) benefit need to draw it for any length of time. No payment is made for the first three "waiting" days of incapacity; 60% of those who qualify for sickness benefit are back at work by the end of a fortnight, 80% within a month and 90% within six weeks. Yet the effort put in by DHSS in dealing with these short-term claims is considerable': White Paper, n 361, para 3.

[365] White Paper, n 361, para 3.

tax month the employer pays out SSP exceeding 13% of his liability to pay NI contributions in that month, he can recoup that excess.[366] This is a far cry from the original scheme under which the employer merely administered the payment of SSP.

Before looking at the details of the scheme, two important points must be noticed. First, the scheme does not in any way directly affect contractual sick pay terms which remain matters between the employer and the employee or his union. Thus, contractual sick pay is still to be paid on top of SSP if there is a contractual term to that effect; likewise, if an employer is not contractually obliged to pay sick pay, there is nothing in the statutory scheme to alter that—he will merely be obliged to discharge what was previously the function of the DSS to pay SSP. Secondly, the abolition at the same time as the introduction of SSP of the separate claim for industrial injury benefit (for those injured at work or contracting a prescribed industrial disease) should be seen in the light of this scheme for the administration of sick pay—employees are now eligible simply for sickness benefit when incapable of work whether or not they are injured in a work-related accident (or incapacitated by an industrial disease), and the SSP scheme will apply to any claim for such benefit by a person in employment.

Turning to the elements of the scheme, there is a legal obligation on all employers to pay SSP, with no contracting out by agreement with his employees.[367] There are three qualifying conditions for payment:

(1) the day in respect of which payment is sought must form part of a 'period of incapacity for work', ie a period of four or more consecutive days (thus preserving the former rule that the claimant had to wait for three days before state sickness benefit was payable); any two periods of incapacity for work which are separated by not more than eight weeks are treated as one single period;[368]

(2) the day must fall within a 'period of entitlement', ie a period starting with the illness and ending with (a) the end of the illness, (b) the expiry of the maximum entitlement of 28 weeks, (c) the termination of the contract of employment, or (d) the 11th week before the expected date of confinement in the case of a pregnant employee;[369]

(3) the day must be a 'qualifying day', ie a day when the employee would normally be required to work.[370]

---

[366] Statutory Sick Pay Percentage Threshold Order 1995, SI 1995/512.

[367] Social Security Contributions and Benefits Act 1992, s 151. SSP may not be paid in kind, or by provision of board, lodging, services or other facilities: Statutory Sick Pay (General) Regulations 1982, SI 1982/894, reg 8.

[368] Section 152. All days of the week are counted for this purpose.

[369] Section 153. An employer may not evade paying statutory sick pay by dismissing the employee in order to end the period of entitlement prematurely: SI 1982/894, reg 4.

[370] Section 154; see R (SSP) 1/85, para 10 for a summary of the method of establishing qualifying days. This requirement is here to prevent a sick employee claiming payment in respect of a day on which he would not normally have worked anyway. Under s 3(2), the definition of an employee's 'qualifying days' is primarily a matter for agreement between employer and employee, with detailed statutory rules in reg 5 in default of such agreement.

There are three main disqualifications:[371]

(1) where the employee has not yet started work,

(2) where the 28-week maximum entitlement is exhausted, and

(3) where at the time when the employee falls sick there is a trade dispute at his place of work; this last disqualification is the same as the well-known trade dispute disqualification from jobseeker's allowance, for it is provided that the employee can avoid it if he can prove that at no time on or before the date his sickness began did he participate in, or have a direct interest in, that trade dispute.[372]

The amount of statutory sick pay which is payable after the first three days is fixed by the Act, subject to a power for the Secretary of State to increase the amount by statutory instrument.[373]

The method by which a sick employee must notify that sickness to his employer is basically a matter for agreement, with residual provisions laid down by regulation.[374] In fact, it was in this sphere of the procedure for making a claim that developments had already obliged employers to consider making changes even before the introduction of the SSP scheme in 1983; this was because of the emphasis being placed on 'self-certification',[375] ie allowing the employee to certify himself as incapable of work through illness without the need for a medical certificate, at least until the beginning of the second week of a period of sickness (thus avoiding the need for a doctor to certify short-term illness which is often of such a nature, for example the classic cold or flu, that such certification was of little practical value). One possible problem with self-certification is how to prevent abuse; it may well be that in most cases this will not be a significant problem,[376] but in a case of persistent illnesses by one employee

---

[371] Schedule 11, para 2. Also excluded are employees who are over retirement age, or pregnant (and past the eleventh week before the expected date of confinement).

[372] Schedule 11, para 7; R (SSP) 1/86.

[373] Section 157. At the time of writing it stands at £85.85 pw. To be eligible at all, the employee must earn over the lower limit for the payment of NI contributions.

[374] SI 1982/894, reg 7.

[375] The old system was that in order to claim state sickness benefits (after the three waiting days) the employee needed a medical certificate, which could then be used in a claim for contractual sick pay from his employer. In 1982 the DHSS went over to self-certification for the first week of illness for the purposes of claiming sickness benefit (SI 1982/699). Theoretically this did not affect employers and contractual sick pay schemes (and it tended to be presented by the DHSS as merely a change in internal administrative procedure), but such was the interrelationship between state and private schemes (as pointed out by the White Paper, n 361) that this immediately put pressure on employers to follow suit (especially as doctors are no longer obliged to give medical certificates until the second week of illness). Thus, self-certification was a separate development from the introduction of SSP in 1983, but naturally in practice the two went hand-in-hand and constituted (along with the fusion of injury and sickness benefits) a major alteration to previous procedures.

[376] In fact, the experience of many employers was that self-certification actually *decreased* short-term illness absences, due to the employee having to declare in writing that he had been incapable of work on each of the days on which he was away (rather than just being signed off for the week by his doctor). One possible administrative remedy for persistent absence is that if an employee has self-certified himself four times within a year, an employer may refuse to pay SSP on the fifth occasion and refer him to the DSS for formal investigation and medical checks: Employers' Guide to Statutory Sick Pay (NI 227, DSS) paras 92–5.

for periods of less than a week it may be necessary for the employer to investigate and ultimately even to treat it as a disciplinary matter,[377] with deliberate fraud presumably a potentially fair ground for dismissal.

The last point to note about the SSP system is that, as stated above, it was viewed by the previous Conservative government (if not by employers who have to administer it) as a considerable success; this meant not only its major expansion by the Social Security Act 1985 but also the further possibility that it could be used as a model for other forms of income maintenance. The Social Security Bill 1986 as originally drafted was not only going to convert family income supplement into family credit, but also make family credit payable through the employer in the same way as SSP. This second proposal was dropped because of employer opposition, *but* the Social Security Act 1986 as eventually passed did of course introduce the system of payment of maternity pay through the employer—statutory maternity pay (SMP).[378] The successor New Labour government took the matter further in the legislation on tax credits (replacing family credit and extending similar ideas to areas of low pay generally) which are payable through the employer, as are statutory paternity pay and statutory adoption pay (introduced by the Employment Act 2002) and additional statutory paternity pay (introduced by the Work and Families Act 2006).

The whole question of income maintenance during sickness or injury has thus been the subject of important developments, which should hopefully be properly reflected in well-drafted contracts of employment, though in the nature of things there will still be cases which arise partly or wholly because contractual terms do not adequately reflect current law or actual working practices. Finally, the general point should be noted that receipt of any form of sick pay normally presupposes that the person claiming it is still in employment and there is of course the possibility of the sick employee being dismissed. The statutory scheme provides that an employer cannot evade paying statutory sick pay by dismissing the claimant employee,[379] but does not go further and declare such a dismissal to be in law unfair. However, there is no reason why such a dismissal should not be unfair on general principles, as considered in Chapter 7.

---

[377] This would be aided by the approach of the EAT to persistent absence through illness in *International Sports Co Ltd v Thomson* [1980] IRLR 340.

[378] See Ch 4, heading 3(v), p 270.

[379] SI 1982/894, reg 4 states that where the contract of employment is brought to an end by the employer solely or mainly for the purpose of avoiding liability for SSP, the employer remains liable to pay it for as long as it would have been payable but for the dismissal. It would appear, however, that reg 4 would not apply if the employer could claim successfully that the contract had been *frustrated* by virtue of the illness, because then it would have been brought to an end by law automatically, not by any action of the employer; in the light of the case law, there is still a distinct possibility that a contract could be frustrated by a serious illness, see Ch 6, heading 1(ii), p 412.

(iii) WAGES DURING LAY-OFF OR SHORT TIME

(a) Generally

Turning to the question of wages during a lay-off or short time, in any employment where this is relevant this too is likely to be covered in some way by a relevant contract or collective agreement, which might define or limit the employer's right to lay off, or provide a guaranteed minimum wage or minimum number of hours per week.[380] In the absence of some express provisions or definite custom, however, the common law position is unclear. The starting point is that, unless it consisted of a dismissal by the employer followed by re-engagement later,[381] a lay-off would be a suspension without pay, and there is no general common law power to do this.[382] This approach would favour the continuance of wages, and indeed in *Devonald v Rosser & Sons*[383] the Court of Appeal held that the employer had no right to close down his work and fail to provide remunerative work for his pieceworkers simply because of a lack of profitable orders. However, in *Browning v Crumlin Valley Collieries*[384] Greer J held that there was an implied term that the employer could lay off without pay where the reason for the suspension (in that case closure of the colliery for necessary repairs) was outside his control. Moreover, although the employer's argument in *Devonald v Rosser & Sons* that there was a custom allowing lay-offs in the circumstances in question failed, there may well be cases where such a custom could be shown, particularly in an industry where lay-offs are common and accepted (whatever be the usual common law position) and in such a case the court might well find suspension without pay impliedly allowed,[385] thus at least bringing the law into line with the practical position. In *Puttick v John Wright & Sons (Blackwall) Ltd*[386] the NIRC held that where the employee had been available to do specific jobs for the same employer over a long period of time, being paid for the work done and then laid off until the next work was ready, the correct legal construction was that there existed an ordinary contract of employment for the whole of that period, including an implied term allowing the employer to lay him off without pay in the periods between available work. It is therefore difficult to state any particular common law rule, but this is of little significance, since most aspects of

---

[380] See, eg, *Powell Duffryn Wagon Co Ltd v House* [1974] ICR 123.

[381] In which case continuity of employment is preserved if it is a 'temporary cessation of work': Employment Rights Act 1996, s 212(3).

[382] *Hanley v Pease & Partners Ltd* [1915] 1 KB 698; *Gorse v Durham County Council* [1971] 2 All ER 666, [1971] 1 WLR 775; *Neads v CAV Ltd* [1983] IRLR 360.

[383] [1906] 2 KB 728, CA.   [384] [1926] 1 KB 522.

[385] *Bird v British Celanese Ltd* [1945] KB 336, CA; *Marshall v English Electric Co Ltd* [1945] 1 All ER 653, CA.

[386] [1972] ICR 457. The question whether on the facts there is a series of individual contracts or one global contract in such a case may cause difficulties; this has arisen in the context of trawlermen and the question whether they have continuity of employment between voyages; in *Hellyer Bros Ltd v McLeod* [1987] ICR 526, [1987] IRLR 232, CA it was held that there was not sufficient mutuality of obligations to establish a global contract (and so there was no continuity for redundancy payment purposes). However, in the present context it will not help the employee if the court finds a global contract but then proceeds to imply into it a lay-off clause.

lay-offs will normally be covered (in a unionized industry) by a collective agreement (which may, for example, give a guaranteed minimum week, subject to safeguards for the employer who may be relieved from this obligation in the case of industrial action or events totally beyond his control, thus approximating to what may be the common law position anyway) or by a statutory provision in the modern legislation. Such provisions affect lay-offs in four main ways:

(1) by preserving continuity of employment;[387]

(2) by allowing an employee subject to lay-offs or short time (in certain circumstances) to treat himself as dismissed and apply for a redundancy payment;[388]

(3) by allowing an employee on short time or lay-off to claim jobseeker's allowance, even though technically the contract of employment subsists; and

(4) by providing certain minimal statutory rights to lay-off pay, either generally or in relation to certain particular forms of lay-off.[389]

It is this last category that must now be considered here, ie the general right to a guarantee payment and the specific right to pay if laid off for certain health and safety reasons.

(b) Guarantee payments

Where an employer is obliged to lay off employees, or is unable to provide them with work at a particular time, the salaried and weekly paid employees may not be affected in the short term, but those paid by the hour or by output (and those whose contracts provide for suspension without pay) may lose wages. To meet this situation, an obligation to make guarantee payments was introduced in 1975, and is now to be found in the Employment Rights Act 1996, sections 28–35. These provisions are a good example of the 'floor of rights' argument for providing statutory minima, for the amounts which may be received are meagre, but the principle is established, presumably in part to encourage the establishment and extension of more generous private schemes (for example to give a guaranteed minimum number of hours per week to hourly paid workers). This approach can be seen in two particular aspects of the statutory scheme. The first is that any contractual payments referable to the workless day are set off against the statutory right (often to the point of extinguishing it), *not* additional to it.[390] The second is that the minister may make exemption orders, exempting from these provisions employers who are parties to a collective agreement or wages order which covers the question of guaranteed remuneration to his satisfaction.[391]

---

[387] See n 381.

[388] Employment Rights Act 1996, s 148; see Ch 8, heading 1(iv), p 595.

[389] On the various statutory and contractual possibilities in this difficult area, see Szyszczak *Partial Unemployment: The Regulation of Short-time Working in Britain* (1990).

[390] Employment Rights Act 1996, s 32.

[391] Section 35; as at 2006, there were 26 such orders (see *Harvey* Q [659]).

To qualify for a guarantee payment, the employee must have been continuously employed under a contract of employment for the month ending with the last complete week before the workless day in question.[392] This may disqualify casual workers, as in *Mailway (Southern) Ltd v Willsher*[393] where the EAT held that a woman who was registered as a part-time packer with the employers who offered her work as and when they needed her, and who on average worked more than 16 hours per week (though she had not in fact done so in the four weeks in question), was not eligible for a guarantee payment as this relationship was only a contract to pay for services rendered, not a contract of employment. If an employee is in fact qualified he is entitled to a guarantee payment under section 28 when he is not provided with work by his employer on a day on which he would normally be required to work; the failure to provide work must be due to either (1) a diminution in the requirements of the employer's business for work of that kind, or (2) any other occurrence affecting the normal working of the employer's business in relation to that work (for example a power failure or natural disaster affecting the factory; it will not extend to extraneous matters such as factory holidays).[394] The requirement that the workless day be one on which he would normally be required to work means that this right cannot be used as a back-door method to gain remuneration for days not in fact envisaged in the contract; for example where a contract is only to work four days a week (possibly varied from an original five-day contract as an alternative to redundancy) an employee cannot claim a guarantee payment for the fifth day,[395] nor can he claim one for days during an agreed annual shutdown of a factory.[396]

The employee will lose his right to payment in three cases. The first is where the failure to provide work is in consequence of a strike, lockout or other industrial action involving his employer or an associated employer.[397] The second is where the employee refuses the offer of suitable alternative work for that day, which may be work outside his contract, provided it is suited to his skill, aptitude, etc.[398] The third is where the employee fails to comply with a reasonable attendance requirement, so that the employer can in certain circumstances hold his workforce together, at least for part of the day, for example if he is still hoping that vital supplies will be delivered in time.[399]

As stated above, the amount of the statutory guarantee payment is small, for although the principle is that the employee is to receive the number of working hours on that day

---

[392] Section 29(1).

[393] [1978] ICR 511, [1978] IRLR 322; aliter where the employer may *oblige* the employee to attend work when he requires him, rather than just offering him work: *Miller v Harry Thornton (Lollies) Ltd* [1978] IRLR 430, IT. In relation to the decision in *Mailway*, note that the employee now does not have to work a minimum of 16 hours per week in order to have continuity of employment.

[394] *North v Pavleigh Ltd* [1977] IRLR 461, IT.

[395] *Clemens v Richards Ltd* [1977] IRLR 332, IT; *Daley v Strathclyde Regional Council* [1977] IRLR 414, IT.

[396] *York v Colledge Hosiery Co Ltd* [1978] IRLR 53, IT.

[397] Employment Rights Act 1996, s 29(3).

[398] Section 29(4); *Purdy v Willowbrook International Ltd* [1977] IRLR 388, IT.

[399] Section 29(5); *Meadows v Faithful Overalls Ltd* [1977] IRLR 330, IT.

multiplied by the 'guaranteed hourly rate' (as defined), this is all subject to a maximum of £23.50 per day at the time of writing, and any individual may only claim for a total of five workless days in any period of three months.[400] Where an employer fails to pay all or part of a guarantee payment, an employee may complain to a tribunal within three months of the last workless day (longer if the tribunal finds that it was not reasonably practicable to complain within that period), and if the tribunal upholds the claim it may order the employer to make the necessary payment.[401]

(c) Suspension from work on medical grounds

Where an employee is suspended from work because of the operation of one of several specified health and safety provisions (for example where the employer has to close down his factory or that part of it where the employee works), he is entitled to be paid a 'week's pay' (as defined in the Employment Rights Act 1996, Part XIV, Chapter II) for each week of suspension, up to a maximum of 26 weeks.[402] It is thus more generous than the more general provisions on guarantee payments, because of the specialized nature of the reason for the suspension; the relevant health and safety provisions have been considerably shortened and simplified, so that they now only cover parts of the Control of Lead at Work Regulations 2002, the Ionising Radiations Regulations 1999 and the Control of Substances Hazardous to Health Regulations 2002. Two general points should be noted. The first is that these sections do not give the employer a positive right to suspend when one of these provisions applies; to suspend lawfully the employer must have contractual authority to do so, and only in such a case do these sections apply to give the employee a limited right to further payments. If there is no contractual right to suspend, the employee may have an ordinary contract action for his wages in full anyway, and indeed it is specially provided that any contractual payments received during the relevant period go towards discharging the employer's obligations under the statute, and vice versa.[403] The second point is that these provisions apply to suspension through the effect of the relevant health and safety legislation on the employer's undertaking, not on the health of the employee himself. Thus, if the employee is in fact incapable of work through disease or injury during the relevant time he cannot claim payment under section 64 for that period of incapacity.[404] It seems that this exclusion would even apply where the employee was ill because of the same health risk that caused the shutdown (eg if he was suffering from lead poisoning after the factory had been closed because of contraventions of the relevant lead regulations),

---

[400] Section 30. This includes any such workless days in respect of which contractual remuneration has already been paid—the employee cannot claim five *further* days of guarantee pay if five or more days have already been paid for under the contract within the three-month period: *Cartwright v G Clancey Ltd* [1983] ICR 552, [1983] IRLR 355.

[401] Section 34.

[402] Employment Rights Act 1996, ss 64–65; the specified provisions may be in either statutes, regulations or codes of practice issued under the Health and Safety at Work etc Act 1974, s 16.

[403] Section 69(3).   [404] Section 65(3).

which may seem inequitable and could cause problems if ever there was added to the list of specified provisions a health and safety requirement which operated by reference to the individual employee and not to the nature of the undertaking (eg a regulation that noone with a particular skin disease should bake bread), for then the employee would have to be suspended but, on the strict wording of the Act, would be ineligible for section 64 payments because of his incapacity for work.

As well as the illness exclusion, an employee will also be disqualified from payment if he refuses suitable alternative work or fails to comply with a reasonable attendance requirement, as in the case of guarantee payments. Complaint lies to a tribunal within three months of the last day of suspension (longer if the tribunal finds that it was not reasonably practicable to complain within that period) and the tribunal may order the employer to make the relevant payment.[405]

A further form of statutory protection requiring the continuation of wages through suspension, this time where it occurs on maternity grounds, was added by the Trade Union Reform and Employment Rights Act 1993. As this is an integral part of the new rules on maternity enacted by that statute, it is dealt with along with those rules in Chapter 4.

(iv) CALCULATION OF NORMAL WORKING HOURS AND A WEEK'S PAY

The concepts of 'normal working hours' and 'a week's pay' are important in several contexts throughout modern industrial legislation. The principal significance of 'normal working hours' was originally in deciding whether an employee worked more than the magic 16 hours per week and so could claim statutory rights, but that hours limit was abandoned in 1995.[406] However, it is still necessary to know whether an employment has 'normal working hours' for the purpose of ascertaining what the 'week's pay' is and, in turn, it is necessary to know what the 'week's pay' is for the purpose of computing, inter alia, the amount of a redundancy payment, guarantee payment or basic award for unfair dismissal. Rather than being defined individually for the purpose of each statutory right where they are relevant, these two concepts are each covered for all statutory purposes in one place, namely sections 220–229 and 234 of the Employment Rights Act 1996. However, it must be added that these have always been difficult provisions and have required a considerable amount of statutory interpretation.

(a) Normal working hours

In many cases it will be obvious what an employee's normal working hours are, in the sense of the number of hours which the employee is *obliged* to work by his contract; there is no overall statutory definition of this, and it is essentially a matter of

---

[405] Section 70.   [406] See Ch 2, heading 5, p 102.

interpreting the contract. Thus, where the contract expressly states the number of hours this will usually be conclusive of the matter,[407] and the employee should ensure that the contractual term correctly reflects the practical position, for he will be held to that term (for example for the purpose of calculation of a redundancy payment) even if in practice he works longer hours and regards himself as bound to work those longer hours, *unless* the facts in his case are such as to support an argument that the term of the contract relating to hours has actually been varied by the parties to include the longer hours.[408] This possibility apart, however, it will normally be to no avail that the employee in fact works longer hours than those stipulated in the contract. In *ITT Components (Europe) Group v Kolah*[409] a clerk was employed under a contract specifying 20 hours per week (at a time when the necessary minimum for qualification for an unfair dismissal claim was 21 hours per week), but she regularly worked a further three hours each week; the EAT, reversing the tribunal decision in her favour, held that this was not in itself a contract for 21 hours or more per week because of the express term for 20 hours, but remitted the case to the tribunal to discover what the correct interpretation of the contract should be, since the clerk had in fact been promoted to a supervisor ten months before she was dismissed, and there was at least the possibility that the relevant contractual term might have been varied on the promotion (that being a question of fact for the tribunal to consider).

If there is no express term covering the normal working hours (in spite of the statutory obligation to give written particulars of this, under the Employment Rights Act 1996, section 1(4)), the tribunal must consider the facts and what happens in practice to decide what is the correct term to infer. This may be a difficult exercise where the employee has in fact been working fluctuating hours. In *Dean v Eastbourne Fishermen's and Boatmen's Protection Society Ltd*[410] a barman worked certain set sessions and at other times when requested to do so by his employer; this produced fluctuating hours, and as the set sessions amounted to less than the 21 hours per week at that time required for qualification for redundancy rights the tribunal rejected his claim for a redundancy payment when he was dismissed. However, the EAT allowed his appeal, holding that as the contract was silent on the matter, the tribunal had to infer the relevant term and in a case such as this, where that term was essentially to work the hours required of him, that meant looking at what happened in practice during a period before the dismissal. The appropriate period appears to be the period required to qualify for the particular right being claimed (in particular two years for redundancy or one year for unfair dismissal);[411] in *Dean's* case the EAT held that as in the qualifying period of the

---

[407] *Gascol Conversions Ltd v Mercer* [1974] ICR 420, [1974] IRLR 155, CA; *Fewell v B & B Plastics Ltd* [1974] IRLR 154; *Lake v Essex County Council* [1979] ICR 577, [1979] IRLR 241, CA.

[408] For a case in which it was held that there had been such a variation, see *Armstrong Whitworth Rolls Ltd v Mustard* [1971] 1 All ER 598, 9 KIR 279.

[409] [1977] ICR 740, [1977] IRLR 53.

[410] [1977] ICR 556, [1977] IRLR 143. See, to like effect, *Green v Roberts* [1992] IRLR 499.

[411] *Larkin v Cambos Enterprises (Stretford) Ltd* [1978] ICR 1247.

last two years the employee had worked for more than 21 hours in 86 weeks the proper interpretation was that his normal working hours exceeded 21 per week and so he was eligible for a redundancy payment.

Whether 'normal working hours' are expressed in the contract or left to be inferred when the need arises, one overall consideration is that in general they will *not* include overtime. This proposition may help to simplify the question, for even if a contract of employment is not specific on the normal working hours (or, to put it another way, the minimum number of obligatory hours), it might well state that overtime is payable after a certain number of hours per week have been worked and where this is the case the Employment Rights Act 1996, section 234, provides that normal working hours shall be that number of hours to be worked before overtime becomes payable. Thus, in *Fox v C Wright (Farmers) Ltd*[412] an agricultural worker was employed under a contract which did not specify a minimum number of hours to be worked, and he often worked 50 or 60 hours per week as the job demanded; the contract did, however, provide that overtime was payable for hours worked in excess of 40 per week, and when he claimed a redundancy payment the EAT held that he was caught by this provision, and his normal working hours were therefore 40 (for the purposes of calculating the redundancy payment). Section 234 does, however, create an exception to this in a case where the contract sets a fixed number of obligatory hours which includes a number of hours in fact payable at overtime rates (eg an obligatory week of 40 hours, but with overtime rates payable from 35 hours). In such a case, the normal working hours will remain the obligatory figure even though that includes some overtime. The predecessor of this provision was considered by the Court of Appeal in *Tarmac Roadstone Holdings Ltd v Peacock*[413] where Lord Denning MR said that for overtime to be included under this exception it must be fully obligatory under the contract, in the sense that the employee must work it *and* the employer must provide it; it is not sufficient if the overtime is voluntary on both sides or if the employer is obliged to work it when requested but the employer is not obliged to provide it in any particular week. Thus, this exception is restrictively construed (in line, it is submitted, with the clear wording of the provision), and so overtime will only be included in the normal working hours if it is clearly obligatory on both sides under the contract.

(b) A week's pay[414]

The rules governing the calculation of a weeks' pay for statutory purposes are laid down in Part XIV, Chapter II of the Employment Rights Act 1996 (sections 220–229). There are four different methods of calculation, depending upon the category into which the employee concerned falls; the first three cover cases where there are normal working

---

[412] [1978] ICR 98.

[413] [1973] 2 All ER 485, [1973] ICR 273, CA, followed in *Lotus Cars Ltd v Sutcliffe* [1982] IRLR 381, CA.

[414] These longstanding rules were adopted for the purpose of calculating statutory holiday pay: Working Time Regulations 1998, reg 16(2).

hours (as defined in the previous paragraphs) but differing or specialized forms of payment for the work done during those hours, and the fourth covers the case where there are no discernible normal working hours. These are now considered in turn.

(i) *Where there are normal working hours and the remuneration does not vary with the amount of actual work done* This is the simplest case where, essentially, the employee is paid on a time basis, ie for the hours during which he is at work, and here the 'week's pay' is the amount payable under the contract of employment when the employee works throughout the normal hours of the week, the relevant contractual provision being that in force on the calculation date.[415] This may be simply the basic rate for a time worker, but not necessarily since it could include any further payments if they are paid on a regular basis, for example a night shift rate or a regular bonus.[416]

(ii) *Where there are normal working hours, but the remuneration varies with the amount of actual work done* This obviously covers pieceworkers, but also extends to persons basically on a time rate but eligible for variable bonuses or commission.[417] Here the 'week's pay' is the remuneration for the normal working hours payable at the *average hourly rate*, which is calculated by working out the total numbers of hours actually worked in a period of 12 calendar weeks preceding the calculation date, then the total amount of remuneration actually paid for those hours over that period (excluding any overtime premia paid), and then working out the average payment per hour.[418]

(iii) *Where there are normal working hours but they are to be worked at varying times and in varying amounts in different weeks* This category primarily covers employees working rotating shifts, where the pattern of work is set, but alternates from week to week, so that here it is necessary to average *both* the rate of remuneration *and* the number of hours worked in a week, once again over a period of 12 calendar weeks preceding the calculation date. The 'week's pay' here is therefore the average weekly number of normal working hours payable at the average hourly rate.[419]

(iv) *Where there are no normal working hours* In this residual category, which would cover, for example, the case of a university lecturer, the tribunal must determine the 'week's pay' simply by calculating the amount of the average weekly remuneration received by the employee over the period of 12 calendar weeks preceding the calculation date.[420] This form of calculation could well be the most favourable for the

---

[415] Employment Rights Act 1996, s 221(2); calculation dates vary with the particular statutory rights involved, and are laid down individually in ss 225 and 226. This could cause injustice if, for example, the contractual term had been varied downwards by the calculation date (eg because of the firm's economic difficulties).

[416] *A & B Marcusfield Ltd v Melhuish* [1977] IRLR 484. See the inclusion of a site bonus in *Donelan v Kerrby Constructions Ltd* [1983] ICR 237, [1983] IRLR 191.

[417] Section 221(4); *Jones v Shellabear Price Ltd* (1967) 2 ITR 36. Where, however, commission is based on the success of work (rather than on a greater amount of work being done) then, if it can still be said that remuneration does not vary with the amount of work done, the employee remains under head (i) above, which may be financially disadvantageous: *Evans v Malley Organisation Ltd* [2003] ICR 432, [2003] IRLR 156, CA.

[418] Section 221(3).   [419] Section 222.   [420] Section 224.

employee since it looks at overall remuneration, and is not tied to concepts such as basic hours, so that, for example, in *Fox v C Wright (Farmers) Ltd*[421] the agricultural worker who regularly worked 50 to 60 hours per week was trying to argue that he had no normal hours in order to put the question of averaging at large, but the EAT held that as his contract provided for overtime rates to be paid after 40 hours' work per week, he was caught by section 234 (considered above) and so he was deemed to have normal working hours of 40 per week.

Those being the four categories of employee covered by the provisions, four general qualifications should be noticed:

(1) The 12-week period referred to must consist of weeks during which the employee actually worked in order to earn some pay, and it is that earned pay which is used for the purpose of calculation even if in any given week he worked (and therefore earned) considerably less than usual for some reason; this leads to a possible gap in the legal coverage in the case where work is consistently run down in the 12 weeks (or more) immediately prior to dismissal—as long as the employee actually earned *something*, those weeks will be used for calculation purposes even if they are in fact untypical and decrease what would otherwise have been his statutory entitlement. This requirement of looking at the pay actually earned in any given calculation week excludes matters such as payment during rest days[422] and the payment of fall-back or guaranteed pay for periods when not actually working.[423] If, however, the period of 12 calendar weeks includes a week when *no* work is done to earn remuneration, the tribunal must ignore that week and take an earlier week instead to bring the number up to 12 again.[424] If the employee has not been employed long enough for calculation over 12 weeks, the tribunal must apply the above provisions as nearly as it can, looking at certain other factors, such as the remuneration of other persons in comparable employment, though if the employee has just joined the employer in question from another employer and his employment with both is deemed to be continuous, a period of employment with the previous employer can be taken into consideration if necessary.[425]

(2) The emphasis remains against the inclusion of overtime rates. As seen above, overtime other than fully obligatory and guaranteed overtime is not counted towards 'normal working hours' in the first place. However, for the purpose of calculating the 'average hourly rate' under categories (2) and (3) above the tribunal must look at the hours *actually worked* during the 12-week period, and this may include some hours worked at overtime rates; where this is so, however, section 223(3) provides that the amount of overtime premia earned is to be ignored when calculating the total remuneration for that period for the purpose of calculating the average; the employee

---

[421] Discussed above; see n 412.   [422] *Mole Mining Ltd v Jenkins* [1972] ICR 282.
[423] *Adams v John Wright & Sons (Blackwall) Ltd* [1972] ICR 463.
[424] Employment Rights Act 1996, s 223(2). *Secretary of State for Employment v Crane* [1988] IRLR 238.
[425] Sections 228 and 229; on continuity of employment, see Ch 2, heading 5, p 101.

therefore cannot take advantage of the overtime premia to increase the average,[426] but this only applies to actual overtime, and does not disallow the inclusion of amounts under incentive or bonus schemes which may be built into the wage structure, for these are not to be treated as analogous to overtime.[427]

(3) The word used throughout the scheme is 'remuneration', but its definition has been left to the case law. It obviously includes wages and salaries, and has been held to include commission;[428] moreover, the tribunal must look at the realities of an employee's pay, which may be significant in the case of certain more complicated payment systems:

> It is not possible for an employer, as a matter of law, to represent that a worker who is paid £1 as remuneration for doing an hour's work is really paid 50p for an hour's work because the parties choose to specify that the rate shall be 50p an hour but one hour's work shall count as two hours' work in calculating pay.[429]

Contractually binding bonuses will be included, in whatever guise they are presented,[430] and it is specifically provided that if such a bonus is only payable at a time outside the calculation period (for example once per year), it may be apportioned for calculation purposes in such manner as may be just, and taken into account accordingly.[431] In addition to such matters, an employee may in fact receive further indirect benefits which may cause more difficulty. He may, for example, receive an amount labelled 'expenses' which may be simply genuine reimbursement for money of his own actually expended, or may instead be a none-too-subtle form of giving increased remuneration. If the former, it is not to be included, but if the latter it may be brought into account according to the leading case of S & U Stores Ltd v Wilkes;[432] such an arrangement may sometimes raise a suspicion of tax evasion, but the general approach has been to ignore this, as being basically a matter for HM Revenue and Customs, not the employment tribunals.[433] The case of S & U Stores Ltd v Wilkes also establishes that two other indirect benefits are *not* to be taken into account when quantifying remuneration; these are payments in kind, such as free accommodation or a firm's car, and payments from a person other than the employer. The latter means that a waiter cannot include cash tips in his remuneration for the purpose of calculating his 'week's pay', since these are

---

[426] This exclusory rule is now particularly important in not allowing overtime premia to count when computing statutory holiday pay under the Working Time Regulations 1998: *Bamsey v Albon Engineering and Manufacturing plc* [2004] ICR 1083, [2004] IRLR 457, CA.

[427] *Ogden v Ardphalt Asphalt Ltd* [1977] ICR 604; the possible intricacies of bonus and overtime schemes in this context are well illustrated by *British Coal Corpn v Cheesbrough* [1990] ICR 317, [1990] IRLR 148, HL.

[428] *Weevsmay Ltd v Kings* [1977] ICR 244.

[429] *Mole Mining Ltd v Jenkins* [1972] ICR 282 at 284, per Sir John Brightman.

[430] *Amalgamated Asphalte Companies Ltd v Dockrill* (1972) 7 ITR 198.

[431] Employment Rights Act 1996, s 229(2); *J & S Bickley Ltd v Washer* [1977] ICR 425.

[432] [1974] 3 All ER 401, [1974] ICR 645.

[433] *S & U Stores Ltd v Lee* [1969] 2 All ER 417, [1969] 1 WLR 626; cf *Jennings v Westwood Engineering Ltd* [1975] IRLR 245, IT.

discretionary payments by a third party.[434] On the other hand, this has been held not to apply to a fixed service charge shared out between the employees, since that is obligatory payment in fact payable by the employer.[435] Likewise, gratuities on credit cards or cheques paid out to waiters (under Inland Revenue pressure) directly through the employer as 'additional pay' may count as part of the week's pay.[436] In recent years, this topic has been complicated by the overlap with the national minimum wage legislation, under which a similar question has arisen (do tips count towards observing the minimum NMW hourly rate?) *but* with the caveat that in the case of 'a week's pay' the employee wants them to count (eg to increase a redundancy payment) but in the case of the NMW it is the *employer* who wants them to count (so that less can be paid by way of basic wages). At first, the above distinction (paid directly by the customer or paid through the employer) was applied in the NMW cases. One middle ground was where gratuities on credit cards or cheques are paid through the employer into a 'tronc' (independent fund) controlled and distributed by the employees themselves. In *Annabel's (Berkeley Square) v HMRC*[437] the Court of Appeal held that such gratuities were *not* paid by the employer and so could not be counted by the employer towards the NMW. At the same time, however, the government altered the NMW legislation (pursuant to a political pledge) to state that *no* tips or gratuities are to count. However, that change does *not* apply to rules such as 'a week's pay', where presumably (a) the above distinction continues to apply and (b) *Annabel's* will govern tronc systems and continue to exclude tronc-based tips (but this time potentially to an employee's disadvantage).

(4) If the week's pay calculated as above turns out to be below the applicable rate of the national minimum wage (NMW), then as a matter of policy it is the NMW rate that is to be used when working out any statutory entitlement (particularly a redundancy payment or compensation for unfair dismissal).[438]

(v) PROTECTION OF WAGES

(a) The repeal of the Truck Acts and the effect on cashless pay

One of the longest standing pieces of social legislation in English law was the Truck Acts 1831–1940, designed and basically put into place early in the nineteenth century

---

[434] *Hall v Honeybay Caterers Ltd* (1967) 2 ITR 538; *Palmanor Ltd v Cedron* [1978] ICR 1008, [1978] IRLR 303.

[435] *Tsoukka v Potomac Restaurants Ltd* (1968) 3 ITR 259; *Keywest Club Ltd v Choudhury* [1988] IRLR 51.

[436] *Nerva v RL & G Ltd* [1997] ICR 11, [1996] IRLR 461, CA (a case on the repealed Wages Councils legislation, but applying the same principle); the waiters' ultimate action before the ECtHR failed: *Nerva v United Kingdom* [2002] IRLR 815.

[437] [2009] EWCA Civ 361.

[438] *Paggetti v Cobb* [2002] IRLR 861; this obviously applies to the basic award for unfair dismissal which is mathematically based on the week's pay, but less obviously it also applies to the compensatory award which is to be based on a calculation of what the employee's net wage would have been if paid at the NMW level.

to protect the employee in his free enjoyment of his earnings.[439] They served two distinct purposes:

(1) the original Act of 1831 gave a legal right to payment in 'current coin of the realm', designed to prevent abuse of the then prevalent 'tommy shop' system whereby an employer might pay at least part of the employee's wages in tokens to be spent at the employer's own shop;[440]

(2) the later legislation (particularly the Truck Act 1896) then placed restrictions on the making of deductions from wages, principally in respect of the provisions of goods and services by the employer, fines or bad workmanship; these were of great complexity, but in essence they usually provided that the deduction had to be authorized in writing and be fair and reasonable in the circumstances.

The principal limitation of the legislation was that it only applied to *manual* workers[441] (with certain limited extensions to shop assistants). Persons not covered were therefore left to their contractual rights on both payment methods and deductions.[442] It was recognized for years that the legislation was in need of, at the least, revision, and indeed the last major case on it showed just how unpredictable and unreliable its coverage was.[443] However, the previous Conservative government became interested in the area not because of anything concerning deductions, but rather because of the first of the above two effects, that of the right to payment in cash. Britain had long lagged behind other western countries in the move towards cashless pay (ie pay by cheque or credit transfer).[444] It is true that the strict requirement in the 1831 Act of current coin of the realm had been qualified by the Payment of Wages Act 1960 which permitted cashless pay with the employee's written agreement, but the problem was that that agreement could always be revoked by written notice and so a manual worker could reinvoke his rights under the Truck Act. Banks had for a long time been interested in extending cashless pay, and sometimes they and employers had offered cash incentives to go over

---

[439] For the details of this legislation, see the third edition of this book, at pp 389–94. The archaic meaning of 'truck' was to exchange or barter; one of the few current usages is the phrase 'to have no truck' with something, in the sense of not wishing to have any dealings with it. The word 'truck' was not actually used in the wording of the legislation.

[440] Such a system was not necessarily vicious, since the employer might have the benefit of discount buying, but obviously it was open to abuse.

[441] This distinction caused great difficulties and a considerable amount of old case law; for a modern example of the problem, see *Brooker v Charrington Fuel Oils Ltd* [1981] IRLR 147, Co Ct.

[442] On deduction, however, there was at least the statutory right to have deductions notified, as part of the statutory itemized pay statement under the Employment Rights Act 1996, s 8.

[443] In *Bristow v City Petroleum Ltd* [1988] ICR 165, [1987] IRLR 340 the House of Lords finally held that a deduction from a shop worker's wages in respect of a stock or till deficiency could be a 'fine' within the Truck Act 1896, s 1, thereby resolving a conflict of opinion between different Divisional Courts on the issue. This final decision came too late to affect the decision to repeal the legislation.

[444] In the early 1980s it was estimated that 50% of all workers in Britain and 78% of manual workers were still paid in cash. This compared with 20% of all workers in Holland and Sweden, 10% in France, 5% in West Germany and Canada and 1% in the USA. Approximately 400,000 workers in Britain were changing to cashless pay each year, but this was considered slow progress.

to it; the problem with the 1960 Act was that any such agreement was *not* irrevocable. The previous government therefore decided to deregulate this area by the repeal of the Truck Acts and the Payment of Wages Act 1960. However, to do so simpliciter would also remove all protection with regard to deductions and eventually this was thought to be too sweeping, particularly in the light of media coverage of certain cases of highly inequitable deduction clauses in employment contracts, particularly in certain areas of retailing.[445] The compromise was contained in Part I of the Wages Act 1986 which repealed the truck legislation (and other related statutes)[446] but also enacted entirely new provisions giving at least partial protection in relation to deductions; the principal feature in favour of this scheme is that it applies to *all* employees, not just to manual workers; one criticism of it, however, is that (with the exception of certain extra protection for retail workers, considered below) these provisions largely relate to the *mechanics* of making deductions (the principal requirement normally being the employee's written consent), rather than any concept of the substantive *fairness* or otherwise of the deductions. In this sense, they are not as interventionist as the old Truck Act provisions, and the question of the reason for the deduction in question is left largely as a matter of contract.

As seen above, however, the matter of deductions was (if not an afterthought) at least a subsidiary matter in the eyes of the government. The principal point was the removal of blockages to cashless pay, and this has been achieved. The repeal of the Truck Acts means that there is now no freestanding legal right to payment in cash and so an employer taking on an employee (manual or otherwise) may lawfully make it a term of the contract that payment will be by cheque or credit transfer.

The Wages Act 1986 was repealed by the Employment Rights Act 1996, and the provisions relating to deductions are now contained in Part II (sections 13–27) of that Act; in employment lawyers' jargon, however, there remains a tendency to refer to an action before a tribunal to recover an unlawful deduction from wages as 'a Wages Act claim'.

(b) Deductions from wages

Section 13 provides that an employer shall not make deductions from the wages of a worker employed by him unless the deduction is (1) required or authorized by statute (for example PAYE, NI contributions or an attachment of earnings order), (2) required

---

[445] One area much in the news at the time was petrol stations, where contracts of employment often included a term requiring the attendant to refund out of his wages any stock or till deficiencies arising during his shift *whether through his default or not*, thus covering the motorist who deliberately drove off without payment. In *Bristow v City Petroleum Ltd*, n 443, the deductions had averaged 17% of net pay over a period of five weeks but there was anecdotal evidence of far greater deductions in some cases, even to the extent of leaving little pay left after the deductions. See Goriely 'Arbitrary Deductions from Pay and the Proposed Repeal of the Truck Acts' (1983) 12 ILJ 236.

[446] The Payment of Wages Act 1960; the Shop Clubs Act 1902; the Payment of Wages in Public-houses Prohibition Act 1883; the Checkweighing in Various Industries Act 1919; and various older statutes concerning coal mines.

or authorized by a provision in the contract of employment which has either been given to him or notified to him previously in writing, or (3) agreed to by the employee in writing prior to the making of the deduction.[447]

(i) *Application* From such humble beginnings, these provisions became subject to quite remarkable development, for one procedural reason which had little to do with their origins. Until 1994, we were afflicted with a split jurisdiction, so that in the past employment tribunals could not deal with common law matters such as non-payment of wages, which had to go to the ordinary courts (doubly annoying if, for example, the ex-employee was already bringing a tribunal action for unfair dismissal). However, a way round this was discovered—if an employee was complaining about a refusal to pay wages, holiday entitlements etc, could that be *called* a 'deduction'? If so, the employee could (on the assumption that there was no prior written consent) complain to a tribunal under the Wages Act for its 'recovery'. This reasoning has been largely successful, as can be seen from the very high number of 'Wages Act cases' brought in recent years;[448] it has operated as a de facto transfer of certain common law, contractual claims to tribunals. It had been hoped that when an order was finally made by the government giving common law jurisdiction to tribunals, this would be in general terms, and would end the need to extend what is now Part II of the 1996 Act to perform a function it was probably not intended for. However, this simple hope did not come about, for two reasons: (1) the order[449] in fact only gives common law jurisdiction to tribunals in cases arising on or out of *termination* of employment, and so challenges to non-payment or under-payment of wages or other benefits *during* employment can still only be brought before a tribunal by squeezing them under Part II; (2) even on termination, it may still be tactically advantageous to the ex-employee to claim amounts not paid under Part II rather than directly under the order, since the latter is subject not only to a monetary limit of £25,000 but also, and far more importantly, to an express power of counterclaim by the employer which can be avoided by claiming under Part II (leaving the employer to pursue any claim he may think he has through the ordinary courts, which

---

[447] Section 15 has equivalent provisions concerning the making of payments by workers to employers, instead of operating by way of deduction. 'Worker' is defined widely in s 230(3), as covering not only a person under a contract of service or apprenticeship, but also under a contract to do or perform personally work or services for another party (other than in a professional–client relationship). The requirement of *prior* written agreement means prior to the event causing the deduction, not just to the deduction itself: *Discount Tobacco and Confectionery Ltd v Williamson* [1993] ICR 371, [1993] IRLR 327; *York City and District Travel Ltd v Smith* [1990] ICR 344, [1990] IRLR 213. To be relied on, a contractual provision must be notified to the employee individually, not just by a factory notice: *Kerr v Sweater Shop (Scotland) Ltd* [1996] IRLR 424.

[448] In 2010/11 ACAS received 27,260 cases from the tribunal service under Part II for individual conciliation. Taken together with the 27,692 cases under the Extension of Jurisdiction Orders (n 449), these cases comprised 33% of all tribunal applications referred to ACAS for conciliation: *ACAS Annual Report 2010/11*.

[449] The Employment Tribunals Extension of Jurisdiction (England and Wales) Order 1994, SI 1994/1623; the Scottish Order is SI 1994/1624. A further point of difference is that Part II applies to the wider category of 'worker' (including some self-employed) but the Extension Order only applies to 'employees' properly so called: *Robertson v Blackstone Franks Investment Management Ltd* [1998] IRLR 376, CA.

in practice is highly unlikely to happen). Thus, claims under Part II are likely to continue at their present high level, and the reported cases show that such an action can be used as a relatively quick and certainly effective way of challenging an attempt by an employer to force through a unilateral variation of contractual terms.[450]

As a matter of law, this development raised two questions of interpretation of the Act—what is a 'deduction' and what are 'wages'? On the first question, section 13(3) gives a broad definition[451] and certain cases have shown an equally broad approach, so that for example there can still be a deduction even if it is so large that it actually extinguishes the wage payment altogether,[452] and the phasing out of a special bonus from a payment system was held to qualify as a deduction.[453] However, the crucial question was whether simple non-payment would qualify—on a straightforward application of section 13 it would, but it could also be argued as a matter of English that non-payment was different in kind from a deduction from wages paid. On the second question, section 27 gives a lengthy inclusive and exclusive definition,[454] although not specifically covering one of the most contentious areas, wages in lieu of notice on a dismissal; could such amounts, if kept by the employer, be recovered under the Act?

Both of these questions caused major disagreements between different divisions of the EAT, but the matter was largely settled by the decisions of the Court of Appeal and House of Lords in the leading case of *Delaney v Staples*.[455] The facts were refreshingly simple. The employee was dismissed, being owed £55.50 commission and holiday pay and £82 in lieu of notice. She claimed both of these amounts, not in the county court, but before a tribunal under the Wages Act. This neatly raised both of the above questions. The Court of Appeal held that the £55.50 could be recovered, because a simple non-payment such as this *does* qualify as a 'deduction', on a literal interpretation

---

[450] *Bruce v Wiggins Teape (Stationery) Ltd* [1994] IRLR 536 (withdrawal of shift bonus); *Morgan v West Glamorgan County Council* [1995] IRLR 68 (disciplinary salary cut in breach of contract); *Saavedra v Aceground Ltd* [1995] IRLR 198 (employer allocating part of waiters' tronc for tips to himself). In each case the employers' actions were held to be unlawful 'deductions'. See Miller (1995) 24 ILJ 162. In addition, it has been held that a Wages Act claim can be used to recover unpaid holiday pay under the Working Time Regulations 1998, even though those Regulations contain their own specific tribunal procedure: *HMRC v Stringer* [2009] UKHL 31.

[451] 'Where the total amount of any wages that are paid on any occasion by an employer to any worker employed by him is less than the total amount of the wages that are properly payable by him to the worker on that occasion'.

[452] *Alsop v Star Vehicle Contracts Ltd* [1990] ICR 378, [1990] IRLR 83.

[453] *McCree v Tower Hamlets London Borough Council* [1992] ICR 99, [1992] IRLR 56.

[454] 'Wages' means 'any sums payable to the worker by his employer in connection with his employment'; there are then six categories specifically included and five specifically excluded. The first included is 'any fee, bonus, commission, holiday pay or other emolument referable to his employment, whether payable under his contract or otherwise'. The last two words meant that the Act's procedure could be used to challenge non-payment of a *discretionary* or ex gratia payment, provided the making of such a payment was clearly anticipated by contract, custom or ad hoc undertaking: *Kent Management Services Ltd v Butterfield* [1992] ICR 272, [1992] IRLR 394; *New Century Cleaning Co Ltd v Church* [2000] IRLR 27, CA; *Farrell Matthews & Weir v Hansen* [2005] ICR 509, [2005] IRLR 160. Ultimately, however, the amount being claimed by the employee must be quantifiable: *Coors Brewers Ltd v Adock* [2007] IRLR 440, CA.

[455] [1991] ICR 331, [1991] IRLR 112, CA; affd [1992] ICR 483, [1992] IRLR 191, HL.

of section 13(3), and there was here no prior agreement. That point was not subject to further appeal and so remains governed by the Court of Appeal's decision. However, the matter of the £82 in lieu went on further appeal to the House of Lords and raised the second question—are payments in lieu of notice 'wages'? Here, the matter was resolved not primarily by the wording of the Act, but by a broader consideration of the nature of payments in lieu. Lord Browne-Wilkinson said that the essential characteristic of wages (at common law and under the Act) was as 'payments in respect of the rendering of services during the employment'. He then analysed 'wages in lieu' as covering four different possibilities;[456] in only one (where the employer formally gives the correct notice, pays during that period, but does not actually require the employee to work during it, for example in a 'garden leave' case) does the payment still constitute wages during employment, to which the Act could apply. In the case itself, the in lieu payment came into the much more common category of anticipatory *damages* for the employer's breach of contract in dismissing the employee instantly, without proper notice. It was therefore not 'wages' and so the non-payment could not be challenged before a tribunal. Thus, the end result is that non-payment of wages accrued during the employment can be subject to a statutory action under Part II before a tribunal, but in most cases non-payment of wages in lieu cannot be (though of course, as such a case by definition arises on termination, such amounts outstanding *can* now be claimed before a tribunal quite separately under the Transfer of Jurisdiction Order).

One further class of case deserves mention. If it is the *employee* who is in breach of contract by leaving without giving his contractual notice, the employer may be very tempted to hang on to any final wages, contractual holiday pay etc, still owing to that employee, as 'damages'. In the light of *Delaney*'s reasoning and two earlier cases[457] this is likely to be unlawful in the absence of prior written consent. The moral is simple; if the employer wants a power to retain accrued wages in the event of the employee leaving in breach of his notice obligation (especially where the employer wants to be able to rely on that obligation, for example so as to have time to find a replacement) the employer should ensure that there is a clear written term to that effect in the employee's contract.

(ii) *Exceptions* Section 14 contains a series of exceptions:[458] thus the provisions of section 13 do not apply to deductions in respect of—

(1) overpayment of wages, or expenses;[459]

(2) disciplinary proceedings held by virtue of any statutory provision;

---

[456] These are set out at Ch 6, heading 2, p 427, in the discussion of dismissal by notice.

[457] *Pename Ltd v Paterson* [1989] ICR 12, [1989] IRLR 195; *Chiltern House Ltd v Chambers* [1990] IRLR 88. A similar rule applies to statutory holiday pay under the Working Time Regulations 1998; an employer may only claim back overpaid holiday pay (where an employee leaves partway through the year) if there is a pre-existing 'relevant agreement' in writing allowing this to be done: *Hill v Chapell* [2003] IRLR 19.

[458] There is also an exception in s 13(4) relating to errors of computation of wages, but this is to be construed narrowly: *Yemm v British Steel plc* [1994] IRLR 117; *Morgan v West Glamorgan County Council* [1995] IRLR 68.

[459] One problem here is that what started out as an amount genuinely supposed to cover actual expenses can, over time, simply become an element of pay; see, eg *Mears Ltd v Salt* UKEAT/0552/11.

(3) a statutory requirement to deduct from wages and pay over to a public authority;

(4) payments agreed to by the worker which are to be made over by the employer to a third party;

(5) a strike or other industrial action in which the worker took part; or

(6) the satisfaction of a court or tribunal order requiring the worker to pay something to the employer.

The primary point to notice about these exceptions is that they do *not* establish an independent, unilateral right for the employer to make such deductions; they only state that deductions made on these grounds do not infringe the procedural requirements of section 13. In any given case, the question of the overall legality of a deduction may well depend on the contractual or other common law propriety of making it at all. If there is no contractual authority to make the deduction, the employee can sue for it in the county court in the normal way. However, the question again arose whether an action could be brought instead in a tribunal. At first that seemed possible, for in *Home Office v Ayres*[460] it was held that the exclusions in section 14 only apply to deductions *lawfully* made on the above grounds; it was therefore open to the employee to argue that the deduction was unlawful at common law and so did not come within the relevant exclusion in section 14. However, this reasoning was later repudiated by the EAT in *Sunderland Polytechnic v Evans*[461] where it was held, by exercising the courts' power to consider *Hansard*,[462] that Parliament's intention was that section 14 and its exceptions were to be applied literally, leaving any question of the contractual lawfulness of the deduction in question to be fought over in the ordinary courts.[463] There is, however, middle ground; if the employee is merely denying that the relevant ground existed on the facts (eg that he had not actually been overpaid or that he had not actually been on strike) the tribunal can hear the claim and adjudicate on that point, without trespassing into the forbidden territory of the contractual lawfulness of the deduction.[464]

(iii) *Retail employment* Due to the discussions prior to the introduction of the 1986 Act and concerns expressed as to certain inequitable deductions made in certain service industries, sections 17–22 of the 1996 Act impose a further limitation on deductions from the wages of workers in retail employment.[465] Where such a deduction is made in respect of cash shortages or stock deficiencies, the maximum that may be deducted

---

[460] [1992] ICR 175, [1992] IRLR 59.

[461] [1993] ICR 392, [1993] IRLR 196, applied in *SIP Industrial Products Ltd v Swinn* [1994] ICR 473, [1994] IRLR 323.

[462] *Pepper v Hart* [1993] AC 593, [1993] 1 All ER 42, HL.

[463] The case itself concerned a deduction for taking part in industrial action (s 14(5)), where this policy consideration is perhaps particularly strong; however, the reasoning should apply to all the heads of s 14.

[464] *Gill v Ford Motor Co Ltd* [2004] IRLR 840.

[465] 'Retail employment' is defined in s 17(2), referring principally to the direct supply to the public or other individuals in a personal capacity of goods or services (including financial services).

is 10% of the gross amount of wages for that particular pay day. While such an extra provision is to be welcomed, two further points should be noticed:

(1) this limitation only applies to the *amount* deductible, not to the grounds for deduction, since there is still no requirement that those grounds be fair and reasonable;[466]

(2) there is nothing to stop the full amount of a contractually recoverable deficiency being carried forward over successive pay days until fully recovered, provided that only 10% is taken on each occasion and indeed section 22 states that the 10% rule does not apply to the final pay day if the employee's employment is terminated, when the whole of any outstanding deficiency could be set against the wages payable.

(iv) *Remedies* A complaint that deductions have been made (or payments demanded) in contravention of section 13 may be presented to an employment tribunal within three months of the date of the last deduction or payment, or if that is not reasonably practicable within such further period as the tribunal thinks reasonable.[467] If the tribunal finds the complaint well-founded, it is to make a declaration to that effect and order the repayment of amounts improperly deducted.[468] In addition (by virtue of an amendment by the Employment Act 2008) a tribunal may award an amount 'to compensate the worker for any financial loss sustained by him' due to the making of the deduction, thus putting the damages at large and no longer restricted to a refund of the deduction. Four final points should be noted on these provisions. The first is that section 205(2) states that '[t]he remedy of a worker in respect of any contravention of [sections 13ff] shall be by way of a complaint under section 23 *and not otherwise*'. At first sight, that may appear to rule out a common law action for wages (the traditional remedy to recover improper deductions). However, that is not so since, as pointed out above, all that the Act does is to apply to deductions from wages certain (albeit important) procedural requirements, particularly as to prior written agreement to the making of such deductions. There may well still be cases where the employee is objecting not just to the procedure adopted (which may have complied with section 13), but rather to the legality of making a deduction at all in those circumstances. In such a case the employee retains the option of a common law action in the county court.[469] The second point is that there is a measure of overlap between these provisions and the right in section 11 of the 1996 Act to bring tribunal proceedings against

---

[466] It is therefore still lawful to incorporate a contractual term requiring the refunding of, for example, till deficiencies at a petrol station, even where those deficiencies are not the attendant's fault (as, for example, where caused by fraud by a customer).

[467] Section 23. One useful point to note (s 23(3)) is that, where there has been a *series* of deductions (eg each pay day) the time limit only flows from the *last* deduction, so that the worker does not have to contemplate a legal complaint after every deduction (see *HMRC v Stringer* [2009] ICR 985, [2009] IRLR 677, HL).

[468] Moreover, those amounts are *not* then to be treated as properly recoverable by further deductions (by whatever means) or by action in the ordinary courts, ie the employer loses the right to them altogether: s 25; *Potter v Hunt Contracts Ltd* [1992] ICR 337, [1992] IRLR 108.

[469] *Rickard v PB Glass Supplies Ltd* [1990] ICR 150, CA.

an employer for failing to give proper notification of deductions from wages in the statutory-required itemized pay statement;[470] section 26 provides that both actions can be brought, but that if that happens there is not to be double recovery of the deduction. The third point is that, in potentially an important extension of the tribunal's powers under the Act, the EAT have held that even if the employer does have prior written consent to make a deduction on a particular ground, the employee can argue that the *amount* deducted was excessive and not justified by the written consent; this permits the tribunal to consider whether that particular deduction was sustainable in fact.[471] The fourth point is that special protection is given to an employee making a complaint under Part II. One initial problem was that, although such a complaint is not subject to any qualifying period and so may be brought by a new employee, if such an employee did not have the necessary qualifying period for unfair dismissal he could be dismissed because of the complaint without protection. Now, however, the Employment Rights Act 1996 provides that if an employee is dismissed for asserting certain statutory rights (which include those under Part II), not only is that dismissal automatically unfair, but (crucially) the normal qualifying period does not apply.[472]

6 RIGHTS ON THE EMPLOYER'S INSOLVENCY

Where an employer becomes bankrupt or insolvent, the general rule is that wages or salary due to an employee in respect of the four months before the bankruptcy or insolvency are a preferential debt, subject to a maximum of £800.[473] Beyond that, they constitute an unsecured debt. The Employment Protection Act 1975 introduced new measures to improve the position of the employee of a bankrupt employer in two ways; they are now in the Insolvency Act 1986 and Part XII of the Employment Rights Act 1996. First the Insolvency Act 1986, Schedule 6 provides that certain other amounts are to be treated as wages and so preferential debts. These are amounts owed by the employer in respect of a guarantee payment, remuneration during suspension on medical grounds, payment for time off for union duties, to attend antenatal care and to look for other work and remuneration under a protective award.[474] Secondly, the Employment Rights Act 1996, section 182 gives the employee rights to claim certain amounts due to him from his employer from the Secretary of State instead, who is to

---

[470] Section 8.

[471] *Fairfield Ltd v Skinner* [1992] ICR 836, [1993] IRLR 4.

[472] See Ch 7, heading 5(iv), p 525. These provisions were introduced by the Trade Union Reform and Employment Rights Act 1993.

[473] Insolvency Act 1986, s 386, Sch 6, para 9; para 10 covers holiday pay. Where the employer goes into administration or receivership and the employee is kept on, there may be a continuing liability on the administrator or receiver for 'qualifying liabilities' (wages, holiday pay, sick pay and pension contributions) *if* his contract is adopted by the administrator or receiver, and only from the *date* of adoption: Insolvency Act 1994. This Act (amending the 1986 Act) was rushed through Parliament to negative the effects of the decisions of the Court of Appeal and then the House of Lords in *Powdrill v Watson* [1995] 2 AC 394, [1995] 2 All ER 65, HL.

[474] Insolvency Act 1986, Sch 6, para 13.

pay them out of the National Insurance Fund.[475] The amounts in question are those relating to arrears of pay (up to a maximum of eight weeks), wages during the statutory minimum notice period,[476] holiday pay (up to a maximum of six weeks), a basic award for unfair dismissal and a reasonable sum to reimburse all or part of any fee paid by an apprentice or articled clerk; further, 'pay' is deemed to include any outstanding amounts by way of guarantee payment, remuneration during suspension on medical grounds, payment for statutory time off work or remuneration under a protective award. Where any of these sums is to be computed by reference to weekly pay (for example arrears of wages) the maximum amount that can be used for computation purposes at the time of writing is £430.[477] The employee may also request the Secretary of State to make up any contributions to his occupational pension scheme left unpaid due to his employer's insolvency. Any further sums outstanding can still be claimed by the employee as unsecured debts.

Where the Secretary of State makes one of the above payments to the employee, the rights and remedies which the employee had in the employer's bankruptcy in respect of that amount become vested in the Secretary of State.[478] However, the employee may still be the ultimate beneficiary from this statutory scheme (apart from gaining from its administrative convenience for him) for the amount which he can claim from the

---

[475] The Secretary of State may also make redundancy payments directly out of the Fund where he is satisfied that the employer is insolvent; Employment Rights Act 1996, s 167.

[476] Laid down in the Employment Rights Act, s 86. If for any reason wages during the notice period would not have been payable by the employer, they are not payable by the Secretary of State under s 182; *Secretary of State for Employment v Wilson* [1978] ICR 200, [1977] IRLR 483; this imports the common law notion of mitigation of damage, so that if the ex-employee in fact earns money during what should have been his notice period, those earnings are deducted from the amount payable by the Secretary of State: *Secretary of State for Employment v Jobling* [1980] ICR 380. The major practical problem that arose was whether unemployment benefit received during what should have been the notice period should be deducted—application of the doctrine of mitigation would suggest that it should, but this would lead (in the case of an ex-employee becoming long-term unemployed) to the ex-employee's (then) one-year entitlement to unemployment benefit running out sooner than it would have done if he had received proper notice, without any recompense. After protracted litigation, the House of Lords finally held in *Westwood v Secretary of State for Employment* [1985] ICR 209, [1984] IRLR 209, HL, that the amount recoverable from the Secretary of State, though by a statutory right, represented damages for wrongful dismissal, so that the duty to mitigate applied, and this included deducting unemployment benefit (though they suggested a method of doing so that in fact recompensed the ex-employee). After this decision the position was altered to allow the employee to get the (net) s 182 payment, but then receive what would otherwise have been his full entitlement to unemployment benefit (now jobseekers allowance).

[477] This figure is subject to annual review under the Employment Relations Act 1999, s 34. Applying the principle in *Westwood* (n 476), the amount to be paid by the Secretary of State is the amount of the employee's *net* loss, so that from gross wages owed there is to be deducted the amounts normally payable as tax and NI contributions, and any mitigating amounts such as benefit received and/or any amounts earned elsewhere during the period in question: *Secretary of State for Employment v Cooper* [1987] ICR 766. However, for the purpose of applying the statutory maximum for a week's pay, the Secretary of State is correct to apply that maximum to the *gross* loss, and only then deduct the above amounts: *Morris v Secretary of State for Employment* [1985] ICR 522, [1985] IRLR 297; heads, the Secretary of State wins, tails ... ?

[478] Employment Rights Act 1996, s 189.

Secretary of State may be greater than that which the Secretary of State can then claim as a preferential debt in the bankruptcy, for two reasons. First, the amount claimable from the Secretary of State may be greater than the £800 maximum preferred debt for wages and salaries; second, certain items in respect of which the employee can claim from the Secretary of State are still not deemed to be preferred debts (for example the amount of a basic award for unfair dismissal). In the case of any such amounts, the Secretary of State must pay them to the employee, claim as much as possible as a preferred debt and then claim the balance simply as an unsecured debt; it is thus the NI which bears the risk in such a case, not the individual employee.

4

THE WORK–LIFE BALANCE RIGHTS

OVERVIEW

This chapter addresses a number of legislative regimes creating rights that affect the balance between work and life outside of work. Specifically, the discussion focuses on rights to a guaranteed minimum wage; to rest breaks, paid leave and a maximum 48-hour working week; to maternity, paternity, adoption and other parental leave; and to request flexible working arrangements. Although not all of these rights can claim work–life balance as their original policy driver, they have come to be seen as representing a loosely coherent programme for ensuring that the process of earning a living does not preclude any worker from enjoying other aspects of life, especially family life.[1] The guarantees of the Part-time Workers (Prevention of Less Favourable Treatment) Regulations 2000 and the Fixed-term Employees (Prevention of Less Favourable Treatment) Regulations 2002 also deserve mention as part of this programme, but because they have stronger doctrinal links with discussions about employment status (Chapter 2) and proof of less favourable treatment in discrimination (Chapter 5) they do not receive separate attention here.

The work of this chapter involves considering, one at a time, each of these work–life rights and the policies and legislation behind them. However, because the rights originated and function (however disappointingly) as components of an integrated (again, however disappointingly) response to an interconnected set of social and economic challenges, the right-by-right treatment must build upon an understanding of the nature of those challenges and the logic behind the response. This chapter will begin, therefore, with a brief introduction of the work–life balance programme and the issues it sought, and seeks, to address. The rights will then be analysed in two groups: first the 'floor' of rights regulating the minimum wage and working time, and then the more overtly 'family-friendly' guarantees relating to parental rights and flexible working.

---

[1] Bogg 'Paid Annual Leave and the Long-Term Sick: Third Time Lucky for the UK' (2007) 36 ILJ 341, 344; Collins *Employment Law* (2003) 76.

1 INTRODUCTION

Work–life balance is a slippery concept, and it seems to mean different things depending on whom the user of the phrase hopes to persuade. In its simplest sense it refers to the idea that preventing downward pay flexibility and exploitative working hours, and requiring appropriate accommodation for caring and other duties outside the workplace, will improve the quality of life for most people and possibly productivity for business as well. The New Labour government under Tony Blair, seeking (understandably) to please both business and workers, promised just such a model of work–life balance in a 1998 White Paper, 'Fairness at Work', which ushered in all of the rights under consideration in this chapter. The White Paper emphasized that fairly treated employees, not worn out and demoralized by an impossible struggle to build a career in the face of competing childcare responsibilities, would be more productive and better able to form constructive relationships with employers.[2] Also, like much of the debate at the time, the White Paper treated work–life balance as implying, and in some ways essentially meaning, 'family-friendly'. However, this paradigm masks the inherent tension between work–life and family-friendly agendas, and places too little emphasis on the most morally insistent basis for the work–life programme: gender imbalance.

The right-by-right discussions in this chapter show that most of the work–life measures introduced by the White Paper have loopholes or unintended consequences that should attract criticism at face value. However, the most significant weaknesses (or strengths, depending on one's project) emerge from the interaction of the measures, and their failure as a whole to deliver on some of the meanings given to work–life balance by different stakeholders and voices in the debate. To start with an easy one, family-friendly policies do not actually afford work–life balance to those who conceive of it as a promise that all workers, whether they have children or not, should be supported in their efforts to pursue a fulfilling life outside the workplace. The extension of the right to request flexible working arrangements to carers for adults (meaning in practice the old and/or infirm) by the Work and Families Act 2006 (as from April 2007) broadened the reach of 'family friendly' beyond parents, but still failed to constitute a *general* flexibility right which might be available to those simply harbouring a desire to spend more time gardening or following the Barmy Army around the cricketing venues of the southern hemisphere. What assistance do maternity leave, a right for carers to request flexible working arrangements, and parental childcare leave provide to a 40-year-old single woman who wants to pursue an advanced degree while still supporting herself? Although nothing suggests that

---

[2] 'Fairness at Work' (Cm 3968, 1998) ch 5; the White Paper also somehow contrives to suggest that more rights will make workers more willing to tolerate 'a flexible and efficient labour market in which enterprise can flourish, companies can grow and wealth can be created' through greater use of casual, part-time and fixed-term work as well as 'businesses being able to adapt quickly to changing demand' (paras 2.10 and 2.13).

a government *ought* to assist people in such a position, this government clearly has chosen to support people in a specific position: that of bearing or raising children and, latterly, of caring for incapacitated adults. That leaves the minimum wage and the regulation of working time to do the heavy lifting of work–life balance for non-carers.

At a superficial level, this looks only mildly unsatisfactory. Yes, it is heavily slanted in favour of those who have caring responsibilities, but it could be argued that caring responsibilities represent the greatest societal obstacle to work–life balance, making it facially legitimate to choose that as a focus for regulation. Non-carers can rest safe in the guarantee of a living wage (for full-time work) and the right not to work more than 48 hours a week (unless they want to get promoted). Meanwhile, the emphasis on support of child-bearing and rearing should ameliorate gender imbalance, as it is women who, as a result of societal assumptions about caring responsibilities, struggle the most with caring-related work–life balance issues. In response to complaints of unfairness from non-carers, under this conception of the work–life balance problem, one need only observe that the family-friendly rights only partially redress the significant career advantages enjoyed by non-carers.

While this analysis makes no errors, strictly speaking, it (1) assumes that extensive maternity leave and unpaid parental leave are likely or even intended to help level the playing field for women in the workplace, (2) trivializes the extent to which work–life balance obstacles disproportionately confront women and (3) misconceives the role of the long-hours culture in erecting those obstacles. The parental rights go beyond merely providing more work–life help to carers than to non-carers: they provide more help to families where the mother stays home for at least 20 weeks.[3] The rights to request flexible working, to adoption leave and to parental leave are not openly gendered, but the maternity and paternity arrangements clearly subsidize a particular vision of whose career should be put on hold when a child arrives. Even the other apparently neutral family-friendly rights have a similar tendency to entrench the role of women as carers, because they are unpaid. Before the advent of work–life balance rights, women made in general much less than men: less than 80% (mean) for the same work, but even less overall because far more women than men worked part time.[4] In this situation, when one parent needed to take time off for caring responsibilities, the only economically sensible course of action was for the woman to do it. The unpaid family-friendly rights do nothing to alter this. They prevent whichever parent takes time off from getting sacked, but they leave in place the grinding logic of having the lower paid partner do the caring. Of course, women are more often in lower paid or part-time work as a

---

[3] Maternity and Parental Leave etc Regulations 1999, as amended, regs 4 and 7, the Paternity and Adoption Leave Regulations 2002, regs 4 and 5, and the Additional Paternity Leave Regulations 2010 provide mothers with 52 weeks of maternity leave, while fathers get two weeks of paternity leave to 'support the child's mother' and whatever leave is transferred to him by the mother at least 20 weeks after the birth of the child.

[4] Carley 'Widening of Gender Pay Gap Triggers Calls for Action' (European Industrial Relations Observatory Online, 1 January 2009), available at <http://www.eurofound.europa.eu/eiro/2008/12/articles/uk0812029i.htm> (last accessed 6 January 2013).

result of an existing social norm that puts pressure on women to be carers. Thus the family-friendly rights could be accused of doing nothing to change the stereotype of women as carers, and of granting state approval and economic support to a traditional gendered division of responsibility for parenting newborn children.

The foregoing seems to support the claim of our earlier, superficial analysis that caring duties, and their disproportionate allocation to women, are the single greatest obstacle to a true work–life balance for people of all genders. This, alas, ignores the other side of the coin: caring responsibilities amount to a problem only because they often conflict with the unnecessarily intractable demands of the traditional workplace. Many carers would insist that they could balance work and caring if they could work flexibly—arranging their caring and work hours around each other—and get jobs commensurate with their skill level, thereby earning higher pay. This so seldom actually happens, however, because of what is known as the long-hours culture. This refers to an attitude, prevailing in most male-dominated professions like law practice, corporate management, manufacturing and construction, that the more continuous hours workers commit to the enterprise, the more valuable they are. This view has a shrewd arithmetic appeal, based on the idea of getting the most hours for a single salary. However, as salaries tend to rise for the most time-committed workers, and because overtime hours tend to be the least productive hours, this simplistic calculation probably yields a feeble dividend. More compelling within the long-hours culture is the conviction that workers cannot deliver seriousness, commitment and competence without an around-the-clock presence and the subordination of all home-life concerns. While not a shred of evidence supports this belief, it persists probably because the predominantly male members of these work communities understandably associate success with the successful (male) mentors and associates they have known, almost all of whom will have assimilated with the long-hours culture. It falls beyond the scope of this discussion to prove that an enterprise could derive just as much value from two people working 20 skilled, efficient and refreshed hours per week as from one exhausted person working 55 hours a week.[5] It suffices to note that because certain professional cultures hold unshakeable beliefs to the contrary, a person who can only work part time, or can work full time but needs to go home at 5pm every day, will generally not go far in those professions. Male or female, people who turn down extra work to care for their children will, in business cultures like these, either fail or languish at the lowest levels. This means that the carer will not get both high-skill/high-pay and a flexible or part-time schedule: the long-hours culture

---

[5] Pozen, 'Stop working all those hours' *Harvard Business Review* (15 June 2012) available at <http://blogs.hbr.org/hbsfaculty/2012/06/stop-working-all-those-hours.html> (last accessed 6 January 2013); *The Return of the Long Hours Culture* (Trade Unions Congress June 2008) available at <http://www.tuc.org.uk/extras/longhoursreturn.pdf> (last accessed 6 January 2013); Moyes 'Long-hours culture hitting productivity' *The Independent*, 26 October 1995, available at <http://www.independent.co.uk/news/uk/longhours-culture-hitting-productivity-1579453.html> (last accessed 6 January 2013); Ferguson 'Long-hours culture saps tech productivity' (ZDNet UK, 19 February 2008) available at <http://news.zdnet.com/long-hours-saps-tech-productivity-3039303406/> (last accessed 6 January 2013).

forces a choice between part-time and low pay on one hand, or married-to-your-work commitment and minimal family time on the other.

So it could be said that caring responsibilities are not the greatest societal obstacle to work–life balance: the long-hours culture is. If so, that makes the Working Time Regulations 1998 (WTRs), heralded in the 1998 White Paper as a measure 'to tackle excessively long working hours', the lynchpin of the work–life balance project. In theory, the WTRs limit the average working week to 48 hours. However, many conceive the problem as exclusively one of companies requiring workers to work excessive hours. This has led to widespread support for an exception in the WTRs that allows individual employees to 'opt out' of the 48-hour week. In other words, the WTRs only prohibit workers from being required to work over 48 hours *against their will*. While any self-respecting work–life balance programme would certainly try to put a stop to this kind of thing, there is little evidence that coercion is at the heart of the larger, structural problems already discussed. The problem is a long-hours *culture*, and the culture is perpetuated by the participants whose interests the culture serves: those who can or will work long hours. There is not a great deal in it for employers to make hourly paid workers work too much: for the same money they can pay someone less exhausted. Meanwhile, hourly paid workers often work long hours because they will earn more. They may not enjoy it, but they choose to do it because it enlarges their pay-packet. Employers have some incentive to coerce salaried employees to work extra hours, so it helps to have a prohibition on that. However, employers can 'coerce' or encourage long-hours work without threats of dismissal or direct orders. They need only make it clear that those who 'opt out' get promoted or get pay rises. Then we are back to where we always were: those who can choose to work long hours and ignore caring responsibilities—usually men—will do so because it advances their careers. This sets the bar for all workers, and those with intractable caring duties—usually women—will struggle to clear that bar and will settle for low-paid part-time work.

One view of the big picture, then, shows the long-hours culture as the primary obstacle to work–life balance—and one faced especially by women—and a legislative programme that makes a feint at dismantling this obstacle while investing its real energy into making mothers and other carers feel a little less put upon by the unequal situation. While we should be grateful for any amelioration of the plight of the working mother, we are left to shake our heads at a regime that openly endorses traditional gender roles, even putting economic pressure on families to do things the old-fashioned way. Of course, like the earlier superficial analysis this assessment, in its turn, minimizes a crucial consideration: choice. The current government and the Trades Union Council (representing, to an extent, the interests of workers) place choice at the centre of their agendas for work–life balance.[6] In particular, they cleave to the more 'common sense' view that the long-hours culture threatens work–life balance

---

[6] 'Fairness at Work' (Cm 3968, 1998); *The Return of the Long Hours Culture* (Trades Union Congress, June 2008) 9, available at <http://www.tuc.org.uk/extras/longhoursreturn.pdf> (last accessed 6 January 2013).

by *requiring* workers to commit excessive time to their jobs. From this perspective, those who wish to work longer hours, either because this reflects their own work–life priorities or because they want the financial rewards that flow from working longer, do not have a work–life balance problem, and should therefore not face regulatory intervention. Meanwhile, those who either cannot or will not prioritize work in this way must confront the stark reality that as long as enough people choose to commit 60 hours a week to their work, workers who cannot match that commitment will fall behind economically. This conflict encapsulates the dilemma: must the longer-hours workers surrender their advantage, or must the shorter-hours workers accept their fate as also-rans? Resolving this apparent zero-sum game hinges on the question of whether longer-working represents a real, objective virtue, or merely a preference common to a currently empowered group that alone can exercise that preference. One could hardly celebrate a 'work–life balance' achieved by suppressing the desires of some workers to give greater value to their employers. If, on the other hand, social constructs place only certain people in a position to work long hours, and long-hour commitment in itself does not add value over what can be achieved by a more diverse workforce working fewer hours, then perhaps unfettered choice should give way to a playing field in which the available choices are accessible by all, or most, workers. This is the kind of question that should inform discussion of the work–life balance rights considered in this chapter.

Meanwhile, it should be remembered that, as in other areas of employment law, the statutory provisions outlined in this chapter represent a minimum entitlement which may in practice be replaced by more generous contractual arrangements, and while the law may give preferential treatment to working parents, it is clear that many employers with flexibility policies extend the benefit of those schemes to all employees, not just to working parents. One leading example is Asda, which had its efforts in promoting flexible working and equal pay recognized by the government through a Castle Award in 2002, and by its own employees voting it top of the *Sunday Times 100 Best Companies to Work For* in that same year. Asda provides a wide range of flexible working practices and family-friendly policies, including shift-swapping, job-sharing, childcare leave, term-time working and (we note enviously) 'Benidorm' leave, in the form of a three-month unpaid winter holiday. Such policies have since become more widespread as employers wake up to the economic and business case for flexibility, and as firms increasingly see cutting-edge flexibility policies as a cost-effective means of recruiting, retaining and motivating the best staff.

More recently, information technology has spurred the development of work–life balance policies that emphasize flexibility of place rather than flexibility of time. Many leading firms, especially law firms, who often argue that the nature of their services to clients calls for a kind of continuity inconsistent with part-time work or job-sharing, have begun letting their employees perform their work wherever their non-work responsibilities force them to be. For example, Eversheds, a large law firm that was the runner-up for Opportunity Now's *Advancing Women in Business Award* in 2009, offered the following explanation for its success:

The firm's investment in technology has made flexible working a realistic option for a significant proportion of its people and has also proven to enhance its service to clients. Over 30% of its employees now have a laptop, most of those also have a 3G card which allows them to work online in any location. 46% of its people have a Blackberry and 25% of its people have the facility to access their office desktop from home. Flexible working is now becoming integral to the firm's culture, and as more men are taking advantage of it, Eversheds is finding that there is no longer a perception that it is only aimed at women.[7]

Addleshaw Goddard, another law firm and the winner of the same award in 2008, likewise cited 'IT infrastructure' as key to more employees working from home and other locations. This kind of approach is increasing in popularity, because businesses find that flexible working not only does not harm productivity but improves it, and 20% of workers in the UK in 2008 said they would relinquish 5% of their pay to be able to work from home or elsewhere even for one or two days a week.[8] If regulation, education, or a combination of the two can maintain pressure on businesses to keep moving in this kind of direction, perhaps neither worker choice nor equality of opportunity need give way.

2 STATUTORY REGULATION OF WAGES AND HOURS

(i) BACKGROUND

For many years the state, in pursuance of its economic policies, sought to play a role in wage regulation, though normally this was done indirectly through extra-legal devices such as white papers, social compacts/contracts or exhortation. Statutory regulation (outside wartime) has been rare. There have been incidents of legislative intervention to try to protect employees receiving inadequately low pay, though these have been on a specific basis applying to particular industries, persons or activities, as opposed to the current legislation on the national minimum wage which puts in place a general 'floor' right.

An early device relating to low pay was the establishment in 1909 of trade boards,[9] later to become known as wages councils. These covered specific industries or trades where unionism was low, as were wages, and consisted of a statutory board (equal numbers of employers and workers, with independent members and chairman) charged with setting minimum wages and (later) other basic terms and conditions

---

[7] Opportunity Now Awards 2009 case studies, available at <http://www.opportunitynow.org.uk>.

[8] *The Web Commuting Imperative* (Citrix Online, 2008) available at <http://www.workshifting.com/citrix_online_w3c_report.pdf> (last accessed 6 January 2013).

[9] Trade Boards Act 1909; the first four boards covered the so-called 'sweated traders' of tailoring, box-making, lacemaking and chain-making.

which were enforceable in the civil courts (and backed by criminal sanctions) through the administrative means of a wages inspectorate. Although the councils were supposed to be a temporary expedient (pending the growth of normal collective bargaining) they proved to be longlasting and their coverage spread,[10] though of course they always remained the exception rather than the rule in industrial relations. With the election of a Conservative government in 1979 espousing laissez-faire free market economics, the wages council system fell into official disapproval, as being a statutory limitation on a free market in labour. Their powers were first curbed in the Wages Act 1986 (taking youth workers out of their jurisdiction and limiting them to setting basic rates) and they were finally abolished by the Trade Union Reform and Employment Rights Act 1993. The only survivor (and now the only example of a statutory minimum wage in a particular industry) was the Agricultural Wages Board which was set up under separate legislation;[11] although technically not a 'wages council' it operates in the same way and continues to set minimum wages, terms and conditions for those employed in agriculture, horticulture and growing.[12] Revival of the wages council system generally has not figured in the plans of the present government.

A second form of low pay provision was the Fair Wages Resolution, a resolution of the House of Commons in 1891 (repeated in 1946) that employers receiving government contracts should be required to pay fair wages, ie the going rate for the job, in order to prevent undercutting by driving down wages.[13] Workers or their trade union could complain of breach of the Resolution to (initially) the Industrial Court (since 1976 the Central Arbitration Committee) which resolved the matter by arbitration, the result of which was legally binding on the employer. This was supplemented by other forms of unilateral arbitration on wages for either the resolution of disputes or for the maintenance of the going rate of pay. The system of arbitration that applied during the Second World War lasted until its abolition in 1959,[14] whereafter the legislation retained vestiges whereby a claim could be made to the Industrial Court that an employer was not observing the terms and conditions established in that industry. This eventually became embodied in Schedule 11 to the Employment Protection Act 1975, enforced by the Central Arbitration Committee. This 'Schedule 11 claim' procedure was widely used in the 1970s;[15] its primary aim was to attack pockets of low pay within an industry, though towards the end of that decade it was criticized as being

---

[10] The largest industries covered were retail, hotels and restaurants. In addition, there were certain rather more rarified examples, such as the ostrich feather and fancy hat council and the pin, hook and zip fasteners council. Shortly before their abolition, there were 24 councils covering 2.5 million workers.

[11] Agricultural Wages Act 1948.

[12] The previous government consulted on abolishing it but, to their surprise, the farmer employers strongly favoured its retention. Its continued role, however, is uncertain because of the existence now of a national minimum wage.

[13] Bercusson Fair Wages Resolution (1978).

[14] Terms and Conditions of Employment Act 1959.

[15] ACAS Annual Reports show conciliation in 3,092 cases between 1976 and 1980, with 1,970 arbitration by the CAC.

used for other, less noble purposes because a Schedule 11 award was not subject to the then government's pay restraint policy. With the change of government in 1979 and the radical change in economic policy, these forms of statutory and quasi-statutory inter-vention quickly became viewed as anachronistic, for two reasons: (1) they presupposed the clear establishment by collective bargaining of comprehensive national terms and conditions across an industry, whereas that model was rapidly breaking down; and (2) in any event the Conservative economic orthodoxy of the time denied outright that there was any such thing as a 'fair' or 'going' rate for a job—the only rate for the job was increasingly to be that set by a deregulated market. Thus, Schedule 11 was repealed immediately, in the Employment Act 1980, and the Fair Wages Resolution was rescinded two years later.[16] Once again, restitution of specific provisions such as these has not been suggested by the present government, and indeed would be difficult if not impossible in the current flexible, devolved and localized labour market.

With regard to hours of work, these too have not been subject to wide-ranging statutory control in mainstream employment law. Of course, the movement to restrict maximum hours, especially in factories, was a major factor in nineteenth-century social history and was eventually successful in a consistent series of factories statutes, aimed at improving what we would now call the health and safety of the workforce.[17] These provisions were, however, specific to certain places and/or industries and, although eventually extended to men, the initial thrust of them was to give extra protection to women and young persons. It was this that fed through into the modern factories legis-lation, and came increasingly under attack. In relation to women, the restrictions (for example on night working or overtime) were seen as unacceptably paternalistic and discriminatory (affecting questions of equal pay if women could not earn certain pre-mium payments)[18] and they were repealed in the Sex Discrimination Act 1986. With regard to young persons, the restrictions were repealed as a deregulatory measure in the Employment Act 1989.

One unusual case where there are highly specific limitations on working hours is that of Sunday shop opening and betting. This was a highly contentious matter and, as part of the eventual political trade-off, the legislation[19] creates a category of 'protected' workers who cannot be obliged to work on Sundays. Initially, this protection was only meant to be transitional, so that those already in employment when the change came in could not be forced to work on Sundays. However, due to pressure in Parliament,

---

[16] The delay was due to the need for the government to denounce an International Labour Organization Convention which underpinned the Resolution.

[17] For an excellent description of this legislation, see Cornish and Clark 'Law and Society in England 1750–1950' (1989) ch 4.

[18] EOC 'Health and safety legislation: should we distinguish between men and women?' (1979).

[19] The main controversy was over the Sunday Trading Act 1994, which gave rise to the provisions governing 'protected shop workers'. When Sunday betting was legalized by the Deregulation and Contracting Out Act 1994, similar provisions were inserted into the Betting, Gaming and Lotteries Act 1963. All of these protective provisions are now in the Employment Rights Act 1996, Pt IV; the anti-victimization and dismissal provisions are in ss 45 and 101, see Ch 7, heading 5(iv), p 522.

it was extended and so in fact enacts a legal regime covering Sunday working into the future too. It gives the right to opt out of Sunday working by giving three months' notice, and not to be prejudiced thereby; there is also provision for a protected shop or betting worker to opt back into Sunday working. Any provision in a contract which contravenes these rules is declared to be unenforceable.

Thus, in spite of a somewhat varied history, by 1997 and the change of government statutory intervention in questions of wages and hours had been restricted to the setting of wages and conditions in agriculture and the specific rules on Sunday working in the retail and betting industries. That position has now been significantly altered by the National Minimum Wage Act 1998 (a New Labour election commitment) and the Working Time Regulations 1998 (an EC law requirement).

(ii) THE NATIONAL MINIMUM WAGE ACT 1998

The advantages and disadvantages of a national minimum wage have been a controversial matter in this jurisdiction for some time; it is a device that is widely used in Europe and some states in the US, and an early International Labour Organization (ILO) Convention[20] encouraged such action by states. Its introduction was an election issue in 1997, and immediately on coming into office the government established a Low Pay Commission, at first on an informal basis and then put on to a statutory footing by the legislation, to investigate and make recommendations. The government proceeded to pass the National Minimum Wage Act 1998 (NMWA) which operates in significant areas by giving regulation-making powers; when the Low Pay Commission made its first report,[21] its recommendations were incorporated into the National Minimum Wage Regulations 1999,[22] which contain much of the detailed law—while obviously the most politically contentious question is the rate at which the minimum wage is set, the most difficult questions legally tend to be those of definition (what is pay? what can be disregarded? how to average? who is covered?) which are particularly acute in a piece of legislation intended to apply to employment across the board, in all its varieties.

The Act sets out a basic entitlement for any worker (working, or ordinarily working, in the UK under his contract) to be remunerated by his employer in any pay reference period at a rate not less than the national minimum wage fixed by regulations by the Secretary of State.[23] The ambit of this duty is deliberately broad through the use of the

[20] Convention No 26 (1928) 'Minimum wage-fixing machinery'.

[21] Cm 3976, 1998. For the Commission's observations on other countries' legislation, see Cash 'Lessons from the International Experience of Statutory Minimum Wages' [1998] Labour Market Trends 463.

[22] SI 1999/584. For detailed guidance, see the DTI 'Guide to the National Minimum Wage' (1999). Simpson 'Implementing the National Minimum Wage' (1999) 28 ILJ 171 and 'The National Minimum Wage Five Years on: Reflections on Some General Issues' (2004) 33 ILJ 22.

[23] National Minimum Wage Act 1998, s 1. The pay reference period is a month or, in the case of a worker who is paid by reference to a period shorter than a month, that period: reg 10. This could cause problems with 'annualized hours' contracts.

wide term 'workers' which covers employees and any other person under a contract (whether express or implied, written or not) whereby the individual undertakes to do or perform personally any work or services for another party to the contract whose status is not that of a client or customer of any profession or business undertaking carried on by the individual.[24] Any attempt to contract out of the protection of the legislation is void.[25] However, *Walton v Independent Living*[26] appears to have allowed a kind of contracting out. In that case a live-in care worker, whose services were required at unpredictable times and in unpredictable amounts, was categorized as doing 'unmeasured work', and could therefore agree a specific number of notional hours to represent a pay basis. This had the effect of removing the question, usually applicable in cases of workers on-call on-site, of whether the on-call time amounted to working time requiring the minimum wage. In effect, Ms Walton and her employer contracted out of the ordinary rules for on-call periods.

Although the introduction of the national minimum wage in 1999 was the honouring of an important commitment by New Labour, the rate at which it was set (the principal rate was £3.60 per hour) was substantially below what the unions had argued for. By the time of writing the rates had risen to:

(1) £6.19 per hour generally;[27]

(2) £4.98 per hour for a worker aged 18 but under 22;[28]

(3) £3.68 per hour for a worker who has not attained the age of 18.[29]

A worker under 26 employed under a contract of apprenticeship and in the first 12 months of his employment or who has not attained the age of 19 does not qualify.[30] A survey in spring 1998 had estimated that between 1.9m and 2.4m employees (ie between 8.4% and 10.4% of the workforce) earned below the projected level of £3.60 (£3.00 for those aged 18–22), and that by commencement in April 1999 between 1.7m and 2.1m were likely to be affected.[31] This fitted the Low Pay Commission's own estimate that

---

[24] Section 54 (see Ch 2, heading 1(vi), p 53): there are subsidiary provisions in ss 34 and 35 to ensure (if necessary) that agency workers and home workers are covered. Voluntary workers (eg for a charity or similar organization) are specifically excluded: s 44. At a late stage, under media pressure, au pairs and family workers were exempted: reg 2(2)–(4).

[25] Section 49. The Secretary of State has power to exclude or modify the right in relation to particular persons but, in response to concerns expressed about the width of this when the Bill was going through Parliament, it is specifically stated that this cannot be on the basis of specifying different areas, sectors of employment, sites of undertakings or occupations: ss 3, 4. In the event, this power has been used in relation to workers of certain ages.

[26] [2003] ICR 688, [2003] IRLR 469.   [27] Regulation 11.   [28] Regulation 13(1).

[29] Regulation 13(1A). The Employment Equality (Age) Regulations 2006 repealed another special rate but did *not* equalize the other age-related rates (considering them to be objectively justified and so not contrary to the Equal Treatment Directive).

[30] Regulation 12(2). Being under a contract of apprenticeship includes being engaged in a Modern Apprenticeship. Workers participating in certain designated training or employment schemes also do not qualify: reg 12(5).

[31] Wilkinson 'Who Are the Low Paid?' [1998] Labour Market Trends 617. Over half of those affected are women working part time; the percentage is highest in hotels and restaurants, with the highest actual numbers in wholesale and retail.

about 2m employees should benefit, with a total recurring cost to industry of £2.4bn (0.6% of the national average wage bill); however, the government were keen to argue that there would be significant offsetting savings to business in lower absenteeism and staff turnover costs, both of which tend to be higher in sectors of low pay.[32] This sanguinity appears to have been justified, as subsequent studies indicate that the National Minimum Wage has had either no effect or a positive effect on employment and productivity, and has narrowed the pay gap between men and women.[33]

In order to determine whether the legal minimum is being paid, it is of course necessary to work out the current hourly rate for the particular individual, which may be easier said than done where the contracting and/or pay arrangements are complex or flexible. The established formula is to take the total of remuneration for the reference period minus the total of reductions to be made, and divide it by the total hours worked in that period.[34] However, the question of 'total hours' is a potential stumbling block, and to try to cover this, the legislation divides work into four possible categories:

(1) 'time work', ie work that is paid for by reference to the time worked (even if depending on the worker's output per hour);[35]

(2) 'salaried hours work', ie where there are ascertainable basic hours in return for an annual salary, not varying with hours actually worked (except for any performance bonus);[36]

---

[32] 'The Low Pay Commission have confirmed the view taken by Government that sustainable economic growth and job creation cannot hinge on low pay alone. The rates introduced by these Regulations should encourage fairer competition by preventing undercutting based on unduly low wages and will reinforce companies which compete through quality, service and timeliness of delivery rather than just price and wage costs': Consultation Document URN: 98/885 (September 1998) Annex 5, para 13. This argument primarily relates to competition with other *national* firms who are also subject to the minimum wage; international competition is another matter.

[33] Metcalf 'Britain's minimum wage: what impact on pay and jobs?', Winter 2006–07 *CentrePiece* 10, available at <http://cep.lse.ac.uk/pubs/download/CP217.pdf> (last accessed 6 January 2013).

[34] Regulation 14.

[35] Regulation 3. In relation to time work, time spent while available for work and required to be available (eg on a standby arrangement at or near the employer's premises) is to count (reg 15(1)). Time when a worker may sleep has caused problems: reg 15(1A) appears to exclude it but the courts have construed this narrowly to apply only where the worker may sleep while waiting to work, not applying where the worker's job is to be available on shift in case of need, eg a nightwatchman or person available to answer requests for help: *Burrow Down Support Services v Rossiter* [2008] All ER (D) 49; *British Nursing Association v Inland Revenue* [2002] IRLR 480; *Scottbridge Construction Ltd v Wright* [2003] IRLR 21, Ct of Sess (IH). On the other hand, a 24-hour carer living in the client's home in case of problems was held to be on 'unmeasured work' and so able to enter a 'realistic average' agreement for only certain hours to count for NMW purposes: *Walton v Independent Living* [2003] ICR 688, [2003] IRLR 469. The potential conflict between these cases could cause problems. Time when the worker is absent from work does not count, and this is expressed to include rest breaks and industrial action: reg 15(5)–(7). Time spent on training counts: reg 19.

[36] Regulation 4. This heading was added to the original draft Regulations, and gives rise to some of the most complex provisions in the Regulations. There may be a difficult borderline with 'unmeasured work', eg in the case of a worker resident on employer's premises: *McCartney v Oversley House Management* [2006] ICR 510, [2006] IRLR 514.

(3) 'output work', ie work that is paid for wholly by reference to the number of pieces made or processed by the worker, or to some other measure of output (for example number or value of sales or transactions);[37]

(4) 'unmeasured work', ie work not within the previous categories, in particular where there are no specified hours and the worker is required to work when needed or when work is available.[38]

Calculating the hours worked is simplest in the case of time work, where it is simply the number of hours actually worked in the relevant pay reference period. Likewise, there is a simple averaging process over the salary year in the case of salaried hours work if only the basic hours are worked. *If*, however, the salaried worker actually works more than this, a more complicated calculation is set out to take the extra hours into account.[39] More generalized problems are bound to arise with output work and unmeasured work because of the variability of the hours put in by the worker in discharging the duties. Prima facie, the measure here has to be the total number of hours *actually* worked in the reference period, but this could be administratively difficult where there are significant fluctuations, and so the Regulations permit the worker and employer to agree in writing what the worker's *normal* hours are likely to be, so determining what the 'ascertained hours' are to be for the pay reference period.[40] In the case of output work, this must be a 'fair estimate', bearing some relationship to the speed at which an average pieceworker would work, and backed by records of actual hours kept by the worker. In the case of unmeasured work, it must be a 'realistic average' of the hours likely to be spent on the contractual duties. As will be seen below, this approach is similar to that in the Working Time Regulations, laying down default rules but placing major emphasis on fitting the requirements to individual jobs by agreement (though with the difference that in relation to working time the emphasis is largely on collective forms of agreement, whereas here it is on individual agreement). An employer may have much to gain in entering such agreements, especially where fluctuating or ungovernable work patterns may mean at times being technically in breach of the legislation, in the absence of agreed averages. One final point in ascertaining hours, possibly a problem with any of the four categories, is travelling time; this is dealt with specifically, the general rule being that work-related travelling (and necessary waiting times) are counted, but travelling from home to work is not.[41]

The other variable which has to be calculated in order to determine whether the worker is being paid the legal minimum is of course the pay in the relevant reference period. The 'total of remuneration' is defined as all moneys paid by the employer to the worker in (or in respect of) that reference period, plus any permitted charge for living accommodation.[42]

---

[37] Regulation 5.   [38] Regulation 6.   [39] Regulation 22; see the DTI Guide, paras 155–72.
[40] Regulations 24–29.   [41] See the DTI Guide, para 127.
[42] Regulation 30. Benefits in kind are excluded (including exchangeable vouchers such as luncheon vouchers), as are (1) loans or advances of wages, (2) any pension or compensation for loss of office, (3) any tribunal award or settlement amount (other than for an amount contractually due), (4) any redundancy payment and (5) any amount under a suggestions scheme: regs 8 and 9.

From this gross amount, there are then a series of reductions to be made,[43] essentially in order to comply with the Low Pay Commission recommendation that (however the pay is calculated) it is components that comprise pay for standard working that are to count towards the national minimum wage, not premia or other additions for non-standard work.

The worker has a statutory right of access to the records which the employer must keep.[44] In a case of non-compliance with the minimum, the individual worker is given a statutory entitlement under his contract to 'additional remuneration' representing the shortfall.[45] As a result of amendments enacted through the Employment Act 2008, the amount of remuneration is calculated according to the greater of the minimum wage at the time of underpayment or the rate applicable at the 'time of determination'.[46] This time will usually be either the time of initiating legal proceedings or the time of enforcement by minimum wage inspectors. The legislation does not give any special procedure for recovery, and so this amount would have to be claimed in an ordinary breach of contract action (in the county court or, on termination, in a tribunal) or as an unlawful deduction for wages under Part II of the Employment Rights Act 1996; in any such proceedings there is a reversal of the burden of proof.[47] There is, however, in an interesting parallel with the old wages council system, an alternative form of enforcement which may be to an individual worker's advantage. The Secretary of State is given power to appoint minimum wage inspectors with wide powers to inspect records, require information and enter premises for these purposes.[48] If such an officer finds non-compliance with the minimum, he or she may serve a 'notice of underpayment' on the employer, requiring future compliance, the payment of arrears to the individual(s) concerned, and the payment of a penalty equal to half of the total arrears, subject to a minimum of £500 and a maximum of £5,000.[49] If the

---

[43] These cover—(1) payment for work done in a previous reference period, (2) payment for time absent from work, (3) (crucially) overtime or shift premium, (4) special allowances (eg for dangerous work, antisocial hours or being on standby; however, performance or incentive payments *do* count), (5) tips or gratuities paid directly by customers and not through the payroll, (6) reimbursement of business expenses, (7) certain deductions which have been made by the employer (eg for purchase of tools, equipment or clothing—this may not include deductions to pay for gas and electric bills, as this is deemed duplicative of the allowance for living accommodation, *Leisure Employment Services Ltd v HMRC* [2007] EWCA Civ 92), (8) certain payments by the worker to the employer (similar to the deductions in (7)) and (9) deductions for living accommodation in excess of a set figure per day (£4.82 as of 2012): regs 31–37.

[44] Section 10; the worker may complain of failure to provide access to an employment tribunal (subject to the usual three-month time limit) and if the complaint is upheld the tribunal must make a declaration to that effect and award compensation of 80 times the hourly amount of the minimum wage: s 11. Details of the records to be kept are set out in reg 38, and because of employer pressure at draft stage they are much less onerous than as originally proposed.

[45] Section 17.   [46] Employment Act 2008, s 8 amends NMWA, s 17.

[47] Section 28. Refusal or wilful neglect to pay the national minimum wage is a criminal offence, punishable on summary conviction by a fine not exceeding level 5 on the standard scale: s 31. After the Employment Act 2008 the offence is triable 'either way' (ie in Crown Court or magistrates' court): s 31(9).

[48] Sections 13, 14.

[49] Sections 19–19H. The employer may appeal against the notice to an employment tribunal, but only on certain enumerated grounds.

notice is not complied with within 28 days, the inspector may bring proceedings for the arrears on behalf of the worker in a tribunal (under Part II of the 1996 Act) or by way of other civil proceedings.[50] Finally, the individual worker is given a right not to be subjected to any detriment by his employer because of any action taken by him or on his behalf under this legislation, because the employer has been prosecuted, or because he qualifies for the legal minimum;[51] in line with other areas of specialized protection in other contexts, a dismissal on these grounds is declared to be automatically unfair.[52]

(iii) THE WORKING TIME REGULATIONS 1998

The Working Time Regulations 1998[53] which came into force on 1 October 1998, enact the Working Time Directive (93/104/EC) and certain provisions of the Young Workers Directive (94/33/EC),[54] applying statutory limits or entitlements in four main areas—the 48 hours maximum working week, night working, rest breaks and paid annual holiday. The Working Time Directive had a complicated history, which has had important effects politically and in relation to the drafting of the eventual Regulations.[55] The previous government took part in some of the negotiations on the Directive which eventually took on a much watered-down form, with major 'derogations' which a member state can adopt in order to lessen the effect of the main requirements. However, even in this form it turned out to be politically unacceptable to the previous government who refused to agree it, on the assumption that that meant that it could not be passed. However, the remaining member states proceeded to adopt it under Article 118a (now Article 137) of the Treaty of Rome, which permits the adoption of 'health and safety' directives by qualified majority voting. This meant that the UK government could neither block it nor use the then-existing opt-out; they instead brought proceedings in the European Court of Justice (ECJ) (now referred to as the Court of Justice of the European Union (CJEU)) to have the Directive

---

[50] Section 19D.

[51] Section 23. Complaint lies to an employment tribunal, subject to the same procedure as other classes of detriment (Employment Rights Act 1996, ss 48 and 49): s 24.

[52] Section 25, adding the Employment Rights Act 1996, s 104A. Adopting the usual 'package' approach, a subsequent redundancy on these grounds is also unfair, no qualifying period is required and the upper age limit does not apply. There is, however, no entitlement to higher levels of compensation.

[53] SI 1998/1833.

[54] They do so in relation to young persons (ie between 15 and 18, and over school leaving age); these provisions were tightened by the Working Time (Amendment) Regulations 2002, SI 2002/3128, primarily to restrict a young worker's working time to eight hours in any day or 40 hours in any week, and to ban night working except in restricted circumstances. In relation to children under that age, the Directive was transposed by the Children (Protection at Work) Regulations 1998, SI 1998/276. On this basis it was held by the EAT that a child cannot claim under the Working Time Regulations (eg for paid holidays): *Addison v Ashby* [2003] 3 ICR 667, [2003] IRLR 211.

[55] See Bercusson *European Labour Law* (1996) ch 21.

annulled, arguing that working time was not a health and safety issue. This challenge was, however, eventually rejected by the ECJ[56] who took a broader approach to health and safety generally, pointing in particular to the phrasing of Article 118a itself which refers to 'improvements, especially in the *working environment*, as regards the health and safety of workers'; on this broader, 'welfare' approach, all elements of the Directive were upheld (except for one minor provision relating to Sunday normally being a rest day). The incoming New Labour government immediately made clear its intention to transpose the Directive willingly and, after a consultation exercise,[57] produced the 1998 Regulations.[58] Although that willingness was in contrast to the attitude of their predecessors, the Regulations as drafted are in fact more notable for continuity of approach because they adopt in full all of the derogations negotiated by the previous government. The Regulations are in fact relatively short, largely adopting the 'copy out' technique of implementation, so that (1) much of the wording comes from the Directive itself and (2) the Regulations are quite difficult to use because of the precision of drafting and the (logical but non-user-friendly) sequence of first setting out the obligations and only later the derogations that are adopted. To counteract this, and to give some practical guidance as to the *possible* interpretations and effects in the substantial number of grey areas, the government has issued Regulatory Guidance,[59] initially under the auspices of what was then the DTI (Department of Trade and Industry) and is now the BIS (Department for Business, Innovation and Skills), which aims to be easier to understand in its format; its use is recommended. It remains the case, however, that (as with the minimum wage provisions) this one set of Regulations is meant to apply to the whole diverse workforce, and so the areas of doubt and possible debate are widespread, and likely to remain so for some time. As in other areas of employment law, it may be necessary to adopt the approach that, on any given question of application, it may only be possible to advise or adopt a *possible* or *arguably tenable* interpretation or application, not *the* indisputably correct one. Moreover, as these provisions had no direct predecessors in UK law (unlike in other countries in the EU, apart from Ireland, which have a long history of working time laws) there will be ways in which they are

---

[56] *United Kingdom v EU Council* C-84/94 [1997] ICR 443, [1997] IRLR 30, ECJ; see Fitzpatrick 'Straining the Definition of Health and Safety?' (1997) 26 ILJ 115. The ECJ gave its decision on 12 November 1996 and the Directive came into force 11 days later; there was therefore a considerable period during which the UK was in breach. Not surprisingly, given our litigious nature and literal approach, the first case law on the subject concerned the legal position during this period of non-implementation. In *R v A-G for Northern Ireland, ex p Burns* [1999] IRLR 315 it was held that a private sector worker could bring a *Francovich* action against the government based on the non-implementation. In the public sector, the EAT at first held that a worker could rely directly on the Directive, but this was reversed by the Court of Appeal: *Gibson v East Riding of Yorkshire Council* [2000] IRLR 598.

[57] DTI consultation document URN 98/645, April 1998.

[58] The Regulations are set out at *Harvey* R [1072]. A useful source of discussion in the IDS Employment Law Supplement 'Working Time Regulations 1998' (October 1998); see also Barnard 'The Working Time Regulations 1998' (1999) 28 ILJ 61.

[59] Available on <http://www.direct.gov.uk/en/Employment/Employees/WorkingHoursAndTimeOff/index.htm>, last accessed 6 January 2013.

hard to reconcile with other employment laws. A good example involves the operation of the holiday entitlement where the worker is on long-term sickness leave or maternity leave. In *Stringer v HMRC and Schultz-Hoff v Deutsche Rentenversicherung Bund*[60] the ECJ ruled that paid holiday accrues during long-term sick leave and, if sickness prevents taking the leave, the leave must be carried over into the next year. The House of Lords subsequently confirmed this and ruled that if an employee is terminated at the end of sick leave without being able to take holiday the employer must make payment in lieu of the time off, requiring a change to the Working Time Regulations.[61]

(a) Application

As with the minimum wage provisions, the Regulations use the wide definition of 'worker', as being an individual under a contract of employment *or* any other contract, whether express or implied, oral or written, whereby they undertake to do or perform personally any work or services for another party to the contract whose status is not that of a client or customer of any profession or business undertaking carried out by the individual.[62] As originally enacted, the Regulations contained three general exclusions in relation to the transport industry, doctors in training and the activities of services such as the armed forces, police and civil protection services 'which inevitably conflict with the provision of these Regulations'. However due to amendments to the Directive and amending Regulations, the general exemption of transport was narrowed by special rules relating to certain transport workers[63] and the wholesale exclusion of junior doctors in training was changed to a phased introduction of the 48-hour maximum week by August 2009.[64] The exemption of the armed and emergency services remains in place.[65]

(b) Agreements to vary or exclude

The various powers to vary or exclude the principal obligations (known in the Regulatory Guidance as 'flexibilities') are so important to these Regulations that it is necessary at the outset to set out the three forms of agreement specifically allowed

---

[60] [2009] All ER (D) 147.   [61] *HMRC v Stringer* [2009] UKHL 31.

[62] Regulation 2(1); Ch 2, heading 1(vi), see p 53. Thus, the paid holiday right could be claimed by Sch D paying, self-employed subcontractors working for only one employer on a long-term basis: *Byrne Bros (Farmwork) Ltd v Baird* [2002] ICR 667, [2002] IRLR 96; *Wright v Redrow Homes (Yorkshire) Ltd* [2004] ICR 1126, [2004] IRLR 720, CA. There are subsidiary provisions in regs 36 and 42 to ensure that agency workers and non-employed trainees are covered.

[63] See Council Directive No 2003/88 concerning certain aspects of the organization of working time, OJ 2003, L299/9, the Merchant Shipping (Working Time: Inland Waterways) Regulations 2003, SI 2003/3049, the Fishing Vessels (Working Time: Sea Fishermen) Regulations 2004, SI 2004/1713, the Civil Aviation (Working Time) Regulations 2004, SI 2004/756 and, most significantly, the Road Transport (Working Time) Regulations 2005, SI 2005/639.

[64] Regulation 25A; a maximum of 58 hours was allowed until July 2007, then 56 hours until August 2009.

[65] Regulation 18. There is a further exclusion in reg 19 of domestic service in a private household, which relates to maximum working hours, night work and pattern of work; this does not appear in the Directive but is justified as being part of the general exclusion of such activities from domestic health and safety law.

by the drafting; in ascending order of potential protection for individual workers, these are.

> *individual agreement*: in itself, this only applies in relation to opting out of the maximum 48 hours per week;

> a *'relevant agreement'*: this is defined as a workforce agreement, any provision of a collective agreement which forms part of a contract between the worker and his employer, or any other agreement in writing which is legally enforceable as between the worker and his employer.[66] As this may include an individual agreement (provided in writing and legally binding, eg as part of a contract of employment), this format tends to be used for definitional issues (eg what may constitute working time), rather than outright exclusions;

> a *'collective agreement or workforce agreement'*: this format, importing an obvious collective element of protection, is adopted for some of the major exclusions.

Clearly, the most important development here is the introduction of the concept of the 'workforce agreement' which is meant to apply to workers who do not have any terms and conditions set by a collective bargain.[67] Such an agreement must be in writing, have a specified length of not more than five years, apply to either all the relevant members of the workforce or to all those in a particular group,[68] and be signed by either the representatives of the workforce or group, or (if the employer employs 20 or fewer workers) either by such representatives or by the majority of the workers.[69] Where use is made of representatives, they must have been 'duly elected' and the Regulations provide the basic electoral rules that must be complied with.[70] There could be overlaps here with representatives elected for other consultative purposes, and this development could be seen as a further 'carrot' towards de facto works councils of sorts. There is, however, one possible trap because, although the point is not made expressly in the Regulations, the Regulatory Guidance takes the view that, while dual (or more) use of the same representatives is possible, 'it would have to be made clear to those voting that

---

[66] Regulation 2(1).

[67] To this extent, it follows the precedent of the Health and Safety (Consultation with Employees) Regulations 1996, which only allow consultation with directly elected worker representatives where there is *no* existing representation by a recognized union. This is achieved in these Regulations by defining the 'relevant members of the workforce' as 'all workers employed by a particular employer, *excluding* any worker whose terms and conditions of employment are provided for, *wholly or in part*, in a collective agreement': Sch 1, para 2 (emphasis added).

[68] This is defined as a group undertaking a particular function, working at a particular workplace or belonging to a particular department or unit: Sch 1, para 2.

[69] Schedule 1, para 1(a)–(d); note that a worker disagreeing but in a minority is bound by the agreement. Before making an agreement available for signature, the employer must have provided all the affected workers with copies of the text and such guidance as they may reasonably require in order to understand it fully: para 1(e).

[70] The number of representatives is to be determined by the employer; candidates must be relevant members of the workforce or group; no eligible candidate must be unreasonably excluded from standing; all relevant members of the workforce or group must be entitled to vote, and able to vote for as many candidates as there are to be representatives; there must be secret voting (as far as is reasonably practicable) and the votes must be fairly and accurately counted: Sch 1, para 3.

the representatives were being elected for both purposes'. Thus, technically the use of *existing* consultative machinery for this further purpose might not be lawful (another similarity with the health and safety consultation requirements and difference from those applying to collective redundancies and TUPE). The answer in the longer term is to ensure that next time a consultative body is elected it is made express for what specific purposes the body is being constituted.

(c) Two principal exceptions

In addition to the excluded sectors, the Regulations adopt from the Directive's permissible derogations two broad exceptions which, while not applying across the board, do apply to the majority of the rights and limitations. By virtue of regulation 20 ('Unmeasured working time') the provisions on the 48-hour maximum week, the length of night working and daily/weekly rest and rest periods do not apply 'in relation to a worker where, on account of the specific characteristics of the activity in which he is engaged, the duration of his working time is not measured or predetermined or can be determined by the worker himself'. The interpretation of this extremely vague exception could prove to be crucial to the effectiveness or otherwise of the Regulations, since so many modern forms of flexible working have at least *some* element of unmeasured time, and discretion in working hours. How great that element needs to be proved to be highly controversial. A teacher, for example, will have set teaching hours, but may put in many hours over and above those in preparation and marking. On behalf of a broad construction, the original Regulatory Guidance[71] stressed that it is impossible to lay down comprehensively who is and is not covered. On the other hand, the examples given in the Regulations ('managing executives or other persons with autonomous decision-making powers', family workers and religious celebrants) are very narrow, and the Guidance suggested that only those with *complete* control over their hours would come within the exclusion.[72] This uncertainty caused problems, partly due to assumptions being made in certain sectors that this regulation would apply (for example in law firms) which may or may not have been correct. In addition, employers nationally expressed their concerns over the uncertainty, with a result that (to the annoyance of the unions) the government amended the 1998 Regulations only a year later, to add a paragraph to regulation 20 stating that where *part* of a worker's working time is measured or predetermined or cannot be determined by the worker himself, but the specific characteristics of the activity are such that, *without being required to do so* by the employer, he may also do work which is *not* measured or predetermined (or can be determined by the worker himself), then the provisions on the 48-hour week and night working only apply to the first part, ie the 'voluntary' part will not be subject to those

---

[71] Paragraph 2.2.2.

[72] One interesting question is whether this is to be construed much more narrowly than the provisions in the minimum wage legislation on 'output workers' and 'non-hours workers'; homeworkers, for example, might come under these 'pay' categories, but are a long way from managing executives.

provisions. While considerable problems remained (eg where there is no rule that an employee has to work long hours, but if they want promotion or a partnership …) this was at least an attempt at explanation (along with accompanying DTI guidance). Unfortunately, however, there was no equivalent provision in the Directive and eventually the UK was threatened with infraction proceedings by the EU Commission. As a result, this extra paragraph was revoked in 2006 and so we are left with the distinctly delphic provisions of the original regulation 20.

The second principal exception is contained in regulation 21 ('Other special cases') which again raises as many questions as it answers in relation to its likely breadth of interpretation. It states that the provisions on length of night working and daily/weekly rest and rest periods do not apply in relation to a worker:

(a) where the worker's activities are such that his place of work and place of residence are distant from one another or his different places of work are distant from one another;

(b) where the worker is engaged in security and surveillance activities requiring a permanent presence in order to protect property and persons, as may be the case for security guards and caretakers or security firms;

(c) where the worker's activities involve the need for continuity of service or production, as may be the case in relation to—

   (i) services relating to the reception, treatment or care provided by hospitals or similar establishments (including the activities of doctors in training), residential institutions and prisons;

   (ii) work at docks or airports;

   (iii) press, radio, television, cinematographic production, postal and telecommunications services and civil protection services;

   (iv) gas, water and electricity production, transmission and distribution, household refuse collection and incineration;

   (v) industries in which work cannot be interrupted on technical grounds;

   (vi) research and development activities;

   (vii) agriculture;

   (viii) the carriage of passengers on regular worker transport services;

(d) where there is a foreseeable surge of activity, as may be the case in relation to—

   (i) agriculture;

   (ii) tourism; and

   (iii) postal services;

(e) where the worker's activities are affected by—

   (i) an occurrence due to unusual and unforeseeable circumstances, beyond the control of the worker's employer;

  (ii) exceptional events, the consequences of which could not have been avoided despite the exercise of all due care by the employer; or

  (iii) an accident or the imminent risk of an accident;

(f) where the worker works in railway transport and—

  (i) this activities are intermittent;

  (ii) he spends his working time on board trains; or

  (iii) his activities are linked to transport timetables and to ensuring the continuity and regularity of traffic.'

As derogations, these provisions generally are to be interpreted strictly.[73] The equal vagueness and potential significance of these categories mean that they are likely to be widely claimed and disputed.

(d) Maximum weekly working time

A worker's working time, including overtime, is not to exceed an average of 48 hours for each seven days in any particular reference period.[74] The fact that this is an averaging process is fundamental, because it does not necessarily mean a maximum of 48 hours per week, and up to a point fluctuations can be accommodated. The question becomes over how long a period the averaging can be done, hence the importance of the 'reference period'. In the first instance this is stated to be 17 weeks,[75] but where one of the 'Other special cases' in regulation 21 (above) applies, this is increased to 26 weeks. Further, it can be raised by a collective or workforce agreement to a maximum of 52 weeks 'for objective or technical reasons or reasons concerning the organisation of work'(!), which could be highly advantageous to employers wanting variations in

---

[73] *Gallagher v Alpha Catering Services Ltd* [2005] IRLR 102, CA.

[74] Regulation 4(1). Time on call only counts when the employee is at the place of employment, not when elsewhere (especially at home) but available to be called in: *Sindicato de Médicos de Asistencia Pública (SIMAP) v Conselleria de Sanidad y Consumo de la Generalidad Valenciana* C-303/98 [2000] IRLR 845, ECJ. If this rule in *SIMAP* is satisfied, it does not matter if the employee is allowed to sleep (eg in a rest room or in their own accommodation on the employer's premises): *Landeshauptstadt Kiel v Jaeger* C-151/02 [2003] IRLR 804, ECJ; *McCartney v Oversely House Management* [2006] ICR 510, [2006] IRLR 514. Regulation 4(6), (7) set out the formula for calculating the average, and days of annual, sickness and maternity leave that are not to count. Note that where a worker works for more than one employer, the average applies to the aggregated hours; the Regulations are silent on what the employer(s) is or are to do in these circumstances, but the original Guidance para 2.1.3 intimated that it is up to the employer to find out if a worker is working elsewhere and if necessary to adjust working arrangements accordingly; it did not say on *which* employer any primary responsibility to do so may rest. When the Regulations came into force in 1998 29.8% of male full-time employees and 11.6% of female full-time employees worked more than 48 hours per week: [1998] Labour Market Trends 599. For the initial effects (or lack thereof) particularly in the light of the opt-out, see Barnard, Deakin and Hobbs 'Opting out of the 48 Hour Week: Employer Necessity or Individual Choice' (2003) 32 ILJ 223.

[75] Regulation 4(3); a relevant agreement can lay down *which* 17-week periods are to be used; failing that, the average must be met over '*any* period of 17 weeks in the course of his employment', which could be less advantageous for an employer with predictable variations in hours required.

hours over certain prolonged seasons in the year;[76] protection for the worker lies in the collective nature of the necessary agreement.

The 48-hour average maximum is then further subject to the most striking exception in the Regulations, namely that it does not apply *at all* to a worker who has agreed in writing with his employer that it should not apply in his case;[77] this individual agreement may be either for a specified period or indefinite, but a worker may terminate it by giving written notice (of a maximum of three months in the agreement or, in default of coverage in the agreement, of seven days). The government and business leaders defend this breathtaking exception on the ground that it respects individual choice. Remember, however, that the Regulations are first and foremost a health and safety measure: regulations requiring workers to wear safety goggles, or to earn a licence before operating certain kinds of machinery, could hardly allow workers to opt out of the requirements simply to protect personal choice. The quid pro quo for an exclusion agreement was originally an obligation on the employer to keep specified records of actual hours which were to be open to inspection by a Health and Safety Inspector; however, in another rapid volte-face, the Amendment Regulations in 1999 watered this down very considerably, so that now the only requirement is to keep a record of *who* has signed the opt-out.[78] One possible point of controversy not covered by the Regulations is what is to happen to the worker's wages if he or she does *not* opt out and their hours have to be reduced to meet the 48-hour average? This will be primarily a matter of contract so that if, for example, the worker is paid at a fixed amount per hour the wage will have to go down pro rata to the new number of hours, whereas a worker paid a salary for work done (over however many hours it takes) would have a good argument for breach of contract if the employer reduced that salary (simply because of a new maximum on hours) without his or her consent. One possible complication could arise if most workers agreed to keep existing hours (and pay) but a particular individual refused to agree and insisted on the 48-hour maximum, suffering a pay cut in consequence—could he or she claim that this constituted a 'detriment' (for not entering an agreement) which is outlawed by the Regulations?[79]

The Employment Appeal Tribunal (EAT) has already made the arresting decision that 'detriment' does not include excluding a worker from the allocation of overtime work for refusing to sign an opt-out. In *Arriva London South v Nicolaou*[80] the EAT held that if an employer's motivation for withholding overtime is a desire to avoid the risk that employees who had not opted out might exceed the 48-hour limit, then the employer has not subjected those workers to a detriment for the exercise of their rights.

---

[76] Regulation 23(b).   [77] Regulation 5(1).   [78] Regulation 4(2), as amended.

[79] Regulation 31, adding the Employment Rights Act 1996, s 45A. This could raise complicated issues such as those arising in the context of detriment on union membership grounds in *Associated Newspapers Ltd v Wilson; Associated British Ports v Palmer* [1995] ICR 406, [1995] IRLR 258, HL. Would it be viewed as a 'detriment' by way of a pay cut, or just a natural inability to continue paying the higher wages of those agreeing to the longer hours?

[80] UKEAT/0293/11 (21 December 2011, unreported).

The EAT made it clear that even though the policy openly withdrew overtime from workers *because they would not opt out* this merely satisfied a 'but-for' test, and did not demonstrate that the detriment was motivated by an animus against the exercise of the right. It is difficult to see how workers will effectively enforce their rights not to opt out after this decision. One hopes that subsequent tribunals might draw the line at, for example, employers refusing to assign workers to certain higher-paying work or posts without the opt-out on the ground that the work is likely to tempt or induce them (the workers) to work more than 48 hours. The avoidance of such a result requires that future tribunals demonstrate less credulity than that in *Nicolaou*, because the logic of the *Nicolaou* decision certainly will not prevent it. Of course, the issue might never reach another tribunal, because what employee would now refuse to sign an opt-out when *Nicolaou* authorizes employers openly to announce that negative consequences in terms of hours and pay will result from their doing so?

(e) Limits on night working

A night worker's normal hours of work in any reference period are not to exceed an average of eight hours in each 24 hours.[81] A 'night worker' is defined as a worker who normally works at least three hours of his daily working time during night time, or such proportion of his annual working time as may be specified in a collective agreement or workforce agreement.[82] As with maximum weekly hours, the averaging process is vital, and the reference period is 17 weeks; a relevant agreement can set out *which* succeeding 17-week periods are to be used, but in default it means *any* 17 weeks (ie a rolling period).[83] There is, however, an exception to the averaging process where the night work involves 'special hazards or heavy physical or mental strain', in which case the limit is eight hours in *any* 24-hour period in which night work is done.[84] On the question of night work, much is left to be determined by agreement, and this goes beyond matters of definition because ultimately it is possible for the rules themselves to be modified or excluded completely by a collective agreement or workforce agreement,[85] a particularly striking example of collective protection being thought sufficient.

---

[81] Regulation 6(1).

[82] Regulation 2(1). 'Night time' means a period set out in a relevant agreement, lasting at least seven hours and including the period between midnight and 5am; in default of agreement, it means 11pm to 6am: reg 2(1). An employer could use this to push back the definition so that workers working late (eg up to 2am in a bar or night club) do *not* work the three hours in the period necessary to be a night worker.

[83] Regulation 6(3). The formula for the average is set out in reg 6(5).

[84] Regulation 6(7); the actual circumstances in which this applies are left to be determined by a collective agreement or workforce agreement, or in a risk assessment required by the Management of Health and Safety at Work Regulations 1999, SI 1999/3242. If neither of these avenues is used, there could be a health and safety breach by the employer, though the Regulations do not say so specifically.

[85] Regulation 23(a). This is subject to the requirement of compensatory rest under reg 24 (below), though on its wording (applying where 'a worker is … required … to work during a period which would otherwise be a rest period or rest break') it is more difficult to apply to night working than to the rules on rest breaks.

Arguably, the night-working provisions are most closely related to the health and safety provenance of the Regulations, and the Directive itself makes clear in its preamble the assumption on which this is based, one of the recitals being:

> Whereas research has shown that the human body is more sensitive at night to environmental disturbances and also to certain burdensome forms of work organisation and that long periods of night work can be detrimental to the health of workers and can endanger safety at the workplace.

In the light of this, two further obligations are laid on employers of night workers, going beyond the regulation of hours. The first is that no adult worker is to be assigned to night work without at least an opportunity for a free health assessment (unless there is an existing such assessment still in operation), and each night worker must then have the opportunity of further assessments at regular intervals appropriate to his case.[86] A young worker must have the opportunity of such assessments (as to health *and capacity*) whenever assigned to work during the period from 10pm to 6am.[87] Secondly, the employer must transfer a night worker on to non-night work if a registered medical practitioner advises that he is suffering health problems related to night working and it is possible to transfer the worker to suitable work not at night.[88] Significantly, there are no permissible derogations to these duties.

(f) Rest periods

A worker is entitled to the following rest periods:

(1) a daily rest period of not less than 11 hours in each 24-hour work period;[89]

(2) a weekly rest period of not less than 24 hours in each seven-day work period;[90]

---

[86] Regulation 7(1). This rather stark paragraph was considerably fleshed out by paras 4.1.2 and 4.1.3 of the original Guidance which suggest that (1) while very few people will be unfit to work at night at all, there could be problems with diabetes, heart/circulatory disorders, stomach/intestinal disorders, sleep conditions, chest disorders and others requiring regular medication; (2) the health assessment (undefined) could start with a screening questionnaire carried out by the employer, with professional opinion being involved in the interpreting of the questionnaire and any necessary follow-up action; (3) while the Regulations are silent on how regularly to reassess, a rule of thumb might be to administer the questionnaire annually.

[87] Regulation 7(2); this does not apply where the work is 'of an exceptional nature' (undefined): reg 7(4). As stated above, the emphasis (since the amendment in 2002) is on the young worker normally not working nights at all.

[88] Regulation 7(6). If the health problems constituted a 'disability' within the Disability Discrimination Act 1995, this might be required in any event as a reasonable adjustment.

[89] Regulation 10(1).

[90] Regulation 11(1). The employer may vary this to two 24-hour rests or one 48-hour rest in a 14-day period: reg 11(2). The relevant seven-day period is to be laid down in a relevant agreement, or, in default of that, is to be a week beginning with Monday: reg 11(6). The weekly rest period is not to include any daily rest period, 'except where this is justified by objective or technical reasons or reasons concerning the organisation of work': reg 11(7).

(3) a rest break of at least 20 minutes (subject to any longer time agreed in a collect-ive agreement or workforce agreement) where daily working time is more than six hours.[91]

In the case of young workers, these entitlements are increased to 12 hours daily rest, 48 hours weekly rest and a rest break of at least 30 minutes after four and a half hours work.[92] The EAT has held that the Regulations entitle workers only to one rest period, no matter how many hours they work beyond the relevant threshold (eg six hours).[93]

As well as the normal derogations (including the ability to modify or exclude entirely all the adult entitlements by collective agreement or workforce agreement),[94] there are special provisions relating to daily and weekly rest periods in the case of shift workers being potentially in breach when changing shifts and, more generally, in the case of 'workers engaged in activities involving periods of work split up over the day, as may be the case for cleaning staff'.[95]

(g) Compensatory rest

Although the derogations are of great importance to the overall scheme of the Regulations, there is one complication to some of them that could cause considerable difficulty in practice. This is that it is stated that where the application of any provision is excluded by regulation 21 ('other special cases') or 22 ('shift workers'), or is modified or excluded by a collective agreement or workforce agreement under regulation 23(a) and a worker is accordingly required by his employer to work during a period which would otherwise be a rest period or rest break, the employer must wherever possible allow him to take an *equivalent period of compensatory rest*.[96] The original Guidance stated that an equivalent period of rest should be considered to be a period as long as that the worker was entitled to but not able to take, and that it should be provided within a reasonable time from when the entitlement to rest was modified (in the case of daily rest, this being within a couple of weeks; in the case of weekly rest, within a couple of months).[97] This may help where there are regular fluctuations of work on a

---

[91] Regulation 12(1)–(3). Whether such rest breaks are to be with pay is a matter of contract, as the Regulations are silent on the matter. A rest break must have a definite beginning and end; it is not enough for the employer to say that the employee in fact has significant periods of 'down time' (during which he is subject to recall by the employer): *Gallagher v Alpha Catering Services Ltd* [2004] IRLR 102.

[92] Regulations 10(2), 11(3), 12(4); the derogations applying to adult workers' rest periods do not apply to young workers, but there is a *force majeure* exception applying to them in reg 27 (unforeseen or exceptional circumstances) in relation to daily rest and rest breaks.

[93] *Corps of Commissionaires Management v Hughes* [2008] All ER (D) 225.

[94] Regulation 23(a).   [95] Regulation 22.

[96] Regulation 24(a). In exceptional cases where this is not possible for objective reasons, the employer must 'afford such protection as may be appropriate in order to safeguard the worker's health and safety': reg 24(b); the original Guidance para 6.2.4 stated that such cases will be rare and that this flexibility is not to be used on a routine basis. This raises a question of interpretation—are regs 24(a) and (b) exhaustive, ie can (1) only be disapplied if (2) applies? Or can there be middle ground where it is not possible to give compensatory rest but for reasons which do not activate the requirements of (2)?

[97] Paragraph 5.25.

short cycle (so that rest breaks can be disapplied at the busy peaks and compensatory rest given during the slack periods) but this may not be possible where rest breaks are disapplied because of a sustained *season* of heavy work possibly lasting for several months (as may be envisaged, for example, in several of the 'special cases' set out in regulation 21, for example a 'foreseeable surge of activity' in agriculture or tourism). In such cases there will be important questions of interpretation as to the meaning of 'wherever possible' and whether compensatory rest is legally acceptable if it only comes at the end of an extended season of consistent work.

(h) Annual leave

Along with the 48-hour maximum working week, the aspect of the Regulations to which most publicity was given on their introduction was the entitlement to a statutory minimum period of paid leave in each leave year, set initially at three weeks (utilizing a derogation in the Directive), but rising to four weeks as from November 1999, and to 5.6 weeks (28 days) by April 2009.[98] The leave year is primarily left to be determined by a relevant agreement; in default of that, the general rule is that it runs from the date of commencement of employment,[99] but of course that could be inconvenient for an employer who will normally wish to stipulate a standardized holiday year for all employees.

Given the existing contractual entitlements of most full-time employees in 1998,[100] it may seem that this new entitlement was hardly revolutionary, even after the 2009 increase, but the provisions bite in two particular ways:

(1) This entitlement applies simply to 'workers', which may include certain casual or temporary workers previously without holiday rights by contract. At first the government tried to minimize this effect by providing, in effect, a 13-week qualifying period for a new employee before having the statutory holiday right but there was no authority for this in the Directive; it was successfully challenged in the ECJ by a union representing many workers in broadcasting who were adversely affected because they were kept on separate short-term contracts (often not individually going beyond the 13 weeks)[101] and the government had to amend the Regulations in 2001 to remove the

---

[98] Regulation 13. The worker is entitled to be paid a 'week's pay' for each week of leave, which is to be worked out by applying the Employment Rights Act 1996, ss 221–224 reg 16; One result of this is that over-time premia do not count in calculating holiday pay: *Bamsey v Albon Engineering and Manufacturing plc* [2004] ICR 1083, [2004] IRLR 457, CA. Contractual remuneration is offset against the statutory amount, and vice versa. Regulation 15 covers the case of a worker leaving part of the way through the holiday year.

[99] Regulation 13. Where an employee joins part of the way through a leave year, he or she is entitled to a holiday period on a pro rata basis: reg 13(5).

[100] At the time of enactment in 1998, 85% of permanent full-time staff already had 20 or more working days holiday per annum: Hours and Holidays 1998 (IDS Study No 657).

[101] *R v Secretary of State for Trade and Industry, ex p BECTU* C-173/99 [2001] ICR 1152, [2001] IRLR 559, ECJ.

qualifying period and provide instead that entitlement accrues on a monthly basis in the first year of employment.[102]

(2) Although it was specifically provided in the Regulations that the statutory holiday period must be actually *taken*, in the sense that it may not (in whole or, particularly, in part) be either carried forward into the next holiday year or bought out by a payment in lieu (except on termination of employment), this is no longer applicable.[103] The rule had generally been thought to be in line with the health and safety provenance of the Regulations (ie that people should actually have the holiday period to rest, in spite of some evidence that holidays with the family can in some cases rate on the stress scale as highly as moving house, public speaking or Christmas!) but this was first put into doubt by the ECJ in *Federatie Nederlandse Vakbewingen v Staat der Nederlanden*[104] where it was held that, although buying out the holiday entitlement is contrary to the Directive, carrying forward any unused entitlement may sometimes be 'inevitable'. *HMRC v Stringer*,[105] of course (following on from the ECJ's earlier judgment in the same case), brought this full circle by ruling that if sickness prevents an employee from taking holiday leave it must be carried over to the next year, and the worker must be paid in lieu if terminated before the holiday can be taken. This required a change to the Regulations to emphasize that leave must be taken, but if that is not possible it must be carried over and, if that is not possible, it must be paid in lieu.

In cases where neither of these points arise, the initial temptation for employers was to think that, if they complied with the prescribed length of annual holidays by contract (5.6 weeks or more), they could simply carry on as before. However, the case law to date has shown this to be a dangerous assumption. Ordinary contractual rules continue to apply to any entitlement above the statutory *but* in relation to the first 5.6 weeks the statutory rules must always be complied with; if necessary they will override any inconsistent contractual rules and, given that they are novel and not linked into existing laws, applying them literally can produce strange (if legally logical) results. One of the earliest cases, *Witley and District Men's Club v Mackay*,[106] concerned the interaction of holiday pay and summary dismissal. When the employee was dismissed summarily for fraud the employers refused payment of accrued holiday pay, as was specifically allowed under the collective agreement incorporated into his contract.

---

[102] Working Time (Amendment) Regulations 2001, SI 2001/3256, amending reg 13 and adding a new reg 15A containing the accrual system. Of course, those on genuinely short-term contracts will not normally want to take holidays, so the key change is that they will be due for accrued holiday *pay* at the end of the hiring.

[103] Regulation 13(9). Subject to a relevant agreement, the general rules on the timing of holidays are that a worker may give notice of intention to take a certain period, of a length twice as long as the time to be taken off; equally, an employer may require a worker to take a particular period by similar notice, or may notify the worker of time that is not to be taken as holiday by notice of a length equal to that to be taken off: reg 15. This gives the employer considerable ability to time holidays, either to bunch them (eg for annual shutdowns) or to spread them among employees to ensure continuity of production.

[104] C-124/05 [2006] ICR 962, [2006] IRLR 561, CJEU.

[105] [2009] UKHL 31; this has been confirmed by the CJEU in *KHS AG v Schulte* C-214/10, [2012] IRLR 156.

[106] [2001] IRLR 595.

Regulation 14 governs the payment of accrued pay when a worker leaves part of the way through the holiday year (normally giving them a right to pro rata payment in lieu of holiday) and allows a relevant agreement to fix 'such sum' as is to be payable. That seemed to cover this case but did not. The EAT held (regretfully) that on a plain wording interpretation 'such sum' could not cover 'no sum'. Thus, the collective agreement term expressly covering this eventuality was unlawful under the Regulations and the employee was entitled to the pro-rata entitlement in the regulation, even though dismissed for gross misconduct.[107] These termination provisions also arose in *Hill v Chapell*[108] but in reverse—what is to happen when the worker has taken *more* than his pro-rata entitlement when leaving in the course of the holiday year? Previously, the general law would allow the employer to recoup holiday pay in respect of those unearned days, for example from moneys outstanding to the worker. That was done in this case but the worker successfully sued for it back—regulation 14(4) states that a relevant agreement 'may' provide for recovery by the employer and this was held by the EAT to be exhaustive, ie the employer can *only* recover overpaid holiday pay if there is a relevant agreement (usually meaning an express term in a written contract) to that effect.

Turning to the form of payment, one device historically used by employers, particularly in cases of sporadic employment where there may be administrative difficulties in working out exact holiday entitlements, was to 'roll up' holiday pay into an enhanced basic pay rate. Is this lawful under the Regulations and the Directive (in relation to the mandatory 5.6 weeks)? When tested before the English Court of Appeal[109] it was held that it could be lawful, provided it was made clear to the employees and was a genuine addition to basic pay and could be calculated. However, when the matter came before the Scottish Court of Session[110] the decision was that the practice was unlawful under the Directive because it could act as a disincentive actually to take the holiday, especially for low-paid workers who ought to have the pay separately at the time of taking the holiday. Eventually the matter was remitted to the ECJ who handed down a decision that was strange even by its own standards. The Court held[111] that the Directive precludes staggered payment as a matter of principle (particularly in the light of the health and safety provenance of the holiday entitlement). To that extent the challenge to rolled-up payment seemed to have succeeded *but* a second question had been permitted—what if the employer in fact *had* paid out holiday pay in a rolled-up way? Can the employer then set that off against any later claim by the employee to be paid it again at the time the holiday is taken? Here the ECJ held that the rolled-up pay *can* be set off, provided it has been paid 'transparently and comprehensibly' (note the similarity to the original

---

[107] Perhaps the oddest part of this is that if the agreement had provided for the dismissed worker to receive £1, 1p or a peppercorn that would have been 'such sum' and so lawful.

[108] [2003] IRLR 19.

[109] *Blackburn v Gridquest Ltd* [2002] ICR 1206, [2202] IRLR 604, CA.

[110] *MPB Structures Ltd v Munro* [2004] ICR 430, [2003] IRLR 350, Ct of Sess (IH).

[111] *Robinson-Steele v R D Retail Services* C-131/04 [2006] IRLR 386, ECJ.

decision of the Court of Appeal). The end result was thus that an employer should not use rolled-up holiday pay but that if it did there was no effective sanction because the relevant amount had already actually been paid! Thus, in practice the device could continue to be used for the time being *but* the ECJ added that it was for member states to ensure that the Directive is not breached and so there may well be an amendment to the Regulations during the currency of this edition to ban rolled-up pay.

The question has also arisen over when workers can be required to take their holiday leave. There are many kinds of work where there are natural periods of time that are more suitable for annual leave than others. For example, a university might reasonably request that lecturers take their annual leave out of term time so their leave does not interfere with teaching. The law has yet to decide whether such a reasonable request could be sustained under the Working Time Regulations (WTR), but in a more obvious case the Supreme Court held that oil rig workers, whose pattern of work involved an alternation of two weeks on the rig and two weeks 'field break' on shore, could legally be required by their employer to take their annual leave during 'field break' periods.[112] While this makes good sense in the facts of the case, the implications might not appeal as much taken to their logical conclusion. The Court reasoned that the leave requirement was quantitative, not qualitative, so it did not actually need to be a break from what would otherwise be working time' the WTR called for a simple mathematical allotment of time. The Court noted that this was not controversial for schoolteachers who could be required to take leave out of term time. Lord Hope, for the unanimous Court, also opined obiter, without deciding, that the WTR would not countenance viewing the working week as consisting of six days, Monday through Saturday, and then requiring that workers take their annual leave on Saturday: he distinguished this on the ground that the WTR speak of 'weeks' of leave, meaning that workers could demand their leave in at least weekly increments. Because this question did not arise from the facts of the case the Court did not decide that workers could insist on their leave in weekly chunks, but it did hold they could not demand their leave in a four-week block. This troubling decision leaves open, for example, the possibility that it would be lawful for an employer to operate for only eleven months out of each year and then require that workers all take their leave during the twelfth month. Indeed, it appears that it would be acceptable for a business to shut down for five weeks distributed throughout the year and oblige employees to take their leave during these weeks. If such an arrangement resulted in, say, an eight-month period without any possibility of annual leave it could be argued that the health and safety objectives of the WTR were thus successfully circumvented. In short, some serious questions around this issue remain in need of clarification.

Two final points may be noted, relating to two controversial aspects of the holiday pay entitlement rules. The first is whether the entitlement can be claimed by an employee who is in fact off on long-term sickness leave. At first sight this would appear

---

[112] *Russell v Transocean International Resources* [2011] UKSC 57, [2011] All ER (D) 53 (Dec).

to be ludicrous but when the issue was first tested the EAT took a very purist view of the interpretation of the Regulations and held that there was nothing to stop such a claim.[113] However, when a subsequent case was heard by the Court of Appeal they held that there is no such entitlement because as a matter of common sense a 'holiday' can only be from *work*.[114] The ECJ in *Stringer v HMRC and Schultz-Hoff v Deutsche Rentenversicherung Bund*[115] then settled the matter by holding that domestic law can, but is not required to, allow for the taking of paid leave during sickness; but if it does not it must permit the entitlement to carry over (or be paid in lieu if it cannot be taken before termination). The second point concerns the position of bank holidays. When the Regulations were first enacted the unions were disappointed that the four-week entitlement was *not* in addition to bank holidays, so that the employer could count them towards the entitlement if so minded. However following a lengthy campaign on this issue the government took a power in the Work and Families Act 2006, section 13, to 'make provision conferring on workers the right, except in prescribed cases, to a prescribed amount of annual leave in each leave year'. This has resulted in the increase of the leave entitlement to 5.6 weeks effective from April 2009.

(i) Pattern of work—the loose end

The Working Time Directive, Article 13 contains the rather opaque provision that member states are to take the measures necessary to:

> ensure that an employer who intends to organise work according to a certain pattern takes account of the general principle of adapting work to the worker, with a view, in particular, to alleviating monotonous work and work at a predetermined work-rate, depending on the type of activity, and of safety and health requirements, especially as regards breaks during working time.

This is potentially a wide provision, arguably in line with the modern emphasis on the working *environment* generally. When, however, the government consulted on implementing the Directive they said that they thought the intention of Article 13 was 'unclear'[116] and that it appeared to replicate Article 6(2)(d) of the Health and Safety Framework Directive.[117] In the result, the only attempt at transposition in the Working Time Regulations is in regulation 8, which picks up only on the specific point of rest breaks:

> Where the pattern according to which an employer organizes work is such as to put the health and safety of a worker employed by him at risk, in particular because the work is

---

[113] *Kigass Aero Components Ltd v Brownl* [2002] ICR 697, [2002] IRLR 312. This would obviously be an attractive option if the employee had exhausted the employer's contractual sick pay entitlement.

[114] *CIR v Ainsworth* [2005] ICR 1149, [2005] IRLR 465, CA.

[115] [2009] All ER (D) 147.   [116] URN 98/645, para 117.

[117] Directive 89/391/EEC. Note, however, that originally Art 6(2) was not specifically transposed in the enacting Management of Health and Safety at Work Regulations 1992, being left instead to be covered by the much more general (existing) provisions of the Health and Safety at Work etc Act 1974. Interestingly, it *was* specifically transposed when the Management Regulations were reissued in 1999 (SI 1999/3242, reg 4, Sch 1).

monotonous or the work rate is predetermined, the employer shall ensure that the worker is given adequate rest breaks.[118]

This falls well short of any general obligation to fit the work to the worker; unless it can be argued that Article 13 is transposed in some other way (expressly or impliedly), it could be argued that there has been a failure to transpose, which might be relevant in independent proceedings (eg a civil action for damages for occupational stress), though there may be less scope for this now that it has been held that the Directive (or at least parts of it) does not have direct effect.[119]

(j) Enforcement

The way in which the Regulations effectively straddle employment law and health and safety law is particularly noticeable in the area of enforcement. The so-called 'limitations' relating to the 48-hour maximum working week, night working and patterns of work are enforceable under the health and safety system, with primary responsibility on the Health and Safety Executive.[120] Thus, the principal obligations in these areas are that the employer must 'take all *reasonable* steps' to ensure that the weekly maximum and the night working limit are observed. There is an obligation on employers to maintain records adequate to show compliance, and to keep them for two years.[121] However, as we have seen, the requirement that employers take reasonable steps to ensure that workers do not exceed the 48-hour maximum appears actually to undermine the possibility of enforcement, given that overtime and other benefits can be taken away from those who refuse to opt out so long as the motivation is somehow related to this requirement.[122]

On the other hand, the 'entitlements' to rest breaks and paid annual leave are enforceable by complaint by an individual worker to an employment tribunal (from 6 April 2009, holiday pay claims can be heard by an employment judge sitting alone).[123] The Tribunal or employment judge can make a declaration, award compensation (not subject to a maximum amount) for a refusal to allow one of these rights to be exercised, or where the complaint is of failure to pay holiday pay, order the employer to pay the amount due.[124] The individual worker is not given a

---

[118] The original Guidance, para 6.1.3 merely stated that this may mean *regular* rest breaks.

[119] *Gibson v East Riding of Yorkshire Council* [2000] IRLR 598, CA.

[120] Regulation 28. It is an offence to fail to comply, carrying a fine on either summary conviction or conviction on indictment: reg 29. The HSE (or local authority where that is the enforcing authority) must make adequate arrangements for enforcement (reg 28(2)), but when the Regulations came into force the HSE made clear that they lacked the resources for proactive enforcement by inspector; it may be that enforcement turns out to be reactive, ie following on accidents or other notified events.

[121] Regulation 9.

[122] *Arriva London South v Nicolaou* UKEAT/0293/11 (21 December 2011, unreported).

[123] Employment Tribunals Act 1996 (Tribunal Composition) Order 2009, SI 2009/789.

[124] Regulation 30. The time limit is the usual three-month period, subject to the 'not reasonably practicable' power to extend (reg 30(2)) or the claimant may sue instead under the 'deductions' provisions of the Employment Rights Act 1996, Pt II (p 197) with their more generous time limit (*HMRC v Stringer* [2009] UKHL 31).

statutory right to complain of breach of the maximum working week or night work (or pattern of work) provisions, but it is possible that breach of these obligations could be used *indirectly* by an individual in three ways—first, it could be used as evidence of unreasonable conduct by the employer in another form of claim, such as for constructive dismissal or in a personal injury action (as, for example, in *Hone v Six Continents Retail Ltd*[125] where a pub manager's refusal to sign an opt-out supplied the element of foreseeability of harm necessary for his negligence action against his employer based on excessive workload); secondly, it is possible that the Regulations could be held to support civil liability, so that in a case of non-compliance causing definable harm to the worker he or she could sue the employer for breach of statutory duty;[126] thirdly, in a highly purposive judgment in *Barber v RJB Mining (UK) Ltd*[127] Gage J held that it is an implied term of the contract of employment that the employer will comply with the maximum working week requirement, so that if an employee is made to work past the 48-hour average (without agreeing to do so) by an employer who assumes that this can 'only' be challenged by health and safety procedures, that employee may have a breach of contract action, or may even (according to the judge) calculate when he has done sufficient hours in that reference period to average 48 per week and then *stop* until the beginning of the next reference period. Thus, there are several possibilities here that do not appear on the face of the Regulations.

Any provision in an agreement (whether or not a contract of employment) is void if it purports to exclude or limit the application of the Regulations or to preclude a person from bringing proceedings before an employment tribunal (subject to the usual exceptions for ACAS-conciliated (COT 3) settlements and compromise agreements).[128]

In line with most other recent protective legislation, it is provided that any dismissal because of refusal to comply with a breach of the Regulations, to forgo a right or to sign a workforce agreement, or because of being or seeking to be a worker representative, is automatically unfair;[129] likewise, a worker has a right not to suffer a detriment (short of dismissal) for similar reasons.[130] These guarantees notwithstanding, roughly two-thirds of workers who worked over 48 hours a week under pressure from their employers

---

[125] [2006] IRLR 49, CA.

[126] This possibility was expressly envisaged in the government's consultation document URN 98/645 para 184. Such liability would not be automatic under the Health and Safety at Work etc Act 1974, s 47(2) because the Regulations were passed under the European Communities Act 1972, not under the 1974 Act; it would therefore be necessary to prove parliamentary intent that they should support civil liability in the usual way. Given this possibility, an employer might be advised to keep records for at least *three* years (the limitation period in personal injury actions) not just the statutory two years.

[127] [1999] ICR 679, [1999] IRLR 308.   [128] Regulation 35.

[129] Regulation 32, adding the Employment Rights Act 1996, s 101A. Asserting a right under the Regulations is protected by s 104 of the Act.

[130] Regulation 31, adding the Employment Rights Act 1996, s 45A.

had not signed an opt-out agreement of any kind.[131] It is not hard for employers to get workers either to sign an opt-out or to work long hours without complaint.

(k) Effects and future

The general impression to date has been that the Working Time Regulations have had little effect in practice. The only notable litigation has been over the holiday entitlement and even there it has been primarily about holiday pay. As far as the pursuit of the wider social goals of limiting working hours and patterns are concerned, little change can be discerned and indeed surveys quoted in the media suggest that while long-hours working reduced slightly from 1998 to 2007, it has started to increase in recent years.[132] Health and safety enforcement has not happened. Some of this will no doubt be due to the Regulations simply being ignored. However, it is also the case that the exceptionally wide derogations and exceptions make the Regulations easy to avoid lawfully;[133] the opting out of the maximum working week by simple written agreement is the most obvious example. Is this likely to change? It must be remembered that the negotiation of the Directive by the previous UK government caused some annoyance among our EU partners, in particular in relation to the inclusions of the wide derogations which have made the UK Regulations so weak. There have been moves to restrict the major exceptions, with amendments already to bring seafaring and the transport industry at least partly within the Directive and to bring trainee doctors within the coverage of the Regulations. The original Directive stated that the major derogations were to be reviewed by November 2003. Although behind schedule, this process did occur and there were clear signs that our partners looked with disfavour on the continued existence of the major derogations, with the 48-hour opt-out being a particular target.[134] The reaction of the UK government was to seek to retain the derogation while recognizing that some changes will be necessary to buy off wholesale repeal. It began to look as if it might be pay-back time for perfidious Albion. However, the government stood firm, and talks on amending the Directive collapsed in April 2009, ensuring that UK workers without caring or other non-work commitments will continue to enjoy the right to 'choose' to entrench long-hours working as the gold standard in the UK workplace.

---

[131] *Slaying the Working Time Myths* (Trade Unions Congress, April 2009), available at <http://www.tuc.org.uk/extras/workingtimemyths.pdf> (last accessed 6 January 2013).

[132] *The Return of the Long Hours Culture* (Trade Unions Congress June 2008) available at <http://www.tuc.org.uk/extras/longhoursreturn.pdf> (last accessed 6 January 2013).

[133] See Barnard, Deakin and Hobbs 'Opting out of the 48 Hour Week: Employer Necessity or Individual Choice' (2003) 32 ILJ 223.

[134] One straw in the wind was the decision of the ECJ in *Pfeiffer v Deutsches Rotes Kreuz* C-397/01 [2005] IRLR 137 that, on a matter of principle, any permitted agreement to work beyond the 48-hour limit must be entered into by the employee 'individually, expressly and freely'. The UK opt-out procedure satisfies the first two but not necessarily the third, especially as a job applicant may have to agree in order to get the job.

3 MATERNITY AND PARENTAL RIGHTS; FLEXIBLE WORKING[135]

One of the areas of greatest development in recent years has been that of maternity and parental rights. Starting off from basic protections from dismissal or other detriment, these have seen the growth of positive rights to time off and at least an element of replacement pay during pregnancy and maternity leave. The entitlement to a year of maternity leave is well established, with statutory maternity pay having gone up to nine months in 2007 (with an eventual aim of the whole year). As part of their general social policy, recent governments have extended similar rights to adopters. Parental leave to look after children was in principle an important development, but shows the basic realities that as long as time off is unpaid the take-up rate will be low. The right to request flexible working (often, but not necessarily, to go part time) started off as an offshoot of maternity/parental rights, but it was always arguable that it was really part of a wider 'work–life balance' agenda, and this was borne out in 2007 when it was extended to carers for the elderly and infirm. The following discussion of these parental rights will begin with a background of how the regulation of these rights developed, and will then explain in turn each of the guarantees that are currently in place.

(i) THE DEVELOPMENT OF PARENTAL RIGHTS

The New Labour government came into office in May 1997 committed to a review of the existing law on maternity rights, and the introduction of new 'family-friendly' measures to help workers strike a balance between work and home.[136] Since that time, the law in this area has been transformed almost beyond recognition, first by the Employment Relations Act 1999, which introduced a new framework of maternity rights, replacing the existing substantive provisions in the Employment Rights Act 1996 with a series of enabling powers which were subsequently fleshed out by supporting regulations;[137] secondly by the Employment Act 2002, which brought further major restructuring and extension of maternity rights, new rights to paternity leave and adoption leave, and a right for parents of young children to request flexible working; and thirdly by the Work and Families Act 2006 which extended statutory maternity pay from six months to nine months (with a view to 12 eventually), gave additional maternity leave to all employees, extended the right to request flexible working to carers for adults and gave powers to extend paternity leave and pay. Finally, amendments in 2008 rendered

---

[135] See McRae *Maternity Rights in Britain* (1991); Fredman *Women in Labour: Parenting Rights at Work* (1995); McColgan (2000) 29 ILJ 125; Conaghan (1993) 20 JLS 71; James, 'The Work and Families Act 2006: Legislation to Improve Choice and Flexibility?' (2006) 35 ILJ 272.

[136] Fairness at Work (Cm 3968, 1998) ch 5.

[137] Maternity and Parental Leave etc (MPL etc) Regulations 1999, SI 1999/3312.

additional leave identical to ordinary leave, and included, in the coverage of the right to flexible working, parents of children up to and including 16.

That the existing law on maternity rights was long overdue for reform was not in doubt. The existing provisions had developed piecemeal since the Employment Protection Act 1975 first introduced three statutory rights relating to maternity—the right not to be unfairly dismissed because of pregnancy, the right to return to work after pregnancy or childbirth and the right to maternity pay. A fourth right, to time off work for antenatal care, was introduced in the Employment Act 1980. The right to maternity pay was superseded in April 1987 by the statutory maternity pay (SMP) provisions, introduced in the Social Security Act 1986 and subsequently consolidated in the Social Security Contributions and Benefits Act 1992. The maternity provisions were notorious for their complexity, and were widely criticized, not least because it was possible for a minor, technical slip-up to cost the employee her rights. In one case, the provisions were memorably described as being 'of inordinate complexity exceeding the worst excesses of a taxing statute'.[138] The position was exacerbated by the fact that the qualifications for the different rights differed in several important respects (for example there were different qualifying dates and notice requirements for the right to return and for SMP).

The whole area was the subject of major change in 1993 by the Trade Union Reform and Employment Rights Act 1993, implementing the Pregnant Workers Directive.[139] The 1993 Act introduced a new right to 14 weeks' maternity leave, and gave improved protection against dismissal on grounds of pregnancy or childbirth, in both cases regardless of length of service.[140] It also introduced a right to be suspended from work on maternity grounds where continued employment would be unlawful or contrary to a code of practice. The 1993 Act provided an excellent opportunity for a thorough overhaul of the law in this area and the removal of unnecessary complexity, but unfortunately that opportunity was missed. The new provisions were simply overlaid onto the existing law, and it took a greater than usual degree of fortitude to attempt to unravel them. Some improvement flowed from the consolidation of employment rights in the Employment Rights Act 1996, but as a consolidating statute, that Act was bound to have only limited success in attempting to fashion the proverbial silk purse out of the raw materials. Nearly two decades after Browne-Wilkinson J uttered the remarks quoted above, Ward LJ was moved to state in the Court of Appeal,[141] in a case on the interpretation of the provisions on maternity leave and the right to return to

---

[138] As was illustrated in *Lavery v Plessey Telecommunications Ltd* [1982] ICR 373, [1983] IRLR 180 at 182, EAT, per Browne-Wilkinson J. In *Lavery* the giving of five days' notice of intention to return to work after maternity leave, instead of the seven then required, robbed the employee of her right to return.

[139] Directive 92/85/EC. The Directive, which was agreed in October 1992, was brought forward as a health and safety measure under Art 118A of the Treaty of Rome, and as such required only qualified majority approval; the UK government abstained in the vote on its adoption.

[140] A right to pay during the 14-week maternity leave period was introduced via reforms to the SMP provisions.

[141] *Halfpenny v IGC Medical Systems Ltd* [1999] ICR 834, [1999] IRLR 177, CA.

work (which by that stage had been in force since 1975), that 'it is surely not too much to ask of the legislature that those who have to grapple with this topic should not have to have a wet towel around their heads as the single most important aid to the understanding of their rights'.[142]

As redrawn in the 1999 Act and the associated regulations, the maternity leave provisions were undoubtedly an improvement on what had gone before. The notification requirements, notoriously complicated under the pre-1999 law, were rationalized and simplified, and some notorious grey areas were clarified, in particular the status of the contract of employment during maternity leave. However, there was a groundswell of opinion that the reforms had not gone far enough: 'Employers and employees alike are bewildered by, or unaware of, the existing legislation on maternity pay and leave. As it stands the system is a minefield of qualification periods and dates, variable leave lengths, different calculation periods and short notification requirements.'[143] The reforms that were intended to achieve the other stated objective, that of making employment law more 'family-friendly', also received a lukewarm response. The 1999 Act extended the right to 'ordinary' maternity leave from 14 to 18 weeks, and reduced the qualifying period for 'additional' maternity leave from two years to one, but these were only modest improvements on the previous position. More significant was the introduction of a right to parental leave for mothers and fathers, and a right to emergency leave ('time off for dependants'), implementing the Parental Leave Directive,[144] but here again the new provisions were open to criticism for example in relation to the restriction of the entitlement to parental leave to the parents of children under five, and the fact that there was no provision for any part of the leave to be paid.

No doubt stung by these criticisms, in 2000 the government embarked on yet another major review of maternity and parental rights, this time with a much wider remit. The Green Paper, 'Work and Parents: Competitiveness and Choice',[145] put forward a wide range of options for further reform, designed 'to balance improving choice for parents and enhancing competitiveness for business'. The responses indicated that the greatest levels of support were for further simplification of the arrangements for maternity leave and pay, the introduction of new rights to paid paternity leave[146] and paid adoption leave, and a new right to flexible working for parents. In June 2001 the government set up the Work and Parents Taskforce, headed by Professor Sir George Bain, to consider how best to implement a right to flexible working for the parents of young children, and the Taskforce reported later that year.[147] The Taskforce recommended the introduction of a new right to *apply* for flexible working, falling well short of a

---

[142] To which prescription both authors would probably wish to add a couple of aspirins or a large whisky, or quite possibly both.

[143] DTI *Work and Parents: Competitiveness and Choice, a framework for simplification* (May 2001).

[144] Directive 96/34/EC.

[145] Cm 5005, December 2000.

[146] On work–life balance for fathers, see Hatton, Vinter and Williams 'Dads on Dads: Needs and Expectations at Home and at Work' (EOC, 2002).

[147] Work and Parents Taskforce *About Time: Flexible Working* (November 2001).

right to insist on working flexibly. Legislation underpinning that right was introduced in the Employment Act 2002, along with measures implementing the other reforms mentioned above. The reformed framework for maternity leave and pay deserves a special mention, as it represented a considerable (and long overdue) simplification, rationalization and enhancement of the existing provisions, to the advantage of both employees and employers.[148] The extension of the maternity leave period to one year, followed by the extension of maternity pay from six to nine months under the Work and Families Act 2006 (with a year as the ultimate goal) were obviously important moves in this area, but it must be remembered that most of the pay entitlement remained at a relatively low and flat rate and the pessimist may still argue that even these changes may be an irrelevance to the many employees who simply cannot afford to stay at home for a year.[149]

The most recent move in the piecemeal construction of a parental rights framework has been the introduction of additional paternity leave and pay.[150] Actually initiated by the New Labour government through the Work and Families Act 2006, they were not brought into effect until the Conservative/Liberal Democrat Coalition government. For leave in respect of births after 6 April 2011 these regulations added to the existing two weeks of paternity leave the possibility for a mother to transfer up to 26 unused weeks of her own 52 weeks of maternity leave, so long as this additional paternity leave does not begin before the child is 20 weeks old, and does not extend beyond the period of the mother's entitlement to maternity leave. Fathers may also receive whatever portion of the mother's 39 weeks of Statutory Maternity Pay has not been used by the time the additional leave is transferred to the father. This welcome enhancement looks likely to give way in 2015 to a system that would constitute a real step change: the government proposes to allow the 52 weeks of maternity leave and 39 weeks of maternity pay to be shared between the mother and the father/mother's partner in a dramatically more flexible way. The proposals call for parents to be able to take leave concurrently, or alternately, or switch places altogether, so long as the leave is taken in week-long blocks and does not amount to more leave or pay altogether than the mother would have been entitled to under the present scheme.[151] The same proposals also herald an increase in unpaid parental leave (connected to childcare, not pregnancy) from 13 weeks to 18 weeks in 2013 to comply with the EU Parental Leave Directive.

---

[148] The more generous the maternity provision, the higher the proportion of women returning to work after childbirth: Callender, Millward, Lissenburgh and Forth *Maternity Rights and Benefits in Britain* DSS Research Report No 67 (1997); see also Forth, Lissenburgh, Callender and Millward *Family-Friendly Working Arrangements in Britain* DfEE Research Report No 16 (1997).

[149] Only a quarter of eligible employees took all or nearly all of the maximum entitlement even before the increases: DTI *Work and Parents: Competitiveness and Choice, a Framework for Simplification* (May 2001).

[150] Additional Paternity Leave Regulations 2010, SI 2010/1055 and Additional Statutory Paternity Pay (General) Regulations 2010, SI 2010/1056.

[151] *Modern Workplaces—Government Response on Flexible Parental Leave* (HM Gov Nov 2012) available at <http://www.bis.gov.uk/assets/biscore/employment-matters/docs/m/12–1269-modern-workplaces-response-flexible-working> (last accessed 6 January 2013).

These plans certainly make it appear that the government is moving away from parental leave arrangements that entrench the role of women as child-carers. However, it only appears that way. These measures do not in any way increase the leave that fathers have as of right, so they can only have leave if the mother chooses to relinquish it. More to the point, the fact that Statutory Maternity/Parental Pay will continue to be much less than most parents usually earn and too little on which to support a family means that pressure will continue for the lower earner in the relationship—usually the woman—to take the leave. The government's attitude towards the idea of requiring full pay during parental leave found voice in the UK's fatal opposition to EU proposals to increase fully paid maternity leave to 20 weeks.[152] So while regulatory innovation focuses on new and more flexible ways to use what is basically a year of maternity leave held by the mother, no proposals are on the horizon to improve the affordability of actually taking that leave for those on lower incomes or single mothers. In practice, one of the most important factors for mothers and fathers seeking to find a satisfactory balance between work and family life is the availability of high quality, convenient and affordable childcare. Although this gets discussed, there are no real measures in place. As already mentioned at the beginning of this chapter, employers themselves often adopt innovative work–life balance initiatives and, while they remain a minority, this may represent the best hope for change.

(ii) DISMISSAL AND DETRIMENT FOR FAMILY REASONS

All employees have the right not to be dismissed or subjected to any detriment by their employer for reasons connected with pregnancy or childbirth or for other speci-fied family reasons, regardless of their age or length of service. Until 1993, the protec-tion against dismissal on grounds of pregnancy or childbirth was seriously deficient, in that it only applied where the employee satisfied the normal qualifying period of continuous employment for unfair dismissal (which was still two years at that time). The effect of this was to exclude some 40% of working women from the protection.[153] All was not lost, however, for a woman dismissed for pregnancy within two years of employment could complain that her dismissal was unlawful sex discrimination (such complaints not being subject to any qualifying period of continuous employment). In 1993, the protection against pregnancy dismissal was extended to all employees by the Trade Union Reform and Employment Rights Act 1993, implementing the Pregnant Workers Directive,[154] with the result that a woman dismissed on grounds of pregnancy or childbirth within the first year of employment does not have to claim

---

[152] 'EU maternity leave plans rejected' *The Independent* (17 June 2011) available at <http:www.independent. co.uk/news/world/europe/eu-maternity-leave-plans-rejected-2299051> (last accessed 6 January 2013).

[153] 1989 Labour Force Survey, *Employment Gazette*, December 1990, p 633. The problem was particularly acute for part-time workers (ie those working less than 16 hours per week) who at that time needed to work for five years in order to qualify.

[154] Directive 92/85/EC.

sex discrimination in order to obtain a remedy. There may, however, still be advantages in doing so, not least being the fact that compensation for sex discrimination is not subject to any upper limit. The significance of sex discrimination law in this area is considered later in this chapter.[155]

The provisions on pregnancy dismissal were further amended by the Employment Relations Act 1999, which simplified the existing provisions, and extended the unfair dismissal protection to dismissal for other family reasons (including the fact that the employee took parental leave, or time off for dependants), as required by the Parental Leave Directive; similar provisions prohibiting dismissal for taking paternity or adoption leave were introduced in 2002. The opportunity was also taken in 1999 to introduce for the first time a parallel right not to suffer detriment short of dismissal for family reasons. Section 99 of the 1996 Act, which used to contain the substantive provisions on dismissal for pregnancy and childbirth, is now a framework provision conferring a power to make regulations concerning dismissal for family reasons, and the detailed provisions on dismissal and other detriment are to be found in the Maternity and Parental Leave etc (MPL etc) Regulations[156] and the Paternity and Adoption Leave (PAL) Regulations.[157]

(a) Dismissal for family reasons

The MPL etc Regulations provide that a dismissal will be automatically unfair if the reason or principal reason for the dismissal[158] is connected with: (1) the pregnancy of the employee;[159] (2) the fact that she has given birth to a child;[160] (3) her suspension from work on maternity grounds;[161] (4) the fact that she took, or sought to take, ordinary maternity leave, additional maternity leave, parental leave or time off for dependants; (5) the fact that she availed herself of the benefits of ordinary maternity leave or additional maternity leave;[162] (6) the fact that she failed to return to work after ordinary or additional maternity leave where the employer had failed to notify her of the date of return;[163] (7) the fact that she undertook or refused to undertake

---

[155] See heading xiii, p 290.   [156] MPL etc Regulations 1999, SI 1999/3312, reg 20.

[157] PAL Regulations 2002, SI 2002/2788, reg 29.

[158] As in other unfair dismissal cases, it will be for the employer to show the reason for the dismissal. An employee dismissed while pregnant or during ordinary or additional maternity leave is entitled to a written statement of the reasons for dismissal, without requesting it, and regardless of her length of service: Employment Rights Act 1996, s 92(4), as amended.

[159] For a case to come within this (primary) category, the employer must have known that the employee was pregnant (though with a possible extension to a case where the employer dismissed *in case* she was pregnant): *Ramdoolar v Bycity Ltd* [2005] ICR 368.

[160] The protection under this head only applies during the employee's ordinary or additional maternity leave: MPL etc Regulations 1999, reg 20(4).

[161] Ie under a relevant statutory requirement or relevant recommendation in a Code of Practice, as defined by s 66(2) of the 1996 Act.

[162] Ie that during her ordinary maternity leave period (or additional maternity leave period), she availed herself of the benefit of any of the terms and conditions of her employment preserved under s 71: MPL etc Regulations 1999, reg 20(5), applying reg 19(3) and (3A).

[163] This head was added by the MPL (Amendment) Regulations 2002, SI 2002/2789.

'keep in touch' days; (8) the fact that she refused to sign a workforce agreement in relation to parental leave;[164] or (9) the fact that she performed (or proposed to perform) any functions or activities of a workforce representative (including standing as a candidate) for the purposes of the provisions on parental leave. Similar provision is made for paternity and adoption leave by the PAL Regulations, which provide that a dismissal will be automatically unfair if the reason or principal reason for the dismissal is connected with the fact that: (1) the employee took, or sought to take paternity or adoption leave; (2) the employer believed that the employee was likely to take adoption leave; (3) the employee undertook or refused to undertake 'keep in touch' days; or (4) the fact that the employee failed to return to work after additional adoption leave where the employer had failed to notify the employee of the date of return.[165] Special rules apply in the case of redundancy. First, a dismissal will be unfair if the employee is made redundant and it is shown that he or she was selected for redundancy in preference to other comparable employees for one of the family reasons set out above.[166] Secondly, where a redundancy situation arises during the employee's ordinary or additional maternity or adoption leave which makes it impracticable for the employer to continue to employ her under her original contract of employment, the employee is entitled to be offered alternative employment with her employer (or with a successor, or an associated employer) where there is a suitable available vacancy, ie where the work to be done is of a kind which is suitable in relation to the employee, appropriate for her to do in the circumstances, and on terms and conditions (including the capacity and place in which she is to be employed) not substantially less favourable to her than if she had continued to be employed under her previous contract.[167] If the employer has a suitable alternative vacancy available, but makes the employee redundant during ordinary or additional maternity or adoption leave without first offering it to her, the redundancy dismissal will be unfair.[168] If, however, there is no suitable alternative work available which could be offered to her, she will not be regarded as unfairly dismissed.

The previous Conservative government introduced two sub-rules in 1980 in an attempt to rebalance the maternity rights in an employer's favour. The first of these was a small firm exemption for employers of five or fewer employees, but this was repealed by the Work and Families Act 2006 (as from April 2007). However, under the second sub-rule it remains the case that if any employer can prove that it is not reasonably practicable (for a reason other than redundancy) to permit the employee to return to

---

[164] See this chapter, heading 3(x), p 281.   [165] PAL Regulations, reg 29.

[166] MPL etc Regulations 1999, reg 20(2); PAL Regulations, reg 29(2).

[167] MPL etc Regulations 1999, reg 10; PAL Regulations, reg 23. The offer of alternative employment must be made before the end of her existing contract, and the new contract must take effect immediately on the ending of the previous contract.

[168] MPL etc Regulations 1999, reg 20(1)(b); PAL Regulations, reg 29(1)(b). If the employer offers her a suitable alternative vacancy and she unreasonably refuses it, she may lose her right to a redundancy payment. It was held under previous provisions that whether a vacancy is 'available' is a question of objective fact, not of reasonableness: *Community Task Force v Rimmer* [1986] ICR 491, [1986] IRLR 203, EAT.

her old job or to a similar job which is both suitable for the employee and appropriate for her to do in the circumstances, and an associated employer has offered suitable alternative employment which the employee has accepted or unreasonably refused, then once again the employee will not be regarded as automatically unfairly dismissed when not allowed to return to work at the end of maternity leave or adoption period.[169] This could be a major limitation on the right to return to work after maternity or adoption leave; the only comfort given to an employee in this situation is that the burden of proof is placed squarely upon the employer to show that (1) it is not reasonably practicable to permit the employee to return in the normal way, and (2) he or an associated employer has offered the employee alternative employment 'which is both suitable for her and appropriate for her to do in the circumstances'.[170] The concept of an offer of suitable alternative employment is well known in the law on redundancy[171] and there may be a tendency to apply redundancy precedents to this maternity leave provision (though the wording of the two provisions is not the same), but it is submitted that in construing the maternity provision a tribunal should consider it as very much the exception to the normal rule, for to allow it to apply too readily would be to jeopardize an important employment right.

Under the original formulation of the maternity rights (before the 1993 changes) a pregnancy dismissal was not unfair where the employer could prove that the employee was incapable of doing her job properly because of her pregnancy (for example where her job involved lifting),[172] or that she could not carry on working without contravening some statutory provision (for example the regulations prohibiting the exposure of pregnant women to ionizing radiations or lead).[173] Those exceptions no longer apply, but where the employee's continued employment would be unlawful or contrary to the recommendations of a code of practice, the employee may now be suspended from work on maternity grounds (see later in this chapter), and a dismissal connected with such suspension will be unfair.

In the case law on the pre-1993 provisions, the words 'reason connected with pregnancy' were broadly construed. In *Brown v Stockton-on-Tees Borough Council*,[174] the applicant, a care supervisor on a youth training scheme, was selected for redundancy on the basis that she was pregnant. The employers argued that they were justified in selecting the applicant for redundancy because otherwise they would have had to arrange a replacement for her during maternity leave. The EAT and the

---

[169] MPL etc Regulations 1999, reg 20(7); PAL Regulations, reg 29(5).

[170] MPL etc Regulations 1999, reg 20(8); see also PAL Regulations, reg 29(6). The requirement in redundancy cases that the terms and conditions of the alternative employment be not substantially less favourable to her than if she had continued to be employed under her previous contract does not apply here.

[171] See Ch 8, heading 1(iv), p 589.

[172] See eg *Brear v Wright Hudson Ltd* [1977] IRLR 287.

[173] The only exception was where the employer had failed to offer her a suitable available vacancy, in which case the dismissal was unfair.

[174] [1988] ICR 410, [1988] IRLR 263, HL. See also *Clayton v Vigers* [1989] ICR 713, [1990] IRLR 177, EAT.

Court of Appeal held that this was not a case of dismissal 'for a reason connected with pregnancy', but was instead purely a redundancy situation.[175] However, in a judgment of some importance the House of Lords held that the dismissal fell within the section and was therefore unfair; the section was to be construed in its own terms, as 'part of social legislation passed for the specific protection of women and to put them on an equal footing with men', and it could not have been the intention of Parliament 'that an employer should be entitled to take advantage of a redundancy situation to weed out his pregnant employees' (per Lord Griffiths). As seen above, the redrafted provisions now expressly provide that selection for redundancy for family reasons will be automatically unfair, but the decision is arguably still important, for it shows that the courts will be prepared to interpret the provisions purposively where necessary in order to achieve the social policy objectives of the legislation.

(b) Protection from detriment for family reasons

The statutory protection from detriment for family reasons was introduced in the Employment Relations Act 1999. Before that Act there was no explicit right not to suffer detriment for family reasons, although in practice detrimental treatment on grounds of pregnancy or childbirth will almost invariably constitute unlawful sex discrimination.[176] The present provisions bring the protection from detriment in line with the unfair dismissal protection, although there are some differences between the two.

Section 47C of the Employment Rights Act 1996 (as fleshed out by the MPL etc Regulations[177] and the PAL Regulations)[178] gives an employee the right not to be subjected to any detriment[179] (other than dismissal) by the employer for the reason that the employee: (1) is pregnant; (2) has given birth to a child; (3) has been suspended from work on maternity grounds; (4) has taken, or sought to take, ordinary maternity leave, additional maternity leave, parental leave or time off for dependants, paternity leave or adoption leave; (5) has availed herself of the benefits of ordinary maternity leave or additional maternity leave; (6) has failed to return to work after ordinary or additional maternity leave, or additional adoption leave, where the employer had failed to notify the employee of the date of return; (7) has undertaken or refused to undertake 'keep in touch' days; (8) has refused to sign a workforce agreement in relation to parental leave; or (9) has performed (or proposed to perform) any functions or activities of a workforce representative (including standing as a candidate) for the purposes of the provisions on parental leave.[180]

[175] The argument on behalf of the employer being that cases of unfair redundancy selection were not subject to the Employment Rights Act 1996, s 99.

[176] See Ch 5, heading 2(ii), p 310.

[177] MPL etc Regulations 1999, reg 19, as amended by the MPL (Amendment) Regulations 2002, reg 13.

[178] PAL Regulations, reg 28.

[179] This includes detriment by any act or by deliberate failure to act: MPL etc Regulations, reg 19(1); PAL Regulations, reg 28(1).

[180] For the detailed interpretation of these grounds, see the discussion of the parallel provisions concerning dismissal. As with dismissal, the protection for childbirth only applies where the detriment takes place during the employee's ordinary or additional maternity leave: reg 19(5).

The remedy for an infringement of the right not to be subjected to a detriment for family reasons operates through the usual procedures in Part V of the Employment Rights Act for protection from suffering detriment in employment. Complaint lies to an employment tribunal, within three months of the act, or deliberate failure to act complained of (or within a further reasonable period where not reasonably practicable),[181] and if the tribunal upholds the complaint it must make a declaration to that effect, and may award the employee such compensation as it considers just and equitable in all the circumstances.[182]

(iii) MATERNITY LEAVE

All pregnant employees are entitled to 52 weeks' maternity leave, irrespective of length of service or hours of work, during which the contract of employment continues (unless either party expressly ends it, or it expires), and the employee is entitled 'to the benefit of the terms and conditions of employment which would have applied if she had not been absent'[183] (apart from remuneration, which is specifically excluded).[184] Prior to 2008 maternity leave consisted of 'ordinary' leave and 'additional' leave. Additional leave originally had a six-month qualifying period and afforded less job protection than ordinary leave. Both distinctions have since been removed. As a result of judicial review proceedings brought by the Equal Opportunities Commission (EOC)—now subsumed into the Equality and Human Rights Commission—the High Court held in 2007 that the distinctions between ordinary and additional maternity leave did not properly implement the 2002 amendments to the EU Equal Treatment Directive.[185] The relevant regulations have since been amended but, owing to the vagaries of the legislative process, the two terms, 'ordinary' and 'additional', continue to exist in the regulations and statutes for now, but the two kinds of leave are identical. The distinction between ordinary and additional maternity leave was important before 2008, however, because it was only during 'ordinary' maternity leave that an employee had a statutory right to continue to benefit from all her normal terms and conditions of employment, except those providing for wages or salary[186] (unless, of course, she has a contractual right to receive wages or salary during maternity leave). This right now applies to all 52 weeks of leave. This means that the employee is entitled to continue to benefit

---

[181] Employment Rights Act 1996, s 48, as amended.

[182] Employment Rights Act 1996, s 49, as amended.

[183] Employment Rights Act 1996, s 71(4), as amended by the Employment Relations Act 1999, Sch 4.

[184] Employment Rights Act 1996, s 71(5). Remuneration is defined for these purposes as 'sums payable to an employee by way of wages or salary': MPL etc Regulations 1999, reg 9. On entitlement to pay during maternity leave, see heading v, p 270 later in this chapter.

[185] *Equal Opportunities Commission v Secretary of State for Trade and Industry* [2007] IRLR 327.

[186] MPL etc Regulations 1999, reg 9. There has occasionally been controversy over the width of this exclusion (ie what does 'wages or salary' cover?). In *Hoyland v Asda Stores Ltd* [2006] IRLR 468 the Inner House of the Court of Session held that it could cover a discretionary bonus (based on time served during the bonus year); this meant that the employer could lawfully pro-rate the bonus to reflect the period in the bonus year not actually worked by the employee on maternity leave.

from any terms and conditions concerning, for example, the use of a company car or mobile phone, membership of clubs and societies, reimbursement of professional subscriptions and participation in employee share-ownership schemes. A woman who also enjoys a contractual right to maternity leave may not exercise the two rights separately, but may take advantage of whichever right is, in any particular respect, the more favourable.[187] She is entitled to any other benefits which would have accrued if she had been at work (for example holiday entitlement) as if she had been at work and not on maternity leave. The period of maternity leave counts towards her period of continuous employment for the purposes of qualifying for statutory employment rights and, because the contract continues throughout, the period also counts when assessing matters such as her seniority, pension rights and other similar rights which depend on length of service (for example contractual pay increments). In contrast, prior to 2008, during additional maternity leave a woman was entitled to the benefit of a much narrower range of terms and conditions of employment, unless her contract provided otherwise. For example, seniority did not accrue during additional leave, and those returning from additional leave had a weaker right to get their job back than did those on ordinary leave. The Maternity and Parental Leave, etc and the Paternity and Adoption Leave (Amendment) Regulations 2008 eliminated these differences for parents of children expected or adopted on or after 5 October 2008. Ordinary and additional leave now represent an integrated 52-week leave period, and the distinct terms will likely be removed before long.

(a) Commencement and duration

Within certain limits, an employee is free to choose the date on which her maternity leave starts (the combination of ordinary and additional leave will hereinafter be referred to as 'maternity leave').[188] Unless the employee specifies otherwise, she is assumed to be taking her entire 52-week entitlement. However, she cannot choose a start date earlier than the beginning of the 11th week before the expected week of childbirth (EWC),[189] and her maternity leave period will be *automatically* triggered by any day on which she is absent from work wholly or partly because of pregnancy after the beginning of the fourth week before the EWC.[190] The thinking behind the latter provision is apparently to prevent a woman from delaying the start of her ordinary maternity leave until the last possible moment (thus ensuring the maximum amount of leave after childbirth) by taking sick leave instead of maternity leave, but it could have the unfortunate consequence of encouraging a woman to continue working during the latter stages of pregnancy, even though medically unfit to do so, in order to

---

[187]   MPL etc Regulations 1999, reg 21. This is commonly referred to as a 'composite' right.
[188]   Employment Rights Act 1996, s 71(3). MPL etc Regulations 1999, reg 6.
[189]   MPL etc Regulations 1999, reg 4(2)(b).
[190]   MPL etc Regulations 1999, reg 6(1)(b). Absence from work due to time off for antenatal care does not count. 'Childbirth' is defined as 'the birth of a living child or the birth of a child whether living or dead after 24 weeks of pregnancy': reg 2; the same definition appears in the Employment Rights Act 1996, s 235(1).

prevent her maternity leave period from being automatically triggered. This still seems a strange way of giving effect to a Directive which is intended to protect the health and safety of pregnant women.[191] If childbirth occurs prematurely, the maternity leave period begins with the day following the day of childbirth,[192] and the employer must be notified of the date of birth as soon as is reasonably practicable.

Provision is also made for two weeks' 'compulsory maternity leave',[193] beginning with the day of childbirth, and if the compulsory maternity leave period extends beyond the date on which maternity leave would have ended, the maternity leave period will be deemed to continue until the end of compulsory maternity leave.[194] The maternity leave period is also deemed to continue beyond the normal 26 weeks where the employee is prohibited by law from working, by reason of having recently given birth.[195] The Act specifically provides for a right to return to work at the end of the maternity leave period, but such a provision is arguably unnecessary given that the contract of employment continues to exist throughout that period. An employee who wishes to return to work *before* the end of her maternity leave period may do so, on giving not less than eight weeks' notice to the employer,[196] although she must still observe the compulsory maternity leave period. Dismissal during the maternity leave period brings that period to an end.[197] Such a dismissal will normally be automatically unfair,[198] as will a dismissal at the end of maternity leave (for example where the employee is not given her job back) although special provision is made for redundancy during maternity leave,[199] in that where a redundancy situation arises during the employee's maternity leave which makes it impracticable for the employer to continue to employ her under her original contract of employment, she is entitled to be offered alternative employment with her employer (or with a successor, or an associated employer) where there is a suitable available vacancy. Failure to offer such a vacancy will make the redundancy dismissal automatically unfair.[200]

(b) Notice requirements

To take advantage of her right to maternity leave, the employee must satisfy certain notice requirements. These requirements, long criticized for their complexity, were

---

[191] The employer can of course choose to disregard days of pregnancy-related illness if the employee wishes to defer the start of her maternity leave period.

[192] MPL etc Regulations 1999, reg 6(2).

[193] It is an offence under the Public Health Act 1936 to permit a woman to work in a factory within four weeks after the date of childbirth.

[194] Employment Rights Act 1996, s 72 (as amended) and MPL etc Regulations 1999, reg 8. The requirement is compulsory on *both* sides, and an employer who infringes the prohibition is liable on summary conviction to a fine not exceeding level 2 on the standard scale; there is no provision for any sanction on the employee in such a case.

[195] MPL etc Regulations 1999, reg 7(2).

[196] MPL etc Regulations 1999, reg 11, as amended as from April 2007 to increase the notice from 28 days.

[197] MPL etc Regulations 1999, reg 7(5).

[198] MPL etc Regulations 1999, reg 20. See heading 3(ii), p 258 earlier in this chapter.

[199] MPL etc Regulations 1999, reg 10. See heading 3(ii), p 259 earlier in this chapter.

[200] MPL etc Regulations 1999, reg 20(1)(b).

simplified by the Employment Relations Act 1999 and the regulations issued thereunder, and further modified by the MPL (Amendment) Regulations 2002.[201] The employee is now required to notify her employer, at least 15 weeks[202] before her EWC:[203] (1) that she is pregnant; (2) when the expected week of childbirth will be; and (3) the date on which she intends her maternity leave to start. If she gives birth before she has notified a date, or before the date she has notified, her maternity leave will start automatically on the day following the day of childbirth, and she must notify her employer as soon as is reasonably practicable (in writing, if so requested) that she has given birth, and of the date on which childbirth occurred.[204] Before the 2002 reforms, notification did not have to be given until 21 days before the date on which the employee intended her maternity leave to start, which in practice often gave employers very little opportunity to make alternative arrangements, such as recruiting a temporary replacement. Under the current rules, the employer will usually have more warning, particularly if the employee decides to delay the start of her maternity leave until closer to the expected date of childbirth. She is, however, allowed to vary the intended start-date, provided she does so at least 28 days before the date varied, or 28 days before the new date, whichever is the earlier (or, if this is not reasonably practicable, as soon as reasonably practicable thereafter).[205] Notification does not have to be in writing, but the employer is entitled to ask for written notification of the intended start date of maternity leave, or of any subsequent variation of that date,[206] and may demand to see a medical certificate verifying the expected week of childbirth.[207] One important requirement is that an employer who has received notification of the intended start-date of maternity leave must respond by notifying the employee of the date on which her maternity leave will end.[208] Failure to do so will mean that the employee will be protected against detriment or dismissal if she fails to return to work on the due date.[209] There is no need for the employee to give notice to the employer of her intention to return to work—it is assumed that she will return on the date notified to her by the employer as the end of her maternity leave period—but if she wishes to return to work *earlier* than that date she may do so, on giving the employer at least eight weeks' notice of the date on which

---

[201]   MPL etc Regulations 1999, reg 4, as amended by the MPL (Amendment) Regulations 2002.

[202]   To be precise, notification must be 'no later than the *end* of the 15th week before the EWC': reg 4(1)(a), as amended.

[203]   Or, where this is not reasonably practicable, as soon as is reasonably practicable. Cf *Nu-Swift International Ltd v Mallinson* [1979] ICR 157, [1978] IRLR 537, decided under the old provisions, where it was suggested that a woman may only be allowed to use this exception if she did not know of the time limit and was not put on inquiry about it.

[204]   MPL etc Regulations 1999, reg 4(4), as amended by the MPL (Amendment) Regulations 2002.

[205]   MPL etc Regulations 1999, reg 4(1A).   [206]   MPL etc Regulations 1999, reg 4(2).

[207]   MPL etc Regulations 1999, reg 4(1)(b). There is no longer a requirement for an employee wishing to take additional maternity leave to inform the employer at this stage that she intends to exercise that right.

[208]   MPL etc Regulations 1999, reg 7(6). The notification must normally be given within 28 days of receiving the employee's notification: reg 7(7).

[209]   See heading 3(ii), pp 258 and 261.

she intends to return.[210] If she attempts to return without giving the correct period of notice, the employer is entitled to postpone her return until eight weeks have elapsed (although not to a date after the end of the maternity leave period),[211] although the employer will be unable to prevent her from returning early if he has failed to notify her of the date on which her maternity leave period will end.[212]

The removal of the need to give notice of intention to return to work after maternity leave has helped to reduce the risk of employees losing their rights through failure to comply with technical notice requirements. That this was a very real danger under the old provisions was graphically demonstrated in *Nu-Swift International Ltd v Mallinson*[213] where the employee failed to give notice of her intention to return to work at the correct time because she could not make up her mind whether she wished to return to work or not. The EAT held that it had been reasonably practicable for her to give notice in time and therefore she had lost her right to return. Perhaps Mrs Mallinson was being too conscientious, for under the old provisions the employer had no recourse against an employee who gave notice saying that she intended to return to work but then changed her mind, or who gave notice while still undecided because she wanted to keep her options open. Indeed, pregnant employees were invariably advised to give notice that they intended to return to work, just as a matter of precaution. The removal of the need to give notice reflects the fact that, in practice, the giving and receiving of notice was an empty gesture which served only to trap the unwary or (as in Mrs Mallinson's case) the indecisive.

If an employee is unable to attend work at the end of maternity leave due to sickness, the normal sickness absence procedures under her contract of employment will apply. If the employer decides to dismiss her because of her inability to return to work, the employee will be able to claim that the dismissal was unfair on general principles and, if the employer responds more harshly to her sickness absence than he would to other employees in comparable circumstances, that could amount to sex discrimination.

(iv) ISSUES AROUND RETURNING TO WORK

When the distinction between additional and ordinary leave subsisted, a number of difficulties arose in relation to the return from additional leave. The right to return to the same job after additional leave did not necessarily mean that a woman was entitled to go back into exactly the same job as before. The definition of 'job' for these purposes was 'the nature of the work which she is employed to do in accordance with

---

[210] MPL etc Regulations 1999, reg 11(1). The employee may vary this notified date by giving further notice of at least eight weeks: reg 11(2A).

[211] MPL etc Regulations 1999, reg 11(2), (3), as amended by the MPL (Amendment) Regulations 2002. If the employer has postponed the employee's return, the employer is under no obligation to pay her if she still insists on returning before that date: reg 11(4).

[212] MPL etc Regulations 1999.   [213] [1979] ICR 157, [1978] IRLR 537.

her contract and the capacity and place in which she is so employed',[214] which clearly implied that the employee did not have a right to return to exactly the same post doing exactly the same work in the same department or under the same person.

An employee who was not permitted to return to her old job at the end of additional maternity leave would normally be regarded as unfairly dismissed. However, the right to return was not absolute, for there were three situations in which the employee would not be entitled to return to her old job. The first was where there was some reason (other than redundancy) which made it not reasonably practicable for the employer to permit her to return to her original job. In such a case, her entitlement was to return to another job which was both suitable for her and appropriate for her to do in the circumstances,[215] and on terms and conditions no less favourable to her than if she had continued to be employed in her old job. Secondly, as with ordinary maternity leave, special provision was made for redundancy during additional maternity leave, in that where a redundancy situation arose during the employee's additional maternity leave which made it impracticable for the employer to continue to employ her under her original contract of employment, the employee was entitled to be offered alternative employment with her employer (or with a successor, or an associated employer) where there was a suitable available vacancy.[216] Failure to offer such a vacancy would make the redundancy dismissal automatically unfair.[217] Thirdly, it was not unlawful for an employer to dismiss an employee during or after the end of maternity leave for a reason other than the fact that she had taken or availed herself of the benefits of maternity leave (or any of the other family reasons for which a dismissal would be automatically unfair),[218] unless of course the dismissal was unfair for some other reason.

One of the most significant changes to the provisions on additional maternity leave in the Employment Relations Act 1999 was that it was made clear that the contract of employment continued throughout additional maternity leave. Under the old provisions, the right to return to work after maternity leave operated independently of the contract of employment. In most cases, it did not matter whether the employee's contract continued to exist during maternity absence: the statute gave her a right to return to work, irrespective of the status of her contract during maternity absence, provided she complied with the complex statutory notice requirements. If she was denied her right to return to work, whether by a total refusal to take her back or by being taken back on disadvantageous terms, she was *deemed* to have been dismissed on the 'notified date of return' (ie the date on which she intended to return to work). The provisions worked tolerably well where the employee complied to the letter with all the notice requirements, and was physically able to return to work on the notified date, but serious difficulties arose for the employee if she was not able to satisfy those requirements, in that she lost her statutory right to return (a problem exacerbated by the lack of any

---

[214] MPL etc Regulations 1999, reg 2.
[215] MPL etc Regulations 1999, reg 18(2).
[216] MPL etc Regulations 1999, reg 10.
[217] MPL etc Regulations 1999, reg 20(1)(b).
[218] See this chapter, heading 3(ii), p 258.

saving provision whereby minor or technical defaults could be overlooked). The problems were graphically illustrated by *Lavery v Plessey Telecommunications Ltd*[219] where
the giving of five days' notice of intention to return (instead of the seven days then
required) robbed the employee of her right to return, even though if she had understood the requirement she could in fact have given the required seven days' notice easily.
The case contains strong criticism of the statutory provisions at that time, which were
described as being 'of inordinate complexity exceeding the worst excesses of a taxing
statute'.[220] Happily, these types of problem should no longer arise, as the employee's contract continues throughout maternity leave and return should happen automatically (to
the extent that it is now technically incorrect legally to refer to a 'right to return' at all).

Four further general points should be noted. The first point is that an employer
(particularly in a small business) may need to take on a replacement to take the place of
an employee on maternity leave. Such an employer is given qualified protection by section 106 which provides that if the employer informs the replacement in writing at the
time of engagement that his or her employment will cease when the original employee
returns to work, and then dismisses him or her in order to take that original employee
back, that will constitute half a defence to an allegation of unfair dismissal in that it is
deemed to be a substantial reason capable of justifying dismissal (within section 98),
but the tribunal must still proceed to consider whether he acted reasonably in all the
circumstances in actually dismissing the replacement, which may be difficult if there
was a vacancy available elsewhere that the replacement might readily have filled. This
provision was less important while the qualifying period for unfair dismissal was two
years, as it was unlikely that a replacement would work for long enough to qualify to
bring an unfair dismissal claim, but now that the qualifying period has been reduced
to one year, and the combined ordinary and additional maternity leave period has been
increased to one year, it assumes a much greater practical significance.

The second general point is that one major perceived deficiency of the statutory
scheme is that it does not give a woman the right to return to work on *different* terms
and conditions (eg on a part-time basis or with flexible working hours), yet for many
women this may be the only way of reconciling the competing demands of work and
family responsibilities, especially in view of the limited availability of affordable childcare in certain areas. However, the Employment Act 2002 has given a woman returning
to work after maternity leave the right to request flexible working,[221] and it is possible
that the return-to-work provisions could be outflanked by the argument that a refusal
to allow a woman previously in full-time employment to return to work part time is
indirect sex discrimination. This is what happened in *Home Office v Holmes*[222] where
the woman used the return-to-work provisions to return full time, but also claimed
that the requirement to continue working full time constituted unjustifiable indirect

---

[219] [1983] ICR 534, [1983] IRLR 202, CA.
[220] Per Browne-Wilkinson J [1982] IRLR 180 at 182, EAT. His remarks were endorsed by the Court of
Appeal, [1983] ICR 534, [1983] IRLR 202, CA.
[221] See this chapter, heading xii, p 290.   [222] [1984] ICR 678, [1984] IRLR 299.

sex discrimination (in that compliance with it was particularly difficult for women with children). This argument succeeded in the case, which was widely reported in the press and said by the EOC to be a significant development. However, it does not stretch the imagination to suppose that there could be many circumstances in which a requirement to work full time might be held to be justifiable[223] in economic terms, and the EAT's decision was based very much upon the facts of the particular case,[224] as can be seen from the subsequent case of *Greater Glasgow Health Board v Carey*,[225] where on similar facts it was held that the employer's refusal to allow a full-time health visitor to return on a part-time basis was indirectly discriminatory but was justified by the need for continuity of care by the same visitor. However, the more recent case of *Hardy & Hansons plc v Lax*[226] resulted in an important victory for an employee refused a move to part-time working on her turn (ie following the *Holmes* line); the Court of Appeal held generally that justification has to be judged directly by the tribunal itself (*not* by applying a variant of the 'range of reasonable responses' test in unfair dismissal), which was particularly important here because the tribunal clearly did not believe a word of the employer's evidence as to why they had refused her request. The case suggests that unlawful discrimination in these cases may now be the 'default setting' and that the onus on the employer to prove justification will be a significant one.[227]

The third general point is that in certain sectors (particularly local government, banks, computer companies, the retail sector and oil companies) there have been significant moves towards allowing women employees to take far more substantial 'career breaks' in order to have a family—breaks of anything up to seven years are mentioned, and with the possibility of attending several days' training per year during the break in order to maintain contact with colleagues and keep up with changes. For present purposes the main point to notice is that any such scheme can come about only by agreement and as a matter of contract; such breaks are not provided for in the statutory maternity leave scheme. Employers' schemes which improve upon the statutory entitlement can have a sting in the tail, however, particularly where they involve a lengthy career break, because the effect of the career break may be to break her continuity of employment, with potential disastrous consequences for her employment rights.

---

[223] See Ch 5, heading 2(iii)(b), p 320.

[224] It is important these days not to be too sanguine about cases as precedents; at its most basic, all that the EAT were doing was to say that in this case the tribunal were not manifestly wrong in holding that the requirement to work full time was (1) discriminatory and (2) unjustifiable on the facts before them.

[225] [1987] IRLR 484. In coming to this conclusion, the EAT applied the obiter remarks in *Rainey v Greater Glasgow Health Board Eastern District* [1987] ICR 129, [1987] IRLR 26, HL that administrative efficiency, if sufficiently demonstrated, may be an important factor in the justification defence under the Sex Discrimination Act 1975, s 1(1)(b)(ii).

[226] [2005] EWCA Civ 846, [2005] IRLR 726, CA; the case is of general importance in the area of indirect discrimination and the justification defence.

[227] But see Baker 'Proportionality and Employment Discrimination in the UK' (2008) 37 ILJ 305, for a general discussion of how the tribunals have had a disappointing record with justification in discrimination cases.

This issue arose for consideration in *Curr v Marks & Spencer plc*[228] where the employee was accepted onto a four-year child break scheme, a condition of which was that she resigned from the company. At the end of the break she returned to work, but was subsequently made redundant. She claimed a redundancy payment covering all her years of service, both before and after the career break, but the employers argued that she was only entitled to count the period since her return from the child break. The Court of Appeal held that the terms of the career break did not constitute a contract of employment, so that her continuity was not preserved on the basis that her contract continued throughout, but neither could she claim that continuity was preserved under section 212(3)(c) of the Employment Rights Act 1996[229] because the employer did not regard her as continuing in employment during the child break (an odd conclusion, it must be said, given that the employee maintained contact with the employer during the break, including returning to work for two weeks each year, but reached on the basis that the terms of the career break agreement were quite unlike a contract of employment). The upshot was that Mrs Curr paid a heavy financial penalty for her career break, and the lesson for an employee is to be very cautious about the effect of a career break on her contract of employment, and on her continuity of employment.

Finally, there was for some time a concern that the modern practice of providing 'keep in touch' days for the employee on maternity leave might inadvertently end the leave because they could be seen as constituting 'work' for the employer. The answer in the Work and Families Act 2006 was to introduce a provision stating that 'an employee may carry out up to ten days' work for her employer during her statutory maternity leave period without bringing her maternity leave to an end'.[230] It is clear that there is no *obligation* to attend such days; any question of payment remains a contractual matter.

(v) STATUTORY MATERNITY PAY

A pregnant employee who meets certain qualifying conditions based on her length of service and average earnings is entitled to receive Statutory Maternity Pay (SMP) from her employer for up to 39 weeks, the first six weeks at nine-tenths of the employee's normal pay, and the remaining weeks at a flat rate (currently £135.45 per week). The employer, in turn, is entitled to recover most of the amount paid out as SMP from the state, by deducting it from PAYE and National Insurance contributions. In effect, therefore, SMP can be seen as a state maternity benefit which is administered via

---

[228] [2003] ICR 443, [2003] IRLR 74, CA.

[229] Ie that there was an 'arrangement' by which she was absent from work in circumstances such that she was regarded as continuing in employment: see Ch 2, heading 5(ii), p 108.

[230] MPL etc Regulations 1999, reg 12A. This also states that reasonable contact by the employer from time to time (eg to discuss the employee's return to work) does not terminate the leave either.

employers. To understand how this convoluted state of affairs has come about, it is necessary to delve a little into the history of the current provisions.

Until 1987 a pregnant employee leaving work to have a baby would normally qualify for the state maternity allowance, but on top of that she could qualify (if she had at least two years' service) for maternity pay from her employer; this latter was payable for the first six weeks of absence, at nine-tenths of her week's pay (less the amount of the maternity allowance and any remuneration paid by the employer under a contractual maternity scheme), and was payable whether or not the employee wished to return to work after her maternity absence, ie it was not dependent upon continuation in some form of the employment relationship. From the point of view of drafting this position was neat since the principal conditions for entitlement were the same as for maternity leave, so that the two major rights went hand in hand. However, the system was viewed as wasteful by the government since it involved duplication of administrative effort by the State and the employer, and as the whole amount paid out as maternity pay could be recouped from the state-run Maternity Pay Fund, the employer was in reality simply performing a social security role.

The whole system was reformed in 1987 in order to require the employer to make all the payments, by the introduction of SMP, payable at two levels depending on length of service, but with the employer able to recover the amount paid out by deducting it from National Insurance contributions; the obvious model was statutory sick pay,[231] introduced by the government four years earlier for the same reasons of rationalization and administrative ease (for the government, that is, not for employers). The structure of the SMP scheme was very different from what had gone before, but the end result as far as most employees were concerned was very similar to the pre-1987 position, in that SMP was payable for up to 18 weeks at a lower rate (in effect replacing the state maternity allowance), but an employee with two years' continuous service was entitled to SMP at a higher rate of nine-tenths of her normal weekly earnings for the first six weeks (corresponding to the old maternity pay scheme).

The SMP scheme was subject to major reforms in 1994 to bring it into line with the requirements of EC Directive 92/85 (the Pregnant Workers Directive), which provides for a minimum entitlement of 14 weeks' paid maternity leave for all pregnant employees,[232] during which a woman is entitled to be paid an amount equivalent to the amount of state benefit she would receive if she were absent from work due to sickness. The Directive was implemented in the UK by equalizing lower rate SMP with statutory sick pay, and granting all those entitled to SMP the right to receive it at the higher rate for the first six weeks. To meet the additional cost to the state of this enhanced entitlement, the amount of SMP which employers were able to recover was

---

[231] See Ch 3, heading 5(ii), p 193.
[232] The Directive permits entitlement to pay during the maternity leave period to be made conditional on periods of previous employment of up to 12 months before the expected date of childbirth.

reduced to 92%,[233] albeit with special help for small employers,[234] who are still able to recover the full amount.[235] When the ordinary maternity leave period was increased from 18 to 26 weeks in 2003, the length of the SMP entitlement was similarly increased to bring it into line, and the notice requirements and qualifying periods for maternity leave and SMP were harmonized. The Work and Families Act 2006 raised the maximum SMP entitlement from 26 to 39 weeks (from April 2007) and contains powers to raise it to a year eventually. The SMP provisions are currently to be found in Part XII of the Social Security Contributions and Benefits Act 1992, and the flesh is added to the bones by several sets of Regulations.[236]

(a) Qualification[237]

To qualify at all, the employee must satisfy a number of complex conditions: (1) her earnings must have been at or above the lower earnings limit for the payment of National Insurance contributions;[238] (2) she must have been employed by that employer[239] for a continuous period of at least 26 weeks ending with the week immediately preceding the 14th week before the expected week of childbirth; (3) she must give the employer medical evidence of the expected week of childbirth,[240] and at least 28 days' notice of the date on which she expects his liability to pay SMP to begin (ie the date on which she expects to start her ordinary maternity leave); (4) she must have reached the 11th week before the expected week of childbirth, or have recently given birth (although she does not need to remain in employment beyond the qualifying week); and (5) she must have stopped work.

(b) The right to payment

If she can satisfy these conditions, the employee qualifies for SMP at the higher, earnings-related rate for six weeks, and thereafter at the lower rate for the remainder of the maternity pay period, subject to an overall maximum of 39 weeks. Once entitlement to SMP is established in the qualifying week, the employee is entitled to receive

---

[233] Statutory Maternity Pay (Compensation of Employers) and Miscellaneous Amendment Regulations 1994, SI 1994/1882, amended by SI 2003/672.

[234] Ie those whose National Insurance liability does not exceed £45,000 for the qualifying tax year. Some small employers may now be able to claim funding in advance.

[235] Small employers are also entitled to recover an additional 4.5% of the SMP paid, to compensate for other costs: SI 2002/225 (amending SI 1994/1882).

[236] Principally the Statutory Maternity Pay (General) Regulations 1986, SI 1986/1960, as amended. Practical guidance is given in some detail (with worked examples) in the Employer's Guide to Statutory Maternity Pay (NI 257, DSS).

[237] Social Security Contributions and Benefits Act 1992, s 164.

[238] The EAT has held that the application of the lower earnings limit as a qualifying condition for SMP is not contrary to Art 141 (ex Art 119) of the EC Treaty or the Pregnant Workers Directive: *Banks v Tesco Stores Ltd* [1999] ICR 1141, EAT.

[239] A woman may not count her previous employment with another employer for these purposes; in this respect the system differs from that applying to statutory sick pay.

[240] This should be given not more than 20 weeks before the expected week of childbirth. The employer cannot start paying SMP until the certificate has been received.

her full entitlement to 39 weeks' SMP, even if she leaves the employer's employment before her SMP was due to start. Alternatively, she may continue working right up to the date of childbirth, and still retain her full entitlement to 39 weeks' SMP. The lower rate of SMP is fixed by regulations (at the time of writing, it stands at £135.45pw).[241] The higher rate of SMP is set at nine-tenths of her week's pay (averaged, if necessary, over the eight weeks prior to the 14th week before the expected week of childbirth).[242] Payments of SMP must be offset against any contractual payments for the weeks in question (for example under a contractual maternity scheme) and vice versa. Under the pre-1994 provisions, an employee lost a week of her SMP entitlement for each week that she continued to work beyond the sixth week before the expected week of childbirth, but this rule no longer applies, and the maternity pay period will normally begin when the ordinary maternity leave period starts, and run contemporaneously with it and then half of the additional maternity leave period, for a total of 39 weeks. However, to ensure consistency with the maternity leave provisions, the maternity pay period is automatically triggered where a woman is absent from work wholly or partly because of pregnancy or childbirth after the fourth week before. The SMP period usually lasts for the full 39 weeks, but it is not payable for any week in which the employee does any work for her employer, and if she starts work for a new employer after childbirth, the entitlement to SMP stops completely. To avoid this being triggered by the modern device of 'keep in touch' days for the maternity absentee, the Regulations now contain a provision[243] allowing her to work for the employer for up to 10 days without her SMP entitlement being affected.

An employee who does not qualify for SMP may be entitled to claim the state Maternity Allowance from the Benefits Agency.

(vi) RISK ASSESSMENT AND SUSPENSION FROM WORK ON MATERNITY GROUNDS

All employers have a duty under the Management of Health and Safety at Work (MHSW) Regulations 1999 to assess the risks to health and safety to which their employees are exposed whilst they are at work.[244] In addition, as a result of an amendment to the MHSW Regulations in 1994 (implementing the Pregnant Workers Directive)[245] employers of women of child-bearing age have a specific duty to carry out a further

---

[241] Statutory Maternity Pay (General) Regulations 1986, SI 1986/1960, reg 6. If her earnings related rate is *less* than the prescribed weekly rate, she will receive the lower of the two rates for the remaining weeks.

[242] Social Security Contributions and Benefits Act 1992, s 166, as substituted by the Employment Act 2002, s 19. If the employer subsequently grants a pay rise that covers any part of the maternity leave, it must be taken into account in calculating SMP for the whole period: Statutory Maternity Pay (General) Regulations 1986, reg 2(7), substituted in 2005 to reflect successful challenges to the previous law in *Gillespie v Northern Health Board* C-342/93 [1996] ICR 398, [1996] IRLR 214, ECJ and *Alabaster v Woolwich plc* C-147/02 [2004] IRLR 486, ECJ.

[243] Regulation 9A, added from April 2007.   [244] SI 1999/3242, reg 3.

[245] Directive 92/85/EC.

risk assessment where the work is of a kind which could involve a risk to the health and safety of a new or expectant mother,[246] or to that of her baby, from any processes or working conditions, or from physical, biological or chemical agents.[247] Where that risk assessment identifies a risk to the health and safety of a new or expectant mother or her baby, the employer is under a duty in the first instance to take action to prevent her from being exposed to the risk by following the requirements of any relevant health and safety regulations (for example by removing the hazard or by providing protective clothing). If the risk cannot be avoided by such means, and it is not reasonable for the employer to alter the employee's working conditions or hours of work, or such an alteration would not avoid the risk, the employer must remove the employee from the risk by suspending her from work for as long as is necessary to avoid the risk.[248] An employer must also suspend an employee from work on maternity grounds where the employee is a new or expectant mother who works at night, and she has a certificate from a registered medical practitioner or registered midwife which shows that it is necessary for her health and safety that she should not be at work for any period of night work identified in the certificate.[249]

Under the MHSW Regulations, the duty to take action by altering working conditions or hours of work, or by suspending an employee from work, does not arise until the employee has notified the employer in writing that she is pregnant, has given birth within the preceding six months or is breastfeeding,[250] although even in the absence of written notification of pregnancy, an employer who fails to take reasonable action to protect an employee who is known to be pregnant or breastfeeding might well be in breach of the general duty to protect the health and safety of his employees. The duty to conduct a pregnancy risk assessment in the first place is triggered whenever the employer employs a woman of child-bearing age, and does not depend upon there being an employee who is pregnant.[251]

The employer's duty under the MHSW Regulations is mirrored by a series of rights enjoyed by employees suspended from work on maternity grounds.[252] These rights

---

[246] Defined as employees who are pregnant, have given birth within the preceding six months or are breastfeeding.

[247] MHSW Regulations, reg 16(1). These are said to include the list of agents set out in Annexes I and II of the Pregnant Workers Directive.

[248] MHSW Regulations, reg 16(2), (3). As this constitutes a form of legitimate discrimination, there is a delicate balance to be struck and the employer should not proceed to a suspension too readily: *New Southern Railways Ltd v Quinn* [2006] IRLR 266, EAT.

[249] MHSW Regulations, reg 17.

[250] MHSW Regulations, reg 18. If the employee has given the employer a medical certificate which arguably indicates that she is pregnant, but without expressly stating that fact, the burden may pass to the employer to show that there was no notification: *Day v T Pickles Farms Ltd* [1999] IRLR 217, EAT.

[251] *Day v T Pickles Farms Ltd* n 250. That case also established that an employer's failure to carry out such a risk assessment may amount to sex discrimination if a new or expectant mother can show that she has suffered a detriment. See also *Hardman v Mallon t/a Orchard Lodge Nursing Home* [2002] IRLR 516, EAT.

[252] See the Employment Rights Act 1996, ss 66–68. Suspension must be in consequence of a 'relevant requirement' or a recommendation in a code of practice issued or approved by the Health and Safety

were introduced by the Trade Union Reform and Employment Rights Act 1993, implementing the Pregnant Workers Directive.[253] First, before being suspended from work on maternity grounds, an employee has the right to be offered suitable alternative employment by her employer where there is an available vacancy,[254] with a right to complain to a tribunal if the employer fails to make such an offer.[255] The work must be suitable in relation to the employee, appropriate for her to do in the circumstances, and on terms and conditions which are not substantially less favourable than those under which she normally works.[256] Secondly, an employee who is suspended from work on maternity grounds has the right to be paid her normal remuneration by her employer during the period of suspension, unless she has unreasonably refused an offer of suitable alternative work for the period in question, in which case no remuneration is payable for the period during which the offer applies;[257] once again, there is a right of complaint to a tribunal that the employer has failed to pay the amount due,[258] and where the tribunal finds the complaint well-founded it will order the employer to pay the unpaid remuneration to the employee.

(vii) TIME OFF FOR ANTENATAL CARE

A pregnant employee has a right not to be unreasonably refused time off during working hours to attend antenatal care on the advice of a registered medical practitioner, registered midwife or registered health visitor,[259] irrespective of her length of service. After the first visit, the employer may require the employee to produce a certificate from the doctor, midwife or health visitor confirming that she is pregnant, and an appointment card or other document showing that an appointment has been made,[260] but for obvious reasons this is not necessary for the first visit. Antenatal care is not defined in the Act, but it can include relaxation and parentcraft classes, as well as medical examinations, provided of course that the attendance is on the advice of a doctor, midwife or health visitor. The right to time off is not absolute: the Act states that an employee has the right not to be *unreasonably* refused time off, which implies

---

Commission under s 16 of the Health and Safety at Work etc Act 1974: s 66(1). The Suspension from Work (on Maternity Grounds) Order, SI 1994/2930, specifies reg 17 of the MHSW Regulations as a relevant requirement for these purposes. See also the Suspension from Work on Maternity Grounds (Merchant Shipping and Fishing Vessels) Order, SI 1998/587.

[253] Directive 92/85/EC.   [254] Employment Rights Act 1996, s 67(1).

[255] Employment Rights Act 1996, s 70(4). The right of complaint is subject to the usual three-month time limit, calculated from the first day of suspension: s 70(5); where the tribunal upholds the complaint it may make an award of compensation: s 70(6).

[256] See *British Airways (European Operations at Gatwick) Ltd v Moore and Botterill* [2000] ICR 678, [2000] IRLR 296, EAT, where an offer of ground work to two pregnant cabin crew workers failed the test because it did not include the flying allowances which they received while working as cabin crew.

[257] Employment Rights Act 1996, s 68.

[258] The time limit here is three months (or a further reasonable period where not reasonably practicable) from the day in respect of which the remuneration was not paid: Employment Rights Act 1996, s 70(2).

[259] Employment Rights Act 1996, s 55.   [260] Employment Rights Act 1996, s 55(2).

that there may be circumstances where it would be reasonable for the employer to refuse time off; for example it might be reasonable for an employer to refuse time off to a part-time worker who could reasonably be expected to arrange her ante-natal care outside her working hours.

The employee is entitled to be paid at her normal rate of pay during the period of time off.[261] Complaint of unreasonable refusal to give time off, or of failure to pay wages during time off may be made to a tribunal within three months of the day of the appointment concerned (or within a further reasonable period if the tribunal accepts that it was not reasonably practicable for the complaint to be presented within the three-month period).[262]

(viii) PATERNITY LEAVE AND PAY

While entitlement to maternity leave is now well established, until fairly recently there was no entitlement for fathers to take paternity leave in order to care for the child or support the child's mother in the weeks after childbirth. In the absence of any contractual entitlement to paternity leave, the only option for fathers who wanted some time at home following the birth of a child was to use whatever holiday entitlement they had, or to take parental leave, which is unpaid. The introduction of a right to paid paternity leave was one of a range of possible reforms floated in the New Labour government's review of working arrangements for parents,[263] and it received a very positive response; the new right was duly introduced by the Employment Act 2002. The entitlements were modest—only two weeks' paid leave, to be taken within eight weeks of childbirth, and only at the same flat rate as lower-rate statutory maternity pay (at the time of writing, £135.45pw)—but the provisions were nevertheless significant, as they were the first legal recognition of the fact that fathers have responsibilities around the time of childbirth that are capable of overriding the needs of employers. Paternity leave was also made available to employees following the adoption of a child, although here the adoptive parents may be able to choose which parent takes paternity leave and which takes adoption leave.

That government subsequently introduced, in the Work and Families Act 2006, sections 3–10, provisions allowing for the establishment of new systems of 'additional paternity leave' and 'additional statutory paternity pay'. This power was finally exercised by the next (Coalition) government in 2010, making it so that an employed father, or partner of a mother or adopter, would be able to be absent from work for a maximum of 26 weeks (in addition to the existing paternity leave) to care for a child; this leave can start any time after the 20th week after birth, and must be taken before the child's

---

[261] Employment Rights Act 1996, s 56. See *Gregory v Tudsbury Ltd* [1982] IRLR 267, IT. The amount of pay will usually be calculated by dividing her week's pay by the number of normal working hours in a week.

[262] Employment Rights Act 1996, s 57. Dismissal or redundancy selection for taking time off for antenatal care is likely to be automatically unfair under s 99: see heading 3(ii), p 258.

[263] *Work and Parents: Competitiveness and Choice* (DTI, December 2000).

first birthday.[264] In itself, it is unpaid *but* the novelty of the scheme is that the new Additional Statutory Paternity Pay (ASPP) allows the father or partner to take over any unclaimed SMP from the mother if she has returned to work early.[265] The result is that fathers—or the partners of a mother, or male adopters—may take two weeks of leave as of right within eight weeks of childbirth at the statutory rate of pay, and may also have up to 26 weeks of the mother's leave transferred to them once the child reaches twenty weeks of age, so long as the period thus transferred does not extend beyond the first year of the child's life; they may also receive the statutory rate of pay during that leave for the number of weeks, of her 39-week entitlement, the mother has not used before returning early to work.

(a) Qualification and notice requirements

In order to qualify for paternity leave in relation to the birth of a child, an employee must: (1) have been continuously employed for at least 26 weeks at the 15th week before the expected week of childbirth;[266] (2) be either the child's biological father or the mother's husband, partner or civil partner; and (3) have, or expect to have, responsibility for the child's upbringing.[267] The notice requirements are similar to those applying to maternity leave: the employee must inform his employer (in writing, if the employer so requests) of his intention to take paternity leave by the 15th week before the expected week of childbirth, unless this is not reasonably practicable, and must tell the employer (1) the expected week of the child's birth; (2) the amount of leave which the employee wishes to take (see below); and (3) the date on which he wants his leave to start.[268] After the child is born, he must notify the employer, as soon as reasonably practicable, of the date of childbirth.[269] An employer who wants some evidence of the employee's entitlement to paternity leave is entitled to ask for a signed declaration from the employee (in effect, a self-certificate) that the leave is for the purpose of caring for a child or supporting its mother, and that he meets the eligibility criteria,[270] but the employer is not entitled to ask for any further evidence of entitlement.

There are parallel provisions for paternity leave in relation to adoption, in which case the employee must: (1) have been continuously employed for at least 26 weeks

---

[264] Additional Paternity Leave Regulations 2010, SI 2010/1055 (APL Regulations), reg 5.

[265] Additional Statutory Paternity Pay (General) Regulations 2010, SI 2010/1056, reg 7.

[266] Special provision is made for cases where the child is born prematurely before the 14th week before the expected week of childbirth: Paternity and Adoption Leave Regulations 2002, SI 2002/2788 (PAL Regulations), reg 4(3) (there are parallel provisions in the Additional Paternity Leave (General) Regulations 2010 as well as those on pay).

[267] PAL Regulations, reg 4(2). An employee who is the mother's husband, partner or civil partner but not the child's father must have 'the main responsibility (apart from any responsibility of the mother) for the upbringing of the child'.

[268] PAL Regulations, reg 6. The employee can vary the chosen start-date by giving the employer notice at least 28 days in advance, unless this is not reasonably practicable: reg 6(4).

[269] PAL Regulations, reg 6(7).   [270] PAL Regulations, reg 6(3).

ending with the week in which notice is given of having been matched with a child;[271] (2) be either married to, the partner of or civil partner of the child's adopter; and (3) have, or expect to have, the main responsibility (apart from the responsibility of the adopter) for the child's upbringing.[272] As with paternity leave at the time of childbirth, the employee must inform the employer that he intends to take paternity leave, in this case no later than seven days after notification of being matched with a child, unless this is not reasonably practicable, and the notice must specify (1) the date of notification of being matched with a child; (2) the date on which the child is expected to be placed with the adopter; (3) the length of the leave period which the employee wishes to take; and (4) the date on which he wants his leave to start.[273] The employer can also require the employee to self-certify that the leave is for the purpose of caring for a child or supporting its adopter, and that he meets the eligibility criteria.[274]

(b) Extent of the entitlement

An employee who satisfies the eligibility criteria and notice requirements set out above can choose to take either one week or two consecutive weeks of 'ordinary' paternity leave. There is no option to take odd days, or even two separate weeks, and unlike parental leave (where there is an entitlement for each child) only one period of paternity leave can be claimed in the event of a multiple pregnancy. The employee can choose to start his leave on the date of the child's birth (whenever that occurs), or on a date which is a chosen number of days or weeks after the child's birth, or on a predetermined date,[275] but the leave must be taken within 56 days of the date of childbirth.[276] Similar rules apply where paternity leave is claimed in connection with adoption, except that the timings run from the date on which the child is placed for adoption.[277] During statutory paternity leave, most employees will be entitled to receive Statutory Paternity Pay (SPP) from their employer, for either one or two weeks, depending on the length of paternity leave chosen.[278] This is fixed at the same rate as standard-rate SMP (at the time of writing, £135.45 pw) or 90% of average weekly earnings if this is less. Any paternity pay received under the employee's contract during paternity leave will be offset against the statutory entitlement, and vice versa.[279] Employees whose average

---

[271] This requires notification to the adopter of a match with a child by an approved adoption agency: PAL Regulations, reg 2(4).

[272] PAL Regulations, reg 8(2).   [273] PAL Regulations, reg 10.

[274] PAL Regulations, reg 10(3).

[275] If the employee chooses a predetermined date and the child has not yet been born at that date, he must choose another date and notify the employer as soon as reasonably practicable: PAL Regulations, reg 6(6).

[276] PAL Regulations, reg 5. If the child is born prematurely, leave can be taken within 56 days of the beginning of the expected week of childbirth. Where the employee has chosen the date on which leave is to begin, the notice to the employer must specify that date, reg 6(1)(c).

[277] PAL Regulations, reg 9.

[278] Social Security Contributions and Benefits Act 1992, s 171ZA, as inserted by the Employment Act 2002. Employers can recover SPP in the same way as they can recover SMP, ie 92% of the amount paid out, or more if eligible for small employer's relief.

[279] Social Security Contributions and Benefits Act 1992, s 171ZG.

weekly earnings are below the Lower Earnings Limit for National Insurance purposes will not qualify for SPP, but may be able to claim Income Support while on paternity leave. As seen above, in the case of adoption the adoptive parents can elect whether to take paternity leave or adoption leave, but for obvious reasons a parent who has elected to receive statutory adoption pay cannot receive SPP. During paternity leave a man is in a similar position as regards contractual entitlements as a woman on maternity leave, in that (unless his contract provides otherwise) he will be entitled to the benefit of all his normal terms and conditions of employment, except for terms relating to wages or salary.[280] The similarity with maternity leave continues after the end of paternity leave, in that an employee returning to work after a period of paternity leave is entitled to return to the job in which he was employed before his absence,[281] with his seniority, pension rights etc as they would have been if he had not been absent, and on terms and conditions no less favourable than those which would have applied if he had not been absent.[282] An employee taking paternity leave is also protected against dismissal or detriment for taking or seeking to take paternity leave.[283]

'Additional' paternity leave carries the same protections (relating to contract terms, return to work, etc) as 'ordinary' paternity leave. It can only be taken (not surprisingly) with the cooperation of the child's mother. She must supply a declaration as to when she is returning to work, stating that the claimant father is the only person taking the remainder of her leave, and expressing her permission for him to do so.[284] The leave must be taken in one continuous block of at least two weeks and no more than 26 weeks,[285] so in practice the mother must have at least two weeks of leave remaining. Additional Statutory Paternity Pay (ASPP) is payable at the statutory rate for the number of full weeks during this period that remain of the mother's original 39-week allowance. The numbers can be deceptive so make no mistake about this: there are few circumstances in which this can ever mean that a father actually receives 26 weeks of leave with ASPP. Often a mother will commence maternity leave one or two weeks before birth and will receive SMP from that time, so typically at least 21 or 22 weeks of the 39 will have been used before a father will be allowed to receive APL. There is nothing wrong with this, but in practice the new regulations will seldom afford fathers more than 17 weeks of paid (at the statutory rate) leave, and this only if the mother agrees to relinquish it.

(ix) ADOPTION LEAVE AND PAY

The introduction of adoption leave was another of the reforms introduced by the Employment Act 2002 after the idea received strong support in the review of maternity

---

[280] PAL Regulations, reg 12.
[281] PAL Regulations, reg 13. As with ordinary maternity leave, the position may be different if the paternity leave is not an isolated period of leave, but follows another period of statutory leave.
[282] PAL Regulations, reg 14.   [283] PAL Regulations, regs 28, 29.
[284] APL Regulations reg 6.   [285] APL Regulations reg 5.

rights.[286] The entitlements mirror those of a woman to maternity leave, ie 52 weeks' of combined (and now identical) ordinary adoption leave and additional adoption leave, and 39 weeks' pay, for an adoptive parent when a child is newly placed for adoption.[287] Partners of adopters, or adopters who were not identified as the initial recipient of adoption leave and pay, have the same entitlements to APL and ASPP as fathers and male partners with regard to Maternity Pay.[288] There are, however, some significant differences, particularly in relation to qualification and entitlement to pay during adoption leave. The leave can be taken by an individual person who adopts, or by one member of a couple who adopt jointly. In the latter case the couple may elect which partner takes adoption leave;[289] the other partner may be eligible for paternity leave. To be eligible for adoption leave, an employee must be the child's adopter (ie he or she must have been matched with a child for adoption by an approved adoption agency), and must have been continuously employed by the employer for at least 26 weeks ending with the week in which the employee receives notification of having been matched with a child.[290] The 26-week qualifying period applies both to ordinary and additional adoption leave (which are hereinafter referred to collectively as 'adoption leave'). The adopter can choose to start adoption leave from the date of the child's placement, or from a predetermined date up to 14 days in advance of the expected date of placement.[291] As in the case of maternity leave, the adopter must notify the employer that he or she intends to take adoption leave, and the requirement is a tight one—notice must be given within seven days of being notified by the adoption agency that they have been matched with a child, although this limit can be extended if it was not reasonably practicable for the employee to comply. The notice must specify the date when the child is expected to be placed with the adopter, and when the adopter wishes the adoption leave to start.[292] The employer can also ask for evidence of the employee's entitlement to adoption leave, in the form of a 'matching certificate' issued by the adoption agency,[293] but the employee will need to provide this in any event in order to claim Statutory Adoption Pay. Once the employer has received notification of the intended start-date, the employer must respond within 28 days by writing to the employee setting out the date on which the adoption leave will end (assuming that the

---

[286] DTI *Work and Parents: Competitiveness and Choice* (December 2000).

[287] PAL Regulations, regs 18(1), 20(2). If the placement ends prematurely during the adoption leave period, the entitlement to leave normally continues for another eight weeks after the end of the placement: reg 22.

[288] Additional Paternity Leave (Adoption) Regulations 2010; Additional Statutory Paternity Pay (Adoption) Regulations 2010

[289] PAL Regulations, reg 2(1), (4).

[290] PAL Regulations, reg 15. The employee must also have notified the adoption agency that he agrees to the placement of the child, and the timing of the placement.

[291] PAL Regulations, reg 16.

[292] PAL Regulations, reg 17(1), (2). This date can be varied on giving 28 days' notice, unless not reasonably practicable to do so.

[293] PAL Regulations, reg 17(3). The certificate must contain certain specified information about the agency, the date of notification of being matched with a child and the expected date of placement.

employee takes advantage of the full entitlement).[294] If the employer fails to do so, the employee will be protected against detriment or dismissal if he or she fails to return to work on the due date.

During adoption leave, employees are entitled to the benefit of all their normal terms and conditions of employment, with the exception of terms relating to wages or salary, just as in the case of maternity leave.[295] The adopter will also be entitled to receive Statutory Adoption Pay (SAP) from the employer for 39 weeks at the same rate as standard SMP (at the time of writing, £135.45), or 90% of average weekly earnings if less than that amount—unless the adopter's average weekly earnings are below the Lower Earnings Limit for National Insurance purposes. Unlike SMP, however, in this context there is no higher, earnings-related rate for the first six weeks. Employers are entitled to recover the amount of SAP paid out in the same way and to the same extent as they can recover SMP (ie 92%, or in the case of small employers, 100% plus an additional amount to cover extra National Insurance contributions). The usual rules requiring contractual payments during leave to be offset against entitlement to SAP apply. The employee does not have to notify the employer before returning to work, unless he or she wishes to return early, in which case eight weeks' notice of their intended date of return must be given.[296] Returnees from adoption leave are in a similar position to those returning to work after maternity leave. Adoptive parents are entitled to return to the job in which they were employed before their absence, with their seniority, pension rights etc as they would have been if they had not been absent, and on terms and conditions no less favourable than those which would have applied if they had not been absent.[297] Finally, as with other types of family-related leave, employees taking adoption leave are protected against dismissal or detriment for taking or seeking to take adoption leave.[298]

(x) PARENTAL LEAVE

As seen in the introduction to this chapter, the Employment Relations Act 1999 introduced a new right to parental leave for male and female employees, implementing the Parental Leave Directive.[299] The detailed provisions on parental leave are contained in the MPL etc Regulations 1999,[300] which set out who has a right to parental leave, and certain key elements which apply to everyone. Employers and employees are free to agree a detailed parental leave scheme, via a collective or workforce agreement, which

---

[294] PAL Regulations, reg 17(7).   [295] PAL Regulations, reg 19.

[296] PAL Regulations, reg 25.

[297] PAL Regulations, regs 26, 27. As with maternity leave, if a redundancy situation arises during adoption leave, the employee is entitled to be offered any suitable available vacancy: PAL Regulations, reg 23; see this chapter, heading 3(ii), p 259.

[298] PAL Regulations, regs 28, 29; see this chapter, heading 3(ii), pp 257, 261.

[299] Directive 96/34/EC. The Directive was extended to the UK by Directive 97/75/EC.

[300] MPL etc Regulations 1999.

will be valid provided it does not contradict any of the key elements in the regulations. The regulations also contain a set of 'default' provisions on parental leave, in the form of a 'model' scheme which will automatically come into operation unless the parties agree on their own scheme.

(a) Entitlement to parental leave

The right to parental leave is available to an employee who has been continuously employed for at least one year, and who has, or expects to have, 'parental responsibility' for a child within the meaning of the Children Act 1989.[301] Such an employee is entitled to at least 13 weeks' parental leave in respect of each child, for the purpose of caring for that child[302] (the Coalition government has announced its intention to raise this to 18 weeks by 2013[303]). If the employee works part time, the entitlement to leave is proportionate to the time for which the employee normally works,[304] and if the leave is taken in shorter periods than the employee's normal working week, the individual periods of leave are aggregated together.[305] Employees have a right not to be dismissed or subjected to any detriment by their employer for taking or seeking to take parental leave.[306]

Controversy arose over the way in which the Parental Leave Directive was originally implemented in the UK, because of the requirement that parental leave had to be taken before the child's fifth birthday[307] (under the Directive the government could have allowed leave to be taken up to the age of eight) and could not be claimed in respect of a child born before 15 December 1999.[308] The latter restriction was challenged by the TUC in judicial review proceedings as being in breach of the requirements of the Directive,[309] and the entitlement to parental leave was duly extended to those with children born before 15 December 1999 by the MPL (Amendment) Regulations 2001.[310] The other major bone of contention is that parental leave is unpaid, unless the employer agrees otherwise. In practice, this means that many employees who might wish to take some parental leave may simply be unable to do so because of the financial consequences.

---

[301] MPL etc Regulations, reg 13.

[302] MPL etc Regulations, reg 14(1). In the case of multiple births, an employee is entitled to 13 weeks' leave for each child. Parents of disabled children are entitled to up to 18 weeks' leave: reg 14(1A).

[303] *Modern Workplaces – Government Response on Flexible Parental Leave* (HM Gov Nov 2012) available at <http://www.bis.gov.uk/assets/biscore/employment-matters/docs/m/12–1269-modern-workplaces-response-flexible-working> (last accessed 6 January 2013).

[304] MPL etc Regulations, reg 14(2).   [305] MPL etc Regulations, reg 14(4).

[306] MPL etc Regulations, regs 19, 20.

[307] In the case of an adopted child, the leave may be taken up to the fifth anniversary of the date on which the child was placed for adoption, or the child's 18th birthday, whichever is the sooner; the parent of a child who is entitled to disability living allowance is allowed to take parental leave up to the date of the child's 18th birthday: reg 15.

[308] An exception was made in the case of a child adopted by the employee, or placed with the employee for adoption, on or after that date.

[309] *R v Secretary of State for Trade and Industry, ex p Trades Union Congress* [2000] IRLR 565.

[310] SI 2001/4010.

During the period of parental leave, the employee remains in employment but, in the absence of an agreement to the contrary, is in the same position as an employee under the old additional maternity leave before it was made identical with ordinary leave: the employee is only entitled to the benefit of the employer's implied obligation of trust and confidence, and any terms and conditions of employment relating to notice of termination by the employer, redundancy compensation, or disciplinary or grievance procedures. During that period the employee is bound by the implied obligation to the employer of good faith, and any terms and conditions of employment relating to notice of termination by the employee, disclosure of confidential information, the acceptance of gifts or other benefits, or the employee's participation in any other business.[311] As in the case of maternity, adoption, or paternity leave, an employee who takes parental leave of four weeks or less is entitled to return to work after parental leave to the job in which he or she was employed before taking leave,[312] with seniority, pension rights etc as they would have been if the employee had not been absent, and on terms and conditions not less favourable than those which would have been applicable to the employee had he or she not been absent.[313] If the period of parental leave is more than four weeks, the employee is entitled to return to the old job or, if that is not reasonably practicable, to another job which is both suitable and appropriate for the employee in the circumstances.[314]

(b) Collective or workforce agreements

In line with the current political emphasis on 'partnership' in the workplace, the MPL etc Regulations allow employers and employees to agree a detailed parental leave scheme via a collective or workforce agreement which is incorporated into the contracts of employment of individual employees.[315] Such a scheme may improve upon the entitlements set out in the regulations (for example by allowing parental leave after a child's fifth birthday), but it may not contradict any of the key elements in the regulations (for example by imposing lower age limits, or a later birth or adoption date). The regulations contain a 'model' scheme which automatically comes into operation if the parties do not agree on their own scheme (see below). A 'workforce agreement' is defined for these purposes in similar terms to those used in the Working Time Regulations.[316] To be valid, a workforce agreement must (1) be in writing; (2) have effect for a specified period not exceeding five years; (3) apply to all the members of the workforce, or all the members of a particular group of workers who share a function, workplace or organizational unit (excluding those whose terms and conditions are provided for, wholly or in part, by a collective agreement); and (4) be signed by all the elected workforce

---

[311] MPL etc Regulations 1999, reg 17.   [312] MPL etc Regulations, reg 18(1).

[313] MPL etc Regulations, reg 18A.   [314] MPL etc Regulations, reg 18(2).

[315] MPL etc Regulations 1999, reg 16. A 'collective agreement' is defined for these purposes as an agreement or arrangement made between one or more independent trade unions and one or more employers or employers' associations: MPL etc Regulations, reg 2.

[316] See earlier in this chapter, heading 2(iii), p 236 above.

representatives (although if the employer employs 20 or fewer employees on the date when the agreement is first made available for signature, it is sufficient if the agreement is signed by a majority of the workforce). In addition, before the agreement is made available for signature, the employer must have provided all the employees to whom it was intended to apply with copies of the agreement, together with such guidance as they might reasonably require to help them understand it.[317] The MPL etc Regulations set out the requirements for the election of workforce representatives,[318] including matters such as candidature, entitlement to vote and the conduct of the ballot.[319]

(c) The model scheme

As seen above, the MPL etc Regulations contain a model scheme[320] on parental leave which automatically comes into operation if the parties do not make their own collective or workforce agreement. The key elements of the model scheme are as follows: (1) parental leave may not be taken in periods other than a week or multiple of a week[321] (except in the case of a child entitled to disability living allowance); (2) an employee may not take more than four weeks' leave in respect of any individual child during a particular year; (3) the employee must give the employer at least 21 days' notice of the taking of parental leave, and its duration; (4) fathers wishing to take parental leave immediately after the baby is born must give the employer notice at least 21 days before the beginning of the expected week of childbirth; (5) employees wishing to take parental leave immediately after the date of placement of an adopted child must give the employer notice at least 21 days before the beginning of the week in which placement is expected to occur, or as soon as reasonably practicable thereafter; (6) the employer may ask for reasonable evidence of the employee's entitlement to parental leave (for example evidence of the child's date of birth, or date of placement for adoption); (7) the employer may postpone a period of parental leave (other than leave on birth or adoption) where the employer considers that the operation of the business would be unduly disrupted if the employee took leave during the period identified in the notice; (8) leave may not be postponed for more than six months, and the employer must notify the employee of the postponement in writing within seven days of receiving the employee's notice, giving the reason for the postponement and specifying the dates on which the period of leave will begin and end.

[317] MPL etc Regulations 1999, Sch 1.

[318] Workforce representatives have a right not to be dismissed or subjected to any detriment by the employer for performing (or proposing to perform) any functions or activities as a workforce representative or a candidate for election as a workforce representative: see p 522.

[319] These requirements are similar to those which apply to the election of workforce representatives under the Working Time Regulations: see earlier in this chapter, heading 2(iii), p 237.

[320] MPL etc Regulations 1999, Sch 2.

[321] This condition was applied strictly in *Rodway v New Southern Railways Ltd* [2005] ICR 1162, [2005] IRLR 583, CA to rule out the use of this scheme to cover a single day needed for childcare (even though the employee was willing to trade in a whole week's entitlement for the one day off).

(xi) TIME OFF FOR DEPENDANTS

In addition to the right to parental leave, the Employment Relations Act 1999 also introduced a right for employees to take a reasonable amount of unpaid time off to deal with incidents involving a 'dependant'.[322] Like the provisions on parental leave, the provisions on time off for dependants were designed to implement the Parental Leave Directive, which gives a right to time off in family emergencies. The hope and expectation was that these provisions would lead to a reduction in the number of employees taking odd days off sick in order to care for sick children or to cope when domestic arrangements (for example child-minding arrangements) go awry at short notice.

   Although colourfully (and sometimes mischievously) portrayed in certain sections of the media as giving employees carte blanche to take time off whenever they wish to attend to the needs of leaking washing machines or sick poodles, the right to time off for dependants is in fact more limited than this. An employee has the right to be permitted to take a 'reasonable amount' of time off (not further defined or explained) during working hours to take action which is necessary: (1) to provide assistance when a dependant falls ill, gives birth, or is injured or assaulted; (2) to make arrangements for the provision of care for a dependant who is ill or injured; (3) when a dependant dies;[323] (4) because of the unexpected disruption or termination of arrangements for the care of a dependant; or (5) to deal with an incident which involves a child of the employee and which occurs unexpectedly during school hours or other time when the child's school is responsible for the child.[324] A 'dependant' of an employee is defined for these purposes as a spouse, civil partner, child, parent, or a person who lives in the same household as the employee, otherwise than as an employee, tenant, lodger or boarder.[325] For the purposes of heads (1) and (2) above, 'dependant' also includes a person who reasonably relies on the employee (a) for assistance on an occasion when the person falls ill or is injured or assaulted, or (b) to make arrangements for the provision of care in the event of illness or injury; and for the purposes of head (4), it includes any person who reasonably relies on the employee to make arrangements for the provision of care. Where time off is taken under these provisions, the employee must tell the employer the reason for the absence as soon as reasonably practicable, and how long the employee expects to be absent from work.[326]

   A complaint that an employer has unreasonably refused time off under these provisions lies to an employment tribunal, within three months of the refusal, or within a further reasonable period where the tribunal is satisfied that it was not reasonably practicable for the complaint to be brought within that period.[327] Where the tribunal

---

[322] Employment Rights Act 1996, ss 57A and 57B, added by the Employment Relations Act 1999.
[323] This only covers the making of the necessary arrangements and attending the funeral; it does *not* enact any wider form of bereavement leave: *Forster v Cartwright Black* [2004] ICR 1728, [2004] IRLR 781, EAT.
[324] Employment Rights Act 1996, s 57A(1). No qualifying period of continuous employment is required.
[325] Employment Rights Act 1996, s 57A(3).   [326] Employment Rights Act 1996, s 57A(2).
[327] Employment Rights Act 1996, s 57B.

upholds the complaint, it must make a declaration to that effect, and may order the employer to pay compensation to the employee of such amount as the tribunal considers just and equitable in all the circumstances, having regard to the employer's default, and any loss suffered by the employee which is attributable to the matters complained of. An employee also has the right not to be dismissed or subjected to any detriment by his or her employer for taking or seeking to take time off for dependants.[328]

The extent of the entitlement to time off under this head was considered by the EAT in the leading case of *Qua v John Ford Morrison Solicitors*.[329] In that case, the applicant was dismissed for absenteeism having been absent from work for 17 days over a ten-month period as a result of medical problems suffered by her young son. The employment tribunal dismissed her complaint that she was unfairly dismissed for taking time off for dependants,[330] on the grounds that she had failed to comply with her obligation to tell the employer as soon as reasonably practicable the reason for her absence and how long she expected to be absent, and that her absences went beyond what was reasonable.

The EAT, allowing the appeal, gave useful guidance on the interpretation of the statutory provisions, pointing out that the right is to take a reasonable amount of time off in order to deal with unexpected or sudden events affecting dependants, and to make any necessary longer term arrangements for their care. The right to time off to provide assistance under head (1) 'does not in our view enable employees to take time off in order themselves to provide care for a sick child, beyond the reasonable amount necessary to enable them to deal with the immediate crisis'. The EAT rejected the argument that each individual request for time off should be considered in isolation, confirming that where an employee has exercised the right on more than one previous occasion, the employer can take into account the number and length of previous absences in order to determine whether the time sought to be taken off is reasonable and necessary. However, in determining what is a reasonable amount of time off, the EAT considered that 'the disruption or inconvenience caused to an employer's business by the employee's absence are irrelevant factors, which should not be taken into account', on the grounds that the 'operational needs of the employer cannot be relevant to a consideration of the amount of time an employee reasonably needs' to deal with emergency situations. On the particular issue raised by the case, that of a parent with a child suffering from a chronic illness, the EAT gave the provisions a narrow interpretation: 'The legislation contemplates a reasonable period of time off to enable an employee to deal with a child who has fallen ill unexpectedly and thus the section is dealing with something unforeseen. Once it is known that the particular child is suffering from an underlying medical condition, which is likely to

---

[328] Employment Rights Act 1996, ss 47C(2)(d); 99(3)(d).

[329] [2003] ICR 482, [2003] IRLR 184, EAT, applied in *Truelove v Safeway Stores plc* [2005] ICR 589, EAT.

[330] She argued her case on this ground because she lacked the necessary continuous employment to bring an ordinary unfair dismissal complaint.

cause him to suffer regular relapses, such a situation no longer falls within the scope of ... section 57A at all.' On the issue of whether the applicant had complied with the duty under section 57A(2) to inform the employer, the EAT held that there is no duty on an employee to report to the employers 'on a daily basis' whilst taking time off work; she must tell the employer the reason for her absence, and how long she expects to be absent, but 'there is no continuing duty on an employee to update the employer as to her situation, though of course many employees would no doubt do this as a matter of course.' It should be noted that the 'unexpected' event need not necessarily be the illness of a child. The unexpected cancellation of ordinary childcare qualifies, and even where a disruption to normal childcare arrangements is anticipated, the unavailability of replacement care can count as 'unexpected'.[331]

(xii) FLEXIBLE WORKING

One of the greatest obstacles faced by working parents trying to reconcile the competing demands of work and family life is that they usually have very little control over the pattern of their working lives. This is a particular problem for women returning to work after maternity leave, as the statutory provisions on maternity leave give a woman the right to return to the job in which she was employed before maternity leave; they do not confer any right to change the job specification to make it easier for her to return to work. However, the moves towards laws on flexible working were not restricted to maternity returners. Parents generally were seen as being in need of such laws but after the debate went wider. One view has been that *anyone* should be able to seek flexibility for any purpose, ie that this is an idea that may have arisen initially in a 'maternity rights' context but is really rooted in the government's much wider 'work–life balance' agenda. Short of a right for anyone, however, one other specific category of employee soon became a focus of concern—the employee who is a carer for an elderly or infirm adult.

(a) The original scheme for childcare

As seen in the introduction to this chapter, the idea of a right to work flexibly received a high level of support in the government's review of maternity and parental rights, and provisions on flexible working for childcare purposes were duly brought forward in the Employment Act 2002.[332] However, those measures fell well below expectations, because they do not give employees an automatic right to work flexibly: they merely

---

[331] *Royal Bank of Scotland PLC v Harrison* [2008] All ER (D) 126 (a parent knew for 12 days that her usual childminder would be unavailable on a specific date, but after diligent efforts to find a replacement faced the 'unexpected' circumstance of there being no available replacements; the EAT noted that had the parent not made diligent efforts, the elapsed time between learning of the risk of needing childcare and confirming that risk as fact might call into question whether the time off was 'necessary').

[332] Employment Rights Act 1996, Pt 8A, as inserted by the Employment Act 2002, s 47. Part 8A is supplemented by the Flexible Working (Procedural Requirements) Regulations 2002, SI 2002/3207, and the Flexible Working (Eligibility, Complaints and Remedies) Regulations 2002, SI 2002/3236.

give a right to *apply* to work flexibly, and even that right is very restricted in its scope. The gist of the provisions is that employees who have (or expect to have) responsibility for the upbringing of a child under 17[333] may request a change in their terms and conditions relating to the hours they work, the times when they are required to work or where they are required to work (ie as between home or on the employer's premises), to enable them to care for the child.[334] Until 2009 the right had been restricted to parents of children under 6, but that was changed from 6 April 2009.[335] To be eligible, the employee must be either the mother, father, adopter, guardian or foster parent of the child, or the spouse or partner of any of these, and must have 26 weeks' continuous service with the employer at the date of the application.[336] The procedure for making and responding to requests for flexible working is set out in detail in the Act and the accompanying Regulations. The employee must apply in writing,[337] and the application must explain what effect, if any, the employee thinks making the change applied for would have on the employer and how in the employee's opinion any such effect might be dealt with.[338] The employer's duty is merely to consider the request; there is no automatic right to work flexibly. The Act specifies the grounds on which an employer may refuse a request, viz, (1) the burden of additional costs; (2) detrimental effect on ability to meet customer demand; (3) inability to reorganize work among existing staff; (4) inability to recruit additional staff; (5) detrimental impact on quality; (6) detrimental impact on performance; (7) insufficiency of work during the periods the employee proposes to work; (8) planned structural changes; and (9) any other grounds specified in regulations.[339] It can be seen that this list provides an employer who is minded to resist an application to work flexibly with plenty of ammunition for doing so, particularly when one appreciates that the employer's refusal is not subject to any test of reasonableness or proportionality. The employer must respond to the employee's application within 28 days of receipt, either by agreeing to it (with notification to the employee in writing) or by arranging a meeting with the employee to discuss the application.[340] The employee is entitled to be accompanied at that meeting by a fellow employee.[341] Within 14 days of the meeting the employer must notify the employee

---

[333] Or a disabled child under 18. The application must be made at least 14 days before the child's 17th (or, if disabled, 18th) birthday.

[334] Employment Rights Act 1996, s 80F, as inserted by the Employment Act 2002, s 47.

[335] Flexible Working (Eligibility, Complaints and Remedies) (Amendment) Regulations 2009, SI 2009/595, reg 3A.

[336] Flexible Working (Eligibility, Complaints and Remedies) Regulations 2002, reg 3.

[337] Flexible Working (Eligibility, Complaints and Remedies) Regulations 2002, reg 4. The application must state whether the employee has made a previous application, and if so, when.

[338] Employment Rights Act 1996, s 80F(2).

[339] Employment Rights Act 1996, s 80G, as inserted by the Employment Act 2002.

[340] Flexible Working (Procedural Requirements) Regulations 2002, reg 3.

[341] Flexible Working (Procedural Requirements) Regulations 2002, reg 14. The companion may address the meeting, and may confer with the employee during the meeting, but may not answer questions on behalf of the employee. In the event of a failure to comply, the employee may complain to an employment tribunal, which may award compensation of up to two weeks' pay: reg 15.

in writing of his decision. If the application is rejected, the notice must specify the particular ground or grounds for the refusal from the above list, and explain why those grounds apply in the circumstances,[342] it must also set out the appeal procedure, which gives the employee a right of appeal within 14 days.[343] The appeal process is essentially a rerun of the original meeting, with the employer again required to provide reasons if the application is still refused.[344] The employee has a right to complain to an employment tribunal on the basis that either the employer has failed to follow the procedure properly or that the decision to reject the application 'was based on incorrect facts'.[345] This strange second formulation rules out any determination by the tribunal of the *reasonableness* of the employer's adverse decision, and was deliberate government policy, though when it was first considered by the EAT a wider interpretation was placed on it than the legislators may have intended, by holding that the tribunal *is* entitled to investigate the evidence, which may involve a consideration of what the effects of granting the request would have been on the employer at the time.[346] This more interventionist role still stops short of judging the justification for the decision, but does seem to occupy some middle ground of judging the 'correctness' of the decision (not necessarily just the 'facts'). If the tribunal finds for the employee it may issue a declaration, order the employer to reconsider the request and award compensation of up to eight weeks' pay.[347] The tribunal cannot order the employer to permit an employee to work flexibly. Employees too have a right not to be dismissed or subjected to any detriment for requesting flexible working, or seeking to exercise or enforce any rights thereto.

Modest though they may be, there are some potential pitfalls for employees in these new procedures: first, any contract variation that results from an application under these procedures will be permanent, unless otherwise agreed at the outset; there is no automatic right to revert to the old terms; and secondly, an employee may only make one variation application per year,[348] up to the child's sixteenth birthday, and each application will be considered by the employer in the light of the employer's circumstances at that time. The combination of these two factors means that an employee who succeeds in achieving flexibility in working arrangements in the short term may be unable to revert to his or her original terms and conditions if circumstances change. There are also potential pitfalls for employers, not least the fact that there are potential sex discrimination implications[349] if either applications for flexible working from male and female employees are not treated equally or, more specifically, if the request came from a maternity returner, where disparate impact on women might well be argued in order to establish indirect discrimination, thus putting the employer

---

[342] Flexible Working (Procedural Requirements) Regulations 2002, reg 5.
[343] Flexible Working (Procedural Requirements) Regulations 2002, regs 6, 7.
[344] Flexible Working (Procedural Requirements) Regulations 2002, regs 8–10.
[345] Employment Rights Act 1996, s 80H.   [346] *Commotion Ltd v Rutty* [2006] IRLR 171, EAT.
[347] Employment Rights Act 1996, s 80I.   [348] Employment Rights Act 1996, s 80F(4).
[349] *Starmer v British Airways* [2005] All ER (D) 323 (Jul), [2005] IRLR 862 (basing a refusal of a 50% contract to a female pilot based on insufficient flight hours was indirectly discriminatory).

to proof on justification for the refusal.[350] Needless to say, the remedies for sex discrimination could be in a different universe than those provided under the flexible working rules.

(b) Extension to carers for adults

One key policy aim of the Work and Families Act 2006 was to extend the right to request flexible working to those caring for the elderly and/or infirm. Indeed, this was given priority over extending the right to parents with children as old as 16, which happened later. The drafting changes were relatively simple, requiring only minor amendments to the existing scheme. Thus, all the major qualification and remedy provisions of that scheme (above) apply to this added category of employees. In their case, the principal requirements are (1) that they must be or expect to be caring for a person (aged 18 or over) in need of care who is (a) married to or the partner or civil partner of the employee, (b) a relative of the employee (as defined) or (c) living at the same address as the employee, and (2) that their purpose for applying for the change is to enable them so to care.[351]

(xiii) PREGNANCY, MATERNITY AND SEX DISCRIMINATION[352]

(a) The effect of EU law

In the last two decades, the law on maternity rights in the UK has been completely transformed by a series of landmark ECJ decisions in which it has been held that adverse treatment of a woman on grounds of pregnancy or maternity can constitute unlawful direct[353] discrimination on grounds of sex. The possibility of challenging adverse treatment on grounds of pregnancy as sex discrimination was particularly attractive in the UK because of the gaps in the protection for pregnancy and maternity under the employment rights legislation: until 1993, the statutory protection against dismissal on grounds of pregnancy was significantly weakened by the requirement to satisfy the normal two-year qualifying period of continuous employment, and parallel protection against detriment short of dismissal for reasons of pregnancy was not introduced until December 1999. Since the 1993 reforms, the need to challenge a dismissal under sex discrimination law has been greatly reduced, although there may still be advantages in doing so, as sex discrimination claims are not subject to any upper limit on compensation.

---

[350] The continued availability of this cause of action for those returning from maternity leave was reaffirmed in fairly spectacular fashion in *Hardys & Hanson plc v Lax* [2005] IRLR 726, CA.

[351] Employment Rights Act 1996 s 80F(1); Flexible Working (Eligibility, Complaints and Remedies) Regulations 2002, reg 3B.

[352] See Fredman (1994) 110 LQR 106; Szyszczak (1996) 59 MLR 589; Wintemute (1998) 27 ILJ 23; Honeyball (2000) 29 ILJ 43.

[353] Protection against indirect sex discrimination (eg in relation to a transfer to part-time work after maternity leave) is considered at Ch 5, heading 2(iii), p 319.

Initially, there was some doubt as to whether adverse treatment on grounds of pregnancy fell within the scope of sex discrimination law *at all*. This might seem strange to those uninitiated in the mysteries of the Sex Discrimination Act 1975—after all, one might be forgiven for thinking that adverse treatment on grounds of pregnancy must necessarily be sexually discriminatory, given the inescapable biological fact that men cannot become pregnant. The doubts arose because in determining whether a woman has been treated less favourably than a man on the ground of sex, the 1975 Act requires the comparison between the treatment of the applicant and that of a man to be such that the relevant circumstances in the one case 'are the same, or not materially different, in the other',[354] and so it seemed that in cases involving pregnancy the necessary comparison could not be made.[355] However, in *Hayes v Malleable Working Men's Club and Institute*,[356] the EAT managed to avoid this conclusion by holding that the correct approach under the 1975 Act was to compare the treatment of a pregnant woman with that of a man in comparable circumstances (for example a man suffering from some temporary disability). While this 'sick man' approach was open to the objection that it treated pregnancy as analogous to illness, it did at least succeed in bringing pregnant women within the protection of the Sex Discrimination Act, which was crucially important at the time for those dismissed within the first two years of employment.

It soon became apparent that there was a further highly significant dimension to this issue, in the form of EC Directive 76/207 (the Equal Treatment Directive). In a series of cases, beginning with *Dekker v Stichting Vormingscentrum voor Jong Volwassenen (VJV—Centrum) Plus*,[357] the CJEU held that less favourable treatment of a woman on account of her pregnancy constituted unlawful direct discrimination on the grounds of sex, contrary to the Equal Treatment Directive, irrespective of how a hypothetical male would have been treated in comparable circumstances. In *Dekker*, the employer refused to appoint the complainant on learning that she was pregnant (the reason being that under Dutch law the employer would have been required to pay Mrs Dekker her full salary while on maternity leave, but could not have recovered that amount from its insurers because her pregnancy was known at the time her appointment would have commenced). The ECJ ruled that as pregnancy is a condition unique to women, to refuse a woman employment on the ground of pregnancy constituted direct discrimination on grounds of sex, contrary to the Directive; this was held to be the case even though the refusal of employment was on account of the adverse financial consequences to the employer of her absence due to pregnancy, as the refusal was still based on the fact of pregnancy itself. In *Handels-og Kontorfunktionaerernes Forbund i Danmark (for Hertz) v Dansk Arbejdsgiverforening (for Aldi Marked A/S)*,[358] decided

---

[354] Sex Discrimination Act 1975, s 5(3).
[355] *Turley v Allders Department Stores Ltd* [1980] ICR 66, [1980] IRLR 4, EAT.
[356] [1985] ICR 703, [1985] IRLR 367.   [357] Case C-177/88 [1992] ICR 325, [1991] IRLR 27, ECJ.
[358] Case C-179/88 [1992] ICR 325, [1992] ICR 332, [1991] IRLR 31, ECJ.

on the same day as *Dekker*, the ECJ held that the same principle applied to a dismissal on account of pregnancy, although on the facts the court held that a dismissal some 18 months after the end of maternity leave due to absence for prolonged post-natal illness would not be sexually discriminatory if a man absent from work due to illness for a similar period would have been treated in the same way.

The apparent conflict between domestic and Community law on this issue was first considered by the UK courts in *Webb v EMO Air Cargo (UK) Ltd*.[359] In that case the applicant, recruited to provide temporary cover for another employee who was about to take maternity leave, was dismissed when she discovered shortly after starting work that she too was pregnant. The industrial tribunal dismissed her claim that her dismissal constituted unlawful discrimination on grounds of sex under the 1975 Act, holding that the reason for her dismissal was her anticipated inability to carry out the primary task for which she had been recruited (ie to cover for an absent colleague) and that if a man recruited for the same purpose had told the employer that he needed to be absent for a similar period of time, he too would have been dismissed. The EAT and the Court of Appeal upheld the tribunal's decision, rejecting the argument that the fact that pregnancy is specific to women means that a dismissal for pregnancy must automatically be discriminatory, and applying the comparative approach by comparing the treatment of the pregnant applicant and the treatment which would have been accorded to a man in comparable circumstances (for example a man with a medical condition requiring him to be absent from work for a similar period of time). On appeal to the House of Lords, Lord Keith (giving the leading judgment) conceded that as child-bearing and the capacity for child-bearing are characteristics of the female sex, ' ... in general to dismiss a woman because she is pregnant or to refuse to employ a woman of child-bearing age because she may become pregnant is unlawful direct discrimination', as it involves the application of a gender-based criterion.[360] However, he considered that on the facts the reason for the dismissal was not gender-based, since the applicant was dismissed not because she was pregnant but because of her unavailability for work at the critical period, and it was therefore appropriate to compare her treatment with that of a hypothetical man who would also be unavailable (for whatever reason) at the critical time.[361] As it was unclear whether under Community law the unavailability for work rather than the pregnancy would be regarded as being the real reason for dismissal, the House of Lords referred the case to the ECJ, which

---

[359] [1990] ICR 442, [1990] IRLR 124, EAT; affd [1992] ICR 445, [1992] IRLR 116, CA; [1993] ICR 175, [1993] IRLR 27, HL; refd [1994] ICR 770, [1994] IRLR 482, ECJ; revsd *(No 2)* [1995] ICR 1021, [1995] IRLR 645, HL. The applicant was unable to complain under s 99 because she lacked the (then) necessary period of continuous employment.

[360] Applying the 'but for' test approved by the House of Lords in *James v Eastleigh Borough Council* [1990] ICR 554, [1990] IRLR 288, HL, discussed at Ch 5, heading 2(iii)(a), p 313.

[361] One obvious objection to this line of reasoning is that it could allow a gender-based dismissal to be disguised as gender-neutral, the point being that if the underlying reason for the woman's unavailability for work is her pregnancy, it is strongly arguable that the dismissal is in fact gender-based, as *but for her sex* she would not have been pregnant, and *but for her pregnancy* she would not have been unavailable for work.

rejected the comparative approach, holding that under the Equal Treatment Directive the dismissal of an employee for pregnancy constitutes direct discrimination and is therefore unlawful per se. Significantly, however, the ECJ's ruling indicated two possible limitations on the scope of the protection: first, the ECJ accepted that in the case of a dismissal for an illness attributable to pregnancy which manifests itself after maternity leave, it would be appropriate to adopt a comparative approach with the treatment of a sick man in analogous circumstances;[362] and secondly, the ECJ emphasized that Ms Webb had been engaged under a contract of employment of indefinite duration, the implication being that had she been engaged simply as a temporary replacement on a fixed-term contract, the outcome might have been different. When the case returned to the House of Lords, Lord Keith reinterpreted the 'more precise' test of unlawful discrimination under the 1975 Act so as to accord with the ECJ's ruling:

> It seems to me that the only way of doing so is to hold that, in a case where a woman is engaged for an indefinite period, the fact that the reason why she will be temporarily unavailable for work at a time when to her knowledge her services will be particularly required is pregnancy is a circumstance relevant to her case, being a circumstance which could not be present in the case of a hypothetical man.[363]

As the applicant had been recruited for an unlimited term, her dismissal was unlawful under the 1975 Act. However, Lord Keith indicated that the outcome might have been different if the employment had been for a fixed period during the *whole* of which the employee would have been unavailable for work because of her pregnancy, commenting that if such a situation were not to be distinguished, 'the result would be likely to be perceived as unfair to employers and as tending to bring the law on sex discrimination into disrepute.'[364] The legal basis for a distinction between indefinite and fixed-term contracts in such cases clearly owed more to pragmatism than to principle, and it came as no surprise that the CJEU, when given the opportunity to approve a fixed-term contract exception in *Tele Danmark A/S v Handels-og Kontorfunktionaerernes Forbund i Danmark (for Brandt-Nielsen)*,[365] held the line and refused to do so. In that case the applicant had applied for a temporary job on a six-month contract knowing that she was pregnant, and that she would be unable to perform a substantial part of her contract. She was dismissed for failing to inform the employers of her pregnancy when she was recruited, and the ECJ was asked to rule on whether the dismissal contravened the Equal Treatment Directive. The ECJ's ruling was unequivocal:

> Since the dismissal of a worker on account of pregnancy constitutes direct discrimination on grounds of sex, whatever the nature and extent of the economic loss incurred by the employer as a result of her absence because of pregnancy, whether the contract

---

[362] As in *Hertz* n 358.   [363] [1995] IRLR 645 at 647, HL.

[364] Cf *Caruana v Manchester Airport plc* [1996] IRLR 378, where the EAT held that any special rule for fixed-term contacts must be restricted to cases where the employee would be unavailable for the *whole* of the term of the contract.

[365] [2001] IRLR 853, ECJ.

of employment was concluded for a fixed or an indefinite period has no bearing on the discriminatory character of the dismissal. In either case, the employee's inability to perform her contract of employment is due to pregnancy.[366]

In the cases since *Webb (No 2)*, the extent of the special protection from pregnancy discrimination has been clarified, and a robust approach has been taken. It is now well established that any adverse treatment on grounds of pregnancy will be unlawful per se[367] provided the necessary causal connection can be established. The EAT gave useful guidance on this latter point in *O'Neill v Governors of St Thomas More RCVA School*.[368] In that case, the complainant, a religious education teacher at a Roman Catholic school, was dismissed after becoming pregnant as a result of a relationship with a local Roman Catholic priest. The tribunal had held that the dismissal, although unfair, was not discriminatory, as pregnancy was not the predominant cause of the dismissal, but the EAT allowed the complainant's appeal. According to Mummery J: 'The basic question is: what, out of the whole complex of facts before the tribunal, is the "effective and predominant" cause or the "real and efficient" cause of the act complained of?' He considered that the other factors surrounding the pregnancy which had led to her dismissal ('the paternity of the child, the publicity of that fact and the consequent untenability of the applicant's position as a religious education teacher') were all causally related to the fact that she was pregnant, and so it could be said, on an objective consideration of all the surrounding circumstances, that her pregnancy 'precipitated and permeated the decision to dismiss her'.

The 'special protection' is, however, subject to certain temporal limits, as the decision in *Hertz* showed. In *Handels-og Kontorfunktionaerernes Forbund i Danmark (for Larsson) v Dansk Handel & Service (for Fotex Supermarked A/S)*,[369] the ECJ held that it was lawful for an employer to take into account periods of absence due to pregnancy-related illness outside the maternity leave period in calculating whether there are grounds for dismissal, provided a man with a similar record of sickness absence would also have been dismissed. To the extent that the decision in *Larsson* seemed to imply that an employer could take account of pregnancy-related absence

---

[366] See also *Jimenez Melgar v Ayuntamiento de Los Barrios* [2001] IRLR 848, ECJ (non-renewal of a pregnant worker's fixed-term contract constitutes direct sex discrimination contrary to the Equal Treatment Directive where the reason for the non-renewal is related to the worker's pregnancy).

[367] See, eg, *Mahlburg v Land Mecklenburg-Vorpommern* [2001] ICR 1032, [2000] IRLR 276, ECJ (unlawful to refuse a pregnant woman appointment to a post of unlimited duration on the grounds that a statutory prohibition on her employment because of her pregnancy prevented her from being employed in that post from the outset and for the duration of her pregnancy); see also *Hardman v Mallon t/a Orchard Lodge Nursing Home* [2002] IRLR 516 (failure to conduct a risk assessment in respect of a pregnant woman was unlawful sex discrimination, without the need for a male comparator). Note to the contrary that any beneficial treatment because of pregnancy cannot be challenged as sex discrimination by a man: Sex Discrimination Act 1975, s 2(2); Equal Treatment Directive, Art 2(3); *Abdoulaye v Regie Nationale des Usines Renault SA* [1999] IRLR 811, ECJ.

[368] [1997] ICR 33, [1996] IRLR 372, EAT; see also *Shomer v B & R Residential Lettings Ltd* [1992] IRLR 317, CA; *P & O European Ferries (Dover) Ltd v Iverson* [1999] ICR 1088, EAT.

[369] [1997] IRLR 643, ECJ.

before the beginning of maternity leave, it appeared to conflict with the basic principle established in *Dekker* and *Webb (No 2)*, and it was no surprise that when the ECJ next had an opportunity to reconsider the matter, in *Brown v Rentokil Ltd*,[370] it confirmed that when considering a dismissal for sickness absence, it is unlawful to take account of absences due to pregnancy-related illness that have occurred between the start of pregnancy and the start of maternity leave.[371] Indeed, in that case the ECJ took the rare step of expressly disapproving the distinction drawn in *Larsson* between absence for pregnancy-related illness during pregnancy and during maternity leave. After *Brown v Rentokil Ltd*, it is now possible to state with some assurance that the special protection against dismissal on grounds of pregnancy applies from the start of pregnancy to the end of maternity leave. Within that period, a dismissal (or other adverse treatment) for absence caused by pregnancy-related illness will be unlawful. After the end of maternity leave, the comparative approach applies, so that such treatment will only be unlawful if a man would have been treated more favourably in comparable circumstances (ie the sick man comparison applies).[372] In making that comparison, however, it will be unlawful to take into account any period of pregnancy-related sickness absence occurring between the start of pregnancy and the end of maternity leave.

While the decisions in *Dekker* and *Webb (No 2)* clarified the law in one area, they in turn gave rise to a further, related issue: if adverse treatment on grounds of pregnancy or maternity leave is unlawful, does this mean that a woman on maternity leave is entitled to claim the benefit of the terms and conditions of employment which she would have enjoyed if still at work? This issue first arose for consideration by the ECJ in *Gillespie v Northern Health and Social Services Board*,[373] where it was argued that a woman should be entitled to receive full pay during maternity leave, on the grounds that if the only reason she does not receive full pay is that she is on maternity leave, that must be direct discrimination on the grounds of sex contrary to Community law, since that reason can only affect women. In a decision which owed more to pragmatism than to logic, but which no doubt caused a huge collective sigh of relief amongst employers, the ECJ ruled that women taking maternity leave 'are in a special position which requires them to be afforded special protection, but which is not comparable either with that of a man or with that of a woman actually at work'; consequently it was not unlawful under Community law to pay women on maternity leave at a level which is less than their full pay for the period of the leave. The Court considered that it was for the national legislature to set the amount of maternity pay, provided this was not so low as to undermine the purpose of maternity leave. In subsequent cases on this issue, the ECJ has

---

[370] [1998] ICR 790, [1998] IRLR 445, ECJ.

[371] The fact that her contract contained a term allowing the employer to dismiss after a stipulated number of weeks of absence was held to make no difference.

[372] See, eg, *British Telecommunications plc v Roberts* [1996] ICR 625, [1996] IRLR 601, EAT (request to jobshare after maternity leave not covered by the special protection, but subject instead to the comparative approach).

[373] [1996] All ER (EC) 284, [1996] IRLR 214, ECJ. See also *Alabaster v Woolwich plc* C-147/02 [2004] IRLR 486, ECJ.

maintained a clear distinction between a woman's rights (1) while she is pregnant and still working; (2) during maternity leave; and (3) following her return to work. While pregnant and still working, the *Dekker* principle applies, so that any adverse treatment on grounds of pregnancy will be unlawful per se.[374] During maternity leave, her rights are those set out in the Pregnant Workers Directive (unless enhanced under national law or by her contract of employment); she cannot compare herself with the position of a man or woman actually at work, nor is she entitled to compare herself with a man or woman absent from work on sick leave,[375] or on holiday.[376] Following her return to work, however, the comparative approach applies.

While the basic principles are now tolerably clear (albeit thoroughly muddled conceptually), they can be difficult to apply in practice, particularly where the tricky issue of the pro-rata-ing of benefits in proportion to periods of absence arises. While the ECJ in *Gillespie* stepped back from the brink of accepting a right to full pay during maternity leave, this left open the question of whether an employee continues to build up entitlement to other contractual benefits (for example the accrual of holiday or pension entitlement or annual bonuses) during maternity leave, particularly where those benefits are not dependent on actual performance of work. Subsequent cases have established that it is permissible under Article 141 and the Equal Treatment Directive for entitlement to (or accrual of) such benefits to be limited to the minimum 14-week maternity leave period guaranteed under the Pregnant Workers Directive. In *Boyle v Equal Opportunities Commissions*,[377] the applicant challenged several aspects of the EOC's maternity scheme, including a clause whereby annual holiday leave ceased to accrue during periods of supplementary contractual maternity leave after the end of the minimum 14-week leave period. The ECJ held that such a clause was not precluded by European law, since the period of contractual maternity leave was a special advantage available only to women, so the fact that annual leave ceased to accrue during that period could not amount to less favourable treatment of women.[378] The ECJ also held that a clause requiring the repayment of any contractual maternity pay over and above the level of SMP if a woman did not return to work after maternity leave was not unlawful (rejecting the comparison with a man or woman absent on sick leave, who would not have been required to repay sick pay on not returning to work), nor was a clause providing for the triggering of maternity leave where a woman absent on sick

---

[374] See, eg, *Handels-og Kontorfunktionaerernes Forbund i Danmark (for Pedersen) v Faellesforeningen for Danmarks Brugsforeninger (for Kwickly Skive)* [1999] IRLR 55, ECJ (held to be unlawful to pay a woman absent from work with a pregnancy-related illness *before* the start of maternity leave a lower level of sick pay than was paid to other employees).

[375] *Boyle v Equal Opportunities Commission* [1998] IRLR 717, ECJ; see also *Todd v Eastern Health and Social Services Board; Gillespie v Northern Health and Social Services Board (No 2)* [1997] IRLR 410, NICA.

[376] *Edwards v Derby City Council* [1999] ICR 114, EAT. [377] See n 375.

[378] This, of course, begs the question of whether the benefit in question is one which is awarded retrospectively as a reward for past service (in which case it may be reduced pro rata for periods of maternity leave after the 14-week minimum) or merely depends on the employee being in current employment when the benefit is awarded: see *Lewen v Denda* [2000] ICR 648, [2000] IRLR 67, ECJ (a case on the Parental Leave Directive).

leave gave birth during such absence. A clause prohibiting an employee from taking sick leave during the minimum 14-week period unless she elected to return to work and terminate her maternity leave was held to be unlawful (although not so in relation to a period of supplementary maternity leave), as was a clause limiting the accrual of occupational pension rights during the minimum 14-week period to the period during which the woman received contractual or statutory maternity pay. In *Caisse Nationale d'Assurance Vieillesse des Travailleurs Salaries v Thibault*,[379] the applicant was denied an annual performance assessment (and with it the possibility of qualifying for promotion) because the relevant collective agreement restricted such assessments to employees who had been present at work for at least six months in the relevant year, and she was unable to qualify because she had been away from work on maternity leave. She argued that to deny her the assessment was discriminatory, since if she had not taken maternity leave, she would have qualified for an assessment. In a brief (and unfortunately rather delphic) judgment which is difficult to reconcile with *Boyle*, the ECJ upheld her complaint, on the grounds that a woman who continues to be bound to her employer by an employment contract during maternity leave should not be deprived of the benefit of working conditions which apply to both men and women and which are a result of that relationship. A similar approach was taken in *GUS Home Shopping Ltd v Green*[380] where the applicants were denied payment under a loyalty bonus scheme because they were absent from work during the relevant period. The EAT held that this was unlawful sex discrimination because their absence from work was due to pregnancy-related illness or maternity leave, and the case therefore fell within the mainstream principle established by *Webb* and *Thibault*. It may be, however, that this analysis now has limited application in the light of *Hoyland v Asda Stores Ltd*[381] in which it was held lawful to make a pro-rata deduction from a discretionary annual bonus (based on profits) to reflect the employee's time absent from work on maternity leave during the bonus year. The EAT found *Thibault* and *GUS Shopping* to be weak authorities on particular facts and preferred the more straightforward line in *Gillespie*. Bean J put it thus:

> The European case law indicates that when a woman returns from maternity leave she must be treated for the purposes of future pay and working conditions as though she had never been away. Thus if the workforce has received a pay rise during her absence the pay rise is applicable to her. If she would have moved to a higher seniority band, she must be given that benefit on her return. If she would have been assessed for promotion, she must be assessed anyway. But none of these is the same as saying that she must be paid for the period of maternity leave as if she had never been on leave.[382]

When the case went to the Inner House of the Court of Session, it was subject to a short and to-the-point judgment, dismissing arguments based on *Webb* and *GUS Shopping*,

---

[379] [1998] IRLR 399, ECJ.   [380] [2001] IRLR 75, EAT.
[381] [2005] IRLR 483, EAT, [2006] IRLR 468, Ct of Sess (IH).
[382] *Hoyland* [2005] IRLR 483, para 20.

and resolving the case purely on domestic law (in particular the Sex Discrimination Act 1975, section 6(6) which removes from its ambit 'benefits consisting of the payment of money when the provision of those benefits is regulated by the woman's contract of employment').

(b) The legislative response

The Sex Discrimination Act 1975 was amended in 2005 to make some of the above principles express in the legislation. This was done in two ways. First, the inserted section 3A tried to codify the relationship between pregnancy and sex discrimination. It enacted the idea of the 'protected period' (ie from becoming pregnant up to the end of the ordinary maternity leave, additional maternity leave, earlier return to work or compulsory maternity leave, whichever is relevant to her) and then stated that during that period it is discrimination for the employer to treat her less favourably (on the ground of her pregnancy) than he would treat her had she not become pregnant.[383] Note that the comparison here was a notional one with *herself not pregnant*, thus hopefully avoiding the arguments over hypothetical or actual male comparators that had bedevilled this area for years. Secondly, the inserted section 6A sought to make clear that sex discrimination cannot be used to outflank the statutory rules on maternity leave which contain their own specific provision on what contractual terms do and do not continue to apply. It states that the laws on discrimination in relation to terms and conditions do not make it unlawful to deprive a woman on maternity leave of the benefit of terms and conditions relating to remuneration (the *Gillespie* and *Hoyland* point).

While these moves to produce greater clarity in the law were welcome, arguments persisted over whether those moves had gone far enough, especially where they were meant to transpose EU Directives. In the case of these 2005 amendments, the EOC had participated extensively in the government's consultation exercise, but remained unconvinced that the eventual form of the amendments was entirely in line with EU requirements. They brought judicial review proceedings in *EOC v Secretary of State for Trade and Industry*,[384] where it was held (in this context) that (1) the continued use of a comparator in section 3A (even when that comparator was herself not pregnant and not on maternity leave) should be removed as unjustified under EC law (*Webb* and *Gillespie*) which requires 'special protection'; (2) the exclusions of contractual rights in section 6A went beyond that acceptable under EC law and should be amended to allow claims for loss of discretionary bonus during the compulsory maternity period[385] and to be less prescriptive as to the rights which survive during additional maternity leave.[386] The Sex Discrimination Act 1975 (Amendment) Regulations 2008 put this ruling into

---

[383] Section 3A(1)(a). By subs (1)(b) it is also discrimination to subject a woman to less favourable treatment because of exercising her right to maternity leave.

[384] [2007] IRLR 327.

[385] As in *Lewen v Denda* C-333/97 [2000] IRLR 67, ECJ.

[386] Applying *Land Brandenburg v Sass* C-284/02 [2005] IRLR 147, ECJ, a case primarily about problems aligning rights from the former East and West Germanies.

effect, eliminating from section 3A any reference to a comparison to demonstrate less favourable treatment, and replacing the 2005 section 6A with a new section 6A, which provides that (1) benefits 'relating to remuneration' may be withheld during leave and (2) 'remuneration' does *not* include 'maternity-related remuneration', 'remuneration in respect of times when the woman is not on maternity leave' and 'remuneration by way of bonus in respect of times when a woman is on compulsory maternity leave'. So that's all cleared up then.

5

DISCRIMINATION IN EMPLOYMENT

OVERVIEW

Discrimination law in the UK, in the employment sphere and beyond, entered a new phase in 2010. Up to then anti-discrimination legislation had developed piecemeal, not only in the sense that different grounds of discrimination (eg race or sex) were targeted by separate legislative instruments, but in the sense that some pieces of legislation had domestic roots while others boasted a clearly European provenance. Beginning with very distinct domestic approaches to race and sex discrimination in the late 1960s and early 1970s, through a period of EC influence on sex discrimination but not race discrimination in the 1980s, UK discrimination law stole a march on the EC with the Disability Discrimination Act in 1995, and then found itself scrambling to implement the 2000 EC Race and Employment Directives, requiring the UK to adopt measures to prohibit employment discrimination on grounds of religion or belief, sexual orientation, and age, and to update several existing protections. This led to a state of affairs, prevailing from 2003 to early 2010, where the student of discrimination law, even one concerned only with its employment aspects, needed to learn four separate statutes and three sets of regulations. The regulations (on age, sexual orientation, and religion or belief discrimination) bore the obvious hallmarks of EC implementation measures, while the sex, race and disability statutes consisted of domestic foundations festooned with EC-driven provisions and concepts.

The Equality Act 2010 changed all of that. It brought all of the grounds of discrimination into one statute, extended anti-discrimination protection to a roughly similar scope of coverage (eg, employment, services, public bodies, etc) across each ground, and harmonized definitions and concepts throughout. It also introduced new requirements and concepts, allowing (inter alia) greater scope for positive action (decisions that favour disadvantaged groups), making express provision for discrimination based on more than one protected characteristic (eg sex and race), shoring up weakened disability protections, and increasing the responsibilities of employers to correct gender pay imbalance. As will be seen in this chapter, however, bringing discrimination law into a single act did not eliminate all of its discontinuities, and even introduced a few. The way in which the Act harmonized the legislation that went before it could hardly be called a fundamental rethink. It left unaddressed important questions about the meaning of discrimination that have spawned inconsistent case law, made no more comprehensible by the Act. On the other hand, it kept enough of the concepts from previous legislation (especially the parts required by EC law) to mean that much of the discrimination case law relied on up to 2010 can be relied on in the future. The Act's relatively superficial changes (not to slight the deeply appreciated benefits of harmonization and simplification) mean that only limited areas of case law were obviated by the Act; part of the work of this chapter is to set out which lines of precedent remain relevant and which do not. The main work of the chapter, surveying and analysing the employment aspects of the Equality Act and the relevant case law, will begin with an exploration of the structure, concepts and definitions of the Act as it relates to employment. The remainder of the chapter will consider special issues that arise under the various grounds of discrimination prohibited in employment: sex, sexual orientation, race, religion or belief, disability and age. Gender reassignment and marriage or civil partnership are characteristics protected by the Act, but do not receive separate sections in this book. Gender reassignment receives some discussion in the section on protected characteristics; with regard to marriage or civil partnership, the only case law development of note under the Equality Act 2010 is that different panels of the EAT have issued conflicting judgments as to whether discrimination based on the person with whom the claimant is married or partnered (as opposed to based on the status of being married or partnered) receives protection as discrimination 'because of' marriage or civil partnership.[1]

1 HISTORICAL BACKGROUND

The common law placed no restrictions on an employer's freedom to decide whether to hire a particular individual, an approach deeply rooted in laissez-faire philosophy and encapsulated in the following dictum of Lord Davey in *Allen v Flood*:[2]

> an employer may refuse to employ [an individual] for the most mistaken, capricious, malicious or morally reprehensible motives that can be conceived, but [that individual] has no right of action against him.

Thus, a refusal to employ on grounds of sex, race, marital status, disability or on any other ground was not unlawful,[3] still less did the courts reveal any concern to enforce equality in the terms of employment. Indeed, in *Roberts v Hopwood*,[4] Lord Atkinson in the House of Lords castigated the Poplar Council's policy of providing equal pay to men and women performing the same work as motivated by 'misguided principles of

---

[1] *Dunn v The Institute of Cemetery and Crematorium Management* UKEAT/0531/10, [2012] All ER (D) 173 (holding that it is); *Hawkins v (1) Atex Group (2) Korsvold (3) Malo de Molina (4) Reardon*, UKEAT/0302/11, [2012] All ER (D) 71 (holding that it is not).

[2] [1898] AC 1 at 172.

[3] See, eg, *Weinberger v Inglis (No 2)* [1919] AC 606, HL; *Bebb v Law Society* [1914] 1 Ch 286, CA; *Short v Poole Corpn* [1926] Ch 66, CA.

[4] [1925] AC 578, HL.

socialistic philanthropy'. The merest hint of a willingness to intervene in cases of sex discrimination on grounds of public policy can perhaps be discerned in the decision of the Court of Appeal in *Nagle v Feilden*,[5] where it was held that the Jockey Club's 'arbitrary and capricious' refusal to grant a licence to a woman trainer infringed her 'right to work'. However, the 'right to work' principle is at best of dubious authority, and it is highly unlikely that the courts would have been able (or indeed willing) to develop it into a broad principle capable of combating discrimination in employment generally.

Given the disinterest of the common law in tackling discrimination at work, the victim of discrimination was forced to look to legislation. The first legislative intervention, the Sex Disqualification (Removal) Act 1919, had a narrow scope, removing the restrictions on the employment of women in certain occupations and vocations (for example as civil servants or solicitors); crucially, it did not outlaw discrimination on grounds of sex in the appointment to those occupations or in the terms of employment. The Race Relations Act 1965 tackled discrimination in certain public places, and established the Race Relations Board, but it was a further three years before the Race Relations Act 1968 prohibited discrimination in employment on grounds of colour, race, ethnic or national origins. However, that Act relied for its enforcement on a combination of voluntary procedures and the institution of proceedings by the Race Relations Board, and was widely considered to have been a failure. The Equal Pay Act 1970[6] introduced a new right to equal terms and conditions for men and women in certain circumstances, but did not prohibit other forms of discrimination between the sexes, in particular discrimination at the point of hiring and in the provision of training. The turning point came with the enactment of the Sex Discrimination Act 1975, which introduced broad protection against direct and indirect discrimination in employment (and also in certain other specified areas such as education and the provision of goods and services) on the grounds of sex and marital status, with a right of complaint to a tribunal in employment cases; that Act also established the Equal Opportunities Commission (EOC) to oversee the operation of the legislation and to enforce it by bringing court proceedings or through the issue of non-discrimination notices. The Race Relations Act 1976 closely followed the provisions of the Sex Discrimination Act 1975, and established the Commission for Racial Equality (CRE) with powers similar to those of the EOC.

In the two decades that followed the enactment of the Sex Discrimination Act 1975, the developments in this area mostly occurred as a result of the influence of European law. As will be seen below, European law has had a profound impact on UK sex discrimination law, stretching it into areas which were not originally considered to fall within the scope of the domestic legislation, such as equal pay for work of equal value, benefits on death or retirement, and discrimination on grounds of gender

---

[5] [1966] 2 QB 633, [1966] 1 All ER 689.

[6] Commencement of the Act was delayed for five years to enable employers to remove discrimination in terms and conditions; the Act was heavily amended by the Sex Discrimination Act 1975, and both Acts came into force on the same date.

reassignment. The principal measure is Article 141[7] of the EC Treaty, which provides that 'Each Member State shall ensure that the principle of equal pay for male and female workers for equal work or work of equal value is applied'.[8] In a series of landmark decisions,[9] the ECJ established that Article 141 and its associated Directives (which extend the principle to pay and conditions and to work of equal value)[10] differ from the domestic law in several important respects, not least of which is that the definition of 'pay' under Community law is significantly wider than under domestic law. This is significant for several reasons: first, the supremacy of EC law over the national law of member states means that our domestic equality laws can be measured by the yardstick of Article 141, which prevails over any conflicting provisions of domestic law, in effect overriding them.[11] If domestic law fails properly to implement Community law, the European Commission can bring enforcement proceedings in the European Court in order to enforce compliance,[12] and a person with sufficient standing can bring judicial review proceedings in the Divisional Court for the purpose of securing a declaration that UK primary legislation is incompatible with EC law.[13] Secondly, Article 141 has direct effect,[14] in the sense that a complainant may rely upon it before a domestic court or employment tribunal,[15] which must set aside any incompatible provision of domestic law to give effect to the supremacy of EC law. Thirdly, the two associated Directives have 'vertical' direct effect,[16] meaning a complainant may rely upon them before a

[7] Article 141 was formerly Art 119, but was renumbered in the Amsterdam Treaty. In the interests of readability, this chapter generally refers to Art 141 throughout, irrespective of whether the decisions pre-date the Amsterdam Treaty.

[8] Before the Amsterdam Treaty modifications, Art 119 (as it then was) only mentioned equal pay for *equal work*, not equal pay for *work of equal value*, but it was nevertheless held to cover work of equal value even before the amendment to the wording by the Amsterdam Treaty.

[9] Beginning with *Macarthys Ltd v Smith* Case 129/79 [1980] ICR 672, [1980] IRLR 210, ECJ.

[10] Directives 76/207/EEC (the Equal Treatment Directive) and 75/117/EEC (the Equal Pay Directive).

[11] European Communities Act 1972, s 2(1). See *Amministrazione delle Finanze dello Stato v Simmenthal SpA* [1978] ECR 629, ECJ.

[12] As in Case 61/81 *EC Commission v United Kingdom* [1982] ICR 578, [1982] IRLR 333, where the ECJ held that the existing Equal Pay Act 1970 did not comply with the requirements of the Equal Pay Directive 75/117/EEC by allowing a woman to demand equal pay for work of equal value where there was no job evaluation scheme in force; this led to the introduction into domestic law in 1983 of the concept of equal pay for work of equal value (see later in this chapter under heading 3(iii), p 361). See also Case 165/82 *EC Commission v United Kingdom* [1984] ICR 192, [1984] IRLR 29, ECJ, concerning small firm and private household exceptions, discriminatory collective agreements and midwives.

[13] As in *R v Secretary of State for Employment, ex p EOC* [1995] 1 AC 1, [1994] ICR 317, HL, where the House of Lords declared that the statutory provisions subjecting part-time employees to different qualifying conditions for unfair dismissal from those applicable to full-time employees were incompatible with EC law as they indirectly discriminated against women; this led to the repeal of the offending provisions and the harmonization of qualifying periods for full-time and part-time workers.

[14] *Defrenne v SABENA (No 2)* [1976] ECR 455, [1976] ICR 547, ECJ.

[15] *Secretary of State for Scotland v Wright and Hannah* [1991] IRLR 187, EAT; *Livingstone v Hepworth Refractories plc* [1992] ICR 287, [1992] IRLR 63, EAT.

[16] See *Marshall v Southampton and South-West Hampshire Area Health Authority (Teaching)* [1986] ICR 335, [1986] IRLR 140, ECJ, where the ECJ held that the compulsory retiring of a woman at an earlier age than a man in the same occupation (then lawful under English law) infringed the Equal Treatment Directive. The decision

domestic court or tribunal, but only against the state or an 'organ of the state'[17] (the reasoning being that as it is the state that should have put the Directive properly into effect, the state should not be allowed to rely on its own failure to implement the Directive).[18] Fourthly, the domestic courts and tribunals are obliged to interpret national law as far as possible in such a way as to achieve the result sought by the Directive,[19] if that can be done without unduly distorting the meaning of the domestic legislation;[20] this is so whether or not the national law in question pre-dates the relevant Directive.[21] Finally, the CJEU held in the landmark case of *Francovich v Italy*[22] that an individual who has suffered loss as a result of the failure of a member state fully to implement Community law may in certain circumstances sue the state for damages. This is potentially a highly significant prospect in view of the continuing uncertainty over the requirements of Community law in this area, particularly for private sector employees, who (as seen above) have no remedy against their employer where the state has failed to implement

led to a major revision of the domestic law relating to compulsory retirement ages by the Sex Discrimination Act 1986, but while an employee in the public sector could rely on the Equal Treatment Directive to demand equal compulsory retirement ages even before that Act, an employee in the private sector could not.

[17] Ie 'a body, whatever its legal form, which had been made responsible pursuant to a measure adopted by a public authority, for providing a public service under the control of that authority and had for that purpose special powers beyond those which resulted from the normal rules applicable in relations between individuals'; *Foster v British Gas plc* [1991] 1 QB 405, [1991] ICR 84, ECJ; the House of Lords subsequently held ([1991] 2 AC 306, [1991] ICR 463, HL) that the nationalized British Gas Corporation was an organ of the state against which the Directive could be directly relied upon by its employees to establish discrimination in compulsory retirement ages. Contrast *Doughty v Rolls Royce plc* [1992] ICR 538, [1992] IRLR 126, CA (Rolls Royce was not an organ of the state despite the fact that the state was the sole shareholder prior to its privatization, as it had not been made responsible for providing a public service, nor was there any evidence that it had special powers).

[18] A Directive does not have 'horizontal' direct effect against individuals or non-state bodies (such as a private-sector employer). The ECJ has stated that Directive 75/117 (the Equal Pay Directive) does not extend Art 141 but is simply designed 'to facilitate the practical application' of the principle outlined in the article, and 'in no way alters the content or scope of that principle as defined in the Treaty'. This suggests that Directive 75/117 has both vertical and horizontal direct effect: *Jenkins v Kingsgate (Clothing Productions) Ltd* [1981] ICR 592, [1981] IRLR 228, ECJ.

[19] By this means a domestic court may be able to give indirect effect to a directive even if is not directly effective (eg because the complainant is not employed by an organ of the state); see eg *Pickstone v Freemans plc* [1988] ICR 697, [1988] IRLR 357, HL, where the House of Lords construed s 1(2)(c) of the Equal Pay Act 1970 purposively in order to bring it into line with Art 141; cf Lord Oliver: 'so to construe a provision which, on its face, is unambiguous involves a departure from a number of well-established rules of construction.' See also *Webb v EMO Air Cargo (UK) Ltd* [1992] 4 All ER 929, [1993] ICR 175, HL.

[20] See eg *Duke v GEC Reliance Ltd* [1988] ICR 339, [1988] IRLR 118, HL, where the House of Lords held that it was not possible to construe s 6(4) of the Sex Discrimination Act 1975 (exclusion in respect of provisions in relation to death or retirement) so as to prohibit differential compulsory retirement ages, because s 6(4) was in fact intended to preserve discriminatory retirement ages, and was therefore unambiguously at variance with EC law.

[21] *Marleasing SA v La Comercial Internacional de Alimentación SA* [1990] ECR I-4135, [1992] 1 CMLR 305, ECJ, approved by the House of Lords in *Webb v EMO Air Cargo (UK) Ltd* [1992] 4 All ER 929, [1993] ICR 175, HL.

[22] [1995] ICR 722, [1992] IRLR 84, ECJ. See Curtin (1992) 21 ILJ 74; Parker (1992) 108 LQR 180.

a Directive, although there are a number of demanding hurdles that must be overcome before a claim against the state can succeed.[23]

Domestically, the next big leap forward came with the enactment of the Disability Discrimination Act 1995, the first piece of UK legislation to tackle discrimination against disabled people, which, inter alia, prohibited discrimination against disabled people in relation to employment, the provision of goods, facilities and services, and the sale and letting of property. The tragic death of Stephen Lawrence and the subsequent public inquiry conducted by Sir William Macpherson[24] led to the introduction of the Race Relations (Amendment) Act 2000, which implemented the recommendations of the inquiry report and also placed a positive duty on a wide range of public authorities to promote race equality. The latter development is highly significant, in that it marks a movement away from the traditional, reactive approach to tackling discrimination, which puts the responsibility onto individuals to seek remedies via the courts and tribunals, towards a more proactive approach which 'mainstreams' equality by requiring public authorities to take equality issues into account in the development of their policies and programmes.[25] This wider approach was extended into the field of sex discrimination in 2007,[26] and has now been incorporated in the Equality Act 2010 across all of the protected characteristics other than marriage or civil partnership (it remains, however, limited to the public sector).

As a result of the inclusion into the EC Treaty (by the Treaty of Amsterdam) of Article 13, which provided a new legal basis for Community-wide action to combat discrimination on grounds of sex, racial or ethnic origin, religion or belief, disability, age or sexual orientation,[27] in 1999 the European Commission brought forward two Directives: a Race Directive combating discrimination on grounds of racial or ethnic origin in a wide range of areas, including employment, education, social security, cultural activities and access to goods and services; and a framework Employment Directive dealing with discrimination in employment and occupation on grounds of religion or belief, disability, age or sexual orientation. The Race Directive[28] was adopted in June 2000, and implemented in Great Britain by Regulations amending the Race Relations Act 1976.[29]

---

[23] In *Brasserie du Pêcheur SA v Germany; R v Secretary of State for Transport, ex p Factortame (No 3)* [1996] All ER (EC) 301, [1996] IRLR 267, ECJ, the ECJ set out three conditions: (1) the rule of Community law infringed must be intended to confer rights upon individuals; (2) the breach must be 'sufficiently serious' (ie did the member state 'manifestly and gravely' disregard the limits on its discretion in implementing the requirements of Community law?); and (3) there must be a direct causal link between the breach of the obligation resting on the state and the damage sustained by individuals. Cf *R v HM Treasury, ex p British Telecommunications plc* [1996] IRLR 300, ECJ, where the test was given a narrow interpretation.

[24] *The Stephen Lawrence Inquiry: Report of an Inquiry by Sir William Macpherson* (Cm 4262-I, 1999).

[25] See Fredman 'Equality: A New Generation?' (2001) 30 ILJ 145; Hepple, Coussey and Choudhury *Equality: A New Framework* (2000).

[26] Sex Discrimination Act 1975, s 76A (added by the Equality Act 2006); Sex Discrimination Act 1975 (Public Authorities) (Statutory Duties) Order 2006, SI 2006/2930.

[27] See Waddington (1999) 28 ILJ 133; (2000) 29 ILJ 176.   [28] Directive 2000/43/EC.

[29] Race Relations Act 1976 (Amendment) Regulations 2003, SI 2003/1626.

The Employment Directive[30] was adopted in November 2000, and was implemented by a series of Regulations amending the Disability Discrimination Act (DDA) 1995,[31] and introducing new measures prohibiting discrimination in employment on grounds of religion or belief,[32] sexual orientation[33] and age.[34] The implementing Regulations were preceded by a lengthy consultation process.[35] The amendments to the existing law on race and disability discrimination, and the new measures on sexual orientation, religion or belief discrimination and age, are now integrated into the 2010 Act. Initially, however, the government implemented the Directives by Regulations[36] rather than by primary legislation, which made it impossible to rationalize the old and new provisions (the obstacle being that as parts of the existing anti-discrimination legislation sat outside the scope of EC law, they were not amenable to modification via secondary legislation). The result was a proverbial dog's breakfast, with significant differences *between* the strands, and even differences *within* the strands, depending on whether the provisions related to areas falling within the scope of one of the new Directives. One problem, for example, was that domestic law on disability pre-dated EU intervention, arguably gave greater protection *but* was drafted entirely differently. Similarly, domestic race discrimination law permitted different defences than those authorized by the EC Directives, and thus retained them, alongside the new European defences, but only for the aspects of 'race' specified in the Race Relations Act *but not* in the EC Directives.

The situation was marginally improved by the Equality Act 2006, whose purpose was *not* to consolidate the multiple strands of substantive law, but instead to create the Commission for Equality of Human Rights (now the Equality and Human Rights Commission), to take over from the Equal Opportunities Commission, the Commission for Racial Equality and the Disability Rights Commission from October 2007. This body (the EHRC) fills in the obvious gaps that, prior to its inception, there was no supervisory body for sexual orientation, religion/belief or age discrimination. More fundamentally, however, it has broad, general duties[37] a more specific duty to promote equality and diversity[38] and a specific remit to promote understanding of, and

---

[30] Directive 2000/78/EC.

[31] Disability Discrimination Act 1995 (Amendment) Regulations 2003, SI 2003/1673.

[32] Employment Equality (Religion or Belief) Regulations 2003, SI 2003/1660.

[33] Employment Equality (Sexual Orientation) Regulations 2003, SI 2003/1661.

[34] Employment Equality (Age) Regulations 2006, SI 2006/1031.

[35] *Towards Equality and Diversity: Implementing the Employment and Race Directives* (DTI, 2001); *Equality and Diversity: The Way Ahead* (DTI, 2002); *Equality and Diversity: Making it Happen* (DTI, 2002); *Equality and Diversity: Age Matters* (DTI, 2003).

[36] Under the European Communities Act 1972, s 2.

[37] Equality Act 2006, s 3; these duties relate to the development of a society in which (1) people's ability to achieve their potential is not limited by prejudice or discrimination, (2) there is respect for and protection of each individual's human rights, (3) there is respect for the dignity of each individual, (4) each individual has an equal opportunity to participate in society, and (5) there is mutual respect between groups based on understanding and valuing of diversity and on shared respect for equality and human rights.

[38] Equality Act 2006, s 8; under s 11 there is a duty to monitor the effectiveness of equality and human rights enactments.

encourage good practice in relation to, human rights *generally*,[39] thus going beyond the pre-existing boundaries of discrimination law as such. However, this only brought coherence to some aspects of anti-discrimination enforcement, and did not cure the broader ills afflicting equality law.

This chaotic state of British anti-discrimination legislation, which arguably brought the law into disrepute, has been rendered much more reputable by the 2010 Equality Act. It had been a long time in coming, the idea having received notable attention as early as 2000,[40] and having been a matter of government consultation since 2005.[41] The Bill itself was introduced in April 2009 and the Act came into force in October 2010. The most important changes wrought by the Act, in the area of employment law, were that it (1) treats all grounds of discrimination the same, using uniform and much clearer definitions of concepts, with some specified and already generally accepted exceptions, (2) permits a carefully circumscribed amount of positive discrimination in tie-breaker cases, and (3) corrects a grievous misinterpretation of the DDA by the House of Lords. All of these issues are taken up in the next, and main, section of the chapter on the 2010 Act. The remaining sections deal with issues unique to specific grounds of discrimination, some of which are specified in the Act, but most of which have evolved through pre-Act case law that remains applicable.

2 THE EQUALITY ACT 2010

(i) APPLICATION AND COVERAGE

The aim of the Equality Act 2010 is to prevent discrimination on the basis of protected characteristics in several areas, including employment. The parts which are relevant here apply to discrimination in 'work' (Part 5 of the Act) which includes 'employment' (Chapter 1) and 'equality of terms' (Chapter 3). 'Employment' is defined as working under a contract of employment, of apprenticeship, or under a contract personally to do work;[42] a person outside this definition may not claim the benefit of the relevant provision,[43] except in the case of 'contract workers' (ie people working for A who have in fact been engaged by B and hired to A under a contract of supply of labour)

---

[39] Equality Act 2006, s 9.

[40] The arguments for and against a single Equality Act are considered in Hepple, Coussey and Choudhury *Equality: A New Framework* (2000) ch 2.

[41] *Discrimination Law Review: A Framework for Fairness: Proposals for a Single Equality Bill for Great Britain* (Department of Communities and Local Government, London: 2007).

[42] Equality Act 2010, s 83(2)(a). This is a deliberately extended definition, capable of taking in certain categories of the self-employed as well as employees: *Quinnen v Hovells* [1984] ICR 525, [1984] IRLR 227; *Gunning v Mirror Group Newspapers Ltd* [1986] 1 All ER 385, [1986] ICR 145, CA. The tribunal's jurisdiction is not dependent on the existence of an enforceable contract: *Leighton v Michael* [1995] ICR 1091, [1996] IRLR 67, EAT.

[43] *Knight v A-G* [1979] ICR 194, EAT.

and certain office holders, who are included.[44] The Act prohibits discrimination at all stages of employment, whether in relation to the arrangements which the employer makes for selecting employees, the terms on which he offers employment, access to promotion, transfer, training or other benefits, or dismissal. The Act also gives a trade union member a right not to be discriminated against by the union on the basis of a protected characteristic in matters of admission, expulsion and provision of union benefits, facilities, etc.[45]

However, once the employment has commenced any complaint relating to sex inequality in the terms and conditions of employment must be brought under the 'equality of terms' provisions.[46] It was recently clarified that less favourable treatment in the exercise of discretion authorized under the contract (such as the allocation of share options permitted, but not specified, under the contract) is sex discrimination, not a matter of equality of terms.[47] This reflects the longstanding separate treatment of equal pay between the sexes on one hand and sex discrimination on the other, both in Europe and domestically. The Sex Discrimination Act 1975 came into force in December 1975, at the same time as the Equal Pay Act 1970. While the statutes were clearly complementary and wherever possible were to be construed 'so as to form a harmonious code',[48] they were mutually exclusive in their operation, so that an action had to be brought under the correct statute.[49] The borderline was that the Equal Pay Act 1970 applied to contractual terms of employment, amenable to inclusion in the statutory 'equality clause', whereas the Sex Discrimination Act 1975 applied to discrimination on grounds of sex in matters outside the contract (such as recruitment, promotion and dismissal) and was thus much wider. The Race Relations Act 1976 was modelled on the Sex Discrimination Act (SDA) 1975 (although it made no distinction between pay and other aspects of employment), and cases decided under one Act would normally also be precedents for the other.[50] The existence of two principal Acts concerning sex discrimination gave rise to complexity and confusion in this area, a situation exacerbated by the impact of EC law, and in particular Article 141 of the EC Treaty. As seen above, although ostensibly concerned with 'pay', Article 141 (as explained and expanded by its supporting Directives) was much wider in scope than the Equal Pay Act 1970, and many of the cases decided by the CJEU have concerned matters which, in English

---

[44] Equality Act 2010, ss 41, 49–52. In *Jivraj v Hashwani* [2011] UKSC 40 it was held that an arbitrator held too independent an office, and was insufficiently subordinate, for his selection to be covered by the employment provisions of the Act.

[45] Equality Act 2010, s 57. See Homans (1984) 13 ILJ 262.

[46] Equality Act 2010, s 66.

[47] *Hosso v European Credit Management* [2011] EWCA Civ 1589, (CA).

[48] *Steel v UPOW* [1978] ICR 181 at 186, [1977] IRLR 288 at 290, per Phillips J; *Jenkins v Kingsgate (Clothing Productions) Ltd (No 2)* [1981] ICR 715, [1981] IRLR 388, EAT.

[49] *Oliver v J P Malnick & Co (No 2)* [1984] ICR 458, IT is a good example. For an illustration of the difficulties raised by the distinction, see *Barclays Bank plc v James* [1990] ICR 333, [1990] IRLR 90; the case was subsequently settled on the understanding that the EAT's decision was wrong: [1990] IRLR 499.

[50] Although this may not be the case where the substantive provisions have diverged, eg as a result of the amendments to the Race Relations Act 1976 to implement the Race Directive.

domestic law, would fall within the ambit of the Sex Discrimination Act (SDA) 1975. With hindsight, the law would have been much more straightforward and transparent if the drafters of the 1975 Act had simply torn up the Equal Pay Act 1970 and started again with a clean sheet of paper. The EOC had long recommended the replacement of the two Acts by a single Sex Equality Act, incorporating EC law and based on the principle of a fundamental right to equal treatment between men and women,[51] but the government indicated[52] that it did not believe that major legislative change of that type was appropriate, a view it held until the consultation on the Equality Act 2010. The separation has been maintained in the Act, however, as the provisions relating to 'equality of terms' (essentially the guarantees found in the Equal Pay Act 1970) provide that anything that counts as equality-of-terms discrimination does not count as sex discrimination.[53]

The Act specifies certain exclusions, some of which are particularly relevant to discrimination in employment. Thus, the application of the Act is modified in the case of ministers of religion,[54] and cases where the alleged discrimination relates to the provision of services by the employer to the worker as a member of the public, rather than as an employee, are excluded.[55] It also allows women and transsexuals to be excluded from certain parts of the armed forces. The SDA 1975 previously contained a blanket immunity to sex discrimination for the armed forces, but it was applied to them in 1995, albeit with an exemption for acts 'done for the purpose of ensuring the combat effectiveness of the armed forces'[56] (a dispensation which has been widely and controversially used in order to exclude women from certain sections of the armed forces). This more limited exemption was itself the subject of legal challenge in *Sirdar v Army Board*,[57] where the CJEU held that the Royal Marines were not in breach of the Equal Treatment Directive by not engaging a woman as a cook, despite the seemingly tenuous connection between catering and combat effectiveness, on the grounds that their policy of 'inter-operability' meant that all members of the Marines had to be capable of serving as front-line commandos. The CJEU held that there is no general exception to the principle of equal treatment under Community law permitting the blanket exclusion of women from the armed forces, but that their exclusion from service in special combat units such as the Marines 'may' be justified under Article 2(2), provided the principle of proportionality is observed (ie that the exclusion is within the limits of what is appropriate and necessary in order to achieve the aim of protecting public security).[58] This principle is now expressly provided for in the Equality Act, which

---

[51] EOC *Equality in the 21st Century: A New Sex Equality Law for Britain* (1998).

[52] The government's response was heavily influenced by the Better Regulation Task Force's *Review of Anti-Discrimination Legislation in Great Britain* (May 1999).

[53] Equality Act 2010, s 70.   [54] Equality Act 2010, Sch 9, para 2.

[55] Equality Act 2010, Sch 9, para 19.   [56] Sex Discrimination Act 1975, s 85(4).

[57] [2000] ICR 130, [2000] IRLR 47, ECJ.

[58] Article 2(2) of the Equal Treatment Directive permits a derogation from the principle of equal treatment in the case of occupational activities where the sex of the worker 'constitutes a determining factor'. See *Kreil v*

allows women or transsexuals to be excluded if the exclusion 'is a proportionate means of ensuring the combat effectiveness of the armed forces.'[59]

There was previously an important (and extremely troublesome) exclusion for provisions in relation to death or retirement,[60] which was considered necessary because discrimination in retirement provision (state and private) has historically been firmly entrenched, based on differential state pensionable ages. However, that exclusion became increasingly untenable in the light of the CJEU's rulings on the scope of Article 141 and the associated Directives, culminating in *Barber v Guardian Royal Exchange Assurance Group*,[61] where the CJEU held that a pension paid under a contracted-out, private occupational pension scheme falls within the scope of Article 141. The government was therefore forced to reconsider the whole question of equality of treatment in pensions provision, and the Pensions Act 1995 introduced important new provisions requiring equal treatment in both membership of and rights under occupational pension schemes,[62] repealing the existing exclusion in the sex discrimination and equal pay legislation for provisions in relation to death or retirement.[63] The issue is now dealt with in the Equality Act.

(ii) PROTECTED CHARACTERISTICS

The Equality Act 2010 sets out early on the protected characteristics to which it applies: age, disability, gender reassignment, marriage and civil partnership, pregnancy and maternity, race, religion or belief, sex and sexual orientation.[64] The Act in general seeks to outline protections in a way that refers back to these characteristics and applies the same prohibitions with regard to each. This is deceptive, however, 'marriage and civil partnership' is excluded from the 'indirect discrimination' provisions. Moreover, almost all of the protected characteristics can boast several special provisions that make discrimination on that ground subtly unique. Nevertheless, most provisions can be understood to forbid discrimination roughly the same across all grounds so long as the discrimination happens because the claimant has one or more of the protected characteristics on the list above (other than 'pregnancy and maternity'). This last characteristic has its own singular protection proscribing unfavourable treatment during a defined maternity period or arising from the pregnancy.[65] Another characteristic that receives custom protection is gender reassignment: a person who is absent

---

Bundesrepublik Deutschland Case C-285/98 [2000] ECR I-69, where the ECJ interpreted the derogation very narrowly.

[59] Equality Act 2010, Sch 9, para 4.

[60] Sex Discrimination Act 1975, s 6(4), as substituted by the Pensions Act 1995, s 66(3). The equivalent exclusion in the Equal Pay Act 1970, s 6(1A) and (2), was substituted by s 66(1) of the 1995 Act.

[61] [1990] ICR 616, [1990] IRLR 240, ECJ.   [62] Pensions Act 1995, ss 62–66.

[63] Sex Discrimination Act 1975, s 66(1), (3). Note, however, that s 6(4) (as substituted by the 1995 Act) does not outlaw discrimination in relation to membership of, or rights under, an occupational scheme where such discrimination is not prohibited by the 1995 Act.

[64] Equality Act 2010, s 4.   [65] Equality Act 2010, s 18.

from work as a result of undergoing gender reassignment has a right to be treated no less favourably than would be the case if the absence was due to sickness or injury, or to some other cause such that, having regard to the circumstances, it is reasonable for the treatment to be no less favourable.[66]

The characteristic of gender reassignment, unlike pregnancy and maternity, also enjoys protection from core prohibitions of direct, combined and indirect discrimination (about which more below). Historically this has been a difficult area because UK law traditionally refused to recognize gender reassignment as having any effect on a person's legal gender, which remained as it was at birth.[67] However, in the landmark case of *Goodwin v United Kingdom*[68] the European Court of Human Rights held that by failing to give legal recognition to the gender reassignment of a post-operative male-to-female transsexual, the UK had failed to comply with its obligation to respect her private life under Article 8 of the European Convention. This led to the Gender Recognition Act 2004 which contains the concept of 'acquired gender'. In fact, however, these legislative changes were effectively upstaged (at least in the case of a post-operative transsexual) by the decision of the House of Lords in *A v Chief Constable of West Yorkshire Police*,[69] in which a post-operative male-to-female transsexual was refused employment in the police on the ground that she could not perform the full range of body searches necessary (the Police and Criminal Evidence Act 1984, section 54 stating that the searcher must be of the same sex as the person searched). The House of Lords, however, held that this was unlawful discrimination. Relying on the Equal Treatment Directive 76/207/EEC to thump the 1984 Act, they said that a post-operative transsexual is to be treated in employment law as being of the acquired gender, where that individual is visually and for all practical purposes indistinguishable from non-transsexual members of that gender.

A few more points should be noted about the remaining protected characteristics. First, 'race' in the 2010 Act means colour, nationality, ethnic origin or national origin.[70] Second, disability also attracts special protections, discussed more in the next section and in the later section on disability discrimination. Third, while age ostensibly receives protection from all of the core provisions, it is riddled with exceptions and qualifications (not a change from the Regulations that preceded the 2010 Act) and is thus clearly less protected than other characteristics. Fourth, 'religion or belief' includes philosophical belief as well as the absence of belief.[71] Finally, sexual orientation as a protected characteristic is not so fully protected when to guarantee that protection would require religious groups or employers to modify their practices or tolerate those whom their belief system tells them they should not tolerate (discussed further in the section on sexual orientation discrimination).

[66] Equality Act 2010, s 16.   [67] *Corbett v Corbett* [1970] 2 WLR 1306.
[68] [2002] IRLR 664, ECtHR.   [69] [2004] ICR 806, [2004] IRLR 573, HL.
[70] Equality Act 2010, s 9.   [71] Equality Act 2010, s 10.

(iii) THE MEANING OF 'DISCRIMINATION'

As has been noted above, from the mid-1970s to the mid-1990s UK discrimination law was dominated by the SDA 1975 and the Race Relations Act (RRA) 1976, which were generally interpreted by the courts as calling for consistent application where possible. Subsequent enactments to cover other grounds of discrimination followed the template of those two Acts, with the result that, except in the case of ground-specific variations, precedent for one ground would apply to similar issues relating to other grounds. Interchangeability particularly applied to interpretations of the meaning of discrimination concepts like 'indirect discrimination' and 'detriment', because the theory behind the legal measures in those regards were the same, regardless of how different the factual issues might be between race and sex. This pattern is expected to continue under the 2010 Act, given that few fundamental changes have been made to the core discrimination concepts. Thus, with regard to defining 'discrimination' and other core concepts and issues applicable to discrimination law across all grounds, cases involving race, sex and other characteristics will be cited interchangeably in this chapter. Because of the historical facts that (1) the SDA came first, followed by the RRA and (2) a great many concepts were fashioned by EC sex equality law, most of the cases cited will be sex cases, and most of the rest will be race cases. There are of course some ground-specific issues, so this chapter deals first with the common issues and then with issues specific to each protected characteristic.

Another point needs to be made about the various meanings of discrimination. This chapter describes the concepts based on the language of the statutes, the theories behind that language, and the best of the decided cases. However, no student of this area of law will fail to notice that some cases appear to fly in the face of the theory of anti-discrimination law or the language of the statutes that implement it. This is a fact that students of discrimination law should accept before they try to tackle the concepts discussed below. An underlying truth about equality law is that it seeks to change behaviour. It does not enter into a world where equal treatment is the status quo, and the law need only hold the line against slipping standards. Instead, it enters into a world in which discrimination—not only discriminatory actions but, more importantly, apparently neutral actions that are experienced as discriminatory—happens every day, and more often than not because of attitudes or policies that strike those who hold or adopt them as 'common sense'. There may exist less blatant discrimination now than when the SDA came on the scene in 1975, but what remains is often more difficult to handle because it is not blatant. The issue is not just that it is hard to prove, or that people keep it hidden. It is that some of the most intractable discrimination is perpetrated by accident, by 'good' people who simply cannot or will not accept this truth: just because (1) something has always been a certain way, and (2) nobody has had bad intentions in keeping it that way, does not mean that nobody is getting unfairly and unequally hurt by it. Arrangements that suit, and always have suited, a majority group might unnecessarily but very seriously disadvantage minority or less empowered groups without anyone meaning them to do so. Judges are no worse than other people, but neither are they better. As a result, a great many judicial decisions simply reflect the inability (or unwillingness) of judges to look past practices or assumptions with which they have been comfortable for a lifetime, to see the relative disadvantage those practices and assumptions produce. In other words, some cases are just wrong, at least when measured against what equality law seeks to accomplish and actually expresses through statutory language. Specific examples of this are noted where relevant in this chapter, but the point in noting it here is to free the reader from a sense of responsibility to reconcile all of the case law with the conceptual explanations that follow.

(a) Direct discrimination

The Equality Act 2010 defines several types of discrimination or 'prohibited conduct': direct discrimination, indirect discrimination and discrimination by way of harassment and victimization (there are also special concepts relating to disability discrimination, as well as protections for pregnancy and maternity and for absence from work for gender reassignment, but these are not treated here as separate discrimination concepts, but considered in the ground-specific sections below; the general discrimination types are addressed in turn in this and the following sections). Direct discrimination is defined in section 13 as where the employer, on the ground of a protected characteristic, treats a worker less favourably than a person without that characteristic. The scope of section 13 is wide, particularly as the House of Lords has made clear in the leading case of *James v Eastleigh Borough Council*[72] that in determining whether there has been direct discrimination the motive or purpose or intention of the alleged discriminator is irrelevant. In that case the applicant, a man of 61, complained that he had been discriminated against by the local authority because he had been charged 75p to swim in the municipal swimming baths, while his wife of the same age had been admitted free under the authority's policy of allowing free entry to those who had reached the state pensionable age of 65 for men and 60 for women. The Court of Appeal had held (distinguishing an earlier House of Lords decision to the effect that a subjective motive or intention to discriminate is not a condition of liability)[73] that there had not been less favourable treatment on the ground of sex because the reason for the concession was to benefit pensioners and not to discriminate against men. In the words of Browne-Wilkinson V-C: 'In my judgment there is a clear distinction between the ground or reason for which a person acts and his intention in so acting.' However, on further appeal the House of Lords overturned this decision, rejecting the subjective approach and instead affirming that the correct approach is an objective one: 'Would the complainant have received the same treatment but for his sex?' On the facts it was clear that the less favourable treatment would not have occurred but for the complainant's sex, and so there was direct discrimination. The fact that the council did not intend to discriminate against the applicant, and that its reason for adopting

---

[72] [1990] ICR 554, [1990] IRLR 288, HL; revsg [1989] ICR 423, [1989] IRLR 318, CA.

[73] *Birmingham City Council v Equal Opportunities Commission* [1989] AC 1155, [1989] IRLR 173, HL.

the policy of concessions to pensioners was an honourable one,[74] was considered to be irrelevant.

It follows that a good motive on the part of the employer (for example a belief that the discriminatory action is in the applicant's own best interests) is no excuse for what is, on the wording, an act of discrimination[75] (nor is the fact that the employer has been pressurized to discriminate by a third party, for example a trade union, or the applicant's fellow employees).[76] A particularly good example of this can be seen in *Moyhing v Barts & London NHS Trust*[77] where, to protect male nurses and to reassure patients, the hospital had a rule that male nurses performing intimate procedures on female patients had to be chaperoned; no such requirement applied to female nurses. In spite of the hospital's view that this was a 'common sense' measure, when it was challenged by an aggrieved male nurse it was held to be unlawful direct discrimination. Given that one of the aims of the legislation is to discourage the treatment of groups en masse as capable of certain things and incapable of others, general stereotypical assumptions (for example that women cannot do heavy work or that Christians will not work on Sundays) are likely to be held to be discriminatory, and an employer who acts on such assumptions may well contravene the statute.[78]

For there to be a finding of direct discrimination it must be shown that the employer has treated the applicant 'less favourably' than the employer 'treats or would treat' others, 'because of a protected characteristic'. Unlike the 'equality of terms' provisions of the Act, which work on the basis of a comparison between the treatment of the applicant and that of a named comparator (or comparators), the rest of the Equality Act is based on a comparison with a hypothetical comparator ('treats or would treat'), and the comparison must be such that there is 'no material difference between the circumstances relevant to each case'.[79] The identification of the appropriate comparator, and the determination of which circumstances are to be considered as relevant, are key elements in any discrimination claim, often requiring difficult judgments as to which of the differences between any two individuals are relevant and which are irrelevant,

---

[74] The case is a good illustration of the fact that, other than the specified exceptions, there is no 'justification' defence in a complaint of direct discrimination. Cf Bowers and Moran 'Justification in Direct Sex Discrimination Law: Breaking the Taboo' (2002) 31 ILJ 307.

[75] *Peake v Automotive Products Ltd* [1977] ICR 480, [1977] IRLR 105 (reversed on other grounds, [1977] ICR 968, [1977] IRLR 365, CA); *Grieg v Community Industry* [1979] ICR 356, [1979] IRLR 158; *Din v Carrington Viyella Ltd* [1982] ICR 256, [1982] IRLR 281. While motive is not relevant when determining whether discrimination has occurred, it may be relevant when deciding the level of compensation to be awarded: *Chief Constable of the Greater Manchester Police v Hope* [1999] ICR 338, EAT.

[76] *R v Commission for Racial Equality, ex p Westminster City Council* [1985] ICR 827, [1985] IRLR 426, CA.

[77] [2006] IRLR 860, Taking up the point in n 75, the fact that the rule was not aimed at him and had actually caused little inconvenience led to a small award of compensation.

[78] *Skyrail Oceanic Ltd v Coleman* [1981] ICR 864, [1981] IRLR 398, CA; *Horsey v Dyfed County Council* [1982] ICR 755, [1982] IRLR 395.

[79] Equality Act 2010, s 23. This kind of requirement has been especially problematic in cases involving pregnancy discrimination, where for obvious reasons it is not possible to make the necessary comparison.

and the choice of characteristics 'may itself be determinative of the outcome'.[80] It is important that judges (and the lawyers who brief them) do not lose sight of the point of this exercise: to determine whether the less favourable treatment was 'because of a protected characteristic'. Obviously, if in a dismissal letter an employer writes, 'you have been dismissed because we do not like homosexuals in this company', the dismissed applicant need hardly produce a comparator to prove the point of less favourable treatment. More problematically, tribunals are sometimes tempted to include, as 'circumstances relevant to each case', facts that actually flow necessarily from the alleged ground of discrimination. So, for example, in *James*—where the man paid to swim but his wife of the same age did not—the court might have included pensionable status as a relevant circumstance, thus distinguishing the comparators and disposing of the case. However, the different pensionable statuses of the man and woman were not considered because they were direct consequences of their sex. Similarly, the gender the criminal justice system *deems* a gender reassigned person to have is not a relevant circumstance for comparison, and should not be allowed to prevent comparison with a non-reassigned person who does not face such an institutional deeming. It is important to note, however, that circumstances that are related to a protected characteristic but are not direct and unavoidable consequences of it can and often should be considered, if relevant. Thus, for example, the facts that a woman with caring responsibilities cannot work certain shifts, or that a person with a given religious affiliation refuses to work on certain holy days, should be considered as distinguishing them from people who can or will work those shifts/days; these can exclude direct discrimination claims—because they can show that a challenged decision was based on a neutral rule about working schedules, not on gender or religion—but they cannot exclude indirect discrimination, discussed below. Finally, relevant circumstances must not include facts that did not in reality have any bearing on the challenged decision. A comparison should not be rejected because the comparators have different degrees of work experience if work experience was not a criterion in the challenged hiring/promotion decision: because it was not actually a criterion for the impugned decision, the distinction cannot disprove that the decision was based on a protected characteristic. It may be possible to find an actual comparator whose circumstances are the same or not materially different to those of the applicant, in which case that person can perform the role of the statutory comparator, but in most cases this will not be possible, and in such circumstances the tribunal must[81] make a hypothetical comparison, by considering how the employer would have treated a male employee in comparable circumstances. One way of doing this is to see how the employer acted 'in cases which, while not

---

[80] *Shamoon v Chief Constable of the Royal Ulster Constabulary* [2003] UKHL 11, [2003] IRLR 285 at 292, per Lord Hope.

[81] A tribunal commits an error of law if it does not construct a hypothetical comparator, where one is required, against which to test the alleged discriminatory treatment: *Balamoody v United Kingdom Central Council for Nursing, Midwifery and Health Visiting* [2001] EWCA Civ 2097, [2002] IRLR 288, CA. See also *Chief Constable of West Yorkshire v Vento* [2001] IRLR 124, EAT.

identical, were also not wholly dissimilar',[82] as that evidence may provide a sound basis for inferring how the employer would have treated another employee in the same circumstances as the applicant.

Prior to the 2010 Act, the SDA 1975 based direct discrimination on the sex of the applicant, and the DDA 1995 based discrimination on the disabled status of the applicant, while other legislation (eg, the RRA 1976 and the 2006 Employment Equality Regulations) addressed direct discrimination 'on grounds of' the protected characteristics of, for example, race or sexual orientation. This meant that some legislation was susceptible to the interpretation that it was discriminatory to treat someone less favourably because of their association with a person of a certain race or sexual orientation, while statutes like the SDA expressly ruled this out. Where possible, case law clarified that such 'association' discrimination was actionable, but discontinuities remained. The 2010 Act clears this up by defining all direct discrimination, whatever the ground, as less favourable treatment 'because of a protected characteristic'. This is intended to make the concept of direct discrimination broad enough to encompass, for example, less favourable treatment for caring for a disabled child, or for being married to an Asian man.

Because direct discrimination is based around the concept of 'less favourable' treatment, differential treatment does not in itself amount to discrimination: 'If discrimination is to be established, it is necessary to show not merely that the [comparators] are treated differently, but that the treatment accorded to one is less favourable than the treatment accorded to the other.'[83] The need to show treatment which is 'less favourable', and not merely different, is problematic, not least because it can give rise to the kind of tendentious 'separate but equal' arguments once used to justify racial segregation in the US.[84] On the whole the courts have been robust in resisting such arguments, and have generally accepted that differential treatment is detrimental, although not without the occasional unfortunate lapse. Indeed, in the first case under the SDA 1975 to come before the Court of Appeal, *Peake v Automotive Products Ltd,*[85] the court was prepared to disregard differential treatment on the grounds that it was too minor. In that case, the employer allowed women to leave the factory five minutes before the men, in the interests of safety and to avoid women being caught in the rush to the gates. One of the men complained to a tribunal that this was unlawful discrimination against men. The EAT upheld his claim, but the Court of Appeal unanimously rejected it, on the grounds that the different treatment was in the interests of safety and good administration (in the words of Lord Denning MR: 'it is not discriminatory for mankind to treat womankind

---

[82] *Balamoody v United Kingdom Central Council for Nursing, Midwifery and Health Visiting* [2001] EWCA Civ 2097, [2002] IRLR 288 at 306, per Lord Rodger.

[83] *Smith v Safeway plc* [1996] IRLR 456 at 458, CA, per Phillips J.

[84] Such arguments are excluded in the case of race, as the Equality Act specifically provides in s 13(5) that racial segregation is less favourable treatment.

[85] [1977] ICR 968, [1977] IRLR 365, CA, restrictively interpreted by the EAT in *Grieg v Community Industry* [1979] ICR 356, [1979] IRLR 158.

with the courtesy and chivalry which we have been taught to believe is right conduct in our society'), and that in any event the employer's action was harmless and could be disregarded under the de minimis principle. In the later case of *Ministry of Defence v Jeremiah*[86] the Court of Appeal reconsidered the approach taken in *Peake*. In that case it was held that requiring a man employed in an ordnance factory to perform dirty and unpleasant work making 'colour-bursting' shells when women working in the factory were excused from such work was less favourable treatment within the meaning of the Act, and therefore unlawful. Lord Denning MR stated that the approach to the definition of direct discrimination taken in *Peake* (ie exempting 'sensible administrative arrangements' in the interests of health or chivalry) was wrong and that the decision was only supportable on the alternative ground given (ie that on the facts the discrimination was too minor to be effective, under the de minimis principle). On the facts in *Jeremiah* it was held that requiring only the men to do the work in question was unlawful, and the fact that they were paid extra to do it was irrelevant.

While the approach of the Court of Appeal in *Jeremiah* showed a stronger adherence to the actual wording of the Act, it still seemed to allow some scope for the de minimis defence. In subsequent cases the courts have tended to take a more robust approach, particularly where the alleged less favourable treatment involves the denial of an opportunity afforded to others. In *Jeremiah*, Brightman LJ suggested that as differentiation is not necessarily discriminatory, a mere deprivation of choice might not of itself be unlawful.[87] However, in *Birmingham City Council v Equal Opportunities Commission*[88] (a case involving access to grammar schools), the House of Lords held that in order to establish less favourable treatment on the grounds of sex, it is enough that members of one sex are deprived of a choice which is valued by them and which (even though others may take a different view) is a choice obviously valued on reasonable grounds by many others. A similarly broad approach to the concept of less favourable treatment was taken in *Gill v El Vino Co Ltd*,[89] where the Court of Appeal held that it was unlawful for a wine bar to refuse to serve women at the bar. In that case Eveleigh LJ stated:

> I find it very difficult to invoke the maxim de minimis non curat lex in a situation where that which has been denied to the plaintiff is the very thing that Parliament seeks to provide, namely facilities and services on an equal basis.[90]

There is, however, an important caveat that needs to be entered, as the question of whether there is less favourable treatment is an objective one for the tribunal to decide; the fact that a complainant subjectively considers that he or she has been less favourably treated does not of itself establish that there is 'less favourable treatment' within the meaning of section 13.[91] The House of Lords has confirmed that in order for

---

[86] [1979] 3 All ER 833, [1979] IRLR 436, CA.   [87] [1979] 3 All ER 833 at 840, [1979] IRLR 436 at 440.
[88] [1989] IRLR 173, HL.   [89] [1983] IRLR 206, CA.   [90] [1983] IRLR 206 at 208.
[91] *Burrett v West Birmingham Health Authority* [1994] IRLR 7 at 8, EAT, per Knox J. See this chapter, heading 3, p 351.

treatment to constitute a detriment, the tribunal must find that 'a reasonable worker would or might take the view that the treatment was in all the circumstances to his [sic] detriment'.[92] The test is not wholly objective, in that it must be applied by considering the issue from the point of view of the victim.[93] A similar approach was taken in *Stewart v Cleveland Guest (Engineering) Ltd*,[94] where the EAT refused to overturn the tribunal's finding that the employers had not discriminated against the complainant on grounds of sex by allowing male employees to display nude pin-ups in the workplace, even though they knew that the pictures were offensive to her. According to the EAT, there is room for disagreement as to what is or is not less favourable treatment, and the employment tribunal is best placed to make a decision on the facts of a particular case.

A further difficulty with the need to show 'less favourable' treatment is that it enables an employer to argue that, because all employees receive equally bad treatment, the treatment of one sex, race or other group is no less favourable than his treatment of another.[95] The tribunals in the past were able to circumvent this line of argument, particularly in harassment cases, by holding that conduct which is 'gender-specific' is sexually discriminatory per se, without the need for any comparison.[96] However, in *Pearce v Governing Body of Mayfield Secondary School*[97] (a case decided shortly before the new statutory definition of 'harassment' was introduced) the House of Lords rejected this approach: 'The fact that harassment is gender specific in form cannot be regarded as of itself establishing conclusively that the reason for the harassment is gender-based: "on the ground of her sex".'[98] The 2010 Act now defines harassment as unwanted conduct 'related to a protected characteristic', calling the continuing vitality of *Pearce* into question. Another circumstance in which the courts are prepared to find that conduct is discriminatory per se, without the need for any comparison, is in the context of pregnancy discrimination, where the comparative approach breaks down because of the absence of an appropriate (actual or hypothetical) male comparator.[99]

Finally, it must be remembered that the complainant has to be able to show the necessary causal connection between the less favourable treatment and the protected characteristic of the complainant; if there is some other genuine reason for the less favourable treatment which is untainted by discrimination (for example the employer genuinely needs someone strong or experienced and the worker in question is weak or

---

[92] *Shamoon v Chief Constable of the Royal Ulster Constabulary* [2003] UKHL 11, [2003] IRLR 285 at 301, per Lord Scott; *Chief Constable of West Yorkshire Police v Khan* [2003] UKHL 11, [2001] IRLR 830 at 835, per Lord Hoffmann.

[93] 'If the victim's opinion that the treatment was to his or her detriment is a reasonable one to hold, that ought, in my opinion, to suffice': [2003] IRLR 285 at 301, per Lord Scott.

[94] [1996] ICR 535, [1994] IRLR 440, EAT.

[95] An argument customarily referred to by the authors as the 'bastard' defence (as in 'But I'm a bastard to everyone').

[96] See eg *British Telecommunications plc v Williams* [1997] IRLR 668, EAT.

[97] [2003] IRLR 512, HL.   [98] [2003] IRLR 512 at 516, per Lord Nicholls.

[99] See Ch 4, heading 3(xiii), p 290.

inexperienced), then that is not 'because of a protected characteristic' and discrimination is not established. So for example, in *Bullock v Alice Ottley School*,[100] the employers maintained a retirement age of 60 for teaching and domestic staff (who were primarily female) and 65 for gardeners and maintenance staff (who were all male). The applicant, a domestic worker who was retired at 60, complained that she had been treated less favourably because of her sex, but the Court of Appeal held that there was no direct discrimination on grounds of sex because there was no evidence that a man in the same job would have been treated any differently. Greater difficulties arise where the employer acts from mixed motives, not all of which constitute unlawful discrimination. It is clearly established that the unlawful motive need not be the sole reason for the employer's action. In *Owen and Briggs v James*,[101] a race discrimination case, the Court of Appeal held that where there is more than one operating cause, it is enough if the unlawful motive is an 'important factor' in the employer's decision; in other words, the unlawful motive must be of sufficient weight in the decision-making process to be treated as a cause, but not necessarily the sole cause, of the act thus motivated.[102]

(b) Indirect discrimination

Discrimination can, of course, take more subtle forms than the overt form envisaged above. In particular, it could take the form of a rule, policy, criterion or practice which, while not expressly mentioning a protected characteristic, in practice puts one group at a disadvantage because it has a disproportionate impact on the members of that group; for example a requirement that applicants for a particular post be between 17 and 28, while gender-neutral on its face, may be held to discriminate indirectly against women because in practice many women would be unavailable for work between those ages because of family commitments.[103] Similarly, a rule that a candidate for a job should come from a certain neighbourhood could be said to discriminate indirectly on grounds of race or religion. On the other hand, it could be the case that the factor causing the discriminatory effect is in fact necessary for the efficient performance of the job. In this case, a balance has to be struck so that legitimate business needs are not jeopardized, while at the same time recognizing that the fact that the discrimination is indirect will often make it, if anything, more insidious. The statutory compromise is the concept of indirect discrimination, which enables an applicant to raise an inference of discrimination by showing that a provision, criterion or practice of the employer has an adverse impact on a group defined by a protected characteristic, but then permits

---

[100] [1993] ICR 138, [1992] IRLR 564, CA. The decision confirms that there is nothing unlawful about having different retirement ages for different jobs, provided there is no direct or indirect discrimination based on a prohibited ground.

[101] [1982] ICR 618, [1982] IRLR 502, CA. Compare *Seide v Gillette Industries Ltd* [1980] IRLR 427, where the EAT suggested that the applicant must be able to show that the discrimination was the activating or the substantial cause. Both cases must now, of course, be considered in the light of the objective test laid down in *James v Eastleigh Borough Council*.

[102] *Nagarajan v Agnew* [1995] ICR 520, [1994] IRLR 61, EAT.

[103] *Price v Civil Service Commission* [1978] ICR 27, [1977] IRLR 291.

the employer to rebut that inference by showing that there is some objective justification for the application of that rule, etc, despite its adverse impact.

The 2010 Act (s 19) defines direct discrimination in a way consistent with the definition contained in the Burden of Proof Directive.[104] There is indirect discrimination when the following four conditions are satisfied:

(1)   the employer applies a provision, criterion or practice which applies or would apply equally to those who do not share the claimant's protected characteristic;

(2)   it puts or would put people with the claimant's protected characteristic at a particular disadvantage when compared with those who do not share it;

(3)   it puts the claimant at that disadvantage;

(4)   it cannot be shown to be a proportionate means of achieving a legitimate aim.

Earlier definitions of indirect discrimination gave rise to quarter of a century of complex case law,[105] but the current definition is so different that it is submitted that it must now be construed and applied as it stands, with that old case law merely providing certain interesting comparisons.

If there is one area, however, where there *may* be a greater element of continuity it is the employer defence of 'justification'. That expression was actually used in the original formulation, whereas the current law uses the classic EC law approach of 'a proportionate means of achieving a legitimate aim'. While that terminology must of course now be used, arguably it means much the same as justification; in particular, the existing case law may still give guidance as to how *strict* the test is to be.

Initially, a stringent view of the defence was taken. Phillips J held in *Steel v Union of Post Office Workers*[106] that generally there is a heavy onus on an employer asserting justification, and that in particular she must be able to show that the discriminatory requirement or condition in question was necessary for her business, not merely convenient. However, the strictness of this test was progressively watered down in a series of cases under the equivalent provision in the Race Relations Act 1976, in particular by the Court of Appeal in *Ojutiku v Manpower Services Commission*[107] where the necessity test was rejected in favour of an approach based on the existence of reasons which would be 'acceptable to right-thinking people as sound and tolerable reasons'.[108] It seemed for a time as though the tests of justification in sex and race discrimination cases had diverged as a result of the decision of the House of Lords in the equal pay

---

[104]   Directive 97/80/EC. Article 2(2) of the Burden of Proof Directive defines indirect discrimination as 'an apparently neutral provision, criterion or practice [which] disadvantages a substantially higher proportion of the members of one sex unless that provision, criterion or practice is appropriate and necessary and can be justified by objective factors unrelated to sex'.

[105]   For the old case law, see the 8th edition of this work at pp 286–93.

[106]   [1978] ICR 181, [1977] IRLR 288, followed in *Hurley v Mustoe* [1981] ICR 490, [1981] IRLR 208, EAT.

[107]   [1982] ICR 661, [1982] IRLR 418, CA. See *Singh v Rowntree MacKintosh Ltd* [1979] ICR 554, [1979] IRLR 199, EAT and *Panesar v Nestlé Co Ltd* [1980] ICR 144n, [1980] IRLR 64, CA.

[108]   Per Eveleigh LJ at 421 (see also Kerr LJ to similar effect). Stephenson LJ preferred an approach based on the objective balancing of the discriminatory effect against the discriminator's need for it.

case of *Rainey v Greater Glasgow Health Board*,[109] where the stricter test of objective justification laid down by the CJEU in *Bilka-Kaufhaus GmbH v Weber von Hartz*[110] was applied to the test of genuine material difference under section 1(3) of the Equal Pay Act 1970. In *Rainey*, Lord Keith stated that there was no material distinction in principle between the need to show 'objectively justified grounds' of difference in order to establish a defence under section 1(3) of the Equal Pay Act, and the need to justify a requirement or condition in a case of indirect discrimination under the Sex Discrimination Act, a comment which seemed to lend support to the argument that *Ojutiku* had been impliedly overruled by *Rainey*. However, in *Hampson v Department of Education and Science*,[111] the Court of Appeal said that there was no significant difference between the test adopted by Stephenson LJ in *Ojutiku*[112] and that adopted by the House of Lords in *Rainey*, and ruled that whether a requirement or condition is justifiable requires an objective balance to be struck between the discriminatory effect of the requirement or condition and the reasonable needs of the person who applies it.[113] The test in *Hampson* was subsequently approved by the House of Lords in *Webb v EMO Air Cargo (UK) Ltd*.[114] This is clearly the preferable view now, as the 2010 Act treats race and sex the same in this regard.

In *Cobb v Secretary of State for Employment*,[115] Wood J explained the correct approach to the question of justification in the following terms:

> It was for the respondent to satisfy the Tribunal that the decisions which he took were objectively justified for economic, administrative or other reasons. It was for the Tribunal to decide what facts it found proved, and to carry out the balancing exercise involved, taking into account all the surrounding circumstances and giving due emphasis to the degree of discrimination caused against the object or aim to be achieved—the principle of proportionality.[116]

Cobb involved a challenge to the eligibility criteria for admission to the Community Programme, a government scheme which provided temporary employment for the long-term unemployed. In *R v Secretary of State for Employment, ex p Seymour-Smith*

---

[109] [1987] ICR 129, [1987] IRLR 26, HL.

[110] Case 170/84 [1987] ICR 110, [1986] IRLR 317, ECJ. The *Bilka* test requires the employer to show that the measures chosen correspond to a real need on the part of the undertaking, are appropriate to achieve that objective and are necessary to that end.

[111] [1989] IRLR 69; overruled on other grounds [1991] 1 AC 171, [1990] ICR 511, HL.

[112] [1982] ICR 661, [1982] IRLR 418, CA. Balcombe LJ considered that neither Eveleigh LJ nor Kerr LJ in *Ojutiku* had indicated what they considered the test to be.

[113] This test was approved by the Northern Ireland Court of Appeal in *Briggs v North Eastern Education and Library Board* [1990] IRLR 181, and by the EAT in *Greater Manchester Police Authority v Lea* [1990] IRLR 372.

[114] [1992] 4 All ER 929, [1993] ICR 175, HL. Lord Keith stated expressly that the *Hampson* test must now be regarded as the appropriate one and as superseding that expressed by Eveleigh LJ in *Ojutiku*.

[115] [1989] ICR 506, [1989] IRLR 464, EAT.

[116] At 468. Note also Wood J's observation that the employer 'is under no obligation to prove that there was no other way of achieving his object, however expensive and administratively complicated'.

(No 2),[117] which involved a challenge under Article 141 to the legality of the two-year qualifying period for claiming unfair dismissal, the House of Lords held that where the complaint relates to legislative measures implementing social policy aims, the onus is on the member state to show (1) that the allegedly discriminatory rule reflects a legitimate aim of its social policy, (2) that this aim is unrelated to any discrimination based on sex, and (3) that the member state could reasonably consider that the means chosen were suitable for attaining that aim.[118] It was also held that the test of justification applied in the lower courts was too stringent, and that member states should be afforded a broad measure of discretion ('margin of appreciation') in pursuing their social policy aims (although generalized assumptions, lacking any actual foundation, would not be good enough).[119] Significantly, however, the House of Lords held that if a government introduces a measure which proves to have a disparately adverse impact, it has a duty to take reasonable steps to monitor the working of that measure by reviewing the position periodically, because if the benefits hoped for do not materialize, the retention of such a measure may no longer be objectively justifiable.[120] There is no reason in principle why this duty to keep indirectly discriminatory policies and practices under periodic review should not also be applied to employers in both the public and private sector.

The question of justification is an issue of fact for the tribunal,[121] with the result that a tribunal's decision on the matter will be difficult if not impossible to challenge provided it applies the correct tests.[122] This approach has been criticized for leading to an undesirable level of uncertainty and inconsistent decisions in this sensitive area,[123] but it is very much in line with the 'anti-legalism' approach sometimes seen in the tribunals and courts in employment law generally. A good illustration of the potential for inconsistency may be seen by comparing two decisions of the EAT concerning refusal to allow a female employee to return to work part time after maternity leave.

---

[117] [2000] IRLR 263, HL.

[118] On the facts, the House of Lords held that the Secretary of State had discharged the burden of showing that the increase in the qualifying period in 1985, and its retention in 1991, were objectively justified.

[119] See to like effect *Kutz-Bauer v Freie und Hansestadt Hamburg* [2003] IRLR 368, ECJ. Significantly, the ECJ rejected arguments that budgetary considerations (ie the desire to reduce costs) could constitute an aim pursued by a member state's social policy and thereby justify sex discrimination. Cf also *Jorgenen v Foreningen af Speciallaeger* [2000] IRLR 726, ECJ.

[120] Per Lord Nicholls [2000] IRLR 263 at 271. His Lordship also observed: 'The greater the disparity of impact, the greater the diligence which can reasonably be expected of the government.'

[121] A point stressed by the House of Lords in the important race discrimination case of *Mandla v Dowell Lee* [1983] ICR 385, [1983] IRLR 209, HL.

[122] In *University of Manchester v Jones* [1992] ICR 52 the EAT suggested that the exercise of a judicial discretion 'may be re-examined where irrelevant factors have been taken into consideration or where relevant considerations have been omitted in its exercise'. (The decision of the EAT was affirmed by the Court of Appeal: [1993] ICR 474, [1993] IRLR 218.)

[123] See in particular the remarks of Browne-Wilkinson J in *Clarke v Eley (IMI) Kynoch Ltd* [1983] ICR 165, [1982] IRLR 482.

In the first, *Home Office v Holmes*,[124] the EAT upheld a tribunal decision that a refusal to allow a woman with children to transfer to part-time working constituted indirect sex discrimination (the 'requirement or condition' in question being the obligation to work full time) which, on the facts, was not justifiable. The potential effect of such a decision is considerable, particularly when allied to the woman's statutory right to return to work after maternity leave (the eventual outcome possibly being to leave full-time work and return to part-time work, at least where the employer cannot show good reason to refuse this).[125] However, the case also demonstrates how difficult it can be to predict the outcome of indirect discrimination claims, for while the decision was hailed in the press as a major step forward in women's rights, in fact it was no such thing. At the end of his judgment, Waite P went out of his way to state that the decision was taken entirely on the particular facts of the case ('It is easy to imagine other instances, not strikingly different from hers, where the result would not be the same'), and the point was subsequently reinforced by the decision of the Scottish EAT in *Greater Glasgow Health Board v Carey*,[126] where on facts very similar to those in *Holmes* it was held that a refusal to allow a return to work part time after maternity leave was justified by considerations of administrative efficiency.[127]

One final point on justification has received a great deal of attention in recent years and is likely to receive more. How is a tribunal to *judge* proportionality? The Human Rights Act 1998 and the influence of EC Directives has made the proportionality analysis much more common in UK courts over the last ten years, and the number of times the Equality Act 2010 invokes proportionality ensures that it will remain no stranger to discrimination law. As a result the judiciary have been rapidly formulating guidelines for how to actually perform the proportionality balancing, and the task is not yet finished.[128] In *Hardy & Hansons plc v Lax*[129] an employee successfully challenged her employer's refusal to allow her to work part time on returning from maternity leave as unlawful indirect sex discrimination. It is fairly clear that the tribunal simply did not believe the employer's evidence, but before the Court of Appeal the employer argued that the tribunal had erred in law by applying the wrong test to the defence of justification. They argued that the tribunal should have allowed the employer

---

[124] [1984] ICR 678, [1984] IRLR 299. See also *London Underground Ltd v Edwards (No 2)* [1999] ICR 494, [1998] IRLR 364, CA, where the employer was unable to show that indirectly discriminatory rostering arrangements were justified.

[125] The Part-Time Workers Directive protects part-time workers from less favourable treatment by reason of their part-time status, but it does not give any right to insist on a transfer to part-time work. See Ch 2, heading 1(iv), p 54.

[126] [1987] IRLR 484.

[127] For a further example of conflicting decisions on similar facts (this time in the context of part-timers first redundancy selection procedures), compare *Clarke v Eley (IMI) Kynoch Ltd* [1983] ICR 165, [1982] IRLR 482 with *Kidd v DRG (UK) Ltd* [1985] ICR 405, [1985] IRLR 190.

[128] A Baker 'Proportionality and Employment Discrimination in the UK' (2008) 37 ILJ 305.

[129] [2005] EWCA Civ 846, [2005] IRLR 726, CA. For a good example of this principle (in the sensitive context of air safety) see *British Airways plc v Starmer* [2005] IRLR 862.

a 'margin of appreciation', on analogy with the 'range of reasonable responses' test in unfair dismissal law.[130] However, the Court of Appeal ruled emphatically against this view and said that it is simply for the tribunal to form their own view of the employer's reason:

> The principle of proportionality requires the tribunal to take into account the reasonable needs of the business. But it has to make its own judgment, upon a fair and detailed analysis of the working practices and business considerations involved, as to whether the proposal [by the employer] is reasonably necessary. I reject the [employer's] submission … that, when reaching its conclusion, the employment tribunal needs to consider only whether or not it is satisfied that the employer's views are within the range of views reasonable in the particular circumstances.

While this welcome distinction eliminated one area of difficulty, it left unresolved the question of when a provision, criterion or practice can be deemed 'reasonably necessary', and whether that is itself an accurate expression of the standard. In the *Bilka-Kaufhaus* case, the CJEU ruled that indirect discrimination under Article 141 EC could satisfy the justification defence only where it 'correspond[s] to a real need on the part of the undertaking' and is 'necessary'.[131] This is not exactly the same thing as 'reasonably necessary': is 'reasonably necessary' less demanding than 'necessary' (an important question given that in the eyes of the CJEU 'necessary' means that no less discriminatory alternative was available)? Moreover, the *Bilka* formulation requires that a challenged measure be necessary to meet the 'real needs' of the business, not that it be 'reasonably necessary' to achieve a mere 'legitimate aim'. In the context of assessing necessity, it makes a significant difference whether the tribunal must establish a real need or only a legitimate aim, a point well illustrated in *GMB v Allen*.[132] That case involved a situation where a planned job evaluation scheme would demonstrate that several women workers had been underpaid for years, and several other employees, mostly men, had been overpaid. In other words, some women would wind up reclassified upward, and have Equal Pay Act claims for past underpayment, while several men (a much greater proportion of the GMB union's membership) would be reclassified down, and face pay cuts. The GMB pressured female union members to take risible settlements of their equal pay claims, in order to leave the employer enough money to grant better concessions to protect the pay of those reclassified downward. The Employment Tribunal (ET) found the union's bargaining policy indirectly discriminatory against women, and applied a justification test that called for the policy to pursue a legitimate aim through proportionate means.[133] Because it did not follow the *Bilka* requirement of a 'real need' for the challenged policy, the ET found the aim of the policy—'to avoid or minimise "losers"' in the pay reclassification—legitimate. Nevertheless the ET found that the means—failing to push the equal pay claims harder and using 'spin' to get women to agree to the settlements—were not proportionate.

---

[130] See Ch 7, heading 4(iv), p 505.   [131] *Bilka-Kaufhaus* Case 170/84 [1987] ICR 110, 126.
[132] [2007] IRLR 752.   [133] *GMB v Allen* [2007] IRLR 752, 760.

On appeal the EAT found the discrimination justified, and did not replace the ET's 'legitimate aim' test with a 'real need' requirement, relying instead on the proposition that once the aim has been accepted as legitimate, then any means necessary to meet that end are justified.[134] Leaving aside whether it could ever be a legitimate objective intentionally to favour, in collective bargaining, the interests of mostly male reclassified employees over the interests of exclusively, and not accidentally, female employees with Equal Pay Act claims, the tribunal below had conceded the legitimacy of this aim as an issue of fact. The EAT could hardly fail to have reached a different result had GMB been required to prove a real need for its discriminatory bargaining position. With only a legitimate aim to worry about, it held that the objective at issue could only be achieved through the means employed: pressuring—even by unlawful or deceitful means—women union members to sacrifice their claims. At no point did the EAT even mention, much less weigh or balance, the impact of such a collective bargaining policy on the women claimants, on women in the union other than the claimants, or on gender equality in the workplace. Although the Court of Appeal subsequently rejected the EAT ruling and reinstated that of the ET, no effort was made to correct or strengthen the analysis used.[135] The opinion observed that the EAT incorrectly discounted the ET's finding, that the union's use of 'spin' amounted to a disproportionate means, because the EAT assumed that this conduct was not really a part of the relevant means.[136] This very technical decision corrects one crucial transgression of the EAT—the suggestion that *any* means necessary to a legitimate aim is proportionate. However, it appears to go no further than to say that a tribunal may find that employing dishonesty as a means to a legitimate aim is disproportionate. It leaves in place a test that (1) does not require a 'real need' for the discriminatory policy and (2) fails to acknowledge that not all 'legitimate aims' are created equal. Because the proportionality analysis that remains does not involve a step where impacts are weighed, then weak aims like that of the union can still pass muster as long as the aim cannot be realized through less discriminatory means, and the means do not involve outright dishonesty.

The real problem lies in the fact that proportionality does not, in its purest sense, turn exclusively on a test of necessity. Proportionality comes to European jurisprudence through German law, which developed a doctrine of proportionality requiring that state acts or measures be (1) suitable to achieve a legitimate purpose, (2) necessary to achieve that purpose, and (3) proportional in the narrower sense: they must not impose burdens or 'cause harms to other legitimate interests' that outweigh the objectives achieved.[137] 'Proportionality in the narrower sense' (proportionality stricto sensu), became the foundation of the Article 14 ECHR analysis in the *Belgian Linguistics* case,

---

[134] *GMB v Allen* [2007] IRLR 761.   [135] *GMB v Allen* [2008] EWCA Civ 810, [18]–[34].
[136] *GMB v Allen* [2008] EWCA Civ 810, [29]–[30], [33].
[137] Lord Hoffmann 'The Influence of the European Principle of Proportionality upon UK Law' in Evelyn Ellis (ed) *The Principle of Proportionality in the Laws of Europe* (1999) 107. Lord Hoffmann is a Law Lord in the UK House of Lords.

which was in fact the first mention of the doctrine of proportionality by the ECtHR.[138] This basic European principle of proportionality requires that invasions of a right impose no greater restrictions on the right (or on 'rights interests') than can be balanced out by the need of the state to invade the right; the state's 'need' refers not only to the importance of the objective but to the 'need' for the particular means employed to achieve it. This principle constitutes proportionality in its 'strict sense', while more complicated formulations are essentially structured analyses intended to ensure the observation of the principle. Proportionality stricto sensu is also included in the CJEU understanding of justification of indirect discrimination, but is far less emphasized owing to *Bilka*'s adoption of a structured analysis involving 'real need' and necessity.[139] Such a test rests on a presumption that a discriminatory impact has substantial 'weight' in the balancing exercise. A justification cannot outweigh this impact unless at least (1) the business has a real need to achieve a particular aim, and (2) the measure it employs to achieve it is necessary, in the sense of representing the least restrictive alternative. Nothing in *Bilka* suggests that the test deprives a court of the option of finding that a measure which meets those criteria nevertheless fails to satisfy proportionality stricto sensu. Subsequent CJEU decisions have made it clear that justification of indirect discrimination must be applied consistently with the *Bilka* requirements.[140] Thus the CJEU approach to proportionality, at least with regard to the justification of indirect discrimination, guarantees proportionality stricto sensu by requiring a level of scrutiny that goes beyond striking an ad hoc balance, in effect giving discriminatory impact a presumptively high weight by approving as justified only means necessary to meet a real need of the business. If UK courts and tribunals do not intend to follow the structured *Bilka* approach, requiring necessity *and* 'real need', justification in statutory indirect discrimination cases should turn on impacts as much as on the reasons offered by the employer. Even provisions, criteria or practices necessary to the achievement of legitimate aims should fail the test if the aim is not compelling or the impacts imposed are too strongly inconsistent with the aims of anti-discrimination law.

(c) Harassment

Harassment at work has long been recognized by the law as a problem, and the early case law tended to concentrate on sexual harassment. There was, however, a potential problem in that it was not specifically covered by the legislation and so it had to be squeezed into the ordinary definition of discrimination, with its emphasis on comparison and *worse* treatment. This gave rise to defences on the basis that either a man would have been treated as badly (for example, he would have been as offended by

---

[138] *Belgian Linguistics* (1968) 1 EHRR 252, para 10; M-A Eissen 'The Principle of Proportionality in the Case Law of the European Court of Human Rights' in Macdonald, Matscher and Petzold (eds) *The European System for the Protection of Human Rights* (1993) 140.

[139] *Cadman v Health and Safety Executive* [2006] ICR 1623, 1635–9, 1647 (the ECJ referred specifically to the paragraph of *Bilka* which required that the policy correspond to a 'real need' of the business).

[140] See, eg, *Cadman v Health and Safety Executive* [2006] ICR 1623.

pornographic pictures displayed at work)[141] or, even more perniciously, he would also have been 'harassed' but in a different way because of his different gender (a curious adoption of an otherwise impermissible 'separate-but-equal' argument).[142] The EAT led the way in trying to counter such defences, in particular by evolving the idea[143] that some acts are 'gender-specific' (eg the invasion of personal space in a sexual manner) and so it is to be *assumed* that they are discriminatory per se. While this often worked in the case law,[144] it always sat uncomfortably with the conceptual basis of ordinary discrimination law, and when it was finally considered by the House of Lords in *Pearce v Governing Body of Mayfield School*[145] it was disapproved and the fundamental comparative element reimposed: 'the fact that the harassment is gender-specific in form cannot be regarded as of itself establishing conclusively that the reason for the harassment is gender-based: "On the ground of her sex". While this did not shut the door on proof of a gender basis, it did raise the spectre once again of wider use of the 'equal misery' defence and reintroduced uncertainties as to who the proper comparator would be.

By this time, however, change was on its way in any event because the Equal Treatment Amendment Directive 2002/73/EC contained its own definition of harassment which avoids most of the problems considered above. It had already been written into the Regulations on sexual orientation and religion/belief and, in a series of moves, was introduced into the existing statutes on race, disability and (eventually, in 2005) sex. It is perhaps one of the most successful elements in the move to codify all the major heads of discrimination. This definition has been generally carried over into the 2010 Act.

The conceptual base for the new approach is that harassment is *not* a sub-set of ordinary discrimination, but is instead a freestanding contravention of the legislation, which has been widely amended to outlaw discrimination *or harassment* in its many particular applications. The common definition[146] states that a person commits harassment if she engages in unwanted conduct related to a protected characteristic that has the purpose or effect (1) of violating a worker's dignity or (2) of creating an intimidating,

---

[141] *Stewart v Cleveland Guest (Engineering) Ltd* [1996] ICR 535, [1994] IRLR 440, EAT; *Balgobin v London Borough of Tower Hamlets* [1987] ICR 829, [1987] IRLR 401 EAT.

[142] In *Insitu Cleaning Co Ltd v Heads* [1995] IRLR 4, EAT the defence was (remarkably!) that it was not sexual harassment to address a female colleague with 'Hiya, big tits' because the perpetrator was so generally offensive that he would have addressed a bald male colleague with 'Hiya, slaphead'. The EAT were unimpressed.

[143] This was most obviously applicable in sex discrimination cases, but might also have applied to the other heads.

[144] *Insitu Cleaning* see n 142, where Morison P said of the insults, 'One is sexual, the other is not'. The earliest application of the principle was in *Porcelli v Strathclyde Regional Council* [1986] ICR 564, [1986] IRLR 134, Ct of Sess (sexual nature of the actions meant that a woman was more vulnerable to it than a man would have been). It was taken to its logical condition in *BT plc v Williams* [1997] IRLR 668, EAT where it was said that there was no need for a comparator at all.

[145] [2003] ICR 937, [2003] IRLR 517, HL.   [146] Equality Act 2010, s 26.

hostile, degrading, humiliating or offensive environment for the worker.[147] Crucially, this is then fleshed out with an explanatory provision which states that conduct is only to be regarded as having these effects if, having regard to the circumstances, including in particular the perception of the woman, it is reasonable for the conduct to have that effect.

This statutory definition effectively reverses *Pearce*, removes the trouble-source requirement for a comparator and should prevent some of the stranger defences raised under the previous law. However, although it is a significant development it is not necessarily a panacea. Much of the previous case law is now obsolete *but* there is one aspect on which the previous case law is still relevant. A key element of the definition (seen in the explanatory provision) is the attempt to impose a test which is *both* subjective and objective. This has always been a problem of balance.

The problem with a subjective test is that it enables an over-sensitive complainant who takes offence unreasonably at an innocent comment to bring a claim for discrimination. On the other hand, the use of an objective test could be considered objectionable because it allows scope for value-judgments about the extent to which certain words and conduct are painful or offensive to the members of particular groups. The statutory definition contains both subjective ('unwanted') and objective ('unreasonable') elements, and the existing case law is not wholly clear on the correct balance between these two approaches. In *Reed and Bull Information Systems Ltd v Stedman*,[148] the EAT considered that the test of whether conduct amounts to sexual harassment is a subjective one:

> The essential characteristic of sexual harassment is that it is words or conduct which are unwelcome to the recipient and it is for the recipient to decide for themselves what is acceptable to them and what they regard as offensive.[149]

In contrast, in *De Souza v Automobile Association*[150] the Court of Appeal suggested that the conduct must be such that 'a reasonable worker would or might take the view that he had been thereby disadvantaged in the circumstances in which he had thereafter to work', and in *Driskel v Peninsula Business Services*[151] the EAT observed that if the facts simply disclosed hypersensitivity on the part of the complainant to conduct which was reasonably not perceived by the alleged discriminator as being to her detriment, no finding of discrimination could follow. In that case, the complainant was told the evening before an interview for promotion that she had better turn up the following

---

[147] Section 26 goes on to cover specifically (1) engaging in unwanted verbal, non-verbal or physical conduct of a sexual nature which has a similar effect and (2) treating an employee less favourably because he or she rejected or submitted to any of this unwanted conduct.

[148] [1999] IRLR 299, EAT.

[149] Per Morison J. See also *Wileman v Minilec Engineering Ltd* [1988] ICR 318, [1988] IRLR 144. Lack of intent is not a defence (although cf the comment of Holland J in *Driskel v Peninsula Business Services Ltd* [2000] IRLR 151, EAT, that 'the understanding, motive and intention' of the alleged discriminator is one of the factors to be considered by the tribunal).

[150] [1986] ICR 514, [1986] IRLR 103, CA.   [151] [2000] IRLR 151, EAT.

day 'in a short skirt and see-through blouse, showing plenty of cleavage'. The employ-ment tribunal found in the employer's favour, heavily influenced by the fact that she did not make an immediate complaint, but the EAT questioned the significance of this, pointing out that 'any instinct to complain must perforce be inhibited by the fact that she wanted the promotion that would come from the approval of [the alleged harasser]'.[152] The EAT also stressed that where a number of specific incidents are alleged to consti-tute harassment, the tribunal should not carve up the case into a series of incidents and try to measure the harm in relation to each of them, but should instead consider the cumulative effect of such behaviour, lest it fall into the trap of 'ignoring the impact of the totality of successive incidents, individually trivial'.[153] On the other hand, a single act may be so clearly unwelcome as to be 'unwanted',[154] thus avoiding the argument that conduct cannot be said to be unwanted until it has been tried and rejected: 'A woman does not, for example, have to make it clear in advance that she does not want to be touched in a sexual manner';[155] at the other end of the scale, where a worker appears to be unduly sensitive to what might otherwise be regarded as unexceptional behaviour, the question becomes whether by words or conduct he or she has made it clear that the conduct is unwelcome: 'Provided that any reasonable person would understand her to be rejecting the conduct of which she was complaining, continuation of the conduct would, generally, be regarded as harassment.'[156] These issues will continue to be debatable under the 2010 Act.

At the very least, the effect of the action complained of on the complainant will be highly relevant when assessing compensation, because the amount of compensation will depend on the extent of the detriment that the complainant has suffered as a result of the harassment. Here, the complainant's attitudes and sensitivities will have a direct bearing on the compensation awarded. So, for example, in *Snowball v Gardner Merchant Ltd*[157] the tribunal admitted evidence of the complainant's sexual exploits and that fact that she was in the habit of referring to her bed as a 'playpen', and in *Wileman v Minilec Engineering Ltd*[158] the tribunal took notice of the fact that the complainant sometimes wore what was described as provocative clothing to work. Significantly, however, the EAT held in that case that the complainant's willingness to pose for a national news-paper in a flimsy costume was not inconsistent with a finding that she had been sexually harassed by her employer: 'A person may be happy to accept the remarks of A or B in a sexual context, and wholly upset by similar remarks made by C.'[159]

---

[152] [2000] IRLR 151, per Holland J. Cf also *Wileman v Minilec Engineering Ltd*, above, n 149 (a tribunal should be slow to infer that the conduct was not unwelcome from the mere fact that the complainant does not complain or delays in making her complaint).

[153] [2000] IRLR 151 at 154 ('That which in isolation may not amount to discriminatory detriment may become such if persisted in notwithstanding objection, vocal or apparent', per Holland J).

[154] See eg *Insitu Cleaning Co Ltd v Heads* [1995] IRLR 4; *Bracebridge Engineering Ltd v Darby* [1990] IRLR 3, EAT. The problem is that the word 'unwanted' is itself ambiguous.

[155] [2000] IRLR 151, per Morison J.   [156] [2000] IRLR 151.

[157] [1987] ICR 719, [1987] IRLR 397.   [158] [1988] ICR 318, [1988] IRLR 144.

[159] [1988] ICR 318, [1988] IRLR 144, per Popplewell J.

Finally, two recent developments are mentioned because they reintroduce uncertainty into this whole area. The first is that an employee suffering harassment now has as alternative civil cause of action for damages under the Protection from Harassment Act 1997 which was held to have wide application (not restricted to its original target of stalking) by the House of Lords in *Majrowski v Guy's and St Thomas's NHS Trust*.[160] Not only does an action under the 1997 Act have significant practical advantages (a six-year limitation, not three months; damages merely for 'anxiety'; no 'employer's defence' that it took all reasonable steps to avoid it), but it is conceptually wider because 'harassment' is not defined (and there are no signs at the time of writing of the discrimination law definition being read over into it) and it applies to harassment for *any* reason (not just sex, race, disability, orientation, religion/belief or age). The second development is that, after the major changes in 2005 to bring sex discrimination into the unified system of discrimination law, those changes were themselves challenged by the EOC in judicial review proceedings, on the grounds that they had not implemented the (amended) Equal Treatment Directive properly. In *EOC v Secretary of State for Trade and Industry*[161] the EOC objected to the new statutory regime because it (1) uses a causative requirement ('on the ground of' her sex) which does not appear in the Directive, (2) imposes an objective element ('it should *reasonably* be considered as having that effect') which also does not appear in the Directive, and (3) fails to impose liability on the employer for harassment by a third party such as a client or visitor. Burton J agreed and issued declarations accordingly. The 2010 Act addresses (1) by substituting 'related to' for 'on the ground of' and (3) by including section 38 making employers responsible for third party harassment where the employer (1) is aware that harassment has happened at least twice before and (2) failed to take reasonable steps to avoid it. Unfortunately, this last provision (third party) was enacted by the New Labour government and its successor Coalition government has announced plans to eliminate the provision and remove from employers any responsibility for third party harassment of their workers.[162]

(d) Victimization

Victimization applies where a person is subjected to 'a detriment' because he or she has brought proceedings or given evidence in proceedings against the discriminator under the Act (or prior Acts), or made allegations in good faith of breaches of one of these Acts.[163] However, to benefit from the statutory protection the applicant must show that the reason for the detriment is because he or she has done one of the protected acts. At one time it was thought that in order to establish victimization there had to be some conscious motivation in the mind of the alleged discriminator which caused less

---

[160] [2005] ICR 977, [2005] IRLR 340, HL.   [161] [2007] EWHC 483 (Admin).
[162] Enterprise and Regulatory Reform Bill 2012, s 57 available at <http://services.parliament.uk/bills/2012-13/enterpriseandregulatoryreform.html> (last accessed 8 January 2013).
[163] Equality Act 2010, s 27.

favourable treatment,[164] but in *Nagarajan v London Regional Transport*,[165] the House of Lords held that in complaints of victimization under the Race Relations Act (and by analogy, under the SDA and now the Equality Act) the motive of the alleged discriminator is irrelevant, and the question to be asked is the simple causative one, ie whether the complainant would have been treated in that way but for engaging in the protected activity.[166] Prior to the 2010 Act, a claim of victimization would fail if the employer did not treat the complainant any less favourably than a person who had not done one of the protected acts, and this once again raised the vexed question of who the appropriate comparator is. Put simply, should the treatment afforded to the complainant be compared with the treatment of other employees who have not made discrimination complaints against the employer? Or should the comparison be with other employees who have not made any type of complaint against the employer? This point was considered in *Chief Constable of West Yorkshire v Khan*,[167] in which the House of Lords revisited some of the issues previously considered in *Nagarajan*. The facts were that the complainant had made a number of unsuccessful applications for promotion, which had led him to bring a race discrimination complaint against West Yorkshire Police. While that claim was still outstanding he applied to another force for a more senior post, but West Yorkshire Police refused to provide him with a reference, on the grounds that it might prejudice the case before the tribunal. The complainant then added a complaint of victimization in respect of the refusal of the reference, claiming that he had been treated less favourably than others by reason of having brought his original discrimination complaint, in that references were normally provided on request for those applying for new employment. The victimization complaint succeeded up to the Court of Appeal, which applied a straightforward 'but for' test (would a reference have been provided but for the fact that he had a discrimination complaint pending?), but the House of Lords allowed the appeal, holding that the Court of Appeal had applied the wrong test. On the issue of the comparator, the House of Lords held that the appropriate comparison was with another employee who had not made a tribunal complaint, and so the complainant had in fact been treated less favourably than the employer would have treated other persons; however, their Lordships considered that the complainant's case failed the second part of the test (was the less favourable treatment 'by reason that' the complainant had brought proceedings under the Act?), as this was considered to involve a higher threshold than the 'but for' test. Their Lordships considered that the reference was not withheld 'by reason that' the complainant had brought discrimination proceedings, but rather because the employers wished to preserve their position in

---

[164] See eg *Aziz v Trinity Street Taxis Ltd* [1988] ICR 534, [1988] IRLR 204, CA.

[165] [1999] ICR 877, [1999] IRLR 572, HL, reversing the Court of Appeal.

[166] This is the *James v Eastleigh Borough Council* test which applies in complaints of direct discrimination under s 1: see this chapter, heading 2(iii), p 312. Dicta to the contrary in *Aziz v Trinity Street Taxis Ltd* [1988] ICR 534, [1988] IRLR 204 were said to be incorrect. Cf the strong dissenting judgment of Lord Browne-Wilkinson, who said that he did not understand how one could victimize someone subconsciously.

[167] [2001] IRLR 830, HL.

the pending discrimination proceedings. The Equality Act resets the debate, by replacing 'less favourable treatment' with 'subjects ... to a detriment'—which removes the need for a comparator—and by changing 'by reason of' to 'because'. The latter change almost certainly calls for a 'but for' test.

A final point is mentioned. The protection against victimization in the SDA 1975 for having made an allegation of discrimination only applied where the allegation is that the discriminator had committed an act 'which ... would amount to a contravention' of the anti-discrimination legislation.[168] The implications of this were graphically demonstrated in *Waters v Metropolitan Police Comr*,[169] where the employee alleged that she had been victimized by the employer for alleging sexual harassment by a work colleague. The Court of Appeal held that for the protection against victimization to apply in such a case, the alleged act must be one for which the employer would be vicariously liable, and as the alleged harassment was not committed in the 'course of employment', the employer could not be held vicariously liable for it, and could not therefore be held to have victimized the complainant for making the allegations.[170] The Equality Act now prohibits a detriment for committing a 'protected act', which is defined to include 'making an allegation that [the victimizer] *or another person* has contravened this act'.[171]

(e) Positive discrimination[172]

The Equality Act is generally based on a neutral or symmetrical model of equality. It gives each individual, male or female, majority or minority, the right not to be treated less favourably on protected grounds. As *James v Eastleigh Borough Council*[173] demonstrated, the fact that the defendant acted from a good or worthy motive is no defence to a complaint of unlawful discrimination. It follows that any preferential treatment aimed at redressing the historic disadvantage experienced by women or minority groups and enabling them to compete equally will normally be illegal if it involves the less favourable treatment of a man. Such measures—generally referred to as 'positive discrimination'—must be distinguished from measures which do not involve preferential treatment of one group but which are designed to promote a greater degree of equality of opportunity within the workplace (so-called 'positive action'). While positive discrimination has normally been unlawful, 'positive action' is not prohibited. Measures aimed at promoting equal opportunities which fall short of positive discrimination might include the development of policies and practices

---

[168] Sex Discrimination Act 1975, s 4(1)(d).   [169] [1997] ICR 1073, [1997] IRLR 589, CA.

[170] The practical importance of the decision has arguably been reduced by the broad approach to vicarious liability taken in some recent cases: see this chapter heading 2(viii), p 343.

[171] Equality Act 2010, s 27(2)(d) (emphasis added).

[172] See Fredman 'Reversing Discrimination' (1997) 113 LQR 575; Pitt 'Can Reverse Discrimination Be Justified?' in Hepple and Szyszczak (eds) *Discrimination: the Limits of Law* (1992) ch 16; McCrudden 'Rethinking Positive Action' (1986) 15 ILJ 219.

[173] [1990] IRLR 288, HL. See also *Jepson and Dyas-Elliott v Labour Party* [1996] IRLR 116, IT (women-only shortlists unlawful), although note now the Sex Discrimination (Election Candidates) Act 2002.

designed to assist disadvantaged groups (for example 'family friendly' policies), encouraging applications from under-represented groups, and the setting of targets to reduce under-representation. Indeed, the Equality Act and its predecessors provide for 'positive duties' on public sector bodies to promote equality.[174]

The 2010 Act, however, introduces for the first time in the UK the right to treat a member of an under-represented or disadvantaged group *more favourably* for hiring or promotion. This is an area in which UK law has generally been in step with EC law, although the position is not entirely clear. In general terms, EC law has tended to adopt the same symmetrical approach to equality as English law. Article 2(4) of the Equal Treatment Directive provides that the Directive 'shall be without prejudice to measures to promote equal opportunity for men and women, in particular by removing existing inequalities which affect women's opportunities', which appears to permit preferential treatment for women to enable them to compete more equally, but the CJEU has interpreted this provision narrowly, and has been reluctant to accept it as legitimizing positive discrimination other than within very narrow limits. In *Kalanke v Freie Hansestadt Bremen*,[175] the CJEU considered the legality of a so-called 'tie-break' provision in the relevant domestic provisions, whereby women who had the same qualifications as men for the same post were to be given priority in sectors where they were under-represented. The CJEU held that national rules which guarantee women absolute and unconditional priority for appointment or promotion go beyond promoting equal opportunities and overstep the limits of the exception to the principle of equal treatment in Article 2(4);[176] the exception was interpreted strictly, as permitting national measures relating to access to employment 'which give a specific advantage to women with a view to improving their ability to compete in the labour market and to pursue a career in an equal footing with men'. The decision in *Kalanke* was greeted with dismay (not least by the European Commission), and when the CJEU next had an opportunity to consider the issue, in *Marschall v Land Nordrhein-Westfalen*,[177] there was a noticeable softening of the tone. That case also involved a tie-break provision giving women priority for promotion in the event of equal suitability, competence and professional performance, but with the crucial addition of a 'saving clause' whereby women were not to be given priority if reasons specific to an individual male candidate tilted the balance in his favour. The CJEU noted that even where male and female candidates are equally qualified, male candidates tend to be promoted because of prejudices and stereotypes concerning the role and capacities of women in working life, and the fear that women will interrupt their working lives more frequently, be less flexible in their working hours because of household and family duties and be absent from work more frequently because of pregnancy or childbirth. The CJEU acknowledged that

---

[174] Equality Act 2010, s 149.   [175] [1996] ICR 314, [1995] IRLR 660, ECJ.

[176] The ECJ held that the provisions in question fell outside this exception by substituting for equal opportunity 'the result which is only to be arrived at by providing such equality of opportunity'.

[177] [1998] IRLR 39, ECJ.

because of these factors, the mere fact that male and female candidates are equally qualified 'does not mean that they have the same chances', and held that although a national rule which guaranteed absolute and unconditional priority for women would not be lawful, a rule which counteracted the prejudicial effects of the attitudes and behaviour described above by giving preferential treatment to equally qualified women candidates could be lawful if it contained a saving clause which guaranteed 'that the candidatures will be the subject of an objective assessment which will take account of all criteria specific to the individual candidates and will override the priority accorded to the female candidates where one or more of the criteria tilts the balance in favour of the male candidate' (all of which begs the question of what 'equally qualified' means in this context). A similar approach was taken in the case of *Badeck*,[178] where the CJEU upheld a programme aimed at eliminating the under-representation of women in the public sector which, inter alia, gave priority to equally qualified women applicants in sectors where they were under-represented and allocated at least half the available training places to women in occupations in which they were under-represented, the decisive point being that, as in *Marschall*, the programme did not automatically and unconditionally give priority to women when women and men were equally qualified. One of the more interesting (and, it must be said, ingenious) aspects of the programme in *Badeck* was the approach taken to the evaluation of the candidates' qualifications, in that the scheme in effect sought to redefine 'merit' for the purposes of the comparison by providing that in assessing their qualifications, certain factors were to be taken into account (for example capabilities and experience acquired by looking after children or persons requiring care, in so far as they were of importance for the suitability of applicants), while other factors (for example family status, income of the partner, part-time work, leave or delays in completing training as a result of looking after children or dependants) were to be left out of the equation. Another novel aspect of the scheme in *Badeck* was that instead of leaving the all-important assessment of the individual situations of the candidates at large, the saving clause identified five situations which justified overriding the tie-break rule for the advancement of women, including promoting disabled persons, ending a period of long-term unemployment or giving preferential treatment to those who, for family reasons, worked part time and wished to resume full-time employment. The scheme in *Badeck* probably represents the high-water mark of positive discrimination programmes accepted as valid to date by the CJEU.[179] In contrast, the scheme in *Abrahammsson v Fogelqvist*,[180] which required the appointment of a suitably qualified candidate of the under-represented sex even if they were less highly qualified than a candidate of the opposite sex, was considered to overstep the boundaries of positive discrimination permitted by Article 2(4).

---

[178] *Badeck's Application* [2000] IRLR 432, ECJ.

[179] Although cf *Lommers v Minister van Landbouw, Natuurbeheer en Visserij* [2002] IRLR 430, ECJ, where a scheme giving female employees priority for subsidized nursery places was upheld so long as nursery places were available on the same terms to male single parents.

[180] [2000] IRLR 732, ECJ.

Prior to the 2010 Act, the UK did not have domestic provisions that rose to the *Badeck* high-water mark. There were provisions that allowed for discrimination in favour of one sex in vocational training where it appeared that in the previous 12 months there were no persons of that sex employed in the work in question in Great Britain, or an area within Great Britain, or the number was comparatively small.[181] However, there was no provision for 'tie-break' discrimination until the Equality Act introduced more flexible outlines for positive action, as well as limited 'tie-break' positive discrimination. Section 158(1) employs a threshold for general positive action, whereby an employer may act when persons sharing a protected characteristic (1) suffer a disadvantage connected to the characteristic, (2) have needs different from those without it or (3) are disproportionately represented in an activity. If one or more of these circumstances apply, under section 158(2) the employer may take any action that is a proportionate means of (1) helping overcome the disadvantage, (2) meeting those needs or (3) enabling participation in the activity. Section 159(1) permits tie-break discrimination where either (1) persons who share a protected characteristic suffer a disadvantage or (2) those persons are disproportionately represented in an activity (ie, the list from above except for the 'different needs' threshold). If the section 159(1) threshold is met, section 159(2) allows an employer to overcome the disadvantage or enable participation by treating persons with the protected characteristic *more favourably* in recruitment or promotion; but this is allowed only where (1) the person thus favoured is 'as qualified' as the other to be recruited or promoted and (2) the employer does not have a policy of favouring the group of which the favoured person is a representative. This last condition is almost certainly intended to ensure that this tie-break permission only applies on a case-by-case basis.

(iv) DISCRIMINATION BEFORE EMPLOYMENT

The first and perhaps most difficult stage at which a person may encounter discrimination in employment is in applying for a job. It is unlawful under the Equality Act 2010, section 39(1) for an employer to discriminate in the arrangements[182] for the selection procedure, in the terms offered for employment, or by refusing or deliberately omitting to offer the employment. A certain amount of realism is necessary in construing these provisions, so that for example it is not necessarily unlawful for an employer to ask a woman a question at an interview which would not be asked of a man; the issue is whether, by asking the question, the woman was treated less favourably because of her sex than a man would be treated.[183]

---

[181] See Sacks 'Tackling Discrimination Positively' in Hepple and Szyszczak (eds) *Discrimination: the Limits of Law* (1992). Employers were also permitted to target training on under-represented groups within their organization: Sex Discrimination Act 1975, s 48. There were parallel provisions in the Race Relations Act 1976, ss 37 and 38.

[182] On the meaning of 'arrangements', see *Brennan v J H Dewhurst Ltd* [1984] ICR 52, [1983] IRLR 357 (biased interview).

[183] *Saunders v Richmond-upon-Thames London Borough Council* [1978] ICR 75, [1977] IRLR 362.

Section 1 of Schedule 9 to the Act creates a statutory exemption from liability for unlawful discrimination where a protected characteristic is a genuine occupational requirement (GOR) for the job. A GOR can be applied only where to do so is a proportionate means to a legitimate aim. The GOR defence is an important exception to the normal rule that motive is irrelevant in cases of direct discrimination. It is designed to avoid some of the more obvious absurdities of complete equality, but it is important that the boundaries of the exception are not stretched too far, lest the protection against discrimination be undermined. Of course, the SDA 1975 and the RRA 1976 used an even broader form of defence, Genuine Occupational Qualifications (GOQs) which articulated specific kinds of circumstance in which the defence would apply. While this might appear to have been a more restrictive approach to the defence, the SDA (and the RRA before the Race Directive amendments) did not require that a GOQ satisfy a test of proportionality. Moreover, something could amount to a 'qualification' without being a defining characteristic of the job. Where GORs appeared before the 2010 Act, for instance in the 2003 Employment Equality (sexual orientation/religion or belief) Regulations, the words 'genuine and determining occupational requirement' were used. This language was taken from the Race and Employment Directives of 2000. While it could be argued that removal of the word 'determining' broadens the defence under the 2010 Act and fails properly to implement the Directives, it should be remembered that this apparent gap is readily closed by the proportionality analysis. The less 'determining' a requirement is, the less weight should be given to the employer's need for it. So, for example, a requirement that a putative waiter at an ethnic restaurant share the ethnicity of the food on the menu (and presumably of the other employees in the restaurant) might struggle to satisfy a proportionality test where the defining characteristic of the job is clearly taking orders and serving food to customers, not having a certain ethnicity. If the restaurant is in an ethnically diverse neighbourhood in times of scarce employment opportunities, it seems hard to defend the proportionality of a requirement whose sole 'legitimate' aim is to present customers with an apparently ethnically pure dining experience, when the impact of the non-determining requirement would be to exclude a talented waiter from much needed employment purely on the grounds of race. Given that the legislation that proceeded the 2010 Act used the word 'determining', and the Race and Employment Directives use it as well, it is likely that tribunals will interpret the phrase 'genuine occupational requirement' to mean 'genuine and determining occupational requirement'.

(v) DISCRIMINATION DURING EMPLOYMENT

Under the Equality Act 2010, section 39(2)(b) it is unlawful for an employer to discriminate against a worker during employment in the way he or she affords or refuses to afford access to opportunities for promotion, transfer or training,[184] or to any other

---

[184] This could occur in a redundancy situation where a new job is created but the employer refuses to transfer a person of a particular sex to it (subject to the genuine occupational qualification defence): *Timex Corpn v Hodgson* [1982] ICR 63, [1981] IRLR 530, EAT.

benefits, facilities[185] or services. It is also unlawful to discriminate by subjecting a worker to any 'detriment'. In *Ministry of Defence v Jeremiah*[186] the Court of Appeal held that subjecting to any detriment is to be given its ordinary, common-sense meaning of 'putting under a disadvantage'.[187] Doubt had arisen over whether this was the correct test as a result of the EAT decision in *Coker v Lord Chancellor*,[188] in which the view was expressed that the applicant needed to demonstrate 'some physical or economic consequence' in order to establish 'detriment', but in *Shamoon v Chief Constable of the Royal Ulster Constabulary*,[189] the House of Lords confirmed the orthodox position. Their Lordships also confirmed that the test of detriment contains both subjective and objective elements, approving Brightman LJ's formulation in *Jeremiah* that 'a detriment exists if a reasonable worker would or might take the view that the [treatment] was in all the circumstances to his detriment';[190] according to Lord Scott, the test must be applied 'by considering the issue from the point of view of the victim. If the victim's opinion that the treatment was to his or her detriment is a reasonable one to hold, that ought … to suffice'.[191] The emphasis on the reasonableness of the victim's view of the treatment means that 'an unjustified sense of grievance cannot amount to "detriment"'.[192] The need to establish detriment means that differentiation between sexes is not in itself unlawful discrimination, for there must be some element of disadvantage, although the courts have generally been prepared to find that differential treatment is detrimental;[193] it may also be possible for a tribunal or court to consider a claimed disadvantage to be so minor as to be disregarded on the de minimis principle, although as seen earlier the scope of the de minimis defence is probably very narrow. Once there is a detriment, however, it will not be a defence for an employer to show that the detriment is taken into account by compensating those who experience it (for example where only men are obliged to do certain disagreeable work, but receive an extra payment in respect of it); there may still be unlawful discrimination even though special rates of pay are given for that work.[194]

[185] This refers to facilities which already exist: *Clymo v London Borough of Wandsworth* [1989] ICR 250, [1989] IRLR 241, EAT.

[186] [1979] 3 All ER 833, [1979] IRLR 436, CA, disapproving the reasoning on this point in *Peake v Automotive Products Ltd* [1977] ICR 968, [1977] IRLR 365, CA.

[187] [1979] IRLR 436 at 438, per Lord Brandon.

[188] [2001] IRLR 116, EAT. See also *Jiad v Byford* [2003] EWCA Civ 135, [2003] IRLR 232.

[189] [2003] UKHL 11, [2003] ICR 337, [2003] IRLR 285.

[190] [1979] IRLR 436 at 440.

[191] [2003] UKHL 11, [2003] IRLR 285 at 301. Note also that to amount to a 'detriment', the disadvantage must arise 'in the field of employment': per Lord Hope at 291.

[192] [2003] UKHL 11, [2003] IRLR 285 at 291, per Lord Hope. See also *Barclays Bank plc v Kapur (No 2)* [1995] IRLR 87.

[193] See this chapter, heading 2(iii), p 314.

[194] See *Ministry of Defence v Jeremiah* [1978] ICR 984, [1978] IRLR 402; affd by CA: [1979] 3 All ER 833, [1979] IRLR 436.

(vi) DISCRIMINATION ON, AND AFTER, TERMINATION OF EMPLOYMENT

Under the Equality Act 2010, section 39(2)(c) it is unlawful to discriminate against a worker by dismissal,[195] and this could give rise to a complaint to a tribunal of discrimination in the ordinary way, with the tribunal empowered to give compensation and make a recommendation, which could include reinstatement of the worker. However, it is likely that in such a case the woman would also have a good claim for unfair dismissal,[196] which has three advantages over the straight discrimination claim—the preliminary burden of proof in the unfair dismissal case is on the employer, there can (in theory) be an order of reinstatement or re-engagement and, if the remedy is to be compensation, it will include a basic award. On the other hand, the discrimination claim has the distinct advantage that the one-year qualifying period for unfair dismissal does not apply, the tribunal is expressly empowered to award a sum for injury to feelings,[197] and there is no upper limit on the compensation which can be awarded for discrimination.[198] It may therefore be wise for the dismissed worker to bring the complaint to the tribunal under both heads. If they do so, there can be no double compensation, as the compensation for discrimination cannot take into account any head of loss already included in the compensation for unfair dismissal, and vice versa.

As originally enacted, the SDA 1975 did not expressly refer to discriminatory acts done by an employer after the end of employment, and case law under the Race Relations Act (which was drafted in the same terms as the SDA) appeared to establish that discrimination against a former employee was not unlawful.[199] However, in *Coote v Granada Hospitality Ltd*,[200] the CJEU held that Article 6 of the Equal Treatment Directive requires member states to introduce measures protecting workers from discrimination after the employment relationship has ended, and in the resumed hearing,[201] the EAT reinterpreted the 1975 Act as covering victimization by an ex-employer. That decision was narrowly interpreted by the EAT in *Rhys-Harper v Relaxion Group plc*[202] as only covering post-termination victimization, not other acts of discrimination occurring after the end of employment (in that case, the employer's alleged failure to investigate an allegation of sexual harassment made during an internal appeal against dismissal), and the EAT's decision was upheld by the Court of Appeal. On a further consolidated appeal addressing the same point under the sex, race and

---

[195] Dismissal here includes a constructive dismissal: Equality Act 2010, s 39(7).

[196] A dismissal through an act of unlawful indirect discrimination is not automatically unfair in law, though in practice it is likely to be found unfair: *Clarke v Eley (IMI) Kynoch Ltd* [1983] ICR 165, [1982] IRLR 482, EAT.

[197] Equality Act 2010, ss 124(6); 119(4).

[198] See this chapter, heading 2(ix), p 345.

[199] *Nagarajan v Agnew* [1995] ICR 520, [1994] IRLR 61, EAT (provision of an adverse reference to a former employee); *Adekeye v Post Office* [1997] ICR 110, [1997] IRLR 105, CA (discrimination in the conduct of an internal appeal against dismissal).

[200] [1998] IRLR 656, ECJ (refusal to provide a reference to a former employee).

[201] *(No 2)* [1999] ICR 942, [1999] IRLR 452, EAT.   [202] [2000] IRLR 810, EAT.

disability discrimination legislation, the House of Lords held[203] that it is unlawful for a person to discriminate against former employees 'if there is a substantive connection between the discriminatory conduct and the employment relationship',[204] whenever the discriminatory conduct arises. In the wake of the decision, the government introduced the Sex Discrimination Act 1975 (Amendment) Regulations 2003,[205] which expressly prohibited unlawful discrimination after the end of the employment relationship which 'arises out of and is closely connected to the [employment] relationship'.[206] This approach has now been incorporated into section 104 of the 2010 Act across all grounds of discrimination. The new wording is wide enough to cover a broad range of claims by ex-employees, including the conduct of internal appeals against dismissal, and the provision of references.[207]

(vii) PROVING DISCRIMINATION

Establishing the liability of an employer in a discrimination case can be highly problematic. Proof can be extremely difficult in these cases, as there will usually be little or no direct evidence of discrimination. Traditionally, the burden of proof has been on the applicant to show, on the balance of probabilities, that he or she has been discriminated against,[208] but in practice the courts developed an approach whereby, if the applicant was able to show less favourable treatment in circumstances consistent with discrimination, the tribunal would look to the employer for an explanation, and if no explanation was put forward, or if the tribunal considered the explanation to be inadequate or unsatisfactory, the tribunal could[209] legitimately infer unlawful discrimination.[210] There was no formal reversal of the burden of proof, which remained on the applicant,[211] but in practice the ability of the tribunals to infer discrimination in the absence of reasonable explanation by the employer meant that there was probably little

---

[203] *Rhys-Harper v Relaxion Group plc; D'Souza v London Borough of Lambeth; Jones v 3M Healthcare Ltd* [2003] IRLR 484, HL.

[204] Per Lord Rodger at 510. Cf Lord Hobhouse at 501 ('a substantive and proximate connection between the conduct complained of and … employment by the alleged discriminator'); Lord Nicholls at 489 ('the obligation not to discriminate applies to all the incidents of the employment relationship, whenever precisely they arise').

[205] SI 2003/1657, inserting new ss 20A and 35C into the Sex Discrimination Act 1975.

[206] SI 2003/1657, reg 3, inserting new s 20A.

[207] The House of Lords emphasized that the refusal of an employer to provide a reference to an ex-employee would only be discriminatory if the employer treated the applicant less favourably than other ex-employees on one of the prohibited grounds.

[208] *Oxford v Department of Health and Social Security* [1977] ICR 884, [1977] IRLR 225.

[209] Such an inference was not mandatory: see *Glasgow City Council v Zafar* [1998] IRLR 36, HL.

[210] *King v Great Britain—China Centre* [1992] ICR 516, [1991] IRLR 513, CA, approved in *Zafar v Glasgow City Council* [1998] IRLR 36. See also: *North West Thames Regional Health Authority v Noone* [1988] ICR 813, [1988] IRLR 195, CA; *West Midlands Passenger Transport Executive v Singh* [1988] ICR 614, [1988] IRLR 186, CA; *Baker v Cornwall County Council* [1990] ICR 452, [1990] IRLR 194, CA.

[211] A point stressed by the EAT in *Barking and Dagenham London Borough Council v Camara* [1988] ICR 865, [1988] IRLR 373, and in *Carrington v Helix Lighting Ltd* [1990] ICR 125, [1990] IRLR 6.

difference (other than one of terminology) between the de facto position and a formal reversal of the burden of proof.

In recognition of the difficulties faced by complainants attempting to prove discrimination, and after an extremely long gestation period,[212] all member states other than the UK adopted a Burden of Proof Directive[213] in 1997 which requires the burden of proof to be shifted onto the respondent in sex discrimination cases when the complainant establishes facts from which it may be presumed that there has been direct or indirect discrimination.[214] The UK government acceded to the Directive in July 1998,[215] and it was duly implemented by the Sex Discrimination (Indirect Discrimination and Burden of Proof) Regulations 2001,[216] which introduced a new section 63A into the 1975 Act. This provided that where the complainant proves facts from which the tribunal could conclude, in the absence of an adequate explanation, that the respondent has committed an unlawful act of discrimination against the complainant, the tribunal must uphold the complaint unless the respondent proves that he did not commit that act. This provision is now echoed in section 136 of the 2010 Act. In the first case to come before the EAT on the new provisions (prior to the Equality Act 2010), *Barton v Investec Henderson Crosthwaite Securities Ltd*,[217] the EAT gave useful guidance[218] on how the burden of proof is now to be approached. This was taken up and applied (with slight amendments) by the Court of Appeal in what is now the leading case, *Igen Ltd v Wong*.[219] The Supreme Court was recently asked to give guidance on how this precedent should be interpreted under the Equality Act and it declined to do so, emphasizing that the existing Court of Appeal guidance was clear and needed no adjustments.[220] This sets out the following extensive guidance, which tends to be used as a template by tribunals:

(1)　It is for the applicant who complains of discrimination to prove on the balance of probabilities facts from which the tribunal could conclude, in the absence of an adequate explanation, that the respondents have committed an act of discrimination against the applicant which is unlawful.

(2)　If the applicant does not prove such facts he or she will fail.

(3)　It is important to bear in mind in deciding whether the applicant has proved such facts that it is unusual to find direct evidence of discrimination. Few employers would be prepared to admit such discrimination, even to themselves.

---

[212] A Directive on the burden of proof in sex discrimination cases was first proposed by the European Commission in 1988.

[213] Directive 97/80/EC.

[214] The Race and Employment Directives make similar provision in relation to discrimination on grounds of race, religion or belief and sexual orientation.

[215] Directive 98/52/EC.　　[216] SI 2001/2660.　　[217] [2003] IRLR 332, EAT.

[218] Based heavily on the old law as set out by Neill LJ in *King v Great Britain—China Centre* [1992] ICR 516, [1991] IRLR 513.

[219] [2005] ICR 931, [2005] IRLR 258, CA.

[220] *Hewage v Grampian Health Board* [2012] UKSC 37, [2012] IRLR 870.

In some cases the discrimination will not be an intention but merely based on the assumption that 'he or she would not have fitted in'.

(4)   In deciding whether the applicant has proved such facts, it is important to remember that the outcome at this stage of the analysis by the tribunal will therefore usually depend on what inferences it is proper to draw from the primary facts found by the tribunal.

(5)   It is important to note the word is 'could'. At this stage the tribunal does not have to reach a definitive determination that such facts *would* lead it to the conclusion that there was an act of unlawful discrimination. At this stage a tribunal is looking at the primary facts proved by the applicant to see what inferences of secondary fact *could* be drawn from them.

(6)   In considering what inferences or conclusions can be drawn from the primary facts, the tribunal must assume that there is no adequate explanation of those facts.

(7)   These inferences can include, in appropriate cases, any inferences that it is just and equitable to draw from an evasive or equivocal reply to a questionnaire or any other questions that fall within section 74(2) of the 1975 Act.

(8)   Likewise, the tribunal must decide whether any provision of any relevant code of practice is relevant and if so, take it into account in determining such facts pursuant to section 56A(10) of the 1975 Act. This means that inferences may also be drawn from any failure to comply with any relevant code of practice.

(9)   Where the applicant has proved facts from which conclusions could be drawn that the respondents have treated the applicant less favourably on a protected ground, then the burden of proof moves to the respondent.[221]

(10) It is then for the respondent to prove that he or she did not commit (or, as the case may be, is not to be treated as having committed) that act.

(11) To discharge that burden it is necessary for the respondent to prove, on the balance of probabilities, that the treatment was in no sense whatsoever because of the protected characteristic, since 'no discrimination whatsoever' is compatible with the Burden of Proof Directive.

(12) That requires a tribunal to assess not merely whether the respondent has proved an explanation for the facts from which such inferences can be drawn, but further that it is adequate to discharge the burden of proof on the balance of probabilities that the treatment in question was not because of the protected characteristic.

---

[221] Although this logically establishes a two-stage process, this is not to be applied too technically and so in deciding whether the claimant has made out a prima facie case the tribunal can look at the evidence given by the claimant *and the employers*: *Laing v Manchester City Council* [2006] IRLR 748, EAT, strongly affirmed by the Court of Appeal in *Madarassy v Nomura International plc* [2007] IRLR 246, *Brown v Croydon LBC* [2007] IRLR 259 and *Appiah v Bishop Douglass RC High School* [2007] IRLR 264.

(13)   Since the facts necessary to prove an explanation would normally be in the possession of the respondent, a tribunal would normally expect cogent evidence to discharge that burden of proof. In particular, the tribunal will need to examine carefully explanations for failure to deal with the questionnaire procedure and/or code of practice.

In practice the main hurdle for the applicant will often be the need to provide factual evidence of discrimination sufficient to shift the burden of proof onto the employer. Unreasonable treatment by the employer will not of itself suffice, as the House of Lords has held that the fact that an employer has acted unreasonably towards an employee and that no satisfactory explanation has been given does not oblige the tribunal to infer that there has been less favourable treatment on grounds of sex or race, as the employer could have treated other employees in the same unreasonable manner;[222] having said that, unreasonable behaviour by the employer is likely to require an explanation, and whether the tribunal is satisfied with the explanation 'will depend not on a theoretical possibility that the employer behaves equally badly to employees of all races [sic] but on evidence that he does'.[223] A live issue under the statutory reversal provisions is the *extent* to which the claimant must prove the initial facts. It is clear that what the law does not do is to reverse the burden merely on accusation. Moreover, it is also the case that the claimant must show a prima facie case of less favourable treatment *because of* sex/race, etc. It is not enough to show less favourable treatment *and* a difference in sex, race, etc, a point of particular relevance in allegations of discrimination in selection (where the claimant's suspicions have been raised precisely because they did not get the job *and* it went to a person of another sex, race, etc).[224] The courts have taken a relatively strict view of the extent to which the claimant must establish the prima facie case; when taken along with the strongly held view that the employer's (exculpatory) evidence can also be considered at this first stage in the process, it has been argued that it may now be *more* difficult for the claimant to discharge their evidential burden than it was under the previous law, possibly as a reaction to the fact that the tribunal now *must* reverse the burden if the necessary facts are shown by the claimant (whereas under the previous law the reversal was an *option*, to be dealt with in each case). If this is so, it is deeply ironic. One particularly difficult issue has always been the extent to which the tribunal may draw inferences of discrimination from statistical evidence, for example, that the employer's workforce is composed almost entirely of men.[225] On the

---

[222] *Zafar v Glasgow City Council* [1998] IRLR 36. The important judgment of Elias J in *Bahl v Law Society* [2003] IRLR 640, EAT (affd [2004] IRLR 799, CA) on the pre-statutory-reversal law is commonly cited for the proposition that bad treatment is not per se discriminatory treatment.

[223] *Anya v University of Oxford* [2001] EWCA Civ 405, [2001] ICR 847, [2001] IRLR 377 (a race discrimination case).

[224] *University of Huddersfield v Wolff* [2004] IRLR 534, EAT and *Network Rail Infrastructure Ltd v Griffiths-Henry* [2006] IRLR 865, EAT are particularly good examples. It was thought in the latter that a reversal might be possible if the claimant was one of two applicants, but not on great numbers.

[225] The complainant may use the statutory procedure for 'Obtaining information, etc' to obtain information from the employer; adverse inferences may be drawn from a failure to reply (s 134). This procedure is in

one hand, the fact that in practice within a workplace there is occupational segregation along gender lines, with men doing one kind of work and women another, will not per se contravene the statute, provided that the employer does not give preferential treatment to men in the former occupation or women in the latter. Thus, for example, in *Noble v David Gold & Son Ltd*,[226] the Court of Appeal found nothing discriminatory about the fact that in a packaging plant men in fact did the heavier tasks and women the lighter, even when the employer, faced with a fall-out of work, decided to run down the lighter side, which in practice meant making some of the women redundant. However, in the context of race discrimination the Court of Appeal has accepted that statistical evidence drawn from ethnic monitoring which reveals a discernible pattern in the treatment of a particular group to which the complainant belongs (for example a regular failure of members of the group to obtain promotion to particular jobs, or under-representation in such jobs) may justify the inference that 'the real reason for the treatment is a conscious or unconscious racial attitude which involves stereotyped assumptions about members of that group'.[227] In other words, statistical evidence, although not in itself conclusive, may be sufficient to raise an inference of discrimination which, in the absence of a satisfactory explanation by the employer, will be sufficient for the complainant to succeed on the balance of probabilities.

(viii) VICARIOUS LIABILITY

In at least one respect the complainant in a discrimination case receives some help from the statute, for section 109 makes the employer vicariously liable for discrimination by the complainant's fellow employees in the course of their employment, whether or not done with the employer's knowledge or approval. This could be particularly important in a sexual harassment case where the harassment is coming from fellow employees rather than from a superior.[228] However, the position is qualified by section 109(4), which provides a defence if the employer can prove that she took such steps as were reasonably practicable to prevent the fellow employees' conduct, and it has been held[229] that this defence is made out where it is shown that an employer (with no knowledge of the conduct) has maintained adequate supervision of the employees and publicized a policy of equal opportunities. In *Jones v Tower Boot Co Ltd*[230]

---

addition to the normal power of the tribunal to order discovery, on which see *Science Research Council v Nassé* [1979] ICR 921, [1979] IRLR 465, HL (discovery of confidential documents may be ordered, with suitable safeguards, where necessary to dispose fairly of the proceedings).

[226] [1980] ICR 543, [1980] IRLR 252, CA.

[227] *West Midlands Passenger Transport Executive v Singh* [1988] ICR 614, [1988] IRLR 186, CA, per Balcombe LJ. In that case the Court of Appeal ordered discovery of statistics showing the ethnic origins of those who had applied for the post of inspector in the preceding two years, and those whose applications had been successful.

[228] See, eg, *Porcelli v Strathclyde Regional Council* [1986] ICR 564, [1986] IRLR 134, Ct of Sess.

[229] *Balgobin v London Borough of Tower Hamlets* [1987] ICR 829, [1987] IRLR 401, EAT.

[230] [1997] ICR 254, [1997] IRLR 168, CA.

(a case under the equivalent provisions of the Race Relations Act), the Court of Appeal explained the purpose of the 'reasonable steps' defence as exonerating a conscientious employer who has used his or her best endeavours to prevent harassment, and encouraging all employers to take the steps necessary to make the defence available in their own workplace. It follows that an employer who has not taken reasonably practicable steps will not be exculpated simply because the employee's conduct was such that, even if those steps had been taken, they would not have prevented the discriminatory acts in question from occurring.[231] The correct approach is to identify what steps, if any, have been taken, and to consider whether there were any further reasonably practicable steps that could have been taken, irrespective of whether taking those steps would have been successful in preventing the discriminatory acts.

The principal limitation on the vicarious liability of an employer in this context is the requirement that the person causing the disadvantage to the complainant was acting 'in the course of employment'. In the earlier cases on this provision it was held that the statutory test of vicarious liability was the same as the common law test at that time (ie whether the employee's act was merely an unauthorized or prohibited mode of doing an authorized act, as distinct from an act which was outside the sphere of what she was employed to do).[232] The problem with this approach, particularly in cases involving sexual or racial harassment, was that the worse an employee's acts, the less likely it was that she would be held to be acting in the course of her employment; indeed, taken to its logical conclusion it might even mean that no employer could ever be held responsible for such acts, as no employee is employed to harass other employees. It was therefore to be welcomed that the application of the (then) common law test in this context was comprehensively rejected by the Court of Appeal in *Jones v Tower Boot Co Ltd*.[233] In that case, the complainant had been subjected to a number of extreme incidents of racial harassment by fellow employees, including being branded with a hot screwdriver, whipped across the legs and verbally abused. The EAT had overturned the tribunal's finding that the perpetrators were acting in the course of their employment, holding that the acts complained of could not 'by any stretch of the imagination' be described as an improper mode of performing authorized tasks. The Court of Appeal reversed the EAT's decision and held the employer liable; giving the principal judgment, Waite LJ held that a purposive approach should be taken to the statutory test, and that the words 'in the course of his employment' should be interpreted in the sense in which they are employed in everyday speech, unclouded by any parallels drawn from the common law of vicarious liability. This wide interpretation places heightened emphasis on

---

[231] *Canniffe v East Riding of Yorkshire Council* [2000] IRLR 555, EAT (sexual assaults on a disabled female colleague).

[232] See eg *Irving and Irving v Post Office* [1987] ICR 949, [1987] IRLR 289, CA (on the equivalent provision in the Race Relations Act 1976, s 32).

[233] See n 230. The common law test was then widened to a more generalized 'work relationship' test (particularly relevant in cases of *criminal* acts by employees at work) in *Lister v Hesley Hall Ltd* [2001] ICR 665, [2001] IRLR 472, HL; sequentially, this could be seen as tort law catching up with discrimination law.

the importance for the employer of being able to rely on the 'reasonable steps' defence, discussed above. In subsequent cases, the test has been interpreted as extending even to social activities occurring outside working hours, where those activities are work-related;[234] there are, however, limits, as was shown in *Waters v Metropolitan Police Comr*,[235] where the Court of Appeal held that no tribunal applying the statutory test (as interpreted in *Jones v Tower Boot Co Ltd*) could find that an alleged sexual assault by a male police officer on a female officer was committed 'in the course of his employment', where both parties were off-duty at the time, and the man was a visitor to her room.[236]

Where the employer is held vicariously liable under section 109, the employee responsible for the discriminatory act may be held personally liable under section 110 for committing an act which would make the employer liable by virtue of section 109, regardless of any subsequent application of the section 109(4) defence. By this convoluted process it is possible to hold an employee responsible in law for discriminatory acts even though the statutory duty not to discriminate applies only to employers. This liability is also subject to a defence under section 110(3) where the employer tells the worker that the act was legal (not a contravention of the Act) and the worker reasonably believes this.

(ix) REMEDIES

An employee or ex-employee may bring to a tribunal a complaint of any of the above forms of discrimination in employment;[237] the time limit for the presentation of complaints is three months[238] beginning when the act complained of was done,[239] or, in the case of a deliberate omission, when the person in question decided upon it,[240] although the tribunal has a wide discretion to consider a complaint out of time if it considers that it

---

[234] *Chief Constable of Lincolnshire Police v Stubbs* [1999] ICR 547, [1999] IRLR 81, EAT (police authority held liable for harassment of a female police officer while off-duty at a pub with her work colleagues, and while at a work-related leaving party).

[235] [1997] ICR 1073, [1997] IRLR 589, CA. See this chapter heading 2(iii)(d), p 330. On appeal ([2000] ICR 1064, [2000] IRLR 720), the House of Lords found for the applicant on the grounds that the Commissioner had acted negligently in failing to protect her from victimization and harassment which might cause her physical or mental harm, in breach of the duty of care both under contract of employment and under the common law principles of negligence.

[236] See also *Sidhu v Aerospace Composite Technology Ltd* [2001] ICR 167, [2000] IRLR 602, CA (violence at a social function organized by the employers outside working hours where most of those present were not employees of the employer held to be outside the course of employment).

[237] Equality Act 2010, s 120.

[238] Or six months for those serving in the armed forces, because of the need to follow the service redress procedures before making a complaint to a tribunal: Equality Act 2010, s 121.

[239] Where the act complained of is dismissal, the date of the dismissal for these purposes is not necessarily the same as the 'effective date of termination' for unfair dismissal purposes: *Lupetti v Wrens Old House Ltd* [1984] ICR 348 (under the Race Relations Act 1976); *Gloucester Working Men's Club and Institute v James* [1986] ICR 603.

[240] Equality Act 2010, s 123(3)(b). See *Swithland Motors plc v Clarke* [1994] ICR 231, [1994] IRLR 275, EAT ('decided' means 'decided at a time and in circumstances when he is in a position to implement that decision').

is 'just and equitable' to do so.[241] The courts have on the whole been reluctant to extend the time limit in discrimination complaints where the delay was caused by the applicant awaiting the resolution of internal grievance or appeal procedures before embarking on litigation.[242] Discrimination often takes the form of a continuing act extending over a period of time, in which case the time limit runs from the end of that period.[243] However, a continuing act of discrimination must be distinguished from a single act or event of discrimination which has continuing consequences, where the time limit runs from the act itself.[244] So, for example, in *Calder v James Findlay Corpn Ltd*,[245] the employer's refusal to allow the complainant access to a mortgage subsidy scheme was held to be a continuing act of discrimination, entitling her to bring her complaint more than three months after the refusal. In contrast, in *Sougrin v Haringey Health Authority*,[246] a case under the Race Relations Act, a grading decision was held by the Court of Appeal to be a single act with continuing consequences, not a continuing act of discrimination. The distinction can be extremely difficult to draw, especially where a single act of discrimination is repeated or reaffirmed on subsequent occasions.[247] A succession of specific instances of discrimination (for example a failure to regrade over a number of years, or the reaffirmation of a refusal to allow an employee to job-share) may, however, indicate the existence of a discriminatory policy or regime (formal or informal), which can constitute a continuing act extending over a period.[248] In *Hendricks v Metropolitan Police Comr*[249] the Court of Appeal reviewed the authorities and took a broad view of the concept of a continuing act, holding that the focus should be on whether there is an 'ongoing situation or a continuing state of affairs' in which the alleged incidents of discrimination were linked to one another, rather than on whether it was possible to identify some 'policy, rule, scheme, regime or practice' in accordance with which decisions

---

[241] Equality Act 2010, s 123(1)(b). This is a much wider formulation than the usual 'reasonably practicable' escape clause: see *Hutchinson v Westward Television Ltd* [1977] ICR 279, [1977] IRLR 69, EAT; *Clarke v Hampshire Electro-Plating Co Ltd* [1992] ICR 312, [1991] IRLR 490, EAT; *Hawkins v Ball* [1996] IRLR 258, EAT; *British Coal Corpn v Keeble* [1997] IRLR 336, EAT; *DPP v Marshall* [1998] ICR 518, EAT. Cf *London Borough of Southwark v Afolabi* [2003] IRLR 220, CA (a case under the parallel provisions in the RRA, in which a complaint was allowed nearly nine years after the expiry of the three-month limit).

[242] *Apelogun-Gabriels v London Borough of Lambeth* [2001] EWCA Civ 1853, [2002] ICR 713, [2002] IRLR 116, CA, approving *Robinson v Post Office* [2000] IRLR 804, EAT, and disapproving *Aniagwu v London Borough of Hackney* [1999] IRLR 303, EAT.

[243] Equality Act 2010, s 123(3)(a).

[244] See eg *Amies v Inner London Education Authority* [1977] 2 All ER 100, [1977] ICR 308, EAT (failure to appoint to a particular post held not to be a continuing act of discrimination). See also *Tyagi v BBC World Service* [2001] EWCA Civ 549, [2001] IRLR 465 (alleged discriminatory recruitment policy not a continuing act).

[245] [1989] ICR 157n, [1989] IRLR 55, EAT, approved by the House of Lords in *Barclays Bank plc v Kapur* [1991] ICR 208, [1991] IRLR 136 (under the Race Relations Act). See also *Littlewoods Organisation plc v Traynor* [1993] IRLR 154, EAT (failure to take promised remedial action in relation to a complaint of discrimination was a continuing act of discrimination by the employer).

[246] [1992] ICR 650, [1992] IRLR 416, CA.

[247] See eg *Rovenska v General Medical Council* [1998] ICR 85, [1997] IRLR 367, CA.

[248] *Owusu v London Fire and Civil Defence Authority* [1995] IRLR 574, EAT (re-grading); *Cast v Croydon College* [1998] ICR 500, [1998] IRLR 318, CA (job-share).

[249] [2003] IRLR 96, CA.

affecting the treatment of workers were taken. This is a less demanding approach than that taken in some of the earlier authorities, and should make it easier in practice for applicants to establish that a succession of discriminatory acts are not unconnected or isolated, but constitute an act extending over a period.

If the tribunal finds the complaint well founded, it may make three orders—a declaration that the employee's rights have been infringed, an order for compensation and a recommendation that the employer take action suggested by the tribunal within a specified period in order to remove the discrimination.[250] The latter recommendation is just that; it is not a positive order and should not be framed as such.[251] If the employer fails to comply with a recommendation without reasonable excuse, the complainant may go back to the tribunal which may award increased compensation if it considers it just and equitable to do so.[252] In such proceedings the tribunal must take a realistic approach and one of the main factors in deciding whether the employer had reasonable justification may be whether there has been sufficient time to put matters right, for the provisions relating to the recommendation clearly envisage the possibility of longer term measures.[253]

On the question of compensation, the tribunal is empowered to award it on the same basis as if the complainant had brought an action for damages in tort before an ordinary court, so that, as far as money can do it, the applicants must be put into the position they would have been in but for the unlawful conduct of the employer.[254] There is an express power to award damages for injury to feelings,[255] difficult though this may be to quantify. An award for injury to feelings has been said to be 'almost inevitable' in a discrimination case,[256] but this does not mean that it is automatic, as the applicant must still prove that some injury has been sustained.[257] The Court of Appeal

---

[250] Equality Act 2010, s 124(2).

[251] *Ministry of Defence v Jeremiah* [1978] ICR 984, [1978] IRLR 402; affd [1979] 3 All ER 833, [1979] IRLR 436. The recommendation may not include an increase of salary (*Prestcold Ltd v Irvine* [1981] ICR 777, [1981] IRLR 281, CA) or an instruction to appoint or promote the applicant to the next available vacancy, where he or she has not been appointed or promoted because of discrimination (*North West Thames Regional Health Authority v Noone* [1988] ICR 813, [1988] IRLR 530, CA; *British Gas plc v Sharma* [1991] ICR 19, [1991] IRLR 101, EAT).

[252] Equality Act 2010, s 124(7).

[253] *Nelson v Tyne and Wear Passenger Transport Executive* [1978] ICR 1183.

[254] Equality Act 2010, ss 124(6); 119(2). See *Alexander v Home Office* [1988] ICR 685, [1988] IRLR 190, CA (under the Race Relations Act 1976) and *Ministry of Defence v Cannock* [1994] ICR 918, [1994] IRLR 509, EAT, which contain detailed guidance on the assessment of damages in discrimination cases.

[255] Equality Act 2010, ss 124(b); 119(4). The injury to feelings must arise directly from the sex discrimination, not from other, more remote, consequences: *Skyrail Oceanic Ltd v Coleman* [1981] ICR 864, [1981] IRLR 398, CA.

[256] *Murray v Powertech (Scotland) Ltd* [1992] IRLR 257, EAT.

[257] *Ministry of Defence v Cannock* [1994] ICR 918, [1994] IRLR 509, EAT. In *Cannock*, the EAT suggested that it will often be easy to prove injury, as no tribunal will take much persuading that the anger and distress caused by the discriminatory act has injured the applicant's feelings. In sexual harassment cases, the EAT has held that compensation must relate to the degree of detriment suffered; this has led to an uncomfortably close examination of the applicant's character and antecedents in some cases: see eg *Snowball v Gardner Merchant Ltd* [1987] ICR 719, [1987] IRLR 397; *Wileman v Minilec Engineering Ltd* [1988] ICR 318, [1988] IRLR 144, EAT.

has indicated that while damages for injury to feelings in discrimination cases should not be minimal[258] (since this would tend to trivialize the issue and diminish respect for the law), the awards should be restrained, as to award sums which are generally felt to be excessive would do almost as much harm to the policy of the legislation as to make nominal awards.[259] In the earlier cases, awards for injury to feelings tended to be fairly small; however, in *Armitage, Marsden and HM Prison Service v Johnson*,[260] a race discrimination case, the EAT upheld an award for injury to feelings of £21,000, holding that the award was not grossly or obviously out of line with the general range of awards in personal injury cases. In one race discrimination case, an employment tribunal awarded £100,000 for injury to feelings plus aggravated damages of £25,000, although this award was highly exceptional and reflected the appalling nature of the conduct complained of and the devastating impact on the complainant.[261] In *Vento v Chief Constable of West Yorkshire Police (No 2)*,[262] the Court of Appeal expressed concern at awards of that magnitude, and attempted to limit the size of awards for injury to feelings by identifying three broad bands into which such awards should fall: the top band, for the most serious cases (such as where there has been a lengthy campaign of sexual or racial harassment) should normally be between £15,000 and £25,000; only in 'the most exceptional case' should an award for injury to feelings exceed £25,000; the middle band of between £5,000 and £15,000 should be used for serious cases not meriting an award in the highest band; and awards of between £500 and £5,000 are appropriate for less serious cases, such as isolated or one-off acts of discrimination; awards of less than £500 should be avoided altogether 'as they risk being regarded as so low as not to be a proper recognition of injury to feelings'.[263] The tribunal can also award damages for personal injury (including an award for psychological harm caused by the discrimination),[264] and the Court of Appeal has held that, unlike a common law claim for negligence, a personal injury claim in a discrimination complaint is not limited to harm that is reasonably foreseeable, and that all the applicant need show is a direct causal link between the act of discrimination and their loss.[265] Aggravated damages are available where, for example, the defendant has behaved in a high-handed, malicious, insulting or oppressive manner in committing the discriminatory act,[266] or where the defendant has defended the discrimination claim in a manner which was designed to

---

[258] £500 is 'at or near the minimum': *Sharifi v Strathclyde Regional Council* [1992] IRLR 259.

[259] *Alexander v Home Office* [1988] ICR 685, [1988] IRLR 190, CA.

[260] [1997] IRLR 162, EAT. The EAT also upheld awards of £500 each against two prison officers personally.

[261] *Virdi v Metropolitan Police Comr* (8 December 2000, unreported).

[262] [2002] EWCA Civ 1871, [2003] ICR 318, [2003] IRLR 102. The tribunal's award of £50,000 for injury to feelings plus £15,000 aggravated damages was held to be excessive, and the Court of Appeal substituted awards of £18,000 and £5,000 respectively; damages for psychiatric injury were left at £9,000.

[263] [2003] IRLR 102 at 110, per Mummery LJ.

[264] *Sheriff v Klyne Tugs (Lowestoft) Ltd* [1999] ICR 1170, [1999] IRLR 481, CA (under the parallel provisions in the RRA).

[265] *Essa v Laing Ltd* [2004] ICR 746, [2004] IRLR 313, CA (also under the RRA).

[266] *Alexander v Home Office* above, n 259; *Armitage, Marsden and HM Prison Service v Johnson* above, n 260; *Ministry of Defence v Meredith* [1995] IRLR 539, EAT.

be intimidatory and to cause the maximum unease and distress to the applicant,[267] but it has been held that a tribunal cannot award exemplary damages in sex and race discrimination cases.[268]

Until 1993, compensation under the Sex Discrimination Act (as well as the RRA) was subject to two major limitations: first, it was subject to the same upper limit as the compensatory award for unfair dismissal;[269] and, secondly, in a complaint of indirect discrimination compensation could only be awarded if the employer applied the requirement or condition with the *intention* of discriminating on the ground of sex (although the tribunal could still make a declaration and recommendation). However, as in so many other areas of UK sex discrimination law, EC law has made its mark in this area, and both these limitations have been removed. In *Marshall v Southampton and South-West Hampshire Area Health Authority (No 2)*,[270] the CJEU held that the upper limit on compensation infringed Article 6 of the Equal Treatment Directive, which requires the provision of adequate remedies which compensate the complainant in full for the loss and damage sustained as a result of the discrimination. This decision led to the removal of the upper limit in sex discrimination cases;[271] the limit in race discrimination cases was also subsequently abolished,[272] bringing the two Acts into line once again. The effect of this change was demonstrated in dramatic fashion by the complaints brought against the Ministry of Defence by servicewomen dismissed on the grounds of pregnancy, where awards of compensation in excess of £300,000 were made in some cases.[273] The removal of the upper limit means that it may be preferable to challenge a discriminatory dismissal under the discrimination legislation rather than in a claim for unfair dismissal, although the normal rules concerning mitigation and discounting for future uncertainties will still apply.[274]

The ruling in *Marshall* also brought into doubt the bar on the award of damages for unintentional indirect discrimination, long seen as a significant weakness in the

---

[267] *Zaiwalla & Co v Walia* [2002] IRLR 697, EAT (£7,500 aggravated damages awarded for the way in which the defendant firm of solicitors conducted their defence).

[268] *Deane v Ealing London Borough Council* [1993] ICR 329, [1993] IRLR 209, EAT, following the decision of the Court of Appeal in *Gibbons v South West Water Services Ltd* [1993] QB 507, [1993] 1 All ER 609. See also *Ministry of Defence v Meredith* [1995] IRLR 539.

[269] See Ch 7, heading 6(ii), p 531.

[270] [1994] QB 126, [1993] ICR 893, ECJ.

[271] Sex Discrimination and Equal Pay (Remedies) Regulations 1993, SI 1993/2798. The Regulations also empowered tribunals to award interest on compensation, in line with the ECJ's ruling in *Marshall*; see now the Employment Tribunals (Interest on Awards in Discrimination Cases) Regulations 1996, SI 1996/2803.

[272] Race Relations (Remedies) Act 1994.

[273] See *Ministry of Defence v Cannock* [1994] ICR 918, [1994] IRLR 509, EAT; *Ministry of Defence v Hunt* [1996] ICR 554, [1996] IRLR 139, EAT.

[274] See *Ministry of Defence v Cannock* [1994] ICR 918, [1994] IRLR 509, EAT; *Ministry of Defence v Hunt* [1996] ICR 554, [1996] IRLR 139, EAT. See also *Ministry of Defence v Wheeler* [1998] ICR 242, [1998] IRLR 23, CA.

domestic provisions. In *London Underground v Edwards*,[275] the EAT managed to circumvent this bar by holding that an intention to discriminate could be inferred where the employer applied a requirement or condition with the knowledge of its unfavourable consequences for a woman, but in *MacMillan v Edinburgh Voluntary Organisations Council*,[276] the EAT held that the provisions excluding compensation for unintentional indirect discrimination were unambiguous, and could not be construed to accord with the provisions of the Directive.[277] The uncertainty was subsequently resolved by the introduction of further Regulations allowing the tribunal to award compensation for unintentional indirect discrimination where it is satisfied that the power to make a declaration and recommendation is not sufficient, and it is just and equitable to award compensation,[278] thus bringing domestic law into line with the Directive. This is echoed in section 124 of the 2010 Act.

In addition to the remedies available to the aggrieved employee, the Equality and Human Rights Commission (as successor to the EOC, CRE and DRC) is empowered to take certain direct steps to secure compliance with the statute. In particular it may conduct a formal investigation into any alleged contraventions, which may result in the issue of an unlawful act notice if it discovers breaches of the Act; such a notice may require the recipient to prepare an action plan for the purpose of avoiding any repetition, and it may contain requirements to be met by the employer, who has six weeks in which to appeal against it to a tribunal. If there is no appeal, or an appeal is dismissed, the notice becomes final, and any further contraventions of it may be restrained by injunction at the suit of the Commission.[279] The Commission may also enter into legally binding agreements to rectify the situation. There are also further, more specific powers given to the Commission to take action against discriminatory advertisements,[280] and to give practical help to individuals to bring discrimination claims against their employers.[281]

---

[275] [1995] ICR 574, [1995] IRLR 355, EAT; see also *J H Walker Ltd v Hussain* [1996] ICR 291, [1996] IRLR 11, EAT, a case under the Race Relations Act, where it was held that a person will be taken to have intended the unfavourable consequences to follow from his acts 'if he knew when he did them that those consequences would follow and if he wanted those consequences to follow', per Mummery J at 15.

[276] [1995] IRLR 536, EAT.

[277] The decision in *London Underground v Edwards* was not mentioned in the judgment. As a private-sector employee, the complainant was unable to rely on the direct effect of the Directive.

[278] Sex Discrimination Act 1975, s 65(1B), inserted by SI 1996/438.

[279] Equality Act 2006 ss 20–24. On the nature of an appeal against a non-discrimination notice, see *Commission for Racial Equality v Amari Plastics Ltd* [1982] ICR 304, [1982] IRLR 252, CA; if the formal investigation is not carried out in accordance with the stipulated procedure, any resulting non-discrimination notice is void: *Re Prestige Group plc, Commission for Racial Equality v Prestige Group plc* [1984] ICR 473, [1984] IRLR 166, HL.

[280] Equality Act 2006, s 25.   [281] Equality Act 2006, s 28.

3 SEX DISCRIMINATION[282]

(i) DRESS AND APPEARANCE RULES

It was mentioned above that sometimes courts and tribunals cannot see past time-honoured conventions to give effect to what discrimination statutes clearly require them to do. One such area is dress and appearance rules. It is not uncommon for employers to impose rules on employees concerning their dress and appearance while at work. This may be done for operational reasons (for example in the interests of safety and hygiene), or simply because the employer is seeking to promote a particular corporate image which involves the employees wearing a uniform or observing restrictions on, for example, their hairstyle or the wearing of jewellery. Such rules often impose different requirements on men and women, reflecting current perceptions of conventional appearance, yet it could be argued that under the test of direct discrimination approved by the House of Lords in *James v Eastleigh Borough Council*,[283] any such differentiation necessarily constitutes discrimination on the grounds of sex, because 'but for' a person's sex, the gender-specific appearance requirement would not have been applied.[284] Furthermore, the underlying rationale of the anti-discrimination legislation was to tackle discrimination which results from gender stereotyping, yet arguably what is regarded as 'conventional' in terms of appearance is itself permeated by gender stereotyping, and therefore inherently sexually discriminatory.

The approach of the courts and tribunals to this issue has been to skirt around the problem by holding that there is no infringement of the Act where the employer imposes an appearance code which has different rules for men and women, as long as the code enforces a common principle of smartness or conventionality, and taken as a whole neither gender is treated less favourably. So, for example, in *Schmidt v Austicks Bookshops Ltd*,[285] the employer imposed a rule that women could not wear trousers at work and had to wear overalls, while men were not allowed to wear tee-shirts. A female employee complained that the rule against trousers was unlawful under the Act, but the EAT held against her on the ground that the employer applied rules on clothing to all employees, although in the nature of things the rules were not the same given the difference between the sexes.[286] According to the EAT, an employer is entitled to a large measure of discretion in controlling the image of his establishment, including the appearance of the staff, especially where they come into contact with the public.

---

[282] See McColgan *Just Wages for Women* (1997).   [283] [1990] IRLR 288, HL.

[284] See Cunningham (1995) 24 ILJ 177; Wintemute (1997) 60 MLR 334.

[285] [1978] ICR 85, [1977] IRLR 360, EAT.

[286] See also *Burrett v West Birmingham Health Authority* [1994] IRLR 7, EAT, where it was held that a female nurse who was required to wear a cap as part of her uniform was not less favourably treated on grounds of sex than male nurses who were not required to wear a cap, since the requirement to wear a uniform applied equally to male and female nurses. Her honestly held belief that the requirement to wear a cap was demeaning was held not to be determinative of whether or not there was less favourable treatment.

The *Schmidt* approach was approved by the Court of Appeal in *Smith v Safeway plc*.[287] In that case, the employers' appearance code placed restrictions on hair length which applied to men only; women were allowed to have long hair provided it was tied back. The complainant was dismissed because he refused to cut off his ponytail. The tribunal, following *Schmidt*, held that the treatment of the complainant was not less favourable than that which would have been accorded to a woman because the code, although different for men and women, enforced a common standard of smartness and conventionality, and taken as a whole it could not be said that either gender was treated less favourably. The EAT upheld the employee's appeal,[288] holding that since the employers' rules restricted only the hair length of men, the treatment of the complainant was self-evidently less favourable, and that the employer's requirements with respect to hairstyle were capable of being applied to both men and women in such a way as to take account of convention (for example by allowing men to have a ponytail), without placing a restriction on hair length for men only. The EAT also placed emphasis on the fact that, unlike other appearance requirements concerning uniform, hairstyle and jewellery, a restriction on hair length extends beyond working hours, and thereby affects individual choice detrimentally at all times (the implication being that such a restriction requires a stronger justification). However, the Court of Appeal overturned the EAT in favour of a more conventional interpretation of *Schmidt*. According to Phillips LJ, the starting point of the reasoning in *Schmidt*, which he considered to be 'plainly correct', was that it was necessary to show not merely that the sexes were treated differently, but that the treatment accorded to one was less favourable than the treatment accorded to the other; in his view, the most important element of the *Schmidt* approach was that, looking at the code as a whole, neither sex was to be treated less favourably as a result of its enforcement, and the tribunal's decision to that effect should therefore be upheld.[289]

There are, however, three reasons why the existing case law on dress and appearance codes should be approached with caution. First, the imposition of restrictions on how a person chooses to present himself or herself could be seen as an infringement of that person's right to respect for private and family life under Article 8 of the European Convention on Human Rights; secondly, where a person adopts a particular form of dress in accordance with the customs or requirements of their religion, the imposition of a dress code that conflicts with the requirements of that religion could constitute unlawful discrimination on grounds of religion or belief;[290] and, thirdly, what is regarded as 'conventional' in relation to dress and appearance may change with time, and employers may be expected to modify their dress and appearance rules to

---

[287] [1996] ICR 868, [1996] IRLR 456, CA.

[288] [1995] ICR 472, [1995] IRLR 132, EAT, Pill J dissenting.

[289] According to Phillips LJ, the fact that a restriction applied to permanent characteristics such as hair length or colour, and therefore extended beyond the workplace, was a factor to be taken into account in considering whether a code treats one sex less favourably than the other, but does not affect the test itself.

[290] See this chapter, heading 6, p 381.

reflect those changes. In *McConomy v Croft Inns Ltd*,[291] a case on discrimination in the provision of goods and services under Part iii of the Act, it was held to be unlawfully discriminatory for a public house to refuse to serve a man for wearing earrings where there was no similar objection to women wearing earrings. The court stressed that while account must be taken of certain basic rules of human conduct, such as the ordinary rules of decency accepted in the community, which might permit or require different dress regulations as between men and women, in today's conditions it is not possible to say that the circumstances are different as between men and women as regards the wearing of personal jewellery or other items of personal adornment. Certain employment tribunal decisions in which dress codes prohibiting women from wearing trousers at work have been held to be discriminatory[292] confirm the inherently transient nature of conventions of dress and appearance and indicate that standards of what is 'conventional' in relation to appearance have shifted somewhat in the years since *Schmidt*; but the decision in *Smith v Safeway plc* suggests that the courts are not yet ready to accept as conventional a man who turns up for work wearing a ponytail, let alone lipstick and high heels.[293]

(ii) THE GENDER PAY GAP

The Equal Pay Act 1970, as amended by the Sex Discrimination Act 1975, was aimed at preventing discrimination between men and women as regards terms and conditions of employment. As such, it only applied to cases where a contractual relationship already existed between the complainant and his or her employer; if a case arose concerning alleged discrimination in an area other than terms and conditions of employment (for example advertising vacancies, recruitment, refusal of employment or promotion), that would come under the Sex Discrimination Act 1975.[294] This division is now reflected in the existence of separate provisions in the 2010 Act for 'Equality of Terms', which apply only on the ground of sex. In its early years the Equal Pay Act 1970 led to a significant shift in relative pay levels as between men and women,[295] but after it had been in operation for several years it became clear that it was subject to certain limitations which meant that it could go so far and no further. However, since the early 1980s the whole area has been revitalized by the impact of EC law, and in particular Article 141 of the EC Treaty, which provided (before the Amsterdam Treaty modifications)[296] that each member state shall 'ensure and subsequently maintain the principle that men and women shall receive equal pay for equal work'. As explained earlier in this chapter,[297] this

---

[291] [1992] IRLR 561, NIHC.

[292] See, eg, *Owen v Professional Golfers' Association* (January 2000, unreported), ET.

[293] Cf Cunningham, n 284.   [294] See this chapter, heading 2(i), p 307.

[295] By 1977, women's pay as a proportion of men's had risen to 75.5%, compared with 63% in 1970.

[296] As modified in the Amsterdam Treaty, Art 141 now expressly confers a right to equal pay for work of equal value: 'Each Member State shall ensure that the principle of equal pay for male and female workers for equal work *or work of equal value* is applied' (italics supplied).

[297] See p 303.

is important for a number of reasons, not least that Article 141 prevails over conflicting provisions of domestic law, and if domestic law is found wanting when measured
against the yardstick of EC law, enforcement proceedings can be brought in the CJEU
in order to enforce compliance. In Case 61/81 *EC Commission v United Kingdom*,[298]
the CJEU held that the Equal Pay Act 1970 did not comply with the treaty requirements by allowing a woman to demand equal pay for work of equal value. This led
to the major amendments in 1983 instituting (by Regulations) the 'equal value claim'
which is considered below. More recently, the CJEU's broad interpretation of Article
141, and in particular its landmark decision in *Barber v Guardian Royal Exchange
Assurance Group*[299] that benefits under a contracted-out, private occupational pension
scheme fall within the scope of the word 'pay', led to the repeal of the exclusion in the
1970 Act for provisions made in connection with death or retirement, the enactment
in the Pensions Act 1995 of a new right to equal treatment in occupational pension
schemes, and the equalization of state pensionable ages at 65.[300] Unusually, the CJEU
held in *Barber* that its decision was not to operate retrospectively, so that Article 141
could not be relied upon in order to claim entitlement to equal pension benefits for
periods of service before the ruling in that case; however, the temporal limitation in
Barber was held not to apply to the right to *join* a pension scheme,[301] and the impact
of Community law was graphically illustrated by the CJEU's decision in *Preston v
Wolverhampton Healthcare NHS Trust*[302] (a test case for some 60,000 part-time workers excluded from occupational pension schemes) that workers unlawfully excluded
from such schemes were in principle entitled to backdate their membership to 8 April
1976 (ie the date on which the CJEU first held that Article 141 had direct effect).

While EC law has undeniably revitalized the domestic law on equal pay, the current
position is far from satisfactory. The relevant principles and procedures are extremely
complex and time-consuming (one well-known case involving a group of NHS speech
therapists took 14 years to resolve),[303] yet the statistics indicate that the pay gap
between men and women is stubbornly resistant to further reduction. Despite over
30 years of equal pay legislation, by the turn of the century the average hourly pay of
female full-time workers was still only 82% of that of male full-time workers, and the
gender pay gap for part-time workers was 39%.[304] A 2009 report had women earning
21% an hour less than men, with women making as much as 50% less in some parts of
the country.[305]

---

[298] [1982] ICR 578, [1982] IRLR 333, ECJ.   [299] [1991] 1 QB 344, [1990] ICR 616, ECJ.
[300] See this chapter, heading 3(vi), p 375.
[301] *Vroege v NCIV Institut voor Volkshuisvesting BV* [1995] ICR 635, [1994] IRLR 651, ECJ.
[302] Case C-78/98 [2000] ICR 961, [2000] IRLR 506.
[303] *Guardian*, 8 May 2000, reporting a £12m settlement for 351 NHS staff, negotiated between the Department of Health and MSF union *Enderby v Frenchay Health Authority*; the legal action in the case is discussed
under heading 3(iv), see n 389.
[304] EOC *Equality in the 21st Century: A New Sex Equality Law for Britain* (1998).
[305] 'Gender pay gap still as high as 50%, UK survey says' *Guardian*, 30 October 2009 (available at <http://www.
guardian.co.uk/money/2009/oct/30/gender-pay-gap-still-high> last accessed 9 January 2013).

In October 1999, the EOC set up an independent Equal Pay Task Force[306] to investigate pay discrimination in the workplace. In its report, *Just Pay*, the Task Force analysed the reasons for the continued gender pay gap between women's and men's pay,[307] and found that three main factors contribute to it: occupational segregation (ie the concentration of women in low-paid jobs such as shop assistants, secretaries, nurses and teachers), the unequal impact of women's family responsibilities, and pay discrimination. The Task Force considered that 25–50% of the pay gap was attributable to discrimination, and advised that with concerted action by all the key players, that part of the gender pay gap attributable to discrimination in the workplace could be reduced to 50% within five years, and eliminated entirely within eight years. Five main barriers to closing the gender pay gap were identified in the report: lack of awareness and understanding of the issue; ineffective, time-consuming and cumbersome equal pay legislation; lack of expertise in addressing the problem; lack of transparency and accountability for implementing equal pay; and social and economic measures that have failed to keep pace with women's changing place in the labour market. The Task Force proposed a 'multi-levered' approach to addressing the problem, focused on: raising levels of awareness and developing a common understanding of what the pay gap means; reforming and modernizing the equal pay legislation; capacity-building to ensure that employers and trade unions know how to implement equal pay; enhancing transparency and developing accountability for delivering pay equality; and amending social, economic and labour market policies to complement equal pay measures. The report also contained a series of recommendations for the reform of equal pay legislation, the principal one being a call for the enactment of a legal duty on employers to carry out regular equal pay reviews:

> Our evidence suggests[308] that the vast majority of employers do not believe they have a gender pay gap and therefore do not believe an equal pay review is necessary. We are firmly of the view that there will be little or no progress in closing the pay gap unless employers take the essential first step of examining whether they have gender inequalities in their pay systems. However, the overwhelming evidence to date is that most will not do so voluntarily.

In addition, the Task Force recommended, inter alia, reforms to streamline the tribunal process in equal pay cases, the use of hypothetical comparators, and the extension of the statutory questionnaire procedure for discrimination claims to equal pay cases.

In the wake of the Task Force report, the government commissioned its own review of women's employment and pay, which reported in December 2001. The Kingsmill

---

[306] The 12-member Task Force included senior figures from the private and public sectors, from employers and trade unions, as well as experts in pay equality and gender issues. The Chair was Bob Mason from BT.

[307] The UK has the widest pay gap in Europe: Grimshaw and Rubery *The Gender Pay Gap: A Research Review* (EOC, 2001) ch 3 (international comparisons).

[308] See Morrell et al *Gender Equality in Pay Practices* (EOC, 2001). The report indicated that employers have misplaced confidence that their payment systems lack bias.

Review[309] contained a far more modest set of recommendations, focusing mainly on voluntary measures to improve 'human capital management' by helping employers to appreciate 'the overwhelming business case for the effective use of the talents and abilities of women' which was seen as offering 'the greatest potential for reducing the pay gap'. The one specific recommendation for reform of the law on equal pay was the introduction of a right for individual employees to obtain information about the pay of named colleagues, and predictably on this occasion the government heeded the call for reform by legislating to extend the statutory questionnaire procedure to equal pay claims.[310] The 2010 Act went further, authorizing, in section 78, the government to impose by regulation a requirement that employers publish all of the information necessary to establish the existence of a pay gap. Were it implemented, it would not apply to employers of fewer than 250 workers, and could not come into force until 2013. However, the Coalition government has announced its intention not to implement the provision and instead pursue a voluntary private sectors scheme.[311] A more significant innovation in the 2010 Act is the section 77 extension of victimization protection to those who engage in 'discussions with colleagues about the terms' of their employment. This effectively outlaws contractual confidentiality clauses forbidding employees to discuss their pay with other workers, as any attempt to enforce it would impose a detriment for engaging in a protected act, and thus constitute victimization.

(iii) EQUALITY OF TERMS

Under section 66 of the Act, every worker's contract is deemed to include an 'equality clause' to the effect that (1) if any term in the contract[312] is less favourable than a similar term in the contract of a person of the opposite sex, that term is to be treated as modified so that it is not less favourable than the other term, and (2) if the contract does not include a beneficial term which appears in the other's contract, the contract shall be treated as including that term.[313] For the equality clause to operate one of three principal tests must be satisfied: the worker must be employed either on 'like work' with a person of the opposite sex 'in the same employment', or on 'work rated as equivalent' with that person, or on 'work of equal value' to that of that person.[314] Where this is

---

[309] *Kingsmill Review of Women's Employment and Pay* (2001).

[310] Equal Pay Act 1970, s 7B, inserted by the Employment Act 2002 (now in the Equality Act 2010, s 134).

[311] *The Equality Strategy: Building a Fairer Britain* (HM Gov December 2010), s 2, available at <http://www. homeoffice.gov.uk/publications/equalities/equality-strategy-publications/equality-strategy/equality-strategy> (last accessed 9 January 2013). The authors wonder if the reader begins to recognize a trend with regard to the Coalition government and the implementation of elements of the Equality Act 2010.

[312] Where the contract grants the employer discretion to allocate a benefit, such as stock shares, any less favourable distribution on the ground of gender is sex discrimination, not a question of equality of terms. *Hosso v European Credit Management* [2011] EWCA Civ 1589 [2012] IRLR 235.

[313] The effect of an equality clause was considered by the House of Lords in *Hayward v Cammell Laird Shipbuilders Ltd* [1988] ICR 464, [1988] IRLR 257, considered below.

[314] Three other heads were added in 2005 to deal specifically with equal pay issues in maternity pay.

shown, a presumption will be raised that the difference in terms is due to sex discrimination, and the contract will be modified by the equality clause, unless the employer is able to rebut the presumption by showing that the difference in terms is genuinely due to some material factor other than the difference of sex between the applicant and the comparator, ie that the reason for the difference is not tainted by sex discrimination. The modification via the equality clause operates on a term-by-term basis. The tribunal is not empowered to act as a general wage-fixing body, deciding for example that the person's work is worth 80% of the value of that of a person of the opposite sex and ordering any necessary wage adjustments accordingly. Neither is it possible to offset any disadvantageous terms in the applicant's contract by pointing to other terms in the contract which are more favourable that those enjoyed by the comparator, a point established in *Hayward v Cammell Laird Shipbuilders Ltd*,[315] one of the first cases on the equal value provisions to come before the higher courts. Miss Hayward (supported by her union and the EOC) won on her substantive claim, but then the question arose as to what she was entitled to. She claimed the same basic rate of pay as her male comparator as a term of her contract under the equality clause, but the employers objected to this, pointing out that although her basic rate had been less, she had enjoyed other terms of employment (particularly as to sickness benefits, holidays and meal breaks) which were better than her comparator's, which offset the disadvantage on pay. Thus, if one took a 'term-by-term' approach she could succeed in her claim for the same basic pay, but if one took a broader, 'package' approach to her terms and conditions as a whole she would fail. The Court of Appeal opted for the package approach, but her appeal was allowed by the House of Lords which held, as a matter of construction of section 1(2), that the correct approach is to examine the two contracts term by term; she was therefore entitled to keep the benefit of those terms which were better than those of her comparator, while still being entitled to the equality of basic pay that she had sought all along,[316] Lord Mackay LC adding for good measure that this approach is consistent with EC law.[317] The term-by-term approach may seem counter-intuitive, but one possible rationale for it is the difficulty that a court might face in making an overall assessment and comparison of all the non-wage elements of the two contracts.

---

[315] [1988] ICR 464, [1988] IRLR 257, HL (noted Napier (1988) NLJ 341); revsg [1987] ICR 682, [1987] IRLR 186, CA.

[316] An obvious danger in this approach is the potential disruption of differentials in pay and conditions, particularly where the employer's payment system involves employees in choosing from a menu of non-wage benefits. The scope to be given to the defence of 'genuine material factor' (see heading 3(iv)) could be crucial in such cases (see *Hayward*, per Lord Goff). Also, in *Degnan v Redcar & Cleveland BC* [2005] IRLR 615 the Court of Appeal cut down the scope for 'cherry picking' (by claiming individual benefits from different comparators) by construing 'remuneration' widely as *one* term (and so not allowing the claimant to choose various components from within it).

[317] This was confirmed by the ECJ in *Barber v Guardian Royal Exchange Assurance Group* [1991] 1 QB 344, [1990] ICR 616, ECJ. See also *Jorgenen v Foreningen af Speciallaeger* [2000] IRLR 726 ECJ; *Brunnhofer v Bank der Osterreichischen Postsparkasse AG* [2001] IRLR 571 ECJ.

(a) Like work

This is defined in section 65(2) as work that is 'the same or broadly similar', such that any differences between the things the applicant does and the things done by the comparator 'are not of practical importance in relation to terms of their work'. Three points might be made on this definition. The first is that in deciding whether work is the same or broadly similar, the tribunal should take a wide view. Thus, in *Capper Pass Ltd v Lawton*[318] a female cook who prepared ten to 20 lunches for directors was held to be employed on like work with two male assistant chefs who helped to provide many more meals at more times of the day in the works canteen, particularly as it was a generally similar type of work involved, with similar skill and knowledge required to do it. In deciding upon similarity or otherwise, the tribunal is not confined to the detailed physical processes performed by the employees in question, but may consider more general matters such as differences in responsibility (as in the case of two buyers, where the higher paid male buyer is in fact employed to buy more expensive goods, thereby incurring greater responsibility if he buys poor goods),[319] or the status of the complainant as a 'trainee'.[320] If matters such as these are taken into account in a bona fide grading scheme, under which the man and the women are genuinely on different grades, then the man and the woman will not be held to be on 'like work' and the woman will not be able to claim equality.[321] The second point is that in looking to see whether any differences are of practical importance the tribunal should take an equally broad approach, for the very concept of 'broadly similar' work necessarily implies differences in detail. However, these should not defeat a claim for equality unless they are such as the tribunal would expect in practice to be reflected in different terms and conditions of employment.[322] Also, section 1(4) itself states that in comparing work 'regard shall be had to the frequency or otherwise with which any such differences occur in practice as well as to the nature and extent of the differences'. Thus, the tribunal must look at the duties actually performed, not those theoretically possible. In *Shields v Coomes (Holdings) Ltd*[323] a male counterhand at a betting shop was paid at a higher hourly rate than a female counterhand, the claimed difference being that the man was there partly as a deterrent to potential troublemakers; the Court of Appeal held that the woman was entitled to equal pay, since there was no evidence of the man in question being particularly skilled or specially trained for this extra function or of there in fact ever having been any particular trouble for him to deal with, so that any difference was in practice only one of sex and the tribunal, in finding for the employer, had paid too much attention to bare contractual obligations and too little to the practicalities. The third point is that the tribunal, in making its comparison, must look at the duties performed by the woman and the man, not at the time at which they are

---

[318] [1977] ICR 83, [1976] IRLR 366.   [319] *Eaton Ltd v Nuttall* [1977] ICR 272, [1977] IRLR 71.
[320] *De Brito v Standard Chartered Bank Ltd* [1978] ICR 650, EAT.
[321] *Capper Pass Ltd v Allan* [1980] ICR 194, [1980] IRLR 236, EAT.
[322] *Capper Pass Ltd v Lawton* [1977] ICR 83 at 87H, [1976] IRLR 366 at 367.
[323] [1978] ICR 1159, [1978] IRLR 263, CA; see also *Redland Roof Tiles v Harper* [1977] ICR 349, EAT.

performed. In *Dugdale v Kraft Foods Ltd*[324] female quality control workers performed prima facie similar work to that done by male quality control workers, but the men were paid at a higher basic rate because they worked night shifts and certain Sundays. The tribunal thought that this was a material difference, but the EAT reversed this decision and remitted the case to another tribunal, which eventually awarded equal pay to a majority of the applicants in the case.[325]

However, it must be remembered that the Act is aimed at securing treatment that is not less favourable than that given to a man in the circumstances, not at securing mathematical equality of pay packets at the end of the day, so that if the male comparator does in fact perform similar work but at antisocial hours, or in unfavourable conditions, this may amount to a material difference justifying the payment of extra remuneration (special premia for overtime, night working, Sunday shifts, etc) provided that such premia genuinely reflect the extra inconvenience and are not so large that they are seen as simply a way of indirectly reintroducing a sex-based distinction:

> this does not mean that men, or women, cannot be paid extra for working at night or at weekends, or at other inconvenient times; if the additional remuneration is justified by the inconvenience of the time at which it is done the claim [for equality] will not succeed. For, while every contract of employment is deemed to include an equality clause, it only has to take effect so that the terms of the woman's contract shall be treated as so modified as not to be less favourable than the man's. Thus the industrial tribunal—without falling into the error of setting itself up as a wage-fixing body—may adjust the woman's remuneration upon a claim by her so that it is at the same rate as the man's, discounting for the fact that he works at inconvenient hours, and she does not.[326]

What has been said on this third point so far, however, assumes that there is a sex-based difference in the working patterns. Where, however, both men and women work at inconvenient times, there is no requirement that all those who work, for example at night, shall be paid the same basic rate as all those who work normal day shifts. Thus, a woman who works days cannot use the principle (of disregarding the time of performing similar work) in order to claim equality with a man on a higher basic rate for working nights if in fact there are women working nights on that rate too, and the applicant herself would be entitled to that rate if she changed shifts.[327]

Finally, it is implicit in what has already been said that a claim under this head should not be defeated simply on the grounds that the applicant and her comparator have different qualifications (although that may be give rise to a 'genuine material factor' defence: see below). However, in *Angestelltenbetriebsrat der Wiener*

---

[324] [1977] ICR 48, [1976] IRLR 368. See also *Electrolux Ltd v Hutchinson* [1977] ICR 252, [1976] IRLR 410.

[325] *Dugdale v Kraft Foods Ltd* [1977] IRLR 160, IT.

[326] *National Coal Board v Sherwin* [1978] ICR 700 at 740D, [1978] IRLR 122 at 124 per Phillips J (cf, on the facts, *Thomas v National Coal Board* [1987] ICR 757, [1987] IRLR 451, EAT).

[327] *Kerr v Lister & Co Ltd* [1977] IRLR 259, EAT.

Gebietskrankenkasse v Wiener Gebietskrankenkasse,[328] the CJEU surprisingly held that for the purposes of Article 141 and the Equal Pay Directive, graduate psychologists employed as psychotherapists were not to be regarded as doing the 'same work' as trained doctors employed to do the same job, 'where the same activities are performed over a considerable length of time by persons the basis of whose qualification to exercise their profession is different'. The decision can perhaps be defended on its facts, on the grounds that the difference in the qualifications of the two groups probably meant that their level of performance was qualitatively different, but as a general proposition it is respectfully doubted.

(b) Work rated as equivalent

A claimant is to be regarded as being on work rated as equivalent to that of the comparator if it has been given an equal value with that of the comparator (in terms of the demands made under various headings such as effort, skill and decision) by a job evaluation scheme covering that employment.[329] The Act does not lay down detailed requirements for such a scheme,[330] but it is in mandatory terms, so that where there has been such a study a tribunal should act upon its recommendations, even if the parties who drafted it are no longer happy with it;[331] once the scheme has been worked out, it will be binding for the purposes of the Act and may be relied on by the claimant, even if the employer has not in fact put it into effect.[332] However, to be binding the job evaluation scheme must be a valid scheme, in the sense that it must be non-discriminatory, objective and capable of impartial application:

> subsection (5) [the predecessor to section 64(4)] can only apply to what may be called a valid evaluation study. By that, we mean a study satisfying the test of being thorough in analysis and capable of impartial application. It should be possible by applying the study to arrive at the position of a particular employee at a particular point in a particular salary grade without taking other matters into account except those unconnected with the nature of the work ... One which does not satisfy that test, and requires the management to make a subjective judgment concerning the nature of the work before the employee can be fitted

---

[328] Case C-309/97 [2000] ICR 1134, [1999] IRLR 804, ECJ. See also *Glasgow City Council v Marshall* [2000] ICR 196, [2000] IRLR 272, HL.

[329] Equality Act 2010, s 64(4). In *Springboard Sunderland Trust v Robson* [1992] ICR 554, [1992] IRLR 261, the EAT held that where a job evaluation scheme operates by awarding points for different criteria, what matters is whether the woman and her comparator have been placed in the same grade under the scheme, and not the precise number of points awarded. If necessary, a woman can compare herself with a man rated *lower* than her (but paid more highly): *Redcar & Cleveland BC v Bainbridge* [2007] IRLR 91, EAT.

[330] For some guidance on standard forms of schemes, see *Eaton Ltd v Nuttall* [1977] ICR 272 at 278, [1977] IRLR 71 at 74.

[331] *Greene v Broxtowe District Council* [1977] ICR 241, [1977] IRLR 34, EAT.

[332] *O'Brien v Sim-Chem Ltd* [1980] ICR 573, [1980] IRLR 373, HL. For this principle to apply, however, the scheme must have been worked out and accepted as valid by the parties who had agreed to carry it out: *Arnold v Beecham Group Ltd* [1982] ICR 744, [1982] IRLR 307.

into the appropriate place in the appropriate salary grade, would seem to us not to be a valid study for the purposes of subsection (5).[333]

It may therefore be possible to challenge the validity of a scheme. However, it should be noted that such a challenge might not in practice be of much assistance to the applicant for, having disposed of the scheme as it stood, she may not then rely on what she thinks the scheme should have provided, for no such different scheme ever existed and the tribunal may not undertake its own evaluation exercise under this head.[334]

(c) Work of equal value

The European Court of Justice ruled in Case 61/81 *EC Commission v United Kingdom*[335] that the existing equal pay laws did not comply with the requirement of the Equal Pay Directive[336] that a woman should be able to claim equal pay for work of equal value; this was only permitted under the existing laws if the employer had voluntarily undertaken some form of job evaluation (head (b) above), so did not avail the majority of women in employments not subject to such a study. In order to comply with this judgment, the government introduced by Regulations[337] a right to equal pay for work of equal value,[338] but subjected it to an exceptionally complicated, not to say tortuous, procedure.

The change was achieved by an amendment to section 1 of the Equal Pay Act 1970, adding a third category of entitlement to equal pay, where a worker is employed on work which (though not being like work or work rated as equivalent)[339] 'is equal to [the comparator's] work in terms of the demands made on [the applicant] by reference to factors such as effort, skill and decision), of equal value to that of a man in the same employment'.[340] This language is now found in section 65(6)(b) of the 2010 Act.

---

[333] *Eaton Ltd v Nuttall* [1977] ICR 272 at 277H, [1977] IRLR 71 at 74. In *Bromley v H & J Quick Ltd* [1988] ICR 623, [1988] IRLR 249 the Court of Appeal held that, to be valid under s 1(5) an employer-commissioned job evaluation must be 'analytical' in nature, ie based on the demands made on employees under various discrete headings, rather than on any job 'ranking' or 'felt fair' basis which would be too vague. Article 1 of the Equal Pay Directive (Directive 75/117/EEC) also has a requirement that an evaluation study must be fair, in the sense of being based on the same criteria for men and women, and so drawn up as to exclude any discrimination on the grounds of sex: see *Rummler v Dato-Druck GmbH* Case 237/85 [1987] ICR 774, [1987] IRLR 32, ECJ.

[334] *England v Bromley London Borough Council* [1978] ICR 1, EAT.

[335] [1982] ICR 578, [1982] IRLR 333, ECJ.

[336] Council Directive 75/117/EEC. Before the Amsterdam amendments, Art 141 did not expressly confer a right to equal pay for work of equal value: the only explicit reference to that head was in the Equal Pay Directive.

[337] The Equal Pay (Amendment) Regulations 1983, SI 1983/1794, amending the Equal Pay Act 1970, s 1 and inserting s 2A, dealing with the main substantive changes.

[338] Rubenstein *Equal Pay for Work of Equal Value* (1984); Hepple *Equal Pay and the Industrial Tribunals* (1984); Lester and Wainright *Equal Pay for Work of Equal Value: Law and Practice* (1984); McCrudden 'Equal Pay for Work of Equal Value' (1983) 12 ILJ 197 and (1984) 13 ILJ 50; Szyszczak 'Pay Inequalities and Equal Value Claims' (1985) 48 MLR 139; McCrudden (ed) *Women, Employment and European Equality Law* (1987) ch 7.

[339] See on this requirement *Pickstone v Freemans plc* [1988] ICR 697, [1988] IRLR 357, HL, discussed under heading 3(ii)(d).

[340] In *Murphy v Bord Telecom Eireann* Case 157/86 [1988] ICR 445, [1988] IRLR 267, ECJ the employer raised the astonishing defence in an equal value case that the women who were paid less than the male comparator could not claim equality because they were in fact engaged on work of *higher* value than his; this was

The immediate problem is that this takes the tribunals away from matters of relatively observable fact (Is the work the same or similar? Has the employer got a job evaluation study that applies to this woman?) and into the realm of assessment of value and the almost religious mysteries of job evaluation, for which arguably a tribunal as a judicial body is not particularly well suited. The compromise has been to keep the procedure judicial, but to make it heavily dependent in practice on the opinion of an independent expert, ie a person appointed by ACAS from a panel kept by them of persons knowledgeable in the techniques of job evaluation.

The equal value procedure has been highly controversial, not least because of the excessive delays which have bedevilled it since its introduction. In the early years, the average time taken to resolve equal value cases was over two and a half years, and some claims took far longer, particularly where the employer decided to fight the claim at each stage. It was widely thought that the decline in the number of equal pay complaints during the 1980s was (at least in part) a result of the length and complexity of the tribunal processes concerned,[341] and some even went so far as to suggest that the system was designed to deter claims. By the early 1990s the case for a radical overhaul of the equal value procedures had become overwhelming. The President of the EAT described the procedures as in need of 'urgent review', and as giving rise 'to delays which are properly described as scandalous and amount to a denial of justice to women seeking remedy through the judicial process'.[342] In 1990, the EOC published a series of proposals for the reform of the equal pay laws,[343] designed in part to tackle the inordinate delays in processing equal value cases. Certain limited changes were made in 1994 and 1996, but significant reform had to wait until 2004 when amendments were made to seek to streamline the system, in particular by permitting the tribunal to determine the claim itself and to place emphasis on the setting of timetables and a greater element of case management (though with the quid pro quo that the tribunal lost its power to rule out a claim at a very early stage on the basis that it had no reasonable chance of success).[344] Even with these provisions in place, an equal value action is of necessity complex, and not to be embarked upon by the faint-hearted.

The right to equal pay through work of equal value is contained in the 2010 Act section 66, which is supplemented by section 65. With regard to procedure, section 131 further states that in such a case the tribunal may either proceed to determine the

---

held by the ECJ to be contrary to Art 141 and so, under EC law at least, a woman can claim equal pay for work that is at least of equal value to that of the male comparator.

[341] ACAS Annual Report, 1992, p 23; EOC Annual Report, 1991, p 6.

[342] *Aldridge v British Telecommunications plc* [1989] ICR 790, [1990] IRLR 10, per Wood J.

[343] *Equal Pay for Men and Women: Strengthening the Acts* (EOC, 1990). The proposals included the automatic application of successful decisions to similarly placed employees, the removal of the initial requirement to show that the case has a reasonable chance of success, the appointment of full-time independent experts, and the removal of the bar on equal value claims where there is an existing job evaluation scheme.

[344] Equal Pay Act 1970 (Amendment) Regulations 2004, SI 2004/2352, amending the Equal Pay Act 1970, s 2A; complementary amendments to the ET Rules of Procedure were made by SI 2004/2351. In the light of these changes, much of the previous case law is now of only marginal significance.

question or require an independent expert to prepare a report on it. If the tribunal goes down the latter route, it is provided that it may at any time withdraw the requirement of a report (and request the expert to provide it with any documentation), but on the other hand if no such withdrawal is made the tribunal may not determine the question without the expert's report. Section 131 goes on to draw a clear line between equal value claims and claims on the basis of work rated as equivalent (sub-heading (b) above). If an equal value claim is brought but there has been a job evaluation study giving different values to her and her comparator, the tribunal is to dismiss the equal value claim unless it has reasonable grounds to suspect that the evaluation in the study was either 'based on a system that discriminates because of sex'[345] or 'is otherwise unreliable'.

(d) The area of comparison

Unlike the general prohibition on discrimination, which works on the basis of a comparison between the treatment of the applicant and that of a hypothetical comparator, the equal terms claim is based on a comparison with a named comparator (or comparators). The requirement to identify an actual comparator can be a major hurdle for an applicant, particularly if he or she works for an organization where jobs are de facto segregated along gender lines, as it may be impossible to find an appropriate comparator. The general rule on the area of comparison in the Act is that the comparator must be 'in the same employment' as the applicant, in the sense of being employed by the same employer (or by an 'associated employer', as defined) at the same establishment, or at another establishment at which common terms and conditions of employment are observed, either generally or for employees of relevant classes.[346] In *Leverton v Clwyd County Council*,[347] the House of Lords held that the requirement of common terms and conditions refers to the terms and conditions at the establishment at which the woman is employed and the establishment at which her comparator is employed, rather than to common terms and conditions as between the applicant and her comparator; in that case, the requirement was satisfied since both establishments were covered by the same collective agreement covering male and female employees of the employer, regardless of the establishment at which they worked.[348] 'Common terms and conditions' in this context means 'broadly similar' rather than 'the same'. In *British Coal Corpn v Smith*,[349] some 1,286 women employed as canteen workers

---

[345] According to s 131(7), this is so where a difference, or coincidence, between values set by that system or different demands under the same or different headings is not justified irrespective of the sex of the person on whom those demands are made.

[346] Equality Act 2010, s 79. There is no statutory definition of 'establishment'; for its construction in the context of redundancy consultation (where it is similarly not defined), see Ch 8, heading 1(iii), p 572.

[347] [1989] ICR 33, [1989] IRLR 28, HL. The case is a good illustration of the fact that, where there are common terms and conditions, there need be no male employees at the woman's establishment, and no women need be employed at the establishment where the male comparator works.

[348] A situation described by Lord Bridge as the paradigm case.

[349] [1996] IRLR 404, HL (reversing the Court of Appeal on this point).

or cleaners at 47 different establishments claimed equal pay for work of equal value with 150 male comparators employed as clerical workers or surface mineworkers at 14 different establishments. The House of Lords held that the applicants were in the same employment as their comparators because the terms and conditions of the comparators were governed by national agreements which also applied (or would apply) to men of the same class employed at the applicant's establishment, even though local variations relating to incentive bonuses and entitlement to concessionary coal meant that the terms and conditions at different establishments for the same classes of worker were not the same. Lord Slynn interpreted the phrase 'common terms and conditions' purposively:

> The real question is what the legislation was seeking to achieve. Was it seeking to exclude a woman's claim unless, subject to de minimis exceptions, there was complete identity of terms and conditions for the comparator at his establishment and those which applied or would apply to a similar male worker at her establishment? Or was the legislation seeking to establish that the terms and conditions of the relevant class were sufficiently similar for a fair comparison to be made, subject always to the employer's right to establish a 'material difference' defence.... If it was the former then the woman would fail at the first hurdle if there was any difference (other than a de minimis one) between the terms and conditions of the men at the various establishments, since she could not then show that the men were in the same employment as she was. The issue as to whether the differences were material so as to justify different treatment would then never arise. I do not consider that this can have been intended.[350]

In *Pickstone v Freemans plc*[351] the question arose whether a woman doing job A could claim equality of pay through work of equal value with a man doing job B if the employer simply pointed out that there were in fact other men doing job A, and so on 'like work'. This literal interpretation (which raised the possibility of an employer being able to avoid an equal value claim by employing a token male in an otherwise all-female workforce on job A) was upheld by the Court of Appeal[352] but disapproved on further appeal by the House of Lords, who held that an equal value claim can be brought in such circumstances—all that the wording in section 1(2)(c) means is that the chosen comparator must not be doing like work or work rated as equivalent; the existence of another male doing such work will be irrelevant.

The wording of the Equal Pay Act envisaged a comparison between a man and a woman working together for the same employer (or an associated employer) at the same time. However, under European sex discrimination law the permitted comparison

---

[350] [1996] IRLR 404 at 408.   [351] [1988] ICR 697, [1988] IRLR 357, HL.

[352] [1987] ICR 867, [1987] IRLR 218, CA. The Court of Appeal proceeded to consider the claim under Art 141 of the EC Treaty and upheld it independently on that ground (see [1987] IRLR 218, CA 232). Thus, while the House of Lords disapproved of the Court of Appeal's narrow interpretation of English law, they in fact upheld the eventual decision, and found it unnecessary to pronounce upon the correctness or otherwise of the Court of Appeal's views on EC law.

is wider. In *Defrenne v SABENA*,[353] the CJEU referred to employment 'in the same establishment or service, whether public or private', and this has led to a significant broadening of the scope of the permitted comparison under the Equal Pay Act. So, for example, in *Macarthys Ltd v Smith*[354] the CJEU held, on a reference from the Court of Appeal, that a woman has the right under Article 141 to compare her pay with that of her male predecessor in the same job, a decision which was subsequently applied by the Court of Appeal at the resumed hearing;[355] and in *Diocese of Hallam Trustee v Connaughton*[356] the EAT allowed a comparison to be made with a male successor. It also seems that cross-employer comparisons may now be possible in circumstances where the difference in pay can be traced to a common source, for example where the applicant and her comparator work for the same legal person or group of persons, or for public authorities operating under joint control, or where their pay is covered by the same collective agreement or legislative provision. In *Lawrence v Regent Office Care Ltd*,[357] the CJEU indicated that such comparisons were possible, but would depend entirely on the facts of each case. *Lawrence* was reaffirmed by the decision of the CJEU in *Allonby v Accrington & Rossendale College*[358] where a part-time college lecturer whose services were dispensed with but who was immediately re-engaged through a private educational provider could not make a cross-employer comparison because (close though the engagements were) there was again no 'single source' governing terms and conditions. Significant though this case was in limiting the effect of equal pay legislation in a case of the contracting out of services, arguably the most important decision in this area was *Robertson v DEFRA*.[359] For many years, under both Conservative and Labour governments, it has been official policy to split up the civil service into separate departments and agencies, each being a separate employer (albeit subject to central control ultimately), setting its own terms and conditions (as a way of moving away from centralized collective bargaining, even though ultimately the employer remained 'the Crown'). What would have wrecked this (given that the civil service unions could not prevent it industrially) was an equal pay action enforcing common terms between different departments. This was what was tried in *Robertson* where six male civil servants in DEFRA claimed equal pay with two female civil servants in DETR. The Court of Appeal dismissed their claims, holding that (within *Lawrence*) there was no 'single source', not even the Treasury or the Minister for the Civil Service; moreover, the fact

---

[353] [1976] ECR 455, [1976] ICR 547.   [354] [1979] 3 All ER 325, [1979] ICR 785, CA.

[355] Case 129/79 [1980] ICR 672, [1980] IRLR 210, ECJ; apld [1980] ICR 672, [1980] IRLR 210, CA. Note, however, that in such a case there may not be an order for equality (even under Art 141) if there are genuine economic or other circumstances accounting for the difference in pay between the woman and her predecessor; ie there is under the article a justification defence analogous to the 'genuine material difference' defence to a claim under the Act: *Albion Shipping Agency v Arnold* [1982] ICR 22, [1981] IRLR 525.

[356] [1996] IRLR 505, EAT.   [357] [2003] ICR 1092, [2002] IRLR 822, ECJ.

[358] C-256/01 [2004] ICR 1328, [2004] IRLR 224, ECJ.

[359] [2005] IRLR 363, CA. In *Armstrong v Newcastle upon Tyne NHS Hospitals Trust* [2006] IRLR 124, CA a policy of devolving of management (including pay determination) was so far advanced that there could not be cross-employer comparisons even between hospitals run by the same Trust.

that Ministers *could* reverse the fragmentation policy and re-establish central control was held to be insufficient.

(iv) THE GENUINE MATERIAL FACTOR DEFENCE

Even if there is a prima facie case of inequality, the applicant may still fail if the employer can show, on a balance of probabilities,[360] that the difference in terms is genuinely due to a material factor which is not the difference of sex.[361] The most obvious examples of genuine material factors justifying differential treatment are personal differences between the applicant and her comparator, for example factors such as long service, superior qualifications, higher output or different geographical location,[362] or where the man is on a higher grade under a bona fide, impartial grading scheme, so that, although in fact performing the same sort of work, he is rated more highly at doing it (for example he works more efficiently, or more reliably and so subject to less supervision).[363]

The kinds of problems engendered by the material factor defence are illustrated by *Rainey v Greater Glasgow Health Board.*[364] The issue in *Rainey* was whether a material difference under section 1(3) of the Equal Pay Act 1970 could relate to matters outside the personal equation, such as the operation of 'market forces'. The case concerned the expansion of a national health prosthetics department by the recruitment of prosthetists (all male, as it happened) from the private sector on their existing level of remuneration, which was higher than that paid to the existing National Health Service prosthetists (who were principally female and included the applicant). The applicant sought equal pay with one of the male entrants, who it was accepted was employed on like work with her. The employer's genuine material difference defence had seemed doomed to fail, as the Court of Appeal had previously held in *Clay Cross (Quarry Services) Ltd v Fletcher*[365] that the payment of higher wages to a male clerk than to a longer serving female clerk on the basis that when his job was advertised he was the only suitable candidate and could only be induced to take the job by the offer of a higher salary than that already being paid to her, went outside the bounds of

---

[360] *National Vulcan Engineering Insurance Group Ltd v Wade* [1978] ICR 800, [1978] IRLR 225. This is consistent with EC law, which places the burden of proof on the employer where a pay system is marked by a 'total lack of transparency': *Handels-og Kontorfunktionaerernes Forbund i Danmark v Dansk Arbejdsgiverforening (acting for Danfoss)* Case C-109/88 [1991] ICR 74, [1989] IRLR 532.

[361] Equality Act 2010, s 69(1). The employer must prove (1) that the variation is genuinely due to a material factor, and (2) that this is not due to the difference of sex: *Financial Times Ltd v Byrne (No 2)* [1992] IRLR 163; see also *Barber v NCR (Manufacturing) Ltd* [1993] IRLR 95, EAT.

[362] *Navy, Army and Air Force Institutes v Varley* [1977] ICR 11, [1976] IRLR 408, EAT. In *Danfoss* C-109/88 (n 360) the ECJ held that length of service payments are *inherently* justified. This was challenged 15 years later as too sweeping, but *Danfoss* was reaffirmed: *Cadman v HSE* C-17/05 [2006] IRLR 969, ECJ.

[363] *National Vulcan Engineering Insurance Group Ltd v Wade* [1978] ICR 800, [1978] IRLR 225, CA.

[364] [1987] ICR 129, [1987] IRLR 26, HL.

[365] [1979] ICR 1, [1978] IRLR 361, CA; this case is also authority for the proposition that it is no defence for an act of unlawful discrimination to say that it was unintentional.

permissible personal differentials envisaged in section 1(3), and that any other conclusion could render the statute a dead letter by allowing employers simply to say that they
paid the man more because he asked for more, or that they paid the woman less because
she was willing to work for less. However, in *Rainey*,[366] the House of Lords held that
the genuine material difference defence under section 1(3) is not limited to personal
differences, but is capable of extending to other objectively justified[367] grounds for the
woman being paid less:

> In my opinion these statements [in *Fletcher*] are unduly restrictive of the proper interpreta-
> tion of section 1(3). The difference must be 'material', which I would construe as meaning
> 'significant and relevant', and it must be between 'her case and his'. Consideration of a
> person's case must necessarily involve consideration of all the circumstances of that case.
> These may well go beyond what is not very happily described as 'the personal equation', i.e.
> the personal qualities by way of skill, experience or training which the individual brings to
> the job. Some circumstances may on examination prove to be not significant or not rele-
> vant, but others may do so, though not relating to the personal qualities of the employee.
> In particular, where there is no question of intentional sex discrimination whether direct
> or indirect (and there is none here) a difference which is connected with economic factors
> affecting the efficient carrying on of the employer's business or other activity may well be
> relevant.[368]

On the facts of the case, the House of Lords held that the applicant's case failed because
there was objective justification for putting the male entrant on to a higher scale (given
the need to expand the prosthetic service within a reasonable time), and for not raising
the wages of the applicant and other existing prosthetists to that higher rate (since there
were 'sound objectively justified administrative reasons' for maintaining their existing
position within the overall Whitley Council scale). In so holding, the House of Lords
adopted the 'objective justification' test for indirect discrimination under Article 141
set out by the CJEU in *Bilka-Kaufhaus GmbH v Weber von Hartz*,[369] where it was held
that in determining whether there were any objectively justified grounds for the variation in pay, the court should consider whether the measures adopted by the employer
'correspond to a real need on the part of the undertaking, are appropriate with a view
to achieving the objectives pursued and are necessary to that end'.[370]

---

[366] Above; the Scottish EAT and the Court of Session had distinguished *Fletcher* (though the grounds of
distinction were difficult to see), but the House of Lords reconsidered the whole matter. The case is noted by
McLean (1987) 46 CLJ 224; Schofield (1987) 50 MLR 379 and Townshend-Smith (1987) 16 ILJ 114.

[367] Lord Keith, giving judgment, states that the test here is the same as that under the Sex Discrimination
Act 1975 for the justification of a provision, criterion or practice (as it now is) which indirectly discriminates
against women.

[368] [1987] ICR 129 at 140, [1987] IRLR 26 at 29, per Lord Keith.

[369] Case 170/84 [1987] ICR 110, [1986] IRLR 317, ECJ.

[370] In *Rainey*, Lord Keith added ([1987] ICR 129 at 143, [1987] IRLR 26 at 30) that he considered that the
ECJ's ruling 'would not exclude objectively justified grounds which are other than economic, such as administrative efficiency in a concern not engaged in commerce or business'.

While the decision on the facts in *Rainey* can perhaps be defended on the basis of the employer's need to recruit prosthetists against a specific labour market shortage, by breaching the 'personal equation' rule in such a comprehensive manner it was feared that the House of Lords might have opened something of a Pandora's Box, particularly if the courts and tribunals were to accept too readily the sort of argument put forward in *Clay Cross*, ie that an employer was justified in paying a woman less because she was willing to work for less. The danger of such an approach is that it simply reinforces historic labour market inequalities in pay between men and women, and could render the equal pay laws a dead letter. In subsequent cases the courts have on the whole taken a cautious approach to market forces defences.[371] In *Enderby v Frenchay Health Authority*,[372] the CJEU held, in a case under Article 141, that 'the state of the employment market, which may lead an employer to increase the pay of a particular job in order to attract candidates, may constitute an objectively justified economic ground' for a difference in pay, but crucially also held that 'it is for the national court to determine, if necessary by applying the principle of proportionality, whether and to what extent the shortage of candidates for a job and the need to attract them by higher pay constitutes an objectively justified economic ground for the difference in pay between the jobs in question'. In other words, an employer will not be able to justify the whole of the difference in pay on the basis of market forces (or indeed any other objectively justifiable reason) where only part of the difference in pay is attributable to that reason.[373] Furthermore, in *Ratcliffe v North Yorkshire County Council*,[374] the House of Lords refused to accept that the imposition of a pay cut for a group of predominantly female school catering assistants to enable the employer to tender for work at a commercially competitive rate was due to a material factor which was not the difference of sex. In that case, the council had established a direct service organization (DSO) for the provision of school meals following the introduction of compulsory competitive tendering, but its catering staff were forced to take a pay cut after it became apparent that the DSO was unable to compete for the school dinner contracts with commercial organizations, who employed only women, while continuing to pay the staff on their existing local government rates. The Court of Appeal held that the material factor which led to the lower rates of pay, the need to compete effectively with rival bidders, was genuinely due to the operation of market forces, and that those market forces were gender-neutral in the sense that they were unconnected with the difference of sex. However, the House of Lords upheld the appeal and restored the tribunal's decision that the material factor

---

[371] For an unfortunate lapse, see *Calder v Rowntree Mackintosh Confectionery Ltd* [1993] ICR 811, [1993] IRLR 212, CA.

[372] [1994] ICR 112, [1993] IRLR 591, ECJ.

[373] However, financial and budgetary consideration may still be a consideration, especially where they give support to a decision objectively justified on other grounds: *Cross v British Airways* [2005] IRLR 423, EAT. A particularly important application of this may be to a temporary pay protection scheme to ease in a new pay structure: *Redcar & Cleveland BC v Bainbridge* [2007] IRLR 91, EAT.

[374] [1995] 3 All ER 597, [1995] ICR 883, HL.

was in fact due to the difference of sex, in that the labour market for catering staff was almost exclusively female, whereas the council employees employed on work of equivalent value (road sweepers, gardeners, refuse collectors and leisure attendants) were mostly men:

> Though conscious of the difficult problem facing the employers in seeking to compete with a rival tenderer, I am satisfied that to reduce the women's wages below that of their male comparators was the very kind of discrimination in relation to pay which the Act sought to remove.[375]

It could perhaps be concluded that where an employer pays one group of workers more, for example to combat a specific labour shortage, as in *Rainey*, the difference in pay will be justifiable under section 69 provided the employer can demonstrate that the difference is genuinely gender-neutral; but where the difference in pay between two groups of employees is simply a reflection of historic inequalities in the labour market, for example where the work in question is sex-segregated, as in *Ratcliffe*, the employer will find it difficult to show that paying lower rates of pay to a predominantly female group of employees is genuinely gender-neutral.[376]

One difficult issue here is whether and when an employer must objectively justify a difference in pay as proportional under section 69(1)(b). The balance of authority domestically, prior to the 2010 Act, was to the effect that there was *no* such general requirement, so that normally all that had to be shown was a difference or factor which *actually* explained the pay divergence (on some ground other than sex). However, in *Strathclyde Regional Council v Wallace*[377] the House of Lords held that the requirement to show some objective justification for a variation in terms only arises where the factor which the employer is relying upon to explain the variation is *itself* directly or indirectly sexually discriminatory. Where there is no element of sex discrimination, 'the employer establishes [the section 66 defence] by identifying the factors which he alleges have caused the disparity, proving that those factors are genuine and proving further that they were causally relevant to the disparity in pay complained of'.[378] According to Lord Nicholls in *Glasgow City Council v Marshall*,[379] the requirement that the factor be 'material' simply means that it must be significant and relevant in a causative sense, rather than in a justificatory sense. If this is correct, it follows that where a difference in

---

[375] [1995] 3 All ER 597 at 604, per Lord Slynn. The fact that two men were employed on the same work at the same rate of pay as the applicants did not detract from this conclusion: 'It means no more than that the two men were underpaid compared with other men doing jobs rated as equivalent' ([1995] 3 All ER 597 at 603).

[376] In *Redcar & Cleveland BC v Bainbridge* [2007] IRLR 91, EAT Elias P said that a pay protection scheme (to cushion comparators who were having their pay decreased as part of a reformed pay system) would often come within the s 1(3) defence *but* on the facts here it did not because it was merely carrying on an illegal pay inequality under the old system.

[377] [1998] ICR 205, [1998] IRLR 146, HL.

[378] [1998] ICR 205, [1998] IRLR 146, per Lord Browne-Wilkinson. Cases such as *Rainey*, *Enderby* and *Ratcliffe* can all be explained as cases where the factor relied upon was one which affected a considerably higher proportion of women than men, and which therefore required objective justification.

[379] [2000] ICR 196, [2000] IRLR 272, HL.

pay is genuinely caused by a factor which is not itself tainted by direct or indirect sex discrimination (for example where there is an historic explanation for the variation,[380] or where it resulted from a careless mistake)[381] the employer is under no obligation to prove a 'good' reason for the pay disparity, even if it could not possibly be objectively justified. The problem that arises is that the CJEU decision in *Brunnhofer v Bank der Osterreichischen Postsparkasse AG*[382] as well as generally upholding the EC law test of justification in *Bilka-Kaufhaus*, also contains dicta which are *capable* of being interpreted as requiring the employer to show objective justification for *any* pay disparity between men and women.

The material factor defence has given rise to further particular difficulties in three areas. The first concerns the application of the defence to part-timers,[383] an area of particular significance in the development of the law on equal pay because it was in cases involving part-timers that the legislation was reinterpreted to cover practices which indirectly discriminate against women. In the early cases it appeared to be established that the fact that a woman worked part time was a genuine material difference, so that she could not claim equality of hourly pay rates with a man working full time, even if he was doing exactly the same work.[384] However, in *Jenkins v Kingsgate (Clothing Productions) Ltd (No 2)*,[385] the EAT (following a reference to the CJEU) reinterpreted the defence and held that the fact of being parttime can be a genuine material difference only if the employer can show that the lower rate for part-timers is reasonably necessary to achieve some objective (probably economic) unrelated to sex. The overall effect of this was to introduce into equal pay law a concept of indirect discrimination akin to that in sex discrimination law, in that if the effect of the particular factor claimed to be the genuine material factor operates particularly harshly against women, it will only be permitted as a defence under section 69 if the employer can justify it objectively, on grounds other than sex. Courts have generally been unwilling to accept part-time working as a justification for indirect sex discrimination.[386]

The second area of difficulty concerns collective bargaining, and the extent to which an employer can argue that the separate bargaining processes for two groups of workers constitutes a genuine material factor which justifies a variation in terms

---

[380] As in *Marshall*, where the difference in pay between two groups of very similar gender composition (instructors and teachers) was due to different collective bargaining structures; significantly, the applicants had accepted that there was no sex discrimination.

[381] See eg *Tyldesley v TML Plastics Ltd* [1996] ICR 356, [1996] IRLR 395, EAT.

[382] C-381/99 [2001] IRLR 571, ECJ.

[383] Part-time workers now have a right to equal treatment under the Part-Time Workers Directive and the implementing Regulations (see Ch 2, heading 1(iv), p 53) and are therefore less likely to need to argue indirect sex discrimination in the future.

[384] *Handley v H Mono Ltd* [1979] ICR 147, [1978] IRLR 534.

[385] [1981] ICR 715, [1981] IRLR 388, EAT.

[386] See, eg, *Bilka-Kaufhaus GmbH v Weber von Hartz* [1981] ICR 110, [1981] IRLR 317, ECJ; *Rinner-Kühn v FWW Spezial-Gebäudereinigung GmbH & Co KG* Case 171/88 [1989] ECR 2743, [1989] IRLR 493, ECJ; *R v Secretary of State for Employment, ex p Equal Opportunities Commission* [1995] 1 AC 1, [1994] ICR 317, HL.

between the two groups. On one view, as long as each bargaining process is in itself non-discriminatory, the different bargaining arrangements could be said to represent an objectively justified reason for the difference in outcome;[387] against that, however, it could be argued that the key issue is whether the difference in outcome between the two pay structures can *itself* be justified, so that the mere fact that pay is regulated by separate collective agreements will not of itself justify a difference.[388] The issue arose in stark form in *Enderby v Frenchay Health Authority*,[389] where the applicant, one of a group of predominantly female speech therapists employed by the health authority, claimed that her work was of equal value with the predominantly male pharmacists and clinical psychologists, who were paid substantially more. The employer argued that the variation in pay was due to historical differences in the collective bargaining arrangements for the two groups, and that since those arrangements were not in themselves discriminatory, they constituted a genuine material factor which justified the difference. The EAT found for the employer,[390] holding that if the factor causing the disparate impact has no taint of gender, there is nothing which requires justification. The Court of Appeal referred the matter to the ECJ,[391] which held that the fact that the respective rates of pay of two jobs of equal value, one carried out almost exclusively by women and the other predominantly by men, were arrived at by collective bargaining processes which, although carried out by the same parties, were distinct and which, considered separately, were not in themselves discriminatory, is not sufficient objective justification for the difference in pay between those two jobs. The ECJ considered that if an employer could rely on the absence of discrimination within each of the collective bargaining processes taken separately as sufficient justification for the difference in pay, he could easily circumvent the principle of equal pay by using separate bargaining processes.[392] Under this approach, it is the *result* of the collective bargaining process which has to be justified by objective factors; the fact that the difference in pay arises from separate collective bargaining processes, while relevant,[393] does not of itself constitute an objective justification for that difference. Having said that, the House of Lords has since held[394] that the need for the results of separate bargaining processes to be objectively justified only arises where the difference in terms results from sex discrimination (for example, where there is evidence that the difference in bargaining processes has a disparate adverse impact on women and is therefore prima facie

---

[387] As was held in *Reed Packaging Ltd v Boozer* [1988] ICR 391, [1988] IRLR 333, EAT, where the genuine material factor defence was held to apply as the applicant and her comparator were employed under separate pay structures which were not in themselves discriminatory.

[388] See *Barber v NCR (Manufacturing) Ltd* [1993] IRLR 95, where the EAT held that the fact that the difference in pay had arisen from collective bargaining did not constitute an objective factor which justified the result which had been produced.

[389] [1994] ICR 112, [1993] IRLR 591, ECJ.   [390] [1991] ICR 382, [1991] IRLR 44, EAT.

[391] [1994] ICR 112, [1992] IRLR 15, CA.   [392] [1994] ICR 112, [1993] IRLR 591 at 595.

[393] See *Specialarbejderforbundet i Danmark v Dansk Industri, acting for Royal Copenhagen* [1996] ICR 51, [1995] IRLR 648, ECJ.

[394] See *Glasgow City Council v Marshall* [2000] ICR 196, [2000] IRLR 272, HL.

indirectly discriminatory). If the separate bargaining structures do not impact disproportionately on one sex, there is no obligation on the employer to justify the disparity
in the terms which result from that process.[395]

The third area of difficulty concerns the 'red circling' cases.[396] These arise where
male employees are paid more than female employees on like or equally rated work
because the pay of the men is protected, or 'red circled', because of some event in the
past; examples of this would be where the man was injured and put permanently on to
lighter work but at his previous higher wage, or where the man's job was down-graded
but rather than being made redundant he was kept on at the lesser job but again at
his previous higher wage. In both of these cases there may be women also doing the
lighter or lesser work, but at the ordinary rate for that work, so that they are paid less.
A genuine red circle case may well come within the material factor defence so that a
woman cannot claim to be put on to the man's protected rate, as can be seen from the
judgment of the EAT in *Charles Early and Marriott (Witney) Ltd v Smith and Ball*,[397]
but in the consolidated appeal in *Snoxell v Vauxhall Motors Ltd*[398] the EAT in fact held
that the red circle argument failed, since it appeared that the existence of the men's protection was partly due to past discrimination on sexual grounds. Thus, the important
principle is that the tribunal should inquire into the original reason for the protection
of the man's wages and should only accept the red circle as a genuine material factor
if it had its origins in genuine factors other than any form of direct or indirect sexual
discrimination. While it is clear that in an appropriate case red circling can provide a
defence indefinitely,[399] the EAT has stressed that even where a red circling agreement is
genuine and reasonable at the time of its inception, its continuation indefinitely would
be likely to cause bad feelings among those not thus protected, so that in the light
of good industrial relations practice it might be expected that the employer would
phase it out after a reasonable period, with the implication that if this is not done the
employer might find after the expiry of such a period that he cannot use it as a defence
to a claim for equal pay.[400]

(v) REMEDIES

A claim for equal pay may be brought before an employment tribunal.[401] On such a
claim, the tribunal may declare the existence of the equality clause, to ensure treatment
no less favourable. However, this is dependent upon a finding that there is like work/
work rated as equivalent, or work of equal value; if that is not so, the tribunal has no

---

[395] As in *Glasgow City Council v Marshall* n 394.
[396] Some care is needed, for 'red circle' must not be considered to be a term of art: *National Coal Board
v Sherwin* [1978] ICR 700 at 706F, [1978] IRLR 122 at 125; *Methven v Cow Industrial Polymers Ltd* [1980] ICR
463, [1980] IRLR 289, CA, per Dunn LJ.   [397] [1977] ICR 700, [1977] IRLR 123.
[398] [1977] ICR 700, [1977] IRLR 123.
[399] *Charles Early and Marriott (Witney) Ltd v Smith and Ball* [1977] ICR 700, [1977] IRLR 123.
[400] *Outlook Supplies Ltd v Parry* [1978] ICR 388, [1978] IRLR 12, EAT.
[401] Equality Act 2010, s 120.

jurisdiction to make any order, even if the women concerned are being poorly treated, and the gap in the remuneration between men and women is in no way commensurate to the difference in the work that they do: the Act does not enable a tribunal to act as a general wage-fixing body.[402] On the other hand, once there is a valid claim for equality, the applicant may be awarded arrears of pay or damages for contravention of the equality clause; there is, however, no power to award general damages (eg for injury to feelings) as would be the case in a sex discrimination claim.[403]

As originally enacted, the Equal Pay Act contained two limitation periods which were both successfully challenged as incompatible with EC law. Section 2(4) stated that a claim had to be brought within six months of the end of employment; and section 2(5) placed a limit of two years from the date of commencement of proceedings on any award of arrears of remuneration (ie back pay) or damages. It is a fundamental principle of EC law that in the absence of Community rules on the matter, it is for domestic legal systems to lay down procedural rules governing the enforcement of Community rights, provided they are not less favourable than those governing similar domestic actions (the principle of equivalence), and do not render the exercise of rights conferred by Community law virtually impossible or excessively difficult (the principle of effectiveness). Both time limits were held by the CJEU to infringe these principles, and the limits were duly amended by the Equal Pay Act 1970 (Amendment) Regulations 2003.[404] The original six-month limit in section 2(4) was held by the CJEU to infringe the principle of effectiveness in *Preston v Wolverhampton Healthcare NHS Trust*,[405] because the limit applied at the end of *each* contract of employment, even in cases where there had been a succession of separate short-term contracts in respect of the same employment, and thus made the enforcement of the right conferred by EC law excessively difficult[406] (the problem being that, as originally enacted, the Equal Pay Act contained no provisions analogous to those in the employment rights legislation preserving continuity of employment through a succession of fixed-term contracts).[407] Under section 129, proceedings before an employment tribunal must now be instituted within the 'qualifying period';[408] as before, this is normally six months after the last day of the employment[409] in question, but the limit is now modified in three circumstances; first, where the employer and employee had a 'stable employment relationship', the qualifying date is six months after the end of

---

[402] *Maidment v Cooper & Co (Birmingham) Ltd* [1978] ICR 1094, [1978] IRLR 462.

[403] *Allan v Newcastle-upon-Tyne CC* [2005] NLJ 619, EAT. [404] SI 2003/1656.

[405] Case C-78/98, [2000] ICR 961, [2000] IRLR 506, ECJ. The case was part of the litigation concerning the exclusion of part-time workers from occupational pension schemes.

[406] Surprisingly, the House of Lords subsequently held ([2001] UKHL 5, [2001] ICR 217, [2001] IRLR 237) that the six-month limit did not breach the principle of equivalence, because taken overall it was not less favourable than the six-year limitation period for bringing a claim for breach of contract.

[407] See Ch 2, heading 5(ii), p 103. [408] Equality Act 2010, s 129(2).

[409] Cf *National Power plc v Young* [2001] IRLR 32, EAT, where this phrase in the pre-2003 provisions was held to refer to her employment with the employer, rather than the actual job for that employer in respect of which her claim was made.

that relationship, irrespective of the fact that there may have been more than one contract of employment during that period;[410] secondly, where the employee was under an incapacity,[411] the qualifying date is six months after she ceased to be under that incapacity;[412] and thirdly, where the employer deliberately concealed relevant facts[413] from the employee, the qualifying day is six months after she discovered (or could with reasonable diligence have discovered) the information in question. The provisions on concealment were introduced to meet the point which arose in *Levez v T H Jennings (Harlow Pools) Ltd*,[414] where the CJEU held that the six-month limit infringed the principle of effectiveness because it did not make allowance for an applicant who delayed bringing proceedings as a result of a deliberate misrepresentation by the employer. In *Levez*, the CJEU also considered the two-year limit on arrears of remuneration. The CJEU held that the two-year limit did not in itself infringe the principle of effectiveness,[415] and that it was for the national courts to determine whether the rule in question infringed the principle of equivalence through being less favourable than the rules applying to similar domestic actions. The EAT subsequently ruled[416] that the two-year limit did in fact contravene the principle of equivalence, in that it was less favourable than the six-year limitation period governing similar claims under domestic law (for example for breach of contract or discrimination on grounds of race or disability), and the EAT disapplied the two-year limit as being incompatible with EC law, holding that the normal six-year time limit applied instead. In *Preston v Wolverhampton Healthcare NHS Trust*,[417] the CJEU clarified the position by holding that in relation to those excluded from occupational pension schemes, the two-year limit on the backdating of membership infringed the principle of effectiveness, and the House of Lords subsequently held[418] that an employer could not rely on the two-year limit to prevent an employee from retroactively gaining access to a pension scheme, and that in principle pension rights could be backdated as far back as 8 April 1976[419] (subject to the proviso that in a contributory scheme the employee would have to pay any contributions owing in respect of the period for which retrospective

---

[410] Equality Act 2010, s 129(3).

[411] Ie a minor or of unsound mind: Equal Pay Act 1970, s 11(2A), as amended.

[412] Equality Act 2010, s 129(3). The exception applies if she was under a disability at any time during what would otherwise have been the six-month limitation period.

[413] Ie facts which are relevant to the proceedings, without knowledge of which the woman could not reasonably have been expected to institute the proceedings: Equality Act 2010, s 129(3).

[414] [1999] ICR 521, [1999] IRLR 36, ECJ.

[415] Although on the facts that principle was found to be infringed because of the lack of any provision on deliberate concealment: see n 413.

[416] *Levez v T H Jennings (Harlow Pools) Ltd (No 2)* [1999] IRLR 764, EAT.

[417] Case C-78/98 [2000] ICR 961, [2000] IRLR 506, ECJ.

[418] *Preston v Wolverhampton Healthcare NHS Trust (No 2)* [2001] UKHL 5, [2001] ICR 217, [2001] IRLR 237, HL.

[419] Ie the date of the *Defrenne* judgment, in which the ECJ first held that Art 141 had direct effect.

membership was being claimed). Section 132(4) now provides that if proceedings under the Equal Pay Act are successful, the tribunal may award back-pay or damages back to the 'arrears date',[420] which is normally six years before the institution of proceedings.[421] This is still less generous than the position under the Sex Discrimination Act, where there is no ceiling on the compensation that may be awarded.

(vi) PENSIONS

As originally enacted, the Equal Pay Act contained a blanket exclusion for any provision made in connection with death or retirement,[422] considered to be necessary because of the differential state pensionable age upon which many such provisions have traditionally been based. However, during the 1980s it became increasingly clear that the breadth of the exclusion in the domestic legislation was incompatible with EC law, in that while the differential state pensionable age itself was outside the scope of Article 141,[423] retirement benefits (and indeed retirement ages) which are based on the state pensionable age are not. As a result, the government was forced to introduce legislation outlawing discrimination in provisions made in connection with retirement, initially in relation to promotion, transfer, training, demotion or dismissal,[424] and later in the area of occupational pensions also.[425] These areas have now been brought together in the 2010 Act. The Act contains provisions establishing a non-discrimination rule (section 61) and a sex equality rule (section 67) for occupational pensions, which are the counterpart, generally, to the equality clause relating to other terms of work. Past editions of this book have devoted a great deal of space to this area. However, in light of the arcane nature of the subject generally and the need to devote limited space in the book to core employment matters, the authors have chosen to leave the reader with this tantalizing hint of the pension secrets to be found in Part 5, Chapters 2 and 3 of the Equality Act 2010.

---

[420] Equal Pay Act 1970, s 2ZB, as inserted by SI 2003/1656.

[421] Equal Pay Act 1970, s 2ZB(3). Special provision is again made for cases involving disability and/or deliberate concealment, where the arrears date is the date of the contravention to which the proceedings relate: s 2ZB(2), (4). There are separate rules for claims by service personnel in the armed forces: s 7A.

[422] Equal Pay Act 1970, s 6. There was an equivalent exclusion in the Sex Discrimination Act 1975, s 6(4).

[423] Article 7 of EEC Directive 79/7 on Social Security allows member states to exclude 'the determination of pensionable age for the purposes of granting old-age and retirement pensions' from the principle of equal treatment, but does not in terms extend to provisions which are tied to the state pensionable age. See *R v Secretary of State for Social Security, ex p Equal Opportunities Commission* [1992] ICR 782, [1992] IRLR 376, ECJ.

[424] Sex Discrimination Act 1986, s 2.   [425] Pensions Act 1995, ss 62–66.

4 SEXUAL ORIENTATION DISCRIMINATION IN EMPLOYMENT[426]

As a result of Article 13 of the EC Treaty[427] and the EC Employment Directive,[428] the Employment Equality (Sexual Orientation) Regulations 2003[429] introduced for the first time in the UK a prohibition on discrimination because of sexual orientation in employment and vocational training. The prohibition has since been incorporated into and expanded by the 2010 Act. 'Sexual orientation' is defined as being a sexual orientation towards persons of (1) the same sex (covering gay men and lesbians); (2) the opposite sex (covering straight men and women); or (3) both sexes (covering bisexual men and women).[430] The Act's use of the expression 'because of a protected characteristic' is wide enough to include discrimination based on A's perception of B's sexual orientation, whether right or wrong, and cases where a person is discriminated against by reason of someone else's sexual orientation, for example where a person is discriminated against for associating with gay friends, or for refusing to carry out an instruction to discriminate against gays or lesbians. This breadth was confirmed in *Lisboa v Realpubs, Pring and Heap*,[431] in which the EAT found that where the management of a former gay pub sought to re-position the pub as 'straight' it was associative sexual orientation discrimination to pressure a gay employee to cooperate in efforts to treat homosexual clients less favourably.

A number of exceptions in some way affect the protection afforded to sexual orientation, some of which have already generated controversy. The widest is a general exception for 'genuine occupational requirements' which allows an employer to treat job applicants and, in certain circumstances, employees differently on grounds of sexual orientation where, having regard to the nature of the job or the context in which it is carried out, being of a particular sexual orientation is a 'genuine occupational requirement' (GOR), and it is proportionate to apply it.[432] This GOR defence also applies in other protected characteristics, but in this context there is another, more controversial exception which applies where employment is for the purposes of an organized religion. This exception allows employers to discriminate on the basis of sex, gender reassignment, marital status (including divorce) and sexual orientation, in order to comply

---

[426] Oliver, 'Sexual Orientation Discrimination: Perceptions, Definitions and Genuine Occupational Requirements' (2004) 33 ILJ 1. Stonewall found that 15% of lesbians and gay men had suffered at least one experience of discrimination in their working lives ('Less equal than Others: A Survey of Lesbians and Gays at Work' (1993)), while the National Survey of Sexual Attitudes and Lifestyles (1990) found that over 20% of lesbian and gay workers had been harassed due to their sexuality: DTI 'Regulatory Impact Assessment for the Employment Equality (Sexual Orientation) Regulations 2003'.

[427] Article 13 provides a legal basis for Community legislation to combat discrimination on grounds (inter alia) of sexual orientation; see heading 1, p 305.

[428] Directive 2000/78/EC; see heading 1, p 305.

[429] SI 2003/1661. The Regulations came into force on 1 December 2003.

[430] Equality Act 2010, s 12.   [431] UKEAT/0224/10, [2011] All ER (D) 188.

[432] Equality Act 2010, Sch 9, para 1.

with the doctrines of the religion, or to avoid 'conflicting with the strongly held religious convictions of a significant number of the religion's followers'.[433] The discrimination must be a 'proportionate means' of achieving either doctrinal compliance or avoidance of conflict. This exception, which existed in the pre-2010 regulations, has been strongly criticized by the Lesbian and Gay Christian Movement as institutionalizing homophobia by permitting religious employers to sack gay and lesbian staff, although an organized religion exception is not unprecedented.[434] The government has claimed that the organized religion exception is consistent with Article 4 of the Directive because 'a requirement which meets the criteria … is necessarily a genuine and determining occupational requirement which is applied proportionately',[435] although if this were so the requirement would presumably be covered by the standard GOR exception anyway, making the organized religion exception redundant. Another exception that affects sexual orientation discrimination is one that allows religious discrimination, in the form of excluding non-believers, where that is a proportionate means of preserving a religious ethos in an enterprise or organization.[436] This could easily have the effect of causing indirect sexual orientation discrimination, which is not covered by the exception.

5 RACIAL DISCRIMINATION IN EMPLOYMENT

As has already been seen, 'race' in the 2010 Act includes colour, nationality, or ethnic or national origins, leaving open the question of what counts as ethnic origin. In *Mandla v Dowell Lee*,[437] the complainant, a Sikh boy, was refused entrance to a private school unless he gave up wearing his turban and had his hair cut, a requirement which conflicted with his religion; the House of Lords held that Sikhs constitute an ethnic group within the meaning of the Act, Lord Fraser commenting that for a group to constitute an ethnic group it must regard itself, and be regarded by others, as a distinct community with a long shared history and a cultural tradition of its own. It is clearly established that Jews[438] and gypsies[439] constitute identifiable ethnic groups, but

---

[433] Equality Act 2010, Sch 9, para 2(6).

[434] There is a similar exception in the Sex Discrimination Act 1975, s 19, permitting discrimination on grounds of sex or gender reassignment in the case of employment for purposes of an organized religion 'so as to comply with the doctrines of the religion or avoid offending the religious susceptibilities of a significant number of its followers'.

[435] Explanatory Memorandum to the Draft Regulations, para 24.

[436] Equality Act 2010, Sch 9, para 3.

[437] [1983] ICR 385, [1983] IRLR 209, HL. The decision shows how the 1976 Act could sometimes be used to outlaw discrimination on religious grounds, even though religious discrimination is not directly prohibited under the Act.

[438] *Seide v Gillette Industries Ltd* [1980] IRLR 427, EAT.

[439] *Commission for Racial Equality v Dutton* [1989] QB 783, [1989] 1 All ER 306, CA.

Rastafarians have been held not to, on the grounds that although they have certain identifiable characteristics, they have not established a separate identity by reference to their ethnic origins.[440] The fact that some faith groups have been able to obtain protection against religious discrimination indirectly via the Race Relations Act while others have not has been a source of considerable grievance, hence the importance of the recent prohibition on religious discrimination. 'Nationality' in this context points to citizenship, and to the existence of a recognized state at the material time, but 'national origin' is a wider concept, turning on the existence of a nation at some point in time, established by reference to history and geography. Thus, in *Northern Joint Police Board v Power*,[441] the issue was whether the applicant, who claimed that he had been rejected for a post of chief constable in Scotland because he was English, had been discriminated against on racial grounds. The tribunal held that there was no discrimination on grounds of nationality, as 'within the context of England, Scotland, Northern Ireland and Wales the proper approach to nationality is to categorise all of them as falling under the umbrella of British'; however, discrimination against an English person, or a Scot, was held to constitute discrimination on grounds of national origin, since it could not be in doubt that both England and Scotland were once separate nations.[442] In *BBC Scotland v Souster*,[443] which involved the non-renewal of the contract of an English journalist to a post as a television sports presenter in Scotland, the Court of Session took a broad, subjective view of the concept of 'national origins', holding that it is not limited to 'nationality' in the legal sense, nor to the citizenship acquired by an individual at birth, and that a person can become a member of a racial group defined by reference to 'origins' through adherence (for example by marriage) or adoption, or through being perceived to have become a member of that racial group. The burden of proof is, however, on the applicant to prove he is English, whether by virtue of national origins, or because he has acquired English nationality, or because he is perceived to be English.

The Act's use of the 'because of a protected characteristic' language means that it applies where a person suffers a detriment on the basis of *another* person's race, for example where a white person is dismissed for refusing to apply a colour bar. In *Weathersfield Ltd v Sargent*,[444] the complainant resigned from her job with a vehicle hire firm after being told not to hire vehicles to black or Asian prospective customers. The Court of Appeal held that she had been discriminated against on racial grounds,

---

[440] *Dawkins v Department of the Environment* [1993] IRLR 284, CA.

[441] [1997] IRLR 610, EAT.

[442] The same reasoning naturally applies to Wales and Ireland, although in *Gwynedd County Council v Jones* [1986] ICR 833, the EAT held that the 1976 Act does not apply to discrimination on the grounds of not being able to *speak* Welsh.

[443] [2001] IRLR 150, Ct of Sess.

[444] [1999] ICR 425, [1999] IRLR 94, CA. This is sometimes referred to as the rule in *Showboat Entertainment Centre Ltd v Owens* [1984] ICR 65, [1984] IRLR 7, EAT. However, the Court of Appeal would not allow this rule to be used *by* an active member of the BNP to claim that disciplinary action against him constituted race discrimination: *Redfearn v Serco Ltd* [2006] EWCA Civ 659, [2006] IRLR 623, CA.

even though it was the race of the prospective customers that was at issue, and not her own race.

The Race Relations Act 1976 set out certain exempted categories of employment where being a member of a particular racial group was a 'genuine occupational qualification' (GOQ) for a job, for example where the holder of the job provided persons of that racial group with 'personal services promoting their welfare', and those services 'can most effectively be provided by persons of that racial group',[445] or where the job involves participation in a dramatic performance, working as an artist's or photographic model, or working in a bar or restaurant, where a person of a particular racial group is required 'for reasons of authenticity'.[446] These GOQs have of course been replaced by the 'genuine occupational requirement' defence.[447] This exception allows employers to recruit employees on the basis of their race or ethnic or national origins if it can be shown that, having regard to the nature of the employment or the context in which it is carried out, being of a particular race or of particular ethnic or national origins is a 'genuine occupational requirement', and it is proportionate for that requirement to be applied in the particular case. The new exception is almost certainly narrower than the GOQ exception, and will probably only apply where the employer can show that the employee's race or ethnic or national origin is an essential, defining feature of the job. This is true not only because the Race Directive uses the phrase 'genuine and determining occupational requirement', but because it would hardly ever be proportionate to exclude a person from employment on racial grounds for a reason that was not an essential, defining feature of the job.

The February 1999 publication of the Stephen Lawrence Inquiry Report,[448] which found clear evidence of institutional racism[449] within the Metropolitan Police, contributed significantly to the later adoption of positive duties for public authorities. In the wake of the Inquiry Report, the government introduced the Race Relations (Amendment) Act 2000, which extended the scope of the Race Relations Act to cover all of the functions of all public bodies (not just the police),[450] thus making it unlawful for a public authority to discriminate directly or indirectly on racial grounds when

---

[445] See *Tottenham Green Under Fives' Centre v Marshall* [1989] ICR 214, [1989] IRLR 147, EAT; *(No 2)* [1991] ICR 320, [1991] IRLR 162, EAT; *Lambeth London Borough v Commission for Racial Equality* [1990] ICR 768, [1990] IRLR 231, CA.

[446] See Pitt 'Madam Butterfly and Miss Saigon: Reflections on Genuine Occupational Qualifications' in Dine and Watt (eds) *Discrimination Law: Concepts, Limitations and Justifications* (1996).

[447] Equality Act 2010, Sch 9, para 1.

[448] *The Stephen Lawrence Inquiry: Report of an Inquiry by Sir William Macpherson* (Cm 4262-I, 1999).

[449] Defined in the Inquiry Report as: 'The collective failure of an organisation to provide an appropriate and professional service to people because of their colour, culture or ethnic origin. It can be seen or detected in processes, attitudes and behaviour which amount to discrimination through unwitting prejudice, ignorance, thoughtlessness and racist stereotyping which disadvantage minority ethnic people.'

[450] There are a few exceptions, including the core functions of the intelligence and security services (other than employment, which remains covered), judicial acts by courts and tribunals, and of course immigration and nationality decisions, which by definition involve discrimination on grounds of nationality and ethnic or national origin: Race Relations Act 1976, s 71A.

performing any of its functions. In a new departure for British anti-discrimination law,[451] the Act also imposed a statutory duty on a wide range of public authorities to promote race equality. Section 71(1) of the amended Race Relations Act requires listed[452] public authorities to have 'due regard' in carrying out their functions[453] to the need (a) to eliminate unlawful racial discrimination; (b) to promote equality of opportunity; and (c) to promote good relations between persons of different racial groups. These positive duties have now been incorporated into sections 149–157 of the 2010 Equality Act and extended to all of the protected characteristics in the act except marriage and civil partnership. The general duty to promote equality extends to approximately 60 categories of public bodies, covering around 40,000 organizations. In addition to the general duty, the Secretary of State is also empowered to impose specific duties on some or all of the public authorities covered by the general duty, for the purpose of ensuring the better performance of their general duty.[454] The specific duties already imposed under the Race Relations Act 1976 include the duty to publish a Race Equality Scheme setting out how the authority intends to fulfil its general duty, and the duty to carry out ethnic monitoring of the workforce (referred to as the 'employment duty'). The introduction of these positive duties to promote equality across all protected grounds represent a highly significant shift in thinking as regards the use of the law to tackle discrimination. Unlike the existing anti-discrimination laws, which are essentially reactive, they reflect a more proactive and strategic approach to tackling discrimination. The imposition of a duty to conduct ethnic monitoring is particularly significant, as it has long been argued that monitoring is an essential tool in the identification of inequality and discrimination, and in the assessment of progress (or lack of it) in removing barriers to equality of opportunity.

Positive equality duties were later extended to disability (enforced by the Disability Rights Commission) and sex (enforced by the EOC). Enforcement of the positive equality duties is now the responsibility of the EHRC, with regard to all protected characteristics. With regard to race, sex or disability equality (specific duties have not yet been ordered for the other grounds) the EHRC may issue a compliance notice on an authority if it is satisfied that the authority has 'failed to comply with, or is failing to comply with' any of its specific duties. The notice will instruct the authority to meet its duty, and to inform the EHRC, within 28 days, of what steps it has taken (or is taking) to comply. If after three months the EHRC considers that the authority has not complied with the notice, it can apply to the county court for an order requiring

---

[451] Although not for Northern Ireland, where the fair employment legislation has imposed a duty to promote equality for some time.

[452] Schedule 1A to the 1976 Act lists, inter alia, Ministers of the Crown and government departments, the National Health Service, local government, education and housing bodies and the police. A further range of public bodies were brought within the scope of the general duty by the Race Relations Act 1976 (General Statutory Duty) Order 2001, SI 2001/3457.

[453] Only the public functions of a listed public authority are covered by the duty.

[454] Equality Act 2010, s 153. The specific race duties adopted prior to the 2010 Act are contained in the Race Relations Act 1976 (Statutory Duties) Order 2001, SI 2001/3458, issued under s 71(2).

compliance, and failure to obey such an order may result in the authority being found in contempt of court. There is no similar statutory procedure for enforcement of the general duty, which may be enforced by an application to the High Court for judicial review by a person or group of people with a sufficient interest in the matter, or by the EHRC.

6 RELIGION OR BELIEF DISCRIMINATION IN EMPLOYMENT[455]

There has been legislation tackling race discrimination on the UK statute books since 1965, but apart from Northern Ireland, where discrimination in employment on grounds of religious belief or political opinion has been unlawful since 1976,[456] there has been nothing directly addressing discrimination on grounds of religion. As was seen in Part 5, some religious groups have enjoyed de facto protection against religious discrimination for many years under the Race Relations Act 1976. The Act does not expressly refer to religious discrimination, but some religious groups (for example Sikhs[457] and Jews[458]) have been held to constitute a 'racial group' within the meaning of the Act because their members have a common ethnic origin.[459] However, the fact that some religious groups have been able to claim the protection of the law in this way has merely served to heighten the sense of injustice felt by other faith groups (for example Muslims, Hindus, Buddhists and Christians) whose members may experience religious discrimination and harassment in the workplace but are unable to obtain any remedy via the Act.[460] In theory, human rights law should offer some protection against religious discrimination, as Article 9 of the European Convention on Human Rights declares that 'Everyone has the right to freedom of thought, conscience and religion', including the freedom 'either alone or in community with others… to manifest his religion or belief, in worship, teaching, practice, and observance'. Article 9 does not itself provide for equal treatment on grounds of religion, but Article 14 of the Convention provides that 'The enjoyment of the rights and freedoms set forth in this Convention shall be secured without discrimination on any ground

---

[455] On the incidence of religion discrimination, see Weller, Feldman and Purdam 'Religious discrimination in England and Wales' Home Office Research Study 220 (2001). The 1999 British Social Attitudes Survey estimated that there are about 4.65 million men and women in employment who actively participate in religious activities, and the DTI's Regulatory Impact Assessment assumes that about 2% (roughly 94,000) of those may have experienced some form of employment discrimination.

[456] See now the Fair Employment and Treatment (Northern Ireland) Order 1998, SI 1998/3162.

[457] *Mandla v Dowell Lee* [1983] 2 AC 548, [1983] 1 All ER 1062, HL.

[458] *Seide v Gillette Industries Ltd* [1980] IRLR 427.

[459] See this chapter, heading 5, p 377.

[460] One possible source of protection for religious groups is via indirect race discrimination, but for this to work the action causing a detriment to eg Muslims must amount to indirect discrimination against a racial group that is predominantly Muslim: see eg *J H Walker v Hussain* [1996] ICR 291, [1996] IRLR 11, EAT.

such as ... religion.[461] However, even though these two Articles, in conjunction, appear to provide a basis for tackling religious discrimination (albeit only directly against public authorities), the fact is that the freedom to manifest one's religion in Article 9 is not an absolute right, but may be subject to restrictions which are 'prescribed by law and ... necessary in a democratic society ... for the protection of the rights and freedoms of others',[462] and case law under the Convention has revealed that the requirements of religious observance are likely to take second place to commercial and business considerations, and the primacy of contractual obligations.[463] Those looking for laws that offer reliable and robust protect against religious discrimination must look elsewhere.

As in the case of sexual orientation discrimination, the turning point came with the Treaty of Amsterdam, which introduced Article 13 into the EC Treaty. This provides a legal basis for Community-wide action to combat discrimination on a range of grounds, including 'religion or belief', and in November 2000 the Council adopted the Employment Directive,[464] which required member states to introduce measures prohibiting discrimination, inter alia, on grounds of religion or belief by 2 December 2003. The Employment Equality (Religion or Belief) Regulations 2003[465] first implemented the UK's obligations under the Directive by prohibiting discrimination on grounds of religion or belief in employment and vocational training. Religion or belief is now a protected characteristic under the 2010 Act and enjoys all the protection afforded to other grounds and more. A key issue for tackling religions' equality, and one which presents an extremely difficult challenge to any legislator intruding into this highly sensitive area, is the definition of the protected group. Which faith groups and their members are to benefit from the protection against discrimination?[466] Should an attempt be made to define 'religion', or to draw up a list of officially recognized religions, or, recognizing that any such attempt is likely to be highly invidious, should the protection be extended to all religious beliefs, including the often obscure religious cults that spring up from time to time? And what of those who experience discrimination on account of their atheism or agnosticism, or their adherence to ethical, secular belief systems? Predictably, the approach taken in Article 13 and the Employment Directive is to sidestep these difficult issues by prohibiting discrimination on grounds of 'religion *or* belief', thereby avoiding the need to define religion. That approach is reflected in the Equality Act, which provides that (1) 'religion' means any religion; (2) 'belief' means

---

[461] This is not a freestanding right, but can only be claimed in conjunction with one of the specified Convention rights. The UK government has not yet signed Protocol 12 to the Convention, which would provide a general prohibition on discrimination.

[462] European Convention on Human Rights, Art 9(2).

[463] See eg *Ahmad v Inner London Education Authority* [1978] 1 All ER 574; *Ahmad v United Kingdom* (1981) 4 EHRR 126; *Stedman v United Kingdom* (1997) 23 EHRR CD 168.

[464] Directive 2000/78/EC.

[465] SI 2003/1660. The regulations come into force on 2 December 2003. See Vickers (2003) 32 ILJ 23.

[466] See Hepple and Choudhury 'Tackling religious discrimination: practical implications for policy-makers and legislators' Home Office Research Study No 221 (2000) part 3.

any religious or philosophical belief; (3) a reference to religion includes a reference to lack of religion; and (4) a reference to belief includes a reference to lack of belief.[467] Although this more clearly covers the position of non-believers, the actual definition remains at large. Ultimately it has been for the humble employment tribunals to attempt to make sense of all this, as the government clearly intended: 'Given the wide variety of different faiths and beliefs in this country, we have reached the view that we should not attempt to define "religion or belief", and that it would be better to leave it to the courts to resolve definitional issues as they arise.'[468] As an exercise in legislative buck-passing, this takes some beating. Be that as it may, early indications have favoured a broad interpretation of the statutory language. The EAT in *Grainger plc v Nicholson* agreed with the tribunal below that a belief in man-made climate change, and the ethical obligations that flow from such a belief, can count as the protected characteristic of 'belief'.[469] Similarly, 'spiritualism', involving a belief in life after death and communication with spirits 'on the other side', has the necessary cogency, seriousness, cohesion and importance to fall within the definition of 'philosophical belief' for the purpose of the Act.[470]

Again, the fact that the Act forbids less favourable treatment 'because of a protected characteristic' includes discrimination based on A's perception of B's religion or belief, and discrimination by reason of the religion or belief of someone else, for example where a person is discriminated against for refusing to carry out an instruction to discriminate against Muslims. One potentially very difficult issue is the appropriate comparison to be made in cases of alleged direct religious discrimination. Most workplaces in the UK are still based around a Christian calendar, with employees enjoying Sunday as a rest day, and holidays at the main Christian festivals of Easter and Christmas. It is likely, therefore, that many employees who adhere to the Christian faith are able to follow the observance requirements of their religion without having to request any special treatment from their employer.[471] The question therefore arises, if for example a Muslim employee approaches his employer requesting time off work to celebrate a Muslim holy day, is the appropriate comparator: (1) an employee who has requested time off to celebrate a different religious festival; (2) an employee who has requested time off for some other non-religious purpose, for example to attend a football match; or (3) an employee who does not need to request time off to celebrate his religious festivals because he is a Christian and the employer's workplace already operates according to a Christian calendar?

An employer that applies rules on leave, or on dress and appearance at work, which particularly disadvantage certain religious or belief groups in comparison with others

---

[467] Equality Act 2010, s 10.

[468] DTI *Towards Equality and Diversity: Implementing the Employment and Race Directives* (2001) para 13.4.

[469] UKEAT/219/09; [2009] WLR (D) 315; [2010] IRLR 4 (EAT).

[470] *Greater Manchester Police Authority v Power* [2010] All ER (D) 173 (EAT).

[471] Cf the right of shop workers and betting workers to object to Sunday working: Employment Rights Act 1996, Pt IV.

may be found to have discriminated indirectly, unless the those rules can be objectively justified as being a proportionate means of achieving a legitimate aim. The potential impact of these provisions on working conditions can be seen from the government's own impact assessment:

> Under the new legislation, and in line with best practice, employers may need to accommodate a wide variety of religious and cultural needs of workers such as different dietary requirements and prayer room facilities. Employers may also need to be flexible in order to accommodate cultural or religious holidays and restrictions on hours of work. People should not be discriminated against in recruitment decisions if they cannot work on particular days of the week; particular times of the day; or in particular areas of a business (for example, the meat and alcohol section of a supermarket) unless this can be objectively justified.[472]

The basis of these provisions in traditional discrimination law is of course fundamental; important as these rights are, it is arguably of equal importance that they are not viewed as the reintroduction of some updated form of blasphemy law. The justification defence is likely to be pivotal in holding the necessary balance, as is the requirement of comparison.

An initial hurdle claimants must clear here is that of demonstrating the existence of a disadvantaged group. Even if the asserted religion or belief is accepted as covered, a claimant cannot show indirect discrimination without demonstrating that an identifiable religious or belief-holding group (as well as the claimant himself) was (or would be) placed at a disadvantage by the relevant provision.[473] The principle here is that one person's uniquely zealous interpretation of the requirements of a religion must not be allowed to render discriminatory a policy that would otherwise not trouble most members of that religion. There are dangers, however, behind this simple concern. First, courts might be tempted to over- or under-protect those whose beliefs are part of an organized religion with identifiable precepts. Any ease in identifying such precepts could work against those with minority interpretations or in favour of those who can more readily point to teachings that favour their claim. Second, there is a risk that the success of some claims will turn, as a practical matter if not one of principle, on whether the workforce happens to feature other members of the claimant's religion who also object to the policy. Concerns of this kind have resulted in the *Eweida* case and others (see *Ladele* and *McFarlane* discussed later) being taken to the European Court of Human rights with the EHRC as intervenor. Among the arguments made when the case was heard in September 2012 was that the law of religion or belief discrimination must apply a 'reasonable adjustments' approach similar to that in disability discrimination law, to obviate disputes about the orthodox requirements of a religion, and focus on bespoke accommodation to a reasonable extent.[474] The following cases suggest there are further reasons for considering this.

---

[472] DTI *Regulatory Impact Assessment on the Religion or Belief Regulations* para 6.

[473] *Eweida v British Airways* [2010] EWCA Civ 80, [2010] All ER (D) 144 (CA); *Chatwal v Wandsworth BC* [2011] All ER (D) 69 (EAT).

[474] 'Commission proposes "reasonable accommodation" for religion or belief' (Equality and Human Rights Commission July 2011) available at <http://www.equalityhumanrights.com/news/2011/july/commission-proposes-reasonable-accommodation-for-religion-or-belief-is-needed/> (last accessed 9 January 2013).

In *Azmi v Kirklees MBC*[475] a teaching assistant was suspended for refusing an instruction not to wear a full facial veil when in a class assisting a male teacher. The EAT upheld the tribunal's rejection of her claim of religious discrimination. They held that there was no direct discrimination because any assistant who wanted to hide his or her face for any reason would have been treated in the same way. With regard to indirect discrimination, they agreed that there was a provision, criterion or practice which put the claimant as a Muslim at a particular disadvantage, but upheld the tribunal; finding that this was justified by the school's concerns about the effect that the veil had on her ability to communicate properly with the children and the impracticability of her suggestions for dealing with her requirements in other ways.[476] In a similar vein, dismissing an employee for promoting religious view in the workplace was not direct discrimination in *Chondol v Liverpool CC*, because the dismissal was because of the inappropriate proselytizing conduct, not the beliefs themselves.[477] More controversial, because they involve the intersection of religion and sexual orientation, are the cases of *McFarlane*[478] and *Ladele*.[479] According to these decisions it is neither direct nor indirect discrimination to (a) require employees at a counselling centre to commit to counselling same-sex couples and (b) otherwise require employees to perform duties to which they conscientiously object because of their religious views about homosexual behaviour. This is true even if the employee could be individually accommodated, because it is a legitimate objective to pursue a policy of non-discrimination on the basis of sexual orientation, and the requirements applied, again, to manifestations of religion or belief, not to the holding of that belief. The logic of these decisions is straightforward, but they have attracted controversy because they are claimed to prioritize sexual orientation protections over protections for religion or belief. Suffice it to say in this regard that no judgments have ever suggested that the prohibition on sexual orientation discrimination would preclude employers from regulating sexual encounters at work, so long as the regulation was orientation-neutral. The authors await with interest what the European Court of Human Rights will do with these issues, especially the idea that there might be a call for more individual accommodation at the intersection of religion and sexual orientation.

In addition to the general 'genuine occupational requirements' (GOR) exception discussed with respect to other protected characteristics, there is a highly controversial exception for organizations with 'an ethos based on religion or belief'; this is similar to the general GOR, but *without* the need to show that religion or belief is an occupational requirement.[480] It is unclear what an organization needs to show in order to qualify as having an ethos based on religion or belief (can an organization acquire such an

---

[475] [2007] UKEAT 9/07.

[476] One such suggestion, that she should not be required to work with a male teacher, would have had interesting consequences in sex discrimination law.

[477] [2009] All ER (D) 155.   [478] *McFarlane v Relate Avon* [2009] All ER (D) 233.

[479] *Ladele v LB Islington* [2009] All ER (D) 148.

[480] Equality Act 2010, Sch 9, para 3. The 'religious ethos' GOR is permitted under Art 4(2) of the Directive, which refers to a situation where a person's religion or belief 'constitute a genuine, legitimate and justified occupational requirement, having regard to the organisation's ethos'.

ethos merely by proclamation, or must it be of a certain type, and have a suitable track record, in order to qualify?), and even if it overcomes that hurdle, the employer will still need to show that that religion or belief is a GOR for the job in question, and that it is proportionate to apply it. It remains to be seen how much latitude employers will be granted under this GOR, but it is submitted that it should be interpreted narrowly, as an exception to the principle of equal treatment.[481]

7 DISABILITY DISCRIMINATION IN EMPLOYMENT[482]

Statistics indicate that disabled people account for nearly a fifth of the working-age population in Great Britain, but for only about one-eighth (or 12%) of all people in employment. There are over 6.5 million people in Great Britain with a work-limiting, long-term disability or health problem, but disabled people are only half as likely as non-disabled people to be in employment.[483] Disabled employees earn on average two-thirds of the wages of non-disabled employees,[484] and are more likely to be employed in manual and unskilled occupations than are non-disabled employees.[485] To some extent this can be explained by the effect which a physical or mental impairment might have on a disabled person's capacity to perform the work in question, but there is also strong evidence to suggest that disabled people suffer systematic discrimination in relation to employment, often as a result of ill-informed, stereotypical assumptions on the part of employers about the impact of particular disabilities on the work-capacity of such employees and the difficulty of adapting working arrangements and premises to accommodate them.[486] Until 1995 there was no legislation tackling the problem of discrimination against disabled people in the workplace, successive governments having maintained (in what has become a familiar refrain) that the issue was most appropriately tackled by education and persuasion rather than by anti-discrimination legislation. However, following an intensive and well-organized campaign for the introduction of comprehensive civil rights legislation for disabled people, and no fewer than 14 abortive attempts to introduce Private Members' Bills on the subject, the Conservative government introduced the Disability Discrimination

---

[481] Significantly, Art 4(2) of the Directive states that the religious ethos GOR 'should not justify discrimination on another ground'.

[482] See generally, Lawson, 'Disability and Employment in the Equality Act 2010: Opportunities Seized, Lost, and Generated' (2011) 40 ILJ 359; Thomas *The New Law on Disability Discrimination* (1996), Doyle *Disability Discrimination: Law and Practice* (Jordans, 4th edn, 2003). See also 'Monitoring the Disability Discrimination Act (DDA) 1995' (DfEE Research Series RR119, 1999).

[483] Labour Force Survey (Summer 1999).

[484] Martin, White and Meltzer *Disabled Adults: Services, Transport and Employment* (OPCS, 1989).

[485] Prescott-Clarke *Employment and Handicap* (SCPR, 1990).

[486] Honey, Meager and Williams *Employers' Attitudes towards People with Disabilities* (IMS, 1993).

Act 1995[487] (DDA), the first legislative attempt to tackle discrimination against disabled people. The DDA prohibited discrimination against disabled people in relation to employment, the provision of goods and services, and the sale and letting of property; it also required schools, colleges, universities and LEAs to provide fuller information about their arrangements and facilities for disabled pupils and students,[488] and imposed some modest requirements as regards accessible public transport for disabled people. In the area of employment, the DDA tried to strike a balance between the interests of disabled people (in terms of access to employment and equal treatment in the workplace, etc) and the interests of employers, by making it unlawful for an employer to discriminate against a disabled employee or job applicant by treating that person less favourably than he treats or would treat others for a reason relating to his or her disability, and by placing a duty on an employer to make reasonable adjustments to working arrangements and premises (by providing special equipment, altering working hours, arranging training, adapting premises, etc), in order to accommodate a disabled person who would otherwise be at a substantial disadvantage in comparison with non-disabled persons, while at the same time allowing an employer to claim that discrimination against a disabled person is justified in certain circumstances.

The DDA was given only a qualified welcome by disabled rights campaigners, on account of the perceived deficiencies in its provisions. In particular, concern was expressed at the narrowness of the definition of disability,[489] the extent to which employers were able to claim that discrimination against disabled persons was justified, and (at the outset) the absence of a commission similar to the EOC and the CRE with powers to investigate complaints, assist individuals in enforcing their legal rights or take enforcement action on its own account. By far the greatest criticism was levelled at the exemption of small businesses from the employment provisions of the Act,[490] which was estimated to exclude 96% of employers from the duty not to discriminate against disabled persons. The incoming Labour government addressed some of the main criticisms by establishing a Disability Rights Commission, with powers similar to those of the EOC and CRE,[491] and reducing the small employer threshold from 20 to 15. The government also set up a Disability Rights Task Force to examine the whole question of disability rights legislation, and the Task Force's Report in late 1999 made over 150 recommendations, including key reforms to the

---

[487] The Act was heralded by a consultation document on *Government Measures to Tackle Discrimination against Disabled People* (produced following the furore surrounding the 'talking-out' of the Civil Rights (Disabled Persons) Bill in 1994), and by a White Paper, 'Ending Discrimination against Disabled People' (Cm 2729) which was published on the same day as the Bill.

[488] The DDA did not apply to the provision of educational services, but this omission has since been remedied by the Special Educational Needs and Disability Act 2001.

[489] Although the definition was broadened during the Act's passage through Parliament, it still does not cover some categories who might fall within a broader definition of disability, eg those with a reputation for disability.

[490] Disability Discrimination Act 1995, s 7. The exclusion mirrored the 1944 Act, under which the duty to employ a 3% quota of registered disabled employees only applied to firms employing 20 or more.

[491] Disability Rights Commission Act 1999.

DDA's employment provisions such as the lowering of the small employer threshold to two, extending the scope of the provisions to cover, for example partnerships, police and prison officers, firefighters and the armed forces, restricting disability-related enquiries before the offer of a job is made, removing the justification defence in the case of the duty to make reasonable adjustments, and giving tribunals power to order reinstatement or re-engagement where a disabled person is unlawfully dismissed, and to make recommendations regarding future conduct.[492] The case for reform of the DDA was given a major boost by the reaching of agreement in October 2000 on the Employment Directive,[493] brought forward under Article 13 of the EC Treaty, which requires member states to introduce laws tackling, inter alia, disability discrimination in employment. Implementation of the Directive required some changes to be made to the DDA, many of which were anticipated in the Task Force's report, for example the ending of the exemption for small firms and the extension of the DDA to cover many of those sectors of employment then excluded from its protection, including police officers, prison officers and firefighters. The Directive also necessitated some changes to the DDA's definition of discrimination, and the availability of the justification defence. The Disability Discrimination Act 1995 (Amendment) Regulations 2003[494] implemented as from 2004 the provisions of the Directive so far as it related to disability discrimination and further significant changes were made by the DDA 2005 (an amending Act). One problem is that, as the UK was generally ahead of the field in the EU with disability protection, the *level* of that protection in the DDA was already at least as high as that required by the Directive but it *achieved* it in a way very different from that set out in the Directive. Arguably, one of the purposes of the amending Regulations was to make the DDA *look* more like the EC law model but the reality is that the Act was still based on a different approach.

A notable feature of the DDA was the extent to which it left many fundamental issues and concepts to be clarified and expanded upon by Regulations, ministerial guidance and codes of practice. The Equality Act 2010 maintains this approach. There are regulations relating to disability,[495] the Secretary of State has issued guidance on 'matters to be taken into account in determining questions relating to the definition of disability',[496] and the EHRC has issued an Equality Act 2010 Employment Code of Practice.[497] The Guidance and the Code of Practice are both admissible in evidence in proceedings before a tribunal, and must be taken into account where relevant. Some of the concepts and terminology used in the Act were borrowed from the sex and race discrimination legislation (for example 'less favourable treatment', 'any other

[492] Disability Rights Task Force *From Exclusion to Inclusion* (1999).
[493] Directive 2000/78/EC.   [494] SI 2003/1673, in force as from 1 October 2004.
[495] The Equality Act 2010 (Disability) Regulations 2010, SI 2010/2128, available at <http://www.legislation.gov.uk/uksi/2010/2128/made> last accessed 10 January 2013.
[496] Available at <http://www.odi.dwp.gov.uk/docs/wor/new/ea-guide.pdf> last accessed 10 January 2013.
[497] Available at <http://www.equalityhumanrights.com/uploaded_files/EqualityAct/employercode.pdf> last accessed 10 January 2013.

detriment'), but the Court of Appeal has warned that a textual comparison between the disability discrimination legislation and the legislation relating to sex and race discrimination is not helpful, and may even be misleading:

> Contrary to what might be reasonably assumed, the exercise of interpretation is not facilitated by familiarity with the pre-existing legislation prohibiting discrimination in the field of employment (and elsewhere) on the grounds of sex (Sex Discrimination Act 1975) and race (Race Relations Act 1976). Indeed, it may be positively misleading to approach the 1995 Act with assumptions and concepts familiar from experience of the workings of the 1975 Act and the 1976 Act.[498]

The DDA has now been subsumed in the Equality Act 2010, but the warning remains applicable. Incorporation within the Act has made disability law work more like other discrimination law with regard to direct and indirect discrimination, harassment and victimization. However it remains distinct in terms of disability-specific protections.

(i) THE MEANING OF 'DISABILITY'

The key to disability discrimination is the definition of disability in the Equality Act 2010, section 6, which states that a disability is a physical or mental impairment which has a substantial and long-term adverse effect on the ability to carry out normal day-to-day activities. This definition has been described as a 'common-sense' definition which fits 'a generally acceptable perception of what disability means to employers, service providers, disabled people and the nation at large';[499] however, it has also been criticized for being too narrow, and for adopting a medical as opposed to a social model of disability,[500] by defining disability in terms of impairments rather than focusing on the ways in which disabled people are disadvantaged by the organization, structure and attitudes of the society in which they live and work. In *Goodwin v Patent Office*,[501] the EAT held that the tribunal should adopt a purposive approach to the interpretation of the definition, and should construe the language of the Act in a way which gives effect to the stated or presumed intention of Parliament, but with due regard to the ordinary and natural meaning of the words.

The definition has the following key elements:

(1) There must be a 'physical or mental impairment'; these terms are not defined, but are intended to cover all forms of impairment, including sensory impairments. Mental illness originally only counted as a mental impairment if it was 'a clinically

---

[498] *Clark v Novacold Ltd* [1999] ICR 951, [1999] IRLR 318 at para 30, CA, per Mummery LJ.

[499] Minister of State, *Hansard* HC Standing Committee E, col 73.

[500] See eg Doyle (1996) ILJ 1. Ironically, EC law may be even narrower because the ECJ held in *Chacon Navas v Eurest Colectividades SA* C-13/05 [2006] IRLR 706 that the Directive does not cover an employee who is merely sick, whereas it was always clear that the DDA can cover those suffering from long-term and debilitating sickness.

[501] [1999] ICR 302, [1999] IRLR 4, EAT.

well-recognized illness' but this qualification was removed in 2005, and the EAT has stressed that the existence or not of a mental impairment 'is very much a matter for qualified and informed medical opinion', and that 'some loose description such as "anxiety", "stress" or "depression" of itself will [not] suffice', unless there is credible and informed evidence of a clinically well-recognized illness.[502] Problems have arisen over the dividing line between physical and mental impairment, particularly where an impairment affects a person physically (for example pain) but it is not clear whether the cause of that impairment is physical or mental.[503] The Court of Appeal set out the correct approach to that issue in *McNicol v Balfour Beatty Rail Maintenance Ltd*,[504] holding that the term 'impairment' bears its ordinary and natural meaning, that it 'may result from an illness or it may consist of an illness',[505] and, crucially, that 'it is not necessary to consider how an impairment was caused'.[506] It follows that in applying the statutory definition, the focus should be on whether a physical or mental function or activity is affected, rather than on whether the cause of the impairment is physical or mental (a particularly helpful approach, given how difficult it can be to distinguish between physical and mental conditions, especially where the impairment is multi-factorial in origin). A number of conditions are deemed not to be impairments for the purposes of the Act (for example dependency on alcohol, nicotine or other non-prescribed substance, pyromania, kleptomania, a tendency to physical or sexual abuse of others, exhibitionism, voyeurism and 'seasonal allergic rhinitis'),[507] although it may still be necessary to distinguish between such excluded conditions and impairments which may result from them.[508]

(2) The impairment must have a 'substantial' effect;[509] this is not defined, although the intention is only to include impairments having an effect which is 'more than minor or trivial'.[510] In *Goodwin v The Patent Office*,[511] the EAT emphasized that the

---

[502] *Morgan v Staffordshire University* [2002] ICR 475, [2002] ICR 475, [2002] IRLR 190, EAT. For mental impairment not arising from a mental illness as such, see *Dunham v Ashford Windows* [2005] IRLR 608 EAT.

[503] As in the condition known as psychological or functional 'overlay', where a person experiences pain which has no apparent physical cause.

[504] [2002] EWCA Civ 1074, [2002] ICR 1498, [2002] IRLR 711.

[505] [2002] IRLR 711 at 713, per Mummery LJ. See to like effect Lindsay J in *College of Ripon & York St John v Hobbs* [2002] IRLR 185 at para 32 and *Millar v Inland Revenue Commissioners* [2006] IRLR 112, Ct of Sess (IH).

[506] [2002] EWCA Civ 1074, [2002] ICR 1498, [2002] IRLR 711, citing with approval Part 1 of the Guidance.

[507] The Equality Act 2010 (Disability) Regulations 2010, SI 2010/2128, regs 3 and 4. These exclusions cannot be circumvented by arguing that they are merely symptoms of some other disability: *Edmund Nuttall v Butterfield* [2005] IRLR 751, EAT disapproving *Murray v Newham CAB* [2003] IRLR 340, EAT.

[508] *Power v Panasonic UK Ltd* [2003] IRLR 151, EAT (depression resulting from alcohol addiction still capable of being an impairment within the meaning of the Act).

[509] Equality Act 2010, Sch 1, para 3 provides that a severe disfigurement will be treated as an impairment having a substantial adverse effect; deliberately acquired disfigurements such as tattoos or decorative body piercing are excluded.

[510] *Goodwin v Patent Office* [1999] ICR 302, [1999] IRLR 4; *Vicary v British Telecommunications plc* [1999] IRLR 680, EAT.

[511] *Goodwin v Patent Office* [1999] ICR 302, [1999] IRLR 4, per Morison J (emphasis added).

Act is concerned with the effect of an impairment on a person's *ability* to carry out activities: 'The focus of attention required by the Act is on the things that the applicant either *cannot* do or can only do with difficulty, rather than on things that the person *can* do.' This approach avoids the danger of a tribunal concluding that as there are many things that an applicant can do, the adverse effect of the impairment cannot be substantial.[512] The Guidance suggests that in determining whether the effect of an impairment is substantial, account should be taken of factors such as the time taken to carry out the activity (paragraph B2) and the way in which it is carried out (paragraph B3), in comparison with what might be expected if the person did not have the impairment.[513]

(3) The impairment must have a 'long-term' effect; conditions which are only temporary, such as short-term illness, are not disabilities within the meaning of the Act. An impairment will be treated as having a long-term effect if it has lasted, or is likely to last, for at least 12 months,[514] or if it is likely to last for the rest of a person's life (as in the case of a terminal illness).[515] Where the impairment is intermittent or sporadic (for example epilepsy or multiple sclerosis), it will be treated as continuing to have a long-term adverse effect, even through periods of remission, if it is likely to recur.[516] The extent to which a person has suffered long-term impairment can be considered in light of two impairments so long as one developed from the other.[517]

(4) The impairment must have an adverse effect on a person's ability 'to carry out normal day-to-day activities'. Schedule 1 to the DDA contained an exhaustive list[518] of activities which are to be treated as normal day-to-day activities for these purposes, namely: mobility; manual dexterity; physical coordination; continence; ability to lift, carry or otherwise move everyday objects; speech, hearing or eyesight; memory or ability to concentrate, learn or understand;[519] or the perception of the risk of physical danger. However, the Equality Act does not have such a list, leaving the issue to the Guidance, which says (paragraph D2) that no such exhaustive list is possible. However, it is likely that the old list will retain some influence on judicial thinking. 'Normal day-to-day activities' are the activities of an ordinary average person, not a person with specialized skills or abilities. In deciding whether an activity is a normal day-to-day

---

[512] *Leonard v Southern Derbyshire Chamber of Commerce* [2001] IRLR 19, EAT.

[513] The Guidance also advises that it may be appropriate to consider the cumulative effects of the impairment on a range of normal day-to-day activities (para B4), and the cumulative effects of more than one impairment (para B6).

[514] The material time at which the disability must be assessed is the time of the alleged discriminatory act, not the date of the hearing (*Cruickshank v VAW Motorcast Ltd* [2002] ICR 729, [2002] IRLR 24, EAT), although the Guidance states (at para C3) that in assessing the likelihood of an effect lasting for any period, account should be taken of the total period for which the effect exists, including time before and after the point when the discriminatory act occurred. Cf also *Greenwood v British Airways plc* [1999] ICR 969, [1999] IRLR 600, EAT.

[515] Equality Act 2010, Sch 1, para 2(1).   [516] Equality Act 2010, para 2(2).

[517] *Patel v (1) Oldham MBC (2) Governing Body of Rushcroft Primary School* [2010] IRLR 280.

[518] Disability Discrimination Act 1995, Sch 1, para 4(1).

[519] This can cover Asperger's syndrome, on a wide interpretation of 'understanding': *Hewitt v Motorola Ltd* [2004] IRLR 545, EAT.

activity, the Guidance states that account should be taken 'of how far it is normal for a large number of people and carried out by people on a daily or frequent and fairly regular basis' (paragraph D3). In *Vicary v British Telecommunications plc*,[520] normal day-to-day activities were held to include making beds, doing housework, sewing and cutting with scissors, minor DIY tasks, filing nails, curling hair and ironing, since they are all 'activities which most people do on a frequent or fairly regular basis'.[521] In *Ekpe v Metropolitan Police Comr*,[522] the tribunal at first instance had held that the ability of a woman to put rollers in her hair and to use her right hand to apply make-up were not normal day-to-day activities because they were 'activities carried out almost exclusively by women', but the EAT, allowing the appeal, stated that what is 'normal' for these purposes may be best understood 'as anything which is not abnormal or unusual', and that the exclusion of any activity done by women rather than men (or vice versa) was 'plainly wrong'.[523] The Guidance states that 'normal day-to-day activities' do not include work of any particular form, 'because no particular form of work is "normal" for most people'.[524] This is not to say, however, that the effect of a person's impairment whilst at work is irrelevant, for the following reasons; first, the work they perform may include some normal day-to-day activities, and evidence of how they are able to perform those activities while at work will be relevant to the tribunal's assessment of their case;[525] and, secondly, the effects of an impairment may be exacerbated by conditions at work (for example exposure to fumes), and 'it would risk turning the Act on its head' if the employer were able to avoid any obligations under the Act (for example to make reasonable adjustments) by arguing that the employee was not disabled because the impairment only had a substantial adverse effect on normal day-to-day activities while the employee was at work.[526]

One difficult practical issue for the tribunal is the weight to be placed on medical evidence. It is for the tribunal to decide whether the applicant has an impairment which has a substantial adverse effect on normal day-to-day activities, and the EAT has held that a tribunal makes an error of law if it relies too heavily on medical opinion on those issues.[527] The medical report should be confined to the doctor's diagnosis of the impairment, the doctor's observation of the applicant carrying out normal day-to-day activities and the ease with which he was able to perform those functions, together

---

[520] [1999] IRLR 680, EAT.

[521] [1999] IRLR 680 at 682, per Morison P. See also *Abadeh v British Telecommunications plc* [2001] IRLR 23, [2001] ICR 156, EAT (travelling by Underground and flying held to be normal day-to-day activities because they were normal means of transport used by most people on a daily or frequent or fairly regular basis).

[522] [2001] IRLR 605, EAT.   [523] [2001] IRLR 605 at 609.

[524] Guidance, para D5. See eg *Quinlan v B & Q plc* (EAT 1386/97) (assistant at garden centre not disabled within the meaning of the Act because, although unable to lift heavy objects following heart surgery, he was capable of lifting everyday objects).

[525] *Law Hospital NHS Trust v Rush* [2001] IRLR 611, Ct of Sess.

[526] *Cruickshank v VAW Motorcast Ltd* [2002] ICR 729, [2002] IRLR 24, EAT (occupational asthma exacerbated by exposure to fumes at work).

[527] *Vicary v British Telecommunications* [1999] IRLR 680, EAT.

with any relevant opinion as to prognoses and the effect of medication.[528] On the other hand, while a tribunal is not obliged to accept uncontested medical evidence,[529] it may not disregard such evidence in favour of its own impression of the applicant formed in the course of the hearing.[530]

A number of further points can be made in relation to the definition. First, the statutory protection extends to those who have had a disability in the past, even if they have made a full recovery and are no longer disabled.[531] This is in recognition of the fact that a person with a history of disability (for example a person with a history of mental illness) may continue to experience discrimination even when no longer disabled; it is an example of the Act adopting a more 'social' model of disability. Secondly, the effect of an impairment on normal day-to-day activities must be considered without taking into account any measures (for example medical treatment,[532] or the use of a prosthesis or other aid) which are being taken to treat or correct the impairment,[533] the rationale again being that such a person may experience discrimination even if the potentially disabling condition is controlled; so for example, in the case of a person with diabetes which is controlled by medication, whether or not the effect of the condition is substantial must be decided by reference to what the effects of the condition would be if that person were not taking his or her medication.[534] Difficulties can arise here where it is not clear whether an impairment would in fact have a substantial adverse effect if the medical treatment were to be discontinued, and on this the Court of Appeal has taken a strict line, requiring the applicant to prove his or her alleged disability 'with some particularity':

> Those seeking to invoke [this] particularly benign doctrine … should not readily expect to be indulged by the tribunal of fact. Ordinarily … one would expect clear medical evidence to be necessary.[535]

---

[528] *Abadeh v British Telecommunications plc* [2001] ICR 156, [2001] IRLR 23, per Nelson J.

[529] Eg where the evidence on the basis of which a doctor has formed an opinion is rejected by the tribunal, or where it is clear that the medical witness has misunderstood the evidence which he was invited to consider in expressing his opinion.

[530] *Kapadia v London Borough of Lambeth* [2000] IRLR 699, CA. Cf Pill LJ at 703: by consenting to a medical examination on behalf of the employer, the applicant was consenting to the disclosure to the employer of a report resulting from that examination, so that no further consent for disclosure was required. See also *London Borough of Hammersmith & Fulham v Farnsworth* [2000] IRLR 691, EAT (an occupational health physician was not bound by any duty of confidence owed to the applicant not to disclose details of the applicant's medical history to the employer, because the applicant had consented to medical information about her being provided to the employer).

[531] Equality Act 2010, s 6(4).

[532] This can include attendance at therapy or counselling sessions: *Kapadia v London Borough of Lambeth* [2000] IRLR 699.

[533] Equality Act 2010, Sch 1, para 5. This does not apply to those with impaired sight which is correctable by spectacles or contact lenses or some other prescribed method.

[534] Ie the tribunal must consider the 'deduced effects' of the impairment: *Goodwin v Patent Office* [1999] ICR 302, [1999] IRLR 4.

[535] *Woodrup v London Borough of Southwark* [2002] EWCA Civ 1716, [2003] IRLR 111.

The other limitation on the doctrine is that where the medical treatment creates a *permanent* improvement, the effects of that treatment *should* be taken into account in assessing the disability, as measures are no longer needed to treat or correct it once the permanent improvement has been established.[536] Thirdly, a person suffering from a progressive condition, such as cancer, multiple sclerosis, muscular dystrophy or infection by HIV, will be deemed to fall within the definition of a disabled person from the point in time when, as a result[537] of that condition, that person has an impairment which has some adverse effect (which need not be substantial) on that person's ability to carry out normal day-to-day activities, if the condition is likely to result in an impairment which has a substantial adverse effect.[538] The burden of proof is on the applicant to show, on the balance of probabilities, that the condition is likely to have a substantial adverse effect at some stage in the future,[539] and this may prove difficult where the applicant has a condition which is variable in nature, such as multiple sclerosis, where the prognosis may be uncertain.[540] The provision for progressive conditions is in recognition of the fact that a person who is diagnosed as suffering from such a condition may suffer discrimination as a result of that diagnosis well before the condition can be said to have a substantial adverse effect on that person's ability to carry out normal day-to-day activities. However, as originally enacted the protection only arose from the point when the condition began to have some effect; it did not apply while the condition, although diagnosed, remained latent, and it could therefore be said to provide a positive incentive to discriminate before a person begins to manifest any symptoms. In view of these concerns, the legislation was amended by the DDA 2005 (and remains under the Equality Act) to provide that 'a person who has cancer, HIV infection or multiple sclerosis is to be deemed to have a disability'.[541] Those diagnosed with other progressive conditions will, however, remain unprotected until the condition becomes symptomatic, as will a person diagnosed as having a genetic predisposition to a potentially disabling condition.[542] Finally, the burden of proof in establishing an

---

[536] *Abadeh v British Telecommunications plc* [2001] ICR 156, [2001] IRLR 23, EAT (although note that a person whose disabling impairment has been successfully treated remains protected by virtue of the provisions on past disability).

[537] An impairment which is a result of standard treatment to relieve a progressive condition (eg urinary incontinence resulting from surgery for prostate cancer) rather than a direct result of the condition itself, still falls within this exception: *Kirton v Tetrosyl* [2003] IRLR 353, CA.

[538] Equality Act 2010, Sch 1, para 8. 'Likely' here means 'more probable than not': Guidance, para 87.

[539] Eg by medical evidence of the likely prognosis, or by statistical evidence.

[540] See eg *Mowat-Brown v University of Surrey* [2002] IRLR 235, EAT. Cf Rubenstein at [2002] IRLR 227: 'This decision ... highlights a problem with the drafting of the DDA. Applicants with progressive conditions do not want them to get worse and it seems invidious, both for them and their doctors, to require them to prove that this is more likely than not to happen.'

[541] Equality Act 2010, Sch 1, para 6.

[542] On the potential for genetic discrimination in employment, see the report of the Human Genetics Advisory Council 'The Implications of Genetic Testing for Employment' (1999). The DRC has called for the Act's protection to be extended to those with a genetic predisposition: see *Disability Equality: Making it Happen* (2003).

impairment is on the applicant, but on discrimination the general rules on burden of proof apply. The tribunal does not have a duty 'to conduct a free-standing inquiry of its own',[543] nor is it required to obtain evidence or to ensure that adequate medical evidence is obtained by the parties.[544] It may, however, exercise its discretion to grant an adjournment to enable the applicant to obtain further evidence, particularly where the applicant is not only in person but also suffers some mental weakness.[545]

(ii) THE MEANING OF 'DISCRIMINATION'

The 2010 Act contains two special kinds of protection afforded only to the protected characteristic of disability: discrimination arising from disability (section 15) and the duty to make adjustments (section 20). The Act does not require a like-for-like comparison (and, indeed, gives *no* correlative rights to non-disabled people), it uses a concept of reasonable adjustment in place of indirect discrimination, and it allows positive discrimination in favour of disabled people.

(a) Discrimination arising from a disability

The Equality Act 2010 section 15 provides that an employer A discriminates against a disabled person B if A treats B in a way such that, because of B's disability, the treatment amounts to a detriment, and the treatment is not a proportionate means to a legitimate aim. This deceptively simple definition emerged from a massive confusion caused by the previous DDA definition, which provided that it was discrimination if:

(1) for a reason which relates to the disabled person's disability, the employer treats him less favourably than he treats or would treat others to whom that reason does not or would not apply and

(2) he cannot show that the treatment in question is justified.

The scope of the protection offered by the earlier DDA provision turned on two fundamentally important issues: first, who was the appropriate comparator when determining whether there has been 'less favourable treatment'?;[546] and, secondly, what degree of knowledge of the complainant's disability was required on the part of the employer? The first issue arose for consideration in *Clark v Novacold Ltd*,[547] where

---

[543] *Rugamer v Sony Musical Entertainment UK Ltd* [2001] IRLR 644 at 652, clarifying the comment of Morison J in *Goodwin v Patent Office* [1999] IRLR 4 that the role of the tribunal 'contains an inquisitorial element'. See also *Morgan v Staffordshire University* [2002] IRLR 190 at 194, EAT.

[544] *McNicol v Balfour Beatty Rail Maintenance Ltd* [2002] IRLR 711 at 714, per Mummery LJ. In this respect, the duty of an employment tribunal differs from that of a medical or other tribunal dealing with a disablement issue as part of a benefits claim.

[545] *Morgan v Staffordshire University* [2002] IRLR 190 at 195, per Lindsay P (the President's guidance was approved by the Court of Appeal in *McNicol* [2002] IRLR 711).

[546] Ie in the words of DDA, s 5(1)(a), who are the 'others to whom that reason does not or would not apply'?

[547] [1998] ICR 1044, [1998] IRLR 420, EAT.

the applicant was dismissed for long-term sickness absence following an accident at work. The EAT identified two possible approaches to the comparison required by section 5(1)(a); the first involves a like-for-like comparison between the treatment of the disabled person and the treatment of a person who was also unable to fulfil all the requirements of the job, but for a reason unrelated to disability (ie someone who had been absent from work for the same amount of time as the applicant, but for a reason other than disability); the second involves a comparison between the treatment of the disabled person and the treatment of a person who was able to fulfil all the requirements of the job (ie someone who had not been absent from work at all, or who had the same absence record as the applicant when any disability-related absences were discounted). In practice, the second approach is far more likely to lead to a finding of less favourable treatment, thus putting the onus on the employer to show justification for that treatment; the first approach is unlikely to lead to a finding of less favourable treatment (unless the employer has discriminated against the applicant simply because he has a disability) which means that the need to show justification is less likely to arise. The EAT preferred the first approach, and held that the applicant had not been less favourably treated for a reason which related to his disability, because he was treated no differently than a person in similar circumstances who was not disabled would have been treated. In sharp contrast, in *British Sugar v Kirker*,[548] the EAT held that the DDA does not require a like-for-like comparison, but 'simply requires the applicant to show that he was less favourably treated than other employees where the reason for the treatment, that is a reason related to his disability, does not apply to those other employees' (ie the straightforward causative test of the second approach); it was unnecessary to identify other employees with whom to compare the treatment of the disabled applicant, other than for the purpose of determining the causation question. On appeal, the Court of Appeal in *Clark v Novacold Ltd*[549] reversed the EAT's decision, and applied the second, causative approach:

> The test of less favourable treatment is based on the reason for the treatment of the disabled person and not on the fact of his disability. It does not turn on a like-for-like comparison of the treatment of the disabled person and of others in similar circumstances.

One objectionable aspect of the DDA as originally enacted was that an employer could try to justify direct discrimination even where the less favourable treatment of a disabled person was simply because that person had a disability, rather than on the basis of that person's ability to do the job (ie where the treatment was essentially for reasons of prejudice). This is not permitted by the Employment Directive, and so the DDA was modified (and the modification remains under the Equality Act) to say that less favourable treatment cannot be justified if it amounts to 'direct discrimination' ie if, *on the ground of* the disabled person's disability, the employer treats the disabled person

---

[548] [1998] IRLR 624, EAT. The earlier EAT decision in *Clark v Novacold Ltd* was not mentioned in the judgment.

[549] [1999] ICR 951, [1999] IRLR 318, CA.

less favourably than he would treat a person not having that particular disability 'whose relevant circumstances, including his abilities, are the same as, or not materially different from, those of the disabled person'.[550] Apart from a relatively straightforward case of the employer simply not liking disabled people, it remains difficult to see when this new substantive head of discrimination would apply. The one thing that is clear is that this head *did* require a comparative approach, though the exact nature of the comparison was problematic.[551]

Turning to the second issue, the degree of knowledge required on the part of the employer, in *O'Neill v Symm & Co Ltd*,[552] the first EAT decision on the DDA provisions, the EAT held that the use of the words 'for a reason which relates to the disabled person's disability' means that that the employer must have knowledge of the employee's disability, or at least the material features of it, and not merely knowledge of one or other equivocal symptom. In that case, the employee was dismissed as a result of absences from work due to chronic fatigue syndrome. The EAT held that she had not been discriminated against for a reason which related to her disability, because her employers had no knowledge of her condition, and had dismissed her solely on the grounds of uncertified absence. However, in *H J Heinz Co Ltd v Kenrick*[553] the EAT disagreed with *O'Neill*, and held that it was not necessary for the employer to have knowledge of the disability in order to be said to have acted for a reason 'which relates' to the disability; according to the EAT, the reason may include a 'reason deriving from how the disability manifests itself even where there is no knowledge of the disability as such'. The EAT used the example of a postman who successfully conceals from the employer the fact that he has an artificial leg, and who is dismissed for making his rounds too slowly. If he can show that his slowness is attributable to his artificial leg, then according to the EAT he would have been treated less favourably than others 'to whom that reason does not apply' (ie others who do their rounds at an acceptable pace) for a reason which related to his disability, whether or not the employer knew before the dismissal that the reason for the slowness was that he was disabled.

The decision in *Heinz* was consistent with the approach of the Court of Appeal in *Clark v Novacold Ltd*,[554] in that it applied an objective test of whether or not there is a causal connection between the less favourable treatment complained of and the applicant's disability, rather than a subjective test through the eyes of the employer: 'Unless the test is objective, there will be difficulties with credible and honest yet ignorant or obtuse employers who fail to recognise or acknowledge the obvious.'[555] The effect in practice was to place much greater emphasis on the question of justification, where absence of knowledge of the disability on the part of the employer may be highly material. The importance of establishing a causal connection between the conduct complained of and the applicant's disability has been illustrated in several EAT

---

[550] DDA, s 3A(5); this is reflected in the Equality Act 2010 s 23.
[551] *High Quality Lifestyles Ltd v Watts* [2006] IRLR 850, EAT.
[552] [1998] ICR 481, [1998] IRLR 233, EAT. [553] [2000] IRLR 144, EAT.
[554] [1998] IRLR 420. [555] [2000] IRLR 144 at 147, per Lindsay P.

decisions. For example in *British Gas Services Ltd v McCaull*,[556] the EAT overturned the tribunal's finding that that the applicant had been treated less favourably by the employer's failure to supply him with information about an alternative job because there was no evidence as to the reason for that failure, which could have been the result of managerial oversight or incompetence or some other reason which had nothing to do with the applicant's disability. Similarly, in *London Clubs Management Ltd v Hood*,[557] the EAT held that the employer's refusal to pay sick pay to the applicant was because of a policy not to pay sick pay generally, and was not for a reason which related to the applicant's disability.

The *Novacold* approach was settled law among employment lawyers until the House of Lords decided the housing discrimination case of *Lewisham LBC v Malcolm*.[558] Although the case did not involve an employment matter, it did involve the question of whether a like-for-like comparison was required under the DDA. The Lords decided that it did, despite the fact that this would render the ostensibly less demanding disability-related discrimination indistinguishable from the new 'direct' disability discrimination. The decision was clearly at odds with the intention of the legislation, and one can only hope that this was a situation where the Lords felt that the only way to spur Parliament to improve a messy piece of legislation was to give it an intolerable interpretation. Be that as it may, Parliament responded swiftly, introducing in the 2010 Act the definition, set out above, of 'discrimination arising from a disability'. The intention of the new language is expressly to correct the result of *Malcolm*, and to ensure that claimants can make out a disability discrimination claim even if a person without the disability would not have been affected in the same way. Although the definition has different attributes from the one considered in *Novacold*—proportionality to name one—it has the similar result that if the postman with the prosthetic leg cannot do his rounds quickly enough, the employer may dismiss him depending on how badly the employer's business is affected and whether reasonable adjustments would mitigate the effect.

The test of course replaces 'justification' with proportionality. It also makes no express reference to reasonable adjustments, where the prior definition had done so. However, under the 2010 Act the duty to make reasonable adjustments exists in section 20, and is essentially in the background of the proportionality question. Put another way, it cannot be proportionate to treat a person in a way that results in a detriment for them when reasonable adjustments are available to remove the detriment. On the other hand, if no reasonable adjustments are available, or those that are do not prevent the treatment from being detrimental to the claimant, then the question is simply whether it is proportionate to treat the person in the relevant way. This will not be a complicated analysis where the treatment is dismissal for being unable to perform the work required by the job. The analysis gets more difficult, however, if the case is more like the postman working a slow round: how slow does it have to be before it

---

[556] [2001] IRLR 60, EAT.   [557] [2001] IRLR 719, EAT.   [558] [2008] UKHL 43, [2008] IRLR 700.

is proportionate to dismiss? This begins to resemble a classic reasonable adjustments analysis, where the reasonable adjustment is a slight relaxation of standards. Some relaxation is reasonable (as we will see below), depending on the balance of the cost to the employer and the efficacy for the employee. However, it has never been claimed that the reasonable adjustment analysis is the same as proportionality, so the new definition will certainly stir things up. It would be very surprising if this new formulation does not lead to a harmonization of the reasonable adjustments analysis with the proportionality balancing.

(b) The duty to make adjustments

The 2010 Act places a duty on the employer to make reasonable adjustments where a provision, criterion or practice or any physical feature of premises occupied by the employer places the disabled person concerned at a substantial disadvantage in comparison with persons who are not disabled, in order to prevent that effect.[559] Failure to comply with the duty to make reasonable adjustments will constitute unlawful discrimination.[560] As originally enacted, the DDA allowed employers to argue that a failure to make a reasonable adjustment was justified. However, one of the most important changes in 2004 was the removal of the justification defence for failure to make a reasonable adjustment on the grounds that it was entirely covered by the need for adjustments only to be reasonable, and was therefore redundant.

In *Kenny v Hampshire Constabulary*,[561] the EAT held that the duty to make reasonable adjustments only applies to job-related arrangements, and does not extend to a duty to provide a personal carer to assist with the personal needs of a disabled employee. The DDA also listed seven factors,[562] embracing issues of cost, practicability and effectiveness, which must be taken into account in determining whether it is reasonable for an employer to have to take a particular step. The Equality Act did not carry forward this specification approach, leaving the courts and tribunals more freedom to develop the concept of reasonableness in this context. The EHRC Code of Practice (6.28) makes some suggestions about factors to consider which track fairly closely with the considerations found in the DDA: (1) the extent to which taking the step would prevent the effect in question; (2) the extent to which it is practicable for the employer to take the step; (3) the financial and other costs which would be incurred by the employer in taking the step and the extent to which taking it would disrupt any of his activities; (4) the extent of the employer's financial and other resources; (5) the availability to the

---

[559] Equality Act 2010, s 20. The EAT provided useful guidance for a tribunal dealing with an alleged failure to make reasonable adjustments in *Morse v Wiltshire County Council* [1998] ICR 1023, [1998] IRLR 352, but it is not an error of law for a tribunal not to apply that guidance, provided they properly applied themselves to considering whether the statutory requirements were satisfied: *Beart v HM Prison Service* [2003] IRLR 238, CA.

[560] Equality Act 2010, s 21. A complaint of a failure to make a reasonable adjustment does not depend upon showing that there has been less favourable treatment: *Clark v Novacold Ltd* [1998] ICR 1044, [1998] IRLR 420, EAT.

[561] [1999] ICR 27, [1999] IRLR 76, EAT.   [562] DDA, s 18B(1).

employer of financial or other assistance; and (6) the nature of the employer's activities and the size of his undertaking. The 2010 Act (section 22) provides for regulations to specify these matters but no regulations have been as yet forthcoming on this issue.

It is for the employer to satisfy the tribunal that the duty to make reasonable adjustments has been satisfied. It will not be good enough for the employer to show that the applicant was unable to think of any satisfactory adjustments if the employer has given no thought to the matter.[563] On the other hand, if there were no particular steps which the employer ought reasonably to have taken in all the circumstances, the employer will have a defence, even if he gave no consideration to the matter. As the EAT stated in *British Gas Services Ltd v McCaull*,[564] the test under section 6 is an objective one: 'The test of whether it was reasonable for an employer to have to take a particular step … does not relate to what the employer considered but to what he did and did not do'; an employer does not fail to comply with the duty merely because he has not consciously considered what steps might reasonably be taken; it followed that '[an] employer might take all reasonable steps as contemplated by section 6 while remaining ignorant of the statutory provision itself'. The duty to make adjustments does not arise if the employer does not know, and could not reasonably be expected to know, that the person has a disability which is likely to place him at a substantial disadvantage in comparison with non-disabled persons.[565]

In practice, the question of reasonable adjustments tends to be the most important aspect of disability discrimination and it has featured prominently in the recent case law. One of the most fundamental issues here is *how* a tribunal is to judge whether the employer has or has not fulfilled this duty. When it was argued that tribunals should apply a version of the band of reasonable responses (from unfair dismissal law) to the reasonableness of adjustments in *Smith v Churchill Stairlifts plc*[566] the Court of Appeal disagreed. Although there may have been some policy arguments in favour of giving the employer a 'margin of appreciation' (given how broad and ill-defined the whole idea of reasonable adjustment is), the court held that, under the wording of the DDA, the test to be applied by a tribunal was *objective*. This means that the tribunal will simply decide whether *they* consider that all reasonable adjustments were made on the facts of the case. This clearly puts this stage in the proceedings into even higher relief and makes the test potentially more difficult for the employer and more protective for the employee (and quite a bit more like proportionality). Turning to what 'reasonable adjustments' means in substance, we again see a wide and purposive approach by the courts. Any idea that it simply means ramps, wider doors and voice-activated computers is seriously misinformed. This may require a large element of lateral thinking by the employer, looking beyond the nuts and bolts of the job itself, and that approach is also

---

[563] *Cosgrove v Caesar and Howie* [2001] IRLR 653, EAT.   [564] [2001] IRLR 60, EAT.

[565] Equality Act 2010, Sch 8, para 20. See also *Eastern and Coastal Kent PCT v Grey* [2009] All ER (D) 171. In the case of a disabled applicant, the duty only applies in relation to a person who is, or has notified the employer that he may be, an applicant for the employment.

[566] [2006] ICR 524, [2006] IRLR 41, CA, distinguishing *Jones v Post Office* [2001] EWCA Civ 558.

shown in the case law. The leading authority is *Archibald v Fife Council*[567] where a council road sweeper became unable to walk. Considerable effort was put into trying to find alternative employment, but all the available posts were at higher levels, for which she would not normally be eligible. The council made the adjustment of allowing her to *apply*, but insisted on continuing with their normal (statute-backed) policy of open competition for such posts. Although she applied for many of them, there was always a better candidate and (after a considerable period) the decision was eventually taken to dismiss her. The House of Lords took a particularly liberal approach to her position and held that the council had *not* made all reasonable adjustments. They construed the reference in section 18D(2)(c) to 'transferring him to fill an existing vacancy' to mean, where necessary, actually *appointing* her to such a vacancy, in preference to a better-qualified candidate. The decision emphasizes the difference between the SDA/RRA model and the disability discrimination legislation which, as seen above, has *no* correlative rights for non-disabled people; it is also notable for a now well-known remark by Lady Hale that 'to the extent that the duty to make reasonable adjustments requires it, the employer is not only permitted but obliged to treat a disabled person more favourably than others'.[568]

However, even a concept as elastic as reasonable adjustments must have limits; for example, it is not reasonable to expect an employer to allow early, ill-health retirement because the worker's disability no longer allows him to perform his work.[569] In two particular areas the case law has shown an eventual resiling from earlier, more extensive views, showing that this whole area is likely to remain one of continuing efforts to strike the appropriate balance. The first area concerns consultation with the disabled employee. Clearly, this is good practice (if necessary with risk assessments), but earlier case law went further and held that consultation was itself a reasonable adjustment, with failure to comply likely to lead to unlawful discrimination.[570] However, this was reassessed by the EAT under Elias P in *Tarbuck v Sainsbury's Supermarkets Ltd*[571] where it was held that to elevate consultation to this level compromises the essentially objective nature of the test and is legally wrong. The second area has been much debated in the past—given that the employer has to look beyond the physical requirements of the job, can this mean that even the employee's *contractual terms* may have to be reasonably adjusted? This becomes relevant whenever the DDA abuts against an employer's contractual sick pay scheme. Given that such a scheme will tend to allow a fixed period on sick pay, two questions have arisen—(1) in working out the employee's maximum

---

[567] [2004] ICR 954, [2004] IRLR 651, HL. In *Southampton City College v Randall* [2006] IRLR 18, EAT it was even held that the employer should have *created* a job for the disabled employee, but that was on particular facts (in particular that the college was at the time going through a 'blank sheet of paper' exercise in restructuring all jobs).

[568] At para [68].

[569] *Tameside Hospital NHS Foundation Trust v Mylott* UKEAT/0352/09, UKEAT/0399/10 (11 March 2011, unreported).

[570] *Mid-Staffs General Hospitals NHS Trust v Cambridge* [2003] IRLR 566, EAT; *Rothwell v Pelikan Ltd* [2006] IRLR 24, EAT.

[571] [2006] IRLR 664, EAT.

period of entitlement, must the employer 'strip out' any sickness absence due to the employee's disability? (2) going even further, if long-term sickness is because of the disability, should the employer disapply the normal sick pay rules and continue to pay full pay for the whole period? In favour of employees, it was argued that both of these should be viewed as reasonable adjustments (especially after the expansive decision in *Archibald*) and indeed in *Nottinghamshire CC v Meikle*[572] the Court of Appeal considered that version (2) would indeed have been a reasonable adjustment. However, that was on peculiar facts, in that the employee's absence with stress (the disability relied on) had itself been caused by the employer's failure to deal properly with the problem that he had been having with worsening eyesight. *Meikle* was thus always a fragile authority, and the subsequent case law showed a very different approach. With regard to issue (1) above in *Royal Liverpool Children's NHS Trust v Dunsby*[573] the EAT under Judge Richardson held that there is no rule that disability-related absences must be disregarded, thus leaving it as a matter of fact. However, in *O'Hanlon v HMRC*[574] the EAT under Elias P went further in relation to issue (2) and held that an employer will *not* be expected to disapply normal sick pay contractual rules for a disability-related absence; to do so would, they said, act as a deterrent to employing disabled people (thus frustrating the policy behind the legislation), and *Meikle* was distinguished as exceptional, only applying where the employer has caused the disability in the first place. When *O'Hanlon* went on further appeal, the Court of Appeal strongly backed this decision of the EAT.[575]

Employment lawyers have wondered for some time whether the relatively high cost of an adjustment, which clearly can be taken into account, can stand alone as the sole reason for finding a requested adjustment unreasonable. The EAT answered this question in the affirmative in *Cordell v Foreign and Commonwealth Office*.[576] Although the opinion makes it clear that all of the relevant factors such as efficacy, size of undertaking, and even what the employer and similar employers have been prepared to spend in the past must be considered, in the end the decision of the employer turned on its conclusion that the cost of the adjustment was simply unpalatable, even though strictly speaking it could be afforded. The claimant, who was profoundly deaf, needed lip-speakers in order to occupy a post for which she was qualified and otherwise would hold, but the cost of this provision was expressed as 'five times the Claimant's salary' annually. A crucial fact was that the respondent had a policy of paying for the children of its ambassadors to attend private, British-style schools and travel three times a year to visit their ambassador parents, so where an employee had five or more children the costs under that policy could rival those of the necessary lip-speakers. The EAT held that the tribunal had considered the competing factors appropriately, and had taken account of the education expense policy (which would have applied to the claimant had she become a parent), and had reached a lawful decision that the lip-speaker

---

[572] [2004] IRLR 703, CA.   [573] [2006] IRLR 751, EAT.   [574] [2006] IRLR 840, EAT.
[575] [2007] EWCA Civ 283.   [576] [2012] ICR 280, [2012] All ER (D) 97.

expense was unreasonable under the circumstances. This case does not mean that 'five times the claimant's salary' will become any kind of test: the EAT denied any such holding. However, it does supply precedent for the idea that cost can make an adjustment unreasonable even if the employer can afford that cost and has decided to afford it for other objectives. It would not be surprising to find this issue reconsidered in a later case, given that it appears to license employers to place disability adjustments below other employee interests in its budgetary priorities.

8 AGE DISCRIMINATION IN EMPLOYMENT

The final part of this chapter's discussion of discrimination law addresses age discrimination. At the 1997 election New Labour indicated a desire to legislate on this inherently difficult area, but the only result was a low-key and anodyne code of practice that had little effect. One other false start was an attempt to produce a version of age discrimination by the use of existing sex discrimination law attacking the age limit on unfair dismissal of 65 at 'normal retirement age' as being indirectly discriminatory against men.[577] This was eventually disapproved by the House of Lords in *Secretary of State for Trade and Industry v Rutherford*,[578] which at least had the merit of avoiding the daunting prospect of any case-produced age law having retrospective effect.

The pace of change was eventually forced by the inclusion of age in the Equal Treatment Directive 2000/78/EC, which (because of the complexities here) gave member states until October 2006 to comply. This time was taken up in the UK with extensive consultations,[579] leading eventually to the Employment Equality (Age) Regulations 2006.[580] One feature of this relatively long period of introduction was the way that the proposals changed; in two particular ways (both relating to the key area of retirement policy) this amounted to significant watering-down—(1) the original proposals would have allowed the employee to challenge the bona fides of an employer relying on retirement for termination, but that did not appear in the final form of the Regulations (which *deemed* a dismissal to be for retirement, provided the employer goes through the right procedure) and (2) early proposals indicated a pure version of age discrimination with *no* compulsory retirement age, but this was changed to 70 and (in the final form) to 65. These and other issues meant legal challenges to the Regulations (as not transposing the Directive properly). The most significant of these was the so-called 'Heydey application', *National Council on Ageing (Age Concern) v SoS*

---

[577] An adventurous tribunal had accepted this argument in *Nash v Mash/Roe Group Ltd* [1998] IRLR 168 but an intended appeal to the EAT failed to happen because of the claimant's death.

[578] [2006] ICR 785, [2006] IRLR 551, HL.

[579] See particularly *Equality and Diversity: Age Matters* (DTI, 2003) and *Equality and Diversity: Coming of Age* (DTI, 2005).

[580] SI 2006/1031; See *Harvey* R [2313] and Sargeant 'The Employment Equality (Age) Regulations 2006: a Legitimisation of Age Discrimination in Employment' (2006) 35 ILJ 209.

for BERR.[581] The ECJ ruled that the Regulations, which allowed for compulsory retirement and the justification of direct age discrimination, were not necessarily in direct
violation of the Equal Treatment Framework Directive. Both compulsory retirement
and justification of discrimination could be acceptable provided those provisions pursued a legitimate aim proportionately. The case was essentially kicked back to the UK
courts to assess the provisions on the facts. In the High Court Blake J ruled that with
appropriate assessment of proportionality in each case justification of direct discrimination was proportionate to a legitimate aim, and that while a compulsory retirement
age was in principle acceptable, he doubted that an age of 65 could be justified in the
current economic climate (the facts before him related to 2006, so his decision put
pressure on to reconsider the age of 65).[582] Any changes that this decision might have
encouraged the government to make did not make it into the 2010 Act, which followed
the pattern of the 2006 Regulations with regard to retirement, justification and exceptions, but of course used the 'because of' language and the other slight adjustments
applicable to all of the protected characteristics. However, the Coalition government,
elected shortly after the 2010 Act was adopted, soon began a consultation on the
Act's default retirement age provisions, which had been carried over from the 2006
Regulations. This resulted in the repeal of the default retirement age—not just at 65
but at any age—in 2011 with the effect that the last default retirement at 65 should
have been in October 2012.[583] Thus the Equality Act age provision acts much the same
as the 2006 Regulations except that the default retirement age is not more (as will
be discussed, this does not mean that employees may not be compelled to retire at a
given age, just that they must justify this on a case-by-case basis). The most useful aid
to understanding and applying the age discrimination provisions is contained in the
ACAS publication 'Guidance on Age in the Workplace' which contains details of the
legal obligations, specific advice on retirement policies and suggested best practice.
What follows concentrates on three main areas—the meaning of age discrimination,
the exceptions and retirement.

(i) THE MEANING OF AGE DISCRIMINATION

The 2010 Act protects against age discrimination in the standard ways with regard to
direct and indirect discrimination, harassment, and victimization. However, there is
then one *major* difference from all other heads of illegal discrimination. This is that
the Equality Act 2010, section 13(2) prescribes that direct age discrimination is not
discrimination if it is a proportionate means of achieving a legitimate aim: direct discrimination can be justified.[584] How widely this will apply will be a key issue in the
development of this law. It is such a departure from usual discrimination law that it
is possible that the tribunals and courts will give it a narrow interpretation, casting

---

[581] Case C-388/07.   [582] [2009] EWCH 2336 (Admin).
[583] The Employment Equality (Repeal of Retirement Age Provisions) Regulations 2011, SI 2011/1069, s 5.
[584] Swift 'Justifying Age Discrimination' (2006) 35 ILJ 228.

a heavy burden on to the employer to establish it. It has so far been used to justify enhanced redundancy schemes,[585] points for long service in a redundancy selection process,[586] and retirement[587] (this is discussed in the next section, but without a default retirement age requiring a person to retire is in theory direct age discrimination and must be justified). In short, it appears generally possible to justify awarding benefits to older workers to reward long service, which is already provided for by specific exceptions discussed below, and to dismiss them owing to advanced age. One argument in favour of a narrow reading is that the employer also has access to the specific 'genuine occupational requirement' defence in Schedule 9. The ACAS Guidance suggests that this defence will only apply in 'very limited circumstances'. It gives the example of an organization protecting the interests of the elderly which *may* be able to show that it is essential to have a chief executive of a certain age. On the other hand, in one consultation document the DTI suggested that restricting applications for a job working in a shop selling clothing for young people to those of a certain age would *not* come within this defence. The answer here may lie in reliance (at selection stage) on defined 'competences' for the job (eg ability to deal and empathize with the dominant customer group), rather than any age bias. This is not cynicism: a focus on competences may produce the right result without the use of age stereotypes.[588]

(ii) EXCEPTIONS

A specific exception is created for age discrimination in relation to the national minimum wage,[589] to enable the government to continue to have different rates based on age (which they maintain is objectively justified). However, of much greater importance for existing pay systems are two other exceptions found in Schedule 9 of the Equality Act. The first relates to certain benefits based on length of service.[590] Payment by (or, at least, enhancements in respect of) length of service are common and the government were keen not to render them unlawful at a stroke. On the other hand, they do have an indirectly discriminatory effect on younger employees. Even a straightforward justification defence might be difficult, for example where by long practice there has been a lengthy pay spine (with annual increments) but the facts show that it only takes x years to reach a level of competence in that job. Why should the pay continue to increase beyond x years? This issue featured heavily at consultation stage. As it happens, service-related pay was also at the time under attack in equal pay law and, although the government eventually saw off the major challenge to civil service increment-based pay in the CJEU,[591] there has in some areas been emphasis on (at the least) *shortening*

---

[585] *MacCulloch v ICI* [2008] All ER (D) 81.   [586] *Rolls Royce v UNITE* [2008] All ER (D) 174.
[587] *Seldon v Clarkson Wright and Jakes* [2012] UKSC 16.
[588] There could of course still be of challenge on the basis of indirect discrimination, and so the employer would still have to justify the relevant competence.
[589] Equality Act 2010, Sch 9, para 11.   [590] Equality Act 2010, Sch 9, para 10.
[591] *Cadman v HSE* C-17/05 [2006] IRLR 969, ECJ.

pay spines and putting less emphasis on service because of future uncertainties. The eventual compromise reached is, in effect, to give an employer five years' grace. It states that where an employee's length of service exceeds five years, a service-related pay difference will only be lawful if it reasonably appears to the employer that the way in which he uses the criterion of length of service, in relation to the award that puts that employee at a disadvantages, fulfils a business need of his undertaking (for example, by encouraging the loyalty or motivation, or rewarding the experience, of some or all of his workers). Case law on this will be of great interest. The one thing that is clear is that justification in these terms will not be shown simply by the *cri de coeur* that 'we've always done it that way' (even if backed by custom and practice and/or longstanding union agreements). The second exception relates to contractual redundancy payment terms. The government took the view that the existing age-weighting in the statutory redundancy payments scheme[592] was objectively justified; to mirror this, Schedule 9, paragraph 13 provides that a contractual scheme can lawfully give enhanced benefits *provided* that the basic method of calculating entitlement remains in line with the statutory scheme.

(iii) RETIREMENT

Retirement of an employee at 65 or the normal retirement age (if different) was not legally an issue under the pre-Age Regulations law because an employee at or beyond that age could not claim unfair dismissal.[593] That exclusion was repealed, and so an employee of any age can now claim unfair dismissal.[594] One 'pure' version of age discrimination would have been to leave it at that, ie with no compulsory (or even fall-back) retirement age, so that an employee could choose to carry on working to any age (subject to a dismissal for incapability). The government decided not to go for such a radical approach. It floated the idea of a default retirement age of 70, and eventually fixed it at 65 (subject to review in 2011). In doing so, it put in place an exhaustive statutory regime to deal with retirement cases, but split this between the Employment Equality Age Regulations 2006 themselves and (inserted) sections 98ZA to 98ZH into the Employment Rights Act 1996. This arrangement persisted under the 2010 Act until the 2011 repeal of the default retirement age, which eliminated, inter alia, sections 8 and 9 of Schedule 9 and sections 98ZA to 98ZH of the ERA 1996 (confused yet?). The Coalition government deserves credit for the fact that Europe did not impose this repeal on the UK: the CJEU has approved laws that adopt a default retirement age, but in doing so has subjected them to intense scrutiny in connection with the legitimacy of their aims and the proportionality of the laws in achieving them.[595] The

---

[592] See Ch 8, heading 1(iv), p 580.

[593] Employment Rights Act 1996, s 109, repealed by the Employment Equality Age Regulations 2006, SI 20061031 as from 1 October 2006.

[594] Note that this applies whatever the ground of dismissal; it is not confined to retirement cases.

[595] *Fuchs and Kohler v Land Hessen* C-159/10, C-160/10, [2011] All ER (D) 97; *Hörnfeldt v Posten Meddelande* C-141/11, [2012] IRLR 785.

result is not quite the 'pure' position described above because compulsory retirement, which is direct discrimination, can be justified if it is proportionate to a legitimate aim. However, employers can no longer assume that a compulsory retirement at the default age will be lawful so long as they pursue the proper procedure, which was the position from 2006 to 2011: they must justify each retirement, or their retirement policy, based on specific circumstances of their operation.

The 2006 Regulations contained a detailed procedure imposing on an employer a duty to consider a request by an employee to work beyond the date on which the employer wished to retire him or her. An employer wanting to retire an employee compulsorily had to notify him or her in writing of the right to make a request *and* the intended retirement date, between six months and a year before the latter date.[596] The employee was allowed to make a written request to work past the intended date (either indefinitely, for a stated period or until a stated date) in the period from six to three months before that intended date. Now none of this is necessary. Employers are left—subject to advice from the ACAS Guidance—to decide whether to justify each retirement or adopt a company policy (in the employment contract or employee handbook) that sets a compulsory or presumptive retirement age. If they look to adopt a policy, the Supreme Court has provided some helpful signposts in *Seldon v Clarkson Wright and Jakes*.[597] The case involved a law firm's partnership agreement, which called for partners to retire at 65. The case had at its heart the thorny, esoteric question of whether the legitimate aims used by the company to justify direct discrimination had to be the same aims as those used by the government to derogate from the Framework Directive[598] to allow the justification of direct age discrimination. The Court held that the aims of the firm did not need to be the precise aims set out in Article 6 of the Directive (employment policy, labour market and vocational training objectives) nor even the aims identified by the government in taking advantage of the exception. Instead, the employer's aims need only be consistent with those objectives:

> [The firm] identified three aims for the compulsory retirement age, which the Court of Appeal summed up as 'dead men's shoes' and 'collegiality'. [Counsel for the claimant] has argued that these were individual aims of the business rather than the sort of social policy aims contemplated by the Directive. I do not think that that is fair. The first two identified aims were staff retention and workforce planning, both of which are directly related to the legitimate social policy aim of sharing out professional employment opportunities fairly between the generations (and were recognised as legitimate in *Fuchs*). The third was limiting the need to expel partners by way of performance management, which is directly related to the 'dignity' aims accepted in *Rosenbladt* and *Fuchs*. It is also clear that the aims

---

[596] Schedule 6, para 2. If the employer failed to do so, there was a continuing duty to inform up to 14 days before termination: para 4.

[597] [2012] UKSC 16.

[598] Council Directive 2000/78/EC of 27 November 2000 establishing a general framework for equal treatment in employment and occupation.

can be related to the particular circumstances of the type of business concerned ... I would therefore accept that the identified aims were legitimate.[599]

The Court also held that a general policy, as opposed to each retirement on its own merits, could be justified, but that the use of a general policy must be a proportionate means to the legitimate objectives, which in this case it was. Once the use of a general policy has been justified, each individual retirement under it is presumed justified.

This decision seems, to the authors, to take some liberties with the Framework Directive and the CJEU case law. Both seem to suggest that a national law, such as one that adopts a default retirement age under specified circumstances or for specified vocations, can be justified on social grounds. However, it is a big leap to say that, where a government chooses not to go through all of the policy research and democratic processes to create such a law, it can allow individual employers to adopt policies with the same effect as long as their aims are merely consistent with those set out in the Directive. The authors suspect that the members of the Court simply could not face the alternative of requiring that every retirement be individually justified: it is easy to sympathize with that. Whether the CJEU will feel the same remains to be seen. Many think that the subsequent CJEU decision in *Hörnfeldt*[600] has already lowered the bar set in *Seldon*, but *Hörnfeldt* concerned the viability of a legal framework that allowed employers to impose compulsory retirement on their workers at age 67, not the viability of a company policy of doing so in the absence of a legal framework for retirement. Be that as it may, *Seldon* is the law in the UK, and it makes it clear that employers *can* adopt a retirement policy, but that they had better consider very carefully their reasons for doing so, whether they are consistent with the policies in the Directive, and whether a general policy is a proportionate means of achieving them (eg, is there a way of achieving those aims that does not require direct age discrimination?). Given that state of affairs employers will almost certainly (they had better) put a lot more thought into retirement decisions than they have been accustomed to thus far.

---

[599] [2012] UKSC 16 at [67].   [600] C-141/11, [2012] IRLR 785

6

CONTRACTS OF EMPLOYMENT (3): DISCHARGE AT COMMON LAW

OVERVIEW

Before going on to the more high-profile area of unfair dismissal, this chapter looks at termination of employment at common law. Employees have rights to have their contracts terminated properly under contract law, but the common law can also be a threat to employees rather than a help. The chapter first discusses ways (such as frustration, death or mutual consent) in which the contract might untypically end by operation of law rather than the 'dismissal' on which many employee rights (contractual or statutory) rest. It then considers the right of either party to terminate most contracts by giving notice—a major feature of UK employment law—and the ability of the employer (unaffected by modern unfair dismissal law) to dismiss summarily for gross misconduct. The chapter concludes with a detailed analysis of the principal remedy for an employee at common law: the action for wrongful dismissal. This common law action is completely separate and different from the statutory unfair dismissal, despite an unfortunate tendency for the press to treat them as interchangeable. The emphasis will be on showing that for most ordinary employees wrongful dismissal has never been a very worthwhile action, hardly ever leading to reinstatement and often capable of giving only limited damages.

1 MODES OF TERMINATION OTHER THAN DISMISSAL

Dismissal acts as a prerequisite to some important common law and statutory rights, but there are certain ways in which employment may be terminated other than simply by dismissal. One of the themes that runs through them is that they are founded on old common law principles established at a time when an employee had few rights and so the concept of continuity of employment was of little significance. As a result these hoary doctrines are now heavily qualified (though not actually abrogated) by specialized statutory provisions aimed at mitigating their potentially harsh application to modern employment rights. One such provision is the Employment Rights Act 1996, section 136, which (along with section 139) provides that, for the purposes of claiming redundancy payments, where an act of the employer or an event affecting the employer (including his death) has the effect of terminating the contract of employment by operation of law, that is deemed to be a termination by the employer (ie a dismissal) and is further deemed to be by reason of redundancy if that is the real reason behind the failure to continue employing the employee. This will go far towards safeguarding the employee's redundancy rights in most cases of death, dissolution or frustration. However, there remain areas not yet covered by ameliorating statutory provisions where the employment lawyer (particularly when representing the employee) has to beware of the sudden emergence of arguments based on common law notions of discharge of employment which, if accepted, can do great harm to statutory rights; a good example is the effect of the doctrine of frustration on certain unfair dismissal actions.

(i) DEATH OR DISSOLUTION OF THE ENTERPRISE

At common law, death would bring the contract of employment to an end, whether it be the death of the employee[1] or the employer, as in *Farrow v Wilson*[2] where the personal representatives were held not to be liable to continue the engagement of the employee. The employee is discharged from further performance on the death of the employer, not through any breach of contract, but as the result of an implied condition that the continued existence of the parties is an essential of the contract. This position is now qualified by statute in three ways. First, if the business does not carry on after the employer's death, the termination of employment is deemed to be a dismissal for redundancy under the Employment Rights Act 1996, sections 136, 139, so the employee may claim a redundancy payment from the employer's personal representatives.[3] Secondly, if the deceased employer's business is carried on by his personal representatives and the employee continues to work for them there is deemed to be no termination for redundancy purposes,[4] and his continuity of employment for general purposes is not broken.[5] Thirdly, where it is the employee who dies, any pending

---

[1] *Stubbs v Holywell Rly Co* (1867) LR 2 Exch 311; *Graves v Cohen* (1929) 46 TLR 121.
[2] (1869) LR 4 CP 744.   [3] Employment Rights Act 1996, s 206(3).
[4] Section 174. It must be shown on the acts that the personal representatives did renew the contract or re-engage the employee, but in practice the longer he continues to work for them the easier this will be to infer (in the absence of express agreement): *Ranger v Brown* [1978] ICR 603, EAT.
[5] Section 218(4).

proceedings of his before an employment tribunal may be instituted or continued by his personal representatives (or by other persons appointed by the tribunal if there are no personal representatives) and if he dies whilst under notice of dismissal he will be treated for the purposes of unfair dismissal and redundancy as if he had actually been dismissed.[6]

In practice of course most employees will be employed by partnerships or companies which do not die, but they may be dissolved or wound up in certain ways, and the operation of these processes of law upon the contracts of employment concerned must now be considered.

In the case of a partnership, where a partners dies and there is a consequent dissolution of the partnership, the contract of employment will be discharged wherever it is one related to the personal conduct of the deceased person. In *Harvey v Tivoli (Manchester) Ltd*[7] the death of a member of a troupe of three music hall artists was held to discharge the contract though he had been replaced, and the troupe was ready to appear. In *Phillips v Alhambra Palace Co*[8] one of the defendant partners had died after a contract had been entered into with the plaintiffs, who were also music hall artists. In this case it was held that the obligation continued despite the death of the partner, for the obligation was not of a personal character and the partners, when they booked the artists to appear, were not individually known. In the first case the contract was with three specific persons—in the second case it was with a firm and the personal element was not paramount. A dissolution of a partnership on account of the retirement of a partner may operate as a wrongful dismissal at common law but the modern approach is that there is no absolute rule, so that it depends on all the circumstances and the intent and acts of the parties,[9] in particular a continuance of employment under a firm containing some of the old partners may amount to a waiver of common law rights of action.[10] Under statute, even if the dissolution did not constitute a dismissal per se (which it almost certainly does) it would be deemed to be such for redundancy purposes under the Employment Rights Act 1996, section 136, and where the employee continues in the reconstituted firm's employment his continuity of employment is safeguarded by section 218(5) of that Act.

In the case of a company, the legal position is complex.[11] The position seems to be as follows. An order of the court for a compulsory winding up of the company operates

---

[6] Section 206; Employment Tribunals Awards (Enforcement in Case of Death) Regulations 1976, SI 1976/663.

[7] (1907) 23 TLR 592; *Tunstall v Condon* [1980] ICR 786.

[8] [1901] 1 KB 59.

[9] *Rose v Dodd* [2005] ICR 1776, [205] IRLR 977, CA, considering the longstanding authority of *Brace v Calder* [1895] 2 QB 253, CA; see also *Briggs v Oates* [1990] ICR 473, [1990] IRLR 472.

[10] *Hobson v Cowley* (1858) 27 LJ Ex 205.

[11] See Davies and Freedland 'The Effects of Receivership upon Employees of Companies' (1980) 9 ILJ 95; Pollard *Corporate Insolvency: Employment and Pension Rights* (2nd edn, 2000). Questions of continuity of employment may be covered separately by the Transfer of Undertakings (Protection of Employment) Regulations 2006, SI 2006/246; see Ch 8, heading 2, p 604, and *Rose v Dodd* [2005] ICR 1776, [2005] IRLR 977, CA.

as notice of dismissal to its employees.[12] The effect of a voluntary winding up depends upon whether the business is to be carried on in some form (as for example where it has been taken over by another company); if it is to carry on *Midland Counties District Bank Ltd v Attwood*[13] decided that it does not operate as notice of dismissal, but if there is no intention of carrying on, then it may so operate, as in the case of a compulsory order.[14] The appointment of a receiver is a less drastic step than an immediate winding up, but once again the rules are complicated. The appointment of a receiver by the court terminates contracts of employment,[15] but the appointment of a receiver out of court by the debenture holders, as agent for the company, does not have that effect,[16] except perhaps in four cases:

(1)   where the receiver is appointed to act as agent for the creditors only, not for the company;[17]

(2)   where the receiver sells the business, so that there is no continuation;

(3)   where the receiver enters a new contract of employment with the employee in question which is inconsistent with the existence of the old one;

(4)   where the continuation of the contract of employment is inconsistent with the appointment of the receiver because of the nature of the employment; this may be the case with a managing director, but is not necessarily so and will depend upon all the facts of the case.[18]

The case law on these points is at times confusing, for though most of the cases envisage the effect of one of these events, if any, to be the giving of notice, some are capable of pointing to instant dismissal (as by operation of law) which, as has been pointed out,[19] could jeopardize common law rights of the employee.

(ii) FRUSTRATION OF THE CONTRACT

It is a general principle of the law of contract that a contract will be terminated automatically if it is frustrated.[20] A contract is frustrated if a change of law or circumstances

---

[12] *Re General Rolling Stock Co (Chapman's Case)* (1866) LR 1 Eq 346; *Re Oriental Bank Corpn Ltd (MacDowall's Case)* (1886) 32 Ch D 366.

[13] [1905] 1 Ch 357.

[14] *Fowler v Commercial Timber Co Ltd* [1930] 2 KB 1, CA: *Reigate v Union Manufacturing Co Ltd* [1918] 1 KB 592, CA; *Fox Bros (Clothes) Ltd v Bryant* [1979] ICR 64, [1978] IRLR 485, EAT.

[15] *Reid v Explosives Co* (1887) 19 QBD 264, CA; *Re Foster Clark Ltd's Indenture Trusts* [1966] 1 All ER 43, [1966] 1 WLR 125; cf *Pambakian v Brentford Nylons Ltd* [1978] ICR 665, EAT.

[16] *Re Foster Clark Ltd's Indenture Trusts* [1966] 1 All ER 43, [1966] 1 WLR 125; *Re Mack Trucks (Britain) Ltd* [1967] 1 All ER 977, [1967] 1 WLR 780; *Nicoll v Cutts* [1985] BCLC 322, CA.

[17] *Hopley Dodd v Highfield Motors (Derby) Ltd* (1969) 4 ITR 289.

[18] On exceptions (2)–(4), see *Griffiths v Secretary of State for Social Services* [1974] QB 468, [1973] 3 All ER 1184.

[19] *Re Patent Floor Cloth Co* (1872) 41 LJ Ch 476 at 477, per Bacon V-C.

[20] *Davis Contractors Ltd v Fareham UDC* [1956] AC 696, [1956] 2 All ER 145, HL. See Mogridge 'Frustration, Employment Contracts and Statutory Rights' [1982] NLJ 795.

makes the contract impossible to perform or makes the result of performance radically different from what was originally undertaken in the contract. This doctrine of frustration applies to contracts of employment. Thus in *Morgan v Manser*[21] it was held that the calling-up for military service of a music-hall artist frustrated the contract which he had with his manager, and Streatfeild J formulated the test as follows:

> If there is an event or change of circumstances which is so fundamental as to be regarded by the law as striking at the root of the contract as a whole, and as going beyond what was contemplated by the parties and such that to hold the parties to the contract would be to bind them to terms which they would not have made had they contemplated that event or those circumstances, then the contract is frustrated by that event immediately and irrespective of the volition or the intention of the parties, or their knowledge as to that particular event, and this even though they have continued for a time to treat the contract as still subsisting.

The effects of this doctrine on the contract of employment are threefold:

(1) If the contract is frustrated it is terminated automatically, and immediately upon the happening of a frustrating event; there is no need, for example, for the employer to take any steps to terminate the contract or even to indicate that he regards it as terminated.[22]

(2) As a consequence of (1), there is no right to any back pay from the date of frustration until any other date (for example a date, if any, on which the employer indicated that he thought the contract had ended).[23]

(3) If the contract of employment is frustrated, its termination is due to the operation of law, and not to dismissal (either at common law or under the Employment Rights Act 1996, section 95 or 136) which could have a serious effect on certain common law and statutory rights, particularly unfair dismissal, which may only be claimed if the employee is dismissed.[24]

For an event or circumstance to frustrate the contract of employment it must be exceptionally grave. Certain wartime factors have been held to have the effect of frustration,

---

[21] [1948] 1 KB 184, [1947] 2 All ER 666; the passage cited is at 191 and 670 respectively.

[22] *Marshall v Harland & Wolff Ltd* [1972] 2 All ER 715, [1972] ICR 101, disapproving suggestions to the contrary in *Thomas v John Drake & Co Ltd* (1971) 6 ITR 146; it is not necessary to be able to date the frustrating event precisely, which is particularly significant in the case of frustration through illness. See also *Egg Stores (Stamford Hill) Ltd v Leibovici* [1977] ICR 260, [1976] IRLR 376, EAT.

[23] *Unger v Preston Corpn* [1942] 1 All ER 200. However, any wages due up to the date of frustration may be claimed under the Law Reform (Frustrated Contracts) Act 1943, either under s 2(4) if the contract can be regarded as divisible and the employee has fully performed those severable parts before the date of frustration, or under s 1(3) if the wages concerned were not actually due at that date but it would be just in all the circumstances for the court to award a sum representing the work done up to that date.

[24] However, where the frustrating event is one relating to the employer (for example his death or the destruction of his business), s 136(5) of the 1996 Act safeguards the employee's rights to a redundancy payment by deeming that termination to be a dismissal, and this will apply even if the event applies to both employer and employee (for example the passing of new legislation making the whole employment in question illegal), for it is enough that some of the effect is upon the employer: *Fenerty v British Airports Authority* (1976) 11 ITR 1.

such as being called up or interned.[25] However, in practice the most important event is illness on the part of the employee, for if it is sufficiently grave to frustrate the contract the employee will lose any potential rights which he may have to claim unfair dismissal or redundancy (the latter because this is not an event befalling the employer, so not covered by the Employment Rights Act 1996, section 136(5)). In *Poussard v Spiers*[26] an opera singer was ill during rehearsals for the opera for which she was engaged, and could not take part in the first four performances; this was held to frustrate the contract so that her employer was entitled to treat the contract as ended. This was also the case in *Condor v Barron Knights Ltd*[27] where the employee was physically unable to play with the pop group in question for seven nights per week through illness and this was held to be a frustration, particularly as the group could not operate on anything less than full time and could not reasonably operate with a part-time substitute. However, some care may be needed with certain theatrical cases, for a court or tribunal may be more ready to find frustration in the case of a short-term contract entered with a particular performance or set of performances in mind. It may be more difficult to establish in the case of a longstanding employment of a permanent nature,[28] particularly in view of the old common law principle that in general the consideration for wages is readiness and willingness to serve on the employee's part, not necessarily the performance of actual work.[29] As the question of frustration through illness is so important in the context of the statutory rights, it was reviewed by the NIRC in *Marshall v Harland and Wolff Ltd*[30] where Sir John Donaldson P laid down the following factors to be weighed by a tribunal in deciding whether a contract was frustrated:

(1) the terms of the contract, including any provisions as to sick pay;

(2) how long the employment was likely to last in the absence of sickness, for a temporary or specific hiring is more likely to be frustrated;

(3) the nature of the employment, in particular whether the employee was in a 'key post' which had to be filled permanently if his absence was prolonged;[31] or whether it was such that it could be held open for a considerable period;[32]

---

[25] *Horlock v Beal* [1916] 1 AC 486, HL; *Marshall v Glanvill* [1917] 2 KB 87; *Morgan v Manser* [1948] 1 KB 184, [1947] 2 All ER 666; *Unger v Preston Corpn* [1942] 1 All ER 200. However, even something as potentially drastic as internment must have a substantial effect and not be merely transitory: *Nordman v Rayner and Sturges* (1916) 33 TLR 87.

[26] (1876) 1 QBD 410; cf *Bettini v Gye* (1876) 1 QBD 183, where a singer's illness incapacitated her for the rehearsals but not for any of the performances, and this was held not to be a frustration.

[27] [1966] 1 WLR 87.

[28] See eg *Storey v Fulham Steel Works Co* (1907) 24 TLR 89, CA.

[29] *Warburton v Co-operative Wholesale Society Ltd* [1917] 1 KB 663, CA; *Henthorn v Central Electricity Generating Board* [1980] IRLR 361, CA.

[30] [1972] 2 All ER 715, [1972] ICR 101.   [31] *Hebden v Forsey & Son* [1973] ICR 607, [1973] IRLR 344.

[32] *Maxwell v Walter Howard Designs Ltd* [1975] IRLR 77, IT.

(4) the nature of the illness, how long it has continued and the prospects of recovery; this may interact with (3) in that if there is no urgency for a replacement, a more distant prospect of recovery may keep the contract alive;

(5) the period of past employment, for 'a relationship which is of long standing is not so easily destroyed as one which has but a short history'.

Tribunals have regularly followed these guidelines, but in *Egg Stores (Stamford Hill) Ltd v Leibovici*[33] the EAT pointed out that they raise a particular difficulty in the case of short-term periodic contracts of employment, which may be determined at short notice, for although the doctrine of frustration is necessary in longer term contracts if it has become impossible for the employee to perform his part, in the case of the short-term contract the employer has the more ready remedy of dismissal on relatively short notice, which may be more appropriate in the circumstances than reliance upon frustration. In the light of this, although frustration has succeeded in such cases (and the EAT reaffirmed that where this is the case it operates automatically without the necessity of any steps being taken by the employer), in these cases more emphasis may be placed upon whether the employer has thought it right to dismiss the absent employee for, if he has not done so, the tribunal *might* infer that the reason was that he did not think that enough time had elapsed to make it a proper course to take, and that would be a strong inference against frustration. The EAT then said that a short-term periodic contract could be subject to an event (for example a crippling accident) so drastic that it was obvious that it was frustrated, but that in the more normal case of a lingering illness there are further matters to be taken into account along with those in *Marshall*'s case; these are:

(6) the risk to the employer of incurring obligations (in respect of redundancy payments and unfair dismissal) to an employee meant to be a replacement;

(7) whether wages have continued to be paid;

(8) the acts and statements of the employer in relation to the employment, in particular whether there has been a dismissal of sorts and if not, why not;[34]

(9) whether in all the circumstances a reasonable employer could be expected to wait any longer.

All of these factors must be weighed by the tribunal which will probably be loath to find frustration. If the contract is not frustrated and the employer is found to have dismissed the employee, a claim for unfair dismissal may proceed which must be decided in the normal way,[35] and it has been stated that the tests laid down in *Marshall*'s case are those for frustration, *not* those for deciding whether a dismissal for ill-health is

---

[33] [1977] ICR 260, [1976] IRLR 376, further discussed in *Hart v AR Marshall & Sons (Bulwell) Ltd* [1977] ICR 539, [1977] IRLR 51 and *Williams v Watsons Luxury Coaches Ltd* [1990] ICR 536, [1990] IRLR 164.

[34] Emphasized in *Hart v A R Marshall & Sons (Bulwell) Ltd* [1977] ICR 539, [1977] IRLR 51.

[35] See Ch 7, heading 4, p 497.

reasonable,[36] though if the further factors in the *Egg Stores* case are applied, in particular factor (1) above, the two tests do begin to look somewhat similar.[37]

At one point, the whole question of the application of the doctrine of frustration to contracts of employment was thrown into confusion by the decision of the EAT in *Harman v Flexible Lamps Ltd*[38] where it was held not only that the applicant's illness did not frustrate her contract on the facts, but further that the doctrine as a matter of law should only apply to long-term contracts not terminable by notice. However desirable such an approach may be as a matter of policy, the decision was fatally flawed as a precedent since it did not even cite either *Marshall v Harland and Wolff Ltd* or *Egg Stores (Stamford Hill) Ltd v Leibovici* (above), with both of which it was inconsistent. Not surprisingly, therefore, when the issue went to the Court of Appeal in *Notcutt v Universal Equipment Co (London) Ltd*[39] orthodoxy was re-established—it was accepted that Bristow J was correct to state in *Harman* that a court should be *cautious* about applying frustration to contracts easily terminable by notice (particularly if it is being used as a means of avoiding statutory rights), but to go further and suggest that the doctrine itself is not applicable was incorrect. In *Notcutt* itself illness absence of eight months due to a coronary was held to have frustrated the contract of employment of an employee of 27 years' service, who was entitled by law to 12 weeks' notice. The employee's claim was in fact a common law claim in the county court for sick pay (which in the event was not payable due to the frustration of the contract) but it is clear that the decision is also applicable to a statutory action, particularly an action for unfair dismissal. While the court did state that defences of frustration should be treated carefully,[40] it must be accepted that the decision does leave considerable scope for frustration in sickness cases—12 weeks was not an unduly long notice period, and the dominant factor in the case appears to be that the illness led immediately to total and lasting incapacity for work, which is not going to be a rare occurrence in cases of major illness or accident. In such an event, however, the position may now be complicated by a modern tendency in some employments to offer (as part of enhanced terms and conditions) 'permanent health insurance' covering generously employees who are permanently unable to work—in such a case, could this factor be used to defeat an argument for frustration, on the basis that the illness was fully covered by the contract and so not an *unforeseen* frustrating event?[41] If so, could the argument eventually be

---

[36] *Tan v Berry Bros and Rudd Ltd* [1974] ICR 586, [1974] IRLR 244.

[37] *Egg Stores (Stamford Hill) Ltd v Leibovici* [1977] ICR 260 at 264G, [1976] IRLR 376 at 378, per Phillips J.

[38] [1980] IRLR 418.

[39] [1986] ICR 414, [1986] IRLR 218, CA, followed in *F C Shepherd & Co Ltd v Jerrom* [1986] ICR 802, [1986] IRLR 358, CA.

[40] Further, it was accepted by Mustill LJ in *F C Shepherd & Co Ltd v Jerrom* (n 39) that the existence of a disciplinary procedure covering the event in question (in that case, imprisonment) might be a factor against finding frustration.

[41] This argument was accepted in *Villella v MFI Furniture Centres Ltd* [1999] IRLR 468. For the effect of such permanent health insurance schemes on the giving of notice to persons subject to them, see Ch 3, heading 3(vii), p 157.

taken even further and applied to an employment covered by an *ordinary* sick pay term, at least where it is relatively generous and envisages a long period off work while still receiving pay? Given that the original doctrine of frustration relied on the occurrence of an event or consequences not 'contemplated' by the parties, the law in this area appears to have strayed from its roots by accepting the frustration defence in the presence of evidence that the parties made arrangements applicable to the circumstances in question.

Varying views as to the proper approach to be taken to frustration can also be seen in the other major area for its potential application to employment contracts, the effect of imprisonment of the employee. Here the complicating factor is not whether the contract is terminable on short notice, but rather whether imprisonment constitutes 'self-induced frustration', for it is usually said that the frustrating event must not be self-induced.[42] In *Hare v Murphy Bros Ltd*[43] the Court of Appeal held that a contract of employment was automatically terminated when the employee was sentenced to 12 months' imprisonment for an assault unconnected with his employment. Lord Denning clearly said that the contract was frustrated and that it was not a case of self-induction for the frustrating event was the imposition of the sentence (even though that was of course originally caused by the criminal behaviour). The problem was, however, that the other two judgments were not unequivocally in agreement with this approach, and a major disagreement arose between different EATs as to whether the doctrine of frustration should apply to imprisonment cases. In one sense the end result might be much the same since even if frustration does not apply and an unfair dismissal action proceeds, it is likely that the dismissal of an employee who has received an immediate and substantial term of imprisonment will be fair, provided it is sensibly handled by the employer.[44] However, it remains of considerable interest legally whether the employer can go further and stop an unfair dismissal action dead in its tracks in such a case by pleading frustration. A finding of frustration through imprisonment was upheld in *Harrington v Kent County Council*[45] (even though the employee's sentence was under appeal, which was ultimately successful), and was assumed to be possible (though not proved on the facts) in *Chakki v United Yeast Co Ltd*;[46] to the contrary, however, it

---

[42] *Bank Line Ltd v Arthur Capel & Co* [1919] AC 435 at 452, HL, per Lord Sumner; *Denmark Productions Ltd v Boscobel Productions Ltd* [1969] 1 QB 699, [1968] 3 All ER 513, CA, at 736 and 533 respectively, per Harman LJ. It is for the party relying on frustration to prove it, but for the other party to prove that it was self-induced (if that be their allegation): *Joseph Constantine Steamship Line Ltd v Imperial Smelting Corpn Ltd* [1942] AC 154, [1941] 2 All ER 165, HL.

[43] [1974] 3 All ER 940, [1974] ICR 603, CA.

[44] *Kingston v British Railways Board* [1984] ICR 781, [1984] IRLR 146, CA.

[45] [1980] IRLR 353, EAT. Note that this case concerns an actual sentence of imprisonment; merely being placed on bail is unlikely to frustrate the contract, and the employer cannot 'back date' frustration in the event of a later sentence: *Four Seasons Healthcare Ltd v Maughan* [2005] IRLR 324, EAT.

[46] [1982] 2 All ER 446, [1982] ICR 140, EAT.

was held in *Norris v Southampton City Council*[47] that a contract of employment is *not* frustrated by imprisonment, as a matter of law.

The point was eventually resolved by the Court of Appeal in *F C Shepherd & Co Ltd v Jerrom*[48] which concerned an unfair dismissal action by an apprentice who lost his employment when sentenced to borstal training for offences of violence halfway through his apprenticeship. The EAT[49] held that imprisonment can frustrate a contract of employment, that *Hare v Murphy Bros Ltd* (above) does support that proposition and that *Norris* is wrong. However, they upheld the tribunal's decision that there was no frustration here on rather novel grounds—they honoured the underlying logic of frustration. Seeking to restrict the operation of the doctrine, Waite P reminded colleagues that where, as here, the contract contained a prescribed termination procedure covering the event in question (in this case, incorporated from a national joint agreement governing apprenticeship) that event cannot be an *unforeseen* eventuality and so cannot be a frustrating event. This principle, that where the contract actually addresses a set of circumstances those circumstances were clearly 'contemplated' by the parties, was not adopted by the Court of Appeal. The court allowed the employer's appeal and held the doctrine to be applicable to cases of imprisonment simpliciter, though a version of the EAT's reasoning resurfaced in *Four Seasons Healthcare Ltd v Maughan*[50] where one of the factors against frustration was the existence in the employee's contract of a power of summary dismissal for just the misconduct of which he was accused, which the employers had chosen not to use. Thus, the point remains a live one.

Returning to *F C Shepherd & Co Ltd v Jerrom*, the Court of Appeal were faced with one remaining problem—was not this frustration self-induced? Further, was it not the case that frustration must not be the fault of *either* party? This was resolved in two ways—Balcombe LJ accepted Lord Denning MR's view in *Hare v Murphy Bros Ltd* that the frustrating event was actually the imposition of the sentence, not the misconduct by the employee, but Lawton and Mustill LJJ took a more fundamental approach— that, properly understood, the rule against self-induction only meant that neither party could rely on his *own* misconduct to establish a defence of frustration. As the employer was relying on the *employee's* fault here, that requirement was satisfied and frustration could succeed; to hold otherwise would allow a party at fault to benefit from his own misdeeds, which would not be tolerated. As with *Notcutt's* case in the context of sickness, this decision of the Court of Appeal resolved an unfortunate division of

---

[47] [1982] ICR 177 [1982] IRLR 141. The decision in this case involved a strained reading of *Hare v Murphy Bros Ltd*, n 43 above and, arguably, entirely misplaced reliance on *London Transport Executive v Clarke* [1981] ICR 355, [1981] IRLR 166, CA, p 439 below, which concerned a case of clear repudiation of contract, not frustration.

[48] [1986] ICR 802, [1986] IRLR 358, CA.

[49] [1985] ICR 552, [1985] IRLR 275. The case was newsworthy when decided by the EAT; the idea of a boy sent to borstal for offences of violence receiving compensation of £7,000 for being refused his job back was not treated sympathetically in the tabloid press.

[50] [2005] IRLR 324.

opinion on frustration, and did so by applying a fairly straightforward and orthodox approach again. It leaves one (possibly unanswerable) question—how long does the sentence of imprisonment have to be in order to justify a finding of frustration? This presumably remains a question of fact for the tribunal or court. The other question that remains is how long the courts and tribunals will allow employers to avoid the consequences of events clearly contemplated in most employment relationships—like sudden illness—on the basis of what was originally an exceptional doctrine to deal with unexpected and fundamental changes of circumstance.

(iii) EXPIRY OF FIXED-TERM CONTRACTS

There used to be a presumption that a general hiring (ie one with no fixed duration) was a hiring for a year, the significance of this being that it guaranteed agricultural labourers employment through all four seasons. This, however, no longer has any place in employment law, and a general hiring now is regarded as a hiring for an indefinite period, determinable by reasonable notice.[51] However, the employer and employee may agree that a contract shall be for a fixed period only (possibly for a probationary period) and at common law that contract terminates automatically at the expiry of the period.[52] Clearly this point had to be taken into account by the framers of the modern statutory employment law, though for many years this was done in a rather ambiguous way. On the one hand, the expiry of a fixed-term contract has always been deemed to be a 'dismissal' for the purposes of unfair dismissal and redundancy law;[53] to have failed to do so would have left a huge gap in the legal protection by allowing the employer to avoid it simply by making the employee's contract fixed term. On the other hand, for many years the employer was allowed to restrict his liability in defined circumstances, in that an employee could sign away his unfair dismissal rights in a fixed-term contract of one year or more and his redundancy rights in a fixed-term contract of two years or more.[54] The present government have repealed both of these provisions, the first by the Employment Relations Act 1999 and the second by the Fixed-term Worker (Prevention of Less Favourable Treatment) Regulations 2002.[55]

Given this involvement of statute, questions of interpretation not surprisingly arose, and two in particular go to the root of the meaning of fixed term. The first, and most immediately pressing in the early case law, was the possible conflict between a statement

---

[51] *De Stempel v Dunkels* [1938] 1 All ER 238, CA; *Richardson v Koefod* [1969] 3 All ER 1264, [1969] 1 WLR 1812, CA.

[52] *R v Secretary of State for Social Services, ex p Khan* [1973] 2 All ER 104, [1973] 1 WLR 187, CA. See also *Brown v Knowsley Borough Council* [1986] IRLR 102 (contract expressed to be subject to continued external funding held to terminate automatically when that funding ceased).

[53] Employment Rights Act 1996, ss 95(1)(b), 136(1)(b); see Ch 7, heading 2(i), p 477.

[54] Section 197, now wholly repealed.

[55] The main purposes of the 2002 Regulations are to enact a regime of less favourable for fixed-term employees and to place limitations on the length of time that an employer can keep an employee on successive fixed-term contracts; see Ch 2, heading 1(iv), p 57.

that a contract is for a fixed term and the inclusion in it of a provision for termination by notice. In *BBC v Ioannou*[56] the contract in question was for a fixed period, but with a provision for termination by three months' notice, and this was held not to be a 'fixed-term contract', so that the purported written surrender of redundancy and unfair dismissal rights was ineffective. Termination by notice was held to be inconsistent with a fixed-term contract, which had to be for that term and not terminable during it. In this case the Court of Appeal were attempting to safeguard the position of those on fixed-term contracts by ensuring that only those *genuinely* on such contracts could sign away their rights (as the law then allowed). When, however, this reasoning was applied to the statutory definition of dismissal it had potentially dire results for the employee,[57] for it meant that if the employer put him on a contract which was ostensibly for a fixed term but used the ploy of inserting a notice provision of sorts, the employer could then have argued that, under *BBC v Ioannou*, that was *not* a fixed-term contract, and so when it expired that was *not* the expiry of a fixed-term contract under the Employment Rights Act 1996, sections 95(1)(b) and 136(1)(b) and so, as it would not qualify as an ordinary dismissal under sections 95(1)(a) and 136(1)(a), there would have been no 'dismissal' and so no possible claims for unfair dismissal or redundancy. This was argued by an employer in *Dixon v BBC*,[58] but in that case the Court of Appeal recognized the absurdity that would arise from this application of *BBC v Ioannou* and so, not wishing to establish two different definitions for 'fixed term' depending on whether the case concerned (a) or (b) above, they reversed as per incuriam that part of *BBC v Ioannou* which dealt with the definition of 'fixed term', and held that a contract for a set period remains a fixed-term contract for statutory purposes even if it also contains a provision for termination by notice during its currency. Thus *Dixon v BBC* is now the ruling case, and so the employer cannot use this simple device to rule out the employee's action, but must instead accept that when a fixed-term contract expires (whether or not there is a notice provision in it), that is a 'dismissal' under sections 95 and 136 and, in an unfair dismissal case, be prepared to justify his reasons for not renewing the contract.[59]

The second question has become even more fundamental and led to a significant change—what form of expiry is necessary before a contract comes within this category at all? The case law on the legislation as it stood until 2002 made the clear distinction that a fixed-term contract is one which is to expire on a definable *date*, not on the happening of a particular event or the completion of a particular task at some time in the future.[60] There was therefore the possibility of such a 'task' or 'purpose' contract (for example employment until a particular building is demolished) terminating

---

[56] [1975] 2 All ER 999, [1975] ICR 267, CA.

[57] See Hepple and Napier 'Temporary Workers and the Law' (1978) 7 ILJ 84.

[58] [1979] ICR 281, [1979] IRLR 114, CA.

[59] *Terry v East Sussex County Council* [1977] 1 All ER 567, [1976] ICR 536, approved by the Court of Appeal in *Fay v North Yorkshire County Council* [1986] ICR 133, [1985] IRLR 247, CA. This is also the position for the purposes of the 2002 Regulations: *Allen v National Australia Group Europe Ltd* [2004] IRLR 847, EAT.

[60] *Wiltshire County Council v NATFHE* [1980] ICR 455, [1980] IRLR 198, CA.

automatically without there being a dismissal in law, which could, of course, materially prejudice statutory rights.[61] If, however, the event or completion in question (for example the end of a particular course in a short-term teaching contract) could in fact be dated with reasonable precision, then it was held that that should be treated as sufficient for the existence of a fixed-term contract; if it were otherwise, it might be easy for an employer to avoid the statutory definition of dismissal by putting the contract in the *form* of an engagement pending a particular event, even if the date of that event could be discerned. This was, however, subject to major change under the Fixed-term Employees (Prevention of Less Favourable Treatment) Regulations 2002 in order to comply with the wider definition in the Fixed-term Worker Directive 1999/70/EC, which covers task or purpose contracts. Moreover, this change applies not only under the Regulations themselves, but also to the basic definitions in the above sections in the Employment Rights Act 1996. Both the unfair dismissal and redundancy payments provisions now state that there is deemed to be a dismissal where the employee 'is employed under a limited-term contract[62] and that contract terminates by virtue of the limiting event without being renewed under the same contract'. Inserted definitions define 'limited-term contract' as being where '(a) the employment under the contract is not intended to be permanent and (b) provision is accordingly made in the contract for it to terminate by virtue of a limiting event'; 'limiting event' is defined as the expiry of a fixed term, the performance of a specific task in contemplation of which the contract is made or the occurrence or non-occurrence of an event where the contract provides for termination on such occurrence or non-occurrence.[63] Thus, task or purpose contracts are now included in the statutory definitions and, as there has not in the past been any divergence between statute and common law concepts of fixed-term contracts (given that they have been so closely intertwined), it is to be assumed that this new approach would, if ever necessary, be applied at common law too.

(iv) MUTUAL CONSENT

As with other contracts, a contract of employment may in general be terminated by the mutual agreement of the employer and employee so to do (just as they may agree to vary the agreed terms of the contract during its operation, provided that the variation is voluntary and without undue pressure on the employee).[64] Thus in *S W Strange Ltd v Mann*[65] the defendant was employed as the plaintiff company's manager under a contract which included a restraint clause, restricting his post-employment activities. After certain disagreements the parties agreed that the defendant should cease to be manager

---

[61] *Brown v Knowsley Borough Council*, n 52, is an extreme example of this.

[62] This change of terminology here is curious because the Regulations themselves (which of course use substantially the same definition) retain the term 'fixed-term contract'.

[63] Employment Rights Act 1996, s 235(2A), (2B).

[64] *Marriott v Oxford and District Co-operative Society Ltd (No 2)* [1970] 1 QB 186, [1969] 3 All ER 1126, CA.

[65] [1965] 1 All ER 1069, [1965] 1 WLR 629; cf *Cowey v Liberian Operations Ltd* [1966] 2 Lloyd's Rep 45.

and instead take over the running of only one department. When he was eventually dismissed, the plaintiff tried to enforce the restraint clause, but the court held for the defendant on the ground, inter alia, that the original contract had been terminated by mutual consent, and the new contract which was entered did not contain the relevant clause. As with other common law concepts, however, 'mutual consent' gained renewed significance with the advent of the new statutory rights, often dependent upon continuity of the employment, and the fact of dismissal. While the concept of mutual consent in fact worked in the employee's favour in *Strange Ltd v Mann*, it would be more likely to jeopardize an employee's statutory rights if found too readily, for it could break continuity and provide the employer with an argument that there had in fact been no dismissal, only a voluntary parting of the ways. In *McAlwane v Boughton Estates*[66] an employee was given notice to terminate his employment on 19 April, but during the notice period he asked if he could leave on 12 April. The employer agreed, and, when the employee claimed a redundancy payment and unfair dismissal, argued that there was no dismissal because the contract had been terminated by mutual consent on 12 April. The NIRC (the relevant forum for such complaints at the time) rejected this argument, holding that this merely constituted an agreed variation of the notice period, so that the employee was still dismissed by the employer. Sir John Donaldson P said:

> We would further suggest that it would be a very rare case indeed in which it could properly be found that the employer and the employee had got together and, notwithstanding that there was a current notice of termination of the employment, agreed mutually to terminate the contract, particularly when one realises the financial consequences to the employee involved in such an agreement. We do not say that such arrangement cannot arise; we merely say that, viewed in a real life situation, it would seem to be a possibility which might appeal to a lawyer more than to a personnel manager.[67]

This decision, and this dictum in particular, was applied by the Court of Appeal (by a majority) in *Lees v Arthur Greaves Ltd*[68] where, on similar facts, it was once again held that there was no termination by mutual consent.

Mutual consent will therefore be difficult to establish, particularly in a statutory context; this is especially so in an unfair dismissal action, for the Employment Rights Act 1996, section 95(2) provides that where an employee under notice gives his employer notice that he wishes to leave before the expiry of the employer's notice, the employee is deemed still to have been dismissed by the employer for unfair dismissal purposes. The applicants in *McAlwane* and *Lees* could not rely upon the equivalent provisions in the legislation at the time[69] since they then required *written* notice by the employee, and

[66] [1973] 2 All ER 299, [1973] ICR 470.

[67] [1973] 2 All ER 299 at 302, [1973] ICR 470 at 473.

[68] [1974] 2 All ER 393, [1974] ICR 501, CA. See also *Glacier Metal Co Ltd v Dyer* [1974] 3 All ER 21, [1974] IRLR 189.

[69] Industrial Relations Act 1971, s 23(3) (later the Trade Union and Labour Relations Act 1974, Sch 1, para 5(3)) and the Redundancy Payments Act 1965, s 4(2).

this had not been given. The requirement of writing was deleted for unfair dismissal purposes by the Employment Protection Act 1975, but not for redundancy purposes where it is still required.[70] However, termination by mutual consent does remain a possibility as can be seen from *Lipton Ltd v Marlborough*[71] where an employee, faced with the loss of his job in a reorganization, began to look for other employment, but was hindered by his contract which required him to give six months' notice and contained a restraint of trade clause. During negotiations he requested that he be released from his contract immediately and the employer agreed. When he later claimed unfair dismissal the tribunal found that he had been constructively dismissed (on the basis that the employer intended to phase out his job), but the EAT allowed the employer's appeal and held that this was a termination by mutual agreement, not a dismissal, Bristow J stating:

> The whole difference between termination by mutual agreement in this context and constructive dismissal is that in the first case the employee says 'Please may I go?' and the employer says 'Yes'. In the second case the employee says 'You have treated me in such a way that I'm going without a by-your-leave.'

Such a case will, however, remain a rarity (either in the specific context of a cross-notice to end employment or more generally) and the fact that the employee did not object to his own dismissal (for example on an agreed redundancy) will not normally prevent it from still being a dismissal;[72] the usual narrow approach was reaffirmed by the EAT in *Tracey v Zest Equipment Co Ltd*[73] where termination of employment following a failure to return on time from holiday (when the employee, who had been late back before, had agreed beforehand that his employment would be terminated in the event of lateness) was held not to have been terminated by mutual consent, but rather to have been repudiatory conduct leading to dismissal, thus allowing the tribunal to consider the substantive question of fairness.

As against that, termination by mutual consent was subsequently found by the Court of Appeal in *Birch v University of Liverpool*[74] in the case of two academics taking early retirement under a scheme adopted by universities and their relevant unions. The facts were exceptional in that the scheme required a high degree of mutual agreement and clearly envisaged that statutory redundancy payments (which the two applicants were now claiming) would *not* be payable on top; the case does, however, show an important

---

[70] Employment Rights Act 1996, s 136(3).　　[71] [1979] IRLR 179.

[72] *Burton, Allton and Johnson Ltd v Peck* [1975] ICR 193, [1975] IRLR 87. In *Lassman v De Vere University Arms Hotel* [2003] ICR 44 a hotel manager whose job was being down-graded was given the choice (only) of going part time or taking redundancy; when she reluctantly chose the latter, it was held that she had still been dismissed and so could claim unfair dismissal.

[73] [1982] ICR 481, [1982] IRLR 268. The case is in line with the restrictive approach taken at the same time to the analogous area of 'constructive resignation' or 'self dismissal', as seen in *London Transport Executive v Clarke* [1981] ICR 355, [1981] IRLR 166, CA (see below) which is cited in the judgment of the EAT.

[74] [1985] ICR 470, [1985] IRLR 165, CA, distinguishing *Burton, Allton & Johnson Ltd v Peck*, n 72; noted Freedland (1985) 14 ILJ 243.

potential application of the idea of mutual consent in modern circumstances particularly where, as Ackner LJ pointed out, the employer calls for resignations well in advance of decreases in the workforce, there is no compulsion and the employer offers financial inducements well in excess of what would be payable under the ordinary redundancy payments scheme. The decision in *Birch* was taken one step further by the EAT in *Scott v Coalite Fuels & Chemicals Ltd*[75] where it was held that there was mutual termination where employees took voluntary early retirement while already under notice of dismissal for redundancy. While such a decision may make good industrial sense in a case where early retirement (with a lump-sum payment, but a reduced weekly pension) is negotiated as an *alternative* to redundancy, it does call into question the dictum of Sir John Donaldson cited at the beginning of this section that mutual termination during a current notice period would only be found in 'a very rare case indeed'. Perhaps cases involving genuine early retirement schemes should be treated as *sui generis*.

2 DISMISSAL BY NOTICE

Most contracts of employment may be terminated by either party giving the necessary notice of termination. The period of notice may be agreed expressly by the parties[76] and, more unusually, the parties may agree to restrict the reasons behind the giving of notice.[77] In the absence of specific limits on reasons for dismissal in the contract, the common law allows termination of the contract by either party, including the employer, for any reason at all. Usually, however, the right to give notice will not be so restricted and only the mechanics of the period to be given will be laid down. If there is no such express notice provision, and no term can be ascertained from custom or trade usage,[78] the law will read into a contract of employment that it is terminable upon 'reasonable notice'. It may then be a matter of litigation to quantify what is reasonable; as this involves construction of the contract it has in the past been within the jurisdiction of the civil courts, but it can now be raised in proceedings before tribunals, under their common law jurisdiction on termination of employment.[79] There are many reported cases on this question of quantification and all that can be said is that each case must depend upon its own facts such as the position of the employee within the firm, his

---

[75] [1988] ICR 355, [1988] IRLR 131 (see also *Logan Salton v Durham County Council* [1989] IRLR 99, where an employee under threat of disciplinary proceedings negotiated severance terms and was held to them). It remains the case, however, that there will still be a dismissal (even if in form there appears to be mutual agreement) if either (1) all that the employee has done is to volunteer to be dismissed for redundancy, or (2) there has been pressure put on the employee to agree to go (see p 477 below).

[76] Written particulars of the notice period should be given to the employee within two months of commencement: Employment Rights Act, s 1(4)(e).

[77] *McClelland v Northern Ireland General Health Services Board* [1957] 2 All ER 129, [1957] 1 WLR 594, HL. It has been held that there is an implied restriction on giving notice to a long-term sick employee where there is a permanent health insurance scheme in operation under the contract.

[78] *George v Davies* [1911] 2 KB 445.   [79] See Ch 1, heading 4, p 27.

or her professional standing and, in some cases, the intervals for payment.[80] To be effective (since it has such a drastic effect) the notice must be definite and explicit. Thus in *Morris v Bailey*[81] it was held that a notice of termination given to the plaintiff's union but not to him personally was not effective to dismiss him, even though most of his contract of employment (including the notice provisions) consisted of terms incorporated from the union's collective agreement. Moreover, the amount of notice must be made known to the employee, so that a mere warning of impending dismissal (eg for redundancy) will not constitute notice.[82] However, once an effective notice has been given by one of the parties, he may not withdraw it unilaterally, and so withdrawal of the notice may only be by mutual consent.[83]

Under the common law of employment, the availability to the employer of dismissal by notice could in practice negate what rights an employee might have; for example an employee might be justified in refusing to obey an order which was illegal or outside the scope of his employment and the employer could not summarily dismiss him for that refusal, but there was nothing to stop the employer from giving him notice because of the incident, since a dismissal on proper notice was lawful regardless of the motive behind it. If the notice period was only a matter of days or even hours, that could be a powerful threat to the employee. This position is now heavily overlaid by the statutory provisions as to redundancy and unfair dismissal (particularly as the latter entails scrutiny of the merits of the dismissal, not just its technical correctness), but the question of notice was first affected by statute in the Contracts of Employment Act 1963[84] which attempted to alter the common law in two ways—first, by gearing the period of notice to the length of continuous service, not simply to the status of the employee; secondly, by safeguarding certain employee rights during the period of notice. The present provisions relating to these two points will now be considered.

The common law rules proved to be inadequate in that they made no distinction for the long-serving employee. Thus an employee on a weekly contract would only be entitled to a week's notice whether he worked for his employer for one week or 40 years. Large-scale redundancies emphasized this defect, and certain minimum notice periods are now laid down by statute. Under the Employment Rights

---

[80] Thus in *Grundy v Sun Printing and Publishing Association* (1916) 33 TLR 77, CA, an editor was entitled to 12 months' notice, but in *Fox-Bourne v Vernon & Co Ltd* (1894) 10 TLR 647 another editor was only entitled to six months'. For a more modern example of this process of quantification, see *Hill v C A Parsons & Co Ltd* [1972] Ch 305, [1971] 3 All ER 1345, CA.

[81] [1969] 2 Lloyd's Rep 215, CA.

[82] *Morton Sundour Fabrics Ltd v Shaw* (1966) 2 ITR 84; *Pritchard-Rhodes Ltd v Boon and Milton* [1979] IRLR 19; *International Computers Ltd v Kennedy* [1981] IRLR 28; *Doble v Firestone Tyre and Rubber Co Ltd* [1981] IRLR 300; *Haseltine Lake & Co v Dowler* [1981] ICR 222, [1981] IRLR 25. This is particularly important in the context of the giving of counter-notice by an employee, for the purposes of redundancy law; see Ch 8, heading 1(iv), p 580.

[83] *Riordan v War Office* [1959] 3 All ER 552, [1959] 1 WLR 1059 (affd [1960] 3 All ER 774n, [1961] 1 WLR 210, CA); *Harris and Russell Ltd v Slingsby* [1973] 3 All ER 31, [1973] ICR 454.

[84] Later the Contracts of Employment Act 1972, and now to be found in the Employment Rights Act 1996, ss 86–91.

Act 1996, section 86, the minimum notice period for an employee with under two years' continuous employment is one week; where there is over two years' continuous employment, the employee is entitled to one week's notice for each year up to a maximum of 12 weeks. As for the employee, the statutory minimum which he must give to terminate his employment is one week if he has been employed for four weeks or more. The section states that it does not affect the right of either party to terminate the contract through the other party's conduct, and does not prevent either party from waiving his right to notice on any particular occasion.[85] Subsection (3) also states that the section does not prevent a party from accepting a payment in lieu of notice.[86] 'Wages in lieu' is a common phenomenon, whereby the employer gives the employee the wages which he would have earned during the notice period, and instructs him not to work out the notice period, so that the employer is rid of him immediately. This is perfectly lawful if both parties agree to it, and this is as far as the subsection goes. One contentious point, however, is whether the employer has a *right* to give wages in lieu if the employee wishes to work out the notice period. The old tenet of employment law that the employer's only obligation is to provide wages, not work, suggested that dismissal with wages in lieu would be lawful,[87] except in one of the exceptional cases where work also had to be provided.[88] However, the more modern approach has been to look more closely at *how* the dismissal is effected. The renewed interest in this point is not because of its direct effect on wrongful dismissal (since the prima facie measure of damages for wrongful dismissal, the wages themselves, have already been paid),[89] but rather because of three incidental matters which may be affected—(1) whether the protection against unlawful deductions in Part II of the Employment Rights Act 1996 applies to any non-payment of the wages;[90] (2) what is the effective date of termination of the dismissal;[91] (3) whether any restraint of trade clause in the contract survives the termination.[92] In *Delaney v Staples*,[93] the leading case on deductions from wages,

[85] Waiver of notice includes waiver of any right to payment for the notice period (especially in a voluntary severance case): *Trotter v Forth Ports Authority* [1991] IRLR 419, Ct of Sess; *Baldwin v British Coal Corpn* [1995] IRLR 139.

[86] *Staffordshire County Council v Secretary of State for Employment* [1987] ICR 956, [1988] IRLR 3 (reversed on other grounds, [1989] ICR 664, [1989] IRLR 117, CA).

[87] *Konski v Peet* [1915] 1 Ch 530.

[88] See Ch 3, heading 3(ii), p 141. This point was particularly taken up (in the context of garden leave) in *William Hill Organisation Ltd v Tucker* [1999] ICR 291, [1998] IRLR 313, CA which showed a broader approach to who can claim an interest in having the work itself provided.

[89] Though it can still affect whether the nature of the employee's right is damages or debt (in which case there is no obligation to mitigate loss, and so earnings in new employment need not be taken into account): *Gregory v Wallace* [1998] IRLR 387, CA.

[90] If it does, the ex-employee may challenge any non-payment (total or partial) of the wages in lieu before an employment tribunal, instead of before the ordinary courts; see Ch 1, heading 4, p 26.

[91] See Ch 7, heading 2(ii), p 487. This is relevant because (1) by that date the employee must have the necessary qualifying service and (2) the three-month time limit for claiming unfair dismissal flows from that date. It is thus in the employer's interest to have the EDT early, ie when the employment actually ends, not the (later) date on which notice would notionally have expired.

[92] If the dismissal is wrongful, the restraint clause falls: see Ch 2, heading 4(ii), p 90.

[93] [1992] ICR 483, [1992] IRLR 191, HL.

Lord Browne-Wilkinson analysed the law on dismissal with wages in lieu; adopting his classification, the position in relation to the above matters appears to be as follows.

(1) The employer gives the employee proper notice, but then tells him that he need not work it out; in such a case (including an ad hoc 'garden leave' arrangement) the dismissal is lawful, with advance payment of 'wages', the effective date of termination is the end of the notice period, and any restraint clause may continue to apply.

(2) The contract itself provides for termination by notice *or* by wages in lieu (including a formal 'garden leave' clause if it operates this way); here, the dismissal is lawful, the payment is not 'wages' for the purposes of Part II of the 1996 Act (because not paid under a subsisting contract of employment), the effective date of termination is the date the wages in lieu are given (*not* the end of the period of notice) and any restraint clause may continue to apply.[94]

(3) At the end of the employment, the employer and employee agree ad hoc that it will end forthwith, on the payment of the sum in lieu; the results here are as in (2), it being a lawful variation of the normal notice term.

(4) The employer summarily dismisses the employee, without his agreement, but tenders a payment in lieu of notice; here, the employer is in breach of contract and so the dismissal is wrongful, which means that the payment is *damages*, not 'wages' (but they extinguish any *claim* for damages), the effective date of termination remains the date of the summary dismissal and payment in lieu, *but* any restraint of trade clause now becomes invalid because of the wrongful dismissal.

From this analysis, it can be seen that the employer now has much to gain from putting into the contract of employment a term expressly permitting dismissal with wages in lieu, since it provides the optimum position of a lawful dismissal, no challenge to the payment in tribunal proceedings, an early effective date of termination and the preservation of any restraint of trade clause. From the employee's point of view, the existence of an express payment in lieu clause is both advantageous and disadvantageous. On the positive side, as the dismissal is lawful, the employee may claim any unpaid wages in lieu as a debt due under the contract, not as damages for breach of it; this means that the employee is not under a duty to mitigate his loss, which may be of particular importance for a highly paid employee on long notice, who has obtained new employment during what would have been the notice period but who does *not* have to bring those new (equally high?) earnings into account, and so may receive and retain both sums of money in full.[95] On the negative side, however, the fact that the payment in lieu is contractual means that the amount paid is taxable in the employee's hands, since

---

[94] *Rex Stewart Jeffries Parker Ginsberg Ltd v Parker* [1988] IRLR 483, CA, explaining the earlier decision in *Dixon v Stenor Ltd* [1973] ICR 157, [1973] IRLR 28.

[95] *Abrahams v Performing Right Society* [1995] ICR 1028, [1995] IRLR 486, CA. This case also contains some extremely dubious dicta, to the effect that even if the dismissal had been unlawful (ie under category (4)) there

it cannot be construed as 'damages' and hence not subject to income tax (which may be the case with a non-contractual payment, under head (4) above).[96]

In addition to laying down minimum periods of notice, the legislation also safeguards certain employee rights during the period of notice,[97] though it should be noted that these provisions do not apply where the notice to be given by the employer under the contract is more than a week longer than the statutory minimum as laid down in section 86.[98] These provisions differ slightly, depending upon whether or not the employee who is under notice works 'normal working hours'. The construction of that phrase is therefore important, and essentially the test is whether the contract of employment lays down a certain or minimum number of hours which the employee must work; if so, he works 'normal working hours'. Prima facie this might be expected to be exclusive of overtime, but under section 234(3) of the 1996 Act some overtime may count if it is included in the number of hours which the employee must work (for example if he is contractually bound to work 40 hours per week, and overtime rates begin to be payable after 37 hours, then that is still normal working hours of 40 per week); to qualify under this extension, however, the overtime must be compulsory in the sense of being obligatory for the employee and guaranteed by the employer.[99] Where the employee works normal working hours and actually works during the notice period he will be contractually entitled to the correct payment without assistance from the legislation but section 88(1) ensures that he continues to be paid at the relevant rate for any periods when (1) he is ready and willing to work but the employer has no work for him, (2) he is incapable of work through sickness or injury or (3) he is away on proper holiday. It is provided that where the employee draws sickness or injury benefit that is to be taken into account in computing the employer's liability to him, since otherwise he might be doubly entitled, through drawing the benefit and

---

would still have been no duty to mitigate; this is contrary to established principle (on mitigation, see this chapter 4(ii)(d), p 458), contrary to the speech of Lord Browne-Wilkinson in *Delaney v Staples* (n 93, at 493, 194), contrary to dicta in the earlier House of Lords case of *Westwood v Secretary of State for Employment* [1985] ICR 209, [1984] IRLR 209 where mitigation was in issue (see particularly per Lord Bridge at 219, 211), and best tactfully forgotten. It was discreetly ignored subsequently in *Gregory v Wallace* [1998] IRLR 387, CA. According to *Cerberus Software Ltd v Rowley* [2001] ICR 376, [2001] IRLR 160, where there is an in lieu clause but the employer refuses to pay under it, the employee is restricted to an action in damages and so must mitigate (even though this in effect allows the employer to benefit from his own misdeed in dismissing wrongfully, rather than lawfully under the in lieu clause).

[96] *EMI Group Electronics Ltd v Coldicott* [1999] IRLR 630, [1999] STC 803, CA; applied to a negotiated settlement in *Richardson (IT) v Delaney* [2001] IRLR 663. It is, however, now clear that a non-contractual payment in lieu of notice (PILON) will not always be free from tax, because the Revenue have issued new guidance restricting non-taxability to payments which are genuinely damages: Tax Bulletin, February 2003, p 999.

[97] Employment Rights Act 1996, ss 87–91.

[98] Section 87(4); *Scotts Co (UK) Ltd v Budd* [2003] IRLR 145, EAT.

[99] See, in the context of the computation of the number of normal working hours, *Tarmac Roadstone Holdings Ltd v Peacock* [1973] 2 All ER 485, [1973] ICR 273, CA, applied to the present context of the definition of normal working hours in *Fox v C Wright (Farmers) Ltd* [1978] ICR 98. The questions of 'normal working hours' and what constitutes 'a week's pay' are discussed at p 203 above.

receiving full pay from the employer.[100] Where the employee does not work normal working hours, the employer must pay him a week's pay (calculated in accordance with Part XIV of the 1996 Act)[101] for each week of the period of notice, provided that he is ready and willing to do work of a reasonable nature and amount to earn it; once again, the employee is specifically entitled to payment during absence through sickness or injury, or whilst on proper holiday. The legislation contains three main qualifications upon these rights to payment:

(1) the employee is not entitled to be paid during time off which he has requested (including time off governed by statute);[102]

(2) if the employee breaks the contract during the period of notice and is justifiably summarily dismissed, he is not entitled to further payment as from that dismissal;

(3) if it is the employee who has given notice and he goes on strike during the notice period, he is not entitled to payment under these provisions at all; where it is the employer who has given notice this qualification does not apply, so that the employee will be contractually entitled to payment for that part of the notice period when he was not on strike.[103]

If an employer fails to give the statutory notice, the rights laid down in these provisions are to be taken into account in assessing damages, and it is further provided that if the employer breaks the contract of employment during the period of notice (for example by wrongfully terminating it summarily) the benefits that the employee will receive anyway under these provisions are to go towards mitigating any damages payable to the employee.[104]

One final point to notice on the common law doctrine of notice is that it has increasingly been used by employers to safeguard trade secrets or (in businesses which are highly reliant on skilled employees) to prevent head-hunting by other firms, by the incorporation into sensitive contracts of employment of 'garden leave' clauses. These provide for long periods of notice on either side, during which the employee will be remunerated in full (either in the normal way or by an in-lieu payment) but not necessarily required to work. Thus, an employee wishing to leave may be required to give, say, six months' or a year's notice during which time (provided the employer pays him

---

[100] Employment Rights Act 1996, s 90. The rationale behind this was queried by Dillon LJ in *Notcutt v Universal Equipment Co (London) Ltd* [1986] ICR 414, [1986] IRLR 218, CA, since it may mean paying sick pay during notice to an employee not normally entitled to it; however, as the court held that the contract was frustrated by the sickness the matter did not arise.

[101] This calculation is considered at Ch 3, heading 5(iv), p203.

[102] Employment Rights Act 1996, Part VI; Trade Union and Labour Relations (Consolidation) Act 1992, ss 168, 170.

[103] For the effect on redundancy entitlements of a strike during the notice period, see the 1996 Act, ss 140 and 143.

[104] Employment Rights Act 1996, s 91(5).

his full entitlement to wages and benefits) he continues to be subject to the implied term not to compete or breach confidence,[105] or preferably to an express term to like effect. Compared with the traditional restraint of trade clause,[106] this is expensive *but it is probably more reliable* since restraint clauses are notoriously difficult to draft and enforce. In an appropriate case, a garden leave clause may be enforced by injunction,[107] but it must be remembered that ultimately an injunction is a discretionary remedy and may be refused by a court if it appears that the clause is unconscionable as, for example, if there is little or no chance of the employer suffering actual damage if the employee does take up a particular new job (albeit in breach of the clause).[108] Moreover, the efficacy of garden leave clauses generally may now be subject to some limitation because of the decision of the Court of Appeal in *William Hill Organisation Ltd v Tucker*.[109] The ratio of that case is that a court will not *imply* a garden leave clause in any case where it is arguable that the employee has an interest in doing the work not just receiving payment,[110] and to this extent it is unexceptionable (merely stressing the advantage of an express term). However, at the end of the judgment Morritt LJ said obiter that it should not be too readily assumed that a garden leave clause will succeed where a restraint clause might fail; he said that:

> if injunctive relief was sought then it had to be justified on similar grounds to those necessary to the validity of the employee's covenant in restraint of trade. The court should be careful not to grant interlocutory relief to enforce a garden leave clause to any greater extent than would be covered by a justifiable covenant in restraint of trade previously entered into by an employee.

Interestingly, where the evidence clearly demonstrated a threat to protectable interests and the notice period was not excessive, the court in *SG & R Valuation Services v Boudrais*[111] was willing to imply a power to impose garden leave in a contract that only provided for notice. This may mean that in future there may be more emphasis on the

---

[105] See Ch 3, heading 4(iv), p 169.

[106] See Ch 2, heading 4(ii), p 90. It is possible to have both a garden leave clause and (then) a restraint of trade clause in a contract, though a court would need to consider the reasonableness of them taken together: *Crédit Suisse Asset Management Ltd v Armstrong* [1996] ICR 882, [1996] IRLR 450, CA.

[107] *Evening Standard Co Ltd v Henderson* [1987] ICR 588, [1987] IRLR 64, CA (clause requiring a year's notice enforced to prevent a newspaper production manager from taking up employment during that time with a new newspaper venture, the employers undertaking to pay in full during the year); *Euro Brokers Ltd v Rabey* [1995] IRLR 206 (six-month garden leave clause enforced against a money broker wishing to move to a competitor firm); see Freedland (1989) 18 ILJ 112; and Gouldring 'Injunctions and Contracts of Employment: The Evening Standard Doctrine' (1990) 19 ILJ 98.

[108] *Provident Financial Group plc v Hayward* [1989] ICR 160, [1989] IRLR 84, CA (injunction to restrain financial director from taking up new employment towards the end of a long notice period refused because there was little evidence of any actual detriment to the employers).

[109] [1998] IRLR 313, CA; applied in *Symbian Ltd v Christiensen* [2001] IRLR 77, CA.

[110] For this aspect of the case, see Ch 3, heading 3(ii), p 141.   [111] [2008] All ER (D) 141.

extent of the garden leave, what interests it is protecting, and a tougher line on severing or reducing an unreasonably wide clause.[112]

3 DISMISSAL FOR CAUSE (SUMMARY DISMISSAL)

At common law an employer may dismiss an employee summarily (ie without notice) if he has sufficient cause to do so. In old cases, from the nineteenth century and before, this was viewed as a natural and necessary aspect of the relationship between master and man, and of the servant's duty of obedience. The judgment of Parke B in *Callo v Brouncker*[113] was treated for many years as laying down set rules on summary dismissal which, he said, could be for moral misconduct (pecuniary or otherwise), wilful disobedience or habitual neglect. However, with the move in the nineteenth century towards viewing employment in a contractual light, the emphasis changed so that the right to dismiss summarily became explicable on the ground that the conduct of the employee was such that it showed a repudiation by him of the contract of employment which the employer then accepted and treated as terminating the contract immediately.[114] In *Laws v London Chronicle (Indicator Newspapers) Ltd*,[115] Lord Evershed MR said:

> the proper conclusion … is that, since a contract of service is but an example of contracts in general, so that the general law of contract will be applicable, it follows that the question must be—if summary dismissal is claimed to be justifiable—whether the conduct complained of is such as to show the servant to have disregarded the essential conditions of the contract of service.

This will apply as a general principle, not just to the particular categories listed by Parke B, but to any context in which the employee's conduct is sufficiently grave as to be repudiatory, so that, for example, an employee may be summarily dismissed for going on strike.[116] The principal effect of this contractual approach is that every case must be viewed on its own facts to determine whether the conduct in question was grave enough, and the question is not to be solved by searching for absolute rules

---

[112] For example, in *GFI Group Inc v Eaglestone* [1994] IRLR 119 an over-long garden leave clause was saved by being reduced in length by the court (and then enforced for that shorter period), but this is just what a court will not normally do with a restraint clause which usually has to stand or fall as originally drafted.

[113] (1831) 4 C & P 518. Several of the points raised below are considered at greater length in Smith and Randall *Contract Actions in Modern Employment Law: Developments and Issues* (2000) ch 8.

[114] *Boston Deep Sea Fishing and Ice Co v Ansell* (1888) 39 Ch D 339, CA, particularly per Bowen LJ at 364–5; *Laws v London Chronicle (Indicator Newspapers) Ltd* [1959] 2 All ER 285, [1959] 1 WLR 698, CA; *Pepper v Webb* [1969] 2 All ER 216, [1969] 1 WLR 514, CA.

[115] [1959] 2 All ER 285 at 287, [1959] 1 WLR 698 at 700.

[116] *Simmons v Hoover Ltd* [1977] 1 All ER 775, [1977] ICR 61, not following the distinction between those strikes with and those without strike notice drawn in *Morgan v Fry* [1968] 2 QB 710, [1968] 3 All ER 452, CA; the common law position on strikes is now considerably affected by statute.

covering each particular context (with the result that decided cases may be of little or no assistance). Thus:

> the true question is whether the acts and conduct of the party evince an intention no longer to be bound by the contract.[117]
>
> in every case the question of repudiation must depend on the character of the contract, the number and weight of the wrongful acts or assertions, the intentions indicated by such acts and words, the deliberation or otherwise with which they are committed or uttered and on the general circumstances of the case.[118]

Much will therefore depend upon the context and the nature of the reason, so that, for example, a relatively minor instance of dishonesty may warrant summary dismissal, particularly if the employee's job involves dealing with money.[119] By contrast mere negligence may in most cases be amenable only to dismissal by notice and a summary dismissal may be wrongful,[120] unless there are other particular factors, such as endangering life by neglect.[121] Also, while an employer may not be justified in dismissing summarily for a single 'offence', a previous history of similar transgressions, even if not as serious as the one leading to dismissal, may be important evidence in the employer's favour.[122] Any particular case should also be viewed with a certain amount of realism, so that in *Jupiter General Insurance Co Ltd v Shroff*[123] the Privy Council said:

> Their Lordships would be very loath to assent to the view that a single outbreak of bad temper, accompanied, it may be, by regrettable language, is sufficient ground for dismissal. Sir John Beaumont CJ [in the court below] was stating a proposition of mere good sense when he observed that in such cases we must apply the standard of men and not angels and remember that men are apt to show temper when reprimanded.

The court went on to make two observations which might be borne in mind. The first was that summary dismissal is a strong measure justified only in exceptional circumstances; the second was that the test to be applied in determining whether a dismissal was justified must vary with the nature of the business and the position held by the employee and that decisions in other cases are of little value. This variable approach can also be seen more recently in *Neary v Dean of Westminster*[124] where ideas taken

---

[117] *Freeth v Burr* (1874) LR 9 CP 208 at 213, per Lord Coleridge CJ, applied by the House of Lords in *General Billposting Co Ltd v Atkinson* [1909] AC 118, HL.

[118] *Re Rubel Bronze and Metal Co and Vos* [1918] 1 KB 315 at 322, per McCardie J.

[119] *Sinclair v Neighbour* [1967] 2 QB 279, [1966] 3 All ER 988, CA.

[120] See eg *Gould v Webb* (1855) 4 E & B 933.

[121] It has been held, however, that the court should look primarily at the negligent act, and not at the consequences which flowed from it, as the latter could be too harsh and involve too much hindsight: *Savage v British India Steam Navigation Co Ltd* (1930) 46 TLR 294.

[122] See eg *Clouston & Co Ltd v Corry* [1906] AC 122, PC (intoxication); *Pepper v Webb* [1969] 2 All ER 216, [1969] 1 WLR 514, CA (unsatisfactory work), discussed in *Wilson v Racher* [1974] ICR 428 [1974] IRLR 114, CA.

[123] [1937] 3 All ER 67, PC.

[124] [1999] IRLR 288 (Lord Jauncey, sitting as a Special Commissioner for the Visitor to Westminster Abbey).

from the modern law on the implied term of trust and respect were also introduced, looking at whether the employee's conduct was such as to undermine completely that element of the employment relationship. In the light of all these factors (and particularly the number of old or very old cases on the subject), another important factor may be changing attitudes, modes of organization or *mores* in general. Thus in *Wilson v Racher*,[125] Edmund Davies LJ said:

> Reported decisions provide useful, but only general guides, each case turning upon its own facts. Many of the decisions which are customarily cited in these cases date from the last century and may be wholly out of accord with the current social conditions. What would today be regarded as almost an attitude of Czar-serf, which is to be found in some of the older cases where a dismissed employee failed to recover damages would, I venture to think, be decided differently today.

Good examples of responsiveness to new needs are the decision in *Denco Ltd v Joinson*[126] that almost any form of deliberate computer misuse during employment will justify summary dismissal and the decision in *Thomas v Hillingdon London Borough Council*[127] that this is also likely to be the case in most instances of internet and/or email abuse at work, particularly when it concerns downloading pornography.

The advent of the modern statutory rights for employees has of course had an effect on summary dismissal, but usually indirectly, since the presence or absence of notice is a procedural matter and as such only of paramount importance in a common law action for wrongful dismissal; the statutory action for unfair dismissal in theory requires an examination of the substantive fairness of the dismissal, and so any question of the presence or absence of notice will be of secondary importance. Under the legislation, the employer is not deprived of his right to dismiss summarily, and the continuance of this common law concept is clearly envisaged in the Employment Rights Act 1996, section 86(6) (rights to minimum periods of notice not to affect cases where summary termination is justified) and the ACAS Code of Practice, 'Disciplinary and grievance procedures'.[128] However, the existence of the unfair dismissal legislation is likely to make employers more wary of dismissing summarily and may perhaps make them more likely to punish misconduct by action short of dismissal (for example suspension) or by dismissal by notice after exhausting a set procedure of warnings and a hearing; this might particularly be the case where the ground for dismissal is incompetence or negligence. The absence of notice would not per se make the dismissal unfair,[129] but might sway the tribunal against the employer on the question whether he or she acted reasonably. Moreover, the advent of the unfair dismissal action has

---

[125] [1974] ICR 428, [1974] IRLR 114, CA.

[126] [1991] ICR 172, [1991] IRLR 63; see Napier 'Computerisation and Employment Rights' (1992) 21 ILJ 1.

[127] (2002) The Times, 4 October.   [128] Particularly para 22.

[129] *Treganowan v Robert Knee & Co Ltd* [1975] ICR 405, [1975] IRLR 247; *BSC Sports and Social Club v Morgan* [1987] IRLR 391. See the discussion of the different bases for wrongful and unfair dismissal in the judgment of Judge Clark in *Farrant v Woodroffe School* [1998] ICR 184, [1998] IRLR 176.

placed new emphasis on *procedures* and so an employer might be advised to exercise his rights to dismiss summarily in the light of modern personnel management techniques, in particular the desirability of such matters as laying down in the company's rules what conduct may warrant summary dismissal, ensuring that the decision to dismiss is taken at a reasonably high level (certainly higher than immediate superiors), and providing for an appeal structure.[130]

The common law on dismissal for cause is thus heavily qualified by statute and the modern statutory provisions owe little to the existing common law rules. For example at common law a summary dismissal would be lawful if the employer acted on reason A which was quite inadequate, but later found out about reason B which could in fact justify summary dismissal,[131] but under the unfair dismissal legislation the relevant reason is the one upon which the employer acted at the time of dismissal, and not anything that he only discovered later.[132] Moreover, at common law there was no obligation upon the employer to give his reasons, but under the Employment Rights Act 1996, section 92, an employee with two years' continuous service has a statutory right to be provided with a written statement giving particulars of the reasons for his dismissal.[133]

4 WRONGFUL DISMISSAL

(i) MEANING

'Wrongful dismissal', at least in terms of establishing liability, is essentially an action for breach of contract. The action typically alleges that some procedural term of the employment contract, such as a notice provision, has been breached. It can, however, involve a breach of a term relating to permissible reasons for dismissal in the rare instance where a contract specifies such reasons. As can be seen from the earlier discussion, the common law on dismissal looks basically at form, not at substance so that, except in the case of a purported dismissal for cause, the concept of wrongful dismissal is essentially procedural and dependent upon the actual terms of the contract in question. Thus, if a contract is for a fixed term, or expressly stated to be terminable only in certain ways,[134] and it is terminated before the term expires or in an improper

---

[130] ACAS Code of Practice (2009) paras 23, 21 and 25 respectively. Even where the contract or work rules identify a kind of conduct as warranting dismissal, it must be clear that it is summary dismissal that is envisaged, given the gravity of the action to be taken: *Skilton v T & K Home Improvements Ltd* [2000] ICR 1162, [2000] IRLR 595, CA (reference to 'instant dismissal' is not enough to mean summary dismissal in a case of missing quarterly sales targets; employee still entitled to wages in lieu of notice).

[131] *Boston Deep Sea Fishing and Ice Co v Ansell* (1888) 39 Ch D 339, CA; *Cyril Leonard & Co v Simo Securities Trust Ltd* [1971] 3 All ER 1313, [1972] 1 WLR 80, CA.

[132] *W Devis & Sons Ltd v Atkins* [1977] AC 931, [1977] 3 All ER 40, HL.

[133] See Ch 7, heading 4(i), p 497.

[134] This is rare in practice: *McClelland v Northern Ireland General Health Services Board* [1957] 2 All ER 129, [1957] 1 WLR 594, HL is an unusual example. In modern circumstances, it might arise if an employer

way, that may be a wrongful dismissal. More typical, however, is the case where the employer dismissed the employee with no or inadequate notice, or purported to dismiss him for cause where the facts did not justify such action. Wrongful dismissal also includes 'constructive dismissal', discussed further in Chapter 7, which occurs where the employer commits a repudiatory breach of contract which the employee accepts by leaving the employment.[135]

The common law action for wrongful dismissal must be kept separate from the statutory action for unfair dismissal which entails an examination of the substantive merits of the dismissal. For many years, there was also a formal split of forum, with an unfair dismissal claim going to an employment tribunal, but a wrongful dismissal claim having to go to the ordinary civil courts; since 1994, however, tribunals have been given jurisdiction over contractual claims on termination of employment,[136] and so can hear a claim for wrongful dismissal (up to the statutory limit of £25,000).[137]

(ii) REMEDIES

(a) The rule against enforcement

While the idea of wrongful dismissal is explicable on a contractual basis (ie that the employer has repudiated the contract by his actions), it is when one comes to the nature of the remedies open to the dismissed employee that the inadequacies of contract theory and, as a consequence, the practical ineffectiveness of the common law become obvious.[138] The starting point is the general principle that the courts will not enforce a contract of employment, either directly by specific performance or indirectly by injunction or any other means,[139] the principal explanation being that the contract is

---

agreed to a contractually binding 'no compulsory redundancy' deal; any redundancy dismissal during its currency would then be wrongful and arguably the damages should not be restricted (as is usual) to wages for the notice period, but should be for the rest of the period of the agreement, subject to mitigation and a discount for the possibility of lawful dismissal (ie on non-redundancy grounds) during that period.

[135] *Atlantic Air v Hoff* (UKEAT/0602/07/ZT, 26 March 2008) available at <http://209.85.229.132/search?q=cache:AgOSEE4F1z4J>: <http://www.employmentappeals.gov.uk/Public/Upload/07_0602fhLBZT.doc+atlantic+air+hoff&cd=1&hl=en&ct=clnk&gl=uk> last accessed 10 January 2013.

[136] Employment Tribunals (Extension of Jurisdiction) Orders 1994, SI 1994/1623 and SI 1994/1624 (one order applying to England and Wales, another to Scotland); see Ch 1, heading 4, p 26.

[137] This cap has not increased with inflation as other compensation caps have, raising the question of why high earners with long notice periods should be shunted to the county courts. A recent survey of solicitors showed that an overwhelming majority favoured raising or removing this cap (not surprisingly in light of increasing insecurity for high earners in the current economic climate). The survey results are available at <http://www.lawsociety.org.uk/documents/downloads/employ-tribunal-survey-results-May09.pdf> last accessed 10 January 2013.

[138] For an analysis of the difficult case law on remedies and possible developments, see Ewing 'Remedies for Breach of the Contract of Employment' [1993] CLJ 405.

[139] *Whitwood Chemical Co v Hardman* [1891] 2 Ch 416, CA. For a peculiar application of this on the facts (employee not seeking to continue his contract per se, but rather to continue to exercise his contractual rights as a shop steward in spite of being suspended), see *City and Hackney Health Authority v NUPE* [1985] IRLR 252, CA.

of a personal nature, not amenable to enforcement. Thus, in *De Francesco v Barnum*[140] Fry LJ said:

> I should be very unwilling to extend decisions the effect of which is to compel persons who are not desirous of maintaining continuous personal relations with one another to continue those personal relations. I think the courts are bound to be jealous lest they should turn contracts of service into contracts of slavery; and ... I should lean against the extension of the doctrine of specific performance and injunction in such a manner.

Moreover, this is now enshrined in statute as far as such an order against an employee is concerned, for the Trade Union and Labour Relations (Consolidation) Act 1992, section 236 provides that no court shall issue an order compelling an employee to do any work or attend at any place for the doing of any work. This sentiment has been applied by the courts equally to cases where the order is sought against the employer, who may not be made to continue employing a particular individual, and so at common law there has never been any general remedy of reinstatement. If an employee is wrongfully dismissed the general rule is that his remedy lies in damages.[141]

Such a rule (of automatic termination) may, or may not, make practical sense but it is difficult to explain in contractual terms, for in contract law a repudiation is usually of no effect unless accepted by the innocent party— 'an unaccepted repudiation is a thing writ in water and of no value to anybody'[142]—and so in theory an employee faced with wrongful dismissal should be entitled to refuse to accept this repudiation and insist on carrying on in the employment. This, however, used not to be the prevailing view and it was said that contracts of employment form an exceptional category in which the employee has no choice but to accept the repudiation and sue for damages, so that the employer's repudiation automatically terminates the contract.[143] Thus, for example in *Sanders v Ernest A Neale Ltd*[144] Sir John Donaldson P said:

> The obvious, and indeed the only, explanation is that the repudiation of a contract of employment is an exception to the general rule. It terminates the contract without the necessity for acceptance by the injured party.

In *Vine v National Dock Labour Board*[145] a dismissal was held to be invalid on the peculiar facts of the case (considered below), but Viscount Kilmuir LC was at pains to point out that:

> This is an entirely different situation from the ordinary master and servant case; there, if a master wrongfully dismisses the servant, either summarily or by insufficient notice, the employment is effectively terminated, albeit in breach of contract.

---

[140] (1890) 45 Ch D 430 at 438.

[141] Or, in an appropriate case, a quantum meruit action: *Planché v Colburn* (1831) 8 Bing 14.

[142] *Howard v Pickford Tool Co Ltd* [1951] 1 KB 417 at 421, CA, per Asquith LJ. See *White and Carter (Councils) Ltd v McGregor* [1962] AC 413, [1961] 3 All ER 1178, HL.

[143] *Denmark Productions Ltd v Boscobel Productions Ltd* [1969] 1 QB 699, [1968] 3 All ER 513, CA.

[144] [1974] 3 All ER 327 at 333, [1974] ICR 565 at 571.

[145] [1957] AC 488 at 500, [1956] 3 All ER 939 at 944, HL.

and he approved the decision of Jenkins LJ in the Court of Appeal[146] that:

> in the ordinary case of master and servant the repudiation or the wrongful dismissal puts an end to the contract, and the contract having been wrongfully put an end to a claim for damages arises. It is necessarily a claim for damages and nothing more. The nature of the bargain is such that it can be nothing more.

On the other hand, this doctrine of automatic (or 'unilateral') termination was doubted in cases such as *Decro-Wall International SA v Practitioners in Marketing Ltd*;[147] *Hill v C A Parsons & Co Ltd*[148] and *C H Giles & Co Ltd v Morris*.[149] This counter-argument is that the rule against enforcement is not a rule of law, but only a question of fact (albeit frequently recurring fact) in that in nearly all cases the basis of mutual confidence has been destroyed and it would be futile to keep the employment relationship in being. Subsequently, this alternative doctrine of elective (or 'acceptance') termination gained ground, with the result that in some cases it can be argued that the employee did not accept the employer's repudiation of the contract (although in most cases in practice such acceptance will be easy to infer). This can be seen in the judgment of Megarry V-C in *Thomas Marshall (Exports) Ltd v Guinle*,[150] in the majority decision of the Court of Appeal in *Gunton v Richmond-upon-Thames London Borough Council*[151] and in the judgment of Hodgson J in *Dietman v Brent London Borough Council*.[152] In practice the difference in common law claims between the automatic and elective theories may not be great, for in *Gunton*'s case the majority, having clearly decided in favour of the latter, went on to stress (1) that in most cases the employee will have no option in reality but to accept the employer's repudiation and seek a remedy in damages,[153] and (2) that the rule of practice against specific enforcement of contracts of employment remains strong and may operate independently of the elective theory

---

[146] [1956] 1 QB 658 at 674, [1956] 1 All ER 1 at 8, CA.

[147] [1971] 2 All ER 216, [1971] 1 WLR 361, CA, per Salmon and Sachs LJJ; aliter per Buckley LJ. The majority judgments are cogently criticized by Sir John Donaldson P in *Sanders v Ernest A Neale Ltd* [1974] 3 All ER 327, [1974] ICR 565.

[148] [1972] Ch 305, [1971] 3 All ER 1345, CA, per Lord Denning MR and Sachs LJ. The more traditional view that there is a rule of law against enforcement is well set out in Stamp LJ's dissenting judgment at 322 and 1357 respectively.

[149] [1972] 1 All ER 960 at 970, [1972] 1 WLR 307 at 318, per Megarry J.

[150] [1978] 3 All ER 193, [1978] ICR 905.

[151] [1980] ICR 755, [1980] IRLR 321, CA, per Buckley and Brightman LJJ. Shaw LJ dissented on the reasoning, adopting the automatic approach, but concurred in the result on the facts. The later decision of the Court of Appeal in *London Transport Executive v Clarke* [1981] ICR 355, [1981] IRLR 166, CA, though of fundamental importance on the statutory definition of dismissal, was ambiguous on this point of theory.

[152] [1987] ICR 737, [1987] IRLR 259; upheld on appeal [1988] ICR 842, [1988] IRLR 299, CA.

[153] See eg *Dietman v Brent London Borough Council* (n 152 above) where the acceptance theory was applied, but the court found acceptance established on the facts fairly readily. In *Delaney v Staples* [1992] ICR 483 at 489, [1992] IRLR 191 at 193, HL, Lord Browne-Wilkinson spoke of an unequivocal instant (wrongful) dismissal being 'effective to put an end to the employment relationship, whether or not it unilaterally discharges the contract of employment'. Moreover, in *Marsh v National Autistic Society* [1993] ICR 453 it was held that, even if the elective theory is applied, the demise of the employment relationship will mean that the employee may not sue in debt for continuing wages, but will be confined to the (restricted) action for damages.

so that while, for some purposes,[154] an employee may wish to argue that he did not accept the employer's repudiation, he will not normally be allowed to do so in order to claim specific performance (directly or indirectly). These severe limitations on the elective theory can be seen in *Gunton's* case where the theory was invoked to attack the validity of a dismissal which had omitted proper observance of a contractually binding disciplinary procedure, the plaintiff claiming that he never accepted this repudiation by the employer; to that extent it succeeded, but given that the employer could have dismissed lawfully by going through the procedure properly the court held that the normal rule on damages for wrongful dismissal applied and all that the plaintiff was entitled to was his wages until the date on which a proper dismissal could have been achieved after exhaustion of the procedure. The plaintiff thus succeeded in invalidating the original dismissal, but only obtained a short stay of execution and a few weeks' extra pay (representing the time it would have taken to exhaust the procedure). He certainly did not get his job back, though the elective approach would in theory help to allow room for an atypical case where a court might be persuaded to enforce a contract of employment (where the usual factors against enforcement do not apply) as in *Hill v C A Parsons & Co Ltd*, which is considered below. Moreover, swings continue to swing and roundabouts to turn; in *R v East Berkshire Health Authority, ex p Walsh*[155] in the Court of Appeal May LJ stated unequivocally that he preferred the dissenting judgment of Shaw LJ in *Gunton* and the automatic view, and Sir John Donaldson MR was clearly not ecstatic about the overruling by the majority in *Gunton* of his own previous decision in *Sanders v Ernest A Neale Ltd*,[156] and in *Boyo v Lambeth London Borough Council*[157] the Court of Appeal applied the ratio of *Gunton* (to allow wages for a short extra period that it would have taken the employer to go through the contractual disciplinary procedure properly), but stated their unease at doing so, making it clear that they had grave doubts about the reasoning of the majority in that case.

The question of which theory (elective or automatic) is to be preferred remains at best undecided; in the context of common law claims it has the same intellectual fascination as the question as to how many angels may dance on the head of a pin and (except perhaps in a case where some collateral or incidental matter relies upon the technical continued existence of the contract) about as much practical relevance.

---

[154] See eg the continued existence of the contractual term restricting the employee's activities during employment in *Thomas Marshall (Exports) Ltd v Guinle* (n 150) in spite of the employee's wrongful resignation, the desire in *C H Giles & Co Ltd v Morris* (n 149) to put the plaintiff into employment in the first place, if only so that his remedies would be better when then dismissed, and the (unsuccessful) attempt to enforce a shop steward's contractual right to enter the employer's premises in spite of being under suspension in *City and Hackney Health Authority v National Union of Public Employees* [1985] IRLR 252, CA. More recently, there have been attempts to seek specific enforcement of contracts of employment in order to insist on disciplinary procedures being properly applied—see p 440 below.

[155] [1984] ICR 743, [1984] IRLR 278, CA.   [156] See n 144.

[157] [1994] ICR 727, [1995] IRLR 50, CA. Appearing in person, the employee (who was on a month's notice) had initially argued that, as he had not accepted the employer's repudiation, he was entitled to his wages up to the year 2000(!).

However, when one turns to the possible impact of these theories on statutory rights on dismissal, the picture becomes much more complicated, and in fact it is in the statutory context (usually of unfair dismissal) that most of the active dispute has arisen. One problem is that if the automatic theory is applied to the statutory definition of dismissal[158] it can support the idea of 'self dismissal', ie that if an employee misbehaves sufficiently badly he can be said to have repudiated his contract of employment, thus automatically terminating it; if this is so, there is no 'dismissal' by the employer and so the tribunal is denied jurisdiction to hear a claim of unfair dismissal. The elective theory in fact fits the statutory definition of dismissal much better, for if acceptance of a repudiation is required the termination of the misbehaving employee's contract is brought about by the employer's acceptance of the repudiation and *is* thus 'dismissal' by the employer;[159] on the other hand if the *employer* repudiates the contract, termination is brought about by the employee's acceptance, but this is specifically covered by statute which deems it to be a 'constructive dismissal'.[160] The *elective* theory is thus important for the actual definition of dismissal. However, the second problem is that equal difficulties arise if one applies it to the *date* of dismissal. It is important to know precisely the date for the purpose of applying the stringent time limits in the statute (particularly the limitation period for starting an unfair dismissal action of three months from the 'effective date of termination'),[161] but if an employee could claim that he had in fact refused to accept the employer's repudiation he could argue that the time limit either never started to run or, at least, started to run at some time significantly later than the wording of the statutory definition of 'effective date of termination' would suggest. In the interests of certainty, therefore, it is important that the *automatic* theory be applied to questions of limitation.

One commentator has made a strong case for adopting this differential approach in the statutory context,[162] and this now seems to be the position in practice—in *London Transport Executive v Clarke*[163] the Court of Appeal by a majority disapproved of the idea of 'self dismissal', applying the elective theory, whereas in *Brown v Southall and Knight*[164] and *Robert Cort & Son Ltd v Charman*[165] the EAT rejected arguments based upon that theory when determining the effective date of termination, preferring instead an automatic termination approach based on (1) the wording of the statutory definition of effective date of termination and (2) the need for certainty on this vital

---

[158] Contained in the Employment Rights Act 1996, s 95 (in relation to unfair dismissal) and s 136 (in relation to redundancy).

[159] Within ss 95(1)(a) and 136(1)(a).

[160] Within ss 95(1)(c) and 136(1)(c); see Ch 7, heading 2(i), p 477.

[161] See Ch 7, heading 2(ii), 487.

[162] J McMullen in his very useful article 'A Synthesis of the Mode of Termination of Contracts of Employment' [1982] CLJ 110.

[163] [1981] ICR 355, [1981] IRLR 166, CA.

[164] [1980] ICR 617, [1980] IRLR 130.

[165] [1981] ICR 816, [1981] IRLR 437, approved by the Court of Appeal in *Stapp v Shaftesbury Society* [1982] IRLR 326, CA.

concept. As long as this practical compromise is maintained, the position now seems to be satisfactory, but if there were in the future any real danger of the reintroduction of the sort of uncertainty that existed prior to this case law (and which may still exist in the case of a common law claim), the time would surely be ripe for legislative clarification.

Returning to the common law position, and accepting that there is at least a rule of practice (if not an absolute rule of law) against enforcing contracts of employment in most cases, we must now consider certain established exceptions.

(b) Exceptions to the rule against enforcement

(i) *A negative restraint clause* Where the employee has agreed in the contract not to do certain things (for example not to perform for any other theatre owner during the currency of the contract, or not to work for a competitor within a certain period after leaving the employment),[166] the court will hold him to his promise and enforce that negative stipulation (even if it would not enforce the positive obligations in the contract).[167] It is immaterial that this may indirectly persuade the employee to remain in the employment (ie that it may have indirectly a positive effect), but on the other hand it is well established that the clause must be bona fide, in particular that it must not be in reality a positive obligation merely expressed in a negative way.[168] Moreover, an injunction will not be granted if the practical effect would be to compel the employee to perform his side of the contract or starve (for example where the stipulation is that he will not take any employment for a period after leaving the employment).[169]

(ii) *The decision in Hill v CA Parsons & Co Ltd*[170] In this case, the plaintiff refused to join a union which had negotiated a closed shop with his employers, who therefore gave him one month's notice of dismissal. He had been employed by them for 35 years as a chartered engineer, and had two years to go to retirement, so that the dismissal would affect his pension rights; moreover, the unfair dismissal legislation was due to come into force within six months of the dismissal. The plaintiff sued the employers for wrongful dismissal and claimed an interim injunction restraining them for treating the notice as terminating his employment. This could be construed as enforcing the contract of employment, but the Court of Appeal by a majority (Lord Denning MR and Sachs and Stamp LJJ dissenting) granted the interim injunction. The imminence of the new legislation was obviously a strong background factor (and hence the finding that proper notice would have been at least six months for a man in his position), but

---

[166] See Ch 2, heading 4 (ii), p 90.
[167] *Lumley v Wagner* (1852) 1 De GM & G 604.
[168] *Davis v Foreman* [1894] 3 Ch 654; *Warner Bros Pictures Inc v Nelson* [1937] 1 KB 209, [1936] 3 All ER 160.
[169] *Rely-a-Bell Burglar and Fire Alarm Co Ltd v Eisler* [1926] Ch 609; *Warner Bros Pictures Inc v Nelson* [1937] 1 KB 209, [1936] 3 All ER 160; *Page One Records Ltd v Britton* [1967] 3 All ER 822, [1968] 1 WLR 157; *Warren v Mendy* [1989] ICR 525, [1989] IRLR 210, CA.
[170] [1972] Ch 305, [1971] 3 All ER 1345, CA.

to find in the plaintiff's favour the majority had to go against the normal rule against enforcement (the application of which was the basis of Stamp LJ's dissent). To do so they held that that rule is not a fixed rule of law, but a question of fact which therefore permits exceptions in cases where the usual reasons against enforcement do not apply, in particular where there is continued confidence between the parties (as in this case, where both the parties wanted to continue the employment and the pressure to terminate it came from the trade union).[171] Further, Lord Denning said that in this case damages were not an adequate remedy, so it was right that an injunction should be granted, on the principle 'ubi jus ibi remedium'[172] which would allow the court to 'step over the trip-wires of previous cases and to bring the law into accord with the needs of today'. It may certainly be argued that justice was done to the plaintiff in this case, but it left many questions open which would have had to have been solved had this area of law not been effectively superseded by the introduction in 1971 of the unfair dismissal action, particularly as the case cast doubt on the general principle discussed above that when an employer repudiates a contract of employment, that automatically terminates the contract and the employee must accept the repudiation and sue for damages; this raised the problem of what circumstances would put a case into the category in which the employer's repudiation might not have this automatic effect, and opened the way for rather refined arguments based on the concept of repudiation which at times, it is submitted, could stray a long way from the realities of employment.[173] In the event, the case did not lead to a radical reappraisal of enforcement of contracts of employment at common law, and was restrictively construed in subsequent cases as a rare case on its facts, relying upon the continued existence of mutual confidence between the parties, which is unlikely to be so in many cases.[174] However, the case is a decision of the Court of Appeal and at least shows that there may be some scope for enforcement of the contract as a remedy at common law.

At times subsequently, interest has been rekindled to some extent in the possibility of such a common law remedy. In *Irani v Southampton and South West Hampshire Health Authority*[175] Warner J applied *Hill v C A Parsons & Co Ltd* to grant an injunction restraining a dismissal in breach of quasi-statutory disciplinary procedures. A similar result was reached by Mervyn Davies J in *Wadcock v London Borough of Brent*[176]

---

[171] This view of the facts was disputed by Stamp LJ.

[172] 'Where there is a right, there is a remedy', but in this context perhaps best translated as 'where there is a will, there is a way'.

[173] See, eg, *Shields Furniture Ltd v Goff* [1973] 2 All ER 653, [1973] ICR 187, NIRC.

[174] *GKN (Cwmbran) Ltd v Lloyd* [1972] ICR 214; *Sanders v Ernest A Neale Ltd* [1974] 3 All ER 327, [1974] ICR 565; *Chappell v Times Newspapers Ltd* [1975] 2 All ER 233, [1975] ICR 145, CA; *City and Hackney Health Authority v NUPE* [1985] IRLR 252, CA. In *GKN (Cwmbran) Ltd v Lloyd* Sir John Donaldson P suggested (at 221) that a further material factor in *Hill v C A Parsons & Co Ltd* was that the actual dismissal had not taken place, so that the court was restraining a proposed dismissal, not putting an employee back into employment after he had been effectively dismissed. This point was also stressed by Lord Prosser in the Court of Session in *Anderson v Pringle of Scotland Ltd* [1998] IRLR 64.

[175] [1985] ICR 590, [1985] IRLR 203.   [176] [1990] IRLR 223.

and by Morland J in *Robb v London Borough of Hammersmith and Fulham*[177] in the case of contractually binding disciplinary procedures. In *Powell v London Borough of Brent*[178] the Court of Appeal granted an interlocutory injunction restraining the employers from depriving the employee of a promotion for which she had successfully applied. In *Hughes v London Borough of Southwark* [179] Taylor J granted an interlocutory injunction restraining the employers from insisting on the employees taking on work which the latter argued was not within their contractual obligations. In *Anderson v Pringle of Scotland Ltd*[180] Lord Prosser granted an interim interdict to restrain a redundancy dismissal in breach of a LIFO redundancy agreement which was assumed to be part of the employee's individual contract. In *Peace v City of Edinburgh Council*[181] Lord Penrose restrained the disciplining (*short* of dismissal) of the employee under a new procedure which he argued he had not consented to as part of his contract. And in *Gryf-Lowczowski v Hitchingbrooke Healthcare NHS Trust*[182] Gray J restrained a threatened dismissal in breach of contractual procedures which would have prejudiced a doctor's chance of re-employment by a different trust. In these cases, the basis of the court's power to intervene is clearly seen as the (argued) continued existence of mutual confidence between the parties,[183] with the exception of *Gryf-Lowczowski* where mutual confidence had vanished but it was held that this was outweighed by the factors that timely intervention was possible and the claimant's professional future was at stake. However, the point remains that these are *not* ordinary, everyday dismissal cases (indeed, *Powell*, *Hughes* and *Peace* are not dismissal cases at all) and while they may point to interesting and useful developments in the use (or threatened use) of

---

[177] [1991] ICR 514, [1991] IRLR 72.

[178] [1988] ICR 176, [1987] IRLR 466, CA; after the plaintiff's successful application for the senior post, one of the unsuccessful applicants claimed that the council's equal opportunity policy had been infringed and so the council purported to negate the promotion and re-advertise the post.

[179] [1988] IRLR 55. In *Ali v London Borough of Southwark* [1988] ICR 567, [1988] IRLR 100 a challenge to threatened disciplinary proceedings that the plaintiff said would be irregular failed on two grounds: (1) no continued mutual confidence; (2) the court will not normally step in in advance to restrain pending disciplinary proceedings (applying the similar rule in trade union cases, in *Longley v National Union of Journalists* [1987] IRLR 109, CA).

[180] [1998] IRLR 64, OH. Lord Prosser stated that 'such exceptional cases as there have been give no very clear picture of the criteria for intervention', but justified his order on the grounds that (1) there was no evidence of loss of trust in the employee (this being a redundancy case) and (2) court intervention was possible before the dismissal was due to take place.

[181] [1999] IRLR 417, OH. Here it was important that it was a breach of contract during employment that was being restrained, and that both parties were assuming that the contract was to continue.

[182] [2006] IRLR 100.

[183] This means either no loss of confidence on the facts or, possibly, that any such loss by the employer is on irrational grounds, and so rectifiable. In Hughes, Taylor J said that mutual confidence should not be considered to have gone merely because the employer and employee are in genuine dispute as to the construction or application of certain contractual terms or duties. Note, however, that in *Robb* Morland J took a slightly different approach saying that, while continued trust and confidence is important where the employee is trying to get his job back, if (as in that case) the employee was only interested in securing use of the disciplinary procedure in order to air his grievances the test should be whether a court order would actually be workable.

the common law to restrain employer misuses of contractually binding disciplinary procedures,[184] it would be premature to consider them as showing a resurgence of common law actions aimed at preserving employment in wrongful dismissal cases generally, particularly as it is equally possible to point to contemporaneous decisions refusing similar relief for traditional reasons.[185] There is, however, one procedural innovation which might have some influence here. What is now Part 24 of the Civil Procedure Rules (originally Order 14A of the Rules of the Supreme Court) was introduced to allow a court to determine any question of law or construction of any document at any stage in the proceedings where it appears to the court that (1) such question is suitable for determination without a full trial of the action and (2) such determination will finally determine the entire cause or matter or any claim or issue therein. This de facto power to issue a declaration of the meaning of, for example, a contract of employment, was used by Chadwick J in *Jones v Gwent County Council*[186] to declare that a letter of dismissal was not validly issued within the contract and, on that basis, to grant injunctions restraining the employers from acting on it. Technically, this power does not 'enforce' the contract of employment, but if its use became more widespread the question would have to be faced as to whether it constituted unacceptable back-door enforcement.

(iii) *Where the dismissal is a nullity* In certain public sector cases, a dismissed employee may be able to invoke certain administrative law remedies to argue that his dismissal was invalid; if this is accepted, the legal result is that there was no effective dismissal, and so the contract of employment will be indirectly enforced. The two principal bases for challenge are that the dismissal was contrary to the rules of natural justice or was in some way ultra vires.[187] There has been considerable case law on this question, though in the modern case law the emphasis has switched to consideration of how this confusing area of law fits in with the procedure for claiming judicial review under what was originally RSC Order 53 and is now CPR 54. In turn, this has coincided with increased interest in this area of employment law since it is well appreciated now that in unfair dismissal cases tribunals hardly ever order reinstatement or

---

[184] Similar proceedings can be seen in *Deitman v Brent London Borough Council* [1988] IRLR 299, CA.

[185] *Alexander v Standard Telephones and Cables plc* [1990] ICR 291, [1990] IRLR 55; *Jakeman v South West Thames Regional Health Authority and London Ambulance Service* [1990] IRLR 62; *Wishart v NACAB Ltd* [1990] ICR 794, [1990] IRLR 383, CA.

[186] [1992] IRLR 521.

[187] Ganz 'Public Law Principles Applicable to Dismissal from Employment' (1967) 30 MLR 288; Freedland *The Contract of Employment* (1976) pp 278–92; Davidson 'Judicial Review of Decisions to Dismiss' (1984) 35 NILQ 121 (written before the decision in *ex p Walsh*, n 209); Fredman and Lee 'Natural Justice for Employees' (1986) 15 ILJ 15; Ewing and Grubb 'The Emergence of a New Labour Injunction?' (1987) 16 ILJ 145; Fredman and Morris 'Public or Private? State Employees and Judicial Review' (1991) 107 LQR 298; Sedley 'Public Law and Contractual Entitlement' (1994) 23 ILJ 201; Laws 'Public Law and Employment Law: Abuse of Power' [1997] PL 455; Freedland (1990) 19 ILJ 199, (1991) 20 ILJ 72; Carty (1991) 54 MLR 129; Smith and Randall *Contract Actions in Modern Employment Law: Developments and Issues* (2002) ch 10. Presumably other public law grounds of challenge such as perversity would be applicable, though less likely to succeed: see *R v Hertfordshire County Council, ex p NUPE* [1985] IRLR 258, CA.

re-engagement; thus any remedy that may in fact keep the employee in employment such as this may well be worth pursuing, certainly in cases arising in the public sector. The following attempt[188] at explanation proceeds by examining first the older case law and then the more recent case law on what is now CPR 54. It is tempting to think of the former as establishing the principles and the latter as determining the remedy but, as will be seen, that would be an oversimplification.

The older case law   In *Ridge v Baldwin*[189] a chief constable who was dismissed without a proper opportunity to be heard in his own defence was granted a declaration that the decision to dismiss him was a nullity as it was in breach of natural justice.[190] Remedies such as this are familiar in the context of expulsion from a trade union and indeed if a dismissal involved jeopardizing trade union rights (as in *Taylor v National Union of Seamen*[191] where dismissal as branch secretary disqualified the individual from later standing for office in the union) the safer course is to rely upon the denial of those rights, not the dismissal. However, in the ordinary case of dismissal the application of these remedies has been confused and illogical. In *Malloch v Aberdeen Corpn*[192] Lord Wilberforce said:

> A comparative list in which persons have been held entitled or not entitled to a hearing, or to observation of rules of natural justice, according to the master and servant test, looks illogical and even bizarre. A specialist surgeon is denied protection which is given to a hospital doctor; a University professor, as a servant, has been denied the right to be heard, a dock labourer and an undergraduate have been granted it.[193]

This confusion arises because if one thing is certain in this area it is that these remedies are not available in 'ordinary master and servant cases'. Thus, in *Ridge v Baldwin* Lord Reid said:[194]

> The law regarding master and servant is not in doubt. There cannot be specific performance of a contract of service and the master can terminate his contract with the servant at

---

[188] Humility is, it is said, a virtue. Any over-confident lawyer wishing to learn it should consider the case law that follows in some depth. He or she is likely to come away from it feeling at best chastened and at worst an *ursus mentis parvae.*

[189] [1964] AC 40, [1963] 2 All ER 66, HL; applied in *Chief Constable of the North Wales Police v Evans* [1982] 3 All ER 141, [1982] 1 WLR 1155, HL.

[190] One possible limitation on the effectiveness of natural justice (even if locus standi can be shown) may be the decision in *R v Chief Constable of the Thames Valley Police, ex p Cotton* [1990] IRLR 344, CA, that in order to succeed the applicant employee must show not just a breach of the procedural requirements of natural justice, but also actual prejudice caused to him.

[191] [1967] 1 All ER 767, [1967] 1 WLR 532; *Stevenson v United Road Transport Union* [1977] 2 All ER 941, [1977] ICR 893, CA.

[192] [1971] 2 All ER 1278 at 1294, [1971] 1 WLR 1578 at 1595, HL; *Jones v Lee and Guilding* [1980] ICR 310, [1980] IRLR 67, CA.

[193] See *Barber v Manchester Regional Hospital Board* [1958] 1 All ER 322, [1958] 1 WLR 181; *Palmer v Inverness Hospitals Board,* 1963 SC 311; *Vidyodaya University of Ceylon v Silva* [1964] 3 All ER 865, [1965] 1 WLR 77, PC; *Vine v National Dock Labour Board* [1957] AC 488, [1956] 3 All ER 939, HL; *Glynn v Keele University* [1971] 2 All ER 89, [1971] 1 WLR 487.

[194] [1964] AC 40 at 65, [1963] 2 All ER 66 at 71, HL.

any time and for any reason or for none.[195] But if he does so in a manner not warranted by the contract he must pay damages for breach of contract. So the question in a pure case of master and servant does not at all depend on whether the master has heard the servant in his own defence; it depends on whether the facts emerging at the trial prove breach of contract.

The problem therefore becomes to determine how to distinguish between ordinary master and servant cases and those rare cases in which the remedies may be invoked. In *Ridge v Baldwin*[196] Lord Reid envisaged the doctrine of natural justice as applicable to an 'office-holder' who could only be dismissed for some measure of cause, and in *Malloch v Aberdeen Corpn*, where a Scottish teacher whose employment was heavily qualified by statute was held by a majority of the House of Lords to have been entitled to a hearing before dismissal, Lord Wilberforce said:[197]

> One may accept that if there are relationships in which all requirements of the observance of rules of natural justice are excluded …, these must be confined to what have been called 'pure master and servant cases', which I take to mean cases in which there is no element of *public employment or service*, no support by *statute*, nothing in the nature of an *office or a status* which is capable of protection. If any of these elements exist, then, in my opinion, whatever the terminology used, and even though in some inter partes aspects the relationship may be called that of master and servant, there may be essential procedural requirements to be observed, and failure to observe them may result in a dismissal being declared to be void.

It is submitted that this is one of the clearest statements of the position in the older cases, but even here the difficulties are numerous, for although his Lordship talks of 'any' of these elements existing, it is clear that they are not necessarily enough by themselves; for example many employees are in 'public employment' but at too lowly a level to claim protection.[198] This means that there will be some need for additional 'status', as in the third element mentioned, but it is this very 'status' that is the elusive factor. Moreover, the question arises whether an office holder in purely private, commercial employment (for example a company secretary) would be able to challenge his

---

[195] The case was decided before the introduction of the unfair dismissal provisions in the Industrial Relations Act 1971.

[196] [1964] AC 40, [1963] 2 All ER 66, HL.

[197] [1971] 2 All ER 1278 at 1294, [1971] 1 WLR 1578 at 1595, emphasis added. Lord Morris (dissenting) took a narrower view of the application of the remedies to employment cases, as he had done in his decision in *Vidyodaya University of Ceylon v Silva* [1964] 3 All ER 865, [1965] 1 WLR 77, PC, but in his speech in *Malloch's* case Lord Wilberforce doubted the correctness of that case on this point (see at 1295 and 1596 respectively).

[198] See eg *Forbes v Johnston* [1971] NZLR 117. The point is taken up in the case law on CPR 54 discussed later in this chapter. In *R v BBC, ex p Lavelle* [1983] ICR 99, [1982] IRLR 404, Woolf J suggested that any employment protected by procedural rules before dismissal might have the necessary office-holding status; this would have had enormous repercussions since most permanent employments these days would come into that category, with disciplinary rules written into their terms of employment. This idea has not been taken any further in the subsequent case law (see eg the narrow approach to 'office' in *R v Hertfordshire County Council, ex p NUPE* [1985] IRLR 258, CA).

dismissal in this way—in theory there is no reason why not, but so far the cases have all been in the context of public employment of sorts, except in *Stevenson v United Road Transport Union*[199] where the dismissed employee was employed by a trade union as an officer of that union.

The position is little clearer when one turns from questions of natural justice to a challenge on the basis of the dismissal being ultra vires. In *McClelland v Northern Ireland General Health Services Board*[200] the House of Lords appear to have held by a majority that a dismissal for a reason other than one expressly permitted in the particular contract of employment in question was ultra vires in the sense of not being allowed under the contract. Normally, however, such a dismissal would only give rise to an action for damages for wrongful dismissal, and if that case is correct the reasoning can only apply where the contract is particularly explicit on the permissible reasons for dismissal. More normally, a challenge on the basis of ultra vires will be based upon a statutory scheme or requirement governing the employment, as in *Vine v National Dock Labour Board*[201] where a registered dock worker employed by the Board (under the now repealed statutory scheme designed to dispense with casual labour on the docks) was dismissed for refusing a valid order, but his dismissal was effected by a committee which, on the true construction of the statutory scheme, did not have power to do so. The House of Lords held the dismissal to be ultra vires, and gave a declaration that it was a nullity. Viscount Kilmuir LC stressed that the existence of the special statutory scheme took the employee out of the 'ordinary master–servant' category:[202]

> Here, the removal of the plaintiff's name from the register being in law a nullity, he continued to have the right to be treated as a registered dockworker with all the benefits which, by statute, that status conferred on him. It is therefore right that, with the background of this scheme, the court should declare his rights.

Challenge on the basis of ultra vires has, however, been restrictively construed, and will not apply simply because the employment in question is in some way governed by statute; even if it has a 'strong statutory flavour' it may still be deemed to be an ordinary master–servant case,[203] and in *Francis v Municipal Councillors of Kuala Lumpur*[204] Lord Morris said that relief could only be given in such cases if there were 'special circumstances'; in *Vine's* case, those circumstances were the all-embracing nature of the statutory scheme and the fact that the employee could not work as a docker *at all* if dismissed from the Board's employment.

---

[199] [1977] 2 All ER 941, [1977] ICR 893, CA; cf *Taylor v National Union of Seamen* [1967] 1 All ER 767, [1967] 1 WLR 532.

[200] [1957] 2 All ER 129, [1957] 1 WLR 594, HL.

[201] [1957] AC 488, [1956] 3 All ER 939, HL; *Taylor v Furness, Withy & Co Ltd* [1969] 1 Lloyd's Rep 324, 6 KIR 488.

[202] [1957] AC 488 at 500, [1956] 3 All ER 939 at 944.

[203] *Barber v Manchester Regional Hospital Board* [1958] 1 All ER 322, [1958] 1 WLR 181.

[204] [1962] 3 All ER 633, [1962] 1 WLR 1411, PC.

Thus, the cases where a dismissal has been successfully challenged as a nullity have been uncommon in the past, and the principles upon which they have succeeded are uncertain, though usually revolved round some sort of elusive office-holding status. Theoretically that has been no great hardship for we now have the laws relating to unfair dismissal, where matters of natural justice[205] and compliance with internal disciplinary procedures re-emphasized by ACAS Code of Practice. However, the practical position may be slightly different with, as stated above, renewed interest generally in common law and/or administrative law remedies for dismissed employees, given the low instance of reinstatement by tribunals and, in some cases, the desire to use the vehicle of an individual challenge in order to prevent or deter abuse of disciplinary procedures by the employer.[206] We can now turn to the later case law but here we find procedural complications.

The problem of Order 53 Order 53 was introduced into the Rules of the Supreme Court in 1977 (and continued into the current civil procedure rules as CPR 54) in order to simplify procedure, so that now there can be one application for 'judicial review' which can lead, if successful, to the granting of any one of the appropriate remedies (certiorari, mandamus, prohibition, declaration, injunction or, possibly, damages). It contains an anti-technicality rule whereby an application under the rule can, if it transpires that that is the wrong procedure, be deemed to have been commenced instead by writ, and proceed accordingly. Essentially it was a liberalizing reform though it does import certain restrictions (especially a time limit) and, more important here, has led to a position in which the division between 'public law' and 'private law' is thrown into higher relief than previously.[207] This has happened through a series of House of Lords cases[208] in which their Lordships have been concerned to establish the proper relationship between the public law remedy in Order 53/CPR 54 and ordinary private law claims, so that hopefully the rule will be neither abused nor so construed as to restrict unduly (or even prejudice) genuine private law claims. The position basically is that application is to be made under CPR 54 if, but only if, the subject matter of the complaint relates to public law (as that is in the process of being defined). Thus, tests

---

[205] Ideas derived from natural justice permeate the ACAS Code of Practice 1 (2009) 'Disciplinary and Grievance Procedures'. Also, there have been cases where rules of natural justice have been applied directly when considering procedural unfairness; see eg *Ayanlowo v IRC* [1975] IRLR 253; CA; *Khanum v Mid-Glamorgan Area Health Authority* [1979] ICR 40, [1978] IRLR 215; cf *Slater v Leicestershire Health Authority* [1989] IRLR 16, CA.

[206] See heading 4(ii), p 440.

[207] This distinction may now have yet more significance under the Human Rights Act 1998; see Morris 'The Human Rights Act and the Public/Private Divide' (1998) 27 ILJ 293.

[208] *O'Reilly v Mackman* [1983] 2 AC 237, [1982] 3 All ER 1124, HL; *Cocks v Thanet District Council* [1983] 2 AC 286, [1982] 3 All ER 1135, HL; *Davy v Spelthorne Borough Council* [1984] AC 262, [1983] 3 All ER 278, HL; *Wandsworth London Borough Council v Winder* [1985] AC 461, [1984] 3 All ER 976; *Roy v Kensington, Chelsea and Westminster Family Practitioner Committee* [1992] 1 All ER 705, [1992] IRLR 233, HL. For an interesting application in the employment context, see *Doyle v Northumbria Probation Committee* [1991] 4 All ER 294, [1992] ICR 121. A different, less technical, approach applies in Scotland: *West v Secretary of State for Scotland* [1992] IRLR 399, Ct of Sess.

have been evolving as to when the CPR 54 remedy is available but the problem in the employment law field is that those tests may not be exactly the same as the principles that evolved under the previous case law as to when some sort of remedy should be given by the courts to a dismissed employee (usually in the past by way of a declaration or injunction); in other words, the older principles and the new remedy may not be co-terminous.

The leading case is *R v East Berkshire Health Authority, ex p Walsh*[209] in which a senior nursing officer (employed under a contract which pursuant to regulations and with the approval of the Secretary of State incorporated terms and conditions jointly agreed for the health service) sought to challenge his dismissal on the grounds of breach of natural justice (through not being given a proper hearing) and ultra vires (having been dismissed, he argued, by an official who did not have the power to do so under the relevant contractual term). He applied for judicial review under Order 53, seeking an order of certiorari to quash the dismissal; he was successful at first instance but the Court of Appeal unanimously rejected the application. They held that the dismissal did not raise the sort of issues of public law necessary under Order 53 to attract the remedy of certiorari. What is the basis for such a decision? The one thing that is clear is that the fact that the applicant was employed by a public body of sorts is *not* enough without more to attract public law remedies; if it were otherwise a substantial proportion of the workforce would be able to seek remedies on dismissal from the Divisional Court, thus potentially outflanking the employment tribunal system which, according to the Court of Appeal, is a far more appropriate forum for the sort of issues that arise on dismissal. The relevant distinction must therefore lie elsewhere. As seen above, in the older case law the courts tended to look at *the status of the applicant*. In *ex p Walsh*, however, the court clearly looked instead at *the nature of his complaint*—did it raise matters cat-egorizable as public law? It is true that Mr Walsh's contract was made by reference to regulatory provisions and subject (ultimately) to sanctioning by the Secretary of State. However, he was not complaining that his contract had not been made in accordance with the correct statutory procedures; his complaint was in essence quite simply that, having been properly made, his contract had then been *broken* by the health authority by the manner of his dismissal. Breach of contract, said the Court of Appeal, remains a matter of private law (even when the employment is in the public sector with some measure of public control):

> The ordinary employer is free to act in breach of his contracts of employment and if he does so his employee will acquire certain private law rights and remedies in damages for wrongful dismissal, an order for reinstatement or re-engagement and so on. Parliament can underpin the position of public authority employees by directly restricting the freedom of the public

---

[209] [1984] ICR 743, [1984] IRLR 278, CA, noted Cripps [1984] CLJ 214, Collins (1984) 13 ILJ 174; *R v Derbyshire County Council, ex p Noble* [1990] ICR 808, [1990] IRLR 332, CA. Where the applicant is a civil servant, an application for judicial review can raise fundamental questions as to the contractual position for Crown servants: see Ch 2, heading 1, p 36 and in particular *R v Lord Chancellor's Department, ex p Nangle* [1991] ICR 743, [1991] IRLR 343.

authority to dismiss, thus giving the employee 'public law' rights and at least making him a potential candidate for administrative law remedies. Alternatively, it can require the authority to contract with its employees on specified terms with a view to the employee acquiring 'private law' rights under the terms of the contract of employment. If the authority fails or refuses thus to create 'private law' rights for the employee, the employee will have 'public law' rights to compel compliance, the remedy being mandamus requiring the authority so to contract or a declaration that the employee had those rights. If, however, the authority gives the employee the required protection, a breach of that contract is not a matter of 'public law' and gives rise to no administrative law remedies.[210]

The only remedies sought by Mr. Walsh arise solely out of his contract of employment with them as opposed to any public duty imposed upon the health authority.[211]

Thus the requirements for Order 53 were not satisfied. In the subsequent case of *McClaren v Home Office*[212] the doyen of modern administrative law, Woolf LJ, developed this approach into four principles which constitute valuable guidance in this maze.

(1) In relation to a personal claim against the employer, an employee of a public body is normally in exactly the same situation as other employees and can bring proceedings in the ordinary way for damages, a declaration or an injunction (except in relation to the Crown).[213]

(2) An employee of a public body can seek judicial review and obtain a remedy which would not be available to an employee in the private sector where there exists some disciplinary or other body established under the prerogative or by statute to which the employer or employee is entitled or required to refer disputes affecting their relationship.

(3) In addition, if an employee of a public body is adversely affected by a decision of general application by his employer, he can be entitled to challenge that decision by way of judicial review on grounds that it is flawed.

(4) Judicial review will *not* be available where disciplinary procedures are of a purely domestic nature, albeit that their decisions might affect the public.

At first sight, it may appear that what the Court of Appeal was doing in these cases was to lay down new principles to replace those in the older case law as to when any form of remedy is to be given, and to do so restrictively in an attempt to minimize the use

---

[210] Per Sir John Donaldson MR at 752 and 281, respectively.

[211] Per Purchas LJ at 769 and 288, respectively.

[212] [1990] ICR 824, [1990] IRLR 338, CA. The case is primarily of importance as a statement of the contractual status of civil servants: see Ch 2, heading 1, p 36. The following passage is merely a précis; Woolf LJ's erudite judgment deserves reading as a whole.

[213] In the case itself a prison officer was seeking to sue the Home Office for breach of contract; it was therefore the Home Office who were arguing that his remedies properly lay in judicial review (for which his application would have been out of time). The restrictive approach to Ord 53 thus worked in the employee's favour on the facts.

of administrative law remedies and have dismissal cases dealt with before the proper forum of employment tribunals (a strong and potent policy factor). However, the position is not so simple because there is a further stage. As explained above, Order 53 provided that an action wrongly commenced under the Order could be transformed at the court's discretion into an action begun by writ (now claim form). In *ex p Walsh*, the employee applied for this to be done but that application was refused by the Court of Appeal on procedural grounds. Thus although *ex p Walsh* is the leading case on what is now CPR 54 and dismissal cases, it does not answer the further question—if the transforming rule is applied (or indeed if an action is commenced by claim form in the first place seeking a declaration or injunction on the grounds of breach of natural justice or ultra vires), what principles are *then* to apply to determine whether relief should be given? Here it seems that the principles in the older cases still apply, and we are back to the status of the employee. As Purchas LJ put it:

> It is important to remember that the three categories of employment described by Lord Reid in *Ridge v Baldwin* and referred to in *Malloch v Aberdeen Corpn* were directed to the question of the right to be heard and not to the procedural question [ie under Order 53] which is central to the instant appeal.... It is important, in my judgment, to distinguish the two concepts involved. The first is the well-debated problem as to whether or not an obligation to obey the rules of natural justice in master and servant cases encapsulated in the expression 'audi alteram partem' is imported into a contract of employment. The second is whether that invokes of necessity the supervisory powers of the court.[214]

To sum up, an application under CPR 54 to challenge a dismissal will only be successful if the nature of the applicant's complaint is such as to raise issues of public law and *ex p Walsh*, the leading case, establishes that a complaint that is essentially one of breach of contract by the employer is *not* categorizable as a matter of public law. Even if CPR 54 is inapplicable, a court may in its discretion treat the application as if begun by claim form for a declaration or injunction (or indeed the applicant may have proceeded in that manner in the first place). In such a case the court may still have jurisdiction to intervene (even though this leads to the logically unsatisfactory position of applying public law concepts such as breach of natural justice or ultra vires in cases to which ex hypothesi the principal public law procedure of CPR 54 is not applicable). Moreover, the grounds for interfering appear to be wider, for the test to be applied is *not* that contained in *ex p Walsh* of the nature of the complaint (ie the criterion for coming under CPR 54), but rather the old test based upon the status of the employee. The older case law on this (considered above) tended to look for something in the nature of, or analogous to, 'officeholding' and, while it stands independently of the recent case law on Order 53/CPR 54, the tenor of the latter suggests that here too a restrictive approach is likely to be taken, for fear of opening the way for a multitude of cases (especially from the public sector) being brought before the ordinary courts which, in the opinion

---

[214] At 768 and 287, respectively.

of the Court of Appeal in *ex p Walsh*, should be dealt with instead by employment tribunals.[215]

(c) Damages for wrongful dismissal

The remedies for wrongful dismissal are limited not only by the rule against enforcement, but also by the restricted measure of damages recoverable in many cases. The restriction arises once again from the doctrine of notice, for if an employer wrongfully dismisses an employee who should have had, say, two weeks' notice, what has the employee in fact lost? He cannot be said to have lost his long-term livelihood, for at common law he could have been dismissed at any time merely by being given two weeks' notice. Thus, all that he has lost is his two weeks' notice, and so his measure of damage is restricted to his pay during that period.[216] This is backed by the general principle that, in a damages action, the employers must be assumed to have discharged their contractual duties towards the employee in the way least onerous to them, which will usually mean assuming that they would have ended the contract in any event, as quickly as they could lawfully have done so (usually by giving notice).[217] Basically, therefore, a wrongfully dismissed employee is entitled to damages equal to his wages or salary during his notice period.[218] Moreover, the common law was always wary of giving further damages under other heads. Thus, in *Addis v Gramophone Co Ltd*[219]

---

[215] The Scottish courts have shown a consistently strict view on the matter, not allowing judicial review of what are essentially contractual matters: *West v Secretary of State for Scotland* [1992] IRLR 399, Ct of Sess. In *Blair v Lochaber District Council* [1995] IRLR 135 the Court of Session refused review to a chief executive allegedly suspended contrary to the authority's own rules, which was held to remain essentially a contractual matter. Distinguishing *Malloch*, above (itself a Scottish decision, but now apparently out of favour) it was held that even if the older case law had to be considered, the chief executive here did not have the necessary 'status' as an office holder. If he did not, who does?

[216] A gloss here is that if a contractually binding disciplinary procedure has been breached, a court may look at when the contract could lawfully have been terminated, awarding damages for a short period representing the time necessary to have operated the procedure properly and then the notice period: *Gunton v Richmond-upon-Thames London Borough Council* [1980] ICR 755, [1980] IRLR 321, CA; *Boyo v Lambeth London Borough Council* [1994] ICR 727, [1995] IRLR 50, CA. However, a court or tribunal cannot go farther and speculate on the chances of the employee having been kept on if the proper procedure had gone in his favour: *Fosca Services (UK) Ltd v Birkett* [1996] IRLR 325; *Janciuk v Winerite Ltd* [1998] IRLR 63, EAT.

[217] This principle, taken from the majority decision in *Lavarack v Woods of Colchester Ltd* [1967] 1 QB 278, [1966] 3 All ER 683, CA (see n 220), was applied strongly in *Janciuk v Winerite Ltd* (above) and *Morran v Glasgow Council of Tenants' Associations* [1998] IRLR 67, Ct of Sess.

[218] One slight extension here is that the employee may also claim any benefit that he would have qualified for, had he been given and served out the proper length of notice: *Silvey v Pendragon plc* [2001] EWCA Civ 789, [2001] IRLR 685 (proper notice would have taken the employee past the age of 55, which was significant for pension purposes; damages awarded to reflect this). It is of course possible that the contract may itself quantify the amount to be paid on termination (especially in the case of a high earners); a danger with this is that, on ordinary contract principles, it may be attacked as a penalty clause, but in *Murray v Leisureplay Ltd* [2005] IRLR 946, CA the court took an indulgent approach to this and validated such a 'golden parachute' clause.

[219] [1909] AC 488, HL, reaffirmed in *Bliss v South East Thames Regional Health Authority* [1987] ICR 700, [1985] IRLR 308, CA. See *Alexander v Standard Telephones and Cables Ltd (No 2)* [1991] IRLR 286. The employee's remedy lies in damages; he may not sue instead in debt for continuing wages into the future: *Marsh v National Autistic Society* [1993] ICR 453.

an employee who was paid at a fixed salary plus commission was wrongfully dismissed and claimed damages under the following heads—(1) salary for the six-month notice period, (2) reasonable commission for a six-month period, (3) damages for the humiliating manner of dismissal, (4) damages for loss of reputation leading to future difficulty in obtaining employment. The House of Lords held by a majority that only heads (1) and (2) were recoverable. Also, the law only looked at the definite contractual liabilities of the employer in assessing damages, not at what the employee might in fact have received (eg a discretionary bonus which he might have received during the notice period). In *Lavarack v Woods of Colchester Ltd*[220] an employee who was wrongfully dismissed had been on a five-year contract with a fixed salary subject to periodic discretionary bonuses. After he had been dismissed (but during the period for which the contract should have continued) the employers discontinued the bonus scheme and increased the wages of their staff. The Court of Appeal held by a majority that the increase in wages should not be taken into account when assessing the damages, since the only fully contractual obligation upon the employers was to pay the fixed salary and anything on top of that was discretionary (whether a bonus or an increase in wages). Lord Denning MR, dissenting, took the wider view that the dismissed employee was entitled to recover all that he would *in fact* have earned but for the employers' breach of contract.

To this harsh general rule on damages, there are exceptions:

(i) *Fixed-term contracts* Where the contract of employment is for a fixed term, not terminable by notice, the damages recoverable are the amount which the employee would have earned under the contract during the remainder of the term, after the wrongful dismissal (subject to mitigation, which is considered below).

(ii) *Additional benefit work* Certain untypical contracts of employment may be construed as envisaging a greater reward for the employee than the bare wage or salary, so that damages in respect of this further loss can be recovered in addition. Thus in *Marbé v George Edwardes (Daly's Theatres) Ltd*[221] an American actress wishing to establish her reputation in London contracted to play a particular part for the defendant, who undertook to give her full publicity. When she was wrongfully denied the chance to play the part, the Court of Appeal held that she could recover the salary due to her for the period of the contract *plus* an amount representing loss of reputation. The extent of this exception outside the theatre is uncertain (quaere, for example, whether it would apply to any case where the courts found that there was a contractual obligation to provide the employee with actual work, not simply to pay wages),[222] but one case which is at least

---

[220] [1967] 1 QB 278, [1966] 3 All ER 683, CA; *Bold v Brough, Nicholson and Hall Ltd* [1963] 3 All ER 849, [1964] 1 WLR 201. Damages for loss of rights under a share option scheme were refused because of a literal interpretation of the scheme's rules in *Micklefield v SAC Technology Ltd* [1991] 1 All ER 275, [1990] IRLR 218.

[221] [1928] 1 KB 269, CA. See also *Herbert Clayton and Jack Waller Ltd v Oliver* [1930] AC 209, HL; *Withers v General Theatre Corpn Ltd* [1933] 2 KB 536, CA.

[222] See Ch 3, heading 3(ii), p 141.

analogous is *Dunk v George Waller & Son Ltd*[223] where the plaintiff, an apprentice, was wrongfully dismissed during the four-year term in question and was held entitled to his net loss of wages for the rest of the term plus an amount representing loss of tuition and training and diminution of future prospects. One possible variant of this may be where the extra 'benefit' that the employee expects under the contract is so important that the court will imply a term that the employer will not use the normal power to dismiss by notice so as to deprive the employee of that benefit. This has arisen in the 'PHI cases', where a long-term sick employee is deprived of major financial benefits under a permanent health insurance (PHI) scheme, provided by the employer, through the employer dismissing him by notice before he can qualify under the scheme.[224] In such cases, courts have impliedly restricted the power to give notice in sickness absences where the result would be deprivation of PHI rights. Thus, a dismissal (otherwise lawful under the contractual notice provision) may become wrongful, with the prospect opening up of *general* damages for loss of those rights. An open question then becomes whether the PHI cases could be extended to other analogous contexts. This was done in *Jenvey v Australian Broadcasting Corpn*,[225] where damages were awarded for the loss of valuable redundancy rights under the contract due to an unlawful early dismissal held to be wrongful because of its effect. Another interesting possibility might be where an employee is taken on specifically in order to bring with him particular trade, contacts or contracts to the new employer; could it be argued that it is an implied term that he will not be dismissed (other than for gross misconduct) as long as the employer retains that trade, etc, so that general damages for wrongful dismissal could be awarded for any such dismissal?[226]

(iii) *Loss of statutory rights* A third exceptional case seemed to have become established but has recently been disapproved. It concerned the case where the employer breaks the contract of employment by dismissing the employee with no or short notice, thereby depriving him of his statutory rights (especially the right to claim unfair dismissal) by advancing the effective date of dismissal to *within* the qualifying period. In such a case, the employee would be debarred from claiming unfair dismissal (if that were the right in question) but it was suggested that the employee might be able to bring an action in the ordinary courts for *wrongful* dismissal claiming extra damages representing the loss to him of his potential statutory rights.[227] This seemed

[223] [1970] 2 QB 163, [1970] 2 All ER 630. Quaere whether the reasoning in this case applies only to apprenticeship, or might be applicable to any contract of employment envisaging vocational training or retraining.

[224] *Aspden v Webbs Poultry and Meat Group (Holdings) Ltd* [1996] IRLR 521; *Adin v Sedco Forex International Resources Ltd* [1997] IRLR 280, Ct of Sess.

[225] [2003] ICR 79, [2002] IRLR 520; see Ch 3, heading 3(vii), p 157.

[226] General damages could cause particular problems of quantification in a context such as this; a court or tribunal would have to fix some sort of 'multiplier' to assess the likely period of loss, but without the highly developed 'tariff' system available to perform a similar task in personal injury cases.

[227] *Robert Cort & Son Ltd v Charman* [1981] ICR 816, [1981] IRLR 437, per Browne-Wilkinson J, approved by the Court of Appeal in *Stapp v Shaftesbury Society* [1982] IRLR 326, CA. This analysis does not work if there is a express payment in lieu of notice clause in the contract, because then the instant dismissal is not wrongful: *Morran v Glasgow Council of Tenants' Associations* [1998] IRLR 67, Ct of Sess.

to be a practical answer to the possible problem of an employer being able to rely on the relatively rigid rules on dates of termination and qualifying periods through deliberate breach of contract on his own part, and an award of damages on this basis was finally permitted by the EAT in *Raspin v United News Shops Ltd*[228] where a summary dismissal three weeks short of the unfair dismissal qualifying period was held to have been wrongful *and* in breach of a contractually binding disciplinary procedure, proper exhaustion of which would have taken long enough to have allowed the employee to reach the qualifying period. Unfortunately for employees in this position, *Raspin* was reconsidered by the Court of Appeal in *Harper v Virgin Net Ltd*[229] and was held to have been wrongly decided in the light of later developments in the common law. Thus, the wrongful dismissal action now cannot be used to challenge an employer's cynical use of short notice to avoid an unfair dismissal claim.

(iv) *Discretionary benefits* The fourth exception arises from potentially significant applications of the modern term of trust and respect[230] and even wider ideas borrowed from administrative law to the area of damages. In *Clark v BET plc*,[231] a wrongful dismissal claim by a highly paid chief executive on a three-year fixed-term contract, liability was conceded but a major question arose as to quantification of damages because the executive had been heavily reliant for much of his pay package on salary increases and bonuses which, while regularly paid in the past, remained discretionary. On a strict approach (typified by the *Laverack* case considered earlier and the principle that the employer should normally be assumed to have discharged the contract in the way least onerous to himself) the executive would not have been awarded anything for these heads, because technically the employer could have decided to give *nothing* for the remainder of the contract. However, Walker J avoided that harsh result by looking at what the employers were likely to have paid out (given the firm's known performance over the relevant period) if they had continued to exercise their discretion *in good faith*. Although only at first instance, this is clearly an important decision in any case where significant elements of remuneration are discretionary, and it does show a significant departure from the straight *Laverack* approach. A similar result can be seen in *Clark v Nomura International plc*[232] where an employee who had been a highly successful trader, receiving large annual bonuses clearly linked to his trading profits for the company, was dismissed and awarded a nil bonus for his final year, even though his trading had continued to be profitable. Burton J felt able to quantify what the employee should normally have received on past experience and awarded that as damages. However, he did not do so under the term of trust and respect (which he thought could cause problems of application here, especially if cast in terms of 'capriciousness'), but on the other hand to apply an ordinary test of reasonableness to cases like this

---

[228] [1999] IRLR 9.

[229] [2004] IRLR 390, CA; damages such as those in *Raspin* were held now to fall foul of the general principles in *Johnson v Unisys* [2001] ICR 480, [2001] IRLR 279, HL, see Ch 7, heading 6(ii), p 538. *Harper* was applied in *Wise Group v Mitchell* [2005] ICR 896, EAT.

[230] See Ch 3, heading 3(iv), p 151.   [231] [1997] IRLR 348.   [232] [2000] IRLR 766.

would be too low a threshold for controversial legal intervention. His solution was to import the concept of *perversity*, the basis of adjudication being whether the exercise of the employer's discretion was such that no reasonable employer would have behaved in that way (the employer on the facts failing that test here). Of course, any importation of public/administrative law principles into private law will be both significant and controversial.[233] It was therefore important that this line was then adopted by the Court of Appeal in *Mallone v BPB Industries plc*[234] and *Horkulak v Cantor Fitzgerald International*.[235] In *Mallone* an executive, dismissed due to genuine concerns by the company about his performance, subsequently had his (vested) rights to valuable share options cancelled by the company. This was technically within its powers under the terms of the share option rules (ie within the employer's 'absolute discretion') but damages for loss of the options were granted on the basis that the company had acted *irrationally* in coming to this decision (especially as there was no documentation showing *how* it had been reached). In *Horkulak* large damages were awarded under an apparently discretionary bonus scheme (as in the two *Clark* cases) and here the Court of Appeal in effect synthesized the two approaches adopted beforehand by finding an implied term that the employer would exercise the discretion genuinely and rationally. Moreover, the court in this case dealt with the old obstacle of *Lavarack v Woods* more directly than in the previous cases, holding that there is no absolute rule that the employer can always exercise a discretion in any way most favourable to itself (especially in a case where the discretionary element is in practice a major element of the payment system).

Arguably, what we are seeing here is the law on damages being used increasingly to control employer discretion, even where that discretion is clearly and deliberately provided for in the contract. Moreover, the end result is coming close to Lord Denning's dissenting view in *Lavarack v Woods* that the employee should be compensated for what, in some sense, he or she *should* have received in practice. Several implications of this are immediately obvious. The first is that employers may increasingly not just have to justify their actions on the strict wording of the contract, but in the light of how and why they exercised the rights or discretions given by that wording (especially on or after dismissal, if there is any suggestion of motives of revenge). The second is that reliance on ideas of perversity or irrationality can provide a wide form of challenge, possibly going beyond pure breach of contract (note that in both *Clark v Nomura* and *Mallone* the dismissals were lawful, and the damages were awarded for the deprivation of the benefits as such, not as part of a wrongful dismissal action). This could provide a wider range of remedies on termination than under traditional analysis. A third implication could arise from ideas expressed in *Mallone* that the vested share option rights

---

[233] See the discussion of possible public law remedies of enforcement of the contract of employment at p 447.

[234] [2002] ICR 1045, [2002] IRLR 452, CA; see the discussion in Smith and Randall *Contract Actions in Modern Employment Law: Developments and Issues* (2002) at 101–3.

[235] [2005] ICR 402, [2004] IRLR 942, CA.

were akin to property rights. Deprivation of such rights can be seen as validating the importation of administrative law ideas; in which case, need they stop at perversity? If emphasis is to be placed on the rationality of the employer's decision (see the concerns of the Court of Appeal about inadequate records), could the employee argue that he or she has a right to *participate* in the decision-making process (ie a right to be heard)? Might ideas of unlawful *bias* surface here (for example if two of the three directors on the committee deciding on annual bonuses or the exercise of share options had been responsible for the employee's dismissal in the first place)? This whole area will need much more judicial exploration, but for the moment it seems that at least the foundations have been laid.

(v) *Stigma damages* A fifth exception, again possibly opening up wider damages (this time *general* damages for injury to feelings and/or manner of dismissal), recently seemed to arise at the highest level, but was immediately heavily restricted, being seen as the movement too far in this volatile area. In *Malik v BCCI SA (in liquidation)*[236] ex-employees of the failed BCCI bank claimed damages in respect of injury to their reputation and future employment prospects caused by the bank conducting a dishonest or corrupt business. The House of Lords upheld this claim on the grounds that the conduct of the employer was a serious breach of the implied term of trust and respect (to the evolution of which they gave their clear support).[237] *Addis v Gramophone Co*[238] was subject to considerable scrutiny by Lords Nicholls and Steyn, giving the principal judgments, and was sidestepped partly on the basis that it principally concerned a claim for injury to feelings caused by the wrongful dismissal whereas the claim in *Malik* was clearly for future financial loss caused by the employer's conduct, and partly on the basis that *Addis* was decided well before the development of the term of trust and respect which now occupies a central position in employment law. This new genus of 'stigma damages' caused much interest and was enthusiastically pursued by claimants' lawyers because it seemed to open up a vista into general damages for wrongful dismissal, even though (1) the case was *not* in fact one of wrongful dismissal but one of breach of contract during employment, and (2) both Law Lords ended their speeches with warnings that the facts in *Malik* were extreme and that in many, more ordinary cases there could be severe problems of causation, remoteness and mitigation.[239] Thus, the case posed the question—a claimant's Pandora's Box or an interesting decision on unusual facts?

The argument that *Malik* was *not* meant to allow damages for injury merely to feelings was accepted by the Court of Appeal in *French v Barclays Bank plc*,[240] a common law damages claim involving breach of trust and respect where a head of claim relating to

---

[236] [1997] ICR 606, [1997] IRLR 462, HL; see McMullen (1997) 26 ILJ 245.
[237] They added that the trust-destroying conduct did not have to be aimed at the individual, and that it was not necessary that that individual became aware of the conduct while still an employee.
[238] [1909] AC 488, HL.
[239] The claim did indeed finally fail on its facts: *BCCI SA (in liq) v Ali (No 3)* [2002] IRLR 460, CA.
[240] [1998] IRLR 646, CA.

stress and anxiety caused by the breach was disallowed. This was consistent, however, with the view that stigma damages for financial loss would now be claimable, including in a wrongful *dismissal* case, but that view has now been stopped by the further (and very different) decision of the House of Lords in *Johnson v Unisys Ltd*.[241] This was a difficult case on rather unusual facts, since the employee (who had suffered from work-induced stress prior to being summarily dismissed) had already succeeded in an unfair dismissal action, and then brought a substantial claim for damages for wrongful dismissal to the tune of £400,000, alleging that as a result of it he had suffered a nervous breakdown and was unable to work (thus arguably covering both injured feelings *and* future financial loss, through admittedly not in the usual 'stigma' manner). Ruling this claim out, the House of Lords confined stigma damages to the (highly unusual) case of an employee suing the employer for breach of contract *during* employment. Such damages, they said, are *not* available on termination (ie in a wrongful dismissal action) for (it appeared from the logic of the decision) two reasons. The first was that, on an analytical level, the implied term of trust and respect (the basis for *Malik*) was aimed at keeping the contract alive and so, ex hypothesi, was not applicable on termination.[242] The second was the interesting and novel constitutional point that the common law was not to be developed in such a way as to evade or negative statutory employment law. Parliament has provided the law of unfair dismissal to deal with employer abuses of power on termination, but has laid down limitations such as the short time limit and (crucially) the statutory cap on the amount of compensation that can be claimed and awarded. A new law on stigma damages in a common law wrongful dismissal action could be used to sidestep unfair dismissal which, said Lord Hoffmann, was the proper action in which to claim more general compensation for an abusive dismissal.[243]

The *Johnson* ruling has been confirmed and clarified in a number of subsequent cases, but perhaps the most contentious has been *Edwards v Chesterfield NHS and Botham v Ministry of Defence*.[244] The Court of Appeal in the two joined cases had given employees a glimmer of hope by ruling that where the employer failed to apply a disciplinary procedure that was enshrined in an express term of the contract, and but for

---

[241] [2001] ICR 480, [2001] IRLR 279, HL.

[242] This then raised the important question as to the meaning of 'on termination', which governs the width of this exclusion. After the Court of Appeal had split on the point, the House of Lords in *Eastwood v Magnox plc* [2004] ICR 1064, [2004] IRLR 733, HL held that the phrase is to be given a narrow interpretation, restricting the 'Johnson v Unisys exclusion zone' to distress, psychiatric injury, etc arising from the dismissal itself. Thus, if the employee has already suffered this damage prior to the eventual dismissal (eg through harassment or bullying before termination, as in *Gogay v Herts CC* [2000] IRLR 703, CA) he or she can bring a common law claim for damages. If, however, they only suffer it because of the dismissal, no such action lies.

[243] This constitutional approach meant that the old authority of *Addis* was not central to the argument of the majority who accepted that the common law could evolve away from that case but held that it was undesirable to do so. Lord Steyn (dissenting on the reasoning but agreeing with the result on the facts) would have effected such an evolution. Part of Lord Hoffmann's reasoning was that manner of dismissal damages could be awarded for unfair dismissal, but this went against longstanding authority and was strongly disapproved in *Dunnachie v Kingston-upon-Hull CC* [2004] ICR 1052, [2004] IRLR 727, HL.

[244] [2011] UKSC 58.

that failure the dismissal would not have happened, there could be a breach of contract action outside the 'Johnson' zone. This holding was consistent with the first prong of the reasoning in *Johnson*, to the effect that the implied term of trust and confidence had no logical application to a patent dismissal: the breached terms in these cases were express, not implied from the nature of the ongoing employment relationship. However, the Supreme Court, by a four to three majority (with some of the four expressing rationales somewhat divergent from the leading judgment) found that breaches of express terms in the employment contract that lead to dismissal are also within the 'Johnson zone', such that any damages flowing from the dismissal must be dealt with through the unfair dismissal procedure and subject to its caps. All of the judgments (including concurrences and dissents) treated *Johnson* as having been based exclusively on the logic that Parliament occupied the field of damages for dismissal when it enacted the unfair dismissal laws, making no mention of the paradox of claiming that a dismissal could somehow breach the implied term of trust and confidence (given that all dismissals seek not to maintain the relationship of trust and confidence, but to end it). This is clearly significant, given that the dissent, led by Lady Hale, felt that the *Johnson* line should be drawn between implied and express terms of the contract. It is clear that the judiciary want nothing to do with the implications of an intentional ending of the employment relationship juxtaposed with a judicial construct that implies a duty to maintain that relationship. In the end, this decision left the law much where it was before the Court of Appeal decided the cases: any breach of contract, express or implied, that results in or leads directly to a dismissal cannot afford damages at common law other than the notice period and the *Gunton* extension.

(d) Reduction of damages

Once the prima facie amount of damages has been ascertained, it is subject to reduction in three ways:

(i) *Mitigation* The employee is under a duty to mitigate his loss, and in the context of the contract of employment this will mean essentially finding another job. This will be particularly important in the case of the wrongful termination of a fixed-term contract which had several years to run, but will apply generally to all wrongful dismissals.[245] What constitutes reasonable steps to mitigate will be a question of fact in each case, but two general points might be made. The first is that the courts apply a realistic standard, so that the dismissed employee is not expected to take any job immediately, irrespective of his former position; thus, he may be allowed a certain time to look around for a position of equal status before resorting to lesser employment, and it may not be reasonable to expect him to take another

---

[245] If the dismissal is not wrongful, the employee may sue for unpaid wages for the notice period in an action for debt, to which the obligation to mitigate does not apply: *Abrahams v Performing Right Society Ltd* [1995] ICR 1028, [1995] IRLR 486, CA; dicta in this case suggesting that the obligation does not apply even where dismissal is wrongful must be considered to be wrong.

post inside the firm that dismissed him, if that is offered, particularly if it involves a reduction in status.[246] The second point is that issues other than another job could constitute mitigation, but before allowing them as such (with the resultant decrease in the amount of damages to be paid by the defendant employer) the court should be satisfied that they are not too remote to be taken into consideration. In *Lavarack v Woods of Colchester Ltd*, the facts of which are given earlier in this chapter, the employee was debarred by the contract of employment from engaging in, or holding shares in, any other business during his employment. After his dismissal, he became employed by M Ltd (purchasing half of its stock) and invested in V Ltd. The defendant employers claimed that the profits on these investments should be taken into account to mitigate his damages; the Court of Appeal held that the profits from his shares in M Ltd were to be taken into account, since his dismissal had left him free to *partake* in M Ltd and thereby increase the value of those shares, but the profits from his shares in V Ltd were not to be taken into account, since these were too remote, and the mere fact that he could not have invested while in the defendant's employment was not enough to alter that.

(ii) *Taxation* The general rule on the taxation of damages, laid down by the House of Lords in *British Transport Commission v Gourley*,[247] is that where a head of damage is based on an estimate of lost wages, the court should make allowance for the tax that would have been paid, and so deduct that figure and award the damages net of tax. This applies to damages for wrongful dismissal. However, the basis for the rule is that the amount awarded as damages is not taxable in the claimant's hands, and at the time of *Gourley* this was generally the case. Now, however, under the Income Tax (Earnings and Pensions) Act 2003, section 403 (previously, and for many years, the Income and Corporation Taxes Act 1988, section 148) such 'post-cessation receipts' are taxed to the extent that they exceed £30,000. The end result is that the rule in *Gourley*'s case applies to the first £30,000 of damages for wrongful dismissal, which must be awarded net of tax, but not to any amount over and above that, which must be awarded gross (and will then be taxed by the Revenue).[248]

---

[246] *Yetton v Eastwoods Froy Ltd* [1966] 3 All ER 353, [1967] 1 WLR 104; *Shindler v Northern Raincoat Co Ltd* [1960] 2 All ER 239, [1960] 1 WLR 1038. The general principles of mitigation in the employment context were summed up by Potter LJ in *Wilding v BT plc* [2002] ICR 1079, [2002] IRLR 524, CA.

[247] [1956] AC 185, [1955] 3 All ER 796, HL.

[248] *Parsons v BNM Laboratories Ltd* [1964] 1 QB 95, [1963] 2 All ER 658, CA. The tax position must be considered realistically, taking into account any tax rebates due to the employee being unemployed after the dismissal: *Hartley v Sandholme Iron Co Ltd* [1975] QB 600, [1974] 3 All ER 475 (a personal injury case). See also *Bold v Brough, Nicholson and Hall Ltd* [1963] 3 All ER 849, [1964] 1 WLR 201; *Basnett v J & A Jackson Ltd* [1976] ICR 63, [1976] IRLR 154; and *Shove v Downs Surgical plc* [1984] ICR 532, [1984] IRLR 17; *Harvey* A [1076]; Powell 'The Taxation of Payments Received on Termination of Employment' (1981) 10 ILJ 239; Bishop and Kay 'Taxation and Damages: The Rule of Gourley's Case' (1987) 104 LQR 211. This is, of course, all on the assumption that the amount recovered by the claimant is damages; if it is simply a debt under the contract (eg a payment in lieu under an express 'in lieu' clause in the contract), it is taxable in the hands of the claimant anyway: *EMI Group Electronics Ltd v Coldicott* [1999] IRLR 630, [1999] STC 803, CA; *Richardson v Delaney* [2001] IRLR 663.

(iii) *Deduction of other benefits received* Where a person is unable to work and claims damages because of that, it is likely that he will receive benefits from various sources during the period out of employment; the question then arises whether the amount of those benefits should be deducted from the damages which the defendant must pay. This is obviously of great importance in personal injury claims, where it is well established that insurance payments provided by the claimant's own foresight and payment of the premia are not deductible,[249] whereas most social security benefits are now (since the Social Security Act 1989) recoverable in full by the state through the system of civil recoupment.[250] Outside those areas, however, the position is less clear, particularly since the decision of the House of Lords in *Parry v Cleaver*[251] which showed a modern tendency not to deduct benefits[252] and concentrated on public policy and overall fairness rather than the older, more technical test for deductibility, such as remoteness, whether the benefit was received as of right and whether the plaintiff had contributed to the scheme providing the benefit. The problem is that the case itself only concerned a contributory police disablement fund and indeed their Lordships declined to consider the deductibility of other benefits (such as those more relevant to the dismissed employee),[253] so that any effect that this case may have on other benefits must be by implication. While in some respects courts subsequently have taken a more straightforward view of quantifying the claimant's actual loss,[254] the approach in *Parry v Cleaver* was strongly reaffirmed by the House of Lords in *Smoker v London Fire and Civil Defence Authority*[255] where it was held in a personal injury case that private pension benefits were not to be deducted from the plaintiff's damages for loss of earnings and this was applied directly to an action for wrongful dismissal in *Hopkins v Norcros plc*.[256] As the law stands at present, with regard to other benefits particularly applicable to wrongful dismissal cases, it appears that contractual payments by the employer such as sick pay are deductible (even if provided under an insurance policy maintained by the employer),[257] that jobseeker's allowance (previously unemployment

---

[249] *Bradburn v Great Western Rly Co* (1874) LR 10 Exch 1.

[250] Social Security (Recovery of Benefit) Act 1997. This special recoupment system does not apply to damages for wrongful dismissal.

[251] [1970] AC 1, [1969] 1 All ER 555, HL. See generally on this question Lewis 'Deducting Collateral Benefits from Damages: Principle and Policy' (1998) 18 LS 15, and 'The Overlap between Damages for Personal Injury and Work Related Benefits' (1998) 27 ILJ 1.

[252] See also *Daish v Wauton* [1972] 2 QB 262, [1972] 1 All ER 25, CA.

[253] See [1970] AC 1 at 19 and 39, [1969] 1 All ER 555 at 562 and 579, per Lord Reid and Lord Wilberforce.

[254] *Dews v National Coal Board* [1987] ICR 602, [1987] IRLR 330, HL; *Hodgson v Trapp* [1989] AC 807, [1988] 3 All ER 870, HL.

[255] [1991] ICR 449, [1991] IRLR 271, HL; see also *Longden v British Coal Corpn* [1998] 1 All ER 289, [1998] ICR 26, HL.

[256] [1994] ICR 11, [1994] IRLR 18, CA; this meant on the facts of the case that the wrongfully dismissed company chairman received £99,604 twice, once from the pension fund and once as damages for lost income. The judge at first instance had pointed out that provision could be made expressly either in an employment contract or in the rules of a pension scheme to prevent such double recovery.

[257] *Hussain v New Taplow Paper Mills Ltd* [1988] ICR 259, [1988] IRLR 167, HL. In an industrial injury case, one way to prevent the employer (by paying sick pay) effectively subsidizing the tortfeasor is to provide

benefit) received by the dismissed employee during the period by which the damages are calculated is deductible,[258] and after considerable doubt over a long period the Court of Appeal held that the same rule of deductibility applies to supplementary benefit (now income support).[259] The other major benefit which might be relevant is a redundancy payment and while there was some authority in earlier cases[260] against deductibility (on the basis that the payment is due on dismissal anyway, whether or not the dismissal is wrongful) the Court of Appeal have held that such a payment *is* deductible, except possibly in a rare case where it can be shown that the employee would have been made redundant anyway.[261]

(iii) WRONGFUL DISMISSAL AND UNFAIR DISMISSAL

The obvious contrast between the two is that the statutory action for unfair dismissal involves an enquiry into the overall merits of the dismissal (substance and procedure) whereas the common law action for wrongful dismissal is essentially a breach of contract action, and therefore looks typically to the *form* of the dismissal (except in cases where the employer purported to dismiss summarily for cause and the employee alleges that he gave no such cause, or where the contract actually contains terms governing the substantive grounds for dismissal). Thus, at common law an employer could dismiss for any reason provided he gave the correct length of notice (or wages in lieu thereof), but for the purposes of unfair dismissal this previously all-important question of notice is of evidential value only, if that, and the fact that proper notice was given will certainly not mean that the dismissal is necessarily fair. Thus, although a dismissal could be both wrongful and unfair, it could also easily be one but not the other. Fundamental concepts, such as the meaning of 'dismissal', can vary from one to the other and so for example a finding that an employee was unfairly dismissed will not

in the sick pay clause that, in the event of the injured employee later recovering damages from a third party, amounts paid to the employee as sick pay are refundable to the employer; this should enable damages to be awarded to the employee in full, without deduction of sick pay. Such clauses have been used, for example, in agricultural, railway and police contracts.

[258] *Parsons v BNM Laboratories Ltd* [1964] 1 QB 95, [1963] 2 All ER 658, CA; *Foxley v Olton* [1965] 2 QB 306, [1964] 3 All ER 248n; *Cheeseman v Bowater UK Paper Mills Ltd* [1971] 3 All ER 513, [1971] 1 WLR 1773, CA. In *Nabi v British Leyland (UK) Ltd* [1980] 1 All ER 667, CA, the Court of Appeal applied the *Parsons* case, but thought that the rule was due for reconsideration. However, the House of Lords applied *Parsons* without demur in *Westwood v Secretary of State for Employment* [1985] ICR 209, [1984] IRLR 209, HL.

[259] *Lincoln v Hayman* [1982] 2 All ER 819, [1982] 1 WLR 488, CA (a personal injury case).

[260] *Yorkshire Engineering and Welding Co Ltd v Burnham* [1973] 3 All ER 1176, [1974] ICR 77; *Millington v T H Goodwin & Sons Ltd* [1975] ICR 104, [1974] IRLR 379; *Basnett v J and A Jackson Ltd* [1976] ICR 63, [1976] IRLR 154. In each of these cases the decision of Arnold J in *Stocks v Magna Merchants Ltd* [1973] 2 All ER 329, [1973] ICR 530 that a redundancy payment should be deducted was not followed.

[261] *Colledge v Bass Mitchells & Butlers Ltd* [1988] ICR 125, [1988] IRLR 163, CA (another personal injury case, where the judge at first instance had made a finding of fact that it was unlikely that the plaintiff would have been made redundant but for the accident).

necessarily put him at an advantage if he wishes later, in some other context, to claim that the dismissal was also wrongful.[262] Also, constructive dismissal[263] amounts to a dismissal for both wrongful and unfair dismissal, but the implications are very different: the dismissal will almost by definition be without notice and can result in wrongful dismissal damages for the notice period, but will constitute a mere 'dismissal' for the purposes of unfair dismissal, proving nothing about whether the dismissal was 'unfair'. Finally, the separate principles of compensation operate independently[264] and indeed in theory the primary remedy for unfair dismissal is reinstatement or re-engagement, a remedy which, as seen above, the common law would only countenance in highly unusual cases.

There used to be a further difference in the appropriate forum. In *Treganowen v Robert Knee & Co Ltd*[265] an employee was dismissed without notice because of a personality clash between her and her colleagues for which she was to blame; the tribunal held that this reason rendered the dismissal fair, but considered that she should not have been dismissed summarily, but should instead have received six weeks' pay in lieu of notice, though they did not have jurisdiction to award this sum. The employee appealed claiming that they did have jurisdiction since the lack of notice was capable of making the dismissal unfair. The EAT dismissed the appeal, clearly holding that, while lack of notice could possibly be of evidential value in deciding some of the points necessary for an unfair dismissal action, it could not per se make a dismissal unfair that was otherwise fair, since it only gave rise to an action for *wrongful* dismissal which had to be brought in the ordinary courts, not before a tribunal at that time. While this case remains an instructive one on the distinction between the two actions, the forum point was altered by the Employment Tribunals (Extension of Jurisdiction) (England and Wales) Orders 1994[266] which give tribunals the power to hear claims for breach of contract on termination of employment (up to a maximum of £25,000) and at long last have rid us of the previous, very unfortunate, split jurisdiction.

(iv) THE RESIDUAL IMPORTANCE OF WRONGFUL DISMISSAL

The common law doctrine of notice meant that wrongful dismissal was only a theoretical remedy for a large number of employees, since they were on relatively short

---

[262] *Turner v London Transport Executive* [1977] ICR 952, [1977] IRLR 441, CA. There is certainly no question of cause of action estoppel as such as between the unfair and wrongful dismissal actions, but on the other hand there are cases where a finding of fact by a tribunal has been treated as raising an issue estoppel in later civil proceedings: *Green v Hampshire County Council* [1979] ICR 861; *Automatic Switching Ltd v Brunet* [1986] ICR 542, EAT; *Soteriou v Ultrachem Ltd* [2004] IRLR 870.

[263] See Ch 7, heading 2(i), p 477.

[264] *Norton Tool Co Ltd v Tewson* [1973] 1 All ER 183, [1972] ICR 501; *Everwear Candlewick Ltd v Isaac* [1974] 3 All ER 24, [1974] ICR 525; there is, however, a duty to mitigate loss as at common law, imposed specifically by the provisions relating to the compensatory award: Employment Rights Act 1996, s 123(4).

[265] [1975] ICR 405, [1975] IRLR 247, applied in *BSC Sports and Social Club v Morgan* [1987] IRLR 391.

[266] SI 1994/1623 in England and Wales; SI 1994/1624 in Scotland.

notice, so that even if such an employee went to the trouble and expense of bringing a common law action, his damages would be small, since they were so rigidly tied to the amount of wages during the notice period. The statutory action for unfair dismissal, whilst not abolishing wrongful dismissal, is now far more important in practice, with its easier procedure, the possibility (at least in theory) of reinstatement or re-engagement, and the more liberal and realistic approach to compensation. On the other hand, there may still be some atypical cases where wrongful dismissal is still important. One class of case would be where the employee does not qualify for the statutory action, in particular where he is in an excluded category or where he lacks the necessary period of continuous service. The most important case, however, would be that of a highly paid employee either on a fixed-term contract or entitled to a substantial period of notice. For the compensation for unfair dismissal is subject to statutory maxima[267] which, though perhaps adequate for many employees (certainly when compared with the small amounts recoverable by them for wrongful dismissal), may be a real restriction in the case of the high earner who, if dismissed unfairly *and* wrongfully, may have more to gain by an action for wrongful dismissal which is not subject to the statutory maxima. Such an action continues to be governed by the law as set out above, but for most practical purposes a modern dismissal case is likely to proceed on the statutory basis and be subject to the separate body of law on unfair dismissal, to which we must now turn.

---

[267] At the time of writing, the maximum basic award is £12,900; the maximum compensatory was for many years kept at a low level, not keeping up with inflation, so that as late as 1999 it was only £12,000. It was raised to £50,000 by the Employment Relations Act 1999 and at the time of writing stands at £72,300, but that could still be a low ceiling in the case of a very high earner.

7

UNFAIR DISMISSAL

OVERVIEW

The action for unfair dismissal provides a major element of modern employment law, giving greater and more realistic remedies than the common law for most employees. An early success in this area was its effects in putting a fair procedure at the forefront of an employer's mind when contemplating disciplining or dismissing an employee. The chapter starts therefore with consideration of the necessary procedures for a fair dismissal and the vital role of the ACAS Code of Practice. The chapter continues by looking at the statutory definition of 'dismissal' (a vital jurisdictional factor) and then tackles the central question of what the statute means by 'fair' and 'unfair'. Particular cases (such as incapability, misconduct, and redundancy and reorganization) are dealt with in detail, as are the evergrowing categories of automatically unfair dismissals which exist to give extra protection to certain employees (eg whistleblowers and health and safety complainants). The chapter concludes with the complex law on remedies if a dismissal is unfair.

1 PROCEDURES FOR DISCIPLINE, DISMISSAL AND GRIEVANCES

The core principles for the management of discipline and dismissal in UK employment law were introduced (originally in 1977) in the highly influential ACAS Code of Practice No 1 *Disciplinary and Grievance Procedures* and many employers now have definite rules and procedures (often in work-rules or handbooks) drafted in the light of the Code's recommendations. The Code itself (reissued in expanded form in 2000, then again in 2004, and most recently in a revised 2009 version) places great emphasis on involvement of employees and their representatives in the drafting of procedures covering grievances, discipline and appeal structures. Having an agreed procedure greatly adds to its authority, and to the authority which may be exercised by the management when they take action clearly in accordance with the agreed rules; tribunals will naturally tend to pay great attention to an agreed procedure as a question of fact and evidence.[1] Where there are set rules on discipline, grievances and appeals (whether agreed or not) the employer must give the employee written notice of them within two months of the commencement of his employment.[2] For the guidance of employers when drawing up rules and procedures, the Code makes the following general points:

> 2. Fairness and transparency are promoted by developing and using rules and procedures for handling disciplinary and grievance situations. These should be set down in writing, be specific and clear. Employees and, where appropriate, their representatives should be involved in the development of rules and procedures. It is also important to help employees and managers understand what the rules and procedures are, where they can be found and how they are to be used.

When drawing up and applying procedures employers should always bear in mind the requirements of natural justice. This means that employees should be given the opportunity of a meeting with someone who has not been involved in the matter. They should be informed of the allegations against them, together with the supporting evidence, in advance of the meeting. Employees should be given the opportunity to challenge the allegations before decisions are reached and should be provided with a right of appeal.

(i) DISCIPLINARY MEASURES

Although certain forms of disciplinary action may still lie entirely within the managerial prerogative (for example, transferring a general labourer to a different job or refusing to give a discretionary bonus), many other forms will impinge upon the rights and expectations of the disciplined employee (eg fines, suspension, demotion) and so the crucial point about lawful disciplinary measures is that the employer must have the power to impose them, and normally this will involve having the contractual authority (express or implied) to do so. If the employer goes outside this authority the employee may in theory maintain a common law action (for example, to recover the amount of a fine unlawfully deducted);[3] of much greater significance in modern employment law is the possibility that the wrongly disciplined employee may walk out and claim to have been constructively dismissed, for the purpose of bringing an unfair dismissal action. Thus, although some managers remain suspicious of setting down their disciplinary powers in writing on the basis that it restricts managerial prerogative, the modern tendency is to put down in written form the company's policy on discipline (which will of course vary from industry to industry) and the procedures to be adopted, which may then form part of the employment contract either expressly or by implication.

---

[1] *Securicor Ltd v Smith* [1989] IRLR 356, CA.
[2] Employment Rights Act 1996, s 3, see Ch 2, heading 3, p 78.
[3] *Gorse v Durham County Council* [1971] 2 All ER 666, [1971] 1 WLR 775. In the example given, there may also be a statutory action under the Employment Rights Act 1996, s 13.

A leading survey referred to a 'massive spread of formal disciplinary and dismissal procedures across British industry and commerce' in the 1970s as a 'remarkable development in British industrial relations'. Their findings in 1990 showed that 97% of establishments recognizing a union operated a disciplinary and dismissal procedure and (perhaps even more significantly) so did 83% of those not recognizing a union; 93% of procedures were written, 74% provided for union representation of employees and 65% were jointly agreed.[4] On the other hand, *compliance* with procedures was sometimes a different matter and a survey by the DTI (predecessor to the Department for Business, Innovation and Skills (BIS)) in 1998 found that when one looked at cases actually brought to tribunals (itself arguably a sign of failure of the system) they were characterized by a relatively high incidence of lack of procedures or failure to operate them.[5] These findings were influential in the government's decision to enact mandatory standard procedures in 2002 (head (iii) later in this chapter) to try to enforce a higher level of compliance with basic rules. These mandatory procedures came into effect in 2004 but were repealed in 2008 with effect from 6 April 2009. Concluding that the cure had been worse than the disease, the government reinstated the ACAS Code as the key mechanism for ensuring procedural fairness.

Turning to the detailed provisions of the Code, the primary suggestion is that where a disciplinary procedure is established it should be clear and unambiguous so that individual employees may know what is expected of them; in particular, they should be made aware of the likely consequences of breaking the rules and the type of conduct which may warrant summary dismissal.[6] Although it is therefore desirable to lay down the major forms of unacceptable conduct in the circumstances of the particular industry involved, and the likely consequences of each form, the list should not necessarily be exhaustive otherwise novel forms of transgression could be construed as permissible (in the sense of not attracting a valid penalty).

A system of warnings (considered further in this chapter) may be an integral part of a disciplinary system (as well as leading up to a dismissal), but if warnings are ignored and the misconduct repeated the employer, in a case not warranting dismissal, may wish to impose a lesser sanction. Fines or deductions must be permissible under the

---

[4] Millward et al 'Workplace Industrial Relations in Transition' (the ED/ESRC/PSI/ACAS Survey) (1992) ch 6. A similar pattern was found in the preliminary results of the 1998 exercise: Cully et al 'The 1998 Workplace Employee Relations Survey: The First Findings' (ESRC/ACAS/PSI, 1998; URN 98/934).

[5] Earnshaw, Goodman, Harrison and Marchington 'Industrial Tribunals, Workplace Disciplinary Procedures and Employment Practice' (DTI Employment Relations Research Paper, 1998); see Edwards (1998) 27 ILJ 362.

[6] COP paras 2 and 23; a statement that an employee is 'liable to' dismissal for particular misconduct is probably strong enough: *Procter v British Gypsum Ltd* [1992] IRLR 7. If the rules are ambiguous as to the seriousness of a particular matter but then the employer dismisses for the first breach (ie without warning), a tribunal may well consider that unfair: *Trusthouse Forte (Catering) Ltd v Adonis* [1984] IRLR 382. On the other hand, however, the fact that particular conduct is absolutely banned by the rules and stated to warrant mandatory dismissal does not mean that such a dismissal will automatically be fair, for the rules cannot oust the jurisdiction of the tribunal to look into the overall merits: *Laws Stores Ltd v Oliphant* [1978] IRLR 251; *Ladbroke Racing Ltd v Arnott* [1983] IRLR 154, Ct of Sess; *Taylor v Parsons, Peebles NEI Bruce Peebles Ltd* [1981] IRLR 119. This may cause problems in striking a reasonable balance between certainty and flexibility.

contract of employment if they are to be valid, and must also comply with the requirements of Part II of the Employment Rights Act 1996.[7] Suspension with pay will usually be lawful,[8] and may be the proper step to take for a brief period while a serious allegation against the employee is under investigation;[9] for any longer period, however, it is tantamount to a holiday and the more obviously punitive sanction is suspension *without* pay. It is here, however, that the question whether the employer has contractual authority to act becomes particularly vital for, in the absence of express or implied incorporation into the contract, there is *no* common law power to suspend without pay, for this would contravene the employer's basic obligation to pay wages.[10] Thus, as in the case of lay-offs, the employer is clearly allowed to suspend without pay only where he incorporates a clause to that effect in the contract, either directly or via the works rules or a collective agreement. Moreover, the ACAS Code, while not forbidding it, does not give its imprimatur to the use of suspension as a punitive measure. Other discipline may take forms such as reprimands, temporary withdrawal of privileges or demotion or transfer; once again these are in theory only lawful if allowed by the contract though the practical position, particularly in the case of demotion or transfer, may be that even if the legality is dubious the employer may go ahead and then, if the employee walks out and claims constructive dismissal, accept that there was a dismissal but argue that it was fair because of the urgent need to remove the employee from his previous position. These are, however, all matters which are amenable to inclusion in a contract of employment in the first place (possibly via a set disciplinary code for the firm).

The Code of Practice should be considered when drafting a disciplinary procedure, for it states that such procedures should:

be put in writing;

allow for matters to be dealt without undue delay;

tell employees what disciplinary action might be taken;

say what levels of management have the authority to take disciplinary action;

require employees to be informed of the complaints against them and supporting evidence, before a meeting;

give employees a chance to have their say before management reaches a decision;

provide employees with the right to be accompanied;

provide that no employee is dismissed for a first breach of discipline, except in cases of gross misconduct;

---

[7] See Ch 3, heading 5(v), p 203.

[8] Except perhaps in cases where the employee claims a right actually to work, not just to be paid wages: *Langston v AUEW* [1974] 1 All ER 980, [1974] ICR 180, CA. This category of case might expand in the light of *William Hill Organisation Ltd v Tucker* [1998] IRLR 313, CA, which emphasis the advantage to an employer of having an express power to suspend with pay.

[9] COP para 6.

[10] *Hanley v Pease & Partners Ltd* [1915] 1 KB 698; *Bird v British Celanese Ltd* [1945] KB 336, [1945] 1 All ER 488, CA.

require management to investigate fully before any disciplinary action is taken;

ensure that employees are given an explanation for any sanction; and

allow employees to appeal against a decision.

(ii) WARNINGS, HEARINGS AND APPEALS

A system of warnings has become an integral part of modern employment procedures, particularly where there is a possibility of dismissal. Warnings may seem particularly appropriate to cases of misconduct by the employee, but the general requirement for them has also been applied to cases of lack of capacity (such as inefficiency, bad workmanship and incompetence)[11] and, in line with the principle that discipline should be constructive as well as punitive, a warning to the employee should not just point out the unsatisfactory conduct but may also be expected to specify any required improvements. Many employers will have a definite warning procedure built into their disciplinary code (which may be in the firm's rules or jointly agreed with a trade union), and may operate on a 'rule of thumb' basis such as 'one oral and two written'; there is no magic in a particular combination, but the Code does lay down this general advice:

> 18. Where misconduct is confirmed or the employee is found to be performing unsatis-factorily it is usual to give the employee a written warning. A further act of misconduct or failure to improve performance within a set period would normally result in a final written warning.
>
> 19. If an employee's first misconduct or unsatisfactory performance is sufficiently serious, it may be appropriate to move directly to a final written warning. This might occur where the employee's actions have had, or are liable to have, a serious or harmful impact on the organisation.
>
> 20. A first or final written warning should set out the nature of the misconduct or poor performance and the change in behaviour or improvement in performance required (with timescale). The employee should be told how long the warning will remain current. The employee should be informed of the consequences of further misconduct, or failure to improve performance, within the set period following a final warning. For instance that it may result in dismissal or some other contractual penalty such as demotion or loss of seniority.
>
> 21. A decision to dismiss should only be taken by a manager who has the authority to do so. The employee should be informed as soon as possible of the reasons for the dismissal, the date on which the employment contract will end, the appropriate period of notice and their right of appeal.

Further to this general guidance, three particular points should be noted. First, the existence of a warning system places emphasis upon writing and the keeping of

---

[11] *Winterhalter Gastronom Ltd v Webb* [1973] ICR 245, [1973] IRLR 120, NIRC.

detailed personnel records by the employer[12] who must be able, if necessary, to provide documentary proof of previous warnings; this leads, for example, to the practices of giving written confirmation even of an 'oral' warning, and of requiring the employee's signature of acknowledged receipt of a warning. This may lead to an increased personnel function within a firm, but is inevitable with the modern movement towards increased legalization. Second, the employer's system should include some time limit on warnings, so that after a set period they lapse.[13] Third, a warning should be reasonably specific, identifying the precise ground of complaint by the employer. One consequence of this is that a warning on ground A (for example, swearing) should not be used as a step in the procedure to dismiss on ground B (for example, bad workmanship), so that one employee may be subject to more than one series of warnings concurrently if he is deficient in different respects; this must be viewed realistically, however, and there may come a point when a multitude of warnings on different matters add up overall to reasonable grounds to dismiss, particularly if some of the grounds are not dissimilar, and the employer may genuinely issue one final warning on generally unsatisfactory conduct.[14]

The presence or absence of warnings may be a most important factor in determining the fairness or otherwise of a dismissal, though as always on matters of procedure it is not necessarily conclusive. Thus, there may be circumstances in which lack of a warning is reasonable; summary dismissal for gross misconduct is still permissible,[15] and a warning might also be dispensed with where the employee has made it clear that he does not intend to 'improve' (for example, where he is at odds with the company's policy),[16] where his incapability is so bad as to be irredeemable or where (as in the case of senior management) the employee already knows exactly what is required of him, so that a warning would be irrelevant.[17]

In addition to warnings, the employee who is in danger of dismissal should normally be allowed a hearing of sorts, which may be built into the firm's disciplinary procedures, or be arranged ad hoc. This may perform two functions, first to ascertain

[12] The warning should usually be given to the employee personally; giving it to his trade union may not be enough: *W Brooks & Son v Skinner* [1984] IRLR 379, EAT.

[13] This requirement was reaffirmed in *Diosynth Ltd v Thomson* [2006] IRLR 284, Ct of Sess (IH), even in the sensitive area of disciplining for health and safety breaches following a fatal accident. A firm's disciplinary procedure may permit an appeal against a warning; a warning which is under appeal may be considered by an employer when dismissing, but the fact that the appeal has not yet been heard should also be taken into account: *Tower Hamlets Health Authority v Anthony* [1989] ICR 656, [1989] IRLR 394, CA.

[14] *Auguste Noel Ltd v Curtis* [1990] ICR 604, [1990] IRLR 326 is a particularly strong case on this point. One innovation was the concept of a 'first and final' warning, to apply to cases of serious misconduct just falling short of warranting dismissal; this provides more flexibility, with a halfway house between instant dismissal and exhaustion of the full warning system. The idea was finally taken up in the 2000 revision of the Code and is now implicit in the warnings system in the 2009 Code.

[15] COP para 22. Note that summary dismissal means without notice, not without a hearing.

[16] *Retarded Children's Aid Society Ltd v Day* [1978] ICR 437, [1978] IRLR 128, CA.

[17] *James v Waltham Holy Cross UDC* [1973] ICR 398, [1973] IRLR 202. For a particularly good example (involving an NHS Trust financial director) see *Perkin v St George's Healthcare Trust* [2005] IRLR 934, CA where a dismissal for 'awkward personality' was fair even though no warnings had been given.

the true facts of the incident in question and second to allow the employee to make representations on the question whether he ought on those facts to be dismissed (when he may wish to refute the charges against him, or accept them but put forward matters such as length of service or previous good conduct in mitigation); where these two functions are separated (for example, where the second is considered by a higher level of management), the employee should normally be given a proper opportunity to be heard at each stage.[18]

It will usually be of the essence of a fair hearing that the employee must be made aware of the charges against him[19] (unless they are obvious),[20] but the precise form of the required hearing will vary with the circumstances and the emphasis is on the overall failures of the procedure adopted, rather than any rigidly prescribed format.[21] At a minimum, though, a statement of 'charges' must identify a specific act: it is not enough to accuse a worker of dishonesty, they must be accused of a specific act or acts of dishonesty.[22] Although the basic requirement of a hearing is akin to the rules of natural justice (which are sometimes prayed in aid in such cases), it must be remembered that these are *not* court proceedings, and so there is no inalienable right to appear in person,[23] to receive witness statements,[24] or to be allowed to cross-examine 'witnesses'.[25] Article 6 of the European Convention on Human Rights, which guarantees the right to a fair trial, applies only to the tribunal hearing of the unfair or wrongful dismissal case not to the disciplinary proceedings;[26] even where a disciplinary procedure can feed into a procedure where the employee's civil rights are determined (eg, the right to continue working with children) Article 6 only applies to the latter procedure, not to the disciplinary procedure that feeds in.[27] On the other hand, a fair hearing procedure

---

[18] *Budgen & Co v Thomas* [1976] ICR 344, [1976] IRLR 174; *Tesco (Holdings) Ltd v Hill* [1977] IRLR 63. It is normally for the employer to take the initiative in operating the procedure; it is not enough to say that the employee could have used the grievance procedure: *Clarke v Trimoco Motor Group Ltd* [1993] ICR 237, [1993] IRLR 148, EAT.

[19] *Louies v Coventry Hood and Seating Co Ltd* [1990] ICR 54, [1990] IRLR 324; *Spink v Express Foods Group Ltd* [1990] IRLR 320, EAT.

[20] *Fuller v Lloyds Bank plc* [1991] IRLR 336, EAT.

[21] There is, however, a very useful summary of the key points normally expected of a fair hearing in the judgment of Wood P in *Clark v Civil Aviation Authority* [1991] IRLR 412 at 415.

[22] *Celebi v Scolarest Compass Group UK and Ireland* [2010] All ER (D) 136.

[23] *Ayanlowo v IRC* [1975] IRLR 253, CA. Moreover, it has been emphasized that the rules of natural justice do not constitute an independent head of challenge to the fairness of a dismissal in this context: *Slater v Leicestershire Health Authority* [1989] IRLR 16, CA.

[24] *Hussain v Elonex plc* [1999] IRLR 420, CA; on the facts, the tribunal had taken the view that the employee had been made sufficiently aware of the allegations in other ways.

[25] *Khanum v Mid-Glamorgan Area Health Authority* [1979] ICR 40, [1978] IRLR 215; *Santamera v Express Cargo Forwarding* [2003] IRLR 273. There may, in particular, be cases where an informant wishes to remain anonymous for fear of reprisals; Wood P laid down guidance on how to deal with the situation in *Linfood Cash and Carry Ltd v Thomson* [1989] ICR 518, [1989] IRLR 235, EAT though even this may be impracticable in an extreme case, when the ultimate test of reasonableness in all the circumstances will have to be applied: *Ramsey v Walkers Food Ltd* [2004] IRLR 754.

[26] *Mattu v University Hospitals of Coventry and Warwickshire NHS Trust* [2012] EWCA Civ 641, [2012] All ER (D) 153.

[27] *R (G) v Governors of X School* [2011] UKSC 30, [2011] IRLR 756.

(in whatever form) should normally give the employee a reasonable opportunity to hear the allegations against him and to attempt to refute them.[28] One particular aspect of this is that, once the charges have been laid against the employee, the employer should *not* add in more charges (especially of a more serious nature) as the hearing progresses; if evidence of different and/or more serious misconduct arises, the proper procedure is to adjourn and start again with new charges.[29] However, the analogy with the rules of natural justice must not be exaggerated, especially in the difficult area of potential bias, for it may not always be practicable to expect a complete separation of powers between the person dismissing and the person holding the disciplinary hearing (or appeal), since they may both be ordinary line managers; as long as there is substantive fairness in the internal procedure, it is not to be attacked with rules of natural justice on bias which evolved in different contexts.[30] Where the employee is to attend a formal hearing, he should normally be allowed to be represented if he so wishes (by a trade union representative or a fellow employee); this has always been good practice, but in addition the Employment Relations Act 1999, sections 10–13 give a statutory right to be accompanied at a disciplinary hearing[31] by a trade union official or another of the employer's workers; that person is to be permitted to address the hearing (but not answer questions on behalf of the worker)[32] and to confer with him or her during the hearing, and is to be given paid time off work for the purpose.[33] If the chosen companion is not available at the time proposed for the hearing, the employer must postpone it to an alternative time proposed by the worker (provided it is reasonable and falls within the next five working days). Complaint of breach of this right lies to

[28] *Bentley Engineering Co Ltd v Mistry* [1979] ICR 47, [1978] IRLR 437. For subsequent examples of findings of unfair dismissal based on breach of natural justice (in these cases, the rule on potential bias) see *Moyes v Hylton Castle Working Men's Social Club and Institute Ltd* [1986] IRLR 482 and *Campion v Hamworthy Engineering Ltd* [1987] ICR 966, CA; cf, however, *Slater v Leicestershire Health Authority*, n 23.

[29] *Strouthos v London Underground Ltd* [2004] IRLR 636, CA is a modern reaffirmation of this basic rule of natural justice.

[30] *Rowe v Radio Rentals Ltd* [1982] IRLR 177, where the (unsuccessful) ground of challenge was that the person hearing the appeal had been told of the facts beforehand by the person who dismissed the employee, and the latter person had been present at the appeal hearing: *R v Chief Constable of South Wales, ex p Thornhill* [1987] IRLR 313, CA. However, wherever possible (especially in a large organization), it is highly desirable to have separate levels of management dealing with the different stages: *Sartor v P&O European Ferries (Felixstowe) Ltd* [1992] IRLR 271, CA; *Byrne v BOC Ltd* [1992] IRLR 505, EAT.

[31] This means a hearing that could result in a formal warning, the taking of some other action or the confirmation of either: Employment Relations Act 1999, s 13(4); what the employer calls it is not particularly relevant, as it is the statutory definition that must be applied: *London Underground Ltd v Ferenc-Batchelor* [2003] IRLR 252. Note that this right also applies to grievance hearings 'which concern the performance of a duty by an employer in relation to the worker': s 13(5). Guidance on this right is found in section 3 of the ACAS Code of Practice.

[32] The wide definition of 'worker' is used in relation to this right, which is itself extended to cover agency workers and home workers: Employment Relations Act 1999, s 13(1)–(3).

[33] Section 10(6), (7). Section 12 extends the usual package of employment protection measures (concerning detriment and dismissal) to both the worker relying on this right and the chosen companion (when in that employer's employment).

an employment tribunal (subject to the usual three-month time limitation provisions), which may order compensation of up to two weeks' pay.

In addition to a hearing, most disciplinary procedures in other than small firms will include some form of appeal from an adverse decision; this is prescribed by the Code of Practice, paragraph 25, and may take many forms, from a simple further hearing by a more senior manager up to a formal appeal hearing by a joint management-union committee or even ACAS-organized arbitration. The importance of such an appeal as an integral part of the internal procedure (lack or denial of which may per se make the dismissal unfair) has been recognized by the House of Lords.[34] This has been emphasized even further subsequently by the evolution of the rule that a bad initial dismissal may be 'cured' by a fair appeal; for many years it was thought that this only applied if the appeal hearing took the form of a complete rehearing (not just a review of the initial decision) but when this point was reviewed by the Court of Appeal it was held that there is no such limitation and that the only test is the overall fairness and open-mindedness of the appeal process, whatever its form.[35]

As in the case of a warning, a hearing and appeal may well be expected in most cases, but lack of them will not necessarily make a dismissal unfair. There may be definite classes of case where it is highly arguable that a hearing would have been inappropriate, such as where the employee clearly refuses to accept the employer's legitimate requirements, where the employee's conduct 'is of such a nature that, whatever the explanation, his continued employment is not in the interests of the business'[36] (particularly where the employment in question is of a delicate or sensitive nature)[37] or where the employee is already being investigated by the police with a view to criminal charges being brought.[38] More generally, however, this is clearly an area where views may differ, and indeed we have seen definite changes of judicial approach to the whole question of fair procedure over the years. In the 1970s (in the infancy of the unfair dismissal law) great emphasis was placed on proper procedures, but this was then perceived to have gone too far and a reaction set in, from two directions—first, through a generally more relaxed approach to procedural requirements beginning with the decision of the Court of Appeal in *Hollister v NFU*,[39] taking the view that a lapse in procedure (such as failure to give a hearing) is merely one factor to take into account and, secondly and more specifically, through the evolution and widespread application of the rule in *British Labour Pump Co Ltd v Byrne*[40] that an element of procedural unfairness (such as the lack of a hearing) may be 'forgiven' if the employer could show that even if the proper procedure had been carried out it would have made no difference. The potential inroad of the

---

[34] *West Midlands Co-operative Society Ltd v Tipton* [1986] ICR 192, [1986] IRLR 112, HL.

[35] *Taylor v OCS Group Ltd* [2006] IRLR 613, CA, overruling on this point *Whitbread & Co Ltd v Mills* [1988] IRLR 501.

[36] *James v Waltham Holy Cross UDC* [1973] ICR 398, [1973] IRLR 202.

[37] *Alidair Ltd v Taylor* [1978] ICR 445, [1978] IRLR 82, CA.

[38] *Carr v Alexander Russell Ltd* [1979] ICR 469n, [1976] IRLR 220, applied in *Parker v Clifford Dunn Ltd* [1979] ICR 463, [1979] IRLR 56, EAT.

[39] [1979] ICR 542, [1979] IRLR 238, CA.   [40] [1979] ICR 347, [1979] IRLR 94, EAT.

Byrne principle into any general requirement of a hearing hardly needed to be spelled out. That is why its overruling in the leading House of Lords decision in *Polkey v A E Dayton Services Ltd*[41] was of such great importance, and led to a general swing back of the pendulum, with more emphasis again being placed on procedure in general, and hearings in particular. The court emphasized that the task of a tribunal is to assess the reasonableness of what the employer actually did at the time, not what he might have done, and that the question whether at the end of the day the employee actually suffered injustice goes only to compensation, *not* to liability. The case of *McLaren v National Coal Board*[42] is a good example of the result of once again taking procedures seriously. The employee was accused of assaulting a working miner during the strike; normally the matter would have been investigated by the local manager but in the circumstances this was thought to be impracticable and so it was left to the police and the court—once the employee was convicted, he was automatically dismissed without a hearing. The tribunal held that this was fair given the surrounding circumstances of industrial warfare, but the Court of Appeal held that it was unfair, Sir John Donaldson MR stating:

> [N]o amount of heat in industrial warfare can justify failing to give an employee an opportunity of giving an explanation.... You have the position that acceptable reasons for dismissing may change in a varying industrial situation, but *the standards of fairness never change. They are immutable but are applied in a different situation.* (Emphasis added)

The pendulum may therefore be seen as having been swung much of the way back; there will still be cases where lack of a hearing is explained sufficiently to the tribunal's satisfaction to produce a finding of fair dismissal, and it remains ultimately a matter of fact for the tribunal.[43] Moreover, even on general principles, in entertaining an employer's case that it was reasonable to dispense with a hearing a tribunal might do well to bear in mind the words of Megarry V-C in *John v Rees*:[44]

> [T]he path of the law is strewn with examples of open and shut cases which, somehow, were not; of unanswerable charges which, in the event, were completely answered; of inexplicable conduct which was fully explained; of fixed and unalterable determinations that, by discussion, suffered a change. Nor are those with any knowledge of human nature who pause to think for a moment likely to underestimate the feelings of resentment of those who find that a decision against them has been made without their being afforded any opportunity to influence the course of events.

---

[41] [1988] ICR 142, [1987] IRLR 503, HL; see heading 4(iii), p 502 and Collins (1990) 19 ILJ 39.

[42] [1988] ICR 370, [1988] IRLR 215, CA; the passage cited is at 377 and 218 respectively.

[43] This can be seen from the decision of a differently constituted Court of Appeal in *Dillett v National Coal Board* [1988] ICR 218, where on facts similar to those in *McLaren* they confirmed a decision that a dismissal without a hearing in the middle of the miners' strike was fair, but largely on the ground that that had been the view of the tribunal on the particular facts of the case and it was not open to an appellate court to reverse them.

[44] [1970] Ch 345 at 402, [1969] 2 All ER 274 at 309.

(iii) THE RISE AND FALL OF THE 'STANDARD PROCEDURE'

A fundamental part of the government's programme in the Employment Act 2002 to reduce the number of tribunal applications by encouraging alternative dispute resolution was the enactment of a new 'standard procedure' to be used in disciplinary and dismissal cases. This was backed by research commissioned by the Department of Trade and Industry (DTI) which showed a worrying level of tribunal cases in which either no or virtually no use had been made of any form of internal procedures in order to resolve the issue without recourse to a tribunal.[45] The Act itself laid down the outlines of a new system, but a great amount was left to be fleshed out in the Employment Act 2002 (Dispute Resolution) Regulations 2004,[46] and the whole system came into force in October 2004.

The scheme sought to discourage resort to tribunal litigation by requiring that employers go through certain basic disciplinary procedures, and employees go through certain procedures for raising grievances, before either could make or defend a claim in an employment tribunal. It set up statutory discipline and grievance procedures and, with some exceptions, dictated that if an employer failed to follow the discipline procedure any dismissal would be automatically unfair, and if an employee failed to follow the grievance procedure with regard to a complaint (eg of discrimination or denial of a statutory right) the complaint could not form the basis of a tribunal claim. Given that the ACAS Code, coupled with the requirement of reasonable procedures under the unfair dismissal legislation, already imposed a kind of procedural requirement on employers, the most significant change introduced by the system was the erection of a new obstacle for employees seeking to enforce their rights. Meanwhile, although the new disciplinary procedures were more strongly enforced than the ACAS Code (in that, in general, any non-observance made a dismissal unfair), they were also much more skeletal, and offered fewer procedural safeguards than would result from enthusiastic implementation of the ACAS Code.

The standard discipline/dismissal and grievance procedures won few friends. The judiciary's dislike of them was clear and it became almost unknown to come across an employment lawyer with a good word for them. They were widely perceived as being significant complications, of an often technical nature, capable of acting as trip-wires for the unwary rather than a positive contribution to dispute resolution. Indeed, it was arguable that they could have the boomerang effect of *increasing* workplace conflict and litigation. The DTI (predecessor to the BIS) had commissioned a report on them

---

[45] 'Findings of the 1998 Survey of Employment Tribunal Applications (Surveys of Applicants and Employers)' (Employment Relations Research Services, No 13, DTI, 2002). A survey of 2,700 ET cases found that only 58% of employers and 32% of applicants said that existing procedures had been fully followed; 65% of employers and 60% of applicants said that there had been no meeting between them to try to resolve the dispute; 39% of employers and 35% of applicants said that there had been no internal attempts at all to try to resolve the dispute.

[46] SI 2004/752; *Harvey* R [1956].

by an independent observer (possibly as a face-saving device for a department that had been so keen to impose them). The result was the Gibbons Report,[47] accompanied by a DTI consultation document.[48] The report pulled no punches. It accepted the almost total failure of the standard procedures, and in a particularly telling phrase referred to them as 'a classic case of good policy, but inappropriately inflexible and prescriptive regulation'. It recommended their complete repeal. Again in a telling remark, the report said that the law should be changed to ensure that procedures were seen once again as a way of actually settling disputes rather than (as had happened with the standard procedures) as a prelude to litigation.

The Gibbons Report led—in the blink of an eye by legislative standards—to the repeal of the standard procedures scheme and a return to the *Polkey* position,[49] under which the ACAS Code is the presumptive but not strictly required standard. The Employment Act 2008 scrapped the statutory discipline and grievance procedures, and replaced them with a revised ACAS Code of Practice for Discipline and Grievance Procedures. Since April 2009 tribunals have been authorized to adjust compensation in unfair dismissal cases up or down by as much as 25% against any party who unreasonably fails to comply with provisions of the new ACAS Code[50]—this in place of the system that found dismissals automatically unfair where employers failed to follow the standard procedures and barred from the tribunals claims that did not exhaust the statutory grievance procedures. The 2009 ACAS Code is more streamlined than the 2004 version, but more detailed and demanding than the earlier standard procedures. The outright and unqualified repeal of ERA 1996 section 98A, which previously enforced the procedures through the sanction of making dismissals automatically unfair, left the law on procedural fairness in dismissal where *Polkey* and its progeny had brought it before the introduction of the standard procedures. This line of cases, as is explained further later in this chapter, holds that failure to follow reasonable procedures can, by itself, make a dismissal unfair regardless of whether the substantive ground of the dismissal was reasonable, or even whether, in hindsight, observation of the procedure would have made no difference to the outcome. Under this case law, the ACAS Code represents a default of reasonable procedural standards, but an employer can, under certain circumstances, reasonably depart from the guidance of the Code.

It has been argued that the 2008 Act has not turned back the clock to 2004, but that the saga of the standard procedures and their eventual repeal has had the effect of watering down procedural protections for employees.[51] There is no doubt that the 2009 ACAS Code is thinned down—ten pages compared with 45 for the 2004 Code—albeit

---

[47] *Better Dispute Resolution* (DTI, March 2007). Michael Gibbons was a member of the Better Regulation Task Force.

[48] *Success at Work: Resolving Disputes in the Workplace* (DTI, March 2007).

[49] See heading 4(iii), p 502.

[50] TULR(C)A 1992, s 207A. The power to adjust awards applies to jurisdictions other than unfair dismissal, but only to employees, not to workers. *Local Government Yorkshire and Humber v Shah* UKEAT/0587/11, UKEAT/0026/12 (19 June 2012, unreported).

[51] Sanders 'Part One of the Employment Act 2008: "Better" Dispute Resolution?' (2009) 38 ILJ 30.

accompanied by 88 pages of non-statutory guidance. The sausage-making process of legislation clearly required a compromise between the bare-bones of the standard procedures and the best-practice ambition of the previous Code. As a result, much of the detail and nuance has been drawn out of the statutory Code—the one that tribunals are bound to consider—and worked up into a guidance document instead. Whether this amounts to a lowering of the expectations for discipline procedures or a simplification that will make the Code a stronger gold standard for fairness will depend on how the tribunals treat it. It should be harder for employers to argue the reasonableness of departing from a ten-page statement of basic principles of fairness than it might have been in the context of a 45-page articulation of ideal disciplinary practice.

The latest chapter in this saga relates not so much to disciplinary procedures but to other means of reducing the number of tribunal claims. At the time of writing, the Enterprise and Regulatory Reform Bill 2012 is making its way through Parliament. The details are not all clear, but the bill proposes to (1) require conciliation before the institution of tribunal proceedings, (2) allow more cases to be resolved by a single legal member rather than three members, (3) forbid the introduction into evidence of any discussions seeking to settle claims, (4) reduce the cap on the compensatory award for unfair dismissal from the current £72,300 to a significantly lower amount, possibly between one and three years of the employee's pay (so long as that is less than the current limit), and (5) impose a financial penalty on employers in the case of aggravating factors (this, presumably, a response to the suggestion that lowering the compensatory award takes away the penalty for egregious employer misdeeds).[52] The idea is to disabuse claimants of the notion that a tribunal claim offers them a ticket to a big payoff. In the likely event that the power granted by the Bill (it is almost certain to be enacted into law) is exercised to limit awards to one year's pay, this will supposedly discourage claims and encourage realistic settlement negotiations; the package is then rounded out by provisions to facilitate those frank negotiations through conciliation, and to streamline tribunal procedures to lower costs. While this scheme probably will result in fewer claims it represents an entirely one-sided approach to handling the problem. At least the Standard Procedure focused on the actual delivery of employment rights through better pre-claim procedures: this new proposal nakedly relieves employers of the inconvenient effects of affording rights to workers. It gives all the bargaining power to employers and makes it affordable essentially to buy out employees. Employers will now know that for the price of a settlement that is less than a year's pay they can dismiss any employee whenever they want. Put this together with (1) the recent increase in the qualifying period for the right to claim unfair dismissal from one year's continuous employment to two[53] and (2) the announced introduction of fees for making a

---

[52] Enterprise and Regulatory Reform Bill 2012, available at <http://www.publications.parliament.uk/pa/bills/lbill/2012–2013/0045/lbill_2012–20130045_En_7.htm#pt5-pb3-l1g56> (last accessed 10 January 2013).

[53] The Unfair Dismissal and Statement of Reasons for Dismissal (Variation of Qualifying Period) Order 2012, SI 2010/989 available at <http://www.legislation.gov.uk/uksi/2012/989/contents/made> (last accessed 10 January 2013).

claim (as much as £250) and for holding a tribunal hearing (as much as £950),[54] and it becomes clear that the Coalition government is pursuing a scorched-earth assault on any aspect of employment law that inhibits employers' ability to dispense with the services of their workers. It will be interesting to see if instead of merely reducing unfair dismissal claims, these changes foster a more frequent resort to discrimination claims where these restrictions will not apply.

2 THE DEFINITION OF DISMISSAL AND THE DATE OF TERMINATION

(i) DISMISSAL

The existence of a dismissal is a vital jurisdictional factor in the laws relating to unfair dismissal and redundancy. In most cases it is obvious that there has been a dismissal, but in cases of doubt the onus is upon the applicant to prove that he is dismissed; if he fails to do so, he cannot proceed with his claim. In particular, a tribunal will have no jurisdiction to hear the claim if the true construction of the facts is that the termination of employment was brought about by some factor other than dismissal (for example, frustration or mutual consent)[55] or that the employee resigned (see later discussion). Dismissal is therefore a central concept in this area of law and has not been without its problems.[56]

(a) The definition of dismissal

Dismissal is defined for the purposes of unfair dismissal and redundancy in sections 95 and 136 respectively of the Employment Rights Act 1996. These definitions are similar and envisage dismissal arising in one of three situations:

(1) where the contract is terminated by the employer either with or without notice;

(2) where a limited-term contract expires or otherwise terminates without being renewed;

(3) where the *employee* terminates the contract, with or without notice, in circumstances such that he is *entitled* to terminate it without notice by reason of the employer's conduct.

---

[54] Charging Fees in Employment Tribunals and the Employment Appeal Tribunal—consultation response (Ministry of Justice 13 July 2012) available at <https://consult.justice.gov.uk/digital-communications/et-fee-charging-regime-cp22-2011> (last accessed 10 January 2013).

[55] For modes of termination other than dismissal, see Ch 6, p 409.

[56] Elias 'Unravelling the Concept of Dismissal' (1978) 7 ILJ 16 was a seminal early consideration of this area.

Category (1) covers the usual case of dismissal, where the employer clearly dispenses with the employee's services either summarily or by giving him notice (or by giving him wages in lieu thereof). As it means the termination of a particular contract, there can be a category (1) dismissal (and hence a claim for unfair dismissal) even though the employee is still working for the same employer under a new contract (which may be particularly useful for the employee where the employer has unilaterally insisted on radically different terms of employment, sufficient to constitute a 'new' contract, rather than just a modification of the existing one).[57] It has also been held to cover cases where at first sight the employee appears to have resigned, but evidence then clearly establishes that the resignation was procured by the employer either by fraud,[58] pressure[59] or ultimatum ('resign or be sacked');[60] this has been done by concentrating, as a matter of fact, on the question—who *really* terminated the employment. This question may also be of importance where there is an ambiguous or hot-headed 'resignation'; while an employer may rely on a clear statement by the employee, there may be an onus on him to investigate further if there are special factors or circumstances leading up to the employee's actions, and failure to do so may mean that what eventually occurred was actually a dismissal and in all likelihood an unfair dismissal.[61] One point of historical importance to note (explaining certain older cases) is that at one time the tribunals and courts sought to extend this head of dismissal to cover matters now covered by category (3) (ie constructive dismissal), because that category (3) for redundancy purposes used to be more narrowly drafted,[62] and for unfair dismissal purposes was not expressly included in the legislation until 1974;[63] thus in certain cases category (1) was

---

[57] This is the rule in *Hogg v Dover College* [1990] ICR 39 which, while only likely to apply on strong facts (of a major change in terms imposed by the employer on a reluctant workforce), was affirmed and applied in *Alcan Extrusions v Yates* [1996] IRLR 327. Its importance is that, unlike constructive dismissal (the usual possibility in a case of unilateral change by the employer), the employees can claim unfair dismissal while keeping their jobs.

[58] *Makin v Grews Motors (Bridport) Ltd* (1986) The Times, 18 April, CA.

[59] *Caledonian Mining Co Ltd v Bassett* [1987] ICR 425, [1987] IRLR 165, applying *Martin v Glynwed Distribution Ltd* [1983] ICR 511, [1983] IRLR 198, CA; *Hellyer Bros Ltd v Atkinson* [1992] IRLR 540, EAT; *Lassman v De Vere University Arms Hotel* [2003] ICR 44.

[60] *East Sussex County Council v Walker* (1972) 7 ITR 280; *Martin*, n 59. However, these cases must be carefully distinguished from—(1) cases where the employer has merely indicated a general intention to dismiss at some time in the future (eg on a planned future factory closure): *Haseltine Lake & Co Ltd v Dowler* [1981] ICR 222, [1981] IRLR 25; *International Computers Ltd v Kennedy* [1981] IRLR 28, (2) cases where an employee under threat of dismissal reaches acceptable terms on which to leave. These will be ordinary resignations.

[61] *Kwik Fit (GB) Ltd v Lineham* [1992] ICR 183, [1992] IRLR 156. One problem is, of course, that in such extreme circumstances the language used tends not to be that contained in s 95; more often a tribunal will have to decide instead whether telling the employer where to insert the job, in graphic anatomical detail, constitutes an unambiguous resignation.

[62] For category (3) to apply, the employee had to leave without notice (Redundancy Payments Act 1965, s 3(1)(c), now repealed): *Marriott v Oxford and District Co-operative Society Ltd (No 2)* [1970] 1 QB 186, [1969] 3 All ER 1126, CA.

[63] See the Industrial Relations Act 1971, s 23(2), in force between 1971 and 1974; the NIRC filled this gap by construing category (1) as extending to constructive dismissals for unfair dismissal purposes in *Sutcliffe v Hawker Siddeley Aviation Ltd* [1973] ICR 560, [1973] IRLR 304, NIRC.

stretched to cover applicants who would otherwise have fallen outside the legislation for one of these reasons, but there is now no need for this stretching and so such cases should not necessarily be viewed as good law in this context, since the type of dismissal in question should now be considered under category (3).[64]

Where under category (1) an employee is given notice of dismissal, he may wish to leave his job before expiry of that notice (for example, where, being about to be made redundant, he finds another job which he wishes to start immediately). In such circumstances he would normally be in a difficult position for if he gave notice to leave he might be construed as having resigned or terminated the employment by mutual consent with his employer;[65] in either case there would be no dismissal and so he would lose his unfair dismissal and redundancy rights. To avoid this pitfall, the legislation includes the concept of 'early notice',[66] so that if, during the currency of the employer's notice, the employee gives counter-notice to terminate the employment at an earlier date he may leave and still be taken to have been dismissed by the employer. It must be noted here, however, that the provisions relating to early notice for redundancy purposes are narrower than those for unfair dismissal purposes in two ways: (1) the employee must give his counter-notice in writing, and (2) the counter-notice must be given during the *obligatory* period of the employer's notice (ie the period which the employer must by law give, either under the individual contract, or by virtue of the minimum notice requirements,[67] whichever is the longer). These requirements used to exist for unfair dismissal purposes also, but were removed by the Employment Protection Act 1975.

The original version of category (2) existed to safeguard the position of employees under fixed-term contracts and used that terminology. In practice, most cases under this heading will still concern fixed-term (ie time limited) contracts, but in 2002 the wording was altered to cover all forms of limited-term contracts, to be consistent with the Fixed-term Worker Directive (in particular to cover 'task' or 'purpose' contracts). Expiry (whether by time or some other limiting event) without renewal is deemed to be a dismissal, so that in an unfair dismissal action, the employer will have to show that the reason for failure to renew was a fair one.[68] The meaning of 'limited term contract' is considered above.[69]

---

[64] See the explanation of *Marriott's* case by Lord Denning MR in *Western Excavating (ECC) Ltd v Sharp* [1978] ICR 221 at 227, [1978] IRLR 27 at 29, CA.

[65] See Ch 6, heading 2(iv), p 424.

[66] Employment Rights Act 1996, ss 95(2) and 136(3). The counter-notice given by the employee may be of any length; it does not have to be of the length required by his contract (or even the statutory minimum of one week under s 86): *Ready Case Ltd v Jackson* [1981] IRLR 312; quaere what if it was only a few hours, or even minutes? The employer must have given actual notice for these provisions to apply; it is not enough that he has made some general statement of a possible future dismissal.

[67] Employment Rights Act 1996, s 86.

[68] *Terry v East Sussex County Council* [1976] ICR 536, [1976] IRLR 332, approved by the Court of Appeal in *Fay v North Yorkshire County Council* [1986] ICR 133, [1985] IRLR 247.

[69] See Ch 6, heading 1(iii), p 419, under 'Expiry of fixed-term contracts'.

(b) Constructive dismissal

While categories (1) and (2) have not been without difficulties, it is category (3) which has been most contentious. This sets out the statutory definition of 'constructive dismissal' which, as seen above, was always in the redundancy payments legislation and was read into the unfair dismissal provisions[70] before being expressly included in 1974. Constructive dismissal occurs where, although it is the employee who appears to terminate the employment by walking out, it can be said that the real reason for termination was in some way the prior conduct of the employer; it is necessary in order to avoid the employer being able to force or goad the employee to leave his employment and then say that the employee in fact resigned and so was not dismissed. When it is established, it means that for statutory purposes the contract is terminated by the employer. This is clearly the most contentious kind of dismissal, for there is no express act of dismissal by the employer. It must be remembered, however, that a constructive dismissal is *not* necessarily unfair and so a tribunal, even if it finds in the employee's favour on constructive dismissal, has only established the existence of a dismissal, and must still go on to consider fairness in the ordinary way; in many cases there will be little argument on this and the dismissal will, in the nature of things, be unfair, but this is not automatically so and there may be cases where, even though the employee had technically the right to walk out, the employer may be able to show that it was fair to act as he did.[71]

The key element of the definition of constructive dismissal is that the employee must have been *entitled* to leave without notice because of the employer's conduct. What does 'entitled' mean? At the outset of this legislation, there were two possible interpretations of this crucial word—first that the employee could leave when the employer's behaviour towards him was so unreasonable that he could not be expected to stay, and second that the employer's conduct had to be so grave that it constituted a repudiatory breach of the contract of employment, ie that the employee was *contractually* entitled to leave. Clearly the second is a narrower approach, and it was argued that the first was more in line with the overall approach in unfair dismissal cases of looking at the reasonableness of the employer's conduct. Following an initial period of uncertainty, with conflicting decisions, the Court of Appeal held in *Western Excavating (ECC) Ltd v Sharp*[72] that the contractual approach is the correct one, Lord Denning MR defining it as follows:

> If the employer is guilty of conduct which is a significant breach going to the root of the contract of employment, or which shows that the employer no longer intends to be bound

---

[70] *Sutcliffe v Hawker Siddeley Aviation Ltd* [1973] ICR 560, [1973] IRLR 304, NIRC.

[71] *Savoia v Chiltern Herb Farms Ltd* [1982] IRLR 166, CA. Note, however, the unenthusiastic approach taken to this distinction by the EAT in *Cawley v South Wales Electricity Board* [1985] IRLR 89 where it was said that in a case where the two stages (constructive dismissal and then fairness under s 98) raise the same issues a constructive dismissal should almost invariably be held to be unfair.

[72] [1978] ICR 221, [1978] IRLR 27, CA; the passage cited is at 226 and 29 respectively; *Courtaulds Northern Spinning Ltd v Sibson* [1988] ICR 451, [1988] IRLR 305, CA.

by one or more of the essential terms of the contract, then the employee is entitled to treat himself as discharged from any further performance. If he does so, then he terminates the contract by reason of the employer's conduct. He is constructively dismissed. The employee is entitled in those circumstances to leave at the instant without giving any notice at all or, alternatively, he may give notice and say that he is leaving at the end of the notice. But the conduct must in either case be sufficiently serious to entitle him to leave at once.

Thus, in a constructive dismissal case the tribunal is looking primarily for conduct by the employer[73] which is clearly a breach of one of the terms of the contract, and sufficiently important to be repudiatory on the part of the employer.[74] Certain examples may be fairly obvious, such as a refusal to pay wages,[75] an unjustified demotion or suspension,[76] failure to follow a contractually binding disciplinary procedure,[77] unilateral alteration of job content without contractual authority,[78] or insistence upon an unlawful or illegal order or the imposition of a penalty disproportionate to the offence.[79] It may, however, go wider than this, for the breach in question may be of an implied term as well as an express one, and therefore it is important to be able to say exactly which term it is

[73] Conduct by an immediate superior (eg a supervisor) may be enough to justify walking out, even if the employer later argues that that superior did not actually have the power to dismiss: *Hilton Industrial Hotels (UK) Ltd v Protopapa* [1990] IRLR 316.

[74] It has been held by the Court of Appeal that the question of whether a particular breach of contract is sufficient to be repudiatory (for the purpose of establishing constructive dismissal) is one of mixed fact and law, so that the EAT should rarely interfere with a tribunal's decision on this point, provided there was some evidence on which to base that decision: *Pedersen v Camden London Borough Council* [1981] ICR 674n, [1981] IRLR 173, CA. Although the test is contractual, seriously unreasonable conduct by the employer may be powerful evidence of breach of contract (in particular, the implied term of trust and respect): *Brown v Merchant Ferries Ltd* [1998] IRLR 682, NICA. Breach of statute by the employer should not be enough alone to find constructive dismissal: *Doherty v British Midland Airways Ltd* [2006] IRLR 90. However, in *Greenhof v Barnsley MBC* [2006] IRLR 98 such a result was achieved by arguing that the statutory breach (failure to make reasonable adjustments for a disabled employee) broke the implied contractual term of trust and respect.

[75] Even this major term is not sacrosanct, however, as every case must be considered on its facts; even a failure to pay wages might not be repudiatory in exceptional circumstances: *Adams v Charles Zub Associates Ltd* [1978] IRLR 551. Further, there is no implied term of an annual wage rise, so failure to give one will not necessarily amount to repudiatory conduct by the employer: *Murco Petroleum Ltd v Forge* [1987] ICR 282, [1987] IRLR 50; likewise, there is no implied term that there will never be a pay decrease: *White v Reflecting Roadstuds Ltd* [1991] ICR 733, [1991] IRLR 331; on the other hand, the Court of Appeal held in *Cantor Fitzgerald International v Callaghan* [1999] ICR 639, [1999] IRLR 234 (a common law action, but on the same point) that failure to pay any element of remuneration, however minor, will usually be repudiatory. For detailed consideration of matters held to be repudiatory in the past, see *Harvey* DI [425].

[76] *McNeill v Charles Crimm (Electrical Construction) Ltd* [1984] IRLR 179, EAT.

[77] *Post Office v Strange* [1981] IRLR 515, EAT.

[78] *Millbrook Furnishing Industries Ltd v McIntosh* [1981] IRLR 309; where the alteration is only temporary and for pressing business need, it may be arguable that it is not enough to be repudiatory, but such an argument failed in the *Millbrook* case. One practical answer for the employer is to incorporate a flexibility clause in the contract in the first place, but even this may not be a panacea because in *Land Securities Trillium Ltd v Thornley* [2005] IRLR 765 such a clause was interpreted narrowly, not covering a wholesale change in job function.

[79] *BBC v Beckett* [1983] IRLR 43; *Cawley v South Wales Electricity Board* [1985] IRLR 89; this class of case is more interesting, for here the employer may technically have the contractual power to impose the penalty in question, but must still act in accordance with some sort of proportionality which is presumably implied into the contractual disciplinary rules.

claimed that the employer broke, and whether any such term ever actually existed in the contract.[80] The question of definition of contractual terms, considered in Chapter 3, has thus been given statutory significance.

The contractual test as laid down in *Western Excavating (ECC) Ltd v Sharp* appears to be much narrower and more precise than the 'reasonableness' test, and at first seemed to be a significant restriction on constructive dismissal. However, this has not been so, principally for two reasons. The first is that the Court of Appeal, while firmly basing the law upon ideas of contract, did not mean to impose a rigid test and envisaged some flexibility in its application; this can be seen particularly in the judgment of Lawton LJ:

> I do not find it either necessary or advisable to express any opinion as to what principles of law operate to bring a contract of employment to an end by reason of an employer's conduct. Sensible persons have no difficulty in recognising such conduct when they hear about it.... Lay members of the [employment] tribunals ... do not spend all their time in court and when out of court they may use, and certainly will hear, short words and terse phrases which describe clearly the kind of employer of whom an employee is entitled without notice to rid himself. This is what [constructive dismissal] is all about; and what is required for the application of this provision is a large measure of common sense.[81]

The second, and more far-reaching, reason is that in subsequent cases, the EAT has shown itself ready to read into contracts of employment a new term obliging the employer to treat the employee with trust and respect.[82] This has also been called the '*Malik*' term, after the case that articulated it as an implied term of mutual trust and confidence.[83] To a large extent this development has outflanked the more purely contractual approach of the Court of Appeal in *Western Excavating (ECC) Ltd v Sharp*, so that harsh and unreasonable conduct by the employer might be construed by the tribunal as breach of this implied term of mutual trust and confidence, giving rise to

---

[80] A good example is *Dryden v Greater Glasgow Health Board* [1992] IRLR 469 (no implied term allowing smoking); it was also held there that if a change of practice is lawful under the contract (there, the imposition of a no-smoking policy) the fact that it bears more heavily on one employee than on others is not a ground for constructive dismissal.

[81] [1978] ICR 221 at 229, [1978] IRLR 27 at 30, CA. Generally speaking, the test is objective, in that the employer's conduct does not have to be intentional or in bad faith before it may be repudiatory: *Post Office v Roberts* [1980] IRLR 347. In line with this, 'seriously unreasonable' conduct can be evidence of contractual breach: *Brown v Merchant Ferries Ltd* [1998] IRLR 682, NICA. However, one class of case has imported a potentially subjective test—in *Frank Wright & Co (Holdings) Ltd v Punch* [1980] IRLR 217 it was held that where there is a genuine dispute as to the meaning of a contractual term and the employer insists on implementing his genuine (but possibly mistaken) version of it, that it not a repudiatory breach (even if he is later proved to have been wrong). This principle has backing from the normal law of commercial contracts (see *Woodar Investment Development Ltd v Wimpey Construction (UK) Ltd* [1980] 1 All ER 571, [1980] 1 WLR 277, HL) but its application to the specialized area of constructive dismissal could have an unfortunately restrictive effect (see the strong criticisms in *Harvey* D [486]ff); it was treated with caution in *Financial Techniques (Planning Services) Ltd v Hughes* [1981] IRLR 32, CA, but mentioned with approval obiter by Sir John Donaldson MR in *Bridgen v Lancashire County Council* [1987] IRLR 58, CA, and so the point remains unresolved.

[82] See Ch 3, heading 3(iv), p 151.

[83] *Malik v Bank of Credit and Commerce International SA* [1997] ICR 606, 621.

a constructive dismissal.[84] Thus, in the outcome, the contractual approach may differ only subtly from a simple 'reasonableness' approach,[85] and indeed a tribunal or court may now be impatient with an excessively contractual or technical argument by an employer which is aimed at frustrating the protective policy behind constructive dismissal. This breadth of approach can be seen, for example, in the so-called 'last straw doctrine', namely that the employee's resignation can be in response to a long series of actions by the employer, with the result that the actual event over which he walks out need not in itself be a seriously repudiatory one; even a relatively minor event may need to be looked at in context.[86] However, there remain two main qualifications. The first is that if the 'conduct' in question consists simply of the employer exercising one of his definite contractual rights (for example, to make the employee move from site to site, where there is a mobility clause in the contract), the employee who refuses to comply *should* not, under the contractual approach, be able to claim constructive dismissal for there has been no breach of contract;[87] however, it is argued elsewhere[88] that this may be changing, with the development by the courts of possible *overriding* implied terms, particularly that of mutual trust and confidence, which may impose limits on the *way* in which even express terms are applied and in so doing increase the scope for constructive dismissal. The second is that a particularly contractual approach has been taken by the Court of Appeal to the question of *anticipatory* breach by the employer; this is unlikely to occur often in practice but if it does (for example, by an employer announcing that he intends to implement unilateral changes of terms and conditions at some time in the future) it has been held that the employer may retract his intended repudiation as long as he does so before the employee has unequivocally accepted it and terminated the contract in anticipation.[89] However, it is also now clear that once a repudiatory breach goes beyond being anticipatory to being a completed breach, the breach cannot be 'cured' by the employer (through, for example, retraction of an accusation or an apology and attempts at reconciliation) unless the employee chooses to affirm the contract.[90] This is true even if it means that where the employer finds in favour of the employee in a workplace grievance procedure and retracts the

[84]   Conduct which is serious enough to breach the term of trust and confidence will always be serious enough to constitute a repudiatory breach by the employer for the purpose of establishing constructive dismissal: *Amnesty International v Ahmed* UKEAT/0447/08/ZT (2009) (available at <http://www.employmentappeals. gov.uk/Public/Upload/08_0447rjfhZTrevisedAmnestyNU.doc> last accessed 14 January 2013); *Morrow v Safeway Stores* [2002] IRLR 9.

[85]   See *British Aircraft Corpn v Austin* [1978] IRLR 332 at 334, per Phillips J.

[86]   *Omilaju v Waltham Forest LBC* [2005] IRLR 35, CA; although the last event need not be per se repudiatory, it must be serious enough to be a contributory factor to the decision to leave.

[87]   For example, a threat by the employer to give lawful contractual notice of dismissal cannot establish constructive dismissal, so that an employee leaving because of it may be held to have jumped the gun: *Kerry Foods Ltd v Lynch* [2005] IRLR 680, not following *Greenaway Harrison v Wiles* [1994] IRLR 380.

[88]   See Ch 3, heading 2(i), p 127.

[89]   *Norwest Holst Group Administration Ltd v Harrison* [1985] ICR 668, [1985] IRLR 240, CA.

[90]   *Buckland v Bournemouth University* [2010] EWCA Civ 121.

offending conduct it is too late: the contract has been breached and the employee has been constructively dismissed.

Although the theory behind constructive dismissal is that it is the employer who terminates the contract for statutory purposes, in practice it will usually be the employee who takes the final step by resigning and walking out, thus showing that he has accepted the employer's repudiation as concluding the contract. If the employee does not take such action, or does so after a delay, there is the danger (particularly in cases where the employer's conduct consists of a unilateral proposal to change the terms of employment) of this being construed as an agreement by the employee to a variation in the contract; if this is so there is no constructive dismissal, even if the employee later resigns. To avoid this danger, the employee should make up his mind quickly whether to leave,[91] or, if his economic circumstances are such that he feels he has to continue working for a short period following the conduct in question, he should let it be known that he does not agree to that conduct and is working under protest. Those working under protest must comply with any changes imposed, even if they consider the changes repudiatory breaches of contract, because staying under protest but not complying can justify a dismissal for misconduct.[92] The courts and tribunals have taken a realistic view of this,[93] but of course the employee cannot work under protest indefinitely and is expected to decide what his final response is to be within a reasonable period. This is because it remains the legal position that the employee must be able to show that he left *in response to* the employer's conduct (ie the causal link must be shown). However, this itself is to be viewed realistically (given the employee's difficult position), and so it has been held that (1) there can still be a constructive dismissal if the employee waits to leave until he has found another job to go to,[94] and (2) as a matter of law there is no absolute requirement on the employee to tell the employer the real reason for leaving (given that the worse the employer's behaviour, the less likely the employee may be to want to dispute the position before getting out).[95] The latter rule (highly inconvenient

---

[91] *Western Excavating (ECC) Ltd v Sharp* [1978] ICR 221 at 226, [1978] IRLR 27 at 29, respectively per Lord Denning MR; *Land and Wilson v West Yorkshire Metropolitan County Council* [1981] ICR 334, [1981] IRLR 87, CA. Note, however, that even if the employee must be taken to have consented to previous repudiations by the employer, it may be possible to rely on the fact of those repudiations having occurred as evidence of overall breach of the general implied term of trust and respect: *Lewis v Motorworld Garages Ltd* [1986] ICR 157, [1985] IRLR 465, CA.

[92] *Robinson v Tescom Corporation* [2008] IRLR 408, EAT.

[93] *Marriott v Oxford and District Co-operative Society Ltd (No 2)* [1970] 1 QB 186, [1969] 3 All ER 1126, CA; *Shields Furniture Ltd v Goff* [1973] 2 All ER 653, [1973] ICR 187; *Sheet Metal Components Ltd v Plumridge* [1974] ICR 373, [1974] IRLR 86; *W E Cox Toner (International) Ltd v Crook* [1981] ICR 823, [1981] IRLR 443. See too, in the context of wrongful dismissal, *Bliss v South East Thames Regional Health Authority* [1987] ICR 700, [1985] IRLR 308, CA.

[94] *Jones v F Sirl & Son (Furnishers) Ltd* [1997] IRLR 493; *Waltons and Morse v Dorrington* [1997] IRLR 488, EAT.

[95] *Weathersfield Ltd v Sargent* [1999] IRLR 94, CA, overruling on this point *Holland v Glendale Industries Ltd* [1998] ICR 493. Failure to make clear the reason for leaving when that might reasonably be expected could cast doubt on the genuineness of that reason, but only as a question of factual causation, not as a matter of law.

for HR professionals who may not have had reason to know what was going wrong until the employee left, thus giving them no chance to put it right) may in practice now be subject to qualification by the Employment Act 2008's provision for adjustments to compensation awards to penalize failure to exhaust internal grievance procedures. This of course does not prevent a tribunal from finding a dismissal (or ultimately an unfair dismissal) where the employee leaves without a word, as the acceptance of the employer's repudiation need not be express, but can take the form of conduct inconsistent with continued employment.[96]

(c) Resignation by the employee

An employee may resign from his employment for any reason or none; if there is a reason and it is connected with the employer's conduct he may argue that he has been constructively dismissed, but otherwise he may not claim unfair dismissal or a redundancy payment for there is no dismissal.[97] An express resignation may be by unambiguous wording or, if the wording is ambiguous, by a combination of wording and circumstances from which a reasonable employer would understand the employee to be resigning.[98] However, the concept of resignation has caused problems when attempts have been made to apply it in circumstances other than those of express resignation by the employee.

Such problems have arisen in two principal ways. The first occurs where the employee simply walks out or where, as in *British Leyland (UK) Ltd v Ashraf*[99] the employee is allowed a definite period of leave from which he does not return on time. It is arguable that there needs to be a concept of 'resignation by conduct' to cover the first of these examples (ie where the employee never returns), but the problem with the second example was that it was tied in frequently with rather more spurious arguments on mutual termination or termination by agreement, for in such cases the employer

---

[96] *Atlantic Air v Hoff* (UKEAT/0602/07/ZT, 26 March 2008) available at <http://209.85.229.132/ search?q=cache:AgOSEE4F1z4J>: <http://www.employmentappeals.gov.uk/Public/Upload/07_0602fhLBZT.d oc+atlantic+air+hoff&cd=1&hl=en&ct=clnk&gl=uk> last accessed 14 January 2013.

[97] Also a resignation under threat of dismissal may constitute a dismissal, unless the parties reach a mutually satisfactory agreement of terms (usually monetary) upon which the employee agrees to go; in that case it is a genuine resignation in spite of the previous threats—compare *Sheffield v Oxford Controls Co Ltd* [1979] ICR 396, [1979] IRLR 133 with *Thames Television Ltd v Wallis* [1979] IRLR 136. If the employer has already given the employee notice and the employee resigns during that period by giving counter-notice, he may still be 'dismissed' by virtue of ss 95(2) and 136(3) (see this chapter heading 2(i)(a), p 477).

[98] *BG Gale Ltd v Gilbert* [1978] ICR 1149, [1978] IRLR 453; *Sothern v Franks Charlesly & Co* [1981] IRLR 278, CA. There may, however, be problems with a 'hotheaded' resignation which the employee seeks to retract almost immediately—theoretically a retraction would need the consent of the employer, but there have been cases where it has been said that a tribunal should take a broader, more common-sense approach to whether the employee must be taken to have unequivocally resigned (even if, for example, the wording at the time left little to the imagination!): *Barclay v City of Glasgow District Council* [1983] IRLR 313; *Martin v Yeoman Aggregates Ltd* [1983] ICR 314, [1983] IRLR 49; *Sovereign House Security Services Ltd v Savage* [1989] IRLR 115, CA; *Kwik-Fit (GB) Ltd v Lineham* [1992] ICR 183, [1992] IRLR 156, EAT.

[99] [1978] ICR 979, [1978] IRLR 330. For termination by mutual consent generally, see Ch 6, heading 1(iv), p 421.

may have allowed the leave on terms that 'if you do not return on time, your employment will terminate'; when the employee arrived back late, he was then told that his contract had ended automatically, without the need for a dismissal. This argument by the employer succeeded in *Ashraf*'s case, but its wider implications soon became obvious and a very different approach was taken. *Ashraf*'s case was first distinguished by the EAT,[100] and finally overruled by the Court of Appeal in *Igbo v Johnson Matthey Chemicals Ltd*,[101] on the ground that such an agreement for automatic termination (on failure to return from leave of absence) was void for contravening the Employment Rights Act 1996, section 203 which invalidates any agreement (whether in a contract of employment or not) which 'purports ... to exclude or limit the operation of any provision of this Act'[102]—this agreement limited the operation of sections 95 and 98 which give the right to claim unfair dismissal. The advantage from the employee's point of view of this reasoning is that even if he signs such an agreement in full knowledge of what he is signing (for example, because the employer will only grant leave if he does so), the agreement will still be of no legal effect under the anti-contracting-out provisions of the section.

The second way in which problems arose had a far greater potential for driving the proverbial horse-drawn transport through the unfair dismissal legislation. This was the idea (known variously as 'constructive resignation' or 'self-dismissal') that in some cases the employee may commit such a grave breach of contract that he must be considered to have resigned by his own act.[103] Once again, this meant that there was no dismissal, and so no action for unfair dismissal. Moreover, such an agreement might arise not only from unusual or drastic facts, but could also possibly be set up by an employer phrasing a final warning in terms that 'if this happens again, you will be considered as having dismissed yourself'. The employer succeeded in showing self-dismissal in the early case of *Gannon v Firth*[104] where the employees (pursuant to a dispute) walked out without informing the management and leaving the plant in a dangerous state; the EAT held that this repudiatory conduct terminated their employment, they had not been dismissed, and so they could not claim unfair dismissal. This was a short decision, citing no authority, but was followed in subsequent cases.[105] Fortunately, the position was clarified by the Court of Appeal in *London Transport Executive v Clarke*[106]

---

[100] *Midland Electric Manufacturing Co Ltd v Kanji* [1980] IRLR 185; *Tracey v Zest Equipment Co Ltd* [1982] ICR 481, [1982] IRLR 268.

[101] [1986] ICR 505, [1986] IRLR 215, CA.   [102] See *Harvey* Q [827].

[103] The theoretical basis for this in contract law can be found in the previously current idea that contracts of employment formed an exception to the normal rule that a repudiation is only effective when accepted by the innocent party; thus, on this 'automatic termination' theory the contract was in fact ended by the employee's repudiation of it, which did not need any further action on the part of the employer and did not constitute a 'dismissal'.

[104] [1976] IRLR 415.

[105] Particularly *Smith v Avana Bakeries Ltd* [1979] IRLR 423 and *Kallinos v London Electric Wire* [1980] IRLR 11.

[106] [1981] ICR 355, [1981] IRLR 166, CA.

which concerned the taking of unauthorized leave by an employee in the knowledge that if he did so his name would be 'removed from the books'. When he returned the employers refused to take him back and he claimed unfair dismissal. The majority of the Court of Appeal (Templeman and Dunn LJJ) held that he had in fact been dismissed, applied the 'elective theory'[107] to repudiation of contracts of employment so that the employment was terminated by the employer's acceptance of the employee's repudiation, and overruled *Gannon v Firth* and the cases that had followed it; Lord Denning MR, dissenting, would have continued to apply the concept of self-dismissal, but the majority decision is clearly against it. Employers should not, however, throw up their hands in despair at this decision, for it was always arguable that the concept of self-dismissal was not particularly necessary anyway—if the employee's conduct was so drastic as to have been clearly repudiatory, then in most cases a tribunal is going to find his dismissal fair anyway (as was the ultimate conclusion of the Court of Appeal in *Clark's* case, unanimously).[108] The advantage of the majority's decision is that at least the fairness of the employer's conduct can be tested in such cases, rather than the employee's (possibly weak) claim being ruled out altogether on the jurisdictional point that technically there had been no dismissal.[109]

(ii) THE DATE OF TERMINATION

In the law relating to unfair dismissal and redundancy it is necessary for several reasons[110] to know when the employment ended; for unfair dismissal purposes this is known as the 'effective date of termination' and for redundancy purposes the 'relevant date'. The principal rules relating to these dates are found in the Employment Rights Act 1996, sections 97 and 145, and are as follows:

(1) Where the contract is terminated by notice (whether given by the employer or employee)—the date that the notice expires (whether or not the notice was of proper length).[111]

(2) Where the contract is terminated without notice—the date on which the termination takes effect.[112]

(3) Where a fixed-term or other limited-term contract expires without renewal— the date on which the termination takes effect.

---

[107] See Ch 6, heading 4(ii), p 435.

[108] See also more recently *Guernina v Thames Valley University* [2007] All ER (D) 156.

[109] Presumably there is now also the secondary ground that if the purported self-dismissal came from an agreement that 'if you do that again, you will be deemed to have dismissed yourself', that agreement itself will be void under s 203 (applying *Igbo v Johnson Matthey Chemicals Ltd*, n 101).

[110] Eg for calculating the period of continuous employment (for calculation and possibly for qualification purposes) and for determining the date from which the three- and six-month limitation periods run.

[111] *Palfrey v Transco plc* [2004] IRLR 916.

[112] This may even mean a precise time on the date in question: *Octavius Atkinson & Sons Ltd v Morris* [1989] ICR 431, [1989] IRLR 158, CA.

(4) Where the employee under notice gives counter-notice to terminate the employment sooner—the date of expiry of the counter-notice.

These rules are relatively straightforward, except in the case of head (2) above,
which unfortunately has attracted a difference of judicial opinion on one of its most
important applications. It is clear that (2) applies to summary dismissals, and in *Stapp
v Shaftesbury Society*[113] the Court of Appeal affirmed that the simple rule that the date
of termination is the date of the summary dismissal applies even if (a) that summary
dismissal is effected while the employee is already under ordinary notice and (b) the
effect of the summary dismissal bringing the date of termination forward is to deprive
the employee of the qualifying period for unfair dismissal which he would otherwise
have attained. However, summary dismissal is only one aspect of dismissal without
notice.

Far more common as a form of dismissal in practice is dismissal with wages in
lieu of notice whereby the employer is rid of the employee immediately (particularly
vital where the employee under notice would otherwise have access at work to the
firm's computers or confidential information) but with payment of what the employee
would have earned had he worked out his notice period. What is to be the date of
termination—the date when the notice would have expired (ie under (1) above) or
the date when the employee in fact leaves, albeit with a payment in lieu (ie under
(2) above)? This could be particularly material on the question of whether a claim is
brought in time, especially when the notice period is several weeks (for example, from
which date does the three-month limit for bringing an unfair dismissal action run?),
and could also affect whether the employee has satisfied the qualifying period for the
right in question. The interests of certainty would be best served by simply opting
for the date when the employee actually leaves (ie treating it as under (2) above, as
if a summary dismissal), and this was for several years thought to be the case, after
the decision of the Court of Appeal in *Dedman v British Building and Engineering
Appliances Ltd.*[114] However, confusion was caused by the decision of the EAT in *Adams
v GKN Sankey Ltd*[115] where it was suggested that the date of termination depends on
the true construction to be placed on the dismissal—if it was expressed as a dismissal
by notice (but with the employee not actually required to work out that notice), the
date of termination should be the date of expiry of the notice; if, however, it was
expressed as an instant dismissal (but with the payment of wages in lieu of notice as,
in effect, compensation for wrongful dismissal), the date of termination should be
the date the employee left. This distinction seems a thin one on which to base such

---

[113] [1982] IRLR 326, CA. The fact that the summary dismissal was in breach of a contractually binding
disciplinary procedure which would have taken some time to go through properly cannot be used to advance
what is otherwise under the section the effective date of termination: *Batchelor v British Railways Board* [1987]
IRLR 136, CA.

[114] [1974] 1 All ER 520, [1974] ICR 53, CA, the leading case on the extension of time limits for commenc-
ing tribunal actions.

[115] [1980] IRLR 416.

an important concept as the date of termination and in practice may, one suspects, owe more to fortune than reality in its application. It certainly means that letters of dismissal should be drafted carefully, from the employer's point of view.

This 'construction' approach can also be seen in *Chapman v Letheby and Christopher Ltd*[116] where it was stated that the mere fact that a dismissal was stated to be with payment in lieu did not mean that it constituted an instant dismissal, and that the effect of the dismissal depended on the construction which would be placed on it by an ordinary, reasonable employee. However, in *Robert Cort & Son Ltd v Charman*[117] the EAT reverted to the straightforward *Dedman* view, stressing (1) the proper interpretation of the wording of section 97 and (2) the need for absolute certainty on the effective date of termination, especially in the context of limitation periods (though the case itself concerned the question whether the employee had served the necessary qualifying period for an unfair dismissal action). This left the law in an uncertain state. The question was canvassed before the Court of Appeal in *Stapp v Shaftesbury Society*,[118] but that case concerned a different aspect of dismissal without notice (considered earlier in this chapter).[119] However, Stephenson LJ, giving the principal judgment, did allude to the present problem at two stages; at one point he expressly approved of the statement of Browne-Wilkinson J in *Chapman v Letheby and Christopher Ltd* that any ambiguity in a dismissal notice should be construed against the employer (though without commenting on the construction approach generally), but later said:

> But the effect of summary dismissal in fixing the effective date of termination cannot be questioned. The case of *Cort* is a very recent application of what was laid down by this court some years ago in the case which it followed, *Dedman v British Building and Engineering Appliances Ltd.*

The judgment in *Stapp* is therefore at best ambiguous and subsequently in *Leech v Preston Borough Council*[120] the EAT pointed out that the well-worn phrase 'wages in

---

[116] [1981] IRLR 440; the facts in the case were distinctly ambiguous, showing the difficulties that this 'construction' approach can cause, though the EAT did say that ultimately any ambiguity should be construed against the employer, who should have drafted the letter of dismissal more carefully. Quaere—how would this apply to an oral dismissal with wages in lieu where noone can remember exactly what was said?

[117] [1981] ICR 816, [1981] IRLR 437 (*Chapman v Letheby and Christopher Ltd* not referred to). The principal significance of the EAT's emphasis on the statutory interpretation of s 97 was that it enabled them to dispose of the employee's subtle arguments based on contractual ideas of repudiation and acceptance (see heading 2(i), p 477); hopefully this case is authority that the 'elective' theory of repudiation does not apply for the purpose of fixing the date of termination for statutory purposes, so that an employee cannot push forward that date for some unspecified time simply by arguing that he never in fact accepted the employer's repudiation.

[118] [1982] IRLR 326.

[119] The case was principally argued on the point whether an employer could avoid statutory rights by wrongfully dismissing the employee (and after having given him proper notice at that). It was, however, a case of dismissal with wages in lieu (in effect, though not in the usual way), for he had been given notice, then when summarily dismissed during the notice period was told that he would in fact be paid for the whole of the rest of what should have been his notice period.

[120] [1985] ICR 192, [1985] IRLR 337; *Cort's* case is not cited in the judgment.

lieu of notice' has two distinct meanings[121] and applied the 'construction' approach in *Adams* and *Chapman*. That must now be considered to be the correct approach, since it is consistent with the explanation of dismissal with wages in lieu generally by Lord Browne-Wilkinson in the leading case on deductions from wages, *Delaney v Staples*;[122] he in fact isolated *four* possible forms of such a dismissal,[123] but they include the two principal forms alluded to in *Leech* and as, in his judgment, he explained that they operate on different grounds, it is reasonable to conclude that the EDT will be different, as the majority of the case law suggests.

Four further points should be noted. The first is that where the employee is dismissed by being given less notice than the employer is obliged to give him by statute,[124] the date of termination is deemed to be the date it would have been had that statutory minimum been given, for certain purposes. Those purposes are computation of the two-year qualifying period for claiming unfair dismissal and demanding a written statement of reasons for dismissal, calculation of the basic award for unfair dismissal, computation of the two-year qualifying period for a redundancy payment and calculation of the period of continuous employment by which such a payment is determined.[125] The second point is that if the employee has been dismissed, the fact that he is actively pursuing an appeal under the firm's grievance procedure does *not* mean that the date of termination is extended to the completion of that appeal process.[126] Moreover, this is likely to be of most significance when deciding when the three-month time limit for an unfair dismissal action begins to run and the Court of Appeal affirmed strongly that the fact of pursuing an internal appeal will *not* be a good reason to extend the three months' period in the tribunal's discretion.[127] The third point is that sections 97 and 145 do not state what the date of termination is to be in a case of constructive dismissal; it has been held that the EDT is the date of acceptance of the employer's repudiation of the contract, which will normally mean the date when the employee walks out, but it

---

[121] The 'grammatically accurate sense of compensation for summary dismissal without notice' or the 'more colloquial sense of payment to someone who is excused or prohibited from attending the workplace during the notice period'.

[122] [1992] ICR 483, [1992] IRLR 191, HL.

[123] These are set out at Ch 6, heading 2, p 427, along with the suggested EDTs, in the light of this discussion.

[124] Employment Rights Act 1996, s 86. The employee can only claim an extension by the period of his statutory entitlement, not by the period of any more generous notice entitlement agreed in his contract: *Fox Maintenance Ltd v Jackson* [1978] ICR 110, [1977] IRLR 306. Note, however, that s 86(6) preserves the employer's right to dismiss summarily for gross misconduct, and so if an employer does so justifiably there can be no extension under the statute: *Lanton Leisure Ltd v White and Gibson* [1987] IRLR 119, EAT.

[125] Employment Rights Act 1996, ss 97(2) and 145(5). The statutory extension is for these purposes only, it is not of general application: *Slater v John Swain & Son Ltd* [1981] ICR 554, [1981] IRLR 303; *Secretary of State for Employment v Cameron Iron Works* [1988] ICR 297 (revsd on other grounds [1989] ICR 664, [1989] IRLR 117, CA). In particular, note that it does not apply for the purposes of the three-/six-month limitation periods for bringing tribunal proceedings.

[126] *J Sainsbury Ltd v Savage* [1981] ICR 1, [1980] IRLR 109, CA. If, however, the appeal is successful there is no break in continuity, as the appeal decision applies as from the date of the original dismissal: *Howgate v Fane Acoustics Ltd* [1981] IRLR 161, EAT.

[127] *Palmer v Southend-on-Sea Borough Council* [1984] ICR 372, [1984] IRLR 119, CA.

has also been held that an employee cannot use this argument to prolong the EDT past the date the employment *actually* ended.[128] The fourth, final, and perhaps most fundamental point on the EDT is that ultimately it is for the employer to get it right, so that any ambiguity is likely to be construed in the employee's favour.[129] In particular, there is in general no doctrine of *constructive* notice of dismissal, so that a dismissal by letter will only take effect when it is actually received by the employee, even if that is later than expected by the employer (who will thus often be well advised to communicate the dismissal directly to the employee, or at the very least to use registered or recorded post so that the date of service can be ascertained).[130]

3 UNFAIR DISMISSAL—THE RIGHT AND THE EXCLUSIONS

Just over 40% of the cases heard by tribunals each year concern primarily claims of unfair dismissal. As is immediately obvious, such a claim is a much more realistic action to bring in most cases than the common law action for wrongful dismissal, and since its inception in 1971[131] this branch of employment law has given rise to an enormous amount of case law. It is therefore particularly important in this context to bear in mind that the only way to cope successfully with the intimidating case law is to concentrate on those cases which establish principles, points of interpretation or (at least when they are in fashion) general guidelines for the tribunals, and consider the rest as mere illustrations, interesting though they may be. One simple truth, so easy to overlook when surrounded by employment law reports, is that unfair dismissal is *not* primarily a case law subject—primacy must remain with the relevant wording of

---

[128] Contrast *G W Stephens & Son v Fish* [1989] ICR 324 with *BMK Ltd v Logue* [1993] ICR 601. Note, however, that there was introduced in 1982 an extension of time for certain purposes (akin to those in n 117) in the case of a constructive dismissal, the extension period being the amount of notice that should have been given under s 86 if it had been the employer who was terminating the employment: s 97(4).

[129] *Widdicombe v Longcombe Software Ltd* [1998] ICR 710 (ambiguous correspondence between employer and absent employee; EDT fixed as the date of the final, clearest letter, which came within the limitation period). As the EDT is a statutory concept, it cannot be altered by agreement between the parties: *Fitzgerald v University of Kent* [2004] ICR 737, [2004] IRLR 300, CA.

[130] *McMaster v Manchester Airport plc* [1998] IRLR 112 (sick employee not receiving dismissal letter on the expected day of delivery because on a day trip to France; limitation period only flowed from the day of his return); *Barratt v Gisda CYF* [2008] All ER (D) 288 (Nov).

[131] The provisions relating to unfair dismissal were first enacted in the Industrial Relations Act 1971; they were re-enacted in the first Schedule to the Trade Union and Labour Relations Act 1974, amended by the Employment Protection Act 1975, and then consolidated, first in the Employment Protection (Consolidation) Act 1978 and then in the Employment Rights Act 1996. The scheme of the provisions follows ILO Recommendation 119 (1963); revised ILO standards on dismissal worked out subsequently have not been adopted; see (1984) 13 ILJ 130. For detailed consideration of this branch of law, see *Harvey* Division DI, to which more detailed references are made below; also Dickens et al *Dismissed* (1983); Collins 'The Meaning of Job Security' (1991) 20 ILJ 227; and, for a fundamental critique of the existing law, Collins *Justice in Dismissal* (1992) and Pitt 'Justice in Dismissal—A Reply to Hugh Collins' (1993) 22 ILJ 251.

the statute. Further, the statute in most contexts puts matters into the discretion of the tribunals (and expressly gives a restricted right of appeal to the EAT, on points of law only) and so, although for the sake of exposition the following discussion will look at the law under certain headings and will concentrate on the evolving rules relating to certain categories of dismissal of practical importance, it must be remembered that in many instances the seeming rules of law under discussion may only be guidelines to the factors to be taken into consideration by the tribunal in deciding upon what is usually the central issue in an unfair dismissal case, namely whether the employer's conduct in the dismissal was reasonable.

(i) THE RIGHT TO CLAIM

Subject to certain exclusions, the Employment Rights Act 1996, section 94 gives to every employee the right not to be unfairly dismissed. There are two principal qualifications for this right: first, the employee must have been 'dismissed' (a concept which is considered in Section 2 earlier in this chapter) and second, on the effective date of termination the employee must have been continuously employed by his employer for the necessary qualifying period, now two years (unless dismissed for a reason stated specifically not to require such qualifying service, such as one relating to membership or non-membership of a trade union, maternity, health and safety complaints, assertion of statutory rights or acting as an employee trustee of a pension scheme or as an elected employee representative). Initially, this period was six months, but it was raised, first to a year in 1979 and then to two years in 1985.[132] The imposition of any such period had two aims. A long-term aim was to exclude (indirectly) part-timers from the right to claim unfair dismissal; this happened because in order to count time worked towards the required period of continuous employment at all, the employee had to work more than 16 hours per week (or more than eight hours per week for five years). The second aim was to lessen what have been perceived to be the adverse effects of employment law on business and the creation of jobs;[133] this aim was particularly important with regard to the significant lengthening of the period. This, however, was controversial; although it is the case that a qualifying period has the bona fide effect of allowing an employer to operate a fairly lengthy trial period for a new employee and assess suitability without having to face an unfair dismissal application, it was argued that the very long period of two years was operated more as a blanket initial immunity, and when it was in force there was at least anecdotal evidence of some employers cynically using that immunity (particularly in areas of high labour turnover) by taking employees on for only 18 months or thereabouts and then dismissing them as a matter of policy.

Both of these aims of the qualifying period were subject to attack under EC law. The exclusion of part-timers no longer works because the 16-hour rule (and eight

---

[132] Unfair Dismissal (Variation of Qualifying Period) Order 1985, SI 1985/782.
[133] 'Lifting the Burden' (Cmnd 951, 1985) ch 5.

hours for five years rule) had to be removed[134] in order to comply with the ruling of the House of Lords in *R v Secretary of State for Employment, ex p Equal Opportunities Commission*[135] that those hours' limitations had a disproportionate effect on female employees and so constituted indirect sex discrimination (contrary to Article 119 and the Equal Treatment Directive) which was not justified by the government's arguments on economic necessity. Thus, an employee with two years' continuous employment could claim unfair dismissal regardless of their hours of work.[136] However, the matter did not rest there, for the next stage was to attack the two-year qualifying period *itself* as sexually discriminatory (thus negating the second aim). This was done in *R v Secretary of State for Employment, ex p Seymour-Smith*[137] in which the application for a declaration that the increase of the qualifying period in 1985 to two years was contrary to the Equal Treatment Directive was granted by the Court of Appeal; at further appeal, the House of Lords remitted the question to the ECJ which gave an exceptionally Delphic reply.[138] When the House of Lords reconsidered the case in the light of this, they finally held that the 1985 increase was *not* discriminatory (three Lords holding that any adverse effect was justified and two that there was no significant adverse effect in the first place).[139] By this time, however, the New Labour government had lowered the period to *one year* in any event legislatively,[140] a far more satisfactory method of reform. As we saw above the current Coalition government has put things back where they were in 1985, for good or ill. Apparently as part of a general effort to relieve employers as much as possible from constraints on their disposing of their employees when they need to, the government introduced, effective 6 April 2012, an increase of the qualifying period to two years.[141] This will only apply to those whose period of continuous employment began on or after 6 April 2012.

(ii) THE EXCLUSIONS

The right to bring an action has always been subject to exceptions. Part-timers were excluded for many years (indirectly, in that an employee working fewer than 16 hours per week could not count this towards the year qualification period) but this was

---

[134] Employment Protection (Part-time Employees) Regulations 1995, SI 1995/31; see Ch 2, heading 1(iv), p 54.

[135] [1994] ICR 317, [1994] IRLR 176, HL.

[136] In *Colley v Corkindale* [1995] ICR 965 an employee working one five-and-a-half-hour bar shift every other Friday was able to claim unfair dismissal.

[137] [1995] ICR 889, [1995] IRLR 464, CA.   [138] C-167/97 [1999] ICR 447, [1999] IRLR 253, ECJ.

[139] [2000] IRLR 263, HL.

[140] Unfair Dismissal and Statement of Reasons for Dismissal (Variation of Qualifying Period) Order 1999, SI 1999/1436.

[141] The Unfair Dismissal and Statement of Reasons for Dismissal (Variation of Qualifying Period) Order 2012, SI 2012/989 available at <http://www.legislation.gov.uk/uksi/2012/989/contents/made> (last accessed 14 January 2013). This order also increases to two years the qualifying period for the right to receive a statement of the reasons for the dismissal.

repealed in 1995.[142] The exception that always caused the most difficulty and extensive litigation concerned employees over 65 or (if different) their 'normal retirement age'.[143] This exception had to go with the advent of the Employment Equality (Age) Regulations 2006 and so there is now no upper age limit for a claim.[144] This change is somewhat illusory, however, as the Equality Act 2010 does not prohibit employers from adopting policies that require retirement at a specific age so long as the policy is a proportionate means to certain legitimate social aims.

The position on exclusions has thus been a fluid one, and indeed the Employment Relations Act 1999 had already made two important changes. First, it repealed the provisions in the Employment Rights Act 1996, section 197 which used to permit an employer to put into a fixed-term contract of one year or more a clause excluding unfair dismissal rights on termination. There had been longstanding criticisms of this power, on the basis of abuse by employers (especially by the device of putting employees on to successive such contracts, possibly over a long period of time), and the government decided to abolish it altogether. Secondly, the 1999 Act also repealed section 196 of the 1996 Act, which used to disapply most of the rights in the latter (including unfair dismissal) where 'under the employee's contract of employment he ordinarily works outside Great Britain'. There was considerable case law on this wording,[145] which tended to help a British employee sent temporarily to work abroad, but equally tended to prejudice a foreign employee temporarily working in Britain, as was seen particularly in *Carver v Saudi Arabian Airlines*.[146] When the Employment Relations Bill was before the House of Lords, a modest amendment to make this area fairer to foreign employees was proposed, but the government minister undertook (on a withdrawal of the amendment) to consider the matter. In fact, when the matter returned to the Lords the government suggested a far more radical solution, namely to repeal section 196 altogether. By now, the real impetus behind this was the need to comply with the Posted Workers Directive 96/71/EC which requires workers sent to work in another member state to have the same rights as workers in that state. Removal of the territorial bars in section 196 was perceived to be one way of doing this, and so this was done. What is to replace it? The government simply said that the matter would now be satisfactorily covered by the well-known rules of private international law(!), and a DTI (BIS predecessor) press release said that the normal provisions of the Brussels and Rome Conventions should be used. However, it is possible that this was a serious mistake, because while these rules and provisions are capable of governing the proper

---

[142] See Ch 2, heading 5(i), p 101.

[143] For the old case law on this, see the eighth edition of this work at p 559.

[144] The age exclusion used to be contained in the Employment Rights Act 1996, s 109, which was repealed as from October 2006.

[145] The leading cases were *Wilson v Maynard Shipbuilding Consultants AB* [1978] ICR 376, [1977] IRLR 491, CA; *Todd v British Midland Airways Ltd* [1978] ICR 959, [1978] IRLR 370, CA; and *Janata Bank v Ahmed* [1981] ICR 791, [1981] IRLR 457, CA.

[146] [1999] 3 All ER 61, [1999] IRLR 370, CA.

law of, and jurisdiction in relation to, a *contract* (such as a contract of employment) it is arguable that they cannot govern the position in relation to a purely statutory right such as unfair dismissal.[147] If this is correct, what the government actually did was to create a *hole* in the 1996 Act, so that we have a statute giving rights *without* the necessary statutory provisions on territorial jurisdiction.[148] The result was that it became a matter of statutory interpretation (not private international law) as to what was intended with regard to jurisdiction. After a period of uncertainty and conflicting decisions, the matter finally came before the House of Lords in *Lawson v Serco Ltd*,[149] a test case involving three appeals by British nationals working (1) for a British company but wholly on Ascension Island, (2) for the MoD on a base in Germany and (3) as a pilot for a foreign airline but flying out of Heathrow. Accepting the gap in the legislation but declining to go down the route of judicial legislation or declaring it all to be a matter of discretion, the House of Lords laid down the applicable principles by dividing possible claimants into three categories:

(1) *Standard cases* Given that we cannot provide tribunals for the world, the necessary limitation is that the Employment Rights Act 1996 applies to an employee 'working in Great Britain'.[150] This appears to hark back to the pre-1999 law *except* that this current test is no longer based on what the contract says, but rather on what happened in practice (the contract only being a factor). In the context of unfair dismissal, Lord Hoffmann said that 'ordinarily the question should simply be whether he is working in Great Britain at the time when he is dismissed'.

(2) *Peripatetic employees* An example here would be airline staff, and in a peripatetic case the answer according to the House of Lords is in effect to go back to some earlier law in this area and apply what for many years was Lord Denning MR's 'base' test in *Todd v British Midland Airways Ltd*,[151] namely a wide factual test as to where the employee was effectively based (eg where he or she was living, paying tax, operating from, organized from; again the contract could be evidence).

---

[147] There is no implied contractual right not to be unfairly dismissed: *Focsa Services (UK) Ltd v Birkett* [1996] IRLR 325.

[148] Contrast this with the far more sensible amendments to the discrimination legislation in the Equal Opportunities (Employment Legislation) (International Limits) Regulations 1999, SI 1999/3163 (again seeking compliance with the Posted Workers Directive) which simply removed the wording 'or mainly' from the exclusion of employees working 'wholly or mainly outside Great Britain'. There may now be disputes over what is meant by 'wholly' outside GB (eg what level of involvement within GB could be ignored as de minimis), but at least we still have a statutory provision here to apply.

[149] [2006] ICR 250, [2006] IRLR 289, HL, noted Linden (2006) 35 ILJ 186.

[150] Note that these principles apply to any claim under the 1996 Act, even though they are being considered here in the context of unfair dismissal. The actual decision in *Carver v Saudi Arabian Airlines*, n 146, must now be considered wrong.

[151] Note 145. Lord Hoffmann said that to hold otherwise would make airline pilots 'the flying Dutchmen of labour law' (presumably a double danger if employed by KLM).

(3) *Expatriate employees*   Such an employee (eg Mr Lawson on Ascension Island) has caused most problems. The fact of working for a GB company is *not* per se enough, and the 'base' test cannot help. Ostensibly this employee is *not* covered by the 1996 Act and must rely on the employment law (if any) of the country in which he or she is working. There are, however, two exceptions:

  (a) where the employee is *posted* abroad for the purposes of a business carried on in GB (an example being a foreign correspondent reporting for a GB television channel); and

  (b) an expatriate 'operating in what amounts to an extra-territorial enclave in a foreign country' (the prime example being a British military base abroad).

On these principles, the MoD employee and the pilot clearly won their right to complain to an employment tribunal here and, on the facts[152] the security guard on Ascension Island won *just*, on the 'enclave' point. In spite of these successes, however, there can remain serious dangers for an employee working abroad, including those 'on secondment' (a weasel word, having no inherent meaning in employment law), especially as the one thing that is clear is that being British, working for a British-owned concern, is *not* in itself enough to establish jurisdiction. Moreover, those who would not ordinarily attract tribunal jurisdiction under these principles cannot bootstrap jurisdiction through the use of a choice-of-law clause in their employment contracts.[153]

To summarize, therefore, the law on excluded categories has always been difficult, even though the question posed ('who can claim?') appears simple. There are, however, three other exclusions which are longstanding and relatively certain:

(1) two specific categories of share fishermen and the police;[154]

(2) an employee governed by a dismissal procedures agreement between employers and trade unions in the industry, designated by the Secretary of State as operating in substitution for the statutory scheme;[155]

(3) an employee whose dismissal was for the purpose of safeguarding national security.[156]

---

[152] One factor being that Ascension Island, in addition to its odd constitutional position, has no indigenous population and so has never had much employment law.

[153] *Bleuse v MBT Transport and Tiefenbacher* [2008] IRLR 264.

[154] Employment Rights Act 1996, ss 199 and 200 respectively. On the meaning of 'share fisherman', see *Goodeve v Gilsons* [1985] ICR 401, CA.

[155] Section 110. Although this scheme was historically significant in showing a willingness to allow the parties to govern their own affairs, in fact only one industry (electrical contracting) ever used it, and that was discontinued in 2001.

[156] Employment Tribunal Act 1996, s 10.

4 WHAT IS AN UNFAIR DISMISSAL?

Once the employee has proved that he was dismissed (if that is a live issue in the case) the burden of proof then passes on to the employer, under section 98 of the 1996 Act, to show two things:

(1) what was the reason for the dismissal (or the principal reason if more than one);

(2) that it fell within one of the enumerated categories of prima facie fair dismissals, namely that the reason was:

(a) related to the capability or qualifications of the employee for performing his work,

(b) related to the conduct of the employee,

(c) that the employee was redundant,

(d) that the employee could not continue to work in that position without contravention of a legislative provision,[157]

(e) 'some other substantial reason of a kind such as to justify the dismissal'.

It is then for the tribunal to decide whether in the circumstances (having regard to equity and the substantial merits of the case) the employer acted reasonably in treating that reason as a sufficient reason for dismissing the employee (section 98(4)).

This basic structure of an unfair dismissal action should be borne in mind (except in cases where the statute expressly provides that a certain type of dismissal shall be automatically fair or unfair), and the significance of the burden of proof being upon the employer is that if he fails to satisfy the tribunal at either of the first two stages ((1) reason and (2) prima facie fair) the dismissal will be held to be unfair.

(i) STAGE ONE: THE REASON

The first stage is that the employer must show what the real reason was for the dismissal;[158] if she clearly relies upon one particular reason and the tribunal disbelieves

---

[157] Eg where an employee employed wholly or principally to drive a vehicle is disqualified and there is no alternative work for him: *Appleyard v F M Smith (Hull) Ltd* [1972] IRLR 19, IT; *Fearn v Tayford Motor Co* [1975] IRLR 336, IT. The tribunal must still go on to consider whether the dismissal was reasonable under s 98(4), as this is not an automatically fair reason for dismissal: *Sandhu v DES* [1978] IRLR 208. A mistaken belief by the employer that he cannot lawfully continue to employ the employee does not come under this heading, but may qualify as 'some other substantial reason': *Bouchaala v Trust House Forte Hotels Ltd* [1980] ICR 721, [1980] IRLR 382, EAT.

[158] The burden of proof is on the employer; if he leads evidence supporting his contention that he dismissed for reason A, that may cast an evidential burden on the employee to adduce some evidence to doubt reason A

her, the finding should be one of unfair dismissal and she should not normally be allowed to try to rely upon an entirely different reason either at the tribunal hearing (without applying for leave to amend her defence) or on appeal.[159] However, tribunal proceedings are not meant to be as formal as High Court proceedings, and it must be accepted that, in the light of the complexity of certain of these areas of law, the employer may not always initially put the correct legal interpretation on the factors determining her decision to dismiss.[160] The general approach has therefore been that the tribunal's task is to discover the reason actually motivating the employer at the time of the dismissal. In *Abernethy v Mott, Hay and Anderson*,[161] Cairns LJ said:

> A reason for the dismissal of an employee is a set of facts known to the employer, or it may be of beliefs held by him, which cause him to dismiss the employee. If at the time of his dismissal the employer gives a reason for it, that is no doubt evidence, at any rate as against him, as to the real reason, but it does not necessarily constitute the real reason. He may knowingly give a reason different from the real reason out of kindness or because he might have difficulty in proving the facts that actually led him to dismiss; or he may describe his reasons wrongly through some mistake of language or of law.

Thus, a wrong label given by the employer is not fatal to his case and, further, it is clear from the cases that the approach here is basically subjective particularly in cases where it is a *belief* on the part of the employer which led her to dismiss. The obvious example here is a belief that the employee is guilty of a crime (see below, under 'conduct'), for in such cases, as with other 'belief' cases, it has been consistently held that what the employer is required to prove is her genuine belief, *not* that her belief was factually correct.[162] However, in the nature of things the approach cannot be totally subjective, for the employer has to *prove* that she held the belief in question and so in practice will have to go on to adduce some supporting evidence of the facts upon which she based her belief (even though it does not have to amount to clear proof of the correctness of that belief), otherwise there is the danger that the tribunal will not believe her.

---

and/or suggest reason B; if he does so, the legal burden of proof remains with the employer at the end of the day: *Maund v Penwith District Council* [1984] ICR 143, [1984] IRLR 24, CA. If dismissal is with notice, it may be necessary to look at the reason(s) operating both at the giving and expiry of the notice: *Parkinson v March Consulting Ltd* [1998] ICR 276, [1997] IRLR 308, CA; *West Kent College v Richardson* [1999] ICR 511.

[159] *Nelson v BBC* [1977] ICR 649, [1977] IRLR 148, CA; *ASLEF v Brady* [2006] IRLR 576. This is certainly so on appeal as *Nelson* shows, if only because it is contrary to natural justice to decide an appeal on a ground that was not fully argued before the tribunal; a similar rule applies before the tribunal itself, but here a change of label may be permissible where the employee is in fact given a proper opportunity to refute the new ground: *Murphy v Epsom College* [1985] ICR 80, [1984] IRLR 271, CA; *Hotson v Wisbech Conservative Club* [1984] ICR 859, [1984] IRLR 422; *Burkett v Pendletons (Sweets) Ltd* [1992] ICR 407. Likewise, if the employer fails to establish the reason put forward, the tribunal should not cast around to try to find some other dismissible reason: *Adams v Derby City Council* [1986] IRLR 163.

[160] 'Redundancy' for example may cover a multitude of sins in layman's use, but in law it has a precise and restricted meaning.

[161] [1974] ICR 323, [1974] IRLR 213, CA; the passage cited was approved by the House of Lords in *W Devis & Sons Ltd v Atkins* [1977] ICR 662, [1977] IRLR 314, HL. For an example of wrong labelling, see *Hannan v TNT-IPEC (UK) Ltd* [1986] IRLR 165.

[162] *Trust House Forte Leisure Ltd v Aquilar* [1976] IRLR 251; *Ford v Libra Fair Trades* [2008] All ER (D) 106.

At the heart of the matter of labelling lies a question of balance. It is clearly important in practice that a relatively lax approach should be taken to the label applied by the employer. On the other hand, too lax an approach could leave too much leeway for an employer to operate a 'shotgun' defence—to make multiple allegations, under different headings, against the employee and hope that one or two are accepted by the tribunal. A major step towards preventing improper use of such tactics was taken by the House of Lords in *Smith v City of Glasgow District Council*.[163] The employer put forward a mixture of reasons for dismissal, relating to incompetence and misconduct, crystallized into three substantive allegations; the tribunal found that one of them had not been made out but proceeded to find the dismissal generally fair. This reasoning was disapproved by the House of Lords, since what appeared to be an integral part of the reason for dismissal had not been proved (or, at least, proved to have been the subject of reasonable belief by the employer). This case does *not* mean that an employer cannot plead several reasons and win; it does mean, however, that if one of several reasons put forward collapses the employer must go further and show that the collapsed reason was not, or did not form a significant part of, the principal reason for the dismissal (ie that the remaining reasons were more important and justified the dismissal by themselves); according to the House of Lords, that had not been shown on the facts of this case. Clearly, the more reasons the employer loads into the shotgun (and the more she eventually fails to prove), the more difficult this will be to establish.

Two further points on this first stage of the action should also be noticed. The first is that the House of Lords held in *W Devis & Sons Ltd v Atkins*[164] that the employer can only rely on the facts as known to him at the date of dismissal; contrary to the position in a common law action for wrongful dismissal,[165] therefore, the employer cannot rely upon subsequently discovered misconduct (as in a case where there is a dubious dismissal for inefficiency, following which the employer checks the books and finds clear evidence of embezzlement by the ex-employee—there must still be a finding of unfair dismissal in such a case, though the subsequently discovered misconduct may be relevant on the question of compensation, discussed later in this chapter).

There is one major qualification to this fundamental rule. Where an initial decision to dismiss is subject to an internal appeal, further evidence may come to light during the course of the appeal and it has been held that the tribunal can look at this (it being unrealistic to do otherwise) *provided* that the new evidence relates to the original

---

[163] [1987] ICR 796, [1987] IRLR 326, HL

[164] [1977] ICR 662, [1977] IRLR 314, HL. Date of dismissal here means the effective date of termination, so that if the facts change between the giving and the expiry of notice (eg a redundancy situation is affected by the receipt of a new order during that period), the tribunal should look at the facts as known at the expiry date: *Stacey v Babcock Power Ltd* [1986] ICR 221, [1986] IRLR 3. Thus, further evidence coming to light during the notice period can be taken into account: *Alboni v Ind Coope Retail Ltd* [1998] IRLR 131, CA (employer's reasonable conduct looking for an alternative to dismissal during the notice period taken into account); *White v South London Transport Ltd* [1998] ICR 293 (further medical evidence during notice period backed up the original ill-health dismissal).

[165] *Boston Deep Sea Fishing and Ice Co v Ansell* (1888) 39 Ch D 339, CA.

ground of dismissal.[166] However, this must not be taken too far and it has been held that (1) this exception does not allow an employer to use evidence from the appeal to set up an entirely new ground for dismissal[167] and (2) it does not render admissible evidence of matters occurring after the conclusion of the appeal.[168] The series of EAT decisions that established these principles were strongly affirmed by the House of Lords in *West Midland Co-operative Society Ltd v Tipton*,[169] where the approach was taken that internal appeal procedures are an integral part of the dismissal procedure and so should be taken into account; to do so does *not* offend the principle in *W Devis & Sons Ltd v Atkins*. Indeed, the *Tipton* case takes matters one stage further and holds that a *refusal* by an employer to allow an internal appeal may itself be evidence of unfairness.

The second point is that section 107 of the 1996 Act provides that in determining the reason for dismissal the tribunal may *not* take into account any industrial pressure (whether by strike or lesser action) which was exercised on the employer in order to procure the dismissal, or which was such that it was foreseeably likely to lead to dismissal.[170] This might apply where action was taken by a union or group of fellow employees against an employee who had refused to join in a strike, and if the employer sacks him solely because of the pressure, section 107 leads to the artificial position before the tribunal that the only reason for dismissal has to be ignored. The employer will then be found to have dismissed the employee unfairly, no reason having been shown, and, unless there was unreasonable conduct or undue obstinacy on the employee's part during the dispute, the employer may have to pay full compensation.[171] Where, however, the pressure was exercised on the employer because the applicant was not a member of the pressuring union, it is now provided that an action may be brought against the union (or other person exercising the pressure) either by the employer or by the applicant himself and the union or other person may be ordered to pay some or all of the compensation awarded to the applicant.[172] These provisions supplement section 107 without replacing it.

(ii) STAGE TWO: PRIMA FACIE FAIR GROUNDS

The second stage of the action is that the employer must prove that the reason for the dismissal fits into one of the enumerated categories. These are considered below, but it should be noted here that the final residual category, 'some other substantial reason

---

[166] *National Heart and Chest Hospitals v Nambiar* [1981] ICR 441, [1981] IRLR 196; *Sillifant v Powell Duffryn Timber Ltd* [1983] IRLR 91.

[167] *Monie v Coral Racing Ltd* [1981] ICR 109, [1980] IRLR 464, CA.

[168] *Greenall Whitley plc v Carr* [1985] ICR 451, [1985] IRLR 289.

[169] [1986] ICR 192, [1986] IRLR 112, HL.

[170] *Ford Motor Co Ltd v Hudson* [1978] ICR 482, [1978] IRLR 66.

[171] *Hazell Offsets Ltd v Luckett* [1977] IRLR 430; *British United Trawlers (Grimsby) Ltd v Carr* [1977] ICR 622; *Colwyn Borough Council v Dutton* [1980] IRLR 420.

[172] Trade Union and Labour Relations (Consolidation) Act 1992, s 160.

(SOSR) justifying dismissal', is deliberately wide and not to be restricted by being construed ejusdem generis with the previous categories.[173] Dismissal of a replacement for a woman temporarily absent on maternity leave (or for a person subject to compulsory medical suspension)[174] is expressly stated to be for a substantial reason (provided the replacement was told of the temporary nature of the job when engaged),[175] as is a dismissal because of a transfer of the employer's undertaking (see Chapter 8), but other than that all that can be said is that the question of what can be a substantial reason is an open one in respect of which the onus is clearly upon the employer to satisfy the tribunal on the facts of the particular case; the wider it is construed by the tribunals, the wider ostensibly is the area of management prerogative,[176] though of course any particular dismissal still has to be shown to be fair, even if for a substantial reason.[177] It has been held in the past to cover a range of miscellaneous reasons including the irretrievable breakdown of a working relationship,[178] an employer's mistaken belief that he had other fair grounds on which to dismiss,[179] dismissal at the behest of an important customer,[180] personality clashes,[181] awkward personality,[182] refusal to sign a restraint of trade clause,[183] refusal to work Sundays on religious grounds[184] and the dismissal of

---

[173] *RS Components Ltd v Irwin* [1973] ICR 535, [1973] IRLR 239.

[174] Under the Employment Rights Act 1996, s 64.

[175] Section 106. This could be of renewed importance now that statutory maternity leave is a year (meaning that the replacement may have the qualifying period of employment for an unfair dismissal action).

[176] Bowers and Clark 'Unfair Dismissal and Managerial Prerogative: A Study of "Other Substantial Reason"' (1981) 10 ILJ 34.

[177] *Gilham v Kent County Council (No 2)* [1985] ICR 233, [1985] IRLR 18, CA. A defence of some other substantial reason requires the tribunal 'to consider the reason established by the employer and decide whether it falls within the category of reason which could justify the dismissal of an employee—not that employee, but an employee—holding the position which that employee held': *Dobie v Burns International Security Services (UK) Ltd* [1984] IRLR 329 at 331, CA per Sir John Donaldson MR; the next stage is to consider whether the dismissal of that employee was fair on the facts, within s 98(4).

[178] *Ezsias v North Glamorgan NHS Trust* [2011] IRLR 550.

[179] *Klusova v London Borough of Hounslow* [2007] All ER (D) 105, CA (mistaken belief that employee was working contrary to immigration rules); *Taylor v Co-operative Retail Services Ltd* [1981] ICR 172, [1981] IRLR 1; affd [1982] ICR 600, [1982] IRLR 354, CA (mistaken belief that employer obliged to dismiss under a closed shop agreement); *Bouchaala v Trust House Forte Hotels Ltd* [1980] ICR 721, [1980] IRLR 382 (mistaken belief that continued employment would contravene a statutory enactment).

[180] *Scott Packing and Warehousing Ltd v Paterson* [1978] IRLR 166; *Grootcon (UK) Ltd v Keld* [1984] IRLR 302; *Dobie v Burns International Security Services (UK) Ltd* [1984] ICR 812, [1984] IRLR 329, CA. As with pressure from co-workers (s 107) this could be relevant in the dismissal of an AIDS sufferer; on such a dismissal generally, see Napier 'AIDS, Discrimination and Employment Law' (1989) 18 ILJ 84 and Watt 'HIV, Discrimination, Unfair Dismissal and Pressure to Dismiss' (1992) 21 ILJ 280.

[181] *Treganowan v Robert Knee & Co Ltd* [1975] ICR 405, [1975] IRLR 247.

[182] *Perkin v St George's Healthcare NHS Trust* [2006] ICR 606, [2005] IRLR 934, CA; the proper approach is to see first if dismissible misconduct had been caused, but if not the awkward personality can be SOSR in itself, if it has had sufficiently serious effects on the employer's business.

[183] *Willow Oak Developments Ltd v Silverwood* [2006] IRLR 607, CA.

[184] *Copsey v WWB Devon Clays Ltd* [2005] ICR 1789, [2005] IRLR 811, CA. This case arose before the Employment Equality (Religion or Belief) Regulations 2003 came into force, though it is by no means certain that they would produce a different decision on the facts.

the spouse of a person already dismissed where they were engaged as a pair;[185] as will be seen in Chapter 8, it has been particularly important in cases of dismissals following necessary business reorganizations, but apart from this area, the extreme diversity of the examples given shows that there is *no* connecting theme as to what constitutes 'SOSR' in that each case depends on its facts.

(iii) STAGE THREE: FAIRNESS

The third stage is that the tribunal must consider under section 98(4) whether the employer acted reasonably in actually 'activating' the reason in question and dismissing the employee; this demonstrates clearly that it is not enough to show that the employer had a reason which would normally justify dismissal—it has to be shown that, in all the circumstances of the case, it actually justified the particular dismissal in question. Unlike a wrongful dismissal action, this is not a technical exercise, looking at the parties' contractual entitlements and rights, but instead entails examination of the *substance* of the dismissal and consideration of the wider circumstances such as the employer's business needs (for example, in a case of ineffi- ciency or ineptitude by the employee) and any factors in mitigation of the employee's default, such as long service, lack of prior grounds for complaint and the possibilities of improvement. While the burden of proof on this overall question of fairness is technically neutral, the House of Lords in *Smith v City of Glasgow District Council*[186] approved the view of the Court of Session below that it remains logical to expect the employer to prove that the reason in question has been established—it cannot be reasonable to treat that reason as sufficient to justify dismissal unless the employer has shown either that it is true or that she believed it to be true. Although other fac- tors (such as procedural considerations) may have to be considered, this emphasis on isolating the real reason(s) for dismissal may mean that in many cases the issue of overall fairness will tend to merge with the question of establishing the reason (on which the employer does still bear the burden of proof).

In applying the test of fairness, the tribunal must consider the reasonableness of the employer's conduct, *not* the injustice (or lack of it) done to the employee. This funda- mental principle was reaffirmed by the House of Lords in *Polkey v A E Dayton Services Ltd*,[187] probably the most important decision on unfair dismissal since *W Devis & Sons Ltd v Atkins*[188] ten years earlier. An employee dismissed without warning for redun- dancy and sent home immediately had his claim for unfair dismissal turned down by the tribunal because they found that proper consultation would not have made any difference, ie they looked at the eventual lack of injustice to the employee. The House

---

[185] *Kelman v Oram* [1983] IRLR 432 (dismissal of publican's wife after (unfair) dismissal of publican).
[186] [1987] ICR 796, [1987] IRLR 326, HL; *Post Office (Counters) Ltd v Heavey* [1990] ICR 1, [1989] IRLR 513, EAT.
[187] [1988] ICR 142, [1987] IRLR 503, HL.   [188] See n 164.

of Lords clearly held this to be wrong and remitted the case to another tribunal, who were to apply the correct test of looking at the reasonableness of the employer's conduct in deciding not to consult or warn; the question of the amount of injustice done to the employee should only be relevant at the later stages of assessing compensation. This reasonableness test in section 98(4) has two overall effects. The first is that it is primarily responsible for giving the tribunals their wide discretion to reach just and equitable decisions in the light of 'good industrial practice' (the relevant wording in section 98(4) being 'in accordance with equity and the substantial merits of the case'); in the exercise of this discretion the tribunals have considerable freedom of action and in general the EAT will be reluctant to interfere with their decisions on such matters. The second effect is that it is the existence of section 98(4) which has led to the importance attached to the concept of 'procedural unfairness', ie the possibility that a dismissal may be unfair if an unfair procedure is adopted by the employer (for example, no warnings, lack of a hearing), even if there is prima facie a good substantive reason for the dismissal.

This concept, not to be found expressly stated in the legislation, was developed at an early stage in the history of the action[189] and remains a significant element in it. It has been subject to definable fluctuations in the amount of emphasis to be placed on it. Five particular phases can be seen. First, procedural fairness was a dominant factor in the early years of the new unfair dismissal law, during most of the 1970s while it was bedding in; the prospect of almost any lapse in procedure being held unfair concentrated employers' minds and meant that the new law had a rapid and significant normative effect on personnel practices. Secondly, however, procedural fairness suffered a definite wane in the later years of that decade and during the first half of the 1980s for two reasons—(a) a generally less enthusiastic attitude by the Court of Appeal, seen most clearly in *Hollister v NFU*[190] with a tendency to view procedural matters as merely one of the background factors; (b) the evolution and widespread application of the rule in *British Labour Pump Co Ltd v Byrne*,[191] to the effect that even if the employer failed to use the proper procedure on dismissal, it would still be fair if he could prove on a balance of probabilities that even if he had gone through the proper procedure the employee would still have been dismissed (and that dismissal would then have been fair)—ie a lapse by the employer could be forgiven if with hindsight it made no difference. Thirdly, however, we saw a swing back of the pendulum in 1987 with the decision of the House of Lords in *Polkey v A E Dayton Services Ltd*[192] in which *Byrne's* case was overruled[193] for two reasons: (a) it is inconsistent with *W Devis & Sons Ltd v Atkins*[194]

---

[189] *Earl v Slater and Wheeler (Airlyne) Ltd* [1973] 1 All ER 145, [1972] ICR 508; approved by the House of Lords in *W Devis & Sons Ltd v Atkins* [1977] ICR 662, [1977] IRLR 314, HL.

[190] [1979] ICR 542, [1979] IRLR 238, CA. See also *Retarded Children's Aid Society v Day* [1978] ICR 437, [1978] IRLR 128, CA and *Bailey v BP Oil (Kent Refinery) Ltd* [1980] ICR 642, [1980] IRLR 287, CA.

[191] [1979] ICR 347, [1979] IRLR 94.

[192] Note 179 above. In his speech, Lord Mackay LC, giving the judgment of the court, relied heavily on the strong criticisms of *Byrne's* case by Browne-Wilkinson P in *Sillifant v Powell Duffryn Timber Ltd* [1983] IRLR 91.

[193] Also overruled is *W & J Wass Ltd v Binns* [1982] ICR 486, [1982] IRLR 283 in which the Court of Appeal had approved *Byrne's* case, and 'all decisions supporting it'.

[194] See n 41.

since the tribunal should be considering what the employer actually did at the date of dismissal (and with his state of knowledge then), not what he might have done with hindsight; (b) more significantly, the *Byrne* approach was based on consideration of the (lack of) injustice to the employee, not the reasonableness of the employer's actions and, as we have seen above, that is a fundamentally flawed approach. In addition, the case of *Polkey* also shows a generally more favourable approach to procedural unfairness;[195] Lord Mackay LC said that a lapse of procedure will not automatically make a dismissal unfair and accepted that (taking the facts of the case) a redundancy dismissal without consultation or warning might still be fair, *but* that would only be so if the employer could show that the decision not to consult or warn was a positive decision taken reasonably in the circumstances at the time, not justified merely as an ex post facto afterthought once the deed had been done.[196] We saw, therefore, the reinstating of procedural fairness, not just as *a* factor, but as one of *the* factors that are likely to dominate an unfair dismissal action, even if this stopped short of a return in full to its heyday in the early years of the unfair dismissal jurisdiction.

The fourth phase coincides with the relatively short lifespan of the statutory 'standard procedures'. In addressing the perceived problem of too many cases being taken to tribunals, the government took the view that, of those so taken in the unfair dismissal jurisdiction, too many were based on procedural unfairness only (ie where the employer had good cause to dismiss but mishandled it). The Employment Act 2002 therefore attempted to limit procedural cases,[197] but in a relatively subtle way. It made the very minimal standard procedures mandatory, meaning that where an employer failed to comply with them the dismissal would automatically be unfair. However, it also provided that where employers had procedures in place that went beyond the statutory minimum (and many did, not least because the ACAS Code recommended that they do so) these could be ignored where the employer could demonstrate that observing them would have made no difference to the outcome. In short, the 2002 Act effected a statutory reintroduction of the rule in *British Labour Pump Co Ltd v Byrne* (cited earlier): if the employer could prove to the tribunal that she would have dismissed even if a wholly fair procedure had been adopted, the result was not just that little compensation was likely to be awarded (the *Polkey* solution)

---

[195] See also the post-*Polkey* decisions in *McLaren v National Coal Board* [1988] ICR 370, [1988] IRLR 215, CA; *Whitbread & Co plc v Mills* [1988] ICR 776, [1988] IRLR 501; *Spink v Express Foods Group Ltd* [1990] IRLR 320; *Stocker v Lancashire County Council* [1992] IRLR 75, CA; and Collins 'Procedural Fairness after Polkey' (1990) 19 ILJ 39.

[196] The formulation of this exception caused problems. Lord Bridge in *Polkey* said that it should only apply where the employer had actually (subjectively) considered the matter at the time of dismissal and concluded that consultation would be useless. However, in *Duffy v Yeomans & Partners Ltd* [1995] ICR 1, [1994] IRLR 642 the Court of Appeal applied Lord Mackay's view that it can apply where the employer could reasonably have so concluded. This could be seen as capable of reviving at least parts of *Byrne*'s case and the 'it made no difference' defence, if not quite as purely retrospectively as in *Byrne*. See Wynn (1995) 24 ILJ 272.

[197] The government's approach was that these cases, producing a basic finding of unfairness and little by way of compensation, had been a waste of tribunal time. Not all tribunal chairmen agreed.

but that the dismissal would be *fair*. This was a significant change, but as we have seen the Employment Act 2008 ushered in the fifth phase, which amounts to a return to the *Polkey* position, only with a more direct enforcement (through adjustments to compensation) of an arguably watered-down ACAS Code (see earlier in this chapter under heading 1(iii)).

(iv) THE CORRECT APPROACH: THE 'RANGE OF REASONABLE RESPONSES' TEST

One aspect of section 98(4) has caused considerable disagreement in the cases; that is whether the approach of the tribunal should be subjective or objective. To any lawyer versed in criminal law or tort, the concept of 'reasonableness' is clearly objective, and in earlier cases on section 98(4) the approach was indeed objective, viewing the tribunal as an 'industrial jury' with full powers to review the employer's conduct from their standpoint and decide, in the light of standard industrial practice (hence the lay membership), whether on the facts they would have dismissed.[198] Some later cases, however, adopted the view that the approach should be subjective (at least in part) particularly in cases where the employer's belief in a set of facts at the time of dismissal is important, so that the employer's own view that he acted reasonably should have some effect.[199] Thus, in *Alidair Ltd v Taylor*,[200] where an airline pilot's instant dismissal after damaging an aircraft in a faulty landing was held to be fair, Lord Denning MR said:

> it must be remembered that [section 98] contemplated a subjective test. The tribunal have to consider the employer's reason and the employer's state of mind. If the company honestly believed on reasonable grounds that this pilot was lacking in proper capability to fly aircraft on behalf of the company, that was a good and sufficient reason for the company to determine the employment then and there.... They clearly had no further confidence in him. He could not be trusted to fly their aircraft on their behalf. That being their honest belief on reasonable grounds, they were entitled to dismiss him. They acted reasonably in treating it as a sufficient reason for dismissing him.

Reinforcing this, his Lordship then said:

> If a man is dismissed for stealing, as long as the employer honestly believed it on reasonable grounds, that is enough to justify dismissal. It is not necessary for the employer to prove that he was in fact stealing. Whenever a man is dismissed for incapacity or incompetence it is sufficient that the employer honestly believes on reasonable grounds that the man is incapable or incompetent. It is not necessary for the employer to prove that he is in fact incapable or incompetent.

---

[198] *Bessenden Properties Ltd v Corness* [1977] ICR 821n, [1974] IRLR 338, CA.

[199] *Ferodo Ltd v Barnes* [1976] ICR 439, [1976] IRLR 302; *Post Office v Mughal* [1977] ICR 763, [1977] IRLR 178.

[200] [1978] ICR 445, [1978] IRLR 82, CA; the passages cited are at 450–1 and 84–5 respectively; *Vickers Ltd v Smith* [1977] IRLR 11. Cf *ILEA v Lloyd* [1981] IRLR 394, CA.

However, the approach cannot be totally subjective (otherwise the tribunal's discretion would be minimal when faced by an employer unshaken in his assertion that he thought he had acted reasonably), as can be seen from the above references to belief *on reasonable grounds*. Moreover, some later cases reaffirmed an objective element:

> the [employment] tribunal, while using its own collective wisdom, is to apply the standard of the reasonable employer; that is to say, the fairness or unfairness of the dismissal is to be judged ... by the objective standard of the way in which a reasonable employer in those circumstances, in that line of business, would have behaved.[201]

Thus, the correct position must lie in a combined approach, namely that the tribunal must have to gauge the employer's conduct by *some* objective yardstick, but at the same time take into account the honest beliefs of the employer where they are relevant. It may seem unsatisfactory not to be able to give a clear answer to what appears to be a fundamental question—subjective or objective?—but in practice it may in most cases be an empty question in the light of two aspects of section 98 which *are* clear and which may be seen as embodying elements of objectivity and subjectivity respectively:

(1) It is clear that, in all but the most blatant and obvious case of misconduct or incapability, the employer must have made a proper investigation of the grounds of his complaint against the employee and come to proper, tenable conclusions if he is to convince the tribunal that he had reasonable grounds for any belief which he is putting forward as a reason for the dismissal. Thus, in a suspected theft case the employer must show reasonable investigations, reasonably allowing him to point the finger of accusation at the employee. Moreover, the requirement of reasonable investigation means that an employer cannot rely upon his own ignorance at the time of dismissal of a particular point in the employee's favour if a reasonable investigation would have revealed it, ie the tribunal may look at the facts of which the employer knew *or ought to have known*.[202] To this extent at least, the test is objective as can be seen from the formula 'belief on reasonable grounds', and if the employer can show these reasonable grounds he may be in a strong position.[203] The test cannot be wholly objective, however, as can be seen from the second point.

(2) If the tribunal could adopt an entirely objective approach, there would be nothing to stop them looking at the facts of every case de novo and simply applying their own view of those facts, deciding whether they would have done what the employer did in the circumstances. However, the courts have consistently held that this is what a tribunal must *not* do.[204] Instead, they have to look at what the employer in fact did

---

[201] *Watling & Co Ltd v Richardson* [1978] ICR 1049 at 1056, [1978] IRLR 255 and 257, per Phillips J, explaining *Vickers Ltd v Smith* (n 200); see also *Mitchell v Old Hall Exchange Club Ltd* [1978] IRLR 160.

[202] *St Anne's Board Mill Co Ltd v Brien* [1973] ICR 444, [1973] IRLR 309, approved by the House of Lords in *W Devis & Sons Ltd v Atkins* [1977] ICR 662, [1977] IRLR 314, HL.

[203] *Post Office v Mughal* [1977] ICR 763, [1977] IRLR 178.

[204] *Trust House Forte Hotels Ltd v Murphy* [1977] IRLR 186; *Meridian Ltd v Gomersall* [1977] ICR 597, [1977] IRLR 425; *Mansfield Hosiery Mills Ltd v Bromley* [1977] IRLR 301; *Watling & Co Ltd v Richardson* [1978] ICR 1049, [1978] IRLR 255.

and decide whether that was a course of action which a reasonable employer could have taken in those circumstances (applying the standard of the reasonable employer as envisaged in the wording of section 98(4) itself). This becomes of particular significance in a case where in the circumstances the employer had several courses of action open to him, all of which were potentially what a reasonable employer might do, eg where the misconduct was such that he could dismiss, suspend without pay or fine and he chose to dismiss, or where in a redundancy case he could dispense with A or B or C and he chose A. In such a case, the tribunal should not consider which course they would have taken and decide whether the dismissal was fair or not in accordance with that (for example, holding dismissal unfair if they would on balance have decided upon suspension, or holding the dismissal of A unfair if on balance they would have dismissed C). Instead, they should decide whether the course of action in fact chosen was one which a reasonable employer *could* have decided upon, ie whether the employer acted *within the area of discretion covered by what would have been reasonable in the circumstances.* Thus, in *Trust House Forte Leisure Ltd v Aquilar*,[205] Phillips J said:

> when the management is confronted with a decision to dismiss an employee in particular circumstances there may well be cases where reasonable managements might take either of two decisions: to dismiss or not to dismiss. It does not necessarily mean if they decide to dismiss that they have acted unfairly because there are plenty of situations in which more than one view is possible.

In *Watling & Co Ltd v Richardson*[206] the same judge, using the redundancy example given above as a warning to tribunals not simply to apply their own views, said:

> It has to be recognised that there are circumstances where more than one course of action may be reasonable ... In such cases ... if an industrial tribunal equates its view of what itself would have done with what a reasonable employer would have done, it may mean that an employer will be found to have dismissed an employee unfairly although in the circumstances many perfectly good and fair employers would have done as that employer did.

Indeed the development of this 'range of reasonable responses' approach has been a major feature of unfair dismissal law and has had the effect of broadening the area of managerial discretion—it does not apply a test entirely subjective to the respondent employer, but it does enjoin the tribunals to look at the matter from an employer standpoint generally (albeit that of a reasonable employer). This approach was approved by the Court of Appeal in *British Leyland (UK) Ltd v Swift*,[207] where Lord Denning MR said:

> The correct test is: was it reasonable for the employer to dismiss him? If no reasonable employer would have dismissed him, then the dismissal was unfair. But if a reasonable

---

[205] [1976] IRLR 251 at 254.
[206] [1978] ICR 1049 at 1056, [1978] IRLR 255 at 258; *Grundy (Teddington) Ltd v Willis* [1976] ICR 323, [1976] IRLR 118.
[207] [1981] IRLR 91, CA. The principle was well expounded by the EAT in *Rolls-Royce Ltd v Walpole* [1980] IRLR 343 and *British Gas plc v McCarrick* [1991] IRLR 305, CA is a strong decision reaffirming it.

employer might reasonably have dismissed him, then the dismissal was fair. It must be remembered that in all these cases there is a band of reasonableness, within which one employer might reasonably take one view; another quite reasonably take a different view ... if it was quite reasonable to dismiss him, then the dismissal must be upheld as fair: even though some other employers may not have dismissed him.

The 'range of reasonable responses' approach has been universally accepted for years and was particularly well set out by Browne-Wilkinson P in *Iceland Frozen Foods Ltd v Jones*[208] as follows:

[T]he correct approach for the Industrial Tribunal to adopt in answering the question posed by [section 98(4) of the 1996 Act] is as follows: (1) the starting point should always be the words of [section 98] themselves; (2) in applying the section an Industrial Tribunal must consider the reasonableness of the employer's conduct, not simply whether they [the members of the Industrial Tribunal] consider the dismissal to be fair; (3) in judging the reasonableness of the employer's conduct an Industrial Tribunal must not substitute its decision as to what was the right course to adopt for that of the employer; (4) in many (though not all) cases there is a band of reasonable responses to the employee's conduct within which one employer might reasonably take one view, another quite reasonably take another; (5) the function of the Industrial Tribunal, as an industrial jury, is to determine whether in the particular circumstances of each case the decision to dismiss the employee fell within the band of reasonable responses which a reasonable employer might have adopted. If the dismissal falls within the band the dismissal is fair; if the dismissal falls outside the band it is unfair.

A bombshell was dropped in late 1999 by the EAT under Morison P (in one of his final judgments in that court) in *Haddon v Van den Bergh Foods Ltd*,[209] where they stated that in their opinion the range of reasonable responses test is *wrong* (being said to be an unhelpful 'mantra', along with the general point that a tribunal should not substitute its own view for that of the employer). This revisionism was based on the argument that the 'range' test made it too difficult for an employee to succeed in a misconduct case, and that it was too close to the administrative law concept of perversity. However, the reasoning in the case was suspect and its authority weak (going against so much prior case law). The point at issue was so fundamental that the Court of Appeal expedited the hearing of the appeal in another case raising the same point and in *Foley v Post Office*[210] unambiguously disapproved *Haddon*, emphasizing the correctness of the range of

---

[208] [1982] IRLR 439 at 442. The EAT was at pains to point out that this did not mean (as may have appeared from *Vickers Ltd v Smith* [1977] IRLR 11) that a dismissal could only be unfair if perverse (ie no reasonable employer could possibly have decided to dismiss); the test is not as stringent as that. In a case depending on the credibility of a witness, the question is whether the employer could reasonably believe him, not whether the tribunal does: *Linfood Cash and Carry Ltd v Thomson* [1989] ICR 518, [1989] IRLR 235, EAT.

[209] [1999] ICR 1150, [1999] IRLR 672. The tribunal had held that the test forced them to find fair the dismissal of an employee who had been invited to a drinks party to celebrate 15 years of good service, who was then summarily dismissed for not returning for the last one and a half hours of his shift because he had been drinking! Arguably, the EAT could just have reversed this on ordinary grounds of perversity.

[210] [2000] ICR 1283, [2000] IRLR 827, CA.

reasonable responses test. Subsequent case law has followed this line, confirming that the test applies not just to the actual dismissal decision but also to the adequacy of the procedures adopted[211] and, in a misconduct case, to the reasonableness of the investigation carried out by the employer prior to the dismissal.[212]

5 PARTICULAR CASES

Having considered the basis of an unfair dismissal action generally, we can now turn to four particular cases of practical importance. The first three (capability, conduct and redundancy/reorganization) correspond to the major headings contained in section 98(2); the fourth (automatically unfair dismissals) concerns special protection added by subsequent legislation. Some heads of unfair dismissal (maternity dismissal, trade union reasons and dismissal while taking part in industrial action) are treated separately in the context in which they arise elsewhere in the book (in Chapters 4, 9 and 10); they tend to be subject to more specialized rules, though some of the general principles discussed here lie behind them. The following discussion of these headings is, however, subject to the major caveat that the modern approach is to treat the accumulation of case law in these areas circumspectly and to deprecate over-reliance on previous authorities (however venerable) if that either over-complicates the issue before the tribunal, or leads the tribunal to stray from the clear wording of the statute. Put shortly, precedents in this area are, to adapt Noel Coward's saying on wit, to be taken like caviar, not like marmalade.

(i) CAPABILITY OR QUALIFICATIONS[213]

The first category of prima facie fair dismissals in section 98(2) is where the reason for dismissal is related to the capability or qualifications of the employee for performing his work. 'Capability' is defined in section 98(3) as capability assessed by reference to skill, aptitude, health or any other physical or mental quality, and 'qualifications' as any degree, diploma or other academic, technical or professional qualification relevant to the employee's position.[214] Lack of capability is of course the more important of these two categories, though the EAT have said that it should be viewed relatively narrowly as applying principally to cases where the employee is *incapable* of satisfactory work;[215]

---

[211] *Whitbread plc v Hall* [2001] ICR 699, [2001] IRLR 275.

[212] *Sainsbury's Supermarkets Ltd v Hitt* [2002] EWCA Civ 1588, [2003] IRLR 23. In the context of misconduct, *Thomas v Hillingdon London Borough Council* (2002) The Times, 4 October is a particularly interesting (and strong) application of the test to the topical issue of internet abuse and downloading porn.

[213] Practical advice on handling cases of absence (medical and otherwise) and poor work performance is given in the 2009 version of the ACAS Code of Practice on Disciplinary and Grievance Procedures and its accompanying Guide.

[214] *Blue Star Ship Management Ltd v Williams* [1978] ICR 770, [1979] IRLR 16.

[215] *Sutton and Gates (Luton) Ltd v Boxall* [1979] ICR 67, [1978] IRLR 486.

where the employee is capable of it, but refuses to exercise his ability, skills, etc, that should preferably be viewed as a case of misconduct, with the result that the employer should apply his warnings procedure more strictly and with more emphasis on the disciplinary aspect.[216]

In the realm of dismissal for incapability, it is important that the employer's business should not have to suffer, to the detriment of all concerned, through the ineptitude or inefficiency of a particular employee. However, it is also important that the employee whose work is causing dissatisfaction should be treated fairly. The question for the tribunal is whether the employer has satisfied them that she genuinely believed on reasonable grounds that the employee was incapable.[217] The requirement of reasonable grounds means that the employer should make a proper and full investigation into the facts of the case, and give careful consideration to the decision to dismiss;[218] amongst other things, this consideration may include as a factor whether the employee was given proper training for the job, adequate supervision and, where appropriate, proper support from the employer. Also, it is well established that this area is amenable to the application of a warnings procedure,[219] though the emphasis may be different from that in misconduct cases, for here the constructive side of a warning may be more important, not only pointing out the employer's ground for complaint but also instructing the employee how to improve and giving her reasonable time in which to do so. Of course, warnings are not essential in every case, and may perhaps be irrelevant where it is clear that the employee is completely incapable of improvement or where she already clearly knows what is expected of her.[220] That apart, however, the importance of a fair procedure in this area should not be underestimated, and lack of it (particularly if it leads to inadequate investigation by the employer) may make dismissal of an incompetent employee unfair (though it may still be open to the employer to argue that there should be little or no compensation where there was wilful default on the part of the employee, such as failure or refusal to improve).[221] One of the ways in which the ACAS Code of Practice on Disciplinary and Grievance Procedures was expanded in 2000 was by the inclusion of guidance on sub-standard work, which adopted and simplified very much the results of this case law. Much of this guidance is now found in the non-statutory Guide to the 2009 version of the Code.

One particular aspect of incapability which has given rise to much litigation is where the employee is incapable of performing his work due to prolonged and/or frequent illness. Three preliminary points may be made on this subject. The first is that an exceptionally severe and incapacitating illness could have the effect of frustrating the contract

---

[216] *Littlewoods Organisation Ltd v Egenti* [1976] ICR 516, [1976] IRLR 334.
[217] *Alidair Ltd v Taylor* [1978] ICR 445, [1978] IRLR 82, CA.
[218] *Cook v Thomas Linnell & Sons Ltd* [1977] ICR 770, [1977] IRLR 132.
[219] *Winterhalter Gastronom Ltd v Webb* [1973] ICR 245, [1973] IRLR 120, NIRC.
[220] *James v Waltham Holy Cross UDC* [1973] ICR 398, [1973] IRLR 202.
[221] *Sutton and Gates (Luton) Ltd v Boxall* [1979] ICR 67, [1978] IRLR 486, explaining *Kraft Foods Ltd v Fox* [1978] ICR 311, [1977] IRLR 431.

of employment, in which case there would be no dismissal and so no action could be brought; frustration is considered elsewhere,[222] and in general it should not be found readily by a tribunal because of its drastic effect on the employee's rights. The tests for a frustrating illness are therefore stringent, and are not the tests to be applied to the separate question whether a dismissal for illness was fair.[223] The second point is that many employees are covered by contractual sick pay schemes which will provide for payment during sickness up to a maximum period. A sick employee in most cases will expect to remain 'employed' during an illness at least until the sick pay period elapses. There is, however, no necessary link-up in law between the sick pay period and the question of dismissal for illness for (1) a contractual sick pay term only covers payment while still employed and, although it would not normally be reasonable to dismiss before the end of the sick pay period, there may be cases where the employer's business needs are so urgent that dismissal (and replacement) *during* that period could be reasonable; (2) on the other hand, it is not necessarily fair to apply a policy of dismissing automatically once the sick pay period expires.[224] Thus, the two matters are conceptually separate. The third point is that if the medical cause of the absence is likely to be long term and have a significant effect on the employee's life, the employer may now have to consider whether it could constitute a 'disability' within the Equality Act 2010, in which case the following unfair dismissal law considerations may have to be supplemented by others under that Act, in particular any reasonable adjustments that might have to be made to help the employee to return.[225]

Subject to these three points, it is well established by leading cases such as *East Lindsey District Council v Daubney*[226] that the approach of the tribunal in assessing the reasonableness of the employer's decision to dismiss should be to consider whether it was reasonable to expect the employer to wait any longer before dismissing, in the light of such factors as the nature of the illness, the actual and potential length of the absence, the circumstances of the individual employee, the urgency of the need to fill the employee's job and the size and nature of the employer's undertaking. The procedural steps to be taken by the employer will vary widely according to

---

[222] See Ch 6, heading 1(ii), p 412. The applicability of the doctrine of frustration in this context was reaffirmed by the Court of Appeal in *Notcutt v Universal Equipment Co (London) Ltd* [1986] ICR 414, [1986] IRLR 218.

[223] *Tan v Berry Bros and Rudd Ltd* [1974] ICR 586, [1974] IRLR 244, NIRC.

[224] *Hardwick v Leeds Area Health Authority* [1975] IRLR 319. For a later confirmation of this point, on rather unusual facts, see *Smiths Industries Aerospace and Defence Systems Ltd v Brookes* [1986] IRLR 434. In addition, it may be necessary also to consider the rules on statutory sick pay, discussed at Ch 3, heading 5(ii), p 193, which may have an indirect effect particularly if there was evidence that one of the reasons behind the dismissal was the avoidance of payment of sick pay. It is increasingly possible that to dismiss before exhausting sick pay, even if fair on the facts, might be viewed as breach of contract in a common law action, on analogy with the 'PHI cases', see Ch 3, heading 3(vii), p 157.

[225] For disability discrimination law, see Ch 5, heading 7, p 386.

[226] [1977] ICR 566, [1977] IRLR 181. This longstanding approach was reaffirmed (and said to be in line with the leading case on procedure generally, *Polkey v A E Dayton Services Ltd* [1988] ICR 142, [1987] IRLR 503, HL) in *A Links & Co Ltd v Rose* [1991] IRLR 353, Ct of Sess.

the facts of the case but, although a 'warning' as such is hardly appropriate, in most cases the employer will be expected to consult the employee and discuss the nature of his illness and his future prospects, bearing in mind the employer's need to have the work done.[227] The employer may also be expected to make such investigations as are necessary to establish the true facts of the case, which may mean taking further medical advice on the nature of the illness. It has been stressed by the EAT that the eventual decision whether to dismiss remains a managerial one, not a medical one,[228] but in the nature of things the employer may reasonably have to rely heavily upon a medical prognosis (even if it later turns out to have been wrong). Where the employee is likely to be away for a considerable period and his position needs to be filled, the employer may still be expected to consider the possibility of alternative (perhaps lighter) work for the employee instead of dismissal; this may particularly be the case where the employer is a large concern, though even then it probably stops short of an obligation to create an entirely new job for that employee.[229] Some occupational pension schemes include provision for ill-health retirement; where this is true it can be unfair for an employer to dismiss a long-term sick employee without a reasonable investigation into whether such retirement is available to the employee.[230] There is, however, a very different possibility at the other end of the spectrum—if it becomes clear that the work is causing illness in that particular employee and there is *no* other work for him, might the employer argue that there is a common law obligation *to* dismiss, on health and safety grounds, which should make the dismissal fair? Older case law was less paternalistic,[231] but in *Coxall v Goodyear GB Ltd*[232] (concerning occupational asthma) the only ground on which the employer was liable in tort for negligence

---

[227] *Spencer v Paragon Wallpapers Ltd* [1977] ICR 301, [1976] IRLR 373. There may, however, be special factors, perhaps in the nature of the job itself, rendering consultation unnecessary: *Leonard v Fergus and Haynes Civil Engineering Ltd* [1979] IRLR 235; *Taylorplan Catering (Scotland) Ltd v McInally* [1980] IRLR 53. Note also that persistent absenteeism through a series of unrelated medical complaints (often impossible to verify medically) may in fact be more amenable to treatment as misconduct (with warnings and a final decision) than under the illness principles in *Spencer and Lindsey: International Sports Co Ltd v Thomson* [1980] IRLR 340; *Lynock v Cereal Packaging Ltd* [1988] ICR 670, [1988] IRLR 510; this may be particularly so under the current system of self-certification for the first week of sickness.

[228] *East Lindsey District Council v Daubney* [1977] ICR 566, [1977] IRLR 181. The managerial role would be particularly important in the case of an employee either with, or suspected of being with, AIDS, and faced by reaction from fellow employees and/or customers; some practical (and educative) advice has been given in the joint DE/HSE booklet AIDS and Employment.

[229] *Merseyside and North Wales Electricity Board v Taylor* [1975] ICR 185, [1975] IRLR 60.

[230] *First West Yorkshire v Haigh* [2008] IRLR 182.

[231] In *Withers v Perry Chain Co Ltd* [1961] 3 All ER 676, [1961] 1 WLR 1314, CA, Devlin LJ put it pithily that 'The relationship between employer and employee is not that of a schoolmaster and pupil'. See *Munkman on Employer's Liability* (13th edn, 2001) at p 144 for the previous case law.

[232] [2002] EWCA Civ 1010, [2002] IRLR 742, CA. Simon Brown LJ did allude to the paradox that the law here is becoming more paternalistic (in the light of health and safety concerns) at the same time that a human rights approach elsewhere is stressing the autonomy of the individual, including the individual employee.

was in not removing the employee from that work, the judge speculating that in an appropriate case the employer (faced with the desire of the employee to carry on and run the risks) might be 'under a duty in law to dismiss him for his own good so as to protect him against physical danger'.

It will be clear from the above that the obtaining of reliable medical evidence on the sick employee is of great importance. Medical confidentiality could be a problem since the employer may not simply demand a report from the employee's own doctor. He may of course invite the employee to allow such a report to be compiled and released to him; if the employee agrees, that covers the matter of confidentiality. However, there is the further complication that the Access to Medical Reports Act 1988 gives the employee a right to see such a report by his own doctor (provided he follows the prescribed procedure) in advance of its disclosure to the employer and, further, a right to object to part or all of it and, ultimately, to refuse to allow it to be disclosed (though of course in the latter, extreme, case there would be nothing to stop the employer drawing his own adverse inferences from the refusal and so in practice this may not be a realistic option). However, the Act is limited to reports compiled by the employee's *own* doctor, and so does not apply to a report compiled by an in-house company doctor, or an independent doctor nominated by the employer.[233] This factor now gives even more importance to the incorporation of a term into contracts of employment (as is now commonly done) that specifically gives the employer the right to require the employee to undertake a medical examination by a doctor nominated by the employer, with the results divulged to the employer. If there is no such term, the employer may only *request* such an examination.

The above discussion of illness has primarily envisaged physical illness as the incapacitating factor. Similar principles apply to mental illness, though in such a case it may be that the problem is more delicate and requires an even more understanding approach by the employer (particularly if he hired the employee knowing of his actual or potential condition). If, however, the employee actively concealed a mental condition when applying for the job, that may be a good reason for dismissal when the employer finds out (depending perhaps on the nature of the job) for that would not be primarily a dismissal for illness but rather for misconduct, as in other cases where an employee is taken on in some way under false pretences.[234]

---

[233] This limitation is achieved indirectly by the drafting of the definition of 'medical report' in s 2(1), as 'a report ... prepared by a medical practitioner who is or has been responsible for the clinical care of the individual'. Section 3 states that the employer must have the consent of the employee before requesting the report in the first place; s 7 contains exceptions where the doctor may withhold parts of the report if disclosure could cause the employee serious physical or medical harm. On the Act generally, see Pitt (1988) 17 ILJ 239.

[234] *O'Brien v Prudential Assurance Co Ltd* [1979] IRLR 140. Likewise, fraudulent use of a sick note might be good grounds for dismissal for misconduct: *Hutchinson v Enfield Rolling Mills Ltd* [1981] IRLR 318, EAT.

(ii) CONDUCT[235]

As seen above,[236] dismissal for misconduct was an important concept at common law, primarily in the context of wrongful dismissal where the main factor was whether the misconduct was so bad that it repudiated the whole contract and so justified summary dismissal. In the modern context of unfair dismissal, dismissal for misconduct is obviously important (as one of the principal heads of prima facie fair dismissals) but it operates on a much broader base than at common law, so that the misconduct may or may not be dealt with by summary dismissal. The reason for this is that the tribunals can now look into the substantive fairness of any dismissal for misconduct, whereas at common law if an employer wished to be rid of an employee guilty of some lesser form of misconduct than that which would justify summary dismissal, he could just dismiss him with notice and, provided that notice was of the proper length, there could be no legal redress for the employee. Thus, the legal rules relating to the modern and the common law approaches to misconduct are different, so that many dismissals which at common law were unexceptionable can now be challenged as unfair; likewise, a dismissal could be wrongful at common law (because the conduct was not grave enough to warrant the summary dismissal which was inflicted upon the employee) but a tribunal might still hold that in the circumstances it was fair.[237] On the other hand, there will remain a practical relationship between the modern and the common law actions in that certain major heads of misconduct accepted as justifying summary dismissal at common law will remain major categories of fair dismissals, for example failure to obey proper and lawful orders,[238] breach of confidence by the employee by unfairly competing with the employer or prejudicing confidentiality necessary to the business,[239] and computer misuse by the employee.[240] One further influence of the common law could arise in the case of an employee who consistently plays practical jokes or is inclined to show physical aggression, for in such a case there is a common law duty upon the employer to take reasonable care for the safety of that employee's *fellow* employees,[241] which may ultimately require a dismissal.

---

[235] Practical advice on handling disciplinary matters is given in the non-statutory ACAS Code of Practice on Discipline and Grievances at Work (2009) with accompanying guidance notes.

[236] Chapter 6, heading 3, p 431.

[237] *Treganowen v Robert Knee & Co Ltd* [1975] ICR 405, [1975] IRLR 247.

[238] As at common law, the employee may refuse to obey an unlawful order: *Morrish v Henlys (Folkestone) Ltd* [1973] ICR 482, [1973] IRLR 61, NIRC.

[239] *Mansard Precision Engineering Co Ltd v Taylor* [1978] ICR 44; *Golden Cross Hire Co Ltd v Lovell* [1979] IRLR 267; *Nova Plastic Ltd v Frogatt* [1982] IRLR 146.

[240] *Denco Ltd v Joinson* [1991] ICR 172, [1991] IRLR 63; *Thomas v Hillingdon London Borough Council* (2002) The Times, 4 October.

[241] *Hudson v Ridge Manufacturing Co Ltd* [1957] 2 QB 348, [1957] 2 All ER 229. Various statutory duties upon the employer to ensure compliance with safety regulations and the use of safety devices may be an important factor in the dismissal of an employee who consistently acts to the peril of himself and other employees.

These overlaps apart, misconduct in the modern statutory context fits into the overall pattern of unfair dismissal law in being essentially a matter of assessing the reasonableness of the employer's reaction to it in all the varied circumstances of the case, including the seriousness of the offence[242] and any extraneous matters such as length of service and previous good conduct which may act in mitigation of the offence; it is a particularly wide category of dismissal, ranging from gross misconduct (still justifying summary dismissal) such as theft, violence, wilful refusal to obey an order and gross negligence, down to lesser matters such as swearing and poor timekeeping which may only become serious if committed regularly. Faced with this wide diversity, there is sometimes an unfortunate tendency to attempt to over-classify, as if for example the many decided cases established a 'law on fighting at work'. While collecting together all the cases on one kind of misconduct may have some value, it must be stressed that that value is restricted to attempting to point out certain factors which *may* be important in certain of the more typical cases. Further than that, these matters remain clearly within the factual jurisdiction of the tribunals. Swearing is a good example of this, for there are ample cases on it but it remains purely a question of fact whether a particular incident merited dismissal, usually depending on factors such as the nature and place of the employment, the effect upon the recipient, whether it was gratuitous or provoked and any previous incidents; thus, for example, words used to a fellow employee in the course of work on a building site could give rise to different considerations if used to a customer by an assistant at a perfume counter.

Except in cases of dismissal for a single act of gross misconduct, this area of dismissal is a prime one for the application of a warnings system (and in most cases for the granting of a hearing to allow employees to put forward either their view of the facts or mitigating circumstances having a bearing upon the question whether to dismiss).[243] A series of warnings may be particularly important in cases of persistent minor misconduct where it is primarily the fact of repetition which may eventually justify dismissal. Moreover, the emphasis in the warnings in this context will normally be disciplinary and so the employer should ensure that they are given in accordance with any procedure laid down in the employee's contract or in the works rules; to this end, it is usually advisable for such terms or rules to lay down any types of misconduct which are particularly relevant to the job in question and the likely consequences of transgressions.[244] Some employers may feel that by laying down such rules they are

---

[242] This may also be important in determining how intrusively the employer is permitted to investigate the employee without breaching human rights or data protection laws. In *McGowan v Scottish Water* [2005] IRLR 167 a serious offence of timesheet falsification justified 'proportionate' covert surveillance by a private investigator.

[243] The importance of following proper procedures in misconduct cases was given a welcome reaffirmation by the Court of Appeal in *McLaren v National Coal Board* [1988] ICR 370, [1988] IRLR 215 (dismissal without any form of hearing unfair, even though it was impossible to operate the normal procedures in the middle of the miners' strike); cf, however, the different decision on the facts in *Dillett v National Coal Board* [1988] ICR 218, CA (a pre-*Polkey* case).

[244] An important and topical example of this is the desirability of clear policies on email and internet abuse by employees working with computers (given the potential legal difficulties for the employer, eg through

fettering their discretion, but this should not be the case. In general disciplinary rules, if properly phrased, need not be viewed as exhaustive (and so employees cannot claim that they can only be disciplined for matters that fall neatly within a particular category in the rules);[245] moreover, the employer stands to gain, for if she wishes to treat as particularly heinous (in the circumstances) something which normally would not be viewed as serious (such as smoking at work or drinking at lunchtime), she is well advised to say so in the rules—if not she may have difficulty showing that a dismissal is fair when the subject matter of it would not normally be viewed as a dismissable offence in other contexts.[246] Being clear about this has the added advantage of making it easier to identify those dismissals that fall outside the category of conduct altogether: a dismissal resulting from the irretrievable breakdown of a working relationship was found not to be a conduct dismissal, but a dismissal 'for some other substantial reason', which meant that it was not unfair for the employer not to have followed its disciplinary procedure for misconduct, including progressive warnings.[247]

The major conceptual problem here is in trying to achieve the right balance between certainty and flexibility. On the one hand, it is said to be an important principle that people committing like offences should be treated alike (equality is equity), which argues in favour of a consistent application of disciplinary rules, regardless of who the culprit is.[248] On the other hand it is said that the key to unfair dismissal is flexibility by the employer, judging each case on its merits and not simply adopting a 'tariff' approach to misconduct based upon rigid disciplinary rules.[249] In as much as the latter point means the matters of *mitigation* should be considered in each individual case (for example, length of service, previous work record) it is consistent with a more certain approach to the offence itself (as in the former point) and so one possible approach (particularly in a larger organization) is that the employer should *start* by considering from the personnel records whether there have been any similar previous incidents and how they were dealt with, before going on to consider the specific facts and any mitigation in the instant case.[250] One thing that can be stated with some confidence, however, is that tribunals should be wary of simple 'disparity' arguments by applicants

the downloading and misuse of porn, especially if used for harassment of others). Such policies are strongly advised by the Data Protection Code of Practice, Pt III 'Monitoring of Employees'. If the correct procedures are carried out, dismissal for downloading porn at work is likely to be fair: *Thomas v Hillingdon London Borough Council* (2002) The Times, 4 October.

[245] *Distillers Co (Bottling Services) Ltd v Gardner* [1982] IRLR 47; *Macari v Celtic Football & Athletic Co Ltd* [1999] IRLR 787, Ct of Sess. An ambiguous approach by an employer (eg when setting out disciplinary rules) may, however, render a dismissal for a first breach of a particular rule unfair: *Trusthouse Forte (Catering) Ltd v Adonis* [1984] IRLR 382, EAT.

[246] *Dairy Produce Packers Ltd v Beverstock* [1981] IRLR 265. One example might be particularly high standards of hygiene in food-processing establishments.

[247] *Ezsias v North Glamorgan NHS Trust* [2011] IRLR 550.

[248] *Post Office v Fennell* [1981] IRLR 221, CA.

[249] *Taylor v Parsons Peebles NEI Bruce Peebles Ltd* [1981] IRLR 119; *Hadjioannou v Coral Casinos Ltd* [1981] IRLR 352, EAT.

[250] *Procter v British Gypsum Ltd* [1992] IRLR 7; *Harrow London Borough v Cunningham* [1996] IRLR 256.

because, as any lawyer knows, few cases are so similar as to be directly comparable, particularly when the element of mitigation is taken into account.[251]

Suspension pending fuller investigation by the employer may be appropriate in serious cases (provided the employer has contractual authority to do so); the Code of Practice[252] states that normally this should be with pay and only for a brief period and so in reality the employer may not be expected to do so for any great length of time and may reasonably have to take the decision to dismiss once he has had time to make reasonable investigations, even if other eventualities such as a criminal trial of the employee are still pending;[253] indeed, any greater delay before the employer takes decisive action could conceivably make the eventual dismissal unfair.[254] As well as the application of warnings and hearings, dismissal for misconduct is also a prime area for the application of the principle that the function of the tribunal is to decide upon the reasonableness of the action taken by the employer, not simply to substitute their views for his; in a case as heavily dependent upon its facts as a misconduct case, there may well be a considerable area of discretion in which several solutions might have been reasonable and as long as dismissal was within that area the employer is not to be penalized for choosing it in preference to any lesser measure.[255]

The type of misconduct case which has caused most concern is the case where the employee has committed a criminal offence, particularly (though not necessarily) theft. Proved theft from the employer will usually be a clear ground for dismissal (regardless of the amount taken)[256] as will wilful concealment of previous convictions when applying for a job,[257] unless the conviction is 'spent' within the meaning of the Rehabilitation of Offenders Act 1974, in which case the employee is not obliged to disclose it and a dismissal because of it will be unfair.[258] The problems arise in cases where there is only a *suspicion* that the employee has committed an offence, for the employer may feel that he ought to dismiss the employee immediately even though it may be some time before a criminal case can be brought against the employee (which may of course result in his eventual acquittal). Where the criminal offence arose outside the employment (for example, theft from another person or the commission of a sexual or drug offence outside working hours), the employer should not normally dismiss

---

[251] *Paul v East Surrey District Health Authority* [1995] IRLR 305, CA.

[252] Paragraph 8. Where the employee is suspended (and so not able to talk to fellow employees) it is particularly important that the employer's investigations should be even-handed and fair: *A v B* [2003] IRLR 405.

[253] *Conway v Matthew Wright & Nephew Ltd* [1977] IRLR 89, EAT.

[254] Cf *Refund Rentals Ltd v McDermott* [1977] IRLR 59.

[255] *Trust House Forte Leisure Ltd v Aquilar* [1976] IRLR 251; *Trust House Forte Hotels Ltd v Murphy* [1977] IRLR 186. See heading 4(iv), p 505.

[256] *Murphy's* case, n 255.

[257] *Torr v British Railways Board* [1977] ICR 785, [1977] IRLR 184, EAT.

[258] *Property Guards Ltd v Taylor* [1982] IRLR 175. Certain categories of persons, primarily professional or connected with law enforcement, are excluded: Rehabilitation of Offenders Act 1974 (Exceptions) Order 1975, SI 1975/1023; *Harvey* R [40]. These categories were significantly extended in 2001 in relation to employments involving contact with children and vulnerable adults: see Ch 2, heading 4(iii), p 93.

before the employee has been found guilty[259] and even then should only do so if on the facts (looking at the nature of the offence, the type of job and the potential effects on customers and fellow employees) the commission of that offence renders the employee unsuitable for the job in question.[260] The Code of Practice, paragraph 30 puts it thus:

> 30. If an employee is charged with, or convicted of a criminal offence this is not normally in itself reason for disciplinary action. Consideration needs to be given to what effect the charge or conviction has on the employee's suitability to do the job and their relationship with their employer, work colleagues and customers.

There are some enterprises or institutions where the accusation alone, especially if it is something like child sexual abuse, makes it necessary for the employer to dismiss if only to disassociate itself with the scandal. In such cases of 'reputational risk' the reason for the dismissal is not conduct but SOSR, and the employer must identify with particularity why the making of the allegation made it impossible to continue employing the claimant.[261] If this is demonstrated, the employer must test the allegation's reliability by questioning the body making the allegations, but need not carry out its own investigation.

Two possible complicating factors may be mentioned. The first is that the employee's basic argument is that what he or she does outside work is his or her own business and this may now give rise to human rights issues (particularly Article 8 on respect for private life and Article 10 on freedom of expression). However, the signs to date are that this extra element does *not* add much to the existing law on unfair dismissal and is unlikely to render unfair a dismissal that is fair under the general law. In *X v Y*[262] a dismissal for conviction of a sexual offence in a public toilet at a time outside work was upheld by the Court of Appeal in spite of human rights arguments and in *Pay v Lancashire Probation Service*[263] the EAT reached a similar conclusion where a long-serving and well-regarded probation officer was dismissed when his employers discovered his out-of-hours sideline of performing at various hedonist and fetish clubs and acting as a director of a company selling bondage, domination and sado-masochistic products through the internet. In each case it was effectively

---

[259] *Securicor Guarding Ltd v R* [1994] IRLR 633. In the contrary case, where a criminal conviction comes before an internal disciplinary hearing, it will normally be reasonable for the employer to rely on the court's finding of guilt (including where the employee has pleaded), without going behind that finding, even where the employee still maintains his innocence: *P v Nottinghamshire County Council* [1992] ICR 706, [1992] IRLR 362, CA; *Secretary of State for Scotland v Campbell* [1992] IRLR 263, EAT.

[260] See *Nottinghamshire County Council v Bowly* [1978] IRLR 252; *Norfolk County Council v Bernard* [1979] IRLR 220; *Moore v C & A Modes* [1981] IRLR 71; *Mathewson v R B Wilson Dental Laboratory Ltd* [1988] IRLR 512. 'Conduct means actions of such a nature, whether done in the course of employment or outwith it, that reflects in some way on the employer-employee relationship': *Thomson v Alloa Motor Co* [1983] IRLR 403 at 404, per Lord McDonald.

[261] *Leach v Office of Communications (OFCOM)* [2012] EWCA Civ 959, [2012] IRLR 839.

[262] [2004] IRLR 625, CA. One point here was that there is no 'private life' interest in a public offence.

[263] [2004] ICR 187, [2004] IRLR 129. Once again the argument was adopted that he could have little 'privacy' interest when he had put himself on the internet!

the longstanding unfair dismissal rules that determined the case, not the human rights arguments. The second complicating factor, yet to be elaborated upon, is the suggestion that, in a case of misconduct away from work, it may be reasonable to expect a *large* employer at least to consider whether there was any other employment to which the employee could be transferred, rather than being dismissed.[264] The idea of alternative work is, of course, well known in capability and redundancy cases, but could be difficult to apply here.

Where the crime arises within the employment (the obvious example being theft of the employer's property) the employer's need to dismiss may appear to be more urgent, but at the same time the employee under suspicion must not be treated arbitrarily. The position as it has evolved (particularly since the decision of the EAT in *British Home Stores Ltd v Burchell*,[265] approved by the Court of Appeal in *W Weddel & Co Ltd v Tepper*[266] and *Whitbread plc v Hall*[267] and fully in line with the current, post-*Polkey* approach) is that the employer may dismiss if he has a genuine belief in the employee's guilt, which is based upon reasonable grounds; he does not have to be able to *prove* the employee's guilt and so provided the employer has his genuine belief it is irrelevant if the employee is later acquitted of the offence (or indeed if the police decline to bring charges).[268] Thus, it is not the function of the tribunal to try the criminal action against the employee and the employer certainly does not have to prove guilt beyond reasonable doubt—the inquiry is a much more general one than that,[269] looking into the bona fides and reasonableness of the employer's claimed belief. The reasonableness of his belief will depend primarily upon whether the employer made a reasonable investigation to establish the facts and drew tenable conclusions from the results.

What constitutes a reasonable investigation will of course vary with the circumstances, so that in the case of red-handed theft with little attempt at explanation, the

---

[264] *P v Nottinghamshire County Council*, n 259. If the employer does look for other work before dismissing, however, that is not to be used by the employee as an argument that the misconduct could not have been too serious: *Hamilton v Argyll and Clyde Health Board* [1993] IRLR 99, EAT.

[265] [1980] ICR 303n, [1978] IRLR 379; see also *Ferodo Ltd v Barnes* [1976] ICR 439, [1976] IRLR 302; *Alidair Ltd v Taylor* [1978] ICR 445 at 451, [1978] IRLR 82 at 85, CA, per Lord Denning MR. The requirement is of actual belief, not just suspicion. However, a well-founded belief in the employee's intent to commit the offence may suffice, if he has been found out before committing it: *British Railways Board v Jackson* [1994] IRLR 235, CA. The principles in *British Home Stores Ltd v Burchell* apply to all forms of misconduct, not just to dishonesty cases: *Distillers Co (Bottling Services) Ltd v Gardner* [1982] IRLR 47; they were reaffirmed in *ILEA v Gravett* [1988] IRLR 497 and *Whitbread & Co plc v Mills* [1988] ICR 776, [1988] IRLR 501.

[266] [1980] ICR 286, [1980] IRLR 96, CA.   [267] [2001] ICR 699, [2001] IRLR 275.

[268] *Da Costa v Optolis* [1976] IRLR 178; *Harris (Ipswich) Ltd v Harrison* [1978] ICR 1256, [1978] IRLR 382. A difficult case might arise if an employee, having been (fairly) dismissed for theft, was later proved to have been innocent and brought defamation proceedings against the employer. Presumably the defence of justification would not be available and so the employer would have to rely on the protean defence of qualified privilege. For an example of findings of fair dismissal after acquittals by a criminal court, see *Dhaliwal v British Airways Board* [1985] ICR 513, EAT.

[269] The strict rules of criminal evidence do not apply so that, for example, evidence of previous dishonesty is admissible, and indeed may be highly relevant: *Docherty v Reddy* [1977] ICR 365; *Coral Squash Clubs Ltd v Matthews* [1979] ICR 607, [1979] IRLR 390.

requirement may not be onerous. In less obvious cases, the employer should make a careful inquiry, allowing the employee to offer a defence, but there is a major qualification on this for the EAT have suggested that where the employee's actions are being actively investigated by the police with a view to criminal proceedings it may be improper for the employer to hold a full investigation and to expect the employee to explain the conduct.[270] However, on at least one occasion,[271] the EAT have suggested that in such a case the employer might at least give the employee an opportunity to make representations particularly on the question whether the employer ought to go as far as to dismiss (which may involve matters in mitigation, such as long and satisfactory service); in many cases, the employer might in fact gain from doing so, and be seen to be acting in the spirit of a fair procedure; and also any failure by the employee to put forward a defence might be held against him. When carrying out an investigation, the involvement of the police may be important for if they give to the employer definite information about their findings that may go far towards confirming the employer's suspicions;[272] on the other hand, the mere fact of police investigation may not be sufficient in itself to constitute reasonable grounds for a belief in guilt and likewise an employer should not simply 'delegate' the matter to the police and the courts (for example, deciding not to investigate but merely to await the outcome of the court case, dismissing automatically if the employee is found guilty).[273]

The employer must therefore have a genuine belief in the employee's guilt based upon such investigations as were reasonable in the circumstances; primarily the belief must relate to the guilt of the particular individual though it has been held by the Court of Appeal that if the employer can only narrow it down to one of two employees, but holds a genuine belief that it must be one or the other of them, it may be reasonable to dismiss *both*, which seems distinctly hard on the innocent one.[274] This just emphasizes yet again how the emphasis of the unfair dismissal protection is not in fact on the unfairness to any given employee from the experience of dismissal, but on the reasonableness of the employer in deciding to dismiss. Once the employer has the

---

[270] *Carr v Alexander Russell Ltd* [1979] ICR 469n, [1976] IRLR 220; *Conway v Matthew Wright & Nephew Ltd* [1977] IRLR 89; *Tesco (Holdings) Ltd v Hill* [1977] IRLR 63; *Parker v Clifford Dunn Ltd* [1979] ICR 463, [1979] IRLR 56. If the employee chooses to remain silent because of impending criminal charges, it may still be reasonable for the employer to dismiss on the basis of other evidence available: *Harris v Courage (Eastern) Ltd* [1981] ICR 496, [1981] IRLR 153.

[271] *Harris (Ipswich) Ltd v Harrison* [1978] ICR 1256, [1978] IRLR 382.

[272] As in *Carr's* case and *Parker's* case, n 270. However, actual police presence at an internal disciplinary hearing may well be held to render it invalid because of the pressure put on the employee: *Read v Phoenix Preservation Ltd* [1985] ICR 164, [1985] IRLR 93.

[273] *McLaren v National Coal Board* [1988] ICR 370, [1988] IRLR 215, CA. It will, however, normally be reasonable for the employer to rely on the fact of conviction when making his decision.

[274] *Monie v Coral Racing Ltd* [1981] ICR 109, [1980] IRLR 464, CA. This decision was applied to a case of suspected negligence by one of two fitters in *McPhie v Wimpey Waste Management Ltd* [1981] IRLR 316 and to a case of incapability in *Whitbread & Co plc v Thomas* [1988] ICR 135, [1988] IRLR 43. In *Parr v Whitbread & Co plc* [1990] ICR 427, [1990] IRLR 39 it was applied to one of four; the case contains useful guidance from Wood P.

necessary belief, it will normally be considered reasonable to dismiss in the standard case of theft (in the absence of exceptionally strong mitigating factors of which the employer knew or ought to have known). It should be noted, however, that there have been suggestions that, as in the other misconduct cases, it depends upon the facts of the case whether the offence is grave enough to warrant dismissal; in particular, it has been suggested that minor participation in theft, or theft from someone other than the employer (for example, from a fellow employee) *might* not warrant dismissal in some cases,[275] though it remains clear that theft from the employer will be a good ground for dismissal in almost all cases.

(iii) REDUNDANCY AND REORGANIZATION

These two related causes of dismissal receive more thorough attention in Chapter 8, which focuses on issues, including dismissal, surrounding redundancy, transfers of undertakings, and other large changes to the business that have effects on employees. However, they deserve a brief mention here in order to explain how and why they differ from other grounds of dismissal and hence call for separate treatment. The conceptual problem with a dismissal resulting from redundancy or reorganization is that it is a dismissal which is at the same time ostensibly fair (in that the employer has no option but to dismiss) and unfair (in that the employee has done no wrong). A redundancy occurs when some economic circumstance causes the employer to decide to reduce the workforce. This can happen in the context of closing a business, shutting down a part of a business (such as a branch, a department, or a distribution centre), or merely thinning out the ranks of workers. An employer typically makes the decision to take any of these kinds of action based on factors unrelated to the workers, like insolvency, competitive pressure, or changes in demand. The same factors can, alternatively, lead to the decision to reorganize the business, rather than shutting part of it or reducing the workforce. Reorganization can nevertheless result in dismissals, because changes to the organization of work or to job responsibilities can lead to resistance from employees, who might rightly complain that the changes amount to breaches of their employment contracts. It can be reasonable, and hence 'fair', for an employer to dismiss employees who refuse to cooperate with changes called for by the economic needs of the business.

Both redundancy and reorganization are, in different ways, potentially fair reasons for dismissal. Redundancy is specifically identified in section 98(2) as a prima facie fair reason, and then subject to a detailed definition in section 139. If a dismissal falls within the statutory definition of redundancy, then it can still be fair or unfair; however, a redundancy dismissal is generally found unfair only on procedural grounds, such as lack of consultation or a flawed process for deciding which group of employees will be made redundant.[276] In these cases fairness will be assessed according to the 'range of

---

[275] *Johnson Matthey Metals Ltd v Harding* [1978] IRLR 248, EAT.
[276] Chapter 8, heading 1(ii), p 557.

reasonable responses test', meaning that the issue will be whether the procedure, the pool of employees subject to selection, or the selection from that pool, were reasonable from the perspective of the employer.[277] Even if the redundancy is 'fair', the employee is entitled to a redundancy payment, based on years of service, but this is almost always a significantly smaller amount than an employee could expect to receive in a successful unfair dismissal claim. A reorganization dismissal—one that results not from a decision to reduce the workforce but to change the way the work is done—can be analysed as a special category of 'some other substantial reason',[278] or possibly of misconduct.[279] If the employee did not commit any disobedience or lack of cooperation that would support a conduct dismissal, the employer's reason will be that the economic circumstances required not only the reorganization, but the dismissal of those who would not go along with the changes. This being a well-accepted form of 'some other substantial reason', the employee might get nothing at all if the dismissal falls within the range of reasonable responses; if it does not the employer is liable to pay proper unfair dismissal compensation, not a mere redundancy payment. Thus, if a dismissal happens in the context of an employer's response to economic pressures, and not because of something the employee did or did not do, in most cases it will fall within the definition of a redundancy, making it harder to prove unfair dismissal (procedural grounds only), but requiring at least some payment. If, however, the economic circumstances lead to changes that do not satisfy the definition of redundancy but nevertheless result in dismissals, the employee has a chance of winning the unfair dismissal claim on substantive grounds, but has an even better chance of losing altogether, and walking away with nothing.

(iv) AUTOMATICALLY UNFAIR DISMISSALS

We have seen over recent years the addition to the longstanding general rules on unfair dismissal of several specific categories of special protection to meet particular concerns. For example, the Trade Union Reform and Employment Rights Act 1993 gave such protection to health and safety representatives/complainants and to those asserting their statutory rights. In addition, there is now special coverage for (1) protected shop workers and betting workers, who may not be dismissed for refusing to work on Sundays,[280] (2) employees appointed as member-nominated trustees of their pension fund, under the Pensions Act 1995, who may not be dismissed for exercising their functions as such,[281] (3) employees elected (or seeking election) as employee representatives for the

---

[277] *Wrexham Golf Club v Ingham* [2012] All ER (D) 209.

[278] *RS Components Ltd v Irwin* [1973] ICR 535, [1973] IRLR 239; *Robinson v Tescom Corporation* [2008] IRLR 408, EAT; *Hollister v National Farmers' Union* [1979] ICR 542, [1979] IRLR 238, CA; *Genower v Ealing, Hammersmith and Hounslow Area Health Authority* [1980] IRLR 297; *Farrant v Woodroffe School* [1998] ICR 184, [1998] IRLR 176.

[279] *Robinson v Tescom Corporation* [2008] IRLR 408.

[280] Employment Rights Act 1996, s 101; for the status of protected shop or betting workers, see Ch 4, heading 2(i), p 226.

[281] Section 102.

purposes of consultation over collective redundancies or transfers of undertakings, who may not be dismissed for performing, or proposing to perform, any such functions or activities,[282] and (4) employees exercising rights under the Working Time Regulations 1998, the Public Interest Disclosure Act 1998, the National Minimum Wage Act 1998, the Tax Credits Act 2002 or the Employment Act 2002, section 47 (flexible working) who may not be dismissed for any such reason.[283] In addition, the Part-time Worker Regulations 2000 and the Fixed-term Employee Regulations 2002 contain their own provisions rendering automatically unfair a dismissal due to exercising rights under the relevant Regulations.[284] In each case, there is also protection from victimization short of dismissal.

The form of the special protection is becoming familiar (in effect now being adopted 'off the peg' by the draftsman)—a dismissal on these grounds is automatically unfair, as is any later selection for redundancy; the normal qualifying period for unfair dismissal does not apply. In the case of whistleblowing, the statutory cap on compensation is removed (bringing it into line with the special protection for health and safety representatives and complainants with which it shares much ground). In the cases of pension trustees, employee representatives and complaints by whistleblowers or under the Working Time Regulations there are further provisions making interim relief available. The need for the extra protection for employee representatives is presumably strengthened by the fact that it is backed by EC Directives, which could give rise to arguments that any lesser provision failed to enact those Directives fully; with this background, there is a further protective provision in their case, namely that (as in the case of health and safety representatives/complainants and working time complainants who are also covered by EC Directives) the normal exclusions of tribunal jurisdiction in cases of dismissal while taking part in unofficial or official industrial action do not apply, so that the employer cannot use those immunities as a cover for getting rid selectively of elected representatives.

Despite the degree of commonality amongst these protections, some have provisions or raise issues that deserve particular attention: health and safety protection, assertion of statutory rights, and dismissals resulting from the transfer of an undertaking.

(a) Health and safety protection

In order to comply with the Framework Directive on the introduction of measures to encourage improvements in the safety and health of workers at work,[285] the Trade

---

[282] Collective Redundancies and Transfer of Undertakings (Protection of Employment) (Amendment) Regulations 1995, SI 1995/2587, reg 14.

[283] Employment Rights Act 1996, ss 101A, 103A, 104A, 104B, 104C respectively. Dismissal for undertaking jury service is specifically covered by s 98B.

[284] SI 2000/1551, reg 7; SI 2002/2034, reg 6. There are similar protective provisions in the Transnational Information and Consultation of Employees ('European Works Council') Regulations 1999, SI 1999/3323, reg 28 and the Information and Consultation of Employees Regulations 2004, SI 2004/3426, reg 30.

[285] Directive 89/391/EEC; most of the requirements of this Directive were put into domestic law by the Management of Health and Safety at Work Regulations 1992 (reissued in 1999). However, the Directive also

Union Reform and Employment Rights Act 1993 inserted what is now section 100 of the Employment Rights Act 1996. This makes a dismissal automatically unfair if the reason (or, if more than one, the principal reason) was that the employee:

(1) having been designated by the employer to carry out health and safety functions, carries out or proposed to carry out such activities;

(2) being a safety representative or member of a safety committee, performed or proposed to perform such functions, or acted as an elected worker representative of employee safety (or took part in an election for such position);[286]

(3) (where there was no representative or committee, or it was not reasonably practicable to raise the matter with them) brought to his employer's attention, by reasonable means, harmful or potentially harmful circumstances;[287]

(4) left the place of work, or refused to return to it, in circumstances of danger which he reasonably believed to be serious or imminent and which he could not reasonably have been expected to avert;[288] or

(5) in such circumstances, took or proposed to take appropriate steps to protect himself or others from the danger.[289]

In addition to the automatic unfairness, extra protection is achieved in the following ways:

(1) the normal qualifying period does not apply;

(2) any selection for redundancy because of the above factors is automatically unfair;[290]

---

contains (in Arts 7.2, 8.4, 8.5 and 11.4) directions to member states requiring protection for workers and workers' representatives from detrimental treatment and rights to take direct action to counter imminent dangers.

[286] To have this protection, the safety representative must have been acting within the scope of his responsibilities or jurisdiction: *Shillito v Van Leer (UK) Ltd* [1997] IRLR 495 (a case under the parallel provisions of s 44 on victimization short of dismissal on these grounds); once that is the case, the protection is wide, covering the exercise of the functions and the manner of doing so: *Goodwin v Cabletel UK Ltd* [1998] ICR 112, [1997] IRLR 665, EAT.

[287] 'Reasonable means' does not include concerted industrial action because the protection here is on an individual basis: *Balfour Kilpatrick Ltd v Acheson* [2003] IRLR 683.

[288] The danger in question can cover threats from another employee, not just for machinery or chemicals: *Harvest Press Ltd v McCaffrey* [1999] IRLR 778, EAT.

[289] Whether steps were appropriate must be judged by reference to all the circumstances, including the employee's state of knowledge, and the facilities and advice available to him: s 100(2). The special protection in (5) does not apply if the employer shows that it was so negligent for the employee to take those steps that a reasonable employer might have dismissed him for taking them: s 100(3). This derogation is specifically permitted by Art 8(3) of the Directive. The reference to danger to 'others' primarily means other employees but it has been held that it can apply more widely, eg to customers or members of the public: *Masiak v City Restaurants (UK) Ltd* [1999] IRLR 780, EAT.

[290] This protection is neutral; it does not put the representative/complainant into a better position in redundancy selection: *Smiths Industries Aerospace and Defence Systems v Rawlings* [1996] IRLR 656, EAT.

(3) the normal exclusions of tribunal jurisdiction in cases of dismissal while taking part in industrial action do not apply;[291]

(4) interim relief is available;[292]

(5) crucially, the statutory cap on the compensatory award for unfair dismissal does not apply;[293]

(6) in addition to these unfair dismissal provisions, section 44 of the 1996 Act gives an employee a right not to have action *short of* dismissal taken against him on the above grounds, and a right to complain to a tribunal of any such detrimental treatment.[294]

While an employee dismissed for making health and safety complaints had some protection previously under the ordinary unfair dismissal law, it was patchy.[295] These provisions were therefore an important step forward. Unlike most of unfair dismissal law, they are the product of an EC Directive and this may mark them apart for two reasons: (1) arguments may arise that they in fact do not go far enough to meet the standards required by the Directive (in which case an applicant may try to claim rights directly under the directive, if not covered by the new domestic provisions); (2) in any event, in the light of the purposive interpretation to be given to domestic provisions enacting EC Directives,[296] it may be necessary for a tribunal considering a claim under this new law to keep an eye on the wording and intent of the Directive as a guide to interpretation.[297] One further point to note is that a person making health and safety complaints in a more public arena may now also have protection under the Public Interest Disclosure Act 1998, as a protected 'whistleblower'.[298]

(b) Assertion of statutory rights

The Trade Union Reform and Employment Rights Act 1993 inserted a new provision (now section 104 of the Employment Rights Act 1996) making a dismissal automatically unfair if the reason (or principal reason) for it was that the employee had brought proceedings against the employer to enforce a 'relevant statutory right' or had alleged

---

[291] For those exclusions, see Ch 10, heading 2(ii), p 697.

[292] For interim relief see Ch 9, heading 2(i), p 636.

[293] Employment Rights Act 1996, s 124(1A); this also applies to dismissal of a whistleblower under s 103A.

[294] This is closely modelled on the remedy for action short of dismissal taken on union or non-union grounds: see Ch 9, heading 2(i), p 636.

[295] An employee without the necessary continuous employment was unprotected, unless he could show that the dismissal was for trade union reasons; however, a health and safety complaint taken up on an individual basis was unlikely to qualify as 'union activities': *Chant v Aquaboats Ltd* [1978] 3 All ER 102, [1978] ICR 643, EAT.

[296] *Litster v Forth Dry Dock and Engineering Co Ltd* [1989] ICR 341, [1989] IRLR 161, HL.

[297] Smith, Goddard, Killalea and Randall *Health and Safety—the New Legal Framework* (2nd edn, 2000) ch 3.

[298] See Ch 3, heading 4(iv), p 178. The decision in *Parkins v Sodexho Ltd* [2002] IRLR 109 (itself concerning a health and safety complaint) gives a very wide interpretation to this specific protection.

infringement by the employer of such a right;[299] this does not apply if the dismissal was because of an allegation that was false and not made in good faith. The following rights are laid down as 'relevant statutory rights':

(1) any right conferred by the 1996 Act, for which the remedy is by way of a complaint to an employment tribunal;

(2) the right to notice laid down in section 86 of the 1996 Act;

(3) the rights conferred by the Trade Union and Labour Relations (Consolidation) Act 1992 relating to deductions from pay, union activities and time off;

(4) the rights conferred by the Working Time Regulations 1998 and allied provisions;

(5) rights conferred by the Transfer of Undertakings (Protection of Employment) Regulations 2006.

As with health and safety complaints (above), any redundancy selection because of such assertion of statutory rights is made automatically unfair and the normal qualifying period does not apply. The latter point may be particularly significant where the alleged breach relates to the provisions on unlawful deductions (originally in the Wages Act 1986 and now in Part II of the 1996 Act), since that protection has no qualifying period, but in the past the exercise of the employee's rights under it was always dangerous if that employee lacked the qualifying period for ordinary unfair dismissal.

(c) Dismissals resulting from transfers of undertakings

When one firm purchases another, the seller 'transfers the undertakings' of that business to the buyer. Among the undertakings of the selling business are the contracts with its employees. The Transfer of Undertakings (Protection of Employment) Regulations 1981 implement the EC Acquired Rights Directive by imposing rules about the obligations of the buyer of the business to the employees of that business, one of which is the obligation not to dismiss them because of the transfer itself. Regulation 7(1)–(3) in effect creates three categories of affected cases:

(1) where the sole or principal reason for the dismissal is the transfer itself, the dismissal is automatically unfair;[300]

---

[299] There are two gaps in the protection, due to this emphasis on the employee having complained of infringement: (1) if the employer has allowed the right in question (eg to time off for public duties), but then dismisses (before the qualifying period is served) because tired of having to allow it, that is not within the statutory protection; (2) it is not enough that on the facts the employee could have brought a complaint: *Mennell v Newell & Wright (Transport Contractors) Ltd* [1997] IRLR 519, CA.

[300] This could arise where employees are dismissed to 'slim down' the business to facilitate an actual or impending sale: *Morris v John Grose Group Ltd* [1998] ICR 655, [1998] IRLR 499, following on this point *Harrison Bowden Ltd v Bowden* [1994] ICR 186 and disapproving the narrower view in *Ibex Trading Co Ltd v Walton* [1994] ICR 907, [1994] IRLR 564, EAT.

(2) where the sole or principal reason for the dismissal is a reason connected with the transfer that is *not* an economic, technical or organizational reason ('an ETO reason' in the jargon) entailing changes in the workforce, again the dismissal is automatically unfair;

(3) where the sole or principal reason for the dismissal is a reason connected with the transfer that *is* an ETO reason entailing changes in the workforce, then that dismissal is deemed for unfair dismissal purposes to have been for 'some other substantial reason' and so the employer must go on to show that the dismissal was fair in the light of equity and the substantial merits of the case under the Employment Rights Act 1996, section 98(4).[301]

Thus, the employer in a TUPE case is only in the clear if he can show that there is no connection with the transfer, for example where the dismissal was for some unconnected act of misconduct.

6 REMEDIES FOR UNFAIR DISMISSAL

The present statutory rules governing remedies for unfair dismissal were established as long ago as the Employment Protection Act 1975 which split compensation into a basic award and a compensatory award, and sought to strengthen the provisions relating to the direct remedies of reinstatement and re-engagement in an attempt to make them the primary remedies in practice as well as in theory; the figures have consistently shown that this aim has not been achieved,[302] and so compensation remains the prime remedy in most cases. The rules governing remedies are contained in sections 111–132 of the Employment Rights Act 1996. In addition, now that dismissal for trade union reasons is covered by the Trade Union and Labour Relations (Consolidation) Act 1992, there are special provisions in sections 161–166 of that Act relating to 'interim relief' which may serve to keep a contract of employment subsisting while a complaint in such cases is considered; such interim relief was extended by the Trade Union Reform and Employment Rights Act 1993 to the new head of dismissal for health and safety reasons and then to cases involving pension trustees, employee representatives, working time complaints and whistleblowers, and so equivalent provisions now appear in the 1992 and 1996 Acts. The normal remedies are now considered in turn, along with the important concepts of contributory fault and mitigation, either of which may

---

[301] *McGrath v Rank Leisure Ltd* [1985] ICR 527, [1985] IRLR 323. Where the defence works in a redundancy context, reg 7(3)(b) specifically preserves the redundancy option and the tribunal should go on to decide on fairness on the ordinary principles of unfair redundancy selection (above): *Warner v Adnet Ltd* [1998] IRLR 394, CA.

[302] In 2007–08, a total of 8,312 unfair dismissal cases went to a tribunal hearing: 46% were upheld and 54% dismissed. There were only eight orders for reinstatement or re-engagement (0.1% of cases heard). Remedy was left to the parties in 141 cases and compensation was awarded in 2,552 cases: *ETS Annual Report 2007–08*.

decrease an award of compensation. As elsewhere in unfair dismissal law, it must be remembered that, although case law may be important in filling out the legislative bones (particularly in the area of the compensatory award), it is the wording of the statute which remains of paramount importance and the majority of cases are merely illustrations of the application of that wording.

(i) REINSTATEMENT AND RE-ENGAGEMENT[303]

If a tribunal finds that a dismissal was unfair, it then proceeds to hear the parties on the question of remedies and by virtue of section 112 it must explain to the complainant the possible orders for reinstatement and re-engagement and ask whether he wishes the tribunal to make such an order.[304] An order for reinstatement means that the employer must take him back into his job; as he is in effect treated as not having been dismissed this means that he is entitled to any benefits he might reasonably have expected to receive during his period of dismissal, principally back pay (including any *improvement* of terms and conditions which he would have received during that period had he not been dismissed, but deducting any amounts actually received from the employer by way of wages in lieu or ex gratia payments, or from any employment during that period with another employer);[305] further, any other rights and privileges such as seniority and pension rights must be restored to him, and the tribunal must specify the date upon which reinstatement is to take effect. An order for re-engagement means that the employee must be taken back on by the employer (or by a successor or an associated employer)[306] in 'employment comparable to that from which he was dismissed or other suitable employment' on terms which are, so far as reasonably practicable, as favourable as if he had been reinstated; this too carries rights to back pay and preservation of accrued interests, and here the tribunal must specify not only the effective date of the order but also the identity of the re-engaging employer, the nature of the employment and the rate of remuneration. In the case of either kind of order, the employee's continuity of employment is preserved and the time between dismissal and re-employment counts as a period of employment.[307]

---

[303] Dickens, Hart, Jones and Weeks 'Re-employment of Unfairly Dismissed Workers: The Lost Remedy' (1981) 10 ILJ 160; Williams and Lewis 'The Aftermath of Tribunal Reinstatement and Re-engagement' DE Research Paper No 23 (1981).

[304] The mandatory nature of this wording is not what it seems; a tribunal decision will not be rendered void by a failure to comply with this requirement: *Cowley v Manson Timber Ltd* [1995] ICR 367, [1995] IRLR 153, CA.

[305] Employment Rights Act 1996, s 114.

[306] Defined in the Employment Rights Act 1996, s 231; see Ch 2, heading 3(ii), p 78. A tribunal should stick to the wording of the statute and make orders for either reinstatement or re-engagement, not just make an order that the employer should offer to re-employ: *Lilley Construction Ltd v Dunn* [1984] IRLR 483. An order may not be made to re-employ on significantly better terms: *Rank Xerox (UK) Ltd v Stryczek* [1995] IRLR 568.

[307] Employment Protection (Continuity of Employment) Regulations 1996, SI 1996/3147, *Harvey* R [1034]. These regulations apply where either there has been an application to a tribunal, or an agreed re-employment

In a case where an employee expresses a desire for reinstatement or re-engagement, section 116 lays down a definite procedure to which the tribunal must adhere.[308] The tribunal must first decide whether to make an order for reinstatement and only if it decides not to do so should it go on to consider whether to order re-engagement and, if so, on what terms. In both exercises, it must take into account (1) the expressed wishes of the complainant, (2) whether it is *practicable* for the employer to comply with an order for reinstatement or re-engagement and (3) whether the complainant caused or contributed to his dismissal and if so whether it would be just to make an order.[309] An employer who does not wish to take the dismissed employee back may therefore at this stage make representations on grounds (2) and (3) and, although (3) is important in ruling out important remedies for a 'rogue', it is (2) and the question of practicability which is likely to be the most pressing. It is for the employer to show impracticability, and as this is such an important matter he must discharge that onus properly—it is not enough for the tribunal to take a lax approach and decide that perhaps it would not be 'expedient' to put the employee back into employment.[310] Impracticability is a question of fact in each case, but may arise from inability to perform the work, unsuitability for it, definite opposition to his return among the workforce (either collectively or individually),[311] inability to take him back without having to dismiss another employee,[312] continued breakdown of trust and confidence between the parties[313] or through an intervening factor arising since the dismissal such as redundancy or potential overmanning (though in such a case the tribunal should be satisfied that it is genuine).[314] In *Enessy Co SA v Minoprio*[315] the Scottish EAT stated obiter that practicability may depend, inter alia, upon the size of the employer and that reinstatement into a small concern where a close personal relationship has to exist should only be ordered in exceptional cases; this may be a factor, particularly in domestic or quasi-domestic employment as in that case itself, but it is submitted that this approach should not be applied too widely, for as a principle it could come to bear an unfortunate resemblance to the old common law rules against enforcement of contracts of employment.[316]

---

after the involvement of an ACAS conciliation officer or through a compromise agreement; thus an employee negotiating re-employment is advised to do so through ACAS or by a formal compromise agreement, otherwise there may be a break in continuity even if the employer had voluntarily taken the employee back: *Morris v Walsh Western UK Ltd* [1997] IRLR 562, EAT.

[308] *Pirelli General Cable Works Ltd v Murray* [1979] IRLR 190, EAT.

[309] Lewis 'Interpretation of "Practicable" and "Just" in Relation to Re-employment in Unfair Dismissal Cases' (1982) 45 MLR 384. Contributory conduct here is the same in content as contributory fault in a compensation case (see head 6(ii)): *Boots Co plc v Lees-Collier* [1986] ICR 728, [1986] IRLR 485, EAT.

[310] *Qualcast (Wolverhampton) Ltd v Ross* [1979] ICR 386, [1979] IRLR 98, EAT.

[311] *Coleman v Magnet Joinery Ltd* [1975] ICR 46, [1974] IRLR 343, CA; *Langston v AUEW (No 2)* [1974] ICR 510, [1974] IRLR 182; *Meridian Ltd v Gomersall* [1977] ICR 597, [1977] IRLR 425.

[312] *Freemans plc v Flynn* [1984] ICR 874, [1984] IRLR 486, EAT.

[313] *Wood Group Heavy Industrial Turbines Ltd v Crossan* [1998] IRLR 680.

[314] *Cold Drawn Tubes Ltd v Middleton* [1992] ICR 318, [1992] IRLR 160.   [315] [1978] IRLR 489.

[316] See Ch 6, heading 4(ii), p 435.

If an order for reinstatement or re-engagement is made and the employee is taken back but the employer does not comply fully with the terms of the order, the employee may complain under section 117 to the tribunal[317] which is to order such compensation as it thinks fit having regard to the loss caused to the employee by the employer's actions. The more common form of complaint, however, will be that the employer has not complied with the order *at all* and has refused to take the employee back. In this case, section 117(3) provides that the tribunal shall make an award of compensation in the normal way instead[318] *and* an award of 'additional compensation' of between 26 and 52 weeks' pay. A 'week's pay' is subject to the same maximum as that in force at the time for the ordinary basic award[319] and, as the additional compensation is not expressly limited to compensation for loss actually suffered by the employee because of the employer's refusal to comply, it can include a punitive element.[320]

Once again, it is a defence to the granting of the additional compensation if the employer can satisfy the tribunal that it was not practicable to comply with the order; this may seem a strange provision as it allows the employer a second opportunity to plead impracticability. In *Timex Corpn v Thomson*[321] Browne-Wilkinson P held that the test effectively was the same (the latter stage *not* being confined to matters arising since the date of the order), so that it was possible for a tribunal merely to 'have regard' to practicability at the first stage and, if necessary, make the order on a fairly speculative basis and leave it to the employer to raise impracticability as a defence at this second stage if it did not work out in practice. This approach was generally approved by the Court of Appeal in *Port of London Authority v Payne*[322] where it was said that, although a determination of sorts has to be made at the first stage, that will be 'of necessity provisional' and without prejudice to a fuller consideration of practicability at the second stage if necessary, with the burden of proof clearly on the employer (though only to show impracticability, not absolute impossibility). Finally, it should

---

[317] One problem is whether s 117 can be relied upon where an employer uses more subtle tactics, eg taking the employee back but subtly victimizing him; also, where the employer takes the employee back on normally, but then later changes the terms of his employment (eg by downgrading him), that would have to be the subject of a separate unfair dismissal action. The tribunal decision *in Nensi v Vinola (Knitwear) Manufacturing Co Ltd* [1978] IRLR 297, IT that a re-employed employee fell between two stools in such a case is per incuriam since his continuity should in fact have been preserved by the 1996 Regulations, so that he had the necessary qualifying period and so should have been allowed his separate unfair dismissal action.

[318] If the tribunal finds that the employee himself unreasonably prevented the order being complied with, that is to be considered as failure to mitigate his loss, with a view to decreasing the award of compensation: Employment Rights Act 1996, s 117(8).

[319] As from February 2012 the figure is £430. For the calculation of a week's pay, see Ch 3, heading 5(iv), p 203.

[320] *George v Beecham Group* [1977] IRLR 43; IT; *Morganite Electrical Carbon Ltd v Donne* [1988] ICR 18, [1987] IRLR 363.

[321] [1981] IRLR 522, applied in *Freemans plc v Flynn* [1984] ICR 874, [1984] IRLR 486 and *Boots Co plc v Lees-Collier* [1986] ICR 728, [1986] IRLR 485.

[322] [1994] ICR 555, [1994] IRLR 9, CA, reversing the decision of the EAT which had been inconsistent with *Timex*. The case itself held the record for a tribunal hearing, having lasted 189 days.

be noted that the statute provides that the fact that the employer has hired a replace-ment for the dismissed employee is not to be taken into account when deciding upon impracticability (at either stage at which it may arise) unless the employer can show that it was not practicable for him to arrange for the work to be done without engaging a permanent replacement, or (at the first stage, when deciding whether to make an order) that he only engaged the replacement after a reasonable period without hearing from the dismissed employee, and then had to do so in order that the work could be done.[323]

(ii) COMPENSATION

The scheme of the present provisions on compensation is that the employee is eligible for a 'basic award' which is calculated mechanically in the same way as a redundancy payment and so rewards long service, and a 'compensatory award' which aims to put a realistic figure upon the employee's actual loss. The maximum for the basic award is determined by the maximum amount for a 'week's pay' for this purpose, and the compensatory award is subject to a maximum set figure in the statute.[324] This latter figure was allowed to fall behind inflation for much of the 1980s and 1990s, so that by 1999 it still stood at only £12,000, which had a depressing effect on unfair dismissal compensation,[325] and caused problems when the equivalent maximum was removed from discrimination cases, so that it was in an applicant's interests to seek to bring a dis-missal case as a discrimination claim whenever possible. The New Labour government at first proposed in the White Paper 'Fairness at Work' to remove the limit altogether, but were prevailed upon only to raise it instead; this was done in the Employment Relations Act 1999 which increased it to £50,000, and at the same time instituted a system for raising all the award limits annually in line with the Retail Prices Index.[326] However, as we have seen above, a Bill was going through Parliament at the time of writing that would grant the authority to lower the cap to something between a year's pay and three years' pay (so long as that is lower than the present cap), and indications are that the power will be exercised in 2013 to reduce the cap to a year's pay.[327]

(a) The basic award[328]

The calculation method for this is similar to that for a redundancy payment; it is depend-ent upon the length of the employee's continuous employment as at the effective date of

---

[323] Section 116(5), (6).

[324] As at February 2012 the maximum for a week's pay is £430 pw, giving a maximum basic award of £12,900.

[325] Given that the figure stood at £6,250 in 1980, by the late 1990s inflation alone should have raised it to £30,000–40,000. The latter figure was suggested by the CBI and IPD in their responses to 'Fairness at Work'.

[326] As at February 2012 the maximum compensatory award stood at £72,300.

[327] Enterprise and Regulatory Reform Bill 2012, available at <http://www.publications.parliament.uk/pa/bills/lbill/2012-2013/0045/lbill_2012-20130045_en_7.htm#pt5-pb3-l1g56> (last accessed 15 January 2013).

[328] See *Harvey* DI [2503].

termination, and under section 119 the employee is to receive one and a half weeks' pay for each year of employment over the age of 41, one week's pay for each year between 22 and 41 and half a week's pay for each year under the age of 22; a maximum of 20 years may be counted and, as stated above, the maximum week's pay for this purpose is limited to a fixed amount, subject to review. The basic award is subject to reduction (1) by the amount of any redundancy payment received (either under the Act or by virtue of a private scheme),[329] (2) where the tribunal finds that there was contributory fault on the part of the employee[330] (see below), (3) where the ex-employee has refused an offer of, in effect, reinstatement[331] and (4) where the employer has made an ex gratia payment meant to offset or extinguish all legal rights (in as much as that amount may be set off against both basic and compensatory awards, if large enough).[332]

The basic award used to be subject to a minimum of two weeks' pay, but this was abolished by the Employment Act 1980, which also extended the idea of contributory fault to cover any conduct by the employee prior to the dismissal (not just conduct known to the employer and contributing positively to the decision to dismiss). A combination of these two reforms to the basic award ensured that an employee who is unfairly dismissed on ground A (for example, unsatisfactory work) but who is later discovered to have been dismissable on ground 2 (for example, concealed fraud, only coming to light after he left) cannot now claim the minimum basic award of two weeks; the reforms were in response to fears expressed by the House of Lords in *W Devis & Sons Ltd v Atkins*[333] that the minimum basic award could be a 'rogue's charter' in such cases.

(b) The compensatory award[334]

Despite the fact that the cap on the compensatory award could be dropped to one year's pay in 2013, the principles for arriving at an award up to that cap will not be changed, so the jurisprudence developed under a more generous cap still applies. Various aspects of the compensatory award can cause problems of quantification, and it is part of the tribunal's function to ensure that the relevant heads of compensation are considered.[335] However, since this award is meant to constitute realistic recompense and as such has to be approached from first principles in each case, the onus lies primarily upon the employee to adduce evidence of his losses;[336] the tribunal should not speculate unduly,

---

[329] Section 122(4); any excess over the amount of the basic award (which is thereby extinguished) is deducted from the compensatory award: s 123(7).

[330] Section 122(2).   [331] Section 122(1).

[332] *Chelsea Football Club and Athletic Co Ltd v Heath* [1981] ICR 323, [1981] IRLR 73, EAT.

[333] [1977] ICR 662, [1977] IRLR 314, HL.

[334] On the calculation of compensation generally, see Upex *Termination of Employment* (7th edn, 2006); Collins 'The Just and Equitable Compensatory Award' (1991) 20 ILJ 201, Hough and Spowart-Taylor 'Liability, Compensation and Justice in Unfair Dismissal' (1996) 25 ILJ 308; and Crump, Pugsley and Ashtiany *Butterworths Compensation Calculations* (1999).

[335] *Tidman v Aveling Marshall Ltd* [1977] ICR 506, [1977] IRLR 218.

[336] *Adda International Ltd v Curcio* [1976] ICR 407, [1976] IRLR 425; *Lifeguard Assurance Ltd v Zadrozny* [1977] IRLR 56; *Smith, Kline and French Laboratories Ltd v Coates* [1977] IRLR 220.

but on the other hand the EAT has pointed out that only a realistic standard should be expected of the employee (who may have difficulty gaining certain evidence, even with the aid of discovery against the employer) and the tribunal should not hide behind the burden of proof where major problems of quantification arise.[337]

The basis of the compensatory award is contained in section 123(1) which provides that:

> the amount of the compensatory award shall be such amount as the tribunal considers just and equitable in all the circumstances having regard to the loss sustained by the complainant in consequence of the dismissal in so far as that loss is attributable to action taken by the employer.

In a potentially important and expansive decision, the Inner House of the Court of Session held in *Leonard v Strathclyde Buses Ltd*[338] that this statutory language is to be applied as it stands, and is not to have grafted on to it common law tests such as whether damage claimed was foreseeable or too remote; thus, when an unfairly dismissed employee had to sell back 6,000 company shares on leaving at the current price of £1.70, only to see them rise to £5.85 some months later (on a takeover), it was held that it was 'just and equitable' to award the difference on the facts, and that this was not to be defeated by technical arguments on remoteness of damage taken from other areas of the law. Such an expansive approach (leaving much in the discretion of the tribunal) became particularly important with the raising of the statutory limit to £50,000 in 1999 and the subsequent annual up-rating. On the other hand, it must also be remembered that ultimately the aim of an award is to reimburse the employee, not to punish the employer,[339] and this principle can have certain overall effects. In particular, it means that if the employee has in fact lost nothing, he is entitled to no compensatory award (only the basic award) and this may be held to be the case where it is clear that it would have made no difference even if he had not been unfairly dismissed; for example in a redundancy dismissal where it is held to have been unfair through lack of consultation but it is clear that he would have been made redundant anyway, or in an incapacity or misconduct case where the dismissal was unfair because the proper procedure was not followed but it is clear that the employee would have been dismissed in any event.[340] In such a case it has long been clear that there may be a nil compensatory award, or a very limited one (for example where in a case of lack of redundancy consultation it appears

---

[337] *Barley v Amey Roadstone Corpn Ltd (No 2)* [1978] ICR 190, [1977] IRLR 299.

[338] [1998] IRLR 693, Ct of Sess; *Balmoral Group Ltd v Rae* (2000) The Times, 25 January, EAT.

[339] *Clarkson International Tools Ltd v Short* [1973] ICR 191, [1973] IRLR 90; *Lifeguard Assurance Ltd v Zadrozny* [1977] IRLR 56. It was said in *Townson v Northgate Group Ltd* [1981] IRLR 382 that the tribunal could look at how unfair the dismissal was when assessing compensation but this was later disapproved in *Morris v Acco Ltd* [1985] ICR 306.

[340] *Clarkson International Tools Ltd v Short* [1973] ICR 191, [1973] IRLR 90; *British United Shoe Machinery Co Ltd v Clarke* [1978] ICR 70, [1977] IRLR 297; *Barley v Amey Roadstone Corpn Ltd (No 2)* [1978] ICR 190, [1977] IRLR 299; *Clyde Pipeworks Ltd v Foster* [1978] IRLR 313; *Brittains Arborfield Ltd v Van Uden* [1977] ICR 211.

that proper consultation would have lasted for four weeks but then the employee would have been dismissed; in such a case the compensatory award may only reflect four weeks' loss of wages).[341]

As we have already seen (under heading 4(iii)) the decision of the House of Lords in *Polkey v A E Dayton Services Ltd*[342] established as a general principle that it is *not* open to a tribunal to find a dismissal substantively fair merely because with hindsight a procedural lapse in fact made no difference, but on the other hand that decision did accept (and, indeed, emphasize) the important point for present purposes, namely that the injustice (or lack of it) to the employee at the end of the day *is* to be taken into account in fixing compensation, and that approach has been applied strongly in the post-*Polkey* case law,[343] to the extent that this is now widely known in employment lawyers' jargon as 'the *Polkey* reduction'. It means that the tribunals have to be proactive on this point in investigating the likelihood (or lack thereof) of continued employment, which can be done either on the basis of direct evidence as to how much longer the employment would have lasted, or on the basis of a percentage estimate of that likelihood.[344] This adjustment should be distinguished from the adjustment introduced by the Employment Act 2008, allowing a 25% reduction or increase in the compensatory award to reflect the failure of one party or the other to comply with applicable disciplinary or grievance procedures.[345]

Finally, and on an even more fundamental level, an employee may be said to have lost nothing if his *conduct* is such that it is not just and equitable to give any compensatory award, in spite of the finding of unfairness. This would be the case for example where the employer unfairly dismissed the employee on a weak ground (for example, incapability) but then later found out about a cast-iron ground for dismissal (for example, embezzlement) which the employee had kept hidden from him. In such a

---

[341] Note, however, that ultimately this remains a question of fact and what would be just and equitable, so that there is no 'tariff' of two or three weeks: *Elkouil v Coney Island Ltd* [2002] IRLR 174 (employers knew of redundancies ten weeks before telling employees; compensation given for ten weeks' loss of job searching opportunity).

[342] [1988] ICR 142, [1987] IRLR 503, HL.

[343] See particularly *Mining Supplies (Longwall) Ltd v Baker* [1988] ICR 676, [1988] IRLR 417; *Slaughter v C Brewer & Sons Ltd* [1990] ICR 730, [1990] IRLR 426; *Red Bank Manufacturing Co Ltd v Meadows* [1992] ICR 204, [1992] IRLR 209; *Campbell v Dunoon and Cowal Housing Association Ltd* [1993] IRLR 496, Ct of Sess; *Britool Ltd v Roberts* [1993] IRLR 481; *Rao v Civil Aviation Authority* [1994] ICR 495, [1994] IRLR 240, CA.

[344] *Dunlop Ltd v Farrell* [1993] ICR 885; *Wolesley Centers Ltd v Simmons* [1994] ICR 503; *Fisher v California Cake & Cookie Ltd* [1997] IRLR 212. The EAT have suggested two glosses to this rule, where the tribunal should not consider future likelihoods—(1) where the unfairness comes from a defect of substance (eg improper selection criteria) rather than of procedure: *Steel Stockholders (Birmingham) Ltd v Kirkwood* [1993] IRLR 515 (criticized by the Court of Appeal in *O'Dea v ISC Chemicals Ltd* [1996] ICR 222, [1995] IRLR 599, but reaffirmed by the Inner House of the Court of Session in *King v Eaton (No 2)* [1998] IRLR 686); (2) where the unfairness comes from positive steps taken by the employer (eg wrong application of criteria), rather than a sin of omission: *Boulton & Paul Ltd v Arnold* [1994] IRLR 532. Arguably, both of these are unfortunate complications in an already difficult area.

[345] Trade Union and Labour Relations (Consolidation) Act 1992, s 207A.

case, the House of Lords held in *W Devis & Sons Ltd v Atkins*[346] that that subsequently discovered reason could not affect the fairness of the dismissal, or activate the provisions on contributory fault, for both of these matters have to be judged according to the employer's knowledge at the time of the dismissals; it could, however, justify the tribunal making a nil or nominal compensatory award on the ground of justice and equity, quite independently of any question of contributory fault.[347]

Given such general considerations, tribunals have to have a system of dividing up possible heads of loss, and this is well established, principally following the early NIRC case *Norton Tool Co Ltd v Tewson*[348] which also established that the tribunal should set out in their judgment the relevant heads of compensation and the amounts awarded under each, not just one global sum.[349] The emphasis is very clearly upon pecuniary loss, and the following are the major heads:

(i) *Loss up to the date of hearing* This head requires a relatively simple mathematical calculation of the employee's actual loss of income during the period between the dismissal and the hearing; it is aimed at realistic compensation, so, as in the case of future loss (detailed later), the relevant figure is his previous weekly take-home pay (net of tax and National Insurance contributions) which may include matters such as overtime and tips which may *not* be counted under the stricter rules for calculating a 'week's pay' for the purpose of the basic award.[350] From this amount which the employee would have earned but for the dismissal the tribunal must deduct any sums earned in alternative employment during the period, or indeed in self-employment.[351] This is simply an example of the ordinary rules of mitigation of damage. However, there has always been an exception to this where the employee finds alternative employment during what should have been the notice period (in a case where no or short notice was given). Here, 'good industrial relations practice' dictates that mitigation should be suspended and the employee should receive any payments for the notice period without deduction.[352]

---

[346] [1977] ICR 662, [1977] IRLR 314, HL.

[347] [1977] ICR 662 at 680, [1977] IRLR 314 at 319, per Lord Dilhorne. This point was reaffirmed by the Court of Appeal in *Tele-Trading Ltd v Jenkins* [1990] IRLR 430.

[348] [1973] 1 All ER 183, [1972] ICR 501. For a criticism of this whole approach, see Collins (1991) 20 ILJ 201.

[349] See also *Adda International Ltd v Curcio* [1976] ICR 407, [1976] IRLR 425, EAT.

[350] *Brownson v Hire Service Shops Ltd* [1978] ICR 517, [1978] IRLR 73; *Palmanor Ltd v Cedron* [1978] ICR 1008, [1978] IRLR 303. Tax matters should not be considered in too great detail by the tribunal which may, for example, ignore minor tax rebates: *MBS Ltd v Calo* [1983] ICR 459, [1983] IRLR 189. If there is a dispute as to what is the correct amount of wage payable at the date of dismissal, that must be resolved by the tribunal which is deciding upon compensation: *Kinzley v Minories Finance Ltd* [1988] ICR 113, [1987] IRLR 490, EAT.

[351] *Ging v Ellward (Lancs) Ltd* (1978) [1991] ICR 222n; *Lee v IPC Business Press Ltd* [1984] ICR 306. This remains the case, even if the employee obtains new, permanent employment at higher pay, which eats into the compensation: *Dench v Flynn & Partners* [1998] IRLR 653, CA, disapproving on this point *Whelan v Richardson* [1998] IRLR 114.

[352] *TBA Industrial Products Ltd v Locke* [1984] ICR 228, [1984] IRLR 48 (disapproving a contrary decision in *Tradewinds Airways Ltd v Fletcher* [1981] IRLR 272 and reverting to the original rule as laid down in *Norton Tool Co Ltd v Tewson* n 348), approved in *Addison v Babcock FATA Ltd*, n 353.

Problems arose when there were attempts to apply this exception for earnings during the (missing) notice period to the separate question of dismissal with wages *in lieu of notice*. Here, a non-deductibility rule would mean the employer paying twice and could have had a serious effect on the practicability of settlements. It was stopped at an early stage by the important decision of the Court of Appeal in *Addison v Babcock FATA Ltd*[353]—even if it is accepted that non-deductibility applies to earnings during the notice period from elsewhere, it was made clear that it does *not* apply where the ex-employer has properly discharged the contract by paying wages in lieu of notice— there, the normal principle of mitigation applies and the employer is permitted to set that payment off against the compensation otherwise payable under this head; the employer will therefore *not* lose out by having to pay twice by reason of attempting to settle the case by, inter alia, the payment of wages in lieu. Moreover, it is clear that this principle applies to ex gratia payments generally[354]—again, the employer will normally[355] be given credit for such payments and be able to set them off against any compensation awarded later.[356] The effect of *Hardy v Polk* is to make this mitigation-based approach apply across the board.

As well as salary, wages and other monetary receipts, the employee can claim compensation for past (and future) loss of other benefits such as a company car, a low interest mortgage or loan, free or cheap accommodation and other fringe benefits such as medical insurance and school fees; also, section 123(2) expressly includes any expenses reasonably incurred as a result of the dismissal (for example expenses incurred in seeking other employment) though this does not include the expense of bringing the unfair dismissal action itself.

(ii) *Future loss* In contrast to the relative certainties of the first head, compensation for future loss may require the tribunal to perform a highly speculative exercise. The actual loss per week may be easy to quantify (either where the ex-employee has not obtained other employment, or has done so at a lower wage) and it may include the

---

[353] [1987] ICR 805, [1987] IRLR 173, CA, overruling *Finnie v Top Hat Frozen Foods* [1985] ICR 433, [1985] IRLR 365, EAT.

[354] *Horizon Holidays Ltd v Grassi* [1987] ICR 851, [1987] IRLR 371, EAT.

[355] The word 'normally' is used because there is an exception—if an ex gratia payment is made on dismissal which would have been made to the employee anyway even if no unfair dismissal had taken place (eg where a redundancy dismissal is unfair for lack of warning, but the facts show that the same ex gratia payment would have been made even if proper warning had been given), then it may be argued that that particular payment should not be taken into account as mitigation: *Roadchef Ltd v Hastings* [1988] IRLR 142; one complication in *Addison* was that there was (in addition to the payment in lieu) an ex gratia payment which was not taken into account, but it was for this reason.

[356] Though even here the employer may lose out, for if the eventual amount of compensation is going to be over the statutory maximum, it has been held that the tribunal must deduct the ex gratia payment and then apply the maximum to what is left, which means that the employer may end up paying in total more than the statutory maximum: *McCarthy v BICC plc* [1985] IRLR 94; for the order of making deductions, see later under this head, p 544. Thus the employer must be careful with ex gratia payments and, certainly in the case of higher earners, might be better advised to seek a binding settlement (either under the aegis of ACAS or under the rules on binding compromise agreements) rather than attempting a simple pay-off.

extra matters and perks mentioned above, but the tribunal has to fix a 'multiplier' (as in personal injury cases) of a number of weeks, months or even years during which this loss might continue;[357] the state of the local labour market and conditions in the industry concerned will be factors, but there will be other discounting factors, such as the possibilities that the employee might have resigned in the future anyway, moved from the area, had a child, etc. Also, the principle mentioned above that the employee will not be compensated if he has in fact suffered no loss must be borne in mind, so that if he would probably have lost his employment in the near future anyway (for example, through impending redundancies) he may only be compensated in respect of that short extra period of likely employment.[358] The number of factors in any particular case may thus be considerable and so, although as in other aspects of compensation the tribunal should explain in its decision how it arrived at the multiplier it used,[359] this is not an exercise in precision; that multiplier may be one general approximation of several different factors and, unless very clearly misguided, will not usually be altered by the EAT. In the past, even rough calculations could soon reach the low statutory maximum, rendering further precision unnecessary, but the raising of that maximum to £50,000 in 1999 was expected to mean much more argument on exact calculation, in order to maximize compensation within (and up to) that limit, especially in cases of higher earners and/or likely long-term unemployment; in the large majority of cases, however, this will not be so and the multiplier will be relatively modest.[360]

(iii) *Loss of accrued rights* When an employee is dismissed and takes other employment, he loses any statutory (or other) rights against the dismissing employer which depend upon continuous service (for example, redundancy and the employment protection rights) and must begin to accrue new rights against his new employer. This head of loss established in *Norton Tool Co Ltd v Tewson*, was meant to reflect that disadvantage and initially caused some problems. Now, however, the major loss (of accrued redundancy rights) is in effect taken into account by the institution of the basic award and so any further compensation under this head will be less, though the EAT held in *Daley v A E Dorsett (Almar Dolls) Ltd*[361] that the right to the longer notice

---

[357] See, eg, *Cartiers Superfoods Ltd v Laws* [1978] IRLR 315. This must be viewed in the context of that individual claimant so that if his personal circumstances render new employment more difficult, the compensation may reflect that: *Fougère v Phoenix Motor Co Ltd* [1976] ICR 495, [1976] IRLR 259; *Gilham v Kent County Council (No 3)* [1986] ICR 52, [1986] IRLR 56, EAT.

[358] *Young's of Gosport Ltd v Kendell* [1977] ICR 907, [1977] IRLR 433.

[359] *Qualcast (Wolverhampton) Ltd v Ross* [1979] ICR 386, [1979] IRLR 98. There is no 'conventional sum' of between six and 12 months—the period is to be determined by the tribunal in the light of all the evidence, subject only to the statutory maximum amount that can be awarded: *Morganite Electrical Carbon Ltd v Donne* [1988] ICR 18, [1987] IRLR 363 (impossible to say that an award covering 82 weeks was excessive).

[360] In 2007–08 the median award was £4,000 and the average award was £8,058. 42% of awards were for under £3,000; 77% were for under £10,000; less than 10% were for over £20,000: *ETS Annual Report 2007–08*.

[361] [1982] ICR 1, [1981] IRLR 385. Compensation may also reflect the loss of any extra redundancy rights that the ex-employee may have had under this contract over and above his ordinary statutory entitlement: *Lee v IPC Business Press Ltd* [1984] ICR 306.

that accrues with service is itself valuable so that, independently of the power that a tribunal now has to award common law damages for loss of wages during the notice period, it is open to it to make an award including an amount reflecting the employee's loss of accrued statutory rights to longer notice.[362]

(iv) *Loss due to the manner of dismissal* It was decided in 1972 (the year after the law on unfair dismissal was introduced) in *Norton Tool Co Ltd v Tewson* (discussed earlier) that the compensatory award was clearly tied to pecuniary loss and so, as at common law,[363] no amount could be awarded for loss of dignity, anguish, etc, simpliciter; an amount could only be granted under this head if the manner of dismissal could be said to affect the employee's future employment prospects, for example by blackening his name in the industry or in some way rendering him unfit for immediate re-employment.[364] This nostrum was followed consistently for three decades, until challenged entirely unexpectedly in a case concerning a very different point of law. *Johnson v Unisys Ltd*[365] was a common law claim for what had become known as 'stigma damages', ie manner of dismissal damages as part of a *wrongful* dismissal action.[366] In a strong decision putting an end to their development, one of the reasons given was that the common law should not be extended in such a way as to outflank or compromise statute law; in this context, that meant that manner of dismissal damages should not be given at common law *because it was the function of unfair dismissal to do so*. This bombshell was contained in Lord Hoffmann's speech, in this short passage:

> I know that in the early days of the NIRC it was laid down that only financial loss could be compensated: see *Norton Tool Co Ltd v Tewson* … It was said that the word 'loss' can only mean financial loss. But I think that is too narrow a construction. The emphasis is upon the tribunal awarding such compensation as it thinks just and equitable. So I see no reason why in an appropriate case it should not include compensation for distress, humiliation, damage to reputation in the community or to family life.[367]

Not unsurprisingly, this was rapidly taken up by claimants' lawyers and representatives as a significant extension to unfair dismissal compensation. However, it split tribunals with some granting such awards and others declining to. Fortunately the matter

---

[362] The EAT quantified this amount as half the wages for the statutory minimum of eight weeks' notice to which he was entitled. However, in the subsequent case of *S H Muffett Ltd v Head* [1987] ICR 1, [1986] IRLR 488 the EAT thought that in most cases it would be more appropriate merely to award a nominal sum of £100 under this head.

[363] *Addis v Gramophone Co Ltd* [1909] AC 488, HL; *Bliss v South East Thames Regional Health Authority* [1987] ICR 700, [1985] IRLR 308, CA; see Ch 6, heading 4(ii), p 451.

[364] *Norton Tool Co Ltd v Tewson*, n 348; *Vaughan v Weighpack Ltd* [1974] ICR 261, [1974] IRLR 105; *Brittains Arborfield Ltd v Van Uden* [1977] ICR 211, EAT. This might be particularly relevant in a whistle-blowing case.

[365] [2001] ICR 480, [2001] IRLR 279.

[366] For this aspect of the case, see Ch 6, heading 4(ii), p 456.

[367] [2001] ICR 480 at 500, [2001] IRLR 279 at 288.

was reconsidered by the House of Lords in *Dunnachie v Kingston-upon-Hull CC*[368] which settled the matter. Giving the principal speech, Lord Steyn had little difficultly in finding that Lord Hoffmann's passage in *Johnson* was obiter, so that the House could consider the matter from first principles. Relying on the wording of section 123 and the longstanding authority of *Norton Tool Co v Tewson* he held that 'loss' in section 123 is indeed restricted to financial loss, so that non-economic loss such as stigma or injury to feelings is *not* to be awarded in an unfair dismissal action.

(v) *Loss of pension rights* Where the dismissed employee cannot find new employment, or can or may find new employment to which he cannot transfer his existing pension rights, this head of compensation may produce a considerable sum. It is, however, perhaps the most complicated head of all and the EAT have stressed that the tribunal should adopt a broad approach so that actuarial evidence, though of considerable help (bearing in mind that the claimant must adduce evidence of loss), is not conclusive. Once again the tribunal is aiming for a realistic, if approximate, estimate of actual loss so that if no loss is sustained overall, nothing is payable under this head; this might occur if the employee has to take, or opts for,[369] a deferred pension from his existing entitlement and can build up a suitable further entitlement from new employment, or if he moves to employment with a better pension scheme (for example, from a contributory to a non-contributory scheme), or if he can simply transfer his pension. In *Copson v Eversure Accessories Ltd*[370] the NIRC said that there is no one correct way to quantify loss of pension rights, but isolated two types of loss—(1) loss of present pension position and (2) loss of future pension opportunity (ie the opportunity, had he not been dismissed, to improve his pension position during further service with that employer). Except in cases where the employee is close to retiring age (where the better approach may be to capitalize the cost of an annuity to produce a sum equal to the likely pension, discounting it for accelerated payment), the starting point for both (1) and (2) will be the contributions already paid to the scheme. The employee may have received back his own contributions, but can also claim (except in cases of transfer or deferment) credit for his legitimate interest in the contributions paid by the employer (plus interest thereon) which may be viewed as an adjunct to his salary.[371] As well as being the primary measure for the detriment to his present pension loss, lack of

---

[368] [2004] ICR 1052, [2004] IRLR 727, HL. This appeal was heard alongside its companion case of *Eastwood v Magnox Electricity plc* [2004] ICR 1064, [2004] IRLR 733, HL which concerned the parallel position at common law, see Ch 6, heading 4(ii), p 451.

[369] Where there is an option the choice lies with the employee, who is not to be penalized by the tribunal if he opts not to take the deferred pension: *Sturdy Finance Ltd v Bardsley* [1979] ICR 249, [1979] IRLR 65. Deferment of pension has been the normal position in the pension scheme since the Social Security Pensions Act 1975, though the amended pensions regime since 1986 puts more emphasis on personal, 'portable' pensions which may go with the person and the present government's intentions in relation to 'stakeholder pensions' remain in line with this, in which case there will be less of a problem of quantification under this head.

[370] [1974] ICR 636, [1974] IRLR 247, NIRC.

[371] *Copson's* case; *Hill v Sabco Houseware (UK) Ltd* [1977] ICR 888; *Smith, Kline and French Laboratories Ltd v Coates* [1977] IRLR 220; *Sturdy Finance Ltd v Bardsley* [1979] ICR 249, [1979] IRLR 65.

the employer's future contributions will be a guide to any future loss when compared with the position under any actual or likely pension scheme in new employment; the factors to be taken into account here may be numerous. Having arrived at a prima facie figure for loss, however, it is incorrect for the tribunal just to apply that for the number of years left to retirement age, because account must be taken of many contingencies, such as future resignation, future dismissal, early death, possible tax advantages and the fact that any capital sum is being paid sooner than normal. This discounting process is achieved by the fixing of the tribunal of a multiplier to take all of these factors into account;[372] this may considerably decrease the possible compensation under this head and inevitably imports an element of uncertainty. In an attempt to lessen the uncertainty generally, a committee of tribunal chairmen in conjunction with the Government Actuary's Department produced in 1991 a report suggesting methods of quantifying loss of pension rights; it contains examples of cases which might be likely to arise in practice, and certain basic actuarial material.[373] It is not necessarily determinative, though in the sea of actuarial uncertainty it may appear to a tribunal to be the only lifeline,[374] and it may prove difficult to introduce independent actuarial evidence based on different calculation methods.[375] However, this remains an area of difficulty and development as the EAT have indicated that, ten years on, there is a need for a further attempt at guidance.[376]

One final point may be noted about the compensatory award. What is the position if the employee has received unemployment benefit (now jobseeker's allowance) or income support prior to the date of the hearing? Before 1977, this was treated in the same way as receipt of income from another source during that period, and so was deductible. However, that meant that the employer was paying less compensation through a 'subsidy' from the state. Under the Employment Protection (Recoupment of Jobseeker's Allowance and Income Support) Regulations 1996,[377] the position now is that the tribunal is not to deduct the amount representing jobseeker's allowance or income

---

[372] *Powrmatic Ltd v Bull* [1977] ICR 469, [1977] IRLR 144, EAT.

[373] Sara, Crump and Pugsley *Employment Tribunals: Compensation of Loss of Pension Rights.*

[374] Its predecessor (by the GAD itself) was relied on in *Manpower Ltd v Hearne* [1983] ICR 567, [1983] IRLR 281 and *Mono Pumps Ltd v Froggatt* [1987] IRLR 368. However, the EAT in *Bingham v Hobourn Engineering Ltd* [1992] IRLR 298 pointed out that a tribunal is not bound to follow it.

[375] See the views of the EAT on this point in *Tradewinds Airways Ltd v Fletcher* [1981] IRLR 272. While a tribunal will properly not expect an employee to come armed with complex actuarial evidence, it is surely another matter actually to exclude it if the employee wishes to put it forward, especially where pension loss is a major factor.

[376] *Clancy v Cannock Chase Technical College* [2001] IRLR 331, where the EAT suggested that the existing guidelines did not cope well with a pension scheme which includes a lump sum entitlement in addition to the weekly amount (as opposed to constituting commutation of part of that weekly amount).

[377] SI 1996/2349, *Harvey* R [1007], replacing the original 1977 Regulations. *Mason v Wimpey Waste Management Ltd* [1982] IRLR 454. The Regulations do not apply to the settlement of an unfair dismissal action, so such a settlement may well take into account the state benefits in fact received, and those benefits will not be recoverable by the state. This may be an inducement to the employer to settle, since he may end up paying less.

support paid up to the date of the hearing, but instead must instruct the employer not to pay immediately that amount of the compensation it has awarded which represents loss of income during the period (ie head (i) above, called in the Regulations the 'prescribed element'). The DTI will then serve upon the employer a recoupment notice (or a notice that no such notice will in fact be served) which requires him to pay back to them from the prescribed element the amount representing jobseeker's allowance or income support paid to the claimant prior to the hearing; after this has been done, the remainder of the prescribed element may be paid to the successful claimant. Thus, the DTI obliges the employer to repay to them amounts made payable by them because of the unfair dismissal and the claimant still only receives what he has in fact lost. If no jobseeker's allowance or income support was in fact claimed during the period, the Regulations do not apply. Thus, the tribunal is relieved of the task of deducting benefits from the award (in return for the administrative chore of explaining the procedure to the parties) and, moreover, need not take the possibility of further receipt of benefit into account when deciding upon future loss (head (ii) above) either, for where compensation is awarded based on future loss for a set period of X weeks, months or years, the claimant is disqualified from receiving benefit during that period.

(c) Contributory fault

If a tribunal, having found in the claimant's favour on liability, considers that the dismissal was to any extent caused or contributed to by any action of the complainant, it must reduce both the basic award and the compensatory award by such proportion as it considers just and equitable.[378] The 'action' of the claimant must constitute blameworthy conduct in some way (so that it will not apply to proper and lawful activity on his part, such as refusing to obey an improper or unlawful order)[379] and this provision is aimed at giving the tribunal discretion to reach a just solution when both parties have been to blame,[380] as in the case of contributory negligence in a tort action.

---

[378] Employment Rights Act 1996, ss 122(2) and 123(6); by a combination of the Employment Acts 1980 and 1982 the contributory fault provision in the case of the basic award was widened to cover any conduct before the dismissal making it just and equitable to decrease that award; the reason for this is discussed below. The procedure to be adopted (especially in a 'split' hearing) is considered by the EAT in *Iggesund Converters Ltd v Lewis* [1984] ICR 544 at 552, [1984] IRLR 431 at 435. There is no requirement that the basic and compensatory awards have to be reduced by the same percentage once contributory fault is found: *Charles Robertson (Developments) Ltd v White* [1995] ICR 349 (reviewing the previous, inconsistent case law); *Optikinetics Ltd v Whooley* [1999] ICR 984.

[379] *Morrish v Henlys (Folkestone) Ltd* [1973] ICR 482, [1973] IRLR 61, approved by the Court of Appeal in *Nelson v BBC (No 2)* [1980] ICR 110, [1979] IRLR 346, CA.

[380] The matter must be looked at between employer and employee, not involving the actions of third parties (eg other employees at fault): *Parker Foundry Ltd v Slack* [1992] ICR 302, [1992] IRLR 11, CA. Contributory fault can be applied even if the dismissal was constructive for, looking at the history of the matter, the employee may have been partly responsible for the employer taking the actual repudiatory action: *Garner v Grange Furnishing Ltd* [1977] IRLR 206; *Morrison v ATGWU* [1989] IRLR 361, NICA; *Polentarutti v Autokraft Ltd* [1991] ICR 757, [1991] IRLR 457 (not following *Holroyd v Gravure Cylinders Ltd* [1984] IRLR 259). 'Fault' on the part of the employee can include fault on the part of his agent, eg his solicitor: *Allen v Hammett* [1982] ICR 227, [1982] IRLR 89.

Contributory fault constitutes a separate stage in the inquiry, once the tribunal has put a figure on the compensation, and should be explained by the tribunal as such.[381] In *Maris v Rotherham Corpn*[382] the NIRC said that the tribunal should approach this question in a broad common-sense manner, looking at all the circumstances of the case and the employee's overall conduct (even if the actual ground of unfairness is a narrow, technical one); a slight change in the wording in 1975 strengthened this view.[383] The actual figure thus lies predominantly within the tribunal's discretion and may be difficult to challenge on appeal, provided that it has been properly considered at the hearing.[384]

Where the ground for dismissal was misconduct, but the dismissal is held to have been unfair (for example, because of lack of warnings or a hearing) in spite of evidence of actual misconduct, that may be a clear case for reduction of compensation. Indeed, in *W Devis & Sons Ltd v Atkins*[385] Lord Dilhorne, disapproving earlier dicta that there may be a limit on the amount of reduction (for example, 80% maximum reduction), held that there is nothing inconsistent in finding unfairness but then using contributory fault in an extreme case to reduce compensation to nil or a merely nominal amount. The position, however, is more difficult in the case of a dismissal for incapacity, for can an employee's unfortunate incapacity ever be considered to be 'fault' on his part? In *Kraft Foods Ltd v Fox*[386] the EAT held that it could not, but in the subsequent case of *Moncur v International Paint Co Ltd*[387] it was explained that that was too sweeping a proposition and that the *Kraft* case envisaged the sort of incapability that was entirely outside the employee's control; even there, the EAT in *Moncur's* case doubted whether it was an absolute rule that such incapability could *never* amount to contributory fault and a reduction in such circumstances was approved subsequently in *Finnie v Top Hat Frozen Foods*.[388] In *Slaughter v C Brewer & Sons Ltd*[389] a different tack was taken; the EAT said that a reduction of contributory fault would be rare in an incapability case *but* if it was clear that, even if the employee had been treated fairly, the employment would have had to end shortly, then compensation can be reduced accordingly under the general 'just and equitable' basis to the compensatory award, thus achieving much the same result. One matter that is well established is that where the incapability is

---

[381] *Nudds v W and J B Eastwood Ltd* [1978] ICR 171.   [382] [1974] ICR 435, [1974] IRLR 147.

[383] *Brown v Rolls-Royce (1971) Ltd* (1977) 12 ITR 382 at 386, per Phillips J. There must still be a causal link between the conduct and the dismissal: *Hutchinson v Enfield Rolling Mills Ltd* [1981] IRLR 318, at least in the case of the compensatory award, though that link has been deliberately loosened in the case of the basic award.

[384] *Sutcliffe and Eaton Ltd v Pinney* [1977] IRLR 349; *Hollier v Plysu Ltd* [1983] IRLR 260, CA.

[385] [1977] ICR 662, [1977] IRLR 314, HL, disapproving in this context dicta in *Kemp v Shipton Automation Ltd* [1976] ICR 514, [1976] IRLR 305 and *Trend v Chiltern Hunt Ltd* [1977] ICR 612, [1977] IRLR 66. See *Marley Homecare Ltd v Dutton* [1981] IRLR 380 and *Chaplin v H J Rawlinson Ltd* [1991] ICR 553.

[386] [1978] ICR 311, [1977] IRLR 431.

[387] [1978] IRLR 223; *Brown's Cycles Ltd v Brindley* [1978] ICR 467.

[388] [1985] ICR 433, [1985] IRLR 365 (overruled later on other grounds in *Addison v Babcock FATA Ltd* [1987] ICR 805, [1987] IRLR 173, CA).

[389] [1990] ICR 730, [1990] IRLR 426.

in any way within the employee's control (for example, where he is negligent, lazy or unwilling to improve), that can clearly be contributory fault and indeed, according to the case of *Sutton and Gates (Luton) Ltd v Boxall*[390] (where a similar view was taken of the *Kraft* case), it may warrant a sizeable reduction.

A particular problem with contributory fault arose where the employer unfairly dismisses on one ground but then subsequently discovers other grounds which would certainly have justified dismissal. The House of Lords in *W Devis & Sons Ltd v Atkins*[391] held that in such a case the subsequently discovered misconduct cannot alter the finding of unfairness under section 57(3) *and* cannot be used as contributory fault for, being unknown at the time of dismissal, it could not have 'caused or contributed to' the dismissal. In such a case, however, justice could be done by giving a nil award under the general 'just and equitable' basis for compensation, *but* in that particular case the House of Lords were applying the old law on compensation which operated *before* the basic award was introduced in 1975. Once that award was introduced, the problem arose that a tribunal could not impose a nil basic award because the calculation is mathematical (not based on what is just and equitable) and it could only be reduced by contributory fault, which did not include subsequently discovered misconduct. Thus, in such a case, the employee whose dishonesty only came to light after being unfairly dismissed for laziness might still get a nil compensatory award but remain eligible for a basic award. Lord Diplock called this a 'rogue's charter' and in the Employment Act 1980 the previous government took steps to prevent it, in two ways. First, the statutory minimum basic award of two weeks' pay was abolished; secondly, the tribunals were given a wider power to decrease (and possibly extinguish) a basic award where the conduct of the complainant before the dismissal was such that it would be just and equitable to reduce the award. This is wider than the previous rule on contributory fault per se (which still applies to the compensatory award) in that it does not require a definite causal link between the conduct and the dismissal.[392] Thus, the undisclosed rogue may now be awarded no compensation at all.

(d) Mitigation

Under section 123(4), the dismissed employee must take the same reasonable steps to mitigate his losses as he would have to at common law;[393] these might include answering job advertisements and going to the local job centre, though of course it might not be reasonable in the circumstances to expect him to take any job that occurs. Refusal of an offer of reinstatement by the same employer can constitute failure to

---

[390] [1979] ICR 67, [1978] IRLR 486.   [391] See n 385.

[392] Employment Rights Act 1996, s 122(2).

[393] See Ch 6, heading 4(ii), p 458. See particularly Potter LJ's summary of the approach to be taken by a tribunal in *Wilding v BT plc* [2002] EWCA Civ 349, [2002] IRLR 524. In that case Sedley LJ suggested that a test akin to the range of reasonable responses test should be applied (so that the employee would only fail to mitigate if no reasonable employee would have acted in that way) but the other two lords justices did not mention or support this idea.

mitigate,[394] but failure to use the company's appeal procedure once dismissed probably will not on general principles;[395] it may be reasonable in certain circumstances to leave one industry altogether and retrain for another, even if that necessarily means a longer period without work.[396] If the employee unreasonably refuses to mitigate, that can lead to a reduction in his compensatory award,[397] though (on general principles) the onus lies upon the employer to prove failure to mitigate.[398] The tribunal is not to account for failure to mitigate by means of a percentage reduction, but instead must determine a date by which the employee would have been expected to secure employment and cut off compensation at that date.[399] The raising of the statutory limit on the compensatory award to its present level can be expected to result in more arguments by respondent employers on failure to mitigate, as part of a generally greater emphasis on calculating compensation.

(e) The order of deductions

In complex cases, where there may be several deductions to be made from an award of compensation (for example, for mitigatory amounts, contributory fault, a *Polkey* reduction and, of course, the statutory limit) a longstanding problem has been the order in which such deductions are to be made. This sounds very technical, but in practice can make a difference of thousands of pounds to the eventual award. It becomes particularly acute where the mitigatory amount in question is an ex gratia payment by the employer who, of course, wants to get full benefit of it when compensation is awarded. This, however, will only happen if that amount is deducted last (ie after the award has been subjected to all the other necessary adjustments). After years of confusing and often inconsistent case law, the EAT reviewed the whole question in *Digital Equipment Co Ltd v Clements (No 2)*[400] and produced a definitive order of deductions,

---

[394] *Sweetlove v Redbridge and Waltham Forest Area Health Authority* [1979] ICR 477, [1979] IRLR 195; *Gallear v J F Watson & Son Ltd* [1979] IRLR 306; cf *Tiptools Ltd v Curtis* [1973] IRLR 276, where the offer of re-engagement included demotion. In *Wilding v BT plc,*n 393, Potter LJ said that a tribunal may have to take into account in such a case the attitude of the former employer, the way the employee was treated and the employee's state of mind. The test may thus be both objective and subjective.

[395] *Seligman and Latz Ltd v McHugh* [1979] IRLR 130; cf *Hoover Ltd v Forde* [1980] ICR 239. The rule was approved (and *Hoover* not followed) in *William Muir (Bond 9) Ltd v Lamb* [1985] IRLR 95.

[396] *Sealey v Avon Aluminium Co Ltd* [1978] IRLR 285, IT. It may also be reasonable to mitigate by setting up in business rather than seeking other employment (even if the initial returns are less): *Aon Training Ltd v Dore* [2005] IRLR 891, CA.

[397] By taking it into account when fixing the multiplier: *Smith, Kline and French Laboratories Ltd v Coates* [1977] IRLR 220; *Peara v Enderlin Ltd* [1979] ICR 804. Note that the basic award is not subject to mitigation (except in the special case where the employee unreasonably refuses an offer of re-employment: s 122(1)), so that if the dismissed employee obtains new employment immediately he may get little or no compensatory award, but he remains eligible for the basic award (reflecting his loss of accrued employment rights).

[398] *Bessenden Properties Ltd v Corness* [1977] ICR 821n, [1974] IRLR 338, CA; *Fyfe v Scientific Furnishings Ltd* [1989] ICR 648, [1989] IRLR 331 (disapproving statements to the contrary in *Scottish and Newcastle Breweries plc v Halliday* [1986] ICR 577, [1986] IRLR 291).

[399] *Roofdec v O'Keefe* [2008] All ER (D) 195.

[400] [1997] ICR 237, [1997] IRLR 140. The case concerned a *Polkey* reduction of 50% and an ex gratia payment of £20,685, against a total loss of £43,136. If the *Polkey* reduction was taken off first, eventual compensation

starting with mitigatory amounts including ex gratia payments (thus meaning that an employer may *not* get the full benefit of such a payment).[401] When the case was appealed to the Court of Appeal,[402] a complication was introduced—on the facts of the case the ex gratia payment was in fact a non-statutory (ie more generous) redundancy payment and the court held that Parliament's intent[403] was that such payments were to be encouraged by being set off in full (subject only to the statutory limit), which could only be done by deducting them later. To that extent they allowed the employers' appeal; however, it is submitted that most of the reasoning of the EAT stands, subject only to this one qualification. On that basis, the order of deduction is:

(1) any mitigatory amounts (from the ex-employer or new employment) *other than* a non-statutory redundancy payment exceeding the statutory amount;

(2) any *Polkey* reduction (ie where a dismissal would have happened even if proper procedure had been observed);

(3) any contributory fault;

(4) any non-statutory redundancy payment;

(5) the statutory limit, if applicable.

It is to be hoped that order has now been introduced into this complex area. There may, however, now be one further complication. If the employee wins but either party is found to have ignored the ACAS Code on discipline and grievance procedures there is to be a decrease or increase in compensation of up to 25%.[404] By virtue of the Employment Rights Act 1996, section 124A, as amended by the Employment Act 2008, section 3(4), this reduction is to be made to the compensatory award 'immediately before' any reduction for contributory fault (so that this punitive reduction applies in full); in the above scheme of things, this presumably means that it would occur between (2) and (3) in an appropriate case.

was £883. If the ex gratia payment was taken off first eventual compensation was £11,225 (reduced to the then maximum of £11,000). The EAT held for the latter approach.

[401] A simple ex gratia pay-off (or attempt thereat) has thus always been inadvisable—it cannot be legally binding (Employment Rights Act 1996, s 203(1) which invalidates any attempt to contract out of the Act); finality can only be achieved by an ACAS (COT 3) settlement or a compromise agreement (s 203(2)–(4)).

[402] [1998] ICR 258, [1998] IRLR 134, CA, awarding compensation of £883.

[403] As evidenced by the Employment Rights Act 1996, s 123(7) which provides that any redundancy payment (statutory or otherwise) exceeding the basic award is to be set off then against the compensatory award.

[404] TULR(C)A 1992, s 207A.

8

REDUNDANCY, REORGANIZATION AND TRANSFERS OF UNDERTAKINGS

OVERVIEW

Redundancy, reorganization and transfers of undertakings all involve significant employment consequences, but happen for reasons unrelated to the affected workers. Wider economic circumstances cause the employer, respectively, to shut down or reduce the size of the workforce, to change the structure or even the nature of the work or to sell all or part of the business enterprise. These upheavals pose serious threats to the interests of the workers while at the same time representing inevitable and desirable business reactions, to be encouraged in a robust and fluid economy. This means that the analysis of dismissals and changes to terms and conditions in this context centres much less than the previous chapters on the relationships among the individual worker, the job and management, and much more on defining the nature of the employer's response to the economic circumstances and the impact of that response on employees as a group. Moreover, the same economic circumstances can, in a given factual scenario, involve combinations of redundancy, reorganization and transfer: a company threatened by hard times or stiff competition may need to sell part of its operation, dismiss some employees and change the terms and conditions of work for other employees. This chapter therefore discusses these situations together both for the practical benefit of grouping issues that arise from similar factual settings and for the analytical coherence of dealing together with protections designed to balance worker interests in job security with the general economic interest in lean, efficient and flexible enterprise. 'Redundancy' is a statutory concept for these purposes, not a common-sense one, and so it is first necessary to devote some time to its statutory definition, which can still cause problems 40 years after the original statutory coverage. The discussion will then focus on distinctions in how tribunals assess the fairness of redundancy dismissals as opposed to other dismissals caused by reorganization. Consideration of the other implications of a finding of redundancy—the duty to consult and inform and the redundancy payments scheme—will follow. Calculation of and claims for the statutory payment are relatively straightforward, but it is then necessary to look at certain more difficult special provisions, such as those applying to offers of alternative employment and redundancy through being laid off. The second half of the chapter then deals with transfers of undertakings. Determining the employees' rights on a transfer has been a matter of quite remarkable complexity ever since EU law required the transposition of the Acquired Rights Directive in 1981. The Transfer of Undertakings Regulations ('TUPE') were updated in 2006. These Regulations made some changes and improvements, but this is likely to remain one of the most complex areas of modern employment law.

1 REDUNDANCY AND REORGANIZATION

Questions of redundancy figure largely in the news in times of recession, often referred to as 'job losses', but resulting also from closures, or as unintended consequences of the reorganization of businesses. However, research has shown[1] that, even in recessionary times with the strong emphasis on 'down-sizing',[2] compulsory redundancy is *not* the first option chosen and that other methods of reduction or reorganization of the workforce are usually considered more desirable, including natural wastage, redeployment, early retirement and voluntary redundancy. Compulsory redundancy tends to be more common in the private sector, particularly where there is no recognized trade union.[3] Although therefore the majority of workforce reductions will be done in ways which, by and large, do not involve litigation (actual or potential) in employment law and will normally be dealt with by agreement (either longstanding or ad hoc), it is now necessary to consider the rights of those not so dealt with.

The difference between a redundancy and a non-redundancy dismissal that happens as a result of a reorganization is, as was already mentioned in Chapter 7, purely a function of the legal definition of redundancy. If company A responds to economic pressure by choosing to dismiss a specific number of employees viewed by the company as redundant, while company B reacts to similar circumstances by restructuring working processes and terms and conditions in such a way that several employees either leave or get dismissed for not cooperating with the changes, both situations could count, legally, as redundancies, fair or unfair; as fair dismissals 'for some other substantial reason'; or as unfair, non-redundancy dismissals. When a company shuts down or closes part of its operation, resulting dismissals will almost invariably qualify as redundancies. However, the mere fact of reductions in the workforce

---

[1] *Reasons for Leaving Last Job, 2011* (office of National Statistics 2011) available at <http://www.ons.gov.uk/ons/dcp171776_241679.pdf> (last accessed 16 January 2013); Millward et al 'Workplace Industrial Relations in Transition' *The ED/ESRC/PSI/ACAS Survey*, (1992) ch 9.

[2] Large sections of British management no longer communicate in English.   [3] See n 1.

begs the question of whether those reductions satisfy the statutory redundancy definition by resulting from a diminished need for work of a particular kind. The answer to this question determines (1) what kind of unfair dismissal analysis should apply to the case, (2) the employer's consultation and information obligations and (3) whether the case can involve a claim for a redundancy payment. Therefore this half of the chapter addresses first the statutory definitions of redundancy, then the distinct unfair dismissal frameworks for redundancy and non-redundancy reorganization dismissals, and finally the other redundancy protections, including consultation and redundancy payments.

(i) THE DEFINITION OF REDUNDANCY[4]

The word 'redundancy' can mean different things to different people and in different contexts. For the purposes of unfair dismissal and the redundancy payments scheme, however, it is defined in the Employment Rights Act 1996, section 139, and this definition is exhaustive.[5] Whether redundancy is the principal reason for a dismissal is determined not by whether the employer claims it as the reason and can prove it, but by whether the definition applies to the factual circumstances. An employee is dismissed by reason of redundancy if the dismissal is attributable wholly or mainly to:

(1) the fact that his employer has ceased, or intends to cease (a) to carry on the business for the purposes of which the employee was employed by him, or (b) to carry on that business in the place where the employee was so employed, or

(2) the fact that the requirements of that business (a) for employees to carry out work of a particular kind, or (b) for employees to carry out work of a particular kind in the place where the employee was employed by the employer have ceased or diminished or are expected to cease to diminish.

This definition applies in two principal cases—where the whole business closes down and where the business carries on (in some cases actually expanding) but its requirements for the people to perform certain services cease or diminish. In either case, this can happen either generally or just in the place where the applicant was employed to work. These major elements will now be considered.

(a) Closure of the business

This type of case is usually easy from the legal point of view (though it may be particularly appropriate for the compulsory consultation procedures which are discussed below). Some problems may arise, however, in defining the 'business' and the 'employer', although 'business' is widely defined in the Employment Rights Act

---

[4] See *Harvey* E [601].
[5] *Hindle v Percival Boats Ltd* [1969] 1 All ER 836, [1969] 1 WLR 174, CA (Lord Denning MR dissenting). Per Widgery LJ at 847 and 187 respectively; 'It is not the policy of this Act to reward long service and good

1996, section 235 as including a trade or profession or any activity[6] carried on by a body of persons, whether corporate or unincorporated. Moreover, if the business is a company which has other associated companies[7] and the economic factors in question affect that group as a whole or some other part of it, that too can be taken into account to satisfy the definition. It is also established that it is not necessary to show that the employer was the legal owner of the 'business' in question, only that that person was generally in control of it prior to its closure. Thus, when a sub-postmistress gave up the business of the sub-post office upon her retirement it could not be argued that the 'business' was that carried on by the post office (which of course had not ceased), and so her ex-employee was able to claim a redundancy payment.[8]

(b) Diminished requirements for employees to do work of a particular kind

Section 139 is designed to cover the case where the business remains (or even expands), but the functions of particular employees disappear; the obvious case of this would occur when the function is automated or, on the same principle, if the work is given instead to independent contractors,[9] or if work previously done by two employees is amalgamated and done by one, the other being dismissed.[10]

The question whether there has been a diminution in the requirements for employees to do work of a particular kind has caused problems for years. For years courts and tribunals treated this as being a question of whether the work of the claimant employee had disappeared. To decide whether an individual employee came within this wording, two tests evolved—the factual test (ie has the work he or she was actually doing gone?) and the contract test (has all the work that he or she *could* be required to

---

conduct as such, but only to compensate an employee who is dismissed for redundancy as defined in [s 139]'. The function of the tribunal is to apply the statutory definition to the facts, *not* to seek to look behind the facts and assess the rights and wrongs of the employer's decision to make the redundancy: *Moon v Homeworthy Furniture (Northern) Ltd* [1977] ICR 117, [1976] IRLR 298; *AUT v Newcastle-upon-Tyne University* [1987] ICR 317, [1988] IRLR 10; *James W Cook & Co (Wivenhoe) Ltd v Tipper* [1990] ICR 716, [1990] IRLR 386, CA; this is subject to the point made above, in the context of reorganization, that the tribunal may look into the reasons at least to the extent of being satisfied that they are genuine and not just a sham.

⁶ *Dallow Industrial Properties Ltd v Else* [1967] 2 QB 449, [1967] 2 All ER 30.
⁷ Defined in the Employment Rights Act 1996, s 231: 'any two employers are to be treated as associated if one is a company of which the other (directly or indirectly) has control, or if both are companies of which a third person (directly or indirectly) has control'. See Ch 2, heading 1(v), p 63.
⁸ *Thomas v Jones* [1978] ICR 274, EAT.
⁹ *Bromby & Hoare Ltd v Evans* [1972] ICR 113, 12 KIR 160; *Amos v Max-Arc Ltd* [1973] ICR 46, [1973] IRLR 285. Contracting out of services or activities has been a dominant theme in modern employment relations: 'The 1998 Workplace Employee Relations Survey—First Findings' (DTI/ACAS/ESRC/PSI; URN/98/934) p 7. Where the employee takes a job knowing that the work is subject to steady decline so that his employment can only be temporary, there may still be a redundancy when he is eventually dismissed: *Nottinghamshire County Council v Lee* [1980] ICR 635, [1980] IRLR 284, CA; this case must cast doubt on the correctness of the EAT's decision in *O'Hare v Rotaprint Ltd* [1980] ICR 94, [1980] IRLR 47.
¹⁰ *Sutton v Revlon Overseas Corpn* [1973] IRLR 173; *Carry All Motors Ltd v Pennington* [1980] ICR 806, [1980] IRLR 455. The fact that the total amount of work to be done remains constant is irrelevant; there is a redundancy provided the number of employees required to do it has diminished: *McCrea v Cullen & Davison Ltd* [1988] IRLR 30, NICA.

do under the contract gone?). It was the latter that eventually gained ground,[11] based on two decidedly ambiguous Court of Appeal decisions,[12] which in some cases had the effect of making it more difficult to establish redundancy where the contractual obligations were drafted to include a level of flexibility. However, on this point we have seen a major change of approach. This began with the judgment of Judge Clark in *Safeway Stores plc v Burrell*[13] which went back to the pure wording of the section and held that both the factual and contractual tests are wrong, and unnecessary glosses on that wording. It was pointed out that the wording considers the need for employees (plural), not that particular employee, and so what matters is whether a redundancy situation has arisen and whether he or she has lost employment because of it. Shortly afterwards another division of the EAT in *Church v West Lancashire NHS Trust*[14] disagreed strongly, but when the matter went to the House of Lords in *Murray v Foyle Meats Ltd*[15] it was *Safeway Stores* that was unequivocally approved. Giving the principal speech, Lord Irvine LC said:

> the language of [section 139(1)(b)] is in my view simplicity itself. It asks two questions of fact. The first is whether one or other of various states of economic affairs exists. In this case the relevant one is whether the requirements of the business for employees to carry out work of a particular kind have diminished. The second question is whether the dismissal is attributable, wholly or mainly to that state of affairs. This is a question of causation. In the present case, the Tribunal found as a fact that the requirements of the business for employees to work in the slaughter house had diminished. Secondly, they found that that state of affairs had led to the appellants being dismissed. That, in my opinion, is the end of the matter. This conclusion is in accordance with the analysis of the statutory provisions by Judge Peter Clark in *Safeway Stores plc v Burrell* and I need to say no more than that I entirely agree with his admirably clear reasoning and conclusions.

He went on to disapprove of the cases said to establish the contract test, and for good measure Lord Clyde giving the other speech castigated both previous tests as unnecessary.

This reinterpretation is very welcome and of great importance generally. However, it arose in the two EAT cases in a specialized and difficult area, known as a 'bumping' redundancy. This occurs where, for example, within a department employee A's job disappears, but A (thought to be a good worker) is retained and given B's job, with B being dismissed instead. Is B redundant? Under the old tests, B's job is still there, and so he is not redundant, but under the new approach there is a diminution in the need

---

[11]   *Cowen v Haden Ltd* [1983] ICR 1, [1982] IRLR 314, CA; *Pink v White* [1985] IRLR 489.

[12]   *Nelson v BBC* [1977] ICR 649, [1977] IRLR 148, CA and *Nelson v BBC (No 2)* [1980] ICR 110, [1979] IRLR 346, CA.

[13]   [1997] ICR 523, [1997] IRLR 200, EAT.   [14]   [1998] ICR 423, [1998] IRLR 4.

[15]   [1999] ICR 827, [1999] IRLR 562, HL. Arguably, the broader approach in this case brings the definition more into line with that now used in the Trade Union and Labour Relations (Consolidation) Act 1992, s 195 (on collective redundancies), ie 'dismissal for a reason not related to the individual concerned or for a number of reasons all of which are not so related'.

for employees (plural) to carry out a particular kind of work and B's dismissal is causally linked ('attributable') to it, and so now B is indeed redundant. Given the curious
agendas behind some of these cases this is in fact usually to the *employer's* advantage,
redundancy often being the easier and cheaper option, whereas the employee may
want *not* to be redundant, in order to open up an unfair dismissal action. Arguably,
this is why the EAT in *Church* were so against this development especially when allied
to what they saw as an objectionable *way* of bumping by the employer, namely sacking
all employees and 'inviting' them to reapply for the jobs left (where, the EAT feared,
there would be too much scope for subjective choice and favouritism by the management). However, *Church* must now be considered wrong, and in a bumping case there
now will normally be a redundancy. However, it may be that this will have the effect of
increasing the importance of an unfair dismissal challenge based on the methods and
procedures used to effect the eventual shedding of labour, especially the process for
deciding whom to select for redundancy.[16] This may be the real answer to the problems
faced in *Church*.

There remains, however, one further element of the definition of redundancy which
is not affected by *Murray* (not being relevant on the facts of the case, and so are not
addressed). This is the question of what is meant by 'work of a particular kind', a particularly crucial concept where for example, the numbers involved remain much the
same (or indeed may even be increasing overall) but the *skills* required change. There
is much case law on this, and the law clearly looks at the *work function* of the employee
within the organization, not necessarily at his particular job at the time, still less at
any particular job title. Thus, the job may change over time in its organization (and
thereby, in some cases, in its suitability for, and attractiveness to, a particular employee)
but, as long as the function remains, an employee who is dismissed for refusing to
accept the changes (or who walks out because of them and then claims constructive
dismissal under section 136(1)(c)) is *not* 'redundant'. In *Chapman v Goonvean and
Rostowrack China Clay Co Ltd*[17] ten employees were provided with free transport to
work; when three were made redundant during a trade recession the transport became
uneconomic and the employer discontinued it for the remaining seven who, though
offered continued employment with the employer, gave in their notice, left the employment and claimed redundancy payments. The Court of Appeal held that they were
not redundant since the work that they performed had not ceased or diminished (the
employer had shown that the seven were replaced by other employees taken on to do
their work); the only change was in the organization and attractiveness of the jobs for
the time being. The facts of this case concern a relatively incidental aspect of employment, but the principle goes further and can apply to changes in the job structure itself,
for there is no definite right to have employment continued indefinitely on the same

---

[16] For unfair redundancy, see heading 1(ii), p 557.
[17] [1973] 2 All ER 1063, [1973] ICR 310, CA, overruling *Dutton v C H Bailey Ltd* [1968] 2 Lloyd's Rep 122, 3
ITR 355; see also *Arnold v Thomas Harrington Ltd* [1969] 1 QB 312, [1967] 2 All ER 866.

terms and the courts and tribunals have ensured that an employer can take necessary steps to increase the efficiency of his enterprise without being liable to make redundancy payments unless there is a genuine diminution in the work function in question. In *Johnson v Nottinghamshire Combined Police Authority*[18] two clerks, whose work had been reorganized from a five-day week to a shift system operating over six days per week to increase overall efficiency, refused to accept this and claimed redundancy pay (in spite of the fact that they had been replaced by two new employees), but this was refused by the Court of Appeal on the ground that the kind of work remained the same and so the reorganization was not due to redundancy:

> It is settled ... that an employer is entitled to reorganise his business so as to improve its efficiency and, in doing so, to propose to his staff a change in the terms and conditions of their employment; and to dispense with their services if they do not agree. Such a change does not automatically give the staff a right to redundancy payments. It only does so if the change in the terms and conditions is due to a redundancy situation.[19]

A similar result was achieved in *Lesney Products Ltd v Nolan*[20] where the work of machine setters was altered from a day shift and a night shift to a double day shift system, with a consequent decrease in overtime payments; when six of the setters refused to work the new system and claimed redundancy payments, the Court of Appeal held against them since the amount of work to be done remained constant, though reorganized on to a daytime basis (the undoubted overall 'redundancy situation' having been dealt with by the company by discontinuing the night shift worked by another class of employees who were not parties to the action). Moreover, this principle is not restricted to alterations in the structure or pattern of working hours and conditions, but may also apply to necessary changes in the discharging of the employee's function, for, as long as that function remains the same overall, the employer may introduce new methods and technology to increase the efficiency of the function and if the employee is either unwilling or unable to adapt to them, he may be dismissed without being redundant.[21] These reorganization dismissals could still be unfair, but they will be analysed either as misconduct dismissals (refusal to obey a lawful instruction) or 'some other substantial reason'.

It can be seen from the above discussion that, under this head of redundancy, much will depend on the difficult question of fact—how radical does a change in the job, or the reorganization of it, have to be before it can be said that the function itself has

---

[18] [1974] 1 All ER 1082, [1974] ICR 170, CA.

[19] Per Lord Denning MR [1974] 1 All ER 1082 at 1084, [1974] ICR 170 at 176; the phrase 'redundancy situation' is clarified in his Lordship's judgment in *Lesney Products Ltd v Nolan* (n 20). The last two sentences in the dictum are important, for they make it clear that there *could* be a redundancy in certain circumstances; the EAT reaffirmed that there is no rule of law that a change of hours or shifts cannot produce a redundancy—it remains ultimately a question of fact for the tribunal: *MacFisheries Ltd v Findlay* [1985] ICR 160.

[20] [1977] ICR 235, [1977] IRLR 77, CA.

[21] *North Riding Garages Ltd v Butterwick* [1967] 2 QB 56, [1967] 1 All ER 644; *Hindle v Percival Boats Ltd* [1969] 1 All ER 836, [1969] 1 WLR 174, CA. It is argued above that the courts might be willing to apply in such cases an implied term of reasonable adaptation to new methods and techniques: see Ch 3, heading 4(ii), p 165 and *Cresswell v Board of Inland Revenue* [1984] 2 All ER 713, [1984] ICR 508.

changed? To put it in the language of section 139—what *is* work of that 'particular kind'? If the change is great enough to turn it into work of a different kind, then the employee who is unwilling or unable to perform the new function can claim that he is redundant since his old function has disappeared.[22] In the earlier cases, this was not easy since the courts and tribunals in general took a fairly wide view of what constitutes one type of work (thus allowing the employer more scope for reorganization without having to make redundancy payments); thus, the function of 'barmaid' remained the same, even when an older style public house was transformed into a 'road house' requiring barmaids with certain attributes which no amount of retraining could possibly have produced in the original incumbent,[23] and the function of 'boatbuilder' remained the same even though the boatyard went over to fibreglass boats instead of the wooden ones which the dismissed employee was by long practice used to making.[24] Such questions may raise difficult borderline cases,[25] and the approach in the later case of *Murphy v Epsom College*[26] shows a narrower approach to 'kind of work' and emphasizes that if that changes there may be a redundancy even if the redundant employee is immediately replaced by someone else skilled in the new kind of work (ie where there is no net decrease in the workforce). In that case the college's heating system was modernized, calling for new skills to maintain it. One of the existing two plumbers said that he was unwilling/unable to perform all the necessary new functions; he was dismissed and replaced with a heating technician. The Court of Appeal upheld the tribunal's decision that the dismissed employee was redundant since the employer's need for *plumbers* was reduced from two to one on the reorganization (with its corresponding requirement for a heating technician instead). However, more recently the EAT reminded employees that even extensive changes to the terms and conditions of work will not amount to a redundancy if the underlying work (in this case selling insurance) remains the same.[27]

This whole problem flows from the emphasis in section 139 on the overall work function and not the particulars of the job as organized at the material time; it has been argued that this should not be so, as it puts the financial risk of a particular job becoming uneconomic upon the employee, rather than upon the employer.[28] However, the courts have consistently adopted the view that this legislation is not meant to be a brake upon necessary reorganization, and it can be argued that the harsher result of this may be mitigated by two factors: first, it has been stated by the courts that

---

[22] *Robinson v British Island Airways Ltd* [1978] ICR 304, [1977] IRLR 477, a case where the employee was arguing that he was *not* redundant, in order to claim the more generous remedies for unfair dismissal. A redundancy can arise from a change in specialisms within an overall job: *BBC v Farnworth* [1998] ICR 1116, EAT.

[23] *Vaux and Associated Breweries Ltd v Ward* (1968) 3 ITR 385.

[24] *Hindle v Percival Boats Ltd* [1969] 1 All ER 836, [1969] 1 WLR 174, CA.

[25] See, eg, *European Chefs (Catering) Ltd v Currell* (1971) 6 ITR 37.

[26] [1985] ICR 80, [1984] IRLR 271, CA.

[27] *Martland and Others v Cooperative Insurance Society Ltd* [2008] All ER (D) 166.

[28] See Freedland (1977) 6 ILJ 237.

a bogus reorganization is not to be used by an employer as a cover for dismissals which are in fact due to redundancy;[29] secondly, since 1971 it has been possible for an employee dismissed because of changing work patterns (or resigning because of them and claiming constructive dismissal) to bring an action for unfair dismissal against the employer if he thinks he has been harshly treated over the change or reorganization (or if he has grounds to doubt the bona fides of the employer's actions), and this action may lead to more generous remedies (especially since the major increase in the compensation limit in the Employment Relations Act 1999), so that in many cases it may be in the employee's favour *not* to be in law redundant, since that would prima facie be a *fair* ground for dismissal.[30] Therefore there can easily arise (especially in reorganization cases) the topsy-turvy situation of the employee (wanting more than the statutory redundancy payment) arguing that his dismissal was *not* for redundancy and the employer (happy to keep the labour-related cost of the reorganization down to statutory redundancy payments) arguing that it was, as indeed was the case in *Murphy v Epsom College*.[31] Thus, the narrower approach to 'kind of work' in that case, with its easier finding of redundancy, paradoxically may operate *against* the employee's wider interests.[32]

(c) In the place where the employee was so employed'

Both of the above heads of redundancy envisage the relevant economic factors producing effects either generally or only in the place where the employee worked. It may therefore be vital to know what that 'place' is. It could cover the whole of the UK or be as small an area as one part of one city.[33] The problem often arises in cases where the employer orders the employee to move to a new workplace, for example if the company wishes to close down a factory in Ipswich, telling its employees there to work in its other factory in Norwich. The approach generally adopted here in the past has been that the question of law involved is whether the employer has *contractual* authority to give the order to move, so that 'in the place where the employee was so

---

[29] *Johnson v Nottinghamshire Combined Police Authority* [1974] 1 All ER 1082 at 1087, [1974] ICR 170 at 179, per Stephenson LJ.

[30] Employment Rights Act 1996, s 98(2)(c).

[31] See n 26. This may blur the edge between a redundancy dismissal and a dismissal because of a business reorganization; it is important for the employer to decide which route to go down, see eg *Shawkat v Nottingham City Hospital NHS Trust* [2001] EWCA Civ 954, [2001] IRLR 555, CA. This kind of perverted logic can also occur in TUPE cases (see heading 2(vi), p 610) with the employees arguing that they have *no* TUPE protection, in order to cash in their redundancy rights against the transferor employers and start afresh with the transferee employer.

[32] Though it is not necessarily so simple—even if the employee succeeds in showing (in an unfair dismissal case arising from a reorganization) that he was *not* dismissed for redundancy, but rather for refusing to agree to changes insisted upon by the employer, contrary to his contractual rights, there is still the danger that the tribunal might hold the dismissal *fair*, as for 'some other substantial reason' (see heading 1(ii), p 557). In such a case he would receive *neither* a redundancy payment *nor* unfair dismissal compensation.

[33] *Rowbotham v Arthur Lee & Sons Ltd* [1975] ICR 109, [1974] IRLR 377; *Air Canada v Lee* [1978] ICR 1202, [1978] IRLR 392, EAT.

employed' means in the place where he could be obliged to work under the terms of his contract of employment, not simply where he had in fact been working prior to the order to move.[34] If the contract envisages working in the new location (for example, in the example used, a term that the employee would work anywhere in East Anglia), then the employee who refuses is dismissed for failure to comply (even if he had in fact been working solely in Ipswich for years); if the contract does not envisage this (ie Ipswich only), then the employee has prima facie a redundancy claim based upon the closure of the Ipswich factory.

Questions have therefore often arisen as to the construction of the individual's contract of employment. The contract may contain an express term[35] which will usually dispose of the matter as the traditional view is that a clear express term should not normally be subject to extension or restriction by any claimed implied term.[36] If there is no such express term the tribunal must consider whether a term should be implied in the contract[37] by looking at all the relevant evidence. In *O'Brien v Associated Fire Alarms Ltd*[38] two electricians worked for a company at its Liverpool office, working exclusively in that city (although the company operated throughout the United Kingdom and the Liverpool office controlled the whole of the north west); when the company's business in Liverpool diminished and they were asked to work in Cumberland, they refused because it would have meant working away from home and they were dismissed. Their claims for redundancy payments were upheld by the Court of Appeal on the basis that, there being no relevant express term in their contracts, there was no implied term obliging them to work outside daily travelling distance from their homes, particularly as they had never been called upon to do so before and there was no clear evidence of any implied agreement to do so.[39] However, in *Stevenson v Teesside Bridge and Engineering Ltd*[40] a steel erector who refused to move to another site when work on the existing site (which was close to his home) finished was not entitled to a redundancy payment since travelling from site to site was found by the Divisional Court to be an integral part of that trade (which there was evidence he had accepted when interviewed for the post) and the contract of employment, though

---

[34] *Sutcliffe v Hawker Siddeley Aviation Ltd* [1973] ICR 560, [1973] IRLR 304, NIRC; *Rank Xerox Ltd v Churchill* [1988] IRLR 280, EAT.

[35] As eg in *Sutcliffe v Hawker Siddeley Aviation Ltd* (above) and *United Kingdom Atomic Energy Authority v Claydon* [1974] ICR 128, [1974] IRLR 6. If the employer wishes to rely on a mobility clause, he should do so clearly, and not as an afterthought: *Curling v Securicor Ltd* [1992] IRLR 549, EAT.

[36] *Nelson v BBC* [1977] ICR 649, [1977] IRLR 148, CA. However, modern cases have shown movement towards a concept of *overriding* implied terms (especially the term of trust and respect); it is possible that this development (if it continues) could spread into redundancy law.

[37] *GEC Telecommunications Ltd v McAllister* [1975] IRLR 346. For the implication of terms into contracts of employment, see Ch 3, heading 2, p 124.

[38] [1969] 1 All ER 93, [1968] 1 WLR 1916, CA; *Mumford v Boulton and Paul (Steel Construction) Ltd* (1970) 5 ITR 222; *Managers (Holborn) Ltd v Hohne* [1977] IRLR 230, EAT.

[39] While each case must depend on its facts, it is likely that a term that an employee may be required to work *within* reasonable daily travel will be easy to imply where the contract is silent on the matter: *Courtaulds Northern Spinning Ltd v Sibson* [1988] ICR 451, [1988] IRLR 305, CA.

[40] [1971] 1 All ER 296, 10 KIR 53.

not containing an express mobility clause, was held to envisage such mobility through terms relating to travelling and subsistence allowances, and the transfer of contracts.

However, this whole contractual approach had long been criticized on the ground that a practical and geographical test (where was the employee *actually* working?) would fit better the purpose and intent of the legislation. The EAT in *Bass Leisure Ltd v Thomas*[41] agreed with that approach, held that the authority in favour of the contractual approach was only persuasive, and applied a geographical test. Thus, an employee whose work at a Coventry depot had ceased with its closure *was* redundant, even though the employers had a contractual right (which they had sought to exercise) to require her to work at another depot 20 miles away, where she did not wish to work. In this particular case, the geographical approach was in the employee's favour, but this is an area ripe for boomerang effects of decisions, and the overall result of this approach (if generally followed) is that it may make it easier for an employer to make an employee redundant (a prima facie fair ground of dismissal) at one location, even where there is a mobility clause in the contract. This could be significant where an employer wants to close down one whole location (where perhaps productivity and labour relations have not been good), dispense with the workforce there and build up production elsewhere by taking on new staff. Something of this sort occurred in *High Table Ltd v Horst*[42] where waitresses dismissed by a service company when the client no longer wanted their work were held to be redundant, in spite of a mobility clause in their contracts. The Court of Appeal approved *Bass Leisure*, on the basis that a factual approach to the actual place of work will normally resolve the question, subject to the caveat that if the employee has in fact been mobile it may well be necessary to consider the terms of the contract (as in the older case law considered above). Thus, their approach is an amalgam, though with a normal bias towards the factual/geographical test, applied by the good sense of the tribunal. Two points are worth noting: (1) the court seemed to view this decision as pro-employee (ie redundancy rights are not to be prejudiced by the inclusion of a mobility clause), but as seen above it will often be in the employer's interests to establish a redundancy (and indeed, the end result of the case was to allow the *employers'* appeal); (2) the employer may now have the best of both worlds with a mobility clause, in that if he tries to enforce it and the employee refuses to go, the latter is potentially subject to fair dismissal through disobedience to a lawful order, whereas if the work dries up in one area but the employer decides *not* to enforce the mobility clause and simply dismisses those working there, the result may well be a simple redundancy (which is *not* defeated by the existence of the clause).

There is, however, whatever the test, one further factor that may cloud the issue; as will be seen below, a redundant employee may be under an obligation to accept suitable alternative work if it is offered by the employer[43] and it is possible that although an employee may have a right to refuse to transfer elsewhere (as in *O'Brien*'s case, or if the

---

[41] [1994] IRLR 104.   [42] [1998] ICR 409, [1997] IRLR 513, CA.
[43] Employment Rights Act 1996, s 141.

geographical test is widely applied), in certain cases where the distance is not great the offer to work at the new location may constitute an offer of suitable alternative work which the employee would be advised to accept.

(ii) DISMISSAL IN REDUNDANCY AND REORGANIZATION

Redundancy is a prima facie fair ground for dismissal. Dismissals can also be fair for 'some other substantial reason' (SOSR) if the dismissal results from an employee's refusal to acquiesce to changes made by an employer, in response to economic pressures, that a reasonable employer would make in the circumstances despite knowing that workers would object. Only redundancy is in play if the employer reacts to difficult times by going out of business or shutting down part of the operation, leading to job losses. Similarly, little controversy attaches to the traditional 'downsizing' scenario where, for example, a drop-off in demand for the company's product requires that several workers lose their jobs: this clearly gets analysed as a redundancy. However, when the employer reorganizes the business and thereby causes job losses, or simply chooses to dismiss several people in response to pressing financial circumstances, the dismissals might not satisfy the 'diminished need for work of a particular kind' definition, and would need to be defended on a SOSR basis, or might enjoy no defence at all. For example, if an employer were to respond to competitive pressure by dismissing 20 workers and immediately hiring 10 new workers with greater skill, experience and industry to do precisely the same amount of work previously performed by 20, it is not clear whether all 20, or even any, of the dismissals could be attributed to a diminished need for work of a particular kind. A more interesting and more common question arises, however, in the scenario where a reorganization of the business arguably either results in or results from a diminished need for work of a particular kind. In this kind of situation, what makes dismissals redundancies, as opposed to SOSR dismissals, is not how the employer conceives of its decision, but whether the dismissals can be factually 'attributed to' a diminished need for work of a particular kind (WOPK). Thus, even if the employer thinks it is making workers redundant, and supplies all of the appropriate consultation and notice, the dismissals will need to be defended under SOSR logic if the evidence does not support a causal link with diminished WOPK. Similarly (and more likely), if the employer reorganizes, and employees are dismissed for refusing to comply with unilateral contract changes effected by the reorganization, the dismissals will be unintended redundancies if they are factually attributable to a diminished need for WOPK; indeed, this situation can even give rise to constructive redundancies, which will almost certainly be unfair owing to a lack of consultation and other procedural steps.

In an unfair dismissal case, as discussed in Chapter 7, the employer must establish the principal reason for dismissal. However, proving the reason for an economic dismissal works somewhat differently from, for example, proving that misconduct was the reason. The existence of a statutory definition means that it is not a simple matter of the employer identifying the alleged reason and either succeeding or failing to prove that he or she based the dismissal on that reason. Instead, the employer might seek to prove a reorganization SOSR, but the tribunal can find that the facts satisfy the redundancy definition: if so, the dismissal is a redundancy and cannot be something else. If the employer seeks to prove that a dismissal was a redundancy, it will not suffice to prove that the employer believed it was a redundancy and meant to make the employee redundant: if the facts do not show the dismissal to have been attributable to a redundancy situation, it cannot be a redundancy. The statutory presumption of redundancy that exists in the redundancy payments scheme[44] is not applicable in an unfair dismissal claim.[45] Another implication of the redundancy definition is that once the facts are shown to satisfy the definition, a tribunal may not look behind that reason and consider whether the employer really was obliged to make employees redundant and, if so, whose fault it was—that economic decision remains with the employer,[46] and if she succeeds in showing it as the principal reason her primary liability will only be to make the statutory redundancy payments. In a simple redundancy case, for example upon a properly conducted liquidation,[47] that will be the appropriate action to bring, but it is also possible for a dismissed employee to claim both a redundancy payment and unfair dismissal,[48] since a redundancy dismissal is only prima facie fair and may become unfair either under special statutory provisions, or under the general test of reasonableness contained in section 98(4).

(a) Unfair redundancy

A redundancy dismissal is deemed to be unfair by a combination now of section 153 of the Trade Union and Labour Relations (Consolidation) Act 1992 and section 105 of the Employment Rights Act 1996 if the employee can show that the circumstances producing the redundancy applied equally to other comparable employees[49] in the same undertaking who were not dismissed, and the applicant employee was chosen for dismissal because of union membership or activities, or non-membership[50] or for an 'inadmissible reason' (covering the categories where dismissal is made automatically unfair, for example where the reason for dismissal is contrary to the special protection afforded to pregnancy or childbirth, making health and safety complaints, asserting statutory rights, being a protected shop-worker, acting as an employee representative or pension fund trustee, exercising rights to the national minimum wage or under the Working Time Regulations, Part-time Worker Regulations or Fixed-term Employee Regulations or the protection given to whistleblowers). The aim of these provisions is to prevent an employer from using the more subtle technique of getting rid of perceived troublemakers or difficult cases by a later redundancy selection (an immediate dismissal

---

[44] Employment Rights Act 1996, s 170(2).
[45] *Midland Foot Comfort Centre Ltd v Richmond* [1973] 2 All ER 294, [1973] IRLR 141.
[46] *Moon v Homeworthy Furniture (Northern) Ltd* [1977] ICR 117, [1976] IRLR 298; *James W Cook & Co (Wivenhoe) Ltd v Tipper* [1990] ICR 716, [1990] IRLR 386, CA.
[47] *Fox Bros (Clothes) Ltd v Bryant* [1979] ICR 64, [1978] IRLR 485.
[48] Though he cannot receive double compensation: Employment Rights Act 1996, s 122(4).
[49] *Powers v A Clarke & Co (Smethwick) Ltd* [1981] IRLR 483.
[50] This head of unfair dismissal generally is considered at Ch 9, heading 2(i), p 636.

on any of these grounds now being declared automatically unfair: see the further discussion).

There used to be a second ground of statutory unfair redundancy dismissal, where the dismissal was in breach of a collectively agreed redundancy procedure (or arrangement).[51] The aim of this longstanding provision was to give statutory backing to such procedures. However, by 1994 the previous government took the view that it was out of line with their current thinking (being an element of the collective co-determination model of industrial relations that they had spent years dismantling); traditionally, such procedures had been heavily based on LIFO (last-in-first-out) which was seen by unions as, at least, the less unfair way of selecting employees.[52] However, in times of recession and declining union influence and recognition, many managers were seeking to move away from LIFO and towards far more rigorous procedures of selection on merit and ability, regardless of length of service. Redundancy procedures were thus being radically altered or scrapped altogether (at a time when large numbers of redundancies were having to be made, and when selection on merit was seen as an essential aid to business survival)[53] and so the decision was taken to repeal the statutory protection for redundancy procedures altogether.[54] The present government have shown no intention to reinstate it.

This removal of collectively based safeguards in redundancy cases has placed even more emphasis on what has been the most important development in this branch of unfair dismissal law, namely that (in addition to any special statutory provisions) an employee may claim that his dismissal for redundancy was unfair *generally*, ie that, under section 98(4), the employer's conduct was unreasonable having regard to equity and the substantial merits of the case. This significant widening of the approach to redundancy cases was originally approved by the Court of Appeal in *Bessenden Properties Ltd v Corness*[55] and remains an important head of unfair dismissal, primarily because of the greater compensation available than the amount recoverable as a simple redundancy payment. This widening allows a tribunal some discretion to review the overall fairness of the dismissal and has led in the cases to the evolution of three general requirements upon an employer who is about to make an employee redundant.[56] The first is that he must not select that employee unfairly; blatant unfairness may be challenged in this way, but in many cases it will be difficult to establish for many different factors may be involved and so questions such as efficiency and

---

[51] This used to be contained in the Employment Protection (Consolidation) Act 1978, s 59(1)(b).

[52] In 1990 length of service as the criterion was found in 70% of workplaces with a recognized union but in only 35% of workplaces without such recognition: Millward et al *Workplace Industrial Relations in Transition* (1992) 325. The survey also found that, where redundancy procedures still existed, there was no evidence of LIFO becoming less common.

[53] This was commented on particularly in the *ACAS Annual Reports* 1991 p 16 and 1992 p 12.

[54] Deregulation and Contracting Out Act 1994, s 36.   [55] [1977] ICR 821n, [1974] IRLR 338, CA.

[56] These three requirements are now so well established that they should automatically be considered by a tribunal in an unfair redundancy case, even if not specifically raised by an applicant (eg where he or she is a litigant in person): *Langston v Cranfield University* [1998] IRLR 172, EAT.

suitability of the employee may arguably be just as reasonably relied upon as a general LIFO principle. The second is that the employer should make reasonable efforts where practicable to look for alternative employment within the firm (or possibly within the group to which the firm belongs),[57] though tribunals should not expect unrealistic efforts to be made in what may be difficult circumstances.[58] The third is that, as a rule, the employer should consult the employee and give him reasonable warning of impending redundancy;[59] this requirement has been said to increase in importance the more the employer moves away from easily applied criteria for selection such as LIFO, towards more judgemental criteria based on work performance and company need.[60] On a general level, its importance was strengthened by the renewed emphasis on procedure in *Polkey* (below), itself a redundancy dismissal case, in the light of which it has been subsequently said by the EAT that 'the importance of such consultation cannot be over-emphasised'.[61]

These guidelines were reaffirmed and recast by the EAT in *Williams v Compair Maxam Ltd*,[62] giving additional emphasis to two further criteria. The first is that where the employer recognizes a union the necessary consultations will normally of course be with that union, and where this is the case the employer should give as much warning as possible of the impending redundancies, seek to agree criteria for selection with the union, review the eventual selection with the union to consider

---

[57] *Vokes Ltd v Bear* [1974] ICR 1, [1973] IRLR 363; *Modern Injection Moulds Ltd v Price* [1976] ICR 370, [1976] IRLR 172. However, a requirement to look within the group, not just within the firm itself, was looked on with disfavour by the Scottish EAT in *Barratt Construction Ltd v Dalrymple* [1984] IRLR 385, and by the English EAT in *MDH Ltd v Sussex* [1986] IRLR 123, EAT.

[58] *British United Shoe Machinery Co Ltd v Clarke* [1978] ICR 70, [1977] IRLR 297. In *Thomas and Betts Manufacturing Ltd v Harding* [1980] IRLR 255, CA, it was said that s 98 is so wide that this may mean looking for other jobs for A to do, even if that means dismissing B instead (if B has less seniority than A), ie a 'bumping' redundancy (though cf the problems with this concept, heading 1(i), p 550); once again, however, the Scottish EAT was unwilling to apply this wider approach: *Green v A&I Fraser (Wholesale Fish Merchants) Ltd* [1985] IRLR 55. Note that statutory preference (in finding other work) is given to (1) women on maternity leave when made redundant (Maternity and Parental Leave etc Regulations 1999, SI 1999/3312, reg 10), (2) employees on adoption leave when made redundant (Paternity and Adoption Leave Regulations 2002, SI 2002/2788, reg 23) and (3) disabled employees, where the employer is making reasonable adjustments; *Kent County Council v Mingo* [2000] IRLR 90).

[59] *Clarkson International Tools Ltd v Short* [1973] ICR 191, [1973] IRLR 90; *Kelly v Upholstery and Cabinet Works (Amesbury) Ltd* [1977] IRLR 91; *British United Shoe Machinery Co Ltd v Clarke* [1978] ICR 70, [1977] IRLR 297; cf *Atkinson v George Lindsay & Co* [1980] IRLR 196, Ct of Sess. The importance of this factor was reaffirmed by the EAT in *Freud v Bentalls Ltd* [1983] ICR 77, [1982] IRLR 443 and *Holden v Bradville Ltd* [1985] IRLR 483. The requirement is for warning and consultation, not just one: *Rowell v Hubbard Group Services* [1995] IRLR 195, EAT.

[60] *E-Zec Medical Transport Service Ltd v Ms S A Gregory* UKEAT/0192/08/MAA (redundancy dismissal unfair because of insufficient consultation on subjective selection criteria); *Graham v ABF Ltd* [1986] IRLR 90; *Ferguson v Prestwick Circuits Ltd* [1992] IRLR 266. Small size of an enterprise may affect the level of consultation, but cannot excuse total lack of it: *De Grasse v Stockwell Tools Ltd* [1992] IRLR 269, EAT.

[61] *Dyke v Hereford and Worcester County Council* [1989] ICR 800 at 807, per Wood J. A particularly useful summary of the consultation requirements is to be found in the judgment of Judge Clark in *Mugford v Midland Bank plc* [1997] ICR 399, [1997] IRLR 208.

[62] [1982] ICR 156, [1982] IRLR 83.

whether it is in accordance with those criteria and consider union representations on selection. This point will now have to be expanded to include the case where there is no recognized union but, because of the added rules requiring consultation with employee representatives,[63] there are collective redundancies requiring by law such consultation; lack of it may affect the fairness of any eventual individual redundancies. One major point of difficulty is whether there has to be *double* consultation, ie with both union or employee representatives and individual employee. In *Walls Meat Co Ltd v Selby*[64] the Court of Appeal declined to lay down any principle requiring such two-stage consultation; on the other hand, Balcombe LJ did say that in a particular case good industrial practice might require it. The court did uphold a tribunal decision of unfair dismissal based on failure to consult the individual as well as the union, and other cases have assumed the need to involve the individual as well.[65] This will therefore be a matter heavily dependent on the circumstances of a particular case, with much discretion given to a tribunal, and resulting uncertainly for an employer in knowing whether he has done enough to resist an individual challenge of unfair dismissal. The second is that when working out criteria for selection (whether or not with union agreement) the emphasis must be on criteria which leave as little as possible to subjective assessments by the people making the selection, but rather are capable of being objectively applied on the basis of matters such as length of service, experience and efficiency.[66] It has more recently been clarified, however, that the mere fact that individual judgement, as opposed to purely quantifiable metrics, plays some role in the decision does not make it unfair, and that so long as the decision is not completely subjective, there is no need for selection decisions to be reduced to 'box-ticking exercises'.[67]

The reaction to *Williams v Compair Maxam Ltd* has been mixed. It initially fared badly in the Scottish courts with the Scottish EAT showing itself unwilling to apply it to redundancies in smaller firms, especially when they are not unionized,[68] and the Court of Session in *Buchanan v Tilcon Ltd*[69] taking a broader, less specific approach to redundancy cases, assuming that it will be relatively easy for an employer to show a redundancy dismissal to have been fair generally, once he has shown compliance with

---

[63] See heading 1(iii), p 572.   [64] [1989] ICR 601, CA.

[65] In *Huddersfield Parcels Ltd v Sykes* [1981] IRLR 115 it was held that union consultation was not enough if the employee himself is left in the dark, and the general guidance on handling redundancies by Wood P in *Dyke v Hereford and Worcester County Council* [1989] ICR 800 assumes that, at least in most cases, consultation will be with both; *Rolls-Royce Motor Cars Ltd v Price* [1993] IRLR 203 is to like effect.

[66] Thus, in *Williams v Compair Maxam Ltd* the redundancy was held to be unfair, partly on the ground that the criteria established by the employer (that those retained would be those 'who, in the opinion of the managers concerned, would be able to keep the company viable') lacked the necessary objectivity. See also *E-Zec Medical Transport Service Ltd v Ms S A Gregory* n 60.

[67] *Mitchells of Lancaster (Brewers) v Tattersall* UKEAT/0605/11/SM, available at <http://www.bailii.org/uk/cases/UKEAT/2012/0605_11_2905.html> (last accessed 20 January 2013).

[68] *Meikle v McPhail (Charleston Arms)* [1983] IRLR 351; *A Simpson & Son (Motors) v Reid and Findlater* [1983] IRLR 401; *Gray v Shetland Norse Preserving Co Ltd* [1985] IRLR 53.

[69] [1983] IRLR 417, Ct of Sess.

the specific statutory requirements. The English EAT, however, applied it,[70] but subject to the qualification that this is an area in which it is particularly important that the tribunal should apply the 'range of reasonable responses' test[71] and not simply impose its own view as to how its members might have handled the redundancy.[72] As seen several times already, *Polkey v A E Dayton Services Ltd*,[73] with its emphasis on the continuing importance of procedures, was a landmark case generally, and in this context it is useful to remember that it was in fact an unfair redundancy case. Curiously, *Williams v Compair Maxam Ltd* was not specifically approved but, although Lord Mackay LC did not hold that a breach of normal procedure would invariably make a dismissal unfair, the overall effect of *Polkey* in reinstating procedural fairness as a central factor must be taken as backing for *Williams*. This was certainly the tenor of subsequent reported cases,[74] a point of some significance given the generally high level of unfair redundancy claims in recent years.

However, possibly as a reaction to that high level of claims, two later Court of Appeal decisions have shown yet another potential change in emphasis, placing qualifications on findings of unfairness, and demonstrating again the volatility of this area of law. The first qualification concerns those cases where the normal procedures can reasonably be dispensed with. As stated above, *Polkey* does not require slavish adherence to procedures in cases where they could have no effect. The tendency was to look to Lord Bridge's speech for the exceptional case,[75] which he described as being where the employer (subjectively) thought reasonably *at the time* that to go through the usual procedures would be meaningless; in such a case, the dismissal could still be fair. However, in *Duffy v Yeomans & Partners Ltd*[76] the Court of Appeal held that the proper description of the exception is that given by Lord Mackay LC, ie an objective test of whether the employer *could reasonably have concluded* at the time that to go through the usual procedures would be meaningless. This is more than semantics because the latter, objective, test could (if applied too loosely) come to bear an unfortunate resemblance to the old 'but it made no difference' test in *British Labour Pump Co Ltd v Byrne*,[77] which was disapproved in *Polkey*. There is a difference in principle (under *Duffy* the tribunal must still look at the date of dismissal, whereas *Byrne* allowed the unrestrained use of hindsight), but it is a point that may need careful handling by the tribunals.

---

[70] *Grundy (Teddington) Ltd v Plummer* [1983] ICR 367, [1983] IRLR 98.

[71] See Ch 7, heading 4(iv), p 505.

[72] *Grundy (Teddington) Ltd v Willis* [1976] ICR 323, [1976] IRLR 118; *Watling & Co Ltd v Richardson* [1978] ICR 1049, [1978] IRLR 255.

[73] [1988] ICR 142, [1987] IRLR 503, HL.

[74] *Walls Meat Co Ltd v Selby* [1989] ICR 601, CA; *Dyke v Hereford and Worcester County Council* [1989] ICR 800; *Ferguson v Prestwick Circuits Ltd* [1992] IRLR 266; *De Grasse v Stockwell Tools Ltd* [1992] IRLR 269; *Rolls-Royce Motor Cars Ltd v Price* [1993] IRLR 203, EAT.

[75] See *Robertson v Magnet Ltd* [1993] IRLR 512, EAT.

[76] [1995] ICR 1, [1994] IRLR 642, CA.

[77] [1979] ICR 347, [1979] IRLR 94; see Ch 7, heading 4(iii), p 502.

The second qualification poses an even more fundamental question—given that (1) a tribunal cannot rule upon the business need for the redundancy, (2) it is therefore confined to judging the fairness of the *handling* of the situation by the employer and (3) the modern tendency has been to replace more simple LIFO-based criteria with more complex and judgmental assessments of skill and worth (often on a points-scoring, 'brownie points', system), how closely should a tribunal investigate the fairness of the *application* of such a system? Should it just look at the general fairness of the system set up by the employer, or should it (as the applicant will probably want) investigate in detail the scoring of *all* the employees involved, in order to decide whether the applicant had been wrongly scored or harshly treated, and so unfairly selected? One point of procedure which may act as the focus for this whole question is the power of the tribunal to order discovery; if the employee chosen has been given his score, but the employer has refused to divulge the scores of the other employees under consideration, should a tribunal accede to that employee's request for an order for discovery of that further information (without which a detailed analysis of the application of the employer's selection scheme probably cannot be made in practice)? In *Eaton Ltd v King*[78] a selected employee was not given the scores of others not selected; moreover, at the tribunal hearing the only employer witness was the plant manager who had *reviewed* all the employee assessments but had not carried them out and could not say why any particular scores had been awarded. In spite of this, the Scottish EAT held that the dismissal was not unfair, commenting that all that the employer has to prove is that the method of selection was fair, and was generally applied reasonably by the responsible manager(s); moreover effective consultation did not require the divulging of information on other employees. In itself, this case could merely have been an example of the more trenchant approach normally taken by the Scottish courts to redundancy dismissal cases.[79] However, the same approach was taken (and the case approved) subsequently by the Court of Appeal in *British Aerospace plc v Green*,[80] where an order for discovery was refused and, on the substantive point at issue, Waite LJ summed up the view of the whole court as follows:

> Employment law recognises, pragmatically, that an over-minute investigation of the selection process by the tribunal members may run the risk of defeating the purpose which the tribunals were called into being to discharge, namely, a swift, informal disposal of disputes arising from redundancy in the workplace. So in general the employer who sets up a system of selection which can reasonably be described as fair and applies it without any overt sign of conduct which mars its fairness will have done all that the law requires of him.[81]

---

[78] [1995] IRLR 75 (revsd on other grounds by the Court of Session: sub nom *King v Eaton Ltd* [1996] IRLR 199).

[79] In particular, the EAT relied on the decision of the Court of Session in *Buchanan v Tilcon Ltd* [1983] IRLR 417.

[80] [1995] ICR 1006, [1995] IRLR 433, CA. There may be a novel complication, given recent developments, concerning the lawfulness of disclosing information on other employees and whether to do so might contravene the data protection legislation; see particularly the Data Protection Employment Code of Practice, Part II: Employee Records.

[81] [1995] ICR 1006 at 1010, [1995] IRLR 433 at 434.

It must be said at the outset that there was indeed a 'pragmatic' reason for refusing discovery in this case because of its very scale—it involved the making redundant (following the cancellation of a fighter contract) of 530 employees out of a workforce of approximately 7,000. However, only one judge (Stuart-Smith LJ) made any reference to the court's approach being restricted to mass redundancy cases, and the two other judgments are in broad terms, which are capable of causing severe problems because their premise is a denial that redundancy selection operates on a comparative and competitive basis at all:

> Documents relating to retained employees are not likely to be relevant in any but the most exceptional circumstances. The question for the industrial tribunal, which must be determined separately for each applicant, is whether the applicant was unfairly dismissed, *not whether some other employee could have been fairly dismissed.*[82]

This cannot, with respect, be correct; given that X redundancies have to be made (which cannot be challenged) and that an inherently competitive points-scoring system has been put into place to effect that, any consideration of the fairness of selecting employee A *must* involve their comparison with those not chosen, and whether the criteria have been properly applied; however distasteful it may be, a challenge to the fairness of selecting A must include within it at least an implied assertion that B or C should have been chosen instead. *British Aerospace* denies this completely. Moreover, only two months later the EAT in *FDR Ltd v Holloway*[83] effectively ignored *British Aerospace* and upheld an order for discovery of information on employees not selected,[84] stating that this was essential in order to dispose of the issue of whether the selection criteria had been applied fairly, and that a tribunal was *not* to take at face value an employer's assertion that it had all been done properly. These decisions are, quite simply, conflicting and, in spite of the pure argument of precedent that the decision of the Court of Appeal should always apply, it would be dangerous for an employer to assume that simple reliance could be placed on that decision in order to refuse disclosure of other scores as a matter of course.

---

[82] [1995] ICR 1006 at 1019, [1995] IRLR 433 at 438, per Millett LJ (emphasis added).

[83] [1995] IRLR 400. Quantitatively the case is at the opposite end of the scale, involving the making redundant of one employee out of eight.

[84] On the question of discovery, the case is distinguishable—in *British Aerospace* the employees wanted the information to see if there were any faults in the selection, and this was disallowed on the ordinary principle of discovery that the court will not allow it for a 'fishing expedition'; in FDR the EAT held that 'an issue' had already arisen (to which discovery could be attached) because the employee's suspicions were aroused by the retention of an employee with less service and a poorer record. In spite of this, it must be said that the EAT's treatment of *British Aerospace* is on the cavalier side of brusque—the judgment is short, citing hardly anything of the Court of Appeal judgments, and dismissing their ratio decidendi as 'certain observations' which had been 'misread' by counsel for the employers. Lord Denning himself could hardly have done better. Where a recognized trade union is involved, it may be able instead to seek the information required on a collective level, under TULR(C)A, s 181, since the CAC have held that redundancy selection methods may remain in the sphere of collective bargaining, for the purpose of disclosure of bargaining information: see Ch 9, heading 4, p 673.

The Scottish EAT in *John Brown Engineering Ltd v Brown*[85] upheld a tribunal decision of unfair dismissal where the employers had refused to divulge scores (either to individuals or their representatives), stating that such a refusal may make individual consultation worthless, and the Court of Session in *King v Eaton Ltd (No 2)*[86] (the remedies stage of the original decision) simply stated in passing that 'the general reasons for trying to avoid that kind of inquiry [ie into individual scores] do not seem to us to be absolute'. As far as one can gather, the general approach in the tribunals has been to continue to order discovery of other employees' scores where appropriate, though it must be accepted that there is a problem of law here because of the uncompromising language in *British Aerospace*, which may eventually have to be referred to the House of Lords (for further guidance to follow on from that given in *Polkey*).

In addition to these general developments, there has been another, quite different, specific development which might add a further layer of complexity to redundancy cases. This was the decision of the EAT in *Clarke v Eley (IMI) Kynoch Ltd*[87] that a woman who is unjustifiably prejudiced on the grounds of sex by a selection procedure for redundancy may complain of indirect discrimination under the Sex Discrimination Act 1975 (this would now apply to the Equality Act 2010).[88] In that case, the EAT held that a selection procedure based on part-timers going first was unlawful sexual discrimination (even though it was a procedure jointly agreed with a union and, under the unfair dismissal rules *alone*, probably fair), because of the predominance of women in part-time work. Thus, a redundancy selection may now have to be judged according to the sex discrimination legislation as well as the unfair dismissal provisions; if unlawful under the former, it will probably be unfair under the latter (even if ostensibly in line with the ordinary rules on fair and unfair redundancies). However, the volatility and indeed unpredictability of this area of law (particularly when allied to the modern approach of treating almost everything as a question of fact) is shown by the subsequent decision of the EAT in *Kidd v DRG (UK) Ltd*[89] upholding, on similar facts, a decision of a tribunal that the dismissing as redundant of part-timers first was *not* unlawful discrimination (on the grounds of either sex or marital status) and that, even if it was, it was justified. However, even if *Clarke* is now thought generally applicable the effect in practice on redundancy might not be as disruptive as at first sight, for two reasons. First, in the course of his judgment, Browne-Wilkinson J took

---

[85] [1997] IRLR 90; analytically, the case is less than helpful, because all it does is to rehearse the arguments for both sides and then decide it as a question of fact; arguably it is the actual decision that is significant.

[86] [1998] IRLR 686; see particularly para 21.   [87] [1983] ICR 165, [1982] IRLR 482.

[88] See Ch 5, heading 2(iii), p 319.

[89] [1985] ICR 405, [1985] IRLR 190. Waite J stressed the flexibility (a euphemism for unpredictability?) of the concept of indirect discrimination and added, 'It would be unwise and unsafe, therefore, for anyone with a taste of drawing generalised conclusions to set the decision in the present case beside, for example, … the earlier decision of the appeal tribunal in *Clarke v Eley (IMI) Kynoch Ltd* for the sake of deriving supposed differences of principle from the fact that in apparently similar contexts they have arrived at opposite results. Any difference follows only from the application by the tribunals in those cases of flexible criteria to the varied circumstances confronting them' ([1985] ICR 405 at 417, [1985] IRLR 190 at 196).

pains to point out that, while 'part-timers first' may be of dubious legality (unless the company can clearly show justification), an ordinary application of LIFO will not be held to constitute unlawful sex discrimination; even if it may have some discriminatory effect (in that women often have been employed for shorter periods than men), that effect is too limited to be unlawful and, in any event (as was pointed out by Wood P in *Brook v London Borough of Haringey*),[90] would readily be held to be justifiable in the light of the hitherto widespread acceptance of LIFO in industrial relations.[91] Even here, though, the matter is not static because questions have been raised as to whether any heavy reliance on LIFO could now be challenged under the law on age discrimination. Use of long service in a selection matrix was recently held lawful under the Employment Equality (Age) Regulations 2006 (effectively the same provisions as are now found in the Equality Act 2010), but the court emphasized that while long service could be a legitimate factor in a formula, selection based exclusively on LIFO would be unlikely to pass muster.[92] The ECJ more recently confirmed that age discrimination legislation need not forbid long service as a factor in employment decisions (in this case pay scales) so long as the link to service, as opposed to age, was justified.[93] Secondly, a simple 'part-timers first' policy now comes within the Part time Workers (Prevention of Less Favourable Treatment) Regulations 2000 and so there would be an obligation on the employer to justify it, presumably on grounds similar to those required by sex discrimination law. A similar development has taken place in relation to any 'fixed-termers first' policy because of the Fixed-term Employees (Prevention of Less Favourable Treatment) Regulations 2002.[94]

(b) Reorganization SOSR dismissals

Although cases where employees are dismissed consequent upon a reorganization are not treated separately in the legislation, they are subject to being treated as potentially fair under the head of 'some other substantial reason'. This recognized subset of SOSR has evolved through the cases and demonstrates how difficult it is to draw the line between fairness and unfairness where there is a clear conflict between the employer's legitimate business interests and the employee's contractual rights. The problem arises

---

[90] [1992] IRLR 478, EAT.

[91] In the case itself, the (part) LIFO arrangement which was being challenged as discriminatory had been agreed by employer, union and ACAS. On the other hand, the case does perhaps show that if, in difficult times, employers (and unions) fall back on 'tried and tested' solutions, that may negate any advances made in other contexts towards greater equal opportunities.

[92] *Rolls Royce plc v Unite the Union* [2008] EWHC 2420.

[93] *Tyrolean Airways Tiroler Luftfahrt Gesellschaft v Betriebsrat Tiroler Luftfahrt Gesellschaft* C-132/11, [2012] All ER (D) 38.

[94] This has, of course, been a common policy in the past (especially where fixed-term contracts were due to expire anyway) but it had not been challenged under discrimination law in the way that 'part-timers first' had been. Ironically, shortly before the 2002 Regulations came in, there arose the first major, successful challenge to a 'fixed-termers first' policy on the basis of sex discrimination: *Whiffen v Milham Ford Girls' School* [2001] EWCA Civ 385, [2001] ICR 1023, [2001] IRLR 468. For the Part-time Worker Regulations, see Ch 2, heading 1(iv), p 53; for the Fixed-term Employee Regulations, see Ch 2, heading 1(iv), p 57.

where the employer wishes to reorganize his operation in such a way that there will have to be changes in the employee's job, or in the way he carries it out (for example, changes relating to hours, shifts, wages, job content or location); the employee's contract, however, is static and so prima facie he can insist upon continued performance of it as it stands. To achieve a sensible balance, the employer must somehow be allowed to make changes necessary for the efficiency (and in an extreme case the survival) of the enterprise,[95] but in ordinary contract law he may not make unilateral alterations to existing contracts of employment. If he attempts to do so the employee has a common law action for breach of contract[96] and, more significantly, may under the legislation walk out because of it and claim to have been constructively dismissed through the employer's breach;[97] alternatively, the employer may dismiss the employee who refuses to change by giving him proper notice, which is lawful at common law but is of course a dismissal for statutory purposes and so either way the employer lays himself open to an unfair dismissal claim. From the decided cases, it appears that there are three possibilities in such a case:

(1) It may be that the proposed changes are such that, on a proper construction, they fall within the permissible range of managerial discretion to organize the work[98] or indeed within the proper ambit of the contractual job description for that employee anyway. This will be particularly so if the changes are minor or of an administrative nature, if they can be construed merely as an updating of essentially the same job (seen in the light possibly of an implied term of the contract that the employee will adapt to new methods and techniques reasonably required of him),[99] or if the job description in fact covers jobs A and B but the employee, used to doing only A in practice, refuses to do B instead, for it is the contractual term which counts, not any particular practice which evolved; so a skilfully drafted contractual job description (and/or a flexibility clause) could perhaps anticipate and cover subsequent re-organizations. If this is the case, the changes are not sufficiently major to constitute a breach of contract and so if the employee still refuses to accept them and is dismissed, that will be a dismissal for refusal to obey a lawful order and so will

---

[95] This has been recognized in the context of redundancy law: *Chapman v Goonvean and Rostowrack China Clay Co Ltd* [1973] 1 All ER 218, [1973] ICR 50; *Johnson v Nottinghamshire Combined Policy Authority* [1974] ICR 170, [1974] IRLR 20, CA; *Lesney Products & Co Ltd v Nolan* [1977] ICR 235, [1977] IRLR 77, CA.

[96] This can take the form of an action for wages due under the old contract, on the old terms, and can be an effective tactic: *Burdett-Coutts v Hertfordshire County Council* [1984] IRLR 91 (concerning unilateral changes to dinner ladies' terms and conditions, a fruitful source of important case law in the mid-1980s); *Rigby v Ferodo Ltd* [1988] ICR 29, [1987] IRLR 516, HL. Unless the employer can show a variation of contract, assented to by the employee, he will lose the common law action, and will then have to force the issue by dismissing those who refuse to accept the changes and taking his chances in an unfair dismissal action (discussed later in the chapter).

[97] *Greenaway Harrison Ltd v Wiles* [1994] IRLR 380, EAT.

[98] See Ch 2, heading 6, p 113.

[99] *Cresswell v Board of Inland Revenue* [1984] ICR 508, [1984] IRLR 190 (computerization of PAYE system still within the ambit of the existing contracts of those operating the system, who were expected to adapt).

probably be fair on conduct grounds; likewise, if the employee walks out because of such changes, it will not constitute constructive dismissal (unless there was something seriously objectionable about the way it was handled, capable of independently producing a breach of contract). He will therefore not receive a redundancy payment or compensation for unfair dismissal.[100]

(2) If the changes are more major and would actually cause a decrease in the employee's work, that may constitute redundancy within the definition in the Employment Rights Act 1996, section 139.[101] If so, the dismissed employee may be eligible for a redundancy payment but, as redundancy is a prima facie fair ground for dismissal, he may not be able to claim unfair dismissal[102] (unless the redundancy was itself unfair—see (iii) 'Redundancy', below). This solution (probably highly acceptable to the employer) is more likely to occur now, with the emphasis of the Court of Appeal in *Murphy v Epsom College*[103] on looking at the 'kind of work' that the dismissed employee was employed to do; if on the reorganization it can be said that the kind of work changed and the employee was incapable of performing the new kind of work, then he may be dismissed as redundant even though a new employee (skilled in the new kind of work) is taken on to replace him, ie where there is *no* net loss in the number of employees required at the end of the day.

(3) If the changes are major but do not produce in law a redundancy (for example, where the work is undiminished but the hours and remuneration have to change), it is well established that the reorganization *can* constitute 'some other substantial reason' within section 98(1), in which case there will be no redundancy payment and the employee may not be able to succeed in a claim for unfair dismissal.[104] This is the type of case which causes most problems, for to reach that result the tribunal in effect has to give precedence to the employer's business needs over the employee's normal contractual and statutory rights, and allow the employer to insist upon a unilateral variation

---

[100]   *George Wimpey & Co Ltd v Cooper* [1977] IRLR 205; *Glitz v Watford Electric Co Ltd* [1979] IRLR 89. In the latter case the EAT pointed out that in a small firm or unit the job descriptions may necessarily be more vague, allowing the employer to expect greater flexibility and adaptability from his employees. Note also, more generally, the successful attack on an unconscionable reliance on an apparently wide flexibility clause in *Land Securities Trillium Ltd v Thornley* [2005] IRLR 765; see Ch 3, heading 1, p 119.

[101]   See heading 1(i), p 548.

[102]   *Wilson v Underhill House School Ltd* [1977] IRLR 475; *Robinson v British Island Airways Ltd* [1978] ICR 304, [1977] IRLR 477, EAT.

[103]   [1985] ICR 80, [1984] IRLR 271, CA (dismissal of plumber held to be for redundancy where a modern heating system installed and a heating engineer appointed to replace him). The case also shows that an employer can run both redundancy and, in the alternative, some other substantial reason (through reorganization) as defences, provided both are properly considered at the tribunal hearing.

[104]   *RS Components Ltd v Irwin* [1973] ICR 535, [1973] IRLR 239; *Wilson's* case and *Robinson's* case, n 102; *Hollister v National Farmers' Union* [1979] ICR 542, [1979] IRLR 238, CA; *Genower v Ealing, Hammersmith and Hounslow Area Health Authority* [1980] IRLR 297; *Farrant v Woodroffe School* [1998] ICR 184, [1998] IRLR 176. Cf, however, *Labour Party v Oakley* [1988] ICR 403, [1988] IRLR 34, CA where the reorganization was shown on the facts to be a pretext for dismissing someone they had already decided to dispense with.

of the contract without incurring a finding of unfair dismissal.[105] It is the section 98(4) concept of reasonableness which holds the balance: given that the reorganization is a substantial reason which *can* justify dismissal, was the dismissal of the recalcitrant employee *in fact* justified on the facts of the particular case? The tribunal is therefore looking at the reasonableness of the employer's handling of the change, and in essence looking to see whether the time had come when the employer had no further option but to dismiss the employee in order to put into effect the necessary changes. In doing so, the tribunal may have to consider three questions:

(a) Was the reorganization necessary? Although it is not for the tribunal to decide how the employer ought to run his business and the employer's genuine belief in the necessity for changes is likely to be paramount, a tribunal may expect the employer to lead evidence showing why he thought change necessary and how he reached the particular decisions in question.[106] In one of the original cases, *Ellis v Brighton Co-operative Society Ltd*,[107] the EAT seemed to assume that in order to justify eventual dismissals for non-compliance, the changes had to be so vital that if they were not put into effect the whole business would be brought to a standstill, but this was held by the Court of Appeal to be too restrictive in *Hollister v National Farmers' Union*[108] where it was said that it is sufficient if there is a good, sound business reason for the reorganization. This approach leaves a great deal in the employer's discretion and, indeed, the area of business reorganizations has produced many findings of fair dismissal. In *Evans v Elemeta Holdings Ltd*[109] the EAT appeared to move in the direction of redressing this imbalance by concentrating more upon examining the changes imposed by the employer and considering whether it was *reasonable for the employee to reject them* (the case itself concerning major changes to overtime obligations, disadvantageous to the employee). However, in the event this case did not lead to a significant development in this area, for it did not decide what was to happen in the most difficult class of case, ie where it was reasonable for the employee to reject the changes because of their effect on his livelihood, but equally it was reasonable for the employer to insist upon

---

[105] The existence of a 'dismissal' will normally be clear, through either (1) an express dismissal by the employer of the refusenik, (2) a constructive dismissal if the employee leaves or (3) an application of the rule that a unilateral change can be so fundamental as the constitute termination of the old contract by the employer, even where the employee in fact carries on working (under, in effect, a new contract), as in *Hogg v Dover College* [1990] ICR 39, affirmed in *Alcan Extrusions Ltd v Yates* [1996] IRLR 327, EAT.

[106] *Banerjee v City and East London Area Health Authority* [1979] IRLR 147; *Ladbroke Courage Holidays Ltd v Asten* [1981] IRLR 59; in *Orr v Vaughan* [1981] IRLR 63 it was said that, while business reorganizations are basically for the employer to decide upon, the tribunal must be satisfied that, at the least, the employer came to his decision on reasonable information reasonably acquired.

[107] [1976] IRLR 419.

[108] [1979] ICR 542, [1979] IRLR 238; *Bowater Containers Ltd v McCormack* [1980] IRLR 50. Outside pressure for change, eg from customers or insurers, may be a relevant factor, but the employer must still establish that he handled the pressure reasonably: *Scott Packing and Warehousing Ltd v Paterson* [1978] IRLR 166; *Dobie v Burns International Security Services (UK) Ltd* [1984] ICR 812, [1984] IRLR 329, CA.

[109] [1982] ICR 323, [1982] IRLR 143.

them because of the needs of his business; the fact that one party was acting reasonably does *not* mean that the other was therefore acting unreasonably. On those grounds, a differently constituted EAT soon afterwards refused to follow *Evans* in *Chubb Fire Security Ltd v Harper*.[110] In that case, a middle way of sorts was suggested, namely that a tribunal might consider whether the employer had acted reasonably in deciding that the advantages of the reorganization to him outweighed the disadvantages to the employee. This is an interesting approach but it was stressed subsequently that this is only a *factor* (not a test) for a tribunal to consider when deciding whether the dismissal was fair within section 98(4) (as being within the range of reasonable responses that an employer faced with the employee's refusal to change might have adopted);[111] this is ultimately the test and its application, here as elsewhere, is a question of fact for the tribunal, as the Court of Appeal has emphasized.[112]

(b) Given the reorganization plan, was it necessary to insist upon changing the employee's job in order to put that plan into effect? In many cases, the answer may simply be 'Yes', particularly where the employee is in a key position. It may be, however, that if only one or two employees are holding out, and their concurrence is not absolutely vital, the employer may be expected to consider any minor alterations to his plan which might accommodate those employees without frustrating the reorganization.[113]

(c) Was there sufficient consultation? Consultation with the employee and perhaps his union has been seen in the past as one of the major requirements of a fair dismissal in these cases and it is clear that if the employer does negotiate a reorganization with the relevant union or with the majority of the employees and one employee still holds out, that agreement will considerably strengthen his hand if he then dismisses that employee. Thus, it has been said by the EAT that there must be proper consultation, not just the presentation of a fait accompli or ultimatum,[114] and that the employer should consider any counter-proposals put forward by the employee, and should bear in mind the position of the individual employee, which may not be done if he treats all cases as one, for example by just consulting a weak union or staff association.[115] However, in *Hollister v National Farmers' Union*[116] the Court of Appeal

---

[110] [1983] IRLR 311; applied in *Catamaran Cruisers Ltd v Williams* [1994] IRLR 386.

[111] *Richmond Precision Engineering Ltd v Pearce* [1985] IRLR 179. One point in this case had to be rectified subsequently, for it was suggested that the test is the reasonableness of the employer's offer; in fact, the correct test (under s 98) is the reasonableness of the decision to dismiss because of the employee's refusal of the offer: *St John of God (Care Services) Ltd v Brooks* [1992] ICR 715, [1992] IRLR 546. Further factors to consider may include how many other employees had accepted the changes and the attitude of any trade union involved: *Catamaran Cruisers Ltd v Williams* [1994] IRLR 386. The existence of a financial inducement to 'buy out' the old terms may also be relevant.

[112] *Gilham v Kent County Council (No 2)* [1985] ICR 233, [1985] IRLR 18, CA.

[113] *Martin v Automobile Proprietary Ltd* [1979] IRLR 64.

[114] *Ellis v Brighton Co-operative Society Ltd* [1976] IRLR 419.

[115] *Martin v Automobile Proprietary Ltd* [1979] IRLR 64. Presumably this would require some form of individual consultation in the case of a non-unionist.

[116] See n 108.

held that too much emphasis had been placed upon consultation in past cases, to the point that the EAT was in danger of putting a gloss upon the simple reasonableness test in section 98(4)—consultation is only one of the factors to be considered when looking at the circumstances of the case, and so lack of it (as in that case, where the changes were just announced to the employee) is not necessarily fatal to the employer's case. It is possible, however, that (if and when the matter is tested again) there will be a move back towards more emphasis on consultation in this area in the light of (a) the decision of the House of Lords in *Polkey v A E Dayton Services Ltd*,[117] which concerned consultation in the context of redundancy dismissals, but in the subsequent case law has taken on wider significance and (b) legislative developments around the Information and Consultation Directive[118] which requires (at least in firms of 50 or more employees) mechanisms for informing and consulting the workforce on, inter alia, 'decisions likely to lead to substantial changes in work organization as in contractual relations'—this operates directly only at a collective level, but it might well have an indirect effect at this individual level in helping to define reasonable handling of one of these difficult cases in the future.

Thus, to recap, the employer who wishes to reorganize parts of the business should first attempt to gain the agreement of the affected employees to variations in their contractual terms. If this is not forthcoming but the changes are still necessary, the employer may order unilaterally such changes as are permissible within the scope of the contracts of employment (and the amount of managerial discretion reserved under their terms); if an employee refuses to accept this category of change this could result in dismissal for disobedience. Alternatively, if the changes alter the kind of work required and lead to a definite diminution in the requirements for the kind of work that the employee was engaged to perform, then the employee may be made redundant (with a redundancy payment but, provided a proper procedure was adopted, no compensation for unfair dismissal). However, if the case falls outside these two possibilities (ie where there is no redundancy, but the changes are major enough to involve definite variations of contract) the employer should usually follow some consultative procedure (depending on the facts of the case), but if an employee still refuses to change this could justify a dismissal, or the employer could insist upon the changes and be prepared to concede that that employee was constructively dismissed; in either event, the employer can then argue that the dismissal (actual or constructive)[119] was fair in the light of the necessity for change, the need to alter the employee's job within the scheme of the reorganization, and the consultative procedure adopted. However, it must be remembered in these cases that a finding of fairness jeopardizes what would normally be the employee's contractual and statutory rights, and so should not be arrived at lightly.

---

[117] [1988] ICR 142, [1987] IRLR 503, HL; see Ch 7, heading 4(iii), p 502.
[118] See Ch 9, heading 5(ii), p 681.
[119] The fact that a dismissal is constructive does not automatically mean that it is unfair: see Ch 7, heading 2(i), p 477, and particularly *Savoia v Chiltern Herb Farms Ltd* [1982] IRLR 166, CA.

(iii) REDUNDANCY PROCEDURES FOR CONSULTATION AND INFORMATION

The redundancy payments legislation gives to individuals rights to payments upon redundancy, but does not itself lay down any particular procedures for handling redundancies. However, pursuant to two European Directives on collective redundancies,[120] procedural requirements were established and are to be found in the Trade Union and Labour Relations (Consolidation) Act 1992, sections 188–198, as amended by the Trade Union Reform and Employment Rights Act 1993 and the Collective Redundancies and Transfer of Undertakings (Protection of Employment) (Amendment) Regulations 1995 and 1999.[121] In many industries, it appears that these provisions have had little effect due to more sophisticated approaches to necessary reductions in manpower, such as voluntary redundancies, redeployment and natural wastage; in some 'problem' industries of greater labour fluctuations, such as the construction industry, the provisions are more relevant.[122] There are two obligations laid upon the employer who is about to make employees redundant—first, to consult employee or trade union representatives and, second, to notify the Secretary of State.

(a) Consultation with employee or trade union representatives

It was enacted in the Employment Protection Act 1975 that where an employer proposes to dismiss as redundant[123] an employee of a class in respect of which the employer recognizes an independent trade union, he or she must consult officials of that union, with a set time framework in the case of collective redundancies; these provisions are now contained in the Trade Union and Labour Relations (Consolidation) Act 1992, section 188. They were updated by the 1993 Act to take into account the 1992 amending Directive, but the whole basis of their enactment of the original 1975 Directive was severely shaken in enforcement proceedings brought by the EC Commission in *EC Commission v United Kingdom*.[124] The problem was the restriction

---

[120] Directives 75/129/EEC and 92/56/EEC, consolidated in Directive 98/59/EC. The 1975 Directive was held not to be directly applicable in *Griffin v South West Water Services Ltd* [1995] IRLR 15, and so cannot be used as the basis of a separate legal action.

[121] SI 1995/2587 and SI 1999/1925. On the latter, see Hall and Edwards 'Reforming the Statutory Redundancy Consultation Procedure' (1999) 28 ILJ 299.

[122] See n 1.

[123] The definition of redundancy for these purposes in s 195(1) was substituted by the Trade Union Reform and Employment Rights Act 1993, and now refers more simply and widely to 'dismissal for a reason not related to the individual concerned or for a number of reasons all of which are not so related'; under s 195(2) there is a rebuttable presumption that a dismissal or proposed dismissal is for redundancy. It was because of this wider definition in s 195(1) that an employer tactic (for forcing through changes in terms) of dismissing all employees and hiring them on the new terms was held to be a collective redundancy; as (not surprisingly!) there had not been the obligatory consultation, the employer was liable for hefty protective awards: *GMB v Man Truck and Bus UK Ltd* [2000] ICR 1101, [2000] IRLR 636.

[124] C-383/92 [1994] ECR I-2479, [1995] 1 CMLR 345, ECJ. Other infringements by the UK were found, but these had been dealt with by the 1993 Act, as well as taking the new Directive into account.

of the consultation requirement to cases where there was a recognized union, whereas the Directive was held in that case to require far more general consultation with 'the workers' representatives'.[125] Given that this country does not have any mandatory system of works councils, this caused a problem as to *whom* to consult where there is no recognized union. The previous government's response came in the 1995 Regulations, which retained the possibility of consultation with a recognized union, but added the alternative route of consultation with elected employee representatives.[126] This system was subject to further refinement by the present government in the 1999 Regulations. As a combined result of the 1993 Act and the 1995 and 1999 Regulations, section 188 now requires the following.

Where an employer is proposing to dismiss as redundant 20 or more employees at one establishment within a period of 90 days or less, he must consult about the dismissals all the persons who are appropriate representatives of any of the employees who may be affected by the dismissals or measures taken in relation to them. Appropriate representatives are defined as (1) if the employees are of a description in respect of which an independent trade union is recognized by their employer, representatives of that union; or (2) in any other case employee representatives already appointed or elected who have authority from the affected employees in relation to the proposed dismissals, or such representatives elected specifically for these purposes.[127] It is specifically provided that existing elected representatives can be used if 'it is appropriate (having regard to the purposes for which they were elected) for the employer to consult them about dismissals proposed by him';[128] taken together with other consultation requirements (especially on TUPE) and increasing advantages to be gained from workforce agreements (for example in relation to the Working Time Regulations and the law on parental leave), this may argue strongly in favour of the employer having *standing* elected machinery for all of these purposes, even where no union is recognized.

---

[125] There is a political irony here, because the Conservative government ended up defending the result of a Labour government's pro-union policies; the aim of the restriction to recognized unions in 1975 was to concentrate industrial power in the latter's hands (see also the health and safety and pension legislation of that period). This of course backfired when the membership and influence of the unions declined dramatically, along with union recognition, so that the consultation requirements applied to fewer and fewer employees.

[126] This was not purely defensive on the previous government's part, as they also viewed the need to change as an opportunity for some deregulation. Thus, the cut-off number was raised from ten to 20 employees and the requirement still to consult under that number was dropped. These changes have not been reversed by the present government.

[127] Trade Union and Labour Relations (Consolidation) Act 1992, s 188(1B), as substituted in 1999. The previous government's provisions had allowed the employer to choose to use directly elected representatives even if there was a recognized union, to allow the employer if desired to sideline the union; that has now been stopped by the current wording. Where elections are held specifically for this purpose, they must comply with rules ensuring fair elections, laid down in s 188A.

[128] Section 196(1). They must be employed by the employer at the time when they are elected or appointed: s 196(2).

The consultation must begin in good time,[129] and in any event 90 days before the first dismissal takes effect (if the employer is proposing to dismiss 100 or more within the 90 days), or at least 30 days beforehand otherwise. It is likely that this will change by 2013: the Coalition government closed, in September 2012, a consultation on its plans to reduce the 90-day period for 100 or more redundancies to 30 or 45 days.[130] Details of the proposals were not out at the time of writing, but some reduction in the period should be expected by spring 2013. According to the statute, the consultation must include ways of avoiding the dismissals, reducing the numbers and mitigating the consequences; these three requirements are to be construed disjunctively (ie the employer must consult on each of them)[131] and this must be undertaken by the employer with a view to reaching agreement with the appropriate representatives. The case law also establishes that as a matter of general principle 'consultation' requires (1) consultation while the proposals are still at a formative stage, (2) adequate information, (3) adequate time in which to respond and (4) conscientious consideration of the responses to the consultation.[132]

With regard to information, section 188(4) specifies that an employer must disclose in writing to the appropriate representatives (1) the reason for the proposals, (2) the numbers and descriptions of employees proposed to be dismissed, (3) the total number of such employees at the establishment, (4) the proposed method of selection, (5) the proposed method of carrying out the dismissals and (6) the proposed method of calculating any non-statutory redundancy payments to be made to those selected.

Four problems of definition have arisen under this section. The first is when it can be said that the employer is 'proposing' to make an employee redundant (as it is this that sets the wheels in motion); under the existing law, it appears that the word 'proposing' requires a certain amount of planning and resolution on the part of the employer, not just speculation:

> a proposal to make redundant within the meaning of [section 188] connotes a state of mind directed to a planned or proposed course of events. The employer must have formed some view as to how many are to be dismissed, when this is to take place and how it is to be arranged. This goes beyond the mere contemplation of a possible event.[133]

---

[129] Where an ad hoc election is being carried out, 'in good time' means as soon as reasonably practicable after the representatives are elected: s 188(7A). If the employees fail to elect representatives within a reasonable time, the employer can give each affected employee the information required by law, but is absolved from the requirement to consult collectively: s 188(7B).

[130] *Collective Redundancies: Consultation on Changes to the Rules* (BIS June 2012) available at <http://www.gov.uk/government/uploads/system/uploads/attachment_data/file/31361/12–808-collective-redundancies-consultation.pdf> (last accessed 20 January 2013).

[131] *Middlesbrough Borough Council v TGWU* [2002] IRLR 324.

[132] *R v British Coal Corpn and Secretary of State for Trade and Industry, ex p Price* [1994] IRLR 72, Div Ct (one of the 'pit closure' cases). Even if time limits are technically met, it may still be argued that in substance the whole exercise was a sham: *Transport and General Workers' Union v Ledbury Preserves (1928) Ltd* [1985] IRLR 412.

[133] *Association of Pattern Makers and Allied Craftsmen v Kirvin Ltd* [1978] IRLR 318 at 320 per Lord McDonald. *Union of Shop, Distributive and Allied Workers v Leancut Bacon Ltd* [1981] IRLR 295; *Hough v Leyland DAF Ltd* [1991] ICR 696, [1991] IRLR 194. It may be enough to trigger these provisions if the

However, this use of the word 'proposing' has led to the argument that the UK provisions do not enact the original 1975 EC Directive properly. The latter states that an employer should begin consultation when 'contemplating' collective redundancies, which may be construed as meaning *before* the employer has formed any definite views on the need for redundancies, whereas the domestic provision appears to apply only once that decision has been taken and therefore to apply principally to the question of *how* to deal with the proposed redundancies. This argument was accepted by Glidewell LJ in the Divisional Court in *R v British Coal Corpn and Secretary of State for Trade, ex p Vardy*[134] (the highly publicized decision declaring the previous government's original coal-mine closure programme to be unlawful), which was ironic because at the very time that the 1993 Act was being enacted with provisions stated to be bringing the UK legislation into line with the new 1992 Directive, that legislation was considered to be out of line in this fundamental way with the original 1975 Directive all along. Subsequently Blackburne J in *Griffin v South West Water Services Ltd*[135] was unimpressed with this argument but when the matter was considered by the EAT in *MSF v Refuge Assurance plc*[136] (a case where it was directly relevant because the union was trying to get domestic law changed to reflect the Directive's approach) it was held (approving *Ex p Vardy*) that there is indeed a conflict but it was not possible to resolve it by reconstruing section 188 (and, moreover, there could not be reliance on any arguments for direct effect because the employer was in the private sector). It is at least established now that if it is reasonably clear that closure of an operation will 'almost inevitably' result in dismissals, the employer is deemed to have 'proposed dismissals' at the time of proposing closure.[137]

The second problem concerns the timing of the consultation and ironically (in the light of the theoretical problem above over proposing/contemplating) it is this matter which has revitalized redundancy consultation. The 30- and 90-day periods are a matter of UK implementation (not the Directive itself) and the wording of section 188(1A) is that the consultation must begin 30/90 days 'before the first of the dismissals *takes effect*'. This was always thought to mean that, provided any notice of dismissal *expired* after this period, the notice itself could be *given* at any time, even before consultation had finished (even though this could cast doubt on the meaningfulness of that consultation). This assumption, however, is now wrong and section 188 must be read in the light of the decision of the ECJ in *Junk v Kuhnel*[138] where it was held that the (differently

---

employer has decided *either* to go down the redundancy route *or* to adopt some other solution (eg sale of the business): *Scotch Premier Meat Ltd v Burns* [2000] IRLR 639.

[134] [1993] IRLR 104; the issue had been previously (understandably!) ducked in *Re Hartlebury Printers Ltd* [1992] ICR 559, [1992] IRLR 516. Another interesting facet of *Ex p Vardy* is that it shows that a collective redundancy might be subject to challenge, not just under the employment legislation, but also by way of judicial review if there is a sufficient element of public law involved.

[135] [1995] IRLR 15.   [136] [2002] ICR 1365, [2002] IRLR 324.

[137] *UK Coal Mining Limited v National Union of Mineworkers (Northumberland Area)* [2008] IRLR 4.

[138] C-188/03 [2005] IRLR 310 ECJ; the Court also stressed the requirement in the Directive that the consultation should be undertaken 'with a view to reaching agreement'. On the question of timing, *Junk* means that *Middlesbrough BC v TGWU* [2002] IRLR 332 must now be considered wrong on this point.

worded) Directive requires that notice should not be *given* until the necessary consultation is *completed*. This strong decision, stressing that consultation is actually meant to be effective, has effected something of a sea change here, though its interaction with the UK provision for the 30/90-day period remains uncertain. One school of thought is that it does *not* mean that the 30/90-day period must elapse before notice can be given, provided that whatever *is* the consultation period in practice has finished. Thus, if consultation actually finishes early (or, indeed, if the parties have agreed that it shall last for a period less than the 30/90 days) the employer can proceed to give any necessary notice of dismissal. However, another school of thought is that the only safe way to comply with *Junk* is indeed to let the 30/90-day period elapse before giving any necessary notice. Either way, this is significantly different from the pre-*Junk* position and arguably puts the significance of proper consultation onto a higher level.

The third problem concerns the nature of an 'establishment', for the purpose of applying the statutory time limits. The word appears in the Collective Redundancies Directive, but once again there is no statutory definition, even though the width of its construction could have an important effect on section 188 in cases where the employer operates at several locations; if each location is a separate 'establishment' and there are fewer than 20 redundancies at each, the requirements of the section will not apply, even if the overall number of redundancies is high. In *Barratt Developments (Bradford) Ltd v Union of Construction, Allied Trades and Technicians*[139] the EAT said that what constitutes an 'establishment' is a question for the employment tribunal to decide, as an industrial jury using its common sense, on the particular facts of the case and upheld the tribunal's decision that 14 house-building sites administered from one central base in fact constituted one establishment. A similar decision was reached by the tribunal in *Baker's Union v Clarks of Hove Ltd*[140] where a firm employing 368 employees in their factory, bakery and 28 retail shops was held to constitute one establishment. It might be different, however, where one organization is split into smaller parts which in fact have considerable autonomy, as for example in the case of one education authority in overall control of many different schools. However, the ECJ have stated that in interpreting the term the protective intent of the Directive must be kept in mind, and not frustrated by the technicalities of corporate structure.[141] This was later clarified, by the ECJ, to mean that three distinct production units for three kinds of paper, each with its own chief production officer, equipment and specialized workforce, were separate establishments despite the fact that the head office made financial decisions for all three.[142]

---

[139] [1978] ICR 319, [1977] IRLR 403.

[140] [1977] IRLR 167. The tribunal's decision was later affirmed by the Court of Appeal: [1978] ICR 1076, [1978] IRLR 366, CA.

[141] *Rockfon A/S v Nielsen* Case C-449/93 [1996] ICR 673, [1996] IRLR 168, ECJ. In particular, they held that a company in a group can still be an 'establishment' even if the power to make redundancies as a matter of policy lies elsewhere in the group. On the other hand (applying *Rockfon*), central management is not enough in itself to constitute one establishment where the organization emphasis remains at the branch level: *MSF Refuge Assurance plc*, [2002] ICR 1365, [2002] IRLR 324.

[142] *Athinaiki Chartoposia AE v Panagiotidis* (C-270/05) [2007] IRLR 284.

The fourth problem is the converse of the third. Even where the 'establishment' has been discerned, it may still be necessary to decide who is the 'employer' and here there may be a problem because the concept of 'associated employers', so important elsewhere in employment law,[143] is surprisingly *not* adopted by section 188 and the EAT has held that it will not unilaterally lift the veil of incorporation in this context. Thus, in *E Green & Son (Castings) Ltd v Association of Scientific, Technical and Managerial Staffs*[144] three companies were making redundancies of 97, 36 and 24 employees respectively but the relevant consultation period was 30 days (not 90) since they were each separate employers even though (1) they were all subsidiaries of one holding company (and so would be associated employers in other contexts) and (2) they all operated from the same physical 'establishment'.

The sanction for failure to consult is a special device, the 'protective award'. This may be sought by employee representatives, the trade union or in any other case (including where no machinery at all has been set up) by any of the employees affected or dismissed. Where employees are represented by a trade union or elected representatives, only those representatives can bring the claim;[145] trade unions in multi-union workforces cannot bring a claim regarding parts of the workforce they do not represent.[146] The matter is referred to a tribunal which, if it finds the complaint established, must make a declaration to that effect and may make a protective award, which is an order that the employer shall continue to pay wages to the employees concerned for a 'protected period'.[147] This period is within the tribunal's discretion, subject to a maximum of 90 days. The employee is entitled to a 'week's pay'[148] for each week of the protected period; if the employer fails to make any or all of the payments due for this period, the individual employee may complain within three months to a tribunal which may order payment. The employee may be disqualified from claiming under the protective award if he is fairly dismissed for a reason other than redundancy, unreasonably resigns during the period or unreasonably refuses suitable alternative employment.[149]

The only guidance given to the tribunals by the statute on the way to apply a protective award is that it should be 'just and equitable in all the circumstances having regard to the seriousness of the employer's default'; this, however, could mean either a compensatory approach (looking at the employee's actual loss) or a punitive one (looking at the seriousness of the employer's default and its effect on industrial relations). Although this has long been an arguable point, the balance of authority for many

---

[143] See Ch 2, heading 1(v), p 65.   [144] [1984] ICR 352, [1984] IRLR 135.

[145] *Northgate HR Ltd v Mercy* [2008] IRLR 222.

[146] *Transport & General Workers' Union v Brauer Coley Ltd* [2007] IRLR 207.

[147] Trade Union and Labour Relations (Consolidation) Act 1992, ss 189, 190. The period starts with the *proposed* date of the first dismissal, whether or not the *actual* date is different: *E Green & Son (Castings) Ltd v Association of Scientific, Technical and Managerial Staffs* [1984] ICR 352, [1984] IRLR 135, applied in *Transport and General Workers' Union v Ledbury Preserves (1928) Ltd* [1986] ICR 855, [1986] IRLR 492.

[148] As defined in the Employment Rights Act 1996, Pt XIV, Ch II.

[149] Trade Union and Labour Relations (Consolidation) Act 1992, s 191; where there is an offer of alternative employment, the 'trial period' provisions are specially applied.

years was that the award was meant to be compensatory. Thus, the burden was on the employee to bid it up from nil by proving actual loss, an approach which could lead to relatively inexpensive awards for employers. However, all this changed in *Susie Radin Ltd v GMB*[150] where the Court of Appeal held that the purpose of the award is punitive and to act as a deterrent to employers. On that basis, advice was given to tribunals to start in each case at the 90-day maximum, thus putting the burden on to the employer to bid it down by proving mitigation. The significance of this can be seen from the subsequent case of *AMICUS v GBS Tooling Ltd*[151] where there was quite substantial mitigation (based on prior consultations and the sudden loss of a major contract) and the EAT approved a reduction in the length of the award, but only to 70 days. If this is to be the norm, this significant change should mean that an employer is less likely to view the threat of a protective award as merely a 'business expense'. Taking this together with the renewed emphasis on genuine consultation in *Junk* (above), collective redundancy law has arguably been given a higher profile than it has had for some years previously.

(b) Notification to the Secretary of State

Where an employer proposes to dismiss as redundant 20 or more employees at one establishment within 30 days, he must give the Secretary of State written notice of the proposal at least 30 days before the first dismissal takes effect; where he proposes to dismiss 100 or more within 90 days, he must give 90 days' notice.[152] A copy of the notice must be sent to the appropriate representatives. If the employer fails to give this notice, the Secretary of State may prosecute the employer summarily (the maximum fine being level 5 on the standard scale).[153]

(c) The 'special circumstances' defence

It is expressly provided, in the case of both consultation and notification, that if there are special circumstances rendering it not reasonably practicable for an employer to comply with the statutory requirements, he need only take such steps towards compliance as are reasonably practicable.[154] The burden of proof is upon the employer to establish special circumstances, but if she can do so, and can show that she did what was reasonably practicable (which may in some cases be nothing), she has a good case that there should be *no* protective award, not just a reduction in it. The meaning of 'special circumstances' has been left to the tribunals and courts, and will be a question of fact

---

[150] [2004] ICR 893, [2004] IRLR 400, CA.

[151] [2005] IRLR 683. The punitive and deterrent approach is so strong that there should still be an award in full, even if the respondent employer is insolvent (so that the Secretary of State may have to fund it): *Smith v Cherry Lewis Ltd* [2005] IRLR 86.

[152] Trade Union and Labour Relations (Consolidation) Act 1992, s 193; the requirement of notice does not apply where less than 20 are dismissed. The wording of s 193 was amended in 2006 to require that the notice is also given before giving any notices of dismissal; this was to bring it into line with *Junk v Kuhnel* (n 138).

[153] Section 194.   [154] Sections 188(7) and 193(7).

in each case. The Court of Appeal in *Clarks of Hove Ltd v Bakers' Union*[155] held that the employer's insolvency and collapse were not in themselves special circumstances:

> insolvency is, on its own, neither here nor there. It may be a special circumstance, it may not be a special circumstance. It will depend entirely on the cause of the insolvency whether the circumstance can be described as special or not. If, for example, a sudden disaster strikes a company, making it necessary to close the concern, then plainly that would be a matter which was capable of being a special circumstance; and that is so whether the disaster is physical or financial. If the insolvency however were merely due to a gradual run-down of the company, as it was in this case, then those are facts on which the industrial tribunal can come to the conclusion that the circumstances were not special. In other words, to be special the event must be something out of the ordinary, something uncommon.[156]

Thus, although insolvency itself may not be special, the employer has been held to have a good defence where the company carried on trading in the face of insolvency in the genuine hope that it would be able to sell the company as a going concern and so prevent redundancies, but had to appoint a receiver (without any consultation) when the last prospective purchaser disappeared.[157] In such a case, extensive consultation could be fatal to delicate negotiations, but on the other hand it may still be reasonable to expect *some* consultation and if that is the case the employer will not have shown that she did all that was reasonably practicable and so will remain liable.[158] The requirement of doing all that is reasonable puts a considerable onus on the employer to know and understand these legal requirements, so that in general a mistaken view of the law and its application will not be a 'special circumstance' unless it was a reasonable mistake,[159] even if the employer was acting upon wrong advice, though in such a case the facts may support an argument for reduction of the protective award if the 'employer's default' is considered less.[160]

The 1992 Directive sought to increase the protection for employees of transnational concerns who may be made redundant by decisions taken at higher levels than their immediate employer; this was put into effect in domestic law by the Trade Union Reform and Employment Rights Act 1993, which added to the 'special circumstances' defences a provision declaring that where the decision leading to the proposed dismissals is that of a person controlling the employer, a failure on the part of that person to provide information to the employer does *not* constitute special circumstances.

[155] [1978] ICR 1076, [1978] IRLR 366, CA.

[156] [1978] ICR 1076 at 1085, [1978] IRLR 366 at 369, per Geoffrey Lane LJ. Sudden financial deterioration following collapse of negotiations to sell the firm's shares to a third party was held to constitute a special circumstance in *USDAW v Leancut Bacon Ltd* [1981] IRLR 295; the shedding of labour normal on an insolvency was held not to in *GMB v Rankin and Harrison* [1992] IRLR 514.

[157] *APAC v Kirvin Ltd* [1978] IRLR 318.

[158] *Hamish Armour v ASTMS* [1979] IRLR 24; cf *USDAW v Leancut Bacon Ltd*, n 156.

[159] *Joshua Wilson & Bros Ltd v USDAW* [1978] ICR 614, [1978] IRLR 120.

[160] *UCATT v Rooke & Son Ltd* [1978] ICR 818, [1978] IRLR 204, applied in *Secretary of State for Employment v Helitron Ltd* [1980] ICR 523.

(d) Protection of representatives

Where the 'appropriate representatives' are officials of a recognized trade union, then they will have the ordinary protection for such offices when taking part in union activities, and the ordinary right to time off work for these duties.[161] However, these provisions would not apply to the new category of elected employee representatives, and so the 1995 and 1999 Regulations enacted parallel provisions for them. Thus, an elected representative (or candidate for that office) has a statutory right not to be victimized (short of dismissal), dismissed or later selected for redundancy on the grounds of having performed or proposed to perform such duties, and similar protection is extended to employees participating in the election of representatives.[162] A representative or candidate also has the right to paid time off work in order to perform such duties or to undergo training.[163]

(iv) THE REDUNDANCY PAYMENTS SCHEME

The scheme requiring employers to make compulsory payments to redundant employees was introduced by the Redundancy Payments Act 1965; this Act was repealed and the relevant provisions are now found in Part XI of the Employment Rights Act 1996. A first basic point to make about the scheme is that it is entirely separate from the dismissed employee's right to claim benefit; in one of the early cases on the 1965 Act Lord Denning MR said:

> As I read the Act, a worker of long standing is now recognised as having an accrued right in his job, and his right gains in value with the years. So much so that, if the job is shut down, he is entitled to compensation for loss of the job ... It is not unemployment pay. I repeat 'not'. Even if he gets another job straightaway, he nevertheless is entitled to full redundancy payment. It is, in a real sense, compensation for long service.[164]

There has been some controversy over the overall purpose of the legislation; ideas of increasing mobility of labour, giving greater job security, reducing the number of strikes over redundancies and rewarding long service have been advanced, but none are complete answers and all are open to doubt.[165] Moreover, one major criticism from a legal point of view is that the legislation is arguably far too complicated for its modest aims, particularly as it is subject to a relatively low maximum payment and in practice yields on average much lower amounts than that.[166] The argument that the whole scheme is itself redundant is now supported by the existence of compulsory

---

[161] See Ch 9.   [162] Employment Rights Act 1996, ss 47, 103, 105(6).

[163] Section 61.

[164] *Lloyd v Brassey* [1969] 2 QB 98 at 102, [1969] 1 All ER 382 at 383, CA. Thus, receipt of a redundancy payment does not disentitle a person from jobseeker's allowance.

[165] See Fryer 'The Myths of the Redundancy Payments Act' (1973) 2 ILJ 1.

[166] As at February 2012 the maximum for a week's pay is £430 pw, giving a maximum basic award of £12,900.

consultation procedures in cases of impending redundancy[167] and the redundancy aspects of the law on unfair dismissal (which of course did not exist in 1965), which is now a more important claim than one for straightforward redundancy pay. On the other hand many employers now have private redundancy schemes,[168] often more generous than the legislative scheme, and it may be that it was the legislation which gave the spur to these improved schemes, while retaining some residual importance in ensuring that an employee who is not subject to such a scheme at least receives *something* if he is fairly dismissed because of economic conditions outside the control of himself or his employer.

In order to claim a redundancy payment, the ex-employee must have been 'dismissed', and that dismissal must have been 'by reason of redundancy'. The statutory definition of dismissal has already been considered,[169] but three particular points may be noted. The first is that dismissal may not be necessary in certain cases if there has been instead a lay-off or short-time working; this matter is considered at the end of this section. The second is that 'dismissal' cannot be stretched to include failure to employ in the first place. Thus, in *North East Coast Shiprepairers Ltd v Secretary of State for Employment*[170] it was argued that an apprentice was redundant for statutory purposes when he could not be taken on by the employer as a journeyman fitter at the end of his contract of apprenticeship, because there was no such work available. The EAT held, however, that there was no dismissal, only a refusal to employ him in a different capacity upon the proper termination of the previous contract. The third point is that the legislation attempts to safeguard the position of an employee under notice of dismissal who wishes to leave early (for example, to take up other employment). The Employment Rights Act 1996, section 136(3) provides that he is still deemed to have been dismissed if he leaves during the obligatory period of the employer's notice and gives written[171] counter-notice of his intention to do so during that period. If, however, the employer has good reason to want him to stay for the full period and

---

[167] See heading 1(iii).

[168] Also, certain specific redundancy schemes have in the past been established by statute in the public sector, eg the steelworkers' redundancy scheme, that relating to British shipbuilders and the scheme for dock workers, following the abolition of the national dock labour scheme; the scheme relating to the coal mining industry was of considerable importance in a time of contraction, but has been discontinued.

[169] Ch 7, heading 2, p 477. See *Harvey* E [401]. As seen at p 421 above, termination of contract by mutual consent will rarely be found in employment law, for it robs tribunals of jurisdiction; however, one application of it is particularly important here, namely a finding of mutual termination (not dismissal) on a voluntary early retirement/severance on satisfactory terms; in such a case, the volunteer *cannot* claim a redundancy payment as well: *Birch v University of Liverpool* [1985] ICR 470, [1985] IRLR 165, CA; *Scott v Coalite Fuels and Chemicals Ltd* [1988] ICR 355, [1988] IRLR 131, EAT.

[170] [1978] ICR 755, [1978] IRLR 149.

[171] In s 95(2), the equivalent provision for unfair dismissal purposes, there is no longer the requirement of writing; before the requirement was dropped it caused problems in cases where there was no notice in writing and the employer then contended that termination of the contract was in fact due to mutual agreement, not dismissal: *Lees v Arthur Greaves (Lees) Ltd* [1974] 2 All ER 393, [1974] ICR 501, CA; *McAlwane v Boughton Estates Ltd* [1973] 2 All ER 299, [1973] ICR 470. There appears to be no good reason why the requirement should remain in the redundancy provision.

gives him a further written notice to that effect, but the employee still leaves early, he will only be eligible for a payment if the tribunal thinks it just and equitable that he should receive some or all of his entitlement, after considering the strength of the employer's reasons for wanting to prolong the employment and the employee's reasons for wanting to leave early.[172] One major restriction on these provisions is that the employee's counter-notice is only effective if given during the 'obligatory' period of the employer's notice; this means the amount of time which, by statute[173] or under the individual contract of employment, the employer *has* to give to terminate the contract and so if the employer is generous and in fact gives longer notice than in law is required, the employee must wait until the start of the obligatory period before giving the counter-notice, otherwise that counter-notice is invalid and the employee may be deemed to have resigned, not to have been dismissed.[174] This is a potential trap for the employee who, under longer notice than the contractual entitlement, finds a new job and needs to leave immediately to take it up, thus not being able to rely on section 136(3) if still outside the obligatory period. However, the EAT has suggested[175] a possible way round in one class of case; this is where the employee *requests* to be allowed to leave early and the employer *agrees*. This is not a section 136(3) case (which is where the employee serves formal notice of his *intention* to leave early) and so can be construed on wider principles; in particular, it may be construed as a consensual variation of the employer's original notice, meaning that the employee leaves at the earlier date, is still 'dismissed' by the employer, and can claim his redundancy payment. However, it must be remembered (1) that the employer must still have given *actual notice* in the first place (not just made vague statements about future job losses),[176] and (2) that this alternative approach only works if there is definite agreement between employer and employee—if the employee wants to (or has to) act unilaterally she must still comply with section 136(3) and beware the 'obligatory period' trap.

A dismissed employee may present a claim for a redundancy payment to an employment tribunal within six months of the 'relevant date' of dismissal, though the tribunal may also hear the claim if presented during the six months following that period if it appears just and equitable to do so, having regard to the employee's reasons for failing to comply with the normal time limit.[177] In such proceedings, one

---

[172] Employment Rights Act 1996, s 142.   [173] Section 86.

[174] *Armit v McLauchlin* (1965) 1 ITR 280; *Pritchard-Rhodes Ltd v Boon and Milton* [1979] IRLR 19; *Doble v Firestone Tyre and Rubber Co Ltd* [1981] IRLR 300, EAT.

[175] *CPS Recruitment Ltd v Bowen* [1982] IRLR 54, approving *Tunnel Holdings Ltd v Woolf* [1976] ICR 387.

[176] Thus, certain previous cases such as *Pritchard-Rhodes Ltd v Boon and Milton* (n 174) remain good law and are reconcilable with *Bowen's* case on the ground that the employer had not actually given notice, and so there was no notice there to be varied by agreement. On the requirement of notice, see heading 1(iii)(a), p 572.

[177] Section 164; 'relevant date' is defined in s 145 as (1) the date the employer's notice takes effect, (2) the date the dismissal takes effect, if no notice is given, (3) the date of termination of a limited-term contract, (4) the 'relevant date' (as already defined) of the last contract where there has been one or more trial periods, or (5) the date of expiry of the employee's notice where he has given valid early notice under s 136(3). Where, however,

crucial factor is that there is in section 163(2) a statutory presumption that the dismissal was for redundancy, so that the burden of proof is upon the *employer* to prove, on a balance of probabilities, that the dismissal was for some other reason.[178] This leads to one problem of at least theoretical importance to which there is no definite answer, and that is—is the test to be applied subjective (what the employer *thought* was the dominant reason for dismissal) or objective (what the overall facts suggest)? The problem arises where there was on the facts prima facie a 'redundancy situation', but the employer claims to have acted on a genuine belief at the time that some other ground for dismissal existed (for example, incompetence, suspected dishonesty); does that discharge his burden of proof and defeat the claim, or should the tribunal look at the facts objectively? The majority decision of the Court of Appeal in *Hindle v Percival Boats Ltd*[179] has been said to be clear authority in favour of the subjective approach and indeed Sachs LJ said:

> once the tribunal is satisfied that the ground put forward by the employer is genuine and is the one to which the dismissal is mainly attributable the onus is discharged—and it ceases to be in point that the ground was unwise or based on a mistaken view of facts.[180]

However, Lord Denning MR's dissent (on the decision and on this point) is a strong one, clearly favouring an entirely objective test[181] and the third judgment, that of Widgery LJ, is less than clear on the point, for although he expresses agreement with Sachs LJ, he states that he finds the distinction between objective and subjective tests neither helpful nor conclusive, and later says:

> the lesson of the *MacLaughlan* case in my opinion is that the tribunal must not accept the explanation put forward by the employer however honestly, without looking at the whole of the evidence to see if it positively established that the dismissal was not mainly due to a diminution in the requirement of the business for employees on work of a particular kind.[182]

---

any notice given (including the case where no notice is given) is shorter than the legal minimum which is required by s 86, the relevant date may be deemed to be the later date of the notional expiry of that legal minimum period, for three purposes—the calculation of the two years' qualifying period, the computation of the length of service for calculation of the payment and the determination of the relevant statutory maximum on a 'week's pay' for calculation purposes (ie where that maximum has been raised by Regulations between the dismissal and the claim). The purpose of this complicated provision is to prevent an employer gaining an advantage in these three areas by wrongfully dismissing the employee with short or no notice.

[178] He may then have to prove that that other reason, if accepted by the tribunal, was fair, if unfair dismissal is also being claimed. However, the presumption of redundancy will *not* apply to the latter claim: *Midland Foot Comfort Centre Ltd v Richmond* [1973] 2 All ER 294, [1973] ICR 219. For a relatively rare example of a case being decided by recourse to the statutory presumption, see *Willcox v Hastings* [1987] IRLR 298, CA.

[179] [1969] 1 All ER 836, [1969] 1 WLR 174, CA.

[180] [1969] 1 All ER 836 at 842, [1969] 1 WLR 174 at 182, CA.

[181] Approving the decision of the Court of Session in *MacLaughlan v Alexander Paterson Ltd* (1968) 3 ITR 251; see also his Lordship's judgment in *Mumford v Boulton and Paul (Steel Construction) Ltd* (1971) 6 ITR 76, CA.

[182] [1969] 1 All ER 836 at 848, [1969] 1 WLR 174 at 188, CA.

Moreover, Sachs LJ actually imports objectivity into his test by requiring that the non-redundancy reason be 'the one to which the dismissal is mainly attributable'. This must be considered in light of the rule in *Murray v Foyle Meats Ltd*,[183] redundancy is defined, objectively, as the redundancy situation coupled with causation, or a factual finding that the dismissal was 'attributable to' the redundancy situation. If the tribunal finds as a matter of fact that a dismissal is mainly attributable to another genuinely believed ground, then there has been, objectively, a redundancy.

Even if a general subjective test could be constructed from *Hindle*, it would certainly not be an unqualified one, and in practice the following qualifications would make the gap between it and an objective approach unimportant in many cases—first, the tribunal clearly does not have to take the employer's word at face value and may look behind it, at the very least to confirm that it is supported by facts (per Widgery LJ, above); second, the tribunal may look behind it to ensure that the employer has not 'misdirected' himself[184] or used the wrong label[185] in calling it redundancy; third, in reorganization cases (which can prove some of the most difficult) the tribunal can clearly investigate whether it is a genuine reorganization and not just a cover for redundancies;[186] fourth, in any case where the tribunal is left in real doubt as to the truth of the employer's assertions (especially if they are at variance with some of the facts) the statutory presumption can decide the case in the employee's favour. There may, however, remain cases where none of these qualifications apply, where an employer who is faced with a diminution of work still genuinely thinks (without misdirection) that she is dismissing for a reason other than redundancy, and it is submitted that in such a case the approach of the tribunal should be objective in the *Murray* sense: if a redundancy situation applies, and the dismissal is not, as a matter of fact, mainly attributable to that situation, it is not a redundancy; if the dismissal is mainly attributable to that situation, it is a redundancy.

(a) Qualification: transfer of business or undertaking

In order to qualify for a redundancy payment, the dismissed employee must have been continuously employed for at least two years on the 'relevant date'.[187] Continuity of employment is considered in detail in Chapter 4; one particular point needs to be added to the general discussion there, relating to a case where there has in fact been a change of employer and a question arises as to continuity through a transfer of business or undertaking. This is covered by the general rules under the 1996 Act and also by

---

[183]   [1999] ICR 827, [1999] IRLR 562, HL.

[184]   Per Widgery LJ [1969] 1 All ER 836 at 847, [1969] 1 WLR 174 at 187.

[185]   On analogy with the unfair dismissal case of *Abernethy v Mott, Hay and Anderson* [1974] ICR 323, [1974] IRLR 213, CA, see Ch 7, heading 4(i), p 487; this may be a particular danger in this area, since the word 'redundancy' in common usage in industry may mean much more than its restricted legal meaning.

[186]   *Johnson v Nottinghamshire Combined Police Authority* [1974] 1 All ER 1082, [1974] ICR 170, CA.

[187]   Section 155, for the 'relevant date' see Ch 7, heading 2(ii), p 498.

special rules under Regulations; as these unfortunately apply independently of each other, it is necessary to consider them separately.

(i) *Transfers of business under the 1996 Act* Continuity of employment through a transfer of business (where the employee in fact remains with that business) is preserved by section 218 of the 1996 Act,[188] so that if the employee is later made redundant by the new employer he can count his time with the old employer for the purposes of qualification for and computation of a redundancy payment. These provisions related solely to questions of continuity of employment and did not prejudice the general common law rule that an employee could not be made to change employer without his consent.[189] Further, these longstanding provisions meant that if the transferor employer sold the business to the transferee who did not keep on the workforce, it was clear that the transferor employer, dismissing the workforce on the transfer, was liable for the redundancy payments.

(ii) *Transfers of undertaking under the Regulations* The above position was, however, materially complicated by the provisions of the Transfer of Undertakings (Protection of Employment) Regulations 1981, re-enacted in 2006,[190] which apply where there has been a 'transfer of undertaking'. It is particularly unfortunate in this context that these changes were enacted by extraneous regulations, rather than by amendments to the existing provisions of the legislation, for the position is subject to a separate set of legislative provisions, on the assumption that there is a 'transfer of undertaking'.[191] On that assumption, the continuity of employment of those transferring to the employ of the transferee is preserved by regulation 4. To this extent, the regulation is in most cases otiose since (assuming it also to be a 'transfer of business') this will be the case anyway under section 218. However, regulation 4 goes considerably further, for it states that a relevant transfer automatically transfers the employee's contract of employment from the transferor employer to the transferee employer.[192] This means that the employee's previous right to claim a redundancy payment from the transferor is no longer applicable and, contrary to the position at common law and under the 1996 Act, if the transferee does not take the workforce

---

[188] Provided that there is a genuine transfer of business, and not just the sale of one of its assets; *Melon v Hector Powe Ltd* [1981] ICR 43, [1980] IRLR 477, HL.

[189] *Nokes v Doncaster Amalgamated Collieries Ltd* [1940] AC 1014, [1940] 3 All ER 549, HL.

[190] SI 2006/246, see *Harvey* R [2290] and heading 2(i), p 589.

[191] For the meaning of this phrase (and 'relevant transfer'), see heading 2(ii), p 600.

[192] This was irrespective of the wishes of the parties (*Newns v British Airways plc* [1992] IRLR 575, CA) and meant that the old common law rule in *Nokes* (n 189) no longer applied to a case covered by the regulations. However, serious confusion was caused by the decision of the ECJ in *Katsikas v Konstantinidis* C-132/91 [1993] IRLR 179 that Directive 77/187/EEC does not *oblige* member states to legislate for automatic transfer against the employee's wishes. In the light of this, the Trade Union Reform and Employment Rights Act 1993 added a right to object to transfer, but for reasons given in (heading 2(v), p 607) it appears that this may be an empty right for many employees, and so automatic transfer will continue to be the norm.

on he may still find that it is he, not the transferor, who has to pay the redundancy payments.[193] The original version of regulation 4 applied wherever an employee was employed by the transferor employer 'immediately before' the transfer. It was originally the case that the regulation could be avoided relatively easily by the device of the transferee requiring the transferor to dismiss the workforce at some point before the transfer; this was possible because in *Secretary of State for Employment v Spence*[194] the Court of Appeal held that 'immediately before' meant 'at the time of' the transfer, so that an employee dismissed before that time (possibly by only a few hours) could not claim the protection of regulation 4, ie any gap was fatal (leaving the employee to pursue remedies, including a redundancy payment, against the original employer who might well be insolvent). However, this position changed radically in the light of two decisions—that of the ECJ in *P Bork International A/S (in liquidation) v Foreningen of Arbejdsledere i Danmark*[195] on the meaning of Directive 77/187/EEC on which the regulations were based, and that of the House of Lords in *Litster v Forth Dry Dock and Engineering Co Ltd*,[196] which followed and applied the decision of the ECJ. The end result was that if the transferor dismissed the employee because of the transfer (for example, at the transferee's request) and that dismissal was unfair under regulation 7 (which it would be unless it came within the 'economic, technical or organizational reasons' defence in regulation 7(2)),[197] then for the purposes of the Transfer Regulations the employee would be deemed to have been still employed by the transferor immediately before the transfer, so that automatic transfer of his contract to the transferee would apply. The decision in *Litster* was specifically adopted in the 2006 Regulations which provide that automatic transfer applies to those employed by the transferor immediately before the transfer 'or who would have been so employed if ... not dismissed in the circumstances described in regulation 7(1)'. Thus, it is doubly clear that prior dismissal will therefore no longer be effective in itself in most cases.

(iii) *The inapplicability of estoppel* Normally questions of continuity (for qualification and computation purposes) will be solved by applying the provisions of Part XIV of the 1996 Act or the Regulations but one judicial gloss was added in the case of a change from one employer to another where there has been no 'transfer of business' or 'transfer of undertaking' (so that the above provisions do not apply). In such a case, there is normally a break in continuity, but the Court of Appeal held in *Evenden v Guildford City AFC Ltd*[198] that where

---

[193] As in *Premier Motors (Medway) Ltd v Total Oil Great Britain Ltd* [1984] ICR 58, [1983] IRLR 471, in which Browne-Wilkinson P made it clear that the position had changed from that under the old law, a fact that had not been realized when the parties negotiated the transfer deal.

[194] [1986] ICR 651, [1986] IRLR 248, CA.   [195] 101/87 [1989] IRLR 41, ECJ.

[196] [1989] ICR 341, [1989] IRLR 161, HL.   [197] See Ch 7, heading 5(iv)(c), p 526.

[198] [1975] 3 All ER 269, [1975] ICR 367; *Rastill v Automatic Refreshment Services Ltd* [1978] ICR 289, EAT.

at the time of the change the new employer gave the employee an assurance that he would regard the employment as unbroken, so that time with the previous employer would count for redundancy purposes, the new employer should not be allowed to go back on that later and claim that continuity was in fact broken by the change. This meant that the presumption of continuity, now contained in section 210(5), was not rebutted and so the whole period could be counted; this principle was accepted by the whole court and Lord Denning MR (with the support of Browne LJ) added the further ground that such conduct by the new employer gives rise to a promissory estoppel[199] in the employee's favour. However, in the case of *Secretary of State for Employment v Globe Elastic Thread Co Ltd*,[200] a case primarily concerned with the (now repealed) redundancy rebate aspect of this problem, the House of Lords over-ruled *Evenden*'s case and held that questions of continuity through a change of employment are governed by the statutory provisions alone; thus, if continuity is not preserved by a statutory provision such as that relating to a 'transfer of business' or the regulations on transfers of undertakings, it is broken by the change of employment and any agreement to the contrary between the parties at the time of the change can only be viewed, if at all, as a separate contract (with a view to which the transferred employee would be advised to demand a formal written agreement).[201]

(b) Exclusions

The following classes of employees are excluded from the redundancy payments scheme:

(1) employees with less than two years' continuous employment;[202]

(2) employees dismissed for misconduct (see under head (f));

(3) redundant employees refusing suitable alternative employment (see under head (e));

(4) share fishermen,[203] employees of foreign governments,[204] civil servants and certain public officials;[205]

(5) classes of employees specifically excluded by order of the Secretary of State, where a collective agreement covers the question of redundancy.[206]

---

[199] *Central London Property Trust Ltd v High Trees House Ltd* [1947] KB 130, [1956] 1 All ER 256.

[200] [1979] 2 All ER 1077, [1979] IRLR 327, HL.

[201] Though even this would not help if, eg, the employee was dismissed by his new employer before serving the qualifying period for unfair dismissal.

[202] Section 155. There used to be a further, frequently used, exclusion where, in a fixed-term contract of two years or more the employee signed away his or her redundancy rights (or, in practice, was obliged to do so by the employer as a condition of getting the job) but this was abolished by the Fixed-term Employees (Prevention of Less Favourable Treatment) Regulations 2002, SI 2002/2034 because it constituted institutional discrimination against fixed-termers.

[203] Section 199(2).   [204] Section 160.   [205] Section 159.   [206] Section 157.

(c) Computation of a redundancy payment

The procedure for calculating a payment is contained in section 162; it is calculated by reference to the period of whole years, ending with the relevant date, during which the employee has been continuously employed. He then receives (1) one and a half week's pay for each year in which the employee was over 41 years old; (2) one week's pay for each year not covered by (1) but in which he was over 22 years old; (3) half a week's pay for each other year (over the age of 18). The maximum number of years which may be counted is 20, and a 'week's pay' is calculated in accordance with Part XIV, Chapter II of the 1996 Act, subject to a statutory maximum figure for computation purposes.[207]

When the laws on age discrimination were being framed, it was at first thought that the above sliding scale would have to go (being indirect discrimination against younger employees) but as eventually enacted the Employment Equality (Age) Regulations 2006 did not do so, the government taking the view that, although discriminatory, these provisions were still objectively justified. This state of affairs is not changed by the Equality Act 2010. Likewise, an employer can still lawfully have an enhanced contractual redundancy scheme provided it is based on the qualification provisions for the state scheme.[208] What did go was the previous exclusion from redundancy rights of those under 20 or over the normal retirement age (as there no longer is one).

(d) Procedure for claiming a redundancy payment

A claim for a payment is subject to a prima facie time limitation of six months from the relevant date, in that the employee will lose his entitlement unless during that period the payment has been agreed and paid or the employee has made a claim in writing to the employer, or has referred the question to an employment tribunal (either directly, or indirectly through making a complaint of unfair dismissal).[209] However, the employee is given a further six-month period in which to submit a claim, but in such a case the awarding of a payment is put into the discretion of the tribunal, which must have regard to whether an award would be 'just and equitable' in the light of the employee's reason for failure to claim during the first six months.[210]

The claim in writing to the employer does not have to be in any particular form, the test being that it must be such that the employer could reasonably appreciate the employee's intention to claim;[211] however, it has been held that it must be submitted during the six-month period *beginning with* the relevant date, so that a claim submitted

---

[207] As at February 2012 the maximum for a week's pay is £430 pw, giving a maximum basic award of £12,900. For the purpose of calculation, actual pay as at the 'relevant date' is used, even if there is a later pay rise back-dated to before that date: *Leyland Vehicles Ltd v Reston* [1981] ICR 403, [1981] IRLR 19.

[208] Employment Equality (Age) Regulations 2006, SI 2006/1031, reg 33, see generally Ch 5, heading 8, p 403.

[209] Section 164(1). Provided the employee has taken one of these steps (and so safeguarded his entitlement) he may still dispute the amount of the payment even after the expiry of the six months: *Bentley Engineering Co Ltd v Miller* [1976] ICR 225, [1976] IRLR 146.

[210] Section 164(2).

[211] *Price v Smithfield and Zwanenberg Group Ltd* [1978] ICR 93, [1978] IRLR 80, EAT.

earlier than the date of termination of employment is invalid,[212] which seems to be an unnecessary complication capable of amounting to a trap for an unwary employee.

When an employer voluntarily gives the payment to which an employee is entitled, the employer must give a written statement to the employee showing how the amount has been calculated.[213] The consequences of failure are, first, that the employer may be fined and, second, may in fact have to pay the sum again in a proper manner, particularly if, for example, the employer just gives the employee one unspecified lump sum upon termination with a vague indication that it is meant to include something for redundancy.[214]

Finally, two points should be noted about the potential role of the Secretary of State. The first is that the Secretary of State has a right to appear in any redundancy proceedings before a tribunal[215] (because of an interest as guardian of the National Insurance Fund). The second is that if the employer either refuses to pay after the employee has taken all reasonable steps (short of legal proceedings) to recover payment, or is insolvent, the employee may apply to the Secretary of State for payment of the amount directly out of the National Insurance Fund; when such a payment is made, the Secretary of State may exercise the employee's rights against the employer to attempt to recover the amount for the fund.[216]

(e) Offers of alternative employment

If the employer makes an offer to an employee before the termination of his contract of employment to renew the contract or re-engage him on suitable alternative work,[217] two consequences may flow. The first is that if the employee accepts that renewal or re-engagement (and there is either no gap, or a gap of less than four weeks between the contracts), there is in law no 'dismissal' at the end of the first contract[218] (subject to the rules on trial periods, considered below). The second is that if the employee unreasonably refuses to accept the offer he is disqualified from claiming a redundancy payment.[219]

Cases of 'renewal' are not likely to cause many problems, for the word means renewal on the *same* terms (including possibly cases where any differences are negligible).[220] 'Re-engagement' may prove more difficult, for this envisages the new terms differing

---

[212] *Watts v Rubery Owen Conveyancer Ltd* [1977] ICR 429, [1977] IRLR 112; *Pritchard-Rhodes Ltd v Boon and Milton* [1979] IRLR 19, EAT.

[213] Section 165. This can be done by using the final page of form RP 1.

[214] It depends on the facts: *Barnsley Metropolitan Borough Council v Prest* [1996] ICR 85.

[215] Employment Tribunals (Constitution and Rules of Procedure) Regulations 2004, SI 2004/1861, rule 51.

[216] Employment Rights Act 1996, s 166.

[217] In *SI (Systems and Instrumentation) Ltd v Grist* [1983] ICR 788, [1983] IRLR 391 the EAT stated obiter that on the strict wording of the subsection, there is a distinction between 'renewal' (which automatically operates to deem there to have been no dismissal) and 're-engagement' (which only so operates if in pursuance of a formal offer, whether in writing or not, made before the end of the first contract).

[218] Section 138(1).   [219] Section 141.

[220] *Devonald v J D Insulating Co Ltd* [1972] ICR 209, NIRC.

from the old ones, and raises two questions—first, was the alternative employment on offer suitable; second, was the employee's refusal of it reasonable? In theory, the tribunal should start with the first question which entails consideration of the nature of the new employment in relation to the employee's skills and abilities. In many cases the offer will be of a similar type of employment, and it has been said that the mere offer of the same salary may not be enough if the job is totally different.[221] However, this is not an invariable rule, and an offer of a completely different job may on the facts be suitable, even for a skilled employee, particularly if it is part of a larger, generally beneficial scheme, and particularly if it is of a temporary nature.[222] Naturally questions of pay may loom large, and difficulties may arise. Opportunities to earn overtime make a comparison of basic rates unreal, but on the other hand overtime may not be certain; the same problem applies to future prospects which might soon recoup and perhaps surpass an initial drop in earnings. Thus, the tribunal must take a realistic view of the question of pay,[223] while at the same time accepting that the matter may be complicated by relevant changes in status and promotion prospects consequent upon acceptance of the new employment.[224] Two further matters which might be material are the expected duration of the new employment and its location. If the new employment is likely to last only for a short time, it has nevertheless been held that it may be suitable provided that it is full-time and regular during that time.[225] Once again, however, this is not a definite rule, for potential duration could be material in some cases, for example where the redundant employee, fearing a general recession in that particular industry if he stays in it, has found another job in another industry, particularly if he is approaching retirement age when employment for his last few years is not easy to find anywhere.[226] The fact that the employment on offer is in a different location, necessitating a move of home or increased travelling, does not necessarily render it unsuitable; obviously this is very much a question of fact, but it is an important qualification on the employee's right, discussed earlier, not to be required to move to a new locality not covered by his contract of employment—he can insist upon that right and refuse an *order* to move, but if in fact the *offer* of work elsewhere is considered 'suitable' by a tribunal, he may still lose his redundancy payment.

The second question, the reasonableness of a refusal, requires consideration of a wider range of different factors, looking at the matter more subjectively from the

---

[221] The judgment of Lord Parker CJ in *Taylor v Kent County Council* [1969] 2 QB 560, [1969] 2 All ER 1080 is often cited on this point, as to whether the offer is of 'employment which is substantially equivalent to the employment which has ceased'. However, this is not part of the statutory wording, and ultimately the question is one of fact for the tribunal: *Standard Telephones and Cables Ltd v Yates* [1981] IRLR 21, EAT.

[222] *Dutton v Hawker Siddeley Aviation Ltd* [1978] ICR 1057, [1978] IRLR 390, EAT.

[223] *Kennedy v Werneth Ring Mills Ltd* [1977] ICR 206, EAT.

[224] *Harris v E Turner & Sons (Joinery) Ltd* [1973] ICR 31, NIRC; *Kane v Raine & Co Ltd* [1974] ICR 300, NIRC.

[225] *Morganite Crucible Ltd v Street* [1972] 2 All ER 411, [1972] ICR 110, NIRC.

[226] *Thomas Wragg & Sons v Wood* [1976] ICR 313, [1976] IRLR 145; *Paton Calvert & Co Ltd v Westerside* [1979] IRLR 108; cf *James and Jones v NCB* (1969) 4 ITR 70.

point of view of the employee who may have certain pressing reasons of a personal nature which make it reasonable to refuse what appears at first sight to be suitable alternative work (for example, health problems, family commitments); in addition, the employee may have personal objections to the job offered (for example, perceived lack of status), even though under the first test the job is objectively 'suitable'.[227] This produces a test that is a mixture of subjective and objective factors, as required by the legislation itself; it has been held that this is sufficient for that purpose and that it is *not* necessary to go further and import an equivalent of the 'range of reasonable responses test', on analogy with unfair dismissal law.[228] One effect of the test being partly subjective is that even where several employees of the same type are made redundant (where possibly one general offer of the same type of alternative work is made to them collectively by the employer),[229] a tribunal must look into the particular circumstances of each individual employee before disqualifying anyone for refusal.[230] The factors which may arise under this second question may be even more various than those under the first, so that the one overall point about the law relating to suitable alternative employment is that each case is heavily dependent upon its own facts, with the results that the tribunal has a wide discretion to use its common sense, precedents from decided cases are of little use[231] and the EAT will only reverse a decision if it is clear that the tribunal completely misdirected itself.[232] Moreover, although the questions of suitability and reasonableness of refusal are in theory separate, they may often be run together in practice in the process of reaching a fair and common-sense decision, particularly as it is well established that the employer bears the burden of proof on *both* questions.[233] Separate or not, the extent to which the alternative employment is suitable has bearing on the question of whether the employee acts reasonably in refusing it.[234]

The above discussion has tended to assume that the employee has either unequivocally accepted or refused the offer. However, it may be the case that the employee is unsure about the new employment because it differs from the old employment in material ways, but wishes to give it a try. To improve the position of such a person, there is

---

[227] *Cambridge and District Co-operative Society Ltd v Ruse* [1993] IRLR 156, EAT.

[228] *Hudson v George Harrison Ltd* (2003) The Times, 15 January. For the range test in unfair dismissal law, see Ch 7, heading 4(iv), p 505.

[229] *McCreadie v Thomson and MacIntyre (Patternmakers) Ltd* [1971] 2 All ER 1135, [1971] 1 WLR 1193, HL; cf *E & J Davis Transport Ltd v Chattaway* [1972] ICR 267, NIRC.

[230] *John Fowler (Don Foundry) Ltd v Parkin* [1975] IRLR 89.

[231] In *Spencer and Griffin v Gloucestershire County Council* [1985] IRLR 393, CA, the EAT had stated as a principle that an employee could not reasonably object on the grounds that the quality of the work was not up to his or her standards, the setting of standards being a matter for the employer (the case concerned the dismissal of school cleaners and the offer to re-engage them on new, inferior contracts which would diminish the standard of cleaning). The Court of Appeal reversed this decision, holding that there is no room for any such principle and that reasonableness remains a question of fact for the tribunal.

[232] *Collier v Smith's Dock Co Ltd* (1969) 4 ITR 338.

[233] *Jones v Aston Cabinet Co Ltd* [1973] ICR 292.

[234] *Commission for Healthcare Audit and Inspection v Ward* [2008] All ER (D) 107 (Jun).

now a statutory 'trial period' of four weeks from the end of the old employment;[235] if during that period the employee terminates the contract for any reason or the employer terminates it for a reason connected with the change of employment, the employee is treated as having been dismissed at the date of termination of the old contract, and for the reason or reasons prevalent at that date, and so may still bring redundancy proceedings on that basis. In the ordinary case where the employee is dismissed by the employer, but with the offer of other employment, this means that she has the next four weeks in which to make up her mind, without prejudice to her rights.[236] However, one problem has arisen in the case of 'constructive dismissal' within section 136(1)(c), ie where the employer, instead of dismissing the employee, is not prepared to carry on employing her in her present capacity, but expects her to change to something different. In this case, the employee could leave and claim to have been constructively dismissed. What happens, however, if the employee is unsure whether to do so and in fact carries on with the employer, performing the new work on a trial basis and only resigns at a later date having decided that she does not like it? In such circumstances it was held (in cases decided before the Employment Protection Act 1975 introduced the statutory trial period) that mere continuance at work did not show acceptance of the new terms and that the employee dismissed under section 136(1)(c) had, in effect, a 'common law trial period' of an agreed or reasonable length during which the employee could still decide that she did not like the new work, leave and still claim to have been constructively dismissed.[237] With the introduction of the statutory trial period, the question arose whether it replaced the common law period, or supplemented it (the practical point being that this period could be *longer* than the statutory four weeks—if a constructively dismissed employee left the new job more than four weeks after the change, could this still be within the common law's 'reasonable period' instead?). The EAT have clearly held that the common law period is *not* abrogated and that the statutory period is in addition.[238] Thus, where the employee is dismissed in the ordinary way it is just a question of applying the statutory period, but where she claims to have been constructively dismissed she may claim to have a period at common law to decide whether to take on the new work (either an agreed period or, in the absence of agreement, a period which is 'reasonable' in all the circumstances), plus a further statutory

---

[235] Employment Rights Act 1996, s 138(2); the trial period may be longer than four weeks if there is a written agreement to that effect, and there may be more than one trial period, in which case the same rules apply with necessary modifications. The four weeks of the trial period are to be applied on a simple calendar basis; the period cannot be extended merely because there was no work available for part of the time (eg because of a Christmas closure): *Benton v Sanderson Kayser Ltd* [1989] ICR 136, [1989] IRLR 19, CA.

[236] If all that has happened is that the employee (already under notice) has agreed to work on temporarily, eg to finish a job, and is then dismissed, that remains an ordinary dismissal for redundancy, without the need to invoke those specialized provisions: *Mowlem Northern Ltd v Watson* [1990] ICR 751, [1990] IRLR 500, EAT.

[237] *Marriott v Oxford and District Co-operative Society Ltd (No 2)* [1970] 1 QB 186, [1969] 3 All ER 1126, CA; *Shields Furniture Ltd v Goff* [1973] 2 All ER 653, [1973] ICR 187; *Sheet Metal Components Ltd v Plumridge* [1974] ICR 373, [1974] IRLR 86, NIRC.

[238] *Air Canada v Lee* [1978] ICR 1202, [1978] IRLR 392; *Turvey v C W Cheyney & Son Ltd* [1979] ICR 341, [1979] IRLR 105.

four-week period (if she decides to try the new work) during which her right to leave and claim constructive dismissal is still protected:

> This is an improvement in the position of the employee who is dismissed in [ordinary dismissal] circumstances. It is also an improvement in the protection of the employee in [constructive dismissal] circumstances. He has a period X in which to make up his mind. If his decision is not to take the new job, he is treated as dismissed at the moment he brings period X to an end by leaving the new job. If his decision is to take the new job and he brings period X to an end by making a new contract or renewing the old one with variations he then has the further trial period created by [section 138] in which to make up his mind, before losing his right to say, 'You dismissed me by repudiating the old contract' ... So he has his common law period X protection plus his statutory trial period protection.[239]

In practice, the addition of four weeks may be of little significance; it is the fact that, in constructive dismissal cases, the common law trial period may be *longer* than four weeks which may be crucial in a particular case.

(f) The effects of misconduct and industrial action

Although an employee may be prima facie redundant, the employee may still commit misconduct (whether by going on strike or otherwise) so that the employer would in fact be justified in dismissing summarily because of that misconduct. In such a case, section 140 provides that the employee shall lose entitlement to a redundancy payment *provided* that the employer dismisses either (1) without notice, (2) with shorter notice than the employee is entitled to, or (3) with full notice which must include a statement in writing that the employer would have been entitled to dismiss without notice (this last possibility being referred to in the cases as 'special notice'). This subsection has caused problems in its interpretation, particularly as it is clear that, if the employer dismisses for cause, that is *not* a dismissal for redundancy anyway, so in theory there is no need in such a case for section 140 in order to disentitle the employee. Two principal interpretations have been put forward. The first, following on from this basic point, is that section 140 is meant to apply where the employee is dismissed for redundancy, but in circumstances where the employer could have dismissed for cause (and makes this known to the employee, either impliedly by giving no or short notice, or expressly by giving special notice). The second is that the subsection applies to dismissals for cause, in order to add the procedural rider that the employer must have given no, short or special notice if he is to rely on 'cause' to rebut the presumption of redundancy. There is still no clear decision as to which view is right; the most important case so far, *Sanders v Ernest A Neale Ltd* ,[240] clearly leans towards the first view, though at the same time stressing the importance of the procedural requirement of special notice:

> We agree ... that neither section [now section 140(1) and (3), discussed below] has any application if the dismissal is neither wholly nor mainly attributable to redundancy ... It

---

[239] *Turvey v C W Cheyney & Son Ltd* [1979] ICR 341 at 346, [1979] IRLR 105 at 108.
[240] [1974] 3 All ER 327 at 336, [1974] ICR 565 at 574.

seems therefore that, subject to [section 140(3)], a man who is dismissed solely on account of redundancy may lose his right to a redundancy payment if, by reason of the employee's conduct, his employer was actually entitled to dismiss him without notice.

Sir Diarmid Conroy [in *Essen v Vanden Plas (England) Ltd*[241]] says he finds it difficult to understand why [section 140] provides for a special notice to be given to the employee if she is allowed to work out her notice and what sanction there is for not giving the notice. We suggest that the answer to the first question is that Parliament thought that an employer should not be allowed to resist a claim for a redundancy payment upon the ground that the employee could have been dismissed without notice, unless the employee was warned of the facts upon which this defence is based at the time of the dismissal ... The answer to the second question is that if the employee is dismissed wholly or mainly on account of redundancy and receives full notice of dismissal, the employer cannot rely on [section 140] unless she has given a notice complying with [section 140(1)(c)]. This is not an insignificant sanction.

This dual approach can also be seen in the judgment of the EAT in *Simmons v Hoover Ltd*:[242]

Certain matters can be stated with a fair amount of confidence:

(1) [section 140] operates only by way of exclusion and, accordingly, has no effect in the case of an applicant who is not prima facie entitled to a redundancy payment, eg where, although there is a redundancy situation, his dismissal is not attributable wholly or mainly to redundancy but to some other cause such as misconduct; (2) the requirements of [section 140(1)(a), (b) or (c)] are presumably designed to ensure that the employee is put on notice that he is being dismissed otherwise than in the ordinary course of the contract'; (3) a failure to serve such a notice under (a), (b) or (c) prevents the employer from relying on [section 140].

Whichever is the preferable interpretation in theory, the practical point is that an employer is advised take the safe position by giving no, short or special notice when dismissing an unsatisfactory employee for redundancy or, ex abundanti cautela, even when dismissing for misconduct in circumstances where the employee may claim to have been redundant.

The exclusory effect of section 140, however it is construed, is subject to two main qualifications, found in that section. The first is that under subsection (2), where an employee under notice of dismissal for redundancy is in fact dismissed during the obligatory period[243] of that notice because of misconduct, the complete exclusion does not apply and a tribunal has discretion to award all or only part of the payment to which he would otherwise have been entitled. This is a wide discretion, not likely to be altered on appeal unless the tribunal has clearly made an error in principle in exercising it.[244]

The second qualification applies where the misconduct in question is the participation in a strike. This is classed as misconduct, entitling the employer to dismiss without

---

[241] (1966) 1 ITR 186.   [242] [1977] ICR 61 at 79, [1977] 1 All ER 775 at 787.
[243] Defined in s 136(4), see heading 1(iii), p 572.
[244] *Lignacite Products Ltd v Krollman* [1979] IRLR 22.

notice, and so the exclusion in section 140(1) is applicable.[245] However, subsection (2) provides that where the strike and dismissal take place during the obligatory period of an existing notice of dismissal for redundancy the exclusion does not apply, and so the employee may still seek a redundancy payment, subject to the employer's statutory right to serve a written notice of extension on the employee requiring him to work extra days after the expiry of the notice, equivalent to the number of days lost due to the strike;[246] if he fails to comply with such a notice, he loses his right to claim. Thus, the position of the redundant employee on strike during his notice period is safeguarded, but only if he is within the scheme of section 140(2). In *Simmons v Hoover Ltd*[247] the unusual situation arose where the employee was already on strike when he was dismissed for redundancy (ie the opposite of the facts envisaged by section 140(2)); the EAT held that this fell outside the wording of the section, so that the employee remained disqualified under subsection (1) and could not claim a redundancy payment. Finally on industrial action, it should be noted that there is no concept of 'self-induced redundancy' (operating to disqualify an employee); thus, even if the employee is a member of a group which has precipitated redundancies by continued industrial action, the employee will remain entitled to payment unless and until clearly disqualified in some way under the legislation:

> The court would like to take this opportunity of exorcising the ghost of self-induced redundancy. It can certainly occur, but as such it has no legal significance ... the mere fact that the employee's action created the redundancy situation does not disentitle them to a redundancy payment. The entitlement depends upon the words of the statute and there is no room for any general consideration of whether it is equitable that the employee should receive a payment.[248]

(g) Lay-off and short time

An ordinary claim for redundancy depends upon the existence of a 'dismissal'. In some cases of shortage of work, however, the employer may not dismiss, but instead may lay off the employee who has no work to do, or put the employee on to short time. If there is no contractual right to do so, this may constitute constructive dismissal so that the employee may walk out and still claim dismissal rights.[249] However, where the employer *has* such a contractual right this will not apply[250] and if the employee, short

---

[245] *Simmons v Hoover Ltd* [1977] 1 All ER 775, [1977] ICR 61. Notice that the exclusion also applies, indirectly, to the case where an employee walks out because of a lockout: s 143.

[246] Employment Rights Act 1996, s 143.   [247] See n 245.

[248] *Sanders v Ernest A Neale Ltd* [1974] 3 All ER 327 at 335, [1974] ICR 565 at 573.

[249] *Powell Duffryn Wagon Co Ltd v House* [1974] ICR 123; *Jewell v Neptune Concrete Ltd* [1975] IRLR 147, IT; *Kenneth MacRae & Co Ltd v Dawson* [1984] IRLR 5. This may be an important argument if for some reason the employee cannot rely on the statutory procedure about to be described (eg owing to failure to comply with the detailed requirements); the employee can try to prove that there was *no* contractual right to lay off, resulting in a constructive dismissal on ordinary principles.

[250] This conclusion was avoided in *A Dakri & Co Ltd v Tiffen* [1981] ICR 256, [1981] IRLR 57 by arguing that even an express lay-off term is subject to an implied term that any lay-off would only last for a reasonable

of money, walks out that will prima facie be a resignation not a dismissal, to the prejudice of dismissal rights. To protect such a person, the legislation contains complicated
provisions allowing the employee to claim a payment, though it is emphasized that
to take advantage of these provisions the employee must qualify strictly under their
wording—it is not necessarily enough to say there was a 'lay off' in common parlance.
For statutory purposes, an employee is 'laid off' during any week when she receives
no remuneration under this contract, and is on 'short time' if she receives during the
week in question less than half her normal week's pay;[251] thus, if she receives more
than half (for example, under a guaranteed minimum wage clause in his contract) she
is not within the statutory scheme.[252] These definitions will be primarily applicable to
piecework employees, but are not restricted to this class.[253] The employee may claim
a redundancy payment where she has been laid off or on short time (as defined) for a
period of four consecutive weeks, or for a total of six weeks in a 13-week period; the
procedure is that she must give written notice to the employer of her intention to claim
a redundancy payment by virtue of the lay-off or short time (within four weeks of the
end of either of the specified periods) and must terminate her employment by giving
the amount of notice required under the contract.[254] The employer may contest the
claim by giving the employee a written counter-notice within seven days of receiving
the employee's notice and by seeking to show that it could reasonably be expected (as
the date of the employee's notice) that within four weeks the employee would enter a
period of at least 13 weeks without any lay-offs or short time;[255] this question is then
decided by the employment tribunal. The period of work without lay-offs or short time
refers to work of the same type as that previously performed by the employee; this provision is not to be confused with the separate provisions on offers of alternative work
of a different kind.[256] Finally, the legislation provides that if the lay-off or short time in
question is caused by a strike or lockout in *any* industry *anywhere*, these special provisions do not apply.[257]

period (so that if it lasted longer an employee could still leave and claim constructive dismissal). This reasoning
was disapproved in *Kenneth MacRae & Co Ltd v Dawson* (n 249) but surfaced again in *McClory v Post Office*
[1992] ICR 758, [1993] IRLR 159 (in the context of a disciplinary suspension) and it can be seen to be consistent with other modern moves towards giving the implied term of trust and confidence overriding effect: see
Ch 3, heading 3, p 151.

[251] Employment Rights Act 1996, s 147. An employee is not on short time if he refuses work that is offered
(eg because he thinks it too poorly paid): *Spinpress Ltd v Turner* [1986] ICR 433.

[252] *Powell Duffryn Wagon Co Ltd v House*, n 249, at 126.

[253] *Hulse v Perry* [1975] IRLR 181, IT; *Powell Duffryn Wagon Co Ltd v House*, n 249; cf *Hanson v Wood*
(1967) 3 ITR 46.

[254] Employment Rights Act 1996, s 148. Note the time limit on giving notice: s 150.

[255] Section 152; if the tribunal finds with hindsight that the employee was in fact laid off or on short time
during the whole four weeks following the date of the notice, that is conclusively deemed to decide the case
against the employer on this point: s 152(2).

[256] *Neepsend Steel and Tool Corpn Ltd v Vaughan* [1972] 3 All ER 725, [1972] ICR 278.

[257] Section 154.

2 TRANSFERS OF UNDERTAKINGS

(i) INTRODUCTION

This part of the chapter considers the rules relating to transfers of undertakings which, like redundancy, may also be relevant in a case of radical business changes, especially if new ownership of the business (or, crucially in many of the cases, part of it) is seen as an alternative to closure and redundancies. Domestic law has had rules since 1963 preserving continuity of employment through a business transfer but these only operated if the new owner took on the existing staff; EC law has, since the early 1980s, required laws going much further to enact a system of compulsory transfer—which is quite a different matter—with accompanying consultation and information obligations. The compulsory transfer rules were contained for quarter of a century in the Transfer of Undertakings (Protection of Employment) Regulations 1981, which were finally amended and reissued in 2006. In that time they have caused legal difficulties out of all proportion to their original, rather limited aims. They have also been one of the areas where employment law can come closest to acting as an adjunct to commercial law, with the possible liabilities to be inherited by an acquiring organization often being a serious consideration in the commercial dealings. In turn, redundancy rights may be a significant element in this, and so the topics dealt with in this chapter may again have a close connection in any given case.

Domestic employment law rules on continuity of employment capable of applying on the acquisition of firm A by firm B, that have been in existence since 1963, only apply *if* the employee in question is kept on by firm B. The novelty contained in the Acquired Rights Directive[258] was a regime of *automatic* transfer of an affected employee, whether anyone wanted it or not. This was transposed into domestic law in the Transfer of Undertakings (Protection of Employment) Regulations 1981, along with equally novel provisions on information and consultation of employees, the continuation of collective agreements and recognition[259] and the dismissal of employees by reason of the transfer.[260] These Regulations (invariably referred to as 'TUPE' in the employment lawyer's jargon) have acquired a not-undeserved reputation as one of the most complex and potentially difficult areas of modern employment law. This may be partly owing to the way that they were introduced. It was a Labour government that agreed to the Directive in 1977, but by the due date for implementation in 1981 there was a Conservative government of very different views. Quite simply, these new laws were not wanted by that government and this affected their eventual form—they took the form of specific Regulations, simply placed on top of existing UK law with little or no attempt to integrate them (even in the major consolidation of the Employment Rights Act 1996). Moreover, in an exercise of minimum compliance, the government adopted

---

[258] Originally Directive 77/187/EEC; now 2001/23/EC.
[259] This is now provided for in regs 5 and 6.   [260] See heading 2(vi), p 604.

the 'copy-cat' technique of drafting, lifting large parts directly from the Directive with no attempt to 'translate' them into concepts more akin to existing law.[261]

At first, this status as an unloved and unwanted child seemed to matter little because, apart from an early flurry of case law on who paid redundancy payments (transferor employer or transferee?), it was generally thought that these new Regulations added little to existing law. This now curious state of affairs lasted for ten years until a series of ECJ decisions[262] (in the context of 'contracting-out' cases, which are considered separately under this heading) suddenly made it clear that these Regulations *had* made important changes, great enough to be seen as challenging at the time one whole plank of the Conservatives' economic policy, namely the compulsory contracting-out of services to the private sector as a form of quasi-privatization. Although the original purpose of the Acquired Rights Directive had been to attack the practice of 'asset stripping' (ie taking over an ailing firm, removing any valuable assets then letting it become insolvent, leaving its employees with legal rights only against its shell), the fact that this by the early 1990s was no longer a major concern was of no consequence; the Regulations had taken on a life of their own and now started to assume a commercial importance in mergers and acquisitions far greater than the original (limited) aims of the Directive. As further case law clarified the width of the liabilities that automatically pass on a TUPE transfer[263] and that the new employer could not simply dismiss the transferring employees as redundant[264] or insist on a change in their terms and condition[265] the 'cost' of the inherited employees (immediate and future) became a significant consideration in many commercial negotiations.

Reform of the Regulations was on the agenda for several years, in the light of amendments made when the Acquired Rights Directive was renegotiated.[266] Consultation began in 2001 but was bedevilled by the conundrum of how to legislate for the TUPE transfer of occupational pension rights, which the government had originally intended to form part of any new Regulations.[267] This caused serious delays, with reform only

---

[261] The best example is the transposition of the 'economic, technical or organisational reasons' defence to unfair dismissal, which had and still has no counterpart in domestic law. It remains a mystery a quarter of a century later.

[262] Particularly important were the decisions in *Dr Sophie Redmond Stichting v Bartol* C-29/91 [1992] IRLR 366, ECJ and *Rask v ISS Kantineservice A/S* C-209/91 [1993] IRLR 133, ECJ which together demonstrated (1) the applicability of TUPE to the public sector, not just the private and (2) their potentially dire effect on the Conservative government's compulsory commercial tendering policy for local government services.

[263] Going well beyond the automatic transfer of basic terms and conditions such as pay and holidays, this meant that, for example, the transferee employer could find itself the respondent in a pre-existing discrimination claim by a transferring employee, or even as the defendant in a pre-existing industrial accident claim.

[264] As the theory is that the transferring employees are deemed always to have been employed by the transferee, any excess numbers can only be fairly dealt with in a redundancy by putting into the redundancy pool *all* employees of that description, original and transferred.

[265] This is the infamous *'Wilson v St Helens'* problem that any transfer-related changes to the employees' terms and conditions are *void*, see heading 2(vii), p 612. This remains the position under the 2006 Regulations.

[266] This was done in Directive 98/50, with the results being consolidated into Directive 2001/23; see Davies 'Amendments to the ARD' (1998) 27 ILJ 365.

[267] See the Detailed Background Paper (URN 01/1158, DTI) and Sargent 'New Transfer Regulations' (2002) 31 ILJ 35.

coming in the Transfer of Undertakings (Protection of Employment) Regulations 2006[268] which ironically did not include pensions transfer. It would be nice to think that the 2006 Regulations constituted a fresh start, addressing all the areas of uncertainty, and allowing the tribunals to take a 'year zero' approach of starting again, unencumbered by the voluminous existing case law. Sadly, this is not the case. In making changes the government did not have a free hand because they could only make amendments permitted by the new Directive, and in its renegotiation the UK government had *not* managed to incorporate many of the changes it sought. It is true that there are some substantive changes in the 2006 Regulations (relating to contracting-out cases, insolvency cases, employee liability information and a small element of joint liability) but in other areas all that has happened is that the *wording* has been updated, often to reflect the position reached in the case law under the old Regulations. While this is to be welcomed for any improvement in clarity (and possibly less need to refer back to the case law), it means that in several key areas the basic *law* remains the same. This can be seen in the transfer of terms and conditions of employment, the transfer of recognition and collective agreements, the dismissal of employees, the identification of which employees transfer, the exclusion of pensions and the duty to inform and consult. Moreover, there remain certain key problems in practice that are not addressed at all, simply because the Directive did not permit it; these are considered at the end of the chapter. While the discussion in the rest of this chapter will of course concentrate on the new wording of the 2006 Regulations, it will still therefore be necessary in places to consider the previous case law; arguably, the only area where there is a serious chance of a completely fresh start and a 'year zero' approach is in the new provisions on contracting-out cases, where such an outcome is fervently to be hoped for.

Two final points may be noted by way of introduction. The first is that the genesis of the Regulations in an EU Directive may well be important in any case requiring their interpretation, because it means that a purposive interpretation is permitted (indeed, required), resolving any ambiguity in the light of the protective intent of the Directive. It is no coincidence that the leading case on the interpretation of TUPE is also a leading case on the interpretation of EC law generally.[269] The second point is that there may be further considerations than the 2006 Regulations in the public sector. Transfers within and from the Civil Service (widely defined) have for many years been governed by the Cabinet Office Statement of Practice: Staff Transfers in the Public Sector[270] which seeks to ensure that TUPE principles are always the norm and which does require protection of pension position. These rules were also 'suggested' for application by local authorities, but here the government has gone further. In response to union

---

[268] SI 2006/246 which came into force on 6 April 2006. For comprehensive discussion, see Wynn-Evans *The New Transfer of Undertakings Regulations* (Blackstone, 2006), Upex and Ryley (Jordans, 2006) and McMullen 'An Analysis of TUPE 2006' (2006) 35 ILJ 113.

[269] *Litster v Forth Dry Dock and Engineering Co Ltd* [1989] ICR 341, [1989] IRLR 161, HL; see heading 2(v), p 607.

[270] January 2000; *Harvey* S [1751].

opposition to public-private finance initiatives and its strong concerns about such initiatives creating a 'two-tier workforce', the government issued to local authorities a code of practice governing contracting-out cases under its 'Best Value' programme.[271] Under this an authority is to require a potential contractor to agree not only to preserve existing terms and conditions for any staff going from authority to contractor with the work, but also to extend those protected terms and conditions to any *new* employees taken on to perform the work under that contract, ie a form of TUPE-plus.

(ii) WHAT IS A TUPE TRANSFER?

The 2006 Regulations are expressed to apply to the transfer of an undertaking, business or part of an undertaking to another person where there is a transfer of an economic entity which retains its identity.[272] 'Economic entity' means 'an organised grouping of resources which has the objective of pursuing an economic activity, whether or not that activity is central or ancillary'.[273] This formulation is taken primarily for the leading and often-cited ECJ decision in *Spijkers v Gebroeders Benedik Abbattoir BV*[274] and has two principal effects. The first is that it places emphasis on the continued viability of that which is transferred; the DTI guidance refers to the transfer of a business 'as a going concern' (a useful phrase, though it does not appear in the Regulations) and this may be particularly important where (as in *Spijkers* itself) it is a *part* that is being transferred, raising possibly the question whether it was the transfer of part of a business or merely the sale of an asset. The second effect is that the test concentrates on the reality of the situation (potentially from the employees' standpoint) rather than requiring any particular form of legal transfer.[275] Thus, early ECJ case law upheld the application of the Directive to the transfer merely of some form of business lease or franchise, with the employees going into the employment of the new lessee or franchisee.[276]

---

[271] *Code of Practice on Workforce Matters in Local Authority Service Contracts* (ODPM, February 2003); *Harvey* S [3182]. ACAS have established an arbitration procedure to deal with any disputes under this Code. In the NHS a different approach has been adopted (the 'Retention of Employment Model') whereby NHS staff can be 'loaned' to a private service provider on a long-term secondment; for the employment law issues arising, see Davies 'Contracting out and the Retention of Employment Model in the National Health Service' (2004) 33 ILJ 95.

[272] Regulation 3(1)(a). The reference to a transfer 'to another person' imposes the major limitation (coming from the Directive) that TUPE has never applied to the takeover of a business by the purchase of its shares. This remains so, even if such a tactic is adopted deliberately to avoid the Regulations: *Brooks v Borough Care Services* [1998] ICR 1198, [1998] IRLR 636.

[273] Regulation 3(2).

[274] 24/85 [1986] ECR 1119, [1986] 2 CMLR 296, ECJ. See also, at ECJ level, *Franciso Hernandez SA v Gomez Perez* C-127/96 [1999] IRLR 132, *Sanchez Hidalgo v ASEN* C-173/96 [1999] IRLR 136 and *Allen v Amalgamated Construction Ltd* C-234/98 [2000] IRLR 119.

[275] For example, reg 3(6)(b) states that a transfer may take place whether or not any property is transferred.

[276] *Foreningen af Asbejdslederei i Danmark v Daddy's Dance Hall A/S*: 324/86 [1988] IRLR 315, ECJ; *Landsoganisationen i Danmark v Ny Molle Kro* 287/86 [1989] ICR 330, [1989] IRLR 37, ECJ; *Berg v Besselsenn*: 144/87 [1990] ICR 396, [1989] IRLR 447, ECJ. A much-reported case showing such an approach in a more mainstream context is the *Christel Schmidt* case: C-392/92 [1994] ECR I-1311, [1995] 2 CMLR 331, ECJ; see Ch 9, heading 2(ii), p 652.

One area where this can get particularly complicated is when a company under contract to provide a service to another company loses that contract to one or more competitors. This kind of 'service provision'[277] transfer means that the employees carrying out the work of providing the service are transferred to the new company or companies who are now under contract to provide the service. Where the service is transferred from one transferor to more than one transferee, the transferee who absorbs the largest portion of the service must take on all of the employees who previously did the work on that service for the transferor.[278] The ECJ has also held that the Acquired Rights Directive applies, to transfer employees from transferor to transferee, 'where the part of the undertaking or business transferred does not retain its organisational autonomy, provided that the functional link between the various elements of production transferred is preserved, and that that link enables the transferee to use those elements to pursue an identical or analogous economic activity.'[279] In other words, a transferee cannot avoid the application of the Directive (and hence TUPE) by breaking up the transferred undertaking and integrating it into the transferee's existing management structure.

In addition to the general definition, there are subsidiary rules stating that the undertaking, business or part must have been situated immediately before the transfer in the UK,[280] that the Regulations apply to public and private undertakings engaged in economic activities whether or not they are operated for gain,[281] but that an administrative reorganization of public administrative authorities or the transfer of administrative functions between public authorities does not constitute a transfer for these purposes.[282] It is further specifically provided that a relevant transfer may be effected by a series of two or more transactions,[283] but some care may be needed here because the ECJ have held that ultimately a transfer must take place at one moment, ie it is not possible to have it take place over an extended period.[284]

There can even be a relevant transfer between two companies in the same group: *Allen v Amalgamated Construction Ltd* C-234/98 [2000] ICR 436, [2000] IRLR 119, ECJ. However, the definition is not infinitely elastic, and domestic courts have held that there was no transfer on the redeployment of a bank's staff from a subsidiary to a new department (*BIFU v Barclays Bank plc* [1987] ICR 495) or where employees were changed from direct staff to agency workers (*Wynnwith Engineering Co Ltd v Bennett* [2002] IRLR 170).

[277] See heading 2(viii), p 615.

[278] *Kimberley Group Housing v Hambley and others* [2008] All ER (D) 408.

[279] *Klarenberg v Ferrotron Technologies* [2009] All ER (D) 133 (Feb).

[280] Regulation 3(1)(a). Note, however, that if this is the case the Regulations apply even if the transfer or the employment of the employees is governed by foreign law (reg 3(4)(b)) and/or persons employed by the undertaking transferred ordinarily work outside the UK (reg 3(4)(c)).

[281] Regulation 3(4)(a). The original 1981 Regulations excluded undertakings of a non-commercial nature but ECJ case law showed that this was contrary to the Directive (particularly in *Dr Sophie Redmond Stichting v Bartol* C-29/91 [1992] IRLR 366) and it was removed in 1993.

[282] Regulation 3(5); this codifies the decision in *Henke v Gemeinde Schievke* C-298/94 [1996] IRLR 701, ECJ.

[283] Regulation 3(6)(a); *Longden v Ferrari Ltd* [1994] ICR 443, [1994] IRLR 157. This may be particularly relevant on a re-tendering of a contracted-out service: *Dines v Initial Health Care Services Ltd* [1994] IRLR 336, CA.

[284] *Celtec Ltd v Astley* C-478/03 [2005] IRLR 647, ECJ. On a partial privatization in 1990, civil servants went on secondment to the new body for three years before formally taking employment with it. The ECJ

(iii) CONSULTATION ON TRANSFERS OF UNDERTAKING

If a projected transfer of undertakings does qualify as a 'TUPE transfer', regulation 13 imposes duties to inform and consult and regulation 15 contains enforcement provisions similar in part to those applying to redundancy consultation, but in one crucial respect falling far short of them. However, it was the basic obligation to consult and inform that fell foul of EC law in *EC Commission v United Kingdom*,[285] in the same way as the obligation to consult and inform on collective redundancies (above), through being confined to cases where there was a recognized trade union, whereas the Directive refers to workers or their representatives. Again, this had to be rectified by the Collective Redundancies and Transfer of Undertakings (Protection of Employment) (Amendment) Regulations 1995 and 1999;[286] the amended provisions largely mirror those that now apply to collective redundancies.

(a) The duty to inform and consult

Long enough before a relevant transfer to enable the employer of any affected employees[287] to consult all their appropriate representatives, the employer must give those representatives information of (1) the fact that the relevant transfer is to take place, when, and the reasons for it, (2) the legal, economic and social implications[288] for the affected employees, (3) the measures the transferor envisages will be taken in relation to those employees in connection with the transfer and (4) if the employer is the transferor, the measures which the transferee envisages will be taken.[289] As with collective redundancies, the concept of appropriate representatives was materially widened by the 1995 Regulations to cover not just the officials of a recognized trade union, but also employee representatives directly elected, either ad hoc for this purpose[290] or having been elected for other purposes but being appropriate for this purpose too; as with

---

ruled against any 'continuing' transfer over three years. Applying this, a divided House of Lords held that they had actually transferred in 1990, even though no one had realized(!); see [2006] ICR 992, [2006] IRLR 635, HL.

[285]   Case C-382/92 [1994] ECR I-2435, [1995] 1 CMLR 345, ECJ.

[286]   SI 1995/2587 and SI 1999/1925.

[287]   An affected employee is defined as an employee of either the transferor or transferee who may be affected by the transfer or may be affected by measures taken in connection with it: reg 13(1). This is a very wide definition, particularly as it also says that the employee does not have to be employed in the undertaking or part thereof to be transferred. As such, it seems open-ended, given that a transfer 'may' affect practically anyone in the two businesses in some way, which could cause problems of line drawing in businesses which recognize several unions (particularly if they know their Donne: no man is an island; any man's transfer diminishes me).

[288]   It suffices for the employer to tell employees what she genuinely believes will be the legal, economic and social implications of the transfer, even if she is wrong: *Royal Mail Group v Communication Workers Union* [2009] All ER (D) 07.

[289]   Regulation 13(2). In order to fulfil the transferor's obligation under (4) the transferee must give him the necessary information: reg 13(4).

[290]   If elected ad hoc, the election must satisfy the requirements for a fair election set out in reg 14, as to numbers, constituencies, tenure of office, candidature, voting rights, secret voting and accurate counting.

collective redundancies, the 1999 Regulations removed the employer's choice of route, by providing that where a union is recognized in respect of affected employees, that is the proper channel. One possible problem relates to the timing. The Regulation says that the information must be given 'long enough before a relevant transfer to enable consultations to take place', which is not further defined or qualified (contrast this with the provisions on collective redundancies); moreover, as has been pointed out,[291] head (1) of the information to be given concerns the *fact* that the transfer is to take place, ie there need be no information or consultation at the stage of *proposals* for a transfer.[292] The transferee's (and logically the transferor's) obligation to consult does not extend past the date of transfer.[293]

Where an employer of affected employees envisages that she will be 'taking measures' in relation to them in connection with the transfer, she must enter into consultations with the appropriate representatives with a view to seeking their agreement to measures to be taken, and in doing so must (1) consider any representations and (2) reply to them, giving reasons for any rejections.[294] If there are special circumstances making it not reasonably practicable for an employer to inform or consult as required, she must take all steps as are reasonably practicable in the circumstances to comply; this means that an employer cannot say that, merely because full compliance was impossible, she did not need to do anything at all.[295]

As in the case of consultation on impending collective redundancies, special legal protection is given to employee representatives from victimization, dismissal and subsequent selection for redundancy, on the grounds of having fulfilled those functions; there is also a statutory right to time off work with pay for fulfilling them or for training.

(b) Enforcement provision

As in the case of a failure to consult on impending redundancies, a complaint of failure to comply with regulation 13 may be presented to a tribunal by the employee

---

[291] Hepple (1982) 11 ILJ at 38.

[292] Again this may be contrasted with the provisions on collective redundancies where the Trade Union and Labour Relations (Consolidation) Act 1992, s 188 requires an employer 'proposing' to make redundancies to consult recognized unions; see heading 1(iii)(a), p 602. Regulation 10(10) provides that where the employer is going through the process of electing representatives, the employer complies with the time requirement if he acts as soon as reasonably practicable after the representatives are elected. If the employees fail to elect representatives within a reasonable time, the employer may give individual affected employees the information required by law, and is then absolved from collective consultation: reg 10(11).

[293] *AMICUS and others v City Building (Glasgow) LLP and others* [2009] IRLR 253.

[294] Regulation 13(6), (7). In *Institution of Professional Civil Servants v Secretary of State for Defence* [1987] IRLR 373 (decided under the Dockyard Services Act 1986 which adopted and applied the provisions of this regulation), Millett J emphasized that although the obligation to give information applied to all four heads above, the obligation to consult only applies to head (3), the measures which are envisaged; his judgment gives guidance on the meaning of 'measures', which is not defined in the Regulations.

[295] Regulation 13(9). This establishes a 'special circumstances' defence in similar terms to that applying to collective redundancies. Presumably the case law which has arisen in that context will be applied here.

representatives, or the recognized trade union or, in any other case, by any affected employee.[296] Where employees are represented by a trade union or elected representatives, only those representatives can bring the claim;[297] trade unions in multi-union workforces cannot bring a claim regarding parts of the workforce they do not represent.[298] The employer may raise the 'special circumstances' defence (ie that there were such circumstances making performance of the obligations not reasonably practicable *and* that she did all that was reasonably practicable in the circumstances), in which case the burden of proof is upon her.[299] If the tribunal finds the complaint well, founded it must make a declaration to that effect and award compensation to affected employees.[300] The maximum amount was raised from four to 13 weeks' pay by the 1999 Regulations.[301] This became of particular significance when it was subsequently held in *Sweetin v Coral Racing*[302] that (in line with the protective award in collective redundancy law) this award is punitive (not merely compensatory) and meant to act as a deterrent; the result is that a tribunal should start in each case at the maximum and only reduce it if the employer proves mitigation.

(iv) WHAT TRANSFERS?

Regulation 4(1) lies at the heart of the statutory regime and provides that a relevant transfer does not terminate the contract of employment of an employee of the transferor, but instead that contract is to 'have effect after the transfer as if originally made between the person so employed and the transferee'. This has been described as a form of statutory novation of the contract, which overrides the basic common law tenet that an employee may not be transferred to a new employer without his or her consent.[303] The ECJ have strongly affirmed the automatic nature of the transfer, irrespective of the views or even the wishes of the parties,[304] and the EAT have held that a transfer can

---

[296] Regulation 15(1). The complaint must be brought within three months of the date on which the transfer was completed (undefined): reg 15(12); it may be brought *before* the transfer is effected: *Banking Insurance and Finance Union v Barclays Bank plc* [1987] ICR 495; *South Durham Health Authority v UNISON* [1995] ICR 495, [1995] IRLR 407.

[297] *Northgate HR Ltd v Mercy* [2008] IRLR 222.

[298] *Transport & General Workers' Union v Brauer Coley Ltd* [2007] IRLR 207.

[299] Regulation 15(2). If the complaint is against the transferor, who maintains that the reason for default was that the transferee had not provided the necessary information, the transferor cannot raise the special circumstances defence unless the transferee is joined as a party to the proceedings: reg 15(5).

[300] Regulation 15(8). If it is not paid, the employee may complain to the tribunal within three months of the date of the order: reg 15(10)–(12). One innovation in the 2006 Regulations was to make the transferor and transferee employers jointly and severally liable (reg 15(9)); it will be interesting to see how this works.

[301] Regulation 16(3). 'Week's pay' is calculated in accordance with the Employment Rights Act 1996, Pt XIV, Ch II.

[302] [2006] IRLR 252, applying *Susie Radin v GMB*.

[303] *Nokes v Doncaster Amalgamated Collieries* [1940] AC 1014, HL.

[304] *Berg and Busschers v Besselsen* C-144/87 [1989] IRLR 447, ECJ; *Celtec Ltd v Astley*, n 284.

occur even if the employee has no knowledge of the facts or the identity of the new employer.[305]

Regulation 4(2) expands on this by stating that on completion of the transfer 'all the transferor's rights, powers, duties and liabilities' are to be transferred to the transferee and (following the logic of regulation 4(1)) any act or omission (before the transfer is completed) of the transferor is to be deemed to be an act or omission of the transferee. Criminal liabilities are not to be transferred (being considered personal to the transferor);[306] nor, after the years of delay on this point, are rights or duties under occupational pension schemes.[307] The 2006 Regulations made two changes to the automatic transfer regime. The first was that, instead of liability for a failure by the transferor to consult on an impending transfer being wholly transferred to the transferee (as had previously been the case),[308] there is now joint liability on transferor and transferee;[309] the policy behind this is to stop the transferor deliberately flouting the requirement in the knowledge that the transferee would pick up the bill if challenged. The second was that if at the time of the transfer the transferor was subject to insolvency proceedings, any liabilities in respect of which the Secretary of State would be liable under the 'guaranteed debts' provisions[310] (if the employee had in fact lost his employment) are not to transfer to the transferee, but instead these amounts (eg unpaid wages or holiday pay) are to be met by the Secretary of State;[311] the policy behind this is to allow a transferee to acquire the business without debts, thus encouraging the government's 'rescue culture' for insolvent businesses.

Subject to these specific instances, the automatic transfer provisions are of wide, general application. They obviously cover the transferred employee's existing terms and conditions of employment, along with accrued rights such as those in relation to redundancy payments and continuity of employment generally. However, one of the themes of the case law at one point was the discovery of *less* than obvious liabilities that could pass to a transferee. Thus, the transferee could find itself the respondent before a tribunal in a case involving a pre-transfer dispute such as a discrimination claim,[312] or even the defendant in a personal injury action where the accident happened before the

---

[305] *Secretary of State for Trade & Industry v Cook* [1997] IRLR 150.

[306] Regulation 4(6).

[307] Regulation 10. Instead of incorporating pension rights into the 2006 Regulations, the government opted to give a much more basic level of pension protection under the Pensions Act 2004, which could leave the employee with a much lesser pension entitlement after the transfer. The exclusion of pensions under reg 10 is a derogation and so, according to the ECJ, is to be construed narrowly; it only applies to old age, invalidity or survivors' benefits, so that any other aspect of a pension scheme (eg early retirement) *can* transfer: reg 10(2), codifying *Beckman v Dynamco Whicheloe Macfarlane Ltd* C-164/00 [2002] IRLR 578, ECJ. See Pollard 'Pensions and TUPE' (2005) 34 ILJ 127.

[308] *Alamo Group (Europe) Ltd v Tuckes* [2003] ICR 829, [2003] IRLR 266.

[309] Regulation 15(9).   [310] Employment Right Act 1996, Pt XII.   [311] Regulation 8.

[312] *DJM International Ltd v Nicholas* [1996] ICR 214, [1996] IRLR 76 (transferee inheriting a sex discrimination claim).

transfer.[313] To provide some protection to the transferee, regulations require transferors to inform transferees about any disciplinary or grievance procedures taken against them in the last two years, an obligation which is now triggered by the applicability of the ACAS Code under TUPE, regulation 11.[314] It has also been held (logically but oddly) that where an employee dismissed for misconduct before the transfer brought an appeal which was heard after the transfer, the transferor could still reinstate him, even though they were reinstating him into the *transferee's* employment.[315] Similarly, if a transferee instructs a transferor to dismiss an employee before a transfer, because that employee had previously pursued a tribunal action against that transferee, the transferee will be held liable for the automatically unfair dismissal (for exercising statutory rights) after the transfer.[316] On the 'rights' side, it has been held that the transferee employer can exercise rights under a restraint of trade clause imposed by the transferor.[317] Problems have arisen where the employee was entitled under the contract to some form of performance-related pay—the right transfers, but based on whose performance? If the claim relates to back-pay before the transfer, the transferee owes the amount based on the transferor's performance,[318] but in the problematic case of the employee's future entitlement the EAT have attempted to square the circle by suggesting that the transferee might be required to establish an *equivalent* payment system, based on its own performance.[319]

One particular issue relating to the continuance post-transfer of a term relating to the previous employment has caused problems only recently resolved. In *Whent v T Cartledge Ltd*[320] local authority employees whose wages were directly related by their contracts to an NJC agreement in the public sector were TUPE transferred to a private company. When pay rates were increased post-transfer by a new agreement, the EAT held that they were entitled to the increase because their transferred contracts retained the reference to the agreement, in spite of the fact that their new employer was not a party to it at all and indeed had derecognized the union. However, when the ECJ considered this matter in *Werhof v Freeway Traffic Systems GmbH*[321] they held that the Directive only protects the rights of the transferred employees under any *existing* collective agreement at the time of the transfer; it does not bestow rights under any *future* collective agreement (ie they held against any 'dynamic' interpretation of the

---

[313] *Bernadone v Pall Mall Services Group* [2001] ICR 197, [2000] IRLR 487, CA. Where the transferor was in the private sector and obliged to insure under the Employers' Liability (Compulsory Insurance) Act 1969, the transferee also inherited the benefit of that insurance. Certain public employers are not obliged to insure under the Act; in such a case, reg 17 now provides that there is to be joint liability for the transferor and transferee.

[314] Transfer of Undertakings (Protection of Employment) (Amendment) Regulations 2009, SI 2009/592.

[315] *G4S Justice Services (UK) Ltd v Austey* [2006] IRLR 588. The case was given an extra frisson because the transferee was the transferor's *competitor*, to which it had just lost the contract!

[316] *Perry's Motor Sales v Lindley* [2008] All ER (D) 32.

[317] *Morris Angel & Son Ltd v Hollande* [1993] ICR 71, [1993] IRLR 169, CA.

[318] *Unicorn Consultancy Services Ltd v Westbrook* [2000] IRLR 80.

[319] *MITIE Managed Services Ltd v French* [2002] IRLR 512.   [320] [1997] IRLR 153.

[321] C-499/04 [2006] IRLR 400, ECJ.

protection). As this was a pronouncement on the meaning of the Directive, arguably it meant that it was not open to argue that *Whent* still applied, giving more protection in domestic law; it simply meant that *Whent* was wrongly decided. However, in *Alemo-Herron v Parkwood Leisure*[322] the EAT ruled that under TUPE, as opposed to the Acquired Rights Directive, a contractual term in the contracts of transferred employees linking their pay to a collective agreement as negotiated from time to time *does* continue to oblige the transferee to pay according to new pay increases under the collective agreement, even if the transferee does not recognize the agreement or the union.

Other case law on what transfers has been similarly expansive, even where the TUPE logic leads to a result which in other ways is illogical. Indeed, as the case law stands at the time of writing, the only matters which have been held not to transfer (because they do not arise under the employee's contract) are liability under an order for interim relief,[323] an employee's normal (as opposed to contractual) retirement age,[324] and a lease on working premises held by the transferor, even where termination of the lease upon transfer could result in the dismissal of the employees.[325] Finally, separate provisions in regulations 5 and 6 transfer to the transferee employer any existing collective agreement and trade union recognition affecting the transferor. Traditionally, that did not in fact give much protection to the relevant union or its members because in this jurisdiction neither a collective agreement nor a recognition agreement is legally enforceable, so a transferee with the necessary industrial power would be able to withdraw from the agreement and/or derecognize the union after the transfer. However, the position might now be different in the case of recognition if that recognition had been obtained by the union by invoking the statutory recognition procedure[326] against the transferor; in that case, any limitations on derecognition by the transferor would presumably continue to apply to the transferee.

(v) WHO TRANSFERS?

In many cases, the question of who transfers is simple; it is the whole workforce of the acquired undertaking, with the transferee having no power to pick or choose. However, in an untypical case, three issues may arise that are now specifically covered by the 2006 Regulations, namely whether the law can be evaded by dismissals before the transfer, who transfers if only a part of the undertaking is acquired and what happens if an employee objects.

The question of 'early dismissal' arose early in the history of this legislation, when it was perceived as a possible way for the transferee to exercise selection by getting the transferor to dismiss those employees the transferee did not want in *advance* of

---

[322] UKEAT/0456/08/ZT.   [323] *Dowling v ME Ilic Haulage* [2004] ICR 1176.
[324] *Cross v British Airways plc* [2006] ICR 1239, [2006] IRLR 804, CA.
[325] *Kirtruna SL, Elisa Vigano v Red Elite de Electrodomesticos SA and others* Case C-313/07, ECJ.
[326] See Ch 9, heading 3(ii), p 666.

the transfer. At first, this seemed to succeed because of the decision in *Secretary of State for Employment v Spence*[327] that automatic transfer only applied to those in the employment of the transferor at the time of the transfer. On that exact point, *Spence* technically remains good law, but this potentially serious gap in the protection was soon closed by the House of Lords by holding that the reasoning in *Spence* did not go far enough. In *Litster v Forth Dry Dock and Engineering Co Ltd*[328] employees of the transferor had been dismissed only an hour before the transfer but the transferee still disclaimed liability for them because they had not been employed 'immediately before the transfer' (thus leaving them to exercise any remedies against what remained of the transferor company which was in liquidation). Picking up on an ECJ decision that had emphasized that under the Directive any dismissal because of the transfer is to be ineffective[329] the House of Lords adopted a highly purposive interpretation and held that in such a case the plain wording of the regulation effecting the transfer of those employed immediately before it was to be read as if there were inserted the words 'or would have been so employed if he had not been dismissed in the circumstances described in regulation [7(1) now]'.[330] Although UK law does not follow the Directive in making a transfer-related dismissal void, this formulation deals with the issue effectively as a matter of interpretation and renders ineffective the tactic of early dismissal. The wording from *Litster* now appears expressly in the 2006 Regulations in regulation 4(3).

Regulation 4(1) covers the second question of who transfers when only a part of the undertaking is acquired. Once again, it does so by adopting wording from what was previously the leading case authority of *Botzen v Rotterdamsche Droogdok Maatschappij BV*,[331] stating that the transfer affects any person 'assigned to the organized grouping of resources or employees that is subject to the relevant transfer'; regulation 2(1) states that 'assigned' means 'assigned other than on a temporary basis'. The *Botzen* 'assignment' test is thus codified, but it can still lead to considerable problems in applying it to the facts, especially where what is being transferred is a part of a complex organization or group of companies; given that the remainder may be facing financial disaster, can an employee who worked for several or all parts of the organization or group claim to be attached to the part transferred, and so 'jump ship' to the employment of the financially viable transferee/purchaser (at least for the purposes of bringing any redundancy or unfair dismissal claims against the latter if not kept on)? In *Sunley Turriff Holdings*

---

[327] [1986] ICR 651, [1986] IRLR 248, CA. Ironically, *Spence* was a case where it was the employees who wanted it *not* to be a transfer (in order to cash in their accrued redundancy rights against the transferor and start afresh with the transferee) but in winning they appeared to worsen the position of employees in more normal cases.

[328] [1989] ICR 341, [1989] IRLR 161, HL.

[329] *P Bork International A/S (in liquidation) v Foreningen of Arbejdsledere i Danmark* C-101/87 [1989] IRLR 41, ECJ.

[330] For the unfair dismissal regime applying to a transfer-related dismissal under reg 7, see Ch 7, heading 5(iv), p 526.

[331] 186/83 [1985] ECR 519, [1986] 2 CMLR 50, ECJ.

Ltd v Thomson[332] two companies (LC Ltd and LC Scotland Ltd) went into receivership and the latter was sold to Co X. The employee had been company secretary and chief accountant for both companies. Although his contract had been with LC Ltd, he had done substantial work for LC Scotland Ltd and so, when made redundant by the receivers the EAT held that he was able to claim that he was covered by the Regulations and so technically taken on by Co X, against whom he could claim unfair dismissal. On the other hand, in *Michael Peters Ltd v Farnfield*[333] when receivers were called in to a group of a holding company and 25 subsidiaries, the EAT held that the chief executive of the group could not invoke the Regulations and claim to go with the transfer when (only) four viable subsidiaries were sold to Co Y. In both cases, the court applied the *Botzen* test, ie to look as a question of fact at 'to which part of the undertaking or business the employee was assigned' or allocated. It is clear from the first of the two EAT cases that this will not be resolved simply by looking at the technicalities of where the contract of employment lay. Other than that (which presumably must at least be a factor) this is a wide question of fact and degree with (so far) no attempt to lay down rules of thumb, such as at least X% of work being done for the part transferred, which could make advising on this point in advance of a transfer very difficult, especially as the EAT subsequently added that tribunals should be astute to ensure that protection of the individual (and the intent of the Directive and Regulations) should not be prejudiced by too formalistic an emphasis being placed on the intricacies of the corporate structure of the transferor organization.[334]

What is the position if it is the employee who does not want to transfer? We have seen that the old common law principle that an employee could not be transferred without consent has been abrogated here. The Regulations do give the employee two powers to object, but they are in restricted format. Regulation 4(9) states that where a transfer involves or would involve a 'substantial change in working conditions to the material detriment' of a person threatened with transfer, he or she may treat the contract as having been terminated, resulting in a dismissal by the employer; this enacts a specific form of constructive dismissal[335] which may lead to an unfair dismissal, though regulation 4(10) then states that where regulation 4(9) applies no damages are to be awarded in respect of any unpaid notice pay, ie there is to be no *wrongful* dismissal action, which seems odd.[336] Even odder, however, are the provisions then giving a *general* right to object to being transferred.

---

[332] [1995] IRLR 184.

[333] [1995] IRLR 190. See also *CPL Distribution Ltd v Todd* [2003] IRLR 28 where a manager's PA was held not to transfer, on similar grounds.

[334] *Duncan Web Offset (Maidstone) Ltd v Cooper* [1995] IRLR 633.

[335] Under the (differently worded) version in the 1981 Regulations it had been held that, like ordinary constructive dismissal, this required the employee to prove a repudiatory breach of contract by the employer. The current, more generalized, wording aims to remove that requirement. Where, however, there *is* a repudiatory breach reg 4(11) preserves the employee's ordinary right to claim constructive dismissal.

[336] For discussion of reg 4(9) and (10) and this oddity, see Wynn-Evans, n 268. The validity of these provision has been called into question by the delphic ECJ decision in *Juuri v Fazer Amica Oy* [2008] All ER (D) 302 (Nov), which appears to say that (1) member states need not provide any compensation remedy for employees who elect not to transfer owing to substantial changes in conditions but (2) they must at least award whatever

Regulation 4(7) states that there is not to be automatic transfer if the employee informs the transferor or the transferee that he objects to becoming employed by the transferee.[337] However, regulation 4(8) then goes on to state that where such objection is made 'the relevant transfer shall operate so as to terminate his contract of employment with the transferor *but he shall not be treated, for any purpose, as having been dismissed by the transferor*'. The result of this bizarre provision is that the employee has a theoretical right of objection but if he exercises it he may be left in a state of legal limbo, with no rights against the transferee (because there is no automatic transfer of his contract), but also no recourse against the transferor for any cause of action that requires him to have been 'dismissed' (because regulation 4(8) deems there to have been no dismissal). The potential harshness of this situation led the Court of Appeal to add a major qualification, in a particularly purposive decision[338] holding that if an employee leaves by exercising his right to do so under regulation 4(9) (above) (substantial detrimental changes being proposed/threatened by the transferee employer), then regulation 4(8) does *not* apply and the employee retains any remedies he may have against the transferor (which remain personal to that employer and do not pass to the transferee, because of regulation 4(7)). This is a good example of both the complexity of these Regulations and the need occasionally for creative interpretation to avoid some of their more notable absurdities.

(vi) UNFAIR TUPE DISMISSAL

An unfair dismissal in connection with a transfer of an undertaking can arise under regulation 7, which operates a regime of possible *automatic* unfairness, subject to a defence whose wording was taken straight from the backing Acquired Rights Directive and which has caused problems consistently in its interpretation. The original form of regulation 7 (which was regulation 8 of the 1981 Regulations) itself raised problems and so when this law was updated in 2006 the opportunity was taken to rephrase it, arguably with little change in substance but some clarification. Regulation 7(1)–(3) delineates three kinds of TUPE dismissal cases:

(1) where the sole or principal reason for the dismissal is the transfer itself, the dismissal is automatically unfair;[339]

---

compensation is awarded under national law for termination of the employment contract. So it seems that reg 4(10) must be disapplied for excluding compensation for the notice period (unless of course it is treated as representing the national law on compensation in such situations). It is nice to get that cleared up.

[337] No particular form is laid down for objection, which may therefore be inferred from words or conduct: *Hay v George Hanson (Building Contractors) Ltd* [1996] IRLR 427, though notice the more cautious approach in *Senior Heat Treatment Ltd v Bell* [1997] IRLR 614.

[338] *University of Oxford v Humphreys* [2000] IRLR 305, CA.

[339] This could arise where employees are dismissed to 'slim down' the business to facilitate an actual or impending sale: *Morris v John Grose Group Ltd* [1998] ICR 655, [1998] IRLR 499, following on this point *Harrison Bowden Ltd v Bowden* [1994] ICR 186 and disapproving the narrower view in *Ibex Trading Co Ltd v Walton* [1994] ICR 907, [1994] IRLR 564, EAT.

(2) where the sole or principal reason for the dismissal is a reason connected with the transfer that is *not* an economic, technical or organizational reason ('an ETO reason' in the jargon) entailing changes in the workforce, again the dismissal is automatically unfair;

(3) where the sole or principal reason for the dismissal is a reason connected with the transfer that *is* an ETO reason entailing changes in the workforce, then that dismissal is deemed for unfair dismissal purposes to have been for 'some other substantial reason' and so the employer must go on to show that the dismissal was fair in the light of equity and the substantial merits of the case under the Employment Rights Act 1996, section 98(4).[340]

TUPE cases therefore essentially treat all dismissals as automatically unfair unless the employer shows that the dismissal is unconnected with the transfer, as in the case of misconduct unrelated to the sale, or for ETO reasons.

The 'ETO' formulation of the employer's statutory defence was transposed directly from the Directive in 1981 and had no prior equivalent in UK law. The potential effect of this, greatly to the transferee employer's disadvantage, was disclosed at an early stage by the decision of the Court of Appeal in *Berriman v Delabole Slate Ltd*[341] that 'changes in the workforce' in the defence means changes in the *composition* of the workforce; mere changes in the terms and conditions of the workforce are not enough. On the other hand, if there are actual changes to the jobs of those transferred (for example, as part of a reorganization, but with a knock-on effect on terms and conditions) it was subsequently held in *Crawford v Swinton Insurance Brokers Ltd*[342] that that *can* constitute a 'change in the workforce' and so give rise to the regulation 7 (ETO) defence. Clearly, there could be a thin line between these two outcomes, with allegations by the employees that the job changes were a sham, aimed at avoiding the Regulations. If, however, a transferee employer falls on the wrong side of the line, he will face the problem that if he buys the undertaking wishing to keep the existing workforce (or, indeed, simply *having* to take them because of the provisions in regulation 4 on automatic transfer of contracts), but then proceeds to alter their terms and conditions (in particular to bring them into line with terms and conditions in the establishments that he already runs), the workforce could walk out, claim constructive dismissal and the defence in regulation 7 would *not* apply.[343] The boomerang effect of this could have been that, far from *protecting* the employment of those in the transferred undertaking,

---

[340] *McGrath v Rank Leisure Ltd* [1985] ICR 527, [1985] IRLR 323. Where the defence works in a redundancy context, reg 7(3)(b) specifically preserves the redundancy option and the tribunal should go on to decide on fairness on the ordinary principles of unfair redundancy selection: *Warner v Adnet Ltd* [1998] IRLR 394, CA.

[341] [1985] ICR 546, [1985] IRLR 305, CA, noted McMullen (1986) 49 MLR 524.

[342] [1990] ICR 85, [1990] IRLR 42, EAT.

[343] For example, in *Manchester College v Hazel* [2012] All ER (D) 46, UKEAT/0642/11, UKEAT/0136/11, choosing as part of a reorganization to dismiss and rehire some workers on new terms for the purpose of harmonizing terms and conditions between existing and transferred employees was not ETO and was automatically unfair.

it put the emphasis on the transferee employer making it a condition of purchase that the transferor dismisses the workforce as redundant before the sale, in an attempt to ensure that the transferee did not 'inherit' them at all.[344] However, as pointed out at in Chapter 9 at heading 2(i), this form of evasion has been effectively countered by the decision of the House of Lords in *Litster v Forth Dry Dock and Engineering Co Ltd*.[345] The end result is a considerable level of legal protection through the actual transfer for employees covered by the Regulations, and their existing terms and conditions, and indeed the decision in *Litster* has now been written directly into the 2006 Regulations.[346]

(vii) WHAT CAN BE CHANGED AFTER THE TRANSFER?

Given that the transferee employer has to take on all the transferred employees on their existing terms and conditions of employment, what can that employer then do if that cohort of new employees are on different terms and conditions from those of his existing employees doing similar work? The obvious economic need is to rationalize the newcomers' terms and conditions on to those applying generally (if only to avoid a future equal pay issue) but employers suffered an early shock in *Berriman v Delabole Slate Ltd*[347] where the Court of Appeal held that the employer's 'economic, technical or organisational reason' (ETO) defence had to involve a change in the *composition* of the workforce on transfer, not just a change to their terms and conditions, so that it could *not* apply to a straightforward rationalization. At that time the ETO defence only arose in the unfair dismissal provisions (see under heading (vi) earlier), but this decision did give the transferred employees' existing terms and conditions considerable protection

---

[344] This appeared possible in the light of the decision in *Secretary of State for Employment v Spence* [1986] ICR 651, [1986] IRLR 248, CA that the continuity of employment provisions only apply to those in employment with the transferor at the moment of transfer.

[345] [1989] ICR 341, [1989] IRLR 161, HL, applying the decision of the ECJ in *P Bork International A/S (in liquidation) v Foreningen af Arbejdsledere i Danmark: 101/87* [1989] IRLR 41, to the effect that the continuity provisions in reg 5 must be read subject to these provisions in reg 8, so that if a dismissal is contrary to the latter the employee is to be deemed still in the transferor's employment at the time of transfer, for the purposes of reg 5. According to the Scottish EAT in *Anderson v Dalkeith Engineering Ltd* [1985] ICR 66, [1984] IRLR 429 the transferor employer may have the reg 8(2) defence ('economic, technical or organisational' reasons), if he shows that he was obliged to sack the workforce by the intending purchaser as a condition of sale; however, this was not followed by the English EAT in *Wheeler v Patel* [1987] ICR 631, [1987] IRLR 211 for two reasons: (1) it did too much violence to the employee's rights under reg 8(1); (2) 'economic' was to be read ejusdem generis with 'technical' and 'organisational', so that the reason must relate to the conduct of the business itself, not just its attractiveness to a buyer; this decision was subsequently followed by the Scottish EAT (rather than *Anderson*) in *Gateway Hotels Ltd v Stewart* [1988] IRLR 287. There is nothing in the decision of the House of Lords in *Litster* to contradict this later interpretation of the defence; indeed, it is entirely in line with their Lordships' views in that case as to the interpretation of the Regulations generally.

[346] Regulation 4(3). The emphasis therefore tends to be on when subsequently the transferee employer can lawfully change the terms and conditions, which involves the difficult case of *Wilson v St Helens BC* [1998] ICR 1141, [1998] IRLR 706, HL.

[347] [1985] ICR 546, [1985] IRLR 305, CA.

because it meant that any threat to dismiss an employee who would not change was legally dangerous under TUPE (even if it might have been a potentially fair dismissal under ordinary unfair dismissal law: see under heading 1(ii)).

For some time after *Berriman* it was assumed that the answer therefore lay in negotiation. In the straightforward world of domestic contract law, it would be possible for the transferee to take on the transferred employees on their existing terms and conditions and then to negotiate changes in the normal way. However, it was then held that the protection of the Directive (and hence the Regulations) is intended to be stronger than that, with the result that a transferee may *not* lawfully change the existing terms and conditions *if* the change is 'transfer-related', and that any attempt to do so will be void, even if for good consideration and with the ostensible agreement of the employees. This particular bombshell was dropped by the EAT in *Wilson v St Helens Borough Council*[348] (with the laconic comment that this may be 'surprising … to English legal tradition'), with the result that employees who had agreed changes to their terms on a transfer for a buy-out payment could demand restoration of the original terms over a year later.[349] By the time that this case reached the House of Lords the basic principle seemed to be accepted, and the argument at that stage was over the circumstances in which the principle might be avoided (and a contractual change lawful).[350] Two such circumstances were accepted: (1) where either transferor or transferee dismisses the employees and re-engages them on the new terms (this being effective because domestic law does not acknowledge the possibility of a dismissal being void, even under the Directive); (2) where the transferee can break the chain of causation by showing that the changes were *not* 'transfer-related', ie that they were made for some other, independent reason such as a reorganization of the whole workplace involving all employees (longstanding and transferred), in which case the ordinary rules of contract law apply. Category (1) is not as attractive as it seems, because it lays the employer open to unfair dismissal actions by the employees,[351] compensation possibly reflecting the net loss incurred under the new terms and conditions. Category

---

[348] [1996] ICR 711, [1996] IRLR 320; this was based on long-overlooked dicta by the ECJ in *Foreningen of Arbejdsledere i Danmark v Daddy's Dance Hall A/S* 324/86 [1988] IRLR 315, ECJ.

[349] The mechanism used was a claim for unlawful deductions from wages under Pt II of the Employment Rights Act 1996 (see Ch 3, heading 5(v), p 211), where the limitation period (in a case of continuing deductions) only flows from the last pay day, under the new terms, before the date of the proceedings. It was later held that an employee can *choose* to enforce a transfer-related change if it is in his or her favour: *Power v Regent Security Services* [2007] UKEAT/499/06. One unresolved point in a case like *Wilson* is whether the employer can reclaim from the employees the amount paid to buy out the original terms, on the basis of failure of consideration.

[350] [1998] ICR 1141, [1998] IRLR 706, HL; see McMullen (1998) 28 ILJ 76. The reasons for this subtle but significant change in emphasis were that (1) the case was consolidated with the appeal in *Meade and Baxendale v British Fuels Ltd* [1996] IRLR 541 where there had been a dismissal and re-engagement on new terms, not just a contractual variation, and (2) it became apparent that the dismissal tactic had in fact also been used in *Wilson* itself, a factor which had not been thought particularly significant at EAT level.

[351] The employees can claim unfair dismissal from their old *contract*, even though still in the employment of the employer under the new contract, under the rule in *Hogg v Dover College* [1990] ICR 39: see Ch 7, heading 2, p 478.

(2) can be fraught with problems of proof and timing (there being *no* rule of thumb that a change will not be transfer-related after a certain period from the transfer), and assumptions made by employers about their ability to impose or even negotiate changes after the transfer can sometimes be proved to have been entirely wrong.[352]

In two recent cases, however, the need to correct a pay anomaly that could and should have been corrected before the transfer,[353] and a harmonization of terms triggered by the demands of a new contract (even where that new contract came with the transfer),[354] were found by the EAT not to be by reason of the transfer and were therefore permissible. What is currently a difficult economic climate has generated a great deal of business and government interest in loosening up what are seen as 'gold-plated' TUPE provisions; in 2013 the Coalition government intends to consult on a variety of changes to TUPE including, inter alia, the ETO/automatically unfair dismissal regime.[355] There is some reason for optimism that in this climate the decisions will continue to show some degree of flexibility over post-transfer changes to terms and conditions.[356]

When it came to drafting the 2006 Regulations, the government's hands were tied because they had not managed to persuade our EU partners to reverse *Wilson* in the new Directive and so they were unable lawfully to do so unilaterally. All they could do, therefore, was to codify *Wilson* into clearer language and in doing so to read across the ETO defence from the unfair dismissal provisions. Regulation 4(4) states that:

> any purported variation of the [transferred] contract shall be void if the sole or principal reason for the variation is—
>
> (a) the transfer itself; or
>
> (b) a reason connected with the transfer that is not an economic, technical or organisational reason entailing changes in the workforce.

Conversely, regulation 4(5) states that this does not prevent the employer and employee from:

> agreeing a variation of that contract if the sole or principal reason for the variation is—
>
> (a) a reason connected with the transfer that is an economic, technical or organisational reason entailing changes in the workforce; or
>
> (b) a reason unconnected with the transfer.

---

[352] In two cases, restraint of trade clauses negotiated into contracts by the transferee shortly after the transfer were held to be unenforceable because they were transfer-related and therefore void changes: *Crédit Suisse First Boston (Europe) Ltd v Padiachy* [1999] ICR 569, [1998] IRLR 504; *Crédit Suisse First Boston (Europe) Ltd v Lister* [1999] ICR 794, [1998] IRLR 700, CA. In the latter case, this was despite the employee having been paid £625,000 for the change in terms.

[353] *Smith v Trustees of Brooklands College* (UKEAT/0128/11).

[354] *Enterprise Managed Services Ltd v Dance* (UKEAT/0200/11).

[355] *Effectiveness of Transfer of Undertakings (Protection of Employment) Regulations 2006: Government Response to Call for Evidence* (BIS September 2012) available at <http://www.bis.gov.uk/assets/BISCore/employment-matters/docs/E/12–1141-effectiveness-transfer-of-undertakings-response.pdf> (last accessed 18 January 2013).

[356] See generally, McMullen, 'Re-Structuring and TUPE' (2012) 41 ILJ 358.

As long as *Berriman* continues to hold that a simple rationalization is not an ETO reason, the employer cannot rely on regulation 4(5)(a) and so is left with the *Wilson v St Helens* conundrum of trying to work out what might break the claim of causation between the transfer and a later change of terms and conditions, thus activating regulation 4(5)(b). A later change to the terms of *all* employees for definable business reasons may qualify, but one major problem in advising on this known problem is that there is *no* magic period of time after which it is automatically safe to propose changes for the transferred employees.

There was, however, one way in which the renegotiated Directive permitted an amendment to *Wilson v St Helens*, and this was adopted in regulation 9 which applies if (but only if) at the time of the transfer the transferor is subject to certain insolvency proceedings. In such a case, the transferor, transferee or an insolvency practitioner may agree with the transferred employees to make 'permitted variations' to the latter's terms and conditions. These are defined as variations where—

(1)   the sole or principal reason for [them] is the transfer itself or a reason connected with the transfer that is not an economic, technical or organizational reason entailing changes in the workforce; and

(2)   [they are] designed to safeguard employment opportunities by ensuring the survival of the undertaking, business or part of the undertaking or business that is the subject of the relevant transfer.

The key point here is (2) which means that, as part of the government's 'rescue culture' for firms in insolvency, the workforce can lawfully agree different (and, of course, possibly worse) terms and conditions as the 'price' of keeping the undertaking going under new management and so keeping their jobs. The protection given by regulation 9 is that this may not be done on an individual basis; instead, any such agreement must be reached with 'appropriate representatives' of the transferred employees. Where a trade union is recognized, that means representatives of the union. Where there is no recognition, it means directly elected or appointed employee representatives. Important though this new provision is in its own context, it falls far short of the wholesale reversal of *Wilson v St Helens* that had originally been hoped for by employers and their advisers.

(viii) APPLICATION TO CONTRACTING-OUT CASES

(a) Developments before the 2006 Regulations

It has been the policy of successive governments for several years now to encourage or even require bodies in the public sector to put out to tender certain services (such as catering or cleaning), on the basis that such services can be more efficiently and cheaply provided by the private sector. Similarly, large private concerns may decide to do so voluntarily, for similar reasons. When this happens, staff who previously performed these services in-house will often be taken on by the successful contractors, but it was always assumed that this was after a clean break with the old employer, so that (1) the contractor did not assume any responsibility for any accrued rights (in particular, accrued redundancy rights) and (2) he was free to take on only some of the old workforce and/or then to 'adjust' (ie diminish) their old terms and conditions, to reduce labour costs. Clearly, if the Regulations applied, neither of those assumptions would survive and the whole economic basis of contracting-out would be called into question.

It initially seemed clear that under domestic law the 1981 TUPE Regulations could not apply, for two independent reasons. The first was the restriction that they did not apply to non-commercial undertakings. Thus, in *Expro Services Ltd v Smith*,[357] where catering services were contracted-out to a private company by the Ministry of Defence, it was held that the Regulations did not apply (and so there was no continuity of employment for an employee who transferred to the private company and was later dismissed within the magic two years then required for an unfair dismissal claim), because the catering venture had not been a commercial venture when carried out by the Ministry. The second was that, in any event, the domestic courts took the view that merely giving out a contract or tender[358] could not constitute the 'transfer of an undertaking' because it fell short of a going business (even if the employees and certain premises or equipment went with it). Thus, in *Curling v Securicor Ltd*[359] the Home Office had contracted out services at a detention centre to Securicor, but when that contract came up for renewal it was awarded to another company; the employee stayed doing the same job and transferred to the employment of the other company, but it was held that the Regulations did not apply because this mere change of contract did not constitute a transfer of undertaking.

This situation began to change when it became clear that the restriction to commercial undertakings was contrary to the Directive and so had to be removed by the Trade Union Reform and Employment Rights Act 1993.[360] At first, the then government maintained that the Regulations still would not apply to contracting-out because of the second reason above (no 'undertaking' transferred). However, the axe soon fell on that with the decision of the ECJ in *Rask v ISS Kantineservice A/S*[361] that the Directive did apply where a large private company had contracted out the running of a staff canteen to a service company and an existing employee entered the latter's employment; the result was that when the service company changed one of her terms

---

[357]   [1991] ICR 577, [1991] IRLR 156.

[358]   This could happen in two ways: (1) the old employer A could change from performing the service in-house, and contract it out to private firm B (a 'first generation contracting-out') *or* (2) the old employer A could already have contracted it out to private firm B, but on the expiry of that contract retendered and awarded the new contract to private firm C (a 'second generation contracting-out'). Problems of continuity arise if a particular employee carries on doing the same job in the same place, but moves in the first case from A to B, and in the second case from B to C.

[359]   [1992] IRLR 549. This was another case where it was in fact the employees arguing that the Regulations did *not* apply, because they were seeking (successfully) redundancy payments from Securicor.

[360]   See heading 2(i), p 589.   [361]   C-209/91 [1993] IRLR 133, ECJ.

of employment she could claim the protection of the Danish legislation enacting the Directive.[362] Following on from this, it was held by the High Court in *Kenny v South Manchester College*[363] that effect must now be given to this wide approach in domestic law; thus, where prison education had been contracted-out to a local authority but, as a result of re-tendering, was then contracted-out to a college, the staff previously employed by the local authority on that work had to be taken on by the college, on the same terms and conditions. A similar conclusion was reached in *Wren v Eastbourne Borough Council*[364] where a mainstream example of a local authority being obliged to contract-out its street cleaning and refuse collection functions led to the finding of a 'transfer of undertaking' when those functions were taken over by a private company. This approach was then taken further in three ways. First, in *Dines v Initial Health Care Services*[365] the Court of Appeal held that the inescapable logic (resisted, as a matter of policy, by the EAT in that case) was that the Regulations could apply to a subsequent re-tendering exercise; thus, where the original contract for the services (in that case, for hospital cleaning) by Co A ran out and the principal body retendered and Co B won the next contract, there was a transfer of undertaking from A to B (albeit in two stages—the handing back from A to the principal body and then the granting of the new contract to B); the effect was that employees of A were either notionally taken into the employment of B for the purposes of an unfair dismissal claim, or were actually taken on by B but with their existing terms and conditions protected. The counter argument, that all that had been 'transferred' was a contract, not an undertaking, was disapproved. Second, in *Isles of Scilly Council v Brintel Helicopters Ltd*[366] it was held that there was a transfer of undertaking where the firm to which airport support services had been contracted-out went into administration and the council took these services back in-house, ie a contracting *back in*. Third, this broad approach to the contracting of services (and, more generally, to the defining of a transfer of undertaking by looking generally for the continuance of an economic entity or activity with some sort of retained identity, rather than for more concrete matters such as the transfer of assets

---

[362] At least in *Rask* it concerned an employee who wanted to be there and whom the transferee wanted to employ; automatic transfer means that a firm contracting for a service would notionally have to take on *all* the employees currently doing the job (even those it had not planned on keeping), with all their accrued rights.

[363] [1993] ICR 934, [1993] IRLR 265.

[364] [1993] 3 CMLR 166, [1993] ICR 955. There was a transfer even though the council retained overall responsibility for the functions being performed; this point was emphasized in *Birch v Nuneaton and Bedworth Borough Council* [1995] IRLR 518 where there was a relevant transfer when the management of a leisure centre was contracted-out, even though the council built into the contract remarkably detailed controls over its running.

[365] [1995] ICR 11, [1994] IRLR 336, CA. In such a case, the potential problems are unlikely to be sorted out by the parties A and B amicably (eg through price adjustments and indemnity clauses) because they are commercial competitors and indeed, in an extreme case, may not even know who the other is. In fact, the application of the Regulations could give an opportunity for disappointed tenderer A to cause problems for the successful tenderer B—there are apocryphal stories of A's last act being to double their employees' wages, so that B has to take them on at those wage rates! Another possibility is that A could assign to that contract for the last phase of the contract all the employees he most wishes to lose.

[366] [1995] ICR 249, [1995] IRLR 6.

or equipment or goodwill) seemed to be taken to its logical conclusion by the decision of the ECJ in the *Christel Schmidt* case[367] that the Acquired Rights Directive applied where an employee who was the sole cleaner of a bank's premises was dismissed when that service function was contracted-out to the firm that already provided it with other cleaning services; this was so in spite of the facts that (1) all that was concerned was a purely ancillary function (not part of the bank's principal business), (2) only one employee was involved and (3) there was no transfer whatever of any tangible assets. Intervening in the argument of the case, the British government had again tried to draw a distinction between the transfer of a business (or part thereof) and the mere entering of a contractual arrangement, but again this had fallen on deaf ears.

Those involved in contracting-out operations thus had to become accustomed to conducting them against the background of the Regulations, which were therefore giving considerable protection to the employees involved. Unfortunately, however, it could not be assumed that the Regulations would always apply, and the uncertainty caused by two subsequent ECJ cases (appearing to resile from the high point reached in *Christel Schmidt*) meant that this continued to be a troublesome area. *Rygard v Stø Mølle Akustik A/S*[368] caused some ripples by appearing to revive ideas that it may be only a contractual function that was being transferred, but it was on unusual facts and was later restrictively distinguished by the EAT and ECJ[369] and has had little effect. The case that did, however, cause most heartache even to TUPE-hardened employment lawyers was *Ayse Süzen*,[370] in which the ECJ stated (helpfully) that a contracting-out may *or may not* be a relevant transfer, depending in many cases on whether assets and/or a significant part of the workforce were actually transferred by the commercial arrangement. Immediately after this decision the Court of Appeal held in *Betts v Brintel Helicopters Ltd*[371] that there was no relevant transfer (on a second generation contracting-out) where the new contractor for the supply of gas rigs had its own helicopters and facilities and deliberately declined to offer employment to any of the employees engaged on the service by the old contractor. A case such as this exposed the flaw in *Ayse Süzen* from the point of view of employee protection, namely that a cynical transferee could use it to make non-application of the Regulations a self-fulfilling prophecy by refusing to take on either assets or staff. This possibility was, however, considerably lessened by the important case of *ECM (Vehicle Delivery Service) Ltd v Cox* where just such a tactic was used, again on a second generation contracting-out.

---

[367] *Schmidt v Spar und Leihkasse der früheren Ämter Bordesholm, Kiel und Cronshagen* C-392/92 [1994] ECR I-1311, [1995] 2 CMLR 331, ECJ.

[368] C-48/94 [1996] ICR 333, [1996] IRLR 51, ECJ.

[369] *BSG Property Services v Tuck* [1996] IRLR 134; *Allen v Amalgamated Construction Co Ltd* C-234/98 [2000] IRLR 119, [2000] All ER (EC) 97, ECJ.

[370] *Süzen v Zehnacker Gebäudereinigung GmbH Krankenhausservice*: C-13/95 [1997] ICR 662, [1997] IRLR 255, ECJ. A similar approach was taken subsequently by the ECJ in *Francisco Hernández Vidal SA v Gomez Perez*: C-127/96 [1999] IRLR 132, ECJ and *Sánchez Hidalgo v Asociación de Servicios Aser and Sociedad Cooperativa Minerva* C-173/96 [2002] ICR 73, [1999] IRLR 136, ECJ, though (it has been argued) with more emphasis on the importance of the workforce itself as the 'economic entity' in a labour-intensive industry.

[371] [1997] ICR 792, [1997] IRLR 361, CA.

The EAT[372] held that the Regulations did apply on two grounds that, they said, had not been before the ECJ in *Ayse Süzen*: (1) in a labour-intensive industry it may be relevant (as it was in *Christel Schmidt*) that the employee in question was 'dedicated' to the work that was being transferred (rather than merely being a member of staff of a large service company who, on the loss of one contract, will simply be moved on to the next one), which should point to there being a relevant transfer; (2) in any event, as a matter of policy and purposive interpretation, a tribunal may wish to prevent an employer from deliberately using *Ayse Süzen* to avoid the Regulations. On appeal,[373] point (1) was not in issue, and on point (2) the Court of Appeal dismissed the employer's appeal and held in a short judgment that *all* the circumstances of the transfer must be considered, *including* any intent to evade the Regulations, a point subsequently approved and applied in Scotland by the Inner House of the Court of Session.[374] This 'ECM point' has continued to cause problems, splitting the Court of Appeal (2–1 in result, but unhelpfully being in effect a three-way split because of different reasoning between the majority judges) in *ADI (UK) Ltd v Willer*[375] and being subject to a less than enthusiastic analysis by another Court of Appeal in *RCO Support Services v UNISON*,[376] where the refusal to accept existing staff by the transferee was agreed to be a factor in the overall assessment, but only in an objective sense (not in the original, subjective sense of being in effect a punishment for a deliberate attempt to evade TUPE). The ECJ returned to the fray in *Oy Liikenne*,[377] where it was held that there was no TUPE transfer when the public bus service in the Finnish capital was recontracted to a different tenderer, with some of the staff being taken back on but no buses being transferred. One interpretation of this case was that (under *Ayse Süzen*) there would not be a TUPE transfer in an assets-reliant industry if there was not transfer of 'significant tangible assets'. On the other hand, such was the diversity of the case law by then, it was also arguable that this was merely the leading EU case authority on the bus industry in Helsinki.

By this time, both the domestic and EU case law seemed to be progressing in wide circles, around concepts of asset transfer, staff transfer and motive, with a sense that the courts had in effect argued themselves to a standstill and could not progress the matter much further. When Lindsay P made a brave attempt in *Cheeseman v R Brewer Contracts Ltd*[378] to sum up the position reached in all the judgments, the question of whether there had been a transfer required 15 separate propositions to explain it. Advising on that basis was becoming next to impossible. What in fact happened was

---

[372] [1998] ICR 631, [1998] IRLR 416. [373] [1999] ICR 1162, [1999] IRLR 559, CA.

[374] *Lightways (Contractors) Ltd v Associated Holdings Ltd* [2000] IRLR 247, Ct of Sess (contractor submitting a bid on the basis that TUPE applied was not allowed to insist later to the employees that it did not).

[375] [2001] IRLR 542, CA. Dyson LJ adopted *ECM* positively; May LJ felt bound to apply it, but reluctantly (on the basis that the recent case law had warped the original meaning of the Directive); Simon Brown LJ, in a remarkably strong dissent, said that *ECM* was contrary to EC law, going beyond permissible purposive interpretation.

[376] [2002] ICR 751, [2002] IRLR 401, CA. [377] C-172/99 [2001] IRLR 171, ECJ.

[378] [2001] IRLR 144.

that the hitherto regular case law dried up from about 2001 and all attention turned to legislative reform, in the form of the delayed 2006 Regulations.

(b) The reforms in the 2006 Regulations

As stated at the beginning of this discussion of TUPE, the provisions in the 2006 Regulations on contracting-out cases are the only serious candidate for a 'year zero' approach, ie to treat them as entirely novel and not to seek to construe them by reference to the (dreadful) previous case law. This is because these provisions do *not* draw on previously important concepts such as asset transfer, staff transfer and motive. Instead, regulation 3 adopts the approach of laying down an entirely new definition of a relevant transfer to apply specifically to contracting-out cases, or as they are now known in the Regulations, 'service provision changes'.

Regulation 3(1)(b) applies the statutory scheme to a first-generation contracting-out, a second-generation contracting-out and a contracting-back-in-again, provided that:

(a) immediately before the service provision change—

(i) there is an organized grouping of employees[379] situated in Great Britain which has as its principal purpose the carrying out of the activities concerned on behalf of the client;

(ii) the client intends that the activities will, following the service provision change, be carried out by the transferee other than in connection with a single specific event or task of short-term duration;[380] and

(b) the activities concerned do not consist wholly or mainly of the supply of goods for the client's use.[381]

The overall aim of this new formulation is to avoid the uncertainties of the previous case law,[382] to ensure that TUPE protection will be the norm (protecting all those who need it to retain their employment) but at the same time to ensure that TUPE does not apply where it would be unnecessary and indeed positively harmful. Two examples may illustrate this. In the first, a small cleaning company with three employees loses its one big contract on which employee A has spent all of his or her time; there is no replacement work. In this case A *needs* TUPE protection and the reference in regulation 3(3)(a)(i) to the organized grouping with the principal purpose of serving that client should mean that there is a TUPE transfer, so that A is transferred to the company obtaining that contract. In the second example, employee B is a longstanding

---

[379] This includes a single employee (reg 2(1)) thus covering the position in *Cristel Schmidt*, n 367.

[380] This reference to a single event or task of short-term duration is included because *Rygard* (n 368) remains good law, albeit narrowly interpreted.

[381] Regulation 3(3). Head (b) is there to prevent an 'accidental' TUPE transfer when the client swaps supplier of, for example, a photocopier (ie the engineer who had always serviced it is not inadvertently transferred by law from that supplier to the new one).

[382] Particularly the regrettable decision in *Ayse Süzen*, n 370.

employee of a major security company with many contracts in the town. B happens to be working at one contracted client at the time that contract is lost to a competitor. B simply expects that the following day he or she will be sent to work at another client's premises (as has happened innumerable times before) and has no desire whatsoever to change employment to the competitor company winning the contract. The wording of regulation 3(3)(a)(i) should ensure that there is *no* undesired application of automatic transfer.[383]

One purpose of enacting a regime where TUPE should be the norm is to create the proverbial level playing field so that all parties know the rules (if necessary through a *series* of service provision changes over time) and can tender and contract on that basis (including as to price, which may be sensitive to the liabilities to be taken on by a successful tenderer). However, there remained one area where the playing field might be uneven. On a second-generation service-provision change, company B when tendering for the contract coming to an end with company A had *no* right under the 1981 Regulations to obtain any information from company A as to the numbers of employees dedicated to that contract that they would have to take on (and on what terms and conditions, with what existing liabilities). The government decided to address this problem in the 2006 Regulations, and indeed regulation 11 obliges a transferor to give to a transferee 'employee liability information' covering the identity and age of the employees in question, their basic terms and conditions, any statutory grievances or disciplinary procedures arising in the previous two years, any actual or reasonably apprehended legal actions against the transferor and any transferable collective agreements.[384] So far, so good *but* regulation 11(6) then effectively wrecks this provision as commercially relevant by stating that the provision as to timing is that the only statutory obligation is to give this information 'not less than fourteen days before the relevant transfer'. To be relevant to the economic decision whether to tender and at what price, a potential bidder will in many cases want this information weeks, if not months, earlier. All that this provision may do in reality is to *confirm* the liabilities that the successful bidder has already undertaken.

(ix) CONCLUSIONS

The 2006 Regulations might be viewed as a case of giving two hearty cheers. The parts that codify the existing case law should increase clarity and lessen the need to refer

---

[383] There might be a problem with professional services, eg where the affairs of a major client of a law firm are handled by one 'dedicated' team of lawyers; if that firm loses that client, might that team transfer? Originally the government consulted on excluding certain professional services altogether, but that proved too difficult to draft and so no such exclusion is in the Regulations and the government have said that ordinary principles must apply.

[384] Regulation 11(1), (2). This information must be updated if necessary: reg 11(5). A transferee may complain to a tribunal that this information was not given; if that is established, the tribunal may grant a declaration and award the transferee compensation which should normally be not less than £500 per employee in question: reg 12.

back to those cases, even if they do not actually alter the basic law. The continued exclusion of pensions (after such long discussion) may be seen as a disappointment, and the inability of the government to change the rules on post-transfer changes in terms and conditions (the *Wilson v St Helens* problem) other than in the specific case of an insolvent transferor is bound to be seen as *the* major disappointment. On the other hand, although the provisions on employee liability information are weak, the principal provisions on service-provision changes do offer the prospect of a breach in a major logjam of case law and a new start in the most difficult area of all. All employment lawyers must await with impatience and some degree of trepidation the proposals promised by the government in 2013: most of the problems highlighted here are to be touched on in the new proposals,[385] although it is not clear whether these cures will be worse than the disease.

Naturally, no amount of new law can remove the many problems of *application* of those laws and we can expect TUPE to remain one of the most complex areas in modern employment law. Moreover, there remain certain problems which are not addressed by a Regulations (old or new) at all. Three examples are (1) 'dumping' (ie putting the least desirable employees on to a contract about to be lost to have them transferred to another employer), (2) late changes to employees' terms and conditions before a TUPE transfer (leaving the transferee to pick up the tab) and (3) requiring the divulging of employee information substantially more than 14 days before a service-provision change (so that it actually has commercial value). The position under the 1981 Regulations was, and the position under the 2006 Regulations continues to be, that if a party wants to prevent (1) or (2) or to require (3), the only answer is to try to achieve this by clauses in the relevant commercial contracts, ie to seek a solution outside the Regulations altogether. Similarly, it will remain vital for lawyers advising transferees to use what is referred to in the TUPE jargon as 'due diligence' to isolate *all* the liabilities that might pass on the transfer and, at a general level, this will doubtless remain an important area for the incorporation of indemnity clauses into commercial contracts just in case the basis on which the parties have dealt (as to who bears what liability) proves later to have been horribly wrong.

---

[385] *Effectiveness of Transfer of Undertakings (Protection of Employment) Regulations 2006: Government Response to Call for Evidence* (BIS September 2012) available at <http://www.bis.gov.uk/assets/BISCore/employment-matters/docs/E/12–1141-effectiveness-transfer-of-undertakings-response.pdf> (last accessed 19 January 2013).

9

COLLECTIVE LABOUR LAW

OVERVIEW

This chapter considers the laws that affect trade unions and employment relations at a collective level. Such collective matters largely still operate on a voluntarist ethos, leaving negotiations and settlements primarily to the parties. This exclusion of the law has historically been underpinned by the most basic rule of industrial relations law, namely that in this jurisdiction collective agreements are not legally binding. However, this voluntarist system was traditionally based on high levels of trade union membership (indeed closed shops, ie compulsory membership), so that the reorganized trade union was the natural conduit for workforce matters and disputes. That system has been in decline since the 1980s; although relatively recent figures show an average union density in organizations of over 25 employees at 39%, this hides a very mixed picture (as well as excluding small firms which are inherently less likely to be unionized) and in particular a major divide between the public sector (where majority union membership can often still be seen) and the private sector (where some figures have put average union density no higher than 16%). Even in a subject as rapidly changing as employment law, this major change has come remarkably quickly, with this edition being written almost thirty years after the miners' strike which many now see as a seminal event in the decline of unionism. All of this raises questions as to the extent to which the traditional system will continue to dominate in amenable areas, and what may replace it in more hostile territory.

It is the traditional system that still gives rise to most of the legal intervention which is the subject of this chapter. It starts by considering the legal status of a trade union (a matter still dominated by history as much as law) and the statutory concept of trade union independence. The focus then turns to the question of freedom of association, a fundamental concept in trade unionism (at the very least requiring a measure of protection from hostile employers) but one which immediately raises complex issues; for example, does a right to associate include an equal-and-opposite right to disassociate, and does it also include a right for those associating to deny membership to those of whom they disapprove?

Turning to employment relations, a key element traditionally has been whether a trade union is recognized by an employer for the purposes of collective bargaining; this is largely a question of fact and the realities of industrial power, with the law's involvement being primarily in defining 'recognition' as a key to certain statutory rights, but since 1999 that law has also provided a statutory mechanism for a trade union with a certain level of support to claim recognition. One of the rights which may be claimed by a recognized trade union is the right to certain information from the employer for collective bargaining purposes, which is considered next, though its use is by now at a relatively low level and indeed it could almost be seen as belonging to an earlier era.

All of this may be seen as encouraging the traditional system, and originally two more collective rights (this time of EU provenance) originally did so. These are the rights to be consulted in impending redundancies and TUPE transfers, which were seen in Chapter 8. As first drafted (to fit into the system then dominant in the UK) these were rights for reorganized trade unions only, but as union membership and influence lessened these rights applied less and less. The result was that (in the light of a decision of the ECJ) the UK government had to recast these rights (along with health and safety consultation) to be claimable by either a recognized trade union or directly elected workforce representatives. This movement towards more direct workforce involvement (and at a level of mandatory consultation, short of the co-determination model of collective bargaining) can be seen as filling a gap left by changes in employment relations. It is perhaps best seen in the final topic covered in this chapter, namely the Information and Consultation of Employees Regulations 2004 which, passed to transpose an EU Directive, some saw as a way forward. Although they could of course be used by a trade union to extend its influence in a hitherto hostile environment, what is notable about them is that they use a model of direct employee involvement which might equally well be through workplace representatives and which gives no formal preference to trade unions. Thus, while the statutory regulation procedure seeks to buttress the traditional system of collective bargaining, these ('ICE') Regulations can be seen as contrasting, not complementary.

1 THE LEGAL POSITION OF A TRADE UNION

(i) DEFINITION

A trade union is defined in the Trade Union and Labour Relations (Consolidation) Act 1992, section 1 as an organization which consists wholly or mainly of workers of one or more descriptions and whose principal purposes include the regulation of relations between workers of that description or those descriptions and employers or employers' associations;[1] the definition also extends to organizations which consist of constituent or affiliated trade unions, or the representatives of such organizations. This definition contains three elements: first, there must be an 'organization', whether

---

[1] An employers' association is similarly defined in s 122 as an organization which consists wholly or mainly of employers or individual owners of undertakings and which has among its principal purposes the regulation of relations between employers and workers or trade unions: see, eg, *Greig v Insole* [1978] 3 All ER 449, [1978] 1 WLR 302; this definition also extends to federations of employers' associations.

temporary or permanent, which indicates that there must be some degree of formal structure as opposed to a casual grouping of workers;[2] secondly, the organization must be composed wholly or mainly of workers[3] or their trade unions or federations;[4] and thirdly, the principal purposes of the organization must include industrial relations with employers or their associations.[5] In *Midland Cold Storage v Turner,*[6] a joint shop stewards' committee was held not to satisfy this requirement because it had not itself entered into negotiations with employers, but had merely acted as a pressure group, seeking to influence the decisions of the dock workers' unions on the taking of industrial action. In contrast, in *British Association of Advisers and Lecturers in Physical Education v National Union of Teachers,*[7] a professional association whose objects clause stated that it 'shall be concerned with the professional interests of its members' was held to be a trade union, although to describe industrial relations as one of its principal purposes might seem on the facts to be stretching several points.

(ii) LISTING

In practice, the simplest way to determine whether or not an organization is a trade union is to see whether it is included in the list of trade unions maintained by the Certification Officer.[8] The procedure for listing trade unions is largely a formality, unlike the old requirement of registration under the Industrial Relations Act 1971. Under the 1971 Act, registration was the keystone to much of the rest of the legislation (which in turn meant that the TUC's tactic of non-registration was extremely effective). Now, however, listing is much more mechanical. The operation is carried out by the Certification Officer, who maintains a list (open to the public) of trade unions.[9] Any unlisted organization may apply in prescribed form to be listed; if listing is refused, the organization may appeal to the EAT (on both fact and law).[10] An organization also has

---

[2] *Frost v Clarke & Smith Manufacturing Co Ltd* [1973] IRLR 216; *Weeks v National Amalgamated Stevedores and Dockers' Union* (1940) 67 Ll L Rep 282; *Midland Cold Storage v Turner* [1972] ICR 230.

[3] 'Worker' is defined for these purposes as including those working or seeking to work under contracts of employment and those who contract personally to perform work or services for another, but excluding contracts with professional clients (see, eg, *Carter v Law Society* [1973] ICR 113): Trade Union and Labour Relations (Consolidation) Act 1992, s 296(1). There are specific exclusions for members of the armed forces (s 296(1)) and the police service (s 280).

[4] Trade Union and Labour Relations (Consolidation) Act 1992, s 1(b). This covers union federations such as the International Transport Workers' Federation: see eg *Camellia Tanker Ltd SA v ITWF* [1976] ICR 274, [1976] IRLR 190, CA.

[5] There is an exception in the case of union federations, where the definition is satisfied if the organization's principal purposes include the regulation of relations between its constituent or affiliated organizations: Trade Union and Labour Relations (Consolidation) Act 1992, s 1(b).

[6] [1972] ICR 230.   [7] [1986] IRLR 497, CA.   [8] See Ch 1, heading 3(iii), p 25.

[9] Trade Union and Labour Relations (Consolidation) Act 1992, s 2. The Certification Officer also maintains a list of employers' associations, to which similar rules apply: see s 123. In 2007–08 there were 167 listed trade unions and 80 listed employers' associations; in that year the number of unions fell by 12 (six amalgamations, five dissolutions and one ceasing to qualify), a trend that can be traced back to the early 1980s: *Annual Report of the Certification Office 2007/8.* Membership of the listed trade unions stood at 7,627,693.

[10] Trade Union and Labour Relations (Consolidation) Act 1992, ss 9 and 126.

a right to be removed from the list if it wishes. In deciding whether to list an organization, the Certification Officer has two functions: (1) to decide whether it in fact qualifies as a trade union, under the definitions considered in head (i) above; (2) to ensure that its name is not the same as that of an existing listed organization, or misleadingly similar. Entry on the list is itself declared to be evidence that the organization in fact is a trade union (and the organization may request a certificate from the Certification Officer (CO) to the effect that it is on the list).[11] There are two principal advantages for a trade union in being listed. The first is that it gains certain tax exemptions with regard to its provident benefits funds, the second is that listing is a precondition for the far more important step of gaining a certificate of independence,[12] which is the key which unlocks the door to most of the statutory union rights contained in the modern legislation.

(iii) THE LEGAL STATUS OF A TRADE UNION

Except during the brief currency of the Industrial Relations Act 1971, trade unions have never been bodies corporate, and indeed under the present legislation are forbidden to be so.[13] In law, a trade union is an unincorporated association, a collection of individuals bound together by the contract of membership with no separate legal personality. However, trade unions are invested with some of the most important attributes of legal personality by statute, including the power to make contracts, to sue and be sued and to be prosecuted for criminal offences. A trade union can therefore be seen as a curious hybrid falling somewhere between an unincorporated association and a body corporate—a 'quasi-corporate' body. Until the landmark case of *Taff Vale Rly Co v ASRS*[14] it was thought that a trade union could not be sued because it had no legal personality. In that case the House of Lords held that, whatever the precise juristic basis, a union was a creature known to the law and could therefore be sued. The prospect of union funds (including benefit funds) being taken in satisfaction of judgment led to the enactment in 1906[15] of the blanket immunity for trade unions in tort, but this immunity was in turn removed by the Employment Act 1982.[16] The legal status of a trade union is now

---

[11] Trade Union and Labour Relations (Consolidation) Act 1992, ss 2(4) and 123(4). The fact of being listed is not a necessary precondition of claiming to be a trade union or employers' association (see eg the attempt of the ICC and TCCB to claim the status of employers' associations in *Greig v Insole* [1978] 3 All ER 449, [1978] 1 WLR 302), but it may be useful evidence.

[12] Trade Union and Labour Relations (Consolidation) Act 1992, s 6: see heading 1(iv), p 628.

[13] Trade Union and Labour Relations (Consolidation) Act 1992, s 10; a professional organization which is a 'special register body' as defined in s 117 (eg the British Medical Association) is permitted to have corporate status. An employers' association may be incorporated or unincorporated: s 127.

[14] [1901] AC 426. Not all doubts were cleared away by the case; eg it was not established until the decision of the House of Lords in *Bonsor v Musicians' Union* [1956] AC 104, [1955] 3 All ER 518, that a member could be awarded damages against the union.

[15] Trade Disputes Act 1906, s 4.

[16] Section 15(1), repealing the Trade Union and Labour Relations Act 1974, s 14; see Ch 10, heading 7, p 766.

governed by section 10 of the Trade Union and Labour Relations (Consolidation) Act 1992, which provides that although a union is not a body corporate and is not to be treated as if it were a body corporate,[17] it is capable of making contracts and of suing or being sued in its own name (in any cause of action), and furthermore that criminal proceedings may be brought against the union itself. All property belonging to the union must be vested in trustees[18] in trust for the union and that property may be attached for the satisfaction of any judgment, order or award in the same way as if the union were a body corporate. This vesting in trustees was important during the miners' strike of 1984–85, for when fines imposed on the National Union of Mineworkers for contempt of court were not paid and sequestration was ordered, an application was successfully made to the court to have the union's trustees removed and in their place a receiver appointed, who thus gained control of the union's property.[19] These steps were taken under the general law (though applying it to hitherto unchartered territory), but the position is now covered by statute.[20]

Section 11 of the 1992 Act contains a provision which historically was of great significance when it was enacted,[21] for it removed from unions the threat of being found to be illegal (directly or indirectly) on the basis of constituting a restraint of trade. This provision states that the purposes of a trade union are not, by reason only that they are in restraint of trade, to be regarded as unlawful so as (1) to make any union member liable to criminal proceedings for conspiracy[22] or otherwise, or (2) to make any agreement or trust void or voidable. This protection also extends to the union's rules, which are not to be regarded as unlawful or unenforceable by reason only that they are in restraint of trade. The protection was extended to union rules as a direct result of certain views expressed in *Edwards v SOGAT*,[23] where the Court of Appeal asserted a jurisdiction to supervise the content of union rules, not just to secure their proper enforcement. Sachs LJ based this power on the doctrine of restraint of trade, arguing

[17] On a literal interpretation of s 10 it has been held that a union cannot sue for libel in its own name, as it lacks sufficient legal personality: *EETPU v Times Newspapers Ltd* [1980] QB 585, [1980] 1 All ER 1097. This formulation also gives rise to the argument that the doctrine of ultra vires should not now apply to trade unions: Wedderburn (1985) 14 ILJ 127, commenting on the case of *Taylor v NUM (Derbyshire Area)* [1985] IRLR 99, in which the doctrine was applied; Clayton and Tomlinson 'Vicarious Liability and Trade Unions' [1985] NLJ 361.

[18] Trade Union and Labour Relations (Consolidation) Act 1992, s 12(1). Section 129 applies similar provisions to an unincorporated employers' association.

[19] *Clarke v Heathfield* [1985] ICR 203, CA; the action showed that the concentration of property-holding power in the hands of the trustees gave the union a vulnerability of which the Emperor Caligula would have been envious ('Would that the Roman people had but one neck').

[20] Trade Union and Labour Relations (Consolidation) Act 1992, s 16.

[21] Trade Union Act 1871, ss 2 and 3; s 128 of the 1992 Act gives similar protection to the purposes and rules of an unincorporated employers' association. For an example of the application of this section, see *Goring v British Actors Equity Association* [1987] IRLR 122, Ch D.

[22] Possible liability for conspiracy on more general grounds (where the object of the conspiracy is not itself unlawful) is excluded in the criminal context by the Criminal Law Act 1977, s 1(1) and in the tortious context by s 219 of the 1992 Act.

[23] [1971] Ch 354, [1970] 3 All ER 689, CA.

that if a rule was capricious and oppressive it might not be made pursuant to the proper purposes of the union and so not be validated by the predecessor to section 11.[24] This view is no longer tenable in the light of the extended wording, though it should be noted that that does not necessarily mean the end of the possible legal development contained in *Edwards v SOGAT*, for Lord Denning MR's approach in that case was wider, being based on general public policy and a 'right to work', not tied to restraint of trade; if this approach is correct (which is respectfully doubted), it is not nullified by section 11.

Legal liabilities of unions markedly increased during the 1980s. As already stated, the general tort immunity was removed in 1982, with special statutory rules on when a union is to be liable for the acts of its officers and members (substantially modified in 1990), and statutory maximum amounts of damages recoverable; these matters are considered in Chapter 10. Also, a union may now be made a party to unfair dismissal proceedings (either at the suit of the employee applicant or the employer respondent) where it is alleged that it put pressure on the employer to dismiss the employee because of non-membership, and may be ordered to pay some or all of the compensation (see under heading 2(i)).

(iv) THE INDEPENDENCE OF A TRADE UNION

(a) The importance of independence

For the purpose of the present legislation, the concept of the 'independence' of trade unions was first to be found in the Trade Union and Labour Relations Act 1974, where it was important in the definition of a union membership agreement (closed shop). However, with the advent of the new statutory trade union rights in the Employment Protection Act 1975 (and in other related legislation), the concept took on far greater significance, for the general scheme is that these new rights may only be exercised by *independent* trade unions, not by any bodies which are liable in any way to be under the influence or control of the employer. Thus, only an independent trade union may receive certain bargaining information as of right, demand to be consulted on pending redundancies or a planned transfer of the employer's undertaking, and appoint safety representatives under the Health and Safety at Work etc Act 1974;[25] likewise, only a member of an independent trade union has a right to certain time off work, a right not to have detrimental action taken against him or be dismissed because of his union activities, and, in the case of dismissal, a right to apply for interim relief pending the

---

[24] In spite of the rejection of this argument by the House of Lords in *Faramus v Film Artistes' Association* [1964] AC 925, [1964] 1 All ER 25, HL. For an interesting illustration of the effect of the restraint of trade doctrine in a case where s 11 did not apply, see *Boddington v Lawton* [1994] ICR 478, Ch D.

[25] This refers to the position where a trade union of some sort is involved; however, the consultation requirements or redundancies and business transfers were extended in 1995 to elected worker representatives, in cases where no trade union is being involved, and similar reforms were made in the case of health and safety representatives in 1996.

hearing of an unfair dismissal action. The availability of these rights to such a union and its members may be a significant help in recruiting members and, perhaps more to the point, lack of them could be very damaging to any nascent organization wishing to establish itself as a viable union. In the past this has been particularly important in an area of disputed or growing unionization, for example in the white collar area, where there is competition for members between a larger, established union and a smaller body such as a staff association, for if that smaller body fails to obtain a certificate of independence it may stand little chance of competing effectively. Staff associations (or 'house' unions) have been particularly at risk in this certification procedure, since they may have evolved from little more than social clubs, and as they only operate with one employer they may be inherently more susceptible to interference (although this is by no means conclusive—the NUM and RMT could be said to be one-employer unions). Also at risk would be non-TUC affiliated bodies and breakaway groups from larger unions,[26] where again they may face opposition from established affiliated unions.

(b) The machinery of certification

A listed[27] trade union may apply to the Certification Officer (CO)[28] for a certificate of independence, under the Trade Union and Labour Relations (Consolidation) Act 1992, section 6. He must decide whether the union is in fact 'independent' within the statutory definition; if his decision is favourable he must grant the certificate, and if unfavourable he must give his reasons for refusal. In coming to his decision he is at liberty to make such inquiries as he thinks fit and 'shall take into account any relevant information submitted to him by any person', which will of course include any other union which has an interest in the area in question and may wish to oppose the application for a certificate. If an applicant union is refused a certificate, it may appeal against that decision to the EAT on a point of law.[29] It should be noted, however, that the right to appeal is so worded that only a refused applicant union may appeal; if a certificate is in fact granted, there is no appeal against that decision by another union which may have opposed the application.[30] Finally, an application can be made more than once so that if a union is at first refused a certificate (whether after an appeal or not) it may reconsider its organization etc (possibly in the light of the reasons given for refusal), make any necessary changes and then apply again.[31] In practice, however,

---

[26] A particularly newsworthy example of a breakaway group was the Union of Democratic Mineworkers which split from the NUM after the miners' strike, and was eventually granted a certificate of independence.

[27] Ie listed under the Trade Union and Labour Relations (Consolidation) Act 1992, s 2—see heading 1(ii), p 625.

[28] See Ch 1, heading 3(iii), p 25.

[29] Trade Union and Labour Relations (Consolidation) Act 1992, s 9, as amended by the Employment Relations Act 2004.

[30] *GMWU v Certification Officer* [1977] 1 All ER 771, [1977] ICR 183.

[31] *Blue Circle Staff Association v Certification Officer* [1977] ICR 224, [1977] IRLR 20; *HSD (Hatfield) Employees Association v Certification Officer* [1978] ICR 21, [1977] IRLR 261.

where there is rivalry with an established union this delay might give the latter a considerable tactical advantage.

(c) The tests to be applied

An independent trade union is defined in the Trade Union and Labour Relations
(Consolidation) Act 1992, section 5 as one which (a) is not under the domination
or control of an employer or a group of employers or of one or more employers'
associations, and (b) is not liable to interference by an employer or any such group
or association (arising out of the provision of financial or material support or by any
other means whatsoever) tending towards such control. The CO has evolved certain
criteria, particularly on limb (a), and these were approved by the EAT in the first case
to come before it on certification, *Blue Circle Staff Association v Certification Officer*.[32]
These criteria are the financing of the union (any direct subsidy from the employer
being potentially fatal); any other material support from the employer, such as free
premises, time off work for officials or office facilities;[33] any interference in the running of the union by the employer; the history of the union, particularly if it started
off as the creation of the employer; the union's rules, particularly if they allow intervention by the employer or give much control to senior members of the management;
whether the union only operates within a single company (not a fixed criterion, but of
course a more broadly based union would be more difficult to influence); the organization of the union (its structure, financial position, recruiting ability); and its general
attitude towards the employer in negotiating, for while it would be going too far to
expect industrial chaos as a necessary sign of independence, the nascent union may
be expected to have evolved far enough to show some 'robustness' in its negotiations.
In the *Blue Circle* case the EAT approved the CO's refusal of a certificate on the basis
that the staff association in question had originated as 'little more than a sophisticated
instrument of personnel control' and had not evolved far enough to qualify as independent, in spite of certain changes to its rules and procedures which had, however,
not gone far enough:

> We are not satisfied that the Association has yet attained that freedom from domination
> which it has been pursuing since it first decided to reorganise its constitution last year. When
> the matrix of the new constitution is regarded, it is found to be an organisation whereby
> the association of the salaried staff members was penetrated at every point by the interfer-
> ence and control of the management. There must be a heavy onus on such a body to show
> that it has shaken off the paternal control which brought it into existence and fostered its
> growth, and which finally joined in drafting the very rules by which the control appears to
> be relaxed.[34]

---

[32] See n 31.

[33] After certification, of course, the union might well bargain for such facilities, and indeed in the case of
time off demand it as of right, but before certification it would be wiser not to accept them.

[34] [1977] ICR 224 at 233, [1977] IRLR 20 at 24, per Cumming-Bruce J.

In order to qualify as independent, the union must satisfy limb (b) of the definition too, for it could be the case that limb (a) is satisfied as things stand, but the union might still in some way be liable to interference, perhaps indirectly.[35] This second stage of the test requires a certain amount of speculation and foresight, and raised a question of interpretation—what was meant by 'liable' to interference? The wider view (ie more indulgent to the applicant union) was that 'liable' meant 'likely to suffer in practice', so that even if there were some provisions in the union's rules which might in theory permit interference by the management they should be ignored if in practice that was unlikely to happen. The narrower view was that 'liable' meant 'vulnerable to' or 'exposed to the risk of' interference, so that any factors raising a possibility of interference should disentitle the union to a certificate of independence even if, as things stood at the time of the application, there was little likelihood in practice of it happening. In *Squibb UK Staff Association v Certification Officer*, the applicant association had a proportionally large membership of the employees involved and was recognized by the employer for bargaining purposes; however, it was dependent upon the employer for material support such as accommodation and communications and was in a weak financial position, though there was found to be little likelihood of withdrawal of the employer's support. The EAT gave 'liable' the wider meaning and held that the union was independent[36] but, on the CO's appeal, the Court of Appeal reversed that decision, holding that the correct interpretation was the narrower view so that on the facts the CO's decision to refuse the certificate was correct.[37] Thus, the overall test for independence is more stringent than it might have been, in the light of the practical significance of the certificate of independence, and an applicant union or staff association should be quite sure before applying that none of its rules or procedures leave open a way for interference by an employer, so that it can claim to pass limb (b) as well as limb (a)—it is not enough to say that, although interference may be a theoretical possibility it is not likely to happen because of the present attitude of the employer:

> One has to envisage the possibility that there may be a difference of opinion in the future between the employers and the staff association. It does not matter whether it is likely or not.... It may be a mere possibility. But when it arises the questions have to be asked. What is the strength of the employers? What pressures could they bring to bear against the staff association? What facilities could they withdraw?[38]

---

[35] *HSD (Hatfield) Employees Association v Certification Officer* [1978] ICR 21, [1977] IRLR 261.

[36] [1978] ICR 115, [1977] IRLR 355; see also the *HSD (Hatfield)* case, n 35.

[37] [1979] ICR 235, [1979] IRLR 75, CA. For an application of these principles, see *A Monk & Co Staff Association v Certification Officer* [1980] IRLR 431, EAT. The staff association formed at GCHQ, Cheltenham (after the government's decision in 1984 to ban unions there on the grounds of national security) was refused a certificate of independence on this second limb of the test and that refusal was upheld by the EAT: *Government Communications Staff Federation v Certification Officer* [1993] ICR 163, [1993] IRLR 260.

[38] [1979] ICR 235 at 245, [1979] IRLR 75 at 78, per Lord Denning MR. The staff association was eventually granted a certificate by the Certification Officer (Employment News No 62 (May/June 1979)).

Beneath the legal challenges lies an important principle. The TUC and its affiliated trade unions resist the establishment and growth of non-affiliated unions—often within the one company (the house union). It is difficult for such trade unions to satisfy the criteria of independence and they will rarely, in the early stages of development, be 'effective'.[39]

2 FREEDOM OF ASSOCIATION[40]

Trade unions can only exist where individuals are free to combine together in associations. This freedom to associate was granted in Britain as long ago as 1824 with the repeal of the Combination Acts,[41] which had made it unlawful for workers to combine together in trade unions. At common law, therefore, individuals were free to form and join trade unions.[42] However, the common law did not grant positive *rights* of association, enforceable against others, so that at common law there was no protection against discriminatory action by an employer on grounds of union membership, whether in the form of a refusal to hire, dismissal or some other action aimed at discouraging union membership or participation in union activities; neither did the common law give any enforceable right *not* to associate to non-union members seeking to work in a closed shop; and, with one possible exception,[43] there was no common law right to insist on being admitted to a trade union of one's choice: admission to a union presupposed the willingness of that union to admit the applicant into membership. As Lord Diplock put it in *Cheall v APEX*:[44]

> My Lords, freedom of association can only be mutual; there can be no right of an individual to associate with other individuals who are not willing to associate with him.

Such positive rights to associate as there are in English law have been granted by statute, not in the form of a broad and general right to associate, but instead through the enactment of a complex set of measures (now contained in Part III of the Trade Union and Labour Relations (Consolidation) Act 1992), giving specific protection to those who are refused employment, discriminated against or dismissed for union reasons, and

---

[39] The *Annual Report of the Certification Office 1987* showed a cumulative total of 52 refusals of applications in the important first ten years of operation—a large proportion of these were staff associations; 231 certificates had been issued and were still in force at the end of 1987; 140 had been issued and subsequently cancelled (largely due to union amalgamation). Needless to say, the rate of application slowed dramatically; in 1992 six certificates were granted, and by 1995 none: *Annual Reports 1992, 1995*.

[40] See, generally, Von Prondzynski *Freedom of Association and Industrial Relations* (1987); Wedderburn 'Freedom of Association and Philosophies of Labour Law' (1989) 18 ILJ 1.

[41] Combination Laws Repeal Act 1824. Repeal of the legal restrictions on union activities did not come until much later—see Ch 10.

[42] With the exception of the police and those working in the intelligence services.

[43] Lord Denning's 'right to work' principle in *Nagle v Feilden* [1966] 2 QB 633, CA.

[44] [1983] ICR 398, [1983] IRLR 215, HL.

controlling admission to and expulsion from trade unions. The approach in English law has therefore been to build a collective right to associate 'out of the bricks of certain individual employment rights'.[45] These rights exist against the backdrop of an array of international treaties and conventions guaranteeing the principle of freedom of association (albeit in varying degrees), including Article 11 of the European Convention on Human Rights and Fundamental Freedoms, Article 5 of the European Social Charter and ILO Conventions No 87 (on Freedom of Association and Protection of the Right to Organize) and No 98 (on the Right to Organize and Bargain Collectively).[46] For many years there has been a lively debate over the extent to which the UK law on freedom of association complies with these international standards, fuelled by a number of cases in which the fragility of the right to associate has been graphically demonstrated, for example the ban in 1984 on union membership at the government Communications Headquarters (GCHQ) on grounds of national security.[47] The debate took on an entirely new dimension in the UK as a result of the 'bringing home' to English law of the European Convention on Human Rights,[48] Article 11 of which states:

(1) Everyone has the right to freedom of peaceful assembly and to freedom of association with others, including the right to form and to join trade unions for the protection of his interests.

(2) No restrictions shall be placed on the exercise of these rights other than such as are prescribed by law and are necessary in a democratic society in the interests of national security or public safety, for the prevention of disorder or crime, for the protection of health or morals or for the protection of the rights and freedoms of others.

Until recently, the judgments of the European Court of Human Rights (and of the now defunct European Commission)[49] under Article 11 had given little cause for optimism that the incorporation of the Convention would lead to a strengthening of the right to associate;[50] indeed, individuals seeking to assert a right *not* to associate had had greater success under Article 11 than had trade unions and their members,[51] hence Ewing's comment in 1998 that 'the contribution of Article 11 to date has been

---

[45] Wedderburn (1976) 39 MLR 168.

[46] See generally Ewing *Britain and the ILO* (2nd edn, 1994); Morris 'Freedom of Association and the Interests of the State' in Ewing, Gearty and Hepple (eds) *Human Rights and Labour Law: Essays for Paul O'Higgins* (1994).

[47] *Council of Civil Service Unions v Minister for the Civil Service* [1985] ICR 14, [1985] IRLR 28, HL. See Morris [1985] PL 177. The ban was eventually lifted by the incoming Labour government in 1998.

[48] See Ewing (ed) *Human Rights at Work* (2000); O'Dempsey et al *Employment Law and the Human Rights Act 1998* (2001); Hepple 'The Impact on Labour Law' in Markesinis (ed) *The Impact of the Human Rights Bill on English Law* (1998); Ewing 'The Human Rights Act and Labour Law' (1998) 27 ILJ 275; Palmer 'Human Rights: Implications for Labour Law' (2000) 59 CLJ 168.

[49] The Commission determined the admissibility of applications to the court until the procedures were streamlined by the 11th Protocol in 1998.

[50] See eg *Council of Civil Service Unions v United Kingdom* (1987) 10 EHRR 269, EComHR.

[51] *Young, James and Webster v United Kingdom* [1981] IRLR 408, ECtHR.

disappointing, failing to deliver any meaningful protection for trade union activities, while being used as an instrument for undermining trade union security'.[52] Arguably, that gloomy assessment had to be reconsidered in the light of the landmark decision of the European Court of Human Rights in *Wilson and National Union of Journalists; Palmer, Wyeth and National Union of Rail, Maritime and Transport Workers v United Kingdom*,[53] which has transformed the whole area and has necessitated a fundamental reappraisal of the protection of the right to associate under UK law. Although the actual point at issue is now covered by legislation (discussed in this chapter in more detail), the general tenor and approach may still be important in debates about other aspects of that right.

The facts of the two cases were very similar; in both, the employers had offered a substantial pay increase to those employees who agreed to give up their right to have their terms and conditions negotiated through collective bargaining and sign individual contracts instead. Those who did not sign the new contracts did not get the pay increase. The main difference between the two was that in *Palmer*, the employees who refused to sign personal contracts had the option of continuing to be represented by their union, whereas in *Wilson* the employers had terminated the collective agreement and derecognized the union. The applicants complained that the withholding of pay increases from those who refused to sign individual contracts requiring them to forgo the right to be represented by a union constituted a breach of their statutory right not to have 'action short of dismissal' taken against them for trade union reasons.[54] The House of Lords[55] ruled against the applicants on the grounds, first, that the statutory protection only applied to 'action', and that as the employers' failure to extend the pay increases to those who refused to sign individual contracts was technically an omission, it did not constitute 'action' within the meaning of the section;[56] and secondly, that the statutory protection only applied to action taken for the purpose of preventing or deterring union membership, and that on the facts there was no evidence that the employer's ultimate purpose was to deter union membership.[57] The applicants then took their complaint to the European Court of Human Rights, which ruled in *Wilson and Palmer*[58] that UK law was in violation of Article 11 of the European Convention on Human Rights. In its decision, the Court stressed that the members of a trade union 'have a right, in order to protect their interests, that the trade union should be heard'.[59] According to the Court, 'it is of the essence of the right to join a trade union ... that employees should be free to instruct or permit the union to make representations to their employer or to take action in support of their interests on their behalf', and that 'it is the role of the State to ensure that trade union members

---

[52] Ewing *Britain and the ILO* (2nd edn, 1994) 279.

[53] [2002] IRLR 568, ECtHR (hereinafter referred to as *Wilson and Palmer*).

[54] Then contained in the Employment Protection (Consolidation) Act 1978, s 23; see now the Trade Union and Labour Relations (Consolidation) Act 1992, s 146.

[55] [1995] ICR 406, [1995] IRLR 258, HL.   [56] See heading 2(i), p 640.

[57] See heading 2(i), p 641.   [58] See n 53.   [59] *Wilson and Palmer* at para 42.

are not prevented or restrained from using their union to represent them in attempts
to regulate their relations with their employers'.[60] The Court considered that the UK
had failed this test, because UK law had 'permitted employers to treat less favourably employees who were not prepared to renounce a freedom that was an essential
feature of union membership'.[61] Furthermore, under UK law at the relevant time 'it
was … possible for an employer effectively to undermine or frustrate a trade union's
ability to strive for the protection of its members' interests'.[62] The Court concluded that
'by permitting employers to use financial incentives to induce employees to surrender
important union rights, the respondent State failed in its positive obligation to secure
the enjoyment of the rights under Article 11 of the Convention'.[63]

As will be seen, the decision in *Wilson and Palmer* led to amending legislation on the
specific issue in question ('sweetener payments'), but this is likely to remain a volatile
area generally. One issue in particular over which UK law may be vulnerable to further
challenge is the way in which, as seen above, the *collective* right to associate is protected
under UK law by a means of a series of *individual* rights. In *Wilson and Palmer*, the
European Court held that the UK was in violation of Article 11 'as regards both the
applicant unions and the individual applicants',[64] the clear implication being that 'trade
unions have freedom of association rights in addition to and separate from the rights
of their members'.[65] However, this begs the obvious question: what exactly do these
collective rights amount to, and how, if at all, can a union enforce them?[66] The Court
stated that a union must be 'free to strive for the protection of its members' interests',[67]
and free, 'in one way or another, to seek to persuade the employer to listen to what it
has to say on behalf of its members',[68] but crucially the Court reasserted its consistently
held view that the freedom of a union to make its voice heard does not extend to an
obligation on an employer to recognize a union,[69] and that contracting states 'enjoy
a wide margin of appreciation as to how trade union freedom may be secured'.[70] The
Court pointed instead to 'other measures' available to unions to further their members'

---

[60] *Wilson and Palmer*, at para 46.   [61] *Wilson and Palmer*, at para 47.

[62] *Wilson and Palmer*, at para 48.   [63] *Wilson and Palmer*, at para 48.

[64] See *Wilson and Palmer*, at para 48. According to the court, a trade union 'must … be free to strive for the
protection of its members interests': para 42

[65] Ewing 'The Implications of *Wilson and Palmer*' (2003) 32 ILJ 1.

[66] Ewing observes ((2003) 32 ILJ 1 at p 12) that this dimension of the case 'exposes an important omission
in British labour law … namely that the rights of trade union membership are rights which vest only in the
individual and not also in the union', and suggests that a new right enforceable by a trade union (possibly via
the device of an 'unfair labour practice') may have to be created in order to secure trade union rights under
Art 11.

[67] *Wilson and Palmer* at para 42.   [68] *Wilson and Palmer*, at para 44.

[69] 'Although collective bargaining may be one of the ways by which trade unions may be enabled to protect their members' interests, it is not indispensable for the effective enjoyment of trade union freedom': *Wilson
and Palmer*, para 44.

[70] *Wilson and Palmer*, at para 44. 'Article 11 does not … secure any particular treatment of trade unions
or their members and leaves each state a free choice of the means to be used to secure the right to be heard':
para 42.

interests, and in particular the protection conferred by domestic law on a trade union organizing strike action.[71] In view of the inherently unreliable nature of that protection under UK law, based as it is on a set of legal immunities that are far from watertight, it seems reasonable to conclude that Article 11, as interpreted and applied by the European Court of Human Rights in *Wilson and Palmer*, offers more by way of protection to individuals than it does to trade unions.[72] *Plus ça change* ...

The approach taken in this section will be, first, to examine the legal protection enjoyed by union members against dismissal or other discrimination by employers on the grounds of their union membership or activities, including the right not to be refused employment on grounds of trade union membership; secondly, to examine the circumstances where union officials and members may claim time off work for their trade union duties and activities; and, finally, to consider the legal protection of the right to dissociate, with particular reference to the closed shop. The controversial controls on union admissions and expulsions are considered later in this chapter under Section 4, in the context of the other statutory controls on internal union affairs.

(i) THE RIGHT TO ASSOCIATE

(a) Refusal of employment on grounds of union membership

Union members have for many years enjoyed protection within employment against dismissal and discriminatory action short of dismissal (for example demotion, blocking promotion, etc) for union reasons. However, until 1990 the law offered no redress to a union member who was refused employment on those grounds. That omission was rectified (at least in part) by the Employment Act 1990,[73] which made it unlawful to refuse a person employment on grounds related to union membership.[74] It is generally accepted that the Conservative government's primary aim in introducing these measures was to attack the practice of the pre-entry closed shop, not to provide additional protection for union members (indeed, the Green Paper in which the proposals originally saw the light of day made no mention of extra protection for union members),[75] but in the event the protection was extended to union members and non-members alike. 'Refusal of employment' is defined very widely,[76] and includes a refusal or 'deliberate omission' to entertain and process an application or to offer employment to the applicant (simple oversight will not be enough), causing

---

[71] *Wilson and Palmer*, at para 45.

[72] Although note the extent to which the Strasbourg Court in *Wilson and Palmer* drew on the broader, more pro-union European Social Charter and ILO Convention Nos 87 and 98 in interpreting Art 11.

[73] Employment Act 1990, s 1. The measures are now contained in the Trade Union and Labour Relations (Consolidation) Act 1992, s 137.

[74] This includes a situation where a person is refused employment because he is unwilling to accept a requirement not to join or to cease to be a union member: s 137(1)(b).

[75] 'Removing Barriers to Employment' (Cm 655, 1989).

[76] Trade Union and Labour Relations (Consolidation) Act 1992, s 137(5).

the applicant to withdraw or cease to pursue his application, and making an offer of employment 'the terms of which are such as no reasonable employer who wished to fill the post would offer, and which is not accepted'. It will normally be for the applicant to prove that the refusal of employment was on grounds related to union membership and not for some other reason (for example inferior qualifications or experience), but in certain specific circumstances a refusal of employment will be deemed to be unlawful; in particular, where a job advertisement is published which indicates (or might reasonably be understood as indicating) that a particular job is only open to union members or to non-union members, a person who does not satisfy that requirement and who applies unsuccessfully for that job will be conclusively presumed to have been refused employment unlawfully, whatever the employer's reason for not appointing.[77]

There is an important limitation on the protection afforded by this right, in that it only covers refusal of employment on grounds of union *membership*; it does not expressly cover an applicant who is refused employment because of his or her past union *activities*. It therefore compares unfavourably with the protection against discrimination within employment, where dismissal and detriment for taking part in union activities is specifically prohibited.[78] If membership of a union means no more than the mere possession of a union membership card, the statutory protection against refusal of employment on grounds of union membership would be narrow indeed. Significantly, however, in *Harrison v Kent County Council*,[79] the first reported case on these provisions, the EAT refused to draw a rigid distinction between membership of a trade union and taking part in union activities, holding that if a person was refused employment because he was a trade union activist or because of his union activities, it was open to a tribunal to conclude that he was refused employment because he was a member of a union. This broad, purposive interpretation of section 137 mirrors the approach taken in an earlier case involving dismissal for union membership,[80] where the EAT held that union membership must necessarily imply some degree of participation in union activities. In *Wilson and Palmer*[81] the House of Lords denied the existence of any general principle that a reference to union membership includes union activities, which seemed to place the correctness of the decision in *Harrison* in some doubt. However, in the wake of the European Court of Human Rights' decision in *Wilson and Palmer*, which made it plain that accessing the essential services

---

[77] Trade Union and Labour Relations (Consolidation) Act 1992, s 137(3). A refusal of employment will also be deemed unlawful where it is in pursuance of a union-labour-supply arrangement and the applicant is not a member of the relevant union (s 137(4)), and where the applicant rejects a job offer because he is unable or unwilling to accept or comply with conditions attached to it concerning union membership (s 137(6)).

[78] See heading 2(i), p 639.

[79] [1995] ICR 434, EAT.

[80] *Discount Tobacco and Confectionery Ltd v Armitage* [1995] ICR 431n, [1990] IRLR 15, EAT (a case involving dismissal for union membership under s 152; see heading 2(i), p 644).

[81] [1995] IRLR 258, HL. The case involved action short of dismissal under s 146. The House of Lords was prepared to accept that the decision in *Discount Tobacco* was correct on its facts. See also *Speciality Care plc v Pachela* [1996] IRLR 248, EAT, considered at heading 2(i), p 644.

of a union is intrinsic to exercising the right to belong to a union, this may need to be treated with caution. Complaints of a breach of this right lie to an employment tribunal,[82] which may make a declaration, order the employer to pay compensation (up to the limit of the compensatory award for unfair dismissal)[83] and/or recommend that the respondent take remedial action 'for the purpose of obviating or reducing the adverse effect on the complainant of any conduct to which the complaint relates'.[84]

While the introduction in 1990 of the right not to be refused employment on grounds of union membership went some way towards plugging the gaps in the protection of the right to associate, it did not tackle the controversial practice of compiling 'blacklists' of union officials or members. The practice of blacklisting was well documented in the UK during the 1980s, when organizations such as the Economic League produced and sold blacklists to employers, and the failure of the UK government to prohibit the practice during that period was criticized on more than one occasion by the International Labour Organisation.[85] In subsequent years there was in fact little evidence of blacklisting activity, but the previous government decided to enact section 3 of the Employment Relations Act 1999, which conferred a power on the Secretary of State to make Regulations prohibiting the compilation, use, sale or supply of lists[86] which contain details of trade union members or persons who have taken part in trade union activities, and which are compiled 'with a view to being used by employers or employment agencies for the purposes of discrimination in relation to recruitment or in relation to the treatment of workers'.[87] Enforcement of the anti-blacklisting provisions may be through the employment tribunals and EAT, with the possibility of criminal sanctions.[88] In 2003 the government issued *draft* Regulations on the prohibition of blacklists, modelled in part on the existing law governing dismissal and detriment on grounds of trade union membership and activities. The intention was to leave these provisions simply available in case of need, and that remained the position for several years. However, in 2009 evidence arose of an element of blacklisting in the construction industry and, while the immediate result was a prosecution of the list compiler by the Information Commissioner under the Data Protection Act 1998, the then government decided to bring the draft provisions into force as from March 2010 as the Employment Relations Act 1998 (Blacklists) Regulations 2010.[89]

---

[82] Trade Union and Labour Relations (Consolidation) Act 1992, s 137(2). Complaints must be brought within three months of the conduct complained of, subject to the usual extension where not reasonably practicable: s 139(1).

[83] At the time of writing, £66,200. Compensation is assessed on the same basis as an award of damages in tort for breach of statutory duty, and may include an amount for injury to feelings: s 140(2).

[84] For the interpretation of this formula in the context of complaints of sex and race discrimination, see p 347 above. Failure to comply with such an order without reasonable justification may lead to an increased award of compensation, but still subject to the statutory maximum: s 140(3).

[85] See eg ILO *287th Report of the Freedom of Association Committee* (1992) para 267.

[86] 'List' is defined widely to mean 'any index or other set of items whether recorded electronically or by any other means': Employment Relations Act 1999, s 3(5).

[87] Employment Relations Act 1999, s 3(1), (2).   [88] Employment Relations Act 1999, s 3(3).

[89] SI 2010/493.

The Regulations make it unlawful to compile, use, sell or supply[90] a blacklist (referred to as a 'prohibited list') of trade union members or persons who have taken part in trade union activities, albeit with certain limited exceptions in the case of those who use a blacklist in order to expose its existence (for example investigative journalists), where there would be a public interest defence, and situations where significant trade union knowledge or experience is a necessary requirement of the job.[91] A person who suffers loss due to blacklisting is entitled to seek damages from the county court, which (unlike an employment tribunal) could grant interim relief to prevent further damage from occurring. The Regulations also make it unlawful for an employer to refuse a person employment, or to dismiss a worker or subject a worker to any detriment, because that person's name is, or is not, on a prohibited list. Complaint here lies to an employment tribunal, as under the existing provisions on refusal of employment, detriment and dismissal on trade union grounds.

(b) Detriment short of dismissal on trade union grounds

Under section 146 of the Trade Union and Labour Relations (Consolidation) Act 1992,[92] a worker has a right not to be subjected to any detriment as an individual by his employer, whether by an act or a deliberate failure to act, for the purpose of (a) preventing or deterring him from being or seeking to become a member of an independent trade union, or penalizing him for doing so; (b) preventing or deterring him from taking part in the activities of an independent trade union at an appropriate time, or penalizing him for doing so; (c) preventing or deterring him from making use of trade union services[93] at an appropriate time, or penalizing him for doing so; or (d) compelling him to be or become a member of a trade union.[94] Section 146 has been the subject of some exceptionally difficult and controversial case law, not least the landmark decision of the European Court of Human Rights in *Wilson and Palmer*[95] (discussed in the introduction to this chapter), in which the Court ruled that UK law was in violation of Article 11 of the European Convention on Human Rights.

The first point to note about section 146 is that it now applies where a worker is 'subjected to any detriment' by the employer, whether by an act or a deliberate failure to

---

[90] The requirement in reg 3(4) for a person to sell or supply a prohibited list 'knowingly or recklessly' would clearly provide a defence for organizations such as the Royal Mail that distribute such lists unknowingly or accidentally.

[91] Reg 3(5), (6).

[92] As amended by the Employment Relations Act 1999 and the Employment Relations Act 2004 (which extended the protection from 'employees' to 'workers'). Note the analogous protection in Pt V of the Employment Rights Act 1996, eg, for health and safety representatives and pension scheme trustees.

[93] This means services made available by virtue of his membership; this includes consenting to a matter being raised on his behalf by the union: s 146(2A)–(2C).

[94] Before the Employment Act 1980 altered it, limb (c) was confined to action compelling the employee to join a *non-independent* trade union (such as the employer's 'house' union). The removal of this wording in 1980 altered its meaning completely, so that it now applies wherever there is managerial pressure to join any union; this aspect of s 146 is considered separately at heading 2(iii), p 658.

[95] [2002] IRLR 568, ECtHR.

act (ie an omission). Until 1999, the protection was stated to apply where an employer took '*action short of dismissal*' against an employee. It had long been thought to be established beyond doubt that 'action' in this context included an omission to act, such as a block on promotion or a refusal to extend a pay increase to the members of a particular union[96] (a view which appeared to be confirmed by the statute, which provides an extended definition of 'act' and 'action' as including an omission, 'unless the context otherwise requires').[97] However, in *Associated Newspapers Ltd v Wilson; Associated British Ports v Palmer*,[98] the House of Lords surprisingly held[99] that, for reasons of legislative history, the statutory definition of 'action' as including an omission did not apply in this context, and that as the conduct complained of (the employers' failure to extend pay increases to employees who refused to sign individual contracts) was an omission, it did not constitute 'action short of dismissal' on trade union grounds.

The effect of the House of Lords' decision (which has been described as 'a brilliant example of grammatical pedantry' and a 'singular triumph of the clever mind at the expense of the big picture')[100] was to restrict the statutory protection against victimization on trade union grounds to positive acts, such as the imposition of a financial penalty. In view of the fact that the victimization of union members is in practice very likely to involve the withholding of some benefit which is conferred on other employees, the effect of the decision was to render the statutory protection against action short of dismissal almost worthless. Indeed, Lord Browne-Wilkinson acknowledged that the conclusion 'leaves an undesirable lacuna in the legislation protecting employees against victimisation'.[101] The anomaly was subsequently corrected by the Employment Relations Act 1999, which amended section 146 so that it now applies where an employee is 'subjected to any detriment' by his employer, whether 'by an act or a deliberate failure to act' (ie a deliberate omission).

Turning to the rest of section 146, to benefit from the statutory protection the worker must be subjected to a detriment 'as an individual', and the act or omission must take place 'for the purpose of' preventing or deterring union membership or participation in union activities', etc. The first of these requirements is designed to ensure that the protection cannot be used to claim what are essentially collective rights.[102] Action

---

[96] *National Coal Board v Ridgway* [1987] ICR 641, [1987] IRLR 80, CA. This was so even where the employer was under no obligation to do the act in question, as in *Ridgway*. See also *Carlson v Post Office* [1981] ICR 343, [1981] IRLR 158, EAT (refusal of a parking space).

[97] Trade Union and Labour Relations (Consolidation) Act 1992, s 298; this definition was formerly located in the Employment Protection (Consolidation) Act 1978, s 153(1), with some minor differences in wording.

[98] [1995] ICR 406, [1995] IRLR 258, HL, overruling the Court of Appeal in *National Coal Board v Ridgway* [1987] ICR 641, [1987] IRLR 80. See Simpson (1995) 24 ILJ 235.

[99] By a 3–2 majority (reversing the Court of Appeal), Lord Keith and Lord Browne-Wilkinson agreeing with Lord Bridge on this point; Lord Lloyd and Lord Slynn dissented, preferring a more purposive interpretation of the provisions.

[100] Ewing (1999) 28 ILJ 283 at 287.   [101] [1995] IRLR 258 at 264.

[102] As seen above at heading 2(i), p 635, this may be an area where the UK will have to change in order to comply with the ECtHR ruling in *Wilson and Palmer* (n 101), which confirmed that unions have a right to freedom of association separate from their members.

taken by the employer against a trade union (for example derecognition of the union, or the withdrawal of union facilities) may well have an indirect adverse effect on union members, but it is unlikely to constitute a detriment to them as individuals within the scope of the statutory protection unless it affects them personally, otherwise than merely as union members or officials (for example through their pay packets). A good example of action taken against a union which affected the members personally can be seen in *National Coal Board v Ridgway*,[103] which arose in the aftermath of the 1984–85 miners' strike, and the breakaway of the Union of Democratic Mineworkers from the National Union of Mineworkers. A pay rise was negotiated with the UDM but rejected by the NUM, and at the colliery in question the rise was paid to UDM members but not to NUM members. The Court of Appeal held, inter alia,[104] that this constituted action taken against the applicants (who were NUM members) as individuals, because the action against the union also affected them as individuals through their pay packets. It seems that derecognition of an individual shop steward (as opposed to derecognition of the union) can constitute action taken against that person as an individual, even though it may not directly affect him as an employee.[105] In the context of dismissal for union membership or activities, it has been held that the protection does not apply where action is taken by the employer in retaliation for activities by the union generally, unless those affected were singled out for attention because of their own trade union membership or activities;[106] it is unclear whether the same reasoning would be applied in a case involving detriment short of dismissal.

Once an employee has established that he was subjected to some detriment short of dismissal 'as an individual', it then falls to the employer to show the 'sole or main purpose' for which he acted or failed to act.[107] The courts have tended to take a narrow approach to this issue, and have refused to equate the employer's *purpose* with the *effect* of the action complained of. In *Gallacher v Department of Transport*,[108] the employee, a civil servant who for several years had spent most of his time on trade union duties, was advised by his career development officer that in order to gain promotion he would need to acquire greater line management experience, which would necessitate a sharp reduction in his union activities. The tribunal held that this recommendation was intended to deter him from continuing with his union activities, and that the employers had therefore taken action short of dismissal against him for the purpose

---

[103] *National Coal Board v Ridgway* [1987] ICR 641, [1987] IRLR 80, CA. See also *Cheall v Vauxhall Motors Ltd* [1979] IRLR 253, where the employer's refusal to allow union representation in disciplinary proceedings was held to be action taken against individual employees. Although *Ridgway* was overruled by the House of Lords in *Associated Newspapers Ltd v Wilson; Associated British Ports v Palmer* (n 101) on other grounds, the reasoning of the Court of Appeal on this point still appears to be valid.

[104] The other grounds of decision are discussed at heading 2(i), p 643.

[105] *F W Farnsworth Ltd v McCoid* [1999] ICR 1047, CA, upholding the EAT decision on this point: [1998] IRLR 362.

[106] *Carrington v Therm-A-Stor Ltd* [1983] ICR 208, [1983] IRLR 78, CA; the decision has been heavily criticized, and rightly so.

[107] Trade Union and Labour Relations (Consolidation) Act 1992, s 148(1).

[108] [1994] IRLR 231, CA.

of deterring him from taking part in trade union activities. However, the Court of Appeal, upholding the EAT, held that the tribunal had misconstrued the meaning of the word 'purpose', by failing to distinguish between purpose and effect. According to Neill LJ, in this context the phrase 'for the purpose of' 'connotes an object which the employer desires or seeks to achieve'; on the facts, the employers' purpose was to ensure that only those with sufficient management experience were promoted, not to deter the employee from continuing with his union activities.

The same distinction was also drawn in *Associated Newspapers Ltd v Wilson; Associated British Ports v Palmer*,[109] where one of the main issues was whether the purpose of the employers' actions in offering a pay rise only to those employees who agreed to sign personal contracts was to deter employees from continuing to be union members or to penalize them for doing so, or was instead to achieve a smooth transition from collective bargaining to individual contracting, and to achieve greater flexibility. The House of Lords held that as the employers' purpose in *Wilson* was to smooth the transition from collective bargaining to individual contracting, and in *Palmer* to achieve greater flexibility, there was no unlawful purpose within the meaning of section 146. According to Lord Slynn, there was no evidence 'that the employers' purpose in paying a salary differential was to prevent or deter union membership, even if derecognition in itself might make the union less attractive to members or to potential members'.[110] This part of the House of Lords' decision was unaffected by the redrafting of section 146 in 1999 to include deliberate omissions, but their Lordships' reasoning was undermined by the decision of the European Court of Human Rights in *Wilson and Palmer*[111] that the law should not allow employers to offer financial inducements to workers on condition that they surrender their rights to union representation, or make it a condition of entering individualized contracts that workers must relinquish those rights. The result was an important legislative amendment by the Employment Relations Act 2004 which added sections 145A–145F to deal specifically with sweetener payments. Section 145A provides that a worker has a right not to have an offer made to him by his employer for the sole or main purpose of inducing him (a) not to be or seek to become a member of an independent trade union, (b) not to take part (at an appropriate time—see later discussion) in the activities of an independent trade union, (c) not to make use (at an appropriate time) of trade union services or (d) to be or become a member of any trade union or of a particular trade union or of one of a number of particular trade unions. Section 145B further states that a worker who is a member of a recognized trade union (or one seeking recognition) has a right not to have an offer made to him if acceptance of the offer (together with other workers' acceptance) would lead to his terms of employment not being (or no longer being)

---

[109] [1995] ICR 406, [1995] IRLR 258, HL.

[110] See also Lord Lloyd, at 266, on the importance of distinguishing between the *purposes* and the *consequences* of derecognition.

[111] [2002] IRLR 568, ECtHR.

determined by collective agreement negotiated by or on behalf of the union (the actual *Wilson and Palmer* point). A worker or former worker can complain to a tribunal if such an offer is made.[112] If the complaint is upheld, the tribunal is to make a declaration to that effect and award compensation of £3,500 (at the time of writing). It is further provided that any apparent acceptance by the worker of the offending offer is unenforceable.[113]

Moving on, the statutory protection of union members arises where an employee is subjected to any detriment for the purpose of (a) preventing or deterring him from being or seeking to become a union member, or (b) preventing or deterring him from taking part in union activities, or penalizing him for doing so. Under the first paragraph (preventing or deterring union membership), two particular issues have been especially problematic: the first concerns the possible application of section 146 to cases of inter-union rivalry, such as in *National Coal Board v Ridgway*.[114] As seen already,[115] in that case a pay rise was paid by the employer to members of the UDM but not to those of the NUM, because the NUM had rejected a pay deal negotiated between the employer and the rival UDM. Two of the NUM members complained that this constituted a breach of section 146 because they were in effect being penalized for being members of the NUM rather than the UDM. The EAT ruled against the applicants on the grounds, inter alia, that section 146 only outlawed action to prevent an employee being a member of *any* trade union, not to prevent membership of a *particular* union (a finding which appeared to gain support from the fact that whereas paragraphs (a) and (b) of section 146 refer to preventing or deterring membership or activities 'of an independent trade union', paragraph (c) specifically refers to compelling membership 'of any trade union or of a particular trade union or of one of a number of trade unions'). However, the Court of Appeal allowed the applicants' appeal and held, inter alia,[116] that on its proper construction, the protection in the section applied to penalizing membership of a particular union as well as membership of unions generally.[117] The court therefore accepted the potential application of section 146 to inter-union disputes which lead to differential treatment by the employer.

The second issue which arose under paragraph (a) concerned the scope of the protection of union membership, and in particular whether the right to be a trade union

---

[112] Trade Union and Labour Relations (Consolidation) Act 1992, ss 145A(5) and 145B(5). The complaint must be brought within three months of the offer being made, or a further reasonable period if it was not reasonably practicable to present it within that period: s 145C. The burden of proof on what was the sole or main purpose of the offer is on the employer: s 145D. Note that a worker is also protected against 'detriment' due to his failure to accept the offer: s 146(2C).

[113] Trade Union and Labour Relations (Consolidation) Act 1992, s 145E.

[114] [1987] ICR 641, [1987] IRLR 80, CA; rvsg [1986] IRLR 379, EAT; see Simpson (1987) 50 MLR 639.

[115] At heading 2(i), p 641.

[116] The other issue in the case was whether the action was taken against them 'as individuals' rather than against their union.

[117] Although *Ridgway* was subsequently overruled on other grounds (see n 114), the reasoning of the Court of Appeal on this point would appear still to be valid.

member means anything more than simply having a right to possess a union membership card. In *Discount Tobacco and Confectionery Ltd v Armitage*[118] (a case on the parallel provisions concerning dismissal for union membership), the EAT declined to draw a sharp distinction between union membership and making use of the essential services of a union.[119] However, in *Associated Newspapers Ltd v Wilson; Associated British Ports v Palmer*,[120] the House of Lords held[121] that while the decision in *Discount Tobacco* might have been correct on its facts, it did not establish any general principle that membership of a union was to be equated with making use of the union's services. The statutory protection was intended to protect union membership as such, and in their Lordships' opinion there was no justification for reading in the words 'or making use of the essential services of the union', still less for regarding trade union membership and the use of trade union services as the same thing.[122] This narrow interpretation of 'membership' would have reduced the protection of union membership under limb (a) almost to vanishing point,[123] as in practice employers are far more likely to be concerned about the consequences of union membership than they are about the mere fact of membership. In *Specialty Care plc v Pachela*,[124] the EAT made a bold attempt to salvage something from the wreckage of the House of Lords' decision in *Wilson and Palmer* by distinguishing *Discount Tobacco* on the facts, and holding that it was still open to a tribunal to find that an employee dismissed for engaging the assistance of a union in a dispute with the employer over working hours was dismissed on grounds of union membership. Moreover, it became clear in the light of the European Court of Human Rights' decision in *Wilson and Palmer* that the broader interpretation of 'membership' was to be preferred, and the issue was resolved by the Employment Relations Act 2004 which adds paragraph (ba) which covers detriment for the purpose of preventing or deterring the worker from 'making use of trade union services at an appropriate time, or penalising him for doing so'. Addressing the *Pachela* point, it is specifically provided that 'making use' of union services includes a case where the worker consents to the raising of a matter on his behalf by his union.

Turning to limb (b) (preventing or deterring union activities), it is clear that to be protected, the activities in question must be those of a trade union, in the sense of having a genuine trade union connection rather than just being the type of activity which one might expect a union to engage in. Thus, protected activities would include

---

[118] [1995] ICR 431n, [1990] IRLR 15, EAT.

[119] *Discount Tobacco* was followed in *Harrison v Kent County Council* [1995] ICR 434, where the EAT held that it was open to a tribunal to conclude that a person who was refused employment because he was a trade union activist or because of his union activities was refused employment because he was a member of a union within the meaning of s 137(1).

[120] See, n 109.

[121] The comments of the House of Lords on this point were strictly speaking obiter, as the main ground of the decision was that the statutory protection only applies to actions, not to omissions.

[122] See Lord Bridge at 264; Lord Lloyd at 266. Cf Lord Slynn at 265, taking a somewhat broader view.

[123] Per Knox J in *Discount Tobacco and Confectionery Ltd v Armitage* [1995] ICR 431n, [1990] IRLR 15 at 16.

[124] [1996] IRLR 248.

taking part in union meetings,[125] consulting a shop steward or union official,[126] and attempting to recruit new members or form a workplace union group[127] (particularly if the employee concerned is himself a shop steward or union officer). However, it would not include actions on an individual basis without any union involvement, as in *Chant v Aquaboats Ltd*[128] where the EAT held that the applicant's actions, in personally complaining about woodworking machinery which did not comply with safety standards and organizing a petition of other employees to support the claim, did not qualify as trade union activities and so were not protected.[129]

The section only protects activities which take place during the employment in question, not to previous activities in other employments, so that if the employer takes action against an individual (for example by transferring him to a non-sensitive area) on finding out about his record of union activity in a previous employment, that person may not complain under section 146. So, for example, in *City of Birmingham District Council v Beyer*,[130] a case on the analogous provisions concerning dismissal for union activities, a well-known union activist gained employment with the council by using a false name, and was subsequently dismissed because of the deceit; the EAT held that the employee could not benefit from the statutory protection, because it did not extend to pre-employment activities. However, the protection does apply where action is taken to prevent or deter an employee from engaging in union activity within the current employment,[131] and it may well be difficult for an employer in such a case to persuade the tribunal that he was entirely motivated by the employee's previous conduct and not by fears that it might be repeated in the present employment.[132]

The principal limitation on limb (b), which attempts to hold a balance between the employee's rights and the employer's business interests, is that to be protected the union activities must take place at an 'appropriate time'. This is defined in section 146(2) as either outside the worker's working hours or during his working hours but with the agreement or consent of the employer. 'Working hours' are defined as time

[125] *Miller v Rafique* [1975] IRLR 70, IT; this may apply to attendance at a meeting which is critical of the union: *British Airways Engine Overhaul Ltd v Francis* [1981] ICR 278, [1981] IRLR 9, EAT.

[126] *Marley Tile Co Ltd v Shaw* [1978] ICR 828, [1978] IRLR 238, EAT (rvsd on other grounds: [1980] ICR 72, [1980] IRLR 25, CA).

[127] *Brennan v Ellward (Lancs) Ltd* [1976] IRLR 378, EAT; *Lyon and Scherk v St James Press Ltd* [1976] ICR 413, [1976] IRLR 215, EAT; *Dixon and Shaw v West Ella Developments Ltd* [1978] ICR 856, [1978] IRLR 151, EAT.

[128] [1978] 3 All ER 102, [1978] ICR 643, EAT (an unfair dismissal case); *Gardner v Peeks Retail Ltd* [1975] IRLR 244, IT; *Drew v St Edmundsbury Borough Council* [1980] ICR 513, [1980] IRLR 459, EAT.

[129] An employee raising health and safety concerns today may well be protected under the specific provisions concerning dismissal or other detriment for health and safety reasons in the Employment Rights Act 1996, ss 44 and 100: see Ch 7, heading 5(iv), p 523.

[130] [1978] 1 All ER 910, [1977] IRLR 211, EAT. See Evans and Lewis 'Anti-union Discrimination: Practice, Law and Policy' (1987) 16 ILJ 88.

[131] *Fitzpatrick v British Railways Board* [1992] ICR 221, [1991] IRLR 376, CA.

[132] As seen at heading 2(i), p 636, a *refusal* of employment on grounds of previous union activity is unlikely to be covered by the Act (although the protection may need to be extended to comply with the ECtHR decision in *Wilson and Palmer*).

when the worker is contractually obliged to be at work, which has been construed as meaning when he is actually performing work, so that when an employee takes part in activities during a tea break or lunch break that will be an 'appropriate time', even if he is still on the premises and being paid by the employer during the break.[133] One potentially contentious area is whether the employer has in fact consented to an activity where it takes place during working hours. The case of *Robb v Leon Motor Services Ltd*[134] showed a fairly rigorous approach to the issue, in the employer's favour. The employee, a shop steward, was transferred to a department where he was no longer in contact with other employees (ie 'neutralized') because of his over-enthusiastic pursuit of union activities in working hours. The union was not recognized and there was no express agreement allowing union activities during working hours, but the employee's written statement of terms of employment stated that he would be permitted to take part in union activities 'at the appropriate time', though without defining it. The EAT dismissed the employee's claim under what is now section 146, holding that there was not the necessary agreement or consent to his union activities (the written term being too vague to be construed as such). In contrast, in *Bass Taverns Ltd v Burgess*,[135] the employee, a pub manager who was also a shop steward of the National Association of Licensed House Managers, was regularly permitted by the company to make presentations on behalf of the union at induction courses for new employees. On one occasion he made some remarks which were highly critical of the company, and which led to his demotion; he resigned and claimed constructive dismissal, arguing that his dismissal was for taking part in union activities at an appropriate time, and was therefore automatically unfair under section 152. The Court of Appeal held that the employer's consent to his participation should not be considered as subject to an implied limitation that nothing critical of the company would be said, so that, despite his remarks, he was still taking part in trade union activities at an appropriate time, and his claim therefore succeeded.

It is, however, clear from other cases that consent does not have to be express (and also that recognition is not a prerequisite), though in practice an express agreement is more certain, and it may well be easier to imply consent from a course of conduct if the union is in fact recognized. This possibility of implied consent was accepted by the Court of Appeal in *Marley Tile Co Ltd v Shaw*,[136] but the case also shows that consent will not be readily implied merely from the employer's silence (particularly on an ad hoc basis, where it is being argued that on one particular occasion the employee

---

[133] *Post Office v UPOW* [1974] 1 All ER 229, [1974] ICR 378, HL; *Zucker v Astrid Jewels Ltd* [1978] ICR 1088, [1978] IRLR 385, EAT.

[134] [1978] ICR 506, [1978] IRLR 26, EAT.

[135] [1995] IRLR 596, CA. Cf the suggestion in the case that the activities might fall outside the protection of s 152 if the employee indulged in malicious, untruthful or irrelevant invective; see also *Shillito v Van Leer (UK) Ltd* [1997] IRLR 495, EAT (on the analogous provisions on victimization for health and safety reasons).

[136] [1980] ICR 72, [1980] IRLR 25, CA; *Zucker v Astrid Jewels Ltd* [1978] ICR 1088, [1978] IRLR 385, EAT. In *Marley's* case the Court of Appeal upheld the EAT on the possibility of implied consent, but reversed their decision on the facts, holding that no consent could be inferred in the circumstances.

proposed to do something during working hours and the employer did not strenuously object), and that implied consent is still not easy to establish where the union member is not accredited by the employer, or the union is not recognized. On the other hand, where the union presence is accepted by the employer it is possible that, even in the absence of express agreement, consent might be implied over a period of time on the basis of established workplace practice or good industrial relations practice. To this extent the onus is placed upon the employer, if he wishes to prevent extraneous activities during working hours (and so preserve his right to stop them), to state expressly that he does not agree or consent (either by notice or in contracts).

An employee subjected to a detriment in contravention of section 146 may complain to a tribunal within three months of the act or failure to act (or within such further period as the tribunal thinks reasonable if it was not reasonably practicable for the complaint to be presented within three months).[137] In such a complaint, the onus is upon the employer to show the purpose for which he acted or failed to act.[138] If the tribunal finds the complaint justified, it must make a declaration to that effect and may order such compensation as it thinks just and equitable;[139] the section states that the tribunal is to have regard to the infringement of the employee's rights under section 146 and to any loss sustained by the employee, in particular any expenses incurred by him and any loss of benefits which he might reasonably have expected but for the employer's act or failure to act. In *Brassington v Cauldon Wholesale Ltd*[140] the EAT held that, while the remedy is compensatory rather than penal, the tribunal is not restricted to the employee's pecuniary loss, and may award compensation over and above such pecuniary loss for any non-pecuniary injury such as stress and anxiety caused to the employee and deprivation of benefits which might have come from trade union membership; it is, however, for the employee to establish that he has suffered the type of injury for which he seeks compensation. Section 148(2) states that in determining a complaint the tribunal shall not take into account any pressure exerted upon the employer (by industrial action or the threat of it) by a union, which may mean that the employer is placed in a difficult position, particularly in the case of an inter-union dispute. However, if the pressure is exercised by the union in order to compel the employee to be or become a union member the union may be joined as a party to the action.[141]

---

[137] Trade Union and Labour Relations (Consolidation) Act 1992, s 147. In *British Airways Board v Clark* [1982] IRLR 238 it was held by the EAT that where the disciplinary action complained of was only effective after exhaustion of the employer's disciplinary procedure (including an appeal), time only began to run (for computing the three-month period) from the date when the employee was finally informed of the failure of his appeal. Where the act or failure to act is part of a series of similar acts or failures, time runs from the last of them; where a single action has a continuing effect, time will run from the initial act: *Adlam v Salisbury and Wells Theological College* [1985] ICR 786, EAT.

[138] Trade Union and Labour Relations (Consolidation) Act 1992, s 148(1).

[139] Trade Union and Labour Relations (Consolidation) Act 1992, s 149(2).

[140] [1978] ICR 405, [1977] IRLR 479, EAT. In *Cleveland Ambulance NHS Trust v Blane* [1997] IRLR 332, the EAT confirmed that compensation for insult or injury to feelings may be awarded under this head.

[141] Trade Union and Labour Relations (Consolidation) Act 1992, s 150. The joinder provisions are considered at heading 2(i), p 650.

(c) Dismissal on trade union grounds

In parallel with the previous provisions, section 152 of the Trade Union and Labour Relations (Consolidation) Act 1992 provides that a dismissal will be *automatically unfair* if the reason for it (or, if more than one, the principal reason) was that the employee (1) was, or proposed to become, a member of an independent trade union, or (2) had taken part, or proposed to take part, in the activities of an independent trade union at an appropriate time, (3) had made use, or proposed to make use, of trade union services at an appropriate time or (4) was not a member of any trade union, or of a particular trade union, or of one of a number of particular trade unions, or had refused, or proposed to refuse, to become or remain a member. The section was subject to major amendment by the Employment Acts 1980, 1982 and 1988, and as it now stands it is a curious hybrid, for heads (1)–(3) are there to protect union members in their membership and activities, whereas head (4) serves the totally different purpose of protecting *non*-union members, and is therefore considered below in the context of the closed shop. A dismissal for redundancy will be deemed to be unfair under section 153 of the 1992 Act if it is shown that the circumstances producing the redundancy applied equally to other comparable employees in the same undertaking who were not dismissed,[142] and the employee was selected for dismissal for any of the above reasons.

Apart from rendering a dismissal automatically unfair, the other significant difference (leaving aside for the moment the question of remedies, considered below) between a dismissal for union reasons and an ordinary unfair dismissal action is that the normal requirements as to the qualifying period of continuous employment and the restrictions on those who have reached retiring age do not apply in this context.[143] Establishing that a dismissal or a redundancy selection is on trade union grounds can give rise to considerable evidential problems, particularly where the employer claims that there was some other reason (for example misconduct) for the dismissal. It is clear that an employer does not have to be motivated by malice or a deliberate desire to be rid of a trade union activist in order to fall foul of these provisions,[144] and the EAT has emphasized that the scope of the factual enquiry into the reason for the dismissal should not be restricted.[145]

The provisions in heads (1)–(3) are substantially the same as those in section 146 which protect the employee from detriment short of dismissal for trade union

---

[142] In making the comparison with the position of other employees, anything that the employee did or had a right to do as a trade union official must be left out of account, lest the purpose of the section be defeated: *O'Dea v ISC Chemicals Ltd* [1995] IRLR 599, CA.

[143] Trade Union and Labour Relations (Consolidation) Act 1992, s 154. This section was substituted by the Employment Relations Act 2004, to make it clear that the burden of proof remains on the employer in all complaints of unfair dismissal on trade union related grounds.

[144] *Dundon v GPT Ltd* [1995] IRLR 403, EAT.

[145] See *Driver v Cleveland Structural Engineering Co Ltd* [1994] ICR 372, [1994] IRLR 636, EAT, where the employer's failure to select the applicant, a former shop steward, for alternative employment in a redundancy situation was held to be legally relevant in determining whether he was unfairly dismissed on account of his trade union activities under s 152.

membership, activities or services, so that cases on the one section (for example on the meaning of 'activities of a trade union' and 'appropriate time') apply *mutatis mutandis* to the other. Two further points should be noted here. First, as in the case of detriment short of dismissal, the protection for those dismissed for taking part in union activities only applies to activities during the employment in question, and does not extend to an employee who is dismissed because of participation in union activities before the employment began.[146] However, in *Fitzpatrick v British Railways Board*,[147] the Court of Appeal held that an employee with a reputation as a union activist in her previous employment who was dismissed not because of anything she had done in her present employment but because the employer feared that she might become a disruptive influence at some time in the future was still protected, because a dismissal will be unfair if the reason for it was that the employee was *proposing* to take part in trade union activities. Secondly, although one might be forgiven for thinking that participation in industrial action is a classic example of taking part in trade union activities, and therefore protected under section 152, the EAT has said, obiter, that taking part in industrial action does not count as taking part in the activities of a trade union for present purposes, and that the two situations are mutually exclusive.[148] This was said to be because the legislation makes separate provision for those dismissed while taking part in industrial action,[149] so that if an employee is dismissed while on strike, his complaint will be determined under the special rules which apply in such a case, and not under section 152. It is arguable that there are circumstances[150] where a tribunal might have to consider whether an employee dismissed during industrial action was dismissed for taking part in trade union activities within the meaning of section 152; however, the issue is of limited practical importance, because even if participation in industrial action could in principle constitute an activity of a trade union, it will rarely, if ever, be undertaken at an 'appropriate time', as it is unlikely to be an activity undertaken outside working hours or with the employer's consent.[151] Significantly, the EAT has held that participating in the preliminary planning and organization of industrial action can amount to taking part in trade union activities within the meaning of section 152.[152]

---

[146] *City of Birmingham District Council v Beyer* [1978] 1 All ER 910, [1977] IRLR 211, EAT (discussed at Ch 2, heading 2(ii), p 75).

[147] [1991] IRLR 376, CA.

[148] *Drew v St Edmundsbury Borough Council* [1980] ICR 513, [1980] IRLR 459, EAT.

[149] Trade Union and Labour Relations (Consolidation) Act 1992, ss 237–238A; see Ch 10, heading 2(iii), p 698.

[150] Eg where the employer has sacked or re-engaged some but not all of the strikers, and the dismissal is neither automatically unfair for taking protected industrial action, nor outside the jurisdiction of the tribunal because the industrial action is unofficial.

[151] *Britool Ltd v Roberts* [1993] IRLR 481, EAT. One example of industrial action which could conceivably be held to be at an 'appropriate time' is a ban on voluntary (ie non-contractual) overtime.

[152] *Britool Ltd v Roberts* [1993] IRLR 481, EAT.

Turning to remedies, there are some significant differences between the remedies available in cases of dismissal for trade union reasons and in most other unfair dismissal cases. Where a dismissal is unfair by virtue of being for trade union reasons the amount of compensation is likely to be higher, because provision is made for a minimum basic award (£5,300 at the time of writing) in such cases[153] and, in addition to the compensatory award for a normal unfair dismissal, an 'additional award' of between 26 and 52 weeks' pay if there is a tribunal order for reinstatement or re-engagement which is not complied with by the employer.[154] As in other unfair dismissal cases, compensation awarded in cases of dismissal for trade union reasons may be reduced where there is contributory fault, although it is specifically provided that failure on the part of the employee to comply with a requirement (whether or not contractual) to join or not to join a union, or not to take part in union activities, is not to be regarded as 'fault' for these purposes.[155]

The enhanced levels of compensation were originally introduced by the Employment Act 1982 as part of the attack on the closed shop[156] (the idea being to make an unfair dismissal because of a closed shop very expensive in order to have a deterrent effect), but the increased compensation was extended to *all* employees dismissed for union reasons, and not confined to those dismissed for *non-membership*. Clearly it was no part of the previous Conservative government's intention to put greater liabilities onto *employers* in closed shop cases, however much it wanted to improve the lot of those dismissed for refusing to become union members. The solution adopted[157] was to allow the employer or the dismissed employee to request the tribunal to join a trade union or other person as a party to the tribunal proceedings where it is claimed that (a) the employer was induced to dismiss the complainant by industrial pressure exercised by that third party (whether by strike or otherwise), and (b) that pressure was exercised because the complainant was not a union member.[158] Any award of compensation in those proceedings may then be made wholly or partly against the union or other person joined in the proceedings, as the tribunal considers just and equitable, instead of against the employer. Originally, the joinder provisions only allowed the *employer* to join the union, but the present position is that the *employee* can also join the union (as, in effect, a second defendant) and may be more likely to do so than the employer

---

[153] Trade Union and Labour Relations (Consolidation) Act 1992, s 156. In common with most other statutory compensation limits, the minimum basic award is subject to indexation under the Employment Relations Act 1999, s 34.

[154] Employment Rights Act 1996, s 117.

[155] Trade Union and Labour Relations (Consolidation) Act 1992, s 155. In determining whether there has been contributory fault the tribunal is entitled to take into account the employee's conduct *leading up* to the dismissal, although clearly it must disregard the conduct which in fact led to the dismissal: *TGWU v Howard* [1992] ICR 106, [1992] IRLR 170, EAT.

[156] See heading 2(iii), p 658.

[157] See now the Trade Union and Labour Relations (Consolidation) Act 1992, s 160; similar provisions apply in the context of detriment short of dismissal: s 150.

[158] Such a request must be granted if made before the hearing but thereafter the tribunal has a discretion to refuse it, save that no such request may be made after the tribunal has made a declaration that the complaint is well-founded: s 160(2).

(who may be more inclined to pay up and hope to forget the whole matter). In practice today the joinder provisions are very rarely used, as complaints of dismissal for non-membership of a trade union are extremely uncommon.

Finally on remedies, sections 161–166 of the 1992 Act make special provision for 'interim relief' pending a hearing where an employee complains that he has been unfairly dismissed for trade union reasons.[159] The aim of interim relief is to secure the position of the employee pending the hearing by seeking to ensure that he remains in employment until the tribunal is able to hear the unfair dismissal complaint. An application for interim relief must be presented to a tribunal within seven days of the effective date of termination,[160] and where the complaint is of dismissal for union membership or activities it must be backed by a certificate from an official of the union concerned[161] stating (a) that the applicant is a member of the union (or proposed to become one) and (b) that in the official's opinion there are reasonable grounds for supposing that the dismissal was for union reasons. The tribunal must hear the application as soon as practicable, although the employer must be given at least seven days' notice of the hearing.[162] If the tribunal thinks it likely[163] that the employee's complaint will be upheld at the full hearing, it must ask the employer if he is willing to reinstate or re-engage the employee pending the hearing. If so, the tribunal will make an order to that effect; if not, the tribunal will make an order for the continuation of the employee's contract pending the full hearing.[164] This is an order that the contract shall continue until the hearing, but only for the stated purposes of pay or any other benefits, seniority, pension rights and other similar matters, and continuity of employment;[165] the order must specify the amount to be paid, which will be the amount which the employee could reasonably have been expected to earn (had he not been dismissed) in the period between the date of the dismissal and the date of determination of the complaint.[166] Any payments received from the employer under the contract or by way of damages for breach of contract must be taken into account. The crucial point, however, is that other obligations under the contract, in particular the employee's duty to work, do not continue in force, which means that there is a very strong incentive for the employer to

---

[159] Interim relief has subsequently been made available in certain other unfair dismissal complaints: see the Employment Rights Act 1996, s 128(1).

[160] On which, see Ch 7, heading 2(ii), p 487.

[161] The official must be authorized by the union to act for this purpose: s 161(4). If the authority of the official is challenged, it will be for the union to prove that the official was authorized to sign the certificate: *Sulemany v Habib Bank* [1983] ICR 60, EAT. For obvious reasons there is no requirement of a certificate where an application for interim relief is made in a case of dismissal for non-membership.

[162] Trade Union and Labour Relations (Consolidation) Act 1992, s 162.

[163] Ie the applicant must have a 'pretty good' chance of success, per Slynn J, *Taplin v C Shippam Ltd* [1978] ICR 1068, [1978] IRLR 450, EAT.

[164] Trade Union and Labour Relations (Consolidation) Act 1992, s 163. If the offer is one of re-engagement in another job, the tribunal must ask the employee whether he is willing to accept that job on the terms and conditions specified; if the employee unreasonably refuses the offer the tribunal will make no order: s 163(5).

[165] Trade Union and Labour Relations (Consolidation) Act 1992, s 164(1).

[166] Trade Union and Labour Relations (Consolidation Act 1992), s 164(3).

agree to re-employ the employee pending the hearing. If the employer fails to comply with the order, the applicant may complain to the tribunal which, in a case where the failure consists of non-payment of wages as specified in the order, will determine the amount owed under the order or, in the case of some other failure (for example failure to comply with an order for reinstatement or re-engagement), will order the employer to pay such compensation as it considers just and equitable.[167]

(ii) TIME OFF WORK

Since the Employment Protection Act 1975, trade union officials have had a statutory right to reasonable time off work to carry out trade union duties and to undertake trade union training, and union officials and members have had a statutory right to reasonable time off work to take part in trade union activities. The distinction between the two rights is crucial, as time off for union duties is with pay, whereas time off for union activities is unpaid (unless there is a contractual agreement to pay). In addition to these rights, the Employment Act 2002 introduced a new right for union learning representatives (who need not be union officials) to take paid time off during working hours to undertake their duties and to undertake relevant training. The relevant provisions are contained in sections 168–173 of the Trade Union and Labour Relations (Consolidation) Act 1992, and are supplemented by the ACAS Code of Practice No 3 on *Time Off for Trade Union Duties and Activities*,[168] which recommends the negotiation of specific agreements on the question between employers and unions, to take into account the particular features of each industry, and to provide clear guidelines against which applications for time off can be determined, thereby avoiding misunderstanding, facilitating better planning and ensuring fair and reasonable treatment.[169]

(a) Trade union duties

An employer is obliged by section 168 of the Trade Union and Labour Relations (Consolidation) Act 1992 to allow an employee who is an official of an independent, recognized trade union to have a reasonable amount of paid time off during working hours[170] for the purposes of carrying on official duties concerned with (a) negotiations with the employer over matters falling within section 178(2) (which defines the subject matter of collective bargaining) in relation to which the union is recognized by the employer, or (b) the performance of functions which the employer has agreed to the union performing on behalf of his employees; an official is also entitled to reasonable paid time off for undergoing training in aspects of industrial relations which

---

[167] Trade Union and Labour Relations (Consolidation Act 1992), s 166. There is no statutory limit on the amount which may be awarded under this section.

[168] The Code is admissible in evidence and is to be taken into account when deciding what time off would be reasonable: s 168(3).

[169] COP No 3, s 4. The Code is set out in *Harvey* S [101].

[170] See n 182 for a possible challenge to this restriction.

is relevant to the above duties and approved by the TUC or his union.[171] 'Official' is defined as covering union officers and shop stewards elected or appointed under the union rules.[172] While the right to time off for trade union duties only applies to recognized unions, a union official also has a separate statutory right to a reasonable amount of paid time off to accompany a worker at a disciplinary or grievance hearing, regardless of whether the official belongs to a recognized union, so long as the worker being accompanied is employed by the same employer, and the official has been certified by the union as being capable of acting as a workers' companion.[173]

The ACAS Code of Practice gives guidance on proper purposes for time off under the existing law, and offers a number of examples of trade union duties for which reasonable time off should be allowed, including duties concerned with terms and conditions of employment (for example pay or hours of work), recruitment and selection policies, redundancy and dismissal arrangements, job grading and job evaluation, flexible working practices, disciplinary procedures and arrangements, matters of trade union membership, facilities for union officials, collective bargaining machinery, grievance procedures and other procedures for consultation and communication. The Code also emphasizes that the duties must be connected with or related to negotiations or the performance of agreed functions in time as well as in subject matter, and suggests that reasonable time off may be sought to prepare for negotiations, inform members of progress, explain outcomes to members and prepare for meetings with the employer about matters for which the union has only representational rights. The Code is also concerned with the question of time off for relevant training, suggesting that employers should consider releasing employees for initial basic training in employment relations duties as soon as possible after their election or appointment, and subsequently for further training covering special responsibilities and changing circumstances. The Code makes two other general points which might be noted. The first is that it suggests that the management should consider making available to representatives the facilities necessary for them to perform their duties efficiently and effectively, which might include (where resources permit) accommodation for meetings, telephones, use of noticeboards (which could include other forms of electronic communications such as email and internet/intranet) and possibly even dedicated office space, the irony here being that a small union should only claim such things after it has been certified as independent, since if it obtains them beforehand, that might

---

[171] There are two stages in a claim to this right: (1) is the activity one envisaged by the Act and COP?; (2) if it is, is it reasonable to give time off in all the circumstances? In *Ministry of Defence v Crook and Irving* [1982] IRLR 488, the EAT suggested that the question of reasonableness is to be approached by applying the 'range of reasonable responses' test evolved in the context of unfair dismissal, but this view is not universally accepted. Note that employee trustees (who may well be union officials) also have a right to paid time off to perform their duties or undergo relevant training: Pensions Act 1995, s 42.

[172] Trade Union and Labour Relations (Consolidation) Act 1992, s 119.

[173] Employment Relations Act 1999, s 10. Alternatively, the worker can choose to be accompanied by an official who is employed by the union, or by a fellow worker.

be a factor working against 'independence'.[174] The second point is that where a representative is not himself engaged in industrial action being taken by his constituents, but he is still representing them, he should be allowed time off in the normal way to exercise that function.[175]

Time off under this section is with pay.[176] According to the 1992 Act, the employee is entitled to be paid the amount which he would normally have received during the time off in question, as if he had worked his normal hours (or, where his remuneration varies with the amount of work done, on the basis of an average of his hourly earnings for that work).[177] This causes few problems where paid time off is claimed for duties which take place at a time when the employee would normally have been at work; the position is, however, more problematic where the employee is a shift worker or part-time worker, and the duties in question are carried out at a time when the employee would not otherwise have been at work. In one case, the EAT held that as the right is to paid time off 'during his working hours', an employee who undertook trade union duties outside his working hours had no right under the 1992 Act to paid time off or to payment in lieu.[178] However, the ECJ has held[179] that it may be unlawful indirect sex discrimination not to pay a part-time female worker for the total number of hours spent on trade union duties (including those outside her normal working hours) in circumstances where a full-time male worker would have been paid for all the hours spent undertaking those duties. Such an outcome hinges upon whether the time off in question is for 'work' within the meaning of Article 141. It is clear from the ECJ decisions that time off to attend the employer's staff council, or to undergo training necessary for performing staff council functions, does constitute 'work' for the purposes of Article 141,[180] and after some initial uncertainty[181] the EAT has confirmed[182] that attendance at a union-organized health and safety training course also constitutes 'work', because it is 'by reason of the existence of an employment relationship':[183] 'Attending a training

---

[174] Trade Union and Labour Relations (Consolidation) Act 1992, s 5. See this chapter, heading 1(iv), p 628.

[175] The Code emphasizes that there is no right to time off for trade union activities which themselves consist of industrial action.

[176] It appeared to be self-evident from the section that once it was established that there was a 'duty' and that the time off requested was 'reasonable', the official was automatically entitled to be paid; this was accepted by the EAT in *Beecham Group Ltd v Beal (No 2)* [1983] IRLR 317, but in *Thomas Scott & Sons (Bakers) Ltd v Allen* [1983] IRLR 329, CA, May LJ seems to assume that there may be cases where it is reasonable to allow the time off, but not reasonable to pay the official for it; sed quaere. See Fitzpatrick (1983) 12 ILJ 258.

[177] Trade Union and Labour Relations (Consolidation) Act 1992, s 169.

[178] *Hairsine v Kingston upon Hull City Council* [1992] ICR 212, [1992] IRLR 211, EAT.

[179] *Arbeiterwohlfahrt der Stadt Berlin v Botel* [1992] IRLR 423, ECJ.

[180] *Arbeiterwohlfahrt der Stadt Berlin v Botel* [1992] IRLR 423, ECJ. See also *Kuratorium fur Dialyse Und Nierentransplantation v Lewark* [1996] IRLR 637, where the ECJ considered the scope of the justification defence.

[181] See *Manor Bakeries v Nazir* [1996] IRLR 604, where the EAT, distinguishing *Botel*, held that attendance at a trade union annual conference was not 'work'.

[182] *Davies v Neath Port Talbot County Borough Council* [1999] ICR 1132, [1999] IRLR 769. The EAT acknowledged that the effect of their judgment was that s 169(2) 'is in conflict with Art 119' (now Art 141).

[183] *Davies v Neath Port Talbot Country Borough Council*, per Morison J. Arguably, it would have been open to the EAT in Davies to distinguish Nazir on the basis that while attendance at a union health and safety

course organised by a recognised trade union is still related to the employment relationship and is safeguarding staff interests which is ultimately beneficial to the employer.'
Significantly, the EAT rejected the employer's argument that only paying part-time
workers for their contractual working hours was not indirectly discriminatory because
it was objectively justified: 'The issue is whether part-time workers (predominantly
female) engaged on a full-time course should receive full-time pay. There cannot, it
seems to us, be a justifiable policy or aim which maintains the inequality.' The position of part-timers in relation to time off is now reinforced by the Part-time Workers
(Prevention of Less Favourable Treatment) Regulations 2000,[184] which give part-time
workers the right not to be treated less favourably in relation to terms and conditions of
employment than comparable full-time workers, unless the employer can show some
objective justification for the less favourable treatment. The Regulations do not deal
expressly with time off, but the BIS guidance on the Regulations recommends that
training should be scheduled so that part-time workers can attend so far as possible,
and the ACAS Code of Practice states that while there is no statutory requirement to
pay for time off where the duty is carried out at a time when the official would not
otherwise have been at work, staff who work part time will be entitled to be paid if staff
who work full time would be entitled to be paid.

It may be that, pursuant to the exhortation in the Code or otherwise, the employer
has agreed to allow certain paid time off, in which case the employee may have a contractual right to his pay during the relevant times (in which case, the pay would be
computed according to the contractual terms). Any such contractual remuneration
which is received goes towards discharging (or extinguishing) the statutory liability,
and vice versa.[185]

(b) Trade union activities

An employee is entitled, under the Trade Union and Labour Relations (Consolidation)
Act 1992, section 170, to reasonable time off during working hours to take part in any
activities of an independent trade union to which the employee belongs and which
is recognized by the employer in respect of such employees. In *Luce v Bexley London
Borough Council*,[186] the EAT interpreted this right narrowly, holding that time off may
only be claimed for union activities that are in some way connected with the employment relationship between the employer, the employee and the union. In that case
the employee, a member of the National Union of Teachers, was refused unpaid time
off to attend a TUC lobby of Parliament in protest against the Education Reform Bill.
The EAT held that the tribunal was entitled to take the view on the facts that as the

---

training course is 'work' because it is 'by reason of the existence of an employment relationship', attendance at
a union's annual conference is not 'work' because it lacks sufficient nexus with the employment relationship;
however, the EAT held that the decision in *Nazir* 'should not be followed'.

[184] SI 2000/1551, see Ch 2, heading 1(iv), p 54.
[185] Trade Union and Labour Relations (Consolidation) Act 1992, s 169(4).
[186] [1990] ICR 591, [1990] IRLR 422, EAT.

lobby was intended to convey only political or ideological objections to the proposed legislation, attendance at it could not be regarded as a trade union activity within the meaning of the section. The ACAS Code of Practice suggests that the right should extend to activities such as attending workplace meetings to discuss and vote on the outcome of negotiations with the employer, meeting full-time officials to discuss issues relevant to the workplace, and voting in industrial action ballots and union elections. Where the member is acting as a representative of the union, the activities may also include taking part in branch, area or regional meetings of the union, attending meetings of official policy-making bodies such as the executive committee or annual conference, and attending meetings with full-time officials to discuss issues relevant to the workplace. The section specifically excludes activities which themselves consist of industrial action, whether or not in contemplation or furtherance of a trade dispute. Time off for 'activities' under section 170 is without pay (in the absence of any contractual term to the contrary) and it has been held that what constitutes 'reasonable' time off may include a consideration of how much time off has already been given to the employee on previous occasions.[187]

(c) Union learning representatives

The Employment Act 2002 introduced a new right for an employee to take paid time off during working hours to undertake the duties of a union learning representative, and to undergo relevant training.[188] To qualify for this right, the employee must be a member of a recognized independent trade union, and have been appointed or elected as a union learning representative, in accordance with the union's rules, to analyse learning or training needs, provide information and advice about learning or training matters, arrange learning or training or promote the value of learning and training.[189] A union learning representative is entitled to reasonable paid time off for the above activities, and also for the purpose of consulting the employer about carrying on any of those activities, provided the union has notified the employer in writing that the employee is a union learning representative, and the employee has undergone sufficient training to be capable of fulfilling the role (or will have undergone such training within six months).[190] In addition, union members are entitled to reasonable unpaid time off during working hours to access the services of a union learning representative.[191]

These provisions are designed to help fill the learning and training gap, particularly in small and medium-sized organizations where employer-provided learning and training may be patchy, or even non-existent. The ACAS Code of Practice cautions

---

[187] *Wignall v British Gas Corpn* [1984] ICR 716, [1984] IRLR 493, EAT.

[188] Trade Union and Labour Relations (Consolidation) Act 1992, s 168A.

[189] Trade Union and Labour Relations (Consolidation) Act 1992, s 168A(2).

[190] Trade Union and Labour Relations (Consolidation) Act 1992, s 168A(3), (4). The employee may be entitled to paid time off to undergo training relevant to the functions of a union learning representative: s 168A(7).

[191] Trade Union and Labour Relations (Consolidation) Act 1992, s 170(2B).

that many employers will have in place well-established training and development pro-grammes for their employees, and that union learning representatives should liaise with their employers to ensure that their respective training activities complement one another and that the scope for duplication is minimized.

(d) Remedies for breach by the employer

Where an employer has failed to permit an employee to take time off in accordance with the statutory provisions, the employee may make a complaint to an employment tribunal within three months of the date when the failure occurred (or a longer period if the tribunal is satisfied that it was not reasonably practicable to complain within that period). Union officials and union learning representatives may also complain if the employer has failed to pay them for the time necessary to perform their duties, in which case the tribunal may order payment of the amount due. The EAT has held that in order for a trade union official to show that the employer has failed to permit him to take time off in order to carry out union duties, the request for time off must have come to the notice of the employer's appropriate representative, and it must be established that they have either refused it, ignored it or, in some other way, knowing of it, simply failed to deal with it.[192] In the case of a complaint of failure to permit time off, the tribunal, if it finds it justified, must grant a declaration to that effect and may in addition award such compensation as it thinks just and equitable, having regard to the employer's default and any loss sustained by the employee attributable to the failure to permit time off.[193] This is analogous to the similar provision on compensation for detriment short of dismissal on trade union grounds,[194] which means that it is not viewed as a penal fine on the employer, but at the same time the tribunal is not limited to awarding compensation only for pecuniary loss and will be able to include an amount for non-pecuniary matters such as interference with the employee's rights and desires to participate in the activities in question.[195] It has been decided by the EAT, however, that the tribunal's powers are only those of awarding a declaration and compensation, which are both essentially ex post facto; the tribunal cannot go further and lay down conditions upon which time off shall be allowed in future, and in particular it cannot rewrite any contractual terms which already exist on the question, even if it has decided that the operation of those terms in the past has not constituted 'reasonable' time off.[196] In *Ryford Ltd v Drinkwater*,[197] the EAT confirmed that an employee does not lose the right to receive compensation by taking time off without permission.

---

[192] *Ryford Ltd v Drinkwater* [1996] IRLR 16, EAT.

[193] Trade Union and Labour Relations (Consolidation) Act 1992, s 172(2).

[194] Trade Union and Labour Relations (Consolidation) Act 1992, s 149(2), as explained by the EAT in *Brassington v Cauldon Wholesale Ltd* [1978] ICR 405, [1977] IRLR 479; see heading 2(i), p 647.

[195] *Skiggs v South West Trains Ltd* [2005] IRLR 459, EAT.

[196] *Corner v Buckinghamshire County Council* [1978] ICR 836, [1978] IRLR 320, EAT.

[197] [1996] IRLR 16, EAT.

(iii) THE RIGHT TO DISSOCIATE AND THE CLOSED SHOP[198]

(a) Protection of individual non-members

While the right to associate has been protected since 1974 through the statutory controls on dismissal and action (now 'detriment') short of dismissal for trade union reasons, supplemented in 1990 by the statutory protection against refusal of employment, the protection afforded in English law to those not wishing to associate together with others is of more recent origin. When the Donovan Commission in 1968 examined the relationship between the right to associate and the right to dissociate it concluded that the one did not necessarily entail the other, since the latter was 'designed to frustrate the development of collective bargaining, which it is public policy to promote', whereas no such objection applied to the former.[199] For much of the following decade this reasoning was applied to justify the greater protection afforded by the law to the positive right. The reason why this conceptual riddle has historically been so important is, of course, the longstanding tradition in British industrial relations of the closed shop, defined by McCarthy as 'a situation in which employees come to realize that a particular job is only to be obtained or retained if they become and remain members of one of a specified number of trade unions'.[200] Unlike in certain other jurisdictions where it has long been subject to detailed control or regulation, in Britain the law until comparatively recently adopted a studiously non-interventionist stance on the closed shop, a reflection perhaps of the philosophy of collective laissez-faire which dominated our labour law for much of the twentieth century. However, in the period after the 1979 general election the political climate became increasingly hostile towards the closed shop, and this was reflected in legislation which, while not rendering the closed shop unlawful per se, made it increasingly difficult for employers and trade unions to enforce a closed shop agreement or arrangement within the law. As a consequence the importance of the closed shop as a social institution declined drastically during the 1980s,[201] and there were many notable examples of employers (for example at British Gas, British Telecom and British Rail) terminating longstanding closed shop agreements, without significant opposition from the unions. This startling turnaround came about in a series of stages, and in order to understand the present position it is necessary to trace those stages, starting with the highpoint of legal protection for the closed shop under the Labour governments of the 1970s.

---

[198] See Davies and Freedland *Kahn-Freund's Labour and the Law* (3rd edn, 1983) 236–70; Millward, Bryson and Forth *All Change at Work? British Employee Relations, 1980–1998* (2000).

[199] Royal Commission on Trade Unions and Employers' Associations (Cmnd 3623, 1968) para 599.

[200] *The Closed Shop in Britain* (1964).

[201] In 1984, it was estimated that some 3.5 to 3.7 million employees were covered by closed shop arrangements: Millward and Stephens *British Workplace Industrial Relations, 1980–1984* (1986); by the time of the follow-up survey, the estimated figure had fallen to somewhere between 0.3 and 0.5 million: Millward, Stephens, Smart and Hawes *Workplace Industrial Relations in Transition* (1992). The most dramatic fall was in the nationalized industries, from 80% of workplaces with manual closed shops in 1984 to less than 1% in 1990.

Before the election of Margaret Thatcher's Conservative government in 1979 the principal legal significance of a closed shop (or 'union membership') agreement lay in the field of unfair dismissal; the relevant law supported the enforcement of the closed shop by providing that a dismissal for non-membership of an independent trade union would be automatically *fair* where there was a union membership agreement in operation which applied to the dismissed employee, unless the employee had a religious objection to union membership, or a genuine objection on reasonable grounds to being a member of a union, in which case the dismissal was deemed automatically *unfair*.[202] The second ground of objection was removed by the Trade Union and Labour Relations (Amendment) Act 1976, leaving religious objection as the only basis for exemption. The Trade Union and Labour Relations Act 1974 had also introduced a statutory right not to be excluded or expelled from trade union membership by way of arbitrary or unreasonable discrimination; however, this too was repealed in 1976, leaving any legal remedies back in the hands of the uncertain common law. As a quid pro quo for the retreat in the 1976 Act, the TUC set up an Independent Review Committee[203] (in consultation with ACAS and the Secretary of State for Employment) to investigate complaints of improper or unreasonable expulsion and exclusion from unions, but the IRC only had jurisdiction (1) where the union was affiliated to the TUC and (2) where there was a closed shop in operation.

Thus, between 1974 and 1980 (and particularly after 1976) the closed shop was well established, with little legal protection for employees who did not wish to be union members, other than under the TUC's own voluntary procedure. The legislation of this period was subsequently challenged before the European Court of Human Rights in *Young, James and Webster v United Kingdom*[204] where the dismissal of three railway workers because of a closed shop was held to have violated Article 11 of the European Convention on Human Rights, which contains the right to freedom of association and to join a trade union.[205] The case was not a total denunciation of the closed shop—the latter was not declared illegal per se, and the Court did not uphold the existence of a negative right to dissociate as strong as the positive right to associate contained in the wording of Article 11.[206] The case was decided on its facts, chief among which were that (1) the employees had already been in employment when the closed shop agreement came into force, and (2) there was already a very high level of union membership without invoking the full rigour of a closed shop; the Court considered that the threat of dismissal for non-membership, involving a loss of livelihood, was 'a most serious form of compulsion' which struck at 'the very substance of the freedom' guaranteed

---

[202] The same rules applied *mutatis mutandis* to the protection against action short of dismissal.

[203] The Donovan Report (Cmnd 3623, 1968) had recommended the establishment of such a body, though not necessarily by the TUC: para 631. See Ewing and Rees 'The TUC Independent Review Committee and the Closed Shop' (1981) 10 ILJ 84.

[204] [1981] IRLR 408, ECtHR; see Forde 'The "Closed Shop" Case' (1982) 11 ILJ 1.

[205] See heading 2, p 633.

[206] Although see *Sigurjonsson v Iceland* (1993) 16 EHRR 462, ECtHR.

by Article 11. On the facts, interference with the employees' limited negative right was not 'necessary in a democratic society' and so the justification defence in Article 11(2) did not apply.[207] If the legal effects of the ruling at that time were difficult to assess,[208] the political effect was of course to give further backing to the incoming Conservative government, who had promised in their 1979 election manifesto to take steps to reform the closed shop.

The period between 1980 and 1990 saw a sustained legislative attack on the closed shop which meant that by the end of that period it was a spent force in British industrial relations. This transformation was achieved not by a frontal assault, but rather by a series of incremental reforms which steadily tightened the legal stranglehold on the closed shop. The starting point was the Employment Act 1980, which introduced a series of what were called 'crucial but limited reforms', with the aim of striking a balance between the collective interest of the union and its members in maintaining a closed shop, and the individual interests of those who did not wish to join. So, for example, dismissal for non-membership remained automatically fair where a closed shop agreement was in operation, but the 1980 Act extended the categories of employees exempted from membership to include, for example, those who had a genuine objection to union membership on the grounds of conscience or deeply held personal conviction, and those already in employment before the closed shop agreement took effect;[209] the 1980 Act also introduced a balloting requirement for the establishment of a new closed shop, whereby dismissal for non-membership would be automatically unfair unless the closed shop had been approved in a secret ballot by not less than 80% of those entitled to vote.[210]

The Employment Act 1982 took matters several stages further, by adding to the categories of exempted employees, and introducing a requirement for five-yearly review ballots of existing closed shops, again with a very high majority required for approval.[211] The 1982 Act also introduced significantly enhanced compensation levels (via a minimum basic award and a 'special' award) in cases of dismissal for trade union reasons, which could be awarded against the union which had pressurized the

---

[207] Compare *Sibson v United Kingdom* (1993) 17 EHRR 193, ECtHR, where the court, distinguishing *Young, James and Webster*, held that the employer's actions in exercising his contractual right to relocate the employee because he had resigned from the union did not violate Art 11, because there was no question of the employee losing his job. In *ASLEF v UK* [2007] IRLR 361 the ECtHR stressed the *lack* of a closed shop as one of the reasons for allowing a union to refuse membership to someone of strongly opposed political views.

[208] The Convention had not then been incorporated into English law.

[209] The existence of this reform in the Employment Act 1980 allowed the Conservative government (defending the previous Labour government's legislation before the European Court of Human Rights in the *Young* case) to argue that even if that previous legislation had been contrary to Art 11, their new legislation met the most serious objection raised by the Court on the facts of the case, ie that the employees had already been in employment with British Rail when the closed shop agreement was concluded.

[210] See Lewis and Simpson 'Disorganising Industrial Relations' (1982) 11 ILJ at 239–44.

[211] 80% of those entitled to vote, or 85% of those actually voting.

employer to dismiss, and introduced a scheme to compensate all those who had lost their employment without remedy during the period 1974–80.[212]

After the Employment Act 1982, the law relating to dismissal for non-membership of a trade union was left in a state of considerable complexity. The combined effect of the 1980 and 1982 Acts was to make it difficult to establish a legally effective closed shop, and arguably even more difficult to enforce it (given the width of the individual exemptions, particularly that relating to conscientious objection), but a dismissal for non-membership could still be automatically fair if there was an approved closed shop agreement in operation, *unless* the employee was within one of the categories of exempted employees, in which case the dismissal would be unfair. However, in 1987 the Conservative government decided to take the further step of removing *all* legal protection from a closed shop,[213] and most of this complexity was duly swept away by the Employment Act 1988, which removed all legal protection from action taken by an employer to enforce a closed shop against existing employees. This was achieved simply by providing that a dismissal for non-membership was automatically unfair in *all* cases if the reason (or principal reason) was that the employee 'was not a member of any trade union, or of a particular trade union, or of one of a number of particular trade unions, or had refused or proposed to refuse to become or remain a member'.[214] Similarly, all discriminatory action short of dismissal against non-members was made unlawful.[215] In short, the position, only reached after three bites of the legislative cherry, was that the protection against dismissal or detriment short of dismissal enjoyed by non-members became co-extensive with that enjoyed by union members.

While the 1988 Act removed the ability of an employer to enforce a closed shop against existing employees (the 'post-entry' closed shop), it remained lawful for an employer to discriminate against non-union members at the point of hiring, and thus to operate a pre-entry closed shop. That final loophole was, however, closed by the Employment Act 1990,[216] which introduced the right not to be refused employment on grounds of union membership or non-membership.[217] It is still technically correct to say that the closed shop has not been 'outlawed', in that a closed shop agreement or arrangement is not illegal or proscribed as such. However, the reforms which were introduced during the period between 1980 and 1990 have made it legally very difficult for an employer to enforce a closed shop against existing or prospective employees.

---

[212] Ewing and Rees 'Closed Shop Dismissals 1974–1980: A Study of the Retroactive Compensation Scheme' (1988) 12 ILJ 148.

[213] Green Paper 'Trade Unions and Their Members' (February 1987).

[214] See now the Trade Union and Labour Relations (Consolidation) Act 1992, s 152(1)(c). It will also be an automatically unfair dismissal to select an employee for redundancy because of his non-membership if other employees holding similar positions were equally affected and have not been dismissed: s 153.

[215] See now the Trade Union and Labour Relations (Consolidation) Act 1992, s 146(1)(c).

[216] White Paper 'Employment for the 1990s' (Cm 540, 1988) para 2.23; Green Paper 'Removing Barriers to Employment' (Cm 655, 1989).

[217] See now the Trade Union and Labour Relations (Consolidation) Act 1992, s 137.

The current position in English law is therefore that, whether or not the right to dissociate is properly seen as the logical corollary of the right to associate, both rights are accorded equal respect.

(b) Other measures restricting the closed shop

In addition to the above measures restricting the enforcement of a closed shop by employers against individual employees, there are a series of further measures restricting its enforcement against employers and third parties through contract compliance or by industrial pressure. Thus, the Employment Act 1982 introduced measures designed to render illegal the practice of encouraging closed shops by making it a condition of contracts or tenders that the contractor or tenderer must use employees who are union members (whether generally, or of a particular trade union). Any such term in a contract is void and any person who refuses to contract or to accept tenders on such grounds may be liable in tort for breach of statutory duty to anyone adversely affected by his actions.[218] Moreover, that Act provided that if any other person (in practice a union) exerts industrial pressure in order to secure a union-labour-only clause in a contract or to induce an unlawful refusal to contract or tender on the ground of the employment of non-union labour, the usual immunities from suit in tort are expressly withdrawn from that industrial pressure,[219] so that the union may be sued for an injunction or damages. The political impetus behind these complicated provisions appears to have come at the time from the insistence on union-labour-only contracts by some Labour-controlled local authorities.[220]

This process was taken an important stage further by the Employment Act 1988, which removed the immunity from suit in tort from any industrial action taken because a particular employer is employing, has employed or might employ a non-union member, or is failing, has failed or might fail to discriminate against such a non-union member.[221] This is aimed principally at the situation where an employer is unwilling to establish or (more likely) continue with a closed shop agreement and the union seeks to bring industrial pressure to bear to require him to do so; any person affected by that industrial action (directly or indirectly) may, if he has been injured tortiously by it, sue

---

[218] Trade Union and Labour Relations (Consolidation) Act 1992, ss 144, 145; s 145 also applies to refusals to contract or tender on the ground that the contractor or tenderer uses union labour. Sections 186 and 187 impose similar restrictions on such refusals where the aim is to oblige the contractor or tenderer to recognize or consult with a particular trade union. It seems that only the term is void, not the whole contract, so that where such a contract has in fact been entered into the contractor may insist on performing (and being paid for) his part of the contract but ignore the void clause.

[219] Trade Union and Labour Relations (Consolidation) Act 1992, s 222(3). For the statutory immunities, see Ch 10.

[220] Lewis and Simpson 'Disorganising Industrial Relations' (1982) 11 ILJ at 227. One practical problem in a claim for wrongful refusal to contract on the ground of union membership would be in proving that that was in fact the real ground for the refusal, when the claimant's was only one of many tenders.

[221] See now the Trade Union and Labour Relations (Consolidation) Act 1992, s 222(1), (2), discussed at Ch 10, heading 4(iii), p 731.

the union for an injunction and for damages without the union having its normal trade dispute immunity.

3 COLLECTIVE BARGAINING (1): RECOGNITION OF TRADE UNIONS

The question of recognition of unions for collective bargaining purposes is not normally a matter for statute; usually it is a question of practical industrial relations and most practical consequences of recognition are extra-legal, particularly in the light of the non-enforceability of collective bargains. The same applies to the withdrawal of recognition, which saw a considerable increase in the 1980s and 1990s. Recognition is expressly covered as a proper subject for a 'trade dispute',[222] and in an appropriate case the parties to such a dispute over recognition may decide to seek the conciliatory help of ACAS in the ordinary way.[223] Other than that, the law has tended to keep out of questions of recognition. However, under the modern legislation, recognition has arisen as a matter of law in two ways. The first, and most obvious, concerns the question whether there should be a residual statutory procedure for a union to claim recognition by an employer (once it has a certain level of membership). Under the Industrial Relations Act 1971 and, more important, during the period from 1976 to 1980 under the Employment Protection Act 1975 there was an attempt to use legal machinery for resolving disputes about union recognition; this was ultimately unsuccessful and the machinery was abolished in the Employment Act 1980, but not before being the source of notable case law going to the root of the problem of how far the courts should control the exercise of its functions by a body such as ACAS when those functions relate to difficult questions of industrial relations.[224] The incoming New Labour government in 1997 were committed to reintroducing a statutory scheme for obtaining recognition, and this featured largely in the 'Fairness at Work' White Paper[225] and the resulting legislation in the Employment Relations Act 1999, which obviously tries to avoid the fatal shortcomings of the pre-1980 legislation.

The second form of legal involvement (always existing independently of the statutory recognition procedures and therefore unaffected by their presence or absence) is that under many provisions of the modern statutes it is necessary to be able to *define*

---

[222] Trade Union and Labour Relations (Consolidation) Act 1992, ss 218(1)(g), 244(1)(g).

[223] Trade Union and Labour Relations (Consolidation) Act 1992, s 210; in 2007–08 it accounted for 9.5% of collective conciliation cases: *ACAS Annual Report 2007–08.*

[224] *Grunwick Processing Laboratories Ltd v Advisory Conciliation and Arbitration Service* [1978] 1 All ER 338, [1978] ICR 231, HL; *United Kingdom Association of Professional Engineers v Advisory Conciliation and Arbitration Service* [1980] ICR 201, [1980] IRLR 124, HL; *EMA v ACAS (No 2)* [1980] ICR 215, [1980] IRLR 164, HL. For details of the repealed procedure, see the early editions of this book; particularly interesting is ch 8 of the *ACAS Annual Report 1980*, giving their own assessment of the operation of the procedure from 1976 until its demise in 1980.

[225] Cm 3968, 1998, paras 4.11–4.20 and Annex 1.

recognition. This is because the key to some of the basic rights is not just that a union is 'independent',[226] but also that it is 'recognized' by the employer in question. Thus, a recognized independent trade union has rights to receive bargaining information,[227] to be consulted on impending redundancies,[228] to appoint safety representatives,[229] to receive information and be consulted about an impending transfer of the employer's undertaking[230] and to be notified about certain matters relating to company pension schemes.[231] Further, the status of a union as recognized also figures in the rights of officers and members to time off work.[232] The general definition of recognition must therefore be considered first, then the statutory recognition procedure and, after that, some incidental aspects of the involvement of the law.

(i) THE DEFINITION OF RECOGNITION

As seen above, the question of whether a union can claim to be 'recognized' in law is an important point of jurisdiction for claiming significant legal rights. The clearest case is where there is an express recognition agreement between employer and union. However, the lack of a written recognition agreement (or disputes procedure involving the union) will not be conclusive, for recognition may also be implied if it exists in practice, no matter what the employer might call it.[233]

The starting point is the statutory definition, which states that a recognized trade union is one which is recognized by an employer, or two or more associated employers,[234] to any extent for the purposes of collective bargaining.[235] The phrase 'to any extent' could have been ambiguous, meaning either (1) that there must be full agreement to recognize the union, though possibly only with regard to certain matters, or (2) that the agreement to recognize might itself only be equivocal or sporadic. However, it has been held that it

---

[226] See heading 1(iv), p 628.

[227] See heading 4, p 673. The right to receive the information is drafted in such a way that, if recognition is less than total, the *extent* of the recognition can determine not only whether a particular union may make a claim but also what information must actually be disclosed: *R v Central Arbitration Committee, ex p BTP Tioxide Ltd* [1981] ICR 843, [1982] IRLR 60. The question is therefore doubly important.

[228] See Ch 8, heading 1(iii), p 572. Most of the case law on the definition of recognition has arisen under this head. As seen above, in this area and in that of transfers of undertakings, equivalent rights have been extended to directly elected worker representatives.

[229] Health and Safety at Work etc Act 1974, s 2, as amended by the Employment Protection Act 1975, s 116. Again, there has been an extension to directly elected worker representatives.

[230] Transfer of Undertakings (Protection of Employment) Regulations 2006, SI 2006/246, reg 13; see Ch 8, heading 3(iii), p 602.

[231] Pension Schemes Act 1993, s 113; Occupational Pension Schemes (Disclosure of Information) Regulations 1996, SI 1996/1655.

[232] See this chapter, heading 2(ii), p 652.

[233] *Joshua Wilson & Bros Ltd v Union of Shop, Distributive and Allied Workers* [1978] ICR 614, [1978] IRLR 120.

[234] For associated employers, see Ch 2, heading 1(v), p 65.

[235] Trade Union and Labour Relations (Consolidation) Act 1992, s 178(3); collective bargaining is itself defined in s 178(1), (2).

means the former[236] and so, although the recognition may only be partial in coverage, there must still be clear evidence of agreement to recognize.

Further than this, the statutes give little guidance in the sort of case where a problem of definition might arise, for example where a union with no express recognition agreement claims for the first time to be recognized in order to insist on one of the statutory rights (usually in the past, in a case such as this, the right to be consulted about threatened collective redundancies). The task of definition has therefore fallen principally on the courts, and the decisions of the Court of Appeal in *National Union of Gold, Silver and Allied Trades v Albury Bros Ltd*[237] and the EAT in *Union of Shop, Distributive and Allied Workers v Sketchley Ltd*[238] are particularly instructive. In the former, the Court of Appeal held that the concept of recognition is so important and so fundamental to the statutory union rights that, in the absence of an express agreement, it should not be held to be established unless there was clear and unequivocal evidence of conduct (probably over a period of time) from which recognition could be inferred; on the facts of the case, evidence of recruitment of a few employees by the union followed shortly after by a letter to the employer raising the question of rates of pay, leading to one inconclusive meeting, was held to be too insubstantial to establish the recognition that would have obliged the employer to consult the union over subsequent redundancies. In addition to this general point, the case established a further point of considerable importance in any case where the employer observes terms and conditions negotiated at a higher level—the employer in the case was in fact a member of an employers' association which *did* conduct collective bargaining with the union in question but it was held that that could not of itself be construed as recognition by that employer; this reinforces the point that recognition is ultimately a matter of agreement between a union and an individual employer, which could cause problems for unions in industries which are composed of many small firms, even if there is established bargaining at a higher level, for example nationally.[239]

So far, discussion has been as to whether a union is recognized or not, and in many industries it is obvious which unions are recognized and that that recognition will cover all foreseeable industrial relations contexts. However, it must be remembered that the statutory definition talks of recognition 'to any extent' and this means that

---

[236] *Transport and General Workers' Union v Dyer* [1977] IRLR 93; *National Union of Gold, Silver and Allied Trades v Albury Bros Ltd* [1978] ICR 62, [1977] IRLR 173 (upheld on appeal by the Court of Appeal—n 237).

[237] [1979] ICR 84, [1978] IRLR 504, CA; *National Union of Tailors and Garment Workers v Charles Ingram & Co Ltd* [1977] ICR 530, [1977] IRLR 147. The *NUGSAT* case was applied in *Cleveland County Council v Springett* [1985] IRLR 131, EAT (concerning health and safety representatives) where it was held that the addition of the union to the Burnham Committee by the Secretary of State did *not* per se mean that the union became recognized by one of the employers represented on that committee.

[238] [1981] ICR 644, [1981] IRLR 291.

[239] A prime example of this is the agriculture industry, where terms and conditions are worked out centrally each year before the Agricultural Wages Board in negotiations between the agricultural section of the TGWU and the NFU, but where any question of union recognition would have to be determined on a farm-by-farm basis.

the definition may be satisfied even if the employer has agreed to bargain and negotiate with the union only on certain topics. As long as the necessary level of agreement can be shown, this form of partial recognition will be sufficient in law.[240] However, an important distinction must be drawn here, for there also exists in practice a form of 'recognition' involving only the right of a union to represent its members in individual matters, for example under a grievance or discipline procedure.[241] This may perhaps be granted while a union recruits a sufficient number of members to warrant full recognition, or may be all that is left after an employer has derecognized the union for most purposes; however it arises, it falls short of an agreement to negotiate and bargain and so does *not* qualify as recognition in law. This can clearly be seen in *USDAW v Sketchley Ltd*,[242] where an agreement between the employer and the union in 1978 granting recognition for representation purposes was held by the EAT to be insufficient in itself to entitle the union to be consulted in 1980 about impending redundancies, particularly as the 1978 agreement expressly stated that it did not confer recognition on USDAW for negotiation of terms and conditions. However, the case also shows that recognition is not a static concept, because the evidence showed that in February 1980, when the employer began to select candidates for redundancy, the union threatened strike action if they were not given information about this, as a consequence of which a meeting took place at which it was agreed that, in return for the union calling off the strike threat, the employer would give the union certain advance information on redundancies, adopt a procedure involving the union and in certain cases make redundancy payments above the legal minimum. While the 1978 agreement could not constitute recognition, the EAT thought it possible that the subsequent events in February 1980 were capable of showing that the union had indeed become accepted as having sufficient negotiating rights (at least in the area of redundancy) to satisfy the definition of recognition, and so they remitted the case to the tribunal for determination of that question.

(ii) THE STATUTORY RECOGNITION PROCEDURE

In its manifesto for the 1997 election, the Labour Party stated its intention to reintroduce a statutory recognition procedure. On coming into power, the new government in typical fashion sought to achieve agreement among the 'social partners' (TUC and CBI) on such a procedure, but consultations merely reinforced existing deep divisions.

---

[240] It will be sufficient to claim to be consulted about impending redundancies or transfer and to claim to appoint safety representatives; however, to claim bargaining information the union must be able to go further and show that the information requested is relevant to one of the purposes for which the union is recognized (*R v Central Arbitration Committee, ex p BTP Tioxide Ltd* [1981] ICR 843, [1982] IRLR 60); and this now also applies to the right to time off for union duties (Trade Union and Labour Relations (Consolidation) Act 1992, s 168(1)(a)).

[241] This is now backed by the employee's statutory right to be accompanied by a trade union official (or fellow worker) before a disciplinary or grievance procedure: Employment Relations Act 1999, ss 10–15.

[242] See n 238; this distinction can also be seen in the *BTP Tioxide* case.

Thus, the government themselves had to take the initiative in the White Paper 'Fairness at Work' and propose a scheme. The failure to discern an agreed version had two principal effects: (1) in an attempt to steer a middle path, the government introduced certain limitations or qualifications to which strong objection was taken by the unions (leading to arguments that there had been resiling from the manifesto pledge of recognition where a simple majority of the workforce voted for it); (2) the prospect of legal enforcement (raising spectres of the failed 1970s version) meant that there had to be a satisfactory forum, eventually meaning a revamped Central Arbitration Committee (CAC).[243] In relation to (1), the White Paper introduced the qualifications that the procedure should not apply to employers of fewer then 20 and that in a ballot those voting in favour of recognition should comprise not just over 50% of those taking part, but also at least 40% of those *eligible* to vote. There was added later the further qualification that, even where there is already a majority union membership the CAC may still insist on a ballot if it considers it necessary to gauge 'real' support.

The new statutory recognition procedure was introduced by the Employment Relations Act 1999, which adds a new Schedule A1 to the Trade Union and Labour Relations (Consolidation) Act 1992.[244] This in turn was subject to review after three years, leading to several relatively technical amendments being made by the Employment Relations Act 2004. The level of detail in the Schedule is stunning; the Schedule entered Parliament 88 paragraphs long and left 172. The intention to avoid the fatal pitfall of its 1970s predecessor (based on broad discretions) is obvious, and was made express by the government minister steering the Bill. He described the main features of the Bill as follows: (1) the legislation would provide the greatest scope for voluntary arrangements to be reached, with compulsion only as a last resort; (2) the threshold for frivolous complaints would be set at 10% of the relevant workforce; (3) the crucial test when determining the appropriate bargaining unit would be effective management, with fragmentation to be avoided; (4) if more than 50% of the workforce were already members of the relevant union, there would be a simplified procedure; (5) if no voluntary arrangement was reached, the dispute would be determined by the CAC; (6) the CAC's determination would be binding *but* would only relate to procedural matters;[245] (7) existing arrangements should, where possible, be left untouched.[246] For most purposes, these statements of principle were adhered to

---

[243] See Ch 1, heading 3(ii), p 24.

[244] For a critical and comparative analysis of these provisions, see Wood and Goddard 'The Statutory Union Recognition Procedure in the Employment Relations Bill: A Comparative Analysis' (1999) 37 BJIR 203; Simpson (1998) 27 ILJ 253 and Wedderburn 'Collective Bargaining or Legal Enactment' (2000) 29 ILJ 1 at 33 ff; Dukes, 'The Statutory Recognition Procedure 1999: No Bias in Favour of Recognition' (2008) 37 ILJ 236. For detailed consideration of the CAC case law, see *Harvey* Div NI7.

[245] The government strongly resisted amendments aimed at going further and providing for either a legal duty to bargain in good faith or some form of binding arbitration on substantive claims: HL Committee, 7 June 1999, cols 1276–80.

[246] See the ministerial statements at HC SC E, 16 March 1999, cols 344–410.

(though with many technical amendments), as was the point that statutory recognition per se would only cover pay, hours and holidays, unless widened by agreement.[247]

Part 1 of the Schedule contains the principal provision on statutory recognition, which may be requested by one or more independent trade unions. In keeping with the voluntarist approach, the request is made in the first instance to the employer.[248] If there is agreement (possibly involving ACAS help), that is the end of the procedure.[249] If, however, the employer rejects the request or negotiations fail, the union(s) may apply to the CAC to decide (1) what is to be the appropriate bargaining unit for these purposes and (2) whether the union has the support of the majority of workers in the appropriate bargaining unit.[250] In order to proceed, the CAC must be satisfied that at least 10% of the workers in the bargaining unit are union members.[251] Moreover, the application may not proceed if 'there is already in force a collective agreement under which a union is … recognised as entitled to conduct collective bargaining on behalf of any workers falling within the relevant bargaining unit'.[252] This important exception (obviously meant to avoid fragmentation of existing procedures) is drafted very widely and may well stop recognition by the applicant union even if the *level* of bargaining under the existing arrangement is substantially lower than that sought by the applicant union,[253] or the applicant union has (or might recruit) substantially more members in the bargaining unit than the existing union, and thus be more representative.[254] As a 'first-in-the-field' rule, it is strong and indeed might be open to manipulation by an employer and an existing union, however unrepresentative.

Determination of the bargaining unit may clearly be a crucial factor. Once again, the initial emphasis is on encouraging the parties to agree it, but in default of that the CAC must determine it, taking into consideration the need for effective management,

---

[247] Schedule A1, para 3(4). The CAC held that 'pay' could include employer contributions to company pension schemes (*UNIFI v Union Bank of Nigeria plc* [2001] IRLR 712, CAC) but this was specifically reversed by the 2004 Act, inserting a new para 171A into the Schedule. Questions of industrial training were originally mooted too, but are now dealt with separately by the Employment Relations Act 1999, s 5.

[248] Paragraph 4. The exclusion of employers with 20 or fewer employees is contained in para 7, which contains a calculation method; employees of any associated employer are included.

[249] Paragraph 10. The CAC may, however be subsequently involved in any dispute over operating the agreement; also, such an agreement may not be unilaterally terminated by the employer for three years: paras 52–63.

[250] Paragraphs 11, 12. The term used here is 'worker', as defined in the Trade Union and Labour Relations (Consolidation) Act 1992, s 296(1); for an example on marginal facts, see *R (on the application of the BBC) v CAC* [2003] IRLR 460.

[251] Paragraph 14.

[252] Paragraph 35. The Schedule adopts the *wide* definition of collective bargaining for this particular purpose (para 3(6); s 178), and note the reference to *any* workers, not a majority.

[253] *TGWU v ASDA* [2004] IRLR 836, CAC ('partnership' agreement with union A covering only facilities for shop stewards was held to rule out an application by union B wanting to represent on pay etc).

[254] *R (NUJ) v CAC* [2005] ICR 493, [2005] IRLR 28, Admin (existing arrangement with (breakaway) journalist union A kept out an application by the NUJ, even though (1) union A only had one member in the bargaining unit and (2) union A had only been recognized by the employer after negotiations with the NUJ had started).

the views of the parties, existing national and local arrangements, the need to avoid fragmentation, the characteristics of the relevant workers and their location.[255] Once this is determined, the CAC is to proceed to the main question, namely whether there is the necessary support for collective bargaining to make an order for recognition. This can be determined in two ways. The short method is that if the CAC is satisfied that a majority of workers in the unit are union members, it may make the order, *unless* it considers that (1) it would still be in the interests of good industrial relations to hold a ballot, (2) a significant number of members in the unit inform the CAC that they do not want collective bargaining or (3) there are doubts about the membership evidence.[256] The longer method (where membership numbers are insufficient to trigger the first method) is for the CAC to go straight to a ballot.[257] If the ballot shows that a majority of those voting support the union *and* that those voting in favour constitute at least 40% of the workers in the bargaining unit, the CAC must issue a declaration that the union is entitled to recognition; if not, the application is dismissed.[258]

On the making of a declaration, the parties are given a period of 30 working days (or longer by agreement) to negotiate a method by which they will conduct collective bargaining. If no agreement is reached, either side may apply to the CAC for assistance.[259] A further period is determined for CAC-assisted negotiations, but then the CAC is to specify a method,[260] which has effect as if in a legally enforceable agreement between the parties, subject to specific performance.

Two further significant matters are covered by the Schedule (in addition to a plethora of highly detailed subsidiary and explanatory provisions). The first concerns subsequent

---

[255] Paragraphs 18, 19, 19B. The CAC's function at this stage is to determine whether the unit sought by the union is 'appropriate'; while it must consider the employer's representations (including any alternative unit proposed), it is not to consider whether such an alternative is *more* appropriate: *R v CAC, ex p Kwik-Fit (GB) Ltd* [2003] IRLR 395, CA. In general, a court may be reluctant to interfere with a CAC decision on a point such as this, given the deliberately wide discretion allowed to it by Parliament: *R (Cable & Wireless Services Ltd v CAC* [2008] IRLR 425, Admin. The doctrine of associated employers does *not* apply at this stage, so that there cannot be a bargaining unit spanning more than one employer unless (per the CAC in an inventive judgment) there are 'exceptional' circumstances showing that in reality two or more employers are one: *Graphical Paper and Media Union v Derry Print Ltd* [2002] IRLR 380, CAC.

[256] Paragraph 22. The CAC discretion here, as elsewhere in the Schedule, is wide and difficult to challenge; as there is no obligation to give reasons there can be no challenge on the basis of inadequacy of reasons, only on the basis that any reasons that are given are erroneous in law or perverse: *Fullarton Computer Industries Ltd v Central Arbitration Committee* [2001] IRLR 752. In fact, the incidence of judicial review applications has been low, even in the early years, causing few problems for the CAC (see the *CAC Annual Report 2001/02* at p 3 and the *CAC Annual Report 2002/03* at p 2).

[257] Paragraph 23. Procedure for the ballot is set out in paras 24–8; it must be conducted by an appointed independent person, and may be either workplace or postal. The employer must cooperate, in particular by allowing access to the workforce; this is backed by a DTI code of practice.

[258] Paragraph 29.   [259] Paragraph 30.

[260] Paragraph 30. Obviously the hope must be that this power would rarely have to be operated, because compulsion at this stage is an odd concept (analogous to the ancient family law order for restitution of conjugal rights!). To ease the situation in such a case, the Secretary of State has exercised his power under para 168 to issue a model form of collective bargaining, to be taken into account by the CAC. By 2012 this power had only had to be exercised in 20 cases: *CAC Annual Report 2011/12*.

changes in the bargaining unit. Part III (paragraphs 64–95) sets out complex procedures for dealing with circumstances which necessitate changes to the established collective bargaining structure. The second matter is, of course, derecognition. Normally, this is simply a question of industrial realities, but where recognition has been obtained under the statutory scheme there are special procedures for its removal. These fall into six main categories: (1) where voluntary agreement has been reached under the procedure (where derecognition is not permitted in the first three years); (2) where the relevant employees fall below the threshold of 21; (3) where the employer applies for derecognition even though the threshold requirement is still met;[261] (4) where the request comes from employees; (5) where recognition was originally granted under the short method (ie more than 50% membership);[262] (6) where the union is not independent.[263]

As stated above, the complexity of these provisions is remarkable. At the time of implementation, views varied as to the significance of this new procedure. A restrictive view was that this innovation was more important politically than industrially, and was principally aimed at a restricted number of firms which did not recognize unions (or, indeed, may have positively derecognized them in the last decade or more) but where union membership remained quite high. A more expansive view was that the very existence of the procedure may have a normative effect on the renewed acceptability of union involvement more generally. As evidence for this, the TUC stated that in the last three quarters of 1999 (with the statutory procedure imminent) their members negotiated voluntarily over 70 recognition agreements. While this may be significant (though subject to the cynical view that such agreements may have been in order to stave off the inevitable, in a way not involving the complexities of Schedule A1, and thus basically defensive), the question still arose whether this return to formal union recognition would be of major practical significance. This gave rise to two main views on their likely impact. The wider view was that they could stem and reverse the decline of union membership and representation that had marked the 1980s and 1990s. The narrower, more cynical, view was that these provisions remain largely explicable on political grounds, as a debt owed by the government to the trade unions which has been honoured in a restricted way and not with a view to any across-the-board reversion to a collective bargaining system.

The figures at the time of writing could give support to either view. By March 2012 there had been 785 applications; of these, 57 were in the first year of operation (2000–01), 118 in 2001–02, 80 in 2002–03, 106 in 2003–04 and 83 in 2004–05 This then seemed to stabilize to, for example, 64 in 2006–07 and 43 in 2011–12. Thus, an initial hump can be seen, in line with the narrower view, but on the other hand, the absolute numbers are probably higher than the cynic might have expected. Of the 785

---

[261] This is the most significant category; the procedure to be adopted is set out in paras 104–11, and requires a secret ballot.

[262] Part V (paras 122–33); this again requires a secret ballot. As with voluntary recognition, a request by an employer may not be made until the expiry of three years.

[263] Part VI (paras 134–48). Part VII (paras 149–55) applies where a union loses its certificate of independence.

cases handled, 101 were not accepted and 213 withdrawn; 106 cases ended in recognition without a ballot, and where ballots were ordered they ended in recognition in 126 cases and no recognition in 77.[264] One study of the first ten years of the scheme (ie up to 2010) found that the total number of workers to whom recognition had been extended by the statutory scheme was only about 56,000. However, the study went on to estimate a far larger figure of 750,000 workers covered by 2,800 new *voluntary* recognition agreements entered into in this period.[265] The difficulty is of course to know to what extent such agreements have in effect been *prompted* by the existence of the statutory scheme in the background. With an apparent decrease in voluntary agreements after an initial 'hump' (as with statutory applications), the jury is still out on the key question—will the statutory procedure eventually be seen as an integral part of the industrial relations system, or as a short-term solution to a level of imbalance in union recognition as a legacy of the 1980s and 1990s?

Two final points are offered in relation to the future of the procedure. The first is that it was subject to review by the government as part of their commitment to the unions to review the working of the Employment Relations Act 1999. The principal finding of this review (published by the DTI in February 2003) was that 'the Act has been a resounding success'; one result of this wholly objective opinion was that very few changes were suggested, those that were being of a technical nature (enacted in the Employment Relations Act 2004). Thus anyone wanting to see serious changes in the recognition procedure to rectify what they saw as its limitations when introduced will have been disappointed. In particular, there were no proposals to drop the small firm exemption, extend the areas for negotiation beyond pay, hours and holidays, or to abandon the 'super majority' (ie the requirement not just of a majority of those voting, but also of 40% of those *entitled* to vote being in favour of union representation). The second point is that, if the procedure does turn out to be more than of short-term significance, a question may arise whether a return to formal union recognition was really the New Labour government's preferred route towards 'partnership' (a key feature of the White Paper 'Fairness at Work'), rather than the arguably more modern and 'Third Way' concept of EU-inspired consultation with and involvement of the workforce *as such*, with more emphasis on the direct election of representatives. This potential conflict may well be seen if the provisions in the Information and Consultation of Employees Regulations 2004 start to bed in (see later under heading 5(ii)). These Regulations (transposing the Information and Consultation Directive) give little by

---

[264] *CAC Annual Report 2011/12.*

[265] Gall 'The First Ten Years of the Third Statutory Union Recognition Procedure in Britain' (2010) 39 ILJ 444. The 2004 Workplace Employment Relations Survey found that between 1998 and 2004 the proportion of workplaces employing 25 or more which recognized unions had stayed stable at 39%, suggesting at least a 'bottoming out' of the decline of the 1980s and 1990s up to that point. However, taking smaller firms into account there remained an overall decrease and a Labour Force Survey in 2010 found that by 2009 recognition had fallen again to 32.7%. For an assessment of CAC adjudication on the procedure in its first five years, see Bogg 'Politics, Community, Democracy; Appraising CAC Decision Making in the First Five Years' (2006) 35 ILJ 245.

way of preference to existing recognized trade unions, and indeed might even constitute a threat to existing structures. Further tensions between these two models of
employee representation may be expected.

(iii) FURTHER LEGAL PROVISIONS

In addition to the legal definition of recognition and the new statutory recognition
procedure, three other areas of legal involvement should be noted at this point—one of
general importance and two specific points, one supporting the concept of recognition
and the other possibly restricting it.

The general point is that the abolition of the previous statutory recognition procedure in 1980 did not mean the end of all ACAS involvement in such matters. This is
because a recognition dispute can of course still be a valid subject for voluntary conciliation by ACAS. This should not be underestimated, and it is interesting to note that
according to ACAS during the period 1976–80 (when the previous statutory procedure
was in force) collective bargaining was extended to more workers through voluntary
conciliation than by the use of that statutory procedure.[266]

The second point is that by virtue of the Transfer of Undertakings (Protection of
Employment) Regulations 2006, where an undertaking or part of one is transferred by
the original employer to a new employer and it retains an identity distinct from the rest
of the transferee employer's business, then if the original employer recognized a particular union, that recognition continues through the transfer and the new employer
is deemed to recognize the union to the same extent.[267] This was not the case before
the Regulations were originally introduced in 1981, for a recognition agreement was
viewed as personal to the employer and was not protected on a transfer.[268]

The third, restrictive, point is that by virtue of the Trade Union and Labour Relations
(Consolidation) Act 1992, sections 186 and 187 it is unlawful to insert into a contract for the supply of goods or services a condition that a party to that contract must
recognize a particular union or unions in relation to persons employed by him; any
such clause is declared to be void. Likewise it is unlawful to refuse to contract with or
accept tenders from an employer on the ground that he does not recognize a particular
trade union. This is to be read along with the wider provisions in sections 144 and
145 aimed at outlawing union-labour-only contracts and tenders[269] and is presumably

---

[266] During that period, 2,292 recognition cases were completed through voluntary conciliation leading
to full recognition in 726 cases (concerning 55,500 employees) and partial recognition in 255 cases (concerning 22,000 employees); this total figure of 77,000 employees exceeds the figure of 64,000 employees to
whom collective bargaining was extended by virtue of the statutory procedure: *ACAS Annual Report 1980*. In
2010–11, 112 recognition disputes were dealt with by ACAS on a voluntary basis (comprising 10.6% of collective conciliation cases in the year): *ACAS Annual Report 2010/11*.

[267] SI 2006/246, reg 6. Of course, there is nothing to stop the transferee employer later rescinding the
deemed recognition agreement.

[268] *UCATT v Burrage* [1978] ICR 314.   [269] See Ch 10, heading 4(iii), p 731.

included to prevent much the same result being reached, not by a direct requirement that contractors or tenderers must employ members of a particular union, but instead by making recognition of the union in question a condition of obtaining the contract. These provisions do not create criminal offences, but the imposition of such a condition or the refusal to contract or accept tenders on the ground of non-recognition is made tortious as a breach of statutory duty (actionable at the suit of the contracting party against whom it is aimed, or 'any other person who may be adversely affected' by it) and section 225 removes the statutory immunities from actions aimed at inducing the incorporation of such a condition or such refusal and from industrial action aimed at disrupting the supply of goods and services because of non-recognition of a particular trade union by the supplier. Thus, not only did the previous government remove the possibility of obtaining recognition through a legal procedure, they also attempted to place legal limits on the ways in which a union may try to obtain it as a matter of practical industrial relations. In practice, these provisions have not had much direct effect—as in the case of industrial dispute cases generally, all that the new legislation does is to remove bars to legal action, but that legal action must be taken, if at all, by individual claimants and therefore must be seen by them to be worthwhile; perhaps it was thought that this may be the case more often with disappointed commercial tenderers (particularly for local government contracts) than in the more usual case of an employer simply being affected generally by industrial action which under the legislation is now illegal (eg as being unlawful secondary action or without the necessary ballot—see Chapter 10), where actual litigation still remains relatively uncommon or, at most, confined to notable exceptions.

4 COLLECTIVE BARGAINING (2): DISCLOSURE OF BARGAINING INFORMATION

One vestige of earlier times when the law actively encouraged rational collective bargaining is the imposition upon an employer of a duty to disclose certain information to an independent trade union which is recognized by him, for the purpose of facilitating the conduct of collective bargaining by that union. This duty was first enacted in the Industrial Relations Act 1971, and is now contained in the Trade Union and Labour Relations (Consolidation) Act 1992, sections 181–185 and the Code of Practice No 2 'Disclosure of information to trade unions for collective bargaining purposes', produced by ACAS pursuant to section 181(4).[270]

---

[270] See Kahn-Freund *Labour and the Law* (3rd edn, 1983) 106–18; Gospel 'Disclosure of Information to Trade Unions' (1976) 5 ILJ 223; Gospel and Williams 'Disclosure of Information: The CAC Approach' (1981) 10 ILJ 10; Gospel and Lockwood 'Disclosure of Information for Collective Bargaining: The CAC Approach Revisited' (1999) 28 ILJ 233.

(i) THE DUTY TO DISCLOSE

Section 181 lays upon an employer the general duty to disclose information which is in his possession and relates to his undertaking or that of an associated employer, if it is (a) information without which the union would be impeded to a material extent in carrying out collective bargaining with him, *and* (b) information which he ought to disclose in the interests of good industrial relations. This formulation by itself is so vague as to be meaningless, indeed head (a) tends to ignore the fact that effective bargaining is possible (some would say easier) with virtually no information. The scheme is to explain it further in the Code of Practice, which states that the detail, form and depth of information in any given case will vary with the level of bargaining to which it may be relevant, and goes on in paragraph 11 to give particular examples of information which may be amenable to compulsory disclosure. These are under the headings of 'pay and benefits' (including pay systems, job evaluation and grading schemes; total pay bill, fringe benefits and the way that the overall pay bill is analysed); 'conditions of service' (recruitment, training, promotion and redundancy policies; appraisal systems; health and safety matters); 'man-power' (analysis of workforce, manpower and investment plans, any planned changes); 'performance' (productivity, efficiency and their savings; return on capital; state of order book); and 'financial' (cost structures, gross and net profits, sources of earnings, assets, liabilities, allocation of profits, government aid, transfer prices, loans within the group and interest charged). The aim of the Code is to show the *sort* of information within the ambit of section 181; it is at pains to point out that these examples are not an exhaustive checklist.[271] Further, the Code stresses the desirability of reaching joint agreement on what should be disclosed, possibly including an agreement to disclose certain information on a regular basis. Where a union wishes to resort to the statutory duty, it must make its request in writing if the employer so wishes, and any information disclosed must also be in writing if the union so wishes.

There is one possible limitation on the right to bargaining information which is inherent in the wording of section 181. As seen above, the union must be 'recognized' in order to make a claim, but that recognition might only be partial (for example restricted to negotiating rights only in respect of certain matters). If that is the case, section 181(1) applies to restrict the disclosure of information to matters 'in respect of which the trade union is recognized by him' and so, although the partial recognition is sufficient to qualify the union as 'recognized', the union will not be able to claim information relating to matters outside the scope of that partial recognition. Thus, in *R v CAC, ex p BTP Tioxide Ltd*[272] the union, ASTMS, had bargaining rights in respect of

---

[271] One marginal area of interest is redundancy selection; in *Rolls Royce plc and AEEU* (CAC Award 94/1) the CAC upheld a union request for further information on how a points-based selection system had been applied, accepting that this process fell within the sphere of collective bargaining. In the individual context, this question has caused severe difficulties to the tribunals and courts (see Ch 8, heading 1(ii), p 557); see the *CAC Annual Report 1994* for a contrasting of the CAC and the tribunal approach.

[272] [1981] ICR 843, [1982] IRLR 60. In his judgment, Forbes J said that there were three categories of case where a union would not be entitled to information, on the wording of s 181—(1) where the bargaining

certain terms and conditions of employment, but in respect of a particular job evaluation scheme it only had the right to make representations on behalf of its members
seeking re-evaluation of their job,[273] not the right to negotiate over the scheme itself.
Because of this, the Divisional Court held that the CAC had exceeded its jurisdiction in
ordering disclosure by the employer of information relating to the scheme.

(ii) EXCEPTIONS TO THE DUTY TO DISCLOSE

The duty is not an absolute one, for it is subject to certain exceptions which are contained in section 182, and which should be known to the prudent employer. Three obvious exceptions are where disclosure would be against the interests of national security
or in contravention of other legislation, and where the information was obtained by the
employer for the purpose of bringing or defending legal proceedings (eg resisting an
unfair dismissal action). The most important exceptions are likely to be:

(1) Information which has been communicated to the employer in confidence, or
     in some way in consequence of a confidence; this is not further defined, either
     in the Act or the Code, and could lead to litigation.[274]

(2) Information relating specifically to an individual (unless he has consented to its
     disclosure); thus, while the union may be able to require disclosure of the wages
     bill for a whole department, the employer may resist a request for details of each
     individual's salary. This exception has caused some difficulties in areas where
     the trend has been towards individual contracting and performance-related
     pay.[275]

(3) Information the disclosure of which could cause 'substantial injury' to
     the employer's undertaking for reasons other than its effect on collective
     bargaining.

This last category is perhaps the most contentious—what is likely to be substantial
injury? Clearly an employer cannot rely on this on the ground simply that he has hitherto as a matter of policy kept the information secret, but on the other hand there will
be cases where the employer's genuine interest in preserving secrecy will outweigh the

---

between employer and union does not meet the statutory definition of 'collective bargaining' because it does
not relate to matters referred to in the Trade Union and Labour Relations (Consolidation) Act 1992, s 178(2);
(2) where dealings between employer and union do not amount to 'collective bargaining' because they cannot
properly be described as 'negotiations' (s 78(2)); (3) where there is 'collective bargaining' but it does not relate
to matters in respect of which the union is recognized. For a good example, see *Babtie Shaw & Morton and
UKAPE* (CAC Award 82/4).

[273] This form of recognition for representation is not sufficient to qualify as 'recognition' for the purpose of
claiming statutory union rights; see heading 3(i), p 666.

[274] This exception was held to apply to information included in a commercial tender submitted to the
employer in confidence: *Civil Service Union v CAC* [1980] IRLR 274.

[275] *CAC Annual Report 1991* p 3.

benefits to the union of disclosure. The Code gives some further guidance in para-graphs 14 and 15. It gives as examples of information possibly under this exception—cost information on individual products, detailed analysis of proposed investment, marketing or pricing policies and price quotas or tender prices. It further states:

> Substantial injury may occur if, for example, certain customers would be lost to competitors, or suppliers would refuse to supply necessary materials, or the ability to raise funds to finance the company would be seriously impaired as a result of disclosing certain information. The burden of establishing that disclosure of certain information would cause substantial injury lies with the employer.

Section 182(2) gives some practical protection to an employer by providing that he need not produce original documentation (so that an abstract or precis will suffice) and that he need not compile or assemble information where to do so would involve work or expenditure 'out of reasonable proportion to the value of the information in the conduct of collective bargaining' (a positive invitation to litigation).

One final point concerns the use made of the information by the union. Even if an employer has to divulge information which he would rather have kept secret, the statute only obliges disclosure to the union officials concerned, and then only for the purposes of conducting collective bargaining with that employer; it is thus an open question whether an employer could restrain further use (or, from his point of view, misuse) of that information by the union by the threat of an action for breach of confidence.

(iii) ENFORCEMENT PROVISIONS

If a union considers that an employer is refusing to disclose information which he ought by law to disclose, it may complain to the CAC under section 183. If the CAC thinks that a solution may be reached by conciliation, it must, and most often does, refer the matter to ACAS for that purpose. This is the opposite of the normal ACAS system of conciliation *first*, with arbitration only if that fails; it has been argued that this approach is more effective, with the initial approach to the CAC concentrating the parties' minds on possibilities for conciliation, and this view certainly appears to be supported by the figures, though the statistical basis is small since use of the procedure remains generally low.[276] If the matter is not referred to conciliation (or if it is but no settlement is reached), the CAC must hear and determine the complaint, giving the reasons for its decision. If it upholds the complaint, its declaration to that effect must specify the material which ought to be divulged, the date on which the employer failed to do so, and a period during which the employer should comply by disclosure. If at the expiry of this period the employer has still failed to disclose the specified information, the union may make a further complaint to the CAC under section 184, and this time may attach a substantive claim on behalf of some or all of the employees in question

---

[276] In 2011–12 there were four references to the CAC under these provisions; taken together with cases carried forward from the previous year, 13 cases were disposed of : *CAC Annual Report 2011/12.*

(for higher pay, better benefits, etc). It is this substantive claim which gives the teeth to this enforcement procedure, for if the CAC finds the union's further complaint well founded (in whole or in part) it may make a declaration to that effect *and* award all or part of the attached claim. Any terms and conditions granted in the CAC's award are automatically incorporated into the contracts of employment of the employees concerned, and are then enforceable in the ordinary courts.

One unfortunate limitation upon the power of the CAC under this procedure is that, as it is drafted, the committee is limited to deciding upon information which has in fact already been refused by the employer; this means that it cannot go on to give guidance on information which should be divulged in the future, even if to do so might avoid future litigation on linked matters where it is foreseeable that disputes may well arise.[277]

(iv) OTHER OBLIGATORY DISCLOSURE

The employer must also disclose information to a recognized trade union concerning pending redundancies, under the statutory provisions covering the procedure for handling redundancies.[278] This covers the reasons for the proposed redundancies, the numbers and descriptions of employees involved, the total number affected at each establishment, the proposed method of selection, timing, and the proposed method of calculating any redundancy payments. Further, the employer must publish to his employees a statement of his health and safety policies[279] and divulge certain information relating to such matters to the Health and Safety Commission upon request[280] and to safety representatives appointed under Regulations.[281] Also, in a more specialized but linked context, an employer who intends to establish a contracted-out occupational pensions scheme must issue notices to that effect to earners who are to be covered by the scheme, giving certain basic information, and must also convey this information to 'all independent trade unions recognised to any extent for the purpose of collective bargaining in relation to the earners concerned', with whom the employer is then under a statutory obligation to consult on the proposed scheme.[282] Likewise, there are regulations providing for the disclosure of more information generally about the

---

[277] *R v CAC, ex p BTP Tioxide Ltd* [1981] ICR 843, [1982] IRLR 60.

[278] Trade Union and Labour Relations (Consolidation) Act 1992, ss 188–192 (see Ch 8, heading 1(iii), p 572); this has also been extended to elected worker representatives.

[279] Health and Safety at Work etc Act 1974, s 2(3).

[280] Health and Safety at Work etc Act 1974, ss 2(3), 27; note that s 28 imposes statutory restrictions on further publication of this information by the recipient officials.

[281] Safety Representatives and Safety Committees Regulations 1977, SI 1977/500, reg 7; this contains grounds upon which an employer may refuse to disclose similar to those in the Trade Union and Labour Relations (Consolidation) Act 1992, s 182. See also the Health and Safety Commission's Code of Practice on Safety Representatives (1978) para 6. Again, there has been an extension to elected worker representatives: Health and Safety (Consultation with Employees) Regulations 1996, SI 1996/1513.

[282] Occupational Pension Schemes (Contracting-Out) Regulations 1996, SI 1996/1172.

running of occupational pension schemes; in the first instance, such disclosure is envisaged as being to the members themselves, but the relevant provisions also mention disclosure to independent trade unions recognized to any extent for the purposes of collective bargaining in relation to members and prospective members of the scheme in question.[283]

A further category of compulsory disclosure was enacted in the case of transfers of business by the Transfers of Undertakings (Protection of Employment) Regulations 2006, considered separately in Chapter 8 above, and of course there are major developments on information that must be given to the workforce of larger undertakings on economic matters generally under the Information and Consultation of Employees Regulations 2004, which are considered next.

5 INFORMING AND CONSULTING THE WORKFORCE GENERALLY—THE NEW APPROACH?

British employment relations have been subject to major changes in the last three decades, and that has been reflected in some of the legal changes explored in this chapter. As already discussed, the statutory recognition laws may have seen at least a bottoming-out of the level of collective negotiation in certain well-unionized industries which has been missing for some time. However, large parts of the economy are likely to remain untouched by it, but it may be that we are seeing the emergence of an alternative legal form of, at least, employee *involvement* in decision taking which, while falling significantly short of the old model of co-determination with recognized unions, could at least start to fill the void left in many areas by the demise of that old model and its replacement by ideas of 'human resource management', which a cynic might argue can be a euphemism for managerial discretion. The question is—are we seeing the beginnings of movements towards a consultation regime not dissimilar to the works council system that is common in much of the rest of the EU (to the extent that its existence is often implicitly assumed in certain employment-related EU Directives)?

We have seen the advent of consultation requirements (and their extension to firms not recognizing unions, through the concept of directly elected employee representatives), largely driven by EU law requirements, which suggest a *via media* (or even Third Way?) of treating the workforce as possessing legal expectations of involvement, not just as a managerial resource.[284] Moreover, to these sticks (requiring consultation with elected

---

[283] Occupational Pension Schemes (Disclosure of Information) Regulations 1996, SI 1996/1655. The Pensions Act 1995, passed in reaction to the Maxwell scandal, had provisions for obligatory member trustees, but not surprisingly this was cast in terms of individual appointment, *not* in terms of any formal involvement of recognized trade unions.

[284] The previous New Labour government's ideas of 'partnership at work' and the involvement of the workforce suffused the White Paper 'Fairness at Work' (Cm 3968, 1998), especially ch 2 'Modern business at work'.

representatives where there is no union recognition, in relation to collective redundancies, TUPE and health and safety) we have now seen added certain legal carrots. Thus, the Working Time Regulations 1998 lay down prima facie relatively strict rules on hours, night work and breaks, but then allow very major 'derogations' from them, in ways that can be highly advantageous to the employer.[285] In the case of most of them, the safeguard is that the derogation in question must be agreed; in the case of a non-unionized workplace, the mechanism established for this is the 'workforce agreement', ie a written agreement with elected employee representatives. A similar regime can be seen in relation to parental leave under the Maternity and Parental Leave etc Regulations 1999,[286] where the 'default rules' on some of the principal administrative requirements for parental leave are to apply unless supplemented by a collective agreement or workforce agreement.[287] Moreover, a collective or workforce agreement can be used under the Fixed-term Employees Regulations 2002[288] to amend the rules relating to the use of successive fixed-term contracts.[289] However, these specific matters are now supplemented by two Directives requiring an element of information and consultation more generally. The first dealt with large organizations operating across member states; the second applies to larger organizations within the member state.

(i) EUROPEAN WORKS COUNCILS

The European Works Council Directive[290] applies to a 'community scale undertaking', meaning one with at least 1,000 employees within the EU and at least 150 employees in each of at least two member states. Initially, the Directive did not apply in this country because of the previous Conservative government's opt-out, but the incoming New Labour government stated their intention to adopt it. Thus, a further Directive extended it to this country, and it was implemented as from January 2000 by the Transnational Information and Consultation of Employees Regulations 1999.[291] These complex Regulations largely follow the Directive and provide for an undertaking covered by them to set up a special negotiating body, either of its own motion, or in response to a written request from at least 100 employees or their representatives in at least two member states. The purpose of this body is to negotiate on the establishment of a European Works Council (EWC) or, as a lesser form, an 'information and consultation procedure'.[292] It is primarily for the parties to agree the

---

See generally Hyman 'The Future of Employee Representation' (1997) 35 BJIR 309 and Pollert 'The Unorganized Worker: The Decline in Collectivism and New Hurdles to Individual Employment Rights' (2005) 34 ILJ 217.

[285] See Ch 4, heading 2(iii), p 234.   [286] SI 1999/3312.   [287] See Ch 4, heading 3(x), p 281.
[288] SI 2002/2034.   [289] See Ch 2, heading 1(iv), p 57.
[290] 1 Directive 2009/38 (replacing the original Directive 94/45); *Harvey* PII [1150]. See Wedderburn 'Consultation and Collective Bargaining in Europe: Success or Ideology' (1997) 26 ILJ 1 at 21.
[291] SI 1999/3323.
[292] The central management and the special negotiating body are under a duty to 'negotiate in a spirit of co-operation with a view to reaching a written agreement': reg 17(1). There is then a further statutory obligation to *work* in such a spirit once the relevant body is set up: reg 19.

composition and procedure of the relevant body. If, however, the central management refuse to commence negotiations within six months of a request, or if negotiations are still fruitless after three years, the 'default' provision of Schedule 1 to the
Regulations apply, ie there will be imposed a 'statutory EWC'.[293] These provisions lay
down the basic rules for composition (between three and 30 members, with minimum
numbers for each member state involved), appointment or election of UK members,
conduct of ballots, the competence of the EWC,[294] yearly information and consultation
meetings on the progress of the business,[295] exceptional information and consultation meetings[296] (where exceptional circumstances affect the employers' interests to a
considerable extent, particularly in the event of relocations, closure of establishments
or undertakings, or collective redundancies) and procedures. Provision is made for
certain information not to be divulged by the central management where it would
cause serious harm to the undertaking,[297] and any disclosure by an individual representative of information given to him by the central management on the basis that
it is to be held in confidence is declared to be a breach of statutory duty.[298] The usual
series of employment protection laws (paid time off and protection from detriment or
dismissal) are extended to members of the body in question. Disputes over procedural
matters in setting up an EWC are heard by the CAC; complaints of failure to establish a
EWC (or information and consultation procedure), or of failure to operate the system
properly once it is set up are heard by the EAT;[299] employment protection disputes go
to an employment tribunal in the ordinary way.

The impact of these Regulations has been a matter of some speculation. Their use
is limited by two factors. The first is that many UK supranationals have already been
covered by the original Directive for some time because of their activities elsewhere in
the EU; they could have set up an EWC only in relation to employees in other member
states but in practice they have strongly tended to include UK employees as a matter of good practice, and so have pre-empted the Regulations. The second is that in

---

[293] Regulation 18.

[294] This is 'limited to information and consultation on the matters which concern the Community-scale
undertaking or Community-scale group of undertakings as a whole or at least two of its establishments or
group undertakings in different member states: Sch 1, para 6(1).

[295] This relates particularly to 'the structure, economic and financial situation, the probable development of
the business and of production and sales, the situation and probable trend of employment, investments, and
substantial changes concerning organisation, introduction of new working methods or production processes,
transfers of production, mergers, cut-backs or closures of undertakings, establishments or important parts
thereof, and collective redundancies': para 7(2).

[296] This may be done through a 'select committee' of the EWC, comprising no more than three members
acting on its behalf: para 2(6).

[297] Regulation 24; the operation of this exception may be challenged before the CAC (this matter being
similar to its longstanding jurisdiction over the disclosure of bargaining information, see heading 3(ii)).

[298] Regulation 23. Again, a declaration by the management that information is confidential may be challenged before the CAC. Further, the normal provisions of the Public Interest Disclosure Act 1998 on 'protected
disclosures' apply.

[299] Regulations 20, 21. The EAT may declare what steps are to be taken to remedy the default and issue a
penalty notice on the employer, to pay a penalty up to £75,000 to the Secretary of State: reg 22.

any event the Directive extending the EWC Directive to the UK allowed undertakings here (not already covered) until December 1999 to reach voluntary agreements on transnational information and consultation, in which case the Regulations did not apply; again, a significant number of these 'Article 13' agreements were entered. At the time of writing, the 1999 Regulations have not caused any significant litigation; for example, in 2011–12 there was only one reference to the CAC under them.

(ii) THE INFORMATION AND CONSULTATION OF EMPLOYEES REGULATIONS 2004

Not surprisingly, there were moves within the European Commission to build on the above transnational provisions and move towards a European obligation to have consultative machinery at the member state level, ie to have a *domestic* works council requirement. This has resulted in the Information and Consultation Directive[300] which, though stopping short of any institutional requirement of works councils as such, has the effect of widening the level of consultation with the workforce (in some form or other) well beyond that currently required in the individual areas of collective redundancies, TUPE transfers and health and safety. When the Directive was negotiated, the UK government were successful in having it drafted in such a way as to leave most questions of detail and implementation to the member states (the much-vaunted 'subsidiarity'). Moreover, it had a phased introduction, coming into force in relation to undertakings of 150 employees or more in 2005, 100 or more in 2007 and 50 or more in 2008; there are currently no plans for it to apply to smaller firms.

The Directive was transposed into UK law in the Information and Consultation of Employees Regulations 2004[301] which set out the statutory scheme and are supplemented by detailed DTI (now BIS) guidance.[302] When an employer comes within these Regulations it does not have to do anything immediately because they operate on a 'trigger' mechanism of 10% of the employees in the undertaking submitting a written 'employee request' for an information and consultation system.[303] This request will normally be to the employer but can also be directly to the CAC if more confidentiality

---

[300] Directive 2002/14/EC; Bercusson 'The European Social Model Comes to Britain' (2002) 31 ILJ 209; Young 'Common Sense or Nonsense' [2002] NLJ 794.

[301] SI 2004/3426; *Harvey* N III [101]; see Hall 'Assessing the ICE Regulations' (2005) 34 ILJ 103 and Hall et al 'Implementing Information and Consultation—Early Experience under the ICE Regulations: Interim Update Report' (BERR Employment Relations Occasional Paper, October 2008).

[302] The ICE Regulations 2004: DTI Guidance (January 2005). ACAS have also issued their own practical guidance on their website (<http://www.acas.org.uk>). The Regulations complete with annotations from the guidance are set out at *Harvey* R [2195].

[303] Regulation 7(1), (2); the 10% can be in a single request, or as an aggregate of requests over a six-month period. One key point is that this trigger works on an 'undertaking' basis (even though an eventual ICE system could be wider); 'undertaking' means a public or private undertaking carrying out an economic activity, whether or not operating for gain. The BIS advice makes clear that, in the commercial sector, this operates on a *company* basis (even if that company is itself part of a larger group); the concept of associated employers does not apply.

is wanted.[304] One initial source of dispute could be whether the undertaking is covered at all because of the numbers limits (now 50). Rules are set out for calculating numbers and an employee or employees' representative has a right to information from the employer to establish the relevant number.[305] Any dispute as to whether a valid request has been made may be referred to the CAC.[306]

If a valid employee request has been made, this leads to three possibilities under the Regulations: (1) the employer must proceed to negotiate an information and consultation (ICE) system; (2) the employer may resist having to do so on the basis of a pre-existing agreement(s) (PEA); or (3) there is no PEA and negotiations either do not start or fail, in which case the employer becomes bound by the 'standard information and consultation provisions' set out in the Regulations (which thus operate as the default option). These are now considered in turn.

(a) Negotiated agreements

As soon as reasonably practicable, the employer must make arrangements for the election and appointment by the employees of negotiating representatives, inform the employees in writing of the identity of those representatives and invite them to enter into negotiations to reach a negotiated agreement.[307] The employer is in effect given three months to do this, because it is then provided that the negotiations are (subject to certain exceptions) to last for a maximum of only six months, beginning three months from the date of the request.[308] Any negotiated agreement must satisfy certain statutory requirements, namely that it (1) sets out the circumstances in which the employer must inform and consult the employees, (2) is in writing and dated, (3) is signed by the employer and (4) provides for the appointment or election of 'information and consultation representatives' (or provides that the employer must inform and consult the employees directly).[309] However, the most important requirement is that the negotiated agreement must be approved by the workforce. This means that it must be (1) signed by all the negotiating representatives *or* (2) signed by a majority of the negotiating representatives and either approved in writing by at least 50% of the

---

[304] Regulation 7(4)–(6). Under reg 11, an employer can start the process too.

[305] The Regulations apply to 'employees', not 'workers'. An average of numbers employed is taken over the previous 12 months. An employer may count a part-timer working for 75 hours or less per month as a half: reg 4.

[306] Regulation 13. Note that where an existing ICE system has been set up (or the employees have voted against one, see below) there is a three-year moratorium before another request can be made, unless there have been material changes in the undertaking: reg 12.

[307] Regulation 14(1). All employees must eventually be represented; no numbers are set out for representatives, but advice on coverage in given in para 35 of the BIS guide, which includes the potentially significant point that the fact that a trade union is recognized does *not* raise any presumption that union representatives should be used for those purposes.

[308] Regulation 14(3). *Darnton v Bournemouth University* [2009] IRLR 4, CAC. The parties may agree to extend this period: reg 14(5). A complaint about the election on appointment of representatives may be made to the CAC: reg 15.

[309] Regulation 16(1). There is no presumption that the negotiating representatives will eventually became the ICE representatives.

undertaking's employees or approved in a ballot of those employees (in which at least 50% of those voting voted in favour of approval).[310] Although the Regulations contain these definite procedural requirements, what is striking is the lack of regulation of the *substance* of the agreement. There are no (minimal) requirements of compliance with the default rules, and the eventual form of the agreement is left entirely to the parties (the state's role being confined to advice in the BIS guidance as to what an agreement *might* cover). This could be particularly important where the parties (particularly the employer) want to *tailor* the eventual system, for example to apply it across several 'undertakings' or to have separate systems for different parts of one undertaking.

(b) Pre-existing agreements

One key concern when drafting the Regulations was that the new system should not be allowed to wreck existing systems or agreements too easily. However, as already seen, these new provisions operate very differently from traditional collective bargaining and do *not* entrench trade unions (even recognized ones) as the proper conduit for employee representation. The Regulations attempt to square this circle by the 'pre-existing agreement' (PEA) defence, stating that the employer need not proceed with an employee request if there exists one or more such agreements. However, the requirements are complex. First, the initial request must have been made by fewer than 40% of the undertaking's employees.[311] Secondly, the agreement or agreements must be in writing, cover all the employees in the undertaking, have been approved by the employees and set out how the employer is to give information to the employees or their representatives and seek their views.[312] Thirdly, if these conditions are met, the employer (on receipt of the request) may proceed to hold a ballot to see if the request is endorsed by the employees.[313] This will only be so if at least 40% of the undertaking's employees *and* the majority of the employees voting vote in favour of endorsing the request. Note the use of the 'super-majority' once again. If this is not attained by those seeking a new system, the employer can refuse to proceed to negotiate a new ICE system.[314] Some of the difficulties that might arise under these requirements were seen in the first case to be heard by the EAT under the Regulations, *Stewart v Moray Council*.[315] Faced with

---

[310] Regulation 16(3). If a ballot is used it must be secret and fair: reg 16(5). The DTI guidance para 40 suggests the use of an independent scrutineer but this is not a legal requirement. A complaint about a ballot may be made to the CAC: reg 17.

[311] Regulation 8(1). Thus, if that request was made by 40% or more, the PEA defence does not apply and a new system must be negotiated (or the default rules applied).

[312] Regulation 8(1). The Regulations do not specify how employee approval is to be gauged, but the BIS guidance para 20 suggests support by a simple majority in a workforce ballot, a majority of the workforce expressed through signatures or the agreement of employee representatives who represent a majority of the workforce; different agreements covering the undertaking could be approved in different ways. The agreement or agreements in question must pre-date the employee request under reg 7: *AMICUS v Macmillan Publishers Ltd* [2007] IRLR 378, CAC.

[313] Regulation 8(2). The usual rules apply as to the fairness of the ballot: reg 8(3)–(5). Complaint about irregularities lies to the CAC: reg 8(7)–(9).

[314] Regulation 8(5)(b).   [315] [2006] IRLR 592.

an employee request for a new ICE system, the council relied on three existing union agreements for a PEA defence. This failed because one of the three agreements did not actually specify how information and consultation was to work (possibly a general problem where the employer is relying on longstanding collective bargains which are largely about terms and conditions). The EAT under Elias P held that where several agreements are being used, each one of them must satisfy this requirement. The judge then went on to give guidance on two of the other requirements, particularly in cases of existing trade union involvement. With regard to the requirement of full coverage of all employees, he said that this could be shown by the existence of trade union recognition agreements covering the workforce (even if there are large numbers, possibly a majority of non-members). This shows a traditional 'IR' view that what matters is the scope of recognition, not membership numbers. *However*, there was then a considerable shot across the bows. With regard to prior approval of the pre-existing agreement(s) this analysis was not used so comprehensively. While trade union 'approval' might be effective, this will only be so if (1) trade union members are a majority of the workforce and (2) there is no evidence of any split within the union itself on the issue. Thus, 'coverage' can be purely collective, but 'approval' is based on an individualistic model. Thus, while the Regulations as a whole might be an opportunity for a trade union trying to establish itself in a non-union organization, the vagaries of the PEA defence might be a *threat* to established trade unions which retain longstanding recognition with the employer but on a reduced membership base (in particular where it is now less than a majority);[316] even a shared desire by employer and union to continue the existing system might be overtaken by a request for something new by non-members or dissidents.

(c) The standard ICE provisions

If there is no PEA defence but no agreement is reached on the scheme to apply, the standard provisions apply. The employer must arrange for a ballot to elect a set number of ICE representatives[317] and the substantive provisions apply from their election (with a time limit of six months from the expiry of the original six months for negotiations).[318] Those substantive provisions set out the requirements on the employer which are, in an ascending order of obligations:

(1) to inform the representatives on 'the recent and probable development of the undertaking's activities and economic situation';[319]

---

[316] The Workplace Employment Relations Survey 2004 showed that (taking all workplaces with ten or more employees) while 38% recognized trade unions (16% in the private sector; 90% in the public sector) only 18% had union density of 50% or more (8% in the private sector; 62% in the public sector).

[317] Regulation 19(1). The ballot must be conducted under rules set out in Sch 2. The set number of representatives is one per 50 employees (with a minimum of two and a maximum of 25): reg 19(3). Complaint of breach of these requirements lies to the CAC: reg 19(4).

[318] Regulation 18.

[319] Regulation 20(1)(a). Information under reg 20 must be given in such a manner as to allow the representatives to conduct an adequate study and prepare for consultation: reg 20(2).

(2) to inform and consult the representatives on 'the situation, structure and probable development of employment within the undertaking, and on any anticipatory measures envisaged, in particular where there is a threat to employment within the undertaking';[320] and

(3) to inform and consult the representatives with a view to reaching agreement on 'decisions likely to lead to substantial changes in work organisation or in contractual relations'.[321]

This contains much that is novel to domestic employment law, and is fleshed out in paragraphs 55–61 of the BIS Guidance. One limitation is that, as pointed out there, none of this applies to issues of pay or benefits with a monetary value.[322] Apart from that, however, these default requirements are in broad terms and it is suggested that they could have at least three effects on established tenets of employment law. *First*, the reference in (2) to 'anticipatory measures envisaged, in particular where there is a threat to employment' could be important in redundancy situations—we have already seen (in Chapter 8) that the law on collective redundancies only requires consultation on how they are to be handled (ie the primary economic decision making has always been managerial), but this could be altered if the standard provisions apply because they appear to push the consultation obligation backwards into the area of the economic need for the redundancies.[323] *Secondly*, the requirement in (3) to consult (with a view to agreement) on 'decisions likely to lead to substantial changes in work organisation' might well cover changes to non-contractual matters (traditionally called 'works rules' and now often found in company handbooks)[324] which employers have often kept in their prerogative, precisely in order *not* to have to involve the workforce in any changes. *Thirdly*, the reference in (3) to consult (with a view to agreement) on changes in 'contractual relations' could be used to counter certain employer tactics to force through changes in terms and conditions, in particular by suddenly 'proposing'

---

[320] Regulation 20(1)(b). Consultation under reg 20 must be appropriate in its timing, method and content; it must be on the basis of the information supplied and any opinion expressed by the representatives; it must permit the representatives to meet an appropriate level of management and to obtain a reasoned response from the employer: reg 20(4)(a)–(c); DTI guidance, para 61.

[321] Regulation 20(1)(c), (4)(d). A legal requirement to consult 'with a view to reaching agreement' is novel in domestic law, and seems to lie somewhere between consultation and negotiation. In addition, reg 21 puts a duty on the parties (when negotiating or implementing either a negotiated agreement or the standard provisions) to 'work in a spirit of co-operation and with due regard for their reciprocal rights and obligations, taking into account the interests of both the undertaking and the employees'.

[322] BIS Guidance para 55. This is because the Directive's treaty base is Art 137 which itself excludes matters of pay as an area of EU competence.

[323] This was expressly envisaged in the government's original consultation document on the Directive. One point of interpretation is that head (3) specifically includes issues coming within the existing laws on collective redundancies and TUPE consultation, with reg 20(5) allowing the employer to disapply the ICE requirement if he notifies the representatives in writing that he intends to go down one of those routes instead. However, the 'threat to employment' limb is contained in head (2) which is *not* covered by reg 20(5) and so cannot be disapplied in this way.

[324] Ch 3, heading 2(ii), p 138.

changes on a 'take-it-or-leave-it' basis, putting the onus on to the employees to object or face the prospect of having consented by acquiescence;[325] it may be that the language of head (3) will cover this directly and diminish significantly the scope for change by employer ambush.

(iii) ENFORCEMENT

Finally, what is to happen if the Regulations are breached? Two preliminary points are (1) that there are duties on employees (as well as employers) not to misuse information received from the employer in confidence, breach of which are declared to be actionable in a civil suit for breach of statutory duty[326] and (2) that the normal panoply of rights (to time off and not to be dismissed or subjected to a detriment) are applied to employees acting as negotiating or ICE representatives.[327] However, the principal significance of the enforcement provisions is the remedies for breach by the employer of the collective obligations under the Regulations. In addition to the specific form of complaint already seen (eg in relation to ballots), regulation 22 provides that an ICE representative (or an employee or employee representative if there are no ICE representatives) can present a complaint to the CAC that the employer has failed to comply with the terms of a negotiated agreement or the standard ICE provisions (whichever are applicable). If the CAC finds for the complainant, it must make a declaration to that effect and may make an order requiring the employer to take specified steps to comply.[328] The complainant may in addition (within three months of the CAC making the declaration) apply to the EAT for a penalty notice. This is to be issued unless the EAT is satisfied, on hearing representations for the employer, that the failure resulted from a reason beyond the employer's control or that he has some other reasonable excuse for the failure. Regulation 23 sets out the factors to be taken into account when fixing the penalty (which is to be paid to the Secretary of State), and sets the maximum penalty at £75,000.[329]

---

[325] Ch 2, heading 6, p 113.

[326] Regulation 25. Advice on this vital issue for employers is given in the ACAS advice and the DTI guidance, with the latter going out of its way to state that (contrary to early employer concerns) the giving of information under these Regulations should *not* involve the employer in breaches of the UK Listing Rules or the City Code on Takeovers and Mergers (see para 77). Regulation 26 permits the employer to withhold information where its disclosure 'would seriously harm the functioning of, or would be prejudicial to, the undertaking'. Where the parties disagree over this exemption, the matter may be referred to the CAC for adjudication.

[327] Regulations 27–33.

[328] The level of this form of enforcement remains low. In 2011–12 the CAC received only four complaints; only two formal CAC determinations were necessary: *CAC Annual Report 2011/12.*

[329] In *AMICUS v Macmillan Publishers Ltd* [2007] IRLR 885, EAT a fine of £55,000 was imposed in a case of consistent failure by the employer to abide by the procedure, showing a 'cavalier attitude'; on the other hand, in *Darnton v Bournemouth University* UKEAT/0039/09 the university's default was largely due to a misunderstanding and the fine was only £10,000.

10

INDUSTRIAL ACTION

OVERVIEW

The law relating to industrial action has always been one of the most difficult areas of employment law. There has never been any positive right to take strike or other action, and any such action has always been potentially illegal at common law, under one or other of the 'economic torts' such as conspiracy or inducement to breach of contract. The key issue has always been, therefore, the extent to which such action is then legalized by statutory immunities. The subject is thus a particularly good example of the interplay between case law and legislation (often being passed to deal with novel liabilities discovered by the courts). One result of this, as will be seen in this chapter, is that in order to understand the current legislation it is necessary to look at its history, rather than just taking a snapshot of it as it now is. After a brief introduction to the development of the law here, this chapter looks first at the effect of industrial action on the individuals involved (in particular, whether they can be lawfully dismissed) and then passes on to the relevant economic torts (as fundamentally recast by the House of Lords in a case in 2007), the statutory immunities and the ways in which liability can be restored if the union gets it wrong (the notoriously complex balloting requirements being the prime example). Potential criminal liability is then considered, in particular the laws on picketing—when, where and for what purposes. The union's vicarious liability then becomes an important issue and the chapter closes by looking at what may ultimately be the sharp end here, the law relating to the granting of injunctions in employment cases.

1 INTRODUCTION[1]

In this country, the right to strike has never been much more than a slogan or a legal metaphor. What has happened is that ... legislation has provided limited immunities from a liability in tort.[2]

---

[1] See generally, Ewing *The Right to Strike* (1991); Auerbach *Legislating for Conflict* (1992); Davies and Freedland *Labour Legislation and Public Policy* (1993); Millward, Bryson and Forth *All Change at Work? British Employee Relations, 1980–1998* (2000); Morris and Archer *Collective Labour Law* (2000) ch 6.

[2] *Metrobus v UNITE* [2009] EWCA Civ 829, per Maurice Kay LJ.

Until the last quarter of the nineteenth century, important aspects of trade union aims and methods were in danger of being construed as criminal, either under certain statutes which outlawed certain forms of combination,[3] or under the general law relating to conspiracy which was capable of rendering an agreement criminal even if the object of the agreement was in fact lawful. The Trade Union Act 1871 provided that the purposes of a union should not be deemed unlawful merely because they were in restraint of trade so as to render members liable to criminal prosecution for conspiracy or otherwise.[4] This, however, only covered one possible head of illegality, and the Criminal Law Amendment Act which was passed in the same year to liberalize the law relating to the use of non-violent means in a dispute was soon found to be ineffective. Thus, as late as 1872, servants of a gas company who had come out on strike as a protest against the dismissal of a fellow employee and who, in striking, had broken their contracts, could still be held guilty of criminal conspiracy.[5] The agitation which followed this decision led to the appointment of a Royal Commission, which in turn led to the passing of the Conspiracy and Protection of Property Act 1875, which repealed the master and servant legislation, codified the law relating to the use of intimidation and violence during industrial action and, most importantly in the present context, removed the possibility of a lawful combination of workmen constituting a criminal conspiracy by providing, in section 3, that an agreement or combination by two or more persons to do or procure to be done any act in contemplation or furtherance of a trade dispute was not to be indictable as a conspiracy if such an act when committed by one person alone would not be punishable as a crime.[6] Thus, the mere fact of combination or agreement is not criminal.[7]

While the Conspiracy and Protection of Property Act 1875 had removed persons engaged in a trade dispute from the fear of prosecution for criminal conspiracy, it had no application to civil actions and so did not protect unions or their members from the payment of damages in a civil suit, and so, not unnaturally, it was to the civil remedy that aggrieved persons now turned. In *Allen v Flood*,[8] the House of Lords prevented the evolution of one general tort of intentionally causing harm to a person without justification, by holding that an act lawful in itself is not converted by a malicious or bad motive into an unlawful act leading to civil liability. However, in this same period

---

[3] Combination Act 1800; Molestation of Workmen Act 1825. For the history of the intervention of criminal law, see Wedderburn *The Worker and the Law* (3rd edn, 1986) 513–21. On the history of trade union law generally, see Orth *Combination and Conspiracy: A Legal History of Trade Unionism, 1721–1906* (1991).

[4] See now the Trade Union and Labour Relations (Consolidation) Act 1992, s 11.

[5] *R v Bunn* (1872) 12 Cox CC 316. See generally Wallington 'Criminal Conspiracy and Industrial Conflict' (1975) 4 ILJ 69.

[6] This is still the criminal law position, though s 3 was repealed by the Criminal Law Act 1977 as being no longer necessary, for s 3 of that Act extends the principle to all conspiracies by restricting criminal conspiracies to agreements to commit crimes (with two exceptions, neither of which is relevant in industrial cases).

[7] Agreements to commit acts which are themselves criminal are not protected, although summary offences may be disregarded in certain circumstances. See heading 6, p 754.

[8] [1898] AC 1, HL.

the courts did create or approve the specific torts of conspiracy[9] and inducement of breach of contract,[10] so that if there was an element of combination (the 'magic of plurality') or contractual breach (both of which were missing in *Allen v Flood*), there could indeed be civil liability.

Moreover, in the famous *Taff Vale* case[11] the House of Lords held that a trade union could be sued in tort (in spite of not being a body corporate) and its assets could be taken in satisfaction of judgment. On one view this may have been no more than a refusal to put trade unions into a preferential position, but it created a genuine dilemma since all the funds of the union became attachable, including those to which members had subscribed for the receipt of benefits. A Royal Commission was set up under the chairmanship of Lord Dunedin which, in its report published in 1906, did not go as far as to recommend the reversal of the *Taff Vale* case, but instead made the more modest proposal that separate benefit funds should be established which would be protected from seizure. However, the government went further and passed the Trade Disputes Act 1906 which (1) gave complete immunity to unions in respect of actions in tort, (2) gave immunity from liability for conspiracy and inducement of breach of contract to officers and members of unions provided they acted in 'contemplation or furtherance of a trade dispute' (a phrase dubbed the 'golden formula' by Wedderburn in recognition of the crucial role which it plays in determining the existence of the statutory immunities), and (3) gave statutory backing to *Allen v Flood* by declaring, for the avoidance of doubt, that an act done in contemplation or furtherance of a trade dispute is not actionable in tort simply because it interferes with the legitimate interests of another person. This statutory protection was extended in the Trade Disputes Act 1965 to give immunity (within the golden formula) from liability for the tort of intimidation which was exhumed and applied by the House of Lords in *Rookes v Barnard*.[12]

The whole scheme was then altered by the Industrial Relations Act 1971 which removed the union's complete immunity and introduced certain 'unfair industrial practices' based on the old heads of civil liability.[13] In 1974, however, the pre-Industrial Relations Act law was reinstated by the Trade Union and Labour Relations Act 1974 and the immunities were further extended by the Trade Union and Labour Relations (Amendment) Act 1976, which widened the immunity from the tort of inducement of breach of contract to cover commercial contracts as well as contracts of employment (thereby removing possible liability for secondary boycotts and 'blackings'), and extended the immunity to cover the possible development of a new head of tortious liability, that of interference with contract (ie short of an actual breach). By 1976, therefore, the immunities appeared almost watertight. For a time in the late 1970s it

---

[9] *Mogul Steamship Co v McGregor, Gow & Co* [1892] AC 25, HL; *Quinn v Leathem* [1901] AC 495, HL.

[10] *South Wales Miners' Federation v Glamorgan Coal Co* [1905] AC 239, HL.

[11] *Taff Vale Rly Co v ASRS* [1901] AC 426, HL.

[12] [1964] AC 1129, [1964] 1 All ER 367, HL.

[13] For a discussion of the law under the 1971 Act, see Cooper's *Outlines of Industrial Law* (6th edn, 1972) ch XI.

seemed that the Court of Appeal had succeeded in restricting the scope of the immunities, not by finding loopholes in the individual immunities themselves, but instead by taking a more stringent approach to what fell within the golden formula, upon which the immunities depend; however, his approach was subsequently disapproved by the House of Lords in three landmark cases.[14]

The incoming Conservative government, elected in 1979 in the wake of the notorious 'winter of discontent', embarked on a relentless 'step-by-step' reform of the law on industrial action which lasted for 14 years and produced a remarkable transformation of industrial relations law. During that period there were no fewer than six Acts of Parliament affecting the law on industrial action, beginning with the Employment Act 1980, which contained complex provisions removing the immunities from most forms of secondary industrial action (ie action against employers not directly concerned in the dispute). This was accomplished by the notorious section 17 of the Employment Act 1980, which in effect reinstated much the same position as that reached by the Court of Appeal in the late 1970s. The Employment Act 1982 constituted a further stage in this process, with the narrowing of the definition of 'trade dispute' and the withdrawal of the immunities from union pressure to have union labour only and union recognition requirements inserted into commercial contracts and tenders. However, the most far-reaching reforms in that Act related to the position of a union itself. As stated above, the Trade Disputes Act 1906 made a union itself immune from an action in tort; any possible action by an employer lay against union officers and members (who themselves have specific immunities). However, the 1982 Act abolished that total immunity,[15] so that a union now only has the same immunity as its individual officers and members, and introduced special rules as to when a union can be liable for the acts of its officials and committees, how much for, and from what funds.

This process was taken a stage further by the Trade Union Act 1984 but, unlike section 17 of the 1980 Act, which limited the scope of lawful industrial action, the 1984 Act concentrated on the machinery for calling the strike or other industrial action. It did this by making a strike ballot mandatory in the case of official action; industrial action without such a ballot was thus made litigable at the suit of any employer (or, semble, any person) adversely affected, by a simple device of withdrawing the statutory immunities altogether. This step, no less radical for its being so simple, has had a considerable effect, and in the years since the introduction of the 1984 Act a significant proportion of actions brought or threatened by employers against unions in relation to industrial action (actual or impending) have been under the strike ballot provisions rather than under the provisions of the earlier Acts.[16]

---

[14] *NWL Ltd v Nelson* [1979] ICR 867, [1979] IRLR 478, HL; *Express Newspapers Ltd v McShane* [1980] 1 All ER 65, [1980] IRLR 35, HL; *Duport Steels Ltd v Sirs* [1980] 1 All ER 529, [1980] IRLR 116, HL.

[15] Employment Act 1982, s 15.

[16] It has been argued that the frequent use of the strike ballot provisions by employers may initially have been at least partly due to the perceived effectiveness of legal sanctions during the miners' strike (albeit at the suit of working miners rather than employers): Benedictus (1985) 14 ILJ 176.

The next stage in this seemingly inexorable process was the Employment Act 1988 which, in addition to imposing extensive controls on internal union affairs (discussed in the previous chapter), removed the statutory immunities from industrial action taken to support or enforce union membership, thereby restricting a union's ability to defend a closed shop by means of industrial pressure. That Act also introduced a further refinement to the strike ballot provisions by requiring separate ballots to be held at each workplace unless certain stringent conditions were satisfied. Hard on the heels of the 1988 Act, the Employment Act 1990 contained a formidable series of measures designed to discourage secondary industrial action and unofficial industrial action. It removed the statutory immunities from virtually all forms of secondary action (repealing section 17 of the 1980 Act), significantly extended the range of circumstances where a union could be held responsible (and therefore potentially liable in tort) for the acts of its officials, committees and members, and completely removed the right to complain of unfair dismissal from those dismissed while taking part in unofficial industrial action.

To describe the state of the law on industrial action following the 1990 Act as confusing would be a considerable understatement. To gain a complete picture it was necessary to consult no fewer than nine statutes, stretching back as far as 1875, five of which had been enacted since 1980, all overlaid on a common law (ie the industrial torts) which was itself of great complexity. The decision to consolidate the whole of trade union law into one massive statute, the Trade Union and Labour Relations (Consolidation) Act 1992, was therefore greeted with relief by those toiling in the field, but in such a volatile area it was too much to hope that the consolidation would survive for long without further amendment. The Trade Union Reform and Employment Rights Act 1993 Act contained several very significant and (needless to say) highly controversial reforms of the law on industrial action, some of which had been considered during the passage of earlier legislation and rejected as either unworkable or undesirable. Thus, there were major changes to the law on industrial action ballots, including compulsory postal ballots, independent scrutiny of the ballot process, and a requirement to give notice of a ballot, and of any subsequent industrial action, to the employers of those involved; furthermore, in a move influenced by the 'Citizen's Charter', the 1993 Act gave individuals a right (the Citizen's Right) to seek an injunction restraining unlawful industrial action where that action affects the supply of goods or services to that person. The potential impact of this development cannot be overestimated, for its effect is to extend the range of potential claimants to embrace anyone adversely affected by unlawful industrial action, even those with no direct cause of action in tort (for example because the unlawful act was not directed at them). Having said that, to date very little use has been made of the Citizen's Right in practice, and it therefore remains something of an unexplored (unexploded?) weapon.

After 18 years of Conservative rule, any lingering hopes that a change of government might herald a return to the collective laissez-faire of the 1970s were dashed by the 1997 Labour general election manifesto, which made it clear that a new Labour government would not repeal the key elements of the Conservative trade union laws.[17] In his foreword to the 1998 White Paper, 'Fairness at Work', Tony Blair stated: 'There will be no going back. The days of strikes without ballots, mass picketing, closed shops and secondary action are over'.[18] However, in that document the government also signalled its intention to simplify the law on industrial action ballots and to extend unfair dismissal protection to those dismissed for taking part in lawfully organized official industrial action, and the Employment Relations Act 1999 duly enacted measures implementing those proposals. It soon became clear that the attempt to simplify the strike ballot provisions had backfired spectacularly as a result of restrictive judicial interpretation,[19] and yet another step was taken in the Employment Relations Act 2004 to achieve a greater element of balance here, though without in any way affecting the legal *requirement* of a strike ballot. The measures protecting workers from dismissal for taking part in lawful, official industrial action were arguably of much greater significance, for while they cannot be said to guarantee a 'right to strike' as such (on account of the qualified nature of the protection against dismissal, and the absence of any protection against victimization short of dismissal), they are undoubtedly the closest that UK law has ever come to such a right.

On the change of government in 2010, the incoming Coalition government launched a wide-ranging review of employment law, but this did not include further measures in relation to industrial action. However, one matter has arisen, at least in the Conservative half of the Coalition, and that is whether the law on balloting should be tightened further in relation to the necessary majority. Under the present law, a union only has to secure a majority *of those voting*. If the voting turnout is low, that majority can be obviously short of anything like a majority of those *entitled* to vote. This has led to calls to enact a requirement of some form of *absolute* majority in order to prevent what is seen in some quarters as the (non-voting) bulk of union members being led into strike action by the votes of a distinct minority of members (especially where the majority in favour of those voting is itself slim); one version of this is a requirement that the majority voting in favour of action must also be at least 40% of those entitled to vote[20] but some of the calls have been for a straightforward 50% requirement. A certain head of steam seemed to build up in favour of such a change in the law in the run-up to the 2012 London Olympics when there were some threats of disruptive strike action.

---

[17] *New Labour: Because Britain Deserves Better* (1997) 17.   [18] Cm 3968, 1998.

[19] See, eg, *London Underground Ltd v National Union of Rail, Maritime and Transport Workers* [2001] IRLR 228, CA (noted by Wedderburn (2001) 30 ILJ 206); *National Union of Rail, Maritime and Transport Workers v Midland Mainline* [2001] EWCA Civ 1206, [2001] IRLR 813. For a different and, it is submitted, more realistic approach, see *P v National Union of Schoolmasters/Union of Women Teachers* [2003] UKHL 8, [2003] 1 All ER 993.

[20] This would echo the qualified majority required in a ballot for union recognition; see Ch 9, heading 3(ii), p 669.

However, that did not materialize and since then the matter seems to have gone to sleep again.

There is one further dimension to this issue, and that is the impact of the Human Rights Act 1998 on the law on industrial action.[21] As seen in the previous chapter, Article 11 of the European Convention on Human Rights confers a right to freedom of association with others, including the right to form and join trade unions. Unlike the European Social Charter, Article 11 does not expressly include a right to strike, but the European Court of Human Rights has held that Article 11 safeguards the freedom of trade unions to protect the occupational interests of their members,[22] and that '[t]he grant of a right to strike represents without any doubt one of the most important of [the] means' by which a state could seek to secure the protection of the Article 11 rights.[23] Crucially, however, Article 11 leaves each state a free choice of the means to be used for safeguarding the freedom of unions to protect their members,[24] and the court has acknowledged that a right to strike may be subject to restrictions under national laws.[25] It would seem therefore that any attempt to use Article 11 to challenge the restrictions on industrial action under national law is probably doomed to failure, although in a potentially significant shift in approach, the European Court of Human Rights held in *UNISON v United Kingdom*[26] that the prohibition of the strike in that case was a restriction on the union's power to protect the interests of its members, and therefore a restriction on the freedom of association guaranteed by Article 11(1). The court's ruling was not as significant as might at first appear, however, because on the facts the court dismissed the union's application as inadmissible, holding that the restriction under national law was justified under Article 11(2) as being 'necessary in a democratic society for the prevention of disorder or crime, for the protection of the health or morals or for the protection of the rights and freedoms of others' (in this

---

[21] See Hendy 'Article 11 and the Right to Strike' in Ewing (ed) *Human Rights at Work* (2000); O'Dempsey et al *Employment Law and the Human Rights Act 1998* (2001) ch 4.

[22] *UNISON v United Kingdom* [2002] IRLR 497, ECtHR; see also *Swedish Engine Drivers' Union v Sweden* (1976) 1 EHRR 617, ECtHR; *National Union of Belgian Police v Belgium* (1975) 1 EHRR 578. It was accepted in *Gate Gourmet London Ltd v TGWU* [2005] IRLR 881, QBD that Convention rights are relevant in an industrial dispute case when deciding on the 'balance of convenience' test for an injunction.

[23] *Schmidt and Dahlström v Sweden* (1976) 1 EHRR 632, ECtHR.

[24] In *Gustafsson v Sweden* (1996) 22 EHRR 409, the ECtHR emphasized that states enjoy 'a wide margin of appreciation' in the choice of means to be employed.

[25] *Schmidt and Dahlström v Sweden* (1976) 1 EHRR 632. See eg *NATFHE v United Kingdom* (1998) 25 EHRR 122, where the Commission held that the then requirement under ss 226A and 234A of the 1992 Act to disclose to an employer the names of those to be balloted or to take part in industrial action was not 'a significant limitation on the right to take collective action'. Likewise, reliance on Art 11 failed at a domestic level in *Ministry of Justice v Prison Officers Association* [2008] IRLR 380, QBD.

[26] [2002] IRLR 497, ECtHR. The union had threatened industrial action against the employer, University College London Hospitals NHS Trust, because it refused to give an undertaking that the terms and conditions of staff to be transferred to a consortium which was to build and run a new private finance initiative hospital would be maintained for a period of 30 years at an equivalent level to employees who were not transferred. The application to the ECtHR followed the issue of an injunction by the Court of Appeal ([1999] IRLR 31) restraining the industrial action on the grounds that the dispute was not a trade dispute: see under heading 3(vi), p 720).

case, the economic interests of the employer). The decision does, however, lend support to the argument that Article 11 may confer a right to strike as a weapon of last resort where a union has no other means of protecting the occupational interests of its members.[27] In addition to the right of association, Article 11 also gives a right to freedom of peaceful assembly, which could conceivably be used to challenge some of the existing legal restrictions on picketing (for example the common law of trespass, and the recommendation in the Code of Practice on Picketing that pickets be limited to six at each entrance), as could the right to freedom of expression in Article 10, though to date this has not been a serious issue.

The complexity of the law on industrial action has in the past attracted adverse judicial comment on the basis that this is an area where it is particularly important that the players (the union leaders and managers) should know what the rules are and what is 'offside'.[28] The 1992 Consolidation Act helped to tidy up the structure of the legislation, but the law itself is still extremely difficult and complex.

Fortunately, the House of Lords had the opportunity in *OBG Ltd v Allan*[29] to review the essentials of the economic torts, which may make their exposition here a little simpler. However, as one door closes another opens and case law has recently given rise to another complication, namely that certain forms of industrial action may be illegal under EC laws relating to freedom of establishment and freedom to provide services.

The approach adopted in this chapter is to look first at the effect of industrial action on the individual participants, and then to consider the position of the organizers of the industrial action, including the economic torts that may be committed during a trade dispute, the statutory immunities which apply where those torts are committed within the 'golden formula', and (most importantly in practice) the restrictions on those immunities enacted by successive Conservative governments during the 1980s and early 1990s. We then turn to the potential criminal liability for industrial action, and the law on picketing, including the specific statutory immunity for 'peaceful picketing'; we assess the extent to which a union is vicariously liable for the acts of its officials and committees; and, finally, we examine the use of injunctions in industrial disputes. While it is necessary for the sake of exposition to split the subject up in this way, it must be remembered that any particular case may depend on the effect and interaction of several of these factors. Indeed, the reforms introduced by the Employment Relations Act 1999 added to the complex interplay of issues by linking the protection against unfair dismissal to the legality of the industrial action. On the latter issue, it

---

[27] See Hendy [1998] EHRLR 583. In *Demiru v Turkey* [2009] IRLR 766 the ECtHR took a broader view generally of the right of association (stating that the *Swedish Engine Drivers* case (n 22) and *Schmidt and Dahlström* (n 23) had been too narrowly decided, but that was in relation to the right including the right to collective bargaining, not the right to strike. That decision was discussed in *Metrobus Ltd v UNITE* [2009] EWCA Civ 829 where it was held that the technical rules on strike ballots (heading 4(vi), p 733) did not contravene Art 11, being within the margin of appreciation left to states in complying with the convention.

[28] *Merkur Island Shipping Corpn v Laughton* [1983] ICR 178, [1983] IRLR 26, CA, per Sir John Donaldson MR, echoed by Lord Diplock in the House of Lords, n 30.

[29] [2007] IRLR 608, [2007] 4 All ER 545, HL.

may help, when looking at the detail, to remember the three basic stages in an action in tort adopted by the House of Lords in *Merkur Island Shipping Corpn v Laughton*:[30] (1) does the industrial action in question give the claimant a cause of action in tort?; (2) if so, is that cause of action covered by the immunities in section 219 or 220 of the Trade Union and Labour Relations (Consolidation) Act 1992?; (3) is the cause of action restored by anything in sections 222–234A of the Trade Union and Labour Relations (Consolidation) Act 1992?

2 THE EFFECT OF INDUSTRIAL ACTION ON THE INDIVIDUAL

As was seen in the introduction to this chapter, the approach traditionally taken in the law on industrial action has been to preserve the freedom to strike by providing immunities at the collective level (albeit within increasingly narrow boundaries) rather than by conferring any positive right to strike on the individual participants. At the collective level, the effect of industrial action on individual contracts of employment is of central importance because it may render the action 'unlawful' in the sense required by certain forms of the industrial torts, so opening the way to a successful civil action to stop the strike in any case where it can be argued that the statutory immunities do not apply.[31] Before turning to the collective dimension, however, it is necessary to examine more closely the effect of industrial action on the individual participants.

(i) THE EFFECT OF INDUSTRIAL ACTION ON INDIVIDUAL CONTRACTS OF EMPLOYMENT

As the most fundamental contractual obligation of an employee is to be ready and willing to serve the employer, the action of going on strike is likely to be regarded as constituting a breach of contract, giving the employer the right to dismiss summarily. In theory it may also entitle the employer to sue the employee for damages,[32] although in practice the employer's common law power to withhold wages in respect of non-performance (or indeed partial performance) of contractual obligations is likely to be of far greater significance.[33] The orthodox view is that industrial action will be unlawful (as a breach of contract) however it is organized, and even if strike notice is

---

[30] [1983] ICR 490, [1983] IRLR 218, HL. Elements of this decision were later disapproved by the House of Lords in *OBG Ltd v Allan* n 29, but this basic approach appears still to be useful.

[31] Immunities are necessary because the very fact that a strike involves a breach of contract means that prima facie those organizing it will be guilty of inducing a breach of contract, which may be tortious in itself and/or may constitute the tort of causing loss by unlawful means; if the immunities are withheld (eg where there is no strike ballot), tortious liability will, in most cases, be easy to establish.

[32] *National Coal Board v Galley* [1958] 1 All ER 91, [1958] 1 WLR 16, CA; *Neil v Strathclyde Regional Council* [1984] IRLR 14 (not an industrial dispute case).

[33] See Ch 3, heading 5(i), p 190.

given it will be construed merely as notice of an impending breach.[34] However, this orthodox view was challenged by Lord Denning MR in *Morgan v Fry*[35] where he suggested that where strike notice of adequate length (ie at least equal to the length required to terminate the contracts of employment) was given, the strike was not unlawful, since the notice had the effect of suspending the contracts, not breaking them:

> The truth is that neither employer nor workmen wish to take the drastic action of termination [of the contracts of employment] if it can be avoided. The men do not wish to leave their work for ever. The employers do not wish to scatter their labour force to the four winds. Each side is, therefore, content to accept a 'strike notice' of proper length as lawful. It is an implication read into the modern law as to trade disputes. If a strike takes place, the contract of employment is not terminated. It is suspended during the strike and revives again when the strike is over.[36]

The Donovan Commission considered the possibility of introducing the concept of suspension through strike notice, but thought it surrounded by problems;[37] in spite of this, it was introduced by the Industrial Relations Act 1971, section 147, but disappeared with the repeal of that Act in 1974. The whole question arose (obliquely) for consideration by the EAT in *Simmons v Hoover Ltd*[38] where, in reaffirming that an employer has a right to dismiss a striking employee (who is thereby disentitled to a redundancy payment), Phillips J held that there is no common law doctrine of suspension by strike notice, and refused to apply Lord Denning's views in *Morgan v Fry*. He considered that those views were out of line with the modern statutory provisions relating to strikes (in contexts such as unfair dismissal, redundancy claims and continuity of employment), which operate on the assumption that participation in a strike is repudiatory conduct entitling the employer to dismiss, and then graft on special rules (depending on the context). *Simmons v Hoover Ltd* showed a clear move back to the original view of strikes as breaches of contract,[39] and any mitigation of the potential harshness of this must be found in the legislation.

While it is clear that strike action will be a breach of contract, the position as regards industrial action short of a strike is less certain. Where the industrial action is inconsistent with contractual obligations, there is little doubt that it will be in

---

[34] See principally *Rookes v Barnard* [1964] AC 1129, [1964] 1 All ER 367, HL, at 1204 and 396 respectively, per Lord Devlin; *Stratford & Son Ltd v Lindley* [1965] AC 269 at 285, [1964] 2 All ER 209 at 217, CA, per Lord Denning MR.

[35] [1968] 2 QB 710, [1968] 3 All ER 452, CA; Davies LJ supported Lord Denning's view, but Russell LJ did not and decided the case on other grounds.

[36] [1968] 2 QB 710 at 728, [1968] 3 All ER 452 at 458.   [37] (Cmnd 623, 1968) para 943.

[38] [1977] ICR 61, [1976] IRLR 266, EAT; applied in *Wilkins v Cantrell and Cochrane (GB) Ltd* [1978] IRLR 483, EAT and *Haddow v ILEA* [1979] ICR 202, EAT.

[39] This view could be said to be implicit in the Trade Union and Labour Relations (Consolidation) Act 1992, s 229(4), which requires a ballot paper to point out that a person who takes part in a strike or other industrial action may be in breach of his contract of employment. Note, however, the judgment of Saville J in *Boxfoldia Ltd v NGA (1982)* [1988] ICR 752, [1988] IRLR 383 to the effect that the question of whether a purported strike notice avoids a breach of contract is a matter of interpretation of the notice (which, in order to be effective, would have to be an unambiguous notice of termination of contracts by the strikers).

breach of contract.[40] But what if the industrial action in question is a work to rule, or a ban on voluntary overtime? Will this constitute a breach of the contracts of employment of the participating employees? In *Secretary of State for Employment v ASLEF (No 2)*,[41] the Court of Appeal held that concerted action by a group of workers which involved working strictly in accordance with their contracts of employment nevertheless amounted to a breach of contract where the object of the action was wilfully to disrupt the employer's business. This does not mean, however, that employees necessarily break their contracts whenever they withdraw their goodwill. In *Burgess v Stevedoring Services Ltd*,[42] the Privy Council held that an overtime ban was not in breach of the contracts of the participants, Lord Hoffmann stating that employees are not in breach of their contracts 'for refusing to do things altogether outside their contractual obligations (like going to work on Sunday) merely because they do not have a bona fide reason for refusal. They do not have to have any reason at all'.[43]

(ii) THE EFFECT OF INDUSTRIAL ACTION ON STATUTORY EMPLOYMENT RIGHTS

Participation in a strike or other industrial action is likely to have a highly detrimental impact on an employee's statutory employment rights. The most serious consequence is likely to be the potential loss of the right to bring proceedings for unfair dismissal, discussed in this chapter; but other statutory rights of a striking employee will also be affected, in particular:

(1) the restrictions on deductions from pay do not apply to deductions in respect of a strike or other industrial action in which the employee took part;[44]

(2) a striking employee's rights to a redundancy payment may be jeopardized;[45]

(3) a week during which an employee takes part in a strike will not count for the purposes of calculating that employee's continuity of employment;[46]

(4) an employee is not entitled to a statutory guarantee payment where the failure to provide work is in consequence of a strike, lockout or other industrial action involving his employer or an associated employer;[47]

---

[40] See, eg, *British Telecommunications plc v Ticehurst* [1992] ICR 383, [1992] IRLR 219, CA, discussed at Ch 3, heading 5(i), p 191.

[41] [1972] 2 QB 455, CA.   [42] [2002] UKPC 39, [2002] IRLR 810.

[43] [2002] UKPC 39, [2002] IRLR 810 at 813. Their motive might have been relevant 'if they had been assigned work and, as part of a concerted action, all claimed to be sick or have some other reason for declaring themselves not available'.

[44] Employment Rights Act 1996, s 14(5); see Ch 3, heading 5(v), p 209. For the common law power to withhold wages in such circumstances, see p 190 above.

[45] Employment Rights Act 1996, s 140; see Ch 8, heading 1(iv), p 593.

[46] Employment Rights Act 1996, s 216. See Ch 2, heading 5(iii), p 109.

[47] Employment Rights Act 1996, s 29(3). See Ch 3, heading 5(v), p 209.

(5) an employee may be disqualified from receiving statutory sick pay where there is a stoppage of work due to a trade dispute at his place of work;[48]

(6) rights to state benefits (in particular those relating to unemployment) will be materially affected.

(iii) INDUSTRIAL ACTION AND UNFAIR DISMISSAL

When employees strike, their employer has the contractual right to dismiss them,[49] even if that right is infrequently exercised. However, while a dismissal in such circumstances is probably lawful at common law, it may still be unfair; indeed following the reforms introduced by the Employment Relations Act 1999, a dismissal may be *automatically* unfair where the employee is dismissed for taking 'protected industrial action'. This protection is, however, contingent on the industrial action in question being official (ie authorized or endorsed by the union), lawful (ie covered by the statutory immunities), and normally lasting for no longer than 12 weeks.[50] Where these requirements are not satisfied, the pre-1999 law still applies, which means that in some circumstances an employment tribunal will have no jurisdiction to hear an unfair dismissal complaint, while in others the tribunal will only be able to consider the complaint on its merits if the employer has discriminated between the participants by selectively dismissing or re-engaging them. To gain a clear picture of the current position, it is necessary to explore how this highly intricate state of affairs has come about.

The approach of those responsible for drafting the original unfair dismissal legislation was to seek to protect the neutrality of the industrial (now employment) tribunals by relieving them of the necessity of investigating the rights and wrongs of an industrial dispute, while at the same time preserving the employer's ultimate freedom to dismiss the participants. This was achieved by providing that where, at the date of dismissal, the employee was taking part in a strike or other industrial action, or the employer was conducting or instituting a lockout, the tribunal would have no jurisdiction to hear an unfair dismissal complaint by that employee unless the employer had discriminated between the participants, either by selectively dismissing only some of them, or by selectively offering re-engagement.[51] In *Heath v J F Longman (Meat Salesmen) Ltd,*[52] Sir Hugh Griffiths expressed the policy behind this as follows:

> the manifest overall purpose of [the section] is to give a measure of protection to an employer if his business is faced with ruin by a strike. It enables him in those circumstances,

---

[48] Social Security Contributions and Benefits Act 1992, Sch 11, paras 2(g) and 7.

[49] *Simmons v Hoover Ltd* [1977] ICR 61, [1976] IRLR 266, EAT; *Wilkins v Cantrell and Cochrane (GB) Ltd* [1978] IRLR 483, EAT; *Haddow v ILEA* [1979] ICR 202, EAT.

[50] Action lasting for longer than 12 weeks may still be protected in certain circumstances: see below.

[51] See *Gallagher v Wragg* [1977] ICR 174, EAT, per Phillips J; the neutrality explanation is arguably undermined by the fact that, where a dismissal or re-engagement is selective, the tribunal will have to decide whether the dismissal was fair or unfair.

[52] [1973] ICR 407, [1973] IRLR 214, at 410 and 215 respectively.

if he cannot carry on business without a labour force, to dismiss the labour force on strike; to take on another labour force without the stigma of its being an unfair dismissal.

The Conservative government of Mrs Thatcher considered the principle of non-selectivity to be too restrictive on employers faced with industrial action, and so the relevant provisions were modified to allow some selectivity in dismissals. Thus, the Employment Act 1982[53] confined the non-selectivity principle to those still taking part in the industrial action at the date of the complainant's dismissal (thereby allowing an employer faced with a strike to wait to see who in fact returns to work before dismissing all those still holding out), and introduced a time limit on the re-engagement of dismissed strikers (in effect permitting selective re-engagement after a three-month period); and the Employment Act 1990 took matters much further, by completely removing the right to complain of unfair dismissal from those dismissed while taking part in unofficial industrial action.[54] Taken together, these reforms significantly weakened the protection which the non-selectivity principle had given to those taking part in industrial action. In its 1998 White Paper, 'Fairness at Work', the incoming Labour government signalled a major policy shift in this area by proposing to give employees dismissed for taking part in lawfully organized official industrial action the right to complain of unfair dismissal to a tribunal,[55] and the Employment Relations Act 1999 subsequently enacted the concept of protected industrial action (discussed later in this chapter). The provisions on protected industrial action differ in several respects from the proposals contained in 'Fairness at Work'; for example, the White Paper had not indicated any intention to restrict the protection temporally, whereas under the 1999 Act the protection normally only lasted for eight weeks (raised to 12 by the Employment Relations Act 2004). However, this temporal limit on the protection is offset by the fact that a dismissal during the protected period will be *automatically* unfair. On balance, the protection of an automatically unfair dismissal, albeit for a limited period, is likely in practice to be more advantageous to workers taking part in industrial action than protection for an unlimited period which is dependent on a tribunal finding on the facts that the dismissal was unfair. There are, however, some significant gaps in the protection. As previously mentioned, it is contingent on the industrial action in question being both official and, more controversially, lawful, which may make reliance on the protection something of a gamble, as an individual union member has no way of knowing whether the union has in fact complied with the Byzantine laws governing industrial action;[56] moreover, the protection does not extend to detriment *short*

---

[53] See Wallington 'The Employment Act 1982, S 9—A Recipe for Victimisation?' (1983) 46 MLR 310; Ewing 'Industrial Action: Another Step in the "Right" Direction' (1982) 11 ILJ 209; Townshend-Smith 'Taking Part in a Strike or Other Industrial Action' [1984] NLJ 194, 240.

[54] See now the Trade Union and Labour Relations (Consolidation) Act 1992, s 237.

[55] (Cm 3968, 1998) paras 4.21–4.23. The White Paper confirmed that the government had no intention of changing the position in relation to those dismissed for taking unofficial action.

[56] A satisfactory report on the ballot by the independent scrutineer may provide some reassurance that the union has safely navigated the legal minefield, but it will probably come too late to be of any help, and in any event it does not guarantee that the industrial action is lawful.

of dismissal, so that an employee who is victimized by the employer (for example by being denied promotion) for taking part in lawfully organized official industrial action remains unprotected under English law. The end of result of the above is as follows.

(a) Unofficial action

An employee has no right to bring an unfair dismissal complaint where at the time of the dismissal the employee was taking part in an unofficial strike or other unofficial industrial action.[57] The only exception is where it is shown that the dismissal was for jury service or family reasons, or because the employee has taken certain specified action in relation to health and safety or flexible working, has acted as an employee representative, or has made a protected disclosure under the 'whistle-blowing' provisions.[58] In such cases, the dismissal will be automatically unfair; in all other cases, the reason for the dismissal is wholly irrelevant. As seen above, the removal of unfair dismissal protection from unofficial strikers was introduced in 1990 as part of a series of measures designed to discourage unofficial industrial action.[59] The effect of the provisions is that an employer may selectively dismiss the ringleaders of unofficial action without fear of having to defend an unfair dismissal complaint.[60]

(b) Official action

Where the industrial action is official, the present position is that the dismissal will be automatically unfair[61] if the reason (or, if more than one, the principal reason) for the dismissal is that the employee took 'protected industrial action',[62] and one of the following three conditions is satisfied: (1) the dismissal took place within 12 weeks[63]

---

[57] Trade Union and Labour Relations (Consolidation) Act 1992, s 237. In determining whether action is 'unofficial', the statutory test of vicarious liability in s 20 of the 1992 Act applies (see heading 7, p 766), save that action will not be regarded as unofficial if none of those taking part are members of a trade union: s 237(2). The meaning of 'taking part', 'strike' and 'industrial action' are considered below in respect of s 238.

[58] Trade Union and Labour Relations (Consolidation) Act 1992, s 237(1A). The health and safety exception was introduced to alleviate fears that employees dismissed for refusing to work in circumstances of danger might be held to be taking part in industrial action, and therefore excluded from the protection against unfair dismissal.

[59] The measures were canvassed in the Green Paper, 'Unofficial Action and the Law' (Cm 821, 1989), in which it was argued that the restrictions on selective dismissal impeded the employer's ability to take effective action against unofficial strikers (para 3.3).

[60] Green Paper, para 3.7. Where industrial action is repudiated by the union under s 21 of the 1992 Act, it does not become unofficial for present purposes before the end of the next working day after the day on which the repudiation takes place, in effect giving those involved a day's grace to decide whether to continue with the action.

[61] The usual qualifying period and age restriction for unfair dismissal claims do not apply in complaints under s 238A: s 239(1). No reinstatement or re-engagement order may be made until after the end of the industrial action: s 239(4).

[62] Trade Union and Labour Relations (Consolidation) Act 1992, s 238A.

[63] The period was raised from eight to 12 weeks by the Employment Relations Act 2004 which also added an 'extension period' of any time during the normal time in which the employee is locked out by the employer.

of the day on which the employee started to take protected industrial action;[64] (2) the dismissal took place after the end of that 12-week period, but the employee had stopped taking protected industrial action before the end of that period (thus protecting the participants against victimization by the employer after they have returned to work); or (3) the dismissal took place after the end of the 12-week period and the employee had not stopped taking part in the industrial action before the end of that period, but the employer had failed to take reasonable procedural steps to resolve the dispute. Industrial action is 'protected' for those purposes if the employee is induced to take part in the industrial action 'by an act which by virtue of section 219 is not actionable in tort';[65] in other words, the protection for the individual participants is contingent upon the union having complied with the complex legal requirements governing the organization of industrial action, including the balloting requirements and the restrictions on certain forms of industrial action. As seen earlier, the unfair dismissal protection normally lasts for only 12 weeks. However, a dismissal for taking protected industrial action will still be unfair where the industrial action has lasted for more than 12 weeks, if the employer has failed to take 'such procedural steps as would have been reasonable for the purposes of resolving the dispute to which the protected industrial action relates'.[66] In deciding whether the employer has taken reasonable procedural steps, the tribunal must have regard to whether the employer or the union had complied with the procedures laid down in any applicable collective agreement, and whether, after the start of the protected industrial action, either party had offered or agreed to commence or resume negotiations, had unreasonably refused to a request that conciliation services be used, or had unreasonably refused a request to use mediation services in relation to the procedures to be used to resolve the dispute.[67]

Where the industrial action is official but is *not* 'protected' within the meaning of the new provisions, a tribunal will not have jurisdiction to consider an unfair dismissal complaint[68] where, at the date of dismissal,[69] the employer was conducting or

---

[64] Note that the protected period runs from the day on which the dismissed employee started to take industrial action, not the day when the industrial action began; this has important implications where employees join in the action after it has already begun.

[65] Trade Union and Labour Relations (Consolidation) Act 1992, s 238A(1). On a strict interpretation, this could be taken to mean that if the industrial action is not tortious, or it involves the commission of a tort which is not covered by the s 219 immunities, the unfair dismissal protection does not apply! See Ewing (1999) 28 ILJ 283, at 292.

[66] Trade Union and Labour Relations (Consolidation) Act 1992, s 238A(5).

[67] Trade Union and Labour Relations (Consolidation) Act 1992, s 238A(6). Where the parties have agreed to use a conciliator or mediator, s 238B (added by the Employment Relations Act 2004) sets out matters which must be taken into account when deciding whether each side made proper use of such services. In determining whether the employer has taken reasonable procedural steps, the tribunal must disregard the merits of the dispute: s 238A(7).

[68] The reason for the dismissal in such a situation is usually irrelevant, although again there is an exception where the dismissal was for jury service or family reasons, or because the employee has taken certain specified action in relation to employment rights or health and safety, or has acted as an employee representative: s 238(2A).

[69] This is defined in s 238(5). See *Heath v J F Longman (Meat Salesmen) Ltd* [1973] ICR 407, [1973] IRLR 214, where it was taken to mean that the employee must be taking part in industrial action at the time of dismissal,

instituting a lockout or the complainant was taking part in a strike or other industrial action, unless the employee shows that either:

(1) one or more relevant employees have not been dismissed; or

(2) a relevant employee has, before the expiry of the period of three months beginning with that employee's date of dismissal, been offered re-engagement and the complainant has not been offered re-engagement.[70]

If the dismissals are selective, or only some of the relevant employees are selected for re-engagement, the tribunal will then have jurisdiction to consider the case in the ordinary way, which means that they must consider the reason for the dismissal,[71] and, if it is a prima facie fair one, the reasonableness of the decision to sack or not to re-engage that particular employee in those circumstances (unless the reason for selection concerned union membership or activities, in which case the dismissal may be automatically unfair);[72] a selective dismissal is therefore not automatically unfair as such (unlike a dismissal for taking protected industrial action), and the employer may be able to show that it was reasonable in all the circumstances to dismiss or not to re-engage some of the strikers. If the dismissal is held to be unfair the tribunal is not entitled to take into account the mere act of participating in industrial action in deciding whether to reduce the award of compensation on the grounds of contributory fault, but the award may be reduced where there is individual blameworthy conduct by the applicant, additional to or separate from the mere act of participation in the industrial action, which contributed to the dismissal and which was sufficiently blameworthy to make it just and equitable for the tribunal to reduce the compensation (for example, if the applicant is a strike leader who has contributed to his own dismissal by his over-zealous or inflammatory actions).[73]

The interpretation of the above provisions has proved to be especially problematic, not least because a number of key phrases are not defined. There is no definition of 'lockout' or 'other industrial action', and until 1992 there was no definition of 'strike'

---

and not merely on the same date. A dismissal before the industrial action has started (*Midland Plastics v Till* [1983] ICR 118, [1983] IRLR 9, EAT) or after it has ended (*Seed v Crowther (Dyers)* [1973] IRLR 199) will not fall within the section.

[70] Re-engagement means taking the employee back into the same job or in a different job which would be reasonably suitable in his case: s 238(4); the definition of 'job' (Employment Rights Act 1996, s 235(1)) allows the employer a certain leeway on the precise terms on which he takes the employee back: see *Williams v National Theatre Board Ltd* [1982] ICR 715, [1982] IRLR 377, CA. An advertising campaign offering job vacancies is unlikely to be interpreted as an offer of re-engagement to a particular employee within the meaning of the section: *Crosville (Wales) Ltd v Tracey* [1993] IRLR 60, EAT.

[71] See *Baxter v Limb Group of Companies* [1994] IRLR 572, CA.

[72] Note, however, that the dismissal of a person while taking part in industrial action is unlikely to be automatically unfair under s 152 of the 1992 Act: see heading 2(iii), p 697.

[73] *Tracey v Crosville Wales Ltd* [1997] ICR 862, [1997] IRLR 691, HL, overruling *TNT Express (UK) Ltd v Downes* [1994] ICR 1, [1993] IRLR 432, EAT. Contributory fault in unfair dismissal complaints is considered at Ch 7, p 541.

either. However, as part of the consolidation process, the definition of 'strike' from the strike ballot provisions was extended to the whole of the law on industrial action, so that now 'strike' is defined in this context as 'any concerted stoppage of work'.[74] There are definitions of 'strike' and 'lockout' in section 235 of the Employment Rights Act 1996, but it has previously been held that those definitions are only for the purposes of continuity of employment and so are not to be applied under section 238,[75] although they may provide some guidance to the tribunal in interpreting the section. However, at the end of the day the words should be given their ordinary and natural meaning, and their interpretation remains strictly a question of fact for the tribunal. This is entirely in line with the modern anti-legalism approach and the unpredictability and inconsistency that it can produce was commented on adversely by Browne-Wilkinson P in *Naylor v Orton and Smith Ltd*;[76] however, that approach was reaffirmed by the Court of Appeal in *Express and Star Ltd v Bunday*[77] where May LJ said:

> What are the necessary elements of a lock-out, or for that matter of a bicycle or an elephant, is not in my opinion a question of law. Nor I think is it necessarily a question of law whether a court or tribunal was correct in thinking that the presence of a particular element or ingredient in a given state of affairs is necessary before that can be, for instance, a 'lock-out'. This may be a mixed question of law and fact. Alternatively it may be solely a question of fact, which it is for the expert tribunal to determine.[78]

The dangers inherent in this strongly fact-based approach are graphically illustrated by *Lewis and Britton v E Mason & Sons*,[79] where the EAT upheld the finding of the employment tribunal that one person acting alone was taking part in industrial action. In that case, the employee was dismissed after refusing to drive a heavy goods vehicle with no overnight heater from South Wales to Scotland in mid-December unless he was given an extra £5 for overnight bed and breakfast accommodation. The EAT held that whether the employee was taking part in industrial action was a question of fact for the tribunal alone, and that the tribunal's finding on that point was not perverse, as it was open to the tribunal to find that one person acting alone was taking part in industrial action where that person's conduct was designed to coerce the employer to improve the terms and conditions of employment in some way. Taken to its logical conclusion, this line of reasoning would appear to mean that any employee who refused to carry out a lawful instruction of his employer in order to gain an improvement in

---

[74] Trade Union and Labour Relations (Consolidation) Act 1992, s 246.

[75] *McCormick v Horsepower Ltd* [1980] ICR 278, [1980] IRLR 182, EAT (upheld on other grounds on appeal) [1981] ICR 535, [1981] IRLR 217, CA and *Rasool v Hepworth Pipe Co Ltd* [1980] ICR 494, [1980] IRLR 88, EAT in relation to 'strike'; *Express and Star Ltd v Bunday* [1988] ICR 379, [1987] IRLR 422, CA in relation to 'lockout'.

[76] [1983] ICR 665, [1983] IRLR 233, EAT.   [77] See n 75.

[78] At 388 and 425 respectively; this view can perhaps best be summed up by saying that the law needs a definitive interpretation of 'lock-out' like an elephant needs a bicycle. Glidewell LJ thought that 'the proper construction of a word or words in a statute is a matter of *law*' (at 390 and 427), but was in a minority on this point.

[79] [1994] IRLR 4, EAT. See Dolding (1994) 23 ILJ 243.

his terms and conditions of employment could be held to be taking part in industrial action, thus enabling his employer to dismiss him without fear of having to defend an unfair dismissal complaint. The EAT's ruling sits uneasily with earlier dicta to the effect that industrial action is a collective act which involves the concerted action of more than one person,[80] and it is difficult to reconcile with the wording of the section, which requires a person to be *taking part* in industrial action (implying the involvement of others), rather than merely *taking* industrial action. It is to be hoped that the adoption in 1992 of the definition of 'strike' as a 'concerted stoppage of work' makes it unlikely that the decision in *Lewis and Britton* will be followed in the future.[81]

In some cases, the dominant consideration for the tribunals in determining whether the circumstances amount to a strike or other industrial action within the meaning of the Act has been the purpose for which the action in question was taken, and in particular whether it involved the application of pressure on the employer.[82] So for example, in *Rasool v Hepworth Pipe Co (No 2)*,[83] the EAT held that attendance at an unauthorized union meeting during working hours did not amount to industrial action because the purpose was to discuss wages and not to apply pressure on the employer, even though the meeting did in fact result in some disruption of production. However, while it is undoubtedly true that industrial action will usually be taken for the purpose of putting pressure on the employer, there may be circumstances where action is taken for a social or political rather than an industrial motive (eg in protest at government policy), and it is highly likely that such action would in practice be held to be industrial action. Greater emphasis is therefore likely to be placed on the nature and effect of the action, rather than on the reasons for it.[84]

It is clear that the technical question of whether the action is in breach of contract is not conclusive, although once again it may be taken into account as a factor. Usually a strike will involve a breach of contract, but the lack of a need to show such a breach could be important in the case of a lockout or, more especially, in cases of 'other

---

[80] See *Tramp Shipping Corpn v Greenwich Marine Inc* [1975] ICR 261 at 266, CA, per Lord Denning: 'a strike is a concerted stoppage of work by men (sic) done with a view to improving their wages or conditions, or giving vent to a grievance or making a protest about something or other, or supporting or sympathising with other workmen in such endeavour'; see also *Coates v Modern Methods and Materials Ltd* [1982] ICR 763, [1982] IRLR 318, CA, per Eveleigh LJ: 'for a person to take part in a strike he must be acting jointly or in concert with others who withdraw their labour'; cf *London Underground Ltd v RMT* [1995] IRLR 636, CA, per Millet LJ (on the strike ballot provisions): 'Industrial action is collective action. An individual does not take collective action; he takes part in it.'

[81] *Lewis and Britton* was heard by the tribunal before the enactment of the 1992 Consolidation Act.

[82] Cf Stephenson LJ in *Power Packing Casemakers Ltd v Faust* [1983] ICR 292, [1983] IRLR 117, CA: 'the continued application of pressure is industrial action in the commonsense of the words.' See also *Fire Brigades Union v Knowles* [1996] IRLR 337, EAT (under s 65(2)(a)).

[83] [1980] IRLR 137, EAT. The case is a good illustration of the potentially fine dividing line between union activity and industrial action. The EAT has held that the two situations are mutually exclusive: *Drew v St Edmundsbury Borough Council* [1980] ICR 513, [1980] IRLR 459.

[84] See *Rasool v Hepworth Pipe Co (No 2)*, n 83, where the EAT acknowledged that it was 'probably incorrect to attempt to interpret [industrial action] narrowly in terms of specific intention and that the nature and effect of the concerted action are probably of greater importance'.

industrial action'—a wide phrase which has been held to cover not just actions argu-ably in breach (such as a go-slow, partial refusal of work or a work-to-rule), but also actions clearly *not* in themselves in breach, such as a refusal to work voluntary over-time which, if done collectively and with a coercive purpose, may constitute industrial action even though individually each employee was perfectly entitled to refuse it.[85]

The right to complain of unfair dismissal is only removed from employees who were 'taking part' in a strike or other industrial action at the date of the dismissal. Here again the Court of Appeal has emphasized that the question of whether or not an individual is 'taking part' is ultimately a question of fact for the tribunal,[86] but the cases neverthe-less provide some guidance as to the correct approach. In *Coates v Modern Methods and Materials Ltd*,[87] the employee had stayed away from work during the strike because she was frightened of crossing a picket line. The majority of the Court of Appeal held that the test to be applied is an objective one, focusing on what the employee in fact did, and not on her motivation; as Stephenson LJ put it: 'participation in a strike must be judged by what the employee does and not by what he thinks or why he does it'.[88]

It follows that employees who are absent from work due to sickness or on holiday leave during the industrial action may still be held to be taking part in it, particularly if they associate themselves with the strike (for example by attending at the picket line).[89] However, it seems that clear evidence of participation will be required before an employee who is off sick when the action begins will be found to be participating in it.[90] Just as the employee's subjective motivation is irrelevant, so also is subjective knowledge on the part of the employer, so that an employer's reasonable but mistaken belief that the employee is taking part in the industrial action will not be sufficient if the employee's actions and omissions do not justify the conclusion that he was in fact taking part in that action.[91] A threat to take industrial action does not of itself amount to taking part in industrial action within the meaning of the Act,[92] but where an employee has stated his intention of joining in existing industrial action, he may be held to be taking part in that action before the time when he is contractually due

---

[85] *Power Packing Casemakers Ltd v Faust* [1983] ICR 292, [1983] IRLR 117, CA. The decision has been heavily criticized.

[86] *Coates v Modern Methods and Materials Ltd* [1982] ICR 763, [1982] IRLR 318, CA; *Naylor v Orton and Smith Ltd* [1983] ICR 665, [1983] IRLR 233, EAT.

[87] See, n 85. See also *Bolton Roadways Ltd v Edwards* [1987] IRLR 392, EAT; *Manifold Industries Ltd v Sims* [1991] ICR 504, [1991] IRLR 242, EAT.

[88] Kerr LJ expressed a similar view.

[89] *Bolton Roadways Ltd v Edwards* [1987] IRLR 392, EAT, per Scott J. In *Hindle Gears Ltd v McGinty* [1985] ICR 111, [1984] IRLR 477, the EAT overturned as perverse the tribunal's decision that a sick employee who spent time talking to pickets while handing in his medical certificate was participating in the industrial action.

[90] *Rogers v Chloride Systems Ltd* [1992] ICR 198, EAT.

[91] *Bolton Roadways Ltd v Edwards*, above; in *McKenzie v Crosville Motor Services Ltd* [1990] ICR 172, [1989] IRLR 516, the EAT held that the reasonable belief of the employer that the employee was participating would be sufficient, but this was rejected in favour of the approach in *Bolton* by the EAT in *Manifold Industries Ltd v Sims*, n 87 (followed in *Jenkins v P&O European Ferries (Dover) Ltd* [1991] ICR 652).

[92] *Midland Plastics v Till* [1983] ICR 118, [1983] IRLR 9, EAT.

to work in fact arrives.[93] In *Lewis and Britton v E Mason & Sons*,[94] an employee was dismissed for refusing to drive a heavy goods vehicle which did not have an overnight heater unless he was given an allowance to cover the cost of overnight accommodation. On learning of the dismissal, one of his colleagues threatened the employer that there would be a strike the following day unless the dismissed employee was reinstated. The EAT controversially held that it was open to the tribunal to find that by making a definite threat not to come to work the following day, at a time when further negotiation could not have been expected to take place and where the work for the following day had been allocated by the employer, the employees were taking part in industrial action.[95]

As seen above, where the industrial action is official but not 'protected' under the new provisions, the tribunal will have jurisdiction to determine the fairness of a dismissal where the employer has discriminated between 'relevant employees' by selectively dismissing[96] or selectively re-engaging them. As defined in section 238(3), 'relevant employees' means:

(a)   in relation to a lockout, employees who were directly interested in the dispute in contemplation or furtherance of which the lockout occurred; and

(b)   in relation to a strike or other industrial action, those employees at the establishment of the employer at or from which the complainant works who at the date of his dismissal were taking part in the action.

In the case of strikes and other industrial action, the definition of 'relevant employees' is restricted to those taking part in the action at the date of the complainant's dismissal. Before 1982, the definition of relevant employees included all those who had taken part *at any stage* in the industrial action, so that an employee who had been on strike but had returned to work before the dismissal occurred was still a relevant employee. Accordingly, in *Stock v Frank Jones (Tipton) Ltd*,[97] the House of Lords held that there had been selectivity where the employer had not sacked two employees who had returned to work before the date of the dismissals, so that the applicant could bring her case. The

---

[93] See *Winnett v Seamarks Bros Ltd* [1978] ICR 1240, [1978] IRLR 387, EAT, where an employee who had made clear his intention to join a strike when his next shift began was held to be taking part in industrial action from the time when he made that intention clear.

[94] [1994] IRLR 4, EAT.

[95] The decision goes considerably further than *Winnett v Seamarks Bros Ltd* [1978] ICR 1240, [1978] IRLR 387, because that case involved a threat to join an existing strike, rather than a threat to commence strike action. Cf Browne-Wilkinson J in *Midland Plastics v Till* [1983] ICR 118, [1983] IRLR 9: 'The actual taking of industrial action is ... quite distinct from the stage at which the threat of it is being used as a negotiating weapon.'

[96] The question of whether the dismissals are selective will be determined at the conclusion of the proceedings in which the tribunal determines whether or not it has jurisdiction: *P&O European Ferries (Dover) Ltd v Byrne* [1989] ICR 779, [1989] IRLR 254, CA; in that case the complainant was ordered to disclose the identity of an alleged relevant employee who had not been dismissed, thus enabling the employer to dismiss that employee before the conclusion of the hearing and so prevent the tribunal from acquiring jurisdiction to hear the complainant's case.

[97] [1978] ICR 347, [1978] IRLR 87, HL.

Employment Act 1982 reversed the decision in that case, thus enabling an employer to issue an ultimatum to those taking industrial action to return to work or face dismissal and then to dismiss all those who fail to comply, while still retaining the protection of the section against unfair dismissal proceedings brought by the dismissed employees.[98]

A second significant amendment made by the 1982 Act was to introduce a time limit on the re-engagement of relevant employees, so that the anti-discrimination provisions only apply where a relevant employee is offered re-engagement within three months of his dismissal; thereafter the employer is free to re-engage strikers selectively without conferring jurisdiction on the tribunal.[99] The time limit also enables the employer to make an initial limited offer of re-engagement—in effect sanctioning a 'cooling-off' period and a phased return to work—provided that all those dismissed have been offered re-engagement within three months of their dismissal.[100] The third amendment introduced by the 1982 Act dealt with the situation where there is industrial action at some or all of the plants of a multi-plant employer. Up to that time, if the industrial action all formed part of one dispute, the non-selectivity rule had to apply to all plants, so that an employer could not adopt a different response to the industrial action in different plants, for example by dismissing the workforce at one plant but not another. However, the 1982 Act restricted the definition of 'relevant employees' to those employed 'at the establishment of the employer at or from which the complainant works',[101] so that any application of the selectivity principle has to be done on an establishment-by-establishment basis. One further potential difficulty for a large employer operating from several sites is that an employee dismissed for taking part in industrial action might be mistakenly re-engaged at another site within the three-month period, so opening up the employer to unfair dismissal complaints by those not re-engaged. However, the EAT has held that for there to be an effective offer of re-engagement, the employer must have actual or constructive knowledge (in the sense that he has the means of finding out) of the job from which the employee was dismissed and the reason why he was dismissed.[102]

---

[98] The restrictions in the 1982 Act only applied to strikes etc, not to lockouts, so that in the case of the latter the definition of relevant employees remains considerably wider, and an employee who was locked-out but has returned to work by the time of the dismissal will still be a relevant employee: *Fisher v York Trailer Co Ltd* [1979] ICR 834, [1979] IRLR 385, EAT; *H Campey & Sons Ltd v Bellwood* [1987] ICR 311, EAT.

[99] This could cause limitation problems where the complainant and the relevant employee's dismissals took place at the same time, for the normal limitation period for the claimant to bring his action is also three months. Because of this, the limitation period is extended to six months in a case where the complainant is relying on the re-engagement of a relevant employee as a ground for arguing that the s 238 or s 238A exclusion should not apply: Trade Union and Labour Relations (Consolidation) Act 1992, s 239(2). The six-month limit also applies to complaints under s 238A (protected industrial action).

[100] *Highland Fabricators Ltd v McLaughlin* [1985] ICR 183, [1984] IRLR 482, EAT.

[101] There is no definition here of 'establishment'; it is used elsewhere (again without definition) in the context of redundancy consultation; for the case law there, which could by analogy apply here, see Ch 8, heading 1(iii), p 572.

[102] *Bigham and Keogh v GKN Kwikform* [1992] ICR 113, [1992] IRLR 4, EAT; the EAT also confirmed that a re-engagement resulting from fraud on the part of the employee will not deprive the employer of the protection of the section.

The principle of non-selectivity was clearly weakened by the Employment Acts of 1982 and 1990, and further marginalized by the Employment Relations Act 1999, but where it still applies the basic concept remains that the employer must dismiss all or none if he is to rely on the exclusion. In most cases this narrows the scope of the exclusion in the employee's favour, but it has been argued that the whole concept of the exclusion is potentially too wide in a case where the employer is in fact willing to dispense with one whole group of employees, who may be deprived of their unfair dismissal rights in two ways—first, by the employer instituting a lockout affecting them all, which is now treated in the same way as a strike;[103] and, secondly, because the employer might try to goad the employees in question into taking industrial action and then dismiss them all. In *Thompson v Eaton Ltd*,[104] Phillips J suggested that this second possibility might be countered by the concept of an 'engineered' strike (ie one produced by 'gross provocation' by the employer) which would not fall within the exclusion. However, in *Marsden v Fairey Stainless Ltd*,[105] the EAT disapproved of the idea of an engineered strike, pointing out that the wording of the section simply requires the employee to have been dismissed *while* on strike,[106] so that the exclusion will apply even if the industrial action was provoked by the employer.[107]

3 LIABILITY IN TORT AND THE STATUTORY IMMUNITIES[108]

(i) DEVELOPMENTS, HERESIES AND THE *OBG* CASE

As seen in the introduction, the decision in *Allan v Flood*[109] prevented the evolution of one 'supertort' of injuring someone without justification, for use in determining the borderline between acceptable and unacceptable industrial action. Instead, the

---

[103] Compare the original drafting in the Trade Union and Labour Relations Act 1974, Sch 1, para 7. Note however, that the 12-week protected period (discussed earlier) is now subject to an 'extension period' of the length of any period during which the employee is locked-out by the employer: s 238(7A)–(7D) (added by the Employment Relations Act 2004).

[104] [1976] ICR 336 at 342, [1976] IRLR 308 at 311, EAT.

[105] [1979] IRLR 103, EAT. See also *Wilkins v Cantrell and Cochrane (GB) Ltd* [1978] IRLR 483, EAT.

[106] Phillips J had been able to argue for the concept of an engineered strike because, as originally drafted, the section provided that the real reason for dismissal must be that the employee was on strike; however, the requirement of such a causal link was removed by the Employment Protection Act 1975, Sch 16, Part III, para 13.

[107] A particularly controversial application of the exclusion was in the dispute between the printing unions and News International; see Ewing and Napier 'The Wapping Dispute and Labour Law' (1986) 45 CLJ 285, at 291. For an ingenious attempt to devise an argument avoiding this unfortunate state of affairs, see Elias 'The Strike and Breach of Contract: A Reassessment' in Ewing, Gearty and Hepple (eds) *Human Rights and Labour Law: Essays for Paul O'Higgins* (1994).

[108] See generally *Harvey* N II [701]ff; Elias and Ewing 'Economic Torts and Labour Law: Old Principles and New Liabilities' (1982) 41 CLJ 321; Carty 'Intentional Violation of Economic Interests: The Limits of Common Law Liability' (1988) 104 LQR 250; Sales and Stilitz 'Intentional Infliction of Harm by Unlawful Means' (1999) 115 LQR 411; Carty *An Analysis of the Economic Torts* (2001).

[109] [1898] AC 1, HL.

emphasis was on the development of specific torts. Conspiracy was evolving as a tort as well as a crime and, nearly half a century before, the case of *Lumley v Gye*[110] had established the tort of inducement of breach of contract. It was against the background of these fundamental torts that the widespread immunities in the Trade Disputes Act 1906 were granted, as a result of which there were relatively few developments in this area for a further half a century because the law was largely removed as a means of resolving industrial disputes. That began to change in the late 1950s and 1960s with an increase in industrial action and (at least in some circumstances) renewed interest in use of the law. This was, however, still well before the intervention of Parliament in the 1980s to redefine by statute the limits of industrial action, and what was seen at the time was increased judicial activism in this area instead, though in a piecemeal and unforeseeable form.[111] In particular, (1) the *Lumley v Gye* tort of inducement was said to have a subset of 'indirect inducement' which required 'unlawful means',[112] (2) it was then extended to cover mere 'interference' with contracts (again, because of its extreme width, requiring unlawful means),[113] (3) this in turn was extended to cover interference with 'trade or business',[114] (4) it was then argued that in fact *Lumley v Gye*, indirect inducement and unlawful interference were all subspecies of one 'unified tort' of interference with contractual rights and (5) for good measure the courts had also exhumed the tort of intimidation.[115] These developments continued to be seen through the fraught industrial relations of the 1970s and into the first Conservative government of Mrs Thatcher in the early 1980s.[116] However, as the reforms of her governments started to bed in (particularly in relation to secondary action, discussed below, which most of the economic tort cases had tended to concern) the question of whether the conduct was tortious in the first place became less important—the

---

[110] (1853) 2 E & B 216.

[111] To trade unions, this often seemed to constitute consistent movement of the goal posts. It also caused problems for Labour governments at the time, trying to keep the statutory immunities up to date to cover new forms of liability being evolved by the courts. One result was that sometimes the immunities had to be framed to cover *possible* liabilities.

[112] *Thomson & Co Ltd v Deakin* [1952] CL 646, [1952] 2 All ER 361, CA; *J T Stratford & Sons Ltd v Lindley* [1965] AC 269, [1964] 3 All ER 102, HL; *Associated Newspapers Group v Wade* [1979] ICR 664, [1979] IRLR 201, CA.

[113] *Torquay Hotel Co Ltd v Cousins* [1969] 2 Ch 106, [1969] 1 All ER 522, CA; the issue arose because, although the union had stopped oil supplies to the employer in dispute, the oil supply contract contained a *force majeure* clause applying to labour disputes and so there was no actual *breach* of contract.

[114] *Merkur Island Shipping Corpn v Laughton* [1983] ICR 490, [1983] IRLR 218, HL.

[115] *Rookes v Barnard* [1964] AC 1129, [1964] 1 All ER 367, HL. The tort had last been heard in *Tarleton v M'Gawley* (1793) Peake 270. The Trades Disputes Act 1965 was passed by a sympathetic Labour government to extend the statutory immunities to cover it. This is now contained in the Trade Union and Labour Relations (Consolidation) Act 1992, s 219(1)(b), which may now be otiose because of the *OBG* case, n 117.

[116] See eg *Dimbleby & Sons Ltd v NUJ* [1984] ICR 386, [1984] IRLR 161, HL and *News Group Newspapers Ltd v SOGAT 82* [1987] ICR 181, [1986] IRLR 337 concerning the open warfare in the newspaper printing industry. Curiously, the economic torts did not feature in the substantial litigation during the miners' strike 1984–85, which concerned the civil war within the NUM.

coverage of the torts was so wide that it tended to be a *given* that a strike or other industrial action was tortious, the emphasis being on whether it was legitimized by the (narrowed) immunities.

The definition of the relevant torts had thus taken a back seat for several years when the issue suddenly arose again in what is now the leading case, *OBG Ltd v Allan*.[117] Perhaps significantly by 2007, this was *not* an industrial dispute case, but was in fact three consolidated commercial cases[118] in which the House of Lords took the opportunity to review the economic torts generally. Although the context was the regulation at common law of what are or are not acceptable commercial practices (a matter arguably better left to Parliament, perhaps explaining the cautious nature of the speeches), the principles laid down now form the basis of much of the law on industrial dispute liability too. The decision is long and complex (involving also issues of confidentiality and conversion). On the economic torts, the principal speeches are by Lord Hoffmann and Lord Nicholls which are largely in agreement (though with some differences in terminology), except on one point on the tort of causing economic loss by unlawful means; in the case of any conflict, it is Lord Hoffmann's speech with which the remaining judges agreed. The principal points established are as follows:

(1) The two torts accepted in the case are inducing breach of contract ('the *Lumley v Gye* tort') and causing economic loss by unlawful means;[119] although they are separate, they could both arise on one set of facts.

(2) The idea that these two torts are merely subdivisions of one larger tort (the 'unifying theory') is wrong; inducement is a form of secondary liability (requiring a breach of contract by (theoretically at least) the primary wrongdoer) whereas causing economic loss by unlawful means is a form of primary liability (*Thompson v Deakin* and *Merkur Island Shipping Corpn v Laughton* disapproved on this point).

(3) The extension of the economic torts into areas such as mere interference with contract (direct or indirect) was improper (*Stratford v Lindley* and *Torquay Hotels v Cousins* disapproved on this point).

---

[117] [2007] IRLR 608, [2007] 4 All ER 545, HL. See Simpson 'Economic Tort Liability in Labour Disputes: The Potential Impact of the House of Lords' Decision in *OBG Ltd v Allan*' (2007) 36 ILJ 468, which sets the decision into the context of the existing statutory immunities.

[118] There had been a renewal of interest in the economic torts in this commercial sphere. *OBG* concerned alleged unlawful action by receivers causing loss to the claimant company. The most newsworthy case, *Douglas v Hello! Magazine*, concerned publication of wedding photographs of Michael Douglas and Catherine Zeta-Jones by *Hello!* magazine when they had previously been sold to *OK!* magazine (thus obviously raising deep human rights issues). *Mainstream Properties Ltd v Young* concerned giving finance to two employees to establish a joint venture in breach of their contracts with the employer.

[119] Confusingly, Lord Nicholls refers to this tort as 'interference with the claimant's business by unlawful means'. Lord Hoffmann's terminology is used here.

(4) The tort of intimidation should no longer be considered a separate form of liability, but is instead only a factual example of the tort of causing economic loss by unlawful means.[120] Likewise, a case of what in the past may have been considered the tort of unlawful interference with contract or business will now only be unlawful if it comes within the ambit of that modern tort.

Two final introductory points are made. The first is that nothing in *OBG* addresses the tort of conspiracy, which must be considered (unless we are ever told to the contrary) to have been left unaffected. The second is that Lord Hoffmann cautioned that this radical reappraisal of the tort base must not be read as meaning that on their facts the multitude of previous cases had necessarily been wrongly *decided*; indeed, many of them would have had the same result under the new rules.[121] In practice, therefore, it is likely to remain the case that in an industrial dispute case it will normally by fairly clear that a tort has been committed by the action, with the emphasis remaining on whether it is legitimized by the legislation. For purposes of analysis, however, it is still necessary to set out the requirements of the applicable torts as they now stand, before going on to consider that legislation in detail.

(ii) CONSPIRACY

(a) The cause of action

That conspiracy is a head of civil, as well as criminal, liability was clearly established by the House of Lords at the end of the nineteenth century in the famous 'trilogy' of conspiracy cases.[122] The tort of conspiracy may take either of two forms. The first, 'conspiracy by lawful means',[123] is committed where two or more persons combine together with intent to injure the claimant by the employment of means which are *lawful* in themselves, but with a predominant purpose to harm the claimant rather than to advance the legitimate interests of the combiners. The second, 'conspiracy to use unlawful means', is committed where two or more persons combine together with intent to injure the claimant by the employment of means which are *unlawful* in

---

[120] This is because at paras 6 and 7 Lord Hoffmann uses the old 'intimidation' case of *Tarleton v M'Gawley* (n 115) as an early authority for the modern tort, stating that the confusion had arisen from an early edition of *Salmond on Tort*. Unfortunately, however, he does not directly discuss *Rookes v Barnard* itself, hence Simpson's remark ((2007) 36 ILJ at 476) that 'The potential which the House of Lords' decision in *Rookes v Barnard* has always had for undermining the whole structure on which the legal basis for the right to strike rests in English law has certainly not been diminished by the decision in *OBG Ltd v Allan*'.

[121] For some reason, the old saying comes to mind about the mountain labouring and bringing forth a mouse (Horace—the Latin author, not Rumpole).

[122] *Mogul Steamship Co v McGregor, Gow & Co* [1892] AC 25, HL; *Allen v Flood* [1898] AC 1, HL: *Quinn v Leathem* [1901] AC 495, HL. See the recent discussion of this history in *Revenue and Customs Commissioner v Total Network SL* [2008] 2 All ER 413, HL.

[123] This version of the tort, sometimes referred to as 'conspiracy to injure' or 'simple' conspiracy or 'conspiracy to effect an unlawful purpose', was described as an 'anomalous tort' in *Lonrho Ltd v Shell Petroleum Co Ltd (No 2)* [1982] AC 173, [1981] 2 All ER 456, HL.

themselves. In the case of the latter, its scope is as wide as the scope of unlawful means, and so a conspiracy to injure by means that are criminal[124] or tortious is actionable. At one point it was thought[125] that for both forms of the tort it was necessary to show that the predominant purpose of the combiners must be to injure the claimant. However, the House of Lords in *Lonrho plc v Fayed*[126] made it clear that under the second form there is no such requirement, and that it is sufficient to show that the defendants acted with intent to injure the claimant.

The emergence of the first form, that of conspiracy by lawful means, could have constituted a serious impediment to the lawfulness of industrial action, particularly after *Quinn v Leathem*, for almost any strike will require concerted action and will lead to loss to the employer. This consideration led to the immunity which was first granted in the Trade Disputes Act 1906 (see later), but in fact, as the tort was developed in subsequent cases (in particular by the House of Lords in *Sorrell v Smith*[127] and *Crofter Hand Woven Harris Tweed Co Ltd v Veitch*),[128] it is arguable that the immunity is in fact unnecessary, for the courts have taken a liberal approach to what constitutes the legitimate interests of organized labour. If the union can show a genuine trade union reason for the industrial action,[129] then the conspiracy will not be actionable, in spite of the loss caused to the employer, because the employer will be unable to show that the union's predominant purpose was to harm him;[130] it is this element of the tort of conspiracy by lawful means which has become dominant, whether it be called lack of an improper purpose or, more commonly, a defence of 'justification'. In the light of this, this particular head of liability has played little part in the modern cases.

(b) The immunity

Section 219(2) of the Trade Union and Labour Relations (Consolidation) Act 1992 provides that an agreement or combination to do any act in contemplation or furtherance

---

[124] *Revenue and Customs Commissioner v Total Network SL* [2008] 2 All ER 413, HL (see Mitchell [2008] NLJ 773 where the point is made that the ruling that a crime is enough per se, as long as it was the necessary 'means' is significant given the large expansion in the number regulatory offences in recent years). The House of Lords accepted that the concept of unlawful means is wider in the tort of conspiracy than in the tort of causing economic loss by unlawful means.

[125] Based on a dictum of Lord Diplock in *Lonrho Ltd v Shell Petroleum Co Ltd (No 2)* [1982] AC 173, [1981] 2 All ER 456, HL.

[126] [1992] 1 AC 448, [1991] 3 All ER 303, HL, overruling *Metall und Rohstoff AG v Donaldson Lufkin & Jenrette Inc* [1990] 1 QB 391, [1989] 3 All ER 14, CA. Cf also *Lonrho plc v Fayed (No 5)* [1994] 1 All ER 188, CA (the claimant must prove actual pecuniary or financial loss for both forms of the tort, as opposed, eg, to loss of reputation).

[127] [1925] AC 700, HL.   [128] [1942] AC 435, [1942] 1 All ER 142, HL.

[129] See, eg, *Reynolds v Shipping Federation* [1924] 1 Ch 28 (action to enforce a closed shop); the *Crofters'* case [1942] AC 435, [1942] 1 All ER 142, HL (action to force up wages); *Scala Ballroom (Wolverhampton) Ltd v Ratcliffe* [1958] 3 All ER 220, [1958] 1 WLR 1057, CA (action to stamp out a colour bar operated by the employer).

[130] *Quinn v Leathem* [1901] AC 495, above, is perhaps best explained as a rare case where the jury decided that the defendants' predominant purpose was vindictive; see also *Huntley v Thornton* [1957] 1 All ER 234, [1957] 1 WLR 321.

of a trade dispute is not actionable in tort if the act is one which, if done by one person alone, would not be actionable. This therefore gives protection from liability for conspiracy by lawful means (ie means which would not be actionable if done by only one person), but does *not* give immunity from suit for conspiracy by unlawful means (ie means which *would* be actionable if done by only one person), although in the latter case there may be an indirect immunity if the means are covered by one of the other immunities and are not therefore 'unlawful'. Thus, in most cases conspiracy will be a dead letter, but on the other hand it is not abolished, only held in abeyance while within the golden formula; if the act complained of is outside that formula, for example a personal vendetta or clear misuse of union power for improper purpose, conspiracy could still be used as a cause of action.[131]

(iii) INDUCING BREACH OF CONTRACT

(a) The cause of action

In the light of the relatively innocuous nature of conspiracy, reliance in economic tort cases has tended to be placed largely on the tort of inducing breach of contract, a cause of action established in *Lumley v Gye*[132] where a theatre owner induced an opera singer to break her existing contract so that she could sing for him instead. At a collective level, such an inducement may arise where a defendant union calls upon members to strike in breach of their contracts or (in a secondary action case) where it puts pressure onto one of the suppliers or customers of the employer in dispute to break a commercial contract (of supply or purchase) with that employer. According to *OBG Ltd v Allan*[133] the constituent elements of the tort are that (1) the defendant knows that he is inducing a breach of contract (in the sense of actual knowledge, not what a reasonable person would realize, though subject to possible liability through a Nelsonian blind eye);[134] (2) the defendant intends to procure a breach of contract (again, in the sense of an actual intention as the defendant's end or means, mere foresight that a breach might occur not being enough);[135] (3) there must be an actual breach of contract, mere 'interference' no longer being sufficient.[136] This last point follows strongly from the perceived rationale for the tort, namely the protection by the laws of tort of the sanctity of contract, allowing the victim to sue not only the contract breacher but also any (secondary) third party responsible for procuring the breach.

---

[131] As in *Huntley v Thornton* [1957] 1 All ER 234, [1957] 1 WLR 321.

[132] (1853) 2 E & B 216.   [133] [2007] IRLR 608, [2007] 4 All ER 545, HL.

[134] *Emerald Construction Co Ltd v Lowthian* [1966] 1 WLR 691, CA approved. One tactic historically has been for the employer's lawyers to serve on the union details of commercial contracts that could be breached.

[135] *Millar v Bassey* [1994] EMLR 44, CA disapproved.

[136] *Torquay Hotel Co Ltd v Cousins* [1969] 2 Ch 106, [1969], All ER 522, CA and *Merkur Island Shipping Corpn v Laughton* [1983] 2 AC 570, [1983] 2 All ER 189, HL disapproved. Previous cases decided on interference grounds (such as *Dimbleby & Sons v NUJ* [1984] IRLR 67, [1984] 1 All ER 117, HL) would now have to come (if at all) under the tort of causing loss by unlawful means (see heading 3(iv)).

One final point of possible difficulty is that the conventional wisdom has always been that there is a defence of justification available, but its scope is uncertain, and it is not as wide as that for conspiracy by lawful means. Thus, in *South Wales Miners' Federation v Glamorgan Coal Co Ltd*[137] it was held that there was no defence of justification available on the facts, in spite of the fact that the workers involved were merely acting in genuine furtherance of their own interests and bore no ill will towards the employers. It appears that exercise of a 'duty' may amount to justification, but mere self-interest cannot;[138] in *Brimelow v Casson*[139] the justification defence succeeded in highly unusual circumstances, the defence in that case being that the union had a duty, as a representative association, to secure the payment of reasonable wages by a theatrical manager in order that chorus girls in his employ could live without having to resort to immoral earnings. The idea of a 'duty' to act as providing justification for the tort of inducement is a nebulous one; it is theoretically capable of being extended to cover many union activities on the basis that a union officer may have certain legal and moral 'duties' towards the membership, but in practice the defence rarely succeeds.[140] This point was not addressed in *OBG Ltd v Allan*; it did not arise on the facts and so did not have to be addressed, and so presumably the old case law on it still stands until directly reconsidered.

(b) The immunity

Section 219(1)(a) of the Trade Union and Labour Relations (Consolidation) Act 1992 provides that an act done in contemplation or furtherance of a trade dispute is not actionable in tort on the ground only that it induces another person to break a contract. The immunity was significantly widened by the Trade Union and Labour Relations (Amendment) Act 1976, which extended the immunity to breach of *any* contract, not just a contract of employment, as had previously been the case; the effect of this was to extend the immunity to cover secondary boycotts and blackings aimed at breaking vital commercial contracts of the employer with whom the union is in dispute. Following this change in 1976, it appeared that the immunity itself was almost watertight, *provided* that the acts in question remained within the golden formula. It should be stressed that in spite of the legislative changes since 1980, the actual immunity in section 219(1) has remained unchanged. The rules on secondary action, strike ballots, etc, operate not by altering the basic immunity, but instead by suspending its operation in certain defined circumstances.

---

[137] [1905] AC 239, HL; and see *British Motor Trade Association v Salvadori* [1949] Ch 556, [1949] 1 All ER 208.

[138] See the *South Wales Miners'* case, in the Court of Appeal [1903] 2 KB 545, at 573 per Romer LJ and in the House of Lords [1905] AC 239 at 249 per Lord James; *Greig v Insole* [1978] 3 All ER 449, [1978] 1 WLR 302 at 491 and 340, respectively, per Slade J. See also *TimePlan Education Group Ltd v National Union of Teachers* [1997] IRLR 457, CA, per Peter Gibson LJ.

[139] [1924] 1 Ch 302; *Camden Nominees Ltd v Forcey* [1940] Ch 352, [1940] 2 All ER 1. The suggestion in *British Industrial Plastics Ltd v Ferguson* [1938] 4 All ER 504, CA at 510 per Slesser LJ that a desire not to break the law might amount to justification must be doubtful.

[140] *Posluns v Toronto Stock Exchange* (1964) 46 DLR (2d) 210 at 270, per Gale J. Cf *Pete's Towing Services Ltd v NIUW* [1970] NZLR 32 at 51 per Speight J.

(iv) CAUSING LOSS BY UNLAWFUL MEANS

(a) The cause of action

According to *OBG Ltd v Allan* there are two elements to this tort. The first is that the defendant must commit acts intending to cause loss to the claimant. As with the tort of inducement, this means actual intervention (the loss being the defendant's end or means) and mere foresight of possible loss is not sufficient. The second element is that the defendant must use 'unlawful means'. As this phrase is capable of covering a multitude of sins, Lord Hoffmann was keen to give a definition capable of keeping the tort within reasonable bounds.[141] He did so by limiting it to acts unlawful in the sense of impinging directly on the relationship between claimant and defendant:

> Unlawful means therefore consists of acts intended to cause loss to the claimant by interfering with the freedom of a third party in a way which is unlawful as against that third party and which is intended to cause loss to the claimant. It does not in my opinion include acts which may be unlawful against a third party, but which do not affect his freedom to deal with the claimant.[142]

This should prevent the tort from being committed through some random illegality, unconnected with the dispute.

(b) The immunity

As stated in the introduction, one of the problems in this whole area has been in trying to keep the statutory immunities up to date with the twists and turns in the case law on liabilities. As this particular tort was only put into its present form in *OBG Ltd v Allan* in 2007 it is hardly surprising that the immunities do not cover it specifically by name. However, the immunities have been extended to deal with possible liabilities of a fairly wide nature and it is likely that they will in fact cover the situations likely to arise under the tort,[143] for three reasons. The first is that where industrial action constitutes an 'interference' with contract, this does not now qualify as an independent tort but may come within the new tort, and in 1976 the immunity in (what is now) the Trade Union and Labour Relations (Consolidation) Act 1992, section 219(1)(a) extended the protection to cover not just inducing another person to break a contract, but also any act which 'interferes or induces another person to interfere with its performance'. The second is similar—there may now be no separate tort of 'intimidation'

---

[141] As he put it, not to permit it to extend beyond the original ambit envisaged for it in the foundation cases of *Allen v Flood* [1898] AC 1, HL and *Quinn v Leathem* [1901] AC 495, HL.

[142] At para [51]. This is the one point on which Lords Hoffmann and Nicholls part company—Lord Nicholls would have allowed 'unlawful means' to cover quite simply 'all acts which the defendant is not permitted to do, whether by the civil law or the criminal law' (para [162]). However, Lord Hoffmann's narrower view was approved by Lords Walker and Brown and Lady Hale.

[143] One of the problems of *OBG* concerning commercial disputes rather than industrial ones is that the House of Lords did not have to consider this question of immunity.

but intimidatory conduct could come within the new tort, in which case it would be covered by section 219(1)(b) which was originally enacted in 1965 to deal with the invention of intimidation in *Rookes v Barnard*[144] and which covers an act that 'consists in his threatening that a contract ... will be broken or its performance interfered with, or that [the defendant] will induce another person to break a contract or interfere with its performance'. The third reason is that it has always been assumed that an *indirect* immunity could operate here;[145] if in an industrial dispute a trade union inflicts loss on the claimant by inducing its members to take strike action (eg with a supplier of the claimant), it is likely that that strike call will itself be immune under section 219(1)(a) and so will not constitute the 'unlawful means' necessary for the modern tort. Thus hopefully the effect of the realignment of this tort in *OBG* should *not* be to give rise to yet another judicial bypassing of the statutory immunities, though in this tortious area nothing is ever completely certain.[146]

(v) OUTFLANKING THE IMMUNITIES—FOUR FURTHER POSSIBILITIES

It is clear from the above that much of the stimulus for the development of the economic torts during the twentieth century came from attempts to outflank the statutory immunities. This could be seen in the now disapproved evolution of a 'genus' tort of interference with trade or business and the exhumation of the tort of intimidation but there are four further possibilities, considered here in ascending order of importance. The first concerns the importation into industrial disputes of the contractual doctrine of 'economic duress', ie that if a party to a contract is obliged to enter into it, or to agree to certain terms, because of illegitimate coercion by the other party, he may claim that the contract is voidable for duress and so claim repayment of anything paid under it.[147] In *Universe Tankships Inc of Monrovia v International Transport Workers' Federation*[148] the International Transport Workers' Federation (ITWF), as part of its campaign against ships under flags of convenience, caused the blacking of the claimants' ship until certain demands were met, including the payment of $6,480 to a seamen's welfare fund. Once the ship was released, the claimants sought the return of this amount on the basis that it had been paid under duress. The House of Lords allowed recovery by a

---

[144] See n 12.

[145] Especially where the economic loss being caused is to the claimant's business generally, not via any specific contact.

[146] See Simpson (2007) 36 ILJ at 476–9.

[147] Originally duress in contract law only covered threats of violence, but was widened to economic duress; see *North Ocean Shipping Co Ltd v Hyundai Construction Co Ltd* [1979] QB 705, [1978] 3 All ER 1170; *Pao On v Lau Yiu Long* [1980] AC 614, [1979] 3 All ER 65, PC; *Syros Shipping Co SA v Elaghill Trading Co* [1981] 3 All ER 189; *B & S Contracts and Design Ltd v Victor Green Publications Ltd* [1984] ICR 419, CA; *CTN Cash and Carry Ltd v Gallagher Ltd* [1994] 4 All ER 714, CA.

[148] [1982] 2 All ER 67, [1982] ICR 262, HL, noted (1982) 45 MLR 556; see Sterling 'Actions for Duress, Seafarers and Industrial Disputes' (1982) 11 ILJ 156.

majority of three to two. The first point to note about this application of the doctrine of duress is that it does *not* constitute a new head of tort; rather, it gives rise to an action for restitution of moneys paid over, and given that such arrangements between unions and employers are not common, it is likely that in practice the occasions when such a claim will be brought will be few.[149] However, if a claim is brought, it raises an exceptionally difficult point—when does pressure by a union on an employer overstep the line between hard bargaining on the one hand and illegitimate coercion (giving rise to economic duress) on the other? The answer given by the House of Lords has at least the attribute of neatness—although the doctrine of duress does not give rise to an action in tort, so that the immunities in the Trade Union and Labour Relations (Consolidation) Act 1992, section 219 are not directly applicable, those immunities can be used *indirectly* to draw the line, the reasoning being that it would be contrary to Parliament's intention to hold voidable for duress actions which, had a suit been pleaded in tort, would have been covered by the statutory immunities. Thus, if an action would have been immune from a suit in tort, it will probably not be held to amount to economic duress. The majority went on to hold that the actions of the ITWF in fact would not have come within the statutory immunity, and so the claimants could recover the money paid over by them.

The second possible development is the extension of the tort of inducement of breach of contract to other situations which involve the violation of legal rights, and in particular to inducement of breach of statutory duty.[150] The basis for the new tort was laid by the Court of Appeal in *Meade v London Borough of Haringey*[151] a case concerning the legality (under the Education Act 1944) of a decision by a local authority to close its schools because of strike action by caretakers and ancillary staff. In the course of their judgments, both Lord Denning MR and Eveleigh LJ stated obiter that it was tortious for the union to induce the local authority to be in breach of its statutory duty, and moreover that such tortious action would not be covered by the statutory immunities. The existence of the tort was subsequently confirmed by the Court of Appeal in *Associated British Ports v TGWU*,[152] but with the important caveat that the statutory duty in question must be independently actionable.[153] The tort of inducement of breach of statutory duty could be of particular significance in the public sector, where

---

[149] Although cf *Dimskal Shipping Co SA v International Transport Workers' Federation, The Evia Luck (No 2)* [1992] ICR 37, [1992] IRLR 78, HL.

[150] See also *Prudential Assurance Co Ltd v Lorenz* (1971) 11 KIR 78 (inducement of breach of equitable obligation).

[151] [1979] 2 All ER 1016, [1979] ICR 494, CA. See also *Associated Newspapers Group Ltd v Wade* [1979] ICR 664, [1979] IRLR 201, CA and *Barretts & Baird (Wholesale) Ltd v IPCS* [1987] IRLR 3.

[152] *Associated British Ports v TGWU* [1989] 3 All ER 796, [1989] IRLR 305, CA; revsd on other grounds [1989] 3 All ER 822, [1989] IRLR 399, HL.

[153] This is a matter of construction of the statute; to be independently actionable the claimant will usually need to show that the statute was passed for the benefit of a class which includes him, or that he has suffered some special damage: see *Cutler v Wandsworth Stadium Ltd* [1949] AC 398, HL; *Lonrho Ltd v Shell Petroleum Co Ltd (No 2)* [1982] AC 173, [1981] 2 All ER 465, HL.

employers are more likely to be under a statutory duty to provide and maintain goods or services, not least because there is no statutory immunity covering it.

The third possible development is of more general application, and concerns the central question of what amounts to unlawful means for present purposes. As seen already, while there is no specific immunity for the tort of causing loss by unlawful means, in practice there may be an *indirect* immunity if the means adopted (for example inducing a breach of contract) are covered by an immunity and are therefore not unlawful.[154] An obvious way of outflanking this indirect immunity is by the development of types of unlawful means which are *not* themselves covered by an immunity. One such development was canvassed by Henry J in *Barretts & Baird (Wholesale) Ltd v IPCS*,[155] where fatstock officers staffing private abattoirs took industrial action in a dispute with their employers, the Meat and Livestock Commission. The abattoir owners brought proceedings for injunctions against the union and against an individual fatstock officer. As against the former, the case relied on inducement to breach of statutory duty (above), but against the latter the argument was that the officers had interfered with the claimant's business, the unlawful means being quite simply their own breaches of employment contracts with their employer. If such an action were accepted it would have the astonishing result that the union officials organizing a strike would be immune,[156] but the individual employees could be sued by anyone affected by their action. The problem here is that it has never been authoritatively decided whether or not simple breach of contract could be unlawful means for the economic torts.[157] Henry J was therefore driven to conclude that it was arguable that simple breach could constitute unlawful means.[158] In the event he avoided finding the fatstock officers individually liable, on the basis, first, that they lacked the necessary intention to injure the claimant[159] and, secondly, that the remedy sought could not be granted against the individual employee defendant because of the statutory restrictions on the enforcement of contracts of employment against employees.[160] The result of the case therefore did not cause too much consternation, but the possibility of such an argument

[154] See heading 3(iv), p 715.

[155] [1987] IRLR 3, noted Simpson (1987) 50 MLR 506, Napier (1987) 46 CLJ 222, Benedictus (1987) 16 ILJ 191.

[156] Assuming there had been a ballot and that it remained primary action, the officials would have the protection of s 219(1) covering their inducement of the breaches of contract by the employees; that inducement would therefore not be actionable per se, nor would it constitute unlawful means, eg for the tort of causing loss on their part.

[157] Breach of contract had been held to be unlawful means for the purposes of the (now doubtful) tort of intimidation in *Rookes v Barnard* [1964] AC 1129, [1964] 1 All ER 367, HL, but it was not decided there that the same applied to the other economic torts, where the effect could be more drastic; s 13(3)(b) of the Trade Union and Labour Relations Act 1974 used to state 'for the avoidance of doubt' that such a breach in contemplation or furtherance of a trade dispute was not to be treated as unlawful means, but that subsection was repealed by the Employment Act 1980.

[158] In so deciding (at p 9) the judge cites Wedderburn *The Worker and the Law* (3rd edn, 1986) at 637 where the author pointed out this danger of the repeal of s 13(3)(b).

[159] This aspect was approved by Lord Hoffmann in *OBG Ltd v Allan*, see n 29.

[160] Now contained in the Trade Union and Labour Relations (Consolidation) Act 1992, s 236.

succeeding in the future cannot be discounted.[161] Another form of unlawful means which is of potentially great practical significance is the tort of inducement of breach of statutory duty. As seen above, this tort may provide a cause of action in its own right, but there its impact is restricted by the requirement that the breach of statutory duty be independently actionable at the suit of the claimant. However, in *Associated British Ports v TGWU*,[162] a majority of the Court of Appeal considered that it was 'strongly arguable' that a breach of statutory duty could be relied upon as unlawful means even if not actionable at the suit of the claimant.

Finally and arguably most importantly in the long term, a question has arisen as to the possible relevance of EC law in this area. Although it does not cover industrial disputes directly, one problem might be the interaction between such disputes and the law on freedom of establishment (Article 43) and freedom to provide services across the union (Article 49). These are cornerstones of the single market, but of course produce tensions where a firm from a lower income member state gets work in a higher income member state and wishes to use its own nationals, on wages significantly lower than those payable to nationals of the host state. What to the employer is bona fide competition within the Union is to the national trade union unacceptable undercutting on wage rates. The Posted Worker Directive[163] was meant to counter such 'dumping' by requiring the foreign firm to observe the terms and conditions of the host state, but that has always been arguable.[164] The problem is that the Directive only enforces the home state's *minimum* wage, or collective bargaining rates *if* they are entrenched across the whole industry in question by law or practice (as can be the case in Germany, but not in many other member states including the UK).

This weakness has been exposed in three ECJ cases. In *ITWF v Viking Line ABP*[165] it was held that action by a trade union to prevent a shipping firm in Finland reflagging their ferry in Estonia in order to use lower cost Estonian crew broke Article 43 and was illegal unless the union could objectively justify it. The case was referred back to the Court of Appeal but then settled; however, there are passages in the ECJ's judgment that suggest that there may *not* have been objective justification here. In *Laval Ltd v Svenska Byggadsarbetareforbundet*[166] (decided by the same bench a week later) the ECJ went further and actually held that there was *no* justification for action by a Swedish trade union to stop a Latvian building company using (on contract in Sweden) Latvian

---

[161] It has been referred to as 'a time-bomb in our labour law': Davies and Freedland *Labour Law Texts and Materials* (2nd edn, 1984) 755. The restriction on the enforcement of contracts of employment would not, of course, apply to an action for damages (actual or threatened) against employees taking industrial action.

[162] [1989] 3 All ER 796, [1989] IRLR 305, CA (reversed on other grounds, [1989] 3 All ER 822, [1989] IRLR 399, HL).

[163] Directive 96/7/EC.

[164] One cynical view was that it was actually a piece of German protectionism to defeat EU competition in its then booming construction industry; see 'Auf Wiedersehn, Pet' passim.

[165] C-438/05 [2008] IRLR 143, ECJ. On this case and *Laval* n 166, see Davies 'One Step forward, Two Steps back?' (2008) 37 ILJ 125.

[166] C-341/05 [2008] IRLR 160, ECJ.

labour at rates lower than the negotiated rates in Sweden. This action contravened Article 49 on services and was not rescued by the Posted Worker Directive because there was no minimum wage contravention and Swedish collective agreements were not legally entrenched to apply across the whole industry. In the third case, *Ruffert v Land Niedersachsen*[167] (concerning a dispute between an employer and the state, rather than a trade union, but the issue is the same) a German local authority had given a contract on the basis that the contractor would observe pay rates set out in a local collective agreement (which crucially had *not* been declared of universal application under the German system). When work was subcontracted to a Polish firm paying lower rates to its nationals, the local authority terminated the contract and sought to fine the employer. This was held to be unlawful by the ECJ. Once again, it was stressed that the Posted Worker Directive only protects the *minimum* rates and insistence on actual rates could not be objectively justified.

The results of these cases are worrying for trade unions seeking to protect their national members from outside competition,[168] because in most cases the union will not simply be wanting to enforce the UK national minimum wage, but the *going* rate for the job. This is what the ECJ says will contravene EC law, with apparently little chance of justification on the grounds of union policy. Moreover, the third case is a threat to any local or other authority wanting to use what has in the past in the UK been called 'contract compliance' in order to enforce 'fair' wages.

The fact that these major areas of uncertainty exist (along with the other unresolved questions relating to the nature and extent of the established economic torts, referred to earlier), and are at least capable of development, shows how deeply unsatisfactory and unpredictable our current law on industrial action is, even after the welcome reassessment of the tortious base in *OBG Ltd v Allan*.

(vi) THE GOLDEN FORMULA

For the statutory immunities to apply, the industrial action in question must be within the 'golden formula', ie it must be 'in contemplation or furtherance of a trade dispute'; if it falls outside that, the immunities will not apply, and, in most cases, it will be easy for the claimant employer to show the elements of one or more of the above torts (particularly since the disapproval of the 'strike notice' theory in *Simmons v Hoover Ltd*)[169] and on

---

[167] C-346/06 [2008] IRLR 467, ECJ. In *EC Commissioner v Luxembourg* C-319/06 [2009] IRLR 388, ECJ an attempt at *state* level to 'gold plate' the Posted Worker Directive to require observance by foreign employers of going rates within the country was struck down by the ECJ in enforcement provisions, as an unjustified interference with the freedom to provide services.

[168] Particularly in times of recession when apparently common-sense policies such as 'British jobs for British workers' (a natural for a political soundbite) can in fact be potentially illegal under EC law. In *EFTA Surveillance Authority v Iceland* E-12/10 [2011] IRLR 773, a provision in Icelandic law (purporting to transpose the Posted Workers Directive) which put more onerous employment conditions on non-Icelandic firms than on domestic ones, in order to protect domestic labour, was struck down as contrary to free market principles.

[169] [1977] ICR 61, [1976] IRLR 266, EAT.

that basis claim an interim injunction to stop the industrial action. Thus, a crucial first stage in an employer's action for an injunction is to consider whether the golden formula applies—if it does not, the employer will probably be successful; if it does, the immunities apply, unless they are disapplied (to use the extremely inelegant word commonly adopted in this context) by anything in sections 222–234A of the Trade Union and Labour Relations (Consolidation) Act 1992. Moreover, as will be seen later, the exemption from liability given to pickets by section 220 is also reliant upon the formula.

To be within the protection of the golden formula, two matters must be shown— there must be a 'trade dispute', and the acts in question must be 'in contemplation or furtherance' of it.

(a) Is there a trade dispute?

The statutory definition of a trade dispute is contained in section 244 of the Trade Union and Labour Relations (Consolidation) Act 1992.[170] It is defined as a dispute between 'workers[171] and their employer' which relates 'wholly or mainly to' one or more of the following:[172]

(a) terms and conditions of employment,[173] or the physical conditions in which any workers are required to work;

(b) engagement or non-engagement, or termination or suspension of employment, or the duties of employment,[174] of one or more workers;

---

[170] For the history of the definition, and a clear and detailed investigation of its pre-1982 form, see Simpson '"Trade Dispute" and "Industrial Dispute" in British Labour Law' (1977) 40 MLR 16. On the alterations in the Employment Act 1982, see Simpson 'A Not So Golden Formula' (1983) 46 MLR 463 and Ewing 'Another Step in the "Right" Direction' (1982) 11 ILJ 209. The wider pre-1982 definition is retained by s 218 for the purposes of Part IV of the 1992 Act, in particular for defining the powers of ACAS and Courts of Inquiry. Given that in social security law the trade dispute disqualification for the jobseeker's allowance uses yet another definition (taken from the Trade Disputes Act 1906), we are now graced (or cursed?) with three definitions of trade dispute in our employment and social security laws.

[171] 'Worker' is defined in s 296 and includes an independent contractor, provided he undertakes to perform work or services personally (other than in a professional capacity); *Broadbent v Crisp* [1974] ICR 248; cf *Writers' Guild of Great Britain v BBC* [1974] ICR 234.

[172] A dispute which relates to matters occurring outside the UK qualifies as a trade dispute only if those taking action within the UK are likely to be affected by the outcome of the dispute in relation to one or more of the matters specified in s 244(1)(a)–(g): s 244(3).

[173] The use of the composite expression 'terms and conditions of employment' shows that the phrase was intended to be given a broad meaning, as covering both the rules of employment and the application of those rules: *P v National Association of Schoolmasters/Union of Women Teachers* [2003] IRLR 307, [2003] 1 All ER 993, per Lord Hoffmann; there must, however, be some limitation of it to terms which regulate the relationship between employer and employee, excluding any matters extraneous to that relationship: *Universe Tankships Inc of Monrovia v International Transport Workers' Federation* [1982] 2 All ER 67, [1982] ICR 262, HL.

[174] A trade dispute arising out of fears for jobs in a period of high unemployment (involving, for example, a demand that what work there is should be done by existing employees, not by outside contractors) was said by Lord Diplock in *Hadmor Productions Ltd v Hamilton* [1982] 1 All ER 1042, [1982] ICR 114, HL to be a classic instance of a dispute covered by head (b); the Court of Appeal had held that there was no trade dispute in such a case.

(c) allocation of work or the duties of employment between workers or groups of workers;[175]

(d) matters of discipline;

(e) the membership or non-membership of a trade union on the part of a worker;[176]

(f) facilities for officials of trade unions; and

(g) machinery for negotiation or consultation, and other procedures, relating to any of the above matters, including recognition of a union by an employer or employer's association.[177]

It is further provided in section 244(4) that there can still be a 'dispute' even if the employer in fact submits to the union's demands, so that the initial making of the demands can still be considered as within the golden formula.[178]

'Trade dispute' is thus given a wide definition, capable of covering most disputes between employees and their employer about the job the employees are employed to do or the terms and conditions on which they are employed to do it, and therefore the actual definition will not normally be a significant legal restriction on a union's activities, provided it acts generally within an employment relations context. If, however, it goes outside that and engages in what, for want of a better word, might be called 'political' action, then arguably it might be outside a trade dispute. Thus, industrial action taken *purely* as a protest against government action might be of dubious legality.[179] However, the mere fact that there is a 'political' aspect will not remove a dispute from the statutory definition, so that anti-government action might still be included if there is a genuine trade aspect as, for example, where the government is a significant employer of the

---

[175] This covers demarcation disputes, but note that the employer must be a party to such a dispute for it to qualify under head (c) because of the general requirement that the dispute be between 'workers and their employer'; moreover that requirement means that head (c) only applies to the allocation of work between the employer's own workers—it does not apply to a dispute over reallocation of work from the employer's own workers to an outside company: *Dimbleby & Sons Ltd v NUJ* [1984] ICR 386, [1984] IRLR 161, HL.

[176] While the definition of trade dispute still includes disputes over non-membership, s 222 provides that the immunities will be withdrawn where industrial action is taken to enforce union membership; see under heading 4(iii), p 731.

[177] Recognition disputes also came within the original definition in the 1906 Act: *Beetham v Trinidad Cement Ltd* [1960] AC 132, [1960] 1 All ER 274, PC. However, the action must clearly be connected with the recognition issue, not just an aftermath: *J T Stratford & Son Ltd v Lindley* [1965] AC 269, [1964] 3 All ER 102, HL.

[178] Nullifying statements to the contrary in *Cory Lighterage Ltd v TGWU* [1973] ICR 339, [1973] IRLR 152, CA.

[179] *Associated Newspapers Group Ltd v Flynn* (1970) 10 KIR 17; in *National Sailors' and Firemen's Union v Reed* [1926] Ch 536, Astbury J held that the 1926 General Strike was illegal, sed quaere (see Goodhart (1927) 36 Yale LJ 464). In *Sherard v AUEW* [1973] ICR 421, [1973] IRLR 188, CA, at 433 and 189 respectively, Lord Denning MR stated as his opinion that a dispute between the TUC and the government (simpliciter) would not be trade dispute. See also *Express Newspapers v Keys* [1980] IRLR 247, and *University College London Hospitals NHS Trust v UNISON* [1999] IRLR 31.

union's members,[180] or where those members may be directly affected by government policies in question (for example on questions of nationalization or privatization of the industry concerned).[181] Until 1982 it was possible for industrial action to qualify as a trade dispute even if the action was taken for predominantly political or more widely social reasons, as long as there was some genuine connection with terms and conditions of employment or any of the other matters in (a) to (g). This was because the wording of the trade dispute definition at that time merely required that the dispute be 'connected with' one of the listed matters, and it seemed that the connection might be relatively slight. Only if the industrial action was wholly unconnected with any of the matters would it fall outside the statutory definition. So, for example, in *BBC v Hearn*[182] a threat to disrupt the transmission of a television signal to South Africa during the cup final because of the union's anti-apartheid policy was restrained by the Court of Appeal since it did not constitute a trade dispute; it had nothing to do with the terms and conditions of employment of the workers involved, and did not become a trade dispute merely because those workers were threatening to break their contracts; the union's argument that there should be read into the contracts of employment a term that employees would not be required to do anything to which they had a conscientious objection (thereby making it a trade dispute over terms and conditions) was not accepted. In contrast, Lord Diplock in *NWL Ltd v Nelson*[183] showed greater willingness to allow as a trade dispute a matter of basically a political nature, provided that it has some connection with terms and conditions of employment, and can be framed in such a way.

However, the Employment Act 1982 narrowed the trade dispute definition considerably by requiring that the dispute relate 'wholly or mainly to' one or more of the listed matters, rather than simply be 'connected with' them; this has made it far more difficult to alter the legal nature of a dispute by the way a demand is phrased, and its overall effect has been to throw the industrial/political distinction into much higher relief (rather than leaving it largely fudged, as was the case under the previous wording). The importance of this can clearly be seen in *Mercury Communications Ltd v Scott-Garner*.[184] The case concerned action taken by the union representing British Telecom workers to try to prevent the successful licensing of a private company by

---

[180] *Sherard v AUEW* [1973] ICR 421, [1973] IRLR 188, CA.

[181] *General Aviation Services (UK) Ltd v TGWU* [1974] ICR 35, [1973] IRLR 355. Section 244(2) provides that a dispute between workers and a government Minister who is not their employer will be treated as a trade dispute with their employer where the dispute cannot be settled without the minister's involvement or approval: see, eg, *Wandsworth London Borough Council v NASUWT* [1993] IRLR 344, CA.

[182] [1977] ICR 685, [1977] IRLR 273, CA, approved by Lord Hoffmann in *P v National Association of Schoolmasters/Association of Women Teachers* [2003] UKHL 8, [2003] 1 All ER 993.

[183] [1979] ICR 867, [1979] IRLR 478, HL, at 878 and 483, respectively. In *Universe Tankships Inc of Monrovia v International Transport Workers' Federation* [1982] ICR 262, [1982] IRLR 200, HL, his Lordship stressed that there must still be some connection with one of the enumerated matters, even if it was not the predominant purpose of the defendant; Lord Cross was clearly against the idea of being able to turn a dispute into a trade dispute by insisting that the employer inserted certain terms into contracts of employment.

[184] [1984] ICR 74, [1983] IRLR 494, CA; the judge at first instance had held that the dispute was mainly related to the BT workers' fears of redundancies, and had refused to grant the injunction. The decision of the

BT (a process referred to as 'liberalization'). The company brought proceedings for an injunction to restrain this action. The union pleaded the immunity, on the basis that this was a trade dispute concerning possible job losses. However, the Court of Appeal granted the injunction on the basis that the facts did not show that fear of job losses was the major factor behind the action (particularly as there was in existence a job security agreement with BT), and that on the facts the dispute related wholly or mainly to the union's political objection to liberalization, which was seen as a precursor to the entire privatization of BT (that in the event followed). The case is a good illustration of the difficulties faced by the courts in attempting to determine what a particular dispute is *mainly* about, in circumstances where there are a range of factors and issues involved which are inextricably linked. In practice much is likely to turn upon the way in which the union presents the dispute to its members and to the public at large. In *Wandsworth London Borough Council v NASUWT*,[185] the Court of Appeal had to decide whether industrial action by teachers which included a boycott of testing under the national curriculum was a 'trade dispute' and therefore covered by the statutory immunities. The local authority argued that the main impetus for the dispute was the objection of the union and its members to the principle of testing, so that it was not wholly or mainly related to terms and conditions, etc, but on the facts the Court of Appeal accepted the union's argument that the dispute related mainly to the increased workload on teachers in conducting the tests (a point stressed by union leaders at every turn and also emphasized in the wording of the strike ballot), and held that there was in fact a trade dispute. The court attached 'considerable importance' to the fact that the wording of the question posed in the ballot paper referred to 'protest against the excessive workload and unreasonable imposition made upon teachers' as a result of the new national curriculum assessment and testing requirements.

The second major change to the trade dispute definition by the Employment Act 1982 was to require that the dispute be between 'workers and *their* employer'. Previously it was possible to have a trade dispute between workers and employers (whether or not their own employer), or workers and workers,[186] and there was deemed to be a dispute involving workers if a union was a party to the dispute, even if the actual workers were not.[187] The definition was thus extremely wide on the question of parties. Since

---

Court of Appeal to grant it was seen as a significant factor in the moves towards privatization, which could have been at risk if the union had lawfully managed to frustrate the process of liberalization.

[185] [1994] ICR 81, [1993] IRLR 344, CA. See also *University College London Hospitals NHS Trust v UNISON* [1999] IRLR 31, CA, and *Westminster City Council v UNISON* [2001] EWCA Civ 443, [2001] ICR 1046.

[186] Thus a demarcation dispute between two unions which did not involve the employer directly could be a trade dispute. Presumably such a dispute could still comply if one or both of the unions were to make demands on the employer relating to the performance of the work in question.

[187] This was particularly important in a case where it was the union itself which had a grievance against the employer even if it did not have the backing (or, indeed, the membership) of his employees (as in the case of the ITWF in its campaign against shipowners who use flags of convenience; see *Star Sea Transport Corpn of Monrovia v Slater* [1978] IRLR 507, CA and *NWL Ltd v Nelson* [1979] ICR 867, [1979] IRLR 478, HL). The changes in the 1982 Act were particularly significant in that sort of case.

1982, however, the wording of the definition has required the existence of a dispute 'between workers and their employer', ie a dispute between the employer and workers currently employed by him.[188] The aim of these changes was to reinforce the need for there to be, somewhere along the line, a genuine dispute between an employer and his employees.[189] One unfortunate consequence of the revised wording has been to throw into doubt the legality of industrial action aimed at securing the terms and conditions of employees following a business transfer. In *University College London Hospitals NHS Trust v UNISON*,[190] the union threatened industrial action after the Trust refused to give an undertaking that the terms and conditions of staff to be transferred to a new consortium which was to build and run a private finance initiative hospital would be maintained for a period of 30 years at an equivalent level to Trust employees who were not transferred. The Court of Appeal issued an injunction restraining the action, on the grounds that the trade dispute definition does not cover a dispute about the terms and conditions of employees of an as yet unidentified employer who have never been employed by the employer who is being threatened with industrial action. In so far as the decision relates to the as yet unidentified *future* employees of an as yet unidentified employer, it is perhaps unexceptionable, but the Court of Appeal's suggestion that the trade dispute definition does not include industrial action to protect the terms and conditions of *existing* employees after they are transferred to a new employer is arguably an undesirably narrow interpretation of the trade dispute definition.[191]

At first sight, the tightening up of the trade dispute definition to disputes between an employer and his employees might seem to outlaw all secondary action, by rendering any action other than that taken against the employer in dispute outside the definition of a trade dispute. However, this is not the case, for section 244 only defines when a trade dispute is in existence; the legality of any action away from the centre of that dispute will depend upon whether it is 'in contemplation or furtherance' of that initial dispute, and whether it is lawful under other statutory provisions, particularly the restrictions on secondary action in section 224. So, for example, if employees of employer A take action purely in support of employees of employer B who are in dispute with their own employer, the only trade dispute is that with B, but the actions of

---

[188] Trade Union and Labour Relations (Consolidation) Act 1992, s 244(5). A dispute between workers and their *former* employer will qualify as a trade dispute where their employment was terminated in connection with the dispute or the termination of employment was one of the factors which gave rise to the dispute: s 244(5).

[189] The protection does not extend to disputes with an associated employer (eg another company in the corporate group), even where that employer is in reality making the decisions which are at the heart of the dispute. The effect of this limitation can be seen from *Dimbleby & Sons Ltd v NUJ* [1984] ICR 386, [1984] IRLR 161.

[190] [1999] IRLR 31, CA. See also *UNISON v United Kingdom* [2002] IRLR 497, ECtHR, discussed at p 656 above, where the ECtHR rejected the union's claim that the Court of Appeal's interpretation was an unjustified restriction on the right to freedom of assembly and association in Art 11 of the European Convention on Human Rights.

[191] A dispute over whether a proposed transfer should go ahead would clearly fall within the definition, as the identity of the employer is a term of the contract: see, eg, *Westminster City Council v UNISON* [2001] EWCA Civ 443, [2001] ICR 1046.

A's employees may well be in contemplation or furtherance of that dispute (see next heading (b)), and therefore technically within the golden formula; however, their action is likely to fall foul of the restrictions on secondary action in section 224, and will therefore be unprotected. The significance of the restricted trade dispute definition is that section 224 cannot be sidestepped by arguing that a fresh trade dispute has been created whenever and wherever industrial action is taken in support of the original dispute.[192]

(b) Is the action 'in contemplation or furtherance'? Swings and roundabouts

It is not enough for there to be a trade dispute; to be within the golden formula, the action actually taken must be 'in contemplation or furtherance' of it. This phrase is a term of art, well known in employment law, but at one crucially important time in the development of our modern law it was the subject of a major division of opinion between the Court of Appeal and the House of Lords as to its proper construction. Two preliminary points should be noted. First, it does *not* just mean 'connected with'; it has a more limited meaning than that. Second, it incorporates a time element, so that the trade dispute must either be about to or likely to happen ('contemplation'), or it must already be in existence ('furtherance'); thus, action could be too far in advance of any possible dispute to be in contemplation of it,[193] and action taken after the conclusion of the dispute (for example to 'punish' certain participants in it or to regain prestige for the union) might be too late to be considered in furtherance of it.[194] In *Conway v Wade*,[195] Lord Shaw said:

> The contemplation of such a dispute must be the contemplation of something impending or likely to occur and ... [it does] not cover the case of coercive interference in which the intervener may have in his own mind that if he does not get his own way he will thereupon take ways and means to bring a trade dispute into existence ... With regard to the term 'furtherance' of a trade dispute, I think that must apply to a trade dispute in existence and that the act done must be in the course of it and for the purpose of promoting the interests of either party or both parties to it.

Given that the timing was right and there was arguably a dispute in existence about industrial matters, it was thought at one time that the immunities were so widely drafted (especially after 1976) and the golden formula so widely construed that it was almost impossible for an employer to bring legal proceedings to stop industrial action. However, in a series of cases in the late 1970s (and particularly through the infamous

---

[192] This is confirmed by s 224(4), which provides that an employer shall not be treated as party to a dispute between another employer and workers of that employer, and where more than one employer is in dispute with his workers, the dispute between each employer and his workers shall be treated as a separate dispute.

[193] *Bents Brewery Co Ltd v Hogan* [1945] 2 All ER 570.

[194] *J T Stratford & Son Ltd v Lindley* [1965] AC 269, [1964] 3 All ER 102, HL; *Stewart v AUEW* [1973] ICR 128, [1973] IRLR 57, NIRC.

[195] [1909] AC 506, HL at 522. The case remains good law on this point.

'winter of discontent' preceding the 1979 election)[196] the Court of Appeal sought to alter that (and, in so doing, alter the bounds of permissible union activity) by looking anew at the phrase 'in contemplation or furtherance of a trade dispute' and establishing three requirements for that phrase to apply to industrial action. These were that: (1) the action must be taken for the 'proper motive' of pursuing a legitimate trade object, not for some extraneous motive (such as, for example, a campaign against flags of convenience by a seamen's union); (2) the action must not be too 'remote' from the centre of the dispute; (3) the action must be capable of furthering the trade objectives of one party to the dispute (the 'objective test').

Had they been accepted by the House of Lords, these three requirements, taken together, would have substantially narrowed the meaning of the phrase 'in contemplation or furtherance of a trade dispute', and enabled the judges to take a more active role in deciding what was and what was not within the golden formula. However, the Court of Appeal's innovations were very quickly set at nought when appeals were taken to the House of Lords, and all three requirements were disapproved,[197] the House of Lords confirming in no uncertain terms that the question whether a person acts in contemplation or furtherance of a trade dispute is a subjective one which must be decided in the light of the intentions and beliefs of the actors; if a person has a genuine and honest belief that his actions will further the interests of one party to the dispute, the fact that those actions, considered objectively, are not reasonably capable of furthering the dispute will be relevant only in so far as it casts doubt on the genuineness of that person's subjective belief. In the words of Lord Scarman in *Express Newspapers Ltd v McShane*:

> It follows therefore that, once it is shown that a trade dispute exists, the person who acts, but not the court, is the judge of whether his acts will further the dispute. If he is acting honestly, Parliament leaves to him the choice of what to do. I confess that I am relieved to find that this is the law. It would be a strange and embarrassing task for a judge to be called upon to review the tactics of a party to a trade dispute and to determine whether in the view of the court the tactic employed was likely to further or advance that party's side of the dispute … It would need very clear statutory language to persuade me that Parliament intended to allow the courts to act as some sort of backseat driver in trade disputes.[198]

The result of these three House of Lords decisions was thus to negative completely the developments brought about by the activism of the Court of Appeal, and to establish clearly a subjective and pro-union interpretation of the phrase 'in contemplation or furtherance' of a trade dispute. That interpretation is still valid, and consequently this phrase is no longer a major limitation on the immunities; theoretically, it remains a

---

[196] *Beaverbrook Newspapers Ltd v Keys* [1978] ICR 582, [1978] IRLR 34, CA; *Star Sea Transport Corpn of Monrovia v Slater, The Camilla M* [1978] IRLR 507, CA; *Associated Newspapers Group Ltd v Wade* [1979] ICR 664, [1979] IRLR 201, CA; *Express Newspapers Ltd v McShane* [1979] ICR 210, [1979] IRLR 79, CA.

[197] *NWL Ltd v Nelson* [1979] ICR 867, [1979] IRLR 478, HL (disapproving the 'proper motive' requirement); *Express Newspapers Ltd v McShane* [1980] ICR 42, [1980] IRLR 35, HL (disapproving the objective test); *Duport Steels Ltd v Sirs* [1980] ICR 161, [1980] IRLR 116, HL (disapproving the 'remoteness' test).

[198] [1980] ICR 42 at 64, [1980] IRLR 35 at 78.

stage in an action where it has to be established whether the immunities apply, but it is not normally an important hurdle for the defendant union or union official, except possibly in a rare case where the acts complained of bore no genuine relationship to a dispute whatsoever[199] or where there was no relationship in time between the acts and an existing dispute.[200]

The developments in the Court of Appeal had, however, been very much in line with the political approach to industrial disputes of the incoming Conservative government in 1979, and not surprisingly the re-establishment and strengthening of the previous law by the House of Lords was not to the government's liking. The government's response was to introduce into the 1980 Employment Bill a complicated provision (the notorious section 17, discussed later), which sought to reinstate much the same position as had been reached by the Court of Appeal, using much the same devices—in effect a statutory 'remoteness' test. However, crucially that section operated by imposing *additional* requirements, not by amending the phrase 'in contemplation or furtherance', which remains as the House of Lords left it. Ironically, section 17 was itself repealed by the Employment Act 1990 and replaced with an even narrower provision[201] which takes the restrictions on secondary industrial action considerably further than the Court of Appeal had proposed in those controversial cases a decade earlier.

4 RESTRICTIONS ON THE STATUTORY IMMUNITIES[202]

Even if industrial action passes the tests considered so far and thereby qualifies for protection under one of the statutory immunities, the final stage[203] in this involved progression is that it may still be rendered illegal and restrainable if it falls within one of the categories of industrial action from which the immunities have been removed by the legislation introduced since 1980. The picture is a particularly complicated one, as there are now no fewer than seven separate circumstances where the immunities will be withdrawn; in some cases this will be on the grounds of the *scope* of the industrial action, as in the case of unlawful secondary action (section 224) and (in part at least) unlawful picketing (section 220(3)); in others it will be because the industrial

---

[199] For example, where a defendant acted purely maliciously; *Express Newspapers Ltd v McShane* did retain a residual requirement that a defendant's purpose (whatever it might be in connection with the dispute) must be genuine and honest; if no reasonable person would have thought the acts in question capable of furthering the dispute, that may as a matter of evidence only call into question the defendant's bona fides.

[200] See the dictum from *Conway v Wade* [1909] AC 506, HL, which appears to be still good law.

[201] Now contained in s 224 of the Trade Union and Labour Relations (Consolidation) Act 1992.

[202] See Auerbach *Legislating for Conflict* (Oxford, 1992).

[203] This means the final stage in theory: in practice it may be obvious in a particular case that (1) the action is prima facie tortious and (2) the statutory immunities are applicable, in which case arguments may be almost entirely upon this 'final' point.

action is taken for what is declared to be an impermissible *reason*, for example action to enforce union membership (section 222), action taken because of the dismissal of unofficial strikers (section 223), and pressure to impose union recognition requirements (section 225); and, finally the immunities will be removed where the union has failed to comply with the mandatory *procedures* for official industrial action, for example where official action is taken without the support of a ballot (section 226), or the union fails to give the requisite strike notice to employers (section 234A). These are now considered.

(i) SECONDARY ACTION

Since 1980, the statutory immunities have been severely curtailed in the case of 'secondary action', ie action which is taken against an employer other than the employer in dispute. Such action might be against a supplier or customer of the employer in dispute, with the union instructing its members employed by that supplier or customer not to handle goods to or from the employer in dispute. Sometimes known as 'sympathy' or 'solidarity' action, it became a highly charged political issue in the 1970s, especially during the 'Winter of Discontent' of 1978–79 which preceded the election of Mrs Thatcher's first government. Legislation to restrict it was a major plank of that government's employment policy and reflected its belief that if trade unions must take industrial action at all, that action should be restricted to the employer in dispute, and not extended to other employers at one stage removed from the employer in dispute. Typically of that government's step-by-step approach to employment reform, the changes here came in two stages. The Employment Act 1980, section 17 first restricted secondary action to three defined circumstances, in particular to action against a 'first customer/first supplier', ie trying at least to *contain* widespread secondary action.[204]

The provisions in section 17 proved to be exceptionally difficult and controversial in practice.[205] Although operating only as a restriction, not a ban, the section soon began to have a significant effect and meant for example that a union had to be careful about the exact contractual relations involved if it were to avoid liability and that it had to be equally careful about the exact corporate organization of the employers concerned. Indeed, it was relatively easy for an employer to render union action unlawful under section 17 by the device of creating a 'buffer' organization (such as an associated employer) between itself and its customers or suppliers, thereby breaking the contractual nexus which was necessary for the first exception to operate.[206] On the other hand, there were those who argued that secondary action should *never* be protected, and that 'there is no good reason why employers who are not party to a dispute should be at risk

---

[204] See the ninth edition of this work at pp 738–40.

[205] The section was described by Lord Denning in the Court of Appeal in *Hadmor Productions Ltd v Hamilton* [1981] ICR 690, [1981] IRLR 210, as 'the most tortuous section I have ever come across'.

[206] This happened in the dispute between News International and the print unions: Ewing and Napier 'The Wapping Dispute and Labour Law' (1986) 45 CLJ 285.

of having industrial action organised against them'.[207] In the event the Conservative government took the latter view and so the second stage was the Employment Act 1990 which repealed section 17 and replaced it with the far more restrictive current provision (now contained in section 224 of the Trade Union and Labour Relations (Consolidation) Act 1992), which removes the statutory immunities in all cases of secondary action other than that occurring in the course of 'lawful picketing'.[208]

Section 224(2) provides that there is 'secondary action' in relation to a trade dispute when a person:

(a) induces another to break a contract of employment[209] or interferes or induces another to interfere with its performance; or

(b) threatens that a contract of employment under which he or another is employed will be broken or its performance interfered with, or that he will induce another to break a contract of employment or to interfere with its performance,

and the employer under the contract of employment is not the employer party to the dispute.

The gist of the definition is that to be secondary action the action must be directed against an employer *who is not a party to the trade dispute* and, moreover, must involve *interference with the contracts of employment* of that employer. Action which is in fact aimed at the employer in dispute, but which causes loss to that employer's customers or suppliers (ie 'primary action'[210] which has what might be termed secondary *effects*) is not 'secondary action' within the meaning of the section, and the legality of such action will be decided on ordinary principles.[211] One way of evading the restrictions on secondary action might have been for a union which was in dispute with employer A, but which wished to increase the pressure on employer A by taking action against employer B, to create a *fresh* trade dispute with B, and so avoid the potential application of the restrictions on secondary action. However, as seen already, the redrafting of the definition of 'trade dispute' by the Employment Act 1982 made this much more difficult, as the dispute with B would have to 'relate wholly or mainly' to the terms and conditions, etc, of the employees of B; simply acting in sympathy with, or promoting the cause of, A's employees would not be enough to generate a new trade dispute with B, so that the only dispute would be between the union and employer A, and any action against employer B would have to be judged according to section 224.[212]

---

[207] See the Green Paper 'Removing Barriers to Employment' (Cm 655, 1989), para 3.10; ironically, the complexity of s 17 was one of the justifications advanced in the Green Paper for its repeal (para 3.10).

[208] Defined in s 224(3) as peaceful picketing within the meaning of s 220 by a worker employed (or last employed) by the employer in dispute or by a trade union official lawfully attending the picket line; see heading 6(v), p 761.

[209] Section 224(6) adopts a wide definition of 'contract of employment' which includes self-employed and freelance workers, and others who personally do work or perform services for another.

[210] As defined in s 224(5).

[211] See, for example, *Hadmor Productions Ltd v Hamilton* [1982] ICR 114, [1982] IRLR 102, HL.

[212] Note also s 224(4), which provides that for the purposes of the section an employer shall not be treated as party to a dispute between another employer and workers of that employer.

The result of the tightening of the restrictions on secondary action in 1990 is that, even more than before, the scope of lawful industrial action may be determined by the corporate structure of the employer in dispute;[213] and the refusal of the courts to lift the corporate veil means that action taken against another employer, even one in the same group as (or otherwise closely related to) the employer in dispute will not be covered by the statutory immunities, unless it is possible to identify a separate trade dispute with that employer.

(ii) UNLAWFUL PICKETING

The second removal of the immunities occurs under section 219(3) of the Trade Union and Labour Relations (Consolidation) Act 1992, which removes all the section 219 immunities from acts done in the course of picketing falling outside the scope of the picketing immunity conferred by section 220.[214] Those whose attendance is not lawful within section 220 enjoy no immunity whatsoever for acts done in the course of picketing. As will be seen, many of the potential liabilities of pickets attract no immunity anyway (for example liability for trespass or nuisance), but picketing activity is also very likely to involve the commission of the torts of inducement of breach of contract and causing loss by unlawful means. Normally such liability would be covered by the immunities in section 219; however, one of the aims of the Employment Act 1980 was to curb secondary picketing and to allow employers affected by it to bring actions to stop it. Accordingly, section 219(3) limits the immunities (in relation to the tortious effects of the picketing) to attendance rendered lawful by the 'narrow but real' immunity in section 220, and section 220(1) confines that picketing immunity to attendance *at or near a picket's own place of work*. The combined effect is that any picketing activity other than at the picket's own place of work which has tortious effects is deprived of the immunities and may be restrained by injunction.

(iii) ACTION TO ENFORCE UNION MEMBERSHIP

In an attempt to ensure that the stringent rules on the closed shop were not out-flanked by practical measures designed to produce de facto requirements of union membership (in particular the use of 'contract compliance' by Labour-controlled local authorities to pressurize contractors into employing only union labour), the Conservative government introduced in the Employment Act 1982 a series of restrictions on union membership requirements in commercial contracts. Thus, any term or condition of a contract for the supply of goods or services which requires that some or all of the work to be done under that contract should be done only by members of

---

[213] Note the obvious implications here of the break-up of the public utilities and the creation of NHS trusts.

[214] See heading 6(v), p 761.

a trade union (or of a particular trade union) is rendered void,[215] and it is unlawful to refuse to deal with a supplier of goods or services (eg by the termination of a contract or the refusal to accept tenders or to enter a contract in the first place), on the grounds that the work under the contract would be done by non-union members.[216] Similar restrictions apply to contract terms requiring recognition of a trade union, and to a refusal to deal with a supplier of goods or services on the grounds of non-recognition of trade union.[217] The aim of these measures was to outlaw discrimination against employers employing non-union labour.[218] However, there remained the possibility that unions might seek to attain these goals by taking or threatening to take industrial action against unsympathetic employers, and so the 1982 Act[219] withdrew the statutory immunities from action aimed at inducing an employer to act in contravention of the above restrictions; thus, for example, not only could an excluded tenderer sue the employer for failure to permit him to tender because of his employment of non-union labour, but he could also sue a union that had induced the employer to exclude him.[220]

However, the relevant provisions then go considerably further, beyond issues of contract compliance, because section 222(1) of the Trade Union and Labour Relations (Consolidation) Act 1992 withdraws the immunities where the reason for the industrial action is the fact or belief that a particular employer (a) 'is employing, has employed or might employ a person' who is not a member of a trade union,[221] or (b) 'is failing, has failed or might fail to discriminate against such a person'. This sweeping provision was introduced by the Employment Act 1988 as part of the attack on the closed shop, but while the main target of the 1988 Act was to outlaw industrial action taken in defence of a closed shop, in fact it went a great deal further by removing the immunities from *all* industrial action taken for reasons of non-union membership, irrespective of whether there is a closed shop in operation. By so doing it could be said to have fundamentally altered the boundaries of a lawful trade dispute, by outlawing industrial action on a matter which had previously been regarded as a legitimate basis for a dispute.[222]

---

[215] Trade Union and Labour Relations (Consolidation) Act 1992, s 144. The restriction also applies to a requirement that the work be done by *non*-members of a trade union or of a particular trade union.

[216] Trade Union and Labour Relations (Consolidation) Act 1992, s 145. Failure to comply will be a breach of statutory duty, actionable at the suit of an aggrieved person.

[217] Trade Union and Labour Relations (Consolidation) Act 1992, ss 186 and 187; see heading 4(v), p 733.

[218] Lewis and Simpson 'Disorganising Industrial Relations' (1982) 11 ILJ 227; Evans and Lewis 'Labour Clauses: From Voluntarism to Regulation' (1988) 17 ILJ 209.

[219] See now the Trade Union and Labour Relations (Consolidation) Act 1992, s 222(3).

[220] The tort of causing loss by unlawful means might be particularly significant here.

[221] Whether the person in question is not a member of any trade union or of a particular trade union or of one of a number of particular trade unions: s 222(5).

[222] See the trade dispute definition in s 244, which still includes in subs (1)(e) a dispute relating to 'a worker's membership *or non-membership* of a trade union'. See heading 3(vi), p 720.

(iv) ACTION TAKEN BECAUSE OF THE DISMISSAL OF UNOFFICIAL STRIKERS

As one of a series of measures designed to discourage unofficial industrial action, the Employment Act 1990 removed the right of those taking part in such action to complain of unfair dismissal.[223] In a related move, section 223 of the Trade Union and Labour Relations (Consolidation) Act 1992 aims to discourage a collective response to such dismissals by removing the statutory immunities where the reason (or *one* of the reasons) for the industrial action is the fact or belief that an employer has dismissed an employee taking part in unofficial industrial action. This will be the case even where the action in question has the support of a ballot. The result is that any industrial action taken by a union in support of members dismissed for taking part in unofficial action will be unprotected by the statutory immunities.

(v) PRESSURE TO IMPOSE UNION RECOGNITION REQUIREMENTS

In parallel with the restrictions on union *membership* requirements discussed above, the Employment Act 1982 introduced a similar set of restrictions on union *recognition* requirements in contracts for the supply of goods or services, and made it unlawful to refuse to deal with a supplier of goods or services on the grounds that the supplier does not or is not likely to recognize, negotiate or consult with a trade union.[224] Section 225 of the Trade Union and Labour Relations (Consolidation) Act 1992 removes the statutory immunities from industrial action taken to impose a union recognition requirement, so that action aimed at inducing an employer to breach any of the above restrictions (eg, by inserting a term requiring union recognition in a commercial contract) will be unprotected. That section also withdraws the immunities from industrial action taken against employer A which interferes with the supply of goods or services between that employer and the supplier, employer B (or can reasonably be expected to do so), where the reason or one of the reasons for the action is the fact or belief that the employer B does not or might not recognize, negotiate with or consult with one or more trade unions. This is similar to the restriction in section 222 on industrial action to enforce union membership, but with the important difference that in that context the immunities are withdrawn from *all* action to enforce union membership, whereas here only action aimed at securing recognition, etc, by a *third party* employer is affected.

(vi) ACTION WITHOUT THE SUPPORT OF A BALLOT

Unquestionably the most impenetrable part of the labyrinth of legal requirements facing a union organizing industrial action is the need to hold a secret ballot before

---

[223] See heading 2(iii), p 698, and the Green Paper 'Unofficial Action and the Law' (Cm 821, 1989).
[224] See now the Trade Union and Labour Relations (Consolidation) Act 1992, ss 186 and 187.

taking official industrial action. Section 226 of the Trade Union and Labour Relations (Consolidation) Act 1992 provides[225] that the immunities in section 219 do not apply where an act is 'done by a trade union'[226] to induce a person to take part (or continue to take part) in industrial action,[227] unless the industrial action has the support of a ballot. Thus, the action could in all other respects be perfectly lawful (ie within the immunities and lawful under heads (i) to (v) above), but be rendered immediately unlawful if there is no ballot, or there is a ballot but it does not meet the detailed statutory requirements.[228] Where the immunities are removed the full weight of the common law liabilities will be restored, and so anyone suffering loss or damage through a tort committed by the union could sue, even ordinary customers or suppliers of the employer in dispute.[229]

The balloting provisions were originally introduced in the Trade Union Act 1984, and were further tightened up by the Employment Acts 1988 and 1990 and the Trade Union Reform and Employment Rights Act 1993. By the time of the 1997 general election it had become clear that the balloting requirements were of such complexity that they presented a major hurdle to a trade union attempting to organize lawful industrial action. The legislation specified (often in Byzantine detail) matters such as who was to be entitled to vote in the ballot, what was to be included on the ballot paper, how the ballot was to be conducted, and how the union was to instigate industrial action if the result of the ballot went the union's way. The complexity of the requirements was of particular significance because, as will be seen, the primary objective of a claimant in an industrial dispute case is usually to secure an injunction to stop the industrial action, and it had become clear that the balloting requirements provided ample scope for the employer's lawyers to argue that there had been some technical infringement which justified the granting of an injunction.[230] The incoming Labour government in 1997 signalled its intention to clarify and simplify the law on industrial action ballots, which it described as 'unnecessarily complex and rigid',[231] and the Employment Relations Act 1999 subsequently enacted a series of changes to the balloting provisions which

---

[225] Section 62 of the 1992 Act gives a trade union member the right to a secret ballot before being induced by the union to take official industrial action; the same ballot is capable of satisfying both sets of requirements: see Ch 9, heading 2(iii), p 658.

[226] Ie the immunities are removed only from *official* industrial action; see heading 7, p 766. One very important consequence of the extension of the statutory vicarious liability test in 1990 to cover all officials and committees is that *most* industrial action will now be prima facie 'official', and will therefore need the support of a valid ballot if the immunities are to apply.

[227] This is not defined for present purposes. For its interpretation in the context of dismissal of those taking part in industrial action, see heading 2(iii), p 698.

[228] The mandatory nature of the balloting requirements means that they still apply even if the union physically cannot comply with them; this may be the case with a purely federal union which has no individual members to ballot—according to *Shipping Co Uniform Inc v ITWF* [1985] ICR 245, [1985] IRLR 71 that is irrelevant and the immunities are still removed for failure to ballot.

[229] See for example *Falconer v ASLEF and NUR* [1986] IRLR 331. Since the withdrawal of immunity is so immediate and so total, the only defence a union will have might be that no tort was committed in the first place, an uphill battle at the best of times.

[230] The use of injunctions in employment cases is considered under heading 8, p 770.

[231] 'Fairness at Work' (Cm 3968, 1998) para 4.26.

appeared to relax the requirements in several important respects.[232] Of particular note was the introduction of an express provision allowing certain small[233] accidental failures in the conduct of the ballot to be disregarded,[234] although crucially this dispensation was restricted to certain types of failure (for example in relation to entitlement to vote and the supply of ballot papers). Another highly significant change related to the information which the union was required to give to the employer. Case law under the pre-1999 provisions had established that in certain circumstances a union might have to supply the employer with the names of those members whom it intended to call upon to take industrial action,[235] a controversial ruling which gave rise to understandable concern about the risk of threats and intimidation of the participants. The 1999 Act sought to avoid this possibility by making it clear that a union could not be forced to 'name names' in this way. However, far from of relaxing the requirements, the revised balloting provisions, as interpreted by the courts, appear to impose even greater burdens on unions than had previously been the case.[236] The government undertook a further consultation exercise,[237] resulting in Part 2 of the Employment Relations Act 2004 which made further clarificatory amendments to the balloting provisions, though once again without prejudicing the balloting *requirement* or affecting the draconian effects if the union still gets it wrong. Those effects continue to be controversial, but in *Metrobus v UNITE*[238] the stringent rules survived a direct challenge in the Court of Appeal that they made lawful strike action so difficult to organize that they contravened the right to associate in Article 11 of the European Convention on Human Rights.

The Code of Practice on Industrial Action Ballots and Notice to Employers[239] gives guidance as to 'desirable practices' in relation to industrial action ballots. Previous versions of the code were criticized for going beyond the obvious function of giving practical advice on staying within the law, and seeming to enact *additional* rules which did not appear in the legislation. Given that a code of practice is not primary legislation, this was argued to be back door law making; moreover, it was difficult to see how such additional rules would actually be enforceable. However, the 2005 Code

---

[232] Employment Relations Act 1999, Sch 3.

[233] Ie on a scale which is unlikely to affect the result of the ballot.

[234] Trade Union and Labour Relations (Consolidation) Act 1992, s 232B. The courts have always had a discretion not to grant an injunction where an infringement is very minor or technical (see eg *RJB Mining (UK) Ltd v National Union of Mineworkers)* [1997] IRLR 621; *British Railways Board v National Union of Railwaymen* [1989] ICR 678, [1989] IRLR 349, CA), but the introduction of an express provision made the position more certain.

[235] *Blackpool and Fylde College v NATFHE* [1994] ICR 648, [1994] IRLR 227, CA.

[236] See eg *London Underground Ltd v National Union of Rail Maritime and Transport Workers* [2001] ICR 647, [2001] IRLR 228, CA (noted by Wedderburn (2001) 30 ILJ 206).

[237] *Review of the Employment Relations Act 1999* (DTI, February 2003).

[238] [2009] EWCA Civ 829. The facts of the case well illustrate the complexity here—the union did not give the employer notice of the ballot result (required by the Trade Union and Labour Relations (Consolidation) Act 1992, s 213A) until two days later, when giving actual strike notice (required by s 234A); *held* that these are two separate requirements, the union had not given the s 231A notice 'as soon as reasonably practicable' and an injunction was granted to stop the strike.

[239] Revised in 2005 to reflect the changes made by the Employment Relations Act 2004.

is different. Although it starts with the usual (non-legally binding) exhortation to use ACAS before resorting to the threat or actuality of industrial action,[240] the rest of it is now much more in line with the traditional function of a code of putting flesh on to the legislative bones, without trying to add the odd limb indirectly. It covers preparations for a ballot (including providing notice to the employer, establishing the balloting constituency, balloting at more than one workplace and producing the voting forms), holding the ballot (including independent scrutiny and secrecy) and action to be taken after the ballot (including guidance on continuous and discontinuous industrial action).

(a) Entitlement to vote

Section 227(1) states that:

> Entitlement to vote in the ballot must be accorded equally to all the members of the trade union who it is reasonable at the time of the ballot for the union to believe will be induced by the union to take part ... in the industrial action in question, and to no others.[241]

The union must take great care when defining the balloting constituency, for if a member is not accorded entitlement to vote in the ballot and is subsequently induced to take part in the industrial action, the whole ballot may be invalidated and the immunity lost (subject to the statutory dispensation permitting small accidental failures to be disregarded).[242] There are two major problems with the interpretation of section 227(1), both of which have given rise to some exceptionally difficult case law: first, what is meant by 'entitlement to vote' and being 'accorded' entitlement to vote?; and, secondly, when will a union be regarded as having 'induced' a member to take part in the action? On the first issue, it is necessary to distinguish *entitlement* to vote from *opportunity* to vote. Section 227(1) is concerned with the former; it defines the class of members who must be accorded entitlement to vote—the balloting constituency—but it does not require that every member within that class must be given an opportunity of voting. This is of immense practical significance because, as has been judicially recognized, in the real world it will normally be impossible for a union to compile an accurate list of all its members within a particular balloting constituency:

> It is a fact of life that no trade union of any size can keep completely full and accurate records of the names and addresses of its ever-changing body of members, still less their current places of work, trade categories and pay grades.[243]

---

[240] Paragraph 6.

[241] Trade Union and Labour Relations (Consolidation) Act 1992, s 227(1). A failure to comply will not be condoned simply because a union's complex structure makes full compliance difficult: *RJB Mining (UK) Ltd v National Union of Mineworkers* [1997] IRLR 621, QBD. On the other hand, an attempt by an employer to restrict entitlement to vote only to those due to *work* on the days or shifts affected was rejected: *United Closures and Plastics Ltd* [2012] IRLR 29, Ct Sess (OH).

[242] Trade Union and Labour Relations (Consolidation) Act 1992, s 232B.

[243] *P v National Union of Schoolmasters/Union of Women Teachers* [2003] IRLR 307, [2003] 1 All ER 993, HL per Lord Walker at [65].

A union is required by law to maintain a register of members' names and addresses, and so far as is reasonably practicable to keep it accurate and up to date,[244] but the union's record-keeping duty does not extend to the occupations, grades or workplaces of its members, nor is there any duty on members to inform the union when they change jobs or move house. In practice, therefore, it is very likely that some members who are within the balloting constituency may not be given an opportunity to vote—for example because the union's records are inaccurate, or because mistakes occur during the ballot process (such as ballot papers getting lost in the post), or because members change jobs or indeed join or leave the union during the balloting process. Such failures do not necessarily mean that those members were not accorded entitlement to vote within the meaning of section 227(1). As the House of Lords has confirmed, whether or not such failures invalidate the ballot must be determined by applying the other provisions of the Act, including section 230(2) (which states that 'so far as is reasonably practicable, every person who is entitled to vote in the ballot must … be given a convenient opportunity to vote by post') and section 232B (which makes both sections 227(1) and 230(2) subject to a dispensation for small accidental errors): 'If failure to send a ballot paper to a person within the constituency falls within either of these exceptions, he is not by reason of that failure to be treated as having not been accorded entitlement to vote.'[245]

Even before the introduction of the dispensation for small accidental failures in 1999, it had been recognized that it would be unrealistic to expect a union to achieve total compliance by supplying a ballot paper to every single member of the balloting constituency. In one of the earliest cases on the strike ballot provisions, the Court of Appeal held that an inadvertent failure to give someone the opportunity of voting did not necessarily constitute an infringement of the balloting requirements,[246] and the House of Lords confirmed in *P v National Union of Schoolmasters/Union of Women Teachers*[247] that, despite the changes in the wording of the balloting provisions in 1999,[248] the position remains the same. That case involved a point which has caused difficulty ever since the balloting provisions were first introduced: what is the position of new employees who did not start working for the employer, or working within the balloting constituency, until after the ballot? And what of new members who did not join the union until after the ballot? Can they be induced to take part in the industrial action? In *Post Office v Union of Communication Workers*,[249] Lord Donaldson suggested obiter that, de minimis apart, any call for industrial action should be limited to

---

[244] Trade Union and Labour Relations (Consolidation) Act 1992, s 24.

[245] *P v National Union of Schoolmasters/Union of Women Teachers* [2003] UKHL 8, [2003] 1 All ER 993, per Lord Hoffmann at [44].

[246] *British Railways Board v National Union of Railwaymen* [1989] ICR 678, [1989] IRLR 349, CA.

[247] [2003] IRLR 307, [2003] 1 All ER 993, HL.

[248] Before 1999, s 227(2) stated that the balloting requirements were not satisfied if a member who was induced to take part in the action was 'denied' entitlement to vote. That provision was replaced by s 232A, which used the expression 'not accorded' in place of 'denied'.

[249] [1990] IRLR 143, CA.

those who were employed by the employer and given an opportunity of voting at the time of the ballot, but this dictum was disapproved by the Court of Appeal in *London Underground v RMT*,[250] where the issue was whether the statutory immunities were lost because some 692 members who had joined the union since the date of the ballot were called upon to take part in the industrial action. The Court of Appeal held that the industrial action still had the support of a ballot:

> The union is required to ballot those, *and only those*, of *its members* who *at the time of the ballot* it is reasonable to believe will be called upon to take part in the industrial action. It cannot identify future members, but even if it could it must not ballot them, since the ballot is confined to persons who were members at the time of the ballot.[251]

But what of existing union members who were not working for the employer in dispute at the time of the ballot? Could they also be called upon to take part in the action? On one analysis, the logic of the decision in *London Underground v RMT* applied equally to such members, since it would not have been reasonable *at the time of the ballot* for the union to believe that those members would be called upon to take part in the action, in view of the fact that they were not employed by the employer in dispute at that time. Against that, however, section 227(2) used to state that section 227(1) was not satisfied 'if any person who was a member of the trade union at the time when the ballot was held was denied entitlement to vote in the ballot', which put the matter in doubt. In an attempt to clarify the position, the Employment Relations Act 1999 replaced section 227(2) with new section 232A, which was intended[252] to make clear that a union *can* in appropriate circumstances call upon a new employee who was a member of the union at the time of the ballot to take part in the industrial action. Section 232A states that industrial action will not be regarded as having the support of the ballot if a person (a) was a member of the union at the time when the ballot was held; (b) it was reasonable at that time for the union to believe that he would be induced to take part in the industrial action; (c) he was not accorded entitlement to vote in the ballot; and (d) he was induced by the union to take part in the industrial action.

Unfortunately, section 232A gave rise to a whole new set of interpretative problems, as was shown in *P v National Union of Schoolmasters/Union of Women Teachers*.[253] In that case the union had organized a ballot of its members at a school in connection with a dispute over the expulsion and subsequent reinstatement of an allegedly disruptive pupil. One of the questions before the court was whether the ballot was invalidated

[250] [1995] IRLR 636, CA. Millett LJ also stated, obiter, that nothing in the statutory balloting provisions curtails a union's right to induce *non-members* to support industrial action called by the union, as those provisions are concerned exclusively with the relationship between the union and its members, and are intended for the protection of members, not the protection of the employer or the public.

[251] [1995] IRLR 636 at 639. Millett LJ's emphasis.

[252] See the Explanatory Notes to the Employment Relations Act 1999, para 137.

[253] [2003] IRLR 307, [2003] 1 All ER 993, HL.

because the union had failed to send ballot papers to two of its members who had recently moved to the school, and of whose existence the union only became aware after the ballot papers had been sent out but before the completion of the ballot process. At first blush this might seem like just the type of situation in which the union could expect to be exonerated by the dispensation for small accidental errors not affecting the result of the ballot in section 232B (not least because, of the 30 members balloted, 26 had voted in favour of industrial action, and none against) but, crucially, at the time section 232A was not one of the provisions listed in section 232B. In a landmark ruling which shed some much-needed light on the complex relationship between the various statutory provisions, the House of Lords emphasized the importance of distinguishing between section 227(1), which defines who must be accorded entitlement to vote, and the other provisions of the Act, which define what counts as being accorded entitlement to vote:[254]

> In my opinion, compliance with [those] provisions in respect of the constituency identified by section 227(1) means that the members of that constituency have been accorded entitlement to vote. In the case of the distribution of ballot papers, section 230(2) makes those requirements subject to the proviso of reasonable practicability and section 232B makes both sections 227(1) and 230(2) subject to the disregard of small accidental errors. If failure to send a ballot paper to a person within the constituency falls within either of those exceptions, he is not by reason of that failure to be treated as having not been accorded entitlement to vote.'[255]

Crucially, their Lordships rejected the argument that the use of the expression 'not accorded' in section 232A(c) in place of 'denied' was intended to mark a significant change of effect,[256] even though this interpretation of section 232A seemed to mean that Parliament had enacted superfluous legislation. Lord Hoffmann remarked dryly:

> it would not be the first time. It is certainly more likely than that Parliament intended, at one and the same time, by section 232B to create a proviso for some accidental errors and by section 232A to deprive the union of protection from liability in the case of the accidental error most likely to occur, namely an omission to include a member in the ballot paper mailing list.[257]

This interpretation was made express by an amendment in the Employment Relations Act 2004 which makes it clear that the 'small accidental failures' defence in section 232B *does* apply to the 'entitlement to vote' requirement in section 232A(c).

The second issue arising from section 227(1) also showed the complexity of this area and the continuing interplay between case law and amending legislation. As the

---

[254] Or, as Lord Walker helpfully put it at [68], between entitlement to vote and opportunity to vote.

[255] [2003] IRLR 307, [2003] 1 All ER 993, HL per Lord Hoffmann at [44].

[256] 'I do not think that the concept of being accorded entitlement to vote in section 232A(c) was intended to mean something different from what it meant in section 227 before the [1999 Act]': per Lord Hoffmann, at [45]; similarly Lord Walker at [72].

[257] [2003] UKHL 8, [2003] 1 All ER 993 at [45].

section originally stood, it was held that entitlement to vote must be extended to all those that it was reasonable for the union to believe 'will be induced to take part', and that this was an *objective* test.[258] This meant that if some might be induced to take part by their own conscience or by their colleagues, they had to be given the entitlement to vote, even if the union had no *intention* to bring them out. This potentially extended the union's exposure to legal action alarmingly. To lessen this particular problem, the Employment Relations Act 2004 amended section 227(1) to read 'will be induced *by the union* to take part'.

In spite of this clarification, there is still a heavy onus on a trade union to keep its membership records up to date. It was argued on behalf of the union in *Midland Mainline* that the test of whether it was reasonably practicable for the union to supply ballot papers to members within the balloting constituency must be assessed in the light of the facts as they were on the day that the ballot papers were sent out, ie in the light of the information available to the union at that time. The Court of Appeal rejected that reading:

> It cannot have been intended that a ballot will be regarded as having been properly conducted if the union does not properly record changes of address notified to it. Where, on the other hand, the union has a system for reminding members of the need to keep the union notified of any changes of addresses but a member fails to notify the union of such a change and the union is in fact ignorant of that change of address and sends a ballot paper to the old address then a court would probably find that the union will have done all that is reasonably practicable.[259]

Finally, the Employment Act 1988 added a further refinement to the rules on the balloting constituency by introducing a requirement of separate workplace ballots[260] where a union wishes to organize industrial action at more than one place of work, the aim apparently being to prevent a union from manipulating the outcome of a ballot by creating 'artificial' balloting constituencies, combining different (and perhaps unrelated) groups of workers together so as to ensure an overall vote in favour of industrial action. As an insistence on separate workplace ballots in every case would have been a recipe for industrial relations chaos, the 1988 Act permitted a union to hold one aggregated ballot across several workplaces where those to be balloted had some particular factor in common. The separate workplace ballot provisions, heavily criticized at the outset for their complexity, were revised in 1999 in the

---

[258] *National Union of Rail, Maritime and Transport Workers v Midland Mainline* [2001] EWCA Civ 1206, [2001] IRLR 813.

[259] [2001] EWCA Civ 1206, [2001] IRLR 813, at para 21. The Court of Appeal suggested (at para 45) that a possible way forward for a union which is unable to identify all the members whom it wishes to take part in industrial action is to approach ACAS to carry out a confidential membership check, to confirm that all relevant members have in fact received ballot papers. This is a sensible suggestion, although there is no legal duty on the employer to cooperate in such a process.

[260] See now the Trade Union and Labour Relations (Consolidation) Act 1992, ss 228 and 228A, as substituted by the Employment Relations Act 1999, Sch 3.

interests of greater clarity and simplicity. It is now provided that a union may hold an aggregated ballot across more than one workplace[261] if one of the following is satisfied: (1) where each workplace concerned is the workplace of at least one member of the union who is 'affected by the dispute';[262] (2) where the union reasonably believes that it is balloting all its members of a particular occupational description (or descriptions) who are employed by an employer (or employers) with whom the union is in dispute; or (3) where the union reasonably believes that it is balloting all its members who are employed by an employer (or employers) with whom the union is in dispute.

(b) The voting paper

The content of the voting paper is specified in great detail. There are four requirements: first, the voting paper must contain at least one of the two 'statutory questions', asking the voter to say, by answering 'yes' or 'no', whether he is prepared to take part in a 'strike', or in 'industrial action short of a strike'.[263] If the union contemplates taking both types of action these two questions must be put separately, and separate approval must be obtained for each type of action.[264] In *West Midlands Travel Ltd v TGWU*,[265] the employers argued that where separate questions are put, the union must obtain a majority approval of all those who had participated in the voting process, including those who had abstained, and not just a simple majority in respect of each individual question on the ballot paper;[266] however, the Court of Appeal sensibly held that where separate questions are posed, one relating to strike action and the other to industrial action short of a strike, each question must be regarded as a separate matter to be voted on individually, and the result of the ballot in respect of each question must be considered separately. There is no express requirement that the voting paper must identify the subject matter of the dispute, or that the dispute so identified must fall within the trade dispute definition, but the courts have nevertheless been prepared to hold

---

[261] For these purposes, 'workplace' means, if the person works at or from a single set of premises, those premises, and in any other case, the premises with which the person's employment has the closest connection: s 228(4). On the original (narrower) definition, which defined the place of work in terms of the premises 'occupied' by the employer, see *InterCity West Coast Ltd v RMT* [1996] IRLR 583. Under the pre-1999 provisions, it was held that the freedom to hold an aggregate ballot was not confined to situations where the different workplaces all belonged to the same employer (see *University of Central England v NALGO* [1993] IRLR 81), and this is believed still to be the case.

[262] A member will be 'affected by a dispute' if, eg, the dispute relates wholly or partly to a decision of the employer over a trade dispute matter, and the member is directly affected by that decision: s 228A(5).

[263] Trade Union and Labour Relations (Consolidation) Act 1992, s 229(2). Overtime bans and call-out bans are to be treated as industrial action short of a strike for these purposes: Trade Union and Labour Relations (Consolidation) Act 1992, s 229(2A), inserted by the Employment Relations Act 1999, Sch 3 (reversing the effect of *Connex South Eastern Ltd v RMT* [1999] IRLR 249, CA).

[264] *Post Office v Union of Communication Workers* [1990] ICR 258, [1990] IRLR 143, CA.

[265] [1994] ICR 978, [1994] IRLR 578, CA.

[266] The wording of the statute is certainly ambiguous, in that s 226(2) provides that 'the majority voting in [the] ballot' must have answered the relevant question affirmatively.

that a ballot is invalid if it covers a non-trade dispute matter.[267] Secondly, the voting paper must contain a statement (a type of government health warning?) informing members that industrial action may be unlawful. The statement was amended in 1999 to include information about the enhanced protection against unfair dismissal during the protected period; it now reads as follows:

> If you take part in a strike or other industrial action, you may be in breach of your contract of employment. However, if you are dismissed for taking part in strike or other industrial action which is called officially and is otherwise lawful, the dismissal will be unfair if it takes place fewer than eight weeks after you started taking part in the action, and depending on the circumstances may be unfair if it takes place later.

This statement may not be qualified or commented on by anything else on the ballot paper,[268] even if it is clear that the action in question does not involve a breach of contract (as, for example, in the case of withdrawal from voluntary overtime).[269] Thirdly, the voting paper must identify the person or persons authorized by the union to call upon members to take part in industrial action in the event of a vote in favour (a requirement introduced by the Employment Act 1990 to prevent union officials from jumping the gun unauthorizedly by calling on members to take industrial action before the leadership has give the go-ahead to do so—see below). Finally, the voting paper must give the name of the independent scrutineer.[270] If any of these requirements is omitted the industrial action will not be regarded as having the support of a ballot, and the statutory immunities will be withdrawn. To facilitate a challenge on the ground of a defective ballot, a union is required to provide the employers of those entitled to vote in the ballot with a sample voting paper at least three days before the start of the ballot.[271]

(c) Conduct of the ballot

Until 1993 the requirements of a valid industrial action ballot differed significantly from those which applied to union elections and political fund ballots, for while ballots for either of those purposes have, since the Employment Act 1988, been required to be fully postal (ie ballot papers delivered and returned by post) and subject to independent scrutiny, a strike ballot could be held at the workplace and was not subject to

---

[267] See eg *London Underground v National Union of Railwaymen* [1989] IRLR 341 (noted by Simpson (1989) 18 ILJ 234), where it was held that several issues may not be rolled up in one single question where there are doubts over whether some of those issues are in fact the subject of a trade dispute, and *University College London Hospitals NHS Trust v UNISON* [1999] ICR 204 (noted by Simpson (2002) 31 ILJ 270), where Lord Woolf held that the ballot failed to meet the statutory requirements because it referred to an issue which was not a trade dispute.

[268] There does not appear to be anything to prevent a union from commenting on the statement in material enclosed with the voting paper, provided nothing appears on the voting paper itself.

[269] *Power Packing Casemakers Ltd v Faust* [1983] ICR 292, [1983] IRLR 117, CA.

[270] A requirement added by the Trade Union Reform and Employment Rights Act 1993, s 20(2).

[271] Trade Union and Labour Relations (Consolidation) Act 1992, s 226A(1).

independent scrutiny. However, the requirements of postal balloting and independent scrutiny[272] were finally extended to industrial action ballots in 1993.[273] In retrospect it was perhaps surprising that workplace strike ballots survived for as long as they did, given the previous government's well-known antipathy towards that practice. One of the reasons for their retention was the recognition that postal ballots take time to organize, and so might be inappropriate in an industrial action ballot where speed of response is often of the essence. There is also evidence to suggest that workplace balloting achieves a higher rate of participation than postal balloting.[274] However, by 1993 the government had been persuaded that fully postal voting was less susceptible to malpractice than other forms of balloting and provided the best security against interference and intimidation, and the extension of postal balloting to industrial action ballots became inevitable. There was pressure for an exception to be made in the case of ballots involving relatively few employees (the Green Paper which proposed the extension of postal balloting would not have required a postal ballot where no more than 50 members were involved),[275] but the 1993 Act made no such exception.[276]

Members must be allowed to vote without interference from the union (although interference from other quarters will not invalidate the ballot), and, so far as reasonably practicable, the voting must be secret and at no direct cost to those voting.[277] Votes must be fairly and accurately counted (although accidental errors may be disregarded if incapable of affecting the result), and the detailed results must be made known both to those voting and to their employers as soon as reasonably practicable after the holding of the ballot.[278]

One particularly controversial requirement, introduced in 1993, has been the need for a union to give the employers of those entitled to vote in the ballot at least seven days' notice in writing of the date of the ballot,[279] the apparent aim being to give employers the opportunity to take action to minimize the disruptive effects of the industrial action, and to put the case against industrial action to their employees

---

[272] These were initially introduced in relation to elections to union office.

[273] Trade Union Reform and Employment Rights Act 1993, ss 17 and 20 amending the Trade Union and Labour Relations (Consolidation) Act 1992, s 230 (postal ballots) and inserting new ss 226B and 231B (independent scrutiny). Significantly, the 1993 Act repealed the provisions whereby unions could claim government funding for postal ballots.

[274] See generally Undy and Martin *Ballots and Trade Union Democracy* (1984), and Leopold (1986) Ind Rels J 287.

[275] 'Industrial Relations in the 1990s' (Cm 1602, 1991).

[276] The only exception is for merchant seamen at sea or at a foreign port for some or all of the balloting period, who are allowed to vote on board ship or at the place where the ship is, where it is convenient for them to vote in this way: s 230(2A), as amended by the Employment Relations Act 1999, Sch 3.

[277] Trade Union and Labour Relations (Consolidation) Act 1992, s 230. This means that the union must pay the postage (eg by providing pre-paid envelopes).

[278] Trade Union and Labour Relations (Consolidation) Act 1992, ss 231 and 231A. This applies whether or not the union proceeds with industrial action: *Metrobus Ltd v UNITE* [2009] EWCA Civ 829.

[279] Trade Union and Labour Relations (Consolidation) Act 1992, s 226A, as amended by the Employment Relations Act 1999, Sch 3. Unions must also give notice to employers before taking industrial action: see under heading 4(vii), p 748.

in advance of the ballot. As originally drafted, the ballot notice had to describe the employees to be balloted so that the employer could 'readily ascertain them'. In the first case on the notice provisions to come before the courts, *Blackpool and Fylde College v NATFHE*,[280] the Court of Appeal controversially held that the union had to supply the employer with the names of those to be balloted in order to satisfy its statutory duty (this despite an assurance from the minister during the passage of the 1993 Act that he could 'envisage no circumstances' in which it would be necessary for the union to 'name names').[281] The incoming Labour government gave notice of its intention to change the law to reverse the effect of this decision,[282] and the law was amended by the Employment Relations Act 1999 to remove any requirement of names and to allow the union to give more generalized information. However, when this amended law came again before the Court of Appeal in *London Underground Ltd v NURMTW*[283] their decision (that the union still had not given the necessary information when stating that the ballot was to cover 'all categories at all workplaces' and giving the overall number of union members as 'approximately 4,938') strongly suggested that the 1999 amendment had not worked. After a further consultation[284] a second amendment was made by the Employment Relations Act 2004. An expanded section 226A of the Trade Union and Labour Relations (Consolidation) Act 1992 is now much more specific as to the exact nature of the obligation on the union; written notice must be given of the intention to hold a ballot and its opening date, together with information in the form of lists of the categories of employees and the workplaces affected and figures of the numbers involved (in total and by category/workplace).[285] The lists and figures supplied must be 'as accurate as is reasonably practicable in the light of the information in the possession of the union at the time when it complies' with these requirements, and it is specifically stated that '[n]othing in this section requires a union to supply an employer with the names of the employees concerned'.[286]

---

[280] [1994] ICR 648, [1994] IRLR 227, CA. The union had notified the college that it intended to ballot 'all our members in your institution', but the Court of Appeal held that this was insufficiently precise to enable the employer readily to ascertain the employees involved, because they did not know which employees were in fact members of the union. The move away from the check-off of union subscriptions from pay has increased employer uncertainty over levels of union membership.

[281] *Hansard*, House of Commons, Standing Committee F, 15 December 1992, col 247, thus allaying fears over the risk of employer interference with the ballot and possible intimidation of voters.

[282] (Cm 3968, 1998) para 4.27.   [283] [2001] IRLR 228, [2001] ICR 647, CA.

[284] Review of the Employment Relations Act 1999 (DTI, February 2003).

[285] Section 226A(2)–(2C)—there must be an explanation of how the figures were arrived at; slightly different rules apply where a check-off system is in force; as to both of these points, see *Metrobus Ltd v UNITE* [2009] EWCA Civ 829. In that case it was held that, in spite of their complexity, these provisions do not infringe the right to free association in Art 11 of the European Convention on Human Rights; they are within the margin of appreciation given to states. The notice must be given not later than the seventh day before the opening of the ballot, and a copy of the voting paper must be given not later than the third day before: s 226A(1).

[286] Section 226A(2D), (2G).

(d) The calling of industrial action

Where there has been a vote in favour of industrial action, that action must begin before the ballot ceases to be effective (ie before it reaches its statutory 'sell-by' date), otherwise the union will have to go through the whole process again.[287] An industrial action ballot normally ceases to be effective at the end of four weeks from the date of the ballot,[288] but sensibly the Employment Relations Act 1999 amended the law to enable the employer and the union to agree an extension of up to four more weeks, thereby reducing pressure on a union to commence industrial action simply to prevent the ballot from becoming ineffective in circumstances where further negotiations might enable the parties to reach an agreement.[289] In *Monsanto plc v TGWU*,[290] the Court of Appeal held that, provided the industrial action commences within the statutory time limit, it may continue beyond that point, even if the union lifts the action during negotiations but then reimposes it if the negotiations prove unsuccessful, provided the dispute continues to be the same dispute as that in respect of which the original ballot was held.

Any strike call by the union in advance of the ballot will normally be fatal;[291] however, in determining whether there has been a 'call' by the union, the statutory test of vicarious liability applies.[292] This means that an unauthorized and unballoted call by, for example, a shop steward, will now be regarded as a call *by the union*, and the resulting action will consequently be denied the protection of the statutory immunities. The only way in which the union might avoid liability in such a case would be to repudiate the unauthorized call,[293] but by doing so it exposes those who continue to take part in the action to the risk of selective dismissal.[294] To add to the complication, the Employment Act 1990 introduced the requirement that industrial action be called by a 'specified person'[295] (ie a person specified by the union on the voting paper), to

---

[287] Trade Union and Labour Relations (Consolidation) Act 1992, s 233(3)(b); s 234(1).

[288] See *RJB Mining (UK) Ltd v National Union of Mineworkers* [1995] IRLR 556, CA.

[289] Trade Union and Labour Relations (Consolidation) Act 1992, s 234(1); there is also a discretion in the court to extend the time-limit up to a maximum of 12 weeks from the date of the ballot where the union has been prohibited from calling or organizing industrial action by a court order or an undertaking given to the court, and that order or undertaking has subsequently lapsed: s 234(2).

[290] [1987] ICR 269, [1986] IRLR 406, CA. But cf *Post Office v Union of Communication Workers* [1990] ICR 258, [1990] IRLR 143, CA, where it was stated, obiter, that the action must continue without substantial interruption, so that a gap of nine months was considered too long; see also *Secretary of State for Scotland v Scottish Prison Officers' Association* [1991] IRLR 371, Ct of Sess.

[291] Trade Union and Labour Relations (Consolidation) Act 1992, s 233(3)(a). The prohibition on calling for industrial action before the date of the ballot is not infringed by a union recommendation to its members to vote in favour of industrial action: *Newham London Borough Council v NALGO* [1993] ICR 189, [1993] IRLR 83, CA.

[292] Trade Union and Labour Relations (Consolidation) Act 1992, s 20. See under heading 7, p 766.

[293] Trade Union and Labour Relations (Consolidation) Act 1992, s 21. See under heading 7, p 768.

[294] Trade Union and Labour Relations (Consolidation) Act 1992, s 237. See under heading 2(iii), p 698.

[295] Trade Union and Labour Relations (Consolidation) Act 1992, s 233(1). The union can decide whom to specify, but the person (or description of persons) specified must come within the list of those for whom the union is deemed responsible under s 20.

prevent local officials unauthorizedly 'jumping the gun' by calling on members to take industrial action without waiting for the union leadership to decide whether or not to implement the ballot decision. If action is called by someone *other* than a specified person, that action will not be regarded as having the support of a ballot, even where there is a clear vote in favour of the action and all the other statutory requirements are satisfied. There are, however, signs that this requirement will be interpreted flexibly, and that some limited degree of delegation may be acceptable; in *Tanks and Drums Ltd v TGWU*,[296] the Court of Appeal held that the section was satisfied where the specified person, the union's general secretary, authorized a district official to implement the industrial action if further negotiations with the employer the following day were not successful. Neill LJ stated that:

> in the field of industrial relations it would be impracticable to leave matters in such a way that there was no possibility for the exercise of judgment on the ground. Some matters must be left for the judgment of those on the ground who have to decide how and when as a matter of common sense the call for action is to be put into operation.

However, Neill LJ also considered that a blanket delegation of authority to a local official would not be acceptable, and stressed the need for 'a close link in time between the call for the strike and the event, for example, an unsuccessful meeting which precipitates the final action'.

(e) A rebalancing of the system?

It can be argued that the overall result of these provisions (in effect, the likelihood of an injunction being granted) is as much a matter of the judicial attitude towards their interpretation as of their inherent complexity. A common view among trade unions is that it has been next to impossible to get it all right first time in order to prevent an employer injunction. As late as 2009 the case of *Metrobus Ltd v UNITE*[297] showed the traditional judicial approach that these procedural requirements are in effect absolute, so that any lapse in them puts the union in breach, subject only to the 'small accidental failures' exception. However, within a year (and ironically at a time of renewed industrial action after the election of the Coalition government) two decisions of the Court of Appeal showed a significantly different approach, at the very least demonstrating a running out of patience with highly technical arguments by the employer. In *British Airways plc v UNITE*[298] long-running industrial action by cabin staff had had a noticeably high level of support of the members but the employer applied for an injunction to prevent strike action on a technical point about informing the membership of the results of a ballot. At first instance an injunction was granted but this was discharged on appeal. In a minority, Neuberger MR took the traditional view requiring

---

[296] [1992] ICR 1, [1991] IRLR 372, CA.   [297] [2009] IRLR 851, CA.
[298] [2010] ICR 1316, [2012] IRLR 809, CA.

strict compliance by the union *but* Lord Judge CJ (with the backing of Smith LJ) held to the contrary. He said that the relevant section in the 1992 Act was poorly drafted and that in the light of that it was inappropriate to apply an overly literal approach in order to comply with the overall aims of the legislation. This was a potentially important majority decision, though possibly explicable because of the ambiguities of the individual section. More important was the second case.

Arguably, the decision of the Court of Appeal (again discharging an injunction) in *NURMT v Serco Ltd*[299] shows more clearly a *general* move against granting injunctive relief on the basis of highly technical breaches by a union. Indeed, Elias LJ's complex judgment starts with a general point that this legislation is to be construed and applied in a normal way, without any presumption that it will be applied strictly against a union wishing to claim its statutory protection (or indeed that the employer's interest must prevail), and in a way that will give it a 'likely and workable construction', giving due weight to freedom of association as enshrined in Article 11 of the European Convention on Human Rights.

The principal alleged defaults by the union were that it had informed the employer that there were 21 affected members at one depot instead of 20, and 33 at another depot instead of 32. Moreover, objection was taken to the form in which the union provided the employer with 'an explanation of how those figures were arrived at' (section 226A(2)(c)) which consisted of the statement:

> The lists and figures accompanying this notice were arrived at by retrieving information from the union's database and workplaces of members and the numbers in and at each, the database having been audited and updated for the purpose of the statutory notification and balloting requirements to ensure accuracy.

It was argued that not only was this too anodyne, but it was also inaccurate because there had not actually been an 'audit'. The judge found for the employer on all of these points and also disapproved the union's specific defence of 'small accidental failures' (section 232B) on the basis that these mistakes may not have affected the result but were not accidental because they had been avoidable if steps had been taken to be more accurate, and held against a more general defence of the de minimis principle.

The Court of Appeal disagreed fundamentally. They held as follows:

(1) In relation to the accidental failures defence in section 232B the court accepted the union's argument that in insisting that the failure be both unintentional and unavoidable the judge had erected a test of perfection which could frustrate the whole purpose of the section. This was not a case where the union had known of the mistakes and continued; it had believed it was balloting the relevant members and no one else, and the mistakes were caused by human error. As Elias LJ put it, 's 232B was designed to cater for precisely this kind of case.

---

[299] [2011] ICR 848, [2012] IRLR 399, CA.

(2) In relation to the requirement (section 226A(2D)) that the information must be accurate, again the court's argument that it is the whole of the relevant phrase that must be considered, and that shows that the requirement is to provide information which is 'as accurate as is reasonably practicable *in the light of the information in the possession of the union*'. This materially diminishes the scope for arguing for a positive duty on the union to have gone out and found more such information; essentially the union can draw on such information as it already has.

(3) In relation to the de minimis point, the employer had argued that the enactment of section 232B had left no scope for it as a general defence but the court disagreed.

(4) In relation to the adequacy of the union's explanation, the court took into consideration paragraph 16 of the Industrial Action Ballots Code of Practice to hold that 'the duty on the union is not a very onerous one' and so the statement could be relatively formulaic or anodyne. The fact that more information could have been given did not mean that the union had failed in the statutory obligation.

(5) In relation to the accuracy of the statement, the court held that it was not misleading to use the words 'audit' and 'updating', which could be construed as covering the sort of basic checking that the union had done.

Thus, the claim for the injunction was comprehensively rejected. The decision must diminish the scope for arguments based on technical defaults by a union, especially with its relatively wide interpretation of the accidental failures defence. Of course, a specific question now becomes just *how* inaccurate information (along with other requirements) needs to be to continue to fall foul of what are still complex and difficult procedural requirements. A more general question is whether this decision means that, to précis one commentator, by trial and error we have now reached a workable system.[300]

(vii) NOTICE OF INDUSTRIAL ACTION FOR EMPLOYERS

One of the most controversial of the reforms introduced by the Trade Union Reform and Employment Rights Act 1993 was the requirement for unions to give employers at least seven days' notice of official industrial action.[301] Apparently prompted by the disruption caused by random strikes in the public services (in particular a series of one-day strikes on the London Underground in 1989), the notice requirements apply to all types of industrial action, and across all sectors of employment. As in other contexts above, the original rules were subject to a two-stage series of reforms in the Employment Relations Acts 1999 and 2004. As a result, the Trade Union and Labour Relations (Consolidation) Act 1992, section 234A now contains information

---

[300] Walker, 'Striking a Balance' [2012] NLJ 1171.
[301] Trade Union and Labour Relations (Consolidation) Act 1992, s 234A.

requirements for the relevant notice which closely parallel those applying to the notice of the ballot under section 226A[302] (ie as to the categories, workplaces and numbers involved, with no obligation to give individual names). In this context, however, the notice must go further and state whether the industrial action is intended to be continuous or discontinuous. If the action is to be continuous, the notice must state when it is to start; if intended to be discontinuous (ie if the union does not intend to take action on all the days on which it could do so), the notice must specify the particular *dates* on which it is to take place. The result is that unions are no longer able to use the threat of random, discontinuous action to bring pressure to bear on employers, although there is still some potential for disruption in that, having given notice of the dates on which it intends the discontinuous action to take place, the union does not then have to call for that action to take place on all (or indeed any) of those dates. One potentially unfortunate consequence of the notice requirements in their original form was that where continuous industrial action was suspended, for example to allow further negotiations to take place, the union was required to give a further seven days' notice before resuming the action, which could act as a disincentive to attempts at negotiation during the action. The provisions were therefore amended in 1999 so that where the industrial action has been suspended by joint agreement between the employer and the union, the action can be resumed after an agreed date ('the resumption date') without the need for the union to issue a fresh notice.[303]

The earliest date that notice may be given is the day on which the employer is informed of the result of the ballot.[304] Given that a strike ballot normally only remains valid for four weeks *from the date of the ballot* (ie from the last day of voting), a further delay of seven days after disclosure of the results means that the 'window of opportunity' within which the ballot may be implemented is considerably shortened.[305] If the union fails to give the required notice the statutory immunities are withdrawn, but only as respects the employer of a person who is induced to take part in the action.[306]

5 POTENTIAL CRIMINAL LIABILITY

As seen in the introduction to this chapter, criminal law does not play any significant role in the regulation of industrial action, outside the specialized law relating

---

[302] See heading 4(vi), p 748.

[303] Trade Union and Labour Relations (Consolidation) Act 1992, s 234A(7B). The period of suspension may be extended by joint agreement.

[304] Trade Union and Labour Relations (Consolidation) Act 1992, s 234A(4).

[305] Indeed, the Code of Practice (at para 49) suggests that a call for industrial action following a ballot should be delayed until the union has received the scrutineer's report on the ballot, which would narrow the window of opportunity even further.

[306] Trade Union and Labour Relations (Consolidation) Act 1992, s 234A(1). Note, however, that in such a case the industrial action will still be regarded as an unlawful act for the purposes of the 'Citizen's Right', discussed at heading 8, p 774.

to picketing, and the application of the ordinary laws relating to violence and public order if a dispute gives rise to violence and disruption. Those matters are considered in the next section. Before turning to that, however, there are two contexts in which, in exceptional cases, there might be criminal liability. The first arises where employees occupy their employer's premises, for example by way of a sit-in or work-in. In civil law they become trespassers when they refuse to leave, and the employer may take civil action to regain possession of his factory. However, English law has always been wary of imposing criminal sanctions for trespass, a position strengthened by the Criminal Law Act 1977, which provided that it could not be a criminal conspiracy for people to agree to commit an act which was merely tortious, such as trespass.[307] At the same time, Part II of that Act created several new trespass offences which could conceivably be committed by workers engaged in occupying the employer's premises, and in respect of which the police have powers of arrest and entry on to the property in question. Thus, it is an offence to use violence to secure entry when there is someone already on the premises,[308] or to enter as a trespasser with a 'weapon of offence'.[309] In most sit-ins or work-ins, the former will not arise, as possession of the premises is usually gained by failing to leave (or, at least, by entry by stealth);[310] the occupiers may, however, be at risk under the latter, for many articles (even working tools) can constitute 'weapons of offence' if the person carrying them has the intention of using them to inflict injury on others. It is also an offence to resist bailiffs who are seeking to regain possession of the premises under a court order.[311] The other main trespass offence created by the 1977 Act, that of remaining in adverse possession after being requested to leave, is aimed essentially at squatting in residential property, and is therefore unlikely to be of any significance in an industrial context as it only applies where the person making the request is a 'displaced residential occupier' (or a 'protected intending occupier', as defined), which does not include a factory owner.[312]

The second area of possible criminal liability is under certain remaining (and in some cases anomalous) statutory provisions creating offences which limit the freedom to take industrial action. Thus, industrial action by postal workers may involve the commission of the offence of intentionally delaying a postal packet under the Postal

---

[307] Criminal Law Act 1977, s 1(1), overruling the decision of the House of Lords in *Kamara v DPP* [1974] AC 104, [1973] 2 All ER 1242, HL.

[308] Criminal Law Act 1977, s 6, as amended by the Criminal Justice and Public Order Act 1994, s 72.

[309] Criminal Law Act 1977, s 8.

[310] Indeed, once inside the occupiers could themselves be protected by s 6, which will render criminal any attempt by the factory owner to use violence to enter to evict them! Note, however, the decision of the Scottish High Court of Justiciary that a work-in can constitute 'watching or besetting' (under the Trade Union and Labour Relations (Consolidation) Act 1992, heading 6(ii), p 756) even though the people concerned are inside the premises: *Galt (Procurator Fiscal) v Philp* [1984] IRLR 156; this decision is potentially more damaging to occupations than the Criminal Law Act 1977.

[311] Criminal Law Act 1977, s 10.

[312] Criminal Law Act 1977, s 7, as substituted by the Criminal Justice and Public Order Act 1994, s 73.

Services Act 2000,[313] and telecommunications workers may commit an offence if they intentionally intercept a communication in the course of its transmission;[314] likewise, there are punitive provisions in the merchant shipping legislation which may affect the legality of a strike by merchant seamen,[315] and there are statutory restrictions on union membership[316] and the organization of strike action in the police force,[317] and on inducing prison officers to withhold their services or to commit breaches of discipline.[318] One further provision, dating from the Conspiracy and Protection of Property Act 1875[319] and now contained in the Trade Union and Labour Relations (Consolidation) Act 1992, section 240, makes it an offence for a person:

> wilfully and maliciously [to break] a contract of service or hiring, knowing or having reasonable cause to believe that the probable consequences of his so doing, either alone or in combination with others, will be to endanger human life or cause serious bodily injury, or to expose valuable property, whether real or personal, to destruction or serious injury.

This provision is potentially of significance in industrial disputes, particularly in the context of industrial action by workers in the essential services such as nurses, doctors, firefighters and ambulance workers. The penalty is small, and there appears to be no record of any prosecution under it, but it is conceivable that the main significance of such a provision could lie in its use as the basis of an application for an injunction to restrain a threatened breach of it, rather than in the possibility of prosecution directly under it. In *Gouriet v UPOW*[320] the claimant sought an injunction to prevent a threatened boycott of mail to South Africa, on the basis that the action would contravene the Post Office Act 1953. This was ultimately refused by the House of Lords, which reaffirmed the traditional limitation on this use of a civil law remedy to prevent anticipated breaches of criminal law—ie that an action may only be brought by the Attorney General or by an individual whose private rights were about to be infringed or who would suffer 'special damage'. As the claimant in *Gouriet* had failed to persuade the Attorney General to bring the action, and had brought it himself merely qua member of the general public, he did not have the necessary locus standi. An action for an injunction to restrain a threatened breach of the criminal law would, however, be open to someone who did have the necessary legal interest, and this could conceivably arise

---

[313] Postal Services Act 2000, s 83. The offence is not committed where a postal packet is delayed as a result of industrial action in contemplation or furtherance of a trade dispute (a dispensation which did not apply under the previous provisions in the Post Office Act 1953, ss 58, 68; see *Gouriet v Union of Post Office Workers* [1978] AC 435, [1977] 3 All ER 70, HL).

[314] Regulation of Investigatory Powers Act 2000, s 1.

[315] Merchant Shipping Act 1995, s 59(1).

[316] Police Act 1996, s 64. A person who belonged to a union before becoming a member of a police force may continue to be a union member: s 64(2).

[317] Police Act 1996, s 91.

[318] Criminal Justice and Public Order Act 1994, s 127; the section operates by imposing a statutory duty owed to the Home Secretary, not by imposing criminal liability.

[319] The 1875 Act also created certain offences pertinent to picketing; see heading 6(ii), p 755.

[320] [1978] AC 435, [1977] 3 All ER 70, HL.

in the circumstances envisaged by section 240, for example where someone stands to risk personal injury or property damage as a result of a strike.

Finally, while the possibility of a lawful combination of workers constituting a criminal conspiracy has long since been removed,[321] this protection does not extend to agreements to commit acts which are themselves criminal, and so if persons involved in industrial action agree among themselves to commit offences, for example to assault or intimidate people or destroy property, they may be prosecuted for those offences and also for criminal conspiracy,[322] as in *R v Jones*[323] (the 'Shrewsbury pickets' case). However, there is an exception to this where the offence in question is a summary offence not punishable by imprisonment, as section 242 of the Trade Union and Labour Relations (Consolidation) Act 1992 provides[324] that any such offence which is committed in contemplation or furtherance of a trade dispute shall be disregarded for the purposes of the law of criminal conspiracy. Moreover, the Criminal Law Act 1977 places two significant limitations on the use of criminal conspiracy—first, it ties the penalty for conspiracy to the maximum for the crime conspired at, thus removing the criticism that conspiracy could be used (or misused) to put the penalty at large;[325] second, it requires the consent of the Director of Public Prosecutions before the prosecution may indict someone for conspiracy to commit an act which in itself is only a summary offence (for example intimidation).[326] As a result of these limitations, criminal conspiracy is rarely of any relevance to industrial action in the present day.

6 PICKETING[327]

The act of picketing the premises of another person may not be unlawful in itself,[328] but in reality it can very easily become so, either as a tort, such as public or private nuisance or trespass to the highway, or under one of several specific or general criminal offences. This is recognized in the statutory immunity for peaceful picketing during a trade

---

[321] Originally by the Conspiracy and Protection of Property Act 1875, s 3; see earlier in this chapter at heading 1, p 688.

[322] And perhaps, on the facts, other 'group offences' under the Public Order Act 1986, see under heading 6(iv).

[323] [1974] ICR 310, 59 Cr App Rep 120, CA.

[324] Re-enacting Criminal Law Act 1977, s 1(3).

[325] Criminal Law Act 1977, s 3. In *R v Jones* [1974] ICR 310, 59 Cr App Rep 120, CA, the three defendants found guilty of conspiracy to intimidate received sentences of nine months', two years' and three years' imprisonment, even though intimidation itself (a summary offence under s 7 of the 1875 Act) then only carried three months. One of the defendants, Ricky Tomlinson, has since become better known as, inter alia, the recumbent paterfamilias in the BBC's *The Royle Family*.

[326] Criminal Law Act 1977, s 4(1).

[327] See Wallington 'Policing the Miners' Strike' (1985) 14 ILJ 145; Auerbach 'Legal Restraint of Picketing: New Trends; New Tensions' (1987) 16 ILJ 227; Auerbach 'Injunctions against Picketing' (1989) 18 ILJ 166.

[328] *Hubbard v Pitt* [1975] 3 All ER 1, [1975] ICR 308, CA, per Lord Denning MR (dissenting); the majority decided the case on procedural points relating to interlocutory injunctions, not primarily upon the substantive law on picketing. See Wallington 'Injunctions and the Right to Demonstrate' (1976) 35 CLJ 86.

dispute, now contained in the Trade Union and Labour Relations (Consolidation) Act 1992, section 220. It is necessary, therefore, to consider first the ways in which a picket may prima facie fall foul of the law and then the extent to which he is protected.

Picketing is a form of public demonstration carried on in an industrial context, and the imposition of restrictions on picketing has important civil liberties implications, particularly for freedom of assembly and freedom of speech. As was seen in the introduction to this chapter, the 'bringing home' of the European Convention on Human Rights into English law by the Human Rights Act 1998 could have implications for the law affecting picketing, as the right to freedom of expression in Article 10 and the right to freedom of peaceful assembly in Article 11 could conceivably be used to challenge some of the existing legal restrictions on picketing.[329] Indeed, even before the coming into force of the Human Rights Act, there was evidence that the courts were increasingly aware of the need to preserve these fundamental freedoms. So, for example, in *Middlebrook Mushrooms Ltd v TGWU*,[330] where the claimants, a firm of mushroom growers, sought an injunction restraining the union from distributing leaflets outside supermarkets supplied by the claimants asking customers not to buy their mushrooms, in support of members dismissed by the claimants for taking industrial action, the Court of Appeal emphasized the importance of keeping the civil law constraints on picketing within proper limits, Neill LJ stating that Article 10 should be taken into consideration 'in all cases which involve a proposed restriction on the right of free speech';[331] similarly, in *DPP v Jones*,[332] Lord Irvine LC expressed the view, obiter, that if English law did not give a right of peaceful assembly on the highway, Article 11 of the European Convention might in future require the common law to develop such a right. As in other areas of employment law potentially affected by human rights law, the key issue here will be the extent to which the guarantee of freedom of peaceful assembly in Article 11(1) is found to be qualified by Article 11(2), which permits restrictions on that freedom 'where necessary in a democratic society ... for the prevention of disorder or crime ... or for the protection of rights and freedoms of others'.[333]

(i) POTENTIAL CIVIL LIABILITY

Picketing is not tortious per se, but in common with other forms of industrial action it is likely to involve the commission of one or more of the economic torts discussed, and

[329] See O'Dempsey et al *Employment Law and the Human Rights Act 1998* (2001) 217–23.
[330] [1993] ICR 612, CA.   [331] [1993] ICR 612 at 620.
[332] [1999] 2 All ER 257, HL. The case demonstrates the difficulties in store for the courts in interpreting Art 11, for Lord Slynn and Lord Hope saw no necessary conflict between the common law and the Convention on this point.
[333] There are similar restrictions in Art 10(2). In *Steel v United Kingdom* (1998) 28 EHRR 603, the ECtHR ruled that the detention for breach of the peace of protestors who were merely holding banners and distributing leaflets infringed Art 10, observing that while states have a margin of appreciation in deciding what restrictions are necessary, the overriding consideration was that the measures used should be proportionate to the end to be achieved. See Fenwick (1999) 62 MLR 491.

may therefore be restrainable at the suit of the employer or some other person involved. For example, a picket who persuades a delivery driver to turn around and not to cross a picket line probably induces that driver to break his contract of employment, and may also indirectly induce a breach of (or at least interfere with) the commercial supply contracts of the driver's employer.[334] The presence of pickets may also give rise to the tort of trespass to the highway[335] or nuisance,[336] and in *Thomas v NUM (South Wales Area)*,[337] Scott J granted an injunction against mass picketing on the grounds of a new common law tort of 'harassment' (a variant of private nuisance) at the suit of working miners who were being prevented from going to work, even though they were not the owners of the land being picketed. The case also illustrates that an action can lie at the suit of people other than the employer in dispute. Picketing could also conceivably involve the commission of the statutory tort of harassment under the Protection from Harassment Act 1997, although to date the civil remedy under that Act has not been used in the context of picketing.[338] An injunction to prevent the unlawful picketing may have the effect of stopping the picketing altogether, or may instead impose conditions on picketing activity (for example on the numbers of pickets and their location).

(ii) POTENTIAL CRIMINAL LIABILITY

If picketing is violent, there will of course be criminal liability for (for example) assault, criminal damage and public order offences (see later in this chapter under heading 6(iv)), in the ordinary way, as seen most dramatically in the miners' strike of 1984–85.[339] Even if it is peaceful, however, picketing may constitute an obstruction of

---

[334] In *Union Traffic Ltd v TGWU* [1989] ICR 98, [1989] IRLR 127, the Court of Appeal held that the mere presence of pickets may constitute the tort of inducing breach of contract if it is clear that the presence of the pickets is intended to induce a breach of contract and it achieves its objective.

[335] See *DPP v Jones* [1999] 2 All ER 257, a landmark case on the law on trespassory assemblies arising from a protest at Stonehenge, where the House of Lords held that there is a public right of peaceful assembly on the highway for any reasonable purpose, provided the activity does not obstruct the highway by unreasonably impeding the rights of others to pass and repass, and does not amount to a public or private nuisance.

[336] *Hubbard v Pitt* [1975] 3 All ER 1, [1975] ICR 308, CA.

[337] [1985] 2 All ER 1, [1985] IRLR 136. See Benedictus 'The Use of the Law of Tort in the Miners' Dispute' (1985) 14 ILJ 176. In *News Group Newspapers Ltd v SOGAT '82 (No 2)* [1987] ICR 181, [1986] IRLR 337 Stuart-Smith J expressed obiter reservations about the decision in *Thomas*. In *Khorasandjian v Bush* [1993] QB 727, [1993] 3 All ER 669 (a non-industrial case), the Court of Appeal accepted the existence of a common law tort of harassment as a form of private nuisance available to a person without an interest in land, but that case was overruled on that point in *Hunter v Canary Wharf Ltd* [1997] AC 655, HL.

[338] In *Tuppen v Microsoft Corpn* (2000) The Times, 15 November, it was stated that the 1997 Act has a narrow ambit and breaches of it which give rise to a civil remedy are confined to cases of stalking, behaviour of an antisocial nature by neighbours and racial harassment, but when the matter was considered by the House of Lords (in a work-stress context) in *Majrowski v Guy's & St Thomas's NHS Trust* [2006] UKHL 34, [2006] IRLR 695 it was held that there is no such restriction and so the Act may apply across employment law (see Ch 3, heading 3(iii), p 147).

[339] During the course of the strike, 10,372 criminal charges were brought, including 468 for assaults of sorts, 360 for assaulting a police officer, 137 for riot, 509 for unlawful assembly, 21 for affray, 4,107 for conduct

the highway,[340] and any refusal to obey lawful police orders may constitute the offence of wilfully obstructing a police officer in the execution of his duty, contrary to the Police Act 1996, section 89. Picketing may also constitute the crime of harassment under the Protection from Harassment Act 1997,[341] which makes it an offence for a person to pursue a 'course of conduct'[342] which amounts to harassment of another and which he knows or ought to know amounts to harassment of another.[343] Although primarily aimed at 'stalkers', the crime of harassment is clearly wide enough to apply to pickets; its significance in practice is likely to turn on the extent to which pickets are able to rely on the statutory defence 'that in the particular circumstances the pursuit of the course of conduct was reasonable'.[344]

In addition to the above, section 241 of the Trade Union and Labour Relations (Consolidation) Act 1992[345] makes it an offence for a person 'with a view to compelling[346] another person to abstain from doing or to do any act which that person has a legal right to do or abstain from doing, wrongfully and without legal authority' to:

(a) use violence to or intimidate[347] that person or his wife or children, or injure his property;

(b) persistently follow that person about from place to place;[348]

---

conducive to breach of the peace (Public Order Act 1936, s 5), 1,019 for criminal damage, 352 for theft, 1,682 for obstructing a police officer, 640 for obstruction of the highway and 275 for intimidation. Subsequently, however, many of the major charges (especially those including riot) were not proceeded with.

[340] Highways Act 1980, s 137; see, eg, *Broome v DPP* [1974] 1 All ER 314, [1974] ICR 84, HL. It seems that picketing will only be an offence under the Highways Act where it involves an unreasonable use of the highway: see *Hubbard v Pitt* [1975] 3 All ER 1, [1975] ICR 308.

[341] See Mullender (1998) 61 MLR 236. Section 3 of the Act provides a civil remedy for a person who is harassed or threatened with harassment (see n 338). Section 4 creates a more serious offence of putting people in fear of violence, which applies where a person's course of conduct causes another to fear, on at least two occasions, that violence will be used against him; there is a defence, inter alia, where the accused can show that the pursuit of his course of conduct was reasonable for the protection of himself or another or for the protection of his or another's property: s 4(3)(c).

[342] This must involve conduct on at least two occasions: Protection from Harassment Act 1997, s 7(3); 'conduct' in this context includes speech: s 7(4).

[343] Protection from Harassment Act 1997, ss 1(1), 2(1). 'Harassment' is not defined, save that references to harassing a person include alarming the person or causing the person distress: s 7(2). A person convicted of an offence under these provisions may be subjected to a restraining order for the purpose of protecting the victim (or any other person named in the order) from further harassment: s 5.

[344] Protection from Harassment Act 1997, s 1(3)(c).

[345] Re-enacting the Conspiracy and Protection of Property Act 1875, s 7. The offence is not necessarily restricted to industrial cases: see eg *DPP v Todd* [1996] Crim LR 344 (anti-road protesters).

[346] The defendant must have acted with a view to *compelling* someone to do something he had a right not to do, or vice versa; an intention to persuade is not enough: *DPP v Fidler* [1992] 1 WLR 91 (another non-industrial case involving a picket outside an abortion clinic).

[347] Actual violence or threats of immediate personal injury are not necessary, but there must be some definite element of causing someone to feel afraid: *Judge v Bennett* (1887) 36 WR 103; *Gibson v Lawson* [1891] 2 QB 545; *Curran v Treleaven* [1891] 2 QB 545; *R v Jones* [1974] ICR 310, 59 Cr App Rep 120, CA.

[348] *Smith v Thomasson* (1891) 16 Cox CC 740; *R v Wall* (1907) 21 Cox CC 401. For a rare example of a prosecution under this limb in Scotland, see *Elsey v Smith (Procurator Fiscal)* [1983] IRLR 292.

(c) hide any tools, clothes or other property owned or used by that person, or deprive him of or hinder him in the use thereof;[349]

(d) watch or beset[350] the house or other place where that person resides, works, carries on business or happens to be, or the approach to such house or place;

(e) follow that person with two or more other persons in a disorderly manner in or through any street or road.

The inclusion of the words 'wrongful and without legal authority' means that the acts complained of under heads (a)–(e) above must already be unlawful (ie either tortious[351] or criminal)—the aim of the section is to make them amenable to summary trial in addition to any other unlawfulness:

> [Section 242] legalises nothing, and it renders nothing wrongful that was not so before. Its object is solely to visit certain selected classes of acts which were previously wrongful, ie were at least civil torts, with penal consequences capable of being summarily inflicted.[352]

The offence under section 241 was rarely used until revived during the 1984–85 miners' strike; subsequently, it was upgraded somewhat by the Public Order Act 1986, which made it an arrestable offence and increased the maximum penalty to six months' imprisonment or a level 5 fine, or both.[353]

(iii) THE IMPORTANCE OF AN ANTICIPATED BREACH OF THE PEACE

The discussion so far has centred on substantive offences which might be committed by pickets. However, one concept which, in practice, has tended to be dominant in

---

[349] *Fowler v Kibble* [1922] 1 Ch 487, CA.

[350] This limb is particularly relevant to picketing (see *R v Bonsall* [1985] Crim LR 150), and it is significant that the statutory immunity now contained in s 220 of the 1992 Act was originally a proviso to s 7 of the 1875 Act which deemed attendance for the purpose of obtaining or communicating information not to be watching or besetting. According to the Scottish High Court of Justiciary in *Galt (Procurator Fiscal) v Philp* [1984] IRLR 156 a person can be guilty of watching and besetting from inside the property, ie by occupying it, but this has been doubted.

[351] The converse of this is that the fact that the conduct in question constitutes an offence under this section does not automatically mean that it is an actionable tort: *Thomas v NUM (South Wales Area)* [1985] 2 All ER 1, [1985] IRLR 136. Cf *Galt (Procurator Fiscal) v Philp* [1984] IRLR 156, where it was held that tortious acts protected by the statutory immunities remain 'wrongful' for the purposes of these provisions. If correct, the decision could have profound implications for the legality of picketing.

[352] *Ward Lock & Co Ltd v Operative Printers' Assistants' Society* (1906) 22 TLR 327, CA, at 329 per Fletcher Moulton LJ; *Fowler v Kibble* [1922] 1 Ch 487, CA; cf *J Lyons & Sons v Wilkins* [1899] 1 Ch 255, where the Court of Appeal had previously held that the section created new offences complete in themselves. The approach in *Ward Lock* was preferred by Scott J in *Thomas v NUM (South Wales Area)* [1985] 2 All ER 1, [1985] IRLR 136.

[353] The fact that the s 241 offence is punishable with imprisonment means that it is capable of founding a charge of criminal conspiracy under the Criminal Law Act 1977, s 1(1): Trade Union and Labour Relations (Consolidation) Act 1992, s 242.

the physical control of picketing by the police is that of breach of the peace[354] (either actual or reasonably apprehended), for it is a police officer's duty to prevent such a breach, if necessary by positive action to limit the numbers and placings of pickets. If a picket disregards an instruction from a police officer, and that officer can show grounds for reasonably anticipating[355] a breach of the peace at the time (for example through the imminent arrival of a lorry going into the picketed factory), then that picket is guilty of wilfully obstructing the police officer in the execution of his duty, contrary to section 89 of the Police Act 1996. Thus, breach of the peace acts as an umbrella head of liability which may justify the police in limiting numbers, as in *Piddington v Bates*,[356] or holding back from the factory gates some, or even all, of the pickets[357] even if that means that there is little practical likelihood of the pickets (or their leaders) being able to converse with the lorry driver at all, provided that the drastic nature of any police action is justified by the magnitude of the risk of a breach of the peace. In the past, these powers have been used to control the activities of pickets at the premises being picketed. However, the miners' strike of 1984–85 saw a significant development when the police, faced with major disorders outside pits (particularly working pits in Nottinghamshire) began to close off areas altogether to would-be pickets, preventing them from reaching the premises in question at all, if necessary by the use of roadblocks. Any pickets proceeding past such a barrier risked being arrested for obstruction of the police.[358] The legality of such drastic preventive tactics was questioned in *Moss v McLachlan*[359] in the case of four such would-be pickets charged with obstruction for trying to pass a police cordon. They were convicted by magistrates and their appeal was dismissed by the Divisional Court which held that, on the facts, the police had reasonably anticipated a breach of the peace and so their preventive action was justified. One important holding was that in forming their reasonable anticipation the police were entitled to take into account their common knowledge of the course of the dispute and the likelihood of further major violence.

---

[354] See *R v Howell (Errol)* [1982] QB 416, [1981] 3 All ER 383, CA, per Watkins LJ: 'There is a breach of the peace whenever harm is actually done or is likely to be done to a person or in his presence to his property or a person is in fear of being so harmed through an assault, an affray, a riot, an unlawful assembly or other disturbance.' See also *Percy v DPP* [1995] 1 WLR 1382; *Nicol and Selvanayagam v DPP* (1995) 160 JP 155. The common law offence of breach of the peace was specifically retained by the Public Order Act 1986, s 40(4).

[355] See *Foulkes v Chief Constable of the Merseyside Police* [1998] 3 All ER 705, CA, per Beldam LJ: 'There must … be a sufficiently real and present threat to the peace to justify the extreme step of depriving of his liberty a citizen who is not at the time acting unlawfully.'

[356] [1960] 3 All ER 660, [1961] 1 WLR 162.

[357] *Kavanagh v Hiscock* [1974] 2 All ER 177, [1974] ICR 282.

[358] Arrested pickets were routinely subjected to stringent bail conditions aimed at preventing them from returning; see eg *R v Mansfield Justices, ex p Sharkey* [1985] 1 All ER 193, [1984] IRLR 496, where the Divisional Court upheld the validity of what was then a common bail condition 'not to visit any premises or place for the purpose of picketing or demonstrating in connection with the current trade dispute between the NUM and the NCB other than peacefully to picket or demonstrate at his usual place of employment.'

[359] [1985] IRLR 76. Police powers to use roadblocks are now codified: Police and Criminal Evidence Act 1984, s 4.

The problem with the case as a precedent is that in fact the police cordon was only between one and a half and four miles from four working pits within one area served by that particular road. Thus, the physical nexus between the cordon and the premises was relatively close. It is perhaps unfortunate that the legality of certain more controversial actions taken by the police (such as the stopping of Kent miners on their way to the northern coalfields at the Dartford tunnel) was not properly tested in the courts. Were similar facts to arise today, the courts would have to give due weight to the exercise by the pickets of their Convention rights to freedom of expression and of peaceful assembly in deciding whether a police officer had reasonable grounds for apprehending a breach of the peace.[360]

(iv) PUBLIC ORDER OFFENCES[361]

As we have already seen, picketing which is not 'peaceful' may bring liability not only under specific criminal offences applying to industrial disputes, but also under the general laws relating to public order, which were subject to major amendment by the Public Order Act 1986. That Act had its origins in a review set up in 1979 to consider problems of public order generally, leading to a White Paper in 1985;[362] although the remit was wide, it was given added impetus by certain newsworthy industrial disputes, particularly the events of the 1984–85 miners' strike, and so several of the provisions in the Act were intended to affect picketing. The law on public order was further amended by the Criminal Justice and Public Order Act 1994 and the Crime and Disorder Act 1998, as successive governments of (supposedly) different political persuasions have resorted to increasingly draconian measures in an attempt to assuage public concern over a perceived deterioration in law and order. The measures relevant to picketing lie principally in the following areas: (1) offences against public order, (2) controls over public processions and assemblies.

Considering first the applicable offences, the Public Order Act abolished the common law offences of riot, rout, unlawful assembly and affray, and repealed the well-known statutory offence of 'threatening behaviour', replacing them with five graduated offences, all carrying powers of arrest; a further offence, that of causing intentional harassment, alarm or distress, was added by the Criminal Justice and Public Order Act 1994, and the Crime and Disorder Act 1998 imposed more severe penalties for certain of the offences where racially aggravated. The offences are as follows:[363]

---

[360] See Fenwick 'The Right to Protest, the Human Rights Act and the Margin of Appreciation' (1999) 62 MLR 491.

[361] See Smith *Offences against Public Order* (1987); Wallington [1987] Crim LR 180; Carty 'The Public Order Act 1986: Police Powers and the Picket Line' (1987) 16 ILJ 146.

[362] *Review of Public Order Law* (Cmnd 9510, 1985); also influential was the Law Commission's Report 'Offences relating to public order' (Law Com No 123, 1983).

[363] The following are condensed versions of the offences; for the full wording, see the text of the Act.

(a) Riot

Twelve or more persons present together using or threatening unlawful violence for a common purpose, their conduct being such as would cause a person of reasonable firmness present at the scene to fear for his personal safety.[364] Anyone using unlawful violence for the common purpose is liable on indictment to a maximum of ten years' imprisonment, a fine or both.

(b) Violent disorder

Three or more persons present together using or threatening unlawful violence, their conduct being such as would cause a person of reasonable firmness present at the scene to fear for his personal safety.[365] Anyone using or threatening unlawful violence is liable on indictment to five years' imprisonment and/or a fine, or on summary conviction to six months' imprisonment and/or the maximum scale fine. This offence replaced the old common law offence of unlawful assembly, and is envisaged as being the major offence in practice in the case of serious disorder.

(c) Affray

Using or threatening unlawful violence towards another, such as would cause a person of reasonable firmness present at the scene to fear for his personal safety.[366] The maximum penalty here is three years' imprisonment and/or a fine on indictment, or six months' imprisonment and/or the maximum scale fine on summary conviction.

(d) Violent behaviour

Using threatening, abusive or insulting words or behaviour (or distributing or displaying anything to like effect) to another person with intent to cause that person to fear immediate unlawful violence (to himself or another) or to provoke that person or another to use immediate unlawful violence.[367] This offence is triable summarily only and carries a maximum penalty of six months' imprisonment and/or a level 5 fine.[368]

(e) Intentional harassment

This offence, which was added by the Criminal Justice and Public Order Act 1994, is based on the existing offence of disorderly behaviour (see (f)), but with the additional requirements that the person must intend to cause, and the victim must actually be caused, harassment, alarm or distress.[369] It carries a much stiffer penalty than

---

[364] Public Order Act 1986, s 1.   [365] Public Order Act 1986, s 2.

[366] Public Order Act 1986, s 3.

[367] Public Order Act 1986, s 4. Violence includes violence to property; s 8.

[368] The penalties are more severe in the case of a racially aggravated offence: Crime and Disorder Act 1998, s 31.

[369] Public Order Act 1986, s 4A. Compare the offence of harassment under the Protection from Harassment Act 1997, where it is enough to show that the accused ought to have known that his course of conduct amounted to harassment: see 6(ii), p 755.

the non-intentional version (reflecting the intentional element), being punishable on summary conviction by up to six months' imprisonment and/or a level 5 fine.[370] Although apparently aimed at serious, persistent racial harassment, it is clearly of great potential significance to picketing.

(f) Disorderly behaviour

Using threatening, abusive or insulting words or behaviour, or disorderly behaviour (or displaying anything to like effect) within the hearing or sight of a person likely to be caused harassment, alarm or distress thereby, with the intention or the awareness that the words or behaviour may be threatening, abusive, insulting or disorderly.[371] This offence (perhaps best summed up colloquially as 'generally loutish behaviour') was particularly strongly criticized upon its introduction; it covers a multitude of sins, but is not of great importance in picketing cases since any such behaviour in that context is likely to lead to a breach of the peace (actual or reasonably apprehended), to which the present section probably adds little.[372] The offence is triable summarily only, with a maximum penalty of a level 3 fine.[373]

Turning to the imposition of controls on public processions and assemblies, sections 11–13 of the Public Order Act 1986 allow the police to be given advance notice of public processions, and to impose conditions on them or to prohibit them altogether in order to prevent disorderly or intimidatory conduct. These powers are considered in full elsewhere[374] and are not of immediate application to picketing (except in the case of, for example, marches in support of pickets). Of more obvious relevance to picketing is the power to regulate public assemblies in section 14.[375] This permits a senior police officer to impose conditions on a 'public assembly',[376] either in advance or at the scene, where the officer reasonably believes that:

(a) [the assembly] may result in serious public disorder, serious damage to property or serious disruption to the life of the community, or

(b) the purpose of the persons organising it is the intimidation of others with a view to compelling them not to do an act they have a right to do, or to do an act they have a right not to do

---

[370] Again, the penalties are more severe in the case of a racially aggravated offence: see n 368.

[371] Public Order Act 1986, s 5. The test of intention or awareness here is subjective: see *DPP v Clarke* (1991) 94 Cr App Rep 359.

[372] Section 5 is principally aimed at conduct which is a social nuisance but which falls short of an actual breach of the peace because there is no actual or threatened harm to a person or his property; in that light, note the inclusion of mere 'disorderly behaviour'.

[373] See n 368.   [374] See n 361.

[375] There is also a power to ban trespassory assemblies, introduced by the 1994 Act, which could conceivably be used where picketing (eg persistent mass picketing) results in 'serious disruption to the life of the community': Public Order Act 1986, s 14A; see *DPP v Jones* [1999] 2 All ER 257, HL.

[376] This is defined as 'an assembly of 20 or more persons in a public place which is wholly or partly open to the air' (s 16), which clearly covers a picket line with that number of people (except in the unlikely event of it being entirely on private property). The requirement of advance notice and the power to ban (which apply to processions) do not apply to assemblies, although note the power to ban *trespassory* assemblies: see n 375.

The potential application of this provision to picketing is obvious. If the police officer has such a reasonable belief, he may:

> give directions imposing on the persons organising or taking part in the assembly such conditions as to the place at which the assembly may be (or continue to be) held, its maximum duration, or the maximum number of persons who may constitute it, as appear to him necessary to avoid disorder, damage, disruption or intimidation.

As we have seen above, the concept of breach of the peace (which remains unaffected by the 1986 Act) already gives a police officer on the spot some of these directional powers, but section 14 puts them into a wider, clearer and more comprehensive statutory form[377] (backed by criminal sanctions on those organizing or taking part in an assembly in breach of conditions), and of course allows conditions to be attached in advance. Particularly significant are possible conditions as to place, time (not at times of shift changes for working employees?) and, of course as to numbers, where a provision in the Code of Practice on Picketing suggesting a limit of six pickets per entrance (considered below) assumes great significance.

(v) THE IMMUNITY

In view of the many and varied ways in which picketing can potentially fall foul of the law, the scope of the statutory immunity for picketing becomes of crucial significance, as it in effect defines the extent of the right to picket. Section 220 of the Trade Union and Labour Relations (Consolidation) Act 1992 provides that:

> It is lawful for a person in contemplation or furtherance of a trade dispute to attend—
>
> (a) at or near his own place of work, or
>
> (b) if he is an official of a trade union, at or near the place of work of a member of the union whom he is accompanying and whom he represents,[378]
>
> for the purpose only of peacefully obtaining or communicating information, or peacefully persuading any person to work or abstain from working.[379]

It is important to appreciate that section 220 does not confer a 'right' to picket as such; it gives a limited right to *attend* for the stated purposes of peacefully obtaining or communicating information or peacefully persuading a person to work or abstain from

---

[377] 'The crucial difference is that reasons other than the need to preserve the peace may be relied upon, in particular the reasonable belief of the senior officer present that the picket organizers' purpose is to intimidate others' (Wallington [1987] Crim LR 180, at 190).

[378] An official who is elected or appointed to represent some members of the union is to be regarded as representing only those members: s 220(4). This is to prevent the drafting in of large numbers of union officials, shop stewards, etc, from different parts of the country to do the picketing. A national officer, however, will be regarded as representing all members.

[379] The 'persuasion' limb was introduced by the Trade Disputes Act 1906, s 2; it had not been included in the immunity given by the Conspiracy and Protection of Property Act 1875: *J Lyons & Sons v Wilkins* [1899] 1 Ch 255, CA.

working (ie 'peaceful picketing'), but it does not legitimize the *activities* of pickets. The section 220 immunity has therefore been described as 'narrow but real'[380] in that by protecting attendance for the purposes of peaceful picketing, it ensures that pickets will not incur either tortious liability (for example for nuisance) or criminal liability[381] (for example for obstruction of the highway or watching and besetting) from the mere fact of their attendance. Any liability which arises from the activities of pickets is protected, if at all, under the general trade dispute immunities contained in section 219 of the 1992 Act; the two provisions are, however, inextricably linked, as picketing which falls outside the section 220 immunity loses any protection which it might otherwise have enjoyed under section 219, while picketing which is within section 220 retains the section 219 immunities, even if it constitutes secondary action which would normally not be immune. The interrelationship of the immunities is discussed further below.

As seen above, the section 220 immunity applies to attendance for the purposes of peaceful picketing. It follows that if some other purpose can be inferred from the actions of the pickets (for example intimidation of those seeking to enter the workplace, or blockading the entrance), the immunity does not apply. Thus, in *Tynan v Balmer*[382] where pickets walked in a circle around the factory gates in such a way as to seal off the entrance from traffic, the court was able to infer a purpose other than one of those in the section. Similarly, in *Broome v DPP*[383] the House of Lords held that the defendant's purpose in standing in front of a lorry to prevent its passage (having failed to persuade the driver not to enter the picketed premises) was to obstruct rather than to persuade or communicate; the justices had acquitted the defendant on a charge of obstruction because they thought that he had only spent a reasonable time in trying to exercise his 'statutory right' of peaceful persuasion, a right which they considered would be meaningless if he was not allowed actually to stop the vehicle. The House of Lords held that this was entirely misconceived—the section gives no 'right' to picket, and certainly does not allow a picket to compel someone to stop and listen if that person does not wish to do so (a point reaffirmed shortly afterwards by the Divisional Court in *Kavanagh v Hiscock*).[384] Lord Salmon put it thus,

> [The] words make it plain that it is nothing but the attendance of the pickets at the places specified which is protected; and then only if their attendance is for one of the specified purposes. The section gives no protection in relation to anything the pickets may say or do whilst they are attending if what they say or do is itself unlawful. But for the section, the mere attendance of pickets might constitute an offence under [section 241(1)(b) and (d) of the 1992 Act or under the Highways Act 1980] or constitute a tort, for example, nuisance. The section, therefore, gives a narrow but nevertheless real immunity to pickets. It clearly does no more.

---

[380] *Broome v DPP* [1974] 1 All ER 314, [1974] ICR 84, HL at 325 and 96 respectively, per Lord Salmon.

[381] The Code of Practice of Picketing, para 41, states that there is no immunity from the criminal law, but there are dicta in *Broome v DPP* to the contrary.

[382] [1967] 1 QB 91, [1966] 2 All ER 133. The case is a good example of a trespass committed by an unreasonable user of the highway: see heading 6(ii), p 755.

[383] See n 380.   [384] [1974] 2 All ER 177, [1974] ICR 282.

Before 1980, the statutory immunity for picketing applied so long as the attendance was for one of the stated purposes (ie peacefully obtaining or communicating information or peacefully persuading any person to work or abstain from working), and was within the golden formula. There were no restrictions on who could picket, or where, except that picketing a person's home was outside the immunity. This meant that those who engaged in so-called 'secondary picketing' enjoyed the full protection of the immunity. The phrase 'secondary picketing' is used to connote one of two things, either the attendance on picket lines of people who are not employed by the employer in dispute (sometimes referred to as sympathy picketing), or the placing of picket lines elsewhere than at the premises of the employer in dispute (particularly the use of so-called 'flying pickets'). The incoming Conservative government in 1979 were determined to tackle secondary picketing, which was perceived as a major problem. The approach taken in the Employment Act 1980 was to restrict the scope of the immunity for peaceful picketing to a person picketing at or near[385] his *own* place of work[386] (and to a union representative accompanying such a person), so that the immunity no longer applies to secondary pickets engaged in sympathy picketing, or persons picketing a place other than their own place of work. As was mentioned above, crucially the 1980 Act also linked the immunity for *attendance* under section 220 with the immunities for the *activities* of pickets under section 219, by expressly removing the section 219 immunities from acts done in the course of picketing which falls outside the scope of section 220[387] (for example because it is not at that person's place of work, or is not peaceful). The effect of this is to allow an employer not a party to a dispute to obtain an injunction to stop employees of some other employer in dispute picketing his premises in the course of their dispute.[388] However, in one important respect the immunity for picketing is wider than the immunity for other forms of industrial action, because in certain circumstances pickets enjoy immunity for *secondary* action occurring during picketing;[389] indeed, following the tightening up of the law on secondary action by the Employment Act

---

[385] A realistic approach must be taken to the meaning of 'at or near': *Rayware Ltd v TGWU* [1989] ICR 457, [1989] IRLR 134, CA (pickets at the entrance to a private industrial estate which contained the employer's factory were held to be attending 'at or near' their place of work, even though 1,200 yards from their employer's premises).

[386] Those with no fixed place of work, or whose workplace makes picketing impracticable (eg the proverbial lighthouse keeper), may picket 'any premises' from which they work or from which their work is administered: s 220(2); see *Union Traffic Ltd v Transport and General Workers' Union* [1989] IRLR 127, CA. Workers who have been dismissed because of the dispute (and so who technically have no place of work) may picket their former place of work: s 220(3), although note that if the employer moves production to a new plant, the dismissed workers may not lawfully picket that plant because it was never their place of work: *News Group Newspapers Ltd v SOGAT 1982 (No 2)* [1987] ICR 181, [1986] IRLR 337.

[387] Trade Union and Labour Relations (Consolidation) Act 1992, s 219(3); see heading 4(ii), p 731.

[388] As in *Mersey Docks and Harbour Co v Verrinder* [1982] IRLR 152. One problem for an employer may be to identify the pickets in order to bring civil proceedings against them; it is no part of the police function to do so (see the Code of Practice on Picketing, para 27).

[389] Trade Union and Labour Relations (Consolidation) Act 1992, s 244(3). The protection is, of course, subject to the other restrictions on the statutory immunities, such as the need to hold a valid ballot.

1990, this is now the only form of secondary action which enjoys any statutory protection. This exception exists for the simple reason that without it the immunity for attendance conferred by section 220 would in practice be worthless. Workers peacefully picketing at their own place of work can very easily become involved in secondary action—for example, the actions of a picket who persuades a delivery driver not to cross a picket line (thereby probably inducing that driver to break his contract of employment and also interfering with the commercial supply contracts of the driver's employer) are likely to constitute secondary action if the driver is not employed by the employer in dispute. If there were no immunity for secondary action occurring during picketing, it would be virtually impossible for any lawful picketing to take place. Secondary action committed during peaceful picketing is therefore protected, but *only* as regards those employed (or last employed) by the employer in dispute, and union officials lawfully accompanying them. Those not employed by the employer in dispute (for example sympathy pickets who picket their own place of work in support of other workers) enjoy no protection against secondary action which occurs during picketing.

One other issue which in the past has been the cause of much controversy is mass picketing. Mass picketing is not in itself unlawful, and section 220 places no limits on the numbers of pickets who may lawfully attend. However, the section does require that the picketing be 'peaceful', ie for the stated purposes of obtaining or communicating information or peacefully persuading any person to work or abstain from working. Thus, while mass picketing is not unlawful in itself, it is in the nature of things easier to infer a purpose other than that of peaceful communication or persuasion as the numbers grow larger. In *Broome v DPP*[390] Lord Salmon said that each case would depend on its facts, with the number of pickets being just one of the factors in deciding whether the attendance was for statutory purposes, but Lord Reid said, perhaps more realistically, that in a case of mass picketing 'it would not be difficult to infer as a matter of fact that pickets who assemble in unreasonably large numbers do have the purpose of preventing free passage', ie a purpose outside those permitted in section 220, an approach echoed in the judgment of Scott J in *Thomas v NUM (South Wales Area)*.[391] When the 1980 Employment Bill was going through Parliament, there was some pressure to supplement this general position with a statutory provision limiting numbers of pickets. This was not done in the Act, but an attempt was made to achieve the same result indirectly in the Code of Practice on Picketing, issued later in the year and revised in 1992.[392] Paragraph 47 states that:

> the law does not impose a specific limit on the number of people who may picket at any one place; nor does this Code affect in any way the discretion of the police to limit the number of people on a particular picket line.

---

[390] [1974] 1 All ER 314, [1974] ICR 84, HL.   [391] [1985] 2 All ER 1, [1985] IRLR 136.
[392] The Code of Practice is discussed under heading 6(vi).

However, paragraph 51, after discussing the problems caused by large numbers, goes on to state that 'pickets and their organisers should ensure that in general the number of pickets does not exceed six at any entrance to, or exit from, a workplace; frequently a smaller number will be appropriate'. Although the Code itself is not legally binding it is expressly made admissible in tribunal or court proceedings,[393] and this suggested maximum of six pickets per entrance has in the past been seized upon by the courts as a guide 'to a sensible number for a picket line in order that the weight of numbers should not intimidate those who wish to go to work',[394] the implication being that the presence of pickets in numbers greater than six may be taken to indicate a purpose outside those permitted by the section. It remains to be seen whether attempts to limit the numbers of pickets in this circuitous way can be reconciled with the greater weight which must now be given to the Convention rights of freedom of expression and of peaceful assembly.

(vi) THE CODE OF PRACTICE ON PICKETING

The Code was published in 1980 by the Secretary of State for Employment,[395] and revised in 1992. The Code is not legally binding, and much of it is concerned with explaining the relevant law. However, as seen above, one aspect of the Code, the suggested maximum number of six pickets per entrance,[396] has in the past been given indirect legal effect through being taken into account by the courts when deciding whether the picketing was 'peaceful' and so within the immunity. Other than that, the Code's general exhortations as to prior consultations with the police and proper organization of picketing by officials[397] are of little legal significance. The revised Code includes the following recommendations: (1) where an entrance or exit is used jointly by the workers of more than one employer, pickets should not interfere with those workers or call upon them to join in the dispute; (2) picketing should be confined to a location or locations as near as practicable to the place of work; (3) a picket should not be designated as official unless it is actually organized by a trade union and the union is prepared to accept responsibility for it. Finally, one part of the Code is open to serious objection

[393] Trade Union and Labour Relations (Consolidation) Act 1992, s 207.
[394] *Thomas v NUM (South Wales Area)* [1985] ICR 886, [1985] IRLR 136, per Scott J; see also *News Group Newspapers Ltd v SOGAT 1982 (No 2)* [1987] ICR 181, [1986] IRLR 337, per Stuart-Smith J. In *Thomas v NUM*, the terms of the injunction were clearly drafted with the Code of Practice in mind, for they restrained the organizing of picketing at the colliery in question in numbers greater than six for any purpose other than peaceful persuasion or communication.
[395] Under powers now contained in the Trade Union and Labour Relations (Consolidation) Act 1992, s 203, which allows him to promulgate codes of practice (with parliamentary approval) after consultation with ACAS. The Code of Practice is set out in *Harvey* S [602].
[396] Paragraph 51.
[397] One irony here is that, while the Code stresses the importance of good organization and marshalling by officials, the law has never accepted that 'official pickets' should have any rights (other than the right of attendance) over and above ordinary pickets, eg a right to go through police cordons to talk to lorry drivers (see *Kavanagh v Hiscock* [1974] 2 All ER 177, [1974] ICR 282).

as a misuse of the idea of codes of practice. This is Section G (Essential Supplies and Services) which states that pickets should ensure that such supplies and services are not impeded or prevented.[398] The problem is that it is difficult to see what legal effect this could have—it would be stretching several points to argue that picketing which did interfere with such services or supplies was thereby not 'peaceful', and it is the peaceful or other nature of it which is normally in issue in deciding whether or not the section 220 immunity can be relied upon. If it is correct that Section G has no legal effect, its inclusion can be seen either as merely pious hope or, more objectionably, an attempt to legislate by code of practice. If there are to be measures on something as important as the protection of essential supplies and services, it is surely not expecting too much that they should be properly enacted in a statute.[399]

7 THE LIABILITY OF A UNION IN TORT

So far in this chapter we have been concerned with the legal gymnastics concerning the existence of a cause of action; the simplified position now is that industrial action by a union which has effects on commercial contracts or dealings is likely to be tortious, most of those torts are covered by immunities, but under the present legislation there are several major inroads into those immunities. However, the next major question concerns enforcement, which (criminal law aside) operates entirely in the civil law domain. This means that while the government may legislate to create or permit causes of action, it is up to individuals to bring proceedings. Historically employers have been loath to do so. Perhaps one reason for this has been the nature of the defendant. Until 1982, unions enjoyed a blanket immunity under the Trade Disputes Act 1906, which meant that actions had to be brought, if at all, against named persons (usually senior union officials). If an injunction was obtained against a union official and the union failed to comply with it, the only remedy available to the employer lay against the individual union official for contempt of court, and continued failure to comply could lead ultimately to imprisonment and the creation of union 'martyrs', something which few employers were prepared to risk. The position was fundamentally changed by the Employment Act 1982, which abolished the blanket immunity of a trade union from liability in tort,[400] leaving unions only with the same immunities (now contained in the Trade Union and Labour Relations (Consolidation) Act 1992, sections 219 and 220), as are enjoyed by individual union officers and members. If those immunities

---

[398] Paragraph 62. Paragraph 63 lists such supplies and services as including pharmaceutical and medical products; hospitals; fuel for institutions; supplies needed in a crisis for public health and safety; goods and services necessary to the maintenance of plant and machinery; livestock; food and animal feeding stuffs; the operation of essential public services and mortuaries, burial and cremation services.

[399] On industrial action in the essential services generally, see Morris *Strikes in Essential Services* (1986), and 'Industrial Action in Essential Services: The New Law' (1991) 29 ILJ 89.

[400] See Ewing 'Industrial Action: Another Step in the "Right" Direction' (1982) 11 ILJ 209.

do not apply, the union itself may now be the defendant in an action brought by an employer.[401] This means that there is less chance of the spectre arising of imprisoned union leaders and that, in addition to the usual remedy of an injunction, the remedy of damages is now more than a mere technical possibility (being an action against the union funds, rather than against an individual). This raises three questions as to the legal effects: when is a union to be liable in tort for the acts of its officers and members; what remedies can be sought against it; and out of which union funds can an award of damages be satisfied?

Turning to the first of these points, before 1982 this problem had hardly ever arisen, for a union itself could not be sued. However, the immunity had been temporarily removed by the Industrial Relations Act 1971, and the difficulties that could be caused became apparent, particularly in the case of *Heatons Transport Ltd v TGWU*,[402] where the House of Lords had to decide upon the scope of the implied authority of a shop steward where the union rules were unclear on the point. In an attempt to avoid the problem of applying ordinary common law rules of vicarious liability, the Employment Act 1982 enacted a statutory test of vicarious liability governing when a union is to be liable for one of the economic torts.[403] That test deemed a union to be responsible for acts which had been 'authorised or endorsed by a responsible person', viz: (1) the union's principal executive committee, (2) any other person empowered by the union rules to authorize or endorse such acts, (3) the president or general secretary, (4) any other employed official or (5) any committee of the union to whom an employed official reports. In the case of the last two categories the union was not to be held responsible where the official or committee in question was prevented under the rules from authorizing or endorsing industrial action, or where the action had been repudiated by the principal executive committee, the president or the general secretary. However, in an attempt to force trade unions to carry more responsibility for unofficial industrial action, the Employment Act 1990[404] extended categories (4) and

---

[401] In a further twist, the Trade Union and Labour Relations (Consolidation) Act 1992, s 235A (as inserted by the Trade Union Reform and Employment Rights Act 1993, s 22) gives an individual the right to apply for an injunction restraining unlawful industrial action where an effect (or a likely effect) of that action will be to (1) prevent or delay the supply of goods or services to that individual or (2) reduce the quality of goods or services supplied to him; see heading 8, p 774.

[402] [1972] 3 All ER 101, [1972] ICR 308, HL; see Hepple, 'Union Responsibility for Shop Stewards' (1972) 1 ILJ 197. One problem is that, in ordinary tort cases, one tends to think of vicarious liability operating from the top downwards, whereas within a union power has traditionally tended tends to move upwards from the shop floor, particularly via the shop steward whose constitutional position may not be fully set out in the union's rules.

[403] Trade Union and Labour Relations (Consolidation) Act 1992, s 20. As originally enacted the statutory test applied to the economic torts but did not apply to contempt proceedings arising out of breach of an injunction granted on the basis of one of the economic torts: *Express and Star Ltd v NGA (1982)* [1986] ICR 589, [1986] IRLR 222, CA; however, the Employment Act 1990 applied the test to subsequent contempt proceedings. It still does not apply to any other form of liability, tortious or otherwise: *Thomas v NUM (South Wales Area)* [1985] ICR 886, [1985] IRLR 136 (nuisance). In such cases, the common law rules (as in *Heatons Transport v TGWU* [1972] 3 All ER 101, [1972] ICR 308, HL) continue to apply.

[404] The proposals were advanced in the Green Paper 'Unofficial Action and the Law' (Cm 821, 1989).

(5) so as to make a trade union liable for the actions of *all* its officials and committees, including lay officials such as shop stewards, irrespective of anything to the contrary in the rules of the union. The 1990 Act even went so far as to make a union responsible for the actions of a 'group of persons', or any individual member of such a group, where an official of the union was a member of the group at the material time and the purposes of the group included organizing or coordinating industrial action (for example an ad hoc strike committee).[405]

In view of this immense extension of responsibility, the ability of a union to repudiate unauthorized actions by its officials and committees becomes of crucial importance. The requirements for a valid repudiation are of truly Byzantine complexity:[406] (1) the repudiation must take place as soon as reasonably practicable after the relevant act has come to the knowledge of the repudiator; (2) written notice of the repudiation must be given to the committee or official in question without delay; (3) the union must 'do its best'[407] to give individual written notice of the fact and date of the repudiation, without delay, to every member of the union who the union has reason to believe is taking part (or might otherwise take part) in industrial action as a result of the act which is being repudiated, and to the employer of every such member; (4) the notice to union members must contain the following statement: 'Your union has repudiated the call (or calls) for industrial action to which this notice relates and will give no support to unofficial industrial action taken in response to it (or them). If you are dismissed while taking unofficial industrial action, you will have no right to complain of unfair dismissal';[408] (5) the repudiation will be deemed to be ineffective if the executive, president or general secretary subsequently behave in a manner which is inconsistent with the purported repudiation,[409] or fail to confirm forthwith and in writing on request by a party to a commercial contract whose performance has been interfered with as a result of the act in question that it has been repudiated.

Given that a union may be liable under the above rules, what may it be liable for? Before the 1982 Act allowed an action in tort to be brought directly against a union, the aim of an action by an employer affected by industrial action was generally to

---

[405] Trade Union and Labour Relations (Consolidation) Act 1992, s 20(3)(b). As the section does not specify that the members of the group have to be members of the union, presumably this could render a union liable for the actions of a non-member in circumstances where the official who happens to belong to that group neither knows nor approves of that person's actions!

[406] Trade Union and Labour Relations (Consolidation) Act 1992, s 21. The actions of the principal executive committee, president or general secretary may not be repudiated, nor may those of a person acting under the authority of the rules.

[407] The 'boy scout' test?

[408] The draftsman somehow managed to resist the temptation to include the words 'you have been warned' in large capitals at the end.

[409] For a case where a purported repudiation was held on the facts to have been a sham, see *Express and Star Ltd v NGA (1982)* [1985] IRLR 455 ('nods, winks, turning of blind eyes and similar clandestine methods of approval', per Skinner J); see also *Gate Gourmet London Ltd v TGWU* [2005] IRLR 881.

obtain an injunction against named union leaders restraining them from organizing the industrial action. To obtain such relief a full action for damages had in theory to be available, but in practice the prospect of an employer pursuing union leaders for damages was very remote. After the 1982 Act, an action in tort can be brought against the union itself, which means that an action for damages (or, perhaps more to the point, the threat of an action for damages) is now a definite possibility, as the union is likely to have assets which could satisfy a judgment for damages. While the primary aim in most cases will still be an injunction, the possibility of unions having to pay damages raises one of the principal objections to laying unions open to actions in tort (ever since the *Taff Vale* decision[410] and the Trade Disputes Act 1906), namely that a strike or other industrial action could well cause vast losses by impeding production, losses which, if fully reflected in damages, could bankrupt the union. Section 22 of the Trade Union and Labour Relations (Consolidation) Act 1992 attempts to meet that argument by laying down maximum amounts of damages to be awarded against unions in tort actions (other than actions for personal injury or arising out of the ownership, occupation, possession, control or use of property, or product liability, where the statutory maxima do not apply). The limits are (1) £10,000 if the union has fewer than 5,000 members; (2) £50,000 if over 5,000 but fewer than 25,000 members; (3) £125,000 if over 25,000 but fewer than 100,000 members; (4) £250,000 if over 100,000 members.[411] These amounts may be varied by the Secretary of State by statutory instrument.

Given that an award of damages is made against the union, how is it to be satisfied? It may be remembered[412] that the Royal Commission set up after the *Taff Vale* case did not recommend the total immunity for a union that was later enacted by the Trade Disputes Act 1906, but rather recommended that certain types of union funds should not be liable to seizure to satisfy awards of damages. Section 23 of the Trade Union and Labour Relations (Consolidation) Act 1992 effects a similar compromise, in that it creates a class of 'protected property' which may not be taken to satisfy any award of damages, costs or expenses. This covers any property (1) belonging to trustees of the union in any other capacity (including personally); (2) belonging to any union member (otherwise than jointly or in common with the other members); (3) belonging to

---

[410] See heading 1, the introduction to this chapter.

[411] These are presumably the maximum amounts at the suit of one particular claimant, so that if there are several claimants, damages up to the maximum can be awarded in the case of each successful claimant, even if the actions arise from the same event. The section is not specific on this point, merely referring to 'any proceedings in tort'. It is unclear whether, if two or more actions are consolidated, or one claimant brings separate actions for damages based on separate events during the dispute, those are separate proceedings. Note that the restrictions on amount in s 22 only apply to damages; they do not apply to any interest awarded on damages (*Boxfoldia Ltd v National Graphical Association (1982)* [1988] IRLR 383) or to fines for contempt of court, and neither this section nor s 23 on protected property prevents the sequestration of the whole of a union's property if a fine is not paid.

[412] See heading 1, the introduction to this chapter, p 689.

any union official who is neither a member nor a trustee; (4) comprised in a political fund;[413] or (5) comprised in a provident benefits fund.[414]

8 THE USE OF INJUNCTIONS IN INDUSTRIAL CASES

Although the establishment of a viable cause of action in an industrial dispute case could, in theory, lead to an award of damages against the defendant union or its leaders or members,[415] the practical importance of such an action has always been that it permits the claimant to seek an injunction to *stop* the action. Moreover, as industrial disputes and stoppages may arise very quickly, the pattern has been for the claimant to apply for an interim injunction as quickly as possible. Such an injunction may stop the industrial action; in theory, it only does so in order to preserve the status quo pending the full trial of the substantive action, but in practice the claimant has achieved his aim and so the vast majority of these cases never proceed to trial; the granting of the injunction in effect decides the issue.[416] This raises two problems for a potential defendant. An interim injunction may be sought and granted at great speed,[417] and indeed can be sought without notice[418] in the absence of the defendant, including before the issue of proceedings in cases of urgency.[419] The normal practice is for the claimant to show good reason why the court should proceed, that is, without giving notice to the defendant, and this is reinforced in employment cases by the Trade Union and Labour Relations (Consolidation) Act 1992, section 221(1) which provides that a court shall not grant the injunction (in a case where the defendant is likely to claim that he acted in contemplation or furtherance of a trade dispute) unless it is:

> satisfied that all steps which in the circumstances were reasonable have been taken with a view to securing that notice of the application and an opportunity of being heard with respect to the application have been given to [the defendant].

---

[413] The political fund must be subject to rules of the union which prevent its contents from being used for financing strikes or other industrial action: s 23(2)(d).

[414] 'Provident benefits' are defined in s 23(3) as including payments expressly authorized by the union rules, in respect of sickness, injury or unemployment; superannuation; accidents; loss of tools through fire or theft; funeral expenses; provision for the children of deceased members.

[415] In *Huntley v Thornton* [1957] 1 All ER 234, [1957] 1 WLR 321 the claimant was awarded £500 damages for conspiracy.

[416] See Anderman and Davies 'Injunction Procedure in Labour Disputes' (1973) 2 ILJ 213 and (1974) 3 ILJ 30; Evans 'The Use of Injunctions in Industrial Disputes' (1987) 25 BJIR 419; Gall and McKay 'Injunctions as a Legal Weapon in Industrial Disputes' (1996) 34 BJIR 567.

[417] See, eg, *Barretts & Baird* (see 3(v), p 718), where the injunction that Henry J discharged had originally been granted by another judge over the telephone on a Sunday afternoon. In *Gate Gourmet London Ltd v TGWU* [2005] IRLR 881 the injunction was granted not just against named individual, but also against unnamed persons who could be defined by their unlawful activities.

[418] Civil Procedure Rules 1998, r 25.3 (ex parte, in the pre-Woolf terminology).

[419] CPR 25.2. There is no right of appeal against a grant or refusal of an interim injunction without permission of a judge: CPR 52.3.

It is probable that this provision does little other than repeat the normal procedure, for the avoidance of doubt.

The second problem is of more substance. In theory, an application for an interim injunction does not involve a trial of the issue, merely a decision whether to give certain temporary relief pending the action; if, however, the matter never goes any further (as in most industrial injunction cases) the interim stage is the only one at which the defendant can put forward his case. It used to be thought that, to be granted an interim injunction, the claimant had to show a 'prima facie' or 'strong prima facie' case that he would succeed at trial;[420] while this fell short of proof of his case on a balance of probabilities, it still meant that there was some examination of the substantive merits of the case. However, in *American Cyanamid Co v Ethicon Ltd*[421] the House of Lords held that this was incorrect—all that has to be shown by the claimant is that there is a 'serious question to be tried'—in other words, an arguable case fit to go on trial; once that has been shown, the question whether to grant the injunction will be decided on the 'balance of convenience', ie whether the claimant will suffer more damage in the meantime if it is not granted than the defendant will suffer if it is. In ordinary commercial cases, this may make perfect sense and may be backed up by other devices such as an undertaking in damages by the successful claimant. In employment cases, however, application of the ordinary principles on interim injunctions is likely to favour the employer,[422] as the dominant feature is the balance of convenience test which is usually decided in the employer's favour, for he can usually point to definite pecuniary loss if the strike is allowed to continue, whereas the defendant union can only point to the intangible 'damage' of loss of a tactical advantage in the dispute if the strike is stopped. In an attempt to meet the potential problem, the Employment Protection Act 1975 added a new require-ment, now contained in section 221(2) of the Trade Union and Labour Relations (Consolidation) Act 1992, which provides that where an application is made to a court for an interim injunction pending the trial of an action, and the party against whom the injunction is sought claims that he acted in contemplation or furtherance of a trade dispute:

> the court shall, in exercising its discretion whether or not to grant the injunction, have regard to the likelihood of that party's succeeding at the trial of the action in establishing any matter which would afford a defence to the action.

---

[420] *J T Stratford & Son Ltd v Lindley* [1965] AC 269, [1964] 3 All ER 102, HL.

[421] [1975] AC 396, [1975] 1 All ER 504, HL. See *Hubbard v Pitt* [1975] 3 All ER 1, [1975] ICR 308, CA, the judgment of Henry J in *Barretts & Baird (Wholesale) Ltd v IPCS* [1987] IRLR 3 and Gray 'Interlocutory Injunc-tions since *Cyanamid*' (1981) 40 CLJ 307.

[422] As was acknowledged by Lord Diplock in *NWL Ltd v Nelson* [1979] ICR 867, [1979] IRLR 478, HL. Moreover, in *British Airways plc v UNITE* [2010] IRLR 423 Cox J in granting an injunction to restrain strike action at airports over Christmas took the interests of the travelling public into account too, in deciding on the balance of convenience.

Section 221(2) was first considered by the House of Lords in *NWL Ltd v Nelson*,[423] where Lord Diplock said that the section was enacted to enable judges to take into account the practical reality of employment disputes when applying the 'balance of convenience' principle:

> [Section 221(2)] ... appears to me to be intended as a reminder addressed to English judges that where industrial action is threatened that is prima facie tortious because it induces a breach of contract they should in exercising their discretion whether or not to grant an interim injunction, put into the balance of convenience in favour of the defend-ant those countervailing practical realities and, in particular, that the grant of an injunc-tion is tantamount to giving final judgment against the defendant ... My Lords, when properly understood, there is in my view nothing in the decision of this House in *American Cyanamid Co v Ethicon Ltd* to suggest that in considering whether or not to grant an interim injunction the judge ought not to give full weight to all the practical realities of the situation to which the injunction will apply ... Cases of this kind are exceptional, but when they do occur they bring into the balance of convenience an important additional element ... it was clearly prudent of the draftsman of the section to state expressly that in considering whether or not to grant an interim injunction the court should have regard to the likelihood of the defendant's succeeding in establishing that what he did or threatened was done and threatened in contemplation or furtherance of a trade dispute.[424]

In practice section 221(2) has placed little restraint upon the granting of interim injunc-tions in industrial disputes. It only exhorts the court to 'have regard to the likelihood' of an immunity defence, which in practice it will almost certainly do anyway: if there is little chance of the claimant employer succeeding, an injunction will not be granted, but otherwise the odds seem to be stacked in the employer's favour, particularly as it appears that the 'public interest' may in appropriate cases be taken into account at this stage[425] (a factor that could be particularly influential where the dispute may give rise to significant disruption to the public). A judge hearing an application for an interim injunction will usually give some (albeit often hurried) consideration to the points of law involved, particularly on the applicability or otherwise of the immunities, but the relevant law is so complex that it is usually not difficult for the employer's counsel to put together an arguable case that there may have been some (perhaps technical) infringement by the union that renders the immunities inapplicable,[426] and that the balance of convenience favours the granting of an injunction.

---

[423] [1979] ICR 867, [1979] IRLR 478, HL.

[424] [1979] ICR 867 at 879, [1979] IRLR 478 at 484.

[425] *Beaverbrook Newspapers Ltd v Keys* [1978] ICR 582, [1978] IRLR 34, CA; *United Biscuits (UK) Ltd v Fall* [1979] IRLR 110; *Express Newspapers Ltd v McShane* [1980] 1 All ER 65, [1980] IRLR 35, HL; *Associated British Ports v TGWU* [1989] 3 All ER 822, [1989] ICR 557, HL.

[426] This is much more likely as a result of the narrowing of the immunities since 1980, particularly with the introduction of the highly complex balloting and notice requirements; see earlier in this chapter at heading 4. The development of torts *not* covered by an immunity (eg inducing breach of statutory duty) is also highly significant here. See, eg, *Associated British Ports v TGWU* [1989] 3 All ER 796, [1989] IRLR 305, CA (reversed on other grounds, [1989] 3 All ER 822, [1989] IRLR 399, HL).

Finally, four points should be noticed; the first is that an appeal against the granting or refusal of an interim injunction will only be allowed where the decision of the trial judge was wrong, or was unjust because of a serious procedural or other irregularity in the proceedings,[427] or where there has been a change of circumstances since the order was made. The issue was considered in *Hadmor Productions Ltd v Hamilton*[428] where Lord Diplock emphasized that the appellate court's function is one of review only; an interim injunction is a discretionary remedy, lying essentially within the discretion of the trial judge, so that the appellate court should not on appeal treat the matter de novo and substitute its own view on the facts.[429] Thus, not only is it likely that the initial application for an injunction will succeed, but also the trial judge's decision may be difficult to challenge on appeal.[430]

The second point is that events during the miners' strike of 1984–85 showed how potent a weapon an injunction[431] can be when it is granted against a union itself, not a named individual, for breach of or failure to comply with it is a contempt of court[432] for which the union may be fined (the fine not being subject to the statutory maxima on damages); if the fine is not paid, the claimant may apply for sequestration of the union's assets, and the fact of sequestration could give rise to a claim by disaffected union members for the union to be placed in receivership. Indeed, it has been argued that sequestration and, to a lesser extent, receivership can be viewed as remedies in their own right (especially as sequestration is not merely an administrative means of gathering the fine, since even after the fine is recovered by the sequestrators the sequestration continues until the union purges its contempt).

The third point is that it must be remembered that an employment dispute is an employment relations problem, and at some stage the two sides will have to try to resume normal relations; this is unlikely to be helped by the service of claim forms, and a delicate balance may have to be preserved between the enforcement of legal rights in the short term, and the resolution of issues in the employment relations context in the long term. ACAS have certainly found their collective conciliation efforts

[427] CPR 52.11(3). There is no right of appeal against a grant or refusal of an interim injunction without the permission of a judge: CPR 52.3.

[428] [1982] 1 All ER 1042, [1982] ICR 114, HL, applied in *Dimbleby & Sons Ltd v NUJ* [1984] ICR 386, [1984] IRLR 161.

[429] Under the Civil Procedure Rules, the court can hold a rehearing if it considers that it would be in the interests of justice to do so in the circumstances: CPR 52.11(1).

[430] The terms of the injunction may give the defendant the right to apply to the court to discharge or vary the injunction, particularly where it was granted without notice, but there will usually be a delay, and the court may be reluctant to interfere with an injunction which has already been granted.

[431] The principal injunctions during the strike were in fact granted to working miners, not employers, but the principles are the same. See Ewing (1985) 14 ILJ at 170; Lightman (1987) 40 CLP 25.

[432] On contempt of court and its remedies, see *Harvey* N II [4162] and Kidner 'Sanctions for Contempt by a Trade Union' (1986) 6 LS 18. Exactly which funds are subject to sequestration may have to be worked out with care in the case of a union with a diverse or decentralized constitution: *News Group Newspapers Ltd v SOGAT 82* [1986] ICR 716, [1986] IRLR 227, CA. For an example of a contempt fine for half-hearted and delayed compliance with a court order, see *Kent Free Press v NGA* [1987] IRLR 267.

materially complicated in cases where there is the threat or actuality of legal proceedings, and at one point suggested that there should be some procedure whereby legal
proceedings in industrial dispute cases could be temporarily stayed by the courts to
allow at least an attempt at conciliation before final steps are taken,[433] but the idea has
not been taken up.

Finally, many employers faced with industrial action which is unlawful, and therefore potentially restrainable, choose not to pursue legal remedies for fear of inflaming
an already difficult situation and reducing the chances of an early negotiated settlement.
However, such a strategy on the part of an employer could in practice be frustrated
by the Trade Union and Labour Relations (Consolidation) Act 1992, section 235A,[434]
which gives an individual who is deprived of goods or services[435] as a result of unlawful industrial action a right (dubbed the 'Citizen's Right') to apply for an injunction
restraining that action.[436] The right arises where 'an effect, or a likely effect, of the
unlawful industrial action is or will be to (i) prevent or delay the supply of goods or
services, or (ii) reduce the quality of goods or services supplied, to the individual
making the claim'.[437] While the industrial action must be unlawful,[438] it does not have
to be actionable in tort on the part of the applicant, and it seems that he need not
have suffered any quantifiable financial loss or damage as a result of it; moreover, it is
immaterial whether or not the applicant is *entitled* to be supplied with the goods or
services in question (this apparently designed to ensure that frustrated commuters
stranded on station platforms are not denied the protection of the section by technical arguments over whether they have a contractual entitlement to travel on any
particular train). The potential impact of this procedure was graphically illustrated in
P v National Association of Schoolmasters/Union of Women Teachers,[439] which arose
out of the refusal of NASUWT members to accept the 'unreasonable direction' of the
head teacher to teach a disruptive pupil who had been permanently excluded from
school, only to be reinstated following a successful appeal to the school governors.
The pupil sought an injunction restraining the industrial action on the grounds that
it was unlawful, and that the separate tuition arrangements which had been made for
him interfered with the provision of educational services to him and placed him at a

---

[433] *ACAS Annual Report, 1983* paras 1.16–1.18.

[434] Introduced by the Trade Union Reform and Employment Rights Act 1993, s 22.

[435] The original proposals in the Green Paper 'Industrial Relations in the 1990s' (Cm 1602, 1991), would
have confined the right to customers of the public services within the scope of the Citizen's Charter, but as
enacted the right goes considerably further.

[436] The section does not give a right to damages.

[437] Trade Union and Labour Relations (Consolidation) Act 1992, s 235A(1)(b).

[438] Trade Union and Labour Relations (Consolidation) Act 1992, s 235A(2), which provides that an act of
inducement is unlawful if it is actionable in tort by any one or more persons (eg by the employer in dispute), or
it could form the basis of an application by a member under s 62 of the 1992 Act (which gives union members a
right to be balloted before industrial action). The effect of this is that any non-excusable failure to comply with
the detailed statutory requirements (eg on balloting) will render the industrial action restrainable by anyone
adversely affected by it.

[439] [2003] IRLR 307, [2003] 1 All ER 993, HL.

disadvantage. In fact, the application was rejected on the facts,[440] and that decision was upheld on appeal by both the Court of Appeal and the House of Lords, but the fact that the application was made at all is significant.

The Citizen's Right is significant on two levels: first, it represents a breathtaking extension of liability, and could be said to render much of the earlier discussion on the scope of the economic torts irrelevant, for as long as the industrial action is in theory actionable by at least one person, anyone else adversely affected by that action may seek an injunction to restrain it; secondly, it could have a damaging effect on attempts to reach negotiated settlements to industrial disputes. In explaining the rationale of the Citizen's Right, the then minister of state posed the question, 'Why should citizens be inconvenienced because a gutless and spineless employer fails to see a remedy for unlawful action which results in loss?',[441] a view which arguably fails to recognize the employment relations realities of the situation.

---

[440] The claimant had alleged (1) that the dispute was not a trade dispute because it did not relate wholly or mainly to terms and condition of employment; and (2) that the statutory balloting requirements had not been complied with because two members of staff to whom ballot papers should have been sent did not receive them. Morison J at first instance found for the union on both points.

[441] Minister of State, Mr Michael Forsyth, *Hansard*, HC (Standing Committee F).

INDEX